THE POEMS OF
SHELLEY

Volume Two
1817–1819

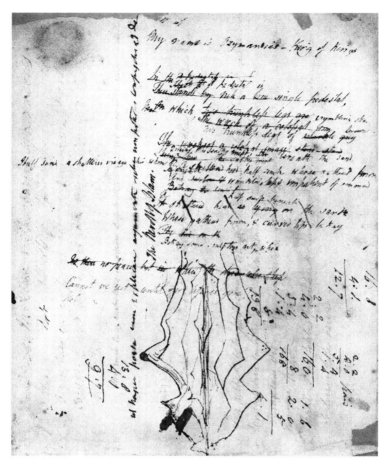

Shelley's rough draft of 'Ozymandias', from a manuscript in the
Bodleian Library (see Note on Illustrations, p. viii).
Reproduced by kind permission of the Bodleian Library, Oxford.

THE POEMS OF
SHELLEY

Volume Two
1817–1819

Edited by
KELVIN EVEREST
and
GEOFFREY MATTHEWS

Contributing Editors:
JACK DONOVAN, *Laon and Cythna*
RALPH PITE, *Julian and Maddalo*
MICHAEL ROSSINGTON, *The Cenci*

Longman

An imprint of Pearson Education

Harlow, England · London · New York · Reading, Massachusetts · San Francisco
Toronto · Don Mills, Ontario · Sydney · Tokyo · Singapore · Hong Kong · Seoul
Taipei · Cape Town · Madrid · Mexico City · Amsterdam · Munich · Paris · Milan

Pearson Education Limited

Edinburgh Gate
Harlow
Essex CM20 2JE
England

and Associated Companies throughout the world

Visit us on the World Wide Web at:
http://www.pearsoned.co.uk

First published 2000

© Pearson Education Limited 1989, 2000

ISBN-13: 978-0-582-03082-4

British Library Cataloguing-in-Publication Data
A catalogue record for this book is available from the British Library

Library of Congress Cataloging-in-Publication Data
A catalog record for this book is available from the Library of Congress

10 9 8 7 6 5 4 3 2
07

Typeset by 35 in 9/11.5pt Stone Serif
Printed and bound by Henry Ling Limited, at the Dorset Press, Dorchester, DT1 1HD.

CONTENTS

NOTE ON ILLUSTRATIONS

The illustration facing the title page shows the *verso* side of folio 85 in Bodleian MS Shelley e. 4 (*Nbk 5*). This is Shelley's original rough draft of 'Ozymandias', probably written under timed conditions in competition with Leigh Hunt and Horace Smith. The illustration on page 306 [i.e. facing the Headnote to Ozymandias] shows the *recto* side of folio 85 in Bodleian MS Shelley e.4, containing Shelley's neat copy of 'Ozymandias'. See poem no. 145, pages 307–311.

PREFACE TO VOLUME TWO

The first volume in this edition, published in 1989, drew attention in its Introduction to the then recent scholarly editions which, coupled with the enhanced access to manuscript collections relating to the text of Shelley, appeared to have eased the path for a new and inclusive edition of Shelley's poems. That was indeed the case, at least in the main part for that earlier period of Shelley's career covered by the first volume. I did however certainly underestimate the difference to the study of Shelley's text that would soon be made by the full appearance, in successive volumes throughout the 1990s, of the Garland series of facsimiles of manuscript materials which is now complete under the general editorship of Donald H. Reiman. This project has produced a truly vast amount of new scholarship and commentary, including minute inspection and assessment of literally every known line and word of Shelley's poetry in manuscript; and all of it directly relevant to the concerns of the present edition.

Many of the volumes in the Garland series deal with manuscript material which is included in the first volume of the present edition, and there has naturally been extensive discussion of datings and editorial decisions, including a good deal of reasoned disagreement. I am in the main content to let the first volume stand without further detailed reference to this body of commentary; readers and scholars will wish to judge for themselves in matters which will always involve varying interpretation. There are however two matters of fact which it is appropriate to acknowledge here. Poem no. 107 in the first volume, Shelley's translation from Moschus beginning 'When winds that move not its calm surface sweep', is a translation not of Moschus's Idyll v, as stated in the headnote, but Idyll iv; Shelley did subsequently translate Idyll v, which is no. 200 in the present volume, entitled 'Retribution: from Moschus'. More significantly, I am persuaded by the arguments advanced by Tim Webb and Paul Dawson in *BSM* xiv (Introduction pp. xviii–xix) that Shelley's poem 'To the [Lord Chancellor]', no. 131 in the first volume of this edition, was not composed 'soon after 27 March 1817', as argued in the headnote, but in the second half of 1820.

The necessity to absorb and judge the implications of the thirty-one Garland volumes which comprise *BSM* and *MYR* meant, not just that progress on the remaining volumes of the present edition would inevitably be slowed, but also that the task had grown effectively beyond the capabilities of a single person to complete within a reasonable period of time; or, at least, a single person also employed full-time in a British university in the 1990s, and working to the deadlines which now dominate all research, however long-term. The new scale of the task, which had never from the start appeared less than daunting, has been further augmented since 1989 by the appearance of good scholarly editions of all or most of the relevant works by Mary Shelley, Mary Wollstonecraft, William Godwin, and a number of other figures whose lives and work are central in Shelley's intellectual and social milieu.

These sobering circumstances necessitated a reconsideration of basic working methods, which led in due course to agreement with three British scholars of Romanticism, Jack Donovan of York University, my colleague Ralph Pite at Liverpool, and Michael Rossington of Newcastle University, that they would join me in working to complete the second volume of the present edition. This assistance has involved each of these contributing editors in taking responsibility for work on one major poem: Jack Donovan has edited *Laon and Cythna*, together with its important discarded opening sequence beginning 'Frail clouds arrayed in sunlight lose the glory'; Ralph Pite has edited 'Julian and Maddalo'; and Michael Rossington has edited *The Cenci*, and has also produced an account of the history of the Cenci story and Shelley's knowledge of it, which appears as Appendix B of this volume. These three colleagues have also provided advice and criticism of my own work in the present volume, and have suggested numerous improvements, corrections, and supplementary annotations. Without their commitment and support, I doubt that this edition of Shelley, which has now been long in the preparation, and first began to take shape in the work of Geoffrey Matthews some thirty-five years ago, would ever have continued to appear.

The principles of the edition remain those set forth in the Introduction to Volume One. That Introduction also makes clear that the basic conception of the edition, and most of its decisions in matters of dating and editorial approach, originate with Geoffrey Matthews. Geoffrey died in 1984, and the enormous growth since then in available materials relevant to Shelley's text, and in the number of scholars and critics interested in working with them, has brought significant changes of theory and practice in the editorial problem. There have also been larger changes and shifts of emphasis in the place of editing as a scholarly activity, in its relation to questions of literary and cultural theory. The work of such commentators as Jerome McGann and D. F. Mackenzie has transformed our understanding of the nature and value of editing. I have nevertheless sought to keep always in mind, as I take it that Geoffrey would wish to have stressed, the editor's responsibility to shape an image of a body of texts, and to attempt a coherent representation of the literary past which can live for the present.

Kelvin Everest
Liverpool, February 1999

ACKNOWLEDGEMENTS

I have many friends, colleagues and scholars to thank for generous assistance in the preparation of this volume. Like all students of Shelley, I am indebted to Donald H. Reiman, whose depth of Shelley scholarship is without parallel. I have also leaned heavily on the work of Dr Reiman's colleagues in the Garland series of facsimiles of Shelley's manuscripts, and here acknowledge a general debt to their work; the present volume has benefited most of all from the work of Paul Dawson and Neil Fraistat. Dr Bruce Barker-Benfield of the Bodleian Library has responded with unfailing courtesy, and unique authority, to numerous detailed questions about Shelley's manuscripts. The annotations in this volume to Shelley's translations from the Greek have drawn extensively on notes made by the late Jamie Matthews. My General Editor, John Barnard, has maintained his, and my, confidence in what has become an alarmingly long-term project; his sharp eye, zeal for accuracy and sound judgement have helped to unpick countless problems and errors.

For advice, information, and patient encouragement, I must also thank Drummond Bone, Marilyn Butler, Judith Chernaik, Nora Crook, Stuart Curran, Paul Foot, Stephen Gill, William Keach, Peter Kitson, Lisa Leslie, James McLaverty, Jim Mays, Andrew Motion, Michael O'Neill, Sharon Ouditt, Adrian Poole, Charles E. Robinson, Nick Roe, Francesco Rognoni, Rick Rylance, Martin Stannard, and Tim Webb. Various stages of preparation were ably and intelligently assisted by Jagori Banerjee, Simone Batin, Deborah Cartmell, Roger Fallon, Shirley Farrell, Sara Haslam, Cathy Rees, Sharon Ruston, and Barbara Smith. I, and the contributing editors, have received substantial financial support from the British Academy, the Leverhulme Trust, the Open University, St John's College, Oxford, Wolfson College, Oxford, the University of Leicester, the University of Liverpool, the University of Newcastle upon Tyne, and the University of York. Colleagues in the Faculty of Arts at Liverpool have provided much tactful criticism and information: I am grateful in particular to those colleagues in Classics, John Davies, Fred Jones, and especially Gillian Clark, whose advice on matters Greek and Latin has been both improving and wittily entertaining; and to my colleagues in the English Department, particularly Jonathan Bate, Nigel Bawcutt, Nick Davis, Julian Ferraro, Hester Jones, Brian Nellist and Karl Simms. I owe a special debt to the constructively frank and searching criticisms of Bernard Beatty. Faith, Lucy, Sophie and Grace Everest have helped in more ways than I care to remember.

The staff of various libraries and institutions have provided invaluable services and advice: the Biblioteca Nazionale Centrale di Firenze, the Bibliothèque Nationale de France, Bloomsbury Book Auctions (especially Justin Philips), the Bodleian Library (especially Mary Clapinson, Keeper of Special Collections and Western Manuscripts), the British Library, the Brotherton Library of the University of Leeds, Cambridge University Library, the Huntington Library, Leicester University Library, the Library of the Taylorian Institution, the Literary and Philosophical Society of Newcastle upon Tyne, Liverpool Public Library, Liverpool University Library, the London Library, the National Library of Scotland, the

National Library of Wales, the New York Public Library, the Open University Library, the Pierpont Morgan Library (especially Robert Parks), Reading University Library, and York University Library.

I am grateful to the following for granting permission to reproduce poems from manuscript material in their possession: the Bodleian Library (nos. 142, 143A–J, 145, 146, 147, 148, 149, 150, 151, 152, 153, 154, 156, 157, 158, 159, 160, 161, 165, 166, 167, 168, 169, 170, 171, 172, 174, 175, 176, 177, 178, 179, 180, 181, 182, 184, 185, 186, 187, 188, 189, 190, 191, 192, 193, 195A, 195B, 195C, 195D, 195F, 195H, 199, 200, 202, 203, 204, 205, 206 and 207); the British Library (nos. 164 and 201); the Carl and Lily Pforzheimer Foundation, Inc. (nos. 146 and 162), the Huntington Library, San Marino, California (nos. 183, 194, 195E, 195G, 195I, 195J, 196, 197 and 208), the Isabella Stewart Gardner Museum, Boston (no. 163), the Pierpont Morgan Library, New York (no. 198), and the Tinker Library, Yale (no. 183).

CHRONOLOGICAL TABLE OF SHELLEY'S LIFE AND PUBLICATIONS

1792   Born at Field Place, near Horsham, Sussex, 4 August, eldest son of Timothy Shelley, landowner and Whig M. P. (Baronet, 1806).

1802–4   At Syon House Academy, Isleworth, near London.

1804–10   At Eton, where he is bullied. Develops scientific as well as literary interests.

1808   Begins correspondence with Harriet Grove, his cousin; relationship ended in 1810 by religious prejudices of her family.

1810   Publishes two Gothic novels, *Zastrozzi* (spring) and *St Irvyne* (December). Publishes *Original Poetry by Victor and Cazire* (September), written with his sister Elizabeth. At University College Oxford (from October); meets Thomas Jefferson Hogg. Publishes *Posthumous Fragments of Margaret Nicholson* (November).

1811   Meets Harriet Westbrook (January). Expelled in his second term at Oxford (25 March) for refusing to answer questions about a sceptical pamphlet written with Hogg, *The Necessity of Atheism* (published February). Hogg also expelled. Elopes with Harriet Westbrook, and marries her in Edinburgh, 29 August. Quarrels with Hogg over his attempted seduction of Harriet. Meets Southey in the Lake District.

1812   Campaigns for political reform in Ireland (February–March); publishes two pamphlets, *Address to the Irish People* and *Proposals for an Association . . . of Philanthropists* (February). Prints *Declaration of Rights*. Adopts vegetarianism (March). Returns to Wales, 6 April, then moves to Devon where he is kept under surveillance by Government agents; writes *Letter to Lord Ellenborough*; his servant is imprisoned for distributing the *Declaration* and S.'s *The Devil's Walk* (August). To Tremadoc, North Wales, where he is involved in further political activity, and where, from September, he works on *Queen Mab*. Meets William Godwin (October) and Thomas Love Peacock (November). Copies out the 'Esdaile Notebook' (November–December).

1813   Flees from Tremadoc (27 February) after mysterious incident at Tanyrallt in which S. is apparently attacked at night. Visits Dublin and Killarney (March), then returns to London (April). Publishes *A Vindication of Natural Diet*, one of the notes to *Queen Mab*. *Queen Mab* privately published in May. Ianthe Shelley born, 23 June. Moves to Bracknell in Berkshire (July). Writes *A Refutation of Deism* (published 1814).

1814   Visiting Godwin in London (May–June); growing estrangement from Harriet. Elopes with Mary Godwin, daughter of William Godwin and Mary Wollstonecraft, 27 July. They travel to Switzerland accompanied by Mary's step-sister Claire Clairmont (daughter of Godwin's second wife by her previous husband). Returns to England 13 September. Problems with debt and ill-health. Charles Shelley born to Harriet, 30 November. S.'s review of Hogg's *Memoirs of Prince Alexy Haimatoff* published (December).

1815 Mary's first child born, 22 February (dies two weeks later). S.'s grandfather Sir Bysshe Shelley dies 5 January; by June S. is receiving annual income of £1000 (of which £200 is made over to Harriet). Gives large sums of money to Godwin. Moves to cottage at Bishopsgate, Windsor Park (August). River excursion up the Thames with Mary Godwin and Peacock (August–September); writes *Alastor*.

1816 William Shelley born to Mary, 24 January. *Alastor . . . and Other Poems* published (February). Visit to Switzerland with Mary and Claire (25 May–29 August); meets Byron; writes 'Hymn to Intellectual Beauty' (June) and 'Mont Blanc' (July). Returns to England, 8 September. Suicide of Mary's half-sister Fanny Imlay (daughter of Mary Wollstonecraft by her lover Gilbert Imlay), 9 October. Suicide of Harriet Shelley, by drowning in the Serpentine, 9 November (discovered, 10 December). Meets Keats, Horace Smith, through friendship with Leigh Hunt (December). Receives news of Harriet's suicide, 15 December. Marries Mary Godwin, 30 December.

1817 Allegra, Claire Clairmont's daughter by Byron, born at Bath, 12 January. Meetings with Keats (February). Writes *A Proposal for Putting Reform to the Vote* (published in March). Lord Eldon, Lord Chancellor, denies S. custody of his two children by Harriet, 27 March. Moves to Marlow (March); close friendship with Peacock. Writes *Laon and Cythna* (April–September). Works on *Rosalind and Helen* (September). Clara Shelley born, 2 September. *History of a Six Weeks' Tour*, by S. and Mary, published anonymously (winter). Writes *An Address to the People on the Death of Princess Charlotte* (November; not published until c. 1843). *Laon and Cythna* published and suppressed (December). Writes 'Ozymandias' (December).

1818 *Laon and Cythna* re-issued in a revised version as *The Revolt of Islam* (January). Leaves England for Italy, 13 March. Sends Allegra to Byron, 28 April. Meets Maria and John Gisborne, with Maria's son Henry Reveley, at Livorno (May). Moves to Bagni di Lucca, 11 June; finishes *Rosalind and Helen*, translates Plato's *Symposium*, writes 'On Love', 'Discourse on the Manners of the Ancient Athenians'. Travels to Venice with Claire to meet Byron (August). Stays at the Villa I Capuccini in Este, near Venice. Mary follows with William and Clara (early September). Clara Shelley dies at Venice, aged 1, 24 September. At Este, begins *Julian and Maddalo*, 'Lines Written among the Euganean Hills', writes Act I of *Prometheus Unbound* (August–October). Travels to Rome, visiting Ferrara and Bologna *en route*; in Rome, 20–27 November. Goes on to Naples, 1 December. Visits volcanic scenery around Naples, writes 'Stanzas Written in Dejection . . . near Naples' (December).

1819 Visits Pompeii and Paestum (February). Returns to Rome, arriving 5 March. Writes *Prometheus Unbound* Acts II and III (March–April). Finishes *Julian and Maddalo* (May). *Rosalind and Helen . . . with Other Poems* published (spring). William Shelley dies aged 3½, 7 June. Moves to Livorno (arrives 17 June). *The Cenci* completed at Villa Valsovano, Livorno, 8 August. Receives news of the Peterloo massacre, 5 September; writes *The Mask of Anarchy* (not published until 1832) and other political poems (September). Moves to Florence, 2 October. Writes 'Ode to the West Wind', *Peter Bell the Third* (October–November); letter to *The Examiner* on the trial of Richard Carlile (not published until 1880); 'On Life', and *A Philosophical View of Reform*

(November–December; not published until 1920). Completes a fourth act of *Prometheus Unbound* (August–December). Percy Florence Shelley born, 12 November. Meets Sophia Stacey (November). Writes 'England in 1819' (December).

1820 Moves to Pisa, 29 January. *The Cenci* published (spring). Writes 'The Sensitive-Plant'. Moves to Livorno, 15 June. Writes *Letter to Maria Gisborne*, 'To a Sky-Lark', 'Ode to Liberty'. Moves to Casa Prinni in the Baths of San Giuliano, near Pisa (August). Writes *The Witch of Atlas, Swellfoot the Tyrant*, 'Ode to Naples'. *Prometheus Unbound . . . with Other Poems* published (September). Returns to Pisa, 31 October. Friendship with Emilia Viviani (from December). *Swellfoot the Tyrant* published and suppressed (December).

1821 Edward and Jane Williams arrive in Pisa (January). Writes *Epipsychidion* (January–February). Writes *A Defence of Poetry* (February–March; not published until 1840). Receives news of Keats's death, 23 February in Rome, on 11 April. *Epipsychidion* published (May). Writes *Adonais* (May–June; published in July). Travels to Ravenna to meet Byron (August). Writes *Hellas* (October). Byron moves to Pisa, 1 November.

1822 Writing *Charles the First*. Edward Trelawny arrives in Pisa, 14 January. Writes lyrical poems to Jane Williams, translations from Goethe, Calderón. *Hellas* published (February). Death of Allegra Byron in a convent, 19 April. Moves with his family and Edward and Jane Williams to Casa Magni at San Terenzo on the Bay of Spezzia, near Lerici, 30 April. Takes delivery of his boat, the *Don Juan*, at Lerici, 12 May. Writing *The Triumph of Life* (May–June). Sails to Livorno with Williams to meet Leigh Hunt, 1 July. Drowns with Williams on return voyage, 8 July. Cremated on the beach between La Spezia and Livorno, in the presence of Trelawny, Byron, and Hunt, 15 August (his ashes are interred in the Protestant Cemetery in Rome in 1823).

ABBREVIATIONS

Poems and Prose Works by Shelley

Alastor = *Alastor: or, the Spirit of Solitude*

Daemon = *The Daemon of the World*

DMAA = *Discourse on the Manners of the Ancient Athenians*

DP = *Defence of Poetry*

J&M = *Julian and Maddalo*

L&C = *Laon and Cythna; or, The Revolution of the Golden City: A Vision of the Nineteenth Century*

PU = *Prometheus Unbound*

PVR = *Philosophical View of Reform*

Q Mab = *Queen Mab*

R&H = *Rosalind and Helen. A Modern Eclogue*

RofI = *The Revolt of Islam*

TL = *The Triumph of Life*

WJ = *The Wandering Jew*

Manuscript Sources

CHPL = The Carl H. Pforzheimer Library.

Esd = The Esdaile Notebook, Carl H. Pforzheimer Library SC 372: 1810–14 (fair copies).

L&C (PM) = The copy of *L&C* with S.'s MS alterations made to transform the poem into *RofI*. This copy, once owned by H. Buxton Forman, and described by him in *The Shelley Library* (1886) pp. 83–6, is now in the Pierpont Morgan Library (W25A 37292).

SDMS = The Scrope Davis Notebook, BL Loan 70/8: 15 May–29 August 1816 (fair copies).

Nbk 1 = Bod. MS Shelley adds. e. 16: June 1816 through July 1817.

Nbk 2 = Bod. MS Shelley adds. e. 19: early April 1817.

Nbk 3 = Bod. MS Shelley adds. e. 10: May through September 1817.

Nbk 4 = Bod. MS Shelley adds. e. 14: October 1817.

Nbk 4a = Bod. MS Shelley d. 3: October 1817.

Nbk 5 = Bod. MS Shelley e. 4: November 1817 through June 1817.

Harvard Nbk 2 = Harvard MS Eng. 258.3: mainly 1817 (fair copies).

Nbk 6 = Bod. MS Shelley adds. e. 11: July 1818 through April 1819.

Nbk 7 = Bod. MS Shelley e. 1: April–May 1819.

Nbk 8 = Bod. MS Shelley e. 2: April–May 1819.

Nbk 9 = Bod. MS Shelley e. 3: April–May 1819.

Nbk 10 = HM 2177 (Huntington Library): May through September 1819.

Nbk 11 = Bod. MS Shelley adds. e. 12: various dates, mainly August 1819 through March 1820.

Harvard Nbk = Harvard MS Eng. 258.2: September 1819 through July 1820 (fair copies).

Nbk 12 = HM 2176 (Huntington Library): October 1819 through mid-January 1820.

Nbk 13 = Bod. MS Shelley adds. e. 15: late October 1819.

Nbk 14 = Bod. MS Shelley adds. e. 6: April through mid-August 1820.

Nbk 15 = Bod. MS Shelley adds. e. 9: mid-June through July 1820, and mid-November 1820 through mid-January 1821.

Nbk 16 = Bod. MS Shelley d.1: mid-August 1820 through January 1821.

Nbk 17 = Bod. MS Shelley adds. e. 8: December 1820 through March 1821.

Nbk 18 = Bod. MS Shelley adds. e. 18: April 1821, and February through April 1822.

Nbk 19 = Bod. MS Shelley adds. e. 17: May 1821 through January 1822.

Nbk 20 = Bod. MS Shelley adds. e. 20: June 1821.

Nbk 21 = Bod. MS Shelley adds. e. 7: October through December 1821.

Nbk 22 = HM 2111 (Huntington Library): December 1821 through April 1822.

Box 1 = Bod. MS Shelley adds. c. 4: various dates.

Box 2 = Bod. MS Shelley adds. c. 5: various dates.

Relation = 'Relation of the death of the family of the Cenci' in Bodleian MS Shelley adds. e. 13, pp. 1–72.

The following abbreviations designate MS collections, now dispersed, originally in the possession of H. B. Forman, C. W. Frederickson, the Gisbornes, Elizabeth Hitchener, T. J. Hogg, Leigh Hunt, Charles Madocks, Thomas Medwin, Charles Ollier, Sophia Stacey, E. J. Trelawny: *Forman MSS, Frederickson MSS, Gisborne MSS, Hitch. MSS, Hogg MSS, Hunt MSS, Madocks MSS, Medwin MSS, Ollier MSS, Stacey MSS, Trelawny MSS*.

Printed Sources

1816 = Percy Bysshe Shelley, *Alastor: or, the Spirit of Solitude, and Other Poems*, 1816.

1817 = [Anon.], *History of a Six Weeks' Tour through a Part of France, Switzerland, Germany and Holland*, 1817 [by Shelley and Mary Shelley].

1819 = Percy Bysshe Shelley, *Rosalind and Helen: A Modern Eclogue; with Other Poems*, 1819.

1820 = Percy Bysshe Shelley, *Prometheus Unbound: A Lyrical Drama in Four Acts, with Other Poems*, 1820.

1824 = Percy Bysshe Shelley, *Posthumous Poems*, 1824 [edited by Mary Shelley; edition suppressed].

1829 = *Poetical Works of Coleridge, Shelley, and Keats* (the Galignani edition), Paris 1829.

1839 = *Poetical Works*, ed. Mary Shelley, 4 vols, 1839.

1840 = *Poetical Works*, ed. Mary Shelley, 1840 [a revised one-volume edition of *1839*, dated '1840' on the title-page but actually published November 1839].

1907 = *Poetical Works*, ed. A. H. Koszul, 2 vols, 1907 (the 'Everyman' edition).

1951 = *Selected Poetry, Prose and Letters*, ed. A. S. B. Glover (the 'Nonesuch' edition), 1951.

1972 = *Complete Poetical Works*, ed. Neville Rogers [4 vols, only two published], vol. 1, 1802–13, Oxford 1972.

1975 = *Complete Poetical Works*, ed. Neville Rogers [4 vols, only two published], vol. 2, 1814–17, Oxford 1975.

Baker = Carlos Baker, *Shelley's Major Poetry: The Fabric of a Vision*, Princeton, N.J. 1948.

Barthelemy = L'Abbé Jean Jacques Barthélemy, *Travels of Anacharsis the Younger in Greece* (1788), [trans. William Beaumont] 2nd edn, 7 vols, 1794.

Bates = E. S. Bates, *A Study of Shelley's Drama The Cenci*, New York, 1908, reprinted 1969.

BSM = *The Bodleian Shelley Manuscripts* (D. H. Reiman, general editor):
   vol. 1, *Peter Bell the Third and The Triumph of Life*, ed. D. H. Reiman, 1991 (= *Box 1* and *Box 2*);
   vol. 2, *Bodleian MS Shelley adds. d. 7*, ed. Irving Massey, 1987;
   vol. 3, *Bodleian MS Shelley e. 4*, ed. Paul Dawson, 1988 (= *Nbk 5*);
   vol. 4, *Bodleian MS Shelley d. 1*, ed. E. B. Murray, 2 Parts, 1988 (= *Nbk 16*);
   vol. 5, *The Witch of Atlas Notebook: Bodleian MS Shelley adds. e. 6*, ed. Carlene Adamson, 1994 (= *Nbk 14*);
   vol. 6, *Shelley's Pisan Winter Notebook (1820–1821): Bodleian MS Shelley adds. e. 8*, ed. Carlene Adamson, 1992 (= *Nbk 17*);
   vol. 7, *'Shelley's Last Notebook': Bodleian MSS Shelley adds. e. 20 together with Bodleian MS Shelley adds. e. 15 and a related section of MS Shelley adds. c. 4*, ed. D. H. Reiman and Hélène Dworzan Reiman, 1990 (= *Nbk 13, Nbk 20* and *Box 1*);
   vol. 8, *Bodleian MS Shelley d. 3*, ed. Tatsuo Tokoo, 1988 (= *Nbk 4a*);
   vol. 9, *The Prometheus Unbound Fair Copies: Bodleian MSS Shelley e. 1, e. 2, and e. 3*, ed. Neil Fraistat, 1991 (= *Nbk 7, Nbk 8* and *Nbk 9*);
   vol. 10, *Mary Shelley's Plays and her Translation of the Cenci Story: Bodleian MSS Shelley adds. d. 2 and adds. e. 13*, ed. Betty T. Bennett and Charles E. Robinson, 1992;
   vol. 11, *The Geneva Notebook of Percy Bysshe Shelley: Bodleian MS Shelley adds. e. 16 and [part of] adds. c. 4*, ed. Michael Erkelenz, 1992 (= *Nbk 1* and *Box 1*);
   vol. 12, *Shelley's 'Charles the First' Notebook: Bodleian MS Shelley adds. e. 17*, ed. Nora Crook, 1991 (= *Nbk 19*);
   vol. 13, *Drafts for Laon and Cythna: Bodleian MSS Shelley adds. e. 14 and adds. e. 19*, ed. Tatsuo Tokoo, 1992 (= *Nbk 2* and *Nbk 4*);
   vol. 14, *Shelley's 'Devils' Notebook: Bodleian MS Shelley adds. e. 9*, ed. Paul Dawson and Timothy Webb, 1993 (= *Nbk 15*);
   vol. 15, *The Julian and Maddalo Draft Notebook: Bodleian MS Shelley adds. e. 11*, ed. Steven E. Jones, 1990 (= *Nbk 6*);

vol. 16, *The Hellas Notebook: Bodleian MS Shelley adds. e. 7*, ed. D. H. Reiman and Michael C. Neth, 1994 (= *Nbk 21*);

vol. 17, *Drafts for Laon and Cythna, Cantos v–xii: Bodleian MS Shelley adds. e. 10*, ed. Steven E. Jones, 1994 (= *Nbk 3*);

vol. 18, *The Homeric Hymns and Prometheus Drafts Notebook: Bodleian MS Shelley adds. e. 12*, ed. Nancy Moore Goslee, 1994 (= *Nbk 11*);

vol. 19, *The Faust Translation Notebook: Bodleian MS Shelley adds. e. 18*, ed. Nora Crook and Timothy Webb, 1996 (= *Nbk 18*);

vol. 20, *The Defence of Poetry Fair Copies: Bodleian MSS Shelley e. 6 and Shelley adds. d. 8*, ed. Michael O'Neill, 1994 (= *Nbk 14*);

vol. 21, *Miscellaneous Poetry, Prose, and Translations from Bodleian MS Shelley adds. c. 4*, ed. E. B. Murray, 1995 (= *Box 1*);

vol. 22, *Additional Materials in the Hand of Mary Shelley: MSS Shelley adds. c. 5 and adds. d. 6*, ed. Alan Weinberg, 2 Parts, 1997 (= *Box 2*);

vol. 23, *Indexes to The Bodleian Shelley Manuscripts, with Addenda, Corrigenda, Lists of Watermarks, and Related Bodleian Materials*, ed. Tatsuo Tokoo and B. C. Barker-Benfield, [not published yet].

Butter (1954) = Peter Butter, *Shelley's Idols of the Cave*, Edinburgh 1954.

Butter (1970) = *Shelley: Alastor, Prometheus Unbound, Adonais, and other poems*, ed. Peter Butter, 1970.

Byron L&J = *Byron's Letters and Journals*, ed. Leslie Marchand, 12 vols, 1973–82.

Byron PW = Lord Byron, *Complete Poetical Works*, ed. Jerome McGann, 5 vols, Oxford 1980–86.

Cameron (1951) = Kenneth Neill Cameron, *The Young Shelley: Genesis of a Radical* (New York 1950), 1951.

Cameron (1974) = Kenneth Neill Cameron, *Shelley: The Golden Years*, Cambridge, Mass. 1974.

Cenci (1819) = *The Cenci*, 1819.

Cenci (1821) = *The Cenci*, 1821.

Chernaik = Judith Chernaik, *The Lyrics of Shelley*, 1970.

Clairmont Correspondence = *The Clairmont Correspondence: Letters of Claire Clairmont, Charles Clairmont and Fanny Imlay Godwin*, ed. Marion Kingston Stocking, 2 vols, Baltimore, Md. 1995.

Claire Jnl = *Journals of Claire Clairmont*, ed. Marion Kingston Stocking, Cambridge, Mass. 1968.

Concordance = *A Lexical Concordance to the Poetical Works of Shelley*, compiled by F. S. Ellis, 1892 [based on *Forman 1882*].

Curran (1970) = Stuart Curran, *Shelley's 'Cenci': Scorpions Ringed with Fire*, Princeton 1970.

Curran (1975) = Stuart Curran, *Shelley's Annus Mirabilis*, San Marino, California 1975.

Darwin = Erasmus Darwin, *The Botanic Garden*, 1791 (comprising Part 1, *The Economy of Vegetation*, Part 2, *The Loves of the Plants* (1789)).

Dowden 1891 = *Poetical Works*, ed. Edward Dowden, 1891.

Dowden Life = Edward Dowden, *Life of Percy Bysshe Shelley*, 2 vols, 1886.

Enquirer = William Godwin, *The Enquirer, Reflections of Education, Manners, and Literature, in a Series of Essays*, 1797.

Esd Nbk = *The Esdaile Notebook: A Volume of Early Poems*, ed. K. N. Cameron (New York 1964), slightly revised, 1964.

Esd Poems = *The Esdaile Poems*, ed. Neville Rogers, Oxford 1966.

Eustace = J. C. Eustace, *A Classical Tour Through Italy*, 4th edn, 4 vols, 1817.

Forman 1876–7 = *Poetical Works*, ed. Harry Buxton Forman, 4 vols, 1876–77.

Forman 1880 = *Works of Percy Bysshe Shelley in Verse and Prose*, ed. Harry Buxton Forman, 8 vols, 1880.

Forman 1882 = *Poetical Works*, ed. Harry Buxton Forman, 2 vols, 1882.

Forman 1892 = *Poetical Works*, ed. Harry Buxton Forman, 5 vols (the 'Aldine' edition), 1892.

Gisborne Jnl = *Maria Gisborne and Edward E. Williams, Shelley's Friends: Their Journals and Letters*, ed. F. L. Jones, Norman, Okla. 1951.

GM = G. M. Matthews.

GM = *Gentleman's Magazine*.

Godwin Novels = *Collected Novels and Memoirs of William Godwin*, ed. Mark Philp, 8 vols, 1992.

Grabo (1930) = C. H. Grabo, *A Newton Among Poets: Shelley's Use of Science in Prometheus Unbound*, Chapel Hill, N.C. 1930.

Grabo (1935) = C. H. Grabo, *Prometheus Unbound: An Interpretation*, Chapel Hill, N.C. 1935.

Harvard Nbk (Woodberry) = *The Shelley Notebook in the Harvard College Library. Reproduced with Notes and a Postscript* by G. E. Woodberry, Cambridge, Mass. 1929 (= *Harvard Nbk*).

Hazlitt Works = William Hazlitt, *Works*, ed. P. P. Howe, 21 vols, 1930.

Hogg = Thomas Jefferson Hogg, *Life of Shelley*, 2 vols [two further volumes announced on title page but never published], 1858.

Holmes = Richard Holmes, *Shelley: The Pursuit*, 1974.

Hughes = A. M. D. Hughes, *The Nascent Mind of Shelley*, Oxford 1947.

Hughes 1820 = *Shelley: Poems Published in 1820*, ed. A. M. D. Hughes, Oxford 1910.

Hunt Autobiography = *The Autobiography of Leigh Hunt; with Reminiscences of Friends and Contemporaries*, 3 vols, 1850.

Hunt Correspondence = *The Correspondence of Leigh Hunt*, ed. [Thornton Hunt], 2 vols, 1862.

Huntington Nbks = *Notebooks of Percy Bysshe Shelley, From the Originals in the Library of W. K. Bixby*, ed. Harry Buxton Forman, 3 vols, Boston, Mass. 1911 (= *Nbk 10, Nbk 12*, and *Nbk 22*).

Hutchinson = *Complete Poetical Works*, ed. Thomas Hutchinson, Oxford 1904.

Julian = *Complete Works*, ed. R. Ingpen and W. E. Peck, 10 vols, 1926–30 (the 'Julian' edition).

KSJ = *Keats–Shelley Journal*.

KSMB = Keats–Shelley Memorial Bulletin.

L = Letters of Percy Bysshe Shelley, ed. F. L. Jones, 2 vols, Oxford 1964.

L about S = Edward Dowden, Richard Garnett, and William Michael Rossetti, *Letters about Shelley,* ed. R. S. Garnett, 1917.

Locock Ex = C. D. Locock, *An Examination of the Shelley Manuscripts in the Bodleian Library,* Oxford 1903.

Locock 1911 = Poems, ed. C. D. Locock, 2 vols, 1911.

Mac-Carthy = Denis Florence Mac-Carthy, *Shelley's Early Life,* 1872.

Mary Jnl = The Journals of Mary Shelley, ed. Paula R. Feldman and Diana Scott-Kilvert, 2 vols, Oxford 1987.

Mary Jnl (Jones) = Mary Shelley's Journal, ed. F. L. Jones, Norman, Okla. 1944.

Mary L = Letters of Mary Wollstonecraft Shelley, ed. Betty T. Bennett, 3 vols, vol. 1, 'A part of the Elect', 1980; vol. 2, 'Treading in unknown paths', 1983; vol. 3, 'What years I have spent', 1988.

Massey = I. Massey, *Posthumous Poems of Shelley,* Montreal 1969.

Medwin = Thomas Medwin, *Life of Percy Bysshe Shelley,* 2 vols, 1847.

Medwin (1913) = Thomas Medwin, *Life of Percy Bysshe Shelley* (2 vols, 1847), ed. Harry Buxton Forman, 1913.

MSW = The Novels and Selected Works of Mary Shelley (Nora Crook, general editor), 8 vols, 1996:
vol. 1, *Frankenstein,* ed. Nora Crook;
vol. 2, *Matilda, Prefaces etc.,* ed. Pamela Clemit;
vol. 3, *Valperga,* ed. Nora Crook;
vol. 4, *The Last Man,* ed. Jane Blumberg with Nora Crook;
vol. 5, *Lodore,* ed. Fiona Stafford;
vol. 6, *Perkin Warbeck,* ed. Doucet Devin Fischer;
vol. 7, *Falkner,* ed. Pamela Clemit;
vol. 8, *Travel Writing,* ed. Jeanne Moskal.

MWW = The Works of Mary Wollstonecraft, ed. Janet Todd and Marilyn Butler, 7 vols, 1989.

MYR = The Manuscripts of the Younger British Romantics: Shelley (D. H. Reiman, general editor), 8 vols:
vol. 1, *The Esdaile Notebook,* ed. D. H. Reiman, 1985 (= *Esd*);
vol. 2, *The Mask of Anarchy,* ed. D. H. Reiman, 1985;
vol. 3, *Hellas: a lyrical drama,* ed. D. H. Reiman, 1985;
vol. 4, *The Mask of Anarchy Drafts: Shelley's 1819–1820 Huntington Notebook (HM 2177),* ed. Mary A. Quinn, 1990 (= *Nbk 10*);
vol. 5, *The Harvard Shelley Manuscripts,* ed. D. H. Reiman, 1991 (= *Harvard Nbk*);
vol. 6, *Shelley's 1819–1821 Huntington Notebook (HM 2176),* ed. Mary A. Quinn, 1994 (= *Nbk 12*);
vol. 7, *Shelley's 1821–1822 Huntington Notebook (HM 2111),* ed. Mary A. Quinn, 1996 (= *Nbk 22*);
vol. 8, *Fair-Copy Holographs of Shelley's Poems in British and American Libraries,* ed. D. H. Reiman and Michael O'Neill, 1997 (includes *SDMS*).

New SL = *New Shelley Letters*, ed. W. S. Scott, 1948.

Notopoulos = James A. Notopoulos, *The Platonism of Shelley: A Study of the Poetic Mind*, Durham, N.C. 1949.

Paine Writings = *Writings of Thomas Paine*, ed. M. D. Conway, 4 vols, New York 1894–96.

Peacock Works = *The Works of Thomas Love Peacock*, ed. H. F. B. Brett-Smith and C. E. Jones, 10 vols, 1924–34.

Peck = Walter Edwin Peck, *Shelley, His Life and Work*, 2 vols, Boston, Mass. 1927.

PFMN = Percy Bysshe Shelley, *Posthumous Fragments of Margaret Nicholson*, Oxford 1810.

Political Justice = William Godwin, *Enquiry Concerning Political Justice* (1793) 3rd edn 1797, ed. F. E. L. Priestley, 3 vols, Toronto 1946.

Prose = *Shelley's Prose; or, The Trumpet of a Prophecy*, ed. David Lee Clark (Albuquerque 1954), corrected edition Albuquerque 1966.

Prose Works = *The Prose Works of Percy Bysshe Shelley*, vol. 1, ed. E. B. Murray, Oxford 1993.

Recollections = E. J. Trelawny, *Recollections of the Last Days of Shelley and Byron*, 1858.

Records = E. J. Trelawny, *Records of Shelley, Byron and the Author*, 2 vols, 1878.

Reiman (1969) = D. H. Reiman, *Percy Bysshe Shelley*, New York 1969.

Reiman (1977) = *Shelley's Poetry and Prose*, ed. D. H. Reiman and Sharon B. Powers, 1977.

Relics = *Relics of Shelley*, ed. R. Garnett, 1862.

Ricci = C. Ricci, *Beatrice Cenci*, 2 vols, Milan, 1923.

Ricci (1926) = C. Ricci, *Beatrice Cenci*, trans. M. Bishop and H. L. Stuart, 2 vols, 1926.

Robinson = Charles H. Robinson, *Shelley and Byron: The Snake and Eagle Wreathed in Fight*, 1976.

Rogers = Neville Rogers, *Shelley at Work: A Critical Inquiry*, Oxford 1956.

Rognoni = *Shelley: Opere*, trans. and ed. Francesco Rognoni, Turin 1995.

Rossetti 1870 = *Poetical Works*, ed. W. M. Rossetti, 2 vols, 1870.

Rossetti 1878 = *Poetical Works*, ed. W. M. Rossetti, 3 vols, 1878.

Ruins = Constantin-François Chasseboeuf, Comte de Volney, *Les Ruines, ou Méditations sur les Revolutions des Empires* (Paris 1791) [there were many English editions; references are to chapters, and quotations are from the English translation of 1796].

S in Eng = R. Ingpen, *Shelley in England: New Facts and Letters from the Shelley–Whitton Papers*, 1917.

S Memorials = *Shelley Memorials*, ed. Lady Jane Shelley [and R. Garnett], 1859.

SC = *Shelley and his Circle 1773–1822* (an edition of the manuscripts of Shelley and others in The Carl H. Pforzheimer Library), ed. K. N. Cameron (vols 1–4, Cambridge, Mass. 1961–70), D. H. Reiman (vols 5–8, Cambridge, Mass. 1973–86). SC followed by a number = the Pforzheimer's classification of a manuscript in its collection.

Shelley Revalued = *Shelley Revalued: Essays from the Gregynog Conference*, ed. Kelvin Everest, Leicester 1983.

Shelley's Guitar = B. C. Barker-Benfield, *Shelley's Guitar: an Exhibition of Manuscripts, First Editions and Relics, to Mark the Bicentenary of the Birth of Percy Bysshe Shelley*, Oxford 1992.

Shepherd 1871–5 = *Poetical Works*, ed. R. H. Shepherd, 4 vols, 1871–75.

St Irvyne = Percy Bysshe Shelley, *St Irvyne or The Rosicrucian*, 1811.

Système de la Nature = Baron D'Holbach, *Système de la Nature* (Paris 1770; attributed to Mirabaud), 1774 edition.

Taylor = C. H. Taylor, *The Early Collected Editions of Shelley's Poems*, New Haven, Conn. 1958.

TL (Reiman) = D. H. Reiman, *Shelley's 'The Triumph of Life': A Critical Study based on a Text Newly Edited from the Bodleian MS*, Urbana, Ill. 1965.

TL (GM) = 'The Triumph of Life: a New Text', ed. G. M. Matthews, *Studia Neophilologica*, xxxii (1960).

Unextinguished Hearth = *The Unextinguished Hearth: Shelley and His Contemporary Critics*, ed. Newman Ivey White, Durham, N.C. 1938.

V&C = *Original Poetry by Victor and Cazire*, Worthing 1810 [by Shelley and his sister Elizabeth].

V&C (1898) = *Original Poetry by Victor and Cazire* (Worthing 1810), ed. Richard Garnett, 1898.

V&P = *Verse and Prose from the Manuscripts of Shelley*, ed. J. C. E. Shelley-Rolls and R. Ingpen, 1934.

Walker = Adam Walker, *A System of Familiar Philosophy*, 1799.

Wasserman = Earl R. Wasserman, *Shelley: A Critical Reading*, Baltimore, Md. 1971.

Webb = Timothy Webb, *The Violet in the Crucible: Shelley and Translation*, Oxford 1976.

White = Newman Ivey White, *Shelley*, 2 vols, New York 1940.

Woodberry 1893 = *Complete Poetical Works*, ed. G. E. Woodberry, 4 vols (Boston, Mass. 1892), 1893.

Woodberry (1909) = *The Cenci*, ed. G. E. Woodberry, Boston, Mass. 1909.

Zillman Text = *Shelley's Prometheus Unbound: The Text and the Drafts*, ed. L. J. Zillman, 1968.

Zillman Variorum = *Shelley's Prometheus Unbound: A Variorum Edition*, ed. L. J. Zillman, Seattle, Wash. 1959.

THE POEMS

142
'Frail clouds arrayed in sunlight lose the glory'

Edited by Jack Donovan *

The drafts for the first two cantos of *L&C* (I i–xxv, lix–lx; II i–xxxvii) in *Nbk 2* begin with a sequence of stanzas, numbered 1 to 8 and occupying pp. 4 to 8, which S. apparently intended to serve as a meditative opening to the poem but which he did not include in final version. Excepting the fifth and eighth stanzas, which show much cancellation and revision, as if drafted directly into the nbk, the copy is comparatively clean and looks like a transcription from an earlier draft. The manuscript presents no major problem, apart from the few doubtful readings that remain here and there, up to the end of stanza 7 which reaches the bottom of page 7. On page 8 it becomes confused and S.'s intentions a puzzle that requires some working out.

At the top of the page the first three lines of a stanza numbered 8 are roughly drafted:

> Even as my soul is [   ] in the hope
> Of overshadowing power I rest the time
> Of my young [   ] beneath the cope

The lines then break off, the middle of the page is left blank, and the rest filled with a draft, as far as line 6, of the stanza which was to become the first of Canto I in the finished poem, under the number 9, which is cancelled. The first three (partially-drafted) lines of this stanza are also cancelled – and were later discarded – but from line 4 onward the manuscript conforms fairly closely to Canto I in the poem as printed until it stops abruptly at stanza xxv 3. Both the fragmentary stanzas, numbered 8 and 9, S. would seem to have copied with minor alterations from a loose sheet, now in *Box 1* (C 4, f. 2v), where they are numbered 7 and 8 and where a similar gap is left between them. The new numbering in *Nbk 2* (8 and 9) would be accounted for if, as seems likely, he had added the heavily-revised stanza 5 as he transcribed the others. In the space left between the fragmentary stanzas on p. 8, together with some miscellaneous notes, 'Canto I' is pencilled in, evidently signalling an intention to change the manner of the poem's beginning to the abrupt onset of vision that was ultimately adopted. Though it is probable that S. at first wished to preserve the stanzas that occur before his pencilled note as an overture to the narrative in the manner of *Alastor* 1–49, with which they show detailed similarities of thought and language, his plan can only be regarded as fluid at this very early stage of composition. Neither the Preface nor the Dedication, both of which take up the theme of inspiration that is explored here, had yet been written;

* For help with various problems Jack Donovan would like to thank Jacques Berthoud, John Birt-whistle, Greg Dart, Stephen Minta, John Pickles, John Walker, P. G. Walsh, Timothy Webb and David Duff. The Leverhulme Trust granted a fellowship which provided relief from teaching and administrative duties in the autumn term 1997.

3

when they were finished, there would have been some redundancy in retaining the opening that he had initially drafted.

So much seems clear. At some later moment, however, S. turned the nbk and wrote at 90 degrees across the page the first seven and a half lines of an unnumbered stanza (the eighth in the text given below) over the pencilled notes and the three lines of draft numbered 8 which are quoted above. *V&P* and *1975* print this stanza as though S. had meant it to take the place of the part-drafted stanza 8 in the series, and their editorial decision may be the correct one in the circumstances. It is followed here, though not without some hesitation, because of the difficulty of inferring S.'s intentions from the uncertain state of the manuscript. The position of the stanza in the nbk, written as it is across the first attempt at an eighth stanza, would seem to argue for including it as S.'s preferred continuation of the poem at this point. On the other hand, the fact that he numbered '11' the first full stanza (corresponding to I ii in the finished poem) on the next page (9) suggests rather that he planned, at least initially, to complete and include *all three* of the stanzas left unfinished on p. 8. Against regarding it as part of the sequence at all is its grammatical shift to a narrative mode using the first person and preterite when the seven previous stanzas form a continuous reflection largely in the present tense and adopt the first person only occasionally, without establishing a developed authorial 'I'. An explanation for the changed person and tense, not in itself implausible, might be that the two efforts at drafting an eighth stanza, and the condition of page 8 generally, represent S.'s tentative endeavours to effect a transition between the meditation of stanzas 1–7 and the first-person narrative of the vision that he had decided to have follow on from it. But there is a further complication to be considered.

The crossways stanza, which is written in a darker ink and with a differently-cut pen than the rest of the page, S. completed and included with minor alterations in the first edition of the poem as stanza xx of Canto II. Between the stanzas, consecutive in the draft, that were to become II xix and II xxi, he wrote in *Nbk 2* (p. 63) 'a stanza to be inserted'. He may then have decided to adopt the already-drafted crossways stanza from the original opening sequence. But the possibility that he happened to use the blank middle of p. 8 simply as an available space to draft the stanza required to become II xx before transcribing fair copy for Canto II cannot be excluded. Certainly its narrative mode is more appropriate to its final home in Canto II, Laon's autobiography recounted in the first person and in the preterite, than it is to the original beginning, though it has to be remarked that there are several other blank spaces in the nbk nearer to p. 63 than p. 8, in any of which the extra stanza might have been drafted. A firm decision between the alternatives seems precluded, as conjecture from a manuscript in so incoherent a state, reflecting a phase of composition when the author's designs were still forming, can be no more than provisional. On balance it has seemed better to include the crossways stanza as the final one of the rejected opening, though subject to the reservations expressed above.

The prelude to *L&C* formed by the present stanzas develops a theory of inspiration which S. entertained through the greater part of his writing life and which he had already articulated as an invocation in *Alastor* 1–49 and as a secular prayer in *Hymn to Intellectual Beauty*. All three instances rest upon the persuasion that human power for good, and pre-eminently the creation of poetry of enduring greatness, results from the intervention of a Spirit that selects the human instruments of its purposes as it wills and whose operations are as discontinuous as the appearances of nature and as unstable as human thought and feeling. In the present meditation S. lays particular stress upon the exemplary literary masterpieces of the past which, themselves the product of such cosmic–human intercourse, constitute both a secondary source of inspiration and an ideal audience for the poet who creates after their example. The identity of the 'mighty dead' (line 59) who have kindled these 'lamps of mind' (line 37), is not specified, though the name Homer is cancelled in the draft of the stanza which is here numbered 8; his example was to be later cited in the Preface, which elaborates upon the relation of the poet to his predecessors, together with those of Lucretius, Spenser, Shakespeare and Milton, among others. S. makes his fullest statement of this intuitive and animistic conception of genius, which is one of the foundation-ideas of his poetics, in a religious context. His unfinished essay 'On Christianity', which he did not publish but which has been dated to the period in mid to late 1817 when he was composing and revising *L&C* (*Prose Works* 460–1), provides this gloss on the beatitude 'Blessed are the pure in heart: for they shall see God' (Matthew v 8):

We live and move and think, but we are not the creators of our own origin and existence, we are not the arbiters of every motion of our own complicated nature, we are not the masters of our own imaginations and moods of mental being . . There is a power by which we are surrounded, like the atmosphere in which some motionless lyre is suspended, which visits with its breath our silent chords, at will. Our most imperial and stupendous qualities, those on which the majesty and power of humanity is erected are, relatively to the inferiour portion of its mechanism indeed active and imperial; but they are the passive slaves of some higher and more omnipresent Power. This power is God. And those who have seen God, have, in the periods of their purer and more perfect nature, been harmonized by their own will, to so exquisite a consentaneity of powers, as to give forth divinest melody when the breath of universal being sweeps over their frame. (*Prose Works* 251–2)

S. may have sensed the incompatibility between such a conception of the inner life and human creativity in relation to the unforeseeable visitings of divinity, clearly implied in stanzas 3 and 4, and the dualistic cosmology and psychology which are expounded in *L&C* I xxv–xxxiv, which would have provided another reason not to include the present self-reflexive overture. At least not in the form in which he had first written it; for several of its major themes and images do appear at various points in *L&C*. As composition advanced, S. would seem to have decided to absorb them into other parts of the poem: some can be found in the Dedication and in the autobiography of the young Laon, who is himself a poet, in Canto II; while others make up part of S.'s own autobiography as poet in the Preface. But not all is accounted for in this way. The unadopted opening, though left in a decidedly unfinished state, retains considerable interest in its own right, as well as displaying S.'s earliest attempt at representing the grand movements of inspiration appropriate to the epic project of *L&C*.

Wasserman 186–90 provides a reading of the first six stanzas as an example of S.'s continuing efforts to develop his 'intellectual philosophy'.

Text from *Nbk 2* pp. 4–8; slight alterations and additions have been made to MS punctuation. Published in *V&P* 17–20; *1975* 268–70; *Wasserman* 186–8 (stanzas 1–6 only); *BSM* xiii 13–21 (facsimile and transcription).

142
'Frail clouds arrayed in sunlight lose the glory'

1

Frail clouds arrayed in sunlight lose the glory
Which they reflect on Earth — they burn and die
Revive and change like genius, and when hoary
They streak the sunless air, then suddenly
5 If the white moon shine forth, their shadows lie
Like woven pearl beneath its beams — each tone
Of the many-voicèd forest doth reply
To symphonies diviner than its own
Then falls and fades, — like thought when power is past and gone.

2

10 The hues of Sea and Sky, and Moon and Sun —
The music of the desert and the deep
Are dark or silent — have their changes run
Thus soon? or, pale enthusiast, dost thou weep
Because all things that change and wake and sleep

1–6. S.'s substitution of 'sunless' for 'twilight' in line 4 can obscure the fact that these lines describe the dramatic changes in the appearance of clouds between sunset and moonrise, a moment habitually associated with inspiration in his poetry.

1. glory] splendour, magnificence.

2. reflect on Earth] *reflect* here signifies 'throw down upon' rather than 'return an image to'. Cp. T. L. Peacock's *Melincourt* (1817) xix: 'the clouds over-head spreading, like an uniform veil of network, through the interstices of which the sky was visible, caught in their turn the radiance [of sunset], and reflected it on the lake'.

4. sunless] twilight *canc.*

> many voiced   doth
7. 'Of the ~~many voiced~~ forest's ~~many voiced depths~~ reply' *Nbk 2* 4. S. must have forgotten to alter 'forest's' to 'forest' when he cancelled 'many voiced depths' and restored his original 'many voiced' above the line.

10. Moon] moon *Nbk 2* 4.

13. enthusiast] In S.'s day the word denoted one given to excess of religious exaltation or political zeal, as well as its sense here: 'one carried away by ardent imagination' (*Concordance*). The lone enthusiast strolling in a rural scene, usually at sunset, and peopling fields and sky with 'romantic' visions was a commonplace in late eighteenth- and early nineteenth-century poetry which S. had appropriated in *Q Mab* i 46–9: 'the wondrous strain / That round a lonely ruin swells, / Which, wandering on the echoing shore, / The enthusiast hears at evening'. Cp. J. Beattie, *The Minstrel* (Bk I 1771, Bk II 1774) I liii–liv; T. L. Peacock, *The Genius of the Thames* (1810, 2nd edn 1812) ii 248–59 (1812). S. introduces the figure in this stanza to enforce a critical distinction between the fanciful animation of nature by one's own desires and the inspiration of genius which results from the divine possession described in stanzas 3–4.

6

15 Tell thine own story? like the altered glance
   Of a dear friend are they? — like thoughts that keep
   Their dwelling in a dying countenance
   Or like the thronging shapes of some tempestuous trance?

3

   There is a Power whose passive instrument
20 Our nature is — a Spirit that with motion
   Invisible and swift its breath hath sent
   Amongst us, like the wind on the wide Ocean —
   Around whose path though tumult and commotion
   Throng fast — deep calm doth follow, and precedeth.
25 This Spirit, chained by some remote devotion,
   Our choice or will demandeth not nor heedeth
   But for its hymns doth touch the human souls it needeth.

4

   All that we know or seek, our loves and hopes,
   Those sweet and subtle thoughts that do entwine
30 Swift gleamings with the shade that interlopes
   Between their visitings, we may repine
   To lose; but they will pass — thou must resign
   Joy, hope, love, power and life when that which gave
   The Shadow and the God, has need of thine,
35 Abandoning thee; then no mercy crave
   But bow thyself in dust, take shelter in the grave.

---

18. shapes] shapes was written first; it is underlined in pencil; 'dreams' is written below the line, cancelled in ink and underlined twice in pencil (*Nbk 2* 5). S. may not have decided finally between them. *tempestuous]* tumultuous *canc.*

19. passive] subtle *canc. Nbk 2* 5.

25. chained by some remote devotion] In the service of, controlled by a (divine) force both far-off and inscrutable. The stanza is rather a statement of faith than a metaphysical argument, in which both *Power* and *Spirit* seem to designate a divine presence whose breath (Latin *spiritus*) appears unpredictably, like the wind, to act upon man but which is itself subject to direction from beyond the realm of human action. Cp. 'One word is too often profaned' (1821) 15–16: 'The devotion to something afar / From the sphere of our sorrow'.

28. All that we know or seek] Our purposes & fears *canc. Nbk 2* 5.

32–6. The syntax of these lines is awkward and the meaning less than perfectly clear. The sense appears to be: When the (remote) Power which, in inspiring man also actuates what he can experience of the divine, selects you for its instrument you must submit all, even life itself, to its demand. Your individuality must be sacrificed when your vitality is required for a purpose beyond your ken.

33. Joy, hope, love, power and life] All that is not thine own *canc. Nbk 2* 6.

7

5

The lamps of mind which make this night of earth
So beautiful, were kindled thus of yore. —
All streams of mortal hope hence drew their birth,
40 Those lyres of ancient song which evermore
Through silent years their kindling music pour
Have thus been fed with sweetness; mighty lyres
Whose sounds awaken thoughts that sleep no more
Which that immortal Spirit, which respires
45 In visioned rest, has breathed upon their silent wires.

6

It is not then presumption if I watch
In expectation's mute and breathless mood
Till it descend — may not the fountain catch
Hues from the green leaves and the daylight wood
50 Even if blank darkness must descend and brood
Upon its waves? — each human phantasy
Hath such sweet visions in the solitude
Of thought, that this drear world like heaven would be
Could words invest such dreams with immortality.

7

55 A colourless and shapeless mist that hovers
Over the morning's birth — a vale outspread
Beneath the gathering rainbow — gloom that covers

---

37. which make this night of earth] which in the hope of man *canc. Nbk 2 6.*

39. mortal hope] living joy *canc. Nbk 2 6.*

40–5. Cp. *Alastor* 41–9; and 143 Appendix: A: 'We are lyres'.

41. Through silent years] To listening worlds *canc. Nbk 2 6.*

45. visioned] Stored with visions. In S.'s poetry the word typically signifies intense imaginings of desired ideals, as in *Q Mab* i 68–73; *Alastor* 681–2; *Hymn to Intellectual Beauty* 64–7; *L&C* 3562–7.

51. phantasy] S. regularly uses the word in the sense, close to that of 'visioned' in line 45 (see previous note), of a mental image of a wished-for good; e.g. in *J&M* 446; *Epipsychidion* 165.

53–4. Cp. *Hymn to Intellectual Beauty* 39–41.

53. this drear world] human life *uncanc. Nbk 2 7*; 'this drear world' is written above the line as if S. had intended to substitute it for 'human life', which is uncancelled, in order to avoid repeating *human* so soon after line 51. But as neither phrase is cancelled, no confident choice between them can be made.

54. invest such dreams with immortality] clothe such sweet thought with their eternity *canc. Nbk 2 7.*

The widely-glancing meteor, ere 'tis sped —
Such is the splendour of the mighty dead;
60   Such, and no more, is living man — yet One
Seeks ere the doubtful paths of death he tread,
If love and truth be not forever gone,
To melodize one song to them and them alone.

8

With deathless minds, which leave when they have ?[passed]
65   A path of light, my soul communion knew,
Till from that ceaseless intercourse at last
As from a mine of magic store I drew
Words which were weapons; round my heart there grew
The adamantine armour of their power
70   And from my fancy wings of golden hue
Sprang forth, whose [

58. *widely-glancing*] Flashing across a broad expanse of sky.

61. This line is drafted in two other places in *Nbk 2*: 'Seeks ere the shadowy paths of death he tread' (2); 'Seeks ere the doubtful future's path he tread' (inside of back cover). See note to *L&C* 89–90.

63. *them alone*] ?[thee] ?[alone] *BSM xiii* 19. The much-cancelled and untidy draft of this line renders the final two words very difficult to decipher. The reading 'them alone' is supported by another draft of the passage in *Nbk 2 2* which ends with the line: 'To melodize one strain which shall be thiers [sic] alone'. S. would appear to be revising the earlier draft at lines 61–3 of this one.

64. *minds*] words *BSM xiii* 21. Just above and to the left of this line, of which three other attempts are cancelled in *Nbk 2 8*, is the cancelled name 'Homer'.

67. *mine*] The draft reads 'mind', the 'd' written clearly over an 'e'. Earlier on the page S. cancelled the phrase, 'As from a mine of magic power'; and in *L&C* II xx, where he later inserted a completed version of the stanza, he restored the reading 'mine', which is adopted here. Cp. *L&C* 40–2.

143
Laon and Cythna[*]

Edited by Jack Donovan[†]

Composition and Publication

In March 1817 S. took up residence in Albion House, Great Marlow, Buckinghamshire where he lived until February 1818 with Mary (his wife since the previous December), their one-year-old son William and, from her birth on 2 September, their daughter Clara. For most of this period Mary's step-sister Clare Clairmont and Alba (later Allegra), Clare's infant child by Byron, also made part of the household. Thomas Love Peacock was a close neighbour and regular visitor. Leigh Hunt and his family stayed at Albion House from 10 April until 25 June, Hunt continuing to act as editor of the liberal weekly *The Examiner* during this time. From the home of Peacock and his mother, where the Shelleys were guests while preparing to enter their own, Mary had written on 2 March to Hunt: 'Our house is very political as well as poetical and I hope you will acquire a fresh spirit for both when you come here' (*Mary L* i 29). It was among this circle of friends and working writers and in an atmosphere of anxious concern over public affairs, widely perceived to be in crisis over the question of parliamentary reform, that the epic romance *L&C* was composed in draft through the spring, summer and early autumn. Finished, transcribed, and seen through the press by about mid-November, it was on sale at the beginning of December. This is not a long period of time to spend on a poem of its length (4818 lines) and claims to high seriousness of purpose; to bring it to completion strenuous effort had to be kept up right through a season of intense imaginative creation which was, moreover, continually marked by the stress of personal adversity. Both S.'s first wife Harriet and Mary's half-sister Fanny had committed suicide the previous autumn. At the end of March S. was deprived as morally unfit of the custody of the two children of his first marriage, while in late June/early July his exertions were clouded with foreboding by a recurrence of what were feared to be consumptive symptoms (*L&C* lines 89–90 and note). Replying on 11 December to a letter from his father-in-law Godwin, to whom a copy of *L&C* had been sent as soon as printing was finished, and who had returned 'admonitions' and 'censures', S. recalled the apprehensions he had experienced during the writing:

---

[*] *The poem has more usually been known by its revised title* The Revolt of Islam: *see pp. 15–17 and note on the full title, p. 31.*

[†] *For help with various problems Jack Donovan would like to thank Jacques Berthoud, John Birtwhistle, Greg Dart, Stephen Minta, John Pickles, John Walker, P. G. Walsh, Timothy Webb and David Duff. The Leverhulme Trust granted a fellowship which provided relief from teaching and administrative duties in the autumn term 1997.*

The Poem was produced by a series of thoughts which filled my mind with an unbounded & sustained enthusiasm. I felt the precariousness of my life, & I engaged in this task resolved to leave some record of myself. Much of what the volume contains was written with the same feeling, as real, though not so prophetic, as the communications of a dying man. I never presumed indeed to consider it anything approaching to faultless, but when I considered contemporary productions of the same apparent pretensions, I will own that I was filled with confidence. (*L* i 577)

The personal urgency and the writer's self-assurance were attended by keen anxiety that *L&C*, a heroic poem boldly assuming a prophetic stance at a moment of national emergency, should attract the readers that S.'s earlier works had failed to find: 'I have the fairest chance of the public approaching my work with unbiassed and unperverted feeling; the fruit of reputation (and you know for *what purposes* I value it) is within my reach', he wrote to his publisher Charles Ollier in December (*L* i 580). Another circumstance must have further sharpened the urgency with which he wrote. S.'s cousin Thomas Medwin remembered: 'Shelley told me that he and Keats had mutually agreed, in the same given time, (six months each,) to write a long poem, and that the *Endymion*, and *Revolt of Islam* [as *Laon and Cythna* was entitled after being withdrawn and reissued: see below p. 16] were the fruits of this rivalry' (*Medwin (1913)* 178–9). It may be in private acknowledgement of this friendly competition with Keats – it is surely out of the anxiety expressed to Ollier and Godwin – that, in the Preface to *L&C*, S. duly forewarns his readers that the 300-page octavo volume he is introducing had been written rapidly: 'The Poem now presented to the Public occupied little more than six months in the composition'; a few lines later he varies the time slightly: 'the mere composition occupied no more than six months'. When considered together with two other pieces of evidence, S.'s statement appears to fix the dates of this six-month period quite precisely. Mary entered in her jnl for 29 September 1817: 'S. finishes his poem and goes up to town with Clare Teusday [sic] 23' (*Mary Jnl* i 180). The next day S. wrote from Leigh Hunt's in Paddington to Byron in Venice: 'I have completed a poem which, when it is finished, though I do not tax your patience to read it, I will send you' (*L* i 557). Taking the discrepancy in the Preface between 'little more than' and 'no more than' as an indication that S. is not counting to the day – and allowing, on the more generous of his calculations, perhaps a week or so beyond six months – a date around the middle of March 1817 would be the earliest that he could have begun to write the poem. Composition would then have started within a few days of the Shelleys' taking possession of Albion House on 18 March (*Mary Jnl* i 166).

Although the period during which the poem was written can be, and has traditionally been, thus closely determined, some notations in *Nbk 2*, apparently an early calendar of composition, need also to be considered. On the first complete page of the nbk, which contains drafts for *L&C* Cantos I and II, S. wrote in a vertical column: 'April 4–May–June–July–August 4'. 4 August 1817 would be his twenty-fifth birthday, and it may be that at this early stage he aimed to complete the poem which he described in the Preface as 'my first serious appeal to the Public' on that anniversary. Above and to the right of the column of months a series of figures begins with 5 and descends by doubling the figure until the number 320 is reached opposite the centre of the column of months. The figure 320 is multiplied, above and to the left of the dates, by 9 (the number of lines in the Spenserian stanza in which the poem is written) to give the total 2880; while below this figure the number 120, the approximate number of days in the 4 April–4 August span, is enclosed in a box. Other faint calculations in pencil would indicate that S. returned to this page at points later in the composition to record his progress. From these dates and figures it could be conjectured that S. originally, or at some early stage, planned that *L&C* should comprise 320 Spenserian stanzas and be finished on his twenty-fifth birthday. The conjecture seems to be supported by a letter addressed to Leigh Hunt in London written on the eve of that birthday, 3 August, and which contains – perhaps prompted by the date – the only reference in S.'s surviving correspondence to *L&C* in the course of its composition: 'I have arrived at the 380th stanza of my Poem' (*L* i 551). On the hypothesis of 320 projected stanzas *L&C* would have grown as it was written well beyond the original estimate to its final length (including the Dedication) of 525 stanzas; and when the interpolated ode of Canto V and the three extra lines of V li are added, the final line-count of 4818 would augment the estimate in *Nbk 2* by nearly 40 per cent. It may well be that S. had already begun *L&C* when he set down the 4 April–4 August scheme. Could he have begun to compose on 4 April, intending to bring the work to completion in four months which were prolonged to six? Possibly, if by 'composition' in the Preface he means to include the not inconsiderable labour required to transcribe a fair copy from the frequently untidy and sometimes incomplete drafts in his working nbks. This would extend the period of composition of just over six months as far as mid-October. Mary's jnl entry for Sunday 12 October, covering the weekend from the preceding Friday, 'S. transcribes his poem' (*Mary Jnl* i 181), could well refer to *L&C*. But, as it seems probable that the work of transcription continued even beyond that date (*SC* v 187–9; vii 74–80), and since both Mary's jnl entry and S.'s letter to Byron evidently regard 23 September as bringing the writing, as opposed to the finishing and transcribing, to a distinct term, mid-to-late March rather than early April must be regarded as the more likely beginning of composition.

S. wrote his poem – frequently out of doors, sometimes while on the water in his boat – in a series of nbks. Four of them, now held in the Bodleian Library, contain almost all the extensive surviving drafts. Facsimiles, transcriptions and codicological analyses of the MSS are provided in *BSM* xiii (*Nbks 2* and *4*), *BSM* xvii (*Nbk 3*), *BSM* viii (*Nbk 4a*). In order of composition, the contents of the nbks are as follows. *Nbk 2* comprises drafts for: 1. the rejected opening to the poem in seven stanzas and part of an eighth (see no. 142 and headnote); 2. Canto I i–xxv line 3 and lix–lx, these last two stanzas having been initially intended as the first two of Canto II; and 3. Canto II i–xxxvii, line 5, continuing to line 6 when the loose sheet Bodleian MS Shelley Adds *c*. 4 (fol. 185v) is restored to its original position in the nbk (*BSM* xiii 158–9). On another loose sheet (Bodleian MS Shelley adds. *c*. 4 folio 2) are incomplete drafts, perhaps first drafts, for Canto I i–iii (see headnote to no. 142 and facsimile in *BSM* xiii 168–71). It seems likely that the drafts for Canto II xxxvii line 7 to Canto V xviii were made in a nbk now lost: see *SC* v 149. *Nbk 3* includes drafts for Canto V xix to Canto XII xxxi, line 3. Drafts for the Dedication and for Canto X xlvii are contained in *Nbk 4*. Finally, *Nbk 4a* contains the MS, originally a set of loose sheets, of what appears to be both first draft and printer's copy for the Preface: see the description in *BSM* viii, pp. xii–xiv.

By comparison, relatively little fair copy for *L&C* has survived, in fragments held in various libraries, chiefly the Bodleian. All those portions that have come to light are given in facsimile with transcription in *BSM* viii. Apart from the printer's copy for the Dedication lines 1–20 and 95–126, the extant fair copy is from Cantos I and IX. The fragments of Canto I, from an intermediate fair copy, comprise lines 151–209 (transcription and analysis of 151–71 in *SC* v 170–82), 241–97, 298–301, 313–15, 327–491, 518–652 (transcription and analysis of 573–99 in *SC* vii 74–6, 79–80). The fragments of Canto IX, which almost certainly served as printer's copy, include the following lines: 3469–517, 3546–71, 3599–726 (lines 3469–91 are transcribed and analysed in *SC* vii 76–80; lines 3625–74 in *SC* v 182–9).

For further consideration of the MSS, see the introduction and commentaries in the three *BSM* volumes cited above, as well as: *Locock Ex*; *V&P* 12–23, 142–3; *1975* xi–xxi, 360–77; Benjamin W. Griffith, Jr., 'The Writing of the *Revolt of Islam*: a Study of Percy Bysshe Shelley's Methods of Composition' (unpublished dissertation, Northwestern University 1952); Donald J. Ryan, 'Percy Bysshe Shelley's "Laon and Cythna": a Critical Edition of the Manuscripts in the Bodleian Library' (unpublished dissertation, New York University 1972); Claude C. Brew, *Shelley and Mary in 1817: The "Dedication" of The Revolt of Islam* (1971); *SC* v 141–89; vii 74–80; *Shelley's Guitar* (Catalogue of the Bicentennial Shelley Exhibition at the Bodleian Library by Bruce Barker-Benfield, 1992), 80–6. See also the headnotes to poems 132, 133, 134, and 137 in volume I of this edition which are edited from the *L&C* nbks listed above, as well as *143 Appendix*.

The surviving MSS, S.'s letters, and MWS's letters and jnl provide few indications as to the rhythm at which the writing of *L&C* proceeded. The rough draft of two lines evidently intended for Canto VI xlv on a letter from Godwin dated 27 June (W. St. Clair, *The Godwins and the Shelleys* (1989) 429) suggests that S. had probably composed to that point by about the end of the month. The letter to Hunt of 3 August in which he says that he has reached the 380th stanza has already been noted: calculating the number of stanzas S. had actually drafted by that date is complicated by the order in which he drafted them. He began a numbered sequence in *Nbk 2* with seven stanzas and most of an eighth, later rejecting the first seven and incorporating the eighth into Canto II of the poem (no. 142 and headnote). That sequence continues until the beginning of what was to become stanza xxv of Canto I when the draft breaks off just as the Woman Guide is about to recount the cosmic events that accompanied the emergence of divinity from chaos and expound their significance for the course of history. The moment is of central importance for the coherence of the mythic dimension of *L&C*, and it would seem that S. had not yet decided how he should proceed with it. He would not return to the topic until the poem was nearly complete.

From a consideration of S.'s occasional calculations of completed stanzas in *Nbk 2* and *Nbk 3*, Donald Reiman (*SC* v 150) demonstrates that as late as page 186 of *Nbk 3*, almost at the end of Canto XI, S. had probably not drafted the remaining stanzas of Canto I. It is probable that he waited to do so until he had completed Canto XII, in the latter part of which Laon, Cythna and Cythna's child journey in a boat to the temple of the Spirit, the equivalent voyage to the one taken by the narrator in Canto I stanzas xxiii–li. Pencilled calculations on page 39 of *Nbk 2* tend to confirm this evidence. The page is one of a series carrying drafts, sketches and notes between the interrupted Canto I and the beginning of Canto II, a point to which S. needed to return to pick up the thread of Canto I where he had left it. Here he has added the number 460 (corresponding to Canto XII xxxviii, three stanzas from the end of the poem) to 30 (apparently the number, or approximate number, of stanzas he had by then decided to use among the 35 drafted or partially drafted for Canto I in *Nbk 2*) and multiplied the total by the nine lines of a stanza, suggesting that he had not yet begun the missing portion of Canto I although the draft of Canto XII was all but complete. Having broken off composition at I xxv, S. turned forward several pages in *Nbk 2* and began Canto II with two stanzas, which he later incorporated as stanzas lix–lx in Canto I, numbering them in a new series from 1. If the 380th stanza mentioned in the letter to Hunt is the 380th in the new series, it would be stanza xxix of Canto X (the page bearing it is torn from *Nbk 3*); if S. is including in his count 30 of the already-drafted stanzas of Canto I, then he had arrived at stanza xxxv of Canto IX. This seems the likelier possibility as there would be no reason to leave out of the reckoning he makes to Hunt stanzas which he had drafted and which he includes in his total in the nbk. On either calculation some three-quarters of the poem had been drafted by 3 August.

Having gone to London on 23 September, S. remained to consult the physician Dr William Lawrence (*Mary L* i 41) and to try to arrange loans for himself and for Godwin (*L* i 560–2), as well as to correct proofs for *Frankenstein*, then being printed. Arrested for debt and detained for two days (note to *L&C* line 69), on 10 October he returned to Marlow where during the weekend he was transcribing 'his poem', which seems likely to have been *L&C* (*Mary Jnl* i 181). Back in London on Monday the 13th, he wrote from Hunt's to a publisher: 'I send you the 4 first sheets of my Poem, entitled "Laon & Cythna, or the Revolution of the Golden City"' (*L* i 563). Since S. suggests in the letter that the sample of the poem should be sent to Thomas Moore, the publisher he adresses could have been Longman & Company who had published Moore's *Lalla Rookh* in May of that year, or Sherwood, Neely and Jones who became co-publishers of *L&C*, or perhaps Taylor and Hessey (*SC* vi 533, *Shelley Revalued* 191). The first four printed sheets, or gatherings, of the main text (excluding the Preface and Dedication) comprise 64 pages carrying 1116 lines, about a quarter of the whole. In view of S.'s illness and the variety of business he had to transact in London from 24 September, it is very unlikely that he could have transcribed and had such a quantity of pages printed unless he had been transcribing the early cantos of the poem (though probably not Canto I) before completing composition. He may even have been sending them to be printed before he finished writing on 23 September. Considering the length of the remainder of the volume, including the Dedication and Preface which he composed in the period October–mid-November, he must have continued transcribing the later cantos as the earlier ones were going through the press (*SC* v 151–4).

Before the end of October C. and J. Ollier, through the offices of their friend Leigh Hunt, had agreed to be the principal publishers of *L&C* (*SC* v 154–5; *Shelley Revalued* 217 n. 35) in association with Sherwood, Neely and Jones, a firm with a tradition of publishing authors of independent and liberal views. The Olliers had published S.'s pamphlet *A Proposal for Putting Reform to the Vote* the previous March. Since *L&C* was being printed even as S. finished transcription, neither of these firms could have seen the entire poem before agreeing to publish it. The Preface must have been written by 13 November when, at lodgings in London, S. read it aloud to an audience that included Mary, William Baxter (the father of her friends Isabel and Christy Baxter) and Isabel's husband David Booth (*Mary Jnl* i 184, *SC* v 390). The printer's bill (reproduced in *SC* v 160) is dated 21 November: 750 copies were printed at the author's expense. They were to sell at 10s. 6d. Four days later S. wrote to Charles Ollier: 'I have not yet seen the announce of Laon & Cythna in the public papers. – Be so good as not to let it be delayed a day longer, as the books are now ready' (*L* i 568). He began to read the entire poem aloud at Marlow on Saturday 29, finishing on Sunday 30 November, the day *The Examiner* (No. 518: 761) printed eight stanzas of *L&C* (II xxi–xxviii) as 'A Poem, Just Published, by Percy Shelley'. That week Ollier's advertisements in *The Morning Chronicle* for 1 and 4 December promise the poem for the following Monday, the 8th (*Shelley Revalued* 191).

In the course of the printing S. had been compelled by the printer Buchanan McMillan to alter in the Preface at least one passage whose frankly irreligious tone had given offence (notes to Preface lines 42, 249). A master printer long established in his trade – he produced the catalogues for Royal Academy exhibitions in the early nineteenth century, for example – McMillan had a reputation to defend and custom to lose. The nature of his interference and S.'s response to it can be gauged by the tone of S.'s letter to Ollier of 3 December about the list of Errata he had by now compiled and asked to be inserted: 'That McMillan is an obstinate old dog as troublesome as he is impudent. 'Tis a mercy as the old women say that I got him thro' the poem at all – Let him print the errata, & say at top if he likes, that it was all the Author's fault, & that he is as immaculate as the Lamb of God. Only let him do it directly, or if he wont, let some one else' (*L* i 571). More serious objections were to follow. Before 11 December some customers of the Olliers had both abused and threatened them on account of the celebration of incestuous love in *L&C* and its attack on established religion as the collusive partner of political oppression – and the alarmed Charles Ollier had written to Shelley withdrawing as principal publisher (*L* i 578–9). He had good reason to be apprehensive. The vigorous political agitation for reform which had gained momentum since the end of the previous summer was being met with measures to control and repress the expression of opinion. Habeas Corpus had been suspended since early March; a recent prosecution for blasphemous libel had ended in conviction (*SC* v 163–4). In early May the journalist and publisher William Hone had been arrested and detained for publishing blasphemous and seditious libels in the form of satirical parodies of the Catechism, the Litany and St Athanasius's Creed (*The Examiner* No. 489: 303–4; No. 491: 335; No. 495: 399–400). Hone would be acquitted of the charges in three celebrated trials on 18–20 December (*The Examiner* No. 521: 811–16, 806–7; No. 522: 830–2), but a week before the trials began this would have seemed a most unlikely outcome. S. replied to Ollier urging him to stand firm for liberty of expression against 'the murmurs of a few bigots'. The terms of his more practical remonstrances to the publisher specify both the readers to whom he addresses *L&C* and the nature of the forces that he supposes to be ranged against it:

> I don't believe that if the book was quietly and regularly published the Government would touch anything of a character so refined and so remote from the conceptions of the vulgar. They would hesitate before they invaded a member of the higher circles of the republic of letters. But if they see us tremble, they will make no distinctions; they will feel their strength. You might bring the arm of the law down on us both by flinching now. Directly these scoundrels see that people are afraid of them, they seize upon them and hold them up to mankind as criminals already convicted by their own fears. You lay yourself prostrate and they trample on you. How glad they would be to seize on any connexion of Hunt's by this most powerful of all their arms – the terrors and self-condemnation of their victim! (*L* i 579)

This shrewd advice was no doubt prompted by a report in *The Examiner* of 30 November (No. 518: 764–5) of the prosecution for blasphemous libel in the Court of King's Bench of a printer, publisher and bookseller of Portsea for printing and selling parodies of the Litany and of St Athanasius's Creed. The bookseller offered no defence against the charge, was convicted, fined and imprisoned, the court expressing particular disapproval of the likely effect of such profanity on the 'uninformed and illiterate' and the 'lower orders', from which S., whose poem was aimed at other readers, might have derived some small reassurance (see further: D. Thomas, *The Library*, 5th Series xxxii (1977) 324–5). Ollier responded to S.'s letter by return of post to propose a compromise. Arriving in Marlow at S.'s invitation the following day (*L* i 581–2) with a marked copy of *L&C* (*Mary Jnl* i 187; *Peacock Works* viii 107) he requested the alteration of those passages that identified the lovers Laon and Cythna as brother and sister, as well as those expressing the poem's aggressively critical estimate of the political implications of Christian doctrine. Forty years later Peacock remembered the tense and sour confrontation that ensued:

> Mr. Ollier positively refused to publish the poem as it was, and Shelley had no hope of another publisher. He for a long time refused to alter a line: but his friends finally prevailed on him to submit. Still he could not, or would not, sit down by himself to alter it, and the whole of the alterations were actually made in successive sittings of what I may call a literary committee. He contested the proposed alterations step by step: in the end, sometimes adopting, more frequently modifying, never originating, and always insisting that his poem was spoiled. (*Peacock Works* viii 141)

Charles Ollier left Marlow on Monday 16 December with the copy of the poem bearing the revisions which had emerged from the sessions of the 'literary committee', a body that evidently included himself, Peacock and Shelley. As copies of *L&C* had already been sold and given to friends, S. found himself in a decidedly awkward position. Later that day he wrote to Thomas Moore, to whom a signed copy of the poem had been sent in acknowledgement of his favourable comments on the specimen S. had submitted to a publisher in October (see above p. 14), in order to explain his reasons for the alterations. The motives he attributes to himself, at odds with the ones that Peacock recorded, read like those pressed upon him by his friends during the previous weekend and which he had now adopted to save face.

> The present edition of 'Laon & Cythna' is to be suppressed, & it will be republished in about a fortnight under the title of 'The Revolt of Islam', with some alterations which consist in little else than the substitution of the words *friend* or *lover* for that of *brother* & *sister*. The truth is, that the seclusion of my habits has confined me so much within the circle of my own thoughts, that I have formed to myself a very different measure of approbation or disapprobation for actions than that which is in use among mankind; and the result of that peculiarity, contrary to my intention, revolts & shocks many who might be inclined to sympathise with me in my general views. –
> As soon as I discovered that this effect was produced by the circumstance alluded to, I hastened to cancel it – not from any personal feeling of terror, or repentence, but from the sincere desire of doing all the good & conferring all the pleasure which might flow from so obscure a person as myself. I don't know why I trouble you with these words, but your kind approbation of the opening of the Poem has emboldened me to believe that this account of my motives might interest you. (*L* i 582)

The letter misrepresents the nature of the alterations, most of which do not concern incest but rather remove matter considered likely to outrage religious sensibilities and constitute grounds for prosecution. Neither does S. mention Charles Ollier's fears or his part in the affair. An action which had been taken on practical grounds and as a last resort is disguised as a prudent decision adopted in the interest of a greater good. S. was not unaware of the real nature of his dilemma, however, and quickly took measures to recover the copies of *L&C* in circulation while urging Ollier to do the same (*L* i 585–6). At the printer's, the alterations to the poem were carried out by substituting 26 cancel-leaves for those on which offending passages occurred; the title-page and fly-title were also replaced (note to *L&C* title). H. B. Forman lists the affected pages of the volume and describes in detail the copy of the poem in which the alterations were entered by hand and from which *RofI* was printed (*Forman 1876–7* 391–9; *The Shelley Library* (1886) 83–6). This copy – abbreviated here as *L&C* (PM) – was once owned by Forman himself and is now in the J. Pierpont Morgan Library in New York. On 27 December S. had not yet received 'the remainder of the proofs', i.e. those of the cancel-pages for *RofI*, his phrase suggesting that he may already have corrected some of them. If so, he must have finished correcting them by 2 January 1818 when he requested Ollier to 'send me copies as quickly as you can' (*L* i 586, 591). Ollier announced *RofI* for 12 January 1818 and, at S.'s insistence, advertised the poem regularly throughout the early months of the year (*L* i 586–96; *Shelley Revalued* 218). The name of the original co-publisher Sherwood, Neely and Jones does not appear on the new title-page. Few copies of *RofI* were sold. As a result of the subsequent disposal of unsold stock of bound copies and unbound sheets, *L&C/RofI* can be found in five different states which are described by Forman in *The Shelley Library* (1886) 71–3.

While S. saw *L&C* through the press and later supervised the alterations that turned it into *RofI*, it is unclear whether he read all the proofs himself or had portions of them read by a friend or friends. Evidence has been adduced that it was Leigh Hunt who read those for gathering O (Canto IX i–xxxi): several of the surviving fragments of what is almost certainly the press-copy for that part of the poem, against which he would have required to examine the proofs, have been traced back to him (*SC* v 188). But, however the proof-reading was managed, to the author's chagrin a considerable number of errors survived the process. The extract from a letter to Ollier given above indicates that Buchanan McMillan had refused to insert the list of errata that S. had compiled unless it carried a disclaimer of the printer's part in them. In the event, a page correcting 22 errata was printed with the following heading: 'The Author deems it right to state, that the following Errata are not attributable to the Printer', thus advertising that the errors listed were either mistakes of printing which were not identified in author's proofs, or had been accurately printed from MS but which the author now belatedly wished to correct or alter. McMillan's insistence was not unjustified. Of the three errata for which draft, press-copy, and first edition can be compared, the fault lies with S. in each case. The lines in question are 3547, 3565 and 3662, all in Canto IX and in gathering O, for which it is quite possible that he did not himself read the proofs. In the first instance S. has transcribed 'Thier' [sic] in a form all but indistinguishable from 'Then'; in the other two he has miscopied the draft so as to duplicate a word from another line in a rhyming position. In setting all three lines the compositor has simply reproduced the inaccurately-transcribed fair copy. In other cases the error is of a kind more likely to be the compositor's, though in the absence of press-copy for these it is impossible to be certain. Examination of the whole of the errata confirms the obvious difficulty of producing an accurate text of a long work like *L&C* when transcription and proof-reading are rapidly carried out.

Four years after publication S. wrote in pencil below the Errata in a copy of *RofI* which he presented to a friend (note to Preface line 249): 'with about fifty more'. Although this may be an exaggeration, it is true that from *1839* editors have intervened to correct what they have identified as errors in *L&C* in addition to those in the Errata; these and other instances where correction appears to be called for are considered in the notes to this edition. But collation with the surviving MSS that very probably served as press-copy for the Preface, the Dedication and Canto IX shows that the parts of the volume that are represented are accurately printed apart from the variations in punctuation and capitalization noted below; and there is no reason to suppose that the rest of the text has been corrupted in any considerable degree. In particular, care needs to be exercised in interpreting a letter of 16 February 1821 to Charles Ollier in which S. asks: 'Is there any expectation of a second edition of "The Revolt of Islam"? I have many corrections to make in it, and one part will be wholly remodelled' (*L* ii 263). At first reading, S.'s 'corrections' might be taken to mean errors resulting from faulty transcription or printing; but when the larger context of this letter, as well as that of S.'s letter of 25 September of the same year to Ollier (in which he says of *RofI*: 'I could materially improve that poem on revision'), are allowed for, it seems clear that by 'corrections' he means improvements rather than the putting right of mistakes. He undoubtedly uses the word in this sense in letters of 25 September and 23 October 1817 to the publishers Lackington and Allen *à propos* of the proofs of *Frankenstein* (*L* i 558, 565).

Fair-copy MSS, which have every appearance of having served as printer's copy, have survived for the Preface, for nearly seven stanzas of the Dedication and for 202 lines of Canto IX. Comparison of these with the printed text of *L&C* reveals that the compositors altered S.'s capitalisation and punctuation freely. The rule holds true in all three cases, though with variations, the punctuation of *L&C* being generally more elaborate and more rhetorical than the sparser practice of syntactical pointing in the MSS. While the *L&C* punctuation sometimes clarifies the syntax, it can on occasion obscure or alter meaning as well as imposing on the verse or prose a rhythm which the MS punctuation has not defined. The differences in capitalisation between MS and print in Canto IX show particular inconsistency. S.'s own capitalising of nouns or pronouns for emphasis or personification is neither uniform in the MS nor consistently respected by the compositor of that part of the text. In line 3650, for example, MS 'Earth' is printed as 'earth', while in line 3693 MS 'Earth' is printed with a capital 'E'. In line 3660 MS 'Winter's' becomes 'winter's', whereas in 3700 'winter' is printed as 'Winter'. The instances of such variation in the MS and between the MS and *L&C* are sufficiently numerous to make it impossible to say that S. followed a settled practice in capitalising. In this edition, therefore, both the punctuation and the capitalisation of *L&C* have been respected except where good reason, usually confirmed by the surviving MSS, exists for departing from them. Such exceptions are explained in the notes where the *L&C* reading is also displayed.

The present edition is based on *Laon and Cythna* (1818), the version of the poem that conforms to S.'s original and unconstrained intention. The alterations that transformed *L&C* into *RofI* are of interest as the direct result of the exceptionally coercive circumstances described above. They represent what S. needed to do to ensure publication but, as Peacock's reliable testimony shows, he only consented to those changes against his will and as a last resort. This view of the matter is borne out by the character of the alterations themselves. On examination, they appear (with one exception: lines 3624–7 and note) no more than functional expedients produced for the occasion and without either intellectual integrity or artistic merit. They are displayed in this edition in the notes to the words and lines of *L&C* that they replaced in *RofI*. The lines affected are: 847, 884, 1108, 1680, 2138, 2549, 2610, 2682–5, 2686, 3234, 3235, 3244, 3251–2, 3253–6, 3262, 3264–5, 3309–10, 3584, 3591, 3598–3600, 3624–7, 3990, 4024, 4036, 4063, 4072, 4075, 4080, 4094–5, 4107, 4138, 4148, 4188, 4196, 4212, 4360, 4447, 4539, 4548, 4554–6, 4705, 4714. Other alterations to the *L&C* text in the cancel-leaves for *RofI* than the ones imposed are considered to be introduced by S. on the proofs of the pages in question. Some of these changes are supported by S.'s MS alterations in *L&C* (PM), others by the draft and fair-copy MSS. Of those without MS support, not all recommend themselves equally, but in view of the evidence that S. examined the proofs of the cancel-leaves, their readings have been followed. Where other variations between *L&C* and the fair-copy or draft MSS are judged to be interesting in themselves or to throw light on the evolution of the text or to clarify its sense, they are recorded in the notes.

Sources and Influences

The French Revolution was among the earliest of S.'s literary concerns and continued as one of the most persistent. *PFMN* (1810) includes the sensational *Fragment. Supposed to be an Epithalamium of Francis Ravaillac and Charlotte Corday* (no. 33) in which the visionary frame and celebratory eroticism, as well as the apotheosis of the virtuous tyrannicides of the title, can seem like a lurid rough sketch for *L&C*; and towards the end of that year or early in 1811 S. made a suitably rousing translation of the *Marseillaise Hymn* (no. 52). It was evidently later in 1811 that he undertook his first large-scale narrative treatment of the theme, for on 2 January 1812 he writes of having completed 200 pages of 'a tale in which I design to exhibit the cause of the failure of the French Revolution, and the state of morals and opinions in France during the latter years of its monarchy. – Some of the leading passions of the human mind will of course have a place in its fabric. I design to exclude the sexual passion & think the keenest satire on its intemperance will be complete silence on the subject' (*L* i 218). Five days later he enumerates the causes which this unromantic novel, now entitled 'Hubert Cauvin', will assign to the Revolution's failure: '*expediency, insincerity, mystery* adherence to which I do not consider the remotest occasions of violence and blood in the French revolution' (*L* i 223). In the long autobiographical letter he addresses to Godwin on 10 January he further nuances the novel's aim, in Godwinian language, as 'an inquiry into the causes of the failure of the French revolution to benefit mankind' (*L* i 229); and the following week he has determined that 'The Novel will be printed cheaply', obviously in order to reach a broad popular readership. While reference to the fictional project disappears from his extant correspondence after 26 January, the conviction that the tragic shortcomings of the Revolution are to be sought in the intellectual and moral life of late eighteenth-century France as well as in the motives and passions of the principal actors on the political scene are topics that S. develops in an important passage of *Proposals for An Association of Philanthropists* (March 1812) which he was writing in February. Here the defeat of the Revolution's ideals is traced to the limitations of the very thinkers whose works laid its foundations; although subsequent analysts who benefited from observing the course of revolutionary events – Paine and Godwin are mentioned – are credited with showing the way forward (*Prose Works* i 50–2). A particular point is made of extolling the example of those few revolutionaries whose selfless devotion might serve as 'germs of excellence' to promote 'the gradual and peaceful regeneration of the world' (52).

The critical backward glance that extracts from history a pattern for future action and the power of exemplary figures to germinate in the public imagination and thereby promote moral and political renewal – these are the ethical and aesthetic bases of *L&C*, and they are fully formulated in S.'s mind as early as February 1812. When he returned to England from Switzerland in September 1816, the country seemed to him to be in need of just such a sense of direction as his view of the Revolution might provide. He develops his assessment of the situation in a series of letters to Byron, reporting on 11 September that although shortages of food had caused severe distress, 'Most earnestly do I hope that despair will not drive the people to premature and useless struggles' (*L* i 505–6). By 20 November the state of affairs seemed to him to have worsened dramatically:

> The whole fabric of society presents a most threatening aspect. What is most ominous of an approaching change is the strength which the popular party have suddenly acquired, and the importance which the violence of demagogues has assumed. But the people appear calm, and steady even under situations of great excitement; and reform may come without revolution . . . I earnestly hope that, without such an utter overthrow as should leave us the prey of anarchy, and give us illiterate demagogues for masters, a most radical reform of the institutions of England may result from the approaching contest. (*L* i 513)

Early in September, as they travelled across France to reach the Channel, S.'s party had visited the royal palaces at Versailles and Fontainebleau which brought to mind 'some of the most interesting events of what may be called the master theme of the epoch in which we live – the French Revolution', as he informed Byron when they reached Portsmouth (*L* i 504). The allusion means to recall some earlier discussion during the summer in Switzerland in which the idea of a major poetic project taking the Revolution as its topic was raised. A long and interesting letter to Byron written three weeks later makes this clear. S. tentatively invites the older poet to consider undertaking a modern epic poem and elaborates upon his idea of the high talents necessary to make the literary response that current circumstances seemed to demand. His design for *L&C* is forming, and it reveals much about his sense of what that design would entail that he should test it as a deferential proposal to the most celebrated poet of the day, who is invited to gather and concentrate his 'powers . . . astonishingly great' in order to create 'a fountain from which the thoughts of other men shall draw strength and beauty':

> I hope for no more than that you should, from some moment when the clearness of your own mind makes evident to you the 'truth of things', feel that you are chosen out from all other men to some greater enterprise of thought; and that all your studies should, from that moment, tend towards that enterprise alone: that your affections, that all worldly hopes this world may have left you, should link themselves to this design. *What* it should be, I

am not qualified to say. In a more presumptuous mood, I recommended the Revolution of France as a theme involving pictures of all that is best qualified to interest and to instruct mankind. But it is inconsistent with the spirit in which you ought to devote yourself to so great a destiny, that you should make use of any understanding but your own – much less mine. (*L* i 507–8)

In his twenty-fifth year and as yet without literary reputation, the audacity of assuming the public role of epic poet and producing a poem 'exemplary to a nation' (in Milton's phrase) leads him to articulate his aim as the culminating destiny of a Byron in comparison to whom, he would write in January 1817, 'I still feel the burden of my own insignificance and impotence' (*L* i 530). The union in *L&C* of the 'master spirit' of the age (note to epigraph to Dedication) with its 'master theme' is an ideal rooted in S.'s anxiously tentative relation to Byron.

Although in the Preface to *L&C* S. makes it plain that the revolution of his subtitle is intended to stand as an image of the French Revolution, in the poem he does not attempt any close approximation of historical events in France. Had he wished to do so, the materials were at hand. He apparently began to read the six volumes of J. P. Rabaut Saint-Etienne's *Précis Historique de la Révolution Française* (1792) and its continuation by C. J. D. Lacretelle (1801–6) on the eve of his departure from Geneva (28 August 1816) for the journey across France, finishing it a month later; he was reading it again in June 1817 (*Mary Jnl* i 97, 102, 132, 173). Rabaut and Lacretelle provide a detailed chronolgy and narrative of political and military developments in France from May 1789; but rather than a historical narrative S. chose to construct a meta-historical type, which he qualified to a prospective publisher in October 1817 as:

a tale illustrative of such a Revolution as might be supposed to take place in an European nation, acted upon by the opinions of what has been called (erroneously as I think) the modern philosophy, & contending with antient notions & the supposed advantage derived from them to those who support them. It is a Revolution of this kind, that is, the *beau idéal* as it were of the French Revolution, but produced by the influence of individual genius, & out of general knowledge. (*L* i 563–4)

Chateaubriand's practical definition of the aesthetic term *beau idéal*, or ideal beauty, in *Le Génie du Christianisme* (1802, II ii 11) as 'l'art de choisir et de cacher' is apt here. Selection and concealment are the principles that govern the representation of the historical Revolution in *L&C* and which allow S. to reconcile his progressive view of history with the manifest imperfections of the event which had promised dramatically to realise its ideals. No violent or retributory acts are laid to the charge of the insurgent patriots in the poem. Only Laon himself bears the guilt of having shed blood. The great motifs of siege, mass assembly, epidemic disease, and public execution can be variously related to well-known moments of the Revolution, but they are also established features of the European epic tradition that begins with Homer. Only two major episodes of *L&C*, both in Canto V, are presented unequivocally as having a specific basis in history. The penetration of the patriot army into the imperial palace, which conflates the entry of the Parisian mob into the palace of Versailles on 5–6 October 1789 with the overrunning of the Tuileries palace on 10 August 1792, reveals S.'s debt to a controversial tradition of revolution narrative. Burke, in a notorious passage of *Reflections on the Revolution in France* (1790) had set the agenda by making of the earlier entry a dramatic emblem of outrage and pollution; Mary Wollstonecraft, in both *A*

Vindication of the Rights of Men (1790) and *A Historical and Moral View . . . of the French Revolution* (1794), and Paine in *Rights of Man* (1791) had been moved to offer alternative versions of the event. S. aligns *L&C* with their apologetic practice by having Laon persuade the crowd to treat the fallen tyrant with the forbearance that Christ bestowed on the woman taken in adultery in St John's Gospel (note to V xxxii–v). A second important revision is carried out in the great set-piece of Canto V, the vast gathering before which Cythna (now known as Laone) conducts the ceremonies of mass dedication to ideals recalling those of the Revolution's Liberty, Equality, Fraternity. The scene explicitly advertises itself as a re-enactment of the Fête de la Fédération celebrated in Paris on 14 July 1790 (notes to lines 2072, 2074). S. has purged the event of both the Christian and the military character that it had, investing it instead with significant elements from Volney's *Ruins*, a seminal text of Revolutionary prophecy. The Preface, in which the Revolution is recovered as moral and civic paradigm, is largely beholden to the defence of the French experience as mounted in Paine and (differently) in Mary Wollstonecraft, as well as, more generally, to the sceptical examination of institutions and opinion and the doctrine of perfectibilty in Godwin's *Political Justice*.

Ruins is one of three major sources that deserve special consideration. A chief formal and intellectual model for *Q Mab*, its similar function for *L&C* was methodically demonstrated by K. N. Cameron (*PMLA* lvi (1941) 175–206). Besides its structure as a vision of an idealised future granted by a supernatural messenger to dispel the narrator's despair at the calamities of history, S. borrows a number of images and narrative motifs from Volney which are indicated in the notes to the passages concerned. He follows *Ruins* closely too in estimating the central role of religious institutions and factionalism in maintaining oppressive political systems in place and ensuring perpetual strife among them. Conversely, *Ruins* is a principal source for the myth of divine origins in Canto I which informs all of *L&C*. This derives from Volney's conspectus of universal religious history in *Ruins* xxii in which the idea of the divine is held originally to have arisen from the elemental and ambiguous confrontation between natural phenomena and human want. In process of time, the productive and destructive powers of nature that alternate in summer and winter have been abstracted and become moral ideas related to the phases of the heavens that seem to govern them. These have in turn become personified as spirits or genii invested with the beneficent or maleficent character of the annual cycle of nature and its presiding constellations. Such are the underlying idea and the celestial theatre that S. has adapted for the brief revelation that the Woman delivers to the narrator in Canto I xxv–vi, and which retrospectively discloses the significance of the earlier combat between the eagle and the serpent (viii–xiv). But as well as sharing with the revolutionary theorist Volney a rationalist and secular appreciation of the rise of the human religious impulse, Canto I of *L&C* asserts a belief in the value of religious myth to inspire human endeavour for good. Hence S.'s adoption of the Zoroastrian inflection of the dualistic narrative of cosmic history in which the eventual triumph of the good spirit Ormusd or Oromaze over his evil counterpart Ahriman is ensured after ages of struggle (I xxxiv). *Ruins* does not attribute this prophetic faith to Zoroaster but other readily available accounts of his teaching did (note to lines 431–2); from these, and through the intermediary of Peacock's *Ahrimanes* (see the following paragraph), S. has supplemented Volney's meagre exposition of Zoroastrian doctrine with a crucial element. His purpose in thus reviving what was regarded, by Volney and other contemporary mythographers, as the earliest conception of divinity is to underwrite a degree of religious feeling in the poem by returning to religion's primitive springs in natural and pre-sectarian experience. But this mythical dimension of *L&C* needs to be read with circumspection; it is hardly S.'s purpose to solicit an uncritical acceptance of dualistic theology, Zoroastrian or otherwise. He clearly expresses his view of divided divinity as metaphor in the essay 'On Christianity', which he may have been composing in mid to late 1817 (*Prose Works* i 255–6, 459–60). The fuller consideration of the position in 'On the Devil, and Devils' (1819–20) may serve as a retrospective gloss on the Woman's revelation in *L&C* I xxv–xxxiv:

> The Manichaean philosophy respecting the origin & government of the world, if not true is at least an hypothesis conformable to the experience of actual facts. To suppose that the world was created, & is superintended by two Spirits of a balanced power & opposite dispositions is simply a personification of the struggle we experience within ourselves, & which we percieve in the operations of external things, as they affect us between good and evil. – The supposition that the good Spirit is, or hereafter will be superiour, is a personification of the principle of hope, & that thirst for improvement without which, present evil would be intolerable. (*Nbk 15* 34–6; *BSM* xiv 41–5)

This sober view of things makes a concession, though a slender one, to the poem's perfectibilian ideal of human destiny while satisfying, with minimal apparatus, the traditional requirement that the epic should include a supernatural plane on which the operations of divine beings, as they affect human events, are revealed. Moreover, the controversial position that a dualistic model of divinity more adequately accounts for our objective and subjective experience of the world than biblical, or koranic, monotheism had entered modern European theological criticism as early as Pierre Bayle's *Dictionnaire Historique et Critique* (1697). S. clearly intends Canto I of *L&C* to open an evaluative perspective on orthodox Christianity, especially as it was deployed to buttress patriotic simplifications such as the laureate Robert Southey's in the 'Argument' to *The Poet's Pilgrimage to Waterloo* (1816):

> To the Christian philosopher all things are consistent and clear . . . The contest in which this country was engaged against that Tyrant [Napoleon], was a struggle between good and evil principles, and never was there a victory so important to the best hopes of human nature as that which was won by British valour at Waterloo.

Between about summer 1813 and autumn 1815 Peacock worked at *Ahrimanes*, a narrative poem in Spenserian stanzas and of epic scale which he neither completed nor published. The surviving MSS include: 1. a fair copy of the first canto in 30 stanzas and 14 stanzas of the second, together with a prose outline for the whole in twelve cantos (*Peacock Works* vii 265–86); 2. sixteen stanzas of an apparently later version of the first canto and a different prose outline for the remainder of the poem in two cantos (*Peacock Works* vii 420–32; *SC* iii 218–33); 3. drafts for a few stanzas that seem to be intermediate between the two fair-copy versions (*SC* iii 211–18). Extensive verbal and structural parallels establish that S. drew freely on *Ahrimanes* in composing *L&C* (K. N. Cameron, *MLQ* iii (June 1942) 287–95; *SC* iii 233–44). He may have known at least the 12-canto version as early as summer 1814, and similarities between *Manfred* and the 2-canto version suggest that he could have shown or recited at least some part of *Ahrimanes* to Byron in Switzerland in summer 1816 (*SC* iii 237–40). S.'s remarks in a letter to Peacock of 23 July 1816 seem clearly to refer to *Ahrimanes*:

> Do you who assert the supremacy of Ahriman imagine him throned among these desolating snows, among these palaces of death & frost, sculptured in this their terrible magnificence by the unsparing hand of necessity, & that he casts around him as the first essays of his final usurpation avalanches, torrents, rocks & thunders – and above all, these deadly glaciers at once the proofs & the symbols of his reign. – (*L* i 499)

By the time he began to compose his poem, Peacock had acquired something of S.'s outlook and poetic aims and there are echoes of *Q Mab* in *Ahrimanes* and of *Ahrimanes* in *Alastor* (*SC* iii 237–8), so that turning the poem over to Shelley, as he seems to have done, would be a recognition of their common interest in it. The relation between *L&C* and the two versions of *Ahrimanes* is complex and intricate; frequent similarities of phrase and image exist between the stanzas that Peacock completed and *L&C* Canto I, and there is a large set of common narrative events. The latter include: supernatural notification of a divine mission, sea voyages, the separation of the lovers, the confinement of the heroine in a seraglio, the instruction of the hero by a sage, the desolation of a city by plague and famine, the oppression of an innocent nation. That such or similar elements feature in any number of epic and romantic narratives that S. is known to have read illustrates the hazards of relating *L&C* too exclusively to a given source. Among modern texts Southey's *Thalaba the Destroyer* (of which the 12-canto *Ahrimanes* seems an ironic variant) and *The Curse of Kehama* furnish ample parallels with both *L&C* and *Ahrimanes*; and there are less extensive ones in, for example, C. M. Wieland's Hellenistic romances *Agathon* and *Peregrinus Proteus* which S. read in 1814 (*Notopoulos* 139–43), C. A. Vulpius's *The History of Rinaldo Rinaldini* (note to line 1361), Sir James Lawrence's *The Empire of the Nairs* (W. E. Peck, *MLN* xl (1940) 246–9). But the shared feature that marks the originality of *Ahrimanes* and *L&C* alike is the hypothesis that the course of history is more truly explained by the existence of opposed good and evil deities than by monotheism. This supposition also furnishes in the reign of an evil deity a metaphor for the oppressive character of contemporary political systems inasmuch as these are deemed to rest upon an alliance between royal power and institutional religion. In his notes to the 2-canto *Ahrimanes* Peacock details the sources of his mythical material, which include what he calls the 'astronomical mythologists', Volney, Charles François Dupuis (another supporter of the French Revolution) whose *Origine de Tous Les Cultes* (1795) was dedicated to the National Assembly, Sir William Drummond (note to Preface line 102) and J. F. Newton (note to line 647). In the works of these authors Peacock encountered the view that religious myth arises from such elemental natural experiences as light and darkness, growth and decay, and frequently gives narrative form to the phenomena of the heavenly bodies as they are configured in the zodiac. This conviction was the subject of lively controversy in early nineteenth century England (M. Butler, *KSMB* xxxvi 57–8); its embodiment in imaginative form gives Peacock's poem a distinctly polemical edge. In *L&C* S. dispenses with much that gives *Ahrimanes* its specific texture: complex theogonies, strangely-named deities, the regular intervention of genii as agents of plot. The Indian zodiacal mythology that Peacock acquired from the eccentric J. F. Newton (*Curran (1975)* 87–90; *Peacock Works* viii 71–3) and which contributes to an unwieldy frame of cosmic history in the 2-canto *Ahrimanes*, is also notably absent from *L&C*. S. evidently judged that such exotic impedimenta would be misplaced in a poem that engages more particularly with contemporary history than Peacock's by looking backward to the French Revolution and forward to a Greek one. In his letter to a publisher of October 1817 he insists that most events in *L&C* occur on a strictly natural plane: 'The whole poem, with the exception of the first canto & part of the last is a mere human story without the smallest intermixture of supernatural interference' (*L* i 563). Peacock's notes on his sources include references to Jacob Bryant's *A New System, or, an Analysis of Ancient Mythology* (1774) which pursues the euhemerist programme of uncovering in the 'pagan idolatry' of the ancient world references to the Deluge in *Genesis* which confirm its historicity. An interesting resemblance between a plate in Bryant (ii 342) representing Samian Juno clothed in a 'mystic veil' (note to line 538) standing upon and crowned with a crescent moon (for Bryant a recollection of Noah's Ark) and the Woman guide in Canto I of *L&C*, who escorts the narrator in a boat shaped like a crescent moon, need not suggest that S. has borrowed the image directly from Bryant. The sequence of stanzas from xx to lvii in Canto I nonetheless reveals an acquaintance with the broad tradition of investigation within which the orthodox and old-fashioned Bryant worked and which had gained some currency by the second decade of the nineteenth century. S. could, for example, have found summarised in J. M. Good's bilingual edition (1805, i 353–60) of Lucretius's *The Nature of Things*, which he owned (*Mary Jnl* i 75), the conclusions of Bryant and other mythographers that the entire body of ancient non-biblical mythology originated in the worship of the sun, of the crescent-shaped ark or of the serpent ('an emblem of providence and protection' ii 358) and that these, sometimes in the subordinate emblems of the mother-goddess, the moon or the pyramid, must all be understood as deformed memories of Noah's Flood. The elementary symbolic language thus defined by comparative mythographers furnishes S. with the chief poetic figures of I xx–lvii: the supernatural woman guide, the serpent, the boat in the shape of the crescent moon, the planet Venus as the morning-star, the pyramid in the temple. S. combines these, in representing the journey to the Temple of the Spirit and its attendant revelations, with allusions to both the Old and the New Testaments and incorporates reminiscences of Mary Wollstonecraft's residence in Revolutionary Paris in order to create a mythic idiom of syncretic character and contemporary resonance which is typical of his practice in *L&C*.

S. was taking up another topic of contemporary religious controversy when he adopted the Roman poet Lucretius as his exemplar in the Preface. J. M. Good's edition, which is cited in the previous paragraph, had presented Lucretius as the ancient philosopher whose ideas had been most fully confirmed by modern thinkers (note to Preface lines 215–16), subject only to minor qualifications and the necessity of supplementing his teachings by those of divine revelation on a future state. Good's *Preface and Life of Lucretius* insist on his rigorously virtuous life, the love of liberty conspicuous in his poem, and on the attachment to the republican constitution of the young men of distinguished family who gathered round him. An analogy between Rome of the late Republic and post-revolutionary Europe is implicit: in both, a corrupt society which is prey to religious confusions and anxieties is losing its attachment to liberty in favour of the cult of the heroic military man which will soon issue in tyranny. S. explicitly develops a similar comparison in the Preface lines 219–31 and describes the political crisis that ensued in the early

Roman Empire in 'On Christianity' (*Prose Works* 247–8). A response to Good's two substantial quarto volumes appeared in 1813 in the form of Thomas Busby's equally weighty *The Nature of Things*. Busby's edition, which had the Prince of Wales as patron and was dedicated to Lord Grenville, Chancellor of the University of Oxford, boasted a list of subscribers that descended through the ranks of the nobility to members of Parliament and highly-placed representatives of the professions. Its aim is to recover an authorised place for *De Rerum Natura* in the established classical canon by challenging, dismissing, excusing or explaining away whatever in the poem is perceived as impugning revealed Christianity. There remains for 'refined and elegant gratification' the 'raptures of poetry' and the curious 'eccentricities to which the brightest mind, unaided by divine illumination, is ever liable'. 'The scholar who should receive Lucretius for his religious guide, would be deemed insane' though no harm need come to those 'who are armed against his sophistry by arguments derived from inspiration, and covered with the impenetrable shield of Christian faith' (i pp. x–xi). The dangers of Lucretius's Epicureanism as professed by both Shelley and Hunt were to be chastised in the *Quarterly Review* xviii (January 1818) 326–7. In Good's virtuous republican, speaking from his philosophical retirement in defiance of venal criticism against the superstition and fear that have hoodwinked his countrymen into losing sight of their true political interests, S. found powerful classical precedent for the critical position on religion that he adopts in *L&C*.

L&C is the most richly and variously autobiographical of S.'s works. He told Godwin that he wished the poem to stand as 'some record of myself' (*L* i 577) and Mary S. strongly indicates in her 'Note on The Revolt of Islam' in *1839* that in Laon's life-story S. was idealising his own. The substantial personal dimension of the text is disposed according to the decorum governing each of its major divisions: public character of the poet (Preface), affective and domestic confession (Dedication), symbolic narrative of history (Cantos I–XII). The pattern had been broadly established in such contemporary works as Byron's *Childe Harold's Pilgrimage* I and II (1812), Wordsworth's *The White Doe of Rylstone* (1815), and Southey's *Joan of Arc* (1796; later editions include a sonnet to the poet's wife Edith) and *The Poet's Pilgrimage to Waterloo* (1816). *L&C* observes the conventional divisions while displaying such obvious correspondences between them as implicitly to question the validity of the distinctions they maintain. The self-representation in the poem's principal narrative clearly both encodes personal events for private motives and makes poetry out of the matter of an individual life. Such a procedure results in passages which typically retain an element of the imponderable about them. The parentage of the child who first enters the poem at V xxi is a case in point. The child is presented both as the offspring of Cythna and the Tyrant Othman and of Cythna and Laon, and no explanation is offered for the discrepancy. The details of its birth and disappearance which are recounted by Cythna (notes to lines 3022–3, 3044) recall Mary's experience of the birth and death of the premature infant, her and Shelley's first child, which lived only a few days in February–March 1815. After the child in the poem dies of the plague it reappears in angelic guise to conduct the spirits of Laon and Cythna to the Temple of the Spirit in an episode that S. has constructed by borrowing details from various literary sources (note to line 4644). The conspicuous mystery that remains around the child must finally be explained by its function as a monument of private consolation.

L&C is a highly self-conscious continuation of the grand European tradition of heroic poetry. As such it displays broad structural and thematic resemblances to, as well as local echoes of, the classical epic narratives of Homer, Virgil and Lucan, through Renaissance Italian romance, especially Tasso's *Gerusalemme Liberata*, to *Paradise Lost* and *Faerie Queene*. Many of these poems figure on the lists of S.'s reading in *Mary Jnl* during and for the two years preceding the composition of *L&C*. The list for 1817 (*Mary Jnl* i 98–102) shows that he undertook a particular course of reading for the representation of the plague in Cantos X and XI. The works he read included Defoe's *Journal of the Plague Year* and John Wilson's verse tragedy *The City of the Plague* (1816), the Christian sentiments of whose hero and heroine contrast with those of Laon and Cythna; although the details in Cantos X and XI also owe much to older accounts of the affliction in, for example, Thucydides, Lucretius and Ovid. In the early nineteenth century the plague was both a traditional poetic figure and a real contemporary menace to public health. Endemic in the southern and eastern Mediterranean, it was considered a threat to western Europe. In 1813 between 100,000 and 250,000 had died of the disease in Constantinople, and *The Annual Register* for 1816 had included extracts from the correspondence of the British Consul Tully published that year which describe the ravages of the plague in Tripoli in 1785. S. wrote to Byron on 23 April 1817: 'We hear that the plague rages in Albania, and hope that you will thus be delayed from proceeding into a country from which it is always questionable whether an European will ever return' (*L* i 540). S.'s treatment of the plague dramatically reverses the Biblical and Homeric conception of epidemic disease as divine retribution by presenting it as a consequence of despotism, a relation tersely expressed in the line, 'The Pestilence, the Tyrant, and the throng' (4595). He may also intend a riposte to Burke's metaphor for the threat of French Revolutionary politics spreading abroad: 'If it be a plague, it is such a plague, that the precautions of the most severe quarantine ought to be established against it' (*Reflections on the Revolution in France*, ed. L. Mitchell (Oxford 1993) 89).

S. remarked in his letter of 13 October 1817 to a publisher: 'The scene is supposed to be laid in Constantinople & modern Greece, but without much attempt at minute delineation of Mahometan manners' (*L* i 563). He is taking care to distinguish *L&C* from such successful oriental poetry as Southey's *Thalaba*, Byron's *Childe Harold* I and II and 'Turkish Tales' and Thomas Moore's *Lalla Rookh*, which appeared in May 1817 and was the current bestseller in the mode. The complex process of assimilation and revision of Southey's and Byron's poems in *L&C* purges them of the layering of oriental detail which contributes to their characteristic style. Neither does *L&C* make any very elaborate localisation of Cantos II to IV which take place in Greece. On several occasions Greek place-names in the drafts have been cancelled or have not been transcribed into the copy from which the poem was printed. The process is consistent with S.'s simplification of his mythical sources and has the same purpose, to create in *L&C* an appropriately generalised and elevated poetic idiom for an epic representation of contemporary history. Such a practice translates the idealised Hellenism of the writers who formed a group round Shelley in Marlow in 1817, which included Hunt, Peacock and T. J. Hogg. The inspirational portrayal of a reviving modern Greece is surely intended as an antidote to the gloomy perception of the country as abject and stifled in the second canto of Byron's *Childe Harold's Pilgrimage*. Images of storm and forest fire combine with cataclysmic evocations of earthquake and volcanic eruption, mediated through Erasmus Darwin's *The Botanic Garden* (1791) and *The Temple of Nature* (1803), to link political evolution to the larger and longer perspectives of change that were being opened up by contemporary geology. The resulting style and epic theatre are meant to create the literary texture and scope for another important opposition, to what S. regarded as the political hopelessness that marked contemporary works such as Wordsworth's *The Excursion*, Coleridge's *Lay Sermons*, and Southey's *The Poet's Pilgrimage to Waterloo* (note to Preface lines 11–12). The conviction that these former friends of liberty were now addressing the country from a narrowly religious standpoint which denied to the revolutionary experience of France its status as a rallying point for liberal aspiration is an essential premise for *L&C*. It is also a regular theme in contemporary issues of the *Examiner* (e.g., leading articles for 22 December 1816 and 12 January 1817) and is summed up in Leigh Hunt's review of *L&C* on 22 February 1818 which qualifies the Lake School as 'dogmatic in their despair as they used to be in their hope' (122).

The atmosphere of polemical controversy from which *L&C* emerges can be appreciated in Leigh Hunt's notices of the poem in the *Examiner* for 1 (no. 527) and 22 February (530) and 1 March 1818 (531), which put the liberal case, and J. T. Coleridge's review in the *Quarterly Review* xxi (April 1819) which argues the conservative one. The latter, the most important review of S.'s work to appear in his lifetime, had a direct influence on some of his major poetry from autumn 1819. Hunt responds to its *ad hominem* vituperation in the *Examiner* (nos. 613–15) for 26 September, 3 and 10 October 1819. There were few other reviews: extracts are given in *Unextinguished Hearth* 117–50 and full texts in *The Romantics Reviewed*, ed. D. H. Reiman (1972) Part C.

Studies, in addition to those mentioned above, which give an important place to sources of *L&C* are: Brian Wilkie, *Romantic Poets and Epic Tradition* (1965) 112–44; *Baker* (64–83); F. L. Jones, 'Shelley and Spenser' *Studies in Philology* xxxix (1942) 662–9; *Notopoulos* 139–44, 213–23; J. L. Ruff, *Shelley's Revolt of Islam* (1972); Paul Turner, 'Shelley and Lucretius' *RES* n.s. x (1959) 269–82; Eleanor Sickels, 'Shelley and Charles Brockden Brown' *PMLA* xlv (1930) 1116–28 (which also suggests several sources for the plague in cantos X–XI); E. H. King, 'Beattie and Shelley: The Making of the Poet' *English Studies* lxi (1980) 338–53; G. McNiece, *Shelley and the Revolutionary Idea* (1969) gives an interesting overview of S.'s reading in 'The Literature of Revolution' (10–41) as well as considering the poem in the light of it (190–217). P. Clemit's 'Shelley's Godwin, 1812–1817' *Durham University Journal* lxxxv (July 1993) 189–201 is informative on a fundamental topic.

Politics is the central concern of: C. Woodring, *Politics in English Romantic Poetry* (1970) 254–8; K. N. Cameron's chapter on *L&C* in *Shelley: The Golden Years* (1974) 311–41; P. M. S. Dawson, *The Unacknowledged Legislator: Shelley and Politics* (1980) 68–75; R. Cronin, *Shelley's Poetic Thoughts* (1981) 94–108; K. Grimes, 'Censorship, Violence, and Political Rhetoric: *The Revolt of Islam* in its Time' *KSJ* xliii (1994) 98–116. Both M. H. Scrivener, *Radical Shelley* (1982) 108–39 and S. C. Behrendt, *Shelley and His Audiences* (1989) 15–38 consider the poem in political context together with S.'s contemporary 'Hermit of Marlow' pamphlets *A Proposal for Putting Reform to the Vote* and *An Address to the People on the Death of the Princess Charlotte*. D. Duff's *Romance and Revolution: Shelley and the Politics of a Genre* (1994) extends beyond generic considerations to an important study of *L&C* in its literary and political context. N. Leask, *British Romantic Writers and the East* (1992) considers the poem in relation to contemporary orientalism.

The controversial treatment of sexual experience in *L&C* is considered in: N. Brown, *Sexuality and Feminism in Shelley* (1979) 181–6; J. Donovan, 'Incest in *Laon and Cythna*: Nature, Custom, Desire' *KSR* ii (1987) 49–90; P. Finch, 'Shelley's *Laon and Cythna*: The Bride Stripped Bare . . . Almost' *KSR* iii (1988) 23–46; Timothy Webb, 'Naming "I-t": Incest and Outrage in Shelley' in *Shelley 1792–1992* ed. J. Hogg (1993) 186–204; S. Sperry, *Shelley's Major Verse* (1988) 41–64 (which also considers the poem as autobiography); W. Ulmer, *Shelleyan Eros* (1990) 51–77. The large topic of feminism in *L&C* and its relation to contemporary feminist thinking is treated in G. Kelly, 'From Avant-Garde to Vanguardism: The Shelleys' Romantic Feminism in *Laon and Cythna* and *Frankenstein*' in *Shelley: Poet and Legislator of the World*, ed. B. Bennet and S. Curran (1996) 73–87. The enigma of the parentage of Cythna's child is addressed by E. B. Murray in ' "Elective Affinity" in *The Revolt of Islam*' *JEGP* lxvii (1968) 570–85.

The use of myth in *L&C* is illuminated by: Curran *(1975)* 3–32; M. Butler, 'Druids, Bards and Twice-Born Bacchus: Peacock's Engagement with Primitive Mythology' *KSMB* xxxvi (1985) 57–76; M. Butler, 'Romantic Manichaeism: Shelley's "On the Devil and Devils" and Byron's Mythological Dramas' in *The Sun is God: Painting, Literature and Mythology in the Nineteenth Century*, ed. J. B. Bullen (1989) 13–37; D. Reiman, *Intervals of Inspiration: The Skeptical Tradition and the Psychology of Romanticism* (1988) 213–61; R. Woodman, *The Apocalyptic Vision in the Poetry of Shelley* (1964) 88–102; Bryan Shelley, *Shelley and Scripture* (1994) 56–74, 185–6 investigates biblical sources.

Text from *Laon and Cythna* (1818). Some readings, which are signalled in the notes, have been adopted from the cancel-leaves for *The Revolt of Islam* (1818) and from those surviving portions of the fair-copy MSS which probably served as press copy for *Laon and Cythna* (see headnote pp. 17–19). As the proportion of the full text that is represented by these MSS is so slight, their capitalization and punctuation, except in the few instances referred to above, have not been reproduced in the present edition.

143
Laon and Cythna;
Or,
The Revolution of the Golden City:
A Vision of The Nineteenth Century.

In the Stanza of Spenser.

ΔΟΣ ΠΟΥ ΣΤΩ ΚΑΙ ΚΟΣΜΟΝ ΚΙΝΗΣΩ.
ARCHIMEDES.

¶ *143. Title.* S. had not yet settled on a title when he left Marlow for London on 23 September 1817, having completed *L&C* subject to alterations and additions (*Mary Jnl* i 180; *Mary L* i 47) – apart from the Preface and Dedication. A version of the title he eventually adopted is written vertically across the draft for stanza xxv of Canto V in *Nbk 3* 4: 'Laon & Cythna / or / The Revolution of the Golden City / A Vision of the 19th Century'; then, separated by a bar, 'The Mirror of Time'. The stanza was drafted in pencil probably in late May/early June but shows signs of revision in both darker pencil and ink so that the title (in a darker pencil) could have been written later. The final phrase may have been meant as an alternative to 'A Vision of the 19th Century', and set aside when that was preferred, or as a third subtitle, and dropped as redundant. It declares the prophetic function that in *PVR* and *DP* S. attributes to poets as 'the mirrors of the gigantic shadows which futurity casts upon the present' (*DP*).

Laon and Cythna] Commentators have derived the name *Laon* from the Gk λαος = the people, the resemblance being closest in the accusative singular λαον (laon) or the genitive plural λαων (laōn) = of the peoples. J. L. Ruff, *Shelley's The Revolt of Islam* (1972) 61, points out that Diogenes Laertius's *Lives of the Eminent Philosophers*, which S. owned and annotated (*Mary Jnl* i 49, 87; Male and Notopoulos *MLR* liv (1959) 10–21), contains a brief biography of Philolaos ('friend of the people') a Pythagorean of Croton who was put to death for aspiring to be tyrant. St. Clair, *The Godwins and the Shelleys* (1989) 430, notices the word λαων in *Iliad* xii 201 in a passage that S. may well have drawn upon: see notes to lines 193, 209. *Cythna* is written vertically in the margin alongside the draft of stanza xv of Canto II (*Nbk 2* 60) several stanzas before its appearance in the draft for II xxi. The heroine's name has been likened to Cythera, the island near which Aphrodite (surnamed Cytherea) was born from the ocean foam (see note to *PU* II v 20–32), but it would seem more exactly to be a feminine formation from the island Cythnos (also called Thermia in S.'s day), one of the northern Cyclades, situated off the southern coast of Attica due east of the southeastern tip of Laon and Cythna's native region of Argolis (lines 676 and note, 1492). (The name also recalls Mount Cynthos on the island of Delos, another of the northern Cyclades, the birthplace of both Artemis and Apollo, to whom the epithets Cynthia and Cynthios were attached). In the draft for Canto II *Cythna* was first called Zia (see note to line 855), a contemporary name for the island of Ceos (also then called Zea, and now Kéa) which lies just to the north of Cythnos. Byron landed there from Constantinople in July 1810 before travelling on to Athens (*Byron L&J* ii 5, 8).

The Revolution of the Golden City] S. identified the city that is the theatre of 'such a Revolution as might be supposed to take place in an European nation' (*L* i 563) as Constantinople. *Golden* would refer variously to the situation of Constantinople on the Golden Horn and to its celebrated wealth and magnificence, but also to the Byzantine imperial monuments of the Golden Milestone and Golden Gate as well as to Byzantium's renowned golden mosaics and artifacts. D. King-Hele, *Shelley: His Thought and Work*, 2nd ed. (1971), finds a similarity to 'The Recovery of Jerusalem', Fairfax's rendering of the title of Tasso's *Gerusalemme Liberata* (1581). The reference to the celestial Jerusalem of *Revelation* xxi 8, 'and the city was of pure gold, like unto clear glass', is to be set against another to the Babylon which is cursed in *Isaiah* xiv 4: 'How hath the oppressor ceased! the golden city ceased!'. See further note to lines 359–60.

Stanza of Spenser] The nine-line stanza of Edmund Spenser's *The Faerie Queene* (1590–6). The conspicuous display of the poem's Spenserian pedigree recalls a point of contemporary literary politics which had been established by Leigh Hunt's polemical review in the *Examiner* 445 and 446 (7 and 14 July 1816) of Robert Southey's *The Lay of the Laureate, Carmen Nuptiale* (1816). In the Proem to the *Lay* Southey had written of: 'That laureate garland [which] crowns my living head. / That wreath which . . . / My master dear, divinest Spenser, wore', before recording the great public events he had commemorated as poet laureate, which include: 'Proudly, I raised the high thanksgiving strain / Of victory in a rightful cause achieved . . . Exulting as became me in such cause, / I offered to the prince his People's just applause'. Hunt retorted: 'As to Spenser, whom he puts in the list of great men who have preceded him in his office, his laureatship has been bestowed on him by Mr. Southey; it did not "crown his living head". We all remember his being refused the hundred pounds [the laureate's annual stipend] for his *Fairy Queen*. Poets were not wanted in those days to celebrate the triumphs of Princes over the People' (7 July 1816, 427). The *Examiner* of 4 August 1816 published a parody of Southey's Proem entitled 'The Laureate Laid Double' which further mocked his enrolling of Spenser among his predecessors. Cp. the ironic supposition in *DP*: 'Let us assume that . . . Spenser was a poet laureate' (*Reiman 1977* 506). Southey closes the Proem to *The Poet's Pilgrimage to Waterloo* (1816) by binding 'The laurel which my master Spenser wore' round his temples.

ΔΟΣ . . . ΚΙΝΗΣΩ] 'Give me a place to stand and I will lift the world'. S. had already borrowed Archimedes' celebrated boast for one of the epigraphs to *Q Mab*. There, as here, its figurative use by radical writers – and in particular by Paine in the first sentence of the Introduction to *Rights of Man*, Part II (1792) – to express the natural force of reason and liberty to effect change, is recalled.

In *RofI* the title was altered to *The / Revolt of Islam; / A Poem, / In Twelve Cantos*. 'The Revolt of Islam' is written along the margin of a draft of *Ozymandias* in *Nbk 5* (fol. 85v) which S. probably used from late summer or early autumn 1817. In *L&C* (PM) the title *Laon and Cythna* is deleted on the fly-title, and 'Othman' written above it in S.'s hand. This, apparently S.'s first attempt at a substitute title, is deleted in its turn and 'The Revolt of Islam' written above it in a hand that *Forman 1876–7* identified as that of the poem's publisher Charles Ollier. 'Othman', adjective and noun signifying 'Ottoman', from the founder of the dynasty, Othman or Osman I, is the name of the tyrant in the poem (see lines 2002, 2010). On the evidence of the fly-title, S. could have requested Ollier to replace the first alternative title with the second either at the time of the other alterations on 15 December 1817 (*Mary Jnl* i 187) or later by letter. The new title-page is consistent with the changes made in the text of the poem at Ollier's insistence, and seems likely to have been urged on S., as they were, to moderate its political attack. The meaning of the new title, as A. C. Swinburne observed (*Essays and Studies* (1875) 193–4), is far from evident. The primary sense of *Islam*, the religious creed and political authority that govern Muslims, is the sense the word has in its only occurrence in the poem (line 4095) as well as throughout *Hellas* (1822); but *Revolt of* can hardly be construed as 'revolt against'. Inasmuch as the revolt is *of* Islam, the meaning is: 1. collectively, those muslims (*OED* Islam b.) of the Ottoman Empire who are inspired to revolution by the modern Greeks Laon and Cythna; 2. in muslim religious usage, 'resignation, submission' (of the believer to the will of God). The latter meaning conceals its revolutionary import beneath a recondite play on words. S. described the ideal revolution in the poem as proceeding by 'the unveiling of the religious frauds by which they [the citizens of a hypothetical modern nation] had been deluded into submission' (Preface, lines 33–4.) 'The Revolt of Islam' encodes for 'the higher circles of the republic of letters' (*L* i 579) that the poem addresses the link between religious authority and political submissiveness which is one of its leading contentions.

PREFACE

The Poem which I now present to the world, is an attempt from which I scarcely dare to expect success, and in which a writer of established fame might fail without disgrace. It is an experiment on the temper of the public mind, as to how far a thirst for a happier condition of moral and polit-
5 ical society survives, among the enlightened and refined, the tempests which have shaken the age in which we live. I have sought to enlist the harmony of metrical language, the etherial combinations of the fancy, the rapid and subtle transitions of human passion, all those elements which essentially compose a Poem, in the cause of a liberal and comprehensive morality,
10 and in the view of kindling within the bosoms of my readers, a virtuous enthusiasm for those doctrines of liberty and justice, that faith and hope in something good, which neither violence, nor misrepresentation, nor prejudice, can ever totally extinguish among mankind.

For this purpose I have chosen a story of human passion in its most uni-
15 versal character, diversified with moving and romantic adventures, and appealing, in contempt of all artificial opinions and institutions, to the common sympathies of every human breast. I have made no attempt to recommend the motives which I would substitute for those at present governing mankind by methodical and systematic argument. I would only
20 awaken the feelings, so that the reader should see the beauty of true virtue,

---

Pref. 3. experiment] Cp. Wordsworth's Advertisement to *Lyrical Ballads* (1798): 'The majority of the following Poems are to be considered as experiments' – repeated with slight modification in the Preface to the enlarged editions of 1800, 1802 and 1805; also Byron's Preface to *Childe Harold's Pilgrimage* I and II (1812): 'these two cantos are merely experimental'.

Pref. 3. temper] Disposition, inclination.

Pref. 5. enlightened and refined] The readers particularly addressed by *L&C*: S. described the poem as immune from government prosecution because 'of a character so refined and so remote from the conceptions of the vulgar' in a letter to the publisher Charles Ollier of 11 December 1817 (*L* i 579). Cp. the Preface to *PU* lines 122–30.

Pref. 5–6. tempests . . . live] The political and military upheavals of the years from the beginning of the French Revolution to the battle of Waterloo and the restoration of the Bourbon monarchy in France (1815), which the Congress of Vienna (1814–15) had translated into a redistribution of sovereignty and reshaped national borders in western and central Europe.

Pref. 9. liberal and comprehensive morality] St. Clair, *The Godwins and the Shelleys* (1989) 431 notes the echo of the Preface to the first edition of Godwin's *Political Justice* (1793) – 'He [the author] conceived politics to be the proper vehicle of a liberal morality' (*Political Justice* i p. vi) – as well as other interesting similarities between the two prefaces. See also note to Preface lines 234–5.

Pref. 11–12. faith and hope in something good] S.'s later assertion of the central role of hope in his moral psychology is apt here: 'Hope, as Coleridge says is a solemn duty which we owe alike to ourselves & to the world – a worship to the spirit of good within, which requires before it sends that inspiration forth, which impresses its likeness upon all that it creates, devoted & disinterested homage' (*L* ii 125). See *Q Mab* vi 11–22 (and note) and headnote *Sources and Influences*, p. 28.

and be incited to those enquiries which have led to my moral and polit-
ical creed, and that of some of the sublimest intellects in the world. The
Poem therefore, (with the exception of the first Canto, which is purely intro-
ductory), is narrative, not didactic. It is a succession of pictures illustrat-
25 ing the growth and progress of individual mind aspiring after excellence,
and devoted to the love of mankind; its influence in refining and making
pure the most daring and uncommon impulses of the imagination, the
understanding, and the senses; its impatience at 'all the oppressions which
are done under the sun;' its tendency to awaken public hope and to enlighten
30 and improve mankind; the rapid effects of the application of that tendency;
the awakening of an immense nation from their slavery and degradation
to a true sense of moral dignity and freedom; the bloodless dethronement
of their oppressors, and the unveiling of the religious frauds by which they
had been deluded into submission; the tranquillity of successful patriotism,
35 and the universal toleration and benevolence of true philanthropy; the
treachery and barbarity of hired soldiers; vice not the object of punish-
ment and hatred, but kindness and pity; the faithlessness of tyrants; the

Pref. 24. didactic] Aiming to instruct by the 'methodical and systematic argument' that S. declines
to employ in the Preface line 19. S. considered, in reference to Q *Mab*, that 'A poem very
didactic is I think very stupid' (*L* i 350), and declared, 'Didactic poetry is my abhorrence', in
the Preface to *PU* lines 122–3 where he elaborates on the aversion here expressed.

Pref. 24. pictures] The unusual word – as a description of narrative – has the rhetorical sense
given to it by Godwin: 'There are two modes, according to which the minds of human beings
may be influenced, by him who is desirous to conduct them. The first of these, is a strong
and commanding picture, taking hold of the imagination, and surprising the judgement; the
second, a distinct and unanswerable statement of reasons' (*Political Justice* ii 134).

Pref. 25. individual mind] an *canc.* individual mind *Nbk* 4a f. 2v. By cancelling his original
'an' S. typifies and generalises the revolutionary aspirations of the poem's title-characters.

Pref. 28–9. 'all . . . sun'] 'So I returned, and considered all the oppressions that are done under
the sun: and behold the tears of *such as were* oppressed, and they had no comforter; and on
the side of their oppressors *there was* power; but they had no comforter': *Ecclesiastes* iv 1.
T. L. Peacock quotes the same phrase *à propos* of the satirical aim of his novel *Maid Marian*
in a letter to S. of 29 November 1818, suggesting that it was a watchword between them
(*Peacock Works* viii 209). Both he and S. will have recalled Southey's use of the biblical phrase
in his defence of his youthful political opinions in *A Letter to William Smith, Esq. M.P.* (1817):
'I wrote *Wat Tyler* as one who was impatient of "all the oppressions that are done under the
sun"' – quoted in *The Examiner* 489 (11 May 1817) 300, which comments: 'he now thinks
it his bounden duty to justify them all'.

Pref. 29. public hope] See note to Preface lines 11–12 and headnote *Sources and Influences*, p. 28.

Pref. 34. submission] See note to the title of the poem, on the revised title *The Revolt of Islam*.

Pref. 36. hired soldiers] i.e. a professional standing army, as opposed to a citizens' militia or
to patriot volunteers 'who war but on their native ground / For natural rights' (lines 2445–6).
Cp. S. to Byron (23 April 1817): 'As to this country, you will have heard that the ministers
have gained a victory [the suspension of Habeas Corpus and the passing of the Seditious
Meetings Act in the previous month], which has not been disturbed by a single murmur; if
I except those of famine, which they have troops of hireling soldiers to repress' (*L* i 540).

confederacy of the Rulers of the World, and the restoration of the expelled
Dynasty by foreign arms; the massacre and extermination of the Patriots,
40 and the victory of established power; the consequences of legitimate
despotism, civil war, famine, plague, superstition, and an utter extinction
of the domestic affections; the judicial murder of the advocates of Liberty;
the temporary triumph of oppression, that secure earnest of its final and
inevitable fall; the transient nature of ignorance and error, and the etern-
45 ity of genius and virtue. Such is the series of delineations of which the
Poem consists. And if the lofty passions with which it has been my scope
to distinguish this story, shall not excite in the reader a generous impulse,
an ardent thirst for excellence, an interest profound and strong, such as
belongs to no meaner desires – let not the failure be imputed to a natural
50 unfitness for human sympathy in these sublime and animating themes. It
is the business of the Poet to communicate to others the pleasure and the
enthusiasm arising out of those images and feelings, in the vivid presence
of which within his own mind, consists at once his inspiration and his
reward.

Pref. 38–9. confederacy of the Rulers of the World . . . foreign arms] An unmistakable allusion to
the restoration of the Bourbon dynasty in France in 1814 and 1815 by a coalition of
European powers including Austria, Prussia, Russia and Great Britain.

Pref. 42. domestic affections] The fair copy in *Nbk 4a* continues: 'The belief in Hell becoming
an epidemic madness which grows furious & cruel with the increase of public calamity'
(f. 3v). This phrase is partially underlined in pencil, suggesting that it attracted attention,
perhaps in the printing-house. It is possible that the printer either removed it himself or
insisted that the author do so, though in a copy of *RofI* annotated by S. in which he indicates
that the printer did remove a similarly provocative phrase (see note to Preface line 249) he
does not signal that this one was interfered with. Contagious public fear of Hell is graph-
ically represented in the poem in lines 4117–215; 4288–338. See also note to Preface line 55.
Respect for the *domestic affections* guarantees political liberty according to Victor Frankenstein
in *Frankenstein* (1818), the proofs of which S. was correcting around the time he composed
the Preface: 'if no man allowed any pursuit whatsoever to interfere with the tranquillity of
his domestic affections, Greece had not been enslaved; Caesar would have spared his country;
America would have been discovered more gradually; and the empires of Mexico and Peru
had not been destroyed' (Ch. 3; *MSW* i 38).

Pref. 44–5. eternity of genius and virtue] A leading idea of the poem which unites its poetic
and political themes and is elaborately figured in S.'s representation of the Temple of the
Spirit (559–666) as well as being reasserted after the death of Laon and Cythna: 'For a deep
shade was cleft, and we did know, / That virtue, though obscured on Earth, not less / Survives
all mortal change in lasting loveliness' (4780–2). Rousseau had defined the role of virtue,
with its republican and secular resonances, as a stimulus to creation – 'l'exercice des plus
sublimes vertus élève et nourrit le génie' – a sentence that S. would have encountered as the
epigraph to Mary Wollstonecraft's *Mary, A Fiction* (1788): see *Mary Jnl* i 15, 22 (17, 31 August
1814). The relation between the two qualities, which is developed at length by Godwin in
Political Justice, Book IV, Ch. V and Appendix, has a temporal as well as an eternal aspect in
L&C. S. would specify this sense in November 1818, referring to the persecution and impris-
onment of the sixteenth-century Italian poet Tasso by the Duke of Ferrara, as the inescapable
result in human life of 'the alliance between virtue & genius' (*L* ii 47).

Pref. 46. scope] Object, intention. Cp. *L&C* lines 1182–5.

55   The panic which, like an epidemic transport, seized upon all classes
of men during the excesses consequent upon the French Revolution, is
gradually giving place to sanity. It has ceased to be believed, that whole
generations of mankind ought to consign themselves to a hopeless inher-
itance of ignorance and misery, because a nation of men who had been
60 dupes and slaves for centuries, were incapable of conducting themselves
with the wisdom and tranquillity of freemen so soon as some of their
fetters were partially loosened. That their conduct could not have been
marked by any other characters than ferocity and thoughtlessness, is the
historical fact from which liberty derives all its recommendations, and false-
65 hood the worst features of its deformity. There is a reflux in the tide of
human things which bears the shipwrecked hopes of men into a secure
haven, after the storms are past. Methinks, those who now live have sur-
vived an age of despair.
      The French Revolution may be considered as one of those manifesta-
70 tions of a general state of feeling among civilized mankind, produced by
a defect of correspondence between the knowledge existing in society and
the improvement, or gradual abolition of political institutions. The year
1788 may be assumed as the epoch of one of the most important crises
produced by this feeling. The sympathies connected with that event
75 extended to every bosom. The most generous and amiable natures were
those which participated the most extensively in these sympathies. But such

Pref. 55. epidemic transport] An epidemic disease is specific to a time and place and the result
of a cause not normally present; *transport* is the state of being carried out of one's usual mind,
as in frenzy or trance. S.'s phrase insists that the panic reaction to the extremes of the French
Revolution was a local and temporary visitation, as of a contagious illness, which has now
nearly run its course. The frenzy in question is vividly exhibited in lines 4162–215, 4288–
338, 4450–566. See also note to Preface line 42.

Pref. 65. reflux] A refluence or flowing back, as in lines 4528–9.

Pref. 69–72. The French Revolution . . . political institutions] Apologists for the French Revolu-
tion maintained that it had followed naturally from improvements in social and political
understanding: 'it is no more than the consequence of a mental revolution priorly existing
in France' (Paine, *Rights of Man* in *Paine Writings* ii 333), a view which S. had adopted in
the pamphlet *Proposals For An Association* (1812) where he wrote of 'the discoveries in the
sciences of politics and morals, which preceded and occasioned the Revolutions of America
and France' (*Prose Works* 50; see also *PVR* (1819) *Prose* 235). By subsuming this position under
the larger Godwinian premiss of ceaseless human progress towards the perfection of know-
ledge, S. presents the French Revolution as the exemplary modern episode of an historically
inevitable process in accord with which the institutions of state must alter to reflect the
current phase of a perpetually advancing opinion.

Pref. 73. 1788] The year that saw the economic and political situation in France arrive at a
crisis following unsuccessful attempts at fiscal reform which led Louis XVI to dismiss the Paris
parlement and remove effective power from it and from its provincial counterparts. The result-
ing widespread public disorder and political dissatisfaction persuaded the king to call the Estates
General for the following May, so setting the scene for the conflict between the third estate
and the clergy and nobles which precipitated the decisive events of 1789.

Pref. 73. epoch] A date initiating a distinctive era in history.

a degree of unmingled good was expected, as it was impossible to realize.
If the Revolution had been in every respect prosperous, then misrule and
superstition would lose half their claims to our abhorrence, as fetters which
80 the captive can unlock with the slightest motion of his fingers, and which
do not eat with poisonous rust into the soul. The revulsion occasioned
by the atrocities of the demagogues and the re-establishment of successive
tyrannies in France was terrible, and felt in the remotest corner of the civil-
ized world. Could they listen to the plea of reason who had groaned under
85 the calamities of a social state, according to the provisions of which, one
man riots in luxury whilst another famishes for want of bread? Can he who
the day before was a trampled slave, suddenly become liberal-minded, forbear-
ing, and independent? This is the consequence of the habits of a state of
society to be produced by resolute perseverance and indefatigable hope,
90 and long-suffering and long-believing courage, and the systematic efforts

Pref. 78. prosperous] Successful, fortunate.

Pref. 82–3. atrocities of the demagogues . . . successive tyrannies in France] The excusing of the
violent retribution of the revolutionaries in France in the next few sentences conforms in
essentials to Paine's in *Rights of Man*: 'These outrages were not the effect of the principles of
the Revolution, but of the degraded mind that existed before the Revolution, and which the
Revolution is calculated to reform' (*Paine Writings* ii 297). S. had adapted this view in *Proposals
For An Association* (1812) so as to explain not only the crimes of the revolutionaries but the
reversal of their ideals: 'The murders during the period of the French Revolution, and the
despotism which has since been established, prove that the doctrines of Philanthropy and
Freedom, were but shallowly understood' (*Prose Works* 51); he developed this position fur-
ther in PVR (*Prose* 235–6).

Pref. 85–6. one man riots . . . want of bread?] Rehearsing a long-standing grievance of re-
formers, e.g. the final phrase of Rousseau's *Discours sur l'inégalité* (1755) – 'une poignée de
gens regorge de superfluités tandis que la multitude affamée manque du nécessaire' – which
S. had transformed into a principle of natural law in *Declaration of Rights* (1812): 'No man
has a right to monopolize more than he can enjoy; what the rich give to the poor, whilst
millions are starving, is not a perfect favour, but an imperfect right' (*Prose Works* 59). Many
contemporary readers will also have detected a reference to the *The Examiner*'s current cam-
paign against the disastrous effects of social inequality, which it conducted in five leading
articles from 12 October to 2 November, and 30 November 1817 under the headline 'Fellow-
Creatures Suffered to Die in the Streets'. The series was prompted by the death of a destitute
discharged seaman in Covent Garden Market which Leigh Hunt took as the occasion for broad
political reflection: 'the subject of men starving, or otherwise dying from want, in the streets,
is unfortunately too much connected with politics in these times' (No. 511, 12 October 1817,
641). On 14 October MWS wrote to S., who was then staying with Hunt in London, 'Hunt
was hardly <u>strong</u> enough in his paper today – The horror of a man's dying in the street was
represented as terrible but was it enough impressed on his reader the superabundant capa-
city of . . . the spectators to have relieved him' (*Mary L* i 54).

Pref. 86–91. Can he . . . intellect and virtue] S. consistently held that a gradual improvement
in political understanding and civic discipline was the precondition for a responsible exer-
cise of power by those long denied it under a tyrannical and brutalising regime. See *Proposals
For An Association* (1812, *Prose Works* 51–2), *A Proposal For Putting Reform To The Vote*
(February–March 1817, *Prose Works* 175–6), and PVR (1819, *Prose* 229–61). Godwin's formula-
tion of the position in *Political Justice* and its restatement in the *Examiner* for 16 March 1817
are cited in *Prose Works* 427.

of generations of men of intellect and virtue. Such is the lesson which ex-
perience teaches now. But on the first reverses of hope in the progress of
French liberty, the sanguine eagerness for good overleapt the solution of
these questions, and for a time extinguished itself in the unexpectedness
95 of their result. Thus many of the most ardent and tender-hearted of the
worshippers of public good, have been morally ruined by what a partial
glimpse of the events they deplored, appeared to show as the melancholy
desolation of all their cherished hopes. Hence gloom and misanthropy have
become the characteristics of the age in which we live, the solace of a dis-
100 appointment that unconsciously finds relief only in the wilful exaggera-
tion of its own despair. This influence has tainted the literature of the
age with the hopelessness of the minds from which it flows. Metaphysics*,
and enquiries into moral and political science, have become little else than
vain attempts to revive exploded superstitions, or sophisms like those† of
105 Mr. Malthus, calculated to lull the oppressors of mankind into a security

* I ought to except Sir W. Drummond's 'Academical Questions;' a volume of very acute and
powerful metaphysical criticism.

† It is remarkable, as a symptom of the revival of public hope, that Mr. Malthus has assigned,
in the later editions of his work, an indefinite dominion to moral restraint over the princi-
ple of population. This concession answers all the inferences from his doctrine unfavourable
to human improvement, and reduces the 'ESSAY ON POPULATION' to a commentary illus-
trative of the unanswerableness of 'POLITICAL JUSTICE'.

Pref. 92–5. But . . . result] The obstacles and practical difficulties attending the revolutionaries'
efforts at reform in France disappointed their most optimistic supporters and temporarily
changed their confident hope into premature despair.

S.'s note [Metaphysics]. Sir William Drummond, (1770?–1828) MP, FRS, diplomat, translator,
political philosopher, archaeologist, dramatist and poet, had recently come to notice as a
biblical critic and writer on general philosophy. *Oedipus Judaicus* (1811), in which he argued
that some episodes in the Old Testament should be understood not as historical records but
as astronomical allegories, aroused a controversy with the Reverend George D'Oyly which
was amply reported from an orthodox standpoint in the *Quarterly Review* ix (1813) 329–46.
S. declared himself unpersuaded by *Oedipus Judaicus* (*L* i 350) but both he and Peacock greatly
admired *Academical Questions* (1805) which develops its own position of sceptical idealism through
a rigorously critical survey of ancient and modern metaphysics and epistemology. (The *Edinburgh
Review* vii (1805) 163–85 bestows both guarded praise and some acerbic criticism on it.) S.
records his specific debt to Drummond in his own intellectual development in the prose frag-
ment 'On Life' (1819, *Reiman* (1977) 476–77) and his opinion of him as 'the most acute meta-
physical critic of the age' in *L* ii 142. The democratic sympathies that Drummond displayed
in his *A Review of the Governments of Sparta and Athens* (1794) and the religious scepticism he
demonstrated in both *Oedipus Judaicus* and *Academical Questions* lend a polemical edge to S.'s
reference to him here. Especially, the citation aligns the Preface and the poem to follow with
the sceptical tradition of unfettered intellectual investigation which Drummond emphatically
characterises in the Preface to *Academical Questions* as: 'that love of enquiry, which is the
promise of genius . . . that freedom of thought, which is the right, and the proof, of intelli-
gence . . . he, who will not reason, is a bigot; he, who cannot, is a fool; and he, who dares
not, is a slave' (xiii–xv).

Pref. 104–5. those of Mr. Malthus] S.'s note [those of Mr. Malthus]. *An Essay on the Principle of
Population, as It Affects the Future Improvement of Society* (1798) by the Rev. Thomas Robert
Malthus (1766–1834) argued that human improvement was severely restricted by the
inevitable disparity between population, which tended to increase geometrically, and the means

of everlasting triumph. Our works of fiction and poetry have been over-shadowed by the same infectious gloom. But mankind appear to me to be emerging from their trance. I am aware, methinks, of a slow, gradual, silent change. In that belief I have composed the following Poem.

110   I do not presume to enter into competition with our greatest contem-porary Poets. Yet I am unwilling to tread in the footsteps of any who have preceded me. I have sought to avoid the imitation of any style of language or versification peculiar to the original minds of which it is the character, designing that even if what I have produced be worthless, it should still

115   be properly my own. Nor have I permitted any system relating to mere

---

of subsistence which increased only arithmetically; and that therefore human ills such as dis-ease, hunger, poverty and war – 'vice and misery' – had a necessary function in curbing human numbers. Moreover these checks must operate most extensively among the lower classes of mankind, so preventing any significant amelioration of their lot. Malthus acknowledged that his investigation of the population problem had been prompted by his disagreement with Godwin's essay 'On Avarice and Profusion' in *The Enquirer* (1797), and throughout the *Essay* he takes issue with Godwin's arguments for perfectibility in *Political Justice*. In the second edition of the *Essay* (1803), revised and much enlarged, Malthus allowed that a third factor (in addition to vice and misery) might operate to check the growth of population, 'moral restraint', or the 'duty of each individual not to marry till he has a prospect of supporting his children' (Book IV, Chapter I). This version of the *Essay*, incorporating the possibility of virtuous human intervention, in the form of a socially-responsible sexual abstinence, to mit-igate the laws of population went through four further editions, incorporating additional changes, in the author's lifetime: 1806, 1807, 1817 and 1826. In common with other advo-cates of social justice, S. regarded the *Essay* as pernicious. In both *Proposals for an Association* (*Prose Works* 52–3) and *PVR* (*Prose* 247–8) he castigates Malthusian principles as tending to perpetuate the evils of an unequal social system by throwing the burden of it upon the poor and by furnishing the powerful with a 'sophism' with which to deny in advance the efficacy of necessary reform. See also *L* i 267; ii 43 (where S. moderates his view of Malthus), 261, 303, 364, *A Ballad: Young Parson Richards* (no. 309) and headnote, and note to *PU* III i 19.

Pref. 107. infectious gloom] S. is thinking principally of Byron whose *Manfred*, he wrote to the author on 9 July 1817, 'made me dreadfully melancholy, and I fear other friends in England, too. Why do you indulge this despondency?' (*L* i 547). On 24 September 1817 he passed on to Byron Leigh Hunt's view that *Manfred* 'administers to a diseased view of things', adding, 'I should say that some of your earlier writings had that tendency, but that "Manfred" was free from it' (*L* i 557). S.'s opinion on the altered tenor of Wordsworth's and Coleridge's poetry is also relevant: see 'O! there are spirits of the air' (no. 106), 'To Wordsworth' (no. 111) and 'Verses written on receiving a Celandine in a letter from England' (no. 117) and the head-notes thereto.

Pref. 110–11. our greatest contemporary Poets] Early in Nbk 2 S. recorded his anxieties on this score: 'Is this an imitation of L⁴ Byron's poem? It is certainly written in the same metre. Coleridge & Wordsworth to be considered' (3). S. had carried the MS of the 3rd canto of Byron's *Childe Harold's Pilgrimage*, which like *L&C* was written in the Spenserian stanza, from Switzerland to the publisher John Murray in September 1816.

Pref. 114. designing] desiring Nbk 4a f. 8r.

Pref. 115–22. Nor have I . . . that familiarity.] The passage acknowledges, while pointedly refusing to join, the contemporary debate on poetic diction and the best models for it among older writers, as carried on in, for example, Wordsworth's Advertisement (1798) and Preface (1800, 1802, 1805) to *Lyrical Ballads* and its Appendix (1802, 1805), Leigh Hunt's Preface to *The Story of Rimini* (1816) and Chapters 16–20 of Coleridge's *Biographia Literaria* (July 1817).

words, to divert the attention of the reader from whatever interest I may
have succeeded in creating, to my own ingenuity in contriving to disgust
them according to the rules of criticism. I have simply clothed my thoughts
in what appeared to me the most obvious and appropriate language. A per-
120 son familiar with nature, and with the most celebrated productions of the
human mind, can scarcely err in following the instinct, with respect to
selection of language, produced by that familiarity.

There is an education peculiarly fitted for a Poet, without which, genius
and sensibility can hardly fill the circle of their capacities. No education
125 indeed can entitle to this appellation a dull and unobservant mind, or one,
though neither dull nor unobservant, in which the channels of commun-
ication between thought and expression have been obstructed or closed.
How far it is my fortune to belong to either of the latter classes, I cannot
know. I aspire to be something better. The circumstances of my accidental
130 education have been favourable to this ambition. I have been familiar from
boyhood with mountains and lakes, and the sea, and the solitude of forests:
Danger which sports upon the brink of precipices, has been my playmate.
I have trodden the glaciers of the Alps, and lived under the eye of Mont

Pref. 115. system] Predetermined scheme or theory: 'In poetry I have sought to avoid system
& mannerism; I wish those who excel me in genius, would pursue the same plan' (S. to Keats,
27 July 1820, *L* ii 221).

Pref. 118. them] Regularised to 'him' in *Rossetti 1870, 1878; Dowden 1891; 1975. Nbk 4a* f. 8r
reads 'them'. Cp. Preface line 151 and note.

Pref. 119. appropriate language] A traditional commonplace which was enjoying renewed cur-
rency in recent critical debate. Coleridge had placed 'a perfect appropriateness of the words
to the meaning' first among the 'excellencies' of Wordsworth's poetry in *Biographia Literaria*
(July 1817), Chapter 22; cp. also Leigh Hunt, Preface to *The Story of Rimini* (1816): 'All the
merit I claim is that of having made an attempt to describe natural things in a language
becoming them.'

Pref. 120–21. the most celebrated productions of the human mind] i.e. the greatest poems, as in
S.'s remark in a letter of 6 July 1817 to T. J. Hogg: 'that production [*The Iliad*] . . . surpasses
any other single production of the human mind' (*L* i 545). Cp. also *L* i 507 (to Byron,
29 September 1816): 'those unequalled achievements of mind [the works of Homer and
Shakespeare] by which we are so deeply benefitted'.

Pref. 129–30. accidental education] *Education* is here to be understood in the comprehensive
Godwinian sense of any experience that gives rise to ideas and reflections, and *accidental
education* as 'the education of accident, or those impressions we receive independently of
any design on the part of the preceptor' (*Political Justice* i 45). The experiences recounted
combine with the innate qualities of *genius and sensibility*, tentatively claimed by S. at the
beginning of the paragraph, and with the power of awakening sympathetic response that he
aspires to at the end, to form the complete poet. He conspicuously leaves out of the reckon-
ing his formal education at school and university.

Pref. 133–34. I have trodden . . . Mont Blanc] S., Mary and Claire Clairmont made an expedi-
tion from Geneva to the valley of Chamonix between 21 and 26 July 1816 during which
they were able to inspect several Alpine glaciers, walk upon the surface of the one known as
la mer de glace at Montanvert, and view Mont Blanc from various perspectives. S.'s letter to
Peacock of 22–26 July 1816 (*L* i 495–502, included in *1817*) describes the expedition, as does
Mary Jnl i 112–21.

Blanc. I have been a wanderer among distant fields. I have sailed down
135 mighty rivers, and seen the sun rise and set, and the stars come forth, whilst
I have sailed night and day down a rapid stream among mountains. I have
seen populous cities, and have watched the passions which rise and
spread, and sink and change amongst assembled multitudes of men. I have
seen the theatre of the more visible ravages of tyranny and war, cities and
140 villages reduced to scattered groups of black and roofless houses, and the
naked inhabitants sitting famished upon their desolated thresholds. I have
conversed with living men of genius. The poetry of ancient Greece and
Rome, and modern Italy, and our own country, has been to me like ex-
ternal nature, a passion and an enjoyment. Such are the sources from
145 which the materials for the imagery of my Poem have been drawn. I have
considered Poetry in its most comprehensive sense, and have read the
Poets and the Historians and the Metaphysicians* whose writings have been

* In this sense there may be such a thing as perfectibility in works of fiction, notwithstand-
ing the concession often made by the advocates of human improvement, that perfectibility
is a term applicable only to science.

Pref. 134–36. I have sailed down mighty rivers . . . among mountains] Recalling the ten days'
journey by water that S., Mary and Claire Clairmont made in late August and early Septem-
ber 1814, which took them from Lake Lucerne in Switzerland, down the Reuss and the Rhine
to Bonn; they continued by road to Rotterdam whence they sailed for England, landing
at Gravesend on 13 September. See *1817* 55–71, *Mary Jnl* i 20–3, *Claire Jnl* 31–7.

Pref. 138–41. I have seen the theatre . . . desolated thresholds] S., Mary and Claire Clairmont
observed just such scenes of destruction, the consequences of the invasion of France by an
Austrian and Russian army earlier in the year, in several of the towns and villages they passed
through on their way to Switzerland in August 1814. See *L* i 392, *1817* 19–28, *Mary Jnl* i
12–14, and note to lines 2743–7.

Pref. 141–42. I have conversed with living men of genius] I have listened to the conversation of
men of genius *canc. Nbk 4a* f. 9r–9v. The more active formulation *conversed with* (including
the sense: associated with, kept company with) refers pre-eminently to Godwin and Byron
with whom S. had regularly spoken and corresponded.

Pref. 143. modern Italy] In contrast to ancient Rome; S. decribes Shakespeare, Dante and Milton
as 'modern writers' in *DP*; here he probably means Dante (1265–1321), Petrarch (1304–74),
and the writers of heroic romance Ariosto (1474–1535) and Tasso (1544–95).

Pref. 147. Historians] Historians, *L&C/Rof1*; historians *Nbk 4a* f. 10r. Later *eds* have usually removed
the comma, which *Locock 1911* considered 'erroneously printed'. If left in place it restricts
the reference of the phrase *whose writings have been accessible to me* to *the Metaphysicians* alone,
whereas the sense requires that it refer to *the Poets and the Historians* as well.

S.'s note. S. tentatively puts forward Godwin's principle of general improvement – 'There is
no science that is not capable of additions; there is no art that may not be carried to a still
higher perfection' (*Political Justice* i 119) – before acknowledging the qualification in Hazlitt's
recent essay 'Why the Arts are Not Progressive? – A Fragment' (*The Morning Chronicle*, 1814)
reprinted with modifications in *The Round Table* (1817) by Hazlitt and Leigh Hunt which
MWS records reading in February 1817 (*Mary Jnl* i 99, 165): 'the analogy appealed to in sup-
port of the regular advances of art to higher degrees of excellence, totally fails; it applies to
science, not to art' (*Hazlitt Works* iv 160). The appropriateness of S.'s note to its passage is
hardly evident at first glance, and *Locock 1911*, following A. C. Bradley, wondered whether
it had been wrongly placed. But in both *Nbk 4a* f. 10r and *L&C/Rof1* the footnote is clearly
keyed by an asterisk to the phrase ending with *Metaphysicians*, and it is difficult to imagine

accessible to me, and have looked upon the beautiful and majestic scenery of the earth as common sources of those elements which it is the province
150 of the Poet to embody and combine. Yet the experience and the feelings to which I refer, do not in themselves constitute men Poets, but only prepares them to be the auditors of those who are. How far I shall be found to possess that more essential attribute of Poetry, the power of awakening in others sensations like those which animate my own bosom, is that which,
155 to speak sincerely, I know not; and which with an acquiescent and contented spirit, I expect to be taught by the effect which I shall produce upon those whom I now address.

   I have avoided, as I have said before, the imitation of any contemporary style. But there must be a resemblance which does not depend upon
160 their own will, between all the writers of any particular age. They cannot escape from subjection to a common influence which arises out of an infinite combination of circumstances belonging to the times in which they live, though each is in a degree the author of the very influence by which his being is thus pervaded. Thus, the tragic Poets of the age of Pericles;
165 the Italian revivers of ancient learning; those mighty intellects of our own country that succeeded the Reformation, the translators of the Bible, Shakespeare, Spenser, the Dramatists of the reign of Elizabeth, and Lord Bacon*; the colder spirits of the interval that succeeded; – all, resemble

---

* Milton stands alone in the age which he illumined.

where else it might have been positioned. Its development of the text emerges distinctly enough if one bears in mind: 1. that in the MS, after the word *Metaphysicians*, S. cancelled the phrase, 'of antiquity & of our own coun', thereby removing from the passage as printed the idea of a long historical development which evidently remained in his mind as he composed the footnote; 2. that the historical progression intended is that of *Poetry in its most comprehensive sense*, which includes history, philosophy and creative expression generally whether in verse or in prose. This enlarged idea of poetry is already present in Francis Jeffrey's review of Weber's edition of John Ford's *Dramatic Works* (*Edinburgh Review* xxxvi (August 1811) 276; see note to Preface line 170) where prose writers as diverse as Barrow, Hooker, Jeremy Taylor and Francis Bacon are declared to be poets in the 'highest and most comprehensive sense of the word'. S. developed this notion fully in *DP*, where he considers both Plato and Bacon as poets in common with 'all the authors of revolutions in opinion'. If S.'s *fiction* is also taken broadly, to signify imaginative creation rather than merely 'fanciful invention', then the note appears as a speculation whether works of poetry thus inclusively defined might exhibit the same progressive tendency through history as do works of science – in the sense of systematised knowledge of any subject.

Pref. 149. sources] Referring to the reading mentioned earlier as well as to *scenery*.

Pref. 151. prepares] prepare *1839; Rossetti 1870, 1878; Forman 1876–77; Locock 1911*; prepares *Nbk 4a* f. 10r. An example of S.'s occasionally casual practice in the matter of agreement between subject and verb. Cp. Preface line 118 and note.

Pref. 164. age of Pericles] The chief statesman (*c.* 495–29 BC) of fifth-century Athens gives his name to the age in which the great dramatists Aeschylus (525–456), Sophocles (*c.* 496–406/05) and Euripides (*c.* 485–06) flourished.

S.'s note. Keyed by means of an asterisk after *Bacon* and referring to the phrase *those . . . Bacon*, the note also looks forward to the following phrase: *the colder spirits of the interval that succeeded*, which describes the temper (according to S.) and time in which Milton's major poetry

each other, and differ from every other in their several classes. In this view
170 of things, Ford can no more be called the imitator of Shakespeare, than
Shakespeare the imitator of Ford. There were perhaps few other points of
resemblance between these two men, than that which the universal and
inevitable influence of their age produced. And this is an influence which
neither the meanest scribbler, nor the sublimest genius of any era can escape;
175 and which I have not attempted to escape.

I have adopted the stanza of Spenser, (a measure inexpressibly beauti-
ful) not because I consider it a finer model of poetical harmony than the
blank verse of Shakespeare and Milton, but because in the latter there is
no shelter for mediocrity: you must either succeed or fail. This perhaps
180 an aspiring spirit should desire. But I was enticed also, by the brilliancy
and magnificence of sound which a mind that has been nourished upon
musical thoughts, can produce by a just and harmonious arrangement of
the pauses of this measure. Yet there will be found some instances where
I have completely failed in this attempt, and one, which I here request
185 the reader to consider as an erratum, where there is left most inadvertently
an alexandrine in the middle of a stanza.

But in this, as in every other respect, I have written fearlessly. It is the
misfortune of this age, that its Writers, too thoughtless of immortality,

---

was published. Cp. *DP*: 'The period in our own history of the grossest degradation of the
drama is the reign of Charles II when all forms in which poetry had been accustomed to be
expressed became hymns to the triumph of kingly power over liberty and virtue' (*Reiman*
(*1977*)   491).

Pref. 168–69. all, resemble . . . several classes] 'Every writer of a given period resembles every
other, while each differs from all other writers of the same kind but of another period'.

Pref. 170. Ford] The *Dramatic Works* of John Ford (1586–after 1639), author, in whole or in
part, of eighteen plays, including '*Tis Pity She's A Whore* and *The Broken Heart*, had recently
been edited by Henry Weber (Edinburgh and London, 1811). Francis Jeffrey's review of Weber's
edition in the *Edinburgh Review* xxxvi (August 1811) anticipates S.'s ideas in this paragraph
by discovering a 'common character' (276) in the writers of Shakespeare's age; as does Charles
Lamb who found that the Elizabethan, Jacobean and Caroline dramatists 'all . . . spoke nearly
the same language, and had a set of moral feelings and notions in common' (*Specimens of
English Dramatic Poets, Who Lived About the Time of Shakespeare* (2nd edn, 1813) 459). See
note to epigraph to the Dedication.

Pref. 173–75. And this . . . to escape] In a letter to Charles Ollier of 15 October 1819 S. wrote,
in reference to the review of *L&C/RofI* in the *Quarterly Review* for April 1819: 'The only remark
worth notice in this piece is the assertion that I imitate Wordsworth. It may as well be said
that Lord Byron imitates Wordsworth, or that Wordsworth imitates Lord Byron, both being
great poets, and deriving from the new springs of thought and feeling, which the great events
of our age have exposed to view, a similar tone of sentiment, imagery, and expression' (*L* ii
127). S. developed this idea of 'the spirit of the age' more fully in the Preface to *PU* and in *DP*.

Pref. 186. alexandrine in the middle of a stanza] In fact an alexandrine (or twelve-syllable line)
occurs as the fifth, or middle, line of the nine-line Spenserian stanza in two places: 1652,
3788; two others, 2537, 2555, are near-alexandrines.

Pref. 187–90. But . . . before their eyes] Cp. Hazlitt, 'On Different Sorts of Fame' (*The Examiner*,
21 April 1816; *The Round Table*, 1817): 'The spirit of universal criticism has superseded the

are exquisitely sensible to temporary praise or blame. They write with the
190 fear of Reviews before their eyes. This system of criticism sprang up in that
torpid interval when Poetry was not. Poetry, and the art which professes
to regulate and limit its powers, cannot subsist together. Longinus could
not have been the contemporary of Homer, nor Boileau of Horace. Yet this
species of criticism never presumed to assert an understanding of its own:
195 it has always, unlike true science, followed, not preceded the opinion of
mankind, and would even now bribe with worthless adulation some of
our greatest Poets to impose gratuitous fetters on their own imaginations,
and become unconscious accomplices in the daily murder of all genius either
not so aspiring or not so fortunate as their own. I have sought therefore
200 to write, as I believe that Homer, Shakespeare, and Milton wrote, with
an utter disregard of anonymous censure. I am certain that calumny and

anticipation of posthumous fame, and instead of waiting for the award of distant ages, the
poet or prose-writer receives his final doom from the next number of the *Edinburgh* or *Quarterly
Review*' (*Hazlitt Works* iv 95). S.'s formulation in *DP* of the role of time in the creation of true
fame is also apt: 'Even in modern times, no living poet ever arrived at the fulness of his
fame; the jury which sits in judgement on a poet, belonging as he does to all time, must be
composed of his peers: it must be impanelled by Time from the selectest of the wise of many
generations' (*Reiman* (1977) 486).

Pref. 190. This system of criticism] Prescriptive criticism in general rather than reviewing in
particular. Immediately before this sentence in *Nbk 4a* f. 12v S. wrote: 'There is a species of
criticism which presumes to instruct the world, by other rules than those which are found
in the'. Cancelling what he had written and continuing as in the printed text, he obscured
his meaning by leaving *This system* without a clear antecedent.

Pref. 192–93. Longinus . . . Horace] 'An age of poetic creation and one of critical codification
are fundamentally opposed in character'. The implication is that S.'s age, being one of cre-
ation, is inapt to conform to the prescriptions of criticism. 'Longinus' was the presumed author
of *On the Sublime*, a treatise of the first century AD which examines the means of achieving
intense and elevated effects in poetry and oratory. Nicolas Boileau-Despréaux (1636–1711)
translated Longinus into French and was himself the author of an *Art Poétique* which com-
prehensively defined a set of poetic canons for his age.

Pref. 197. greatest Poets . . . their own] S. is no doubt recalling the fulsome praise bestowed on
Byron's poetry, person, character and rank in society by Walter Scott in a review of *Childe
Harold's Pilgrimage III* and *The Prisoner of Chillon* in the *Quarterly Review* xvi (October 1816).
Scott expresses some disapprobation of Byron's political opinions, following this with a
prediction that 'his future writings may probably shew that he thinks better of the morals,
religion, and constitution of his country, than his poems have hitherto indicated' (194) as
well as suggestions on how such an improvement might be brought about: 'he must regulate
and tame the fire of his fancy, and descend from the heights to which she exalts him, in
order to achieve ease of mind and tranquillity . . . Let the patient submit to the discipline
of soul enjoined by religion, and recommended by philosophy, and the scar will become
speedily insensible to their stings' (207–8). The same review renders homage to Coleridge's
'high poetical genius' while deploring his 'wild, unbridled, and fiery imagination' which
has 'too frequently for his own popularity, wandered into the wild and mystic' (204). The
October 1816 number of the *Quarterly* appeared in February 1817; MWS records reading it
on 29 and 30 May (*Mary Jnl* i 172).

Pref. 201. anonymous censure] Both articles and reviews were unsigned in the major period-
icals of the day.

misrepresentation, though it may move me to compassion, cannot disturb my peace. I shall understand the expressive silence of those sagacious enem-
ies who dare not trust themselves to speak. I shall endeavour to extract
205 from the midst of insult, and contempt, and maledictions, those admoni-
tions which may tend to correct whatever imperfections such censurers may discover in this my first serious appeal to the Public. If certain Critics were as clear-sighted as they are malignant, how great would be the benefit to be derived from their virulent writings! As it is, I fear I shall be malicious
210 enough to be amused with their paltry tricks and lame invectives. Should the Public judge that my composition is worthless, I shall indeed bow before the tribunal from which Milton received his crown of immortality, and shall seek to gather, if I live, strength from that defeat, which may nerve me to some new enterprise of thought which may *not* be worthless. I can-
215 not conceive that Lucretius, when he meditated that poem whose doctrines are yet the basis of our metaphysical knowledge, and whose eloquence has been the wonder of mankind, wrote in awe of such censure as the hired sophists of the impure and superstitious noblemen of Rome might affix to what he should produce. It was at the period when Greece was led captive,

Pref. 205. insult . . . maledictions] S. anticipated an outraged response to the poem in a letter to Byron of 24 September 1817: 'As to me, I can but die; I can but be torn to pieces, or devoted to infamy most undeserved; and whether this is inflicted by the necessity of nature, and circumstances, or through a principle, pregnant, as I believe, with important benefit to mankind, is an alternative to which I cannot be indifferent' (*L* i 557).

Pref. 207. my first serious appeal to the Public] S. is according himself the period of appren-
ticeship traditionally allowed to the author of a heroic poem, such as Virgil, Milton and Spenser, and asking to be judged thereby rather than on *Q Mab* (1813) or the *Alastor* volume (1816), the two previously-published works that might enter into account in estimating his *serious* contribution to contemporary literature. The youthful efforts of the year 1810 – *V&C*, *PFMN*, and his two gothic romances *Zastrozzi* and *St. Irvyne* – as well as his later controversial prose pamphlets, he will have regarded as of a lower order of importance. He described *Alastor* sim-
ilarly on 7 March 1816 (*L* i 462).

Pref. 213. nerve] Encourage, embolden.

Pref. 215–16. that poem . . . metaphysical knowledge] S. is following the Preface to John Mason Good's edition of *De Rerum Natura* (1805), which he bought on 18 April 1815 (*Mary Jnl* i 75) and which claims that the Epicurean system embodied in Lucretius's poem and propagated by the French metaphysician Pierre Gassendi (1592–1655) 'was embraced by the most emin-
ent modern philosophers, and at last appears to have obtained an eternal triumph, from its application, by Newton and Huygens, to the department of natural philosophy, and, by Locke and Condillac, to that of metaphysics' (i cxxix–cxxx). See further note to Preface lines 231–2 and headnote *Sources and Influences*, pp. 25–6.

Pref. 218. impure and superstitious] The licentiousness and intemperance of the Roman nobility of the late republic was proverbial; traditionally Greek and Asian influences were accounted a principal cause of its moral decline. The situation was severely censured in Sallust's *Bellum Catilinae* x–xiii which S. read in 1815 (*Mary Jnl* i 97) and developed with numerous examples in *Memoirs of the Court of Augustus* 3 vols (1753–63) by Thomas Blackwell and John Mills which he read in 1816 (*Mary Jnl* i 97): see further J. P. V. D. Balsdon, *Romans and Aliens* (1979) chs 3–4. On the superstition of the nobles of the period see, for example, Plutarch's Life of Sulla v 4–vi 7; Life of Marius xvii 1–3, xlii 4–5.

Pref. 219. It was at the period] See headnote *Sources and Influences*, p. 25.

220 and Asia made tributary to the Republic, fast verging itself to slavery and
ruin, that a multitude of Syrian captives, bigoted to the worship of their
obscene Ashtaroth, and the unworthy successors of Socrates and Zeno, found
there a precarious subsistence by administering, under the name of freed-
men, to the vices and vanities of the great. These wretched men were skilled
225 to plead, with a superficial but plausible set of sophisms, in favour of that
contempt for virtue which is the portion of slaves, and that faith in por-
tents, the most fatal substitute for benevolence in the imaginations of men,
which arising from the enslaved communities of the East, then first began
to overwhelm the western nations in its stream. Were these the kind of
230 men whose disapprobation the wise and lofty-minded Lucretius should have
regarded with a salutary awe? The latest and perhaps the meanest of those
who follow in his footsteps, would disdain to hold life on such conditions.

The Poem now presented to the Public occupied little more than six
months in the composition. That period has been devoted to the task with

Pref. 222. obscene Ashtaroth] S. could have encountered the collective form *Ashtaroth*, the plu-
ral of Ashtoreth (or Astarte) the Syrian moon-goddess, in the Bible; e.g. *Judges* x 6: 'And the
children of Israel did evil again in the sight of the Lord, and served Baalim, and Ashtaroth,
and the gods of Syria', as well as in *Paradise Lost* i 419–23. Cicero (*De Natura Deorum* iii 59)
mentions Astarte as a Syrian manifestation of Venus. *Ashtaroth* seems here to be used broadly
to include Atargatis, the Dea Syria, who is identified with the Phrygian mother-goddess of
fertility Cybele in Lucian's *De Dea Syria* 15. The statue of Cybele was brought from Phrygia
to Rome at the end of the third century BC and placed in a temple on the Palatine Hill. The
obscene behaviour of the priests (Galli) of the Syrian goddess is described in *De Dea Syria*
50–60 and in Apuleius's *Metamorphoses* (*The Golden Ass*) viii 25–9. S. cites both texts in his
review (February 1818) of Peacock's *Rhododaphne* (*Prose Works* i 285; see also *L* i 542; *Mary
Jnl* i 102, 169–70). Lucretius's *De Rerum Natura* ii 600–60 describes the image and ceremo-
nial worship of Cybele as an example of a false conception of deity.

Pref. 222. unworthy successors of Socrates and Zeno] Asian Greeks who, taken as slaves by the
Roman armies, taught philosophy in Rome – as Socrates (469–399 BC) and Zeno of Citium
(*c*. 333–262 BC), founder of the Stoic school, had done at Athens. Greeks from Asia were
regarded with suspicion by their Roman captors as having learned habits of submission and
sycophancy under tyrannical regimes (*Romans and Aliens* 40; Cicero *Pro Flacco* 61–6, 100).

Pref. 223–24. freedmen] Slaves who had been released from servitude and acquired citizen-
ship, a very numerous class in the late Roman republic.

Pref. 228–29. enslaved communities . . . stream] It was a commonplace of Roman literature (e.g.
Lucan, *Pharsalia* vii 442–3) that Asians, and Syrians pre-eminently, being ruled by despots,
were born slaves. The corrupting Oriental influence that is traced here was deplored in *Memoirs
of the Court of Augustus* iii 398: 'When . . . foreign uncouth Deities were received and wor-
shipped; – when *Slavery* had entailed *Superstition* . . . and Superstition came in its Turn to sup-
port its baneful Parent; – then every Thing great or valuable was effaced in *Rome*'. See also
Romans and Aliens 67.

Pref. 231–32. The latest . . . footsteps] i.e. S. himself, alluding to Lucretius's celebrated claim
(*De Re. Nat.* iv 1–2) which S. had borrowed for one of the epigraphs to *Q Mab*: 'Avia Pieridum
peragro loca, nullius ante trita solo' (I wander through a pathless region of poetry, trodden
by no other foot before). Lucretius says of his own relation to his philosophic master Epicurus:
'Cuius ego ingressus vestigia' (I follow in his footsteps), *De Re. Nat.* v 55; also iii 3–4.

Pref. 233–34. six months] The dating of the poem's composition is discussed in the headnote
Composition and Publication, pp. 11–12.

235 unremitting ardour and enthusiasm. I have exercised a watchful and earnest
criticism on my work as it grew under my hands. I would willingly have
sent it forth to the world with that perfection which long labour and
revision is said to bestow. But I found that if I should gain something in
exactness by this method, I might lose much of the newness and energy
240 of imagery and language as it flowed fresh from my mind. And although
the mere composition occupied no more than six months, the thoughts
thus arranged were slowly gathered in as many years.

I trust that the reader will carefully distinguish between those opinions
which have a dramatic propriety in reference to the characters which they
245 are designed to elucidate, and such as are properly my own. The erroneous
and degrading idea which men have conceived of a Supreme Being, for
instance, is spoken against, but not the Supreme Being itself. The belief
which some superstitious persons whom I have brought upon the stage,
express in the cruelty and malevolence of God, is widely different from
250 my own. In recommending also a great and important change in the spirit
which animates the social institutions of mankind, I have avoided all flattery

Pref. 234–35. That period . . . enthusiasm] St. Clair, *The Godwins and the Shelleys* (1989) 431,
notes the echo of the 1793 Preface to Godwin's *Political Justice*: 'This period [sixteen months]
was for the most part devoted to the purpose with unusual ardour' (*Political Justice* i, p. vii).
See also note to Preface line 9.

Pref. 242. as many years] As the thoughts would have been gathered by the time composi-
tion began in late March/early April 1817, S. dates the period of personal education that issued
in the poem from the day of his expulsion from Oxford: 25 March 1811.

Pref. 249. express in the cruelty and malevolence of God] 'entertain of the Deity, as injurious to
the character of his benevolence' *L&C/RofI*. The reading of *Nbk 4a* f. 16r is adopted here
on the evidence of two printings of the passage carrying significant MS notations. The first
is the single proof-leaf of *L&C* known to survive – pp. xix–xx of the Preface – which is bound
into *L&C* (PM) – see headnote *Composition and Publication*. The proof-leaf carries the *Nbk 4a*
reading, which is cancelled in ink, and the *L&C/RofI* reading written at the bottom of the
page in the form: 'entertain of the Deity, as injurious to the character of his *mercy canc.* and
canc. benevolence'. The alteration is signed 'B. McM.', i.e. Buchanan McMillan the printer.
From McMillan's note it cannot be concluded that he was exclusively responsible for the
change, nor whether he or S. cancelled the words 'mercy and'. *Forman 1876–7* notes that
the cancellation was made in a lighter ink than that in which the rest of the phrase is writ-
ten, though in itself this is inconclusive too. The fact that the proof-leaf shows no sign of
the other alterations that S. introduced in proof suggests that it was part of the proof-copy
kept at the printer's and not sent to the author. The second notation occurs in the copy of
RofI which was once owned by S.'s friend George William Tighe – evidently presented to
him by S. himself – and which is now in the Harry Hunt Ransom Humanities Research Center
of the University of Texas at Austin. In this copy S. has bracketed the two sentences running
from *The erroneous* to *from my own.* and written in ink at the bottom of the page (xxi): 'The
Printer's insertion. PBS'. In fact S. has bracketed too generously; the only difference between
Nbk 4a and *L&C/RofI* in these sentences is the substitution of the phrase already noted. S.'s
MS note can only mean that McMillan made that change on his own authority. But even if
S. did agree to the change, rather than simply accepting it when accomplished, it seems prob-
able that he would have done so under the same sort of coercion that induced him to remove
the incest between the two title-characters and tone down the anti-religious sentiments of
the poem. The MS reading has therefore been restored.

to those violent and malignant passions of our nature, which are ever on
the watch to mingle with and to alloy the most beneficial innovations.
There is no quarter given to Revenge, or Envy, or Prejudice. Love is celeb-
255 rated everywhere as the sole law which should govern the moral world.

In the personal conduct of my Hero and Heroine, there is one circum-
stance which was intended to startle the reader from the trance of ordin-
ary life. It was my object to break through the crust of those outworn
opinions on which established institutions depend. I have appealed there-
260 fore to the most universal of all feelings, and have endeavoured to
strengthen the moral sense, by forbidding it to waste its energies in seek-
ing to avoid actions which are only crimes of convention. It is because
there is so great a multitude of artificial vices, that there are so few real
virtues. Those feelings alone which are benevolent or malevolent, are essen-
265 tially good or bad. The circumstance of which I speak, was introduced, how-
ever, merely to accustom men to that charity and toleration which the
exhibition of a practice widely differing from their own, has a tendency to
promote*. Nothing indeed can be more mischievous, than many actions
innocent in themselves, which might bring down upon individuals the
270 bigotted contempt and rage of the multitude.

* The sentiments connected with and characteristic of this circumstance, have no personal
reference to the Writer.

Pref. 256–70. The final paragraph was removed from *RofI.* J. Donovan, *Keats–Shelley Review*
ii (1987) 70–4 comments on it in detail.

Pref. 256–57. circumstance] The incest between Laon and Cythna.

S.'s note. This note is not present in the draft in *Nbk 4a*, and was probably added in proof.
It is clearly an afterthought aiming to prevent the inference, potentially damaging to the
poem's reception, that the sexual love between the brother and sister Laon and Cythna ide-
alises S.'s own experience. As such it responds to a rumour then current that Byron, S., Mary
W. Godwin (as her name then was) and Claire Clairmont had formed a promiscuous sexual
community during the period they spent together near Geneva in summer 1816. This sup-
posed 'League of Incest' drew its specifically illicit character from the fact that Claire and
Mary, though unrelated by blood, were sisters in law; i.e. one of the parents of each had died
and the surviving two had later married. The imputation of incest may well have been made
through a mistaken belief that the sisters in law were sisters, but no doubt also on a strict
interpretation of the principle that affinity by marriage counts as consanguinity in determining
persons between whom sexual relations were prohibited. The 'Table of Kindred and Affinity,
Wherein Whosoever Are Related Are Forbidden In Scripture and Our Laws to Marry
Together' that occupied the final page of *The Book of Common Prayer* enumerated the prohi-
bitions, which included a man's wife's sister and a woman's sister's husband. In summer 1816
Byron (widely believed to have had an incestuous relationship with his half-sister Augusta)
was married though separated from his wife by legal agreement; Shelley remained married
to, although he lived apart from, his first wife Harriet. He and Mary had lived together as
man and wife from summer 1814. Moreover, for much of the time since then Claire had
made part of their household and continued to do so during her pregnancy and after the
birth in January 1817 of Allegra, her child by Byron. Their attempts to conceal the child's
parentage only contributed to the view that S. maintained sexual relations with both
women. See *L* i 540, ii 326; *SC* v 390–1; *Quarterly Review* xviii (January 1818) 328 and xxi
(April 1819) 467–8; Byron *L&J* vi 76, 82–3, 126; *Clairmont Correspondence* i 53, as well as J.
Donovan, *Keats–Shelley Review* (1987) ii 69–70.

DEDICATION

THERE IS NO DANGER TO A MAN, THAT KNOWS
WHAT LIFE AND DEATH IS: THERE'S NOT ANY LAW
EXCEEDS HIS KNOWLEDGE; NEITHER IS IT LAWFUL
THAT HE SHOULD STOOP TO ANY OTHER LAW.

CHAPMAN

TO

MARY ⸺ ⸺

Dedication. Epigraph. From George Chapman's tragedy *The Conspiracy of Charles Duke of Byron* (1608) III iii 140–3 (act and scene division of modern *eds*), evidently by way of Charles Lamb's *Specimens of English Dramatic Poets, Who Lived About the Time of Shakspeare: with Notes* (1808, 1813), which S. and MWS were reading on 11–12 November 1817 (*Mary Jnl* i 183–4) and where the title is given as *Byron's Conspiracy*. The *Specimens* gives the following extract under the heading *The Master Spirit* (p. 95): 'Give me a spirit that on life's rough sea / Loves to have his sails fill'd with a lusty wind, / Even till his sail-yards tremble, his masts crack, / And his rapt ship run on her side so low, / That she drinks water, and her keel ploughs air. / There is no danger to a man, that knows / What Life and Death is: there's not any law / Exceeds his knowledge; neither is it lawful / That he should stoop to any other law: / He goes before them, and commands them all, / That to himself is a law rational'. The four lines that S. excerpts form part of a long speech directed by the title-character, marshall of France and conspirator against Henry IV, to an astrologer who has predicted that he will lose his head, as he does in the second part of the play, *The Tragedy of Charles Duke of Byron*. The series of passages from both plays included in the *Specimens* leaves no doubt that pride and ambition bring about Byron's execution. Removed from its context the epigraph is deprived of its intended political application and its irony; its aptness to the epic project of *L&C* will rather have been suggested by the peculiar associations the name 'Byron' in the play's title had for S. S. had paid homage to Lord Byron's powers in a letter of September 1816 in terms interestingly like those of the passage from Chapman before going on to recommend that he consider the French Revolution as the theme of an epic poem, with this condition: 'But it is inconsistent with the spirit in which you ought to devote yourself to so great a destiny, that you should make use of any understanding but your own – much less mine' (*L* i 508). Francis Jeffrey uses the phrase 'the master spirits of their age' in a review of Byron's *Childe Harold's Pilgrimage III* and *The Prisoner of Chillon* in the *Edinburgh Review* liv (December 1816) 299. The epigraph announces that exemption from common rule and convention which S. deemed necessary to an adequate treatment of what he had qualified in a letter to Byron earlier in the month as 'the master theme of the epoch in which we live – the French Revolution' (*L* i 504), as well as to the celebration of 'Love . . . the sole law which should govern the moral world' (Preface, lines 254–5). Two years later, in his satirical portrait of the poet Peter Bell in *Peter Bell the Third* (1819), S. recalled the theme of the 'master-spirit' to cast a sceptical glance at Wordworth's (and his own) pretensions to poetic power: 'Yet his was individual mind, / And new created all he saw / In a new manner, and refined / Those new creations, and combined / Them, by a master-spirit's law' (lines 303–7). See headnote *Sources and Influences*, p. 21.

MARY ⸺ ⸺] 'Mary Wollstonecraft Shelley' is cancelled in the fair copy in *Nbk 4a* f. 18r; the Christian name and two dashes are substituted beneath it. S. and Mary Wollstonecraft Godwin were married on 28 December 1816.

48

1

So now my summer task is ended, Mary,
And I return to thee, mine own heart's home;
As to his Queen some victor Knight of Faëry,
Earning bright spoils for her enchanted dome;
5   Nor thou disdain, that ere my fame become
A star among the stars of mortal night,
If it indeed may cleave its natal gloom,
Its doubtful promise thus I would unite
With thy belovèd name, thou Child of love and light.

2

10   The toil which stole from thee so many an hour,
Is ended, — and the fruit is at thy feet!
No longer where the woods to frame a bower
With interlacèd branches mix and meet,

---

3. *Knight of Faëry*] Knight of fairyland, the sense of *faëry* in Spenser's *Faerie Queene*, which approximates one of MWS's affectionate names for S., 'Elfin Knight' (*Mary Jnl* i 80 and n). Spenser's Red Cross Knight is regularly so styled in *Faerie Queene*, as is a character in popular ballads. 'Elfin Knight' also served S. as a *nom de plume*; together with his own name it was attached to the first publication of *Hymn to Intellectual Beauty* in the *Examiner* for 19 January 1817, and his review of Godwin's *Mandeville* in the *Examiner* for 28 December 1817 was signed 'E. K.' (*Prose Works* 276–9).

4. *dome*] (stately) house, mansion.

5. 'No more beside the river's sunny [waterfalls sparkling] foam' *Nbk 4* 36.

6. *star . . . stars*] The classical figure for the poet's fame as in Ovid, *Metamorphoses* xv 875–9.

8–9. In marrying Mary Wollstonecraft Godwin S. united his name to those of her parents Mary Wollstonecraft (1759–97) and William Godwin (1756–1836) who achieved fame in the 1790s as progressive writers on politics and morals.

Stanza 2. In her 'Note on the Revolt of Islam' in *1839* MWS records that: 'The poem was written in his boat, as it floated under the beech-groves of Bisham, or during wanderings in the neighbouring country'. Peacock recalled in 'Memoirs of Percy Bysshe Shelley' (1860) that: 'he wrote the *Revolt of Islam*, chiefly on a seat [see note to line 13] on a high prominence in Bisham Wood, where he passed whole mornings with a blank book and a pencil' (*Peacock Works* viii 106–7). Leigh Hunt's recollections, set down earlier, and relating to the period *c.* 10 April–25 June when he was staying with the Shelleys in Marlow, modify the account of outdoor composition: 'He was up early; breakfasted sparingly; wrote this *Revolt of Islam* all the morning; went out in his boat or into the woods with some Greek author or the *Bible* in his hands . . .' *Examiner* 615 (10 October 1819) 652–3.

12–17. The cancelled draft for these lines (*Nbk 4* 36) provides a more idyllic and circumstantial sketch of the poet in composition: 'Beneath the emerald woods [ ] roam . . . / Weaving a heaven [ ] / Weave from the light of thoughts a Fan / Shall I be seen like an unconscious child / . . . to build / A resting place for truth, [ ] / Wearied with play, return to [ ]'.

12. 'Or where the woods an emerald hall' *Nbk 4* 36.

13. Cp. *Nbk 4* 7: '[High in the Heavens above ?[one] ?[ivied] seat]'.

15
Or where with sound like many voices sweet,
Waterfalls leap among wild islands green,
Which framed for my lone boat a lone retreat
Of moss-grown trees and weeds, shall I be seen:
But beside thee, where still my heart has ever been.

3

20
Thoughts of great deeds were mine, dear Friend, when first
The clouds which wrap this world from youth did pass.

14–17. Two sketches of a lone figure in a small boat with a sail on water bordered by trees and vegetation decorate the page (*Nbk 4* 16) on which S. drafted stanza 6 of the Dedication. Similar images are interspersed among the drafts for Cantos I and II in *Nbk 2*, and among those for Cantos V–XII in *Nbk 3*, as well as occurring on the front and back pastedowns of *Nbk 5*, which he began to use in the latter months of 1817.

15. Waterfalls] When he visited Marlow in 1835 Thomas Medwin described 'the fall of the river, over an artificial embankment immediately above the town, where the eye crossing the richest meadows, rests on the lovely beech groves of Bisham Abbey' (*Medwin (1913)* 190).

Stanzas 3–5. Although many of S.'s biographers have treated these stanzas as evidence that such a conversion-experience actually took place during his schooldays, either at Syon House Academy, Isleworth, near Brentford (1802–4) or at Eton (1804–10), persuasive evidence to locate and date solitary and inward events such as the one represented here is always difficult to come by and in this case has not been adduced. Moreover, S. provided other versions of an early and dramatic mental awakening leading to the self-dedication which he felt had given direction to his adult life in *L* i 227–8, 517–18, *Hymn to Intellectual Beauty* Text B 59–72 (and see note thereto) – as well as furnishing two characters recognised as in some measure autobiographical, Laon in *L&C* II xv and the Maniac in *Julian and Maddalo* 380–2, with youthful moments of self-consecration. Whether in these texts he is variously rewriting a particular experience of his own or investing a gradually-acquired moral and political awareness with specific imaginative form according to the needs of the moment seems impossible to decide. What is clear is that the nature and effects of the crisis delineated here conform in essentials to those he recounts to Godwin in a letter of 10 January 1812 (*L* i 227–8) as a consequence of his reading of *Political Justice* at Eton. The testimony of those who knew him well – MWS (Note on *Q Mab* in *1839*), Medwin (*Medwin (1913)* 15–33), Hunt (*Autobiography* ch. xv), Peacock (*Peacock Works* viii 52) and *Hogg* (ch. 2) – concurs in insisting on his unhappy relations with the masters at Eton and profound abhorrence of the regime of fagging enforced by the senior boys. It seems likely therefore that the personal drama evoked in these stanzas derives principally from his memory of those years. It should be noted, however, that while the tyranny deplored in stanzas 3 and 4 could include that of older over younger boys (see the following note, iii), the *tyrants* of stanza 5 are schoolmasters whose oppression of their pupils is presented as a type of wider social injustice.

Stanza 3. Several rough and incomplete versions of this stanza (*Nbk 4* 7–13), much revised and cancelled, provide details not included in the final version. The draft at first continued from line 21: 'By dreams divine my youthful soul was nursed / And tho no mate it [ ] / So that I stood alone among my kind / In happy solitude [ ] . . . / Alas a blight *alt.* storm came on my sunny heart / A clinging darkness that would not [ ] end'. The lines were then revised: '. . . and dreams divine my heart had nursed / Till it grew strong on night-dividing wings / To visit thought's most unimagined springs / And I remember well the day & hour / One amongst many of lone wanderings / When Truth first came upon me; & that power / Which doth the mists [ ] – to outsoar'. There follow three partially-drafted stanzas: i. 'I feared not those who ruled, nor did I hate / Mine equals, but was lone, untameable / Like some wild beast that cannot find its mate / A solitary [ ] gazelle/Which in the desert wilderness doth dwell / Secure in its own swiftness . . .'; ii. 'I feared or hated none but wept to find / That

I do remember well the hour which burst
My spirit's sleep: a fresh May dawn it was,
When I walked forth upon the glittering grass,
And wept, I knew not why; until there rose
25   From the near schoolroom, voices, that, alas!
Were but one echo from a world of woes —
The harsh and grating strife of tyrants and of foes.

4

And then I clasped my hands and looked around —
But none was near to mock my streaming eyes,
30   Which poured their warm drops on the sunny ground —
So without shame, I spake: — 'I will be wise,
And just, and free, and mild, if in me lies
Such power, for I grow weary to behold
The selfish and the strong still tyrannise
35   Without reproach or check.' I then controlled
My tears, my heart grew calm, and I was meek and bold.

5

And from that hour did I with earnest thought
Heap knowledge from forbidden mines of lore,
Yet nothing that my tyrants knew or taught
40   I cared to learn, but from that secret store
Wrought linkèd armour for my soul, before

---

none did love me ?[tho] a gentle child / Thus solemn feelings on my soul did dwell / Mine
equals shunned a boy so sad & wild / And those who ruled me, found untameable / The
spirit of a meek & gentle child; / Nor with a bitter scorn of wrong I smiled'; iii. 'When hoary
men or youths of strength mature / Struck me with fruitless blows; thus undefiled / By awe
or by submission, did endure / In its own [?] [   ] my spirit [?]/And hate grew with me of the
law of crime / In its own [   ] free & pure'.

22. spirit's] spirits' *L&C/RofI*; the draft in *Nbk 4* has no apostrophe; the fair copy in *Nbk 4a*
lacks this stanza; *1839* and later *eds* have emended to *spirit's*. The singular is S.'s regular usage
for an individual's powers of mind. Cp. line 675 and note, and lines 1444–5: 'did my spirit
wake / From sleep . . . ?'

25. schoolroom] an important detail which S. inserted (*Nbk 4* 11) only after earlier attempts
at drafting the stanza. See note to stanzas 3–5.

29. But] – But *L&C/RofI*. The draft in *Nbk 4* has no dash, nor does any other line in *L&C/RofI*
begin with one; evidently a printer's error.

37–40. 'I have known no tutor or adviser not excepting my father from whose lessons and
suggestions I have not recoiled with disgust. – The knowledge which I have whatever it may
be . . . has been acquired by my unassisted efforts' (S. to Godwin 16 January 1812 *L* i 230).

41. armour for my soul] The image associates the figure of the knight in line 3 with the spir-
itual warfare recommended by St Paul in *Ephesians* vi 11–17 where the Christian is urged to
'put on the whole armour of God'. This is the armour worn by Red Cross Knight, as Spenser
explains in a 'Letter of the Authors' (to Sir Walter Raleigh) appended to the *Faerie Queene* –
which S. follows and secularises.

It might walk forth to war among mankind;
Thus power and hope were strengthened more and more
Within me, till there came upon my mind
45   A sense of loneliness, a thirst with which I pined.

6

Alas, that love should be a blight and snare
To those who seek all sympathies in one! —
Such once I sought in vain; then black despair,
The shadow of a starless night, was thrown
50   Over the world in which I moved alone: —
Yet never found I one not false to me,
Hard hearts, and cold, like weights of icy stone
Which crushed and withered mine, that could not be
Aught but a lifeless clog, until revived by thee.

47. *one*] One beloved person.

51–2. Yet never found I one not false to me, / [but rather] *Hard hearts, and cold* . . . The ellipsis in the sense is a residual awkwardness owing to frequent revision; see the following note.

51–4. Two tentative and heavily-cancelled attempts to draft these lines in *Nbk 4* contain details that were not retained. One follows on from the draft of the earlier part of the stanza: 'The dedicated foe of tyranny / The lonely one I wandered blindly on . . . / Not love or will, but hope & power in me / Withered & died away, until revived by thee' (16). The other develops through three stages in blank spaces from p. 28 back to p. 26: 'And one was fair but faithless . . . / The other heart was like a heart of stone / Whose touch made all my hopes & be / Withered [ ] until revived by thee'; S. then modified this to: 'One whom I found was dear but false to me / The other's heart was like a heart of stone / Which crushed & withered mine [ ]' – before arriving at a final draft almost identical to the printed version. The suppressed allusions, as *Forman 1876–7* and *Locock 1911* point out, are to Harriet Grove and Harriet (Westbrook) Shelley. With the approval of their families and a possible marriage in prospect, S. and his first cousin Harriet Grove shared a romantic attachment which developed through 1809 until autumn 1810 when his uncle and aunt Grove intervened to break it off. The Groves had taken alarm at S.'s sceptical and anti-Christian views; he himself reacted vehemently to the enforced rupture, attributing it to the baleful influence of religion (*L* i 27–47; headnotes to Poems 14–18, 20, 23–6, 49, 53, 63, and Desmond Hawkins, *Shelley's First Love* (1992)). Harriet Grove married in October 1810; S. married Harriet Westbrook in August 1811. S. learned of his wife Harriet's suicide in December 1816 and by January 1817 had become persuaded that she had been unfaithful to him four months before he eloped with Mary Godwin in July 1814 (*L* i 528).

54. clog] clod *Rossetti 1870, 1878, Hutchinson, Locock 1911, 1975; clog* L&C/*Rofl*. There is no textual authority for the emendation 'clod'. Neither word occurs in the two attempts to draft the stanza in *Nbk 4* 16, 28; and those parts of the fair copy preserved in *Nbk 4a* do not include this stanza. *Forman 1876–7* considered the emendation 'doubtful'; it is that at least. Arguments in its favour – of which *Hutchinson's* is the most vigorous – have been based solely upon a preference for 'clod' as consistent with the natural metaphor likening the *heart* (line 55) to a plant that has *withered* (line 53), then to a *plain* (line 56) where growth is renewed. But the comparison of a *crushed* (line 53) heart to a *clog* might just as well develop from *weights of icy stone* (line 52) which approximates the original meaning of the word – a block or weight attached to an animal or man to impede escape – and so be understood as an encumbrance or impediment to love.

7

55   Thou Friend, whose presence on my wintry heart
    Fell, like bright Spring upon some herbless plain;
    How beautiful and calm and free thou wert
    In thy young wisdom, when the mortal chain
    Of Custom thou didst burst and rend in twain,
60   And walked as free as light the clouds among,
    Which many an envious slave then breathed in vain
    From his dim dungeon, and my spirit sprung
    To meet thee from the woes which had begirt it long.

8

    No more alone through the world's wilderness,
65   Although I trod the paths of high intent,
    I journeyed now: no more companionless,
    Where solitude is like despair, I went. —
    There is the wisdom of a stern content
    When Poverty can blight the just and good,

58–63. The sixteen-year-old Mary Godwin declared her love for S. on 20 June 1814 at her mother's grave in Old St. Pancras Churchyard.

60. *walked*] *Rossetti 1870*, *Dowden 1891* and *1975* emend to 'walk', taking the verb to be governed by the auxiliary *didst* in the previous line; *Forman 1876–7* regards *walked* instead as S.'s euphonious alternative to 'walkedst'. *Walked* certainly sounds better than either.

60–2. The sense of the passage is obscured by a double ambiguity: the meaning of *breathed* and the referent of *his*, which can be either *Custom* or *slave*. *Rossetti 1870*, taking the antecedent of *his* to be *Custom*, repunctuated: 'And walk (as free as light the clouds among / Which many an envious slave then breathed in vain) / From his dim dungeon'. But *Forman 1876–7*, Bradley *MLR* i (1905) 25–6 and *Locock 1911* have persuasively defended the original punctuation, considering *which* to refer to *clouds* and *breathed* to mean 'breathed forth' – which gives the sense: 'The slaves of Custom abuse Mary for her breach of convention, though they secretly envy her courage' (Bradley 26). This reading is reinforced by lines 2890–2 which recount the effects of Cythna's denunciation of the tyrant Othman on the slaves of the harem: 'And sympathy made each attendant slave / Fearless and free, and they began to breathe / Deep curses . . .'.

63. *woes which had begirt it long*] Recalling Campbell, *Gertrude of Wyoming* (1809) III vi: 'When Transatlantic Liberty arose, / Not in the sunshine and the smile of heaven, / But wrapt in whirlwinds and begirt with woes'.

65. *high intent*] A rejected line in the draft in *Nbk 4* 17, apparently intended as the initial line of this stanza, indicates the nature of the *intent*: 'And so the youthful foe of tyranny'.

68. 'The sober happiness of the sage is yet possible'. Cp. lines 4699–701: 'then is lent / To man the wisdom of a high despair, / When such can die, and he live on and linger here'.

69. *Poverty*] From the time of his expulsion from Oxford in March 1811 S.'s expenditure continued in excess of his allowances, occasioning a succession of financial crises and obliging him to negotiate loans on unfavourable terms. His supply of ready money increased after the settlement of his grandfather's estate in May 1815 when many of his debts were paid and he received a substantial cash sum together with an annuity of £1000. But by autumn 1817 he was again desperately short of funds, his creditors were pressing their claims, and he had been arrested for debt and detained briefly in early October. (*S in Eng* 522–6). S. will

70   When Infamy dares mock the innocent,
     And cherished friends turn with the multitude
     To trample: this was ours, and we unshaken stood!

9

     Now has descended a serener hour,
     And with inconstant fortune, friends return;
75   Though suffering leaves the knowledge and the power
     Which says: — Let scorn be not repaid with scorn.
     And from thy side two gentle babes are born
     To fill our home with smiles, and thus are we
     Most fortunate beneath life's beaming morn;
80   And these delights, and thou, have been to me
     The parents of the Song I consecrate to thee.

---

also have had in mind the chronic want of money of his father-in-law Godwin and his friends Hunt and Peacock, all of whom he had generously relieved.

70. Infamy] S. described himself in a letter to Leigh Hunt of 8 December 1816 as 'an outcast from human society; my name is execrated by all who understand its entire import' (*L* i 517). The major practical consequence of the *infamy* that resulted from his conduct and published writings took effect on 27 March 1817 when, on the petition of his father-in-law John Westbrook in the Court of Chancery, he was deprived of the custody of his two children by Harriet Westbrook on a decision of the Lord Chancellor Eldon. The judgment cited the immorality of the principles which had led S. to leave his wife and cohabit with Mary W. Godwin and the necessity of shielding his children from an education in which those principles would be inculcated. John Westbrook and his daughter Eliza had alleged S.'s unfitness to be the children's guardian because he was an avowed atheist, had blasphemed in *Q Mab* and other works, and, in a *Letter to Lord Ellenborough*, had defended Daniel Isaac Eaton against his conviction for having published a work condemned as a blasphemous libel. For his part S. was persuaded that, as he wrote to Byron on 11 January 1817, 'I am here, dragged before the tribunals of tyranny and superstition, to answer with my children, my property, my liberty, and my fame, for having exposed their frauds, and scorned the insolence of their power' (*L* i 530).

71–4. S. will have had chiefly in mind MWS's (and his own) relations with the family of William Thomas Baxter of Dundee. Mary had visited the Baxters for two long periods in the years 1812–14, developing intimate friendships with the daughters Christina and, especially, Isabel. After Mary's elopement with S. the Baxters discontinued correspondence with her, but from spring 1817, following her marriage to S. the previous December, communication between the two families was renewed. W. T. Baxter stayed with the Shelleys in Marlow for most of September; Christina was invited to visit them there and Isabel to accompany them to Italy. The Shelleys met both Baxter and Isabel's husband David Booth in London during the first half of November, by which time the Dedication to *L&C* had been written; but thereafter relations between the families again deteriorated because of David Booth's long-standing objections to S.'s views on the institution of marriage. See headnote to *R&H*; *L* i 575, 587–9, *Mary L* i 58–61; *SC* v 332–42, 345–7, 371–92.

77–8. Cp. Milton, *Comus* 1009–11: 'And from her [Psyche's] fair unspotted side / Two blissful twins are to be born, / Youth and Joy . . .'. MWS gave birth to William Shelley on 24 January 1816 and to Clara Everina Shelley on 2 September 1817. Her first child, a girl, was born on 22 February and died on 6 March 1815.

80–1. '[And the first fruits of this sweet peace to thee / I consecrate, the blest & innocent & free]': *Nbk 4* 19.

10

Is it, that now my inexperienced fingers
But strike the prelude of a loftier strain?
Or, must the lyre on which my spirit lingers
85   Soon pause in silence, ne'er to sound again,
Though it might shake the Anarch Custom's reign,
And charm the minds of men to Truth's own sway
Holier than was Amphion's? I would fain
Reply in hope — but I am worn away,
90   And Death and Love are yet contending for their prey.

11

And what art thou? I know, but dare not speak:
Time may interpret to his silent years.
Yet in the paleness of thy thoughtful cheek,
And in the light thine ample forehead wears,
95   And in thy sweetest smiles, and in thy tears,
And in thy gentle speech, a prophecy
Is whispered, to subdue my fondest fears:
And through thine eyes, even in thy soul I see
A lamp of vestal fire burning internally.

86. '[tho it might charm the slave to burst his chain]' *Nbk 4* 21. *Anarch Custom's reign*] The dominion of misrule which is maintained by blind adherence to established ideas and practices. The title *Anarch* associates the empire of *Custom* with the darkness and chaos over which an *anarch* rules in both *Paradise Lost* ii 988 and *The Dunciad* iv 653 as well as with the violent folly of imperial ambition Byron had designated by the title in *Childe Harold's Pilgrimage* II xlv 8.

88. *Amphion's*] i.e. Amphion's lyre. In Greek myth Amphion, the son of Zeus and Antiope, had been given the lyre by Hermes and was renowned as poet and as the father of music. He helped build the walls of Thebes by playing so sweetly that the stones were charmed to move of their own accord to take their places in it.

89–90. In late June / early July 1817 S. fell ill with what he called his 'constitutional disease', pains in his side and general weakness and lethargy (*L* i 543–4, 47), suffering a relapse in late September which he feared threatened his life (*L* i 556). Having consulted a physician, he was told that his symptoms indicated consumption (*L* i 570, 73) – which had already been diagnosed in 1815 (MWS's Notes on Alastor and The Early Poems in *1839*) – and that he must seek a warmer climate. He wrote to Godwin on 1 December 1817: 'I am strongly impelled to doubt whether Italy might not decide in my frame the contest between disease & youth in favour of life' (*L* i 570). See also headnote *Composition and Publication*, p. 10.

91–2. S.'s successive cancelled drafts for the end of line 92, 'the listening Earth / a thousand years / his listening years' (*Nbk 4* 22) suggest that he was thinking of MWS's as yet unrealised fame as an author. *1817*, jointly written with S., was to be published in December, and *Frankenstein* (completed May 1817), in January 1818 – both anonymously.

97. *fondest fears*] Those expressed in lines 89–90.

99. *vestal fire*] Vesta was worshipped by the Romans as the goddess of the hearth. In her temple the vestal flame, upon which the prosperity of the state was held to depend, was perpetually tended by an order of women consecrated from girlhood to the task and vowed to strict chastity. Although *vestal fire* derives from the common stock of neoclassical poetic diction,

12

100 They say that thou wert lovely from thy birth,
     Of glorious parents, thou aspiring Child.
     I wonder not — for One then left this earth
     Whose life was like a setting planet mild,
     Which clothed thee in the radiance undefiled
105 Of its departing glory; still her fame
     Shines on thee, through the tempests dark and wild
     Which shake these latter days; and thou canst claim
     The shelter, from thy Sire, of an immortal name.

13

     One voice came forth from many a mighty spirit,
110 Which was the echo of three thousand years;
     And the tumultuous world stood mute to hear it,

---

the resemblance is nonetheless marked between this line and the previous one and Peacock's
Rhododaphne vii 28–32 which attribute the human erotic impulse to the divinity Primordial
or Creative Love: 'He kindles in the inmost mind / One lonely flame – for once – for one – /
A vestal fire, which, there enshrined, / Lives on, till life itself be done' (*Peacock Works* vii 78).
MWS transcribed *Rhododaphne* between 4 and 10 December 1817 (*Mary Jnl* i 186); S. had already
informed Hogg on 28 November that Peacock had finished the poem, adding: 'I have not
heard it all, but in a few days he will send it to the Press' (*L* i 569). This is several weeks after
the Dedication was completed but it is possible that the lines quoted formed part of what S.
had heard Peacock read – and this may have been early enough for him to have recalled it
when composing the Dedication. On 25 November S. had still not received copies of *L&C*
(*L* i 568) which would seem to preclude the possibility that Peacock had seen the finished
book and that it was S.'s lines which had influenced his. It is not impossible that he had
seen the Dedication either in MS or in proof or had heard S. read it, but, as the phrase *vestal
fire* and its variants ('vestal flame', etc.) are habitual in his poetry before 1817 (e.g. 'Truth's
vestal torch and love's Promethean lamp' in *Ahrimanes*, Longer Verse Fragment (II iii 5) which
S. had certainly read), such influence as may have been exerted is likelier to be his on S.

102. One] Mary Wollstonecraft, who died on 10 September 1797, eleven days after giving
birth to MWS.

106–7. See Preface, lines 5–6: 'the tempests which have shaken the age in which we live',
and note.

108. thy Sire] The fair copy of this stanza (*Nbk 4a* 19v) identifies the *Sire* in a footnote: 'The
Author of "An Enquiry concerning Political Justice"'. The draft in *Nbk 4* 25 gives a similar
note but keys it to *spirit* in the first line of the next stanza.

Stanzas 12–13. Between the drafts for these two stanzas in *Nbk 4* 23–4 S. made and cancelled
successive attempts at what was apparently intended as another stanza developing MWS's
nature as deriving from her parents: 'Thus thou art wise & beautiful . . . / Wert nourished by
the fountains of the streams . . . / Which slake, as thro the desart world they flow / A thousand
thirsting spirits, whom high dreams / Of justice truth & joy, & all that seems / & is eternal'.

109. 'A voice went forth from that unshaken Spirit' *Nbk 4* 25. When S. revised the line in
the fair copy in *Nbk 4a*, he keyed the footnote identifying the 'Spirit' as Godwin to line 108
(see note thereto). The first attempt at drafting this stanza, heavily cancelled and revised,
attributes more specifically political effects to Godwin's writings: '& Kings were filled / And
Earth grew wan with supernatural fears / at the sound. [ ] / And thou who loved good, but
were without a law / And the oppressed in thee a champion saw'.

As some lone man who in a desert hears
The music of his home: — unwonted fears
Fell on the pale oppressors of our race,
115   And Faith, and Custom, and low-thoughted cares,
Like thunder-stricken dragons, for a space
Left the torn human heart, their food and dwelling-place.

14

Truth's deathless voice pauses among mankind!
If there must be no response to my cry —
120   If men must rise and stamp with fury blind
On his pure name who loves them, — thou and I,
Sweet Friend! can look from our tranquillity
Like lamps into the world's tempestuous night, —
Two tranquil stars, while clouds are passing by
125   Which wrap them from the foundering seaman's sight,
That burn from year to year with unextinguished light.

115. 'And The free leapt forth in joy' *Nbk 4* 26. *low-thoughted cares*] Cp. Milton, *Comus* 5–8: 'this dim spot, / Which men call earth, and, with low-thoughted care, / Confined . . . / Strive to keep up a frail, and feverish being'.

118. The cancelled draft for the line in *Nbk 4* 3, 'There is a pause & I would wake', suggests that the sense is: 'there is an interval in the eternal expression of truth (which I would fill)'.

121. '[Till thou art dead *alt.* we are dead,] yet, Mary, thou & I' *Nbk 4* 3.

121–6. Combining two of the leading images of Lucretius, *De Re. Nat.*: that of the sage who stands aloof from the blind struggles of humankind as if observing another in danger on the raging sea (ii 1–14, quoted by S. as a note to *Q Mab* v 58), and that of the philosopher who illuminates the darkness of human ignorance and passion (e.g. i 146–8; iii 1–2; v 10–12). S. similarly adapts this favourite source in, e.g. *Q Mab* viii 53–7, *Daemon* i 282–92, *Athanase* 150–9. See Paul Turner *RES* x (1959) 269–73.

122. Friend] friend *L&C/RofI*; Friend *Nbk 4a* f. 20r. Cp. lines 19 and 55 of the Dedication where the word, used as here to apostrophise MWS, is capitalised.

124–6. The first draft of these lines poses a question: 'How should the star when storms are passing by / Which wraps it from the foundering seamans sight / [Mourn for aught] but his dark fate for whom it burneth bright' *Nbk 4* 3. The final line was then redrafted: 'That grieve for his deep fate, but burn for others bright' before approaching its printed form (*Nbk 4* 2).

LAON AND CYTHNA

ΟΣΑΙΣ ΔΕ ΒΡΟΤΟΝ ΕΘΝΟΣ ΑΓΛΑΙΑΙΣ 'ΑΠΤΟΜΕΣΘΑ,
ΠΕΡΑΙΝΕΙ ΠΡΟΣ ΕΣΧΑΤΟΝ
ΠΛΟΟΝ· ΝΑΥΣΙ Δ'ΟΥΤΕ ΠΕΖΟΣ ΙΩΝ ΑΝ ΕΥΡΟΙΣ
ΕΣ 'ΥΠΕΡΒΟΡΕΩΝ ΑΓΩΝΑ ΘΑΥΜΑΤΑΝ 'ΟΔΟΝ.

PIND. *Pyth.* X.

Epigraph. From the tenth Pythian Ode of Pindar (27–30), an epinicion, or victory song, in honour of the winner in a foot race at the Pythian Games at Delphi in 498 BC. S. extracts part of a passage linking Pindar's praise of the victor to an account of a mythical exploit of Perseus who, guided by Athene, reached the land of the Hyperboreans and feasted with them. The bridge-passage begins, 'The brazen heaven he [the victor blessed with victorious children] cannot climb', then continues as in the epigraph: 'But as for all the bright achievements that we mortals attain, he reaches the utmost limit of that voyage. Neither by ships nor by land can you find the wondrous road to the place where the Hyperboreans assemble' [modified from Loeb trans.]. The Hyperboreans were a mythical people who inhabited a tem-

Canto First

I

When the last hope of trampled France had failed
Like a brief dream of unremaining glory,
From visions of despair I rose, and scaled

---

perate climate in the far north – their name signifies 'those who live beyond the north wind' (Boreas) – where they enjoyed an idyllic existence, surviving to an uncommonly advanced age free from all pain and strife. Apollo was supposed to have spent part of his early life among them and to return regularly in winter. Their devotion to the god took the form of continual dancing and singing in his praise. S. adapts details from their legendary dwelling-place and ceremonies in the voyages to the Temple of the Spirit in Cantos I and XII: see notes to I xlviii, liii–iv and to line 4813. The persistent legend of a temperate polar region fascinates the arctic explorer Walton in *Frankenstein* (1818) Vol. I, Letter I (*MSW* i 10). In setting before his poem a passage that qualifies victory in relation to an imaginative paradigm of blessedness and harmony, S. intends to bring forward the '*beau ideal* . . . of the French Revolution' (*L* i 564) as against the recent triumph of what he regarded as the forces of reaction in Europe. The signal example of a contemporary poem proposing the opposite view, the laureate Robert Southey's *The Poet's Pilgrimage to Waterloo* (1816), which celebrates the allied victory over France as the triumph of civilising Christian principles, also borrows its epigraph from a Pythian Ode of Pindar, the second, in praise of the success in a chariot-race of Hieron, tyrant of Syracuse from 478–67 BC: εὐανθέα δ'ἀναβάσομαι στόλον ἀμφ' ἀρετᾷ / κελαδέων ('I shall embark upon a ship crowned with flowers loudly singing the praise of valour', 62–3). The nautical image, appropriate both to the passage of Pindar's ode in a ship to Sicily and to Southey's return voyage across the channel, together with the theme of victory, invite comparison with S.'s epigraph as an effective reply to Southey's whether or no he meant it specifically as such.

Canto I. Nbk 2 4–8 contains a meditative opening to the poem in seven stanzas and most of an eighth (see no. 142) which S. drafted then rejected in favour of the sudden onset of vision of the published early stanzas. Some of the important images and themes of these rejected stanzas are developed in the Preface, the Dedication and in Canto II, especially xii–xx. The draft of what was to become the present stanza i (*Box 1* f. 2v) signals the visionary character of the narrator's experience unequivocally:

A vision

1

The [   ] were short & transitory
When sudden all became distinct & clear —
Methought on an aerial promontory
Whose caverned base with the vext surge was hoary
I stood & saw the golden dawn awaken

The lines are recopied with much cancelling in *Nbk 2* 8. The published version of stanza i, curtailing the perceptual detail and adding a reference to the defeat of France in 1814 and 1815 (drafted much further on in *Nbk 2* 38), effectively assimilates the narrator's despair to the mood of liberal Europe after the Bourbon Restoration, to which the succeeding ideal revision of recent revolutionary history is particularly addressed. See headnote *Sources and Influences*, p. 28. S. considered the opening canto to be 'in some measure a distinct poem, tho' very necessary to the wholeness of the work', adding that 'if it were all written in the manner of the first Canto, I could not expect that it should be interesting to any great number of people' (*L* i 563). Critical commentary on Canto I has focused on the associated questions of the significance and coherence of its symbolic action and its relation to the rest of the poem.

127. trampled France] S. habitually uses 'trampled' as an epithet for the victims of tyranny as in the 'trampled multitude' of line 403 or in *Q Mab* iv 201. See also note to line 142. The

130 The peak of an aerial promontory,
  Whose caverned base with the vexed surge was hoary;
  And saw the golden dawn break forth, and waken
  Each cloud, and every wave: — but transitory
  The calm: for sudden, the firm earth was shaken,
135 As if by the last wreck its frame were overtaken.

---

political sympathies set out in the Preface lines 69–109 are prominently displayed in the poem's first line.

129. visions of despair] Cp. Preface lines 67–8: 'Methinks, those who now live have survived an age of despair', and see headnote *Sources and Influences*, p. 28. *R&H* (691–779) vividly portrays the wasting effects on both the public temper and the individual mind of loss of hope in the progress of political reform. Traditionally the testing of heroic stature requires the hero to overcome the failing of despair, as in Redcross Knight's encounter with Despair in *Faerie Queene* I ix 33–45 or the imprisonment of Christian and Hopeful by the Giant Despair in *The Pilgrim's Progress*. The revisions S. made to the stanza leave some uncertainty as to the narrator's state of consciousness. *From visions of despair I rose* might seem to indicate that he is awakening from a sleep of dreams, an interpretation which appears to be confirmed when the woman-guide tells him in lines 311–12 that 'the despair / Was weak and vain which led thee here from sleep'. But it could also suggest a waking reverie like Darassah's as he stands on the shore at the beginning of Peacock's *Ahrimanes* (ii 6–9): '[his] eyes these forms survey / As phantoms of a half-remembered dream: / His eyes are on the water's glittering play: / Their mental sense is closed – his thoughts are far away' (*Peacock Works* viii 266).

130. aerial promontory] S. wrote 'aetherial' above the line in *Nbk 2* 8. Two senses of *aerial* seem to be intended: 1. lofty, rising high into the air; 2. ideal, imaginary. For the latter sense compare *PU* i 778: 'Dream visions of aerial joy'. The elemental symbolism of the scene, bringing together earth, air, fire and water, resumes the cosmos as do the 'etherial cliffs of Caucasus' in *Alastor* 352–7. Both biblical and classical literary tradition make of the mountain or elevated vantage-point the scene of revelation and inspiration. Important precedents for the promontory in S.'s opening passage are the hill in Paradise from which the archangel Michael reveals to Adam the providential course of history in *Paradise Lost* xi 376 ff. and the 'sea-cliff's verge' in Coleridge's *France: An Ode* (1798), a poem S. knew well, which identifies the natural sublime of ocean, sky, forest and hill as the element in which Liberty inheres permanently despite historical reverses. *L&C* recalls the sentiments and phrases of Coleridge's ode frequently; e.g. in lines 465, 471, 527, 716, 1272, 3609. Interesting correspondences of landscape and mood also exist between the first stanza of *L&C* and Peacock's *Ahrimanes* I i: 'In silver eddies glittering to the moon, / Araxes rolls his many-sounding tide. / Fair as the dreams of hope, and past as soon, / But in succession infinite supplied, / The rapid waters musically glide. / Now, where the cliff's phantastic shadow laves, / Silent and dark, they roll their volumed pride: / Now, by embowering woods and solemn caves, / Around some jutting rock the struggling torrent raves' (*Peacock Works* viii 265). The poet in Southey's *The Poet's Pilgrimage to Waterloo* (1816) receives his visionary enlightenment on a 'sacred mountain' which displays affinities with both the hills of Calvary and of Paradise.

131. vexed surge] The angry sea, a poeticism: cp. 'the raging surges' of *Faerie Queene* II xii 2 or the 'fierce winds' which 'vexed the Red Sea coast' in *Paradise Lost* i 305–6.

135. the last wreck] The violent natural convulsions traditionally foreseen as accompanying the end of the world; for example, in *Revelation* vi 12–14, xvi 18–21. *frame*] sustaining structure; cp. *Paradise Lost* ii 924–7: 'if this frame / Of heaven were falling, and these elements / In mutiny had from her axle torn / The steadfast earth'.

II

So as I stood, one blast of muttering thunder
Burst in far peals along the waveless deep,
When, gathering fast, around, above and under,
Long trains of tremulous mist began to creep,
140   Until their complicating lines did steep
The orient sun in shadow: — not a sound
Was heard; one horrible repose did keep
The forests and the floods, and all around
Darkness more dread than night was poured upon the ground.

III

145   Hark! 'tis the rushing of a wind that sweeps
Earth and the ocean. See! the lightnings yawn
Deluging Heaven with fire, and the lashed deeps
Glitter and boil beneath: it rages on,
One mighty stream, whirlwind and waves upthrown,
150   Lightning, and hail, and darkness eddying by.
There is a pause — the sea-birds, that were gone

136. *So as I stood*] 'As I stood thus' *Forman 1876–7*. Cp. *Faerie Queene* IV x 20: 'So as I entred'.
muttering] smothered *Nbk 2* 9.

137. *waveless deep*] At first sight contradicting lines 131–3 above; but the sequence of changes in the elements in stanzas i–v appears to be: at dawn the natural agitation of the waves is interrupted, first by earthquake, then thunder; a moment of calm and darkness follows (stanza ii) before the onset of the storm which then continues in the heavens while the earth and sea grow calm again.

140. *complicating*] Intermingling (*Concordance*). *steep*] envelop.

142. *keep*] Pervade, hold possession of (*Concordance*); *Locock 1911* compares *R&H* 930–1: 'The fierce despair and hate which kept / Their trampled bosoms almost slept'.

145. *rushing of a wind*] A traditional motif of spiritual awakening by supernatural agency, as in *Q Mab* i 45: 'Hark! whence that rushing sound?', announcing the arrival of the Fairy Queen's chariot; or in *Acts* ii 2: 'And suddenly there came a sound from heaven as of a rushing mighty wind, and it filled all the house where they were sitting', preceding the descent of the Holy Ghost as tongues of fire upon the apostles. S.'s draft in *Box 1* f. 2r reads: 'the rushing of a [mighty] wind'.

146. *the lightnings yawn*] 'sweeps', 'gush', 'falls', 'yawns', 'gapes' are all cancelled in the draft in *Box 1* f. 2r; the sense appears to be that the bolts of lightning gape as wide as chasms from which fire spills through the heavens. Cp. *Othello* V ii 108–10: 'Methinks it should be now a huge eclipse / Of sun and moon, and that th'affrighted globe / Should yawn at alteration'. S. may be remembering *The Rime of the Ancient Mariner* (1798): 'Like waters shot from some high crag, / The lightning fell with never a jag, / A river steep and wide' (324–6).

148. *it*] The wind of line 145.

149. Like a dark torrent among mountains lone *canc. Nbk 2* 10.

150. *eddying by*] swirling as it passes by.

151. *There is a pause*] Lo there is light on high *canc. Nbk 2* 10.

> Into their caves to shriek, come forth, to spy
> What calm has fallen on earth, what light is in the sky.

IV

For, where the irresistible storm had cloven
155   That fearful darkness, the blue sky was seen
Fretted with many a fair cloud interwoven
Most delicately, and the ocean green,
Beneath that opening spot of blue serene,
Quivered like burning emerald: calm was spread
160   On all below; but far on high, between
Earth and the upper air, the vast clouds fled,
Countless and swift as leaves on autumn's tempest shed.

151–2. S. may be remembering Southey's *Thalaba* (1801) xii 8: '. . . the entrance of the cave / Darkened the boat below. / Around them from their nests, / The screaming sea-birds fled' (ii 304–5 in 1801 edn).

156. Fretted] Decorated with interlaced ornaments, as a ceiling adorned with fretwork; cp. *PU* III iv 116: 'Beneath a dome fretted with graven flowers'. The complex image developed in lines 148–60 plays on two other senses of the word *fret*: 1. a storm or squall of wind; 2. to form by wearing away. The storm, rushing like a stream, has shaped the clouds into ornamental patterns. This cluster of meanings gathers together thus early some of the poem's fundamental oppositions – between storm and calm, agitation and serenity of mind, elemental natural forces and art.

158. blue serene] *Serene* is apparently here a noun (Latin *serenum*) meaning an expanse of clear and tranquil sky. Cp. *Epipsychidion* 506: 'the day's intense serene' and Byron, *Childe Harold's Pilgrimage* ii 627; Keats, *On First Looking into Chapman's Homer* 7.

159. Quivered] glittered *Nbk 2* 10. *burning emerald*] S. first wrote 'amethyst', then 'liquid emerald' *Nbk 2* 10.

162. Countless and swift as leaves] Introducing a sense of epic amplitude and sombreness by reference to the commonplace which likens the falling of leaves in autumn to the myriad dead: *Iliad* vi 146–7 (quoted by S. in the note to *Q Mab* v 4–6); *Aeneid* vi 309–10; Dante, *Inferno* iii 112–15. *Paradise Lost* i 302–3 describes the legions of fallen angels lying 'Thick as autumnal leaves that strew the brooks / In Vallombrosa'. The motif of numberless leaves is repeated with variations in lines 382, 1530, 2282, 4182–3.

162–3. The draft in *Nbk 2* 11 includes a stanza between these lines which S. recopied fair (MS in CHPL: SC 391) before cancelling it with a vertical stroke of the pen:

> And, as I gazed methought 'twas strange to feel
> The calmness of the Earth grow more profound
> While all the sky & all its clouds did reel
> And shivered & were torn & whirled around
> Like frail foam on the torrent – to resound
> Meanwhile the thunder ceased not, nor the air
> To echo with its deep & sullen sound,
> Nor the red flames to burst – but all did spare
> That spot of eastern Heaven which was so still & fair

Printed in *V&P* 21 (draft version in *Nbk 2*); *1975* (*Nbk 2* version) 270; the fair copy is given in facsimile with transcription in *SC* v 170–4 and in *BSM* viii 152–5. The cancelled stanza reinforces the contrast between the storm in the sky and the calm on earth but otherwise adds little to the development of the scene. Reiman (*SC* v 172) considers that it was 'deleted,

V

For ever, as the war became more fierce
Between the whirlwinds and the rack on high,
165 That spot grew more serene; blue light did pierce
The woof of those white clouds, which seemed to lie
Far, deep, and motionless; while through the sky
The pallid semicircle of the moon
Passed on, in slow and moving majesty;
170 Its upper horn arrayed in mists, which soon
But slowly fled, like dew beneath the beams of noon.

VI

I could not choose but gaze; a fascination
Dwelt in that moon, and sky, and clouds, which drew
My fancy thither, and in expectation
175 Of what I knew not, I remained: — the hue
Of the white moon, amid that heaven so blue,
Suddenly stained with shadow did appear;
A speck, a cloud, a shape, approaching grew,

---

no doubt, because it is very bad poetry'; and indeed the quality of the writing is not remarkable by the standard of the surrounding stanzas.

164. rack] High clouds driven by the wind. 'mists' Nbk 2 11.

166. woof] the fabric of the 'interwoven' clouds of line 156. The Spirit in Milton's *Comus* speaks of 'my sky robes spun out of Iris' woof' (line 83).

167–71. Typically the onset of vision in S.'s poetry coincides with the liminal period of sunset or sunrise, the visionary experience proceeding in concert with the diurnal movement of the heavenly bodies whose appearances figure the mental and spiritual enlightenment of the visionary subject. See, for example, lines 407–504, 562–7, Q Mab i 94–104, ii 1–21, *Lines Written among the Euganean Hills* 66–89. The collocation of sun and moon, as here and for example in *TL* 79–85 and *R&H* 1102–86, marks the threshold of a particularly charged moment of insight.

172. I could not choose but gaze] 'He cannot chuse but hear', Coleridge, *The Rime of the Ancient Mariner* (1798) i 22.

172–80. This stanza and the last four lines of the next draw upon the episode of the spectre-ship in the *Ancient Mariner* iii 139–200 as well as upon the apparition of the Genius Aretina in *Ahrimanes* I iii: 'But central in the flood of liquid light, / A sudden spot its widening orb revealed, / Jet-black amid the mirrored beams of night, / Jet-black, and round as Celtic warrior's shield, / A sable circle in a silver field. / With sense recalled and motionless surprise, / Deeming some fearful mystery there concealed, / He marked that shadowy orb's expanding size, / Till slowly from its breast a form began to rise' (*Peacock Works* vii 266). But S. is also remembering the approaching ship in lines 13–16 of his own unpublished poem *Zeinab and Kathema* (1811?): 'And now the beamless, broad and yellow sphere / Half sinking lingered on the crimson sea; / A shape of darksome distance does appear / Within its semicircled radiancy'.

178. A speck, a cloud, a shape] 'A speck, a mist, a shape, I wist!', *Ancient Mariner* iii 145.

180   Like a great ship in the sun's sinking sphere
       Beheld afar at sea, and swift it came anear.

                        VII

       Even like a bark, which from a chasm of mountains,
       Dark, vast, and overhanging, on a river
       Which there collects the strength of all its fountains,
       Comes forth, whilst with the speed its frame doth quiver,
185   Sails, oars, and stream, tending to one endeavour;
       So, from that chasm of light a wingèd Form
       On all the winds of heaven approaching ever
       Floated, dilating as it came: the storm
       Pursued it with fierce blasts, and lightnings swift and warm.

                        VIII

190   A course precipitous, of dizzy speed,
       Suspending thought and breath; a monstrous sight!
       For in the air do I behold indeed
       An Eagle and a Serpent wreathed in fight: —

179. Cp. *Ancient Mariner* iii 163–8: 'The western wave was all a flame, / The day was well nigh done! / Almost upon the western wave / Rested the broad bright Sun; / When that strange shape drove suddenly / Betwixt us and the Sun'.

181–5. The epic simile recalls *Paradise Lost* ix 513–16 where the Serpent's progress towards Eve is likened to the motion of a skillfully-piloted ship as well as Spenser's comparison of Sir Guyon's combat with a pair of hostile knights to a storm-tossed vessel that meets 'two contrary billowes' (*Faerie Queene* II ii 24); the figure of a ship in a storm is frequent in *Faerie Queene*: e.g. I vi 1; V ii 50; VI iv 1; VI xii 1.

181–4. Even like a bark . . . comes forth] *Locock 1911* calls attention to the ungrammatical use of *like* where one would expect 'as' to introduce a clause, saying that he could not recall another instance of this usage in S.'s poetry.

191. monstrous] portentous *canc. Nbk 2* 13; besides its appropriateness to the astounding apparition of the eagle and the serpent warring in the sky, *monstrous* retains here the obsolete sense: of the nature of a prodigy or marvel (*OED* Monster a 1), from Latin *monstrum*: a divine omen or portent (usually of misfortune).

193. An Eagle and a Serpent] The contest between the serpent and the eagle is the presiding symbolic event of the first canto as well as a major thematic focal point for the entire poem. S. initially elaborates the figure over seven stanzas in poetry supercharged with the energy of elemental conflict, withholding its metaphysical and moral significance until the revelations of the woman-guide to the narrator in stanzas xxv–xxxiii. This visionary encounter reworks an epic motif which has its antecedents in *Iliad* xii 200–7, where it serves as a divine warning to the Trojan army, and in *Aeneid* xi 751–6 and *Metamorphoses* iv 714–17 where it typifies the implacable enmity of two adversaries – as it does also in the aerial contest between a griffin and a dragon of *Faerie Queene* I v 8. The occurrence of a struggling eagle and serpent in *Metamorphoses* iv 361–4 as an analogy for the frenzied passion of the nymph Salmacis for the beautiful youth Hermaphroditus has also been noticed by commentators – Sperry (*Shelley's Major Verse* (1988) 45–6) pointing out that the androgyny with which Ovid's passage concludes represents an ideal of being that *L&C* addresses. See note to I lvi–lvii. (MWS read Francis Beaumont's narrative poem *Salmacis and Hermaphroditus* (1602), based on the passage

And now relaxing its impetuous flight,
195 Before the aerial rock on which I stood,
The Eagle, hovering, wheeled to left and right,
And hung with lingering wings over the flood,
And startled with its yells the wide air's solitude.

IX

A shaft of light upon its wings descended,
200 And every golden feather gleamed therein —

---

from Ovid cited above, on 6 February 1817, *Mary Jnl* i 163.) All these instances express an irreducible principle of passionate natural opposition which S. adopts as the basis for his imaginative overview of the revolutionary pattern of recent European history. Both the narrator's response to the spectacle of the combat and the woman-guide's explanation emphasise profound sympathetic links with the inner life of the individual – S. had already used the snake-eagle struggle as a poetic figure for conflicting impulses within the self in *Alastor* 227-37. Specific commentary on the snake–eagle conflict can be found in: *Baker*, 72–3; Sperry, *Shelley's Major Verse* (1988) 44–6; J. L. Ruff, *Shelley's The Revolt of Islam* (1972) 17–26; *Cameron (1974)* 317–19; D. Bush, *PQ* xii (1934) 299–302; C. W. Lemmi, *MLN* 1 (1935) 165–8; A. H. Gilbert, *MLN* xxxvi (1921) 505–6; D. Richardson, *KSJ* xl (1991) 73–98, Bryan Shelley, *Shelley and Scripture* (1994) 64–6. Rudolf Wittkower's chapter 'Eagle and Serpent' in *Allegory and the Migration of Symbols* (1977) provides a comprehensive account of the antiquity and diffusion of the symbol in myth, literature and the visual arts.

Although S. referred to Byron as an eagle in 1821–22 (*L* ii 289, 442) and Byron to S. as 'the snake' in the same period (*Byron L&J* ix 81, *Records* i 34, 42, 84–5) there is no reason to detect disguised personal references here. Reviewing *Manfred* in the June 1817 number of *Blackwood's* (I iii 289), Lockhart described Byron's poetic vision as able 'to soar upon unflagging wings, – that when he has reached the black and tempestuous elevation of his favourite atmosphere, he will, eagle-like, sail on undisturbed through the heart of clouds, storms, and darkness.' About the time that he drafted the early stanzas of *L&C* S. also drafted the fragment 'Mighty Eagle, thou that soarest' which portrays its subject's flight in terms (conventional enough) similar to those in the *Blackwood's* review, and for which various addressees, including Byron, have been proposed (see no. 136 and headnote). The fragment initiates a series of occurrences of the eagle in S.'s poetry as a type of intellectual and imaginative excellence aspiring to freedom: see, e.g., lines 2182–96; *Ode to Liberty* 5–8; *Hellas* 76–82, as well as the fictional portrait of Byron in *Julian and Maddalo* (1818) 50–2.

Pliny (*Natural History* X v) attributes a settled enmity to the snake and the eagle because of the snake's habit of stealing eggs from the eagle's nest. Both animals are appropriate agents of a perpetual struggle through history as legend supposed each to be self-regenerating. The eagle was imagined as soaring, every ten years, into the fiery regions near the sun and/or plunging into the sea or other body of water only to emerge with fresh plumage ('Thy youth is renewed like the eagle's' *Psalms* ciii 5; see also *Faerie Queene* I xi 34, *Adonais* 147–9, and lines 3688–93). The snake achieved the same end by casting its skin. As the bird of Jupiter the eagle was carried as an ensign by the Roman legions and had been adopted as the symbol of royal / imperial power by many of the adversaries in the recent European wars: Napoleonic France, Austria, Prussia and Russia.

199–204. Forman 1876–7 suggested that the reading of this passage could be clarified by reversing the positions of the dash and the full stop in lines 200–1; but the punctuation at the end of the two lines in the fair copy in *Nbk 4a* f. 21v is identical to *L&C/RofI*; the draft in *Nbk 2* 14 has only a full stop plus dash at the end of line 201. The sense seems clear: 'the shaft of light that illuminated each feather in the eagle's wings also made shine the serpent's scales and coloured skin which were intertwined with the bird's plumes'.

Feather and scale inextricably blended.
The Serpent's mailed and many-coloured skin
Shone through the plumes its coils were twined within
By many a swollen and knotted fold, and high
205   And far, the neck receding lithe and thin,
Sustained a crested head, which warily
Shifted and glanced before the Eagle's steadfast eye.

X

Around, around, in ceaseless circles wheeling
With clang of wings and scream, the Eagle sailed
210   Incessantly — sometimes on high concealing
Its lessening orbs, sometimes as if it failed,
Drooped through the air; and still it shrieked and wailed,

202–6. Scaled, crested and with voluminous constricting coils, the Serpent of stanzas ix–xiv has a literary pedigree reaching back to the serpent of Mars with which Cadmus and his companions fight in *Metamorphoses* iii 28–94, the sea serpent that kills Laocoon and his sons in *Aeneid* ii 199–227, the monsters Errour of *Faerie Queene* I i 14–26 and Sin of *Paradise Lost* ii 648–53 – as well as the serpent (Satan) of the same poem ix 495–531. (See Lloyd N. Jeffrey, *KSJ* vii (1958) 29–46). S. combines classical and Christian traditions to create a serpent with features that express the horrific visage of divine wrath overlaid with the associations of guile and sin deriving from *Genesis* iii with which Spenser and Milton in particular had invested it. The conduct of the foes in the battle as well as the language in which it is reported reinforce a conventionally sinister apprehension of the serpent as wily adversary, like the one in *Alastor* 227–32, so preparing for the reversal of stanzas xxvii–xxviii. Cameron, *PMLA* lvi (1941) 201 indicates a passage in the notes to *Ruins* in which '*Ophioneous serpentinus* [the constellation of The Serpent] had been chief of the rebels against Jupiter', according to Pherecydes the reputed teacher of Pythagoras.

202. mailed] Resembling mail- or scale-armour; composed of overlapping scales. Cp. *Ode to Naples* 68: 'armour of impenetrable scale' and *Mask of Anarchy* 110–11: 'It grew – a Shape in mail / Brighter than the viper's scale'. The serpent in *Metamorphoses* iii 63 is described as 'loricaeque modo squamis defensus' (protected by its scales as by a corslet).

203. plumes] plumes; *1839*.

204. [Even as a waterfall among the woods] *Nbk 2* 14. Cp. line 15 above. The first four words of the line require to be elided so as to give four accents only in the metrical scheme.

206–7. [Shrunk from the eagles broad & burning eye / Fired by the rage of war & hope of victory] *Nbk 2* 14. Cp. *Ancient Mariner* 171–2: 'As if thro' a dungeon grate he [the sun] peer'd / With broad and burning face'.

207. steadfast eye] The unflinching gaze of the eagle, reputed the only creature able to look directly into the sun, was proverbial. Cp. lines 4423–4: 'like an Eagle, whose young gaze / Feeds on the noontide beam'. The draft in *Nbk 2* 15 includes the cancelled phrase: 'His broad eye lit by the reflected flames / Of the small serpents gaze'.

208. ceaseless circles wheeling] Cp. Coleridge, *Kubla Khan* (1816) 17: 'ceaseless turmoil seething', and see note to stanza xxi below.

209. clang] Here suggesting the ringing clash of arms, though not in line 251 below after the snakes's defeat; both instances recall the sense of *clang* as 'the loud harsh resonant cry or scream of certain birds' (*OED* 2), perhaps echoing κλαγξας (klanksas) in *Iliad* xii 207; see note to lines 250–2 and cp. *PU* i 330 and note.

And casting back its eager head, with beak
And talon unremittingly assailed
215   The wreathèd Serpent, who did ever seek
Upon his enemy's heart a mortal wound to wreak.

XI

What life, what power, was kindled and arose
Within the sphere of that appalling fray!
For, from the encounter of those wondrous foes,
220   A vapour like the sea's suspended spray
Hung gathered: in the void air, far away,
Floated the shattered plumes; bright scales did leap,
Where'er the Eagle's talons made their way,
Like sparks into the darkness; — as they sweep,
225   Blood stains the snowy foam of the tumultuous deep.

XII

Swift chances in that combat — many a check,
And many a change, a dark and wild turmoil;
Sometimes the Snake around his enemy's neck
Locked in stiff rings his adamantine coil,
230   Until the Eagle, faint with pain and toil,
Remitted his strong flight, and near the sea
Languidly fluttered, hopeless so to foil
His adversary, who then reared on high
His red and burning crest, radiant with victory.

XIII

235   Then on the white edge of the bursting surge,
Where they had sunk together, would the Snake

213. eager] Both 1. fierce; and 2. sharp, biting.

217. What life what power *L&C/Rofl.* One of the two cancelled drafts of the line in *Nbk 2* 16–17 is punctuated: 'What hate, what life, what power'.

222. bright scales] [the scales of steel] *Nbk 2* 17.

224. as they sweep] *they* could take as antecedent either *talons* (line 223), in which case the sense would be: 'as the eagle's talons strike sweeping blows', or *foes* (line 219), giving the sense: 'as the adversaries sweep through the air'. The latter reading is supported by the cancelled draft in *Nbk 2* 17: '& whence [ ] that [ ] flight did wheel / Blood fell in showers beneath'.

226. Swift chances] the quick succession of incidents in the course of the struggle.

229. adamantine] unbreakable; a poetic hyperbole as is shown by lines 241–2.

233–4. Cp. the sea serpents in *Aeneid* ii 206–7: 'pectora quorum inter fluctus arrecta iubaeque / sanguinae superant undas' (their breasts and blood-red crests rise from the waves and tower above the billows).

236. sunk] sank *L&C/Rofl.* 'Sank' is a rare form of the past participle. S's draft in *Nbk 2* 20 reads 'sunk' which is the form he uses elsewhere. (An identical discrepancy occurs between *A Vision of the Sea* 8 as printed in *1820* and the fair copy in *Harvard Nbk.*) *1839*'s emendation to *sunk* has been followed by almost all later *eds.*

Relax his suffocating grasp, and scourge
The wind with his wild writhings; for to break
That chain of torment, the vast bird would shake
240   The strength of his unconquerable wings
As in despair, and with his sinewy neck,
Dissolve in sudden shock those linkèd rings,
Then soar — as swift as smoke from a volcano springs.

XIV

Wile baffled wile, and strength encountered strength,
245   Thus long, but unprevailing: — the event
Of that portentous fight appeared at length:
Until the lamp of day was almost spent
It had endured, when lifeless, stark, and rent,
Hung high that mighty Serpent, and at last
250   Fell to the sea, while o'er the continent,
With clang of wings and scream the Eagle passed,
Heavily borne away on the exhausted blast.

XV

And with it fled the tempest, so that ocean
And earth and sky shone through the atmosphere —

245. unprevailing] i.e. neither combatant could gain a victory. *the event*] the outcome.

246. portentous] The secondary sense, 'monstrous, prodigious' is the principal one here, though the primary sense, 'ominous, foreboding', is also appropriate: 1. to the narrative sequence which has still to recount (retrospectively) an idealised history of the French Revolution as a manifestation of the serpent-eagle conflict; 2. to the prophetic character of the poem as 'A Vision of the Nineteenth Century'.

248. lifeless, stark, and rent] Forman 1876–7, Locock 1911 and 1975 construe *lifeless* as 'exhausted' in order to account for the serpent's reappearance alive at line 280. This explains an apparent inconsistency in the narrative by adopting a possible meaning of the word, but hardly gives adequate weight to the first two of the three adjectives which suggest that the serpent is dead. 'Stark', in the sense of 'stiff, rigid', would more exactly describe death than exhaustion as well as recalling the phrase 'stark dead'. The word is used below to refer to the dead (2793) and the dying (4454). S. may be exaggerating the serpent's plight here in order to prepare a more surprising reversal in line 280, although death followed by rebirth would be a natural analogy with that casting of its old skin and growing a new one which made the serpent a symbol of immortality. See note to line 280.

250–2. In *Iliad* xii 205–7 the eagle: 'stung with pain, cast it [the serpent] from him to the ground, and let it fall in the midst of the throng, and himself with a loud cry sped away down the blasts of the wind' (Loeb trans.) See following note.

Stanza xv. S.'s much-cancelled drafts for this stanza in *Nbk 2* reveal his original intention of making the narrator undergo a form of psychic death corresponding to the serpent's defeat: 'So I did seem to feel that I was dead' (23). Like those who see 'The dreadful gloomy pageant of their passing bier' (21) in dream, the narrator experiences the weird sensation that he has become separated into two men, one alive and one dead: 'To leave my own corpse *alt.* self moveless lax & sere / . . . Upon the mountain' (23). Such a division of self is a condition of the vision granted to Ianthe in *Q Mab* (i 130–66 and notes) and to the narrator in Volney's *Ruins* ch. iv.

255   Only, 'twas strange to see the red commotion
        Of waves like mountains o'er the sinking sphere
        Of sunset sweep, and their fierce roar to hear
        Amid the calm: down the steep path I wound
        To the seashore — the evening was most clear
260   And beautiful, and there the sea I found
        Calm as a cradled child in dreamless slumber bound.

                        XVI

        There was a Woman, beautiful as morning,
        Sitting beneath the rocks, upon the sand
        Of the waste sea — fair as one flower adorning

Stanza xvi. S.'s cancelled draft of the stanza in *Nbk 2* 25 places another figure in the scene: 'And a fair child who near her, who, adorning / Her hair with seaweed – sometimes sought his home / In her deep bosom; then [ ] would roam / To snatch those wreathes from the receding tide / But, when the serpent fell, that boy f [ ] / Beside, like a fair heart left desolate'. Compare the child that ministers to Othman in V xxi–iv and the report of its death in XII xxiv–v.

262. There was a Woman] The woman who discloses the meaning of the serpent–eagle combat to the narrator and conducts him to the Temple of the Spirit of Good appears from a notation on the draft for stanzas 2 and 3 (*Box 1* f. 2r) and from partial drafts of stanza xvi on pp. 2–3 of *Nbk 2* to have been among S.'s earliest conceptions for Canto I. Her complex role in the narrative over the next forty stanzas includes a pedagogical function in which she bears evident similarities to the Fairy in *Q Mab* and to the Genius in Volney's *Ruins* as well as to Diotima in Plato's *Symposium*; and there are especially detailed resemblances between her and the Genius Aretina in Peacock's *Ahrimanes* who instructs the young man Darassah in the struggles between cosmic powers which have founded the metaphysical and moral condition of the world and encourages him to sail down the river of his native land to the countries beyond. *Baker 72* discusses the relation between Aretina and the Woman as well as listing a number of other female figures in poetry who have been proposed as influences on her portrait. The most interesting of these are: 1. Phaedria in *Faerie Queene* II vi 2–11 who ferries the knight Cymochles to an island in the midst of the Idle lake in a boat that moves without sail or oars; 2. the aged woman with a serpent gnawing at her heart in Southey's *Joan of Arc* (1796) who pilots the dreaming Joan in an 'age-worn bark . . . impell'd / By powers unseen' (ix 21–2) to the regions of Despair where she is tempted to suicide. The symmetry of the oppositions – gnawing serpent: despair / cherished serpent: hope – might suggest a deliberate revision of Southey's figure by S. who recommended *Joan of Arc* in 1811 (*L* i 126). Several minor verbal parallels over the next stanzas make it likely that S. is also recalling the damsel who sits at the helm of the self-propelled boat which carries Thalaba in Southey's *Thalaba* (1801) xi 31–41 (ii 287–96 in 1801 edn), and who sees in the hero 'A hope, alas! how long unknown!' (32. 5, ii 288). Bryan Shelley, *Shelley and Scripture* (1994) 65–6 sees the Woman as S.'s 'subversion' of the 'woman clothed with the sun' of *Revelation* xii in which the Archangel Michael wars with the dragon, who is 'that old serpent, called the Devil, and Satan' in heaven.

264. waste] Desolate, like the *wilderness* in the next line. The rapid change in the state of the sea from *commotion* (line 255) to *calm* (line 261) to *waste* figures the return of the narrator's despair which the Woman will teach him to overcome.

264–5. Locock 1911 cites 'A violet by a mossy stone / Half-hidden from the eye! / Fair as a star, when only one / Is shining in the sky' from Wordsworth's *She Dwelt Among the Untrodden Ways* (1800) as a model for the image in these lines. Cp. also *Athanase* 130–2.

265   An icy wilderness — each delicate hand
                 Lay crossed upon her bosom, and the band
                 Of her dark hair had fallen, and so she sate
                 Looking upon the waves; on the bare strand
                 Upon the sea-mark a small boat did wait,
270   Fair as herself, like Love by Hope left desolate.

XVII

                 It seemed that this fair Shape had looked upon
                 That unimaginable fight, and now
                 That her sweet eyes were weary of the sun,
                 As brightly it illustrated her woe;
275   For in the tears which silently to flow
                 Paused not, its lustre hung: she watching aye
                 The foam-wreaths which the faint tide wove below
                 Upon the spangled sands, groaned heavily,
                 And after every groan looked up over the sea.

XVIII

280   And when she saw the wounded Serpent make
                 His path between the waves, her lips grew pale,

269. sea-mark] The line left at the limit of the rising tide.

270. Love by Hope left desolate] Among her other functions the Woman personifies Hope.

272. unimaginable] Inconceivable (had it not been seen).

274. illustrated] 'Illumined, made lustrous', as is evident from the two following lines.

278. spangled] Interspersed with glittering particles.

280–306. S. recuperated a number of the details in these lines from his unpublished fragment of a prose romance *The Assassins* (1814–15), in the final episode of which two children are observed playing by a lake: 'They had constructed a little boat of the bark of trees, and had given it sails of interwoven feathers and launched it on the water. They sate beside a white flat stone, on which a small snake lay coiled, and when their work was finished they arose and called to the snake in melodious tones, so that it understood their language. For it unwreathed its shining circles and crept to the boat, into which no sooner had it entered than the girl loosened the band which held it to the shore, and it sailed away. Then they ran round and round the little creek, clapping their hands, and melodiously pouring out wild sounds which the snake seemed to answer by the restless glancing of his neck. At last a breath of wind came from the shore, and the boat changed its course and was about to leave the creek, which the snake perceived and leaped into the water, and came to the little children's feet. The girl sang to it, and it leaped into her bosom, and she crossed her fair hands over it, as if to cherish it there. Then the boy answered with a song, and it glided from her hands, and crept towards him. While they were thus employed, Maimuna looked up, and seeing her parents on the cliff, ran to meet them up the steep path that wound around it, and Abdallah, leaving his snake, followed joyfully' (*Prose Works* i 138–9).

280. wounded Serpent] See notes to lines 248, 359, 400–1. The serpent that emerges from the sea resembles the docile creature of *The Assassins* (see previous note) rather than the fierce monster of stanzas ix–xiv; its recovery or rebirth is effected by appropriating the eagle's legendary feat of renewing its plumage by plunging into the ocean, a reversal of traditional roles

Parted, and quivered; the tears ceased to break
From her immovable eyes; no voice of wail
Escaped her; but she rose, and on the gale
285   Loosening her star-bright robe and shadowy hair
Poured forth her voice; the caverns of the vale
That opened to the ocean, caught it there,
And filled with silver sounds the overflowing air.

XIX

She spake in language whose strange melody
290   Might not belong to earth. I heard, alone,
What made its music more melodious be,
The pity and the love of every tone;
But to the Snake those accents sweet were known
His native tongue and hers; nor did he beat
295   The hoar spray idly then, but winding on
Through the green shadows of the waves that meet
Near to the shore, did pause beside her snowy feet.

---

among many others in Canto I. McNiece, *Shelley and the Revolutionary Idea* (1969) 196 cites the Abbé Barruel on the snake as a Jacobin revolutionary emblem because of its powers of rejuvenation, and *Cameron (1974)* 623 points out its symbolic use by American revolutionaries. See note to line 369.

283. immovable] Steadfastly fixed upon the Serpent. At this point in the draft (*Nbk 2* 28) is a cancelled attempt at four lines: 'as when some immortal painter, dips / His pencil in the darkness of eclipse / And feigns among the gloom some figure frail / And beautiful'. S. reworked the image for lines 1925–6; see note thereto.

284. gale] Not a high wind but a gentle breeze. Cp. *Fragment* (no. 33): 'the pause of the summer gale's swell, / O'er the breast of the waveless deep' (lines 12–13).

285. star-bright robe] The Genius Aretina in *Ahrimanes* I iv wears a veil 'Where living flowers of flame inwoven bloomed' as well as a crown: 'Twelve points it bore: on every point upraised / A star – a heavenly star – with dazzling radiance blazed' (*Peacock Works* vii 266–7). Cp. *Revelation* xii 1.

290. Might not belong] = could not belong (*might* is past tense, not subjunctive). *alone*] only.

294. His native tongue and hers] Unintelligible to the narrator's ears (line 300), the language of the Woman and the Serpent is the 'spirit's tongue' which later in the poem expresses the insight that accompanies or follows especially intense moments of sympathetic exchange between lovers. See lines 512, 917, 2622.

297. And lay as dead beside her feet Nbk 2 29; marmoreal feet *canc. ibid.* The serpents of *Aeneid* ii 225–7, after slaying Laocoon and his sons, go and lie at the feet of the statue of Minerva, and statues of the goddess (and of her Greek counterpart Athene) often represent her with a snake at her feet. The snake frequently seen under the feet of statues of the Virgin Mary alludes to *Genesis* iii 15: 'And I will put enmity between thee and the woman, and between thy seed and her seed; it shall bruise thy head, and thou shalt bruise his heel'. J. Rieger (*The Mutiny Within* (1967) 103) has aptly termed the poem's 'emblematic irony' the mutual revision of traditional motifs that results from such combination. See note to I lvi–vii.

XX

Then on the sands the Woman sate again,
And wept and clasped her hands, and all between,
300   Renewed the unintelligible strain
Of her melodious voice and eloquent mien;
And she unveiled her bosom, and the green
And glancing shadows of the sea did play
O'er its marmoreal depth: — one moment seen,
305   For ere the next, the Serpent did obey
Her voice, and, coiled in rest in her embrace it lay.

XXI

Then she arose, and smiled on me with eyes
Serene yet sorrowing, like that planet fair,
While yet the daylight lingereth in the skies
310   Which cleaves with arrowy beams the dark-red air,
And said: 'To grieve is wise, but the despair
Was weak and vain which led thee here from sleep:

299. Cp. lines 28–30 and 449–50.

302–6. In *Metamorphoses* iv 572–603 Cadmus is transformed into a snake and enters his wife Harmonia's bosom before she is similarly transformed, a metamorphosis that horrifies those that witness it.

304. marmoreal] Marble-like. The Genius Aretina in *Ahrimanes* iv 1–2 is: 'A female form: and even as marble pale / Her cheeks' (*Peacock Works* vii 266).

Stanza xxi. 'Demon Lover' is written above the stanza in *Nbk 2* 31. The phrase is from Coleridge's *Kubla Khan* (1816) 16: 'By woman wailing for her demon-lover!', which may be recalled in the action and the details of landscape of 286–8, 298–301. At this point in the narrative it would be natural to think that the woman loves an evil spirit in the form of the serpent; the notation furnishes a clue to her true nature. She assures the narrator of her human form in lines 433–6 but her transformation in lines 616–30 reveals her as a supernatural being. Like the Fairy in *Q Mab*, later renamed *The Daemon of the World*, and the Genius in Volney's *Ruins*, she functions as a daemon (Gk δαίμων); i.e. a being of a kind that mediates between gods and men. See notes to the title of *Daemon* and to *PU* I 1; also *Rogers* (1968) 110–11.

308–10. The *planet fair* is Venus who is *serene* as a heavenly body and *sorrowing* because of her grief at the death of Adonis (*Metamorphoses* x 708–39). As the evening star Venus shows brilliantly in the west after the sun has set and in the east as the morning star just before sunrise: each of these appearances occurs at a different time of year when the orbit of the planet is favourable in relation to the earth's. The Woman has already been compared to morning in line 262, and the dual aspect of Venus is a major symbol of Canto I. See lines 356 (and note), 485, 501. At Marlow, according to Leigh Hunt, S. kept statues of 'the Vatican Apollo and the celestial Venus' in his study: see headnote to *Marianne's Dream* (no. 138). Both S. (*L* ii 25) and MWS (*Mary L* i 77) recalled in 1818 the brilliant views of the planet Venus of the previous summer at Marlow when S. was composing *L&C*. In 1817 Venus was visible in the evening through the month of March until about the end of April, and in the morning from the end of July until the end of October. (Information by courtesy of Jacqueline Mitton of the Royal Astronomical Society.)

311–15. The speech-marks are not present in *L&C/RofI*.

This shalt thou know, and more, if thou dost dare
With me and with this Serpent, o'er the deep,
315 A voyage divine and strange, companionship to keep.'

XXII

Her voice was like the wildest, saddest tone,
Yet sweet, of some loved voice heard long ago.
I wept. Shall this fair woman all alone,
Over the sea with that fierce Serpent go?
320 His head is on her heart, and who can know
How soon he may devour his feeble prey? —
Such were my thoughts, when the tide 'gan to flow;
And that strange boat, like the moon's shade did sway
Amid reflected stars that in the waters lay.

XXIII

325 A boat of rare device, which had no sail
But its own curvèd prow of thin moonstone,
Wrought like a web of texture fine and frail,
To catch those gentlest winds which are not known

313. This shalt thou know, and more] [For good must spring from hope] Nbk 2 31.

315. voyage] monosyllabic in the metrical scheme.

316–17. Inasmuch as the Woman's autobiography idealises some details from Mary Wollstonecraft's life (see notes to lines 522, 525) these lines bear a personal significance for her daughter MWS who cannot have remembered the voice of a mother who died eleven days after giving birth to her, but who was familiar with her mother's writings from childhood.

317. voice] tune Nbk 2 31.

323. moon's shade] The boat, which resembles the moon in shape and substance (line 326), is its *shade* in the sense both of its image and its phantom, being drawn by sympathy with the tidal motion through a sea of reflected stars. This analogy with the passage of the moon through the night sky, which measures the progress of the narrator's vision, may well owe something to S.'s recent reading (*Mary Jnl* i 101) of Thomas Moore's *Epistles, Odes, and Other Poems* (1806) as Ruff (Shelley's *The Revolt of Islam* (1972) 40–1, 48) suggests. A footnote to Moore's *The Grecian Girl's Dream of the Blessed Islands* reads: 'It was imagined by some of the antients that there is an ethereal ocean above us, and that the sun and moon are two floating, luminous islands, in which the spirits of the blest reside' (134). *Epistle IV. To George Morgan, Esq.*, in the same collection, alludes to a visionary voyage to the planet Venus in a boat guided by the genius of the world. See notes to lines 562–7, 604–6, 622–8. S. is no doubt also remembering the 'Ship of Heaven' which carries the maiden Kailyal through the sky in Southey's *The Curse of Kehama* (1810) vii. See headnote *Sources and Influences*, p. 25.

325. A boat of rare device] Cp. *Kubla Khan* 34–5: 'It was a miracle of rare device, / A sunny pleasure-dome with caves of ice!' Like Coleridge's 'pleasure-dome', S.'s boat is a poetic figure for the work of art – its specific character being to mediate those obscure natural impulses which would otherwise pass unperceived. See note to line 579.

326. moonstone] A translucent variety of feldspar, so called because of its milky-blue sheen which varies as the stone is moved; it was supposed to have a special affinity with the moon, its lustre increasing or decreasing as the moon waxed or waned.

To breathe, but by the steady speed alone
330   With which it cleaves the sparkling sea; and now
We are embarked — the mountains hang and frown
Over the starry deep that gleams below
A vast and dim expanse, as o'er the waves we go.

XXIV

And as we sailed, a strange and awful tale
335   That Woman told, like such mysterious dream
As makes the slumberer's cheek with wonder pale!
'Twas midnight, and around, a shoreless stream,
Wide ocean rolled, when that majestic theme
Shrined in her heart found utterance, and she bent
340   Her looks on mine; those eyes a kindling beam
Of love divine into my spirit sent,
And ere her lips could move, made the air eloquent.

330. sea; and now] sea. And now *Rossetti 1870*; sea. And, now *Rossetti 1878, Dowden 1891*. There appears to be no good reason for adding a comma after *and* which makes *now* the equivalent of 'now that'.

331. embarked –] embarked, *L&C/RofI*; most later *eds* have preferred a stronger stop. See note to lines 330–3.

332. below] below, *Rossetti 1870, Hutchinson, 1975.*

330–3. The punctuation of this syntactically awkward passage has been much emended. The stronger stop substituted by many *eds* after *embarked* in line 331 has the support of the draft in *Nbk 2* 32 where there is a semicolon, and the fair copy in *Nbk 4a* f. 22r where there is a dash. Both manuscripts are otherwise lightly punctuated. The decision of several *eds* to insert a comma after *below* follows from taking *A vast and dim expanse* to be in apposition with *starry deep*. While this is a possible reading, two difficulties make against it: 1. it requires adding punctuation which is not present in draft or fair copy or *L&C/RofI*; 2. it makes no better sense of the passage than considering *A vast and dim expanse* to refer to the sky or the overhanging mountains or both. Elsewhere S. uses *expanse* for: the earth (line 705), the sea (*A Vision of the Sea* 46) and Heaven (*Ode to Heaven* 40).

333. as o'er the waves we go] The phrase is underlined and has two question marks underneath it in the draft in *Nbk 2* 32, and is omitted in the fair copy in *Nbk 4a* f. 22r, the latter half of the line being left blank, suggesting that S. intended to replace it but found no preferable alternative.

337. shoreless stream] The ancient Greeks thought of the Ocean as a stream encircling the earth and defining the limits of the known world. Cp. *Hellas* 166–7: 'the stream / Of ocean sleeps around those foamless isles'.

339–42. The lover's glance as the vehicle of metaphysical and moral enlightenment is modelled proleptically on lines 487–504. Cp. lines 98–9; 1383–6; 4579–81.

342. 'Even before she spoke, the love in the Woman's eyes imparted by anticipation an eloquence to the air as the medium which would transmit the sounds of her voice'. Cp. lines 2180–1, 2847; also *Athanase* (no. 146), Detached Passages (b) 5: 'Of whose soft voice the air expectant seems'.

XXV

'Speak not to me, but hear! much shalt thou learn,
Much must remain unthought, and more untold,
345   In the dark Future's ever-flowing urn:
Know then, that from the depth of ages old,
Two Powers o'er mortal things dominion hold
Ruling the world with a divided lot,

Stanzas xxv–xxvi. As the Woman apprises the narrator (line 344) her account leaves much unsaid, offering no more than glimpses of two archaic events to account for the existence of the physical and moral conflict inherent in the world. These broadly conform to the pattern of Theogony (xxv) and Fall (xxvi). Unlike such ancient cosmogonies as those in Hesiod (*Theogony* 115–22), Aristophanes (*The Birds* 693–702), Ovid (*Metamorphoses* i 15–88) and *Genesis* i, which recount the imposition of form upon chaos and the reducing of discord to harmony, the fable of origins related here reaches back only to the appearance of opposed divinities simultaneously with physical and mental life (xxv) and the replication of the material and human world in their image (xxvi). All proceeds from the existence of this conflicting primary relation. It impels the operations of the physical universe and human (including moral) life alike – an essential analogy that S. had already proposed through the Fairy Mab in *Q Mab*, iv 139–50 being especially pertinent to this passage. For the significance of the dualistic theology and metaphysics, see headnote *Sources and Influences*, pp. 22–5. These two stanzas should be set against the contemporary fashion for rewriting the Orphic cosmogony in Aristophanes' *The Birds*, which gives a central place to the harmony established by 'Primogenial Love', in such texts as: *Darwin* I i 413–20, Thomas Moore's *Fragment of a Mythological Hymn to Love* (*Epistles, Odes, and Other Poems* 1806, 191–3), T. L. Peacock's *Rhododaphne* vii 1–37, *Ahrimanes* I xix, *Ahrimanes* (shorter verse fragment) I iii (*Peacock Works* vii 77–8, 272, 423).

343. The speech-marks from here until line 542 are not present in *L&C/RofI.* '*Speak not to me, but hear!*] List Stranger, list, o list! *Nbk 4a* f. 22v. Perhaps altered to avoid a repetition at line 433 where the echo of *Hamlet* I v 22 is attenuated.

344. Neither the Cumaean Sibyl nor the Priestess of Apollo at Delphi was able to reveal more than a minute part of the vast knowledge that she possessed by divine inspiration. See Virgil, *Aeneid* vi 625–7; Lucan, *Pharsalia* v 174–89, as well as the epigraph to *Daemon* (and note) where S. quoted part of the latter passage: *Nec tantum prodere vati, / Quantum scire licet. Venit aetas omnis in unam / Congeriem, miserumque premunt tot saecula pectus* ('Nor is the prophetess permitted to divulge all she knows. The whole of time comes in one mass, and so many centuries press on her afflicted breast').

345. And more which none may know or guess or dream *Nbk 2* 33. *urn*] Water-vessel, used figuratively for the source of a river or stream as in *To the Nile* 7 or *Arethusa* 27. Cp. Peacock, *The Genius of the Thames* (1810, 1812) i 17–20: 'The streams roll on, nor e'er return / To fill again their parent urn; / But bounteous nature, kindly-wise, / Their everlasting flow supplies' (*Peacock Works* vi 109) which S. may be recalling. The image of the urn carries multiple significance in the poem (see notes to lines 647, 1611): here, in view of the cosmic dualism expounded in the following stanzas, S. is probably also remembering *Iliad* xxiv 527–33 where by Zeus's throne two great jars (Gk πιθοι, pithoi, often translated as 'urns', e.g. by Pope) stand, one containing the good, the other the ill to be meted out to humankind. S. described his reading of the latter books of the *Iliad* to T. J. Hogg on 6 July 1817 (*L* i 545). See note to lines 365–7.

347–8. The sense is not that each *Power* (i.e., celestial being, deity) reigns separately over half the world but that together and in opposition they exercise the sway over all things which is theirs equally.

350   Immortal, all-pervading, manifold,
       Twin Genii, equal Gods — when life and thought
       Sprang forth, they burst the womb of inessential Nought.

                              XXVI

       'The earliest dweller of the world alone,
       Stood on the verge of chaos: Lo! afar
       O'er the wide wild abyss two meteors shone,
355   Sprung from the depth of its tempestuous jar:
       A blood-red Comet and the Morning Star
       Mingling their beams in combat — as he stood,

349. manifold] Assuming various forms and features: see line 363 and note.

350. Genii] Superintending spirits, the plural of 'genius'. In *Ahrimanes*, the term designates both powerful divinities and their ministers; S. adopts the first but reserves the secondary usage for the ministers of the Spirit of Good as in lines 407, 603. The Spirit of Good (line 373) is styled 'the better Genius of this world's estate' in line 4724. The term also suggests an affinity with the belief in a good and an evil genius supposed in various religious traditions to attend an individual from birth.

351. womb of inessential Nought] Rather than a state of nothingness or non-being (*OED* Nought 2a) which is *ipso facto* without substance, immaterial (*OED* Inessential a 1 citing this passage), it seems likelier that *nought* is synonymous with *chaos* of line 353 in the sense of the 'formless void' (*OED* Chaos 2) which was the 'womb of nature' (*Paradise Lost* ii 911), and that *inessential* here qualifies a state that is indeterminate and so without defining properties or constituent elements (*OED* Essence 7a and b) as in Ovid, *Metamorphoses* i 5–20 or Lucretius, *De Re. Nat.* v 432–48. See also *Faerie Queene* III vi 36: 'For in the wide wombe of the world there lyes, / . . . An huge eternall *Chaos*, which supplyes / The substances of natures fruitfull progenyes'. Having declared the atomism of Lucretius, which assumes the eternity of matter, to be 'yet the basis of our metaphysical knowledge' in the Preface line 216, S. could hardly intend the Woman to assert a pre-original condition of non-being. Elsewhere S. consistently adopts the tradition of creation from chaos; e.g. *Adonais* 166–7, *Prologue to Hellas* 112–13, *Ode to Naples* 137–8.

353–7. The language and images of these lines bear clear resemblances to two passages in *Paradise Lost* – 1. Satan's journey through Chaos (ii 890–1044): 'here nature first begins / Her farthest verge, and Chaos to retire' (1037–8); 'Into this wild abyss, / the womb of nature and perhaps her grave' (910–11); 2. the battle between Satan and the archangel Michael: 'such as to set forth / Great things by small, if nature's concord broke, / Among the constellations war were sprung, / Two planets rushing from aspect malign / Of fiercest opposition in mid sky, / Should combat, and their jarring spheres confound' (vi 310–15).

355. depth] depths *Nbk 4a* f. 22v (*fair copy*); no doubt altered for euphony.   *jar*] discordant strife, as in Dryden, *A Song for Saint Cecilia's Day, 1687* 3–4: 'When Nature underneath a heap / Of jarring Atomes lay'.

356. The *Comet's* colour recalls the planet Mars; the *Morning Star* is the planet Venus. See lines 308–10 and note. S. had used the opposition of these two heavenly bodies as long ago as the poem *Zeinab and Kathema* (?1811; no. 58) which remained unpublished in 1817: 'Therefore against them she [Zeinab] waged ruthless war / With their own arms of bold and bloody crime, / Even like a mild and sweetly-beaming star / Whose rays were wont to grace the matin prime / Changed to a comet horrible and bright / Which wild careers awhile then sinks in dark-red night'.

All thoughts within his mind waged mutual war,
In dreadful sympathy — when to the flood
360   That fair Star fell, he turned and shed his brother's blood.

XXVII

'Thus evil triumphed, and the Spirit of evil,
One Power of many shapes which none may know,
One Shape of many names; the Fiend did revel
In victory, reigning o'er a world of woe,

359–60. Combining allusions to: 1. *Isaiah* xiv 12: 'How art thou fallen from heaven, O Lucifer, son of the morning!', where the reference is to the King of Babylon; the Latin form Lucifer ('light-bearer') came in Christian tradition (from *Luke* x 18) to designate the rebel angel Satan, as well as being applied to Venus as the morning star, which is associated with Christ in *Revelation* xxii 16: see previous note and lines 586–90 and note; 2. Cain's murder of Abel in *Genesis* iv: 'the voice of thy brother's blood crieth unto me from the ground. And now art thou cursed from the earth, which hath opened her mouth to receive thy brother's blood from thy hand' (9–10).

359. flood] 'The sea' (*Concordance*) could not be the sense intended here if S. were adhering to a strict definition of *chaos* in which there can be no sea, matter remaining undifferentiated; in that case *flood* might indicate the flow (its etymological sense) or random movement of primary matter, an ocean of sorts, lying below the struggling planets. But a rigorous chronology of creation is hardly to S.'s purpose, and he may be condensing his images after the model of Erasmus Darwin's *The Temple of Nature* i 227–32: 'Ere Time began, from flaming Chaos hurl'd / Rose the bright spheres, which form the circling world; / Earths from each sun with quick explosions burst, / And second planets issued from the first. / Then, whilst the sea at their coeval birth, / Surge over surge, involv'd the shoreless earth'. See note to lines 400–1.

Stanzas xxvii–xxx. The account of the triumph of evil is closely indebted to *Ahrimanes* (shorter verse fragment) I x–xii (*Peacock Works* vii 425–6).

361. evil . . . evil] Evil . . . Evil *Nbk 4a* f. 23r (*fair copy*).

362. The meaning may be either: 'The *Power* of evil cannot be known directly but only through the *shapes* he assumes'; or 'the *shapes* assumed by the *Power* of evil are so numerous that no one can know them all'.

363. One Shape of many names] The phrase, which is repeated at line 3276, translates part of line 212 of Aeschylus, *Prometheus Bound*; the original Gk is jotted on the back pastedown of *Nbk 3* (*1975* 390). Responding to the demand of the chorus to say how he has come to be punished by Zeus, Prometheus mentions that his mother is Themis or Earth: she has many names but one shape. S.'s purpose in adapting the phrase to describe the pervasiveness of evil tyranny is that of Paine in a celebrated passage of *Rights of Man*, Part One: 'When despotism has established itself for ages in a country, as in France, it is not in the person of the king only that it resides . . . Every office and department has its despotism, founded upon custom and usage. Every place has its Bastille, and every Bastille its despot. The original hereditary despotism resident in the person of the king, divides and sub-divides itself into a thousand shapes and forms, till at last the whole of it is acted by deputation' (*Paine Writings* ii 284–5). Lines 730–5 and Cythna's speech to the mariners in Canto VIII (3274–6, 3280–2, 3379–81) elaborate the significance of this, one of the poem's cardinal assertions. Cp. *Ahrimanes* (shorter verse fragment) I xv: 'frantic myriads hailed with loud acclaim / The power of ill, in many a mystic name / His name disguising, which they feared to breathe' (*Peacock Works* vii 427).

365 For the new race of man went to and fro,
 Famished and homeless, loathed and loathing, wild,
 And hating good — for his immortal foe,
 He changed from starry shape, beauteous and mild,
 To a dire Snake, with man and beast unreconciled.

XXVIII

370 'The darkness lingering o'er the dawn of things,
 Was Evil's breath and life: this made him strong
 To soar aloft with overshadowing wings;
 And the great Spirit of Good did creep among
 The nations of mankind, and every tongue
375 Cursed, and blasphemed him as he passed; for none
 Knew good from evil, though their names were hung
 In mockery o'er the fane where many a groan,
 As King, and Lord, and God, the conquering Fiend did own, —

365–7. The fate of those whose lot is chosen by Zeus from the jar of evil fortune that stands by his throne is to be famished, outcast and cursed (*Iliad* xxiv 531–4). See note to line 345.

368. He] The Fiend of line 363.

368–9. Cameron (*PMLA* lvi (1941) 201) notes an interesting passage in *Ruins* xxii, section iv, which traces the origin of the Persian-Zoroastrian, Jewish and Christian emblem of the serpent as the evil principle to the ancient practice of identifying the constellations of winter (among them The Serpent) with the pains and woes of humankind. It is certainly possible that S. intended to reverse this tradition as well as the usual biblical and Miltonic ones in making his serpent represent Good, though the leading rationale of his revision, the substitution of Greek for Hebraic sources, is formulated in the prose essay 'On the Devil, and Devils' (late 1819 to mid-1820): 'I can sufficiently understand why the author of evil should have been typified under the image of a Serpent, that animal producing merely by its sight, so strong an associated recollection of the malignity of many of its species. But this was eminently a practise confined to the Jews, whose earliest mythology suggested this animal as the cause of all evil. [A]M[o]ng the greeks the Serpent was considered an auspicious & favourable being. He attended on Asculapius & Apollo . . . The Christians have turned this [the biblical] serpent into their Devil, & accomodated the whole story to their new scheme of sin & propitiation' (*Nbk 15 (BSM xiv)* 98–101).

369. Jeffrey, *KSJ* vii (1958) 36 notes the resemblance to Dante, *Purgatorio* xiv 37–8: *virtù così per nimica si fuga / da tutti come biscia* ('virtue is shunned as an enemy by all as if it were a snake'). *dire*] Inspiring terror and dread, as in *Paradise Lost* ii 628: 'Gorgons and Hydras, and Chimeras dire'.

377. In mockery] In derisory inversion of their true meaning. Cp. *Q Mab* vii 215–20: 'And friends to friends, brothers to brothers stood / Opposed in bloodiest battle-field . . . / Whilst the red cross, in mockery of peace, / Pointed to victory!'; and *Ahrimanes* (shorter verse fragment) I xv–xvi: 'And priests, prepared in human heart to sheathe / The steel, their victim twined with mockery's myrtle-wreath . . . Wherever priests awake the battle strain, / And bid the torch of persecution glare, / And curses ring along the vaulted fane, – / Call on what name they may, – their god is Ahrimane' (*Peacock Works* vii 427). *fane*] temple.

378. own, –] own. *L&C/RofI*. Since *Rossetti 1870 eds* have substituted a comma and dash to mark the continuity between stanzas xxviii–xxix. The fair copy in *Nbk 4a* f. 23 lacks punctuation at this point. *Own* = Acknowledge as sovereign, profess obedience to (*OED* 6c).

XXIX

'The fiend, whose name was Legion; Death, Decay,
380   Earthquake and Blight, and Want, and Madness pale,
Wingèd and wan diseases, an array
Numerous as leaves that strew the autumnal gale;
Poison, a snake in flowers, beneath the veil
Of food and mirth, hiding his mortal head;
385   And, without whom all these might nought avail,
Fear, Hatred, Faith, and Tyranny, who spread
Those subtle nets which snare the living and the dead.

XXX

'His spirit is their power, and they his slaves
In air, and light, and thought, and language dwell;
390   And keep their state from palaces to graves,
In all resorts of men — invisible,
But when, in ebon mirror, Nightmare fell
To tyrant or impostor bids them rise,
Black-wingèd demon forms — whom, from the hell,
395   His reign and dwelling beneath nether skies,
He loosens to their dark and blasting ministries.

Cp. *A Summer-Evening Churchyard, Lechlade, Gloucestershire* 9: 'Light, sound, and motion own the potent sway'.

379. Legion] The unclean spirits possessing the Gadarene man in *Mark* v 9 respond to Jesus: 'My name is Legion: for we are many'. See also *Luke* viii 30.

382. See note to line 162.

383–4. Combining two well-known sources: 1. Virgil, *Eclogues* iii 92–3: *Qui legitis flores et humi nascentia fraga, / frigidus, o pueri, fugite hinc, latet anguis in herba* (O boys who gather flowers and strawberries springing from the earth, run away! a cold snake is lurking in the grass); 2. Lucretius, *De Re. Nat.* iv 1131–4: *eximia veste et victu convivia, ludi, / pocula crebra, unguenta coronae serta parantur, / nequiquam, quoniam medio de fonte leporum / surgit amari aliquid quod in ipsis floribus angat* (Banquets are prepared with lavish trappings and choice dishes, entertainments, abundance of drink, perfumes, garlands, festoons; but all in vain: from the very fountain of delight arises a drop of bitterness to torment even amidst the flowers). S. especially recommended the fourth book of *De Re. Nat.* to Hogg on 6 July 1817 (*L* i 545).

390. state] Office or position of power.

392. But when,] But, when *L&C/RofI*; But when, *Nbk 4a* f. 24v (*fair copy*); almost all *eds* have moved the comma to after *when*.

394. Black-wingèd] *Nbk 4a* f. 24r (*fair copy*); Black winged *L&C/RofI*. In Aristophanes, *The Birds* 595 'black-winged Night' lays an egg from which Eros (Love) springs in Erebos (darkness) later associated with the infernal regions or Hades. See note to stanzas xxv–xxvi.

395. reign] Realm. *beneath nether skies*] in the underworld, the *nether* regions.

396. blasting] Blighting, as by divine curse. Cp. line 698 and *Q Mab* iv 100: 'Blasted with withering curses'.

XXXI

'In the world's youth his empire was as firm
As its foundations — soon the Spirit of Good,
Though in the likeness of a loathsome worm,
400   Sprang from the billows of the formless flood,
Which shrank and fled; and with that fiend of blood
Renewed the doubtful war — thrones then first shook,
And earth's immense and trampled multitude,
In hope on their own powers began to look,
405   And Fear, the demon pale, his sanguine shrine forsook.

XXXII

'Then Greece arose, and to its bards and sages,
In dream, the golden-pinioned Genii came,
Even where they slept amid the night of ages,
Steeping their hearts in the divinest flame,
410   Which thy breath kindled, Power of holiest name!
And oft in cycles since, when darkness gave

398. its] The world's.

398, 402. foundations – war –] foundations . . . war . . . *Nbk 4a* f. 24v. The suspension points in the fair copy have been adopted by *Hutchinson, Locock 1911* and *1975* because they seem to mark a longer pause judged appropriate here.

400–1. The Spirit of Good in the form of the serpent leaps from the *formless flood* of chaos, which quails and draws back from the combat to come, to do battle again with the Spirit of Evil. Some confusion is caused by stanza xxx being written in the present tense and describing things as they are. Stanza xxxi returns to the narrative of mythical time that begins at the end of xxv, at a point in the chronology later than *the dawn of things* (xxviii) though apparently still close enough – *the world's youth* (397) – for chaos to remain proximate as it was when man first appeared (xxvi).

405. sanguine] Sanguinary, bloody; the usual sense in S.

406. S. adopts the commonplace of the eighteenth-century 'progress poem' which made political liberty a necessary condition of the artistic and philosophical achievements of ancient Greece, e.g. Gray's *The Progress of Poesy* II. 3. Cp. *Ode to Liberty* iv–vi and Peacock's sonnet *'The bards and sages of departed Greece'* which is set before *Rhododaphne* (1818) (*Peacock Works* vii 8).

407. golden-pinioned] *Nbk 4a* f. 24v (*fair copy*); golden pinioned *L&C/RofI*. Eros (Love) is so called in Aristophanes, *The Birds* (697): cp. *The Witch of Atlas* 298–9, *The Two Spirits. An Allegory* (no. 182) 14.

409–10. The play on the senses of *breath* (with reference to Gk πνεῦμα (pneuma) and Latin *spiritus* = wind, breath, spirit) aims to make a secular revision of the inspiration of the Holy Spirit in the form of tongues of fire (*Acts* ii 1–4).

411–14. The meaning of the passage turns on two senses of *save* (line 413): 1. preserve (by directing aright) as in lines 3291–3: 'Justice, or truth, or joy! those only can / From slavery and religion's labyrinth caves / Guide us, as one clear star the seaman saves'; 2. admit to eternal happiness. The deathless example and fame of the Greek poets and philosophers guides those who battle for Liberty rather than the illusion of perpetual bliss in *Paradise* which is promised to the soldier who dies in a religious war.

New weapons to thy foe, their sunlike fame
Upon the combat shone — a light to save,
Like Paradise spread forth beyond the shadowy grave.

XXXIII

415 'Such is this conflict — when mankind doth strive
With its oppressors in a strife of blood,
Or when free thoughts, like lightnings are alive;
And in each bosom of the multitude
Justice and truth, with custom's hydra brood,
420 Wage silent war; — when priests and kings dissemble
In smiles or frowns their fierce disquietude,
When round pure hearts, a host of hopes assemble,
The Snake and Eagle meet — the world's foundations tremble!

XXXIV

'Thou hast beheld that fight — when to thy home
425 Thou dost return, steep not its hearth in tears;
Though thou mayst hear that earth is now become
The tyrant's garbage, which to his compeers,
The vile reward of their dishonoured years,
He will dividing give. — The victor Fiend
430 Omnipotent of yore, now quails, and fears
His triumph dearly won, which soon will lend
An impulse swift and sure to his approaching end.

417. Paragraphs 5 and 6 of the Preface to *PU* provide an extensive commentary on the image in this line, especially: 'The cloud of mind is discharging its collected lightning, and the equilibrium between institutions and opinions is now restoring, or is about to be restored'.

419. *hydra brood*] The Lernaean Hydra was a monstrous snake with venomous breath and blood and numerous heads which grew back when Heracles cut them off in slaying it. Cp. 'struggling fears and cares, dark custom's brood' (line 3501). In *Q Mab* v 195–6 venereal disease 'has filled / All human life with hydra-headed woes'.

420–3. 'In an act of mythical recollection only attainable by the most exalted artistic intuition Shelley showed a clear perception of the cosmic grandeur of the symbol and of its universal significance in the history of mankind': R. Wittkower, *Allegory and the Migration of Symbols* (1977) 44, citing these lines.

422. *When*] Where *Nbk 4a* f. 25r.

427. *garbage*] 'The offal of an animal used for food' (*OED*), perhaps in reference to the eagle's predatory habits, with a suggestion of the wider sense, 'refuse, filth'. Cp. 'Plague, a wingèd wolf, who loathes alway / The garbage and the scum that strangers make her prey' (4007–8). *compeers*] associates, henchmen.

431–2. The Woman's prophecy of the eventual return of the reign of good is modelled upon Peacock's *Ahrimanes* (see headnote *Sources and Influences*). Her conviction is not expressed with the assurance of permanence that S. would have found in Gibbon's account of Persian theology in *The History of the Decline and Fall of the Roman Empire* (1776–88) viii: 'At that decisive period, the enlightened wisdom of goodness will render the power of Ormusd

XXXV

'List, stranger list, mine is an human form,
Like that thou wearest — touch me — shrink not now!
435   My hand thou feel'st is not a ghost's, but warm
With human blood. — 'Twas many years ago,
Since first my thirsting soul aspired to know
The secrets of this wondrous world, when deep
My heart was pierced with sympathy, for woe
440   Which could not be mine own — and thought did keep
In dream, unnatural watch beside an infant's sleep.

XXXVI

'Woe could not be mine own, since far from men
I dwelt, a free and happy orphan child,
By the seashore, in a deep mountain glen;
445   And near the waves, and through the forests wild,
I roamed, to storm and darkness reconciled:
For I was calm while tempest shook the sky:
But when the breathless heavens in beauty smiled,
I wept, sweet tears, yet too tumultuously
450   For peace, and clasped my hands aloft in ecstasy.

XXXVII

'These were forebodings of my fate — before
A woman's heart beat in my virgin breast,
It had been nurtured in divinest lore:
A dying poet gave me books, and blessed

---

superior to the furious malice of his rival. Ahriman and his followers, disarmed and subdued, will sink into their native darkness: and virtue will maintain the eternal peace and harmony of the universe'. See note to *PU* I 12.

433. 'List, stranger list,] See note to line 343.   *human form*] The woman appears to be a daemon, i.e. a heroic spirit who has once lived (*OED* Demon 1a) and who has been sent as a messenger from the temple of the Spirit of Good in the physical form of a human being. See notes to line 262, stanza xxi and stanzas lvi–lvii.

441. unnatural] Because an infant's natural sleep is untroubled by dreams as in line 261: 'Calm as a cradled child in dreamless slumber bound'.

449. I wept, sweet tears] I wept sweet tears *Nbk 4a* 26r (*fair copy*).

450. Cp. the response to the beauty of spring in *Hymn to Intellectual Beauty* (B) 60: 'I shrieked, and clasped my hands in ecstasy!'.

454–8. Commentators have recognised the *dying poet* of *Alastor* (whose hair is 'withered' and 'thin') in these lines which recall 'And virgins, as unknown he passed, have pined / And wasted for fond love of his wild eyes' (62–3) as well as the episode of the Arab maiden (129–39) in the same poem. S. used the phrase *A youth with hoary hair* in the poem *They die – the dead return not* (no. 129), which was probably written some months earlier, to describe 'Misery'

455   With wild but holy talk the sweet unrest
           In which I watched him as he died away —
           A youth with hoary hair — a fleeting guest
           Of our lone mountains — and this lore did sway
           My spirit like a storm, contending there alway.

XXXVIII

460   'Thus the dark tale which history doth unfold,
           I knew, but not, methinks, as others know,
           For they weep not; and Wisdom had unrolled
           The clouds which hide the gulf of mortal woe:
           To few can she that warning vision show,
465   For I loved all things with intense devotion;
           So that when Hope's deep source in fullest flow,
           Like earthquake did uplift the stagnant ocean
           Of human thoughts — mine shook beneath the wide emotion.

XXXIX

           'When first the living blood through all these veins
470   Kindled a thought in sense, great France sprang forth,
           And seized, as if to break, the ponderous chains
           Which bind in woe the nations of the earth.
           I saw, and started from my cottage hearth;
           And to the clouds and waves in tameless gladness,
475   Shrieked, till they caught immeasurable mirth —
           And laughed in light and music: soon, sweet madness
           Was poured upon my heart, a soft and thrilling sadness.

---

who beckons 'parent, friend, and lover' to the grave; and again in *R&H* 151 to describe the ghost of a brother who is his sister's incestuous lover. Cp. Laon's appearance in lines 1668–73, and see *Chernaik* 8–31.

465. Recalling Coleridge, *France: An Ode* (1798): 'Possessing all things with intensest love' (104).

466. See note to line 647.

468. emotion] commotion *Nbk 4a* 27r; the fair-copy reading has been adopted by *Locock 1911*, *Hutchinson* and *1975*, but the rhyme *ocean / emotion* is common in S. in similar contexts, e.g. lines 2265–7, *PU* IV 42–5, 96–7.

469–70. 'When first I felt a conviction passionately'. Cp. *PU* I 542–5. The imagery takes up that of stanza xxxii as well as signalling the awakening of sexual desire which is developed over the next three stanzas.

475. mirth —] mirth *Nbk 4a* 27r. Several *eds* substitute a comma for the dash in *L&C/RofI*, *Locock 1911* considering it 'misleading', presumably because it dramatically separates the two consecutive effects of *shrieked*.

476. laughed in light and music] S. reused the phrase to express a similar phenomenon in *Ode to Naples* 107–8.

XL

'Deep slumber fell on me: — my dreams were fire,
Soft and delightful thoughts did rest and hover
480 Like shadows o'er my brain; and strange desire,
The tempest of a passion, raging over
My tranquil soul, its depths with light did cover,
Which passed; and calm, and darkness, sweeter far
Came — then I loved; but not a human lover!
485 For when I rose from sleep, the Morning Star
Shone through the woodbine wreaths which round my casement were.

XLI

''Twas like an eye which seemed to smile on me.
I watched, till by the sun made pale, it sank
Under the billows of the heaving sea;
490 But from its beams deep love my spirit drank,
And to my brain the boundless world now shrank
Into one thought — one image — yes, for ever!
Even like the dayspring, poured on vapours dank,
The beams of that one Star did shoot and quiver
495 Through my benighted mind — and were extinguished never.

XLII

'The day passed thus: at night, methought in dream
A shape of speechless beauty did appear:
It stood like light on a careering stream
Of golden clouds which shook the atmosphere;
500 A wingèd youth, his radiant brow did wear
The Morning Star: a wild dissolving bliss
Over my frame he breathed, approaching near,
And bent his eyes of kindling tenderness
Near mine, and on my lips impressed a lingering kiss,

---

485. *Morning Star*] See note to lines 308–10.

493. *dayspring*] Dawn, daybreak. Bryan Shelley, *Shelley and Scripture* (1994) 185 detects a reference to *2 Peter* i 19: 'We have also a more sure word of prophecy; whereunto ye do well that ye take heed, as unto a light that shineth in a dark place, until the day dawn, and the day star arise in your hearts'.

497. *speechless*] Unutterable, indescribable as in lines 944 and 4257.

504. *kiss,*] kiss. *L&C/RofI*. Many *eds* have emended the punctuation to mark the continuation of the sentence into the next stanza. The fair copy in *Nbk 4a* is defective here.

XLIII

505 'And said: "a Spirit loves thee, mortal maiden,
How wilt thou prove thy worth?" Then joy and sleep
Together fled, my soul was deeply laden,
And to the shore I went to muse and weep;
But as I moved, over my heart did creep
510 A joy less soft, but more profound and strong
Than my sweet dream; and it forbade to keep
The path of the seashore: that Spirit's tongue
Seemed whispering in my heart, and bore my steps along.

XLIV

'How, to that vast and peopled city led,
515 Which was a field of holy warfare then,
I walked among the dying and the dead,
And shared in fearless deeds with evil men,
Calm as an angel in the dragon's den —
How I braved death for liberty and truth,
520 And spurned at peace, and power, and fame; and when
Those hopes had lost the glory of their youth,
How sadly I returned — might move the hearer's ruth:

505–6. The double speech-marks are not present in *L&C/RofI*. As well as translating the annunciation of the angel Gabriel to the Virgin Mary in *Luke* i 26–35 into terms of secular dedication, the words of the *wingèd youth* clearly resemble those of the Genius Aretina to Darassah in *Ahrimanes* I xv 6–7: 'The monarch of the world hath chosen thee / High trust, and power, and dignity to bear' (*Peacock Works* vii 271).

512. Spirit's tongue] See note to line 294.

Stanza xliv. Though the details are idealised, the stanza refers, as H. S. Salt (*A Shelley Primer* (1887) 55) suggested, to Mary Wollstonecraft's residence in revolutionary Paris between December 1792 and April 1795.   *517. men,*] men. *L&C/RofI*.

518. A composite biblical image deriving from a conventional formula of divine wrath menacing cities with desolation, as in 'I will make Jerusalem heaps, and a den of dragons' and 'make the cities of Judah desolate, and a den of dragons' (*Jeremiah* ix 11, x 22); as well as from the episode of Daniel in the lions' den in *Daniel* vi 16–24: 'My God hath sent his angel, and hath shut the lions' mouths, that they have not hurt me' (22).

522. How sadly I returned] William Godwin's *Memoirs of the Author of A Vindication of the Rights of Woman* (1798) portrays Mary Wollstonecraft as returning from Paris in April 1795 'with a heavy heart' (*Godwin Novels* i 121), though more on account of the complications of her personal life than because of her disappointment at the disorder and bloodshed she witnessed there. This disappointment was frequently expressed in print, for example in her *Historical and Moral View of the Origin and Progress of the French Revolution* (1794) where the Preface prominently advertised her conviction that, 'The rapid changes, the violent, the base, and nefarious assassinations, which have clouded the vivid prospect that began to spread a ray of joy and gladness over the gloomy horizon of oppression, cannot fail to chill the sympathizing bosom, and palsy intellectual vigour' (*MWW* vi 6).   *ruth*] compassion.

85

XLV

'Warm tears throng fast! the tale may not be said —
Know then, that when this grief had been subdued,
525   I was not left, like others, cold and dead;
The Spirit whom I loved, in solitude
Sustained his child: the tempest-shaken wood,
The waves, the fountains, and the hush of night —
These were his voice, and well I understood
530   His smile divine, when the calm sea was bright
With silent stars, and Heaven was breathless with delight.

XLVI

'In lonely glens, amid the roar of rivers,
When the dim nights were moonless, have I known
Joys which no tongue can tell; my pale lip quivers
535   When thought revisits them: — know thou alone,
That after many wondrous years were flown,
I was awakened by a shriek of woe;
And over me a mystic robe was thrown,
By viewless hands, and a bright Star did glow
540   Before my steps — the Snake then met his mortal foe.'

XLVII

'Thou fear'st not then the Serpent on thy heart?'
'Fear it!' she said, with brief and passionate cry,
And spake no more: that silence made me start —

523. *the tale may not be said*] See note to line 344.

525. *like others, cold and dead*] The natural details of lines 527–8 are those of stanza i of Coleridge's *France: An Ode* (1798); together with the echoes of Wordworth's *Ode* (1807) in lines 530–1 they suggest that the two older poets are the *others* especially intended. See headnote *Sources and Influences*, p. 28. Despite her disillusionment with events in France (see note to line 522) Mary Wollstonecraft remained an advocate of progressive reform, persuaded that 'the revolution was neither produced by the abilities or intrigues of a few individuals; nor was the effect of sudden and short-lived enthusiasm; but the natural consequence of intellectual improvement, gradually proceeding to perfection in the advancement of communities' (*Historical and Moral View: MWW* vi 6–7).

526. *loved,*] Nbk 4a f. 28r; loved *L&C/RofI*: the comma in the fair copy clarifies the sense and has been widely adopted by *eds.*

530. *sea was*] seas were Nbk 4a f. 28r (*fair copy*).

530–1. 'The Moon doth with delight / Look round her when the heavens are bare; / Waters on a starry night / Are beautiful and fair' (Wordsworth, *Ode* (1807, 'Intimations of Immortality' added to the title in 1815)) 12–15. See note to line 525.

538–9. *mystic robe*] Presumably her 'star-bright robe' of line 285, the garb of the seer and prophet as in *I Kings* xix 19, *Isaiah* lxi 10 or in *Ahrimanes* I iv 3–5. Cp. *Hellas* 41–4: 'If Liberty / Lent not Life its soul of Light, / Hope its iris of delight, / Truth its prophet's robe to wear'. *viewless*] invisible. See headnote *Sources and Influences*, p. 25.

545 I looked, and we were sailing pleasantly,
     Swift as a cloud between the sea and sky;
     Beneath the rising moon seen far away
     Mountains of ice, like sapphire, piled on high
     Hemming the horizon round, in silence lay
     On the still waters — these we did approach alway.

XLVIII

550 And swift and swifter grew the vessel's motion,
     So that a dizzy trance fell on my brain —
     Wild music woke me: we had passed the ocean
     Which girds the pole, Nature's remotest reign —
     And we glode fast o'er a pellucid plain
555 Of waters, azure with the noontide day.
     Etherial mountains shone around — a Fane
     Stood in the midst, girt by green isles which lay
     On the blue sunny deep, resplendent far away.

XLIX

     It was a Temple, such as mortal hand
560 Has never built, nor ecstasy, nor dream,
     Reared in the cities of enchanted land:
     'Twas likest Heaven, ere yet day's purple stream
     Ebbs o'er the western forest, while the gleam
     Of the unrisen moon among the clouds

545–6. sky; . . . away] sky, . . . away; L&C/RofI. The punctuation of the fair copy in Nbk 4a f. 29r is adopted here because far away and horizon (line 548) seem clearly to belong to the same viewpoint. Locock 1911 and 1975 reverse the position of the comma and semicolon of L&C/RofI.

Stanza xlviii. The stanza shares circumstantial details with The Rime of the Ancient Mariner Part V: the mysteriously moving vessel, the trance or swoon, the strange music, the time of day (noon).

552–8. Ancient legend located the temperate country of the Hyperboreans in the remote northern seas where they maintained a temple dedicated to the worship of Apollo. See Diodorus Siculus ii 47 and the notes to the epigraph before Canto I, to stanzas liii–liv and to line 4813.

553. the pole] In a poem written from a European perspective the phrase Nature's remotest reign would indicate the South Pole, and the borrowings from The Ancient Mariner as well as the location of the dwelling of Oromaze (the good spirit of preservation) in Ahrimanes (shorter verse fragment) I xiii, 'Far [in] the south's impenetrable bowers', might seem to confirm this. By contrast the Hyperboreans' land was in the northern polar seas. The voyage not being plotted according to actual geography, the location of the pole is left ambiguous.

560. ecstasy] Prophetic rapture or poetic frenzy.

562–7. These lines condense the analogy between the spectacle of sunset over the ocean and the vision of the Fairy Mab's palace in Q Mab ii 1–34. The additional presence of the rising moon provides a link to the poem's initiating visionary moment in lines 167–71. For the calculated ambiguity between sky and ocean, see the note to line 323.

565   Is gathering — when with many a golden beam
The thronging constellations rush in crowds,
Paving with fire the sky and the marmoreal floods;

L

Like what may be conceived of this vast dome,
When from the depths which thought can seldom pierce
570   Genius beholds it rise, his native home,
Girt by the deserts of the Universe.
Yet, nor in painting's light, or mightier verse,
Or sculpture's marble language can invest
That shape to mortal sense — such glooms immerse
575   That incommunicable sight, and rest
Upon the labouring brain and overburdened breast.

LI

Winding among the lawny islands fair,
Whose blosmy forests starred the shadowy deep,
The wingless boat paused where an ivory stair
580   Its fretwork in the crystal sea did steep,
Encircling that vast Fane's aerial heap:
We disembarked, and through a portal wide
We passed — whose roof of moonstone carved, did keep
A glimmering o'er the forms on every side,
585   Sculptures like life and thought; immovable, deep-eyed.

567. floods;] floods. *L&C/RofI*. Several *eds* substitute a briefer stop at the end of the stanza to mark continuity with the next stanza. The fair copy in *Nbk 4a* f. 29v is unpunctuated at this point.

568. this vast dome] The arching vault of the heavens, a synecdoche for the earth, with a play on *dome* = stately building, here a temple: cp. 'religion's tottering dome' (line 1053).

569–71. Genius can sometimes attain a vision of the earth as a planet among the infinite spaces of the universe like that which is granted to the spirit of the virtuous Ianthe from the celestial palace of the Fairy Mab in *Q Mab* ii 68–108: 'None but a spirit's eye / Might ken that rolling orb' (85–6).

578. blosmy] Blossomy, blooming: Cp. Coleridge, *The Nightingale* (1798) 79: 'blosmy twig'. Cp. line 1700.

579 wingless] Without sails. The phrase may have been suggested by Phaedria's boat in the *Faerie Queene* II vi 5, which was 'More swift, then swallow sheres the liquid skie, / Withouten oare or Pilot to guide, / Or winged canuas with the wind to flie'. See note to line 325, and cp. lines 1412 and 4624.

581. Encircling] Sustaning [sic] SC 576 (*BSM* viii 168–9): *fair copy*. *aerial heap*] the phrase can signify both an elevated and a visionary structure. See note to line 130 and cp. the palace composed of the four elements in Southey's *The Curse of Kehama* (1810) vii 10.

583. We] I SC 576 (*BSM* viii 168–9): *fair copy*. *moonstone*] see note to line 326. *did keep*] maintained.

585. immovable, deep-eyed] following my silent guide SC 576 (*BSM* viii 168–9): fair copy.

LII

We came to a vast hall, whose glorious roof
Was diamond, which had drank the lightning's sheen
In darkness, and now poured it through the woof
Of spell-inwoven clouds hung there to screen
590   Its blinding splendour — through such veil was seen
That work of subtlest power, divine and rare;
Orb above orb, with starry shapes between,
And hornèd moons, and meteors strange and fair,
On night-black columns poised — one hollow hemisphere!

LIII

595   Ten thousand columns in that quivering light
Distinct — between whose shafts wound far away
The long and labyrinthine aisles — more bright
With their own radiance than the Heaven of Day;
And on the jasper walls around, there lay
600   Paintings, the poesy of mightiest thought,
Which did the Spirit's history display;
A tale of passionate change, divinely taught,
Which, in their wingèd dance, unconscious Genii wrought.

586–90. Many diamonds are phosphorescent, glowing in the dark after exposure to sunlight. S. could have read of the phenomenon in W. Nicholson's *British Encyclopaedia* (1807–9) which he ordered on 17 December 1812 (*L* i 343). See R. A. Hartley (*N&Q* n.s. (20 Aug. 1973) 293–4) who suggests a possible pun: Phosphor ('light-bearer') = Lucifer, both names for the morning-star. See also *Darwin* note to I ii 228, and note to *PU* II iii 86–7.

587. drank] As *Locock 1911* points out, S. regularly uses both this and the modern form of the past participle.

Stanzas liii–iv. Cp. the Hyperboreans' ceremonies in praise of Apollo as recounted in Diodorus Siculus (ii 47) which S. ordered on 24 December 1812 (*L* i 344): 'And there is also in the island both a magnificent sacred precinct of Apollo and a notable temple which is adorned with many votive offerings and is spherical in shape. Furthermore, a city is there which is sacred to this god, and the majority of its inhabitants are players on the cithara; and these continually play on this instrument in the temple and sing hymns of praise to the god, glorifying his deeds' (Loeb translation). See notes to epigraph before Canto I, lines 552–8, 4813. Pindar's tenth Pythian Ode, an extract of which is set as epigraph before Canto I, also describes the Hyperboreans' celebrations (37–44).

599. jasper walls] 'And the building of the wall of it was of jasper: and the city was pure gold, like unto clear glass': *Revelation* xxi 18, describing the heavenly Jerusalem.

600. poesy] *Locock 1911* construes as 'creation' (Gk ποίησις), which is a possible meaning.

602–3. The Genii, presumably the same beings as those who inspired the ancient Greek poets and philosophers in stanza xxxii, spontaneously represent the *Spirit's history* (line 601) through the medium of their aerial dance, themselves unaware of what they are creating. This form of inspiration resembles that granted to Cythna in dream (965–8): 'Cythna taught / Even in the visions of her eloquent sleep, / Unconscious of the power through which she wrought / The woof of such intelligible thought'.

LIV

Beneath, there sate on many a sapphire throne,
605 The Great, who had departed from mankind,
A mighty Senate; — some, whose white hair shone
Like mountain snow, mild, beautiful, and blind.
Some, female forms, whose gestures beamed with mind;
And ardent youths, and children bright and fair;
610 And some had lyres whose strings were intertwined
With pale and clinging flames, which ever there
Waked faint yet thrilling sounds that pierced the crystal air.

LV

One seat was vacant in the midst, a throne,
Reared on a pyramid like sculptured flame,
615 Distinct with circling steps which rested on
Their own deep fire — soon as the Woman came
Into that hall, she shrieked the Spirit's name
And fell; and vanished slowly from the sight.
Darkness arose from her dissolving frame,
620 Which gathering, filled that dome of woven light,
Blotting its spherèd stars with supernatural night.

604–6. J. Ruff, *Shelley's Revolt of Islam* (1972) 41 notes the resemblance to Thomas Moore's *The Grecian Girl's Dream of the Blessed Islands* (*Epistles, Odes, and Other Poems* (1806) 134–42) in which a dream-voyage through the ocean of the heavens reaches the moon, 'an isle of love', where the souls of Aristotle, Socrates, Epicurus and Pythagoras, together with the women they have loved, repose forever. See notes to lines 323, 622–8.

607. blind] *Concordance*, apparently taking the adjective to refer to *hair* in the previous line, glosses as 'without colour', but it is more likely that it qualifies *some* and alludes to the sightless poets Homer (see note to 'Frail clouds arrayed in sunlight lose the glory' (no. 142) 64, *The Witch of Atlas* 319) and Milton who in *Adonais* 31–6 is described as 'blind, old, and lonely' (a phrase that S. jotted near the end of the drafts for *L&C* in *Nbk 3* 215, perhaps as early as March 1817) but whose 'clear Sprite / Yet reigns o'er earth; the third among the sons of light'.

614. pyramid like sculptured flame] The word *pyramid* was formerly thought to derive from the Gk word for fire, πυρ. In *Paradise Lost* ii 1013–14 Satan 'Springs upward like a pyramid of fire / Into the wild expanse [of chaos]'. Cp. line 2076 and note.

615. Distinct with] Decorated or adorned with so as to be distinctive, a poetic usage from the Latin *distinctus*. S. used the phrase and the image again in lines 2076–7.

618. sight.] sight . . . *Nbk 4a* f. 30v. The suspension points in the fair copy mimic the action.

621. spherèd] *Concordance* glosses as 'rounded, formed as orbs', but the meaning here is rather 'set high in the *hollow hemisphere*' (line 594) that forms the temple's sky. In older astronomy the fixed stars occupied the eighth sphere of the heavens; see note to line 630. Cp. *Fiordispina* 26: 'But thou art as a planet sphered above'. *with*] in *Nbk 4a* f. 30v: *Locock 1911* adopts the reading of the fair copy, conjecturing that 'the printer, mistaking "night" for "might", changed "in" to "with"'; but this fair copy did not serve as printer's copy, and in any case the hypothesis is a complicated one where the *L&C/RofI* reading is hardly a solecism.

LVI

Then first, two glittering lights were seen to glide
In circles on the amethystine floor,
Small serpent eyes trailing from side to side,
625   Like meteors on a river's grassy shore,
They round each other rolled, dilating more
And more — then rose, commingling into one,
One clear and mighty planet hanging o'er
A cloud of deepest shadow, which was thrown
630   Athwart the glowing steps and the crystàlline throne.

Stanzas lvi–lvii. 'A magic and obscure circumstance then takes place, the result of which is, that the woman and the serpent are seen no more, but that a cloud opens asunder, and a bright and beautiful shape, which seems compounded of both, is beheld sitting on a throne, – a circumstance apparently imitated from Milton' (Leigh Hunt, *The Examiner* xxxix No. 527 (1 February 1818) 75). Hunt refers to the episode of Satan's return to Pandemonium after the Fall in *Paradise Lost* x 441–584 in which both he and the other fallen angels are transformed into serpents, a process that S. reverses here. There is some resemblance of detail between these stanzas and *PL* x 444–50: 'invisible / Ascended his high throne, which under state / Of richest texture spread, at the upper end / Was placed in regal lustre. Down a while / He sat, and round about him saw unseen: / At last as from a cloud his fulgent head / And shape star-bright appeared'. More intricate similarities are shared, in these stanzas as well as in stanzas lii–v, with Spenser's account of Scudamore's visit to the 'inmost Temple' of Venus in *Faerie Queene* IV x 41 as well as with the description of Cynthia's (the Moon's) palace in the *Two Cantos of Mutabilitie* vi 8–10. (See Ruff, *Shelley's The Revolt of Islam* (1972) 37–40, following Baker, *The Influence of Spenser on Shelley's Major Poetry* (1939) 106). Cynthia's page is '*Vesper,* whom we the Euening-starre intend' (vi 9). Also interesting is the veiled statue of Venus Hermaphroditus: 'And both her feete and legs together twyned / Were with a snake, whose head and tail were fast combyned . . . they say, she hath both kinds in one, / Both male and female, both vnder one name: / She syre and mother is her selfe alone, / Begets and eke conceiues, ne needeth other none' (*Faerie Queene* IV x 40–1). This source together with the language of lines 633–8 reinforce Hunt's suggestion that the figure on the throne in stanza lvii is meant to be perceived as androgynous. See note to line 193.

622–8. Ruff, *Shelley's The Revolt of Islam* (1972) 41 cites Thomas Moore's *The Grecian Girl's Dream of the Blessed Islands*; lines 75–6 are pertinent here: 'The One that's form'd of Two who dearly love, / Is the best number heaven can boast above!' (*Epistles, Odes, and Other Poems* (1806) 140). See notes to lines 323, 604–6.

625. meteors] The term 'meteor' could be applied to other luminous phenomena than atmospheric ones, and the movement described in 624–5 resembles an appearance of marsh gas, the *ignis fatuus* or will-o-the-wisp. Cp. Byron, *The Prisoner of Chillon* (1816) 31–5: 'A sunbeam which hath lost its way, / . . . Creeping o'er the floor so damp, / Like a marsh's meteor lamp'. S. could have read in *Darwin* (note to I i 189) that the phenomenon was 'supposed to originate from the inflammable air, or Hydrogene, given up from morasses', though Darwin himself was sceptical of this. The same element when risen into the upper atmosphere and ignited by electricity was thought by some to appear as meteors or falling stars. See *Grabo (1930)* 172–4; *Butter (1970)* 284–5. Cp. lines 2615–32 and *PU* II ii 71–82 (and note).

630. crystàlline] Formed of crystal; in the present cosmic context perhaps alluding to the substance of the ninth or crystalline sphere imagined in Ptolomaic astronomy as lying between the sphere of the fixed stars and the *primum mobile*. The altar on which the statue of Venus stands in *Faerie Queene* IV x 39 is 'like to christall glasse'; and the palace of Cynthia in the *Cantos of Mutabilitie* vi 10 is supported by 'thousand Crystall pillors of huge hight'. See note to stanzas lvi–vii.

LVII

The cloud which rested on that cone of flame
Was cloven; beneath the planet sate a Form,
Fairer than tongue can speak or thought may frame,
The radiance of whose limbs rose-like and warm
635   Flowed forth, and did with softest light inform
The shadowy dome, the sculptures, and the state
Of those assembled shapes — with clinging charm
Sinking upon their hearts and mine — He sate
Majestic, yet most mild — calm, yet compassionate.

LVIII

640   Wonder and joy a passing faintness threw
Over my brow — a hand supported me,
Whose touch was magic strength: an eye of blue
Looked into mine, like moonlight, soothingly;
And a voice said — 'Thou must a listener be
645   This day — two mighty Spirits now return,
Like birds of calm, from the world's raging sea,
They pour fresh light from Hope's immortal urn;
A tale of human power — despair not — list and learn!'

LIX

I looked, and lo! one stood forth eloquently,
650   His eyes were dark and deep, and the clear brow
Which shadowed them was like the morning sky,

635. *inform*] 'Pervade as a spirit, inspire, animate' (*OED* Inform II 3b). Cp. lines 1336–7: 'what radiance did inform / Those horny eyes?', and *Paradise Lost* iii 593–4: 'informed / With radiant light, as glowing iron with fire'.

636. *state*] The exalted and dignified condition of the *mighty Senate* of stanza liv.

644–8. The speech-marks are not present in *L&C/RofI*.

647. *Hope's immortal urn*] *The Urn* was an old name for the constellation Aquarius, and S. may be recalling a detail from J. F. Newton's letter on the 'Hindoo Zodiac' published in the *Monthly Magazine* xxxiii (1812) 107–9, which interprets an ancient Indian representation of the constellations divided into four compartments as an allegory of the natural life-cycle from impregnation, through creation and destruction, describing the final phase thus: 'But, as Hope has never abandoned the earth, that precious gift which the Almighty in his beneficence has conferred upon mankind, the great dew of India, Dhanavantara [Aquarius], presents himself with his urn of amreeta [ambrosia], and dominates in the last compartment of the circle'. Peacock included a reference to the *Monthly Magazine* for the first half of 1812 (when three further articles by Newton appeared) among the notes to the shorter verse fragment of *Ahrimanes* (*Peacock Works* vii 423). Both S. and Peacock had met Newton in 1813 (*Peacock Works* viii 71–3). See notes to lines 345, 1611.

Stanzas lix–lx. After breaking off the composition of Canto I at stanza xxv, S. drafted these two stanzas further on in *Nbk 2* (41–3) as the first two stanzas of Canto II.

649. *one*] Laon, who is first named in line 791.

The cloudless Heaven of Spring, when in their flow
Through the bright air, the soft winds as they blow
Wake the green world — his gestures did obey
655   The oracular mind that made his features glow,
And where his curvèd lips half open lay,
Passion's divinest stream had made impetuous way.

LX

Beneath the darkness of his outspread hair
He stood thus beautiful: but there was One
660   Who sate beside him like his shadow there,
And held his hand — far lovelier — she was known
To be thus fair, by the few lines alone
Which through her floating locks and gathered cloak,
Glances of soul-dissolving glory, shone: —
665   None else beheld her eyes — in him they woke
Memories which found a tongue, as thus he silence broke.

Canto Second

I

The starlight smile of children, the sweet looks
Of women, the fair breast from which I fed,
The murmur of the unreposing brooks,
670   And the green light which shifting overhead,
Some tangled bower of vines around me shed,
The shells on the sea-sand, and the wild flowers,
The lamplight through the rafters cheerly spread,
And on the twining flax — in life's young hours
675   These sights and sounds did nurse my spirit's folded powers.

659. One] Cythna, who is first named in line 855.

662–4. If *lines* is understood as 'rays of light' and *glances* as 'beams of light' and in apposition to *lines*, then the meaning appears to be: 'Her beauty could be discerned by means of the light radiating from her, and by no other light' (*Locock 1911*) – a construction that is supported by the draft of line 664 in *Nbk 2* 43: 'Like sunrise ?[thro] a forest struggling, shone'.

670. Locock 1911 points out that it is the *bower* of the next line that shifts.

673. rafters] cottage *canc. Nbk 2* 44.

675. spirit's] spirits' *L&C/RofI*. In *Nbk 16* S. made an Italian translation of the beginning of this Canto down to line 698, probably in the period December 1820–early February 1821 (*BSM* iv Part Two f. 103v rev.). The translation of this line on f. 103v reads: 'del spirito' (sic, for 'dello spirito'), the Italian singular confirming the justness of an emendation made by many *eds*.

II

In Argolis, beside the echoing sea,
Such impulses within my mortal frame
Arose, and they were dear to memory,
Like tokens of the dead: — but others came
680   Soon, in another shape: the wondrous fame
Of the past world, the vital words and deeds
Of minds whom neither time nor change can tame,
Traditions dark and old, whence evil creeds
Start forth, and whose dim shade a stream of poison feeds.

III

685   I heard, as all have heard, the various story
Of human life, and wept unwilling tears.
Feeble historians of its shame and glory,
False disputants on all its hopes and fears,
Victims who worshipped ruin, — chroniclers
690   Of daily scorn, and slaves who loathed their state
Yet flattering power had given its ministers
A throne of judgement in the grave: — 'twas fate,
That among such as these my youth should seek its mate.

676. *In Argolis*] In rocky *canc.* Argolis; in Lemnos *canc. Nbk* 2 44. Above the line is the cancelled phrase: 'There was a grey old man, who'. *Argolis* is a mountainous district of the northeastern Peloponnesus, its eastern part forming a broad isthmus with an irregular coastline and numerous islands. S. probably acquired an impression of it from Edward Daniel Clarke's *Travels in Various Countries of Europe, Asia and Africa* (1814), which MWS was reading between 9 and 19 May 1817 (*Mary Jnl* i 169). A memorandum in *Nbk* 2 1 – 'See Clarke's travels Peloponnese p. 614' – refers to the author's passage through Argolis which is described in lyrical terms: 'the fields, and the groves, and the mountains, and the vales of *Argolis*, surpassed all that we had imagined . . . To render the effect of the landscape still more impressive, shepherds, upon the distant hills, began to play, as it were an evening-service, upon their reed pipes; seeming to realize the ages of poetic fiction; and filling the mind with dreams of innocence, which, if it dwell anywhere on earth, may perhaps be found in these retreats, apart from the haunts of the disturber, whose "whereabout" is in cities and courts, amidst wealth and ambition and power. All that seems to be dreaded in these pastoral retreats are the casual and rare visits of the *Turkish* lords' (Part II, Section ii, pp. 613–14). Clarke goes on to recount the brutal mistreatment of a group of Greek villagers by his party's Turkish guide. See note to the name *Cythna* in the title. Lemnos is a large island in the northern Aegean.

677. *Such impulses*] The phrase is more appropriate to the last line of the previous stanza as originally drafted: 'All [thoughts] a child can love or feel or understand' (*Nbk* 2 44).

690–2. 'Although they hate their condition, the oppressed, in order to court favour with established power, accept the authority which the priests who are its ministers exercise in the name of a divine judgement which will be given after death'.

IV

The land in which I lived, by a fell bane
695 Was withered up. Tyrants dwelt side by side,
And stabled in our homes, — until the chain
Stifled the captive's cry, and to abide
That blasting curse men had no shame — all vied
In evil, slave and despot; fear with lust,
700 Strange fellowship through mutual hate had tied,
Like two dark serpents tangled in the dust,
Which on the paths of men their mingling poison thrust.

V

Earth, our bright home, its mountains and its waters,
And the etherial shapes which are suspended
705 Over its green expanse, and those fair daughters,
The clouds, of Sun and Ocean, who have blended
The colours of the air since first extended
It cradled the young world, none wandered forth
To see or feel: a darkness had descended
710 On every heart: the light which shows its worth,
Must among gentle thoughts and fearless take its birth.

VI

This vital world, this home of happy spirits,
Was as a dungeon to my blasted kind,
All that despair from murdered hope inherits
715 They sought, and in their helpless misery blind,
A deeper prison and heavier chains did find,

---

694. *fell bane*] *Q Mab* iii 176–8 provides an exact gloss: 'Power, like a desolating pestilence, / Pollutes whate'er it touches; and obedience, / Bane of all genius, virtue, freedom, truth, / Makes slaves of men'. See also note to this passage. S.'s Italian translation of the phrase is 'amara peste' = grievous pestilence (*BSM* iv Part Two f. 103r rev.).

706. *of Sun and Ocean*] In *The Clouds*, Aristophanes says that the clouds are the daughters of Ocean; S. has the cloud in *The Cloud* say that she is the 'daughter of Earth and Water' (line 73). *blended*] By filtering sunlight cloud produces the tints of the sky as a painter mixes colours on a palette. Cp. *Darwin* I i Additional Note III to i 119: 'Colours are produced from clouds or mists by refraction, as well as by reflection'.

710–11. The sense of the lines appears to be, taking (with *Locock 1911*) the antecedent of *its* to be *Earth* (line 703): 'the inner light that allows us to value the beauty of the earth must arise in a mind both *gentle* and *fearless*'.

716–20. Cp. Coleridge, *France: An Ode* (1798 and later versions) 85–8: 'The Sensual and the Dark rebel in vain, / Slaves by their own compulsion! In mad game / They burst their manacles and wear the name / Of freedom, graven on a heavier chain!' Here the *deeper prison and heavier chains* are those of religious fear and the *gulf* that of Hell, as a cancelled fragment of line in *Nbk 2* 48 makes clear: '?[Torment] An everlasting ruin'. The contending fears of passing time and of punishment after death combine to create a storm tide that drives the *shrieking wretch* on to that *gulf* of ocean which is an image of the gulf of fire that he dreads in the afterlife.

And stronger tyrants: — a dark gulf before,
The realm of a stern Ruler, yawned; behind,
Terror and Time conflicting drove, and bore
720   On their tempestuous flood the shrieking wretch from shore.

VII

Out of that Ocean's wrecks had Guilt and Woe
Framed a dark dwelling for their homeless thought,
And, starting at the ghosts which to and fro
Glide o'er its dim and gloomy strand, had brought
725   The worship thence which they each other taught.
Well might men loathe their life, well might they turn
Even to the ills again from which they sought
Such refuge after death! — well might they learn
To gaze on this fair world with hopeless unconcern!

VIII

730   For they all pined in bondage: body and soul,
Tyrant and slave, victim and torturer, bent
Before one Power, to which supreme control
Over their will by their own weakness lent,
Made all its many names omnipotent;
735   All symbols of things evil, all divine;
And hymns of blood or mockery, which rent
The air from all its fanes, did intertwine
Imposture's impious toils round each discordant shrine.

IX

I heard as all have heard, life's various story,
740   And in no careless heart transcribed the tale;
But, from the sneers of men who had grown hoary

721–5. At the head of the stanza S. cancelled the line: 'The grave became the dwelling of their hearts thoughts' (*Nbk 2* 49). The pains of oppression and the guilt fostered by religion have turned the thoughts of the oppressed from this world towards a sombre anticipation of the life to come.

732. one Power] one grim Idol *canc.*; one dread Image *canc. Nbk 2* 53.

734. See note to line 363.

736. See note to line 377.

737. fanes] Temples.

Stanzas viii–ix. Between the drafts for these two stanzas in *Nbk 2* 54 is a partially-drafted stanza with much cancelling which S. did not use: 'The foes who dwelt amongst us were not free / Tho we were slaves – each one did fear the other – / And, when the panic of the Idolatry, / Which they had framed to [ ] one another / Fell on them, all grew pale, nor did the steel / Feed on our tribes alone; but each'.

In shame and scorn, from groans of crowds made pale
By famine, from a mother's desolate wail
O'er her polluted child, from innocent blood
745 Poured on the earth, and brows anxious and pale
With the heart's warfare; did I gather food
To feed my many thoughts: a tameless multitude!

X

I wandered through the wrecks of days departed
Far by the desolated shore, when even
750 O'er the still sea and jaggèd islets darted
The light of moonrise; in the northern Heaven,
Among the clouds near the horizon driven,
The mountains lay beneath one planet pale;
Around me, broken tombs and columns riven
755 Looked vast in twilight, and the sorrowing gale
Waked in those ruins grey its everlasting wail!

XI

I knew not who had framed these wonders then,
Nor, had I heard the story of their deeds;
But dwellings of a race of mightier men,
760 And monuments of less ungentle creeds
Tell their own tale to him who wisely heeds
The language which they speak; and now, to me
The moonlight making pale the blooming weeds,
The bright stars shining in the breathless sea,
765 Interpreted those scrolls of mortal mystery.

XII

Such man has been, and such may yet become!
Ay, wiser, greater, gentler, even than they
Who on the fragments of yon shattered dome
Have stamped the sign of power — I felt the sway
770 Of the vast stream of ages bear away
My floating thoughts — my heart beat loud and fast —
Even as a storm let loose beneath the ray

---

744. *polluted*] violated *canc. Nbk 2* 55. The mother is lamenting a sexual outrage committed on her child.

749. *even*] Evening.

753. *mountains lay*] Athos reposed beneath *canc.*; Hymettus lay *Nbk 2* 55. Athos is a mountain far to the north on the easternmost promontory of Chalcidice; Mount Hymettus, which overlooks Athens, is in Attica, the region immediately to the north of Argolis.

Of the still moon, my spirit onward passed
Beneath truth's steady beams upon its tumult cast.

XIII

775 It shall be thus no more! too long, too long,
Sons of the glorious dead, have ye lain bound
In darkness and in ruin. — Hope is strong,
Justice and Truth their wingèd child have found —
Awake! arise! until the mighty sound
780 Of your career shall scatter in its gust
The thrones of the oppressor, and the ground
Hide the last altar's unregarded dust,
Whose Idol has so long betrayed your impious trust.

XIV

It must be so — I will arise and waken
785 The multitude, and like a sulphurous hill,
Which on a sudden from its snows has shaken
The swoon of ages, it shall burst and fill
The world with cleansing fire: it must, it will —
It may not be restrained! — and who shall stand
790 Amid the rocking earthquake steadfast still,
But Laon? on high Freedom's desert land
A tower whose marble walls the leaguèd storms withstand!

---

776. glorious dead] The ancient Greeks whose achievements Laon discovered in the ruined monuments of the previous stanza.

778. wingèd child] The *Hope* of the previous line, as in *R&H* 798–800: 'And wingèd hope . . . / Like some bright spirit newly born'.

783. impious trust] Ironic, because the *trust* in a false deity would have been imposed upon them as piety.

785. The multitude] my nation *Nbk 2* 59.

785–7. G. M. Matthews (*ELH* xxiv (1957) 199–200) notes that S. may well have derived the image from an account of the eruption of Cotopaxi in 1803 which 'was preceded by a dreadful phenomenon, the sudden melting of the snows that covered the mountain' in Alexandre de Humboldt and Bonpland's *Researches concerning the institutions and monuments of the ancient inhabitants of America*, trans. H. M. Williams (1814) i 119. The passage was quoted in the *Quarterly*'s (July 1816) review of the book which MWS read in August (*Mary Jnl* i 131). Cp. Canto IX iv and note to line 2892.

792. Cp. S.'s letter to Godwin of 7 December 1817: 'Falkland [in Godwin's novel *Caleb Williams*] is still alone: power is in Falkland not as in Mandeville [in Godwin's novel of the same name]. Tumult hurried onward by the tempest, but Tranquillity standing unshaken amid its fiercest rage!' (*L* i 573). S.'s ultimate source is Lucretius *De Re. Nat.* ii 1–14. See note to lines 121–6. *leaguèd*] usually signifying in S. forces united against liberty; e.g. line 3825, *Q Mab* viii 185.

XV

One summer night, in commune with the hope
Thus deeply fed, amid those ruins grey
795 I watched, beneath the dark sky's starry cope;
And ever from that hour upon me lay
The burden of this hope, and night or day,
In vision or in dream, clove to my breast:
Among mankind, or when gone far away
800 To the lone shores and mountains, 'twas a guest
Which followed where I fled, and watched when I did rest.

XVI

These hopes found words through which my spirit sought
To weave a bondage of such sympathy,
As might create some response to the thought
805 Which ruled me now — and as the vapours lie
Bright in the outspread morning's radiancy,
So were these thoughts invested with the light
Of language: and all bosoms made reply
On which its lustre streamed, whene'er it might
810 Through darkness wide and deep those trancèd spirits smite.

XVII

Yes, many an eye with dizzy tears was dim,
And oft I thought to clasp my own heart's brother,
When I could feel the listener's senses swim,
And hear his breath its own swift gaspings smother
815 Even as my words evoked them — and another,
And yet another, I did fondly deem,
Felt that we all were sons of one great mother;
And the cold truth such sad reverse did seem,
As to awake in grief from some delightful dream.

XVIII

820 Yes, oft beside the ruined labyrinth
Which skirts the hoary caves of the green deep,

796–801. Compare Laon's illumination and self-dedication with those S. recounts of him-
self in lines 19–45 and of the woman narrator in lines 478–513.

813. swim] Perceive indistinctly as a result of the agitation of spirit caused by Laon's words.
The analogy is with the sense of sight: 'Then all the scene was wont to swim / Through the
mist of a burning tear' (R&H 194–5). See note to line 1751.

Stanza xviii. S.'s attempts to draft this stanza reveal an initial uncertainty over the character
of Laon's disappointed friendship as well as the tone to adopt in representing it. He first
wrote: 'How bitter & how deep, when one dear friend / Had seemed to shared [sic] my heart

Did Laon and his friend on one grey plinth,
Round whose worn base the wild waves hiss and leap,
Resting at eve, a lofty converse keep:
825 And that this friend was false, may now be said
Calmly — that he like other men could weep
Tears which are lies, and could betray and spread
Snares for that guileless heart which for his own had bled.

XIX

Then, had no great aim recompensed my sorrow,
830 I must have sought dark respite from its stress
In dreamless rest, in sleep that sees no morrow —
For to tread life's dismaying wilderness
Without one smile to cheer, one voice to bless,
Amid the snares and scoffs of humankind,
835 Is hard — but I betrayed it not, nor less
With love that scorned return, sought to unbind
The interwoven clouds which make its wisdom blind.

XX

With deathless minds which leave where they have passed
A path of light, my soul communion knew;
840 Till from that glorious intercourse, at last,
As from a mine of magic store, I drew

& on the morrow / Mocked & betrayed me'. For 'dear friend' he later substituted 'some young associate', then 'one companion', leaving the offence unspecified, before opting for 'his friend' and the philosophical resignation of the final version. Beneath the first partial draft of the stanza he wrote 'some failure here', repeating the phrase at the foot of the page, as if he meant to introduce an instance of personal betrayal. Biographers and commentators have considered T. J. Hogg as the most probable original of the friend. Certainly the rupture between him and S. in November 1811 over Hogg's sexual advances towards Harriet Shelley (*L* i 166–86) would qualify as an appropriate instance of *false* conduct. Laon is reconciled with this same friend in Canto V iii–v, as S. was with Hogg in autumn 1812. Of course this brief sketch may have been inspired by more than one individual and more than one instance of faithless behaviour.

828. *had bled*] *Forman 1876–7, Locock 1911* and *1975* take the sense to be 'would have bled', apparently reading *for* as equivalent to 'in place of'. But *for his own had bled* could just as well be considered as metaphorical for 'suffered in sympathy with his'.

835–7. An obscure passage: the best sense seems to result from taking *it* to refer to the *great aim* of line 829 and *its* to *sorrow* in the same line so that lines 836–7 mean: 'attempt to mitigate the preoccupation with self that accompanies the benefits of sorrow'. *Locock 1911* (who considers that both *it* and *its* refer to *sorrow*) cites *The Sunset* 36: 'wisdom-working grief' and *PU* I 58: 'ere misery made me wise'.

Stanza xx. At this point in the draft in *Nbk 2* (63) S. wrote 'a stanza to be inserted' and went on to draft stanza xxi, later recuperating (with minor alterations) and completing as stanza xx the unfinished stanza 8 of the original opening to *L&C*. See stanza 8 of no. 142 and headnote.

Words which were weapons; — round my heart there grew
The adamantine armour of their power,
And from my fancy wings of golden hue
845   Sprang forth — yet not alone from wisdom's tower,
A minister of truth, these plumes young Laon bore.

XXI

I had a little sister, whose fair eyes
Were lodestars of delight, which drew me home
When I might wander forth; nor did I prize
850   Aught human thing beneath Heaven's mighty dome
Beyond this child: so when sad hours were come,
And baffled hope like ice still clung to me,
Since kin were cold, and friends had now become
Heartless and false, I turned from all, to be,
855   Cythna, the only source of tears and smiles to thee.

XXII

What wert thou then? A child most infantine,
Yet wandering far beyond that innocent age
In all but its sweet looks and mien divine;
Even then, methought, with the world's tyrant rage
860   A patient warfare thy young heart did wage,
When those soft eyes of scarcely conscious thought,
Some tale, or thine own fancies would engage
To overflow with tears, or converse fraught
With passion, o'er their depths its fleeting light had wrought.

XXIII

865   She moved upon this earth a shape of brightness,
A power, that from its objects scarcely drew
One impulse of her being — in her lightness

Stanza xxi. S. drafted and cancelled the first four lines of this stanza on p. 46 of *Nbk 2* between drafts for stanzas iii and iv of Canto II, apparently first intending to introduce Laon's sister at this early stage of his autobiography. The final part-line of the incomplete stanza reads: 'I had a father who was kind'.

847. An orphan with my parents lived, whose eyes *Rofl.*

848. lodestars] A lodestar is one that guides, e.g. navigators at sea, especially the polestar. 'Your eyes are lodestars': *A Midsummer Night's Dream* I i 183.

849. When I might wander] Whenever I wandered.

850. Aught] 'Any', a Shelleyan usage: *Locock 1911* compares *PU* I 70: 'aught evil wish'.

851–5. Compare Laon's experience here with lines 46–72 of the Dedication.

855. Cythna] Zia *canc. Nbk 2* 64. S. hesitated between the two names over the next few stanzas in the draft. See note to the name *Cythna* in the title.

Most like some radiant cloud of morning dew,
Which wanders through the waste air's pathless blue,
870 To nourish some far desert: she did seem
Beside me, gathering beauty as she grew,
Like the bright shade of some immortal dream
Which walks, when tempest sleeps, the wave of life's dark stream.

XXIV

As mine own shadow was this child to me,
875 A second self, far dearer and more fair;
Which clothed in undissolving radiancy,
All those steep paths which languor and despair
Of human things, had made so dark and bare,
But which I trod alone — nor, till bereft
880 Of friends, and overcome by lonely care,
Knew I what solace for that loss was left,
Though by a bitter wound my trusting heart was cleft.

XXV

Once she was dear, now she was all I had
To love in human life — this sister sweet,
885 This child of twelve years old — so she was made
My sole associate, and her willing feet
Wandered with mine where earth and ocean meet,
Beyond the aerial mountains whose vast cells
The unreposing billows ever beat,
890 Through forests wide and old, and lawny dells,
Where boughs of incense droop over the emerald wells.

XXVI

And warm and light I felt her clasping hand
When twined in mine: she followed where I went,
Through the lone paths of our immortal land.
895 It had no waste, but some memorial lent
Which strung me to my toil — some monument

884. *sister*] playmate *Rofl*.

885. *twelve years old*] The chief public actions of the poem, beginning with Laon's journey to the Golden City in Canto V i, take place seven years hence in fictional time when Cythna is nineteen years old, MWS's age in spring 1817 when S. drafted these lines.

888. *cells*] Caves, as in line 2934.

890–1. Cp. Coleridge, *Kubla Khan* (1816) 9–11: 'Where blossomed many an incense-bearing tree; / And here were forests ancient as the hills, / Enfolding sunny spots of greenery'.

895. *lent*] Afforded.

896. *strung*] Braced.

Vital with mind: then, Cythna by my side,
Until the bright and beaming day were spent,
Would rest, with looks entreating to abide,
900   Too earnest and too sweet ever to be denied.

XXVII

And soon I could not have refused her — thus
Forever, day and night, we two were ne'er
Parted, but when brief sleep divided us:
And when the pauses of the lulling air
905   Of noon beside the sea, had made a lair
For her soothed senses, in my arms she slept,
And I kept watch over her slumbers there,
While, as the shifting visions o'er her swept,
Amid her innocent rest by turns she smiled and wept.

XXVIII

910   And, in the murmur of her dreams was heard
Sometimes the name of Laon: — suddenly
She would arise, and like the secret bird
Whom sunset wakens, fill the shore and sky
With her sweet accents — a wild melody!
915   Hymns which my soul had woven to Freedom, strong
The source of passion whence they rose, to be;
Triumphant strains, which, like a spirit's tongue,
To the enchanted waves that child of glory sung,

XXIX

Her white arms lifted through the shadowy stream
920   Of her loose hair — oh, excellently great
Seemed to me then my purpose, the vast theme

904. *pauses*] Cadences, rhythm, as in poetry or music.

905. *lair*] Couch, resting-place.

912. *secret bird*] The nightingale, from its inconspicuous appearance and retiring habits as well as the tradition (inexact) that it sings only by night.

915–16. The inverted syntax has prompted some *eds* to repunctuate – *1839, Rossetti 1870* (but not *1878*) and *1975* suppressing the semicolon after *be* so that the *Hymns* (line 915) swell into *Triumphant strains* by line 917. But *Forman 1876–7*'s construction of the meaning as 'competent to become in others the source of that passion for liberty whence they had arisen in Laon' is surely correct and removes the need for repunctuation, though the awkward word-order requires attentive reading.

917. *spirit's tongue*] See note to line 294. Above several cancelled drafts for the line in *Nbk 2* 70 is the uncancelled word 'prophetic'.

918. *sung,*] sung. *L&C/RofI*. The sentence carries on until the end of line 927, though the dash in line 920 has nearly the force of a full stop.

Of those impassioned songs, when Cythna sate
Amid the calm which rapture doth create
After its tumult, her heart vibrating,
925   Her spirit o'er the ocean's floating state
From her deep eyes far wandering, on the wing
Of visions that were mine, beyond its utmost spring.

XXX

For, before Cythna loved it, had my song
Peopled with thoughts the boundless universe,
930   A mighty congregation, which were strong
Where'er they trod the darkness to disperse
The cloud of that unutterable curse
Which clings upon mankind: — all things became
Slaves to my holy and heroic verse,
935   Earth, sea and sky, the planets, life and fame
And fate, or whate'er else binds the world's wondrous frame.

XXXI

And this belovèd child thus felt the sway
Of my conceptions, gathering like a cloud
The very wind on which it rolls away:
940   Hers too were all my thoughts, ere yet endowed
With music and with light, their fountains flowed
In poesy; and her still and earnest face,
Pallid with feelings which intensely glowed
Within, was turned on mine with speechless grace,
945   Watching the hopes which there her heart had learned to trace.

XXXII

In me, communion with this purest being
Kindled intenser zeal, and made me wise
In knowledge, which in hers mine own mind seeing,
Left in the human world few mysteries:
950   How without fear of evil or disguise

---

927. spring] 'A distance capable of being covered by a spring or leap' (*OED* Spring n. 14d cites this passage).

937–9. The subject of the participle *gathering* is *child*: 'gathering strength from my ideas as a cloud gathers the very wind that carries it away'.

944. speechless] Inexpressible.

946–9. The language in which the brother–sister bond is expressed is derived from Wordsworth's *Lines Written A Few Miles Above Tintern Abbey* (1798); e.g. 'with far deeper zeal / Of holier love' (155–6).

Was Cythna! — what a spirit strong and mild,
Which death, or pain or peril could despise,
Yet melt in tenderness! what genius wild
Yet mighty, was enclosed within one simple child!

XXXIII

955 New lore was this — old age with its grey hair,
And wrinkled legends of unworthy things,
And icy sneers, is nought: it cannot dare
To burst the chains which life forever flings
On the entangled soul's aspiring wings,
960 So is it cold and cruel, and is made
The careless slave of that dark power which brings
Evil, like blight on man, who still betrayed,
Laughs o'er the grave in which his living hopes are laid.

XXXIV

Nor are the strong and the severe to keep
965 The empire of the world: thus Cythna taught
Even in the visions of her eloquent sleep,
Unconscious of the power through which she wrought
The woof of such intelligible thought,
As from the tranquil strength which cradled lay
970 In her smile-peopled rest, my spirit sought
Why the deceiver and the slave has sway
O'er heralds so divine of truth's arising day.

XXXV

Within that fairest form, the female mind
Untainted by the poison clouds which rest
975 On the dark world, a sacred home did find:
But else, from the wide earth's maternal breast,
Victorious Evil, which had dispossessed
All native power, had those fair children torn,
And made them slaves to soothe his vile unrest,
980 And minister to lust its joys forlorn,
Till they had learned to breathe the atmosphere of scorn.

965–8. See note to lines 602–3.

978. *those fair children*] Women.

979. *vile unrest*] Degrading sexual passion. Cp. *Athanase* 11–13: 'Nor evil joys which fire the vulgar breast / And quench in speedy smoke its feeble flame / Had left within his soul their dark unrest'.

XXXVI

This misery was but coldly felt, till she
Became my only friend, who had endued
My purpose with a wider sympathy;
985   Thus, Cythna mourned with me the servitude
In which the half of humankind were mewed
Victims of lust and hate, the slaves of slaves,
She mourned that grace and power were thrown as food
To the hyena lust, who, among graves,
990   Over his loathèd meal, laughing in agony, raves.

XXXVII

And I, still gazing on that glorious child,
Even as these thoughts flushed o'er her. — 'Cythna sweet,
Well with the world art thou unreconciled;
Never will peace and human nature meet
995   Till free and equal man and woman greet
Domestic peace; and ere this power can make
In human hearts its calm and holy seat,
This slavery must be broken' — as I spake,
From Cythna's eyes a light of exultation brake.

XXXVIII

1000   She replied earnestly: — 'It shall be mine,
This task, mine, Laon! — thou hast much to gain;
Nor wilt thou at poor Cythna's pride repine,
If she should lead a happy female train
To meet thee over the rejoicing plain,
1005   When myriads at thy call shall throng around
The Golden City.' — Then the child did strain

982. coldly felt] By me (Laon).

986. mewed] Confined.

988–90. 'To be condemned to feed on the garbage of grinding misery that hungry Hyena mortal life' (*L* i 173): To Elizabeth Hitchener (?11 November 1811) in reference to T. J. Hogg's erotic overtures to Harriet Shelley.

992. flushed] Figurative: flowed over her like rushing water, or passed through her mind like a rush of blood that flushes the skin. Cp. *Adonais* 108: 'It [a dream] flushed through his pale limbs, and passed to its eclipse'. The untidy draft in *Nbk 2* 76 appears to read 'flashed', and the possibility of an uncorrected misprint or mistranscription cannot be excluded. Cp. *R&H* 998: 'The truth flashed o'er me like quick madness'.

997. seat,] seat; *L&C/RofI*: most *eds* have replaced the semicolon with a comma.

1006. The Golden City] See note on the title of the poem.

My arm upon her tremulous heart, and wound
Her own about my neck, till some reply she found.

XXXIX

I smiled, and spake not — 'wherefore dost thou smile
1010   At what I say? Laon, I am not weak,
And though my cheek might become pale the while,
With thee, if thou desirest, will I seek
Through their array of banded slaves to wreak
Ruin upon the tyrants. I had thought
1015   It was more hard to turn my unpractised cheek
To scorn and shame, and this belovèd spot
And thee, O dearest friend, to leave and murmur not.

XL

'Whence came I what I am? thou, Laon, knowest
How a young child should thus undaunted be;
1020   Methinks, it is a power which thou bestowest,
Through which I seek, by most resembling thee,
So to become most good, and great and free,
Yet far beyond this Ocean's utmost roar
In towers and huts are many like to me,
1025   Who, could they see thine eyes, or feel such lore
As I have learnt from them, like me would fear no more.

XLI

'Think'st thou that I shall speak unskilfully,
And none will heed me? I remember now,
How once, a slave in tortures doomed to die,
1030   Was saved, because in accents sweet and low
He sung a song his Judge loved long ago,
As he was led to death. — All shall relent
Who hear me — tears as mine have flowed, shall flow,
Hearts beat as mine now beats, with such intent
1035   As renovates the world; a will omnipotent!

1015. my unpractised] 'I know no other instance in Shelley of so barbarous an elision' (*Locock 1911*).

1028–32. Locock 1911 cites Plutarch's *Life of Nicias* (xxix) which recounts how some of the Athenian freemen who were sold into slavery after the defeat of their forces in Sicily were set free by their masters who were moved when the Athenians recited Euripides' verses. Locock notes the use of the anecdote by Byron in *Childe Harold's Pilgrimage iv* 16, speculating that he and S. might have discussed it in Switzerland in 1816. But S. could have encountered the story in Plutarch or in Peacock's *Philosophy of Melancholy* (1812) Part II (*L* i 325) which also included an extensive note on it (*Peacock Works* vi 201–2; 235–8).

XLII

'Yes, I will tread Pride's golden palaces,
Through Penury's roofless huts and squalid cells
Will I descend, where'er in abjectness
Woman with some vile slave her tyrant dwells,
1040   There with the music of thine own sweet spells
Will disenchant the captives, and will pour
For the despairing, from the crystal wells
Of thy deep spirit, reason's mighty lore,
And power shall then abound, and hope arise once more.

XLIII

1045   'Can man be free if woman be a slave?
Chain one who lives, and breathes this boundless air
To the corruption of a closèd grave!
Can they whose mates are beasts, condemned to bear
Scorn, heavier far than toil or anguish, dare
1050   To trample their oppressors? in their home
Among their babes, thou know'st a curse would wear
The shape of woman — hoary crime would come
Behind, and fraud rebuild religion's tottering dome.

XLIV

'I am a child: — I would not yet depart.
1055   When I go forth alone, bearing the lamp
Aloft which thou hast kindled in my heart,
Millions of slaves from many a dungeon damp
Shall leap in joy, as the benumbing cramp
Of ages leaves their limbs — no ill may harm
1060   Thy Cythna ever — truth its radiant stamp
Has fixed, as an invulnerable charm
Upon her children's brow, dark falsehood to disarm.

XLV

'Wait yet awhile for the appointed day —
Thou wilt depart, and I with tears shall stand

1050–3. 'Should men overcome their tyrants without also liberating women from domestic servitude, women would represent in the home a blight on the new liberty which would in consequence revert to its former wrongs and religious deception'.

1060–2. Recalling the figure that appears in the Woman's dream in lines 500–1: 'A wingèd youth, his radiant brow did wear / The Morning Star'. The verb *charm* can mean 'To mark with a symbol as a charm' (*OED* 2b), in order to protect from ill. An allusion is perhaps intended to *Genesis* iv 15: 'And the Lord set a mark upon Cain, lest any finding him should kill him'.

1060. its] her *Rossetti 1878*, emending for consistency with line 1062.

1065   Watching thy dim sail skirt the ocean grey;
    Amid the dwellers of this lonely land
    I shall remain alone — and thy command
    Shall then dissolve the world's unquiet trance,
    And, multitudinous as the desert sand
1070   Borne on the storm, its millions shall advance,
    Thronging round thee, the light of their deliverance.

XLVI

    'Then, like the forests of some pathless mountain,
    Which from remotest glens two warring winds
    Involve in fire, which not the loosened fountain
1075   Of broadest floods might quench, shall all the kinds
    Of evil, catch from our uniting minds
    The spark which must consume them; — Cythna then
    Will have cast off the impotence that binds
    Her childhood now, and through the paths of men
1080   Will pass, as the charmed bird that haunts the serpent's den.

XLVII

    'We part! — O Laon, I must dare nor tremble
    To meet those looks no more! — Oh, heavy stroke,
    Sweet brother of my soul! can I dissemble
    The agony of this thought?' — As thus she spoke
1085   The gathered sobs her quivering accents broke,
    And in my arms she hid her beating breast.
    I remained still for tears — sudden she woke
    As one awakes from sleep, and wildly pressed
    My bosom, her whole frame impetuously possessed.

XLVIII

1090   'We part to meet again — but yon blue waste,
    Yon desert wide and deep holds no recess,

1069. 'I will multiply thy seed as the stars of the heaven, and as the sand which is upon the sea shore . . . and in thy seed shall all the nations of the earth be blessed' (*Genesis* xxii 17–18); 'I will surely do thee good, and make thy seed as the sand of the sea, which cannot be numbered for multitude' (*Genesis* xxxii 12).

1080. Lloyd N. Jeffrey (*KSJ* vii (1958) 30) discovers here the popular belief that the snake 'charms' its prey, but as lines 1060–2 (and note) show, the *charmed bird* is immune from danger just as the truth of Cythna's words act as a charm to keep her safe. The line recalls the Woman of Canto I who moved through a city at war 'Calm as an angel in the dragon's den' (line 518).

1081. *dare nor tremble*] Dare without trembling.

Stanza xlviii. Remarkably, at twelve years of age Cythna predicts their sacrificial destiny and posthumous existence as exemplary heroes.

Within whose happy silence, thus embraced
We might survive all ills in one caress:
Nor doth the grave — I fear 'tis passionless —
1095   Nor yon cold vacant Heaven: — we meet again
Within the minds of men, whose lips shall bless
Our memory, and whose hopes its light retain
When these dissevered bones are trodden in the plain.'

XLIX

I could not speak, though she had ceased, for now
1100   The fountains of her feeling, swift and deep,
Seemed to suspend the tumult of their flow;
So we arose, and by the starlight steep
Went homeward — neither did we speak nor weep,
But pale, were calm with passion — thus subdued
1105   Like evening shades that o'er the mountains creep,
We moved towards our home; where, in this mood,
Each from the other sought refuge in solitude.

Canto Third

I

What thoughts had sway over my sister's slumber
That night, I know not; but my own did seem
1110   As if they might ten thousand years outnumber
Of waking life, the visions of a dream,
Which hid in one dim gulf the troubled stream
Of mind; a boundless chaos wild and vast,
Whose limits yet were never memory's theme:

1104. *But pale, were calm. —* With passion thus subdued *1839, Rossetti 1870* (with an additional comma after *But*), *Locock 1911*, who cites the final line of *Samson Agonistes*: 'And calm of mind all passion spent'. But the *L&C/RofI* reading is appropriate to a state of devoted resolution following a moment of intensely heightened awareness like that at the close of stanza iv of the Dedication: 'I then controlled / My tears, my heart grew calm, and I was meek and bold'. Without supporting textual authority there is no persuasive reason to emend.

1108. *over my sister's*] o'er Cythna's lonely *RofI*.

1110. *might*] *RofI*; did *L&C*. As *Forman 1876–7* noticed, the change is not made by hand in *L&C* (PM); it was probably introduced by S. when correcting the proof of the cancel-leaf for *RofI* required to make the alteration signalled in the previous note. See headnote *Composition and Publication*, p. 19. The change from *did* to *might* distinguishes the verb from *did* in the previous line and makes it consistent with the use of the same words in the following stanza in which *did* signifies what was experienced in dream and *might*, the past subjunctive, conveys what would have been true if the dream experience had been real.

1113. *vast,*] *RofI*; vast *L&C*. The change is not made by hand in *L&C* (PM) but was introduced on the proof of the *RofI* cancel-leaf. See previous note.

1115 And I lay struggling as its whirlwinds passed,
   Sometimes for rapture sick, sometimes for pain aghast.

II

   Two hours, whose mighty circle did embrace
   More time than might make grey the infant world,
   Rolled thus, a weary and tumultuous space:
1120 When the third came, like mist on breezes curled,
   From my dim sleep a shadow was unfurled:
   Methought, upon the threshold of a cave
   I sate with Cythna; drooping briony, pearled
   With dew from the wild streamlet's shattered wave,
1125 Hung, where we sate to taste the joys which Nature gave.

III

   We lived a day as we were wont to live,
   But Nature had a robe of glory on,
   And the bright air o'er every shape did weave
   Intenser hues, so that the herbless stone,
1130 The leafless bough among the leaves alone,
   Had being clearer than its own could be,
   And Cythna's pure and radiant self was shown
   In this strange vision, so divine to me,
   That if I loved before, now love was agony.

IV

1135 Morn fled, noon came, evening, then night descended,
   And we prolonged calm talk beneath the sphere
   Of the calm moon — when, suddenly was blended
   With our repose a nameless sense of fear;
   And from the cave behind I seemed to hear
1140 Sounds gathering upwards! — accents incomplete,
   And stifled shrieks, — and now, more near and near,
   A tumult and a rush of thronging feet
   The cavern's secret depths beneath the earth did beat.

Stanzas ii–v. The significance of Laon's erotic dream is considered in Sperry, *Shelley's Major Verse* (1988) 49–51 and in Ulmer, *Shelleyan Eros* (1990) 57–60.

1123. briony] Common white bryony, a climbing plant bearing greenish-white flowers and poisonous red berries; it was formerly used in medicinal preparations for the acrid and cathartic properties of its root which is large and sometimes forked; hence the name 'English Mandrake'. S. may well be remembering the sinister erotic journey in Canto II of Leigh Hunt's *The Story of Rimini* (1816) which takes Francesca and Paulo from the wedding at which he has been proxy bridegroom for his elder brother Giovanni to that brother's home at Rimini, and which passes through a forest where grow: 'Wild pear, and oak, and dusky juniper, / With briony between in trails of white' (189–90). See note to line 1287.

V

The scene was changed, and away, away, away!
1145   Through the air and over the sea we sped,
And Cythna in my sheltering bosom lay,
And the winds bore me — through the darkness spread
Around, the gaping earth then vomited
Legions of foul and ghastly shapes, which hung
1150   Upon my flight; and ever as we fled,
They plucked at Cythna — soon to me then clung
A sense of actual things those monstrous dreams among.

VI

And I lay struggling in the impotence
Of sleep, while outward life had burst its bound,
1155   Though, still deluded, strove the tortured sense
To its dire wanderings to adapt the sound
Which in the light of morn was poured around
Our dwelling — breathless, pale, and unaware
I rose, and all the cottage crowded found
1160   With armèd men, whose glittering swords were bare,
And whose degraded limbs the tyrant's garb did wear.

VII

And ere with rapid lips and gathered brow
I could demand the cause — a feeble shriek —
It was a feeble shriek, faint, far and low,
1165   Arrested me — my mien grew calm and meek,
And grasping a small knife, I went to seek
That voice among the crowd — 'twas Cythna's cry!
Beneath most calm resolve did agony wreak
Its whirlwind rage: — so I passed quietly
1170   Till I beheld, where bound, that dearest child did lie.

VIII

I started to behold her, for delight
And exultation, and a joyance free,

1144–5. *Rossetti 1870* emended *Through* [*Thro'* in *L&C/RofI*] to *Thorough* in order to regularise the metre, suggesting instead in *Rossetti 1878* that the positions of *Through* and *over* should be reversed. *Forman 1876–7* recognised instead a 'telling irregularity' which creates a 'marvellous appropriateness [of the lines] to the subject'.

1154. *burst its bound*] Intruded into Laon's dream.

1158. *unaware*] Of what was happening.

1165. *Arrested me*] Caught my attention, making me pause.

1166. See note to lines 1193–5.

1171. *I started to behold her*] Her appearance startled me.

Solemn, serene and lofty, filled the light
Of the calm smile with which she looked on me:
1175 So that I feared some brainless ecstasy,
Wrought from that bitter woe, had wildered her —
'Farewell! farewell!' she said, as I drew nigh.
'At first my peace was marred by this strange stir,
Now I am calm as truth — its chosen minister.

IX

1180 'Look not so, Laon — say farewell in hope,
These bloody men are but the slaves who bear
Their mistress to her task — it was my scope
The slavery where they drag me now, to share,
And among captives willing chains to wear
1185 Awhile — the rest thou knowest — return, dear friend!
Let our first triumph trample the despair
Which would ensnare us now, for in the end,
In victory or in death our hopes and fears must blend.'

X

These words had fallen on my unheeding ear,
1190 Whilst I had watched the motions of the crew
With seeming careless glance; not many were
Around her, for their comrades just withdrew
To guard some other victim — so I drew

1175–6. some . . . wildered her] 'The rapturous excitement she found in her distress had con-
fused her mind'.

1182. scope] Aim, purpose.

1186. our first triumph] 'The triumph we can gain if we maintain hope in the face of this
setback'.

1193–5. 'I have often heard our Shelley relate the story of stabbing an Upper Boy [at Eton]
with a fork – but never as you relate it – He always described it in my hearing as being an
almost involuntary act, done on the spur of anguish, and that he made the stab as the boy
was going out of the room' (Mary L i 475; to Leigh Hunt, 8 April 1825). '. . . on being dared
to the act by the surrounding boys, he pinned a companion's hand to the table with a fork
. . . the incident arose out of his resistance to the seniors among the scholars and to the cus-
toms of the school' (Thornton Hunt, Atlantic Monthly XI lxiv (1863) 192). 'He told me that
he had been provoked into striking a penknife through the hand of one of his young tyrants,
and pinning it to the desk, and that this was the cause of his leaving Eton prematurely: but
his imagination often presented past events to him as they might have been, not as they
were. Such a circumstance must have been remembered by others if it had actually occurred.
But if the occurrence was imaginary, it was in a memory of cordial detestation that the ima-
gination arose' ('Memoirs of Percy Bysshe Shelley' in Peacock Works viii 52). Locock 1911 con-
sidered the incident 'one of the more conspicuous puerilities' of L&C, citing S.'s later remark
on his 'Satire upon Satire' as retrospective self-mockery: 'I meant [it] to be very severe, – it
was full of small knives in the use of which practice would have soon made me very expert'
(L ii 383).

My knife, and with one impulse, suddenly
1195   All unaware three of their number slew,
And grasped a fourth by the throat, and with loud cry
My countrymen invoked to death or liberty!

XI

What followed then, I know not — for a stroke
On my raised arm and naked head, came down,
1200   Filling my eyes with blood — when I awoke,
I felt that they had bound me in my swoon,
And up a rock which overhangs the town,
By the steep path were bearing me: below,
The plain was filled with slaughter, — overthrown
1205   The vineyards and the harvests, and the glow
Of blazing roofs shone far o'er the white Ocean's flow.

XII

Upon that rock a mighty column stood,
Whose capital seemed sculptured in the sky,
Which to the wanderers o'er the solitude
1210   Of distant seas, from ages long gone by,
Had made a landmark; o'er its height to fly
Scarcely the cloud, the vulture, or the blast,
Has power — and when the shades of evening lie
On Earth and Ocean, its carved summits cast
1215   The sunken daylight far through the aerial waste.

XIII

They bore me to a cavern in the hill
Beneath that column, and unbound me there:
And one did strip me stark; and one did fill
A vessel from the putrid pool; one bare
1220   A lighted torch, and four with friendless care
Guided my steps the cavern-paths along,
Then up a steep and dark and narrow stair
We wound, until the torch's fiery tongue
Amid the gushing day beamless and pallid hung.

1195. *All unaware*] The phrase can mean both 'without giving any warning' and 'without being observed'.

Stanza xiii. Several details of Laon's ordeal from here through stanza xxiv S. borrowed from the imprisonment of the character Verezzi in chapter 1 of his Gothic romance *Zastrozzi* (1810). John Cordy Jeaffreson (*The Real Shelley. New Views of the Poet's Life* (1885) i 119–22) pointed out the resemblances which include the cave, the chains, the bread and water, as well as the prisoner's delirium and despair. General and particular similarities to Byron's *The Prisoner of Chillon* are also evident (see notes to lines 1229–30, 1270–1).

1223. *torch's*] torches' *L&C/R of I*: most *eds* have emended for consistency with *torch* in line 1220.

XIV

1225   They raised me to the platform of the pile,
That column's dizzy height: — the grate of brass
Through which they thrust me, open stood the while,
As to its ponderous and suspended mass,
With chains which eat into the flesh, alas!
1230   With brazen links, my naked limbs they bound:
The grate, as they departed to repass,
With horrid clangour fell, and the far sound
Of their retiring steps in the dense gloom were drowned.

XV

The noon was calm and bright: — around that column
1235   The overhanging sky and circling sea
Spread forth in silentness profound and solemn
The darkness of brief frenzy cast on me,
So that I knew not my own misery:
The islands and the mountains in the day
1240   Like clouds reposed afar; and I could see
The town among the woods below that lay,
And the dark rocks which bound the bright and glassy bay.

XVI

It was so calm, that scarce the feathery weed
Sown by some eagle on the topmost stone
1245   Swayed in the air: — so bright, that noon did breed
No shadow in the sky beside mine own —
Mine, and the shadow of my chain alone.
Below the smoke of roofs involved in flame
Rested like night, all else was clearly shown

1229–30. Robinson 259 n. 16 compares Byron's *The Prisoner of Chillon* 37–46: 'That iron is a cankering thing, / For in these limbs its teeth remain, / With marks that will not wear away' (38–40).

1233. were] was *1839, eds.* The widely-adopted emendation simply corrects an absence of agreement between subject and verb which is common enough in S. *Locock 1911* cites numerous examples including lines 2150–1; lines 1369–70 of this canto may be added to his list.

1234–8. The lines have been much discussed and variously emended following Mathilde Blind (*Westminster Review* n.s. xxxviii (1870) 84) who, finding the passage 'absolutely preposterous as it stands', proposed placing a colon at the end of line 1236 and altering *cast* to *past* in line 1237. *Forman 1876–7* followed her example, only preferring a full stop to the colon. But the perceived textual corruption arises from taking *spread* as a preterite; when it is understood as a past participle, *sky* and *sea* being the subject of the preterite *cast*, the need for emendation disappears. Cp. *Julian and Maddalo* 159–60: 'The word you spoke last night might well have cast / A darkness on my spirit'. *Rossetti 1878*'s remark that 'Laon becomes dizzy and light-headed' catches the sense of the lines: the first shock of solitary exposure to the elements above and below briefly deranges his mind.

1250   In that broad glare, yet sound to me none came,
              But of the living blood that ran within my frame.

XVII

              The peace of madness fled, and ah, too soon!
              A ship was lying on the sunny main,
              Its sails were flagging in the breathless noon —
1255   Its shadow lay beyond — that sight again
              Waked, with its presence, in my trancèd brain
              The stings of a known sorrow, keen and cold:
              I knew that ship bore Cythna o'er the plain
              Of waters, to her blighting slavery sold,
1260   And watched it with such thoughts as must remain untold.

XVIII

              I watched, until the shades of evening wrapped
              Earth like an exhalation — then the bark
              Moved, for that calm was by the sunset snapped.
              It moved a speck upon the Ocean dark:
1265   Soon the wan stars came forth, and I could mark
              Its path no more! — I sought to close mine eyes,
              But like the balls, their lids were stiff and stark;
              I would have risen, but ere that I could rise,
              My parchèd skin was split with piercing agonies.

XIX

1270   I gnawed my brazen chain, and sought to sever
              Its adamantine links, that I might die:
              O Liberty! forgive the base endeavour,
              Forgive me, if reserved for victory,
              The Champion of thy faith e'er sought to fly. —
1275   That starry night, with its clear silence, sent
              Tameless resolve which laughed at misery
              Into my soul — linkèd remembrance lent
              To that such power, to me such a severe content.

1270–1. *Robinson* 259 n. 16 compares Byron's *The Prisoner of Chillon* (1816) 147–8: 'Though hard I strove, but strove in vain, / To rend and gnash my bonds in twain'.

1272–4. The sentiments and vocabulary are borrowed and revalued from stanzas iv and v of Coleridge's *France: An Ode* (1798): 'Forgive me, Freedom! O forgive those dreams! . . . Are these thy boasts, Champion of human kind? . . . O Liberty! with profitless endeavour / Have I pursued thee, many a weary hour' (lines 64, 80, 89–90).

XX

To breathe, to be, to hope, or to despair
1280   And die, I questioned not; nor, though the Sun
Its shafts of agony kindling through the air
Moved over me, nor though in evening dun,
Or when the stars their visible courses run,
Or morning, the wide universe was spread
1285   In dreary calmness round me, did I shun
Its presence, nor seek refuge with the dead
From one faint hope whose flower a dropping poison shed.

XXI

Two days thus passed — I neither raved nor died —
Thirst raged within me, like a scorpion's nest
1290   Built in mine entrails: I had spurned aside
The water-vessel, while despair possessed
My thoughts, and now no drop remained! the uprest
Of the third sun brought hunger — but the crust
Which had been left, was to my craving breast
1295   Fuel, not food. I chewed the bitter dust,
And bit my bloodless arm, and licked the brazen rust.

XXII

My brain began to fail when the fourth morn
Burst o'er the golden isles — a fearful sleep,
Which through the caverns dreary and forlorn
1300   Of the riven soul, sent its foul dreams to sweep
With whirlwind swiftness — a fall far and deep, —
A gulf, a void, a sense of senselessness —
These things dwelt in me, even as shadows keep
Their watch in some dim charnel's loneliness,
1305   A shoreless sea, a sky sunless and planetless!

1287. Locock 1911's gloss on the line, 'because the hope was more like despair' (citing the fragment 'Such hope, as is the sick despair of good' (1820)) is broadly accurate. The *one faint hope* is that of reunion with Cythna: Laon's erotic passion for her has begun in 'agony' beside a poisonous plant dropping dew (1123–5) and will resume in 'sickness' (1714, 2115).

1292. uprest] Uprising, apparently a Shelleyan coinage on the model of the obsolete noun 'uprist' = the rising of the sun, and perhaps remembering its use as verb in 'The glorious sun uprist' (*The Rime of the Ancient Mariner* (1798) 94).

1296. Cp. Coleridge, *The Rime of the Ancient Mariner* (1798) 160: 'I bit my arm, I sucked the blood'.

1304. charnel's] A charnel-house is a repository for the dead in a churchyard. Cp. *Alastor* 23–4 and note: 'I have made my bed / In charnels and on coffins'.

XXIII

The forms which peopled this terrific trance
I well remember — like a choir of devils,
Around me they involved a giddy dance;
Legions seemed gathering from the misty levels

1310 Of Ocean, to supply those ceaseless revels,
Foul, ceaseless shadows: — thought could not divide
The actual world from these entangling evils,
Which so bemocked themselves, that I descried
All shapes like mine own self, hideously multiplied.

XXIV

1315 The sense of day and night, of false and true,
Was dead within me. Yet two visions burst
That darkness — one, as since that hour I knew,
Was not a phantom of the realms accursed,
Where then my spirit dwelt — but of the first

1320 I know not yet, was it a dream or no.
But both, though not distincter, were immersed
In hues which, when through memory's waste they flow,
Make their divided streams more bright and rapid now.

XXV

Methought that gate was lifted, and the seven
1325 Who brought me thither, four stiff corpses bare,

1307. choir] A band not of singers but of dancers, as the next line makes clear.

1311–14. 'The real world and the nightmare vision deluded and flouted each other so that I perceived myself in every diabolical shape'. *Bemocked* also carries the sense of the verb 'mock' = to mimic, counterfeit, as in lines 2735–7. S. is perhaps remembering, 'Her [the moon's] beams bemocked the sultry main / Like April hoar-frost spread' (*The Rime of the Ancient Mariner* 261–2).

1317. one] The appearance of the Hermit in stanza xxvii.

1321–3. The meaning is obscure: 'Whatever these visions were' (or perhaps 'whether they were of different kinds'), 'is no plainer now than it was then, but so intensely coloured were they as to render each more brilliant and lively in the remembrance'.

Stanzas xxv–vii. Commentators have recognised the crisis of Laon's inner life that is played out here as one of the poem's important sequences and, taking their lead from his own uncertainty (lines 1319–20), one that both invites and resists interpretation. What is clear is that the episode proceeds by bringing together elements from both the erotic dream and the slaying of the three soldiers in stanzas i–x of this canto and translating them into 'swift phantasmagoria' (Wilson Knight); the significance attached to this varies with the commentary. Interesting explications are provided by E. Murray (*JEGP* lxvii (1968) 572–4); R. Cronin, *Shelley's Poetic Thoughts* (1981) 103–4; W. Ulmer, *Shelleyan Eros* (1990) 57–61. D. Duff, *Romance and Revolution: Shelley and the Politics of a Genre* (1994) 174–7, assesses previous interpretations and considers the nature of the episode as psychic portrayal and its function in the moral development of the hero.

1324. gate] *L&C* and *RofI* both read thus as does *1839*; thereafter most *eds* emend to 'grate' which is used in lines 1226, 1231 and 1358 for the barrier closing the passage between the

And from the frieze to the four winds of Heaven
Hung them on high by the entangled hair:
Swarthy were three — the fourth was very fair:
As they retired, the golden moon upsprung,
1330 And eagerly, out in the giddy air,
Leaning that I might eat, I stretched and clung
Over the shapeless depth in which those corpses hung.

XXVI

A woman's shape, now lank and cold and blue,
The dwelling of the many-coloured worm
1335 Hung there, the white and hollow cheek I drew
To my dry lips — what radiance did inform
Those horny eyes? whose was that withered form?
Alas, alas! it seemed that Cythna's ghost
Laughed in those looks, and that the flesh was warm
1340 Within my teeth! — a whirlwind keen as frost
Then in its sinking gulfs my sickening spirit tossed.

XXVII

Then seemed it that a tameless hurricane
Arose, and bore me in its dark career
Beyond the sun, beyond the stars that wane
1345 On the verge of formless space — it languished there,
And dying, left a silence lone and drear,
More horrible than famine: — in the deep

---

staircase in the cavern below and the base of the column where Laon is bound. The temptation to emend is strong, but as the 'grate' is also a *gate* it makes sense enough to stand.

Stanza xxvi. As Cameron noted in *Esd Nbk* (279), S. anticipated this stanza in lines 130–50 of his then unpublished poem *Zeinab and Kathema* (1811?) in which the Indian youth Kathema discovers the gibbetted and decaying corpse of his betrothed Zeinab who had been taken by force to England from Cashmere whence he has followed her. (For sources and context see N. Crook and D. Guiton, *Shelley's Venomed Melody* (1986) 59–63.) This phase of Laon's hallucination also resembles Victor Frankenstein's nightmare in *Frankenstein* (1818) ch. 4: 'I thought I saw Elizabeth [his cousin], in the bloom of health, walking in the streets of Ingolstadt. Delighted and surprised, I embraced her; but as I imprinted the first kiss on her lips, they became livid with the hue of death; her features appeared to change, and I thought that I held the corpse of my dead mother in my arms; a shroud enveloped her form, and I saw the grave-worms crawling in the folds of the flannel' (*MSW* i 40).

1337. horny] *Concordance* glosses as 'dull, lustreless', but the sense is more precisely that Cythna's eyes are 'semi-opaque like horn' (*OED*) and illuminated eerily from within. Cp. line 2751 and *PU* II i 3.

1339–40. The cannibalism that Laon imagines here is to be compared with that imagined in Cythna's delirium in lines 2961–2.

The shape of an old man did then appear,
Stately and beautiful, that dreadful sleep
1350   His heavenly smiles dispersed, and I could wake and weep.

XXVIII

And when the blinding tears had fallen, I saw
That column, and those corpses, and the moon,
And felt the poisonous tooth of hunger gnaw
My vitals, I rejoiced, as if the boon
1355   Of senseless death would be accorded soon; —
When from that stony gloom a voice arose,
Solemn and sweet as when low winds attune
The midnight pines; the grate did then unclose,
And on that reverend form the moonlight did repose.

XXIX

1360   He struck my chains, and gently spake and smiled:
As they were loosened by that Hermit old,

1348. an old man] In her 'Note on the Revolt of Islam' in *1840* MWS wrote: 'There exists in this poem a memorial of a friend of his youth. The character of the old man who liberates Laon from his tower-prison, and tends on him in sickness, is founded on that of Dr. Lind, who, when Shelley was at Eton, had often stood by to befriend and support him, and whose name he never mentioned without love and veneration'. Dr. James Lind, M. D. (1736–1812), of an Edinburgh family of some distinction, was an astronomer, botanist, geographer, inventor and fellow of the Royal Society who treated some members of the royal household and was appointed physician to Eton College in 1799. He had travelled to India, China and Iceland, maintained a keen interest in contemporary science, collected drawings and antiquities, and printed books on his own press at Windsor. Evidence for Lind's political views is scanty, but from what there is, and from S.'s praise of his tolerance, it seems reasonable to infer that he held humane and progressive ones; it seems likely too that he encouraged S.'s reading in this vein. MWS recorded S.'s generous tribute to Lind in MS notes in *Box 2*: ' "This man" – he has often said' – "is exactly what an old man ought to be. Free, calm-spirited – full of benevolence & even of youthful ardour his eye seemed to burn with supernatural spirit beneath his brow shaded by his venerable white locks – he was tall, vigorous & healthy in his body – tempered as it had ever been by his amiable mind – I owe that man far – oh! far more than I owe my father – he loved me & I shall never forget our long talks where he breathed the spirit of the kindest tolerance & the purest wisdom" ' (incorporated in *Hogg* Chapter II). See *DNB; Hughes* 26–9; W. G. Bebbington, *N&Q* n.s. vii (1960) 83–93; D. King-Hele, *KSMB* xviii (1967) 1–6; N. Crook and D. Guiton, *Shelley's Venomed Melody* (1986) 21–4, 31–2. Interesting resemblances exist between the character who here enters the poem and that of Zonoras in *Athanase*: 125–97; *Cancelled sequence following line 129*, 1–34; *Alternative sequence from line 125*, 1–28. See also headnote to *Athanase* (final paragraph) and notes to stanza xxix, lines 1361, 1387–8.

Stanza xxix. The Hermit's rescue of Laon gives fictional form to a persistent autobiographical reminiscence which MWS recorded in MS notes towards a biography of S. (*Box 2* ff. 113r–113v) probably written in early 1823 (*BSM* xxii Part Two 269–70, 421) and which is incorporated in *Hogg* Chapter II. MWS remembered that on the night S. first declared his love told her that once during Eton school holidays when he was recovering from 'a fever which had attacked my brain', a servant reported overhearing his father say that he had consulted about sending his son to a private madhouse. S. contrived to send a message to Dr. Lind who answered the summons, defied Sir Timothy, and prevented his young friend from being

Mine eyes were of their madness half beguiled,
To answer those kind looks — he did enfold
His giant arms around me, to uphold
1365   My wretched frame, my scorchèd limbs he wound
In linen moist and balmy, and as cold
As dew to drooping leaves; — the chain, with sound
Like earthquake, through the chasm of that steep stair did bound,

XXX

As lifting me, it fell! — What next I heard,
1370   Were billows leaping on the harbour bar,
And the shrill sea-wind, whose breath idly stirred
My hair; — I looked abroad, and saw a star
Shining beside a sail, and distant far
That mountain and its column, the known mark
1375   Of those who in the wide deep wandering are,
So that I feared some Spirit, fell and dark,
In trance had lain me thus within a fiendish bark.

---

confined as insane. *Hogg* considered S.'s disturbed recollections to be those of a recovering patient which should be received accordingly. Peacock drily says that 'the idea that his father was continually on the watch for a pretext to lock him up, haunted him through life' (*Peacock Works* viii 53).

1360. struck] Struck off, removed.

1361. Hermit] The aged recluse who exercises a salutary and instructive office is a commonplace of romantic narrative, but closer resemblances with various figures from S.'s reading have been proposed: the hermit who administers physical and spiritual succour to Timias and Serena in the *Faerie Queene* VI v 35–vi 15 (*Baker* 79); the hermit in James Beattie's *The Minstrel* 1771, 1774 (E. H. King, *English Studies* lxi (1980) 350); the hermit in Christian August Vulpius's *The History of Rinaldo Rinaldini* 1798, English trans. 1800 (W. E. Peck, *PMLA* xlv (1925) 165–71); the magician and sage Orondate in the oriental romance *Le vieux de la montagne* (1799) by J.-B.-C. Izouard, dit Delisle de Salles (Jean Overton Fuller, *Shelley: A Biography* (1968) 157–61, 199).

1364. giant arms] Laon, whose eyes are still only 'half beguiled' (line 1362) of his delirium, perceives the Hermit according to his original impression of his voice as the sound of the night wind through pines (lines 1356–8) which rise to a great height above him. The old man will later stand 'firm as a giant pine' (line 2417) by Laon's side in battle. S. compares trees to giants in, for example, *Mont Blanc* 20: 'Thy giant brood of pines around thee clinging' and in *Alastor* 383: 'mighty trees, that stretched their giant arms'.

1366. linen moist and balmy] 'A phrase with New Testamant associations' (G. Wilson Knight, *The Starlit Dome* (1941) 192). All four evangelists report that Jesus' body was recovered by a disciple and wrapped in linen after the crucifixion.

1369. As lifting me, it fell] As he lifted me, it fell. The awkward syntax presumably results from the attempt to make a fluid passage across the stanzas in imitation of the action.

1371. idly] Gently, lightly *Concordance*. Cp. line 1849: 'Bright pennons on the idle winds were hung' (and note).

1377. lain] *Rossetti 1870* and several later *eds* have corrected to 'laid', either as a misprint or a grammatical lapse. *Lain* is again used as the past participle of 'lay' in line 3124 where it makes a rhyme.

XXXI

For now indeed, over the salt sea billow
I sailed: yet dared not look upon the shape
1380   Of him who ruled the helm, although the pillow
For my light head was hollowed in his lap,
And my bare limbs his mantle did enwrap,
Fearing it was a fiend: at last, he bent
O'er me his agèd face, as if to snap
1385   Those dreadful thoughts the gentle grandsire bent,
And to my inmost soul his soothing looks he sent.

XXXII

A soft and healing potion to my lips
At intervals he raised — now looked on high,
To mark if yet the starry giant dips
1390   His zone in the dim sea — now cheeringly,
Though he said little, did he speak to me.
'It is a friend beside thee — take good cheer,
Poor victim, thou art now at liberty!'
I joyed as those a human tone to hear,
1395   Who in cells deep and lone have languished many a year.

XXXIII

A dim and feeble joy, whose glimpses oft
Were quenched in a relapse of wildering dreams,
Yet still methought we sailed, until aloft
The stars of night grew pallid, and the beams
1400   Of morn descended on the ocean streams,
And still that agèd man, so grand and mild,
Tended me, even as some sick mother seems
To hang in hope over a dying child,
Till in the azure East darkness again was piled.

1387–8. In the Preface to *Recollections* Trelawny says that 'At Eton, after an illness, the doctor who attended him took a liking to him, and Shelley borrowed his medical books and was deeply interested in chemistry from that time'. If Trelawny's memory is accurate, S. was not only befriended by Dr. Lind but was treated by him.

1389–90. The constellation Orion, commonly represented as a hunter with sword and belt (*zone*), took its name from the giant hunter of myth who had been given the gift of walking on the sea by his father Poseidon. The Hermit is watching the progress of the night towards morning. See lines 2328–32 and note.

XXXIV

1405 And then the night-wind steaming from the shore,
Sent odours dying sweet across the sea,
And the swift boat the little waves which bore,
Were cut by its keen keel, though slantingly;
Soon I could hear the leaves sigh, and could see
1410 The myrtle blossoms starring the dim grove,
As past the pebbly beach the boat did flee
On sidelong wing, into a silent cove,
Where ebon pines a shade under the starlight wove.

Canto Fourth

I

The old man took the oars, and soon the bark
1415 Smote on the beach beside a tower of stone;
It was a crumbling heap, whose portal dark
With blooming ivy trails was overgrown;
Upon whose floor the spangling sands were strown,
And rarest sea shells, which the eternal flood,
1420 Slave to the mother of the months, had thrown
Within the walls of that grey tower, which stood
A changeling of man's art, nursed amid Nature's brood.

II

When the old man his boat had anchorèd,
He wound me in his arms with tender care,

1405. *steaming*] 'streaming' *Rossetti 1870*. S. usually employs *steaming* to signify a rising rather than a wafting odour, but the sense here is like that in *R&H* 1089–91: 'And rare Arabian odours came, / Through the myrtle copses steaming thence / From the hissing frankincense'.

1407. And the swift waves the little boat which bore, *1975*. The emendation had previously been considered by *Rossetti 1878* and several later *eds* (following a conjecture in *The Examiner* for 21 October 1876). A similar case arises in line 3281 which reads in *L&C/RofI*: 'All power – aye, the ghost, the shade, the dream', which is corrected in the Errata list to: 'All power – aye, the ghost, the dream, the shade'. The state of the draft in *Nbk 3* 85 suggests that S. or another scribe may have made this latter error in transcribing copy for the printer, and it is possible that such an error of transcription or one of printing has entered the present line, which is tortuously phrased and connects awkwardly with the next one. Despite these suspicions, it remains possible that the line as it stands is an awkward inversion for 'And the little waves which bore the swift boat'.

1417. *ivy trails*] The chapel of the hermit in *Faerie Queene* VI v 35 is 'all with Iuy ouerspred'.

1420. *mother of the months*] The moon.

1422. *changeling*] A child secretly substituted for another in infancy; hence a thing cared for by Nature as its own.

1425   And very few, but kindly words he said,
And bore me through the tower adown a stair,
Whose smooth descent some ceaseless step to wear
For many a year had fallen — We came at last
To a small chamber, which with mosses rare
1430   Was tapestried, where me his soft hands placed
Upon a couch of grass and oak-leaves interlaced.

III

The moon was darting through the lattices
Its yellow light, warm as the beams of day —
So warm, that to admit the dewy breeze,
1435   The old man opened them; the moonlight lay
Upon a lake whose waters wove their play
Even to the threshold of that lonely home:
Within was seen in the dim wavering ray,
The antique sculptured roof, and many a tome
1440   Whose lore had made that sage all that he had become.

IV

The rock-built barrier of the sea was passed, —
And I was on the margin of a lake,
A lonely lake, amid the forests vast
And snowy mountains: — did my spirit wake
1445   From sleep, as many-coloured as the snake
That girds eternity? in life and truth,
Might not my heart its cravings ever slake?

1436. *wove their play*] Linked the motion of their ripples and waves. Cp. line 277.

1441–4. In the final stanza of Canto III the hermit's boat entered a small cove; stanza i of this canto situates his tower on the beach where the sea throws sand and shells on to its floor (1418–21). It is apparently this cove that is protected from the open sea by the *barrier* of line 1441, though this is not made clear. Yet these lines locate the tower on the shore of a remote lake amid *forests vast*. It is possible that S. imagined the tower as standing at the end of a cove reaching deep into these forests and overlooking a lake on its opposite side, but the setting, cursorily sketched, is not meant to be geographically consistent, rather to figure a passage to the tranquil sublimity that will restore Laon's mental balance.

1445–6. Cameron, *PMLA* lvi (1941) 203, cites *Ruins* xxii on a form of ancient pantheist belief that took as emblem 'a great round serpent (representing the heavens where they placed the moving principle, and for that reason of an azure colour, studded with spots of gold, the stars) devouring his tail, that is folding and unfolding himself eternally, like the revolutions of the spheres'. Cp. *Daemon* i 100–1: 'Where the vast snake Eternity / In charmèd sleep doth ever lie' and 'On the Devil and Devils' (*Prose* 274). For the comparison of life to a multi-coloured illusion, see *PU* III iv 190–2 (and note), *Sonnet*: 'lift not the painted veil' (and head-note) and *Adonais* 462–4.

Was Cythna then a dream, and all my youth,
And all its hopes and fears, and all its joy and ruth?

V

1450   Thus madness came again, — a milder madness,
Which darkened nought but time's unquiet flow
With supernatural shades of clinging sadness;
That gentle Hermit, in my helpless woe,
By my sick couch was busy to and fro,
1455   Like a strong spirit ministrant of good:
When I was healed, he led me forth to show
The wonders of his sylvan solitude,
And we together sate by that isle-fretted flood.

VI

He knew his soothing words to weave with skill
1460   From all my madness told; like mine own heart,
Of Cythna would he question me, until
That thrilling name had ceased to make me start,
From his familiar lips — it was not art,
Of wisdom and of justice when he spoke —
1465   When mid soft looks of pity, there would dart
A glance as keen as is the lightning's stroke
When it doth rive the knots of some ancestral oak.

VII

Thus slowly from my brain the darkness rolled,
My thoughts their due array did reassume
1470   Through the enchantments of that Hermit old;
Then I bethought me of the glorious doom
Of those who sternly struggle to relume
The lamp of Hope o'er man's bewildered lot,
And, sitting by the waters, in the gloom
1475   Of eve, to that friend's heart I told my thought —
That heart which had grown old, but had corrupted not.

1449. *ruth*] 'Sorrow, grief' rather than 'compassion', as the paired opposition with *joy* makes clear.

1459–60. 'From the words uttered in my ravings he was able to compose speech that tranquillised me'.

VIII

That hoary man had spent his livelong age
In converse with the dead, who leave the stamp
Of ever-burning thoughts on many a page,
1480   When they are gone into the senseless damp
Of graves; — his spirit thus became a lamp
Of splendour, like to those on which it fed:
Through peopled haunts, the City and the Camp,
Deep thirst for knowledge had his footsteps led,
1485   And all the ways of men among mankind he read.

IX

But custom maketh blind and obdurate
The loftiest hearts: — he had beheld the woe
In which mankind was bound, but deemed that fate
Which made them abject, would preserve them so;
1490   And in such faith, some steadfast joy to know,
He sought this cell: but when fame went abroad,
That one in Argolis did undergo
Torture for liberty, and that the crowd
High truths from gifted lips had heard and understood;

X

1495   And that the multitude was gathering wide;
His spirit leaped within his agèd frame,
In lonely peace he could no more abide,
But to the land on which the victor's flame
Had fed, my native land, the Hermit came:
1500   Each heart was there a shield, and every tongue

1477–82. Cp. II xx; *Fair clouds arrayed in sunlight lose the glory* (no. 142) stanzas 5 and 8; *Athanase, Cancelled sequence following line 129* 1–12.

1482. fed:] fed *L&C/RofI.* Most *eds* have supplied a strong stop here. *like to those on which it fed*] Adapting a favourite idea from Paine's *Rights of Man*: 'It is the faculty of the human mind to become what it contemplates, and to act in unison with its object' (*Paine Writings* ii 350). Cp. *Athanase, Cancelled sequence following line 129* 10 and note.

1483–5. Cp. the characterisation of Odysseus in the *Odyssey* i 3: 'Many were the men whose cities he saw and whose minds he learned' (Loeb trans.) Horace's nuancing of the Homeric formula to include 'customs' (*mores*) in *Epistles* I ii 17–20 and in *Ars Poetica* 141–2 thereafter became a commonplace, as in Chapman's translation of the *Odyssey*: 'The cities of a world of nations, / With all their manners, mindes and fashions, / He saw and knew' (i 5–7). In the *Faerie Queeene* VI vi 3 the hermit 'knew the diuerse went of mortall wayes, / And in the mindes of men had great insight'.

1485. among mankind he read] 'He read among mankind', completing the knowledge gained from books in lines 1477–82.

1492. one] Laon, in III xiii–xxvii.

Was as a sword of truth — young Laon's name
Rallied their secret hopes, though tyrants sung
Hymns of triumphant joy our scattered tribes among.

XI

He came to the lone column on the rock,
1505   And with his sweet and mighty eloquence
The hearts of those who watched it did unlock,
And made them melt in tears of penitence.
They gave him entrance free to bear me thence.
'Since this,' the old man said, 'seven years are spent,
1510   While slowly truth on thy benighted sense
Has crept; the hope which wildered it has lent
Meanwhile, to me the power of a sublime intent.

XII

'Yes, from the records of my youthful state,
And from the lore of bards and sages old,
1515   From whatsoe'er my wakened thoughts create
Out of the hopes of thine aspirings bold,
Have I collected language to unfold
Truth to my countrymen; from shore to shore
Doctrines of human power my words have told,
1520   They have been heard, and men aspire to more
Than they have ever gained or ever lost of yore.

XIII

'In secret chambers parents read, and weep,
My writings to their babes, no longer blind;
And young men gather when their tyrants sleep,
1525   And vows of faith each to the other bind;
And marriageable maidens, who have pined
With love, till life seemed melting through their look,
A warmer zeal, a nobler hope now find;

1509. *In L&C/RofI* the speech-marks do not begin until line 1513. *seven years*] The interval
is a commonplace of romantic narrative but has particular significance in relation to Laon's
role of persecuted national poet as the period of time the Italian heroic poet Tasso (1544–95)
spent confined as a madman on the order of the Duke, Alfonso d'Este. Tasso's harsh treat-
ment, his hopeless love for Leonora d'Este and the madness that resulted in, or from, his
detention had acquired exemplary status, though these incidents in his life had been the
subject of critical reassessment in, for example, John Black's *Life of Torquato Tasso* (1810). See
Scene for Tasso (and headnote) in which Tasso, the Duke and Leonora figure in tense con-
frontation. S. ordered Byron's *The Lament of Tasso* on 24 July 1817 and wrote to Byron with
his opinion of it on 24 September (*L* i 548, 556–7).

1513. 'From the writings of my youth'.

And every bosom thus is rapt and shook,
1530   Like autumn's myriad leaves in one swoln mountain brook.

XIV

'The tyrants of the Golden City tremble
At voices which are heard about the streets,
The ministers of fraud can scarce dissemble
The lies of their own heart; but when one meets
1535   Another at the shrine, he inly weets,
Though he says nothing, that the truth is known;
Murderers are pale upon the judgement-seats,
And gold grows vile even to the wealthy crone,
And laughter fills the Fane, and curses shake the Throne.

XV

1540   'Kind thoughts, and mighty hopes, and gentle deeds
Abound, for fearless love, and the pure law
Of mild equality and peace, succeeds
To faiths which long have held the world in awe,
Bloody and false, and cold: — as whirlpools draw
1545   All wrecks of Ocean to their chasm, the sway
Of thy strong genius, Laon, which foresaw
This hope, compels all spirits to obey,
Which round thy secret strength now throng in wide array.

XVI

'For I have been thy passive instrument' —
1550   (As thus the old man spake, his countenance

1533. *ministers of fraud*] Priests; cp. Preface lines 33–4: 'the religious frauds by which they had been deluded into submission'.

1535. *weets*] Knows.

1537. Cp. Preface line 42: 'the judicial murder of the advocates of Liberty'.

1539. Cp. *Ahrimanes* II iii 1: 'But not in fanes where priestly curses ring'; *Ahrimanes*, Shorter Verse Fragment xvi 8: 'And curses ring along the vaulted fane' (*Peacock Works* vii 278, 427).

1545. *chasm*] Evidently the spiralling gulf of the whirlpool, but there may be an allusion to the theory, which S. could have met in *Darwin* I i (Additional Note xxxi to iii 93), that a whirlpool is caused by a *chasm* in the sea floor into which the sea-water swirls. See note to lines 2888–9, and cp. *Alastor* 369–97.

Stanzas xvi–xvii. The hermit's self-confessed limitations would be more appropriate to S.'s current opinion of another of his mentors, William Godwin, than to Dr. Lind. Godwin held S.'s poetry in low esteem, having told him that *Q Mab* was an example of 'false taste', and privately noted the 'wild' and 'frantic' qualities of S.'s verse as well as the 'drunken, reeling, mystical Pythia form in which [the thought] clothes itself' (P. Clemit, *Durham University Journal* 85 (n.s. 54) No. 2 (1993) 189). S.'s redefinition of the roles of elderly sage and aspiring poet has thus interesting autobiographical resonances. Godwin had written to S. in January 1812:

Gleamed on me like a spirit's) — 'thou hast lent
To me, to all, the power to advance
Towards this unforeseen deliverance
From our ancestral chains — ay, thou didst rear
1555 That lamp of hope on high, which time nor chance,
Nor change may not extinguish, and my share
Of good, was o'er the world its gathered beams to bear.

XVII

'But I, alas! am both unknown and old,
And though the woof of wisdom I know well
1560 To dye in hues of language, I am cold
In seeming, and the hopes which inly dwell,
My manners note that I did long repel;
But Laon's name to the tumultuous throng
Were like the star whose beams the waves compel
1565 And tempests, and his soul-subduing tongue
Were as a lance to quell the mailèd crest of wrong.

XVIII

'Perchance blood need not flow, if thou at length
Wouldst rise, perchance the very slaves would spare
Their brethren and themselves; great is the strength
1570 Of words — for lately did a maiden fair,
Who from her childhood has been taught to bear
The tyrant's heaviest yoke, arise, and make
Her sex the law of truth and freedom hear,
And with these quiet words — "for thine own sake
1575 I prithee spare me;" — did with ruth so take

XIX

'All hearts, that even the torturer who had bound
Her meek calm frame, ere it was yet impaled,
Loosened her weeping then; nor could be found
One human hand to harm her — unassailed
1580 Therefore she walks through the great City, veiled

'you appear to be in some degree the pupil of my writings, and I feel so far as if I were in a manner responsible for your conduct' (L i 233). Although he continued to have high regard for Godwin's intellectual powers, S. is here making an ironic reversal of the positions they had initially adopted towards one another as well as privileging the inspirational power of poetry over discursive reasoning. S. responds to Godwin's 'censures' of L&C in L i 577.

1570–2. The maiden is Cythna who is not formally identified until line 2546 and who after her abduction was confined in Othman's harem.

1575. The line is a foot short.

In virtue's adamantine eloquence,
'Gainst scorn, and death and pain thus trebly mailed,
And blending in the smiles of that defence,
The Serpent and the Dove, Wisdom and Innocence.

XX

1585 'The wild-eyed women throng around her path:
From their luxurious dungeons, from the dust
Of meaner thralls, from the oppressor's wrath,
Or the caresses of his sated lust
They congregate: — in her they put their trust;
1590 The tyrants send their armèd slaves to quell
Her power; — they, even like a thunder-gust
Caught by some forest, bend beneath the spell
Of that young maiden's speech, and to their chiefs rebel.

XXI

'Thus she doth equal laws and justice teach
1595 To woman, outraged and polluted long;
Gathering the sweetest fruit in human reach
For those fair hands now free, while armèd wrong
Trembles before her look, though it be strong;
Thousands thus dwell beside her, virgins bright,
1600 And matrons with their babes, a stately throng!
Lovers renew the vows which they did plight
In early faith, and hearts long parted now unite,

XXII

'And homeless orphans find a home near her,
And those poor victims of the proud, no less,
1605 Fair wrecks, on whom the smiling world with stir,
Thrusts the redemption of its wickedness: —
In squalid huts, and in its palaces
Sits Lust alone, while o'er the land is borne
Her voice, whose awful sweetness doth repress
1610 All evil, and her foes relenting turn,
And cast the vote of love in hope's abandoned urn.

1584. 'Behold, I send you forth as sheep in the midst of wolves: be ye therefore wise as serpents, and harmless as doves' (*Matthew* x 16).

1586. *dust*] Humiliation and misery.

1604–6. The *victims* are recipients of charity ostentatiously bestowed out of a sense of guilt.

1611. Combining the sense of *urn* as a receptacle for votes in an election with an allusion to the myth of Pandora (Hesiod, *Works and Days* 60 ff.) who, when she released into the world all the evils that have since become familiar from her husband Epimetheus's earthenware

XXIII

'So in the populous City, a young maiden
Has baffled havoc of the prey which he
Marks as his own, whene'er with chains o'erladen
1615   Men make them arms to hurl down tyranny,
False arbiter between the bound and free;
And o'er the land, in hamlets and in towns
The multitudes collect tumultuously,
And throng in arms; but tyranny disowns
1620   Their claim, and gathers strength around its trembling thrones.

XXIV

'Blood soon, although unwillingly to shed,
The free cannot forbear — the Queen of Slaves,
The hoodwinked Angel of the blind and dead,
Custom, with iron mace points to the graves
1625   Where her own standard desolately waves
Over the dust of Prophets and of Kings.
Many yet stand in her array — "she paves
Her path with human hearts," and o'er it flings
The wildering gloom of her immeasurable wings.

XXV

1630   'There is a plain beneath the City's wall,
Bounded by misty mountains, wide and vast,

---

vessel (in other versions of the myth she lets all beneficial things escape), replaces the lid to trap Hope, the one good remaining within. See lines 345, 647 and notes.

1623. hoodwinked] Both 'blindfolded' and 'deceived'. S. seems to be recalling the goddess *'Aτη* ('Ruin', apparently intended in the 'havoc' of line 1613) who in *Iliad* xix 85 ff. blinds and deceives men, and transferring her two chief characteristics to Custom. See note to lines 1627–8.

1625. Where] *1839* and *eds*; When *L&C/RofI*. The same error is corrected in the list of Errata at lines 2028 and 2129.

1626. Prophets] Here, those *prophets* who speak flatteringly to kings, as in *1 Kings* xxii 13 or in *Jeremiah* xxxvii 19.

1627–8. 1975 cites S.'s translation of Plato, *Symposium* 195 in which Love is presented in terms borrowed from Homer's description of Ruin (see note to line 1623) which S. renders as 'Calamity'. 'For Homer says, that the goddess Calamity is delicate, and that her feet are tender . . . she walks not upon that which is hard, but upon that which is soft . . . For Love . . . dwells within, and treads on the softest of existing things, having established his habitation within the souls and inmost nature of Gods and men'. Cp. *PU* I 772–9 (and note): 'Ah sister, Desolation is a delicate thing: / It walks not on the Earth, it floats not on the air, / But treads with lulling footstep, and fans with silent wing / The tender hopes which in their hearts the best and gentlest bear' (772–5). The quotation-marks round the sentence in the text do not indicate an exact quotation.

Millions there lift at Freedom's thrilling call
Ten thousand standards wide, they load the blast
Which bears one sound of many voices past,
1635 And startles on his throne their sceptered foe:
He sits amid his idle pomp aghast,
And that his power hath passed away, doth know —
Why pause the victor swords to seal his overthrow?

XXVI

'The tyrant's guards resistance yet maintain:
1640 Fearless, and fierce, and hard as beasts of blood;
They stand a speck amid the peopled plain;
Carnage and ruin have been made their food
From infancy — ill has become their good,
And for its hateful sake their will has wove
1645 The chains which eat their hearts — the multitude
Surrounding them, with words of human love,
Seek from their own decay their stubborn minds to move.

XXVII

'Over the land is felt a sudden pause,
As night and day those ruthless bands around
1650 The watch of love is kept: — a trance which awes
The thoughts of men with hope — as when the sound
Of whirlwind, whose fierce blasts the waves and clouds confound,
Dies suddenly, the mariner in fear
Feels silence sink upon his heart — thus bound,
1655 The conquerors pause, and oh! may freemen ne'er
Clasp the relentless knees of Dread the murderer!

XXVIII

'If blood be shed, 'tis but a change and choice
Of bonds, — from slavery to cowardice
A wretched fall! — uplift thy charmèd voice,
1660 Pour on those evil men the love that lies

1632. Millions] Multitudes, the usual sense in S.

1634. Cp. lines 109–10.

1639–40. Rossetti 1870 and *1878* alter the semicolon at the end of line 1640 to a comma; *Woodberry 1893* alters the colon at the end of line 1639 to a comma; but, as *Locock 1911* remarks, the original punctuation ought to stand as line 1640 goes as well with *guards* in the previous line as with *They* in the following one.

1643. ill has become their good.] Cp. Satan in *Paradise Lost* iv 110: 'Evil be thou my good' and *Isaiah* v 20: 'Woe unto them that call evil good, and good evil'.

Hovering within those spirit-soothing eyes —
Arise, my friend, farewell!' — As thus he spake,
From the green earth lightly I did arise,
As one out of dim dreams that doth awake,
1665 And looked upon the depth of that reposing lake.

XXIX

I saw my countenance reflected there; —
And then my youth fell on me like a wind
Descending on still waters — my thin hair
Was prematurely grey, my face was lined
1670 With channels, such as suffering leaves behind,
Not age; my brow was pale, but in my cheek
And lips a flush of gnawing fire did find
Their food and dwelling; though mine eyes might speak
A subtle mind and strong within a frame thus weak.

XXX

1675 And though their lustre now was spent and faded,
Yet in my hollow looks and withered mien
The likeness of a shape for which was braided
The brightest woof of genius, still was seen —
One who, methought, had gone from the world's scene,
1680 And left it vacant — 'twas her brother's face —
It might resemble her — it once had been
The mirror of her thoughts, and still the grace
Which her mind's shadow cast, left there a lingering trace.

XXXI

What then was I? She slumbered with the dead.
1685 Glory and joy and peace, had come and gone.
Doth the cloud perish, when the beams are fled
Which steeped its skirts in gold? or dark and lone,
Doth it not through the paths of night unknown,

1667. wind] *RofI*; wind, *L&C*: alteration introduced in the cancel-leaf for *RofI*.

1668–73. See lines 454–8 and note.

1671. age;] *RofI*; age; – *L&C*: alteration in the cancel-leaf for *RofI*.

1673. Their] S. may have taken both the flush in the cheeks and the flush in the lips as antecedents of the plural *their* as *Locock 1911* suggests.

1675. was] were *L&C*. The error is both noted in the Errata list and corrected in the cancel-leaf for *RofI*.

1680. brother's] lover's *RofI*. 'An alteration which robs the stanza of half its meaning' (*Forman 1876–7*).

On outspread wings of its own wind upborne
1690 Pour rain upon the earth? the stars are shown,
When the cold moon sharpens her silver horn
Under the sea, and make the wide night not forlorn.

XXXII

Strengthened in heart, yet sad, that agèd man
I left, with interchange of looks and tears,
1695 And lingering speech, and to the Camp began
My way. O'er many a mountain chain which rears
Its hundred crests aloft, my spirit bears
My frame; o'er many a dale and many a moor,
And gaily now meseems serene earth wears
1700 The blosmy spring's star-bright investiture,
A vision which aught sad from sadness might allure.

XXXIII

My powers revived within me, and I went
As one whom winds waft o'er the bending grass,
Through many a vale of that broad continent.
1705 At night when I reposed, fair dreams did pass
Before my pillow; — my own Cythna was
Not like a child of death, among them ever;
When I arose from rest, a woeful mass
That gentlest sleep seemed from my life to sever,
1710 As if the light of youth were not withdrawn for ever.

XXXIV

Aye as I went, that maiden who had reared
The torch of Truth afar, of whose high deeds
The Hermit in his pilgrimage had heard,
Haunted my thoughts. — Ah, Hope its sickness feeds
1715 With whatsoe'er it finds, or flowers or weeds!
Could she be Cythna? — Was that corpse a shade
Such as self-torturing thought from madness breeds?
Why was this hope not torture? yet it made
A light around my steps which would not ever fade.

1689. its own wind] See lines 937–9 and note.

1700. blosmy] See note to line 578. *investiture*] Clothing, covering.

1701. aught] ought *L&C/RofI*; aught *eds*. 'Ought' was an obsolescent alternative spelling of *aught* in the early nineteenth century. Cp. line 54.

Canto Fifth

I

1720 Over the utmost hill at length I sped,
A snowy steep: — the moon was hanging low
Over the Asian mountains, and outspread
The plain, the City, and the Camp below,
Skirted the midnight Ocean's glimmering flow,
1725 The City's moonlit spires and myriad lamps,
Like stars in a sublunar sky did glow,
And fires blazed far amid the scattered camps,
Like springs of flame, which burst where'er swift Earthquake stamps.

II

All slept but those in watchful arms who stood,
1730 And those who sate tending the beacon's light,
And the few sounds from that vast multitude
Made silence more profound — Oh, what a might
Of human thought was cradled in that night!
How many hearts impenetrably veiled,
1735 Beat underneath its shade, what secret fight
Evil and good, in woven passions mailed,
Waged through that silent throng; a war that never failed!

1720. utmost] The furthest in Laon's course.

1722–8. The location of the Golden City in a plain between the sea and *the Asian mountains* marks it as contemporary Constantinople where S. said that 'the scene is supposed to be laid', after the preceding three cantos which are set in modern Greece (*L* i 563). The setting also resembles that of Homeric Troy; here the description of the Trojan camp in *Iliad* viii 540–65 is especially recalled.

1725–7. Cp. the infernal Pandemonium (*Paradise Lost* i 722–30) where suspended from the roof 'starry lamps and blazing cressets . . . yielded light / As from a sky'.

1726. sublunar] Earthly, terrestrial; in older cosmology, 'subject to the moon's influence' (*OED*), hence to alteration and decay.

1728. The image derives from the contemporary theory that earthquakes occur in order to release energy generated by subterranean fires, e.g. pressure built up when water has found a passage underground and been heated into steam. S. could have encountered the idea in *Darwin* I note to i 152 and Additional Note VI, as well as in the note to I ii 68 where the irregularities of the earth's crust are attributed to such primeval convulsions: 'You! who then, kindling after many an age, / Saw with new fires the first Volcano rage . . . / Saw at each opening cleft the furnace glow, / And seas rush headlong on the gulphs below' (ii 67–8, 71–2). See also Darwin, *The Temple of Nature* (1803) i 322: 'Next when imprison'd fires in central caves / Burst the firm earth, and drank the headlong waves' (and Additional Note III to these lines).

1737. never failed] Continued perpetually.

III

And now the Power of Good held victory,
So, through the labyrinth of many a tent,
1740 Among the silent millions who did lie
In innocent sleep, exultingly I went;
The moon had left Heaven desert now, but lent
From eastern morn the first faint lustre showed
An armèd youth — over his spear he bent
1745 His downward face — 'A friend!' I cried aloud,
And quickly common hopes made freemen understood.

IV

I sate beside him while the morning beam
Crept slowly over Heaven, and talked with him
Of those immortal hopes, a glorious theme!
1750 Which led us forth, until the stars grew dim:
And all the while, methought, his voice did swim,
As if it drownèd in remembrance were
Of thoughts which make the moist eyes overbrim:
At last, when daylight 'gan to fill the air,
1755 He looked on me, and cried in wonder — 'thou art here!'

V

Then, suddenly, I knew it was the youth
In whom its earliest hopes my spirit found;
But envious tongues had stained his spotless truth,
And thoughtless pride his love in silence bound,
1760 And shame and sorrow mine in toils had wound,
Whilst he was innocent, and I deluded;
The truth now came upon me, on the ground
Tears of repenting joy, which fast intruded,
Fell fast, and o'er its peace our mingling spirits brooded.

1738. victory,] *1839*; victory *L&C/Rof1*: subsequent *eds* have variously supplied the punctuation that is clearly called for at this point.

1740. millions] Multitudes; cp. line 1632.

1750. led us forth] Brought us to be gathered here.

1751. swim] *OED* cites this passage to illustrate sense 2b of the verb *swim*: 'to be supported [e.g. a particle] in a fluid medium'. Though broadly what is intended, the meaning here seems less precise and resists clear paraphrase, running the sense of recollection and of weeping together to produce a mixed aural and visual perception: in the darkness the speaker's voice strikes Laon as though it passed through the welling tears that he imagines are being shed. Cp. the analogous sense of *swim* in line 813.

1756. youth] The friend who had been false to Laon: see line 825.

VI

1765 Thus, while with rapid lips and earnest eyes
We talked, a sound of sweeping conflict spread,
As from the earth did suddenly arise;
From every tent roused by that clamour dread,
Our bands outsprung and seized their arms — we sped
1770 Towards the sound: our tribes were gathering far,
Those sanguine slaves amid ten thousand dead
Stabbed in their sleep, trampled in treacherous war
The gentle hearts whose power their lives had sought to spare.

VII

Like rabid snakes, that sting some gentle child
1775 Who brings them food, when winter false and fair
Allures them forth with its cold smiles, so wild
They rage among the camp; — they overbear
The patriot hosts — confusion, then despair
Descends like night — when 'Laon!' one did cry:
1780 Like a bright ghost from Heaven that shout did scare
The slaves, and widening through the vaulted sky,
Seemed sent from Earth to Heaven in sign of victory.

VIII

In sudden panic those false murderers fled,
Like insect tribes before the northern gale:
1785 But swifter still, our hosts encompassèd
Their shattered ranks, and in a craggy vale,
Where even their fierce despair might nought avail
Hemmed them around! — and then revenge and fear
Made the high virtue of the patriots fail:

1765–6. *Thus, while . . . We talked*] While we talked thus. Cp. line 136 and note.

1766–7. Various ways of reducing the awkward syntax to order have been proposed. *Rossetti* (*1870* and *1878*), followed by *Woodberry 1893*, repunctuates: 'a sound of sweeping conflict, spread / As from the earth, did suddenly arise'. But *Locock 1911* is surely right in thinking that the *sound* seems rather to *arise* from the earth than to have *spread* from it; he suggests that *spread* should be taken 'as an epithet of *sound*' – i.e. *sound of sweeping conflict* [which had] *spread*. It is also possible to consider *spread* as a preterite and the next line a parallel clause with *sound* as the implied subject. As neither of the two latter readings materially alters the sense of, or is clearly preferable to the other, there is no reason to alter the punctuation of *L&C/RofI*.

1772. *war*] war, *L&C/RofI*. Most modern *eds* have removed the awkwardly-placed comma.

1774. *rabid*] Furious, enraged. The treacherous soldiers are compared to snakes deceived by winter sunshine into waking prematurely from hibernation.

1777. *They*] The *sanguine slaves* of line 1771.

1790   One pointed on his foe the mortal spear —
                I rushed before its point, and cried, 'Forbear, forbear!'

IX

                The spear transfixed my arm that was uplifted
                In swift expostulation, and the blood
                Gushed round its point: I smiled, and — 'Oh! thou gifted
1795   With eloquence which shall not be withstood,
                Flow thus!' — I cried in joy, 'thou vital flood,
                Until my heart be dry, ere thus the cause
                For which thou wert aught worthy be subdued —
                Ah, ye are pale, — ye weep, — your passions pause, —
1800   'Tis well! ye feel the truth of love's benignant laws.

X

                'Soldiers, our brethren and our friends are slain.
                Ye murdered them, I think, as they did sleep!
                Alas, what have ye done? the slightest pain
                Which ye might suffer, there were eyes to weep;
1805   But ye have quenched them — there were smiles to steep
                Your hearts in balm, but they are lost in woe;
                And those whom love did set his watch to keep
                Around your tents truth's freedom to bestow,
                Ye stabbed as they did sleep — but they forgive ye now.

XI

1810   'O wherefore should ill ever flow from ill,
                And pain still keener pain forever breed?
                We all are brethren — even the slaves who kill
                For hire, are men; and to avenge misdeed
                On the misdoer, doth but Misery feed
1815   With her own broken heart! O Earth, O Heaven!
                And thou, dread Nature, which to every deed
                And all that lives, or is, to be hath given,
                Even as to thee have these done ill, and are forgiven.

1797–8. The sense is both obscure and ambiguous. *Locock 1911* paraphrases line 1798 thus:
'For the sake of which alone thou [my blood] wert of any worth' – a possible meaning if *for*
= 'for the sake of'. But if *for* = 'of', then the meaning of the clause *ere . . . subdued* would be
instead: 'rather than the cause, of which my blood might be at all worthy, should know defeat'.
The *cause* is non-violent revolution.

1808. *truth's freedom*] 'And ye shall know the truth, and the truth shall make you free' (*John*
viii 32).

1817. And all that lives, or is to be, hath given *1839*; but the sense of lines 1816–17 appears
to be: 'Thou hast given existence to every action and to all animate and inanimate creatures'.
hath] *Rossetti 1870, 1878* and *1975* correct to 'hast'; it is possible that the error of agreement
is owing to faulty transcription or printing.

XII

'Join then your hands and hearts, and let the past
1820 Be as a grave which gives not up its dead
To evil thoughts' — a film then overcast
My sense with dimness, for the wound, which bled
Freshly, swift shadows o'er mine eyes had shed.
When I awoke, I lay 'mid friends and foes,
1825 And earnest countenances on me shed
The light of questioning looks, whilst one did close
My wound with balmiest herbs, and soothed me to repose;

XIII

And one whose spear had pierced me, leaned beside
With quivering lips and humid eyes; — and all
1830 Seemed like some brothers on a journey wide
Gone forth, whom now strange meeting did befall
In a strange land, round one whom they might call
Their friend, their chief, their father, for assay
Of peril, which had saved them from the thrall
1835 Of death, now suffering. Thus the vast array
Of those fraternal bands were reconciled that day.

XIV

Lifting the thunder of their acclamation,
Towards the City then the multitude,

1819–21. 'Let those who were slain not be resurrected in the mind as motives of ill will'. Cp. 'The past is Death's, the future is thine own' (line 3394) and note to line 3396.

1823. Freshly] Afresh, anew.   shed.] The duplication of the rhyme-word in line 1825 may be a scribal or printer's error (the draft in Nbk 3 is defective here), like the spread of line 2014 in L&C/RofI which is corrected to shed in the list of Errata. Rossetti (1870 and 1878) suggests S. may have written spread in this line, where it would be appropriate. Similar uncorrected duplications stand, e.g. in lines 742 and 745.

1828. one] Forman 1876–7 suggested that one might be a printer's error for 'he'; but one (= the one) seems an awkwardness of diction in the interest of parallelism with one of line 1826 and the contrast with all of line 1829.

1830–3. The language is biblical, as in Exodus ii 22: 'I have been a stranger in a strange land' – though recalling especially the meeting of Joseph and his brothers in Egypt in Genesis xlii 1–7 ('And Joseph saw his brethren, and he knew them, but made himself strange unto them').

1833–4. assay / Of peril] 'Perilous attempt' Locock 1911, citing Spenserian usage; but 'trial' (i.e. initial testing experience) of danger' seems closer to the sense here.

1834–5. thrall/ Of death] The moral bondage that would have been their state had they revenged their comrades by murder. The language of the lines is that of Pauline theology (e.g. 2 Corinthians i 1–10) which S. is revising.

1836. were] See note to line 1233.

And I among them, went in joy — a nation
1840   Made free by love; — a mighty brotherhood
Linked by a jealous interchange of good;
A glorious pageant, more magnificent
Than kingly slaves arrayed in gold and blood,
When they return from carnage, and are sent
1845   In triumph bright beneath the populous battlement.

XV

Afar, the city walls were thronged on high,
And myriads on each giddy turret clung,
And to each spire far lessening in the sky,
Bright pennons on the idle winds were hung;
1850   As we approached a shout of joyance sprung
At once from all the crowd, as if the vast
And peopled Earth its boundless skies among
The sudden clamour of delight had cast,
When from before its face some general wreck had passed.

XVI

1855   Our armies through the City's hundred gates
Were poured, like brooks which to the rocky lair
Of some deep lake, whose silence them awaits,
Throng from the mountains when the storms are there;
And as we passed through the calm sunny air
1860   A thousand flower-inwoven crowns were shed,
The token flowers of truth and freedom fair,
And fairest hands bound them on many a head,
Those angels of love's heaven, that over all was spread.

XVII

I trod as one tranced in some rapturous vision:
1865   Those bloody bands so lately reconciled,

1839. And I among them] 'Now just as the Gates were opened to let in the men, I looked in after them; and behold, the City [of Heaven] shone like the Sun, the Streets also were paved with Gold, and in them walked many men . . . which when I had seen, I wished my self among them'. Bunyan, *The Pilgrim's Progress* (1678) ed. J. B. Wharey, 2nd edn (1960) 162.

1841. jealous] Zealous, eager.

1849. pennons] Narrow flags or streamers.   *idle]* still, inactive; cf. 'the calm sunny air' of line 1859.

1855. hundred gates] Egyptian Thebes is said to have an hundred gates in the *Iliad* ix 383.

1859. Rossetti 1870, 1878 and *Dowden 1891* place a comma after *air*; *Locock 1911* places a comma after *passed*. But the ambiguous reference of *through* is impossible to resolve without the authority of another textual witness.

1865. reconciled] Won over again to brotherhood with the patriots.

Were, ever as they went, by the contrition
Of anger turned to love from ill beguiled,
And every one on them more gently smiled,
Because they had done evil: — the sweet awe
1870   Of such mild looks made their own hearts grow mild,
And did with soft attraction ever draw
Their spirits to the love of freedom's equal law.

XVIII

And they, and all, in one loud symphony
My name with Liberty commingling, lifted,
1875   'The friend and the preserver of the free!
The parent of this joy!' and fair eyes gifted
With feelings, caught from one who had uplifted
The light of a great spirit, round me shone;
And all the shapes of this grand scenery shifted
1880   Like restless clouds before the steadfast sun, —
Where was that Maid? I asked, but it was known of none.

XIX

Laone was the name her love had chosen,
For she was nameless, and her birth none knew:
Where was Laone now? — the words were frozen
1885   Within my lips with fear; but to subdue
Such dreadful hope, to my great task was due,
And when at length one brought reply, that she
Tomorrow would appear, I then withdrew
To judge what need for that great throng might be,
1890   For now the stars came thick over the twilight sea.

XX

Yet need was none for rest or food to care,
Even though that multitude was passing great,
Since each one for the other did prepare
All kindly succour — Therefore to the gate

1877. *one*] Laone; the images in lines 1877–8 anticipate those of her public appearance in V xliv.

Stanza xix. From this point until XII xxxi 3, nearly complete drafts for the poem exist in *Nbk 3*. S. began to draft this stanza on the first page of the nbk thus: 'Laone was the [n]', cancelled what he'd written and noted 'the sister is to be more uncertain', then resumed the draft with the same words below. The sentence, which has been variously interpreted (see J. Donovan, *KSR* ii (1987) 56–7), appears to be S.'s memorandum to himself to proceed so as to keep Laone's private identity as Cythna from becoming too conspicuous after the strong hints in lines 1705–19 as well as in the name 'Laone' itself.

1895   Of the Imperial House, now desolate,
I passed, and there was found aghast, alone,
The fallen Tyrant! — silently he sate
Upon the footstool of his golden throne,
Which starred with sunny gems, in its own lustre shone.

XXI

1900   Alone, but for one child, who led before him
A graceful dance: the only living thing
Of all the crowd, which thither to adore him
Flocked yesterday, who solace sought to bring
In his abandonment! — she knew the King
1905   Had praised her dance of yore, and now she wove
Its circles, aye weeping and murmuring
'Mid her sad task of unregarded love,
That to no smiles it might his speechless sadness move.

XXII

She fled to him, and wildly clasped his feet
1910   When human steps were heard: — he moved nor spoke,
Nor changed his hue, nor raised his looks to meet
The gaze of strangers — our loud entrance woke
The echoes of the hall, which circling broke
The calm of its recesses, — like a tomb
1915   Its sculptured walls vacantly to the stroke
Of footfalls answered, and the twilight's gloom
Lay like a charnel's mist within the radiant dome.

XXIII

The little child stood up when we came nigh;
Her lips and cheeks seemed very pale and wan,
1920   But on her forehead, and within her eye
Lay beauty, which makes hearts that feed thereon
Sick with excess of sweetness; on the throne
She leaned; — the King with gathered brow, and lips

Stanza xxii. The contrast in this stanza and in stanza xxvi between the magnificence of the imperial palace and the desolation of fallen monarchy is just that which S. noticed when he visited the palace of Versailles on 3 September 1816, recording his impressions in *Mary Jnl* i 132–4 and in *L* i 504. It is clear from his account of the visit that some confusion then existed in his mind between the incidents at the palace of Versailles on 5–6 October 1789 which culminated in the escorting of the King and Queen to Paris and those at the Tuileries palace which the rioters of 10 August 1792 entered to seize the royal family.

1914–17. 'The vacant rooms of this palace imaged well the hollow shew of monarchy' (*Mary Jnl* i 134, written by S.). See previous note.

1916. gloom] *Nbk 3* 3 and *eds*; gloom, *L&C/RofI.*

Wreathed by long scorn, did inly sneer and frown
1925   With hue like that when some great painter dips
His pencil in the gloom of earthquake and eclipse.

XXIV

She stood beside him like a rainbow braided
Within some storm, when scarce its shadows vast
From the blue paths of the swift sun have faded;
1930   A sweet and solemn smile, like Cythna's, cast
One moment's light, which made my heart beat fast,
O'er that child's parted lips — a gleam of bliss,
A shade of vanished days, — as the tears passed
Which wrapped it, even as with a father's kiss
1935   I pressed those softest eyes in trembling tenderness.

XXV

The sceptred wretch then from that solitude
I drew, and of his change compassionate,
With words of sadness soothed his rugged mood.
But he, while pride and fear held deep debate,
1940   With sullen guile of ill-dissembled hate
Glared on me as a toothless snake might glare:
Pity, not scorn I felt, though desolate
The desolator now, and unaware
The curses which he mocked had caught him by the hair.

XXVI

1945   I led him forth from that which now might seem
A gorgeous grave: through portals sculptured deep

1924. Wreathed] Curled or twisted. Cp. *Ozymandias* 4–5 and note.

1925–6. The simile had been in S.'s mind from early in the poem's composition; a cancelled draft for I xviii (*Nbk 2* 28) reads: 'as when some immortal painter, dips / His pencil in the darkness of eclipse / And feigns among the gloom some figure frail / And beautiful'. It occurs again in an isolated draft on an otherwise blank page (56) of the same nbk in the form: 'who dip / Its pencil in the darkness of eclipse'. In its present formulation it bears an intriguing similarity to a sketch for a painting by George Jones (1786–1869) exhibited at the Royal Academy from May 1817 and described in *The Examiner* 493 (9 June 1817) 363: '*Earthquake at Sparta – Terror of the Inhabitants, and the assembling of Troops to suppress an Insurrection of the Helolae*'. Details of the sketch are given which include: 'slaves, with horrid but natural vengeance, seeking the lives of their enslavers; congregating soldiers'. MWS records a visit to the exhibition on 24 May 1817, when she and S. were in London, though she does not say specifically that S. accompanied her (*Mary Jnl* i 170).

1926. pencil] A small fine paintbrush.

1934. See lines 4659–65.

1946–9. 'They [the rooms of the palace at Versailles] are lined with marble of various colours whose pedestals & capitals are gilt, & the cieli[n]g is richly gilt with compartments of exquisite painting' (*Mary Jnl* i 133, written by S.). See note to stanza xxii.

With imagery beautiful as dream
We went, and left the shades which tend on sleep
Over its unregarded gold to keep
1950   Their silent watch. — The child trod faintingly,
And as she went, the tears which she did weep
Glanced in the starlight; wilderèd seemed she,
And when I spake, for sobs she could not answer me.

XXVII

At last the tyrant cried, 'She hungers, slave,
1955   Stab her, or give her bread!' — It was a tone
Such as sick fancies in a new-made grave
Might hear. I trembled, for the truth was known,
He with this child had thus been left alone,
And neither had gone forth for food, — but he
1960   In mingled pride and awe cowered near his throne,
And she a nursling of captivity
Knew nought beyond those walls, nor what such change might be.

XXVIII

And he was troubled at a charm withdrawn
Thus suddenly; that sceptres ruled no more —
1965   That even from gold the dreadful strength was gone,
Which once made all things subject to its power —
Such wonder seized him, as if hour by hour
The past had come again; and the swift fall
Of one so great and terrible of yore,
1970   To desolateness, in the hearts of all
Like wonder stirred, who saw such awful change befall.

XXIX

A mighty crowd, such as the wide land pours
Once in a thousand years, now gathered round
The fallen tyrant; — like the rush of showers
1975   Of hail in spring, pattering along the ground,
Their many footsteps fell, else came no sound
From the wide multitude: that lonely man
Then knew the burden of his change, and found,
Concealing in the dust his visage wan,
1980   Refuge from the keen looks which through his bosom ran.

1964. *sceptres ruled no more*] Bryan Shelley, *Shelley and Scripture* (1994) 185 cites 'The Lord hath broken the staff of the wicked, and the sceptre of the rulers' (*Isaiah* xiv 5).

XXX

And he was faint withal: I sate beside him
Upon the earth, and took that child so fair
From his weak arms, that ill might none betide him
Or her; — when food was brought to them, her share
1985 To his averted lips the child did bear,
But when she saw he had enough, she ate
And wept the while; — the lonely man's despair
Hunger then overcame, and of his state
Forgetful, on the dust as in a trance he sate.

XXXI

1990 Slowly the silence of the multitudes
Passed, as when far is heard in some lone dell
The gathering of a wind among the woods —
'And he is fallen!' they cry, 'he who did dwell
Like famine or the plague, or aught more fell
1995 Among our homes, is fallen! the murderer
Who slaked his thirsting soul as from a well
Of blood and tears with ruin! he is here!
Sunk in a gulf of scorn from which none may him rear!'

XXXII

Then was heard — 'He who judged let him be brought
2000 To judgement! blood for blood cries from the soil
On which his crimes have deep pollution wrought!
Shall Othman only unavenged despoil?
Shall they who by the stress of grinding toil
Wrest from the unwilling earth his luxuries,
2005 Perish for crime, while his foul blood may boil,
Or creep within his veins at will? — Arise!
And to high justice make her chosen sacrifice.'

1988. his state] His rank, his greatness.

1993–8. The speech-marks are not present in *L&C/RofI.*

Stanzas xxxii–v. In these stanzas, ripe with biblical allusion, Laon quite explicitly re-enacts the role of Christ in the episode of the woman taken in adultery (*John* viii 3–11), setting mercy above retributive justice while introducing a secular appeal to nature (lines 2013–14) and virtue (lines 2023–5) as standards of right conduct.

1999–2007. The speech-marks are not present in *L&C/RofI.*

1999–2000. 'Judge not, that ye be not judged. For with what judgement ye judge, ye shall be judged' (*Matthew* vii 1–2; also *Luke* vi 37). 'What hast thou done? the voice of thy brother's blood crieth unto me from the ground' (*Genesis* iv 10). See lines 359–60 and note.

2002. Othman] See note on the title of the poem, on the revised title *The Revolt of Islam.*

XXXIII

'What do ye seek? what fear ye?' then I cried,
Suddenly starting forth, 'that ye should shed
2010   The blood of Othman — if your hearts are tried
In the true love of freedom, cease to dread
This one poor lonely man — beneath Heaven spread
In purest light above us all, through earth,
Maternal earth, who doth her sweet smiles shed
2015   For all, let him go free; until the worth
Of human nature win from these a second birth.

XXXIV

'What call ye *justice?* is there one who ne'er
In secret thought has wished another's ill? —
Are ye all pure? let those stand forth who hear,
2020   And tremble not. Shall they insult and kill,
If such they be? their mild eyes can they fill
With the false anger of the hypocrite?
Alas, such were not pure — the chastened will
Of virtue sees that justice is the light
2025   Of love, and not revenge, and terror and despite.'

XXXV

The murmur of the people slowly dying,
Paused as I spake, then those who near me were,
Cast gentle looks where the lone man was lying
Shrouding his head, which now that infant fair
2030   Clasped on her lap in silence; — through the air
Sobs were then heard, and many kissed my feet
In pity's madness, and to the despair
Of him whom late they cursed, a solace sweet
His very victims brought — soft looks and speeches meet.

2013. earth,] earth L&C/RofI; 1839 and later *eds* have supplied the comma. The draft in Nbk 3 is defective here.

2015–16. 'Until the benevolence of nature regenerate his inherent humanity'. Cp. *John* iii 3: 'Except a man be born again, he cannot see the kingdom of God'.

2017–20. 'He that is without sin among you, let him first cast a stone at her' (*John* viii 7); 'Who can say, I have made my heart clean, I am pure from my sin?' (*Proverbs* xx 9).

2031. kissed my feet] 'And [she] stood at his feet behind him weeping, and began to wash his feet with tears, and did wipe them with the hairs of her head, and kissed his feet' (*Luke* vii 38).

XXXVI

2035 Then to a home for his repose assigned,
Accompanied by the still throng he went
In silence, where to soothe his rankling mind,
Some likeness of his ancient state was lent;
And if his heart could have been innocent
2040 As those who pardoned him, he might have ended
His days in peace; but his straight lips were bent,
Men said, into a smile which guile portended,
A sight with which that child like hope with fear was blended.

XXXVII

'Twas midnight now, the eve of that great day
2045 Whereon the many nations at whose call
The chains of earth like mist melted away,
Decreed to hold a sacred Festival,
A rite to attest the equality of all
Who live. So to their homes, to dream or wake
2050 All went. The sleepless silence did recall
Laone to my thoughts, with hopes that make
The flood recede from which their thirst they seek to slake.

XXXVIII

The dawn flowed forth, and from its purple fountains
I drank those hopes which make the spirit quail;
2055 As to the plain between the misty mountains
And the great City, with a countenance pale
I went: — it was a sight which might avail
To make men weep exulting tears, for whom
Now first from human power the reverend veil

2038. ancient state] Former pomp and splendour.

2041. straight] Since *Rossetti 1870 eds* have expressed doubts about the appropriateness of the word, wondering whether it is a printer's error for 'strait', without going so far as to emend. Such an emendation would make the usage here consistent with the 'strait lips' of line 3610 which describe a similarly guileful expression of face, as does the 'strait lip' of *R&H* 426. (The draft in *Nbk 3* is defective at this point.) But that the tyrant's (normally) *straight lips* suggest 'the cruelty of a curveless mouth' (*Forman 1876–7*) may well be the sense intended.

2047. sacred Festival] The *festival* that begins in the next stanza combines elements of the historical *Fête de la Fédération* of 14 July 1790 and of the assembly of the people in *Ruins* xvi–xviii. See notes to lines 2072, 2074, 2076, 2156.

2051–2. One of the effects of the Rajah's curse on Ladurlad in Southey's *The Curse of Kehama* (1810) is that water shrinks from his touch; but as Duff notices in *Romance and Revolution* (1994) 164, the reference reaches back to the mythical punishment of Tantalus.

2060   Was torn, to see Earth from her general womb
               Pour forth her swarming sons to a fraternal doom:

XXXIX

               To see, far glancing in the misty morning,
               The signs of that innumerable host,
               To hear one sound of many made, the warning
2065   Of Earth to Heaven from its free children tossed,
               While the eternal hills, and the sea lost
               In wavering light, and, starring the blue sky
               The city's myriad spires of gold, almost
               With human joy made mute society,
2070   Its witnesses with men who must hereafter be.

XL

               To see like some vast island from the Ocean,
               The Altar of the Federation rear
               Its pile i' the midst; a work, which the devotion
               Of millions in one night created there,

2061. doom] The expansive gloss in *Locock 1911*, 'consummation of happiness', is repeated by *1975*; but the nature of the important episode which commences in this stanza is defined by both of the word's fundamental senses – 'destiny' and 'judgement'. As lines 2058–61 and 2064–5 show, such a spectacle of congregated human power as gathers before the city is accompanied by the awareness that its strength need no longer be attributed to a divine source removed in heaven but can now be relocated in human fraternity itself; this is the *fraternal doom* or destiny of those assembled. Furthermore, the words and images of the lines cited leave no doubt that S. presents the unfolding events as an alternative, in human time, to the 'Day of Doom' or Last Judgement. The specificity of this entry to the Golden City is its egalitarianism and comprehensiveness as opposed to the mysterious determinations of the divine will for inclusion and exclusion in the corresponding scene in *Revelation* xx–xxi.

2063. signs] S. first wrote 'standards' in the draft (*Nbk 3* 9) and that is the sense here.

2066–9. 'The surroundings themselves seemed nearly to join in the infectious joy'.

2070. S. had difficulty with the line in *Nbk 3* 9, leaving the draft incomplete and only including the idea of future men at a later stage. The sense is that the present scene will be a witness of the events taking place to generations to come, perhaps because men will remember the place where they happened. Locock thought that *Its* must refer to the 'warning' of line 2064; a likelier antecedent is 'human joy' in the previous line.

2072. Federation] A clear reference to one of the great public occasions of the French Revolution, the *Fête de la Fédération* which was held on 14 July 1790 on the Champ de Mars at the western outskirts of Paris to commemorate the first anniversary of the taking of the Bastille. The day featured a procession of soldiers, sailors and militiamen from the various departments of France which was joined by the royal family and members of the national assembly. In a great amphitheatre on the Champ de Mars high mass was celebrated on the symbolic centrepiece of the ceremonies, the 'autel de la patrie'. The king and deputies swore an oath to maintain the constitution to the acclamations of a crowd of several hundred thousand citizens.

2074. one night] S. is elevating to the level of poetic miracle the extraordinary collective effort of the citizens of Paris who presented themselves *en masse* to help the workers employed in the task construct the vast amphitheatre for the ceremonies of the Federation on time. See

2075   Sudden, as when the moonrise makes appear
         Strange clouds in the east; a marble pyramid
         Distinct with steps: that mighty shape did wear
         The light of genius; its still shadow hid
         Far ships: to know its height the morning mists forbid!

XLI

2080   To hear the restless multitudes forever
         Around the base of that great Altar flow,
         As on some mountain islet burst and shiver
         Atlantic waves; and solemnly and slow
         As the wind bore that tumult to and fro,
2085   To feel the dreamlike music, which did swim
         Like beams through floating clouds on waves below
         Falling in pauses, from that Altar dim
         As silver-sounding tongues breathed an aerial hymn.

XLII

         To hear, to see, to live, was on that morn
2090   Lethean joy! so that all those assembled
         Cast off their memories of the past outworn;
         Two only bosoms with their own life trembled,
         And mine was one, — and we had both dissembled;
         So with a beating heart I went, and one,
2095   Who having much, covets yet more, resembled;
         A lost and dear possession, which not won,
         He walks in lonely gloom beneath the noonday sun.

---

previous note. J. P. Rabaut (*Précis Historique de la Révolution Française* 6th edn 1813, 288) considered this the largest theatre ever built by the hand of man. In her *Letters Written in France* (1790) Helen Maria Williams reported: 'Twenty days labour, animated by the enthusiasm of the people, accomplished what seemed to require the toil of years' (6).

2076. pyramid] In *Ruins* xvi–xvii the people seat their chosen legislators on a throne in the form of a pyramid and place an altar before it dedicated to equal law. Cp. line 614 and note.

2077. Distinct with] See note to line 615.

Stanza xlii. Like III xxv–vii, this stanza marks a critical moment in the developing narrative of Laon's inner life. Commentary on it is provided by D. Duff, *Romance and Revolution* (1994) 162–5 and J. Donovan, *Shelley Revalued*, ed. T. Clark and J. Hogle (1995) 134–8.

2090. Lethean joy] In classical mythology Lethe is that river of Hades from which the dead must drink to forget their past lives on entering the underworld, or (as in *Aeneid* vi 703–51) from which souls drink to erase their memories before entering the world again in another body. See *R&H* 409 and note and *TL* 463.

2092. Two only bosoms] Laon and the estranged friend with whom he was reconciled in stanza v and upon whom he leans in stanza xlv.

2097. Appropriating a common biblical idiom to characterise the sinner, as in *Job* v 14: 'They meet with darkness in the daytime, and grope in the noonday as in the night'. Also *Psalms* xli 6, *Isaiah* lviii 10, etc.

XLIII

To the great Pyramid I came: its stair
With female choirs was thronged: the loveliest
2100   Among the free, grouped with its sculptures rare;
As I approached, the morning's golden mist,
Which now the wonder-stricken breezes kissed
With their cold lips, fled, and the summit shone
Like Athos seen from Samothracia, dressed
2105   In earliest light by vintagers, and one
Sate there, a female Shape upon an ivory throne.

XLIV

A Form most like the imagined habitant
Of silver exhalations sprung from dawn,
By winds which feed on sunrise woven, to enchant
2110   The faiths of men: all mortal eyes were drawn,
As famished mariners through strange seas gone
Gaze on a burning watch-tower, by the light
Of those divinest lineaments — alone
With thoughts which none could share, from that fair sight
2115   I turned in sickness, for a veil shrouded her countenance bright.

2099. female choirs] Round the altar of Venus in *Faerie Queene* IV x 48 'A beuie of fayre damzels close did lye, / Wayting when as the Antheme should be sung on hye'.

2104. Mount Athos rises some 2000 m. on the easternmost promontory of Chalcidice in the northern Aegean. Sacred to Zeus in ancient times, it was known in the Greece of S.'s day as the 'Holy Mountain' and was the site of several monasteries. Samothrace is an island some 100 km. to the east and north of Athos. E. D. Clarke's *Travels in Various Countries* (Part II, Section i 207–8 1817 edn) describes a view of Athos from Sigeum on the coast of Asia Minor over a distance of some 150 km. See note to lines 676, 753.

2105. vintagers] grape-harvesters; S. first wrote then cancelled 'mariners', no doubt to avoid repetition with line 2111.

2107–10. The *Form* resembles an imaginary being (a Shelleyan variant of the goddess of the dawn Aurora or Eos) given shape by the action of wind and sun on the *silver exhalations* ('the morning mists' of line 2079) of dawn and able to suspend as by enchantment the received religious beliefs of men.

2111–12. See lines 121–6 and note.

2115. a veil] The veil that preserves Laone's private identity as Cythna also functions to shield the face of the inspired prophet from general view as in *Exodus* xxxiv 32–5 where Moses veils his face after speaking with God on Mount Sinai. Other sources that S. may have recalled are: the Indian priestess Luxima in Sydney Owenson's [Lady Morgan's] novel *The Missionary* (1811), which he admired (*L* i 101, 107, 130), who is first 'distinctly seen through the transparent veil of the palanquin' (2nd edn i 78) in which she is carried; the statue of the goddess in the temple of Venus (*Faerie Queene* IV x 40) which is covered by a veil; the countenance of the statue of the goddess Nature in Erasmus Darwin's *The Temple of Nature* (1803) i 133.

XLV

And, neither did I hear the acclamations,
Which from brief silence bursting, filled the air
With her strange name and mine, from all the nations
Which we, they said, in strength had gathered there
2120   From the sleep of bondage; nor the vision fair
Of that bright pageantry beheld, — but blind
And silent, as a breathing corpse did fare,
Leaning upon my friend, till like a wind
To fevered cheeks, a voice flowed o'er my troubled mind.

XLVI

2125   Like music of some minstrel heavenly-gifted,
To one whom fiends enthral, this voice to me;
Scarce did I wish her veil to be uplifted,
I was so calm and joyous. — I could see
The platform where we stood, the statues three
2130   Which kept their marble watch on that high shrine,
The multitudes, the mountains, and the sea;
As when eclipse hath passed, things sudden shine
To men's astonished eyes most clear and crystalline.

XLVII

At first Laone spoke most tremulously:
2135   But soon her voice the calmness which it shed
Gathered, and — 'thou art whom I sought to see,
And thou art our first votary here,' she said:
'I had a brother once, but he is dead! —
And of all those on the wide earth who breathe,
2140   Thou dost resemble him alone — I spread
This veil between us two, that thou beneath
Shouldst image one who may have been long lost in death.

2118. *nations*] *RofI*; nations, *L&C*: alteration in cancel-leaf for *RofI*.

2122. *fare*] Advance, make my way.

2125–6. An allusion appears to be intended to Orpheus who, as the son of Calliope, chief of the nine muses whose hymns delighted the gods, was *heavenly-gifted*. His song not only liberated Eurydice from Hades but also temporarily suspended the punishment of celebrated sinners like Tantalus and Ixion (Virgil, *Georgics* iv 468–84; Ovid, *Metamorphoses* x 40–9). S. refers to his song as the 'heavenly offspring of ambrosial food' in *Orpheus* 66. The allusion signals that the role of inspired poet of liberty is about to pass to Cythna.

2129. *statues three*] See note to line 2156.

2138. *brother*] dear friend *RofI*. In *L&C* (PM) S. first replaced *brother* with 'lover', then deleted that and wrote in 'dear friend', perhaps to avoid repeating his substitution at line 1680. See note on that line.

XLVIII

'For this wilt thou not henceforth pardon me?
Yes, but those joys which silence well requite
2145   Forbid reply; — why men have chosen me
To be the Priestess of this holiest rite
I scarcely know, but that the floods of light
Which flow over the world, have borne me hither
To meet thee, long most dear; and now unite
2150   Thine hand with mine, and may all comfort wither
From both the hearts whose pulse in joy now beat together,

XLIX

'If our own will as others' law we bind,
If the foul worship trampled here we fear;
If as ourselves we cease to love our kind!' —
2155   She paused, and pointed upwards — sculptured there
Three shapes around her ivory throne appear;
One was a Giant, like a child asleep

2151. beat] beats *1839, Rossetti 1870, 1878.* See line 1233 and note for a similar case of lack of agreement between subject and verb. The draft in *Nbk 3* 15 is gramatically regular: 'From both the hearts whose blood in peace here throbs together', so that the possibility of an error of transcription or of printing cannot be excluded.

2152. S.'s cancelled draft in *Nbk 3* 15 glosses the line: 'If our own will we make another's law'; i.e. if we act as the deposed tyrant has done.

2153. See lines 2167–9. The idiom is that of Lucretius, *De Re. Nat.* i 78–9 praising the effects of Epicurus's philosophy: *quare religio pedibus subjecta vicissim / obteritur* (Wherefore Religion is now in her turn cast down and trampled underfoot; Loeb trans.).

2156. Three shapes] The motif of three emblematic sculptures S. appears to have adapted from Southey's *The Curse of Kehama* xxiii 14–15, xxiv 6 where three 'living statues' glowing with inward fire support a golden throne that stands before the seat of Yamen the Lord of Hell. The figures confess themselves damned for practices that can be summed up as avarice, tyranny and religious fraud respectively, each being the initiator of his particular vice. S. reported of a meeting with Southey in Keswick in late 1811 that 'he says he designs his three statues in Kehama to be contemplated with republican feelings – but not in this age' (*L* i 212). The social virtues symbolised by Cythna's three sculptures, unequivocally appealing to republican sentiments, are broadly the converse of the vices punished in Southey. Most commentators have agreed that the three figures represent Equality, Love and Wisdom – following the first three stanzas of Cythna's Ode where they are addressed in the reverse order. Cameron (*PMLA* lvi (1941) 178–80) notes that at the assembly of the people in *Ruins* xvii a standard is raised on which are inscribed the three principles of political renewal: Equality, Liberty, Justice. Volney's, Southey's, and Shelley's own triad all recall the Liberty, Equality, Fraternity of the French Revolution.

2157. Giant] The figure conspicuously revises that of the Giant in *Faerie Queene* V ii 30–50 who addresses levelling doctrines to an assembled crowd, advocating a return to natural equality in all things including the political order: 'Tyrants that make men subiect to their law, / I will suppresse, that they no more may raine' (line 38). The giant is opposed by Sir Artegall,

2160

On a loose rock, whose grasp crushed, as it were
In dream, sceptres and crowns; and one did keep
Its watchful eyes in doubt whether to smile or weep;

L

2165

A Woman sitting on the sculptured disk
Of the broad earth, and feeding from one breast
A human babe and a young basilisk;
Her looks were sweet as Heaven's when loveliest
In Autumn eves. — The third Image was dressed
In white wings swift as clouds in winter skies,
Beneath his feet, 'mongst ghastliest forms, repressed
Lay Faith, an obscene worm, who sought to rise,
While calmly on the Sun he turned his diamond eyes.

---

the champion of Justice, who defends the equity of a divinely-instituted hierarchy throughout nature: 'He maketh Kings to sit in souerainty; / He maketh subiects to their powre obay' (line 41). In Spenser's poem the Giant's views appeal only to the foolish, and he is eventually pushed into the sea and drowned by the iron man Talus. S. wrote to Peacock in January 1819 of his desire to: 'cast what weight I can into the right scale of that balance which the Giant (of Arthegall) holds'. Peacock recalled S. remarking on this passage: ' "Artegall argues with the Giant; the Giant has the best of the argument; Artegall's iron man knocks him over into the sea and drowns him. This is the usual way in which power deals with opinion". I said: "That was not the lesson which Spenser intended to convey". "Perhaps not", he said; "it is the lesson which he conveys to me. I am of the Giant's faction" ' (L ii 71). S. may also be remembering the terms of the ironic analogy for the supposed restraint with which kings have exercised their power in The Examiner No. 484 (6 April 1817) 209: 'They have a giant's strength, but they use it like a child'.

2158. loose rock] The Giant in Faerie Queene stands 'Vpon a rocke' by the seashore (V ii 30). The sense of loose is not perfectly clear. Concordance suggests 'detached from the mass', presumably a single rock that is not part of a group or chain, and this would appear to be what is intended.

2159. one] The Woman of line 2161.

2163. basilisk] A fabulous reptile, also known as a 'cockatrice'; reputed to be hatched by a serpent from a cock's egg, its breath and look were supposed to be venomous. Its title of 'king of snakes' was derived from a mark on its forehead said to resemble a crown: in the draft S. first wrote 'the crowned basilisk' (Nbk 3 16). An allusion is intended to Isaiah xi which describes the age of peace that will be brought about by the 'rod out of the stem of Jesse': 'And the sucking child shall play on the hole of the asp, and the weaned child shall put his hand on the cockatrice' den' (8). See Q Mab viii 84–7 and note.

2165–9. The third sculpture, recalling both the archangel Michael's defeat of Satan and St George's slaying of the dragon, is a traditional image of religious victory turned against Faith.

2169. diamond eyes] S. may be recalling the idol of Jaggernaut, described as having the shape of a serpent with seven heads in the notes to Southey's The Curse of Kehama (1810) XIV (Jaga-Naut) and as having diamond eyes in the initial prose section (and note) of Thomas Moore's Lalla Rookh (1817).

LI

2170 Beside that Image then I sate, while she
Stood, mid the throngs which ever ebbed and flowed
Like light amid the shadows of the sea
Cast from one cloudless star, and on the crowd
That touch which none who feels forgets, bestowed;
2175 And whilst the sun returned the steadfast gaze
Of the great Image as o'er Heaven it glode,
That rite had place; it ceased when sunset's blaze
Burned o'er the isles; all stood in joy and deep amaze,
When in the silence of all spirits there
2180 Laone's voice was felt, and through the air
Her thrilling gestures spoke, most eloquently fair.

1

'Calm art thou as yon sunset! swift and strong
As new-fledged Eagles, beautiful and young,
That float among the blinding beams of morning;
2185 And underneath thy feet writhe Faith, and Folly,
Custom, and Hell, and mortal Melancholy —
Hark! the Earth starts to hear the mighty warning
Of thy voice sublime and holy;
Its free spirits here assembled,
2190 See thee, feel thee, know thee now, —
To thy voice their hearts have trembled

Stanza li. This twelve-line stanza extending the regular Spenserian stanza by a triplet of 2 iambic pentameter lines plus an alexandrine has been variously treated by *eds.* Nearly all have removed or weakened the full stop at the end of line 2178 in *L&C/RofI* to mark a syntax that continues to the end of line 2181. A comma has been substituted here. *1839, Rossetti 1870, Forman 1876–7* and *Locock 1911* leave a space after line 2178, so setting off the final three lines as tail-piece to stanza li and as introduction to the lyric ode following. In *L&C/RofI* the regular ninth line finishes a page, the remaining three lines coming at the top of the following page so that no division is evident; nor is any shown in the draft (*Nbk 3* 16–17).

2181. eloquently fair] Cythna's public role and performance recall the improvisation of verses on Italian history and literature delivered on the Capitol in Rome to great applause by the eponymous female poet of Italian renewal in Madame de Staël's novel *Corinne* (1807) II iii. MWS was reading *Corinne* in February–March 1815 (*Mary Jnl* i 66–8). S. refers to the novel in December 1818 (*L* ii 68); *Mary Jnl* i 243 records his reading of it on 13–15 December 1818. S. may also be remembering the Fête de la Raison celebrated in Notre Dame on 10 November 1793 at which a female singer from the Opéra impersonated the goddess Reason and a hymn to Liberty was sung.

Ode: 2182–271. The six 15-line stanzas of Cythna's Ode follow the syllabic pattern: $6 \times 10 + 6 \times 8 + 2 \times 10 + 1 \times 12$, lines 7–12 of each stanza being indented. Stanza 5 is an exception: the last four lines = $3 \times 10 + 1 \times 12$. In *L&C/RofI* the 10-syllable line 2209 is incorrectly indented and the 8-syllable lines 2248, 2263 and 2268 incorrectly set flush with the left margin; they have been set regularly here, and a full stop supplied at the end of line 2196.

Like ten thousand clouds which flow
With one wide wind as it flies! —
Wisdom! thy irresistible children rise
2195   To hail thee, and the elements they chain
And their own will to swell the glory of thy train.

2

'O Spirit vast and deep as Night and Heaven!
Mother and soul of all to which is given
The light of life, the loveliness of being,
2200   Lo! thou dost reascend the human heart,
Thy throne of power, almighty as thou wert,
In dreams of Poets old grown pale by seeing
    The shade of thee: — now, millions start
    To feel thy lightnings through them burning:
2205   Nature, or God, or Love, or Pleasure,
    Or Sympathy the sad tears turning
    To mutual smiles, a drainless treasure,
    Descends amidst us; — Scorn, and Hate,
Revenge and Selfishness are desolate —
2210   A hundred nations swear that there shall be
Pity and Peace and Love, among the good and free!

3

'Eldest of things, divine Equality!
Wisdom and Love are but the slaves of thee,
The Angels of thy sway, who pour around thee
2215   Treasures from all the cells of human thought,
And from the Stars, and from the Ocean brought,
And the last living heart whose beatings bound thee:
    The powerful and the wise had sought
    Thy coming, thou in light descending
2220   O'er the wide land which is thine own
    Like the spring whose breath is blending

2195. *chain*] Control, direct.

2199. *light of life*] 'He that followeth me shall not walk in darkness, but shall have the light of life' (*John* viii 12).

2207. *drainless*] Inexhaustible.

2212. *Equality*] S. is following *Ruins* xvii where Equality is established as the first principle of all right and law. The difference from the narrative of origins in *Ahrimanes*, where Equality develops after the appearance of Love, is one of S.'s important departures from his principal source. See *Ahrimanes* I xix–xx; Shorter Verse Fragment iii–vi (*Peacock Works* vii 272–3, 423–4). See note to I xxv–vi.

2217. 'The remotest human heart on the utmost limits of thy sway' (*Locock 1911*).

All blasts of fragrance into one,
Comest upon the paths of men! —
Earth bares her general bosom to thy ken,
2225   And all her children here in glory meet
To feed upon thy smiles, and clasp thy sacred feet.

4

'My brethren, we are free! the plains and mountains,
The grey sea-shore, the forests and the fountains,
Are haunts of happiest dwellers; — man and woman,
2230   Their common bondage burst, may freely borrow
From lawless love a solace for their sorrow;
For oft we still must weep, since we are human.
    A stormy night's serenest morrow,
    Whose showers are pity's gentle tears,
2235   Whose clouds are smiles of those that die
    Like infants without hopes or fears,
    And whose beams are joys that lie
    In blended hearts, now holds dominion;
The dawn of mind, which upwards on a pinion
2240   Borne, swift as sunrise, far illumines space,
And clasps this barren world in its own bright embrace!

5

'My brethren, we are free! the fruits are glowing
Beneath the stars, and the night-winds are flowing
O'er the ripe corn, the birds and beasts are dreaming —
2245   Never again may blood of bird or beast
Stain with its venomous stream a human feast,
To the pure skies in accusation steaming,
    Avenging poisons shall have ceased
    To feed disease and fear and madness,

2227. brethren,] brethren *L&C/RofI*. The comma is supplied in conformity with the one in line 2242.

2231. lawless love] Love that knows no law but itself. Cp. Preface, lines 254–5 'Love is celebrated everywhere as the sole law which should govern the moral world'.

2245–52. S. set out his convictions on the benefits of a vegetable diet and the baneful physical and moral effects of animal food in the pamphlet *A Vindication of Natural Diet* (1813) and the MS essay 'On the Vegetable System of Diet' (1814–15?): *Prose Works* i 77–91, 147–55, as well as in *Q Mab* viii 70 ff. and note to 211–12. See also Timothy Morton, *Shelley and the Revolution in Taste* (1994) 110–16.

2247. The image is to be set against the frequent burnt sacrifices offered to God in the Old Testament, especially perhaps that of Noah in *Genesis* viii 21–2 at which 'the Lord smelled a sweet savour' and was pleased.

2250   The dwellers of the earth and air
    Shall throng around our steps in gladness
    Seeking their food or refuge there.
Our toil from thought all glorious forms shall cull,
To make this Earth, our home, more beautiful,
2255 And Science, and her sister Poesy,
Shall clothe in light the fields and cities of the free!

6

'Victory, Victory to the prostrate nations!
Bear witness Night, and ye mute Constellations
Who gaze on us from your cràstàlline cars!
2260 Thoughts have gone forth whose powers can sleep no more!
Victory! Victory! Earth's remotest shore,
Regions which groan beneath the Antarctic stars,
    The green lands cradled in the roar
    Of western waves, and wildernesses
2265 Peopled and vast, which skirt the oceans
    Where morning dyes her golden tresses,
    Shall soon partake our high emotions:
    Kings shall turn pale! Almighty Fear
The Fiend-God, when our charmèd name he hear,
2270 Shall fade like shadow from his thousand fanes,
While Truth with Joy enthroned o'er his lost empire reigns!'

LII

Ere she had ceased, the mists of night entwining
Their dim woof, floated o'er the infinite throng;
She, like a spirit through the darkness shining,
2275 In tones whose sweetness silence did prolong,
As if to lingering winds they did belong,
Poured forth her inmost soul: a passionate speech
With wild and thrilling pauses woven among,
Which whoso heard, was mute, for it could teach
2280 To rapture like her own all listening hearts to reach.

2250–2. Cp. the poet in *Alastor*: 'the doves and squirrels would partake / From his innocuous hand his bloodless food' (100–1).

2255. In the *The Temple of Nature* (1803) i 422 Erasmus Darwin describes as 'virgin Sisters' the two imaginary narrators of the poem: Urania the priestess of Nature (who offers a distinctly scientific survey of the goddess she serves) and the Muse of Poetry. S. may also be remembering the relations established between the Poet and the Man of Science in Wordsworth's Preface to *Lyrical Ballads* (1800). He developed the relation fully in *DP*.

LIII

Her voice was as a mountain stream which sweeps
The withered leaves of Autumn to the lake,
And in some deep and narrow bay then sleeps
In the shadow of the shores; as dead leaves wake
2285   Under the wave, in flowers and herbs which make
Those green depths beautiful when skies are blue,
The multitude so moveless did partake
Such living change, and kindling murmurs flew
As o'er that speechless calm delight and wonder grew.

LIV

2290   Over the plain the throngs were scattered then
In groups around the fires, which from the sea
Even to the gorge of the first mountain glen
Blazed wide and far: the banquet of the free
Was spread beneath many a dark cypress tree,
2295   Beneath whose spires, which swayed in the red flame,
Reclining as they ate, of Liberty,
And Hope, and Justice, and Laone's name,
Earth's children did a woof of happy converse frame.

LV

Their feast was such as Earth, the general mother,
2300   Pours from her fairest bosom, when she smiles
In the embrace of Autumn; — to each other
As when some parent fondly reconciles
Her warring children, she their wrath beguiles
With her own sustenance; they relenting weep:
2305   Such was this Festival, which from their isles
And continents, and winds, and oceans deep,
All shapes might throng to share, that fly, or walk, or creep.

Stanza liii. Cythna's words first clear away then renew the thoughts of the multitude as a stream carries the fallen leaves of autumn to the lake where in spring, though they lie motionless at the bottom, plants shoot up among them.

2287. so] Just in this way.

2295. flame] light *L&C/RofI*. Most *eds* have emended to *flame* because of the necessity of rhyme. In the draft S. first wrote 'light', then cancelled it and substituted 'flames', later cancelling the 's' to rhyme with the last two lines of the stanza (*Nbk 3* 26). The cancelled word 'light' was evidently transcribed into the fair copy for the printer, survived proof-reading and does not appear in the Errata list even though this includes the error 'their' for *her* in line 2304 of the next stanza.

2306. oceans] ocean's *Rossetti 1870, 1878; Dowden 1891*. The draft (*Nbk 3* 27) reads 'And continents, the winds & clouds & Deep'. S.'s first thought was a singular noun, so that an error of transcription or printing cannot be ruled out.

LVI

Might share in peace and innocence, for gore
Or poison none this festal did pollute,
2310 But piled on high, an overflowing store
Of pomegranates, and citrons, fairest fruit,
Melons, and dates, and figs, and many a root
Sweet and sustaining, and bright grapes ere yet
Accursèd fire their mild juice could transmute
2315 Into a mortal bane, and brown corn set
In baskets; with pure streams their thirsting lips they wet.

LVII

Laone had descended from the shrine,
And every deepest look and holiest mind
Fed on her form, though now those tones divine
2320 Were silent as she passed; she did unwind
Her veil, as with the crowds of her own kind
She mixed; some impulse made my heart refrain
From seeking her that night, so I reclined
Amidst a group, where on the utmost plain
2325 A festal watch-fire burned beside the dusky main.

LVIII

And joyous was our feast; pathetic talk,
And wit, and harmony of choral strains,
While far Orion o'er the waves did walk
That flow among the isles, held us in chains
2330 Of sweet captivity, which none disdains
Who feels: but when his zone grew dim in mist
Which clothes the Ocean's bosom, o'er the plains
The multitudes went homeward, to their rest,
Which that delightful day with its own shadow blessed.

2309. *festal*] Feast, festival.

2315. *mortal bane*] 'How many thousands have become murderers and robbers, bigots and domestic tyrants, dissolute and abandoned adventurers, from the use of fermented liquors' (*A Vindication of Natural Diet* (1813): *Prose Works* 82).

2316. *pure streams*] 'Who will assert, that had the populace of Paris drank at the pure source of the Seine, and satisfied their hunger at the ever-furnished table of vegetable nature, that they would have lent their brutal suffrage to the proscription-list of Robespierre?' (*Prose Works* 82: see previous note).

2326. *pathetic*] Passionate, affecting.

2328. *Orion*] That the hunter of the constellation Orion should preside over a vegetarian feast is an irony that is prophetic of the carnage to come in the next canto. See note to lines 1389–90.

Canto Sixth

I

2335   Beside the dimness of the glimmering sea,
    Weaving swift language from impassioned themes,
    With that dear friend I lingered, who to me
    So late had been restored, beneath the gleams
    Of the silver stars; and ever in soft dreams
2340   Of future love and peace sweet converse lapped
    Our willing fancies, till the pallid beams
    Of the last watch-fire fell, and darkness wrapped
    The waves, and each bright chain of floating fire was snapped.

II

    And till we came even to the City's wall
2345   And the great gate, then, none knew whence or why,
    Disquiet on the multitudes did fall:
    And first, one pale and breathless passed us by,
    And stared and spoke not; — then with piercing cry
    A troop of wild-eyed women, by the shrieks
2350   Of their own terror driven, — tumultuously
    Hither and thither hurrying with pale cheeks,
    Each one from fear unknown a sudden refuge seeks —

III

    Then, rallying cries of treason and of danger
    Resounded: and — 'they come! to arms! to arms!
2355   The Tyrant is amongst us, and the stranger

2337. dear friend] The youth from whom Laon had become estranged (820–8) and with whom he was reconciled (1744–64).

2343–5. Since *Rossetti 1870 eds* have commonly substituted a weaker stop after *snapped* to mark the continuation of the adverbial clause that begins with *till* (2341) across the two stanzas, and replaced the comma after *gate* with a semicolon or full stop. Such interventions, aiming to smooth and regularise the syntax, have masked the larger ellipsis in sense between the stanzas. The draft in *Nbk 3* (29) shows that S. hesitated whether to begin the new canto with the conversation between Laon and his friend or with the approach of the patriots to the city walls. He wrote and cancelled, 'We came in joy to where the city gates'; then, after beginning the conversation, imagined that it 'Beguiled our joyous way', which he also cancelled before finishing the stanza as though set on the seashore in the enveloping darkness. He must have had this second cancelled phrase in mind as he composed the first line and a half of stanza II which carries on the narrative the following morning as if from some earlier progress of the patriots towards the city walls. The number (190) of the second stanza in the draft sequence is cancelled and a heavy X written in ink beside it, apparently S.'s reminder to himself to revise. In the event, it was printed essentially as drafted, and the punctuation of *L&C/RofI*, although awkward, accurately reflects the resulting abruptness of the transition.

2355. stranger] Foreigner.

Comes to enslave us in his name! to arms!'
In vain: for Panic, the pale fiend who charms
Strength to forswear her right, those millions swept
Like waves before the tempest — these alarms
2360   Came to me, as to know their cause I leapt
On the gate's turret, and in rage and grief and scorn I wept!

IV

For to the North I saw the town on fire,
And its red light made morning pallid now,
Which burst over wide Asia; — louder, higher,
2365   The yells of victory and the screams of woe
I heard approach, and saw the throng below
Stream through the gates like foam-wrought waterfalls
Fed from a thousand storms — the fearful glow
Of bombs flares overhead — at intervals
2370   The red artillery's bolt mangling among them falls.

V

And now the horsemen come — and all was done
Swifter than I have spoken — I beheld
Their red swords flash in the unrisen sun.
I rushed among the rout to have repelled
2375   That miserable flight — one moment quelled
By voice, and looks, and eloquent despair,
As if reproach from their own hearts withheld
Their steps, they stood; but soon came pouring there
New multitudes, and did those rallied bands o'erbear.

VI

2380   I strove, as drifted on some cataract
By irresistible streams, some wretch might strive
Who hears its fatal roar: — the files compact
Whelmed me, and from the gate availed to drive
With quickening impulse, as each bolt did rive

2358. *millions*] Multitudes.

2361. The line is a foot too long.

2369. *bombs*] Explosive shells.

2370. *red artillery's bolt*] The phrase may involve a transferred epithet = 'the artillery's red bolt', i.e. a red-hot projectile shot from a cannon; or it may describe the flash of the cannon at a distance as in Thomas Campbell's *Hohenlinden* (1802) 10–11: 'And louder than the bolts of heaven / Far flashed the red artillery', which S. is perhaps recalling.

2374. *to have repelled*] *Locock 1911* glosses 'To repel at once', taking the phrase as a Latin idiom; *1975* prefers 'thinking to repel'. The intention to repel is the principal sense.

2385   Their ranks with bloodier chasm: — into the plain
        Disgorged at length the dead and the alive
        In one dread mass, were parted, and the stain
        Of blood, from mortal steel fell o'er the fields like rain.

VII

        For now the despot's bloodhounds with their prey,
2390   Unarmed and unaware, were gorging deep
        Their gluttony of death; the loose array
        Of horsemen o'er the wide fields murdering sweep,
        And with loud laughter for their tyrant reap
        A harvest sown with other hopes, the while,
2395   Far overhead, ships from Propontis keep
        A killing rain of fire: — when the waves smile
        As sudden earthquakes light many a volcano isle.

VIII

        Thus sudden, unexpected feast was spread
        For the carrion fowls of Heaven. — I saw the sight —
2400   I moved — I lived — as o'er the heaps of dead,
        Whose stony eyes glared in the morning light
        I trod; — to me there came no thought of flight,
        But with loud cries of scorn which whoso heard

2390. unaware] Not having been warned.

2395. Propontis] The ancient Gk name for the Sea of Marmara which links Constantinople with the Aegean to the west. In the draft S. first wrote 'Euxine', the ancient Gk name for the Black Sea to the east of the city.

2396. a killing rain of fire] *Forman 1876–7* attributes the incongruous tactics of having the Ottoman cavalry engage the enemy at close quarters while its ships continue to bombard the field to the 'ardour of his [S.'s] narration'. Cp. lines 2455–9.

2396–7. The lines are at first sight puzzling and have been much emended. *Forman 1876–7, Dowden 1891, Woodberry 1893, Hutchinson,* and *1975* substitute a comma for the full stop at the end of line 2397, stressing in this way the analogy between sudden earthquakes and the *unexpected feast* of line 2398. But the terms of the double simile clearly compare the smiling waves to the laughing horsemen of line 2393 and the earthquakes to the fiery bolts of the artillery passing through the air and striking the ground (line 2396). Cp. lines 2370, 2496. This would be more clearly evident if the positions of *when* and *As* were reversed, but is clear enough on consideration. *Hutchinson's* conjecture that *light* could be a misprint for 'lift' might gain support in *Ode to Liberty* (line 125): 'Like rocks which fire lifts out of the flat deep'. But the draft in *Nbk 3* 33 reads 'light', giving an image drawn, like the one in *Ode to Liberty*, from contemporary geological science. S. could have read in Erasmus Darwin, *The Temple of Nature* (Additional Note III to i 322) of the primeval earthquakes which convulsed the globe, then covered entirely by the sea, in order to release the energy generated by the subterranean fires: 'Next when imprison'd fires in central caves / Burst the firm earth, and drank the headlong waves; / And, as new airs with dread explosion swell, / Form'd lava-isles, and continents of shell'. Cp. line 1728 (and note).

2399. sight –] *1839*; sight *L&C/RofI.* Most *eds* have followed 1839 in supplying a dash here.

That dreaded death, felt in his veins the might
2405 Of virtuous shame return, the crowd I stirred,
And desperation's hope in many hearts recurred.

IX

A band of brothers gathering round me, made,
Although unarmed, a steadfast front, and still
Retreating, with stern looks beneath the shade
2410 Of gathered eyebrows, did the victors fill
With doubt even in success; deliberate will
Inspired our growing troop, not overthrown
It gained the shelter of a grassy hill,
And ever still our comrades were hewn down,
2415 And their defenceless limbs beneath our footsteps strown.

X

Immovably we stood — in joy I found,
Beside me then, firm as a giant pine
Among the mountain vapours driven around,
The old man whom I loved — his eyes divine
2420 With a mild look of courage answered mine,
And my young friend was near, and ardently
His hand grasped mine a moment — now the line
Of war extended, to our rallying cry
As myriads flocked in love and brotherhood to die.

XI

2425 For ever while the sun was climbing Heaven
The horsemen hewed our unarmed myriads down
Safely, though when by thirst of carnage driven
Too near, those slaves were swiftly overthrown
By hundreds leaping on them: — flesh and bone
2430 Soon made our ghastly ramparts; then the shaft
Of the artillery from the sea was thrown

2407. *band of brothers*] Alluding to *Henry V* IV iii 60–2: 'We few, we happy few, we band of brothers. / For he today that sheds his blood with me / Shall be my brother'.

2419. *old man*] The hermit of Cantos III and IV.

2421. *friend*] See note to line 2337.

2426. *horsemen*] *1839, Rossetti 1870, 1878*; horseman *L&C/RofI. Locock 1911* and *1975* defend 'horseman' as classical usage. The pencil-draft in *Nbk 3* (33) is very difficult to decipher, *1975* deciding 'horseman' to be the probable reading and *BSM* xvii opting for 'horsemen'. The occurrence of 'horsemen' in lines 2371, 2392 and later in 3885, as well as the awkward reference of *those slaves* (line 2428) and *conquerors* (line 2432) to a grammatically singular noun support the emendation.

More fast and fiery, and the conquerors laughed
In pride to hear the wind our screams of torment waft.

XII

For on one side alone the hill gave shelter,
2435 So vast that phalanx of unconquered men,
And there the living in the blood did welter
Of the dead and dying, which, in that green glen
Like stifled torrents, made a plashy fen
Under the feet — thus was the butchery waged
2440 While the sun clomb Heaven's eastern steep — but when
It 'gan to sink — a fiercer combat raged,
For in more doubtful strife the armies were engaged.

XIII

Within a cave upon the hill were found
A bundle of rude pikes, the instrument
2445 Of those who war but on their native ground
For natural rights: a shout of joyance sent
Even from our hearts the wide air pierced and rent,
As those few arms the bravest and the best
Seized, and each sixth, thus armed, did now present
2450 A line which covered and sustained the rest,
A confident phalanx, which the foes on every side invest.

XIV

That onset turned the foes to flight almost
But soon they saw their present strength, and knew
That coming night would to our resolute host
2455 Bring victory, so dismounting close they drew
Their glittering files, and then the combat grew
Unequal but most horrible; — and ever
Our myriads, whom the swift bolt overthrew,
Or the red sword, failed like a mountain river
2460 Which rushes forth in foam to sink in sands forever.

XV

Sorrow and shame, to see with their own kind
Our human brethren mix, like beasts of blood
To mutual ruin armed by one behind

2451. The line is a foot too long; in the draft in *Nbk 3* (37) it is marked with two Xs as if
for later correction. *invest*] hem in.

2463. *one behind*] The tyrant Othman: see lines 2039–42.

Who sits and scoffs! — That friend so mild and good,
2465 Who like its shadow near my youth had stood,
Was stabbed! — my old preserver's hoary hair
With the flesh clinging to its roots, was strewed
Under my feet! — I lost all sense or care,
And like the rest I grew desperate and unaware.

XVI

2470 The battle became ghastlier — in the midst
I paused, and saw, how ugly and how fell
O Hate! thou art, even when thy life thou shed'st
For love. The ground in many a little dell
Was broken, up and down whose steeps befell
2475 Alternate victory and defeat, and there
The combatants with rage most horrible
Strove, and their eyes started with cracking stare,
And impotent their tongues they lolled into the air,

XVII

Flaccid and foamy, like a mad dog's hanging;
2480 Want, and Moon-madness, and the pest's swift Bane
When its shafts smite — while yet its bow is twanging —
Have each their mark and sign — some ghastly stain;
And this was thine, O War! of hate and pain
Thou loathèd slave. I saw all shapes of death
2485 And ministered to many, o'er the plain
While carnage in the sunbeam's warmth did seethe,
Till twilight o'er the east wove her serenest wreath.

XVIII

The few who yet survived, resolute and firm
Around me fought. At the decline of day
2490 Winding above the mountain's snowy term
New banners shone: they quivered in the ray
Of the sun's unseen orb — ere night the array
Of fresh troops hemmed us in — of those brave bands
I soon survived alone — and now I lay
2495 Vanquished and faint, the grasp of bloody hands
I felt, and saw on high the glare of falling brands:

2469. *unaware*] Reckless.

2480. *Moon-madness*] 'Intermittent insanity such as was formerly supposed to be brought about by the changes of the moon' (*OED* Lunacy 1).

XIX

When on my foes a sudden terror came,
And they fled, scattering — lo! with reinless speed
A black Tartarian horse of giant frame
2500 Comes trampling over the dead, the living bleed
Beneath the hoofs of that tremendous steed,
On which, like to an Angel, robed in white,
Sate one waving a sword; — the hosts recede
And fly, as through their ranks with awful might,
2505 Sweeps in the shadow of eve that Phantom swift and bright;

XX

And its path made a solitude. — I rose
And marked its coming: it relaxed its course
As it approached me, and the wind that flows
Through night, bore accents to mine ear whose force
2510 Might create smiles in death — the Tartar horse
Paused, and I saw the shape its might which swayed,
And heard her musical pants, like the sweet source
Of waters in the desert, as she said,
'Mount with me Laon, now' — I rapidly obeyed.

XXI

2515 Then: 'Away! away!' she cried, and stretched her sword
As 'twere a scourge over the courser's head,
And lightly shook the reins: — We spake no word
But like the vapour of the tempest fled
Over the plain; her dark hair was dispread
2520 Like the pine's locks upon the lingering blast;
Over mine eyes its shadowy strings it spread
Fitfully, and the hills and streams fled fast,
As o'er their glimmering forms the steed's broad shadow passed.

XXII

And his hoofs ground the rocks to fire and dust,
2525 His strong sides made the torrents rise in spray,

2498. *reinless*] Unrestrained. The horse is controlled by reins (line 2517) unlike the super-
natural 'reinless steed' in Southey's *Thalaba the Destroyer* (1801; vi 9, vol. ii 11 in 1801 edn)
which has no bridle and takes its own course.

2499. *Tartarian*] Of Tartary not of Tartarus as lines 2510, 2558–9 and 2714 indicate.

2502–3. For the image of an angel mounted on a horse and brandishing a sword S. seems
to have combined details from *Revelation* vi 5, 8; xix 11–16.

2519. *dispread*] Spread wide, spread out.

2521. *strings*] Strands.

And turbulence, as of a whirlwind's gust
Surrounded us; — and still away! away!
Through the desert night we sped, while she alway
Gazed on a mountain which we neared, whose crest
2530 Crowned with a marble ruin, in the ray
Of the obscure stars gleamed; — its rugged breast
The steed strained up, and then his impulse did arrest.

XXIII

A rocky hill which overhung the Ocean: —
From that lone ruin, when the steed that panted
2535 Paused, might be heard the murmur of the motion
Of waters, as in spots forever haunted
By the choicest winds of Heaven, which are enchanted
To music, by the wand of Solitude,
That wizard wild, and the far tents implanted
2540 Upon the plain, be seen by those who stood
Thence marking the dark shore of Ocean's curvèd flood.

XXIV

One moment these were heard and seen — another
Passed; and the two who stood beneath that night,
Each only heard, or saw, or felt the other;
2545 As from the lofty steed she did alight,
Cythna, (for, from the eyes whose deepest light
Of love and sadness made my lips feel pale
With influence strange of mournfullest delight,
My own sweet sister looked), with joy did quail,
2550 And felt her strength in tears of human weakness fail.

XXV

And, for a space in my embrace she rested,
Her head on my unquiet heart reposing,
While my faint arms her languid frame invested:
At length she looked on me, and half unclosing

2530–1. The cancelled draft reads: 'In the pale starlight showed in thier [sic] decay / Seven columns' (*Nbk 3* 41).

2536–9. *as . . . wild*] The phrase is parenthetical.

2539–40. The cancelled draft reads: 'And the cries might be heard of those who daunted / By our ?[coming]' (*Nbk 3* 41).

2541. *Thence marking*] 'Observing from the hill' (*Locock 1911*).

2549. *sister*] Cythna *RofI*.

2553. *invested*] Enfolded.

2555   Her tremulous lips, said: 'Friend, thy bands were losing
        The battle, as I stood before the King
        In bonds. — I burst them then, and swiftly choosing
        The time, did seize a Tartar's sword, and spring
        Upon his horse, and swift as on the whirlwind's wing,

XXVI

2560   'Have thou and I been borne beyond pursuer,
        And we are here.' — Then turning to the steed,
        She pressed the white moon on his front with pure
        And rose-like lips, and many a fragrant weed
        From the green ruin plucked, that he might feed; —
2565   But I to a stone seat that Maiden led,
        And kissing her fair eyes, said, 'Thou hast need
        Of rest,' and I heaped up the courser's bed
        In a green mossy nook, with mountain flowers dispread.

XXVII

        Within that ruin, where a shattered portal
2570   Looks to the eastern stars, abandoned now
        By man, to be the home of things immortal,
        Memories, like awful ghosts which come and go,
        And must inherit all he builds below,
        When he is gone, a hall stood; o'er whose roof
2575   Fair clinging weeds with ivy pale did grow,
        Clasping its grey rents with a verdurous woof,
        A hanging dome of leaves, a canopy moon-proof.

XXVIII

        The autumnal winds, as if spellbound, had made
        A natural couch of leaves in that recess,
2580   Which seasons none disturbed, but in the shade
        Of flowering parasites, did spring love to dress

2568. See note to line 2519.

2575. ivy] Traditionally regarded as sacred to Bacchus, ivy is commonly associated with erotic experience in S.'s poetry; e.g., *PU* II ii 24–40 (and notes); *The Witch of Atlas* 533–6. S. appears to be chiefly indebted to Spenser for the connection: see Carlos Baker, *MLQ* iv (June 1943) 205–8.

2577. moon-proof] On a mountain sacred to Venus in the Garden of Adonis (*Faerie Queene* III vi 44) is an arbour 'With wanton yuie twyne entrayld athwart, / And Eglantine, and Caprifole emong, / Fashiond aboue within their inmost part, / That nether *Phoebus* beams could through them throng, / Nor *Aeolus* sharp blast could worke them any wrong'.

2580–4. A virtual image: the narrative voice imagines the operation of nature in spring rather than defining the season of narration.

2581. parasites] Climbing plants; see note to *Q Mab* i 43.

With their sweet blooms the wintry loneliness
Of those dead leaves, shedding their stars, whene'er
The wandering wind her nurslings might caress;
2585 Whose intertwining fingers ever there,
Made music wild and soft that filled the listening air.

XXIX

We know not where we go, or what sweet dream
May pilot us through caverns strange and fair
Of far and pathless passion, while the stream
2590 Of life, our bark doth on its whirlpools bear,
Spreading swift wings as sails to the dim air;
Nor should we seek to know, so the devotion
Of love and gentle thoughts be heard still there
Louder and louder from the utmost Ocean
2595 Of universal life, attuning its commotion.

XXX

To the pure all things are pure! Oblivion wrapped
Our spirits, and the fearful overthrow
Of public hope was from our being snapped,
Though linkèd years had bound it there; for now
2600 A power, a thirst, a knowledge, which below
All thoughts, like light beyond the atmosphere,
Clothing its clouds with grace, doth ever flow,
Came on us, as we sate in silence there,
Beneath the golden stars of the clear azure air.

2585. Whose] Refers to the *nurslings* of the previous line which are the *parasites* of line 2581.

2594. Ocean] *Notopoulos* 218 cites Plato, *Symposium* 210d on the passage of the true lover from individual instances of beauty to the love of beauty itself: 'Turning rather towards the main ocean of the beautiful [he] may by contemplation of this bring forth in all their splendour many fair fruits of discourse and meditation in a plenteous crop of philosophy' (Loeb trans.).

2596. To the pure all things are pure!] 'Unto the pure all things are pure: but unto them that are defiled and unbelieving is nothing pure; but even their mind and conscience is defiled' (*Titus* i 15). In the draft S. encloses the sentence in double inverted commas. D. Duff, *Romance and Revolution* (1994) 183 points out the use of St Paul's text in both Godwin's *Enquirer* and Milton's *Areopagitica*. *Notopoulos* 218 compares Orphic notions of purification in Plato; e.g. *Phaedo* 67b, 69c.

2604. air.] Since *Rossetti 1870 eds* have substituted a colon and dash or comma and dash to extend the complex adverbial phrase that begins with *in silence* in the previous line as far as *speech* in line 2608. *Forman 1876–7* retains the full stop after *air*, arguing persuasively that lines 2605–8 are intended to qualify the sentence that runs from 2608 to *voice* in the first line of the next stanza, the sense being that the *youthful years* and so on had *found a voice* in the *silence which doth follow talk*. The strength of the colon and dash in line 2608 might, as Forman thought, indicate a metrical pause; or it might be necessary because of the length and complexity of the adverbial phrases that precede it. The punctuation of the draft (*Nbk 3* 46) appears to be a semicolon.

XXXI

2605 In silence which doth follow talk that causes
The baffled heart to speak with sighs and tears,
When wildering passion swalloweth up the pauses
Of inexpressive speech: — the youthful years
Which we together passed, their hopes and fears,
2610 The common blood which ran within our frames,
That likeness of the features which endears
The thoughts expressed by them, our very names,
And all the wingèd hours which speechless memory claims,

XXXII

Had found a voice: — and ere that voice did pass,
2615 The night grew damp and dim, and through a rent
Of the ruin where we sate, from the morass,
A wandering Meteor by some wild wind sent,
Hung high in the green dome, to which it lent
A faint and pallid lustre; while the song
2620 Of blasts, in which its blue hair quivering bent,
Strewed strangest sounds the moving leaves among;
A wondrous light, the sound as of a spirit's tongue.

XXXIII

The Meteor showed the leaves on which we sate,
And Cythna's glowing arms, and the thick ties
2625 Of her soft hair, which bent with gathered weight
My neck near hers, her dark and deepening eyes,
Which, as twin phantoms of one star that lies
O'er a dim well, move, though the star reposes,
Swam in our mute and liquid ecstasies,
2630 Her marble brow, and eager lips, like roses,
With their own fragrance pale, which spring but half uncloses.

2610. *common blood*] blood itself *RofI*.

2612. *our very names*] Laon and Laone, the name Cythna had taken in her public character as revolutionary leader.

2613. *speechless*] Unexpressed, or inexpressible, in words.

2617. *Meteor*] See note to line 625.

2622. *spirit's tongue*] See note to line 294.

2624. *ties*] 'Bands, plaits' *Concordance*.

2625. *hair,*] *RofI*; hair *L&C*. Alteration in cancel-leaf for *RofI*.

XXXIV

The meteor to its far morass returned:
The beating of our veins one interval
Made still; and then I felt the blood that burned
2635 Within her frame, mingle with mine, and fall
Around my heart like fire; and over all
A mist was spread, the sickness of a deep
And speechless swoon of joy, as might befall
Two disunited spirits when they leap
2640 In union from this earth's obscure and fading sleep.

XXXV

Was it one moment that confounded thus
All thought, all sense, all feeling, into one
Unutterable power, which shielded us
Even from our own cold looks, when we had gone
2645 Into a wide and wild oblivion
Of tumult and of tenderness? or now
Had ages, such as make the moon and sun,
The seasons, and mankind their changes know,
Left fear and time unfelt by us alone below?

XXXVI

2650 I know not. What are kisses whose fire clasps
The failing heart in languishment, or limb
Twined within limb? or the quick dying gasps
Of the life meeting, when the faint eyes swim
Through tears of a wide mist boundless and dim,
2655 In one caress? What is the strong control
Which leads the heart that dizzy steep to climb,
Where far over the world those vapours roll,
Which blend two restless frames in one reposing soul?

2632. *meteor*] See note to line 625.

2633–4. *one interval / Made still*] *Locock 1911*'s construction, 'still made one intermittent rhythm', presumably referring to a space of time intervening regularly between the throbbing of their veins, is difficult to accept because the sense of intermittance is not present in the phrase. It would also strain the musical sense of *interval* as the difference of pitch between sounds in either melody or harmony. 'Ceased beating for one moment' seems closer to what is intended here, as a condition of the intense consciousness of sexual ecstasy in the remaining lines of the stanza. Cp. lines 3038–9: 'in every vein / The blood stood still one moment'.

2638. *speechless*] Indescribable.

2649. *below*] In this world.

XXXVII

It is the shadow which doth float unseen,
But not unfelt, o'er blind mortality,
Whose divine darkness fled not, from that green
And lone recess, where lapped in peace did lie
Our linkèd frames; till, from the changing sky,
That night and still another day had fled;
And then I saw and felt. The moon was high,
And clouds, as of a coming storm, were spread
Under its orb, — loud winds were gathering overhead.

XXXVIII

Cythna's sweet lips seemed lurid in the moon,
Her fairest limbs with the night wind were chill,
And her dark tresses were all loosely strewn
O'er her pale bosom: — all within was still,
And the sweet peace of joy did almost fill
The depth of her unfathomable look; —
And we sate calmly, though that rocky hill,
The waves contending in its caverns strook,
For they foreknew the storm, and the grey ruin shook.

XXXIX

There we unheeding sate, in the communion
Of interchangèd vows, which, with a rite
Of faith most sweet and sacred, stamped our union. —
Few were the living hearts which could unite
Like ours, or celebrate a bridal night
With such close sympathies, for to each other
Had high and solemn hopes, the gentle might
Of earliest love, and all the thoughts which smother
Cold Evil's power, now linked a sister and a brother.

2660

2665

2670

2675

2680

2685

2659–60. Cp. *Hymn to Intellectual Beauty* B. 1–2: 'The awful shadow of some unseen Power / Floats though unseen amongst us'.

2668–71. There are detailed similarities between these lines and lines 22–3 of *To [ ] Nov. 5 1815*: 'The moon made thy lips pale, beloved – / The wind made thy bosom chill'. See no. 127/128 and headnote.

2682–5. 'With such close sympathies, for they had sprung / From linked youth, and from the gentle might / Of earliest love, delayed and cherished long, / Which common hopes and fears made, like a tempest, strong.' *RofI.*

XL

And such is Nature's modesty, that those
Who grow together cannot choose but love,
If faith or custom do not interpose,
Or common slavery mar what else might move
2690   All gentlest thoughts; as in the sacred grove
Which shades the springs of Ethiopian Nile,
That living tree, which, if the arrowy dove
Strike with her shadow, shrinks in fear awhile,
But its own kindred leaves clasps while the sunbeams smile;

2686. modesty] law divine *Rof1*.

2690–705. The elaborate simile in these lines constructs an emblem for the doctrine of natural love which is asserted in lines 2686–90 and which transcends the customary proscription against brother–sister 'incest'. The figure unites two extraordinary phenomena of nature, one spectacular – the fertilising effects of the annual flooding of the Nile, the other curious – the behaviour of the mimosa or sensitive plant. Both were topics of contemporary scientific interest. See the following notes. S. probably also intends a reference to *Paradise Lost* iv 280–3 in which Milton alludes to a mistaken opinion on the situation of Paradise: 'Nor where Abassin kings their issue guard, / Mount Amara, though this by some supposed / True Paradise under the Ethiop line / By Nilus' head'. The image of a tree standing in a *sacred grove* at the source of the Nile both adopts and revises the original radical sexual innocence of Adam and Eve in *Paradise Lost*.

2691. springs of Ethiopian Nile] The springs of the Blue Nile in the mountains of northern Ethiopa were believed by many at the time to be the Nile's principal source, Lake Victoria in Uganda not being identified as the source of the White Nile until decades later. The Blue Nile's source, from ancient times considered one of the tantalising mysteries of nature, had been approximately located by the Portuguese Jesuit Pedro Paez in the early seventeenth century and confirmed by the Scottish nobleman James Bruce who published an account of his explorations in *Travels . . . to Discover the Sources of the Nile* (1790). Bruce's findings had become current, e.g. in the article 'Nile' in The *Encyclopaedia Britannica*, 4th edn 1810. In the notes to *The Genius of the Thames* Peacock refers to Bruce's discovery, though remarking 'that [the source] of the western [or White Nile], which is the principal branch, has never yet been visited by any European' (*Peacock Works* vi 160). This fact and literary tradition preserved the commonplace of the Nile's undiscovered springs. Cp. *To the Nile* (1818): 'Month after month the gathered rains descend / Drenching yon secret Ethiopian dells' (1–2).

2692. living tree] S. is combining characteristics of two members of the genus 'Mimosa': the *mimosa pudica* or sensitive plant and the mimosa tree: the latter's boughs bend to offer hospitable welcome in the bowers of Irem in Southey's *Thalaba the Destroyer* 14, 48; 1801 edn. Vol. I, 12, 58–9. The *mimosa pudica*'s sensitivity to temperature, light and touch appeared to some eighteenth-century botanists to challenge strict division between the vegetable and animal realms, and seemed to bolster Erasmus Darwin's hypothesis that all of nature might share a general animating principle: *living* suggests such a meaning here. Certainly the similarities to *Darwin* II i 247–62, including the bridal analogy, are interesting, and S. may well have had the passage in mind as he composed this one: 'Oft as light clouds o'erpass the Summer-glade, / Alarm'd she trembles at the moving shade; / And feels, alive through all her tender form, / The whisper'd murmurs of the gathering storm; / Shuts her sweet eye-lids to approaching night . . . Veil'd, with gay decency and modest pride, / Slow to the mosque she moves, an eastern bride; / There her soft vows unceasing love record, / Queen of the bright seraglio of her Lord.' See *The Sensitive-Plant* and headnote, R. M. Maniquis, *SiR* viii (1969) 129–55 and *Wasserman* 157.

2694–5. kindred leaves . . . darkness] The *mimosa pudica* is hermaphrodite bearing male and female flowers on the same plant, and folds its leaves at night.

173

XLI

2695 And clings to them, when darkness may dissever
The close caresses of all duller plants
Which bloom on the wide earth — thus we forever
Were linked, for love had nursed us in the haunts
Where knowledge, from its secret source enchants
2700 Young hearts with the fresh music of its springing,
Ere yet its gathered flood feeds human wants,
As the great Nile feeds Egypt; ever flinging
Light on the woven boughs which o'er its waves are swinging.

XLII

The tones of Cythna's voice like echoes were
2705 Of those far murmuring streams; they rose and fell,
Mixed with mine own in the tempestuous air, —
And so we sate, until our talk befell
Of the late ruin, swift and horrible,
And how those seeds of hope might yet be sown,
2710 Whose fruit is evil's mortal poison: well,
For us, this ruin made a watch-tower lone,
But Cythna's eyes looked faint, and now two days were gone

XLIII

Since she had food: — therefore I did awaken
The Tartar steed, who, from his ebon mane,
2715 Soon as the clinging slumbers he had shaken,
Bent his thin head to seek the brazen rein,
Following me obediently; with pain
Of heart, so deep and dread, that one caress,
When lips and heart refuse to part again,

2699. *knowledge*] Both intellectual and sexual as the following two lines make clear.

2701. *gathered flood*] The phrase is illuminated by *To the Nile* (10–14): 'O Nile – and well thou knowest / That soul-sustaining airs and blasts of evil / And fruits and poisons spring where'er thou flowest. / Beware, O Man – for knowledge must to thee / Like the great flood to Egypt, ever be. –' The ancient Egyptians attributed the flooding of the Nile to the tears of Isis for her dead husband, and brother, Osiris.

2702. *Egypt;*] *Rofl*; Egypt, *L&C*. The alteration in the cancel-leaf for *Rofl* is made in ink in *L&C* (PM).

2705. *far murmuring*] far-murmuring *Rossetti 1878*, *Locock 1911*, *1975*. The sense of murmurs arriving from afar seems clear without the hyphen. *streams*] apparently the 'springs' of line 2691.

2710–11. 'Fortunately we could keep watch safely from our secluded ruin'.

2720   Till they have told their fill, could scarce express
    The anguish of her mute and fearful tenderness,

XLIV

    Cythna beheld me part, as I bestrode
    That willing steed — the tempest and the night,
    Which gave my path its safety as I rode
2725   Down the ravine of rocks, did soon unite
    The darkness and the tumult of their might
    Borne on all winds. — Far through the streaming rain
    Floating at intervals the garments white
    Of Cythna gleamed, and her voice once again
2730   Came to me on the gust, and soon I reached the plain.

XLV

    I dreaded not the tempest, nor did he
    Who bore me, but his eyeballs wide and red
    Turned on the lightning's cleft exultingly;
    And when the earth beneath his tameless tread,
2735   Shook with the sullen thunder, he would spread
    His nostrils to the blast, and joyously
    Mock the fierce peal with neighings; — thus we sped
    O'er the lit plain, and soon I could descry
    Where Death and Fire had gorged the spoil of victory.

XLVI

2740   There was a desolate village in a wood
    Whose bloom-inwoven leaves now scattering fed
    The hungry storm; it was a place of blood,
    A heap of hearthless walls; — the flames were dead
    Within those dwellings now, — the life had fled
2745   From all those corpses now, — but the wide sky
    Flooded with lightning was ribbed overhead
    By the black rafters, and around did lie
    Women, and babes, and men, slaughtered confusedly.

2727–9. 'The gleam of Cythna's *garments white* could be seen intermittently as the tempest blew the heavy rain'.

Stanza xlvi. Two lines are cancelled in the draft at the head of the stanza: 'The trophies of a false & bloody King / Falsest & bloodiest of that evil race' (*Nbk 3* 52).

2743–7. Cp. Preface 138–41 (and note): 'I have seen the theatre of the more visible ravages of tyranny and war, cities and villages reduced to scattered groups of black and roofless houses, and the naked inhabitants sitting famished upon their desolated thresholds'.

XLVII

Beside the fountain in the market-place
2750 Dismounting, I beheld those corpses stare
With horny eyes upon each other's face,
And on the earth and on the vacant air,
And upon me, close to the waters where
I stooped to slake my thirst; — I shrank to taste,
2755 For the salt bitterness of blood was there;
But tied the steed beside, and sought in haste
If any yet survived amid that ghastly waste.

XLVIII

No living thing was there beside one woman,
Whom I found wandering in the streets, and she
2760 Was withered from a likeness of aught human
Into a fiend, by some strange misery:
Soon as she heard my steps she leaped on me,
And glued her burning lips to mine, and laughed
With a loud, long, and frantic laugh of glee,
2765 And cried, 'Now Mortal, thou hast deeply quaffed
The Plague's blue kisses — soon millions shall pledge the draught!

2751. horny] See line 1337 and note.

2755. blood] S. may be recalling a detail from the narrative of the siege of Ziget in Croatia in William Godwin's *St. Leon* (1799; xliv): 'we fought the enemy street by street, and inch by inch; the great fountain in the market-place ran with blood'.

2758. one woman] S. would appear to have developed the figure of the mad woman of stanzas xlviii–lii from his reading in preparation for the sequence on the plague in X xiv–xlviii. See headnote *Sources and Influences* p. 27 and E. Sickels, *PMLA* xlv (1930) 1116–28. In particular, Defoe's *A Journal of the Plague Year* (1722) refers to frequent instances of madness from disease, fear and grief during the visitation of the plague in London in 1665, including 'Mothers murthering their own Children, in their Lunacy' (ed. L. Landa and D. Roberts 1990, 81; also 115).

2763. burning lips] S. may well have derived the incident from one in *A Journal of the Plague Year*: 'He was going along the Street, raving mad to be sure, and singing, the People only said, he was drunk; but he himself said, he had the Plague upon him, which, it seems, was true; and meeting this Gentlewoman, he would kiss her; she was terribly frighted as he was only a rude Fellow, and she run from him, but the Street being very thin of People, there was no body near enough to help her . . . she being so near, he caught hold of her, and pull'd her down also; and getting up first, master'd her, and kiss'd her; and which was worst of all, when he had done, told her he had the Plague, and why should not she have it as well as he' (ed. L. Landa and D. Roberts 1990, 160).

2766. blue kisses] S. regularly associates the colour blue with death and disease as in lines 1333, 3964, *Q Mab* i 4, *Alastor* 216. N. Crook and D. Guiton (*Shelley's Venomed Melody* (1986) 163–5) detail the woman's associations with venereal disease citing *Proverbs* vi 26: 'For by means of a whorish woman a man is brought to a piece of bread'. The similarities to *Epipsychidion* 256–66 reinforce the connection. *pledge the draught*] Themselves drink in response to the *draught* Laon has taken from the cup of disease; typically it is someone's health that is pledged in a second draught. For the association of the colour blue with plague, see note to line 3964.

XLIX

'My name is Pestilence — this bosom dry,
Once fed two babes — a sister and a brother —
When I came home, one in the blood did lie
2770   Of three death-wounds — the flames had ate the other!
Since then I have no longer been a mother,
But I am Pestilence; — hither and thither
I flit about, that I may slay and smother: —
All lips which I have kissed must surely wither,
2775   But Death's — if thou art he, we'll go to work together!

L

'What seek'st thou here? the moonlight comes in flashes, —
The dew is rising dankly from the dell —
'Twill moisten her! and thou shalt see the gashes
In my sweet boy, now full of worms — but tell
2780   First what thou seek'st.' — 'I seek for food.' — ''Tis well,
Thou shalt have food; Famine, my paramour,
Waits for us at the feast — cruel and fell
Is Famine, but he drives not from his door
Those whom these lips have kissed, alone. No more, no more!'

LI

2785   As thus she spake, she grasped me with the strength
Of madness, and by many a ruined hearth
She led, and over many a corpse: — at length
We came to a lone hut, where on the earth
Which made its floor, she in her ghastly mirth
2790   Gathering from all those homes now desolate,
Had piled three heaps of loaves, making a dearth
Among the dead — round which she set in state
A ring of cold, stiff babes; silent and stark they sate.

2767. bosom dry] S. may be remembering the portrait of Cleone, the mother who has lost six daughters and her husband to the plague, in *Darwin* II iii 317–42: 'Daughter of woe! ere morn, in vain caress'd, / Clung the cold Babe upon thy milkless breast, / With feeble cries thy last sad aid required, / Stretch'd its stiff limbs, and on thy lap expired!' (331–4).

2768. two babes] two twins *canc. Nbk 3* 55.

2770. three death-wounds] many wounds *Nbk 3* 55. S.'s revisions to this line and to line 2768 introduce a sinister resemblance between the dead children and Laon and Cythna: see III xxv–vii and note.

LII

She leaped upon a pile, and lifted high
2795　Her mad looks to the lightning, and cried: 'Eat!
Share the great feast — tomorrow we must die!'
And then she spurned the loaves with her pale feet,
Towards her bloodless guests; — that sight to meet,
Mine eyes and my heart ached, and but that she
2800　Who loved me, did with absent looks defeat
Despair, I might have raved in sympathy;
But now I took the food that woman offered me;

LIII

And vainly having with her madness striven
If I might win her to return with me,
2805　Departed. In the eastern beams of Heaven
The lightning now grew pallid — rapidly,
As by the shore of the tempestuous sea
The dark steed bore me, and the mountain grey
Soon echoed to his hoofs, and I could see
2810　Cythna among the rocks, where she alway
Had sate, with anxious eyes fixed on the lingering day.

LIV

And joy was ours to meet: she was most pale,
Famished, and wet and weary, so I cast
My arms around her, lest her steps should fail
2815　As to our home we went, and thus embraced,
Her full heart seemed a deeper joy to taste
Than e'er the prosperous know; the steed behind
Trod peacefully along the mountain waste,
We reached our home ere morning could unbind
2820　Night's latest veil, and on our bridal couch reclined.

2795–6. 'Let us eat and drink; for to morrow we shall die' (*Isaiah* xxii 13).

2800. *absent looks*] The imagined looks of the absent Cythna.

2805–8. 'As the steed bore me rapidly by the shore of the tempestuous sea, the lightning grew pallid in the eastern sky'. The awkward punctuation obscures the sense: it is clearer in the draft in *Nbk 3* (57) which shows a comma and perhaps a dash after *pallid* and no comma after *rapidly*. Several *eds* have removed this comma.

2811. *lingering*] Slowly breaking.

LV

Her chilled heart having cherished in my bosom,
And sweetest kisses past, we two did share
Our peaceful meal: — as an autumnal blossom
Which spreads its shrunk leaves in the sunny air,
2825 After cold showers, like rainbows woven there,
Thus in her lips and cheeks the vital spirit
Mantled, and in her eyes, an atmosphere
Of health, and hope; and sorrow languished near it,
And fear, and all that dark despondence doth inherit.

Canto Seventh

I

2830 So we sate joyous as the morning ray
Which fed upon the wrecks of night and storm
Now lingering on the winds; light airs did play
Among the dewy weeds, the sun was warm,
And we sate linked in the inwoven charm
2835 Of converse and caresses sweet and deep,
Speechless caresses, talk that might disarm
Time, though he wield the darts of death and sleep,
And those thrice mortal barbs in his own poison steep.

II

I told her of my sufferings and my madness,
2840 And how, awakened from that dreamy mood
By Liberty's uprise, the strength of gladness
Came to my spirit in my solitude;
And all that now I was, while tears pursued
Each other down her fair and listening cheek
2845 Fast as the thoughts which fed them, like a flood
From sun-bright dales; and when I ceased to speak,
Her accents soft and sweet the pausing air did wake.

2821. *cherished*] Warmed.

2822. *past*] *Rossetti 1870, 1878* and *1975* modernise to 'passed'. The draft reading in *Nbk 3* 59 is 'past'. The phrase *sweetest kisses past* could be a condensation of 'sweetest kisses being (now in the) past' or 'sweetest kisses having (now) been passed between us'.

2827. *Mantled*] Flushed.

2829. *inherit*] Is heir to.

2840–2. Referring to the Hermit's recounting to Laon of the revolution in the Golden City which had been conducted by Cythna: IV xi–IV xxxiv.

2847. *pausing air*] See note to line 342.

III

She told me a strange tale of strange endurance,
Like broken memories of many a heart
2850   Woven into one; to which no firm assurance,
So wild were they, could her own faith impart.
She said that not a tear did dare to start
From the swoln brain, and that her thoughts were firm
When from all mortal hope she did depart,
2855   Borne by those slaves across the Ocean's term,
And that she reached the port without one fear infirm.

IV

One was she among many there, the thralls
Of the cold tyrant's cruel lust: and they
Laughed mournfully in those polluted halls;
2860   But she was calm and sad, musing alway
On loftiest enterprise, till on a day
The Tyrant heard her singing to her lute
A wild, and sad, and spirit-thrilling lay,
Like winds that die in wastes — one moment mute
2865   The evil thoughts it made, which did his breast pollute.

V

Even when he saw her wondrous loveliness,
One moment to great Nature's sacred power

2848. 1975 notes that the first *strange* is deleted in the draft (*Nbk 3* 60) 'indicating an intent
to revise', which was not carried out, but there is no reason why in transcribing fair copy
S. might not have opted to repeat *strange* which has the poetic effectiveness that he achieved
by repetition of the same word in lines 1831–2.

2849. broken] The word is underlined in *Nbk 3* 60; *1975* sees here, as in the previous line,
an uncompleted intention to revise, but S. may just as well have decided against revision.

2849–50. Cythna's tale seems to combine disjointed elements from many women's lives into
a single tale. Cp. Preface to *Julian and Maddalo*: 'His [the Maniac's] story, told at length, might
be like many other stories of the same kind: the unconnected exclamations of his agony will
perhaps be found a sufficient comment for the text of every heart.'

2850–1. 'Her own conviction that they had actually happened was insufficient warrant
for the truth of her wild memories'. S. is preparing the reader for the shift to the mode of
romantic and marvellous adventure that marks Cythna's narrative.

2859. polluted] See note to line 744.

2864. Like winds that die in wastes] Daedal as that of Orpheus *canc. Nbk 3* 61.

2866–8. 'Shelley's mind had become familiarized with the idea of a Spirit ruling throughout
Nature, obedience to which constitutes human power. Most remarkable is the passage in which
the tyrant recovers his faculties through his subjection to this spirit; because it indicates Shelley's
faithful adhesion to the universal, though oft obscurely formed belief, that the ability to receive
influence is the most exalted faculty to which human nature can attain, while the exercise
of an arbitrary power centring in self is not only debasing, but is an actual destroyer of human
faculty' (Thornton Hunt, *Atlantic Monthly* xi (February 1863) 198).

He bent, and was no longer passionless;
But when he bade her to his secret bower
2870 Be borne, a loveless victim, and she tore
Her locks in agony, and her words of flame
And mightier looks availed not; then he bore
Again his load of slavery, and became
A king, a heartless beast, a pageant and a name.

VI

2875 She told me what a loathsome agony
Is that when selfishness mocks love's delight,
Foul as in dream's most fearful imagery
To dally with the mowing dead — that night
All torture, fear, or horror made seem light
2880 Which the soul dreams or knows, and when the day
Shone on her awful frenzy, from the sight
Where like a Spirit in fleshly chains she lay
Struggling, aghast and pale the Tyrant fled away.

VII

Her madness was a beam of light, a power
2885 Which dawned through the rent soul; and words it gave,
Gestures and looks, such as in whirlwinds bore,
Which might not be withstood, whence none could save,

2868. *passionless*] Untouched by any strong feeling; here, those inspired by Cythna's beauty.

2877. *dream's*] eds; dreams *L&C/RofI, 1839. Woodberry 1893* prefers to repunctuate: 'dreams, most fearful imagery,'. The draft in *Nbk 3* (62) shows no apostrophe or commas. The most plausible explanation is that an apostrophe in the fair copy was omitted by the printer and that the error was overlooked in proof.

2878. *mowing*] Grimacing. S. originally wrote 'putrid' (*Nbk 3* 62).

2885–9. This notoriously awkward passage, for which the draft in *Nbk 3* is defective, has been much discussed and repunctuated. The commas at the end of lines 2885, 2886, 2887 are not present in *L&C/RofI*; they have been supplied as the minimal pointing necessary to mark the meaning. As far as *sphere* (line 2888), the sense – although obscured by lack of punctuation in *L&C/RofI* – seems clear enough: 'Cythna's madness inspired her with *words, gestures* and *looks* which like *whirlwinds* carried irresistibly with them all those who drew near to listen'. Line 2887 is to be understood as parenthetical. (*Forman 1876–7*'s reading of *gave* as the equivalent of 'gave to' removes the need to insert a comma and produces a possible meaning though one that appears just too strained to be acceptable.) The reference of *like* (line 2888), however, is not immediately evident. For *Forman 1876–7* it is *sphere*, for *Hutchinson* it is Cythna herself. Forman seems closer to what is intended, the sense of *sphere* as the circle within which Cythna's words operated also suggesting both the *whirlwind* she effectively created and the *whirlpool* into which those who approached were drawn. The meaning of the phrase *like . . . beneath* (lines 2888–9) would then be the equivalent of an adverbial clause having *all who approached* as implied subject: 'just as a calm wave is agitated into whirlpools as it is sucked into the hollow gulfs beneath it'. (For whirlpools resulting from cavities in the ocean floor, see *Darwin* I Additional Note xxxi to iii 93, and cp. line 1545 and note.)

All who approached their sphere, like some calm wave
Vexed into whirlpools by the chasms beneath;
2890　And sympathy made each attendant slave
Fearless and free, and they began to breathe
Deep curses, like the voice of flames far underneath.

VIII

The King felt pale upon his noonday throne:
At night two slaves he to her chamber sent,
2895　One was a green and wrinkled eunuch, grown
From human shape into an instrument
Of all things ill — distorted, bowed and bent.
The other was a wretch from infancy
Made dumb by poison; who nought knew or meant
2900　But to obey: from the fire-isles came he,
A diver lean and strong, of Oman's coral sea.

IX

They bore her to a bark, and the swift stroke
Of silent rowers clove the blue moonlight seas,
Until upon their path the morning broke;
2905　They anchored then, where, be there calm or breeze,

2890. *each attendant slave*] Each inmate of the harem.

2891. *breathe*] See line 61 and note.

2892. *voice of flames far underneath*] Referring to the subterranean fires whose action contemporary geology identified as the cause of both earthquakes and the eruption of volcanoes. Cp. the 'volcano's voice' of line 3498 and see G. M. Matthews, *ELH* xxiv (1957) 191–228 for S.'s use of geological phenomena as poetic figures of human energy for political change, an analogy that he may well have adapted from the Abbé Barruel's *Memoirs Illustrating the History of Jacobinism* (trans. 1797–98): see *L* i 264; *Mary Jnl* i 18–19, 34. Cp. lines 2396–7 and note, and *PU* II ii 1–23 and note.

2895. *green*] Pale or sickly of complexion, 'indicative of fear, jealousy, ill-humour or sickness' (*OED*).

2899. *dumb*] The practice of depriving certain attendants of the power of speech to ensure the secrecy of the sinister acts they were required to perform was traditionally attributed to the Turkish Sultan.

2900. *fire-isles*] Volcanic islands (*OED*). See note to lines 2396–7.

2901. *Oman's coral sea*] A name sometimes applied to the Persian Gulf, according to the note to the first line of 'The Fire-Worshippers', the third of the tales that make up Thomas Moore's *Lalla Rookh* (1817). Pearl divers, coral seas, fire sparkling on mountains, on sands and on ocean all figure in 'The Fire-Worshippers' which was published on 27 May 1817. S. ordered it on 3 August, had not received it by 8 August (*L* i 549, 552) and, according to *Mary Jnl* i 178, began reading it on 23 August – by which time this passage had been drafted. But it is very likely that S. had seen *Lalla Rookh* soon after publication as MWS records reading it on 1 June following a visit they made to London between 23 and 31 May (*Mary Jnl* i 172).

The gloomiest of the drear Symplegades
Shakes with the sleepless surge; — the Ethiop there
Wound his long arms around her, and with knees
Like iron clasped her feet, and plunged with her
2910   Among the closing waves out of the boundless air.

X

'Swift as an eagle stooping from the plain
Of morning light, into some shadowy wood,
He plunged through the green silence of the main,
Through many a cavern which the eternal flood
2915   Had scooped, as dark lairs for its monster brood;
And among mighty shapes which fled in wonder,
And among mightier shadows which pursued
His heels, he wound: until the dark rocks under
He touched a golden chain — a sound arose like thunder.

XI

2920   'A stunning clang of massive bolts redoubling
Beneath the deep — a burst of waters driven
As from the roots of the sea, raging and bubbling:
And in that roof of crags a space was riven
Through which there shone the emerald beams of heaven,
2925   Shot through the lines of many waves inwoven,
Like sunlight through acacia woods at even,
Through which, his way the diver having cloven,
Passed like a spark sent up out of a burning oven.

2906. *Symplegades*] Two islands lying at the entrance to the Black Sea from the Bosphorus and traditionally identified with the 'Clashing Rocks' or 'Blue Rocks' between which the Argonauts had to sail on their voyage to recover the Golden Fleece in Apollonius of Rhodes, *Argonautica* (ii 550–610).

2907. *Ethiop*] Having black, or swarthy, skin.

2911. From this point until line 3782, apart from Laon's brief intervention in lines 2990–5, Cythna narrates her own story. *stooping*] swooping, as if on its prey.

2920. *redoubling*] Re-echoing, resounding.

2922. *roots of the sea*] In the Preface to *Thalaba the Destroyer* Southey claimed that the poem grew from a mention in 'the continuation of the Arabian Tales' of 'the Domdaniel . . . a Seminary for evil Magicians under the Roots of the Sea'. See also ii 2 (i 67 in 1801 edn).

2925. *lines*] The picture evoked by the word is anything put distinct. 'Ripple-marks' (*Concordance*) or 'lines of spray caused by the waves as they suddenly dashed up through the space made in the roof of crags' (*Locock 1911*) is each possible. The next verse makes it clear at least that *beams* of daylight tinted green by the seawater descended through horizontal *lines* created by the movement of the water above Cythna and the diver.

XII

'And then,' she said, 'he laid me in a cave
2930   Above the waters, by that chasm of sea,
A fountain round and vast, in which the wave
Imprisoned, boiled and leaped perpetually,
Down which, one moment resting, he did flee,
Winning the adverse depth; that spacious cell
2935   Like an hupaithric temple wide and high,
Whose aery dome is inaccessible,
Was pierced with one round cleft through which the sunbeams fell.

XIII

'Below, the fountain's brink was richly paven
With the deep's wealth, coral, and pearl, and sand
2940   Like spangling gold, and purple shells engraven
With mystic legends by no mortal hand,
Left there, when thronging to the moon's command,
The gathering waves rent the Hesperian gate
Of mountains, and on such bright floor did stand

2934. *adverse*] Opposite; i.e. in the opposite direction.

2935. *hupaithric*] 'Under the air'; so, without a roof. *1975* cites Peacock's *Rhododaphne* i 2: 'Round Thespian Love's hypaethric fane' (*Peacock Works* vii 9). Cp. *PU* III iv 118 and note.

2936. *aery*] Lofty.

2940–1. Glen O'Malley, *Shelley and Synesthesia* (1964) 193 likens these shells to one imagined in Thomas Moore's *The Genius of Harmony. An Irregular Ode*, included in *Epistles, Odes and other Poems* (1806) which S. read in 1817 (*Mary Jnl* i 101): 'There lies a shell beneath the waves . . . / It bears / Upon its shining side the mystic notes / Of those entrancing airs, / The genii of the deep were wont to swell, / When heaven's eternal orbs their midnight music roll'd!' (47–8).

2943. *Hesperian gate*] i.e. Western gate: S. originally wrote 'western mountains' (*Nbk 3* 65) which provides a clue to the meaning of the phrase. Cythna's cave, situated at the extreme eastern limit of the Mediterranean, is paved with shells dating from that sea's creation. This was attributed in ancient myth to an exploit of Hercules who tore apart the mountains linking southern Spain with North Africa to form the straits of Gibraltar through which the Atlantic rushed to form the Mediterranean. On either side he piled up the high peaks of Calpe and Abyla known as the Pillars of Hercules: these are S.'s *Hesperian gate of mountains*. Darwin I i 325–30 recounts the feat: 'Last with wide arms the solid earth He tears, / Piles rock on rock, on mountain mountain rears; / Heaves up huge ABYLA on Afric's sand, / Crowns with high CALPE Europe's saliant [sic] strand, / Crests with opposing towers the splendid scene, / And pours from urns immense the sea between'. Darwin detected a geological cataclysm behind the myth and it is this that S. alludes to in particular: 'If the passage between the two continents was opened by an earthquake in antient times, as this allegorical story would seem to countenance, there must have been an immense current of water at first run into the Mediterranean from the Atlantic; since there is at present a strong stream sets always from thence into the Mediterranean' (note to I i 297).

2944–5. The cancelled draft (*Nbk 3* 65) includes macabre details which S. did not retain: 'Of mountains; but among them lay a ?[band] / Of human bones [ ] / A youthful female dead, which in that state / The salt air kept a work of [ ] ?[date]'.

2945   Columns, and shapes like statues, and the state
           Of kingless thrones, which Earth did in her heart create.

XIV

           'The fiend of madness which had made its prey
           Of my poor heart, was lulled to sleep awhile:
           There was an interval of many a day,
2950   And a sea-eagle brought me food the while,
           Whose nest was built in that untrodden isle,
           And who, to be the jailor had been taught,
           Of that strange dungeon; as a friend whose smile
           Like light and rest at morn and even is sought,
2955   That wild bird was to me, till madness misery brought.

XV

           'The misery of a madness slow and creeping,
           Which made the earth seem fire, the sea seem air,
           And the white clouds of noon which oft were sleeping,
           In the blue heaven so beautiful and fair,
2960   Like hosts of ghastly shadows hovering there;
           And the sea-eagle looked a fiend, who bore
           Thy mangled limbs for food! — thus all things were
           Transformed into the agony which I wore
           Even as a poisoned robe around my bosom's core.

2945–6. The fancy of a chthonic artistic production from a primeval epoch that is exemplary to the present is repeated in the description of the pleasure-house in *Epipsychidion*: 'in the heart / Of Earth having assumed its form, then grown / Out of the mountains, from the living stone' (494–6). There are also interesting similarities, cited by *Locock 1911*, with the noble ruins pregnant with significance in the valley of Bethzatanai in *The Assassins* (1814–15; *Prose Works* 126–7). See note to *PU* IV 302–14.

Stanzas xiv–xvi. The parallels between the visions of Laon's madness in III xxii–vi and Cythna's in these stanzas, including the imagination of eating the beloved's flesh, are signalled by a number of verbal echoes.

2950. sea-eagle] Pliny, *Natural History* X vi tells of an eagle that was reared by a maiden of the city of Sestos and which in gratitude brought her birds and larger game which it had killed. When she died, it threw itself on her funeral pyre and was consumed with her.

2955–6. Several *eds* have preferred a weaker stop after *brought*, taking the syntax to be governed by apposition between the *misery* of line 2955 and the same word in 2956; but it is also possible to accept the punctuation of *L&C/RofI* by considering the series of clauses beginning at line 2956 as in a relation of loose dependance on the main clause beginning 'thus all things were / Transformed' (2962–3).

2961–2. Cp. lines 1339–40.

2964. poisoned robe] Probably alluding to the tunic poisoned with the blood of Nessus the centaur which, given to Hercules as a love-philtre by his wife Deianeira, caused his death.

XVI

2965 'Again I knew the day and night fast fleeing,
The eagle, and the fountain, and the air;
Another frenzy came — there seemed a being
Within me — a strange load my heart did bear,
As if some living thing had made its lair
2970 Even in the fountains of my life: — a long
And wondrous vision wrought from my despair,
Then grew, like sweet reality among
Dim visionary woes, an unreposing throng.

XVII

'Methought I was about to be a mother —
2975 Month after month went by, and still I dreamed
That we should soon be all to one another,
I and my child; and still new pulses seemed
To beat beside my heart, and still I deemed
There was a babe within — and when the rain
2980 Of winter through the rifted cavern streamed,
Methought, after a lapse of lingering pain,
I saw that lovely shape, which near my heart had lain.

XVIII

'It was a babe, beautiful from its birth, —
It was like thee, dear love, its eyes were thine,
2985 Its brow, its lips, and so upon the earth
It laid its fingers, as now rest on mine
Thine own belovèd: — 'twas a dream divine;
Even to remember how it fled, how swift,
How utterly, might make the heart repine, —
2990 Though 'twas a dream.' — Then Cythna did uplift
Her looks on mine, as if some doubt she sought to shift:

2969. living thing] evil thing *Nbk 3* 67.   *lair*] couch, resting-place, not necessarily the den of a wild beast.

2982. I saw that lovely shape] I bore a female child *canc. Nbk 3* 67.

Stanza xviii. In *L&C* (PM) there are marks in pencil against this stanza, which are partly rubbed out, as though (*Forman 1876–7* conjectures) it had been considered for revision. Once the brother–sister relation between Laon and Cythna had been removed in *RofI*, the stanza no longer implied an incestuous connection between them. See *R&H* 1218–24 and note.

2985. so] Thus.

XIX

A doubt which would not flee, a tenderness
Of questioning grief, a source of thronging tears;
Which, having passed, as one whom sobs oppress,
2995   She spoke: 'Yes, in the wilderness of years
Her memory, aye, like a green home appears,
She sucked her fill even at this breast, sweet love,
For many months. I had no mortal fears;
Methought I felt her lips and breath approve, —
3000   It was a human thing which to my bosom clove.

XX

'I watched the dawn of her first smiles, and soon
When zenith-stars were trembling on the wave,
Or when the beams of the invisible moon,
Or sun, from many a prism within the cave
3005   Their gem-born shadows to the water gave,
Her looks would hunt them, and with outspread hand,
From the swift lights which might that fountain pave,
She would mark one, and laugh, when that command
Slighting, it lingered there, and could not understand.

XXI

3010   'Methought her looks began to talk with me;
And no articulate sounds, but something sweet
Her lips would frame, — so sweet it could not be,
That it was meaningless; her touch would meet
Mine, and our pulses calmly flow and beat
3015   In response while we slept; and on a day
When I was happiest in that strange retreat,
With heaps of golden shells we two did play, —
Both infants, weaving wings for time's perpetual way.

2994. *oppress*] Nbk 3 68; opprest *L&C/RofI*: most *eds* make the emendation.

2996. *aye*] Ever.

2998. *I had no mortal fears*] 'A slumber did my spirit seal; / I had no human fears': Wordsworth, *A slumber did my spirit seal* (1800).

2999. *approve*] 'Demonstrate, attest': Cythna, who has described her experience in the cave as 'madness', 'frenzy', 'vision', and 'dream', remembers suckling the infant as proof that it actually existed.

3002–5. Through the opening in the roof of the cave the stars directly overhead (at the zenith) are mirrored in the waters of the pool whereas the slant beams of the moon or the sun are reflected from the gems on the walls of the cave upon the surface of the pool.

3005. *gem-born*] A Southeyan word; e.g. *The Curse of Kehama* (1810) xvi 11.

XXII

'Ere night, methought, her waning eyes were grown
3020 Weary with joy, and tired with our delight,
We, on the earth, like sister twins lay down
On one fair mother's bosom: — from that night
She fled; — like those illusions clear and bright,
Which dwell in lakes, when the red moon on high
3025 Pause ere it wakens tempest; — and her flight,
Though 'twas the death of brainless fantasy,
Yet smote my lonesome heart more than all misery.

XXIII

'It seemed that in the dreary night, the diver
Who brought me thither, came again, and bore
3030 My child away. I saw the waters quiver,
When he so swiftly sunk, as once before:
Then morning came — it shone even as of yore,
But I was changed — the very life was gone
Out of my heart — I wasted more and more,
3035 Day after day, and sitting there alone,
Vexed the inconstant waves with my perpetual moan.

XXIV

'I was no longer mad, and yet methought
My breasts were swoln and changed: — in every vein
The blood stood still one moment, while that thought
3040 Was passing — with a gush of sickening pain
It ebbed even to its withered springs again,
When my wan eyes in stern resolve I turned

3022–3. from that night / She fled] MWS gave birth to a daughter, two months prematurely, on 22 February 1815; she discovered the infant dead twelve days later on the morning of 6 March (*Mary Jnl* i 65–8; *Mary L* i 10–11).

3025. Pause] The subjunctive is similarly employed in an adverbial clause introduced by *when* in line 2269. There it makes a rhyme; here it seems also to be a grammatical irregularity in the interest of euphony, as *Forman 1876–7* thought. *1975* emended *when* in the preceding line to 'should', so regularising the grammar, on the basis of the draft reading (*Nbk 3* 70) which was 'probably miscopied by Shelley himself'. The draft, in pencil, is both faint and confused at this point. S. cancelled two attempts at completing the line from *Which dwell in lakes*, before writing '?[should] the red moon on high'. The emendation is not without support but two factors make against it: the draft reading '?[should]' is uncertain, and it seems somewhat likelier that S. chose to write *when* than that he miscopied the draft.

3026. brainless fantasy] Irrational imagining.

3041. again,] *Rossetti 1870, 1878, Locock 1911, 1975*; again: *L&C/RofI*. The colon obscures the dependance of the adverbial clause beginning with *When* in the next line on *ebbed* in this one. There is no punctuation after *again* in the untidy draft in *Nbk 3* (71).

From that most strange delusion, which would fain
Have waked the dream for which my spirit yearned
3045   With more than human love, — then left it unreturned.

XXV

'So now my reason was restored to me,
I struggled with that dream, which, like a beast
Most fierce and beauteous, in my memory
Had made its lair, and on my heart did feast;
3050   But all that cave and all its shapes possessed
By thoughts which could not fade, renewed each one
Some smile, some look, some gesture which had blessed
Me heretofore: I, sitting there alone,
Vexed the inconstant waves with my perpetual moan.

XXVI

3055   'Time passed, I know not whether months or years;
For day, nor night, nor change of seasons made
Its note, but thoughts and unavailing tears:
And I became at last even as a shade,
A smoke, a cloud on which the winds have preyed,
3060   Till it be thin as air; until, one even,
A Nautilus upon the fountain played,
Spreading his azure sail where breath of Heaven
Descended not, among the waves and whirlpools driven.

3043. strange delusion] That her breasts were those of a mother who has been nursing a child.

3044. the dream] Of the child she remains uncertain that she had. MWS records dreaming that her dead child had come to life on 19 and 20 March 1815 (*Mary Jnl i* 70–1).

3046. now] Now that.

3061. A Nautilus] The name is applied to two sorts of mollusc: the pearly nautilus and the paper nautilus or Argonaut: both are described in *Darwin* I Additional Note to iii 67. The latter, the one S. describes in this stanza and the next, had been noticed in the Mediterranean since ancient times. It feeds at the surface and was traditionally believed to sail and row in its shell by spreading a membrane attached to some of its feet while using the others as oars. Pope's celebration of the creature as one of those whose instincts instructed man's reason in the state of nature was well known: 'Learn of the little Nautilus to sail, / Spread the thin oar, and catch the driving gale' (*An Essay on Man* (1733–34) iii 177–8). Charlotte Smith had more recently moralised its natural technology for young readers: 'So let us catch life's favouring gale, / But if fate's adverse winds be rude, / Take calmly in th'adventurous sail, / And find repose in Solitude' (*The Nautilus* 25–8 in *Conversations Introducing Poetry: Chiefly on Subjects of Natural History. For the Use of Children and Young Persons* (1804)). In 1821 S. used the word as though it were a familiar name for himself, writing to Claire Clairmont of a boat that was being refitted for him as 'a very nice little shell, for the Nautilus your friend' (*L* ii 288). Cp. *PU* III iii 64–8 and note. The Nautilus's 'boat' of shell has evident relations with the boat of line 4630 in which Cythna's child sails with her and Laon to the temple of the Spirit. Sperry (*Shelley's Major Verse* (1988) 59–63) discusses the nautilus as one of the poem's leading symbols.

XXVII

'And when the Eagle came, that lovely thing,
3065 Oaring with rosy feet its silver boat,
Fled near me as for shelter; on slow wing,
The Eagle, hovering o'er his prey did float;
But when he saw that I with fear did note
His purpose, proffering my own food to him,
3070 The eager plumes subsided on his throat —
He came where that bright child of sea did swim,
And o'er it cast in peace his shadow broad and dim.

XXVIII

'This wakened me, it gave me human strength
And hope, I know not whence or wherefore, rose,
3075 But I resumed my ancient powers at length;
My spirit felt again like one of those,
Like thine, whose fate it is to make the woes
Of humankind their prey — what was this cave?
Its deep foundation no firm purpose knows
3080 Immutable, resistless, strong to save,
Like mind while yet it mocks the all-devouring grave.

XXIX

'And where was Laon? might my heart be dead,
While that far dearer heart could move and be?
Or whilst over the earth the pall was spread,
3085 Which I had sworn to rend? I might be free,
Could I but win that friendly bird to me,
To bring me ropes; and long in vain I sought
By intercourse of mutual imagery
Of objects, if such aid he could be taught;
3090 But fruit, and flowers, and boughs, yet never ropes he brought.

XXX

'We live in our own world, and mine was made
From glorious fantasies of hope departed:
Aye, we are darkened with their floating shade,
Or cast a lustre on them — time imparted

3073. human strength] Cp. the function of the leech-gatherer in Wordsworth's *Resolution and Independence* (1807): 'Or like a Man from some far region sent; / To give me human strength, and strong admonishment' (118–19).

3076. those,] *1839* and *eds*; those *L&C/RofI*. The draft in *Nbk 3* is defective.

3093. Aye,] 'Ever', 'always'. Several *eds* omit the comma to clarify the adverbial function. *Rossetti 1878* emends to 'ay' = 'yes', 'indeed'. The draft in *Nbk 3* is defective here.

3095   Such power to me, I became fearless-hearted,
    My eye and voice grew firm, calm was my mind,
    And piercing, like the morn, now it has darted
    Its lustre on all hidden things, behind
    Yon dim and fading clouds which load the weary wind.

XXXI

3100   'My mind became the book through which I grew
    Wise in all human wisdom, and its cave,
    Which like a mine I rifled through and through,
    To me the keeping of its secrets gave —
    One mind, the type of all, the moveless wave
3105   Whose calm reflects all moving things that are,
    Necessity, and love, and life, the grave,
    And sympathy, fountains of hope and fear;
    Justice, and truth, and time, and the world's natural sphere.

XXXII

    'And on the sand would I make signs to range
3110   These woofs, as they were woven, of my thought;

3095. Such power] The power to *cast a lustre on* (line 3094), and so be strengthened by, the memory of departed hopes rather than allow her mind to be *darkened* (ine 3093) by them. This sense is altered by *Rossetti 1870, 1878* and *Dowden 1891* who remove the comma after *me.*

3103. gave –] The dash signifies 'i.e.'

3104. One mind] Cythna's education by the exploration of her own mind is a narrative figure underpinned by the idealist conception of universal mind in which all individual minds participate and which is subject to neither time nor space. S. summarised the position he had adopted on the matter, citing Sir William Drummond's *Academical Questions* (1805), in late 1819 in the prose fragment *On Life*: 'The words, *I, you, they*, are not signs of any actual difference subsisting between the assemblage of thoughts thus indicated, but are merely marks employed to denote the different modifications of the one mind' (*Reiman (1977)* 477–8). S. cites Drummond in a footnote to the Preface 102. See note thereto and *Wasserman* 145–8.

3106. grave,] *Locock 1911* (followed by *1975*) removes the comma 'in order to bring out the meaning that the grave and sympathy are the fountains of fear and hope respectively'. But 'fountains of hope and fear' could equally well characterise the whole range of ideas and experiences evoked as 'all moving things that are' (line 3105). The draft in *Nbk 3* is defective.

Stanza xxxii. Cythna's mental experiences in this stanza recapitulate and perfect the philosophy that was *dimly taught / In old Crotona*; i.e. by Pythagoras in ancient Croton, the Greek colony on the Calabrian coast of southern Italy where he lived in the sixth century BC. What these are is not specified; in particular neither of two well-known Pythagorean doctrines, vegetarianism and the transmigration of souls, is mentioned. Rather it seems that Cythna achieves intuitive understanding, which she expresses in geometrical symbols, of the Pythagorean conviction that the basis of reality is mathematical. As they form in her mind, she represents her ideas by sketching them in *elemental shapes* on the sand and by rearrangements of these is able to grasp conceptions subtler than those that could be apprehended in language. That her memory then passes to the melodies she would hear in the cave is apt, as Pythagoras had defined musical intervals by means of mathematical ratios. The Pythagorean conception of cosmic harmony is celebrated in Thomas Moore's *The Genius of Harmony. An Irregular Ode* which S. read in 1817 (see note to lines 2940–1).

Clear, elemental shapes, whose smallest change
A subtler language within language wrought:
The key of truths which once were dimly taught
In old Crotona; — and sweet melodies
3115 Of love, in that lorn solitude I caught
From mine own voice in dream, when thy dear eyes
Shone through my sleep, and did that utterance harmonize.

XXXIII

'Thy songs were winds whereon I fled at will,
As in a wingèd chariot, o'er the plain
3120 Of crystal youth; and thou wert there to fill
My heart with joy, and there we sate again
On the grey margin of the glimmering main,
Happy as then but wiser far, for we
Smiled on the flowery grave in which were lain
3125 Fear, Faith, and Slavery; and mankind was free,
Equal, and pure and wise, in wisdom's prophecy.

XXXIV

'For to my will my fancies were as slaves
To do their sweet and subtle ministries;
And oft from that bright fountain's shadowy waves
3130 They would make human throngs gather and rise
To combat with my overflowing eyes,
And voice made deep with passion — thus I grew
Familiar with the shock and the surprise
And war of earthly minds, from which I drew
3135 The power which has been mine to frame their thoughts anew.

XXXV

'And thus my prison was the populous earth —
Where I saw — even as misery dreams of morn
Before the east has given its glory birth —

3115. *lorn*] *Forman 1876–7*; lone *L&C/RofI*. Forman introduced the emendation from *L&C* (PM) where it is made in ink. The draft in *Nbk 3* 73 appears to read 'lorn' but is difficult to decipher with confidence.

3124. *lain*] Cp. line 1377 and note.

3126. *Eds* have variously repunctuated the line but the punctuation of *L&C/RofI* creates significant pairings (*free/equal* – *pure/wise*) as well as imparting a peculiar rhythm to the alexandrine. The sense that is completed by the final adverbial phrase is that in the prophetic wisdom of their joyful youth as recovered in Cythna's dream-vision, mankind appeared in its full social perfection.

3131. *To combat*] 'To contend in argument' (*Locock 1911*).

Religion's pomp made desolate by the scorn
3140 Of Wisdom's faintest smile, and thrones uptorn,
And dwellings of mild people interspersed
With undivided fields of ripening corn,
And love made free, — a hope which we have nursed
Even with our blood and tears, — until its glory burst.

XXXVI

3145 'All is not lost! there is some recompense
For hope whose fountain can be thus profound,
Even throned Evil's splendid impotence,
Girt by its hell of power, the secret sound
Of hymns to truth and freedom — the dread bound
3150 Of life and death passed fearlessly and well,
Dungeons wherein the high resolve is found,
Racks which degraded woman's greatness tell,
And what may else be good and irresistible.

XXXVII

'Such are the thoughts which, like the fires that flare
3155 In storm-encompassed isles, we cherish yet
In this dark ruin — such were mine even there;
As in its sleep some odorous violet,
While yet its leaves with nightly dews are wet,
Breathes in prophetic dreams of day's uprise,
3160 Or, as ere Scythian frost in fear has met
Spring's messengers descending from the skies,
The buds foreknow their life — this hope must ever rise.

XXXVIII

'So years had passed, when sudden earthquake rent
The depth of ocean, and the cavern cracked
3165 With sound, as if the world's wide continent
Had fallen in universal ruin wracked;
And through the cleft streamed in one cataract,
The stifling waters: — when I woke, the flood
Whose banded waves that crystal cave had sacked
3170 Was ebbing round me, and my bright abode
Before me yawned — a chasm desert, and bare, and broad.

3142. *undivided*] Held in common.

3147. *Even*] Specifically, namely.

3160. *Scythian*] In ancient geography Scythia designated the regions northeast of the
Caspian Sea, corresponding to European and Asiatic Russia. See headnote to no. 175.

XXXIX

'Above me was the sky, beneath the sea:
I stood upon a point of shattered stone,
And heard loose rocks rushing tumultuously
3175 With splash and shock into the deep — anon
All ceased, and there was silence wide and lone.
I felt that I was free! the Ocean-spray
Quivered beneath my feet, the broad Heaven shone
Around, and in my hair the winds did play
3180 Lingering as they pursued their unimpeded way.

XL

'My spirit moved upon the sea like wind
Which round some thymy cape will lag and hover,
Though it can wake the still cloud, and unbind
The strength of tempest: day was almost over,
3185 When through the fading light I could discover
A ship approaching — its white sails were fed
With the north wind — its moving shade did cover
The twilight deep; — the mariners in dread
Cast anchor when they saw new rocks around them spread.

XLI

3190 'And when they saw one sitting on a crag,
They sent a boat to me; — the sailors rowed
In awe through many a new and fearful jag
Of overhanging rock, through which there flowed
The foam of streams that cannot make abode.
3195 They came and questioned me, but when they heard
My voice, they became silent, and they stood
And moved as men in whom new love had stirred
Deep thoughts: so to the ship we passed without a word.

Canto Eighth

I

'I sate beside the steersman then, and gazing
3200 Upon the west, cried, "Spread the sails! behold!
The sinking moon is like a watch-tower blazing
Over the mountains yet; — the City of Gold
Yon Cape alone does from the sight withhold;

3181. 'And the Spirit of God moved upon the face of the waters' (*Genesis* i 2).

194

The stream is fleet — the north breathes steadily
3205   Beneath the stars, they tremble with the cold!
Ye cannot rest upon the dreary sea! —
Haste, haste to the warm home of happier destiny!"

II

'The Mariners obeyed — the Captain stood
Aloof, and whispering to the Pilot, said,
3210   "Alas, alas! I fear we are pursued
By wicked ghosts: a Phantom of the Dead,
The night before we sailed, came to my bed
In dream, like that!" — The Pilot then replied,
"It cannot be — she is a human Maid —
3215   Her low voice makes you weep — she is some bride,
Or daughter of high birth — she can be nought beside."

III

'We passed the islets, borne by wind and stream,
And as we sailed, the Mariners came near
And thronged around to listen; — in the gleam
3220   Of the pale moon I stood, as one whom fear
May not attaint, and my calm voice did rear;
"Ye all are human — yon broad moon gives light
To millions who the selfsame likeness wear,
Even while I speak — beneath this very night,
3225   Their thoughts flow on like ours, in sadness or delight.

IV

' "What dream ye? Your own hands have built an home,
Even for yourselves on a belovèd shore:
For some, fond eyes are pining till they come,
How they will greet him when his toils are o'er,
3230   And laughing babes rush from the well-known door!
Is this your care? ye toil for your own good —

3211. *wicked ghosts*] water spirites *Nbk 3* 79. S.'s revision renders less conspicuous the resemblance of this stanza to the exchange between the hermit and the pilot in *The Rime of the Ancient Mariner* vii stanzas 1–6, which S. appears to be adapting.

3222. The double speech-marks to indicate Cythna's address to the mariners, which begins here and continues until line 3397, are not present in *L&C/RofI. Ye all are*] Ye are all *1839, Rossetti 1870, Woodberry 1893*. The draft (*Nbk 3* 80) reads: 'We are all', which agrees with *ours* in line 3225, so that an error of transcription or printing is possible.

3226. *an home*] a home *1839, Rossetti 1870*. The draft (*Nbk 3* 81) reads 'a home', as does the draft (*Nbk 3* 189) for line 4432 which ends as this line does: 'built a home'. The *an* in the present line may well be the compositor's preferred form.

Ye feel and think — has some immortal power
Such purposes? or in a human mood,
Dream ye that God thus builds for man in solitude?

V

3235 ' "What then is God? ye mock yourselves, and give
A human heart to what ye cannot know:
As if the cause of life could think and live!
'Twere as if man's own works should feel, and show
The hopes, and fears, and thoughts from which they flow,
3240 And he be like to them. Lo! Plague is free
To waste, Blight, Poison, Earthquake, Hail, and Snow,
Disease, and Want, and worse Necessity
Of hate and ill, and Pride, and Fear, and Tyranny.

VI

' "What then is God? Some moon-struck sophist stood
3245 Watching the shade from his own soul upthrown
Fill Heaven and darken Earth, and in such mood
The Form he saw and worshipped was his own,
His likeness in the world's vast mirror shown;
And 'twere an innocent dream, but that a faith

3234. that God] some Power *Rofl. in solitude*] In the necessary *solitude* of divinity, which by its nature cannot manifest human social instincts.

3235. What then is God?] What is that Power? *Rofl.*

3235–40. S. has Cythna summarily state the objections of critical scepticism to the supposition of a creative and sustaining deity – that it attributes to its explanation the characteristics of that which it seeks to explain. The case against the rational basis for belief in God is systematically argued by Eusebius in *A Refutation of Deism* (1814) (*Prose Works* i 112–23); e.g., 'There is no attribute of God which is not either borrowed from the passions and powers of the human mind, or which is not a negation' (120).

3237. In *L&C* (PM) there is a cross, itself deleted, against this line as if it too had at first been intended for revision as impious: see *Forman 1876–7*.

3244. What then is God?] What is that Power? *Rofl.*

3244–8. Bryan Shelley (*Shelley and Scripture* (1994) 186) cites *Romans* i 23: 'And change the glory of the uncorruptible God into an image made like to corruptible man'. But Cythna is not seeking to assert any independently-existing divine perfection; the process she describes invents God by projecting human imperfection, as in *Q Mab* vi 94–110. See note to lines 3235–40, and cp. Leigh Hunt's sonnet *To Percy Shelley: On the Degrading Notions of Deity* (1818): 'What wonder, Percy, that with jealous rage / Men should defame the kindly and the wise, / When in the midst of the all-beauteous skies, / And all this lovely world, that should engage / Their mutual search for the old golden age, / They seat a phantom, swelled into grim size / Out of their own passions and bigotries, / And then, for fear, proclaim it meek and sage! / And this they call a light and a revealing! / Wise as the clown, who plodding home at night / In autumn, turns at call of fancied elf, / And sees upon the fog, with ghastly feeling, / A giant shadow in its imminent might, / Which his own lanthorn throws up from himself'.

3250   Nursed by fear's dew of poison, grows thereon,
    And that men say, God has appointed Death
    On all who scorn his will, to wreak immortal wrath.

VII

    ' "Men say they have seen God, and heard from God,
    Or known from others who have known such things,
3255   And that his will is all our law, a rod
    To scourge us into slaves — that Priests and Kings,
    Custom, domestic sway, ay, all that brings
    Man's free-born soul beneath the oppressor's heel,
    Are his strong ministers, and that the stings
3260   Of death will make the wise his vengeance feel,
    Though truth and virtue arm their hearts with tenfold steel.

VIII

    ' "And it is said, that God will punish wrong;
    Yes, add despair to crime, and pain to pain!
    And his red hell's undying snakes among,
3265   Will bind the wretch on whom he fixed a stain,
    Which, like a plague, a burden, and a bane,
    Clung to him while he lived; — for love and hate,

3251. God has appointed Death] that Power has chosen Death *Rofl*.

3252. his will,] it's [sic] laws, *Rofl*; his will *L&C*. The comma added to the altered phrase in the cancel-leaf for *Rofl* has been adopted because its clarification of the ambiguous meaning applies equally to the *L&C* text. That meaning becomes: 'God (that Power) wreaks his wrath on those who scorn his will by condemning them to eternal death', rather than: 'God (that Power) condemns to death all those who dismiss his power to vent his anger'.

3253–6. Men say that they themselves have heard and seen, / Or known from others who have known such things, / A Shade, a Form, which Earth and Heaven between / Wields an invisible rod – *Rofl*.

3259–60. stings / Of death] 'The sting of death is sin; and the strength of sin is the law' (*1 Corinthians* xv 56). Cythna attributes to the civil and religious doctrines of established power a vindictive legalism that St Paul, in the context of the passage alluded to, declares to have been abrogated by the sacrifice of Christ.

3262. that God] this Power *Rofl*.

3264. And deepest hell, and deathless snakes among, *Rofl*. The comma after *among* introduced in the cancel-leaf for *Rofl* has been adopted. Cp. *Isaiah* lxvi 24: 'for their worm shall not die, neither shall their fire be quenched'.

3265. he] is *Rofl*; he *Nbk 3* 84. Forman *1876–7* points out that the *Rofl* reading, which is not entered by S. in *L&C* (PM), might have been introduced by the printer. That the printer's care for religious orthodoxy (see headnote *Composition and Publication*, p. 15 and notes to Preface lines 42, 249) might lead him to remove any remaining suggestion of divine responsibility for sin is possible and a likelier hypothesis than that S. would make this further alteration voluntarily.

3267. for] *Rofl*; for, *L&C*. The *Rofl* reading, introduced on the cancel-leaf, is adopted here and in the next line.

Virtue and vice, they say are difference vain —
The will of strength is right — this human state
3270   Tyrants, that they may rule, with lies thus desolate.

IX

' "Alas, what strength? opinion is more frail
Than yon dim cloud now fading on the moon
Even while we gaze, though it awhile avail
To hide the orb of truth — and every throne
3275   Of Earth or Heaven, though shadow rests thereon,
One shape of many names: — for this ye plough
The barren waves of ocean, hence each one
Is slave or tyrant; all betray and bow,
Command, or kill, or fear, or wreak, or suffer woe.

X

3280   ' "Its names are each a sign which maketh holy
All power — ay, the ghost, the dream, the shade
Of power — lust, falsehood, hate, and pride, and folly;

3268. they say] Rofl; they say, *L&C*. See previous note.

3270. Tyrants,] Rofl; Tyrants *L&C*. See note to line 3267.

3275. shadow] Rofl; shadow, *L&C, 1839*. The removal of the comma after *shadow* in the cancel-leaf for *Rofl*, which was not made in *L&C* (PM), has not been widely accepted by *eds*, even those who adopt the *Rofl* text, because it materially alters the sense of lines 3271–6 in a way that they have found inferior to the meaning that results when the comma is present. This is a very difficult textual crux for which an entirely satisfactory solution is unlikely, given the nature of the case. The problem begins with the draft of the stanza in *Nbk 3* (84–5). There, although much revised, the first three and a half lines, and the final four, exist in a state close to the printed version. Not so the latter half of line 3274 and all of line 3275 which are only roughly sketched with heavy cancellation, so leaving S. the tricky problem of connecting them with the syntactically complete statements that come before and after when he transcribed the fair copy. If the comma after *shadow* in *L&C* is allowed to stand, the resulting sense is: 'Every throne on earth or in heaven rests on opinion, and every one, though no more than shadow, is the same shape whatever name it assumes'. This alternative has the advantage of giving a sense that is coherent and characteristic enough, as well as readily providing the clause that runs between the dashes from line 3274 to line 3276 with a main verb (*rests*). The balance of textual evidence decides against it, however: there is no comma after *shadow* in the (admittedly rough) draft and the comma is removed from the cancel-leaf for *Rofl*, the proofs of which it is probable that S. read (see headnote *Composition and Publication*, p. 17). Without the comma the meaning becomes: 'and every throne on earth or in heaven [is also frail], though shadow rests on them, the same shape whatever name it assume'. This reading, although it relies upon an implied repetition of the verb from line 3271, gives an image of a dark shape on a throne which is a favourite of S.'s, as in lines 629–30, 3311 taken together with 3379–80, or in *PU* II iv 1–6. Neither with the comma nor without it is the transition between the first three and a half and the second three and a half lines of the stanza (which were virtually completed in the draft) especially smooth; nor is the concessive sense of *though* evidently appropriate.

3278. tyrant;] tyrant, L&C: alteration in cancel-leaf for *Rofl*.

3282. power –] Rofl; power, – *L&C*. Alteration introduced in the cancel-leaf for *Rofl*.

198

The pattern whence all fraud and wrong is made,
A law to which mankind has been betrayed;
3285 And human love, is as the name well known
Of a dear mother, whom the murderer laid
In bloody grave, and into darkness thrown,
Gathered her wildered babes around him as his own.

XI

' "O love! who to the hearts of wandering men
3290 Art as the calm to Ocean's weary waves!
Justice, or truth, or joy! those only can
From slavery and religion's labyrinth caves
Guide us, as one clear star the seaman saves, —
To give to all an equal share of good,
3295 To track the steps of freedom though through graves
She pass, to suffer all in patient mood,
To weep for crime, though stained with thy friend's dearest blood.

XII

' "To feel the peace of self-contentment's lot,
To own all sympathies, and outrage none,
3300 And in the inmost bowers of sense and thought,

3285–8. The drafts for the final four lines of the stanza, which continue the thought otherwise than in the printed version, occupy an entire page in *Nbk 3* (86). From the false starts and revisions it is possible conjecturally to reconstruct the incomplete development of a condensed history of the human fall from a happier condition: 'justice, and natural love whose [ ] / Fled far, & Justice who all things had weighed / In equal balance while the world's fair youth / Yet smiled, & holiest love [ ] / Hence blood, & fierce dominions, and [ ] / Hence good & evil [ ]'.

3289. men] man *Rossetti 1870, 1878, Dowden 1891.* Rossetti considered the necessity of rhyme a warrant to emend, also emending *hearts* to 'heart'. The confusion exists in the draft in *Nbk 3* (87) which reads: 'to the hearts of wandering man'. S. would seem to have preferred the plural at the expense of the half-rhyme when preparing the fair copy.

3291. those] thou *Rofl*; these *L&C.* The *L&C* reading is corrected to *those* in the list of Errata. S. did not make the correction in *L&C* (PM). Forman, *The Shelley Library* (1886) 79, conjectured that S. made it on the proof of the cancel-leaf for *Rofl* and that the compositor misread his 'those' as 'thou'. The draft in *Nbk 3* can be read as either 'those' or 'thou'.

3293. saves, –] saves. *L&C/Rofl*; saves, – *Nbk 3* 87. The full stop here and at the end of the stanza in *L&C/Rofl* leave the series of infinitive clauses in between unattached to a main verb. Most modern *eds* have weakened the full stop at the end of 3297 in order to carry the series down to line 3304 in the next stanza and make it in its entirety the subject of *is* in line 3305. *Forman 1876–7* is unusual in preferring to substitute a comma after *saves* (line 3293) so that the infinitive clauses as far as *blood* (line 3297) complement the verb *Guide* in line 3293. One full stop or the other must be altered. Forman's emendation gains support from the draft; its punctuation has been adopted here.

3297. 'To pity (and not revenge) crime, even though it be the murder of thy dearest friend'. *crime,]* *Rofl, Nbk 3* 87; crime *L&C:* alteration on cancel-leaf for *Rofl*.

Until life's sunny day is quite gone down,
To sit and smile with Joy, or, not alone,
To kiss salt tears from the worn cheek of Woe;
To live, as if to love and live were one, —
3305 This is not faith or law, nor those who bow
To thrones on Heaven or Earth, such destiny may know.

XIII

' "But children near their parents tremble now,
Because they must obey — one rules another,
For it is said God rules both high and low,
3310 And man is made the captive of his brother,
And Hate is throned on high with Fear her mother,
Above the Highest — and those fountain-cells,
Whence love yet flowed when faith had choked all other,
Are darkened — Woman, as the bond-slave, dwells
3315 Of man, a slave; and life is poisoned in its wells.

XIV

' "Man seeks for gold in mines, that he may weave
A lasting chain for his own slavery; —
In fear and restless care that he may live
He toils for others, who must ever be
3320 The joyless thralls of like captivity;
He murders, for his chiefs delight in ruin;
He builds the altar, that its idol's fee
May be his very blood; he is pursuing
O, blind and willing wretch! his own obscure undoing.

XV

3325 ' "Woman! — she is his slave, she has become
A thing I weep to speak — the child of scorn,

3309–10. And as one Power rules both high and low, / So man is made . . . *Rofl*.

3311. *her*] *Rofl*; his *L&C*. The change on the cancel-leaf for *Rofl* is not entered in *L&C* (PM). *Eds* have been divided over which reading to adopt. *Forman 1876–7*, opting for 'his', cites lines 4165–6: 'for Fear is never slow / To build the thrones of Hate, her mate and foe'. *Nbk* 3 88 shows that S. originally wrote 'his', cancelled it and substituted what looks like 'her' above the line, perhaps to avoid the jingle 'his brother . . . his mother'. It may then be that S. corrected on the proof of the cancel-leaf an error of transcription from draft which had passed uncorrected on the original proof.

3315. *man,*] *Rofl*; man *L&C*. The alteration in the cancel-leaf for *Rofl*, which is not made in *L&C* (PM), clarifies the meaning of what can seem an enigmatic assertion. S. wrote in the draft (*Nbk* 3 88): 'Woman as the [bond-slave] dwells / Of man who is a slave'. In the context of the entire stanza, the sense of the final two lines would be: 'Man who is already the slave of a tyranny sanctioned by religion, in his turn enslaves woman'.

The outcast of a desolated home,
Falsehood, and fear, and toil, like waves have worn
Channels upon her cheek, which smiles adorn,
3330 As calm decks the false Ocean: — well ye know
What Woman is, for none of Woman born,
Can choose but drain the bitter dregs of woe,
Which ever from the oppressed to the oppressors flow.

XVI

' "This need not be; ye might arise, and will
3335 That gold should lose its power, and thrones their glory;
That love, which none may bind, be free to fill
The world, like light; and evil faith, grown hoary
With crime, be quenched and die. — Yon promontory
Even now eclipses the descending moon! —
3340 Dungeons and palaces are transitory —
High temples fade like vapour — Man alone
Remains, whose will has power when all beside is gone.

XVII

' "Let all be free and equal! — from your hearts
I feel an echo; through my inmost frame
3345 Like sweetest sound, seeking its mate, it darts —
Whence come ye, friends? alas, I cannot name
All that I read of sorrow, toil, and shame,
On your worn faces; as in legends old
Which make immortal the disastrous fame
3350 Of conquerors and impostors false and bold,
The discord of your hearts, I in your looks behold.

XVIII

' "Whence come ye, friends? from pouring human blood
Forth on the earth? or bring ye steel and gold,
That Kings may dupe and slay the multitude?
3355 Or from the famished poor, pale, weak, and cold,
Bear ye the earnings of their toil? unfold!
Speak! are your hands in slaughter's sanguine hue
Stained freshly? have your hearts in guile grown old?

3330–3. 'You understand well the condition of woman because in oppressing her you taste the woe that all human beings experience when they oppress others'.

3337–9. That the great name whose Idol is more hoary / Than fear or crime, shall be a blasphemy / Not heard among mankind – *Nbk 3* 91.

3360

Know yourselves thus! ye shall be pure as dew,
And I will be a friend and sister unto you.

XIX

' "Disguise it not — we have one human heart —
All mortal thoughts confess a common home:
Blush not for what may to thyself impart
Stains of inevitable crime: the doom

3365

Is this, which has, or may, or must become
Thine, and all humankind's. Ye are the spoil
Which Time thus marks for the devouring tomb,
Thou and thy thoughts and they, and all the toil
Wherewith ye twine the rings of life's perpetual coil.

XX

3370

' "Disguise it not — ye blush for what ye hate,
And Enmity is sister unto Shame;
Look on your mind — it is the book of fate —
Ah! it is dark with many a blazoned name
Of misery — all are mirrors of the same;

3375

But the dark fiend who with his iron pen
Dipped in scorn's fiery poison, makes his fame
Enduring there, would o'er the heads of men
Pass harmless, if they scorned to make their hearts his den.

XXI

' "Yes, it is Hate, that shapeless fiendly thing

3380

Of many names, all evil, some divine,
Whom self-contempt arms with a mortal sting;
Which, when the heart its snaky folds entwine
Is wasted quite, and when it doth repine
To gorge such bitter prey, on all beside

3385

It turns with ninefold rage, as with its twine
When Amphisbaena some fair bird has tied,
Soon o'er the putrid mass he threats on every side.

3361. we have one human heart] 'That we have all of us one human heart', Wordsworth, *The Old Cumberland Beggar* (1800) 146. S. appropriates Wordsworth's formulation of a universal impulse to benevolence, redefining it in this stanza and over the next three as the basis of Cythna's counsel to the mariners: they must not allow shame for their past crimes to breed enmity and hate in their hearts for what is common to all hearts.

3368. they] All of humankind, as in line 3366.

3377–8. See note to lines 1627–8.

3379–80. See line 363 and note, and line 3276.

3385. twine] Coil.

3386. Amphisbaena] A fabulous serpent with a head at either end mentioned by Lucan, *Pharsalia* ix 719 and Milton, *Paradise Lost* x 524. Cp. *PU* III iv 119.

XXII

' "Reproach not thine own soul, but know thyself,
Nor hate another's crime, nor loathe thine own.

3390   It is the dark idolatry of self,
Which, when our thoughts and actions once are gone,
Demands that man should weep, and bleed, and groan;
O vacant expiation! be at rest. —
The past is Death's, the future is thine own;

3395   And love and joy can make the foulest breast
A paradise of flowers, where peace might build her nest.

XXIII

' "Speak thou! whence come ye?" — A Youth made reply,
"Wearily, wearily o'er the boundless deep
We sail; — thou readest well the misery

3400   Told in these faded eyes, but much doth sleep
Within, which there the poor heart loves to keep,
Or dare not write on the dishonoured brow;
Even from our childhood have we learned to steep
The bread of slavery in the tears of woe,

3405   And never dreamed of hope or refuge until now.

XXIV

' "Yes — I must speak — my secret should have perished
Even with the heart it wasted, as a brand
Fades in the dying flame whose life it cherished,
But that no human bosom can withstand

3410   Thee, wondrous Lady, and the mild command
Of thy keen eyes: — yes, we are wretched slaves,
Who from their wonted loves and native land
Are reft, and bear o'er the dividing waves
The unregarded prey of calm and happy graves.

3388. know thyself] S. anticipated Cythna's association of the celebrated maxim with love in a letter to MWS of 28 October 1814: 'How divinely sweet a task it is to imitate each others excellencies – & each moment to become wiser in this surpassing love – so that constituting but one being, all real knowledge may be comprised in the maxim γνωθι σεαυτον (know thyself) with infinitely more justice than in its narrow & common application' (L i 414).

3396. S. began to draft another stanza at this point in *Nbk 3* (115a) but broke off without finishing it: 'Each moment is the grave of all the past / And cradle of the things that are to be. – / The dead will waken at no trumpets blast / [The living cannot]'. Cp. lines 3394, 1819–21 (and note).

3414. 'Those who would have been happier in the untroubled grave but that death has neglected to take them'.

XXV

3415 ' "We drag afar from pastoral vales the fairest,
Among the daughters of those mountains lone,
We drag them there, where all things best and rarest
Are stained and trampled: — years have come and gone
Since, like the ship which bears me, I have known
3420 No thought; — but now the eyes of one dear Maid
On mine with light of mutual love have shone —
She is my life, — I am but as the shade
Of her, — a smoke sent up from ashes, soon to fade.

XXVI

' "For she must perish in the tyrant's hall —
3425 Alas, alas!" — He ceased, and by the sail
Sate cowering — but his sobs were heard by all,
And still before the ocean and the gale
The ship fled fast till the stars 'gan to fail,
And round me gathered with mute countenance,
3430 The Seamen gazed, the Pilot, worn and pale
With toil, the Captain with grey locks, whose glance
Met mine in restless awe — they stood as in a trance.

XXVII

' "Recede not! pause not now! thou art grown old,
But Hope will make thee young, for Hope and Youth
3435 Are children of one mother, even Love — behold!
The eternal stars gaze on us! — is the truth
Within your soul? care for your own, or ruth
For others' sufferings? do ye thirst to bear
A heart which not the serpent custom's tooth
3440 May violate? — be free! and even here,
Swear to be firm till death!" they cried, "We swear! we swear!"

XXVIII

'The very darkness shook, as with a blast
Of subterranean thunder at the cry;
The hollow shore its thousand echoes cast
3445 Into the night, as if the sea, and sky,

3415. [And we bring slaves from Caucasus], the fairest Nbk 3 94.

3418. Are stained and trampled] Are turned to uses vile Nbk 3 94.

3438. others'] other's L&C/RofI, 1839, Nbk 3 96. Most modern eds silently correct the singular possessive which is in the draft and seems not to have been corrected in the transcription of fair copy.

And earth, rejoiced with new-born liberty,
For in that name they swore! Bolts were undrawn,
And on the deck, with unaccustomed eye
The captives gazing stood, and every one
3450 Shrank as the inconstant torch upon her countenance shone.

XXIX

'They were earth's purest children, young and fair,
With eyes the shrines of unawakened thought,
And brows as bright as spring or morning, ere
Dark time had there its evil legend wrought
3455 In characters of cloud which wither not. —
The change was like a dream to them; but soon
They knew the glory of their altered lot,
In the bright wisdom of youth's breathless noon,
Sweet talk, and smiles, and sighs, all bosoms did attune.

XXX

3460 'But one was mute, her cheeks and lips most fair,
Changing their hue like lilies newly blown,
Beneath a bright acacia's shadowy hair,
Waved by the wind amid the sunny noon,
Showed that her soul was quivering; and full soon
3465 That Youth arose, and breathlessly did look
On her and me, as for some speechless boon:
I smiled, and both their hands in mine I took,
And felt a soft delight from what their spirits shook.

Canto Ninth

I

'That night we anchored in a woody bay,
3470 And sleep no more around us dared to hover
Than, when all doubt and fear has passed away,
It shades the couch of some unresting lover,
Whose heart is now at rest: thus night passed over
In mutual joy: — around, a forest grew
3475 Of poplars and dark oaks, whose shade did cover
The waning stars pranked in the waters blue,
And trembled in the wind which from the morning flew.

3476. *pranked*] (*OED* Prank v. 4d.) cites this instance of the past participle as an apparently erroneous usage for 'set' (like a gem). Cp. *Hellas* 1048–9: 'mountains and islands inviolably / Pranked on the sapphire sea'.

II

'The joyous mariners, and each free maiden,
Now brought from the deep forest many a bough,
3480   With woodland spoil most innocently laden;
Soon wreaths of budding foliage seemed to flow
Over the mast and sails, the stern and prow
Were canopied with blooming boughs, — the while
On the slant sun's path o'er the waves we go
3485   Rejoicing, like the dwellers of an isle
Doomed to pursue those waves that cannot cease to smile.

III

'The many ships spotting the dark blue deep
With snowy sails, fled fast as ours came nigh,
In fear and wonder; and on every steep
3490   Thousands did gaze, they heard the startling cry,
Like earth's own voice lifted unconquerably
To all her children, the unbounded mirth,
The glorious joy of thy name — Liberty!
They heard! — As o'er the mountains of the earth
3495   From peak to peak leap on the beams of morning's birth:

IV

'So from that cry over the boundless hills,
Sudden was caught one universal sound,
Like a volcano's voice, whose thunder fills
Remotest skies, — such glorious madness found
3500   A path through human hearts with stream which drowned
Its struggling fears and cares, dark custom's brood,
They knew not whence it came, but felt around
A wide contagion poured — they called aloud
On Liberty — that name lived on the sunny flood.

V

3505   'We reached the port — alas! from many spirits
The wisdom which had waked that cry, was fled,
Like the brief glory which dark Heaven inherits
From the false dawn, which fades ere it is spread,

Stanza ii. The rejoicing ship covered with *blooming boughs* recalls Phaedria's mirthful boat
in *Faerie Queene* II vi 2 which is 'bedecked trim / With boughes and arbours wouen cun-
ningly, / That like a little forrest seemed outwardly'.

3486. Doomed] Destined.

3498. volcano's voice] See line 2892 and note.   *3503. contagion*] *PU* III iii 93–5 and note.

Upon the night's devouring darkness shed:
3510 Yet soon bright day will burst — even like a chasm
Of fire, to burn the shrouds outworn and dead,
Which wrap the world; a wide enthusiasm,
To cleanse the fevered world as with an earthquake's spasm!

VI

'I walked through the great City then, but free
3515 From shame or fear; those toil-worn Mariners
And happy Maidens did encompass me;
And like a subterranean wind that stirs
Some forest among caves, the hopes and fears
From every human soul, a murmur strange
3520 Made as I passed; and many wept, with tears
Of joy and awe, and wingèd thoughts did range,
And half-extinguished words, which prophesied of change.

VII

'For, with strong speech I tore the veil that hid
Nature, and Truth, and Liberty, and Love, —
3525 As one who from some mountain's pyramid,
Points to the unrisen sun!— the shades approve
His truth, and flee from every stream and grove.
Thus, gentle thoughts did many a bosom fill, —
Wisdom, the mail of tried affections wove
3530 For many a heart, and tameless scorn of ill,
Thrice steeped in molten steel the unconquerable will.

VIII

'Some said I was a maniac wild and lost;
Some, that I scarce had risen from the grave
The Prophet's virgin bride, a heavenly ghost: —
3535 Some said, I was a fiend from my weird cave,
Who had stolen human shape, and o'er the wave,
The forest, and the mountain came; — some said

3526. *approve*] Confirm, give proof of.

3534. *The Prophet's virgin bride*] Some of the Muslims of the Golden City take Cythna to be the resurrected ghost of Ayesha, the youngest of Mahomet's wives. S. could have read of her in Gibbon, *The History of the Decline and Fall of the Roman Empire* (1776–88) l: 'What is singular enough, they were all widows, excepting only Ayesha, the daughter of Abubeker. *She* was doubtless a virgin, since Mahomet consummated his nuptials (such is the premature ripeness of the climate) when she was only nine years of age. The youth, the beauty, the spirit of Ayesha, gave her a superior ascendant: she was beloved and trusted by the prophet; and, after his death, the daughter of Abubeker was long revered as the mother of the faithful'.

I was the child of God, sent down to save
Women from bonds and death, and on my head
3540   The burden of their sins would frightfully be laid.

IX

'But soon my human words found sympathy
In human hearts: the purest and the best,
As friend with friend made common cause with me,
And they were few, but resolute; — the rest,
3545   Ere yet success the enterprise had blessed,
Leagued with me in their hearts; — their meals, their slumber,
Their hourly occupations were possessed
By hopes which I had armed to overnumber
Those hosts of meaner cares, which life's strong wings encumber.

X

3550   'But chiefly women, whom my voice did waken
From their cold, careless, willing slavery,
Sought me: one truth their dreary prison has shaken, —
They looked around, and lo! they became free!
Their many tyrants sitting desolately
3555   In slave-deserted halls, could none restrain;
For wrath's red fire had withered in the eye,
Whose lightning once was death, — nor fear, nor gain
Could tempt one captive now to lock another's chain.

XI

'Those who were sent to bind me, wept, and felt
3560   Their minds outsoar the bonds which clasped them round,

3538–40. Others in the City take Cythna to be a female Christ who will both liberate women from their servitude and atone for their sins by taking them upon herself. Relevant New Testament references would be *John* viii 32: 'And ye shall know the truth, and the truth shall make you free', and *Romans* v 8: 'But God commendeth his love towards us, in that, while we were yet sinners, Christ died for us'.

3541–2. *human . . . human*] The emphatic repetition insists that Cythna's eloquence is an expression of her humanity and appeals to that of her auditors, rather than deriving from the supernatural sources to which it has been attributed in the preceding stanza.

3548. *overnumber*] *Nbk 3* 104, *1839*, eds; overnumber, *L&C/RofI*. Cythna expresses herself in military metaphor: she has put more troops in the field than the enemy.

3552. *has shaken*] had shaken *Nbk 3* 104, *1975*; has shaken *fair copy = University of Texas MS Shelley, P. B./Works* recto (facsimile in *BSM* viii 176). *Forman 1876–7* suspected that *has shaken* was a misprint, and *1975* emends to 'had shaken' on the strength of the draft in *Nbk 3*. The fair copy shows that if there was an error it was an error of transcription from draft, but it is possible that S. altered the draft reading by preference.

Even as a waxen shape may waste and melt
In the white furnace; and a visioned swound,
A pause of hope and awe the City bound,
Which, like the silence of a tempest's birth,
3565   When in its awful shadow it has wound
The sun, the wind, the ocean, and the earth,
Hung terrible, ere yet the lightnings have leaped forth.

XII

'Like clouds inwoven in the silent sky,
By winds from distant regions meeting there,
3570   In the high name of truth and liberty,
Around the City millions gathered were,
By hopes which sprang from many a hidden lair;
Words, which the lore of truth in hues of fame
Arrayed, thine own wild songs which in the air
3575   Like homeless odours floated, and the name
Of thee, and many a tongue which thou hadst dipped in flame.

3565. wound] *Nbk 3* 105; bound *fair copy* = *University of Texas MS Shelley, P. B./Works* verso (facsimile in *BSM* viii 178); bound *L&C/RofI*; wound *correction in Errata List*. This clear example of mistranscription from draft which is accurately printed from fair copy, then corrected in the Errata List suggests that a similar error of transcription – less conspicuous than here where a duplicated rhyme-word is involved, and so not noticed when the list of Errata was compiled – might account for the state of line 3352 in *L&C/RofI*.

3567. ere . . . forth] Some confusion arises because the adverbial clause appears to be attached to both the preceding relative clause *Which . . . Hung terrible* and the parenthetical simile *like . . . earth*. Better sense seems to be achieved by regarding it as continuing the latter and *Hung terrible* as notionally the final phrase of the syntactical movement that begins after the semicolon in line 3562.

3568–9. 1975 reconstructed a notation in pencil below this stanza in *Nbk 3* 107 as: 'painted by Νεφεληγερετα Ζευς, a partial artist'. The Gk phrase signifies 'Cloud-compelling Zeus'. S.'s note playfully imagines that the image of clouds being brought together by winds in these lines was painted by the father of the gods who controls the sky.

3572. lair;] *RofI*; lair, *L&C*. Alteration in cancel-leaf for *RofI*.

3573. fame] *1975*; grace *L&C/RofI*. The *L&C/RofI* reading has occasioned much editorial intervention. *Forman 1876–7*, followed by *Dowden 1891*, emended to 'flame' even though this duplicated the rhyme-word of line 3576. Considering 'grace' an obvious error, and in the absence of any other textual witness to aid in correcting it, *Locock 1911* preferred to leave a blank space while *Rossetti 1870, 1878* and *Woodberry 1893* print the 'grace' of *L&C/RofI*, *faute de mieux*. In the draft in *Nbk 3* (107) S. first wrote 'glory', cancelled this and substituted what appear to be 'fame' above it and 'grace' below. It seems likely that 'grace' was transcribed into the fair copy by error (see notes to lines 3552, 3565); what is more puzzling is that it was neither listed among the Errata nor corrected when S. altered line 3584 on the same page which is part of a cancel-leaf for *RofI*. As the 'fame' of the draft is the only reading to satisfy the requirement of rhyme, it has been adopted here following the decision of *1975*.

XIII

'The Tyrant knew his power was gone, but Fear,
The nurse of Vengeance, bade him wait the event —
That perfidy and custom, gold and prayer,
3580   And whatsoe'er, when force is impotent,
To fraud the sceptre of the world has lent,
Might, as he judged, confirm his failing sway.
Therefore throughout the streets, the Priests he sent
To curse the rebels. — To their God did they
3585   For Earthquake, Plague, and Want, kneel in the public way.

XIV

'And grave and hoary men were bribed to tell
From seats where law is made the slave of wrong,
How glorious Athens in her splendour fell,
Because her sons were free, — and that among
3590   Mankind, the many to the few belong.
By God, and Nature, and Necessity.
They said, that age was truth, and that the young
Marred with wild hopes the peace of slavery,
With which old times and men had quelled the vain and free.

XV

3595   'And with the falsehood of their poisonous lips
They breathed on the enduring memory

3578. the event] The outcome.

3579. That] So that, in order that.

3580–1. 'When *force* will not serve, kingly authority sanctions every resource of *fraud'*.

3584. God] gods *Rofl.*

3591. God] Heaven *Rofl.*

Stanza xv. The anomaly of a ten-line stanza would seem to have come about in the first place because of the difficulties S. had in composing it. He drafted the first seven lines (up to line 3600) on page 109 of *Nbk 3*, then struggled to complete the final couplet to rhyme with *mankind* (3599). Various attempts at lines ending in 'find' and 'grind' fill the space to the end of the page requiring a leaf to be turned in order to continue, thus concealing the already-drafted seven lines of the stanza from view. He succeeded in completing line 3601 but evidently mistook it for the seventh line of the stanza instead of the eighth and so added two further lines rhyming b–b instead of c–c. So much seems clear. What is puzzling is that the irregular stanza was first transcribed into fair copy and then passed in proof without being corrected. If someone other than S. read the proofs of this part of the poem, which is possible (see headnote *Composition and Publication*, p. 17), then its escaping revision at this stage may be explained by a combination of haste to have the poem appear and his not being on the spot to do the necessary redrafting. S. took the occasion of the revision required by Charles Ollier to reduce the stanza to nine lines by compressing the four lines 3598–3600 into three: 'There was one teacher, who, necessity / Had armed, with strength and wrong against mankind, / His slave and his avenger aye to be;'. This expedient renders the already difficult sense of the

Of sages and of bards a brief eclipse;
3598   There was one teacher, and must ever be,
3598a   They said, even God, who, the necessity
Of rule and wrong had armed against mankind,
3600   His slave and his avenger aye to be;
That we were weak and sinful, frail and blind,
And that the will of one was peace, and we
Should seek for nought on earth but toil and misery.

XVI

' "For thus we might avoid the hell hereafter."
3605   So spake the hypocrites, who cursed and lied;
Alas, their sway was past, and tears and laughter
Clung to their hoary hair, withering the pride
Which in their hollow hearts dared still abide;
And yet obscener slaves with smoother brow,
3610   And sneers on their strait lips, thin, blue and wide,
Said, that the rule of men was over now,
And hence, the subject world to woman's will must bow;

passage even more so, besides creating a different prosodic irregularity in *Rofl* by introducing a c-rhyme instead of a b-rhyme at line five of the stanza. As the imposed alterations and the attempt to regularise the stanzaic form cannot be separated one from the other, the stanza has been printed as it appears in *L&C* with the exception signalled in the note to line 3600.

3598–3600. An obscure passage which seems to yield the sense: 'God had given power to rulers and created the woeful condition of men in order that the ones should serve him unquestioningly and the other wreak his vengeance on humankind'. The obscurity derives in part from the singulars *slave* and *avenger* which refer grammatically to *necessity*. The meaning is clearer in the draft (*Nbk 3* 109) where S. first wrote: 'who the necessity / Of rule & wrong had sent among mankind', then cancelled the final phrase and replaced it with 'placed over mankind'. The draft originally continued: 'His slaves & his avengers'. *1839*, which prints the *Rofl* text, reads: 'whom necessity / Had armed with strength and wrong against mankind'. *Rossetti 1870, 1878* considered *1839*'s 'whom' for 'who' a misprint; it may be that or it may be an attempt to extract another, and quite different, kind of sense from these difficult lines.

3600. aye] *Rofl*; there *L&C*. The alteration in the cancel-leaf for *Rofl* is made in ink in *L&C* (PM), evidently to replace the adverb 'there' which, without a referent in *L&C*, is a survival from the draft (*Nbk 3* 109) where an earlier version of the final phrase of line 3599 read: 'sent into the world'. The fair copy reads 'there': *Trinity College Library MS Cullum* P175r (facsimile in *BSM* viii 180).

3604. L&C/Rofl's double speech-marks enclosing this line appear odd when it seems to continue Cythna's report in indirect speech of what was said by the *hypocrites* which begins in the third person plural in line 3598, shifting to the first person plural (*we* = all human beings) in line 3601. The mood of *might avoid*, which is consistent with *should seek* in the preceding line, hardly resembles direct speech. But the double speech-marks are clearly present in the fair copy; see previous note.

3612. bow;] *Rofl*; bow. *L&C*; bow, *fair copy* = *Trinity College Library MS Cullum* P175r (facsimile in *BSM* viii 180). The *Rofl* reading is not entered in *L&C* (PM) and *Forman 1876–7* doubted whether S. would have made such a change; but there seems no reason why not, especially as the comma in the fair copy signals a continuity between the stanzas. There is no punctuation at this point in the draft in *Nbk 3* 110.

XVII

'And gold was scattered through the streets, and wine
Flowed at a hundred feasts within the wall.
3615 In vain! the steady towers in Heaven did shine
As they were wont, nor at the priestly call,
Left Plague her banquet in the Ethiop's hall,
Nor Famine from the rich man's portal came,
Where at her ease she ever preys on all
3620 Who throng to kneel for food: nor fear nor shame,
Nor faith, nor discord, dimmed hope's newly kindled flame.

XVIII

'For gold was as a god whose faith began
To fade, so that its worshippers were few,
And Hell and Awe, which in the heart of man
3625 Is God itself; the Priests its downfall knew,
As day by day their altars lonelier grew,
Till they were left alone within the fane;
The shafts of falsehood unpolluting flew,

3615–16. steady towers . . . wont] i.e. the earthquake for which the Tyrant's priests prayed in line 3585 did not come about; nor did the famine and plague (3616–20) they called down upon the people.

3617. Plague] *Rofl, fair copy = Trinity College Library MS Cullum* P175v (facsimile in *BSM* viii 182); plague *L&C*. S. capitalised the word in *L&C* (PM) for the *Rofl* cancel-leaf, restoring the fair-copy form no doubt for local consistency with the personified *Famine* of the next line. *Ethiop's hall*] Commentators have agreed that S. alludes to the habit of the Homeric gods of taking time away from their usual involvement in human affairs to go and feast with the Ethiopians. See *Iliad* i 423–5; *Odyssey* i 22–7. The ancient Greeks regarded Ethiopia, broadly the African lands to the south of Egypt, as marking the limits of human habitation. But this is also a specific allusion to the presumed origin of the plague: 'Aethiopia and Egypt have been stigmatised in every age, as the original source and seminary of the plague' (Gibbon, *The History of the Decline and Fall of the Roman Empire* (1776–88) xliii). See note to line 3929.

3622. god] *Rofl, Nbk 3* 111; God *L&C, fair copy = Trinity College Library MS Cullum* P175v (facsimile in *BSM* viii 182). The sequence of readings shows, probably, that the 'god' of the draft was capitalised by mistake in the fair copy, printed as 'God', and the draft reading restored by S. (as it is) in *L&C* (PM) for the *Rofl* cancel-leaf. The change happens also to be consistent with the purpose of toning-down the critical view of religion that dictated the changes for *Rofl. Forman 1876–7* left the capital G in place, expressing surprise that S. had lower-cased it in *L&C* (PM); but the capital G, the conventionally respectful spelling indicating 'The One God', is inconsistent with the indefinite article.

3624–7. And Faith itself, which in the heart of man / Gives shape, voice, name, to spectral Terror, knew / Its downfall, as the altars lonelier grew, / Till the Priests stood alone within the fane; Rofl. In these lines S. has not only opportunely improved on the somewhat routine expression of the corresponding passage in *L&C*, but also helped to clarify its sense: 'Hell and Awe ceased to be worshipped as distortions of the divine'.

And the cold sneers of calumny were vain,
3630   The union of the free with discord's brand to stain.

XIX

'The rest thou knowest — Lo! we two are here —
We have survived a ruin wide and deep —
Strange thoughts are mine. — I cannot grieve or fear,
Sitting with thee upon this lonely steep
3635   I smile, though human love should make me weep.
We have survived a joy that knows no sorrow,
And I do feel a mighty calmness creep
Over my heart, which can no longer borrow
Its hues from chance or change, dark children of tomorrow.

XX

3640   'We know not what will come — yet Laon, dearest,
Cythna shall be the prophetess of love,
Her lips shall rob thee of the grace thou wearest,
To hide thy heart, and clothe the shapes which rove
Within the homeless future's wintry grove;
3645   For I now, sitting thus beside thee, seem

3629. [And custom & authority did wane] *Nbk 3* 111.

3631. Cythna's two sentences serve to re-establish the main temporal progression of the narrative as well as recalling the place of narration. Laon entered the revolution that she had precipitated in Canto V at the point at which her account of events now finishes (*The rest thou knowest*). Her echo of the sentence she addressed to Laon – 'And we are here' (line 2561) – as they reached the ruin above the battlefield, closes the interpolated story of her life since their separation in Canto III; after the next line, which epitomises the disastrous collapse of their revolution, her prophecy introduces the narrative of their end.

3633. fear,] In the draft (*Nbk 3* 116) there is no punctuation after *fear* and a semicolon after *steep* in the next line so that the adverbial phrase *Sitting . . . steep* qualifies *I cannot* rather than *I smile*. The fair copy (SC 392) shows a comma crossed with a short line after *fear* which is read as a full stop in *SC* v 183, but as a comma-plus-dash in *BSM* viii 185, and no punctuation after *steep*. The fair-copy punctuation, on either reading, attaches line 3634 to *I smile* and that is also the effect, if less clearly so, of the punctuation in *L&C/RofI*.

3635. human love] Love for humanity.

3637–8. The cancelled version of these lines in *Nbk 3* (116) makes immediately clear the course of Laon and Cythna's fate, which she develops gradually over the next sixteen stanzas: 'The hours henceforth for us may flee or creep / It is the same, for us there is no morrow'.

3640–4. The phrasing can obscure the sense of this important passage. Cythna is proposing to take as her own the *grace* that is created by Laon's poetic art. In S.'s partially-cancelled draft for line 3642 she characterises herself as 'The Poet who shall steal'. Cp. the poet-witch in *The Witch of Atlas*: 'ever she / Added some grace to the wrought poesy' (255–6). This art conceals Laon's deepest feelings – a point S. emphasised by altering his original 'Around thy heart' (*Nbk 3* 116) to *To hide thy heart* – so she will add to it the love she embodies in order to create a prophetic utterance capable of endowing with imaginative form the otherwise *homeless* shapes of the future.

Even with thy breath and blood to live and move,
And violence and wrong are as a dream
Which rolls from steadfast truth an unreturning stream.

XXI

'The blasts of autumn drive the wingèd seeds
3650 Over the earth, — next come the snows, and rain,
And frosts, and storms, which dreary winter leads
Out of his Scythian cave, a savage train;
Behold! Spring sweeps over the world again,
Shedding soft dews from her etherial wings;
3655 Flowers on the mountains, fruits over the plain,
And music on the waves and woods she flings,
And love on all that lives, and calm on lifeless things.

XXII

'O Spring, of hope, and love, and youth, and gladness
Wind-wingèd emblem! brightest, best and fairest!
3660 Whence comest thou, when, with dark winter's sadness
The tears that fade in sunny smiles thou sharest?
Sister of joy, thou art the child who wearest
Thy mother's dying smile, tender and sweet;
Thy mother Autumn, for whose grave thou bearest
3665 Fresh flowers, and beams like flowers, with gentle feet,
Disturbing not the leaves which are her winding-sheet.

XXIII

'Virtue, and Hope, and Love, like light and Heaven,
Surround the world. — We are their chosen slaves.
Has not the whirlwind of our spirit driven
3670 Truth's deathless germs to thought's remotest caves?
Lo, Winter comes! — the grief of many graves,
The frost of death, the tempest of the sword,
The flood of tyranny, whose sanguine waves

3648. truth] Fair copy = SC 392 (facsimile in *SC* v 183, *BSM* viii 186); truth, *eds.* The absence of a comma after *truth* in both fair copy and *L&C/RofI* indicates that *rolls* is probably to be considered as transitive.

3649. The blasts of autumn] The phrase occurs as the opening of Charlotte Smith's sonnet *Written in October* (1798, 1800): *The Poems of Charlotte Smith*, ed. Stuart Curran (1994) 74–5.

3652. Scythian] See note to line 3160.

3661. sharest?] Fair copy = SC 393 (facsimile in *SC* v 185; *BSM* viii 188); sharest; *L&C/RofI*.

3670. germs] Seeds.

3673. sanguine] Sanguinary.

Stagnate like ice at Faith, the enchanter's word,
3675 And bind all human hearts in its repose abhorred.

XXIV

'The seeds are sleeping in the soil: meanwhile
The tyrant peoples dungeons with his prey,
Pale victims on the guarded scaffold smile
Because they cannot speak; and, day by day,
3680 The moon of wasting Science wanes away
Among her stars, and in that darkness vast
The sons of earth to their foul idols pray,
And grey Priests triumph, and like blight or blast
A shade of selfish care o'er human looks is cast.

XXV

3685 'This is the winter of the world; — and here
We die, even as the winds of Autumn fade,
Expiring in the frore and foggy air. —
Behold! Spring comes, though we must pass, who made
The promise of its birth, — even as the shade
3690 Which from our death, as from a mountain, flings
The future, a broad sunrise; thus arrayed
As with the plumes of overshadowing wings,
From its dark gulf of chains, Earth like an eagle springs.

XXVI

'O dearest love! we shall be dead and cold
3695 Before this morn may on the world arise;
Wouldst thou the glory of its dawn behold?
Alas! gaze not on me, but turn thine eyes
On thine own heart — it is a paradise
Which everlasting spring has made its own,
3700 And while drear Winter fills the naked skies,

3683. *blast*] A sudden destructive infection of plants; figuratively, a curse or withering influence.

3688–91. 'We who have been the harbingers of spring must fade before it arrives just as the shade on a dark mountain disappears when it refelects the sunrise (or when the sun suddenly rises over it)'.

3698. *paradise*] Cythna's elaboration of a secular psychology of hope adapts the traditional internal *paradise* of moral perfection which both compensates for loss and promises to recover it. Cp. *Paradise Lost* xii 585–7: 'then wilt thou not be loath / To leave this Paradise, but shalt possess / A paradise within thee, happier far'; and *Luke* xvii 20–1: 'The kingdom of God cometh not with observation: Neither shall they say, Lo here! or, lo there! for, behold, the Kingdom of God is within you'.

Sweet streams of sunny thought, and flowers fresh blown,
Are there, and weave their sounds and odours into one.

XXVII

'In their own hearts the earnest of the hope
Which made them great, the good will ever find;

3705 And though some envious shade may interlope
Between the effect and it, One comes behind,
Who aye the future to the past will bind —
Necessity, whose sightless strength forever
Evil with evil, good with good must wind

3710 In bands of union, which no power may sever:
They must bring forth their kind, and be divided never!

XXVIII

'The good and mighty of departed ages
Are in their graves, the innocent and free,
Heroes, and Poets, and prevailing Sages,

3715 Who leave the vesture of their majesty
To adorn and clothe this naked world; — and we
Are like to them — such perish, but they leave
All hope, or love, or truth, or liberty,
Whose forms their mighty spirits could conceive

3720 To be a rule and law to ages that survive.

3701. Sweet streams of sunny thought] [It is a bower of bliss] *Nbk 3* 121.

3705–6. S. is recuperating an image from the rejected opening of *L&C*, 'Frail clouds arrayed in sunlight lose the glory' (no. 142): 'Those sweet and subtle thoughts that do entwine / Swift gleamings with the shade that interlopes / Between their visitings' (29–31).

3706. One] *Fair copy = The Texas Christian University MS*, page 3 (facsimile in *BSM* viii 196), draft in *Nbk 3* 122; one *L&C/RofI*.

3708. Necessity] S. set out fully his understanding of the doctrine of Necessity, which he had gathered from his reading of Hume, Holbach and Godwin, in *Q Mab* vi 146–238 and note to vi 198. The operation of Necessity in the mental and moral spheres is there taken to be a correlation between motive and action which is as strict as that between material cause and effect, and in consequence of which no one can act but as he does. Here the principle is extended to underpin an assertion that good actions and evil actions must invariably generate further actions of the same character. *Locock 1911* aptly cites Aeschylus, *Agamemnon*, which S. was reading in late July 1817 (*Mary Jnl* i 177); and it is likely that the new inflection given to Necessity in the final four lines of this stanza derives from that source. Lines 3709–11 could be a restatement in abstract terms of the warning of the chorus that the good and evil deeds of a house continue through the generations: 'It is the deed of iniquity that thereafter begetteth more iniquity and like unto its own breed; but when a house is righteous, the lot of its children is blessed alway' (758–62; Loeb trans.). In late 1819 or early 1820 S. recopied into *Nbk 10* (39v–40r), with approving remarks on the originality of the thought, part of the choral antistrophe from which the above passage is taken, including most of the passage itself (*MYR* iv 328–6).

3714. Heroes, and Poets] [Homer Brutus, & he who slew / His brother] *Nbk 3* 123. *prevailing*] victorious, whose ideas and precepts have prevailed.

XXIX

'So be the turf heaped over our remains
Even in our happy youth, and that strange lot,
Whate'er it be, when in these mingling veins
The blood is still, be ours; let sense and thought
3725   Pass from our being, or be numbered not
Among the things that are; let those who come
Behind, for whom our steadfast will has bought
A calm inheritance, a glorious doom,
Insult with careless tread, our undivided tomb.

XXX

3730   'Our many thoughts and deeds, our life and love,
Our happiness, and all that we have been,
Immortally must live, and burn and move,
When we shall be no more; — the world has seen
A type of peace; and as some most serene
3735   And lovely spot to a poor maniac's eye,
After long years, some sweet and moving scene
Of youthful hope returning suddenly,
Quells his long madness — thus man shall remember thee.

XXXI

'And Calumny meanwhile shall feed on us,
3740   As worms devour the dead, and near the throne
And at the altar, most accepted thus
Shall sneers and curses be; — what we have done
None shall dare vouch, though it be truly known;
That record shall remain, when they must pass
3745   Who built their pride on its oblivion;
And fame, in human hope which sculptured was,
Survive the perished scrolls of unenduring brass.

XXXII

'The while we two, belovèd, must depart,
And Sense and Reason, those enchanters fair,
3750   Whose wand of power is hope, would bid the heart
That gazed beyond the wormy grave despair:

3728. *doom*] Lot, destiny.

3744-7. 'The immaterial monument which we have sculptured from the hopes of humankind will outlive the memory of those tyrants whose pride depends on its being forgotten'. Cythna's claim is a version of the traditonal poet's claim to immortality, as in Ovid *Metamorphoses* xv 871, Horace *Odes* xxx 1–5, Shakespeare *Sonnet* 55.

217

These eyes, these lips, this blood, seems darkly there
To fade in hideous ruin; no calm sleep
Peopling with golden dreams the stagnant air,
3755   Seems our obscure and rotting eyes to steep
In joy; — but senseless death — a ruin dark and deep!

XXXIII

'These are blind fancies — reason cannot know
What sense can neither feel, nor thought conceive;
There is delusion in the world — and woe,
3760   And fear, and pain — we know not whence we live,
Or why, or how, or what mute Power may give
Their being to each plant, and star, and beast,
Or even these thoughts: — Come near me! I do weave
A chain I cannot break — I am possessed
3765   With thoughts too swift and strong for one lone human breast.

XXXIV

'Yes, yes — thy kiss is sweet, thy lips are warm —
O! willingly, belovèd, would these eyes,
Might they no more drink being from thy form,
Even as to sleep whence we again arise,
3770   Close their faint orbs in death: I fear nor prize
Aught that can now betide, unshared by thee —
Yes, Love when wisdom fails makes Cythna wise:
Darkness and death, if death be true, must be
Dearer than life and hope, if unenjoyed with thee.

XXXV

3775   'Alas, our thoughts flow on with stream, whose waters
Return not to their fountain — Earth and Heaven,
The Ocean and the Sun, the clouds their daughters,
Winter, and Spring, and Morn, and Noon, and Even,
All that we are or know, is darkly driven

3752. *seems*] seem *Rossetti 1870, 1878, Dowden 1891.* For lack of agreement between subject and verb, see notes to lines 1233, 2151. *Locock 1911* cites *England in 1819* 8–9 and the Preface to *Alastor* 6–7. The draft in *Nbk 3* 131 could be either 'seem' or 'seems'.

3757–8. Cythna's reflection on the groundlessness of the fear of death derives from Epicurean rational precepts as formulated by Lucretius in *De Re. Nat.*, e.g.: 'For if by chance anyone is to have misery and pain in the future, he must needs himself also exist then in that time to be miserable. Since death takes away this possibility, and forbids him to exist for whom these inconveniences may be gathered together, we may be sure that there is nothing to be feared after death, that he who is not cannot be miserable' (iii 862–7; Loeb trans.).

3767. *willingly,*] *eds*; willingly *L&C/RofI, Nbk 3* 132.

3780   Towards one gulf — Lo! what a change is come
    Since I first spake — but time shall be forgiven,
    Though it change all but thee!' — She ceased, night's gloom
    Meanwhile had fallen on earth from the sky's sunless dome.

XXXVI

    Though she had ceased, her countenance uplifted
3785   To Heaven, still spake, with solemn glory bright;
    Her dark deep eyes, her lips, whose motions gifted
    The air they breathed with love, her locks undight;
    'Fair star of life and love,' I cried, 'my soul's delight,
    Why lookest thou on the crystàlline skies?
3790   O, that my spirit were yon Heaven of night,
    Which gazes on thee with its thousand eyes!'
    She turned to me and smiled — that smile was Paradise!

Canto Tenth

I

    Was there a human spirit in the steed,
    That thus with his proud voice, ere night was gone,
3795   He broke our linkèd rest? or do indeed
    All living things a common nature own,
    And thought erect an universal throne,
    Where many shapes one tribute ever bear?
    And Earth, their mutual mother, does she groan
3800   To see her sons contend? and makes she bare
    Her breast, that all in peace its drainless stores may share?

3788–91. The lines are a free translation of a celebrated epigram attributed to Plato. At the bottom of the page on which the stanza is drafted in *Nbk 3* (134) S. noted 'Apuleius', a reference to his source for the epigram in the *Apologia* (x 24) of that author. A second translation of the same poem, transcribed by MWS, is given as no. 140: see the headnote for the original Gk text and for a discussion of the relation between the two versions. The epigram is also given in Diogenes Laertius' 'Life of Plato' iii 29, a passage that S. marked in his copy of *Lives of the Eminent Philosophers* (Male and Notopoulos *MLR* liv (1959) 17). Diogenes Laertius says that it was addressed to a boy named Aster ('Star') who studied astronomy with Plato. See also *Webb* 133; *1975* 323, 392, 413; *Notopoulos* 508–11.

3793–5. Recalling the breeze that wakens the sleeping hero in Southey's *Thalaba* xii 4: 'Was there a Spirit in the gale / That fluttered o'er his cheek?' (ii 301 in 1801 edn).

3795–8. 'Do all creatures share the sovereign faculty of thought?'

3799. *mutual*] common *canc. Nbk 3* 135. The word cancelled to avoid repetition with line 3796 gives the sense of *mutual* here.

3801. *drainless*] Inexhaustible.

II

I have heard friendly sounds from many a tongue,
Which was not human — the lone Nightingale
Has answered me with her most soothing song,
3805 Out of her ivy bower, when I sate pale
With grief, and sighed beneath; from many a dale
The Antelopes who flocked for food have spoken
With happy sounds, and motions, that avail
Like man's own speech; and such was now the token
3810 Of waning night, whose calm by that proud neigh was broken.

III

Each night, that mighty steed bore me abroad,
And I returned with food to our retreat,
And dark intelligence; the blood which flowed
Over the fields, had stained the courser's feet; —
3815 Soon the dust drinks that bitter dew, — then meet
The vulture, and the wild dog, and the snake,
The wolf, and the hyena grey, and eat
The dead in horrid truce: their throngs did make
Behind the steed, a chasm like waves in a ship's wake.

IV

3820 For, from the utmost realms of earth, came pouring
The banded slaves whom every despot sent
At that throned traitor's summons; like the roaring
Of fire, whose floods the wild deer circumvent
In the scorched pastures of the South; so bent
3825 The armies of the leaguèd kings around
Their files of steel and flame; — the continent
Trembled, as with a zone of ruin bound,
Beneath their feet, the sea shook with their Navies' sound.

V

From every nation of the earth they came,
3830 The multitude of moving heartless things,
Whom slaves call men: obediently they came,
Like sheep whom from the fold the shepherd brings
To the stall, red with blood; their many kings
Led them, thus erring, from their native land;

3809–10. 'Just so did the steed's neigh in the still night speak as a sign or omen'.

3834. land] home L&C/RofI. S. altered the draft in Nbk 3 138 from 'home' to 'land', but must have transcribed 'home' by error into the fair copy. He later made the same correction in ink in the copy of RofI he presented to his friend George William Tighe. See note to Preface line 249.

3835 Tartar and Frank, and millions whom the wings
Of Indian breezes lull, and many a band
The Arctic Anarch sent, and Idumea's sand,

VI

Fertile in prodigies and lies; — so there
Strange natures made a brotherhood of ill.
3840 The desert savage ceased to grasp in fear
His Asian shield and bow, when, at the will
Of Europe's subtler son, the bolt would kill
Some shepherd sitting on a rock secure;
But smiles of wondering joy his face would fill,
3845 And savage sympathy: those slaves impure,
Each one the other thus from ill to ill did lure.

VII

For traitorously did that foul Tyrant robe
His countenance in lies, — even at the hour
When he was snatched from death, then o'er the globe,
3850 With secret signs from many a mountain tower,
With smoke by day, and fire by night, the power
Of kings and priests, those dark conspirators
He called: — they knew his cause their own, and swore

3835. *Frank*] A term in use in the eastern Mediterranean to designate a person of western nationality.

3837. *The Arctic Anarch*] For *Anarch* see note to line 86. A reference is no doubt intended to the Tsar Alexander I (1777–1825) who entered Paris with the allied armies in March 1814 and whose forbearance towards the city was celebrated – on the occasion of his arrival in England together with the King of Prussia – by the laureate Robert Southey in one of the odes of *Carmina Aulica* (1814). Alexander was the chief proponent of The Holy Alliance, which liberals regarded as a cover of pious hypocrisy for an unjust post-war settlement in Europe. *Idumea's sand*] S. first wrote 'Arabys', then '?[Aegypts]' (*Nbk 3* 138). Idumea is the Gk form of Edom, an ancient kingdom lying west and south of the Dead Sea between southern Palestine and Egypt. It bore the name of Esau, also called Edom, who went to dwell there (*Genesis* xxxvi 8). The context, especially lines 3832–3, suggests that S. is recalling the name from the prophecy of divine wrath in *Isaiah* xxxiv: 'For my sword shall be bathed in heaven: behold, it shall come down upon Idumea, and upon the people of my curse, to judgment. The sword of the Lord is filled with blood, it is made fat with fatness, and with the blood of lambs and goats, with the fat of the kidneys of rams: for the Lord hath a sacrifice in Bozrah, and a great slaughter in the land of Idumea' (5–6). Line 3838 indicates that *Idumea* also stands by synecdoche for the lands where the Old Testament, with its accounts of miracles and its (for Shelley) false conception of divine–human relations, originated.

3842. *bolt*] See note to line 2370.

3851. Alluding ironically to *Exodus* xiii 21: 'And the Lord went before them by day in a pillar of cloud, to lead them the way; and by night in a pillar of fire, to give them light; to go by day and night'.

Like wolves and serpents to their mutual wars
3855   Strange truce, with many a rite which Earth and Heaven abhors.

VIII

Myriads had come — millions were on their way;
The Tyrant passed, surrounded by the steel
Of hired assassins, through the public way,
Choked with his country's dead: — his footsteps reel
3860   On the fresh blood — he smiles, 'Ay, now I feel
I am a King in truth!' he said, and took
His royal seat, and bade the torturing wheel
Be brought, and fire, and pincers, and the hook,
And scorpions; that his soul on its revenge might look.

IX

3865   'But first, go slay the rebels — why return
The victor bands?' he said, 'millions yet live,
Of whom the weakest with one word might turn
The scales of victory yet; — let none survive
But those within the walls — each fifth shall give
3870   The expiation for his brethren here. —
Go forth, and waste and kill!' — 'O king, forgive
My speech,' a soldier answered — 'but we fear
The spirits of the night, and morn is drawing near;

X

'For we were slaying still without remorse,
3875   And now that dreadful chief beneath my hand
Defenceless lay, when, on a hell-black horse,
An Angel bright as day, waving a brand

3854. wolves] Nbk 3 139, *eds;* wolves, *L&C/Rof1. Forman 1876–7* moves the comma to follow *serpents* – in effect explaining its position in *L&C/Rof1* as a misplacing, rather than an intrusion, by the compositor.

3862. wheel] A large wheel to which victims were attached to be tortured or executed by having their limbs broken.

3863. hook] Presumably for securing victims or tearing their flesh.

3866. bands?] *eds;* bands, *L&C/Rof1,* Nbk 3 140. *millions yet live]* Noticing that in lines 2493–4 Laon says that 'of those brave bands / I soon survived alone', *Locock 1911* concludes that the rebellion must have gained *millions* of adherents since the slaughter there described. But by *bands* in lines 2493–4 S. may mean those who were defending themselves in proximity to Laon rather than the *multitudes* (line 2346) or *myriads* (line 2458) of the patriots: in the battle-scene (2434–505) the focus regularly shifts from the whole to smaller groups.

3877. brand] Not a torch but a sword as in line 2503. The soldier is recalling the events of VI xix.

Which flashed among the stars, passed.' — 'Dost thou stand
Parleying with me, thou wretch?' the king replied;
3880   'Slaves, bind him to the wheel; and of this band,
Whoso will drag that woman to his side
That scared him thus, may burn his dearest foe beside;

XI

'And gold and glory shall be his. — Go forth!'
They rushed into the plain. — Loud was the roar
3885   Of their career: the horsemen shook the earth;
The wheeled artillery's speed the pavement tore;
The infantry, file after file did pour
Their clouds on the utmost hills. Five days they slew
Among the wasted fields: the sixth saw gore
3890   Stream through the city; on the seventh, the dew
Of slaughter became stiff; and there was peace anew:

XII

Peace in the desert fields and villages,
Between the glutted beasts and mangled dead!
Peace in the silent streets! save when the cries
3895   Of victims to their fiery judgement led,
Made pale their voiceless lips who seemed to dread
Even in their dearest kindred, lest some tongue
Be faithless to the fear yet unbetrayed;
Peace in the Tyrant's palace, where the throng
3900   Waste the triumphal hours in festival and song!

XIII

Day after day the burning Sun rolled on
Over the death-polluted land — it came
Out of the east like fire, and fiercely shone

3888–91. Parodying the seven days of creation in *Genesis* i 1–ii 3.

3894–8. This obscurely-expressed passage has attracted lengthy commentary in *Rossetti 1870, 1878, Forman 1876–7, 1975*, Bradley *MLR* i (1905) 28. Rossetti's suspicion that *fear* (3898) might be a misprint for 'few' would appear to be denied by the draft (*Nbk 3* 142A), where 'fear' seems the likelier reading and where the line, in the form it takes there, 'Be faithless to the ?[fear] they strove to hide', would seem to make against 'few' as without a clear antecedent. The sense appears to be: 'except when the cries of those being led to the stake to be burnt caused to turn pale with anxiety those among the bystanders who feared lest even the kin dearest to them (among those being led to execution) break faith and reveal the fear they strove to conceal (presumably that they too held opinions that might render them subject to the same fate)'.

223

A lamp of Autumn, ripening with its flame
3905   The few lone ears of corn; — the sky became
Stagnate with heat, so that each cloud and blast
Languished and died, — the thirsting air did claim
All moisture, and a rotting vapour passed
From the unburied dead, invisible and fast.

XIV

3910   First Want, then Plague came on the beasts; their food
Failed, and they drew the breath of its decay.
Millions on millions, whom the scent of blood
Had lured, or who, from regions far away,
Had tracked the hosts in festival array,
3915   From their dark deserts; gaunt and wasting now,
Stalked like fell shades among their perished prey;
In their green eyes a strange disease did glow,
They sank in hideous spasm, or pains severe and slow.

XV

The fish were poisoned in the streams; the birds
3920   In the green woods perished; the insect race

3904. A lamp of Autumn] *Locock 1911* detected a rapid change of seasons between the first half of Canto V, which seemed to him to have taken place in late spring or early summer, and this moment, conjecturing that S. was aligning the chronology of the poem with the actual time of writing. But the occurrences of 'spring' in IV xxxii, V xxix and in Cythna's Ode at line 2221 are all metaphorical; the only certain seasonal indications in the Canto, whose action takes place over two days, are Cythna's reference to 'fruits' and 'ripe corn' in lines 2242–4 and the autumnal festival in lv–lvi.

3908–9. rotting vapour . . . unburied dead] Medical theory had for long traced the origin of pestilential infections to miasma or noxious exhalation (cp. the 'green mist' of line 3975) as well as recognising its propagation by various forms of human contact. Defoe's *Journal of the Plague Year* (1722) stresses the latter point. A representative contemporary overview such as Gibbon's account of the plague in sixth-century Constantinople in *The History of the Decline and Fall of the Roman Empire* (1776–88) xliii, which was based on both historical and scientific sources (including Richard Mead's widely-read *A Short Discourse concerning Pestilential Contagion* 1702 and later eds), accepted the contagious nature of the disease while locating its genesis in 'the putrefaction of animal substances'. The temperature and quality of the air were also considered important factors in the rise and progress of plague. Lucretius (*De Re. Nat.* vi 1090–1137) attributes epidemics to airborne miasma. The topic was surveyed in *The Encyclopaedia Britannica*, 4th edn (1810) under Plague. See also 143 Appendix H.

3914. hosts] armies *Nbk 3* 146. The alternative draft reading gives the sense of *hosts. in festival array*] The image is of a following *host* of predators drawn up in order (like an army) and preparing to celebrate a feast.

Stanza xv. Before this stanza S. noted: 'Here shall I say that the beasts are tamed by it – & deer & wolves go together' (*Nbk 3* 146), apparently referring to one of the topics to be developed which he had jotted two pages previously: 'the birds & beasts of prey become mild'. A note before stanza xvi, 'Or here? too abrupt', would seem to refer to the same suggestion. He may well be remembering a passage from the account of the plague at Aegina in Ovid

Was withered up; the scattered flocks and herds
Who had survived the wild beasts' hungry chase
Died moaning, each upon the other's face
In helpless agony gazing; round the City
3925   All night, the lean hyenas their sad case
Like starving infants wailed; a woeful ditty!
And many a mother wept, pierced with unnatural pity.

XVI

Amid the aerial minarets on high,
The Ethiopian vultures fluttering fell
3930   From their long line of brethren in the sky,
Startling the concourse of mankind. — Too well
These signs the coming mischief did foretell: —
Strange panic first, a deep and sickening dread
Within each heart, like ice, did sink and dwell,
3935   A voiceless thought of evil, which did spread
With the quick glance of eyes, like withering lightnings shed.

XVII

Day after day, when the year wanes, the frosts
Strip its green crown of leaves, till all is bare;
So on those strange and congregated hosts
3940   Came Famine, a swift shadow, and the air
Groaned with the burden of a new despair;
Famine, than whom Misrule no deadlier daughter
Feeds from her thousand breasts, though sleeping there
With lidless eyes, lie Faith, and Plague, and Slaughter,
3945   A ghastly brood; conceived of Lethe's sullen water.

Metamorphoses vii: 'The boar forgets his rage, the hind to trust his fleetness, the bears to attack the stronger herds. Lethargy holds all. In woods and fields and roads foul carcasses lie; and the air is defiled by the stench. And, strange to say, neither dogs nor ravenous birds nor grey wolves did touch them' (545–50; Loeb trans.). See also 143 Appendix H.

3929. Ethiopian] See note to line 3617, and cp. Thucydides' account of the plague at Athens (II xlviii): 'The disease began, it is said, in Ethiopia beyond Egypt, and then descended into Egypt and Libya and spread over the greater part of the King's territory' (Loeb trans.).

3934. A pale contagion in each brain did dwell *Nbk 3* 147.

3939. strange and congregated hosts] The foreign armies of stanzas v–vi who are gathered within the walls (3869), together with the inhabitants of the City.

3945. ghastly] The word is cancelled in the draft (*Nbk 3* 148) and 'dragon' substituted below the line. *Lethe's*] See note to line 2090. The allusion here is illuminated by a phrase in the list of topics that S. jotted a few pages earlier in the draft (*Nbk 3* 143): 'In the pestilence – its effects on man – destroying the memory of things'. The anarchy that is both cause and effect of the disastrous conditions that now prevail in the City is sustained by the loss of the memory of the political and intellectual liberation so recently accomplished by the

XVIII

There was no food, the corn was trampled down,
The flocks and herds had perished; on the shore
The dead and putrid fish were ever thrown;
The deeps were foodless, and the winds no more
3950   Creaked with the weight of birds, but as before
Those wingèd things sprang forth, were void of shade;
The vines and orchards, Autumn's golden store,
Were burned; — so that the meanest food was weighed
With gold, and Avarice died before the god it made.

XIX

3955   There was no corn — in the wide market-place
All loathliest things, even human flesh, was sold;
They weighed it in small scales — and many a face
Was fixed in eager horror then: his gold
The miser brought, the tender maid, grown bold
3960   Through hunger, bared her scornèd charms in vain;
The mother brought her eldest-born, controlled
By instinct blind as love, but turned again
And bade her infant suck, and died in silent pain.

XX

Then fell blue Plague upon the race of man.
3965   'O, for the sheathèd steel, so late which gave
Oblivion to the dead, when the streets ran
With brothers' blood! O, that the earthquake's grave
Would gape, or Ocean lift its stifling wave!'
Vain cries — throughout the streets, thousands pursued
3970   Each by his fiery torture howl and rave,

---

revolution. The extreme mental effects of the plague, including loss of memory, are stressed in Thucydides (II xlix) and in Lucretius, *De Re. Nat.*: 'And there were others who fell into oblivion of all things, so that they could not even tell who they were' (vi 1213–14; Loeb trans.). See also 143 Appendix H.

3950. Creaked] *Locock 1911* compares the 'creeking' wings of the rook in Coleridge's *This Lime-Tree Bower My Prison* (1800) 74 (and note), but the creaking of the wings of larger birds in flight can be commonly heard. S. is probably also remembering a detail from Lucretius's account of the plague in Athens in *De Re. Nat.*: 'Yet it was not often in those days that any bird was to be seen at all' (vi 1219–20; Loeb trans.).

3964. blue Plague] A set phrase referring to the colour of plague-spots or 'tokens' (see note to line 3980) which were taken as a characteristic symptom of the disease. Cp. Coleridge, *Fears in Solitude* (1798) 91–2: '(famine or blue plague, / Battle, or siege, or flight through wintry snows,)'. See also note to line 2766.

3967. earthquake's] *1839, eds*; earthquakes *L&C/RofI.*

Or sit, in frenzy's unimagined mood,
Upon fresh heaps of dead; a ghastly multitude.

XXI

It was not hunger now, but thirst. Each well
Was choked with rotting corpses, and became
3975   A cauldron of green mist made visible
At sunrise. Thither still the myriads came,
Seeking to quench the agony of the flame,
Which raged like poison through their bursting veins;
Naked they were from torture, without shame,
3980   Spotted with nameless scars and lurid blains,
Childhood, and youth, and age, writhing in savage pains.

XXII

It was not thirst but madness! many saw
Their own lean image everywhere, it went
A ghastlier self beside them, till the awe
3985   Of that dread sight to self-destruction sent
Those shrieking victims; some, ere life was spent,
Sought, with a horrid sympathy, to shed
Contagion on the sound; and others rent
Their matted hair, and cried aloud, 'We tread
3990   On fire! Almighty God his hell on earth has spread.'

XXIII

Sometimes the living by the dead were hid.
Near the great fountain in the public square,
Where corpses made a crumbling pyramid
Under the sun, was heard one stifled prayer
3995   For life, in the hot silence of the air;
And strange 'twas, amid that hideous heap to see

3980. *nameless scars . . . lurid blains*] The so-called 'tokens' of the plague, symptomatic erup-
tions from subcutaneous bleeding. Their appearance determines that the plague is in London
in Defoe's *A Journal of the Plague Year* (1722): 'finding evident Tokens of the Sickness upon
both the Bodies that were dead, they gave their Opinions publickly, that they died of the
Plague' (ed. L. Landa and D. Roberts (1990) 2). *Blains* are sores, blisters or swellings, espe-
cially those produced by the plague, with which the term was associated from the account
in *Exodus* ix 9 of one of the punishments visited upon the Egyptians by God.

3986–8. See note to line 2763.

3990. *Almighty God*] the avenging Power *Rofl*; *spread.*] *Rofl*; spread! *L&C*.

3996. *'twas,*] *Rofl*; 'twas *L&C*. Alteration in the cancel-leaf for *Rofl*. *Forman 1876–7*, noting
the halting metre of the line, suspected that 'Shelley first noticed the awkwardness of the
line in reading a proof of the cancel, – marked an apostrophe in the margin, [to alter *amid*
to ''mid'] – that the printer mistook it for a comma, and that either poet or printer omitted

Some shrouded in their long and golden hair,
As if not dead, but slumbering quietly
Like forms which sculptors carve, then love to agony.

XXIV

4000   Famine had spared the palace of the king: —
He rioted in festival the while,
He and his guards and priests; but Plague did fling
One shadow upon all. Famine can smile
On him who brings it food and pass, with guile
4005   Of thankful falsehood, like a courtier grey,
The house-dog of the throne; but many a mile
Comes Plague, a wingèd wolf, who loathes alway
The garbage and the scum that strangers make her prey.

XXV

So, near the throne, amid the gorgeous feast,
4010   Sheathed in resplendent arms, or loosely dight
To luxury, ere the mockery yet had ceased
That lingered on his lips, the warrior's might
Was loosened, and a new and ghastlier night
In dreams of frenzy lapped his eyes; he fell
4015   Headlong, or with stiff eyeballs sate upright
Among the guests, or raving mad, did tell
Strange truths; a dying seer of dark oppression's hell.

XXVI

The Princes and the Priests were pale with terror;
That monstrous faith wherewith they ruled mankind,

---

to take out the *a* from *amid'*. This is possible but the simpler hypothesis is to accept *Rofl*'s comma as designed to improve the awkward rhythm of the line. *1975* emends *amid* to "mid'. The draft in *Nbk 3* is defective.

3999. Alluding to the love of the Cyprian sculptor Pygmalion for the ivory statue he had sculptured and which, in answer to his prayer, was endowed with life by Venus (Ovid *Metamorphoses* x 243–97).

4003–8. The rationale of the contrast on which the passage is based has exercised commentators. The sense seems to be: 'Famine is a familiar of the royal household, like an old *courtier* or a *house-dog*, and can be placated by being fed; Plague on the other hand is a wild beast who is relentless, detesting the offal that she travels far to seek out'. S. struggled to draft the lines in *Nbk 3* 152. One of his attempts at the final line of the stanza reads: 'The ?[tainted] food which she perforce must make her ?[prey]', suggesting that the printed phrase *that strangers make her prey* = 'the strangers that she makes her prey'. The image of a *wingèd wolf* that feeds on *garbage* is appropriate to the miasmatic theory that plague originates in rotting animal matter and is carried as vapour in the air. See notes to lines 427 and 3908–9.

4010. *dight*] Clothed, arrayed.

4020 Fell, like a shaft loosed by the bowman's error,
    On their own hearts: they sought and they could find
    No refuge — 'twas the blind who led the blind!
    So, through the desolate streets to the high fane
    Of their Almighty God, the armies wind
4025 In sad procession: each among the train
    To his own Idol lifts his supplications vain.

XXVII

'O God!' they cried, 'we know our secret pride
    Has scorned thee, and thy worship, and thy name;
    Secure in human power we have defied
4030 Thy fearful might; we bend in fear and shame
    Before thy presence; with the dust we claim
    Kindred; be merciful, O King of Heaven!
    Most justly have we suffered for thy fame
    Made dim, but be at length our sins forgiven,
4035 Ere to despair and death thy worshippers be driven.

XXVIII

'O God Almighty! thou alone hast power!
    Who can resist thy will? who can restrain
    Thy wrath, when on the guilty thou dost shower
    The shafts of thy revenge, a blistering rain?
4040 Greatest and best, be merciful again!
    Have we not stabbed thine enemies, and made
    The Earth an altar, and the Heavens a fane,
    Where thou wert worshipped with their blood, and laid
    Those hearts in dust which would thy searchless works have weighed?

XXIX

4045 'Well didst thou loosen on this impious City
    Thine angels of revenge: recall them now;
    Thy worshippers abased, here kneel for pity,
    And bind their souls by an immortal vow:
    We swear by thee! and to our oath do thou
4050 Give sanction, from thine hell of fiends and flame,
    That we will kill with fire and torments slow,
    The last of those who mocked thy holy name,
    And scorned the sacred laws thy prophets did proclaim.'

4023. fane] fane, *RofI*. An alteration in the cancel-leaf for *RofI* which is required by the enforced
alteration of the next line, but unnecessary for *L&C*.
4024. The many-tongued and endless armies wind *RofI*.
4036. O God Almighty] O King of Glory *RofI*.

XXX

Thus they with trembling limbs and pallid lips
4055   Worshipped their own hearts' image, dim and vast,
Scared by the shade wherewith they would eclipse
The light of other minds; — troubled they passed
From the great Temple; — fiercely still and fast
The arrows of the plague among them fell,
4060   And they on one another gazed aghast,
And through the hosts contention wild befell,
As each of his own god the wondrous works did tell.

XXXI

And Oromaze, and Christ, and Mahomet,
Moses, and Buddh, Zerdusht, and Brahm, and Foh,
4065   A tumult of strange names, which never met
Before, as watchwords of a single woe,
Arose; each raging votary 'gan to throw
Aloft his armèd hands, and each did howl
'Our God alone is God!' and slaughter now

4055–6. See note to lines 3244–8.

4059. arrows of the plague] The phrase recalls the arrows which Apollo shoots into the Achaean army to strike them with plague in the *Iliad* i 43–58; but, in view of the location, S. may have more especially in mind an Oriental tradition such as the one described in the *Encyclopaedia Britannica* 4th edn (1810) under Plague: 'The Mahometans believe that the plague proceeds from certain spirits, or goblins, armed with bows and arrows, sent by God to punish men for their sins; and that when the wounds are given by spectres of a black colour, they certainly prove fatal, but not so when the arrows are shot by those that appear white'.

4062. god] *Rof1*; God *L&C*. The page on which the stanza is drafted has been torn out of *Nbk 3*. In *L&C* (PM) S. has altered the capital G to lower case in ink for the *Rof1* cancel-leaf. Whether this was imposed to avoid offence, as was the alteration in the next line, or opportunely made to conform to common usage, the 'God' of *L&C* (perhaps mistakenly capitalised by the compositor, or miscopied from draft) not referring to the One God but to the various deities spoken of by the crowd, is in the nature of the case difficult to determine confidently. The latter possibility seems more likely and the *Rof1* reading has been adopted in conformity with the decision taken in the analogous instance of line 3622. The capital G in 'God' in lines 4027, 4069 and 4101 occurs within speech-marks and should perhaps therefore be considered as different from this line and line 3622.

4063. and Christ] Joshua *Rof1*. Joshua is the Hebrew form of Jesus; the substitution leaves the original name to be discovered by those learned enough to do so. *Oromaze*] See note to lines 431–2.

4064. Foh,] *Rof1*; Foh; *L&C*. The alteration is made in ink in *L&C* (PM) for the *Rof1* cancel-leaf. Cp. Q *Mab* vii 26–30: 'The name of God / Has fenced about all crime with holiness, / Himself the creature of his worshippers, / Whose names and attributes and passions change, / Seeva, Buddh, Foh, Jehovah, God, or Lord'. There, as here, S.'s source is *Ruins* xx where the bewildering variety of human religions and the consequent sectarianism, intolerance and enmity are evoked. *Zerdusht*] Zoroaster. *Brahm*] Brahma, the creator of the universe in Hindu mythology. *Foh*] 'one god, who, under various names, is acknowledged by the nations of the east. The Chinese worship him under the name of *Fôt*' (*Ruins* xx).

4070 Would have gone forth, when from beneath a cowl
A voice came forth, which pierced like ice through every soul.

XXXII

He was a Christian Priest from whom it came,
A zealous man, who led the legioned west
With words which faith and pride had steeped in flame,
4075 To quell the rebel Atheists; a dire guest
Even to his friends was he, for in his breast
Did hate and guile lie watchful, intertwined,
Twin serpents in one deep and winding nest;
He loathed all faith beside his own, and pined
4080 To wreak his fear of God in vengeance on mankind.

XXXIII

But more he loathed and hated the clear light
Of wisdom and free thought, and more did fear,
Lest, kindled once, its beams might pierce the night,
Even where his Idol stood; for, far and near
4085 Did many a heart in Europe leap to hear
That faith and tyranny were trampled down;
Many a pale victim, doomed for truth to share
The murderer's cell, or see, with helpless groan,
The priests his children drag for slaves to serve their own.

XXXIV

4090 He dared not kill the infidels with fire
Or steel, in Europe: the slow agonies
Of legal torture mocked his keen desire:
So he made truce with those who did despise
His cradled Idol, and the sacrifice
4095 Of God to God's own wrath, — that Islam's creed
Might crush for him those deadlier enemies;
For fear of God did in his bosom breed
A jealous hate of man, an unreposing need.

4072. *He was a Christian Priest*] 'Twas an Iberian Priest *Rofl*. The character here introduced bears evident resemblances to the zealous Spanish Jesuit in Volume iii of Lady Morgan's novel *The Missionary* (1811) which S. read and reread in that year (*L* i 101, 107, 112, 130). See note to line 4522. The use S. makes of the novel in *L&C* is discussed in N. Leask, *British Romantic Writers and the East* (1992) 115–18.

4075. *rebel Atheists*] unbelievers *Rofl*.

4080. *God*] Heaven *Rofl*.

4094. *cradled Idol*] creed of Christ *canc. Nbk 3* 157.

4094–5. The expiation, and the sacrifice, / That, though detested, Islam's kindred creed *Rofl*.

XXXV

'Peace! Peace!' he cried, 'when we are dead, the Day
4100 Of Judgement comes, and all shall surely know
Whose God is God, each fearfully shall pay
The errors of his faith in endless woe!
But there is sent a mortal vengeance now
On earth, because an impious race had spurned
4105 Him whom we all adore, — a subtle foe,
By whom for ye this dread reward was earned,
And thrones, which rest on faith in God, nigh overturned.

XXXVI

'Think ye, because ye weep, and kneel, and pray,
That God will lull the pestilence? it rose
4110 Even from beneath his throne, where, many a day
His mercy soothed it to a dark repose:
It walks upon the earth to judge his foes,
And what are thou and I, that he should deign
To curb his ghastly minister, or close
4115 The gates of death, ere they receive the twain
Who shook with mortal spells his undefended reign?

XXXVII

'Ay, there is famine in the gulf of hell,
Its giant worms of fire for ever yawn, —
Their lurid eyes are on us! those who fell
4120 By the swift shafts of pestilence ere dawn,
Are in their jaws! they hunger for the spawn
Of Satan, their own brethren, who were sent
To make our souls their spoil. See! See! they fawn
Like dogs, and they will sleep with luxury spent,
4125 When those detested hearts their iron fangs have rent!

XXXVIII

'Our God may then lull Pestilence to sleep: —
Pile high the pyre of expiation now!
A forest's spoil of boughs, and on the heap
Pour venomous gums, which sullenly and slow,
4130 When touched by flame, shall burn, and melt, and flow,

4107. And kingly thrones, which rest on faith, nigh overturned. *RofI. Forman 1876–7* notes
that in *L&C* (PM) S. has deleted *in God* but not supplied 'kingly', taking this as an indica-
tion among others that S. himself corrected proofs of the cancel-leaves for *RofI*, adding 'kingly'
at that stage.

A stream of clinging fire, — and fix on high
A net of iron, and spread forth below
A couch of snakes, and scorpions, and the fry
Of centipedes and worms, earth's hellish progeny!

XXXIX

4135 'Let Laon and Laone on that pyre,
Linked tight with burning brass, perish! — then pray
That, with this sacrifice, the withering ire
Of God may be appeased.' He ceased, and they
A space stood silent, as far, far away
4140 The echoes of his voice among them died;
And he knelt down upon the dust, alway
Muttering the curses of his speechless pride,
Whilst shame, and fear, and awe, the armies did divide.

XL

His voice was like a blast that burst the portal
4145 Of fabled hell; and as he spake, each one
Saw gape beneath the chasms of fire immortal,
And Heaven above seemed cloven, where, on a throne
With storms and shadows girt, sate God, alone,
Their King and Judge — fear killed in every breast
4150 All natural pity then, a fear unknown
Before, and with an inward fire possessed,
They raged like homeless beasts whom burning woods invest.

XLI

'Twas morn — at noon the public crier went forth,
Proclaiming through the living and the dead,
4155 'The Monarch saith, that his great Empire's worth
Is set on Laon and Laone's head:
He who but one yet living here can lead,
Or who the life from both their hearts can wring,
Shall be the kingdom's heir, a glorious meed!
4160 But he who both alive can hither bring,
The Princess shall espouse, and reign an equal King.'

4138. God] Heaven *RofI.*
4142. speechless pride] His *pride*, the true motive for his imprecations, remaining unexpressed.
4148. Girt round with storms and shadows, sate alone, *RofI.*
4152. invest] See note to line 2451.
4158. Or who the severed heads of both ?[should] bring *Nbk 3* 162.

XLII

Ere night the pyre was piled, the net of iron
Was spread above, the fearful couch below,
It overtopped the towers that did environ
4165   That spacious square; for Fear is never slow
To build the thrones of Hate, her mate and foe,
So, she scourged forth the maniac multitude
To rear this pyramid — tottering and slow,
Plague-stricken, foodless, like lean herds pursued
4170   By gadflies, they have piled the heath, and gums, and wood.

XLIII

Night came, a starless and a moonless gloom.
Until the dawn, those hosts of many a nation
Stood round that pile, as near one lover's tomb
Two gentle sisters mourn their desolation;
4175   And in the silence of that expectation,
Was heard on high the reptiles hiss and crawl —
It was so deep, save when the devastation
Of the swift pest with fearful interval,
Marking its path with shrieks, among the crowd would fall.

XLIV

4180   Morn came, — among those sleepless multitudes,
Madness, and Fear, and Plague, and Famine still
Heaped corpse on corpse, as in autumnal woods
The frosts of many a wind with dead leaves fill
Earth's cold and sullen brooks; in silence, still
4185   The pale survivors stood; ere noon, the fear
Of Hell became a panic, which did kill

4176. reptiles] *Nbk 3* 163; reptiles' *eds*. It is not certain that the apostrophe is required grammatically as *hiss* and *crawl* can be understood as verbs, the phrase being the equivalent of 'the reptiles as they hissed and crawled', and *crawl* reads awkwardly as a noun after *heard* and a possessive. *Concordance*, which accepts the apostrophe, illustrates the difficulty by listing *hiss* as a noun and *crawl* as an intransitive verb – which is not possible. *OED* cites this passage (also with apostrophe) under Crawl sb. la. It seems preferable to leave it as it is in *L&C/RofI*, the more so as this is a cancel-leaf on which a correction might have been made but was not – though that in itself is not a decisive reason for not emending. See note to lines 4213–15.

4178. interval] Regularity, rhythm.

4184. in silence, still] *RofI*; in silence still, *L&C*. The alteration in the cancel-leaf for *RofI* makes the function of *still* as temporal adverb unambiguous.

4186. Hell] *RofI*; hell *L&C*; Hell *Nbk 3* 164. Alteration in cancel-leaf for *RofI*.

Like hunger or disease, with whispers drear
As 'Hush! hark! Come they yet? God, God, thine hour is near!'

XLV

And Priests rushed through their ranks, some counterfeiting
4190 The rage they did inspire, some mad indeed
With their own lies; they said their god was waiting
To see his enemies writhe, and burn, and bleed, —
And that, till then, the snakes of Hell had need
Of human souls: — three hundred furnaces
4195 Soon blazed through the wide City, where, with speed,
Men brought their atheist kindred to appease
God's wrath, and while they burned, knelt round on quivering knees.

XLVI

The noontide sun was darkened with that smoke,
The winds of eve dispersed those ashes grey,
4200 The madness which these rites had lulled, awoke
Again at sunset. — Who shall dare to say
The deeds which night and fear brought forth, or weigh
In balance just the good and evil there?
He might man's deep and searchless heart display,
4205 And cast a light on those dim labyrinths, where
Hope, near imagined chasms, is struggling with despair.

XLVII

'Tis said, a mother dragged three children then,
To those fierce flames which roast the eyes in the head,
And laughed, and died; and that unholy men,

4188. *Hush*] *RofI*; hush *L&C*. Alteration in cancel-leaf for *RofI*. *God, God,*] Just Heaven! *RofI*. S. altered 'Just Heaven!' to 'Great God!' in ink in the copy of *RofI* once owned by George William Tighe, no doubt from a memory of his first intention. See note to Preface line 249.

4191. *their god*] *RofI*; their God *L&C*; that God *Nbk 3* 165. S. substituted the lower-case 'g' in ink in *L&C* (PM). Here, as in lines 3622 and 4062, the *RofI* reading cannot be accepted with entire confidence as S.'s unconstrained preference; but, on an analogy with the two earlier lines, it seems that 'god' here collectively signifies the different supreme beings of the various faiths represented by the priests, and therefore need not be capitalised.

4193. *Hell*] *RofI*; hell *L&C*; Hell *Nbk 3* 165. The alteration on the cancel-leaf for *RofI* is not entered in *L&C* (PM).

4196. *atheist*] infidel *RofI*.

4204. *searchless*] Inscrutable.

4210   Feasting like fiends upon the infidel dead,
        Looked from their meal, and saw an Angel tread
        The threshold of God's throne, and it was she!
        And, on that night, one without doubt or dread
        Came to the fire, and said, 'Stop, I am he!
4215   Kill me!' they burned them both with hellish mockery.

XLVIII

        And, one by one, that night, young maidens came,
        Beauteous and calm, like shapes of living stone
        Clothed in the light of dreams, and by the flame
        Which shrank as overgorged, they laid them down,
4220   And sung a low sweet song, of which alone
        One word was heard, and that was Liberty;
        And that some kissed their marble feet, with moan
        Like love, and died, and then that they did die
        With happy smiles, which sunk in white tranquillity.

4212. The threshold of God's throne] The visible floor of Heaven *Rofl*.

4213–15. The incompatibility of *one* (line 4213) and *both* (line 4215) has occasioned much commentary. *Rossetti 1870, 1878* put forward a series of possible explanations: that, apart from the man who is the *one* of line 4213, *both* might refer to: a. the corpse of the mother of line 4207, or b. her three children; or c. that for *one* (line 4213) we should read 'two'. *Forman 1876–7* preferred to think that to *one* (line 4213) ought to be added either one of the *unholy men* of line 4209 or perhaps another who had simply reported what they had seen. Rejecting both Rossetti's and Forman's hypotheses, A. C. Bradley (*MLR* i (1905) 28) offered instead his brother F. H. Bradley's interpretation of the passage: 'The orthodox are burning the infidels. One infidel, A, is just going to be burned. Another infidel, B, comes up and says, "Stop; that is not A; I am A". The orthodox burn both A and B, and think it an excellent joke'. This brisk formula has been accepted by both *Locock 1911* and *1975*, even though it depends upon inventing the presence of 'infidel B' without any warrant in the text as well as upon the inference that B claims to be A, when the claim of *one* (line 4213) is evidently that he is Laon. As it stands the passage does not seem to admit of any secure reading that assumes it is consistent, even if obscurely so. Its state may, however, be traced to, and to some extent explained by, the surviving draft. The draft sequence in *Nbk 3* stops with stanza xlvi, after which S. has jotted in pencil: 'Another Stanza or ?[two]' (166). He carried out half this intention on p. 40 of *Nbk 4* (which is mostly filled with drafts for the Dedication) where a fairly clean, though not perfectly finished, draft of stanza xlvii is found, the last three lines of which read: 'And on that night friends without doubt or dread / Came to the pile & said – stop I am he / And yet they burned them both with hellish mockery'. The plural 'friends' indicates that S. first imagined two, or more, patriots who wished to save Laon from execution by claiming separately to be he – their attempts resulting in themselves being burned. When S. came to transcribe copy for the printer, he may have decided, seeking to improve on the awkward reference of 'both' to 'friends' of unspecified number, to adopt the singular 'one' in place of 'friends' but neglected to alter 'them both' in the final line, so leaving an inconsistency in the text which passed unnoticed in proof, and was not corrected on this cancel-leaf for *Rofl*.

Canto Eleventh

I

4225 She saw me not — she heard me not — alone
Upon the mountain's dizzy brink she stood;
She spake not, breathed not, moved not — there was thrown
Over her look, the shadow of a mood
Which only clothes the heart in solitude,
4230 A thought of voiceless depth; — she stood alone,
Above, the Heavens were spread; — below, the flood
Was murmuring in its caves; — the wind had blown
Her hair apart, through which her eyes and forehead shone.

II

A cloud was hanging o'er the western mountains;
4235 Before its blue and moveless depth were flying
Grey mists poured forth from the unresting fountains
Of darkness in the North: — the day was dying: —
Sudden, the sun shone forth, its beams were lying
Like boiling gold on Ocean, strange to see,
4240 And on the shattered vapours, which defying
The power of light in vain, tossed restlessly
In the red Heaven, like wrecks in a tempestuous sea.

III

It was a stream of living beams, whose bank
On either side by the cloud's cleft was made;
4245 And where its chasms that flood of glory drank,
Its waves gushed forth like fire, and as if swayed
By some mute tempest, rolled on *her*; the shade
Of her bright image floated on the river
Of liquid light, which then did end and fade —
4250 Her radiant shape upon its verge did shiver;
Aloft, her flowing hair like strings of flame did quiver.

IV

I stood beside her, but she saw me not —
She looked upon the sea, and skies, and earth;
Rapture, and love, and admiration wrought

4254–60. 'The intense emotions that the sudden dramatic appearance of the setting sun inspires in Cythna as she stands on the cliff combine with the inexpressible impulse that led her there to throw a radiance from her eyes so dazzling that all her physical beauty is outshone, and her essential inner loveliness unveiled to Laon'.

4255   A passion deeper far than tears, or mirth,
Or speech, or gesture, or whate'er has birth
From common joy; which, with the speechless feeling
That led her there united, and shot forth
From her far eyes, a light of deep revealing,
4260   All but her dearest self from my regard concealing.

V

Her lips were parted, and the measured breath
Was now heard there; — her dark and intricate eyes
Orb within orb, deeper than sleep or death,
Absorbed the glories of the burning skies,
4265   Which, mingling with her heart's deep ecstasies,
Burst from her looks and gestures; — and a light
Of liquid tenderness like love, did rise
From her whole frame, an atmosphere which quite
Arrayed her in its beams, tremulous and soft and bright.

VI

4270   She would have clasped me to her glowing frame;
Those warm and odorous lips might soon have shed
On mine the fragrance and the invisible flame
Which now the cold winds stole; — she would have laid
Upon my languid heart her dearest head;
4275   I might have heard her voice, tender and sweet;
Her eyes mingling with mine, might soon have fed
My soul with their own joy. — One moment yet
I gazed — we parted then, never again to meet!

4258–9. In the draft in *Nbk 3* 169 there is a comma after *there*, two suspension points after *united* and no punctuation after *eyes* – which clarifies the syntax without materially altering the sense.

4259. far] Laon is beside Cythna, but her eyes show that her spirit is *far* away.

4262–6. In stressing thus the depth and intricacy of Cythna's eyes, S. is suggesting corresponding qualities of mind and feeling in this modern European advocate of women's rights. Ancient Greek women, he wrote in *A Discourse on the Manners of the Ancient Greeks Relative to the Subject of Love* (1818), possessed 'the habits and the qualities of slaves ... They were certainly devoid of that moral and intellectual loveliness with which the acquisition of knowledge and the cultivation of sentiment animates as with another life of overpowering grace the lineaments and the gestures of every form which it inhabits. Their eyes could not have been deep and intricate from the workings of the mind and could have entangled no heart in soul-enwoven labyrinths' (*Prose* 220). See also *PU* II i 114–17 and note.

VII

Never but once to meet on Earth again!
4280   She heard me as I fled — her eager tone
Sunk on my heart, and almost wove a chain
Around my will to link it with her own,
So that my stern resolve was almost gone.
'I cannot reach thee! whither dost thou fly?
4285   My steps are faint — Come back, thou dearest one —
Return, ah me! return' — the wind passed by
On which those accents died, faint, far, and lingeringly.

VIII

Woe! woe! that moonless midnight — Want and Pest
Were horrible, but one more fell doth rear,
4290   As in a hydra's swarming lair, its crest
Eminent among those victims — even the Fear
Of Hell: each girt by the hot atmosphere
Of his blind agony, like a scorpion stung
By his own rage upon his burning bier
4295   Of circling coals of fire; but still there clung
One hope, like a keen sword on starting threads uphung:

IX

Not death — death was no more refuge or rest;
Not life — it was despair to be! — not sleep,
For fiends and chasms of fire had dispossessed
4300   All natural dreams: to wake was not to weep,
But to gaze mad and pallid, at the leap
To which the Future, like a snaky scourge,
Or like some tyrant's eye, which aye doth keep
Its withering beam upon his slaves, did urge
4305   Their steps; they heard the roar of Hell's sulphureous surge.

4279. Never but once] When they are executed on the pyre (XII xv–xvii): a reminder that Laon is narrating retrospectively.

4290. hydra's swarming lair] See note to line 419.

4293–5. The image of the scorpion that stings itself to death when ringed by fire is used variously as a poetic figure by S.: see, e.g., *Q Mab* vi 35–8; *The Cenci* II ii 70–1 (and note).

4296. starting] Loosening, coming away: apparently alluding to the story of the sword suspended by a hair over the head of Damocles by Dionysus I Tyrant of Syracuse.

X

Each of that multitude alone, and lost
To sense of outward things, one hope yet knew;
As on a foam-girt crag some seaman tossed,
Stares at the rising tide, or like the crew
4310   Whilst now the ship is splitting through and through;
Each, if the tramp of a far steed was heard,
Started from sick despair, or if there flew
One murmur on the wind, or if some word
Which none can gather yet, the distant crowd has stirred.

XI

4315   Why became cheeks wan with the kiss of death,
Paler from hope? they had sustained despair.
Why watched those myriads with suspended breath
Sleepless a second night? they are not here
The victims, and hour by hour, a vision drear,
4320   Warm corpses fall upon the clay cold dead;
And even in death their lips are wreathed with fear. —
The crowd is mute and moveless — overhead
Silent Arcturus shines — ha! hear'st thou not the tread

XII

Of rushing feet? laughter? the shout, the scream,
4325   Of triumph not to be contained? see! hark!
They come, they come, give way! alas, ye deem
Falsely — 'tis but a crowd of maniacs stark
Driven, like a troop of spectres, through the dark,
From the choked well, whence a bright death-fire sprung,
4330   A lurid earth-star, which dropped many a spark
From its blue train, and spreading widely, clung
To their wild hair, like mist the topmost pines among.

4321. wreathed] writhed *1839, Rossetti 1870, 1878, Dowden 1891. Nbk 3* 179 appears to read
'writhed', which is cancelled. There are large areas of overlap in meaning between the two
verbs. The sense here, 'to twist, turn, or contort the body or features, as in pain' is that of
Wreathe (*OED* v. trans. 6d and e) and of Writhe (*OED* v. trans. 5a and b). It may be that
S. preferred *wreathed* over the 'writhed' in the draft, or that he transcribed 'writhed' into the
fair copy and that the compositor's preferred form was 'wreathed'. Cp. line 1924 and note.

4323. Arcturus] Both *Locock 1911* and *1975* point out that *Arcturus* (the brightest star in the
constellation Boötes or 'The Ploughman') could not be described as *overhead* in autumn, which
is now the fictional season, as indicated in line 3904.

XIII

And many from the crowd collected there,
Joined that strange dance in fearful sympathies;
4335   There was the silence of a long despair,
When the last echo of those terrible cries
Came from a distant street, like agonies
Stifled afar. — Before the Tyrant's throne
All night his agèd Senate sate, their eyes
4340   In stony expectation fixed; when one
Sudden before them stood, a Stranger and alone.

XIV

Dark Priests and haughty Warriors gazed on him
With baffled wonder, for a hermit's vest
Concealed his face; but when he spake, his tone,
4345   Ere yet the matter did their thoughts arrest,
Earnest, benignant, calm, as from a breast
Void of all hate or terror, made them start;
For as with gentle accents he addressed
His speech to them, on each unwilling heart
4350   Unusual awe did fall — a spirit-quelling dart.

XV

'Ye Princes of the Earth, ye sit aghast
Amid the ruin which yourselves have made,
Yes, desolation heard your trumpet's blast,
And sprang from sleep! — dark Terror has obeyed
4355   Your bidding — O, that I whom ye have made
Your foe, could set my dearest enemy free
From pain and fear! but evil casts a shade,
Which cannot pass so soon, and Hate must be
The nurse and parent still of an ill progeny.

Stanza xiv. S. drafted, then partially cancelled, a note to this stanza in *Nbk 3* 182: 'This somewhat resembles an incident in "The Corsair". The catastrophe & tendency of this involuntary imitation of it is widely different, & an allusion to it might justly be considered as presumptuous'. The incident in question is the appearance of Conrad the Corsair chief disguised as a Dervise at a feast given by the Muslim Pacha Seyd. Wearing (like Laon) a vest, Conrad claims to have escaped from the pirate band that he himself leads (*The Corsair* II ii–iv). His ruse is a strategem to cover a surprise attack by his men.

4343. vest] A loose cloak or robe; here, apparently, either fitted with a cowl or hood or held by Laon so as to cover his face.

4357–9. Cp. lines 3706–11 and note to 3708.

XVI

4360   'Ye turn to God for aid in your distress;
    Alas, that ye, the mighty and the wise,
    Who, if ye dared, might not aspire to less
    Than ye conceive of power, should fear the lies
    Which thou, and thou, didst frame for mysteries
4365   To blind your slaves: — consider your own thought,
    An empty and a cruel sacrifice
    Ye now prepare, for a vain idol wrought
    Out of the fears and hate which vain desires have brought.

XVII

    'Ye seek for happiness — alas, the day!
4370   Ye find it not in luxury nor in gold,
    Nor in the fame, nor in the envied sway
    For which, O willing slaves to Custom old,
    Severe taskmistress! ye your hearts have sold.
    Ye seek for peace, and when ye die, to dream
4375   No evil dreams: all mortal things are cold
    And senseless then; if aught survive, I deem
    It must be love and joy, for they immortal seem.

XVIII

    'Fear not the future, weep not for the past.
    O, could I win your ears to dare be now
4380   Glorious, and great, and calm! that ye would cast
    Into the dust those symbols of your woe,
    Purple, and gold, and steel! that ye would go
    Proclaiming to the nations whence ye came,
    That Want, and Plague, and Fear, from slavery flow;

4360. God] Heaven *RofI*.

4361–5. 'What a pity that you who occupy the seats of strength and wisdom and who are capable of realising in yourselves all the power that you imagine God to possess, should be held in awe by the religious lies you have invented to dupe your subjects'.

4361. the mighty] *Nbk 3* 182, *1839, eds*; tho' mighty *L&C/RofI*. The emendation is perhaps not such an inevitable decision as its wide acceptance would suggest. This is a cancel-leaf for *RofI*, giving S. the occasion to make a correction, which was not made; but the ungainly phrase with 'tho'' and the presence of *the* in the draft weigh heavily against the *L&C/RofI* reading.

4362. ye] *L&C, Nbk 3* 182, *eds*; he *RofI*. This evident misprint in *RofI*, together with the probability of an uncorrected mistake in the previous line, would indicate that this part of the proof for the *RofI* cancel-leaf was not carefully read.

4375. No evil dreams] 'For in that sleep of death what dreams may come / When we have shuffled off this mortal coil / Must give us pause' (*Hamlet* III i 68–70).

4385 And that mankind is free, and that the shame
Of royalty and faith is lost in freedom's fame!

XIX

'If thus 'tis well — if not, I come to say
That Laon' — while the Stranger spoke, among
The Council sudden tumult and affray
4390 Arose, for many of those warriors young,
Had on his eloquent accents fed and hung
Like bees on mountain flowers; they knew the truth,
And from their thrones in vindication sprung;
The men of faith and law then without ruth
4395 Drew forth their secret steel, and stabbed each ardent youth.

XX

They stabbed them in the back and sneered — a slave
Who stood behind the throne, those corpses drew
Each to its bloody, dark, and secret grave;
And one more daring raised his steel anew
4400 To pierce the Stranger: 'What hast thou to do
With me, poor wretch?' — Calm, solemn, and severe,
That voice unstrung his sinews, and he threw
His dagger on the ground, and pale with fear,
Sate silently — his voice then did the Stranger rear.

XXI

4405 'It doth avail not that I weep for ye —
Ye cannot change, since ye are old and grey,
And ye have chosen your lot — your fame must be
A book of blood, whence in a milder day
Men shall learn truth, when ye are wrapped in clay:
4410 Now ye shall triumph. I am Laon's friend,

4385–6. 'The good opinion you would acquire in espousing freedom would dissipate the *shame* that attaches to your present allegiances'.

4387. *If thus 'tis well*] The draft reading (*Nbk 3* 184) imparts a subtler rhythm to the phrase: 'If thus . . . tis well'.

4389. *Council*] *RofI*; council, *L&C*, council. *Nbk 3* 184: alteration on the cancel-leaf for *RofI*.

4399–404. The incident, as St. Clair (*The Godwins and the Shelleys* (1989) 111) points out, is borrowed from Godwin's *Political Justice* (1793, 1796, 1798) VII iii: 'When Marius said, with a stern look and a commanding countenance, to the soldier that was sent down into his dungeon to assassinate him, "Wretch, have you the temerity to kill Marius!' and with these few words drove him to flight; it was that the grandeur of the idea conceived in his own mind made its way with irresistible force to the mind of his executioner . . . Who shall say how far the whole species might be improved, did they cease to respect force in others, and did they refuse to employ it for themselves?' (*Political Justice* ii 338–9).

And him to your revenge will I betray,
So ye concede one easy boon. Attend!
For now I speak of things which ye can apprehend.

XXII

    'There is a People mighty in its youth,
4415   A land beyond the Oceans of the West,
    Where, though with rudest rites, Freedom and Truth
    Are worshipped; from a glorious Mother's breast,
    Who, since high Athens fell, among the rest
    Sate like the Queen of Nations, but in woe,
4420   By inbred monsters outraged and oppressed,
    Turns to her chainless child for succour now,
    It draws the milk of Power in Wisdom's fullest flow.

XXIII

    'That land is like an Eagle, whose young gaze
    Feeds on the noontide beam, whose golden plume
4425   Floats moveless on the storm, and in the blaze
    Of sunrise gleams when Earth is wrapped in gloom;
    An epitaph of glory for the tomb
    Of murdered Europe may thy fame be made,
    Great People: as the sands shalt thou become;
4430   Thy growth is swift as morn, when night must fade;
    The multitudinous Earth shall sleep beneath thy shade.

XXIV

    'Yes, in the desert there is built a home
    For Freedom. Genius is made strong to rear

Stanzas xxii–xxiv. The eulogy of the American republic in these stanzas as political example to Europe, and especially to England, adopts the position of progressive reformers, e.g. Paine's *Rights of Man*, Part Two (1792) which S. reread in 1817 (*Mary Jnl* i 102).

4418. high Athens] See note to line 406.

4419. Queen of Nations] England: here imagined as the political heir of Athenian and the mother of American democracy, though at present rendered unworthy of both ancestor and child by the action of the *inbred monsters* of the next line. S. may be remembering Paine, *Rights of Man*, Part Two (1792): 'What Athens was in miniature America will be in magnitude' (*Paine Writings* ii 424).

4420. inbred] Native.

4424. noontide beam] See note to line 207.

4428. murdered Europe] buried Europe *canc.* Albion *Nbk 3* 188.

4429. See note to line 1069.

4432. desert] Wilderness. *there*] *Nbk 3* 189, *eds*; then *L&C/Rof1, 1839*. No alteration to the word is made in *L&C* (PM) on what was to become a cancel-leaf for *Rof1* even though another

The monuments of man beneath the dome
4435 Of a new Heaven; myriads assemble there,
Whom the proud lords of man, in rage or fear,
Drive from their wasted homes: the boon I pray
Is this, — that Cythna shall be convoyed there —
Nay, start not at the name — America!
4440 And then to you this night Laon will I betray.

XXV

'With me do what ye will. I am your foe!'
The light of such a joy as makes the stare
Of hungry snakes like living emeralds glow,
Shone in a hundred human eyes — 'Where, where
4445 Is Laon? haste! fly! drag him swiftly here!
We grant thy boon.' — 'I put no trust in ye,
Swear by your dreadful God.' — 'We swear, we swear!'
The Stranger threw his vest back suddenly,
And smiled in gentle pride, and said, 'Lo! I am he!'

---

correction was made (see note to line 4438), so that the emendation to *there* rests upon the complex hypothesis of a mistranscription from draft or misprint from fair copy ('then' and 'there' can be difficult to distinguish in S.'s hand even in fair copy) which passed unnoticed – first in proof, then when the alterations at lines 4438 and 4447 were made, and finally on the proof of the cancel-leaf. On the other hand, it is difficult to believe that S., once having written *there* in the draft, would alter it to 'then'. This has decided the question, though in such a case the conclusion can hardly be a confident one.

4435–40. S. nearly completed stanza xxiv in draft in *Nbk 3* 189 before cancelling what he had written after *Heaven* (4435) and drafting alternative lines which are essentially those printed. The cancelled lines read: 'no fanes to Force or Fear, / But shapes of beauty simple grand & clear / Like that from which they spring, the good & free / Shall dwell in peace & love & union there / And deeds be done which those who think ?[on] ?[thee] / *alt. line* And thine are deeds weak tyrant, which must be / Like beacons to'.

4438. Cythna] S. has forgotten that in the Golden City Cythna is known only by her adopted name of Laone. *Rossetti 1870, 1878* went so far as to emend the name to 'Laone' accordingly. *convoyed] Nbk 3* 190, *RofI*; conveyed *L&C*: alteration in *L&C* (PM) for the *RofI* cancel-leaf. The condition that Cythna shall be escorted to America in order to avoid apprehension and punishment can hardly have failed to evoke in contemporary readers the parallel case of William Cobbett. Before sailing for a period of two years' voluntary exile in America in March 1817, Cobbett claimed in an open letter 'To the Public', published on 5 April 1817 (reprinted in *The Examiner* No. 484 (6 April 1817) 219–21) that the suspension of Habeas Corpus earlier in the month represented a threat to freedom of expression such that he could now only write the truth beyond England's shores. His opponents maintained that he was escaping to avoid imprisonment for debt.

4445. Laon?] RofI; Laon? – *L&C*: alteration on the cancel-leaf for *RofI*.

4447. your dreadful God] the Power ye dread *RofI*.

4448. vest] See note to line 4343.

Canto Twelfth

I

4450 The transport of a fierce and monstrous gladness
Spread through the multitudinous streets, fast flying
Upon the winds of fear; from his dull madness
The starveling waked, and died in joy; the dying,
Among the corpses in stark agony lying,
4455 Just heard the happy tidings, and in hope
Closed their faint eyes; from house to house replying
With loud acclaim, the living shook Heaven's cope,
And filled the startled Earth with echoes: morn did ope

II

Its pale eyes then; and lo! the long array
4460 Of guards in golden arms, and priests beside,
Singing their bloody hymns, whose garbs betray
The blackness of the faith it seems to hide;

Stanzas i–xv. Both general and particular resemblances exist between the incidents in these stanzas and the rescue by the female warrior Clorinda of the lovers Sophronia and Olindo from death by burning at the stake in Tasso's *Gerusalemme Liberata* II i–liii. S. read Tasso's epic in 1815 and was rereading Tasso in October 1816 (*Mary Jnl* i 92, 139). On a draft for stanzas ii and iii of Canto I S. noted Clorinda's name together with that of Erminia, the princess and lover of Tancred in Tasso's poem (*Box 4* f. 2r; facsimile in *BSM* viii 170). There are other interesting similarities to the burning of heretics by the Inquisition in six-teenth-century Spain in William Godwin's novel *St. Leon* (1799; xxxii–xxxiii) and to the death of the patriot Hafed in Moore's 'The Fire-Worshippers' (*Lalla Rookh*, 1817).

Stanza i. 'The frenzied movement of mixed horror and exultation – the ululation of vengeance which ascended instantaneously from the individual street, and then by a sub-lime sort of magnetic contagion from all the adjacent streets, can be adequately expressed only by a rapturous passage in Shelley' (Thomas DeQuincey, *Murder Considered as One of the Fine Arts*, 'Postscript' (1854)) – citing this stanza to illustrate the generalised nervous response to the information that the author of a notorious murder was again murdering in a house in an east London neighbourhood.

Stanzas ii–iii. These stanzas incorporate details from the incident of the burning of the athe-ist in *Q Mab* vii 1–13: 'The dark-robed priests were met around the pile; / The multitude was gazing silently; / And as the culprit passed with dauntless mien, / Tempered disdain in his unaltering eye, / Mixed with a quiet smile, shone calmly forth' (3–7).

Stanzas ii–vi. There are resemblances of detail between these stanzas and Sydney Owenson's [Lady Morgan's] novel *The Missionary* (1811) iii 165–76 in which Hilarion, the Apostolic Nuncio of India, is led to the stake to be burned as a heretic by the Inquisition in Goa.

4462. it] The lack of agreement with *garbs* in the previous line prompted *Rossetti 1870, 1878* to emend to 'they'. In the draft in *Nbk 3* 191 S. first wrote 'The blackness of thier [sic] hearts', but, no doubt wishing to avoid repetition with 'their bloody hymns' in the previous line, entered revisions above and below the line which are impossible to decipher confidently. The singular pronoun would be appropriate to 'garb betrays' rather than *garbs betray*, required by the rhyme, and it seems likely that S. had the more idiomatic phrase in mind as he wrote *it*.

And see, the Tyrant's gem-wrought chariot glide
Among the gloomy cowls and glittering spears —
4465   A Shape of light is sitting by his side,
A child most beautiful. I' the midst appears
Laon, — exempt alone from mortal hopes and fears.

III

His head and feet are bare, his hands are bound
Behind with heavy chains, yet none do wreak
4470   Their scoffs on him, though myriads throng around;
There are no sneers upon his lip which speak
That scorn or hate has made him bold; his cheek
Resolve has not turned pale, — his eyes are mild
And calm, and like the morn about to break,
4475   Smile on mankind — his heart seems reconciled
To all things and itself, like a reposing child.

IV

Tumult was in the soul of all beside,
Ill joy, or doubt, or fear; but those who saw
Their tranquil victim pass, felt wonder glide
4480   Into their brain, and became calm with awe. —
See, the slow pageant near the pile doth draw.
A thousand torches in the spacious square,
Borne by the ready slaves of ruthless law,
Await the signal round: the morning fair
4485   Is changed to a dim night by that unnatural glare.

V

And see! beneath a sun-bright canopy,
Upon a platform level with the pile,
The anxious Tyrant sit, enthroned on high,
Girt by the chieftains of the host; all smile
4490   In expectation, but one child: the while
I, Laon, led by mutes, ascend my bier
Of fire, and look around; each distant isle
Is dark in the bright dawn; towers far and near,
Pierce like reposing flames the tremulous atmosphere.

4481. doth draw] In the draft (*Nbk 3* 193) S. has placed a cross above this phrase as a key to
a note written in a space at the top of the page and across the top of the next: 'In this ?[&
in] other occasions, the present has been employed in [speaki] the delineation of past events.
The effect is [?] This is what the imagination perpetually does ?[while] adverting'.

4491. mutes] See note to line 2899.

VI

4495   There was such silence through the host, as when
An earthquake trampling on some populous town,
Has crushed ten thousand with one tread, and men
Expect the second; all were mute but one,
That fairest child, who, bold with love, alone
4500   Stood up before the King, without avail,
Pleading for Laon's life — her stifled groan
Was heard — she trembled like one aspen pale
Among the gloomy pines of a Norwegian vale.

VII

What were his thoughts linked in the morning sun,
4505   Among those reptiles, stingless with delay,
Even like a tyrant's wrath? — the signal-gun
Roared — hark, again! in that dread pause he lay
As in a quiet dream — the slaves obey —
A thousand torches drop, — and hark, the last
4510   Bursts on that awful silence; far away
Millions, with hearts that beat both loud and fast,
Watch for the springing flame expectant and aghast.

VIII

They fly — the torches fall — a cry of fear
Has startled the triumphant! — they recede!
4515   For ere the cannon's roar has died, they hear
The tramp of hoofs like earthquake, and a steed
Dark and gigantic, with the tempest's speed,
Bursts through their ranks: a woman sits thereon,
Fairer it seems than aught that earth can breed,
4520   Calm, radiant, like the phantom of the dawn,
A spirit from the caves of daylight wandering gone.

IX

All thought it was God's Angel come to sweep
The lingering guilty to their fiery grave;

4502. *one aspen*] an aspen *Nbk 3* 195, *1839, Rossetti 1870*. It is possible that *one* is an error of transcription or printing. The original spelling in *L&C/RofI* is 'aspin'.

4520. Cp. lines 2107–10 and note.

4522. *God's Angel*] Cp. lines 4211–12. There are detailed similarities between Cythna's appearance here and a scene late in Sydney Owenson's [Lady Morgan's] novel *The Missionary* (1811), which S. knew well (see note to line 4072), in which the Hindu priestess Luxima joins her lover, the missionary Hilarion, who is being burnt at the stake in Goa by the Inquisition at the instigation of a Spanish Jesuit. The comparison was made by G. E. Woodberry (*The Complete Poetical Works of Percy Bysshe Shelley* (1901) 619–20. '. . . a form scarcely human,

4525

The tyrant from his throne in dread did leap, —
Her innocence his child from fear did save;
Scared by the faith they feigned, each priestly slave
Knelt for his mercy whom they served with blood,
And, like the refluence of a mighty wave
Sucked into the loud sea, the multitude

4530

With crushing panic, fled in terror's altered mood.

X

They pause, they blush, they gaze, — a gathering shout
Bursts like one sound from the ten thousand streams
Of a tempestuous sea: — that sudden rout
One checked, who, never in his mildest dreams

4535

Felt awe from grace or loveliness, the seams
Of his rent heart so hard and cold a creed
Had seared with blistering ice — but he misdeems
That he is wise, whose wounds do only bleed
Inly for self, thus thought that Christian Priest indeed,

XI

4540

And others too, thought he was wise to see,
In pain, and fear, and hate, something divine,

darting with the velocity of lightning through the multitude, reached the foot of the pile, and stood before it in a grand and aspiring attitude . . . thus bright and aërial as it stood, it looked like a spirit sent from Heaven in the awful moment of dissolution to cheer and to convey to the regions of the blessed, the soul which would soon arise, pure from the ordeal of earthly suffering. The sudden appearance of the singular phantom struck the imagination of the credulous and awed multitude with superstitious wonder . . . Luxima, whose eyes and hands had been hitherto raised to Heaven, while she murmured the *Gayatra*, pronounced by the Indian women before their voluntary immolation, now looked wildly round her, and, catching a glimpse of the Missionary's figure, through the waving of the flames, behind which he struggled in the hands of his guards, she shrieked, and in a voice scarcely human, exclaimed, "My beloved, I come! – *Brahma* receive and eternally unite our spirits!" – She sprang upon the pile' (2nd edn, iii 176–9). Luxima's prayer is that of an Indian widow before submitting to suttee on the funeral pyre of her husband. Two young widows are immolated with the dead Arvalan in Southey's *The Curse of Kehama* (1810) I 10–15.

4537. seared] Perhaps an ironic reminiscence of *1 Timothy* iii 2: 'Speaking lies in hypocrisy; having their conscience seared with a hot iron'.

4537–9. The priest's sentiment, elliptically expressed, seems to be: 'He mistakenly considers himself wise who confines his suffering to individual and inward pain (?for his own sins)'. His belief illustrates one of the poem's important contentions – that the torment of a heart wounded by religious fear requires that others too should shed their blood. This is the social corollary of the individual psychology of guilt of lines 3390–2: 'It is the dark idolatry of self, / Which, when our thoughts and actions once are gone, / Demands that man should weep, and bleed, and groan'.

4539. that Christian Priest] the Iberian Priest *RofI*.

4541. divine,] *Nbk 3* 199; divine *L&C/RofI*; divine; *1839*. Most *eds* have supplied punctuation here.

In love and beauty — no divinity. —
Now with a bitter smile, whose light did shine
Like a fiend's hope upon his lips and eyne,
4545 He said, and the persuasion of that sneer
Rallied his trembling comrades — 'Is it mine
To stand alone, when kings and soldiers fear
A woman? God has sent his other victim here.'

XII

'Were it not impious,' said the King, 'to break
4550 Our holy oath?' — 'Impious to keep it, say!'
Shrieked the exulting Priest — 'Slaves, to the stake
Bind her, and on my head the burden lay
Of her just torments: — at the Judgement Day
Will I stand up before God's golden throne,
4555 And cry, O Lord, to thee did I betray
An Atheist; but for me she would have known
Another moment's joy! the glory be thine own.'

XIII

They trembled, but replied not, nor obeyed,
Pausing in breathless silence. Cythna sprung
4560 From her gigantic steed, who, like a shade
Chased by the winds, those vacant streets among
Fled tameless, as the brazen rein she flung
Upon his neck, and kissed his moonèd brow.
A piteous sight, that one so fair and young,
4565 The clasp of such a fearful death should woo
With smiles of tender joy as beamed from Cythna now.

XIV

The warm tears burst in spite of faith and fear,
From many a tremulous eye, but like soft dews
Which feed spring's earliest buds, hung gathered there,
4570 Frozen by doubt, — alas, they could not choose,
But weep; for when her faint limbs did refuse
To climb the pyre, upon the mutes she smiled;
And with her eloquent gestures, and the hues

4548. *God has sent his*] Heaven has sent its *Rofl*.

4554–6. 'Will I stand up before the golden throne / Of Heaven, and cry, to thee did I betray / An Infidel' *Rofl*.

4566. *as*] Such as.

4573. *hues*] Cp. lines 1559–60: 'the woof of wisdom I know well / To dye in hues of language'. S. first wrote 'the hues / Of her fair cheek' (*Nbk 3* 201).

Of her quick lips, even as a weary child
4575 Wins sleep from some fond nurse with its caresses mild,

XV

She won them, though unwilling, her to bind
Near me, among the snakes. When there had fled
One soft reproach that was most thrilling kind,
She smiled on me, and nothing then we said,
4580 But each upon the other's countenance fed
Looks of insatiate love; the mighty veil
Which doth divide the living and the dead
Was almost rent, the world grew dim and pale, —
All light in Heaven or Earth beside our love did fail. —

XVI

4585 Yet, — yet — one brief relapse, like the last beam
Of dying flames, the stainless air around
Hung silent and serene — a blood-red gleam
Burst upwards, hurling fiercely from the ground
The globèd smoke, — I heard the mighty sound
4590 Of its uprise, like a tempestuous ocean;
And, through its chasms I saw, as in a swound,
The tyrant's child fall without life or motion
Before his throne, subdued by some unseen emotion.

XVII

And is this death? the pyre has disappeared,
4595 The Pestilence, the Tyrant, and the throng;
The flames grow silent — slowly there is heard
The music of a breath-suspending song,

4577. there] *Forman 1876–7, Dowden 1891, 1904, 1975*; then *L&C/RofI*; they *Rossetti 1870*; these *Locock 1911*. The draft in *Nbk 3* 202, cited by *1975* as 'there', and transcribed as 'these' in *BSM* xvii 219, can be read as either. 'These' (the mutes) creates a difficulty: *smiled* must then be taken as transitive, which is possible; but *nothing then we said* implies that Cythna has previously spoken the *reproach* rather than *smiled* it. 'Then' is the reading of *L&C/RofI* but has otherwise little to recommend it: *then had fled* sounds very awkwardly as well as jingling with *then* of line 4579. Misreading 'there' as 'then' would be a plausible printer's error as the two words are often difficult to distinguish in S.'s hand, and, although it hardly makes an idiomatic phrase, 'there' does avoid the difficulties of either 'then' or 'these'.

4594. *And is this death?*] The number of incomplete lines of the cancelled draft over half a page in *Nbk 3* (203–4) testifies that S. was at first uncertain how to represent Laon's consciousness of the passage from life: 'we sate among the . . . And we are wandering thro a garden silent *alt.* wild . . . / That echoes voices on the wind are heard . . . And soon a joyous company we meet / With gentle looks & words ?[us two] they greet / As welcome strangers; we with wonder know / They are the same [ ] / The city armed hosts [ ] / I look around, the city & the throng / . . . So we sate down upon a ?[hill].

251

Which, like the kiss of love when life is young,
Steeps the faint eyes in darkness sweet and deep;
4600   With ever-changing notes it floats along,
Till on my passive soul there seemed to creep
A melody, like waves on wrinkled sands that leap.

XVIII

The warm touch of a soft and tremulous hand
Wakened me then; lo, Cythna sate reclined
4605   Beside me, on the waved and golden sand
Of a clear pool, upon a bank o'ertwined
With strange and star-bright flowers, which to the wind
Breathed divine odour; high above, was spread
The emerald heaven of trees of unknown kind,
4610   Whose moonlike blooms and bright fruit overhead
A shadow, which was light, upon the waters shed.

XIX

And round about sloped many a lawny mountain
With incense-bearing forests, and vast caves
Of marble radiance to that mighty fountain;
4615   And where the flood its own bright margin laves,
Their echoes talk with its eternal waves,
Which, from the depths whose jaggèd caverns breed
Their unreposing strife, it lifts and heaves, —
Till through a chasm of hills they roll, and feed
4620   A river deep, which flies with smooth but arrowy speed.

XX

As we sate gazing in a trance of wonder,
A boat approached, borne by the musical air
Along the waves which sung and sparkled under
Its rapid keel — a wingèd shape sate there,
4625   A child with silver-shining wings, so fair,
That as her bark did through the waters glide,
The shadow of the lingering waves did wear
Light, as from starry beams; from side to side,
While veering to the wind her plumes the bark did guide.

Stanza xix. The details of the landscape recall Coleridge's *Kubla Khan* 1–36.

4624. a wingèd shape] The boat propelled by the wind caught by the wings of the child is modelled upon the vessel of souls driven by the wings of an angel in Dante, *Purgatorio* ii 22–36.

XXI

4630   The boat was one curved shell of hollow pearl,
Almost translucent with the light divine
Of her within; the prow and stern did curl
Hornèd on high, like the young moon supine,
When o'er dim twilight mountains dark with pine,
4635   It floats upon the sunset's sea of beams,
Whose golden waves in many a purple line
Fade fast, till borne on sunlight's ebbing streams,
Dilating, on earth's verge the sunken meteor gleams.

XXII

Its keel has struck the sands beside our feet; —
4640   Then Cythna turned to me, and from her eyes
Which swam with unshed tears, a look more sweet
Than happy love, a wild and glad surprise,
Glanced as she spake; 'Ay, this is Paradise
And not a dream, and we are all united!
4645   Lo, that is mine own child, who in the guise
Of madness came, like day to one benighted
In lonesome woods: my heart is now too well requited!'

XXIII

And then she wept aloud, and in her arms
Clasped that bright Shape, less marvellously fair
4650   Than her own human hues and living charms;
Which, as she leaned in passion's silence there,
Breathed warmth on the cold bosom of the air,
Which seemed to blush and tremble with delight;
The glossy darkness of her streaming hair
4655   Fell o'er that snowy child, and wrapped from sight
The fond and long embrace which did their hearts unite.

XXIV

Then the bright child, the plumèd Seraph came,
And fixed its blue and beaming eyes on mine,
And said, 'I was disturbed by tremulous shame

4644. *we are all united*] S. would seem to have designed the reunion of Laon, Cythna and the child after that of Ladurlad, his daughter Kailyal and her dead mother Yedillian in the earthly paradise at the top of Mount Meru whence they are transported in a boat guided by a Glendoveer, or kindly spirit, in Southey's *The Curse of Kehama* (1810) Section X. See notes to lines 325, 4807. Cp. also the final sentence of Peacock's prose outline for the 2-canto *Ahrimanes: Peacock Works* vii 432.

4645. *mine own*] our own *canc. Nbk 3* 208.

4660 When once we met, yet knew that I was thine
From the same hour in which thy lips divine
Kindled a clinging dream within my brain,
Which ever waked when I might sleep, to twine
Thine image with *her* memory dear — again
4665 We meet; exempted now from mortal fear or pain.

XXV

'When the consuming flames had wrapped ye round,
The hope which I had cherished went away;
I fell in agony on the senseless ground,
And hid mine eyes in dust, and far astray
4670 My mind was gone, when bright, like dawning day,
The Spectre of the Plague before me flew,
And breathed upon my lips, and seemed to say,
"They wait for thee belovèd;" — then I knew
The death-mark on my breast, and became calm anew.

XXVI

4675 'It was the calm of love — for I was dying.
I saw the black and half-extinguished pyre
In its own grey and shrunken ashes lying;
The pitchy smoke of the departed fire
Still hung in many a hollow dome and spire
4680 Above the towers like night; beneath whose shade
Awed by the ending of their own desire
The armies stood; a vacancy was made
In expectation's depth, and so they stood dismayed.

XXVII

'The frightful silence of that altered mood,
4685 The tortures of the dying clove alone,
Till one uprose among the multitude,
And said — "The flood of time is rolling on,
We stand upon its brink, whilst *they* are gone
To glide in peace down death's mysterious stream.
4690 Have ye done well? they moulder flesh and bone,
Who might have made this life's envenomed dream
A sweeter draught than ye will ever taste, I deem.

4660–2. The child refers to her meeting with Laon in Othman's palace in V xxiv.
4664. Thy memory with [my mothers now again] that image dear – again *Nbk 3* 210.
4674. death-mark] See line 3980 and note.

XXVIII

' "These perish as the good and great of yore
Have perished, and their murderers will repent,
4695 Yes, vain and barren tears shall flow before
Yon smoke has faded from the firmament
Even for this cause, that ye who must lament
The death of those that made this world so fair,
Cannot recall them now; but then is lent
4700 To man the wisdom of a high despair,
When such can die, and he live on and linger here.

XXIX

' "Ay, ye may fear not now the Pestilence,
From fabled hell as by a charm withdrawn,
All power and faith must pass, since calmly hence
4705 In torment and in fire have Atheists gone;
And ye must sadly turn away, and moan
In secret, to his home each one returning,
And to long ages shall this hour be known;
And slowly shall its memory, ever burning,
4710 Fill this dark night of things with an eternal morning.

XXX

' "For me the world is grown too void and cold,
Since hope pursues immortal destiny
With steps thus slow — therefore shall ye behold
How Atheists and Republicans can die —
4715 Tell to your children this!" then suddenly
He sheathed a dagger in his heart and fell;
My brain grew dark in death, and yet to me

4699. then] there *Forman 1876–7, Dowden 1891, 1904, 1975.* Forman emended, alleging a probable printer's error and pointing out both the difficulty of distiguishing 'then' and 'there' in S.'s hand and the ease with which such an error might be overlooked in proof. *1975* follows his lead, pointing out that 'there' is the likelier reading in the draft (*Nbk 3* 213) and that S.'s first draft phrase, 'they have', would more naturally attract the revision 'there is'. However that may be, it remains that *then* was not corrected either in *L&C* (PM) or on the proof of this cancel-leaf for *Rofl* even though an error listed among the Errata ('mourn' for *moan* in line 4706), itself not corrected in *L&C* (PM), was corrected in *Rofl*. Since *then*, though hardly euphonious, makes coherent sense, it has been allowed to stand. *Locock 1911* takes *then* as emphatic.

4704–5. 'The example of the serene death of the atheists Laon and Cythna demonstrates the transience of a political power and a faith whose sanctions are judicial execution and the menace of eternal punishment in hell'.

4705. In pain and fire have unbelievers gone; *Rofl.*

4714. How those who love, yet fear not, dare to die; *Rofl.*

255

There came a murmur from the crowd, to tell
Of deep and mighty change which suddenly befell.

XXXI

4720 'Then suddenly I stood a wingèd Thought
Before the immortal Senate, and the seat
Of that star-shining spirit, whence is wrought
The strength of its dominion, good and great,
The better Genius of this world's estate.
4725 His realm around one mighty Fane is spread,
Elysian islands bright and fortunate,
Calm dwellings of the free and happy dead,
Where I am sent to lead!' these wingèd words she said,

XXXII

And with the silence of her eloquent smile,
4730 Bade us embark in her divine canoe;
Then at the helm we took our seat, the while
Above her head those plumes of dazzling hue
Into the winds' invisible stream she threw,
Sitting beside the prow: like gossamer,
4735 On the swift breath of morn, the vessel flew
O'er the bright whirlpools of that fountain fair,
Whose shores receded fast, whilst we seemed lingering there;

XXXIII

Till down that mighty stream dark, calm, and fleet,
Between a chasm of cedarn mountains riven,
4740 Chased by the thronging winds whose viewless feet
As swift as twinkling beams, had, under Heaven,
From woods and waves wild sounds and odours driven,
The boat fled visibly — three nights and days,
Borne like a cloud through morn, and noon, and even,
4745 We sailed along the winding watery ways
Of the vast stream, a long and labyrinthine maze.

4737. So lightly does the boat sail that their only sensation of movement is the rapidly-receding shore.

4739. Cp. Coleridge, *Kubla Khan* 12–13: 'But oh! that deep romantic chasm which slanted / Down the green hill athwart a cedarn cover!'

4741. *under Heaven*] 'Into the open air' (*Locock 1911*): the winds mingle *sounds* and *odours* from river and shore.

4743. *visibly*] See note to line 4737.

XXXIV

A scene of joy and wonder to behold
That river's shapes and shadows changing ever,
Where the broad sunrise filled with deepening gold
4750   Its whirlpools, where all hues did spread and quiver,
And where melodious falls did burst and shiver
Among rocks clad with flowers, the foam and spray
Sparkled like stars upon the sunny river,
Or when the moonlight poured a holier day,
4755   One vast and glittering lake around green islands lay.

XXXV

Morn, noon, and even, that boat of pearl outran
The streams which bore it, like the arrowy cloud
Of tempest, or the speedier thought of man,
Which flieth forth and cannot make abode,
4760   Sometimes through forests, deep like night, we glode,
Between the walls of mighty mountains crowned
With Cyclopean piles, whose turrets proud,
The homes of the departed, dimly frowned
O'er the bright waves which girt their dark foundations round.

XXXVI

4765   Sometimes between the wide and flowering meadows,
Mile after mile we sailed, and 'twas delight
To see far off the sunbeams chase the shadows
Over the grass; sometimes beneath the night
Of wide and vaulted caves, whose roofs were bright
4770   With starry gems, we fled, whilst from their deep
And dark-green chasms, shades beautiful and white,
Amid sweet sounds across our path would sweep,
Like swift and lovely dreams that walk the waves of sleep.

Stanza xxxiv. The stanza has been much repunctuated by *eds*, but the sense is clear enough without intervention except in line 4749 where the commas in *L&C/RofI* after *sunrise* and *gold* have been removed.

4749. Where] When *Rossetti 1878, Dowden 1891, Hutchinson, 1975.* Rossetti put forward a parallel with *when* in line 4754 in support of his emendation; 'when' and 'where' can be difficult to distinguish in S.'s hand, but *where* makes adequate sense as it stands.

4762. Cyclopean piles] Monumental buildings constructed by the Cyclops, a giant race of master-builders who, in Greek legend, were credited with erecting the great structures of the heroic age: 'it being usual to attribute to a race of men who, from their power, were considered by after-ages as giants, any result of extraordinary labour' – E. D. Clarke, *Travels in Various Countries of Europe Asia and Africa*, Part the Second, Section the Second, 4th edn (1818) vi 426.

XXXVII

And ever as we sailed, our minds were full
4775   Of love and wisdom, which would overflow
In converse wild, and sweet, and wonderful;
And in quick smiles whose light would come and go,
Like music o'er wide waves, and in the flow
Of sudden tears, and in the mute caress —
4780   For a deep shade was cleft, and we did know,
That virtue, though obscured on Earth, not less
Survives all mortal change in lasting loveliness.

XXXVIII

Three days and nights we sailed, as thought and feeling
Number delightful hours — for through the sky
4785   The spherèd lamps of day and night, revealing
New changes and new glories, rolled on high,
Sun, Moon, and moonlike lamps, the progeny
Of a diviner Heaven, serene and fair:
On the fourth day, wild as a wind-wrought sea
4790   The stream became, and fast and faster bare
The spirit-wingèd boat, steadily speeding there.

XXXIX

Steady and swift, where the waves rolled like mountains
Within the vast ravine, whose rifts did pour
Tumultuous floods from their ten thousand fountains,
4795   The thunder of whose earth-uplifting roar
Made the air sweep in whirlwinds from the shore,
Calm as a shade, the boat of that fair child
Securely fled, that rapid stress before,
Amid the topmost spray, and sunbows wild,
4800   Wreathed in the silver mist: in joy and pride we smiled.

4781–2. Cp. Preface, lines 44–5 and note.

4783–8. The time of the journey is measured subjectively according to earthly habit, since the heavenly bodies move and change to a different rhythm in the celestial dimension through which the boat now travels.

4785. spherèd lamps] Celestial bodies set among the spheres which, in older astronomy, were imagined as forming the heavens. See note to line 621.

4799. sunbows] 'We beheld an immense body of water fall two hundred and fifty feet, dashing from rock to rock, and casting a spray which formed a mist around it, in the midst of which hung a multitude of sunbows, which faded or became unspeakably vivid, as the inconstant sun shone through the clouds' (*1817* in *Prose Works* 222).

XL

The torrent of that wide and raging river
Is passed, and our aerial speed suspended.
We look behind; a golden mist did quiver
When its wild surges with the lake were blended:
4805   Our bark hung there, as on a line suspended
Between two heavens, that windless waveless lake;
Which four great cataracts from four vales, attended

4804. When] *L&C/RofI, 1839, Woodberry 1893, Locock 1911*; Where *Rossetti 1870, 1878, Forman 1876–7, Dowden 1891, Hutchinson, 1975*. Rossetti and Forman defend the emendation on the grounds that it indicates, what they take to be S.'s intention, the place where the *golden mist* occurs. *Locock 1911* considers *When* as the equivalent of 'Whenever', and that a continuing process is the sense intended. A moment of blending that is continually renewed as the surges from the river meet the lake is certainly a possible meaning of *When* in the context.

4805. on a line] *Rossetti 1870, eds*; one line *L&C/RofI*. Rossetti's emendation has been widely adopted. Besides making the poetic line metrically consistent with the previous one, it clarifies an image otherwise hard to visualise distinctly. *Forman 1876–7* cites *Fragment of an Unfinished Drama* (1822) 228–32: 'And thus it lay in the Elysian calm / Of its own beauty, floating on the line / Which, like a film in purest space, divided / The heaven beneath the water from the heaven / Above the clouds'. *Daemon* 192–3 and *Lines Written among the Euganean Hills* 100–104 are also apposite, as is *Hellas* 477–80.

4805–6. The awkward construction seems to result from *on* doing double service as preposition, the boat being suspended both *on a line* and [on] *that windless waveless lake*. *Rossetti 1870, 1878*, reading as parenthetical the sentence *Our bark . . . two heavens*, placed it between dashes and round brackets. *Hutchinson* and *1975* have adopted his dashes, and this is one way of finding syntactical coherence in the passage. Another, requiring no repunctuation, is to consider *that windless waveless lake* as equivalent to '[on the surface of] that windless waveless lake', and in apposition with *line*.

4807. four great cataracts] *Curran (1975)* 211 makes an interesting connection between the lake fed by four cataracts and 'Mansarovara', the lake that Indian legend placed on Mount Meru which was traditionally located at the North Pole. S. read of the lake and mountain in Southey's *Curse of Kehama* (1810) X (see note to line 4644) and of the four rivers that descend from it in the notes to that section of the poem. The identification with the four rivers that flow out of Eden (*Genesis* ii 10–14; *Paradise Lost* iv 230–5) had been suggested, as Curran points out, by the orientalist Francis Wilford. One of Southey's notes, taken from Wilford, specifies that Meru signifies 'hemisphere' and that the Hindus regard the world as divided into a northern one which is a 'seat of delights' and a southern one, 'the dreary habitation of demons . . . In strict propriety, Meru denotes the pole and the polar regions; but it is the celestial north pole round which they place the gardens and metropolis of *Indra* [God of the Elements], while *Yama* [Lord of Hell] holds his court in the opposite polar circle, or the station of *Asuras*, who warred with the *Suras*, or gods of the firmament'. The water of the ocean is said to come down from heaven upon the mountain, circle it in seven channels and then divide 'into four streams, which, falling from the immense height of Meru, rest themselves in four lakes, from which they spring over the mountains through the air, just brushing the summits'. There is an evident compatibility between this mythic dualism and that of *L&C*, as well as suggestive resemblances in the two schemes of moral geography. S. characteristically simplifies his source material; he also reverses the direction of the rivers, which here run into the lake, in order to retain from Southey's poem the ethical symbolism of the place as paradisal destination for the virtuous.

By mists, aye feed; from rocks and clouds they break,
And of that azure sea a silent refuge make.

XLI

4810   Motionless resting on the lake awhile,
I saw its marge of snow-bright mountains rear
Their peaks aloft, I saw each radiant isle,
And in the midst, afar, even like a sphere
Hung in one hollow sky, did there appear
4815   The Temple of the Spirit; on the sound
Which issued thence, drawn nearer and more near,
Like the swift moon this glorious earth around,
The charmèd boat approached, and there its haven found.

Finis

4813. *sphere*] See note to I liii–iv.

4818. The line renders S.'s homage to Spenser who in the celebrated first stanza of *Faerie Queene* I xii compared his poetic enterprise to a 'feeble barke' about to reach 'the hauen nigh at hand'. The gesture had been anticipated by Sir Walter Scott in *The Vision of Don Roderick* (1811) which S. ordered in June of that year (*L* i 98, 110): the final Spenserian stanza of Scott's poem – '(With Spenser's parable I close my tale,)' – follows the progress of his 'skiff' as it approaches land. See note to epigraph before Canto I.

143 Appendix
Fragments from the *L&C* Notebooks

*Edited by Jack Donovan**

A: 'we are lyres'

This rough and much-cancelled draft is written in pencil lengthways from bottom to top of page 2 in *Nbk 2* (which contains drafts for *L&C* Cantos I and II) beneath pencil drafts for 'Fair clouds arrayed in sunlight lose the glory' (no. 142) lines 60–3 and *L&C* lines 267–70. It therefore probably dates from late March/early April 1817 when S. was beginning composition of *L&C*. All three drafts are attempts at the final four lines of a Spenserian stanza. Affinities of thought and language establish a connection between this draft and stanzas 3 and 5 of no. 142, which occupies pages 4–8 of the same nbk, and for which it may at first have been intended. Cp. also *Alastor* lines 42–9. Facsimile and transcription in *BSM* xiii 8–9.

we are lyres
Suspended on a boundless Ocean's shore
Which as the world unseen in sleep respires
[With the inconstant] voice of its own dream inspires

B: 'Like a sunbeam on a tempest streaming'

These lines, drafted in pencil, occupy page 35 of *Nbk 2*, the second of the six pages of miscellaneous drafts that follow those for *L&C* I xxv at which S. interrupted the composition of the poem, resuming on page 40 with I lix. The imagery drawn from the heavenly bodies common to the lines suggests that they may form part of a single conception, though the variation in their length seems to indicate that that conception was still far from being realised in poetic form. The final three lines, written in a darker pencil, and perhaps a late addition to the others, may not be verse as lines 9–10 do not begin with capital letters. Published in *1975* 365–6; facsimile and transcription *BSM* xiii 74–5.

Like a sunbeam on a tempest streaming

And with thy sweet eyes' awful glance
Would wake the world from its cold trance

* *For help with various problems Jack Donovan would like to thank Jacques Berthoud, John Birtwhistle, Greg Dart, Stephen Minta, John Pickles, John Walker, P. G. Walsh, Timothy Webb and David Duff. The Leverhulme Trust granted a fellowship which provided relief from teaching and administrative duties in the autumn term 1997.*

¶B 3. the world] nature *alt. uncanc.*

Hast thou
5   Breathless withdrawn Like the Heaven of night
Over a lake star-paved [   ] azure
Whose columns are the snowbright ?[mountains] round

When the light of the rising moon
10   is in the East and the setting sun
yet in the west

C: 'Who with the Devil doth rage and revel'

These lines are clearly written in pencil above fragment E on page 39 of *Nbk 2*. They approximate the alternating long and short line of ballad metre. The language and style resemble those of *The Devil's Walk: A Ballad* (no. 83), in particular lines 1–4, 132–3. Printed in *1975* 364; facsimile and transcription *BSM xiii* 82–3.

Who with the Devil doth rage and revel
When he keeps his Sabbath of sin

D: 'He ceased – another rose – One pale and [   ]'

Text from *Nbk 2* 37. After breaking off composition of *L&C* at stanza xxv of Canto I, S. made miscellaneous notes and drawings as well as drafting fragments of verse, some of it later incorporated into *L&C*, on the next six pages (34–9) of the nbk before resuming composition of the poem with the first two stanzas of Canto II, which he later made the final two of Canto I. It may be that this draft of a Spenserian stanza is his first attempt at stanza lix of Canto I in which Laon is introduced as narrator of *L&C*. The top right-hand corner of the page is torn away removing the final word of the first line. *1975's* conjecture, 'weak', is plausible. Published in *1975* 366; facsimile and transcription in *BSM xiii* 78–9.

He ceased — another rose — One pale and [   ]
As he had been subdued by sufferings
Too deep and dread to leave upon his cheek
Aught but those lines which high endurance brings
5   And scorn of anguish — [like the peak that flings]
The sunbeam from its snowy rocks
Gently in [innocent pride] while on its wings
His golden locks, the wind spread wide and wild

¶D   *4. those lines*] that wan hue *canc.*
6. The lightning from its rocks he stood, & smiled *canc.*

E: 'He ceased – and approbation like the sound'

Text from *Nbk 2* 39. This much-cancelled draft may have been an alternative to fragment D or intended to come before or after it. Its development of an epic simile for the reaction to an address of a vast assembly is evidently indebted to *Paradise Lost* ii 284–91. The final line, written in pencil, may have been added much later, and may not have been meant as part of the stanza. Below it are some calculations in pencil of completed stanzas such as occur throughout the *L&C* nbks (see *L&C* headnote *Composition and Publication*, p. 4) which must have been made when S. had nearly finished composing Canto XII, probably in September 1817. Published *1975* 364; facsimile and transcription *BSM* xiii 82–3.

> He ceased — and approbation like the sound
> Of wind among a grove of pines was heard
> [Through the vast tem]
> [From the assembly]. as [when a gust has stirred]
> [Ascending the vast]
> Their thousand [   ] another rose
>
> I fear that I am hardly human

F: 'Many shall feel who dare not speak their feeling'

This cancelled line and what may have been intended as the first two words of another are written in ink across the top of page 4 of *Nbk 4* which contains drafts for the Dedication to *L&C*. The fragment therefore probably dates from October 1817, and may at first have been meant for the Dedication. Variations on the sentiment expressed are frequent in S.'s verse; e.g. *L&C* 3742–3. Facsimile and transcription *BSM* xiii 182–3.

> Many shall feel who dare not speak their feeling
> Many shall [

G: 'And hopes like morning dew unshed'

These two lines are written with the page reversed on the otherwise blank page 37 of *Nbk 4* which S. used largely for drafting the Dedication to *L&C*. Three pages previous to this one (starting from the back; S. worked in both directions in the nbk) occurs the draft of *L&C* X xlvii (see note to *L&C* 4213–15) which S. added to the end of Canto X as originally drafted in *Nbk 3* and which could have been written at any time in late summer/early autumn 1817, as these two lines could have been. *1975* 257 considers that they anticipate *L&C* 4568–9, which they resemble; if so, they were perhaps written in early September. Facsimile and transcription *BSM* xiii 242–3.

> And hopes like morning dew unshed
> Trembling on spring's unopened buds

H: 'The wild ?[bull] in the mountain and the horse'

This attempt at a Spenserian stanza is roughly drafted in pencil on page 143 of *Nbk 3*, the second of four pages which interrupt the drafts for *L&C* X between stanzas xii and xiii. The writing is both larger than S.'s usual pencil drafts and the letters crudely formed, as if there was no firm support beneath the nbk when he wrote them. The draft is followed by some notes on the effects of the plague (S. introduces the disease at *L&C* X xiv): 'In the pestilence – its effects on man – destroying the memory of things – the imagination of ghosts – Daphies Thebd – See Senecas'. The notes continue on the following page: 'The dogs become hydrophobic & the wolves – the horse – cold sweat – tear their flesh with their teeth. – the birds & beasts of prey become mild.' *1975* considered that 'Daphies' = Daphnis, one of the principal characters of *Daphnis and Chloe* the Greek romance of the third century AD by Longus which S. praises in 1820 (*L* ii 213); 'Greek Romances' figures in a memorandum in *Nbk 4* 38 which may have been written at this time or shortly after. *1975* further suggests that 'Thebd' refers to the *Thebaid*, the epic poem of the first century AD by Statius. The partially-drafted stanza describes the destruction of animals by the plague, a theme that S. develops in *L&C* X xiv–xv (see note to xv), leading to the formation of the miasma which was thought to carry pestilential infection (see note to *L&C* 3908–9). Most of line 2 is introduced at *L&C* 3919. See also note to *L&C* 3945. Published *1975* 374; facsimile and transcription *BSM* xvii 154–5.

> The wild ?[bull] in the mountain and the horse
> Perished, the fish were poisoned in the streams
> A cloud of ?[horrid] exhalations [?]
> From the Earth [?] to Heaven steams
5 > The birds are killed which float among the [?]
> And winds they have drank poison

I: 'How long has Poesy, the widowed Mother'

This brief fragment is written on page 215, reversed, of *Nbk3* – the page that follows the breaking off of the draft of *L&C* at Canto XII xxxi 3. At the bottom of the page is the memorandum '£5 – March 19 1817' above the figure '5191' – both 'probably in Mary Shelley's hand' (*BSM* xvii 233). Given S.'s practice of writing in a nbk from both directions at once, this fragment may date from mid to late March 1817 but it is impossible to be sure. Reiman (*Sc* v 145) speculated that the three lines might represent S.'s attempt to begin *L&C*, though the connection between the two is not evident. In 1821 S. incorporated the phrase 'he died / Blind old and lonely' into *Adonais* 29–31, where it designates Milton. The childlessness of Poesy also finds its equivalent in *Adonais* where the Muse Urania is imagined as having lost in Keats her youngest child. The lines may be the beginning of an elegiac poem on the state of poetry in England, with Milton as the touchstone of

¶H *4. 1975* conjectured 'up' for the illegible word.

5. 1975 conjectured 'skies' for the illegible word.

departed excellence, in the manner of Wordsworth's *London, 1802* (1807). Published *1975* 374; facsimile and transcription *BSM* xvii 232–3.

> How long has Poesy, the widowed Mother
> Been childless in our land [   ] he died
> Blind old and lonely when

J: '?[Like the] wintry skies of a mountain'

These lines occupy the top third of the same page in *Nbk 3* on which fragment I occurs, and are written with a pencil so worn that some letters are scratched into the paper with its wood. The resulting draft is faint and extremely difficult to decipher; hence the high proportion of uncertain readings in the text offered below. Line 2 was later incorporated into *Lines Written among the Euganean Hills* (no. 183) at line 46. The moment of simultaneous sunset and moonrise described in lines 3–4 is also rendered in lines 8–10 of fragment B. Published *1975* 375; facsimile and transcription *BSM* xvii 232–3.

> ?[Like the] wintry skies of a mountain
> Which the ?[tempests] shake ?[eternally]
> Like the ?[young] moon [   ] which the 1000 fountains
> Which floats ?[on] the sunset's golden ocean
> 5   Above the piny dells of [   ] mountains

¶J   3. Above the space after *moon* is an uncancelled word: 'kissed'?
5. *piny*] *BSM xvii* reads ?[fiery].

144
Rosalind and Helen, a Modern Eclogue

The exact composition-sequence is complex and perhaps undeterminable. Mary S. stated that 'Rosalind and Helen was begun at Marlow, and thrown aside – till I found it; and, at my request, it was completed . . . Rosalind and Helen was finished during the summer of 1818, while we were at the Baths of Lucca' (*1839* iii 159–60). Not all of this statement is correct. The only known MS, a first draft of lines 40–349 with some omissions and additions, is in *Nbk 1*, which also contains jnl entries for S.'s tour of Lac Léman with Byron in June 1816, so Mary S. must have 'found' these lines when she began compiling *1817* at Marlow on 9 August 1817 (*Mary Jnl* i 178). On 26 September she lamented to S., who was in bad health and had just been forbidden by his doctor Sir William Lawrence to write poetry, that 'It is well that your poem [*L&C*] was finished before this edict was issued against the imagination but my pretty eclogue will suffer from it' (*Mary L* i 43), so composition of *R&H* was about to be resumed, or had just been resumed, after the completion of *L&C* at the end of September. Lines 894–901 of *R&H* are an acknowledged quotation of 'The billows on the beach' (no. 139), so those lines cannot be earlier than July–August 1817. The last week of September, moreover, was that in which William Baxter, Isabella Booth's father, told Mary S. on his second visit to Albion House 'that Mr Booth is illtempered and *jealous* towards Isabell – & Mr B[axter] thinks that she half repents her marriage – so she is to [be] another victim of that ceremony'(*Mary L* i 41), a situation greatly developed in lines 219–535. For 18–25 February 1818 Mary S. noted: 'copy Shelley's Eclogue' (*Mary Jnl* i 194), and some at least of the poem went to Ollier for printing before the departure to Italy. The Shelleys were at Bagni di Lucca (15 miles N. of Lucca) from 11 June to 17 August 1818, but for most of this time S. found himself 'totally incapable of original composition'. On 16 August, however, he told Peacock: 'I have finished, by taking advantage of a few days of inspiration . . . the little poem I began sending to the press in London. Ollier will send you the proofs. Its structure is slight and aëry; its subject ideal [i.e. imaginary]. The metre corresponds with the spirit of the poem, and varies with the flow of the feeling' (*L* ii 29). Two days later he wrote to Ollier: 'Voici the conclusion of my little poem, which I took advantage of ten days of dubious inspiration to finish – the terror of your reproaches & the printer's wonder operated as Muse on the occasion. You will observe that the fabric of the composition is light & unstudied, & that if it have little merit it has as much as it aspires to. – I cannot expect that that pig the public will trust itself to desert its cherished mud, & drink a cup of dew so evanescent' (text by Walter Fischer, *Eng. Studien* li (1918) 389). *R&H* was therefore completed about 4–14 August 1818, and the final additions must have been fairly substantial to have taken ten days in writing and three days in transcription (*Mary Jnl* i 223).

Despite Mary S.'s note, however, the poem was probably not begun at Marlow in 1817, but at line 40 in late July 1816, in Switzerland. In *Nbk 1* there is not only an interruption between lines 73 and 74 of the draft to admit that of 'Mont Blanc' but fossil lines are left in the 'Mont Blanc' draft itself on p. 3 (see note to line 73). Ink colour and the layering of texts on the page suggest that the 'Mont Blanc' draft is probably lying over those parts of the *R&H* draft which merge with it. The lines at the top of p. 3 are precisely picked up for continuation after the conclusion of 'Mont Blanc' on p. 13 (see *BSM* xi 6–9, 28–29 for photographic reproductions of the MS with transcription; it is however not possible to determine an order of composition from the reproductions, which are in black and white). That the resumption of the poem on p. 13 also took place in Switzerland is suggested by the fact that the placing of the last two lines of 'Mont Blanc' appears to be cramped by the heading 'Isabel' already on the page; so *R&H* presumably neither skipped an already completed 'Mont Blanc' nor predated it, but was actually interrupted by the writing of that poem. There is nothing in the *R&H* lines drafted in *Nbk 1* specifically to identify an Italian setting, and in the resumed draft on p. 13 S. has replaced his original draft 'is it Linnas seat' with ''tis Fenice's' (see note to line 74), added in thick pencil and obviously at a later date (i.e. to import into the draft its only definitely Italian marker). *BSM* xi argues that 'at least one quire of sixteen pages has been lost from the front of the notebook', and that some of these pages 'must have contained the opening lines of *Rosalind and Helen*' (Introduction, xix). But this hypothesis cannot be definitively tested, nor, if it could, is it possible to determine when the 'missing' pages were first removed. The placement of S.'s draft of *R&H* from line 40 on p. 1 of *Nbk 1* (see *BSM* xi 3) is consistent with an actual beginning, and indeed stylistic evidence might suggest that the first forty lines of the received text of *R&H* are later in manner than the following lines 40–216, and more similar in accomplishment and tone to the seven-syllable line of 'Lines Written Among the Euganean Hills', written of course in Italy in the late summer of 1818. The setting of the printed poem is 'the Shore of the Lake of Como', and Medwin originally thought the work 'glows with all the enchanting scenery of that delicious summer retreat' (*Athenaeum* 248, 28 July 1832, 489); but S. was at Como for three days only, 9–12 April 1818. Clearly the original lake setting of *R&H* was Geneva, which was changed to Como when S. took up his unfinished poem in Italy. Apart from lines 1–40 and 1240–1318, however, the sections of the poem composed in Italy are a matter of guesswork. The temple in the myrtle-wood (lines 1049 ff.), which suggests Italy, might have been influenced by Grecian scenes in Peacock's *Rhododaphne* (e.g. Canto iii 60–129). But the nightingale's song in lines 1102–1130 is described with immediacy and at length, and may well record the impact of S.'s early experience of Italy in April 1818; he could not in fact have heard a nightingale during any other known composition-time of the poem. The following composition-pattern (neglecting brief passages mentioned in the notes) accords with the available evidence:

Lines 40–218 (or 349):	Switzerland, July 1816.
Lines 219 (or 350)–1101 (or 1048):	Marlow, October 1817–*c.* January 1818.
Lines 1–39:	Italy, on or after the visit to Lake Como, 9–12 April 1818.
Lines 1102 (or 1049)–end:	Italy, Bagni di Lucca, first half of August 1818.

Dowden (*Dowden Life* ii 129–31) first connected *R&H* with Mary S.'s broken friendship for Isabella Booth, married daughter of Godwin's friend William Baxter, with whose family Mary had spent more than a year of her adolescence at The Cottage (once on the site of Baffin Street, Dundee). There is no external evidence for the connection beyond Mary S.'s private appropriation of the poem as 'my pretty eclogue' (*Mary L* i 43) and her anxiety for its completion, but real-life relationships were undoubtedly the origin of the poem, as the draft's use of 'Isabel' and 'Robert' (the name of Isabella Booth's brother) helps to confirm. David Booth, an elderly ex-brewer of intimidatingly forceful mind and character, married Isabella Baxter (illegally) after the death of her elder sister Margaret, his first wife, in 1814. S. eloped with Mary Godwin the same year, and Booth made this the pretext for forbidding Isabella to continue the relationship. 'Receive a letter from Mr Booth;' Mary S. wrote in her jnl on 3 November, 'so all my hopes are over there – ah Isabel – I did not think you would act thus' (*Mary Jnl* i 42). The loss of a year of the jnl conceals the course of events; but when Baxter's business failed at the end of 1816 and he came to London, the Shelleys sought to revive the friendship with his daughter. Much impressed by S. during the long visit he paid to Albion House in September 1817, Baxter encouraged Isabella to renew the association, and at Godwin's request Booth permitted his wife to correspond with Mary S. after the latter had legalised her union with S. S., who twice met Booth in person (13, 23 November 1817), judged him to have a 'keen and subtle mind, deficient in those elementary feelings which are the *principles* of all moral reasoning' (*L* i 588). The Shelleys invited Isabella to go with them to Italy, and despite her own prejudice against S. she wanted to accept, but Booth refused (now misinterpreting the presence of Byron's daughter in the S. ménage), and eventually induced even Baxter to break off relations entirely. The friendship with Isabella was renewed only after S.'s death (full details are in *SC* iii 103–105; v 334–42, 371–92). Thus the relationship fluctuated repeatedly between 1814 and 1818, which may account for some stops and starts in composition as well as for changing attitudes to Rosalind/Isabella in the extant draft of the poem. Much is fiction ('its subject is ideal') in both narratives, though that of Helen and Lionel is closer to actuality. The name 'Lionel' derives presumably from that of the hero in Godwin's *Mandeville*, which S. read in the first week of November 1817 (*Mary Jnl* i 185), so that Helen's narrative from line 596 must postdate that reading. S. is not known to have read Charlotte Smith's novel *Desmond* (1792), outspoken in support of the French Revolution and in criticism of the marriage laws, whose hero Lionel Desmond is even closer to the Shelleyan ideal than Lionel Clifford. S. adopted the name for himself in 'The Boat on the Serchio' and in the MS prose fragment beginning 'A strange fellow that Lionel' first published by Neville Rogers (*Rogers* 16–17). The classical eclogue, a dialogue between shepherds, had been modified by Southey in his nine 'English Eclogues' (1799) into what he claimed to be a wholly original kind in English poetry: a short dialogue between native speakers rehearsing some affecting domestic event, and *R&H* is in this kind, considerably expanded. The abrupt original opening at line 40 closely resembles Southey's practice. S.'s poem became 'a great favourite' of Leigh Hunt's, and much pleased those readers who looked for 'human interest' in poetry, but S. himself told Byron it was 'a mere extempore thing, and worth little, I believe' (*L* ii 199). In his Advertisement to *1819*, dated 20 December 1818, he wrote:

> The story of 'Rosalind and Helen' is, undoubtedly, not an attempt in the highest style of poetry. It is in no degree calculated to excite profound meditation; and if, by interesting the affections and amusing [i.e. engaging] the imagination, it awaken a certain ideal melancholy favourable to the reception of more important impressions, it will produce in the reader all that the writer experienced in the composition. I resigned myself, as I wrote, to

the impulse of the feelings which moulded the conception of the story; and this impulse determined the pauses of a measure, which only pretends to be regular inasmuch as it corresponds with, and expresses, the irregularity of the imaginations which inspired it.

Post-Victorian readers have generally accepted S.'s estimate of the poem, and more recent interest has been in its ideology rather than in its appeal to the affections. Cameron holds that 'the story, in fact, is simply a peg used by Shelley to support a passionate exposition of his social beliefs' (*Cameron (1974)* 253), and Paul Foot remarks that the poem is 'one of Shelley's most neglected longer poems, probably because it is so overtly feminist' (*Red Shelley* (1980) 104).

To his publisher on 6 September 1819 (*L* ii 117) S. wrote: 'In the Rosalind & Helen I see there are some few errors, which are so much the worse because they are errors in the sense', but he did not specify, and some errors at least will have been noticed elsewhere in the volume than in the title-poem, so S.'s complaint is no open licence for emendation.

Text from *1819*, pp. 3–68.

Published in *1819*.

144
Rosalind and Helen

Rosalind, Helen and her Child.
Scene, the Shore of the Lake of Como.

Helen
Come hither, my sweet Rosalind.
'Tis long since thou and I have met;
And yet methinks it were unkind
Those moments to forget.
5   Come sit by me. I see thee stand
By this lone lake, in this far land,
Thy loose hair in the light wind flying,
Thy sweet voice to each tone of even
United, and thine eyes replying
10   To the hues of yon fair heaven.
Come, gentle friend: wilt sit by me?
And be as thou wert wont to be
Ere we were disunited?
None doth behold us now: the power
15   That led us forth at this lone hour
Will be but ill requited
If thou depart in scorn: oh! come,

1. *Rosalind*] 'Isabel' throughout *Nbk 1*, Mary S.'s friend's real name. The new name was perhaps borrowed from that of Celia's 'coupled and inseparable' friend in *As You Like It*, a favourite play of S.'s.

And talk of our abandoned home.
Remember, this is Italy,
20 And we are exiles. Talk with me
Of that our land, whose wilds and floods,
Barren and dark although they be,
Were dearer than these chestnut woods:
Those heathy paths, that inland stream,
25 And the blue mountains, shapes which seem
Like wrecks of childhood's sunny dream:
Which that we have abandoned now,
Weighs on the heart like that remorse
Which altered friendship leaves. I seek
30 No more our youthful intercourse.
That cannot be! Rosalind, speak,
Speak to me. Leave me not. — When morn did come,
When evening fell upon our common home,
When for one hour we parted, — do not frown:
35 I would not chide thee, though thy faith is broken:
But turn to me. Oh! by this cherished token,
Of woven hair, which thou wilt not disown,
Turn, as 'twere but the memory of me,
And not my scorned self who prayed to thee.

Rosalind
40 Is it a dream, or do I see
And hear frail Helen? I would flee
Thy tainting touch; but former years
Arise, and bring forbidden tears;
And my o'erburthened memory
45 Seeks yet its lost repose in thee.
I share thy crime. I cannot choose
But weep for thee: mine own strange grief
But seldom stoops to such relief:
Nor ever did I love thee less,
50 Though mourning o'er thy wickedness
Even with a sister's woe. I knew
What to the evil world is due,
And therefore sternly did refuse
To link me with the infamy
55 Of one so lost as Helen. Now

---

24. that inland stream] The river Tay in central Scotland. See note to lines 1277–8.
46. I share thy crime] i.e. by associating with you.
52. Followed in *Nbk 1* by 'And painfully that painful task / I did accomplish –'.

Bewildered by my dire despair,
Wondering I blush, and weep that thou
Should'st love me still, — thou only! — There,
Let us sit on that grey stone,
60   Till our mournful talk be done.

Helen
Alas! not there; I cannot bear
The murmur of this lake to hear.
A sound from thee, Rosalind dear,
Which never yet I heard elsewhere
65   But in our native land, recurs,
Even here where now we meet. It stirs
Too much of suffocating sorrow!
In the dell of yon dark chestnut wood
Is a stone seat, a solitude
70   Less like our own. The ghost of peace
Will not desert this spot. To-morrow,
If thy kind feelings should not cease,
We may sit here.

Rosalind
                    Thou lead, my sweet,
And I will follow.

59. *sit on*] sit down on *Nbk 1*. The pencil insertion *down* was perhaps missed in transcription.

63. *A sound from thee,*] *1819, Nbk 1*; A sound from there, *Rossetti 1870, eds*. A needless emendation. It cannot be supposed that Helen, who has lived many months by Lake Como (lines 196–7, 1245–55), has never yet heard the murmur of it. The meaning is: 'The sound of your sobbing (line 81), which up to now I have heard only at home in Britain, is repeated by the lake here where we sit – come to a place where the sounds of sorrow are not replicated by nature'. 'To recur' in the sense of 'to be reproduced' is used in 'To Ianthe' (no. 95) 9–12 (not in *Concordance*).

73. See headnote. After 'We may sit here', *Nbk 1* names the new speaker, 'Isabel', at the foot of p. 2, and at the top of p. 3, palimpsested beneath the opening of the 'Mont Blanc' draft, continues:
                    well Helen – well
                    You move me strangely
                    I pray thee cease such talk I feel
The canc. resumption on p. 13 on the other hand, although it skips 'Mont Blanc', appears to have been on the page before the final two lines of that poem, suggesting that these lines of 'Mont Blanc' were added at a late stage. It reads:
                    Isabel
                    well Helen well
                    I pray thee talk not thus
                    As I had wronged thee My heart
                    Was once thine own – dear Helen –

Henry

'Tis Fenici's seat.

75   Where are you going? This is not the way,
Mamma; it leads behind those trees that grow
Close to the little river.

Helen

Yes: I know:
I was bewildered. Kiss me, and be gay,
Dear boy: why do you sob?

Henry

I do not know:
80   But it might break any one's heart to see
You and the lady cry so bitterly.

Helen

It is a gentle child, my friend. Go home,
Henry, and play with Lilla till I come.
We only cried with joy to see each other;
We are quite merry now: Good-night.

85   The boy
Lifted a sudden look upon his mother,
And in the gleam of forced and hollow joy
Which lightened o'er her face, laughed with the glee
Of light and unsuspecting infancy,
90   And whispered in her ear, 'Bring home with you
That sweet strange lady-friend.' Then off he flew,
But stopped, and beckoned with a meaning smile,
Where the road turned. Pale Rosalind the while,
Hiding her face, stood weeping silently.

95   In silence then they took the way
Beneath the forest's solitude.
It was a vast and antique wood,
Through which they took their way:
And the grey shades of evening

74. *Henry*] Robert *Nbk 1*. *Fenici's*] Linnas *Nbk 1* canc., then apparently *Fenice's* (see head-note). 'Fenice' is Italian for 'Phoenix', the name of the Venice Opera House.

83. *Lilla*] Presumably Henry's nurse. The name was first left blank in *Nbk 1*, then 'Mary' was tried and canc. for 'Lilla', a German diminutive for Elizabeth which S. borrowed from Gothic fiction.

95–6. *the way/Beneath*] their way / into *Nbk 1*. The repetition of line 95 in 98 is not in *Nbk 1*, and may have been inadvertent.

100 O'er that green wilderness did fling
Still deeper solitude.
Pursuing still the path that wound
The vast and knotted trees around
Through which slow shades were wandering,
105 To a deep lawny dell they came,
To a stone seat beside a spring,
O'er which the columned wood did frame
A roofless temple, like the fane
Where, ere new creeds could faith obtain,
110 Man's early race once knelt beneath
The overhanging deity.
O'er this fair fountain hung the sky,
Now spangled with rare stars. The snake,
The pale snake, that with eager breath
115 Creeps here his noontide thirst to slake,
Is beaming with many a mingled hue,
Shed from yon dome's eternal blue,
When he floats on that dark and lucid flood
In the light of his own loveliness;
120 And the birds that in the fountain dip
Their plumes, with fearless fellowship
Above and round him wheel and hover.
The fitful wind is heard to stir
One solitary leaf on high;
125 The chirping of the grasshopper
Fills every pause. There is emotion
In all that dwells at noontide here:
Then, through the intricate wild wood,
A maze of life and light and motion
130 Is woven. But there is stillness now:
Gloom, and the trance of Nature now:
The snake is in his cave asleep;
The birds are on the branches dreaming:
Only the shadows creep:
135 Only the glow-worm is gleaming:
Only the owls and the nightingales
Wake in this dell when daylight fails,
And grey shades gather in the woods:
And the owls have all fled far away

111. *The overhanging deity.*] The sun.

116–17. Glows with an evanescent hue / Shed from yon domes serener blue *Nbk 1*.

123–4. Recalling *Christabel* i 48–52: 'There is not wind enough to twirl / The one red leaf . . . / . . . hanging so high'.

140   In a merrier glen to hoot and play,
        For the moon is veiled and sleeping now.
        The accustomed nightingale still broods
        On her accustomed bough,
        But she is mute; for her false mate
145   Has fled and left her desolate.

        This silent spot tradition old
        Had peopled with the spectral dead.
        For the roots of the speaker's hair felt cold
        And stiff, as with tremulous lips he told
150   That a hellish shape at midnight led
        The ghost of a youth with hoary hair,
        And sate on the seat beside him there,
        Till a naked child came wandering by,
        When the fiend would change to a lady fair!
155   A fearful tale! The truth was worse:
        For here a sister and a brother
        Had solemnized a monstrous curse,
        Meeting in this fair solitude:
        For beneath yon very sky,
160   Had they resigned to one another
        Body and soul. The multitude,
        Tracking them to the secret wood,
        Tore limb from limb their innocent child,
        And stabbed and trampled on its mother;
165   But the youth, for God's most holy grace,
        A priest saved to burn in the market-place.

        Duly at evening Helen came
        To this lone silent spot,
        From the wrecks of a tale of wilder sorrow
170   So much of sympathy to borrow
        As soothed her own dark lot.

---

142. accustomed] customed *Nbk 1*.

146–55. This silent spot . . . A fearful tale!] A link with the exchange of ghost-stories at the Villa Diodati which produced *Frankenstein* and S.'s lines in this same nbk 'A shovel of his ashes' (no. 119). S. read *Christabel* aloud on 26 August 1816 (*Mary Jnl* i 131).

155. The truth was worse:] Ironical; 'worse' as judged by convention. R. D. Havens argued (*JEGP* xxx (1931) 221note) that the worse truth 'was not incest . . . but the action of the multitude and the priest'. This however ignores line 157 'Had solemnized a monstrous curse' which S. substituted for the *Nbk 1* reading 'Had loved so fondly one another', a change that surely makes the irony unmistakable.

163–4. Whose senseless limbs were rent / By the fury of the bloody rabblement *Nbk 1* canc.

Duly each evening from her home,
With her fair child would Helen come
To sit upon that antique seat,
175   While the hues of day were pale;
And the bright boy beside her feet
Now lay, lifting at intervals
His broad blue eyes on her;
Now, where some sudden impulse calls
180   Following. He was a gentle boy
And in all gentle sports took joy;
Oft in a dry leaf for a boat,
With a small feather for a sail,
His fancy on that spring would float,
185   If some invisible breeze might stir
Its marble calm: and Helen smiled
Through tears of awe on the gay child,
To think that a boy as fair as he,
In years which never more may be,
190   By that same fount, in that same wood,
The like sweet fancies had pursued;
And that a mother, lost like her,
Had mournfully sate watching him.
Then all the scene was wont to swim
195   Through the mist of a burning tear.

For many months had Helen known
This scene; and now she thither turned
Her footsteps, not alone.
The friend whose falsehood she had mourned,
200   Sate with her on that seat of stone.
Silent they sate; for evening,
And the power its glimpses bring
Had, with one awful shadow, quelled
The passion of their grief. They sate
205   With linkèd hands, for unrepelled
Had Helen taken Rosalind's.
Like the autumn wind, when it unbinds
The tangled locks of the nightshade's hair,
Which is twined in the sultry summer air
210   Round the walls of an outworn sepulchre,

185. might stir] 'Happened to stir'.
207–18. Not in *Nbk 1*; presumably composed later.

Did the voice of Helen, sad and sweet,
And the sound of her heart that ever beat,
As with sighs and words she breathed on her,
Unbind the knots of her friend's despair,
215   Till her thoughts were free to float and flow;
And from her labouring bosom now,
Like the bursting of a prisoned flame,
The voice of a long-pent sorrow came.

Rosalind
I saw the dark earth fall upon
220   The coffin; and I saw the stone
Laid over him whom this cold breast
Had pillowed to his nightly rest!
Thou knowest not, thou canst not know
My agony. Oh! I could not weep:
225   The sources whence such blessings flow
Were not to be approached by me!
But I could smile, and I could sleep,
Though with a self-accusing heart.
In morning's light, in evening's gloom,
230   I watched, — and would not thence depart —
My husband's unlamented tomb.
My children knew their sire was gone,
But when I told them, — 'he is dead,' —
They laughed aloud in frantic glee,
235   They clapped their hands and leaped about,
Answering each other's ecstasy
With many a prank and merry shout.
But I sate silent and alone,
Wrapped in the mock of mourning weed.

240   They laughed, for he was dead: but I
Sate with a hard and tearless eye,
And with a heart which would deny
The secret joy it could not quell,
Low muttering o'er his loathèd name;
245   Till from that self-contention came
Remorse where sin was none; a hell
Which in pure spirits should not dwell.

---

211. sad and sweet] As in 'Passion' (no. 66) S. puns on the Bittersweet (*Solanum dulcamara*, the only European climbing Nightshade) of line 208. Cp. also *PU* III iv 78–83 and note.

244. muttering o'er] 'Repeating over to myself'.

I'll tell thee truth. He was a man
Hard, selfish, loving only gold,
250   Yet full of guile: his pale eyes ran
With tears, which each some falsehood told,
And oft his smooth and bridled tongue
Would give the lie to his flushing cheek:
He was a coward to the strong:
255   He was a tyrant to the weak,
On whom his vengeance he would wreak:
For scorn, whose arrows search the heart,
From many a stranger's eye would dart,
And on his memory cling, and follow
260   His soul to its home so cold and hollow.
He was a tyrant to the weak,
And we were such, alas the day!
Oft, when my little ones at play,
Were in youth's natural lightness gay,
265   Or if they listened to some tale
Of travellers, or of fairy land, —
When the light from the wood-fire's dying brand
Flashed on their faces, — if they heard
Or thought they heard upon the stair
270   His footstep, the suspended word
Died on my lips: we all grew pale:
The babe at my bosom was hushed with fear
If it thought it heard its father near;
And my two wild boys would near my knee
275   Cling, cowed and cowering fearfully.

I'll tell thee truth: I loved another.
His name in my ear was ever ringing,
His form to my brain was ever clinging:
Yet if some stranger breathed that name,
280   My lips turned white, and my heart beat fast:
My nights were once haunted by dreams of flame,
My days were dim in the shadow cast
By the memory of the same!
Day and night, day and night,
285   He was my breath and life and light,
For three short years, which soon were past.

---

272. *The babe at my bosom*] An oversight, perhaps from a gap in composition: lines 387–410, 526 etc., make it clear that Rosalind's daughter was her firstborn. Isabella Booth had two daughters (SC v 372).

281. *once*] At this same time, i.e. before her marriage.

On the fourth, my gentle mother
Led me to the shrine, to be
His sworn bride eternally.
290 And now we stood on the altar stair,
When my father came from a distant land,
And with a loud and fearful cry
Rushed between us suddenly.
I saw the stream of his thin grey hair,
295 I saw his lean and lifted hand,
And heard his words, — and live! Oh God!
Wherefore do I live? — 'Hold, hold!'
He cried, — 'I tell thee 'tis her brother!
Thy mother, boy, beneath the sod
300 Of yon churchyard rests in her shroud so cold:
I am now weak, and pale, and old:
We were once dear to one another,
I and that corpse! Thou art our child!'
Then with a laugh both long and wild
305 The youth upon the pavement fell:
They found him dead! All looked on me,
The spasms of my despair to see:
But I was calm. I went away:
I was clammy-cold like clay!
310 I did not weep: I did not speak:
But day by day, week after week,
I walked about like a corpse alive!
Alas! sweet friend, you must believe
This heart is stone: it did not break.

315 My father lived a little while,
But all might see that he was dying,
He smiled with such a woeful smile!
When he was in the churchyard lying
Among the worms, we grew quite poor,
320 So that no one would give us bread:
My mother looked at me, and said
Faint words of cheer, which only meant
That she could die and be content;
So I went forth from the same church door
325 To another husband's bed.
And this was he who died at last,

---

287. *On the fourth*] 'On the arrival of the fourth'.

320. *give us*] i.e. supply us with.

When weeks and months and years had passed,
Through which I firmly did fulfil
My duties, a devoted wife,
330   With the stern step of vanquished will,
Walking beneath the night of life,
Whose hours extinguished, like slow rain
Falling for ever, pain by pain,
The very hope of death's dear rest;
335   Which, since the heart within my breast
Of natural life was dispossessed,
Its strange sustainer there had been.

When flowers were dead, and grass was green
Upon my mother's grave, — that mother
340   Whom to outlive, and cheer, and make
My wan eyes glitter for her sake,
Was my vowed task, the single care
Which once gave life to my despair, —
When she was a thing that did not stir
345   And the crawling worms were cradling her
To a sleep more deep and so more sweet
Than a baby's rocked on its nurse's knee,
I lived: a living pulse then beat
Beneath my heart that awakened me.
350   What was this pulse so warm and free?
Alas! I knew it could not be
My own dull blood: 'twas like a thought
Of liquid love, that spread and wrought
Under my bosom and in my brain,
355   And crept with the blood through every vein;
And hour by hour, day after day,
The wonder could not charm away,
But laid in sleep, my wakeful pain,
Until I knew it was a child,
360   And then I wept. For long, long years
These frozen eyes had shed no tears:
But now — 'twas the season fair and mild
When April has wept itself to May:
I sate through the sweet sunny day
365   By my window bowered round with leaves,
And down my cheeks the quick tears ran

---

366. *ran*] Unrhymed, like *tell* in line 369. *Eds* emend to *fell*, possibly an MS revision unnoticed
by the transcriber.

Like twinkling rain-drops from the eaves,
When warm spring showers are passing o'er:
O Helen, none can ever tell
370   The joy it was to weep once more!

I wept to think how hard it were
To kill my babe, and take from it
The sense of light, and the warm air,
And my own fond and tender care,
375   And love and smiles; ere I knew yet
That these for it might, as for me,
Be the masks of a grinning mockery.
And haply, I would dream, 'twere sweet
To feed it from my faded breast,
380   Or mark my own heart's restless beat
Rock it to its untroubled rest,
And watch the growing soul beneath
Dawn in faint smiles; and hear its breath,
Half interrupted by calm sighs,
385   And search the depth of its fair eyes
For long departed memories!
And so I lived till that sweet load
Was lightened. Darkly forward flowed
The stream of years, and on it bore
390   Two shapes of gladness to my sight;
Two other babes, delightful more
In my lost soul's abandoned night,
Than their own country ships may be
Sailing towards wrecked mariners,
395   Who cling to the rock of a wintry sea.
For each, as it came, brought soothing tears,
And a loosening warmth, as each one lay
Sucking the sullen milk away,
About my frozen heart did play,
400   And weaned it, oh how painfully! —
As they themselves were weaned each one
From that sweet food, — even from the thirst
Of death, and nothingness, and rest,
Strange inmate of a living breast!

376-7. 'Whether in later life it, too, would have to pretend to be happy'.

393. *their own country ships*] 'Ships of their own country'.

398-9. *1819* has a comma after *heart* and not after *away*; making possible sense but depriving *did play* of context and meaning.

405　　　　Which all that I had undergone
　　　　Of grief and shame, since she, who first
　　　　The gates of that dark refuge closed,
　　　　Came to my sight, had almost burst
　　　　The seal of that Lethean spring;
410　　　　But these fair shadows interposed:
　　　　For all delights are shadows now!
　　　　And from my brain to my dull brow
　　　　The heavy tears gather and flow:
　　　　I cannot speak: Oh let me weep!

415　　　　The tears which fell from her wan eyes
　　　　Glimmered among the moonlight dew:
　　　　Her deep hard sobs and heavy sighs
　　　　Their echoes in the darkness threw.
　　　　When she grew calm, she thus did keep
　　　　The tenor of her tale:

420　　　　　　　　　　He died:
　　　　I know not how: he was not old,
　　　　If age be numbered by its years:
　　　　But he was bowed and bent with fears,
　　　　Pale with the quenchless thirst of gold,
425　　　　Which, like fierce fever, left him weak;
　　　　And his strait lip and bloated cheek
　　　　Were warped in spasms by hollow sneers;
　　　　And selfish cares with barren plough,
　　　　Not age, had lined his narrow brow,
430　　　　And foul and cruel thoughts, which feed
　　　　Upon the withering life within,
　　　　Like vipers on some poisonous weed.
　　　　Whether his ill were death or sin
　　　　None knew, until he died indeed,
435　　　　And then men owned they were the same.

　　　　Seven days within my chamber lay
　　　　That corse, and my babes made holiday:
　　　　At last, I told them what is death:

408. *had*] and *1819*. The simplest emendation of a confusing passage that has provoked much ingenuity. The meaning of 397–409 is then: 'a warmth weaned my heart from its longing for death, which all my sufferings – ever since seeing my newborn daughter first made death impossible – had almost opened the way to again'. The only irregularity is the redundant *that Lethean spring*, easily acceptable as poetic repetition. To unseal the Lethean spring is to gain access to oblivion, the *dark refuge* of line 407. *Hutchinson* 895 suggests that 'The obscurity . . . may have been, in part at least, designed; Rosalind grows incoherent before breaking off abruptly'.

The eldest, with a kind of shame,
440 Came to my knees with silent breath,
And sate awe-stricken at my feet;
And soon the others left their play,
And sate there too. It is unmeet
To shed on the brief flower of youth
445 The withering knowledge of the grave;
From me remorse then wrung that truth.
I could not bear the joy which gave
Too just a response to mine own.
In vain. I dared not feign a groan;
450 And in their artless looks I saw,
Between the mists of fear and awe,
That my own thought was theirs; and they
Expressed it not in words, but said,
Each in its heart, how every day
455 Will pass in happy work and play,
Now he is dead and gone away.

After the funeral all our kin
Assembled, and the will was read.
My friend, I tell thee, even the dead
460 Have strength, their putrid shrouds within,
To blast and torture. Those who live
Still fear the living, but a corse
Is merciless, and power doth give
To such pale tyrants half the spoil
465 He rends from those who groan and toil,
Because they blush not with remorse
Among their crawling worms. Behold,
I have no child! my tale grows old
With grief, and staggers: let it reach
470 The limits of my feeble speech,
And languidly at length recline
On the brink of its own grave and mine.

Thou knowest what a thing is Poverty
Among the fallen on evil days:
475 'Tis Crime, and Fear, and Infamy,

---

446. that truth] i.e. the meaning of death (lines 438, 445).

448. response] Normally at this time accented on the first syllable.

463–7. power doth give . . . crawling worms.] 'When the powerful are dead ('pale tyrants') they exploit the workers just as mercilessly by their control of property, because in death they feel no shame'.

And houseless Want in frozen ways
Wandering ungarmented, and Pain,
And, worse than all, that inward stain
Foul Self-contempt, which drowns in sneers
480   Youth's starlight smile, and makes its tears
First like hot gall, then dry for ever!
And well thou knowest a mother never
Could doom her children to this ill,
And well he knew the same. The will
485   Imported, that if e'er again
I sought my children to behold,
Or in my birthplace did remain
Beyond three days, whose hours were told,
They should inherit nought: and he,
490   To whom next came their patrimony,
A sallow lawyer, cruel and cold,
Aye watched me, as the will was read,
With eyes askance, which sought to see
The secrets of my agony;
495   And with close lips and anxious brow
Stood canvassing still to and fro
The chance of my resolve, and all
The dead man's caution just did call;
For in that killing lie 'twas said —
500   'She is adulterous, and doth hold
In secret that the Christian creed
Is false, and therefore is much need
That I should have a care to save
My children from eternal fire.'
505   Friend, he was sheltered by the grave,
And therefore dared to be a liar!
In truth, the Indian on the pyre
Of her dead husband, half consumed,
As well might there be false, as I
510   To those abhorred embraces doomed,
Far worse than fire's brief agony.
As to the Christian creed, if true
Or false, I never questioned it:

497–8. *all . . . just did call;*] i.e. maintained that the deceased was quite right to take precautions against his widow.

500–4. *doth hold . . . eternal fire.*] Lord Eldon's formal order of 27 March 1817 had debarred S. from his children by Harriet on the grounds that he had 'unlawfully cohabited with the said Mary Godwin', and in Q *Mab* had 'blasphemously derided the truth of the Christian Revelation' (*Medwin (1913)* 475). In Rosalind's case, of course, both allegations are untrue.

I took it as the vulgar do:
515   Nor my vexed soul had leisure yet
To doubt the things men say, or deem
That they are other than they seem.

All present who those crimes did hear,
In feigned or actual scorn and fear,
520   Men, women, children, slunk away,
Whispering with self-contented pride,
Which half suspects its own base lie.
I spoke to none, nor did abide,
But silently I went my way,
525   Nor noticed I where joyously
Sate my two younger babes at play,
In the court-yard through which I passed;
But went with footsteps firm and fast
Till I came to the brink of the ocean green,
530   And there, a woman with grey hairs,
Who had my mother's servant been,
Kneeling, with many tears and prayers,
Made me accept a purse of gold,
Half of the earnings she had kept
535   To refuge her when weak and old.

With woe, which never sleeps or slept,
I wander now. 'Tis a vain thought —
But on yon alp, whose snowy head
'Mid the azure air is islanded,
540   (We see it o'er the flood of cloud,
Which sunrise from its eastern caves
Drives, wrinkling into golden waves,
Hung with its precipices proud,
From that grey stone where first we met)
545   There — now who knows the dead feel nought? —
Should be my grave; for he who yet
Is my soul's soul, once said: "'Twere sweet
'Mid stars and lightnings to abide,
And winds and lulling snows, that beat
550   With their soft flakes the mountain wide,
Where weary meteor lamps repose,

---

545. Hutchinson. There, now who knows the dead feel nought? *1819.*

551. Where] *Woodberry 1893.* When *1819.* Rosalind's brother was specifying a *place*; and it is impossible to abide amid lightnings *when* storms cease.

And languid storms their pinions close:
And all things strong and bright and pure,
And ever during, aye endure:
555 Who knows, if one were buried there,
But these things might our spirits make,
Amid the all-surrounding air,
Their own eternity partake?'
Then 'twas a wild and playful saying
560 At which I laughed, or seemed to laugh:
They were his words: now heed my praying,
And let them be my epitaph.
Thy memory for a term may be
My monument. Wilt remember me?
565 I know thou wilt, and canst forgive
Whilst in this erring world to live
My soul disdained not, that I thought
Its lying forms were worthy aught
And much less thee.

Helen
                    O speak not so,
570 But come to me and pour thy woe
Into this heart, full though it be,
Aye overflowing with its own:
I thought that grief had severed me
From all beside who weep and groan;
575 Its likeness upon earth to be,
Its express image; but thou art
More wretched. Sweet! we will not part
Henceforth, if death be not division;
If so, the dead feel no contrition.
580 But wilt thou hear since last we parted
All that has left me broken hearted?

Rosalind
Yes, speak. The faintest stars are scarcely shorn
Of their thin beams by that delusive morn
Which sinks again in darkness, like the light
585 Of early love, soon lost in total night.

568. *lying forms*] False conventions (OED 13). Not 'unreal appearances', for Nature is lovely and enduring (547–54), but man's behaviour makes it an 'erring world' (566).

573–6. *I thought . . . express image;*] 'I thought Grief had singled me out to be its perfect representative'.

579. i.e. if death does separate us it will be by annihilation, and we shall feel no regret.

Helen
Alas! Italian winds are mild,
But my bosom is cold — wintry cold —
When the warm air weaves, among the fresh leaves,
Soft music, my poor brain is wild,
590   And I am weak like a nursling child,
Though my soul with grief is grey and old.

Rosalind
Weep not at thine own words, though they must make
Me weep. What is thy tale?

Helen
               I fear 'twill shake
Thy gentle heart with tears. Thou well
595   Rememberest when we met no more,
And, though I dwelt with Lionel,
That friendless caution pierced me sore
With grief; a wound my spirit bore
Indignantly, but when he died
600   With him lay dead both hope and pride.

Alas! all hope is buried now.
But then men dreamed the agèd earth
Was labouring in that mighty birth,
Which many a poet and a sage
605   Has aye foreseen — the happy age
When truth and love shall dwell below
Among the works and ways of men;
Which on this world not power but will
Even now is wanting to fulfil.

586–91. These lines – almost a stanza – occur in *Nbk 1* f. 29 in an isolated sequence perhaps
originally intended as part of the opening of the poem. Cancellations before these lines include
the following, evidently allotted to Helen:
              [It is past – I]
              [We neer may meet again I fear]
              [Thou art false in heart I fear
                 Cold & selfish & untrue]
After the lines, uncancelled: 'To believe thee will false woman'. The whole group except this
last line is also canc. by a vertical stroke.

590. *a nursling child,*] A child still at nurse.

597. *friendless*] Unfriendly.

602. *then*] i.e. at the beginning of the French Revolution.

610 Among mankind what thence befell
Of strife, how vain, is known too well;
When liberty's dear paean fell
'Mid murderous howls. To Lionel,
Though of great wealth and lineage high,
615 Yet through those dungeon walls there came
Thy thrilling light, O liberty!
And as the meteor's midnight flame
Startles the dreamer, sun-like truth
Flashed on his visionary youth,
620 And filled him, not with love, but faith,
And hope, and courage mute in death;
For love and life in him were twins,
Born at one birth: in every other
First life then love its course begins,
625 Though they be children of one mother;
And so through this dark world they fleet
Divided, till in death they meet:
But he loved all things ever. Then
He passed amid the strife of men,
630 And stood at the throne of armèd power
Pleading for a world of woe:
Secure as one on a rock-built tower
O'er the wrecks which the surge trails to and fro,
'Mid the passions wild of human kind
635 He stood, like a spirit calming them;
For, it was said, his words could bind
Like music the lulled crowd, and stem
That torrent of unquiet dream,
Which mortals truth and reason deem,
640 But is revenge and fear and pride.
Joyous he was; and hope and peace
On all who heard him did abide,
Raining like dew from his sweet talk,
As where the evening star may walk
645 Along the brink of the gloomy seas,
Liquid mists of splendour quiver.
His very gestures touched to tears
The unpersuaded tyrant, never
So moved before: his presence stung
650 The torturers with their victim's pain,

614. Locock compares 'Athanase' (no. 146) 29: 'Although a child of Fortune and of Power . . .'
632–5. Paul Turner notes (RES x (1959) 271) that these lines are indebted to Lucretius, *De Re. Nat.* ii 7–13.

And none knew how; and through their ears,
The subtle witchcraft of his tongue
Unlocked the hearts of those who keep
Gold, the world's bond of slavery.
655 Men wondered, and some sneered to see
One sow what he could never reap:
For he is rich, they said, and young,
And might drink from the depths of luxury.
If he seeks fame, fame never crowned
660 The champion of a trampled creed:
If he seeks power, power is enthroned
'Mid ancient rights and wrongs, to feed
Which hungry wolves with praise and spoil,
Those who would sit near power must toil;
665 And such, there sitting, all may see.
What seeks he? All that others seek
He casts away, like a vile weed
Which the sea casts unreturningly.
That poor and hungry men should break
670 The laws which wreak them toil and scorn,
We understand; but Lionel
We know is rich and nobly born.
So wondered they: yet all men loved
Young Lionel, though few approved;
675 All but the priests, whose hatred fell
Like the unseen blight of a smiling day,
The withering honey dew, which clings
Under the bright green buds of May,
Whilst they unfold their emerald wings:
680 For he made verses wild and queer
On the strange creeds priests hold so dear,
Because they bring them land and gold.
Of devils and saints and all such gear,
He made tales which whoso heard or read
685 Would laugh till he were almost dead.
So this grew a proverb: 'Don't get old
Till Lionel's "Banquet in Hell" you hear,
And then you will laugh yourself young again.'
So the priests hated him, and he
690 Repaid their hate with cheerful glee.

662–4. to feed . . . must toil;] 'Those who want the patronage of the powerful must work to
sustain their traditional privileges with flattery and revenue'.

687. No capitals for this title in *1819.* About October 1819 S. actually began writing a kind
of 'Banquet in Hell': 'Sucking hydras hashed in sulphur'.

Ah, smiles and joyance quickly died,
For public hope grew pale and dim
In an altered time and tide,
And in its wasting withered him,
695 As a summer flower that blows too soon
Droops in the smile of the waning moon,
When it scatters through an April night
The frozen dews of wrinkling blight.
None now hoped more. Grey Power was seated
700 Safely on her ancestral throne;
And Faith, the Python, undefeated,
Even to its blood-stained steps dragged on
Her foul and wounded train, and men
Were trampled and deceived again,
705 And words and shows again could bind
The wailing tribes of human kind
In scorn and famine. Fire and blood
Raged round the raging multitude,
To fields remote by tyrants sent
710 To be the scornèd instrument
With which they drag from mines of gore
The chains their slaves yet ever wore:
And in the streets men met each other,
And by old altars and in halls,
715 And smiled again at festivals.
But each man found in his heart's brother
Cold cheer; for all, though half deceived,
The outworn creeds again believed,
And the same round anew began,
720 Which the weary world yet ever ran.

Many then wept, not tears, but gall
Within their hearts, like drops which fall
Wasting the fountain-stone away.
And in that dark and evil day
725 Did all desires and thoughts, that claim
Men's care — ambition, friendship, fame,
Love, hope, though hope was now despair —

701. *Faith, the Python,*] Locock compares *L&C* V 1 8: 'Faith, an obscene worm'.

708–12. *the raging multitude . . . yet ever wore*] 'Armies – themselves despicable – are sent to distant battlefields to extort through bloodshed ('drag from mines of gore') the conquests that perpetuate tyranny'.

717. *though half deceived,*] i.e. though *only* half deceived.

Indue the colours of this change,
As from the all-surrounding air
730   The earth takes hues obscure and strange,
When storm and earthquake linger there.

And so, my friend, it then befell
To many, most to Lionel,
Whose hope was like the life of youth
735   Within him, and when dead, became
A spirit of unresting flame,
Which goaded him in his distress
Over the world's vast wilderness.
Three years he left his native land,
740   And on the fourth, when he returned,
None knew him: he was stricken deep
With some disease of mind, and turned
Into aught unlike Lionel.
On him, on whom, did he pause in sleep,
745   Serenest smiles were wont to keep,
And, did he wake, a wingèd band
Of bright persuasions, which had fed
On his sweet lips and liquid eyes,
Kept their swift pinions half outspread,
750   To do on men his least command;
On him, whom once 'twas paradise
Even to behold, now misery lay:
In his own heart 'twas merciless,
To all things else none may express
755   Its innocence and tenderness.
'Twas said that he had refuge sought
In love from his unquiet thought
In distant lands, and been deceived
By some strange show; for there were found,
760   Blotted with tears as those relieved
By their own words are wont to do,
These mournful verses on the ground,
By all who read them blotted too.

728. Indue] 'Assume or put on' (*Concordance* 353; OED 4).

739–79. This section has affinities with *J&M*, especially lines 751–5 with *J&M* 286–90 and 476–81; 764–79 with the whole tenor of the Maniac's soliloquy. Parts of the two poems are close in date of composition: Mary S. finished transcribing *R&H* on 16 August 1818 (before Clara S.'s death), *J&M* was begun at Este in September–October. Compare also the fragment 'Alas, this is not what I thought life was' (no. 174), and the 'Song for Tasso' (no. 186) 'I loved – alas, our life is love'.

'How am I changed! my hopes were once like fire:
765   I loved, and I believed that life was love.
How am I lost! on wings of swift desire
Among Heaven's winds my spirit once did move.
I slept, and silver dreams did aye inspire
My liquid sleep: I woke, and did approve
770   All nature to my heart, and thought to make
A paradise of earth for one sweet sake.

'I love, but I believe in love no more.
I feel desire, but hope not. O, from sleep
Most vainly must my weary brain implore
775   Its long lost flattery now: I wake to weep,
And sit through the long day gnawing the core
Of my bitter heart, and, like a miser, keep,
Since none in what I feel take pain or pleasure,
To my own soul its self-consuming treasure.'

780   He dwelt beside me near the sea:
And oft in evening did we meet,
When the waves, beneath the starlight, flee
O'er the yellow sands with silver feet,
And talked: our talk was sad and sweet,
785   Till slowly from his mien there passed
The desolation which it spoke;
And smiles, — as when the lightning's blast
Has parched some heaven-delighting oak,
The next spring shows leaves pale and rare,
790   But like flowers delicate and fair,
On its rent boughs, — again arrayed
His countenance in tender light:
His words grew subtle fire, which made
The air his hearers breathed delight:
795   His motions, like the winds, were free,
Which bend the bright grass gracefully,
Then fade away in circlets faint:
And wingèd hope, on which upborne
His soul seemed hovering in his eyes,
800   Like some bright spirit newly born
Floating amid the sunny skies,
Sprang forth from his rent heart anew.
Yet o'er his talk, and looks, and mien,

764–79. 'The poem appears to be a personal lyric of Shelley's' (*Woodberry 1893* 620), but no trace of it is known outside this text.

Tempering their loveliness too keen,
805 Past woe its shadow backward threw,
Till like an exhalation, spread
From flowers half drunk with evening dew,
They did become infectious: sweet
And subtle mists of sense and thought:
810 Which wrapped us soon, when we might meet,
Almost from our own looks and aught
The wide world holds. And so, his mind
Was healed, while mine grew sick with fear:
For ever now his health declined,
815 Like some frail bark which cannot bear
The impulse of an altered wind,
Though prosperous: and my heart grew full
'Mid its new joy of a new care:
For his cheek became, not pale, but fair,
820 As rose-o'ershadowed lilies are;
And soon his deep and sunny hair,
In this alone less beautiful,
Like grass in tombs grew wild and rare.
The blood in his translucent veins
825 Beat, not like animal life, but love
Seemed now its sullen springs to move,
When life had failed, and all its pains:
And sudden sleep would seize him oft
Like death, so calm, but that a tear,
830 His pointed eyelashes between,
Would gather in the light serene
Of smiles, whose lustre bright and soft
Beneath lay undulating there.
His breath was like inconstant flame,
835 As eagerly it went and came;
And I hung o'er him in his sleep,
Till, like an image in the lake
Which rains disturb, my tears would break
The shadow of that slumber deep:
840 Then he would bid me not to weep,
And say with flattery false, yet sweet,
That death and he could never meet,
If I would never part with him.

810. *when we might meet,*] 'whenever we chanced to meet' (cp. line 185 and note).
825. *animal life*] Vital sensation. See notes to *Q Mab* i 142 and *PU* I 484.
828. 'Sudden sleep' was a habit reported of S. himself at Oxford (*Hogg* i 76–8).

And so we loved, and did unite
845   All that in us was yet divided:
For when he said, that many a rite,
By men to bind but once provided,
Could not be shared by him and me,
Or they would kill him in their glee,
850   I shuddered, and then laughing said —
'We will have rites our faith to bind,
But our church shall be the starry night,
Our altar the grassy earth outspread,
And our priest the muttering wind.'

855   'Twas sunset as I spoke: one star
Had scarce burst forth, when from afar
The ministers of misrule sent,
Seized upon Lionel, and bore
His chained limbs to a dreary tower,
860   In the midst of a city vast and wide.
For he, they said, from his mind had bent
Against their gods keen blasphemy,
For which, though his soul must roasted be
In hell's red lakes immortally,
865   Yet even on earth must he abide
The vengeance of their slaves: a trial,
I think, men call it. What avail
Are prayers and tears, which chase denial
From the fierce savage, nursed in hate?
870   What the knit soul that pleading and pale
Makes wan the quivering cheek, which late
It painted with its own delight?
We were divided. As I could,
I stilled the tingling of my blood,
875   And followed him in their despite,
As a widow follows, pale and wild,
The murderers and corse of her only child;
And when we came to the prison door
And I prayed to share his dungeon floor
880   With prayers which rarely have been spurned,
And when men drove me forth and I

846–8. Presumably these lines mean that Lionel was already married.

866–7. *a trial, / I think, men call it.*] S. had denounced Daniel Eaton's condemnation to pillory and prison on 15 May 1812 for blasphemous libel as 'that mockery of a trial' and his sentence as 'vengeance' on the part of the legislature (*Letter to Lord Ellenborough*, 1812; *Prose Works* i 66, 70).

Stared with blank frenzy on the sky,
A farewell look of love he turned,
Half calming me; then gazed awhile,
885 As if through that black and massy pile,
And through the crowd around him there,
And through the dense and murky air,
And the thronged streets, he did espy
What poets know and prophesy;
890 And said, with voice that made them shiver
And clung like music in my brain,
And which the mute walls spoke again
Prolonging it with deepened strain:
'Fear not the tyrants shall rule for ever,
895 Or the priests of the bloody faith;
They stand on the brink of that mighty river,
Whose waves they have tainted with death:
It is fed from the depths of a thousand dells,
Around them it foams, and rages, and swells,
900 And their swords and their sceptres I floating see,
Like wrecks in the surge of eternity.'

I dwelt beside the prison gate,
And the strange crowd that out and in
Passed, some, no doubt, with mine own fate,
905 Might have fretted me with its ceaseless din,
But the fever of care was louder within.
Soon, but too late, in penitence
Or fear, his foes released him thence:
I saw his thin and languid form,
910 As leaning on the jailor's arm,
Whose hardened eyes grew moist the while,
To meet his mute and faded smile,
And hear his words of kind farewell,
He tottered forth from his damp cell.
915 Many had never wept before,
From whom fast tears then gushed and fell:
Many will relent no more,
Who sobbed like infants then: aye, all
Who thronged the prison's stony hall,

894. 'Fear not] 'Fear not, *1819*. Grammatical punctuation (as in German) at the time, now conveying an opposite sense.

894–901. A borrowing of Stanza 4 from 'The billows on the beach' (no. 139) with minor changes: *shall* for *will* (line 1); *bloody* for *evil* (2); *mighty* for *raging* (3); *depths* for *depth* (5); *in* for *on* (8).

920   The rulers or the slaves of law,
                   Felt with a new surprise and awe
                   That they were human, till strong shame
                   Made them again become the same.
                   The prison blood-hounds, huge and grim,
925   From human looks the infection caught,
                   And fondly crouched and fawned on him;
                   And men have heard the prisoners say,
                   Who in their rotting dungeons lay,
                   That from that hour, throughout one day,
930   The fierce despair and hate which kept
                   Their trampled bosoms almost slept:
                   When, like twin vultures, they hung feeding
                   On each heart's wound, wide torn and bleeding,
                   Because their jailors' rule, they thought,
935   Grew merciful, like a parent's sway.

                   I know not how, but we were free:
                   And Lionel sate alone with me,
                   As the carriage drove through the streets apace;
                   And we looked upon each other's face;
940   And the blood in our fingers intertwined
                   Ran like the thoughts of a single mind,
                   As the swift emotions went and came
                   Through the veins of each united frame.
                   So through the long long streets we passed
945   Of the million-peopled City vast;
                   Which is that desert, where each one
                   Seeks his mate yet is alone,
                   Beloved and sought and mourned of none;
                   Until the clear blue sky was seen,
950   And the grassy meadows bright and green,
                   And then I sunk in his embrace,
                   Enclosing there a mighty space
                   Of love: and so we travelled on
                   By woods, and fields of yellow flowers,
955   And towns, and villages, and towers,
                   Day after day of happy hours.
                   It was the azure time of June,
                   When the skies are deep in the stainless noon,
                   And the warm and fitful breezes shake

---

932. *When,*] *1819*; where, *Woodberry 1893*, *Hutchinson* (an emendation perhaps justified, but not essential). *they*] i.e. despair and hate.

960 The fresh green leaves of the hedge-row briar,
    And there were odours then to make
    The very breath we did respire
    A liquid element, whereon
    Our spirits, like delighted things
965 That walk the air on subtle wings,
    Floated and mingled far away,
    'Mid the warm winds of the sunny day.
    And when the evening star came forth
    Above the curve of the new bent moon,
970 And light and sound ebbed from the earth,
    Like the tide of the full and weary sea
    To the depths of its tranquillity,
    Our natures to its own repose
    Did the earth's breathless sleep attune:
975 Like flowers, which on each other close
    Their languid leaves when daylight's gone,
    We lay, till new emotions came,
    Which seemed to make each mortal frame
    One soul of interwoven flame,
980 A life in life, a second birth
    In worlds diviner far than earth,
    Which, like two strains of harmony
    That mingle in the silent sky
    Then slowly disunite, passed by
985 And left the tenderness of tears,
    A soft oblivion of all fears,
    A sweet sleep: so we travelled on
    Till we came to the home of Lionel,
    Among the mountains wild and lone,
990 Beside the hoary western sea,
    Which near the verge of the echoing shore
    The massy forest shadowed o'er.

    The ancient steward, with hair all hoar,
    As we alighted, wept to see
995 His master changed so fearfully;
    And the old man's sobs did waken me
    From my dream of unremaining gladness;

982–87. *Which, like two strains . . . A sweet sleep:*] Cp. S.'s comparison of a sculptured Bacchus in Florence (October 1819) to 'some fine strain of harmony which flows round the soul and enfolds it in the soft astonishment of a satisfaction, like the pleasure of love with one whom we most love, which having taken away desire, leaves pleasure, sweet pleasure' (*Prose* 348).
997. An echo of *L&C* I i 2: 'Like a brief dream of unremaining glory'.

The truth flashed o'er me like quick madness
When I looked, and saw that there was death
1000 On Lionel: yet day by day
He lived, till fear grew hope and faith,
And in my soul I dared to say,
Nothing so bright can pass away:
Death is dark, and foul, and dull,
1005 But he is — O how beautiful!
Yet day by day he grew more weak,
And his sweet voice, when he might speak,
Which ne'er was loud, became more low;
And the light which flashed through his waxen cheek
1010 Grew faint, as the rose-like hues which flow
From sunset o'er the Alpine snow:
And death seemed not like death in him,
For the spirit of life o'er every limb
Lingered, a mist of sense and thought.
1015 When the summer wind faint odours brought
From mountain flowers, even as it passed
His cheek would change, as the noonday sea
Which the dying breeze sweeps fitfully.
If but a cloud the sky o'ercast,
1020 You might see his colour come and go,
And the softest strain of music made
Sweet smiles, yet sad, arise and fade
Amid the dew of his tender eyes;
And the breath, with intermitting flow,
1025 Made his pale lips quiver and part.
You might hear the beatings of his heart,
Quick, but not strong; and with my tresses
When oft he playfully would bind
In the bowers of mossy lonelinesses
1030 His neck, and win me so to mingle
In the sweet depth of woven caresses,
And our faint limbs were intertwined,
Alas! the unquiet life did tingle
From mine own heart through every vein,
1035 Like a captive in dreams of liberty,
Who beats the walls of his stony cell.
But his, it seemed already free,
Like the shadow of fire surrounding me!
On my faint eyes and limbs did dwell
1040 That spirit as it passed, till soon,
As a frail cloud wandering o'er the moon,

Beneath its light invisible,
Is seen when it folds its grey wings again
To alight on midnight's dusky plain,
1045   I lived and saw, and the gathering soul
Passed from beneath that strong control,
And I fell on a life which was sick with fear
Of all the woe that now I bear.

Amid a bloomless myrtle wood,
1050   On a green and sea-girt promontory,
Not far from where we dwelt, there stood
In record of a sweet sad story,
An altar and a temple bright
Circled by steps, and o'er the gate
1055   Was sculptured, 'To Fidelity';
And in the shrine an image sate,
All veiled: but there was seen the light
Of smiles, which faintly could express
A mingled pain and tenderness
1060   Through that etherial drapery.
The left hand held the head, the right —
Beyond the veil, beneath the skin,
You might see the nerves quivering within —
Was forcing the point of a barbèd dart
1065   Into its side-convulsing heart.
An unskilled hand, yet one informed
With genius, had the marble warmed
With that pathetic life. This tale
It told: A dog had from the sea,
1070   When the tide was raging fearfully,
Dragged Lionel's mother, weak and pale,
Then died beside her on the sand,
And she that temple thence had planned;
But it was Lionel's own hand
1075   Had wrought the image. Each new moon
That lady did, in this lone fane,
The rites of a religion sweet,
Whose god was in her heart and brain:

1045. gathering] 'passing to new existence' (*Concordance*); 'condensing' (Locock). The simile of the thin cloud regaining substance and visibility after crossing the moon explains the force of the adj.

1069. A dog] Possibly this story was suggested by the legend of Beddgelert in Caernarvon, not far from Tremadoc. There is also a heroic dog Charon in Godwin's *St. Leon* (1799) that rescues a boy from drowning (iii chs 1, 3; *Godwin Novels* iv).

The seasons' loveliest flowers were strewn
1080 On the marble floor beneath her feet,
And she brought crowns of sea-buds white,
Whose odour is so sweet and faint,
And weeds, like branching chrysolite,
Woven in devices fine and quaint,
1085 And tears from her brown eyes did stain
The altar: need but look upon
That dying statue, fair and wan,
If tears should cease, to weep again:
And rare Arabian odours came,
1090 Through the myrtle copses steaming thence
From the hissing frankincense,
Whose smoke, wool-white as ocean foam,
Hung in dense flocks beneath the dome,
That ivory dome, whose azure night
1095 With golden stars, like heaven, was bright
O'er the split cedar's pointed flame;
And the lady's harp would kindle there
The melody of an old air,
Softer than sleep; the villagers
1100 Mixed their religion up with hers,
And as they listened round, shed tears.

One eve he led me to this fane:
Daylight on its last purple cloud
Was lingering grey, and soon her strain
1105 The nightingale began; now loud,
Climbing in circles the windless sky,
Now dying music; suddenly
'Tis scattered in a thousand notes,
And now to the hushed ear it floats
1110 Like field smells known in infancy,
Then failing, soothes the air again.
We sate within that temple lone,
Pavilioned round with Parian stone:
His mother's harp stood near, and oft

1081. *sea-buds white,*] Perhaps *Polygonum raii*, Ray's Knotgrass.

1083. *chrysolite*] A green gemstone formed from silicate of magnesia.

1090. *Through*] Though *1819* (a misprint).

1096. *cedar's*] cedars *1819*. i.e. cedar-wood for burning on the altar.

1105. *The nightingale began;*] Even before her voyage south in lines 1197–206 Helen's experiences seem to have a Mediterranean setting. Nightingales do not visit the west coast of Britain.

1115   I had awakened music soft
             Amid its wires: the nightingale
             Was pausing in her heaven-taught tale:
             'Now drain the cup,' said Lionel,
             'Which the poet-bird has crowned so well
1120   With the wine of her bright and liquid song!
             Heardst thou not sweet words among
             That heaven-resounding minstrelsy?
             Heardst thou not, that those who die
             Awake in a world of ecstasy?
1125   That love, when limbs are interwoven,
             And sleep, when the night of life is cloven,
             And thought, to the world's dim boundaries clinging,
             And music, when one beloved is singing,
             Is death? Let us drain right joyously
1130   The cup which the sweet bird fills for me.'
             He paused, and to my lips he bent
             His own: like spirit his words went
             Through all my limbs with the speed of fire;
             And his keen eyes, glittering through mine,
1135   Filled me with the flame divine,
             Which in their orbs was burning far,
             Like the light of an unmeasured star,
             In the sky of midnight dark and deep:
             Yes, 'twas his soul that did inspire
1140   Sounds, which my skill could ne'er awaken;
             And first, I felt my fingers sweep
             The harp, and a long quivering cry
             Burst from my lips in symphony:
             The dusk and solid air was shaken,
1145   As swift and swifter the notes came
             From my touch, that wandered like quick flame,
             And from my bosom, labouring
             With some unutterable thing:
             The awful sound of my own voice made
1150   My faint lips tremble; in some mood
             Of wordless thought Lionel stood
             So pale, that even beside his cheek

1132. like spirit] i.e. like 'animal spirit', nervous vitality.

1144–70. Locock noted the affinity of this singing with Constantia's in 'Thy voice, slow rising' (no. 155).

1149. awful] i.e. awe-inspiring.

The snowy column from its shade
Caught whiteness: yet his countenance
1155 Raised upward, burned with radiance
Of spirit-piercing joy, whose light,
Like the moon struggling through the night
Of whirlwind-rifted clouds, did break
With beams that might not be confined.
1160 I paused, but soon his gestures kindled
New power, as by the moving wind
The waves are lifted, and my song
To low soft notes now changed and dwindled,
And from the twinkling wires among,
1165 My languid fingers drew and flung
Circles of life-dissolving sound,
Yet faint; in aery rings they bound
My Lionel, who, as every strain
Grew fainter but more sweet, his mien
1170 Sunk with the sound relaxedly;
And slowly now he turned to me,
As slowly faded from his face
That awful joy: with looks serene
He was soon drawn to my embrace,
1175 And my wild song then died away
In murmurs: words I dare not say
We mixed, and on his lips mine fed
Till they methought felt still and cold:
'What is it with thee, love?' I said:
1180 No word, no look, no motion! yes,
There was a change, but spare to guess,
Nor let that moment's hope be told.
I looked, and knew that he was dead,
And fell, as the eagle on the plain
1185 Falls when life deserts her brain,
And the mortal lightning is veiled again.

1165–70. Hogg describes how S. would throw a stone into a pond and 'quietly watch the decreasing agitation, until the last faint ring and almost imperceptible ripple had disappeared on the still surface. "Such are the effects of an impulse on the air," he would say' (*Hogg* i 82).

1166. life-dissolving] life dissolving *1819*.

1170. Sunk] Here transitive (*OED* iii 1b), with *mien* its object (e.g. *Cymbeline* V v 413). 'Lionel who, as the music faded, relaxed his bearing in sympathy with the sound'.

1176. words] words, *1819*.

1186. the mortal lightning] The 'spark of life'.

O that I were now dead! but such
— Did they not, love, demand too much,
Those dying murmurs? — he forbade.
1190   O that I once again were mad!
And yet, dear Rosalind, not so,
For I would live to share thy woe.
Sweet boy, did I forget thee too?
Alas, we know not what we do
When we speak words.

1195   No memory more
Is in my mind of that sea shore.
Madness came on me, and a troop
Of misty shapes did seem to sit
Beside me, on a vessel's poop,
1200   And the clear north wind was driving it.
Then I heard strange tongues, and saw strange flowers,
And the stars methought grew unlike ours,
And the azure sky and the stormless sea
Made me believe that I had died,
1205   And waked in a world, which was to me
Drear hell, though heaven to all beside:
Then a dead sleep fell on my mind,
Whilst animal life many long years
Had rescue from a chasm of tears;
1210   And when I woke, I wept to find
That the same lady, bright and wise,
With the silver locks and quick brown eyes,
The mother of my Lionel,
Had tended me in my distress,
1215   And died some months before. Nor less
Wonder, but far more peace and joy
Brought in that hour my lovely boy;

1187–9. *but such . . . he forbade.*]   but such
                Did they not, love, demand too much,
                Those dying murmurs? He forbade. 1819.

1209. *had rescue*] *Forman 1882, Dowden 1891, Hutchinson*; had rescued *1819*. The *1819* text
is barely possible, even admitting an awkward inversion: 'I passed into a mental sleep, dur-
ing which a long stretch of time kept my nervous faculties from suffering'; but either *Whilst*
ought to be *Till*, or *Had* is unwanted. Whereas *Had rescued* for *Had rescue* is an easily under-
stood compositor's error; and the latter makes good sense: 'I slept mentally, while for many
years my sentient being was spared from suffering'. For *animal life* (1208) see note to 825.

1217. *my lovely boy;*] Subj. of *brought*.

For through that trance my soul had well
The impress of thy being kept;
1220 And if I waked, or if I slept,
No doubt, though memory faithless be,
Thy image ever dwelt on me;
And thus, O Lionel, like thee
Is our sweet child. 'Tis sure most strange
1225 I knew not of so great a change,
As that which gave him birth, who now
Is all the solace of my woe.

That Lionel great wealth had left
By will to me, and that of all
1230 The ready lies of law bereft,
My child and me might well befall.
But let me think not of the scorn,
Which from the meanest I have borne,
When, for my child's belovèd sake,
1235 I mixed with slaves, to vindicate
The very laws themselves do make:
Let me not say scorn is my fate,
Lest I be proud, suffering the same
With those who live in deathless fame.

1240 She ceased. — 'Lo, where red morning through the woods
Is burning o'er the dew;' said Rosalind.
And with these words they rose, and towards the flood

1218–24. For through that trance . . . our sweet child.] It was generally believed that strong visual or mental impressions during pregnancy could modify an unborn child, hence the resemblance of a child to its father (see Erasmus Darwin, *Zoonomia* ch. 39.6.3, and *PU* II iv 83–84 and note). Cp. *L&C* VII xviii 2–5 and note. It is Lionel who is addressed in 1219, 1222.

1228–31. An editorial transfer of the comma from after *bereft* to after *me* is needless and weakens the bitter contrast between Lionel's bounty and the law's injustice: 'That Lionel had left me great wealth, and that the law had taken it all away, might well happen to my child and myself'. S.'s own will had recently been executed (18 February 1817), leaving – with other bequests – £6000 for his son William and all his wealth and estates in expectancy to Mary S.

1238–9. 'Lest I start ranking myself with the great martyrs'.

1240. woods] Perhaps a misprint for *wood*, as both this word and *flood* are unrhymed. But so too is *below*, six lines later.

1242–52. This passage parallels S.'s description to Peacock on 20 April 1818 of the woods surrounding the Villa Pliniana on Lake Como: '. . . the immediate border of this shore is composed of laurel trees & bay & myrtle & wild fig trees & olives which grow in the crevices of the rocks & overhang the caverns & shadow the deep glens . . . Here are plantations of olives & orange & lemon trees which are now so loaded with fruit that there is more fruit than leaves . . . immediately over you are clusters of cypress trees of an astonishing height which seem to pierce the sky. On the other side is seen the blue extent of the lake . . . The terraces which overlook the lake & conduct under the shade of . . . immense laurel trees . . . are most delightful.' (*L* ii 6–7).

Of the blue lake, beneath the leaves now wind
With equal steps and fingers intertwined:
1245 Thence to a lonely dwelling, where the shore
Is shadowed with steep rocks, and cypresses
Cleave with their dark green cones the silent skies,
And with their shadows the clear depths below,
And where a little terrace from its bowers,
1250 Of blooming myrtle and faint lemon-flowers,
Scatters its sense-dissolving fragrance o'er
The liquid marble of the windless lake;
And where the agèd forest's limbs look hoar,
Under the leaves which their green garments make,
1255 They come: 'tis Helen's home, and clean and white,
Like one which tyrants spare on our own land
In some such solitude, its casements bright
Shone through their vine-leaves in the morning sun,
And even within 'twas scarce like Italy.
1260 And when she saw how all things there were planned,
As in an English home, dim memory
Disturbed poor Rosalind: she stood as one
Whose mind is where his body cannot be,
Till Helen led her where her child yet slept,
1265 And said, 'Observe, that brow was Lionel's,
Those lips were his, and so he ever kept
One arm in sleep, pillowing his head with it.
You cannot see his eyes, they are two wells
Of liquid love: let us not wake him yet.'
1270 But Rosalind could bear no more, and wept
A shower of burning tears, which fell upon
His face, and so his opening lashes shone
With tears unlike his own, as he did leap
In sudden wonder from his innocent sleep.

1275 So Rosalind and Helen lived together
Thenceforth, changed in all else, yet friends again,
Such as they were, when o'er the mountain heather
They wandered in their youth, through sun and rain.
And after many years, for human things
1280 Change even like the ocean and the wind,
Her daughter was restored to Rosalind,
And in their circle thence some visitings

1277–8. Mary S. later described 'the bleak sides of the woodless mountains' (the Sidlaw Hills) behind the house she shared with Isabella Baxter on the Tay as, for her, 'the eyry of freedom' (Introduction to *Frankenstein* (3rd edn 1831) *MSW* i 176).

Of joy 'mid their new calm would intervene;
A lovely child she was, of looks serene,
1285 And motions which o'er things indifferent shed
The grace and gentleness from whence they came.
And Helen's boy grew with her, and they fed
From the same flowers of thought, until each mind
Like springs which mingle in one flood became,
1290 And in their union soon their parents saw
The shadow of the peace denied to them.
And Rosalind, for when the living stem
Is cankered in its heart, the tree must fall,
Died ere her time; and with deep grief and awe
1295 The pale survivors followed her remains
Beyond the region of dissolving rains,
Up the cold mountain she was wont to call
Her tomb; and on Chiavenna's precipice
They raised a pyramid of lasting ice,
1300 Whose polished sides, ere day had yet begun,
Caught the first glow of the unrisen sun,
The last, when it had sunk; and through the night
The charioteers of Arctos wheelèd round
Its glittering point, as seen from Helen's home,
1305 Whose sad inhabitants each year would come,
With willing steps climbing that rugged height,
And hang long locks of hair, and garlands bound
With amaranth flowers, which, in the clime's despite,
Filled the frore air with unaccustomed light:
1310 Such flowers, as in the wintry memory bloom
Of one friend left, adorned that frozen tomb.

Helen, whose spirit was of softer mould,
Whose sufferings too were less, death slowlier led
Into the peace of his dominion cold:
1315 She died among her kindred, being old.
And know, that if love die not in the dead
As in the living, none of mortal kind
Are blessed, as now Helen and Rosalind.

1291. *shadow*] Replica.

1298. *Chiavenna's precipice*] The town of Chiavenna is at the north end of Lake Como, with Alpine summits behind.

1303. *The charioteers of Arctos*] The stars of Ursa Major, the Great Bear.

1308. *amaranth flowers,*] A family of subtropical annuals, here associated with the 'unfading' Amaranth of legend.

1317–18. The poem concludes in an equivocal tone by recalling the final cadence of *Romeo and Juliet*: 'For never was a story of more woe / Than this of Juliet and her Romeo'.

Shelley's neat copy of 'Ozymandias', from a manuscript in the Bodleian Library
(see Note on Illustrations, p. viii).
Reproduced by kind permission of the Bodleian Library, Oxford.

Ozymandias

Composed probably between 26 and 28 December 1817. The sonnet was first published in *The Examiner* on 11 January 1818 over the name GLIRASTES, and was followed on 1 February by a sonnet of Horace Smith's with the same title, introduced in these words: 'The subject which suggested the beautiful Sonnet, in a late number, signed "Glirastes", produced also the enclosed from another pen, which, if you deem it worthy insertion, is at your service'. The text of Smith's sonnet – which was subsequently reprinted in his *Amarynthus the Nympholept* (1821) under the title 'On a Stupendous Leg of Granite, Discovered Standing by itself in the deserts of Egypt, with the inscription inserted below' – reads as follows (*Examiner* No. 527, p. 73):

OZYMANDIAS

In Egypt's sandy silence, all alone,
        Stands a gigantic Leg, which far off throws
        The only shadow that the Desart knows: –
"I am great OZYMANDIAS," saith the stone,
        "The King of Kings; this mighty City shows
        "The wonders of my hand." – The City's gone, –
Nought but the Leg remaining to disclose
The site of this forgotten Babylon.

We wonder, – and some Hunter may express
Wonder like ours, when thro' the wilderness
        Where London stood, holding the Wolf in chace,
He meets some fragments huge, and stops to guess
        What powerful but unrecorded race
        Once dwelt in that annihilated place.

Smith stayed for two nights after Christmas 1817 at Marlow, and the two sonnets were probably written then in friendly competition. Leigh Hunt's later mistake in sending S.'s 'Ozymandias' to Monckton Milnes as the Nile sonnet written in competition with himself and Keats (see no. 163 and headnote) may have arisen partly from his remembrance that this sonnet had also been the product of a friendly contest. The title 'The Revolt of Islam' is written in ink at right angles to the draft of the poem in *Nbk 5* f. 85ᵛ; this revised name was presumably adopted as a result of the conference with S.'s publisher on 15 December (see headnote to *L&C*), which helps to confirm the date. S.'s pseudonym is a jokey compound of Lat. *Glis* (dormouse) and Gk ἐραστής (lover) to make GLIRASTES, 'dormouse-lover'. 'The Dormouse' was one of S.'s pet names for Mary S. (see no. 104).

Much scholarly effort has been devoted to the question of S.'s sources for his famous poem. 'Ozymandias' is the Greek name for the notorious Egyptian Pharaoh Rameses II. His statue stood across the Nile from Luxor near the funereal temple at Thebes now known as the Ramesseum. It is computed to have been 60 feet high and to have weighed 1,000 tons. It now lies mutilated, and no inscription is visible. According to the Napoleonic Army's 20-volume *Description de l'Egypte* (1809–26), by the early nineteenth century the legs of the statue were completely destroyed. All versions of the lost inscription, whether in late Classical sources or from the accounts of travellers, appear to derive from Diodorus Siculus, whose description in his *Library of History* (i 47) itself paraphrases the historian Hecataeus's *Aigyptiaka*:

> Ten stades from the first tombs, he says, in which, according to tradition, are buried the concubines of Zeus, stands a monument of the king known as Osymandias . . . beside the entrance are three statues, each of a single block of black stone from Syene, of which one, that is seated, is the largest of any in Egypt, the foot measuring over seven cubits, while the other two at the knees of this, the one on the right and the other on the left, daughter and mother respectively, are smaller than the first one mentioned. And it is not merely for its size that this work merits approbation, but it is also marvellous by reason of its artistic quality and excellent because of the nature of the stone, since in a block of so great a size there is not a single crack or blemish to be seen. The inscription upon it runs: 'King of Kings am I, Osymandias. If anyone would know how great I am and where I lie, let him surpass one of my works'. There is also another statue of his mother standing alone, a monolith twenty cubits high . . . (Loeb trans.)

But Diodorus's account has frequently been attributed by travellers to a different Egyptian statue, the Colossus of Memnon at Thebes, renowned in Strabo's account of the sound it was reputed to emit at dawn. This has led to bewildering confusion among the many accounts of travels in the East which may possibly have been in S.'s mind when composing the sonnet. S. is known to have had a taste for travel books since at least as early as his brief undergraduate career (see *Hogg* i 108), and may well have known one or more of the various works which have been proposed as sources. Most plausible among these are Dr Richard Pococke, *A Description of the East and Some Other Countries* (1742; also in vol. x of J. Pinkerton, *General Collection of Voyages* (1808–1814)), which includes striking illustrations and a number of descriptive passages which accord with details in the poem; Dominique Vivant Denon, *Voyage dans la Basse et la Haute Egypte pendant les campagnes du general Bonaparte* (2 vols, Paris 1802; trans. by Arthur Aikin as *Travels in Upper and Lower Egypt* . . . , 3 vols [2 vols in the American edition], 1803); E. Claude Savary, *Letters on Egypt* (English trans., 2 vols, 1787); Count Volney, *Travels through Syria and Egypt* . . . (English trans., 2 vols, 1793); and a number of other works, including Raleigh's *History of the World*, James Bruce's *Travels to Discover the Source of the Nile* (5 vols, 1790), and Robert Walpole's *Memoirs* (1817). In short, the account in Diodorus Siculus had filtered by many routes into the general literary culture in which S. was steeped, and he was undoubtedly familiar with the figure of Ozymandias and his remnants.

What is needed is a stimulus rather than an obvious single source for the poem. S. could not have received his account from a real traveller: there was no such single isolated ruin in the Egyptian desert; the broken figure of Osymandias (Rameses II) is at the entrance to a temple, is seated, and is flanked by two other seated figures (indeed all the surviving large statues are seated, with or without torsos); none of the statues is of marble, brown or grey, which are drafted as alternative possibilities for description of the statue in S.'s working notes in *Nbk 5*; no inscription existed in S.'s day, nor could it have been deciphered if it had existed (Champollion used the Rosetta Stone as the key to Egyptian hieroglyphic script in 1822); sculptors of the nineteenth dynasty did not express character in the faces of their subjects. S.'s draft notes also strongly suggest that the 'Traveller' was not in the original conception of the sonnet; the draft first line reads 'There stands by Nile a single pedestal' (*Nbk* 5 f. 85ᵛ). S.'s sonnet is a composite work, drawing its details from various sources which have been thoroughly investigated, and based on Diodorus Siculus' widely-quoted account of the statue and its inscription.

One immediate stimulus may have been an article in the *Quarterly Review* xvi (October 1816) 1–27 (see especially pp. 10–11), reviewing Thomas Legh, *Narrative of a Journey in Egypt and the Country beyond the Cataracts* (1816). This article mentions all of the important recurring details in descriptions of the statue of Osymandias, including the inscription, together with reflections on the best-known traveller's accounts (including those of Pococke and Denon). The *Quarterly* article seems definitely to be the main source for Horace Smith's sonnet quoted above, and the two poems seem very likely to have shared the same occasion, as they both oddly spell 'Ozymandias' with a 'z' rather than an 's'; no other known source does this. Other possible immediate influences in late December 1817 may have included passages from Godwin's *Mandeville*, which was published on 1 December 1817 (see notes). Suggestions by various commentators that S. may also have been influenced by the arrival at the British Museum of the sculpted head of a 'younger Memnon' are however not persuasive. A colossal excavated head of Rameses II (known to contemporary antiquaries as the Younger Memnon) was sent by Joseph Banks through the agency of Henry Salt, British Consul-General in Egypt, via Alexandria in 1816; but by May 1819 Salt was still negotiating for its sale to the Museum, and it was not exhibited before 1820, though some interest may have been excited by its expected arrival in 1817 and 1818 (see Edward Miller, *That Noble Cabinet: A History of the British Museum* (Athens, Ohio, 1974) 198–200). An account in the *Quarterly Review* xviii (1818) 368 cannot be a source for S.'s poem, as it contains a review of Hunt's *Foliage*, which was published in March 1818.

Commentary on the poem has concentrated almost exclusively on the problem of sources. Interesting discussions include: D. W. Thompson, 'Ozymandias', *PQ* xvi (1937) 59–64; H. J. Pettit, 'Shelley and Denon's "Voyage Dans La Haute et La Basse Egypte"', *Revue de Littérature Comparée*, xviii (1938) 326–34; J. Gwyn Griffiths, 'Shelley's "Ozymandias" and Diodorus Siculus', *MLR* xliii (1948) 80–4; H. M. Richmond, 'Ozymandias and the Travellers', *KSJ* xi (1962) 65–71; see also briefer discussions by Johnston Parr, 'Shelley's "Ozymandias" Again', *MLR* xlvi (1951) 441–2, and 'Shelley's *Ozymandias*', *KSJ* vi (1957) 31–5, and J. Notopoulos, 'Shelley's "Ozymandias" Once Again', *MLR* xlviii (1953) 442–3. Critical discussions of the sonnet, one of the best-known and most widely anthologised of all short poems in English, are extraordinarily few; a helpful reading, clarifying S.'s grammar and discussing the rhyme scheme, is in E. M. W. Tillyard, *Essays Literary and Educational* (1962), and see also K. Everest, ' "Ozymandias": The Text in Time', in K. Everest (ed.), *Percy Bysshe Shelley: Bicentenary Essays* (Cambridge, 1992) 24–42. The rhymes are subtle; six are used, in a pattern approximating to a Petrarchan octave/sestet arrangement but with a late 'turn' after line 11 and a difficult pattern further complicated by half-rhymes. The octave and sestet are connected by the rhyme of line 7 with line 10. The formal handling is in keeping with other Romantic experiments in sonnet form in the Regency period, notably in Keats's work, where the culminating instances are the stanza forms of the Odes. The poem's implicit judgement on its subject is a version of a classical *topos*; cp. e.g. Simonides in *Lyra Graeca* (Book vi, No. 31):

Who that hath understanding would praise Cleobulus the man of Lindus for his pitting of the might of a gravestone against the ever-running rivers and the flowers of the Spring, against the flame of sun and of golden moon, and against the eddies of the ocean-wave? All these are subject to the Gods; but a stone, even mortal hands may break it. This is the rede of a fool. (Loeb trans.)

See also Diogenes Laertius, *Lives* i 89–90.

The choice of text represents a minor problem. There is a carefully-written holograph fair copy in *Nbk 5* f. 85ʳ (S.'s cancelled first draft notes are on the reverse side, f. 85ᵛ; see *BSM* iii for a transcription), but S. evidently made substantive changes in lines 5, 9, and 12 before the sonnet was sent to the *Examiner*. The *Examiner* text, however, is carelessly printed, and Hunt introduced editorial emphases, as he also did with Horace Smith's sonnet. The *1819* text is tidier, but presumably derives from the *Examiner* and was punctuated by Peacock in S.'s absence abroad. A compromise seems unavoidable: the text here reproduces S.'s careful fair copy, but incorporates the three revisions that he must have authorised.

Text from *Nbk 5* f. 85ʳ, with three verbal revisions from *Examiner* No. 524, 11 January 1818, p. 24.

Published in the *Examiner* No. 524, 11 January 1818 (reprinted unchanged in same No., 12 January, same page); *1819*.

145
Ozymandias

> I met a traveller from an antique land,
> Who said — 'Two vast and trunkless legs of stone
> Stand in the desert . . . near them, on the sand,
> Half sunk a shattered visage lies, whose frown,
> 5   And wrinkled lip, and sneer of cold command,

1. *traveller*] Traveller *Examiner*. *land,*] land *1819*. The occasion of the poem cannot have been an actual meeting with a real traveller; see headnote.

2. *said – 'Two*] said – "two *Nbk 5*; said, "Two *Examiner*; said: Two *1819*.

3. *desert . . . near*] desert. Near *Examiner, 1819*.

4–5. Cp. Godwin, *Mandeville* (1817) (Mandeville on Clifford, 'puffer of his own worth'): 'His skin is smooth, and the contour of his body is sleek . . . the emblem of that overweening and venomous self-conceit by which he is inflated. I see the insolence of his gait, assumed to trample on all merit, but his own . . . I see the insidious curl of that lip . . . the hostile gesture, that effectually betrays the secret soul' (*Godwin Novels* vi 173). For similar images elsewhere in S.'s poetry, cp. *Q Mab* ix 26–30; the description of Othman's face in *L&C* V xxiii; and especially *PU* III iv 138, 168–76. *sunk*] sunk, *Examiner, 1819*. *lip*] *Examiner, 1819*; lips *Nbk 5*.

Tell that its sculptor well those passions read
Which yet survive, stamped on these lifeless things,
The hand that mocked them, and the heart that fed;
And on the pedestal these words appear:
10   My name is Ozymandias, King of Kings,
Look on my Works ye Mighty, and despair!
Nothing beside remains. Round the decay
Of that colossal Wreck, boundless and bare
The lone and level sands stretch far away'. —

146
Athanase

Drafted according to Mary S. (*1824* 110, 256) at Marlow in December 1817. The
content of Additional Passages (b) and (c), however, suggests that these stanzas
at least were written in Italy in spring 1818, and Locock argued that the use of
paler-coloured ink indicated corrections or additions in other parts (*Locock Ex* 51–6).
Like all S.'s poems in strict *terza rima* this one was never completed, and on
23 December 1819 S. sent a transcript of lines 1–124 to Ollier, under the present
title and headed by a note explaining its non-completion (see note to line 124).
The mutilated letter is quoted from *SC* vi 1097 with a conjectural reconstruction
approximating the lost text: 'I send you a little poem [for you to print at the end
of 'Julian'] & Maddalo' – which, indeed, was written some time af[ter it, but this

6–8. GM: 'those passions which, preserved on this broken image, still outlive the sculptor's
hand that copied (and derided) them, and the king's living heart that nourished them'; 'them'
in line 8 is a pronoun for 'passions' (from line 6), and the same pronoun is understood after
'fed'. *read*] read, *Examiner*. *them,*] them *1819*. *fed;*] fed: *Examiner, 1819*.

9. *pedestal these words appear:*] pedestal, this legend clear: *Nbk 5*.

10–11. Diodorus Siculus, *Library of History* i 47, records the inscription on the monument of
Osymandias (the Greek name for Rameses II, 1304–1237 BC, 3rd king of the 19th dynasty of
Egypt,) as follows: Βασιλεὺς βασιλέων Ὀσυμανδύας εἰμί. εἰ δέ τις εἰδέναι βούλεται πηλίκος εἰμὶ
καὶ ποῦ κεῖμαι, νικάτω τι τῶν ἐμῶν ἔργων ('King of Kings am I, Osymandias. If anyone would
know how great I am and where I lie, let him surpass one of my works'. Loeb trans.). "My
name is OZYMANDIAS, King of Kings." *Examiner*; 'My name is Ozymandias, king of kings:
1819. *Works*] works *Examiner*; works, *1819*. *despair!*] despair!' *1819*.

12–14. Cp. Peacock, *Palmyra* (2nd edition, 1812):

        Where shattered forms of ancient monarchs lie,
        Mid grass-grown halls, and falling colonnades
        Beneath the drifting sand, the clustering weed,
        Rest the proud relics of departed power.

12. *beside remains.*] remains beside. *Nbk 5*.

13. *colossal Wreck,*] Colossal Wreck, *Examiner*; colossal wreck, *1819*. *bare*] bare, *Examiner*.

14. *away' –*] away. *Examiner, 1819*.

fits the place because it is som]ewhat the same in character as that poem. –' (See also *L* ii 196, letter to Ollier, 14 May 1820.) After Mary S. had used this holograph as copy-text for *1824*, it was given to 'Arthur Brooke' (John Chalk Claris) on 7 June 1824, and was subsequently auctioned by Sotheby, Wilkinson and Hodge on 24 July 1918, whereupon it disappeared. On the publication of *SC* vii and viii in 1986 it emerged that the MS had been purchased anonymously by the Pforzheimer Library in 1973 at the auction of the collection of David Gage Joyce of Chicago (Hanzel Galleries, 23–24 September 1973). *SC* vii prints a transcription of the MS with full commentary and accompanying contextual material as SC 582 (*SC* vii 110–60). D. H. Reiman argues in *SC* that *Athanase*, like *J&M* and roughly contemporarily with it, was composed in the second half of 1819 (see *SC* vii 147–51). These arguments are not convincing; they are largely based on the negative circumstance that the specific dating of items in *Nbk 5* is often debatable, and that the drafts for *Athanase* fall at a point between items certainly datable to the period before S.'s departure for Italy in February 1818 (such as the *Essay on Christianity*, 'To Constantia', and 'Ozymandias') and items definitely written in Italy in the spring and summer of 1818 (such as *Mazenghi* and the translation of *Cyclops*). Dr Reiman's assertion that *Athanase* is, if datable to 1817, the sole example of *terza rima* in S. before his Italian period, is not conclusive; it seems, for example, very probable that the two *terza rima* tercets 'My spirit like a charmèd bark' were drafted before 'To Constantia', and therefore before Italy (see no. 153 and headnote). In stylistic terms *Athanase* does not strongly suggest the work of the second half of 1819: the figure of Zonoras is obviously akin to the conception of *L&C*, as indeed is the use of a broadly narrative manner (a manner uncharacteristic of the months from July–December 1819, when the emphasis falls on social-historical concerns in a symbolic manner more dependent on natural description); perhaps most strikingly, the later, unassimilated fragments of *Athanase* seem to point very clearly to the impact on S. of his first arrival in Italy in spring of 1818. Thus *Detached Passage (b)* suggests a first Italian spring (see note); *Detached Passage (c)* may well bear the influence of S.'s work on his translation of *Cyclops* (see note); and the Platonic interests of lines 185ff., particularly in the *Symposium*, which S. translated at Bagni di Lucca in the summer of 1818, plausibly constitute a continuation and new inflection of the Hellenism cultivated in the Shelley–Peacock circle at Marlow in the summer of 1817, which itself probably gave an initial impetus to many features of the original poem. The evidence points to a poem begun in later 1817, continued sporadically over the first few months in Italy, set aside unfinished, and finally rounded-off as a 'Fragment' for inclusion in the proposed *J&M* volume in December 1819 (the poems have thematic affinities, and without *Athanase* the volume would scarcely have been of viable length). This accords with the implication of the fragmentary letter quoted above that *Athanase* predates *J&M*, and is broadly in agreement with Paul Dawson's commentary on *Nbk 5* in *BSM* iii.

The draft of all the lines is in *Nbk 5* and the apocryphal passages have been arranged in various ways by different editors. However, S. numbered the stanzas which were originally meant to follow the first 41, from 44–66, and there is no interruption in the draft at line 124; consequently that order is preserved in the text below as far as line 197. S. then began a new, abridged version of the poem from line 125 ('*Alternative Sequence*'). When this too petered out, the remaining passages were composed unconnectedly, but apparently in the order printed below. The tradition of dividing the poem into 'Part I' and 'Part II' was an editorial convenience only, with no known basis in the MS. Before the first draft in *Nbk 5* there are three prose notes, widely spaced: on f. 83ᵛ, 'His visiting the Lady in the ship in the disguise of'; at the top of f. 83ʳ, 'to his death bed the Lady who really can reply to his soul comes and kisses his lips. — The death bed of Athanase'; and at the foot of the same page, 'Pandemos & Urania' written above 'Prince Athanase'. Mary S.'s note on the poem (*1839* iii 46) seems to depend on these jottings by S.:

> The idea Shelley had formed of Prince Athanase was a good deal modelled on Alastor. In the first sketch of the Poem he names it Pandemos and Urania. Athanase seeks through the world the One whom he may love. He meets, in the ship in which he is embarked, a lady, who appears to him to embody his ideal of love and beauty. But she proves Pandemos, of the earthly and unworthy Venus, who, after disappointing his cherished dreams and hopes, deserts him. Athanase, crushed by sorrow, pines and dies. 'On his death-bed the lady, who can really reply to his soul, comes and kisses his lips.' This slender note is all we have to aid our imagination in shaping out the form of the Poem such as its Author imaged.

There is nothing in this note which cannot be derived from the jottings quoted, and it is doubtful whether Mary S. had any other knowledge of the poem than what she found in *Nbk 5*; if so, there is no certainty, or even likelihood, that 'Pandemos and Urania' was ever contemplated as a title. Notopoulos (*Notopoulos* 51) claimed that 'The similarity of the plot of *Prince Athanase* to [Peacock's] *Rhododaphne* makes it obvious that Shelley composed this poem after an enthusiastic reading of *Rhododaphne*'. But if Mary S. was only interpreting S.'s jottings, we do not know what the plot would have been (indeed the various different narratives suggest that S. had not himself decided), and it may have been Mary S. whose notes on *Athanase* were influenced by Peacock's poem. In any case a conflict between Uranian and Pandemian love is by no means what *Rhododaphne* is about, as S. recognised (see Marilyn Butler, *Peacock Displayed* (1979) 106–8).

The name 'Athanase' means 'immortality' (Gk ἀθᾰνᾰσία); 'Zonoras', however, seems arbitrarily invented (S.'s first ideas were 'Uberto' and 'Andreas'), possibly suggested by 'Zonaras', a sixth-century Greek historian quoted by Gibbon (see *Decline and Fall*, ed. J. B. Bury, 7 vols (1896) v 508). Zonoras resembles the old man who rescues Laon in *L&C* (III xxvii–xxxii), who as Mary S. tells us was based on the character of Dr James Lind, the Royal Physician, who befriended S. at Eton:

> Free, calm-spirited, full of benevolence, and even of youthful ardour; his eye seemed to burn with supernatural spirit beneath his brow, shaded by his venerable white locks; he was tall, vigorous, and healthy in his body; tempered, as it had ever been, by his amiable mind. I owe to that man far, ah! far more than I owe to my father; he loved me, and I shall never forget our long talks, where he breathed the spirit of the kindest tolerance and the purest wisdom. (*Hogg* i 31–2)

Text from *SC* vii 132–9 (lines 1–124); *Nbk 5* (remainder).

Published in *1824* 105–10 (lines 1–124); 249–50 (lines 125–9; *Cancelled Sequence* lines 1–33); 251–3 (lines 131–96); 254–5 (*Detached Passage (b)* lines 1–30); 255–6 (*Detached Passage (c)* lines 1–19); *1840* 199 (*Detached Passage (d)*); *Locock Ex* 55–56 (*Detached Passage (a)*); 57 (*Alternative Sequence* lines 19–28); 59–60 (*Detached Passage (c)* lines 20–4); 59 (*Detached Passage (b)* lines 36–40).

146

Athanase

There was a Youth, who, as with toil and travel
Had grown quite weak and grey before his time;
Nor any could the restless griefs unravel

Which burned within him, withering up his prime
5   And goading him, like fiends, from land to land.
Not his the load of any secret crime,

For nought of ill his heart could understand
But pity and wild sorrow for the same; —
Not his the thirst for glory or command

10   Baffled with blast of hope-consuming shame;
Nor evil joys which fire the vulgar breast
And quench in speedy smoke its feeble flame

Had left within his soul their dark unrest;
Nor what Religion fables of the grave
15   Feared he, Philosophy's accepted guest.

For none than he a purer heart could have
Or that loved good more for itself alone;
Of nought in Heaven or Earth was he the slave.

What Sorrow deep and shadowy and unknown
20   Sent him, an hopeless wanderer, through Mankind?
If with a human sadness he did groan, —

1. *Youth,*] youth, *1824*. *travel*] travel, *1824*.
6. *crime,*] *1824*; crime *SC*.
10. *shame;*] *1824*; shame, *SC*.
12. *quench*] *1824*; quench, *SC*. *speedy*] *1824*; the transcription in *SC* offers 'specky', an odd reading not justified by the photographic reproduction of the relevant passage, which rather suggests that the *1824* reading is correct; and 'speedy' is unambiguous in the draft in *Nbk 5* (*BSM* iii 330–31).
13. *unrest;*] unrest: *1824*.
14. *Religion*] religion *1824*.
15. *he,*] he, – *1824*. *guest.*] *1824*; guest *SC*.
16. *have*] have, *1824*.
17. *alone;*] *1824*; alone, *SC*.
18. *Heaven or Earth*] heaven or earth *1824*.
19. *deep and shadowy and unknown*] deep, and shadowy, and unknown, *1824*.
20. *an*] a *1824*. *Mankind?*] mankind? – *1824*.
21. *groan, –*] groan, *1824*.

He had a gentle yet aspiring mind;
Just, innocent, with varied learning fed,
And such a glorious consolation find

25 In others' joy, when all their own is dead:
He loved, and laboured for his kind in grief,
And yet, unlike all others, it is said,

That from such toil he never found relief.
Although a child of Fortune and of Power,
30 Of an ancestral name the orphan chief,

His soul had wedded Wisdom, and her dower
Is love and justice, clothed in which, he sate
Apart from men, as in a lonely tower,

Pitying the tumult of their dark estate . . .
35 Yet even in youth did he not e'er abuse
The strength of wealth or thought, to consecrate

Those false opinions which the hard rich use
To blind the world they famish for their pride;
Nor did he hold from any man his dues,

24. such] i.e. 'such minds as these'.

26. grief,] *1824*; grief *SC*.

27. others,] *1824*; others *SC*.

28. such] Such *SC*. *relief.*] relief; *SC, 1824*; 'Consolation for his sadness'.

29. Fortune and of Power,] fortune and of power *1824*; Power *SC*.

30. chief,] chief *SC*; chief. *1824*. The line gave S. problems in the draft. His first attempt read 'Of a long lineage the respected Chief'. Paul Dawson's transcript of the draft (*BSM* iii 327) gives 'And though [And *canc*.] of a high race [*above* long lineage *canc*.] the orphan [*above* respected *canc*.] Chief'.

31. Wisdom] wisdom *1824*.

32–4. he sate . . . their dark estate] Cp. Lucretius, *De Re. Nat.* ii 7–10: 'nil dulcius est bene quam munita tenere / edita doctrina sapientum templa serena, / despicere unde queas alios passimque videre / errare atque viam palantis quaerere vitae' ('nothing is more delightful than to possess lofty sanctuaries serene, well fortified by the teachings of the wise, whence you may look down upon others and behold them all astray, wandering abroad and seeking the path of life' Loeb trans.). *which,*] which *1824*. *estate . . .*] estate – *1824*.

33. lonely tower] Following Milton's *Il Penseroso* 85–6: 'Or let my lamp at midnight hour, / Be seen in some high lonely tower'; Milton's imagery of withdrawal from worldly life is also indebted to Lucretius (see preceding note).

37. hard] harsh *1824*.

40   But, like a steward in honest dealings tried,
           With those who toiled and wept, the poor and wise
           His riches and his cares he did divide.

           Fearless he was, and scorning all disguise,
           What he dared do or think, though men might start,
45   He spoke with mild but unaverted eyes;

           Liberal he was of soul and frank of heart,
           And to his many friends — all loved him well —
           Whate'er he knew or felt he would impart

           If words he found those inmost thoughts to tell;
50   If not, he smiled or wept; and his weak foes
           He neither spurned nor hated, — though with fell

           And mortal hate their thousand voices rose,
           They passed like aimless arrows from his ear —
           Nor did his heart or mind its portal close

55   To those, or them, or any whom life's sphere
           May comprehend within its wide array.
           What sadness made that vernal spirit sere?

           He knew not. Though his life day after day
           Was failing like an unreplenished stream,
60   Though in his eyes a cloud and burthen lay,

---

40. *But,*] But *1824.*

43. *was,*] *1824;* was *SC.*

44. *start,*] *1824;* start *SC.*

45. *but*] yet *1824.*

46. *soul*] soul, *1824.* *heart,*] *1824;* heart *SC.*

48. *impart*] impart, *1824.*

51. *hated, –*] hated, *SC, 1824.*

55. *To those, or them,*] i.e. to his friends (line 47), or to his foes (line 50).

57. *that*] Underlined in the draft, presumably for emphasis.

58–76. *Though his life . . . he knew not*] One single suspended grammatical unit: 'Though his life . . . was failing . . . though his lips seemed like reeds . . . and thoughts were driven within him . . . like fiends . . . he knew not what his grief was'. *wake and feed*] foment and keep active.

58. *life day after day*] life, day after day, *1824.*

Through which his soul, like Vesper's serene beams
Piercing the chasms of ever-rising clouds,
Shone, softly burning; though his lips did seem

Like reeds which quiver in impetuous floods;
65   And through his sleep, and o'er each waking hour,
Thoughts after thoughts, unresting multitudes,

Were driven within him by some secret power
Which bade them blaze and live and roll afar
Like lights and sounds from haunted tower to tower

70   O'er castled mountains borne, when tempest's war
Is levied by the night-contending winds,
And the pale dalesmen watch with eager ear; —

Though such were in his spirit as the fiends
Which wake and feed an everliving woe, —
75   What was this grief, which ne'er in other minds

A mirror found, he knew not — none could know —
But on whoe'er might question him, he turned
The light of his frank eyes, as if to show,

He knew not of the grief within that burned,
80   But asked forbearance with a mournful look;
Or spoke in words from which none ever learned

61. *soul,*] *1824*; soul *SC*.
62. *ever-rising*] ever rising *1824*.   *clouds,*] clouds *SC*.
65. *hour,*] *1824*; hour *SC*.
66. *multitudes,*] *1824*; multitudes *SC*.
67. *him*] him, *1824*.   *power*] power, *1824*.
68. *blaze . . . live . . . afar*] blaze, . . . live, . . . afar, *1824*.
69. *sounds*] sounds, *1824*.
71. *winds,*] *1824*; winds *SC*.
72. *ear; –*] *1824*; ear; *SC*.
73. *such*] i.e. such thoughts.   *spirit*] spirit, *1824*.
74. *an*] on *1824*.
75. *grief,*] *1824*; grief *SC*.
76. *found,*] found, – *1824*.   *know –*] know; *1824*.
77. *him,*] him *1824*.

81–3. *Or spoke . . . or turned pale*] Athanase's symptoms resemble those of Gray's elegist: 'now sitting as in scorn, / Muttering his wayward fancies he would rove, / Now drooping, woeful wan, like one forlorn, / Or crazed with care, or crossed in hopeless love' (*Elegy in a Country Churchyard* 105–8). Gray was a favourite poet of S.'s.

The cause of his disquietude; or shook
With spasms of silent passion; or turned pale;
So that his friends soon rarely undertook

85   To stir his secret pain without avail, —
For all who knew or loved him then perceived
That there was drawn an adamantine veil

Between his heart and mind, — both unrelieved
Wrought in his brain and bosom, separate strife.
90   Some said that he was mad, others believed

That memories of an antenatal life
Made this, where now he dwelt, a penal Hell;
And others said that such mysterious grief

From God's displeasure, like a darkness, fell
95   On souls like his which owned no higher law
Than love, love calm, steadfast, invincible

By mortal fear or supernatural awe;
And others — "Tis the shadow of a dream
Which the veiled eye of memory never saw

100   'But through the soul's abyss, like some dark stream
Through shattered mines and caverns underground
Rolls, shaking its foundations; and no beam

'Of joy may rise but it is quenched and drowned
In the dim whirlpools of this dream obscure,
105 Soon its exhausted waters will have found

83. *pale;*] pale: *1824.*

85. *avail, –*] avail; – *1824.*

86. *or*] and *1824.*

89. *bosom,*] bosom *1824.* *strife.*] *1824*; strife; *SC.*

91. *memories of an antenatal life*] Cp. TL 332–3. OED cites this poem for first use of the word *antenatal*, but *Notopoulos* (226) points out that S. found it in a marginal note of Godwin's argument against innate ideas (*Political Justice* 2nd edn 1796 i 36).

92. *Hell;*] hell; *1824.*

96. *love,*] love; *1824.*

98. *others –*] others, – *1824.*

100. *'But*] *1824*; But *SC.*

103. *'Of*] *1824*; Of *SC.* *rise*] rise, *1824.*

'A lair of rest beneath thy spirit pure,
O Athanase! — in one so good and great,
Evil or tumult cannot long endure.'

So spake they: idly of another's state
110 Babbling vain words and fond philosophy;
This was their consolation; such debate

Men held with one another; nor did he
Like one who labours with a human woe
Decline this talk; as if its theme might be

115 Another, not himself, he to and fro
Questioned and canvassed it with subtlest wit;
And none but those who loved him best could know

That which he knew not, how it galled and bit
His weary mind, this converse vain and cold;
120 For like an eyeless nightmare grief did sit

Upon his being; a snake, which fold by fold
Pressed out the life of life, a clinging fiend
Which clenched him if he stirred with deadlier hold; —
And so his grief remained — let it remain — untold.

106. 'A] 1824; A SC. pure,] 1824; pure SC.

107. Athanase! –] 1824; Athanase! SC. great,] 1824; great SC.

116. wit;] wit, 1824.

120. Like an eyeless nightmare] S. had probably seen one of Henry Fuseli's several striking paintings entitled 'The Nightmare' (c. 1781) which depict a fiend-like shape with uncanny eyes sitting on a woman outstretched in sleep.

123. hold; –] 1824; hold SC.

124. SC and 1824 end at this line which, in different ink, is evidently added in the draft so as to round-off a publishable 'Fragment'. This was done perhaps as late as December 1819 when S. sent the poem to Ollier (see headnote). A note follows at this end-point in 1824:
    The Author was pursuing a fuller development of the ideal character of Athanase, when it struck him that in an attempt at extreme refinement and analysis, his conceptions might be betrayed into the assuming a morbid character. The reader will judge whether he is a loser or gainer by this difference. – Author's Note.
This text is taken from S.'s note at the beginning of the SC manuscript, except that SC has 'diffidence' for 'difference'. Without line 124 the rhyme-pattern in the draft continues regularly, and so does S.'s tercet-count.

125   Prince Athanase had one beloved friend:
      An old, old man with hair of silver white
      And lips where heavenly smiles would hang and blend

      With his wise words; — and eyes whose arrowy light
      Shone like the reflex of a thousand minds
      [   ]

130   Such was Zonoras . . . and, as morning finds
      One amaranth glittering on the path of frost
      When Autumn nights have nipped all weaker kinds,

      Thus through his age, dark, cold and tempest-tossed
      Shone Truth upon Zonoras; — and he filled
135   From fountains pure nigh overgrown and lost

      The spirit of Prince Athanase, a child,
      With soul-sustaining songs of ancient lore,
      And philosophic wisdom clear and mild;

      And sweet and subtle talk they evermore,
140   The pupil and the master, shared; — until
      Sharing that undiminishable store

      The youth, as shadows o'er a grassy hill
      Outrun the winds that chase them, soon outran
      His teacher, and did teach with native skill

145   Strange truths and new to that experienced man.
      Still they were friends, as few have ever been
      Who mark the extremes of life's discordant span. —

      They in the caverns of the forest green
      Or on the rocks of echoing Ocean hoar,
150   Zonoras and Prince Athanase, were seen

---

125. one beloved friend] A character evidently based on that of Dr James Lind, S.'s 70-year-old friend who, (Mary S. wrote) 'when Shelley was at Eton, had often stood by to befriend and support him, and whose name he never mentioned without love and veneration' (*1839* i 376). Lind had died in 1812. See headnote, and note to *L&C* 1348.

126. Perhaps seen as antithetical in his nature to Spenser's Ignaro (*Faerie Queene* I VIII xxx 2), similarly seen as 'An old, old man, with beard as white as snow'.

130. Zonoras] See headnote.

131. amaranth] One of a family of warm-climate flowers which includes the British *Amaranthus Caudatus*, Love-lies-bleeding.

By summer woodmen; and when Winter's roar
Sounded o'er earth and sea its blast of war,
The Balearic fisher, driven from shore

Hanging upon the peakèd wave afar
155   Then saw their lamp from Laian's turret gleam,
Piercing the stormy darkness, like a star

Which pours beyond the sea one steady beam,
Whilst all the constellations of the sky
Seemed reeling through the storm . . . they did but seem —

160   For lo, the wintry clouds are all gone by
And bright Arcturus through yon pines is glowing,
And far o'er southern waves, immoveably

Belted Orion hangs — warm light is flowing
From the young moon into the sunset's chasm.
165   'O summer eve, with power divine bestowing

'On thine own bird the sweet enthusiasm
Which overflows in notes of liquid gladness,
Filling the sky like light — how many a spasm

'Of fevered brains oppressed with grief and madness
170   Were lulled by thee, delightful nightingale, —
And these soft waves murmuring a gentle sadness —

---

152. war] A perfect rhyme in the old pronunciation to 'afar' and 'star' (see H. C. Wyld, *Studies in English Rhymes* (1923) 69–70).

153. The Balearic fisher] Probably a mistake: the Balearic Islands (Majorca, Minorca, Ivica) are more than 1,000 miles West of the Sporades.

155. Laian's turret] Presumably the invented name derives from Laios on the island of Chios in the eastern Aegean.

160–71. Locock (*Locock 1911* i 578) noted that 'The season is changed from summer to winter, and is again summer', and sought with help from the Royal Observatory to attach the occasion to the contemporary date of 20–21 March 1817. Rogers (*1975* 402) quotes King-Hele who endorses the seasonal details as 'all accurate and specific' for the month of March, but warns against Locock's attempt to relate these details to 1817. 'Athanase is a timeless sort of character, so an exact date, determined by the moon, seems inappropriate'. This is true; nevertheless a close correspondence is offered by S.'s visit to Lake Como on 9–12 April 1818: Arcturus, a star of summer, then rose after sunset, with Orion to the south; there had been a new moon on 6 April; nightingales would be singing (impossible in England on the March dates) and S. describes the song as refreshingly new and consoling; while the image of the wind over a 'forest-bosomed lake' (line 179; a cancelled draft for line 167 says that the song 'fills the shore') accords with S.'s impressions of Como (*L* ii 6–7).

'And the far sighings of yon piny dale
Made vocal by some Wind we feel not here —
I bear alone what nothing may avail

175 'To lighten; — a strange load' — no human ear
Heard this lament; but o'er the visage wan
Of Athanase, a ruffling atmosphere

Of dark emotion, with swift shadow ran
Like wind upon some forest-bosomed lake,
180 Glassy and dark — and that divine old man

Beheld his mystic friend's [   ] being shake
Even where its inmost depths were gloomiest —
And with a calm and measured voice he spake,

And with a soft and equal pressure pressed
185 That cold lean hand — 'Dost thou remember yet
When the curved moon then lingering in the West

'Paused in yon waves her mighty horns to wet,
How in those beams we walked, half entered on the sea?
'Tis just one year . . . sure thou dost not forget,

190 '[   ] Plato's words of light in thee and me
Lingered like moonlight in the moonless East,
For we had just then read — thy memory

'Is faithful now — the story of the feast;
And Agathon and Diotima seemed
195 From death, and Dark [   ] released

'To talk with us of all they knew or dreamed,
Of love divine [

188. *half entered*] half resting *1824, eds*; 'entered' is written on top of 'entering', which distorts the orthography. The line is metrically a syllable too long; but S.'s characteristic suspended syntax has given unnecessary trouble. 'We walked in the moonlight, while the moon's crescent, half-setting in the sea, delayed its submergence'. Cp. 'Zeinab and Kathema' (no. 58) 13–14: 'And now the beamless, broad and yellow sphere / Halfsinking lingered on the crimson sea'.

193. the story of the feast] Plato's *Symposium* (συμπόσιον means 'drinking-party', 'banquet').

194. Agathon and Diotima] Agathon was the Greek dramatist for whom the Symposium was a celebration-party, Diotima a Mantinean sage, a woman, whose concept of Love was expounded by Socrates in reply to that of Agathon.

197. Of love divine, and all its sacred symbols dim *Nbk 5* (the last seven words cancelled, but 'divine' reinstated by underlining). Below this line, in different ink, occurs the following line: 'What was his grief? [he loves not.] his heart is deeply laden', which perhaps belongs with Alternative Sequence lines 23–7.

Cancelled Sequence following line 129

He was the last whom Superstition's blight

Had spared in Greece; — the blight that cramps and blinds —
And in his olive bower at Oenoe
Had sate from earliest youth; like one who finds

5   A fertile island in the barren sea,
One mariner who has survived his mates
Many a lone month in a great ship — so he

With soul-sustaining songs, and sweet debates
Of ancient lore there fed his lonely being. —
10   'The mind becomes that which it contemplates,'

And thus Zonoras, by forever seeing
Their bright creations, grew like wisest men.
And when he heard the crash of nations fleeing

From a bloodier power than ruled thy ruins then,
15   O sacred Hellas, many weary years
He wandered, till the path of Laian's glen

Cancelled Sequence

3. *Oenoe*] S. noted 'Lempriere' beside this line in *Nbk* 5. Lemprière's *Classical Dictionary* says only that Sicinus (modern Sikino), one of the Southern Cyclades, was known as Oenoe after the wife of Sicinus, son of the King of Lemnos.

10. 'Said of Shakespeare' – S.'s note in *Nbk* 5. The quotation, adapted by S. in many contexts, is from Paine's *Rights of Man*: 'It is the faculty of the human mind to become what it contemplates, and to act in unison with its object.' The application to Shakespeare may have been Hazlitt's: 'He had only to think of any thing in order to become that thing, with all the circumstances belonging to it' ('On Shakespeare and Milton', in *Lectures on the English Poets* (1818), *Hazlitt Works* v 48). Hazlitt gave this lecture in London on 27 January 1818 (see *Henry Crabb Robinson on Books and their Writers*, ed. Edith J. Morley, 3 vols (1938) i 218) when S. was still at Marlow, but he was in town from 7 February and could have had accounts of it from his friends or from Hazlitt himself. The same idea had already been expressed in 'Antony and Cleopatra', in Hazlitt's *Characters of Shakespeare's Plays* (1817). There is however a difference between the faculty of imaginative empathy in Shakespeare and Paine's notion of adaptive identity, which derives from Plato, e.g. *Republic* (vi 500cd): 'the man whose mind is truly fixed on eternal realities . . . will endeavour to imitate them and, as far as may be, to fashion himself in their likeness and assimilate himself to them . . . Then the lover of wisdom associating with the divine order will himself become orderly and divine in the measure permitted to man' (trans. Paul Shorey). For further commentary on this line see note to *PU* I 450.

14. *a bloodier power*] Napoleon, compared with Turkish domination.

Was grass-grown, and the unremembered tears
Were dry in Laian for their honoured chief
Who fell in Sestos pierced by Moslem spears —

20   And as the lady looked with faithful grief
From her high lattice o'er the rugged path
Where she once saw that horseman toil, with brief

And blighting hope, who with the news of death
Struck body and soul as with a mortal blight,
25   She saw between the chestnuts, far beneath,

An old man toiling up, a weary wight,
And soon within her hospitable hall
She saw his white hair glittering in the light

Of the wood fire, and round his shoulders fall,
30   And his wan visage, and his withered mien
Yet calm and [   ] and majestical. —

And Athanase her child who must have been
Then three years old sate opposite and gazed
And looked in patient silence, whilst [

Alternative Sequence from line 125

Prince Athanase had one beloved friend,
An old old man with hair of silver white
And lips where heavenly smiles would hang and blend

With his wise words, and eyes whose arrowy light
5   Was the reflex of many minds; he filled
From fountains pure nigh overgrown and lost

The spirit of Prince Athanase, a child;
And soul-sustaining songs of ancient lore
And philosophic wisdom clear and mild

19. *in Sestos*] in Byzant *Nbk 5* canc.

Alternative Sequence
An abridged second attempt at lines to follow 125, but the first version was uncancelled.

6. *lost*] A non-rhyme, cancelled in *Nbk 5*; 'Evidently copied mechanically from the earlier version' (*Locock 1911* i 578).

10   And sweet and subtle talk they evermore,
      The pupil and the master, shared, until
      Sharing that undiminishable store

      The youth, as clouds athwart a grassy hill
      Outrun the winds that chase them, soon outran
15   His teacher, and did teach with native skill

      Strange truths and new to that experienced man.
      So they were friends as few have ever been
      Who mark the extremes of life's discordant span;

      And when the old man saw that on the green
20   Leaves of his opening manhood a blight had lighted,
      He said — 'My friend, one grief alone can wean

      'A gentle mind from all that once delighted.
      Thou lovest, and thy secret heart is laden
      With feelings which should not be unrequited.'

25   And Athanase then smiled, as one o'erladen
      With iron chains might smile to talk of bands
      Twined round her lover's neck by some blithe maiden,

      And said . . . 'Then I will tell thee all I know
      [

      Detached Passages

                            (a)
      'Tis often when the eyes are cold and dry
      And the lips calm the Spirit weeps within
      Tears bitterer than the blood of agony

      Trembling in drops on the discoloured skin
5   Of those who love their kind, and therefore die
      In ghastly torture . . . a sweet medicine

      Of peace and sleep are tears, and quietly
      Those soothe from whose uplifted eyes they fall
      But [

Detached Passage (a)
These lines originally skipped a page, later used for lines 629–65 of *The Cyclops*.
1–3. Adapted later for *The Cenci* I i 109–13. See also note to *PU* II iv 27–8.
8. Those soothe] i.e. Soothe those.

(b)

'Twas at that season when the Earth upsprings
From slumber, as a spherèd Angel's child
Shadowing its eyes with green and golden wings

Stands up before its mother bright and mild
5   Of whose soft voice the air expectant seems:
So stood before the Sun, which shone and smiled

To see it rise thus joyous from its dreams,
The fresh and radiant Earth; — the hoar wood grove
Waxed green and flowers burst forth like starry beams;

10   The grass in the warm sun did start and move,
The sea buds burst under the waves serene.
How many a one, though none be near to love,

Loves then the shade of his own soul half seen
In any mirror — or the spring's plumed minions,
15   The forest leaves amid the copses green;

How many a spirit then puts on the pinions
Of fancy, and outstrips the lagging blast
And his own steps, and over wide dominions

Sweeps in his dream-drawn chariot far and fast,
20   More fleet than storms: the wide world shrinks below
When winter and despondency are past:

'Twas at this season that Prince Athanase
Passed the aërial Alps — those wintry mountains
Slept in their shrouds of frost; beside the ways

Detached Passage (b)
This seems evidently to have been written in Italy, reflecting S.'s own elation at the change
of climate expressed in his letter to Peacock of 6 April 1818: 'Our journey was somewhat
painful from the cold & in no other manner interesting until we passed the Alps: of course
I except the Alps themselves, but no sooner had we arrived at Italy than the loveliness of
the earth & the serenity of the sky made the greatest difference in my sensations – I depend
on these things for life . . .' (*L* ii 3). The opening tercets have a strong likeness to those of *TL*.

12–15. How many a one . . . the copses green] Cp. S.'s prose fragment 'On Love' (June–July 1818):
'We dimly see within our intellectual nature a miniature as it were of our entire self, yet
deprived of all that we condemn or despise . . . a mirror whose surface reflects only the forms
of purity and brightness . . . The discovery of its antitype . . . this is the invisible and
unattainable point to which Love tends . . . Hence in solitude . . . we love the flowers, the
grass and the waters and the sky. In the motion of the very leaves of spring in the blue air
there is then found a secret correspondence with our heart' (*Reiman (1977)* 473–4).

25 The streams were voiceless, for their fountain springs
    Were changed to mines of sunless crystal now,
    Or by the curdling winds, like brazen wings

    Which clanged along the mountain's marble brow,
    Warped into adamantine fretwork, hung
30 And filled with frozen light the chasms below.

    Vexed by the blast, the great pines groaned and swung
    Under their load of snow . . . the soil was hard
    And from the step a sound like iron flung.

    On high the dark and purple noon did gird
35 The rayless [
                                                    ]

    Such as the eagle sees when he dives down
    From the grey deserts of wide air, beheld
    Prince Athanase, and o'er his mien was thrown

    The shadow of that scene, field after field,
40 Purple and dim and wide, and many a town,
    Distinct with antique towers and walls, which yield

    Their image in the lucid streams below

                        (c)
    Thou art the wine whose drunkenness is all
    We can desire, o Love, and joyous souls
    Ere from thy vine the leaves of autumn fall

    Catch thee and feed from their o'erflowing bowls
5   Thousands who thirst for thine ambrosial dew;
    Thou art the radiance which where Ocean rolls

    Investeth it, and when the Heavens are blue
    Thou fillest them, and when the earth is fair
    The shadow of thy moving wings imbue

Detached Passage (c)
This passage in celebration of 'Love divine' might have been intended to follow shortly after line 197 of the main text. If *The Cyclops* was being written simultaneously, this could account for the wine imagery, which S., though virtually a teetotaller, often used in a Dionysian sense (cp. *PU* II iii 4–10): Dionysus was 'the greatest among men for joy of life' (*Cyclops* 529).

10 Its deserts and its mountains, till they wear
   Beauty like some light robe; thou ever soarest
   Among the towers of men, and as soft air

   In spring which moves the unawakened forest
   Clothing with leaves its branches bare and bleak
15 Thou floatest among men, and aye implorest

   That which from thee they should implore: the weak
   Alone kneel to thee, offering up the hearts
   The strong have broken . . . yet where shall any seek

   A garment whom thou clothest not? — the darts
20 Of the keen winter storm barbèd with frost
   Which from the everlasting snow that parts

   The Alps from heaven pierce some lone traveller lost
   In the wide-waved interminable snow
   Ungarmented, are not [

(d)

   Her hair was brown, her spherèd eyes were brown
   And in their dark and liquid moisture swam
   Like the dim orb of the eclipsèd moon:

   Yet when the spirit flashed beneath there came
5   The light from them as when tears of delight
   Double the western planet's serene flame

147
To Constantia
('The red Rose that drinks the fountain dew')

Stanza 1 is first drafted vertically on f. 219 of *Nbk 3*, palimpsesting quotations from Plato's *Apology*, which was presumably among the works of Plato read during S.'s first fortnight in Albion House at Marlow, 18 March–2 April 1817. *Nbk 3* is filled with drafts of *L&C*, V xix to the end of the poem, so the need to insert it in this

Detached Passage (d)
Perhaps intended for the lady who, in Mary S.'s account of S.'s proposed continuation of the poem, Athanase was to fall in love with as the embodiment of his ideal of love and beauty.

way strongly suggests that it was written there after the completion of *L&C* on 29 September 1817 but while S. was still working with the draft. The later, fuller, version is in *Nbk 5*, used from the back end, and follows 'Ozymandias' (December 1817, the first piece of writing inside the cover) and a page of notes for an essay 'On the true Nature of Metaphysical Science'; it is followed in turn by 'Athanase'. The fragment therefore dates from the end of 1817, probably December. Mary S. included it among the poems of 1817 in *1839*. For Constantia as the name by which S. called Claire Clairmont at this time, see headnote to no. 155, 'Thy voice, slow rising'. S. associated Mary S. with the moon, the 'cold chaste moon' of *Epipsychidion* 281, as early as October 1814 (*L* i 414), but even if this poem has a biographical meaning it does not concern Mary: the imagery here merely contrasts the noonday of Constantia's fluctuating affection with the changed light of her emotional apostasy.

Text from *Nbk 5*, f. 84ʳ (text of draft lines 1–6 from *Nbk 3*, f. 219).

Published in *1839* iii 63; *Massey* 297 (transcript of *Nbk 5* text), 296 (transcript of *Nbk 3* draft of lines 1–6).

The red Rose that drinks the fountain dew
    In the fragrant air of noon
Grows pale and blue with altered hue
    In the gaze of the nightly moon, —
For the Planet of frost so cold and bright
Makes it wan with borrowed light.

Such is my Heart — Roses are fair
    And that at best a withered blossom —
But thy false care did idly wear
    Its withered leaves in a faithless bosom,
And fed with love, like air and dew,
    Its growth [

5

10

1–6.
    Roses which drink the fountain dew
    Beneath the gazing noon
Are pale & blue, with changed hue
    In the eye of the nightly moon
For the frost has been their
For the planet of frost, so cold & bright
Makes them wan with borrowed light
                      1st draft, Nbk 3

1. An echo of Peacock's *Palmyra* (1812 version) 164–5: 'The flower, that drinks the morning-dew, / Far on the evening gale shall fly' (for 'Roses' S. first had 'Flowers' in his draft in *Nbk 3*).

3. *grows*] *BSM* iii reads 'grown'.

6. *Makes it wan*] Shines over it *canc. MS.*

10. In the warmth of a dear but faithless bosom *canc. MS.*

11. *with love*] *canc. MS.*

148
'arise sweet Mary rise'

Drafted in *Nbk 5*, on the same page as the preceding and following poems; Mary S.'s transcript is in Bodleian MS Shelley adds. d. 9, f. 81 (see also f. 93).

Text from *Nbk 5* f. 84ᵣ.

Published in *Locock Ex* 75, *1975* 322.

> arise sweet Mary rise
> For the time is passing now

149
'My head is heavy, my limbs are weary'

Drafted in *Nbk 5*, on the same page as the two preceding poems. Mary's transcript is in Bodleian MS Shelley adds. d. 9 f. 93.

Text from *Nbk 5* f. 84ᵣ.

Published in *Relics* 1–2; given as part of no. 148 in *1975* 322.

> My head is heavy, my limbs are weary
> And it is not life that makes me move
> And my [?way] [?is]

150
'Serene in his unconquerable might'

Written December 1817/January 1818. In *Nbk 5* the lines follow parts of the prose draft for *A Refutation of Deism* (1814), but are followed after two pages by the 'Essay on Christianity', which is datable to late 1817/early 1818, and all the other contents of the nbk belong to the same period. S. was reading the opening Books of *Paradise Lost* late in December 1817 after revising *L&C* for republication (*Mary Jnl* i 188–9), which might account for the Miltonic style of these lines and for their semi-parody of *Paradise Lost* iii. It is also possible, as Locock surmised (*Locock 1911* ii 498), that they represent an abortive start of S.'s projected poem on Job. Mary S. says in her note on *PU* that at the time of their removal to Italy S. 'meditated

---

1. *arise*] Arise *Massey*.

¶**149**   1. *weary*] weary, *Massey*.

2. *it*] Originally *its* in *Nbk 5*, with the *s* canc.

3. *And my [?way] [?is]*] omitted *Massey*.

three subjects', the first-mentioned being the story of Tasso, the third that of Prometheus, while the second 'was one founded on the book of Job, which he never abandoned in idea, but of which no trace remains among his papers'. This seems to discount the possibility at the moment of raising it; but Mary S. either missed or purposely ignored this fragment, which so far as is known she never even transcribed. Some odd lines on the opposite page (f. 6ʳ) may be associated with it:

> soft pillows for the fiends
> Of power to renovate their blighted pinions
> For

The holograph is unpunctuated except for the dashes and a comma after *King*, but S.'s syntax is plain and has only been made tortuous by editorial pointing.

Text from *Nbk 5* f. 5ᵛ.

Published in *Locock Ex* 71, 73; *1975* 320–21, 322.

> Serene in his unconquerable might
> Endured the Almighty King; his steadfast throne,
> Encompassed unapproachably with power
> And darkness and deep solitude and awe,
> Stood like a black cloud on some aery cliff
> Embosoming its lightning — in his sight
> Unnumbered glorious Spirits trembling stood
> Like slaves before their Lord — prostrate around
> Heaven's multitudes hymned everlasting praise.

5

151
Address to the Human Mind

Drafted in *Nbk 5* ff. 5ᵛ–6ʳ, under the following heading: 'Address to the human mind: representation of its being a perpetual flame. Burning on the altars of Greece & Rome & Egypt. Gods [?] its ministering Powers. Temples. Juganaut. China.' This fragment is perhaps connected with the fragment following (no. 152), 'Great Spirit', drafted on the cover of the nbk.

Text from *Nbk 5* ff. 5ᵛ–6ʳ.

Published in *Locock Ex* 71–72, *1975* 321.

1. Written above a canc. first line in *Nbk 5*: 'Steadfast in his adamantine throne'. *Serene in* is slightly doubtful; 'secure in' is a conceivable reading.

2. Endured] Endued *Locock Ex*, eds. The sense of the word is that in S.'s argument against God's existence in the same notebook: 'Until it is clearly proved that the Universe was created, we may reasonably suppose that it has endured from all eternity' (f. 3ʳ). Line 2 originally began 'Jehovah ruled the universe' (canc.).

4. deep solitude] The loneliness of a tyrant, even amid homage, was soon to be re-emphasised in the 'self-torturing solitude' of S.'s Jupiter (*PU* I 295).

Thou living light, that in thy rainbow hues
Clothest this naked world; and over Sea
And Earth and Air and all the shapes that be
In peopled darkness of this wondrous world
5   The Spirit of thy glory dost diffuse,
[   ] truth [   ] thou Vital Flame,
Mysterious thought, that in this mortal frame
Of things, with unextinguished lustre burnest
Now pale and faint, now high to Heaven upcurled,
10   That e'er as thou dost languish still returnest
And ever [   ]
Before the [   ] before the pyramids,
So soon as from the Earth formless and rude
One living step had chased drear Solitude
15   Thou wert, Thought; thy brightness sealed the lids
Of the vast snake Eternity, who kept
The tree of good and evil. —

152
'Great Spirit whom the sea of boundless mind'

Pencilled inside the front cover of *Nbk 5*, probably in early 1818 (assuming that the cover is more likely to be used when many early pages are occupied). The lines are a fragmentary address to the Power of which Shelley had such frequent

1–2. Cp. 'Mont Blanc' 142–4; 'And what were thou, and earth, and stars, and sea, / If to the human mind's imaginings / Silence and solitude were vacancy?'

3. Air] air; *BSM* iii.   *be*] Conjectured from the rhyme; the short word is hidden by a blot.

5. diffuse,] diffuse. *BSM* iii.

6. Blanks in *Nbk 5.*

9. upcurled,] upcurled *Nbk 5.*

11–12. Blanks in *Nbk 5.*

12. pyramids,] Pyramids *Nbk 5, BSM* (iii 25); S. may have altered the initial p to upper case.

15. sealed] *charmed* is an uncanc. alt. in *Nbk 5,* and *eds* give it as the received reading. The alternative verbs imply that Eternity's eyes were either dazzled or lulled to closure by the brightness of Thought, so that the apple of Knowledge could be taken.

16. the vast snake Eternity] The δράκων ουροβόρος, or snake with tail-in-mouth, symbolising the endlessness of eternity.

and various intuitions in his work, e.g. in the 'Hymn to Intellectual Beauty', the apocryphal opening stanzas of *L&C*, *PU* I 658–61, *Adonais* 373–87, and 'The Zucca' 22–40.

The last lines are very hard to read, including one that is wholly illegible, and almost every word is dubious except in line 8. The holograph is unpunctuated except for a possible semicolon after *caves*. See *BSM* iii 3 for an excellent transcript.

Text from *Nbk 5*, inside front cover.

Published in *Rossetti 1870* ii 362 (lines 1–4, from Mary Shelley's transcript in Bod. MS Shelley adds. d. 9 f. 85); *Locock 1911* ii 188 (lines 1–5, 8, from MS); *Massey* 304 (transcript of MS).

Great Spirit whom the sea of boundless mind
Nurtures within its unimagined caves
In which thou sittest solemnly reclined,
Giving a voice to its mysterious waves
5   Which breathes among the winds that wake mankind,
Thou must   portion be
[   ]
The   surrounding Sea should fail
Like golden winged Love whose footstep paves
10 Like Proteus   in the sea

153
'My spirit like a charmèd bark doth swim'

These lines are written vertically in ink between the last of the 'Essay on Christianity' and stanza 2 of no. 155, 'To Constantia' ('Thy voice, slow rising') in *Nbk 5*, and may have resulted from the initial impulse that was then realised in the poem. At any rate the lines were probably already on the page when S. drafted 'To Constantia', as he did not go back another page in order to write stanza 3 but instead skipped forward two pages and used f. 36ʳ. The concept and some of the phrasing of the lines were incorporated sixteen months later into Asia's song at the end of *PU* II (v 72–81), in an elaborate stanza-form. These lines are in *terza rima*, and are so spaced in MS.

Text from *Nbk 5*, f. 34ʳ.

Published in *1839* iii 69 (lines 1–5); *Locock Ex* 63 (line 6).

1. *mind*] omitted *Massey*.
5. *among*] within *Locock 1911* (an uncanc. alt. in *Nbk 5*).
8. *surrounding*] <soun>ding *BSM* iii; ?resounding *Massey*.
10. *the sea*] their *Massey*.

My spirit like a charmèd bark doth swim
Upon the liquid waves of thy sweet singing
Far far away into the regions dim

Of rapture, as a boat with swift sails winging
5   Its way adown some many-winding river
Speeds through dark forests o'er the waters swinging

154
'To thirst and find no fill'

These couplets are tucked into the top right-hand corner of a page in *Nbk 5* with stanza 2 of 'To Constantia' ('Thy voice, slow rising') drafted round them and covering the last word, 'Sick'. They immediately follow 'My spirit like a charmèd bark', and then the 'Essay on Christianity', which was probably abandoned at the end of 1817. They are therefore likely to date from November or December 1817 and may well, as many readers have assumed, belong to the material associated with Claire Clairmont which surrounds them. Mary Shelley thought that, like 'Athanase', the lines expressed 'the restless passion-fraught emotions of one whose sensibility, kindled to too intense a life, perpetually preyed upon itself' (*1839* iii 69). However, the apparent situation (which Forman labelled 'Unsatisfied Desires' and linked with *J&M* – *1876–7* iii 405 – and which Locock more decorously called 'Igniculus Desiderii' – *Locock Ex* 63) and certain phrases also call to mind Shelley's projected *Tasso* drama, begun six months later in Italy. The unlikely verb *wail* (line 1), which has worried all transcribers but seems correct, suggests a fictional persona. Shelley later used both situation and phrasing from these lines for Orsino's soliloquy at the close of *Cenci* II (ii 133–44).

Text from *Nbk 5* f. 34ᵛ.

Published in *1839* iii 69.

To thirst and find no fill — to wail and wander
With short unsteady steps — to pause and ponder —
To feel the blood run through the veins, and tingle
Where busy thought and blind sensation mingle —
5   To nurse the image of unfelt caresses
Till dim imagination just possesses
The half created shadow — all the night
Sick

155
To Constantia
('Thy voice, slow rising like a Spirit, lingers')

Composed between 29 April 1817, when 'the piano arrives' at Albion House (*Mary Jnl* i 168), and 19 January 1818 when Claire Clairmont recorded 'Copy part of Verses to Constantia' (*Claire Jnl* 79), most likely in December or early January (see head-notes to nos 147 and 153). The poem was drafted in *Nbk 5*, and written out by S. into Claire's nbk (*Harvard Nbk 2*) except for a final line, which he must have supplied when she copied the poem to send to the *Oxford University and City Herald* ('*O*'). This last line is the only important variant between *Harvard Nbk 2* and *O*, and Claire Clairmont, ironically, may not have been shown the only version known to posterity up to 1969. This is because it exists only in the draft, which Mary S. had been compelled to rely on for her reconstruction of the poem in *1824* under her own title 'To Constantia, Singing'. Edward Silsbee, who came to own *Harvard Nbk 2*, noted below this poem – no doubt from Claire herself – 'Written at *Marlowe* 1817 wd not let Mary see it sent it to Oxford Gazette or some Oxford or county paper without his name'. See *MYR* v Introduction xviii for discussion of the pos-sible whereabouts of *Harvard Nbk 2* in the years following the departure of S. and his party from Marlow. The original published text remained undiscovered until Judith Chernaik traced and reprinted it in 1969 (see below). It appeared over the signature PLEYEL, perhaps (as suggested in *1975* 404) from Haydn's living pupil Ignaz Pleyel, who may plausibly have composed the music Claire had been singing, or from Henry Pleyel, the rationalist hero of Charles Brockden Brown's novel *Wieland, or The Transformation* (New York 1798). Certainly S.'s pet name for Claire Clairmont came from Brown's *Ormond; or, the Secret Witness* (New York 1799), for 'The heroine of this novel, Constantia Dudley, held one of the highest places, if not the very highest place, in Shelley's idealities of female character' (*Peacock Works* viii 77). Mary S. had probably read this novel in July (*Mary Jnl* i 177, which however identifies Mary's entry 'Read Miss E's Harrington and ormond – Arthur Mervyn' as a reference to Edgeworth's *Harrington, a tale, and Ormond, a tale*). That Claire accepted the name is proved by the inscription on her former tomb at Antella near Florence, which gave her full name as 'Clara Mary Constantia Jane Clairmont' (*N&Q* 10th series, 8 October 1904, 284). The accomplished musician in *Ormond* was in fact Constantia's rival, Helena Cleves, but 'if ever human tones were qualified to convey the whole soul, they were those of Constantia' when she did sing a ditty to herself in ch. xix. S. was extremely fond of vocal music, and had arranged at Marlow for Claire to resume lessons under a music master. Rogers describes the poem's background and thematic significance in *KSMB* v (1953) 20–5; a good critical account is in *Chernaik* 52–8. Its affinities with Schiller's 'Laura am Klavier' may be coincidental, but the influence of the ninth of Moore's 'Odes to Nea' (1806) is less speculative:

> It felt as if her lips had shed
> A sigh around her, ere she fled,
> Which hung, as on a melting lute,

> When all the silver chords are mute,
> There lingers still a trembling breath
> After the note's luxurious death,
> A shade of song, a spirit air
> Of melodies which had been there! (5–12)

S. is known to have admired these Odes (see Mary S.'s letter to Thomas Moore, 18 January 1839, *Mary L* ii 308). Working from an erratic draft, Mary S. mistook the sequence of the stanzas, so that earlier *eds* have printed them in the order 4,3,1,2.

Text from *The Oxford University and City Herald*, 31 January 1818.

Published in *The Oxford University and City Herald*, 31 January 1818, reprinted in *TLS* 6 February 1969, p. 140; *1824* 143–4 (lines 35–44, 23–33, 1–22, from *Nbk* 5, ff. 36ᵛ–34ᵛ), revised by Locock, *Locock Ex* 60–2 (adding line 34); *Boston Herald*, 21 December 1925, p. 12 (text from *Harvard Nbk*), corrected in *TLS* 17 January 1935, p. 33, and 11 April 1935, p. 244; *Chernaik*, 196–7.

155
To Constantia

> Thy voice, slow rising like a Spirit, lingers
> O'ershadowing me with soft and lulling wings;
> The blood and life within thy snowy fingers
> Teach witchcraft to the instrumental strings.
> 5 My brain is wild, my breath comes quick,
> The blood is listening in my frame,
> And thronging shadows fast and thick
> Fall on my overflowing eyes,
> My heart is quivering like a flame;
> 10 As morning dew, that in the sunbeam dies,
> I am dissolved in these consuming ecstasies.
>
> I have no life, Constantia, but in thee
> Whilst, like the world-surrounding air, thy song
> Flows on, and fills all things with melody:

¶155 *1. Spirit,*] *Harvard Nbk*; spirit, *O*.

1–2. (a) Constantia's voice is on my soul – it lingers / upon the heart like loves oershadowing wings (b) Her voice is hovering oer my soul – it lingers / Oershadowing it with soft & lulling wings (alternative drafts in *Nbk* 5; see *BSM* iii 141).

2. me] it *Harvard Nbk* (An inadvertence in copying the draft).

12. thee] *Harvard Nbk*; thee; *O*. (The listener's dependence on the singer is only while her song lasts, as the draft emphasises; *O*'s semi-colon would make it unconditional).

13. world-surrounding] This adjective predates the earliest usage recorded in *OED*; cp. *PU* I 661.

15   Now is thy voice a tempest, swift and strong,
         On which, as one in trance, upborne
         Secure o'er woods and waves I sweep
         Rejoicing, like a cloud of morn:
         Now 'tis the breath of summer's night
20   Which, where the starry waters sleep
      Round western isles with incense-blossoms bright,
      Lingering, suspends my soul in its voluptuous flight.

      A deep and breathless awe, like the swift change
      Of dreams unseen, but felt in youthful slumbers,
25   Wild, sweet, yet incommunicably strange,
      Thou breathest now, in fast ascending numbers:
         The cope of Heaven seems rent and cloven
         By the enchantment of thy strain,
         And o'er my shoulders wings are woven
30   To follow its sublime career,
         Beyond the mighty moons that wane
      Upon the verge of Nature's utmost sphere,
      Till the world's shadowy walls are past, and disappear.

      Cease, cease — for such wild lessons madmen learn:
35   Long thus to sink — thus to be lost and die
      Perhaps is death indeed — Constantia turn!
      Yes! in thine eyes a power like light doth lie,
         Even though the sounds its voice that were
         Between thy lips are laid to sleep —

16. trance, upborne] *Harvard Nbk, Draft*; trance upborne, *O, Chernaik*.

21. incense-blossoms] *Harvard Nbk*; incense blossoms *O, Chernaik*.

24. slumbers,] slumbers; *O*; slumbers *Harvard Nbk, Nbk 5*. A semicolon is impossible, as *awe*, qualified by the adjectives of line 25, is the object of *Thou breathest*.

26. numbers] 'Lyrical measures' (cp. the 'plaintive numbers' of Wordsworth's 'Solitary Reaper').

27. the cope of Heaven] the deep Earth *Nbk 5 canc*.

29–34. And o'er my shoulders . . . madmen learn:] A Platonic image: 'Such a one [a beauty-lover], as soon as he beholds the beauty of this world, is reminded of true beauty, and his wings begin to grow; then is he fain to lift his wings and fly upward; yet he has not the power, but inasmuch as he gazes upward like a bird, and cares nothing for the world beneath, men charge it upon him that he is demented' (*Phaedrus* 249e).

34. for such wild lessons madmen learn:] for of such things do maniacs tell – *Nbk 5 canc*.

35. to sink] Chernaik notes (*Chernaik* 55) that this 'falling away, which follows ecstasy' anticipates much in S.'s later poetry, e.g. *Epipsychidion* 587–91.

38–9. 'Even though the sounds that constituted the Power's voice are now silent'.

40   Within thy breath and on thy hair
      Like odour it is lingering yet —
      And from thy touch like fire doth leap:
      Even while I write my burning cheeks are wet —
      Such things the heart can feel and learn, but not forget!

156–161
Translations of the Homeric Hymns

S. translated, wholly or in part, seven of the 33 Greek Hymns (songs in honour of gods) ascribed to Homer, six of them in January 1818, but the most considerable, the Hymn to Mercury, two and a half years later. Hogg had recommended the Hymns to S. on 5 April 1817 as 'miraculous effusions of genius' containing 'magical verses' (qu. A. Koszul, *La Jeunesse de Shelley* (Paris 1910) 438); S. read them the same summer (*Mary Jnl* i 176–7), requested them in an edition 'printed distinctly from the Iliad or Odyssey' from Lackington, Allen & Co. in October (*L* i 565) and evidently obtained this as he was billed for it in November (*Nbk 11* f. 9). The edition sent, as *Webb* 350–1 has shown, was G. Hermann's *Homeri Hymni et Epigrammata* (Leipzig 1806); S.'s versions are drafted in *Nbk 11*, in Hermann's order and numbering, working backwards: 'Castor & Pollux' is headed '33' in the MS, 'Earth' '30', and 'Minerva' '28'. 'Vesta' (Hestia, no. 29) was omitted (S. wrote the title in due sequence but crossed it out and passed on to translate 'Minerva'). As was customary at the time, S. used the Latin equivalents of Greek names. Webb is mistaken, however, in suggesting that the final invocation of 'Castor & Pollux' was omitted because S. had not noticed the continuation of the text overleaf in Hermann, as S. did begin to translate the invocation (a mistake compounded in *BSM* xviii, Introduction lv and 272, even though the transcription of *Nbk 11* p. 233 does give the passage, as 'Farewell [?Ty ni iride], who wish'). His drafts suggest that S. may at first have contemplated omitting all the final invocations (see note to lines 25–8 of 'To the Sun'). By 20 January 1818 he was working on his translations (*Mary Jnl* i 191), having probably begun them earlier under the stimulus of Hogg's visit to Marlow (3–19 January) as S. wrote to him three days after his departure to say 'The Hymns go on' (*L* i 595). Composition was interrupted, however, by an attack of ophthalmia announced in the same letter, and then by the move from Albion House, in preparation for Italy, on 10 February. This may be the point at which the work finally broke off, by which time S. had translated the first five Hymns, each with a fair copy, and had drafted a version of the 'Hymn to Venus' up to line 58 of the Greek original. He ordered a copy of George Chapman's translation of the Hymns on 22 January, '*if possible* by tomorrows Coach' (*L* i 594), but even if he received

---

40–1. Cp. Sydney Owenson, *The Missionary: an Indian Tale* (1811) i 161: 'her dark and flowing tresses left an odour on the air, which penetrated his senses'. S. had been deeply influenced by this novel in 1811 (*L* i 107).

44. Omitted in *Harvard Nbk*. Alas that the torn heart can bleed but not forget *Nbk 5*.

this quickly there is no clear evidence of its use here (but see notes to lines 4 and 17 of 'To the Sun'). He does not seem to have referred to Latin translations either, as he did later for the 'Hymn to Mercury'. For further detailed discussion of the circumstances and implications of S.'s translations see *BSM* xviii Introduction liv–lvi.

S.'s translation of the Hymns are skilful and confident, adapting the Gk to English rhyme with impressive fluency. There are critical discussions of the 'Hymns' in *Webb* 63–79, and in Jennifer Wallace, *Shelley and Greece* (1997) 99–104. Among the motivations of S.'s choice of the 'Hymns' for the translation Webb stresses the intrinsic quality of the poems and their likeness to S.'s own work in their empathy with Nature. To which might be added their celebration of 'the graceful religion of the Greeks' (*L* ii 230), which he always found more attractive than Christianity (but see Wallace for a different view of S.'s Romantic Hellenism).

Texts from *Nbk 11* pp. 205–34^{rev}; S.'s punctuation in the fair copies has been lightly supplemented where appropriate.

Published in *1840* (nos 156–160), *Relics* (no. 161; see also T. Webb, 'Shelley's "Hymn to Venus": a New Text', *RES* xxi (1970) 318–21).

156
To Castor and Pollux

Ye wild-eyed Muses, sing the twins of Jove,
Whom the fair-ankled Leda, mixed in love
With mighty Saturn's heaven-obscuring Child
On Taygetus, that lofty mountain wild,
5   Brought forth in joy, mild Pollux void of blame
And steed-subduing Castor, heirs of fame.

These are the powers who earthborn mortals save
And ships, whose flight is swift along the wave.
When wintry tempests o'er the savage sea
10   Are raging, and the sailors tremblingly
Call on the twins of Jove with prayer and vow,
Gathered in fear upon the the lofty prow,
And sacrifice with snow-white lambs, — the wind
And the huge billow bursting close behind

Title. The Gk title is 'To the Dioskouroi'.

1. twins of Jove] The Dioscuri, 'sons of Jupiter', were twin brothers born of Leda, wife of Tyndarus, King of Sparta, after Jupiter had visited her in the form of a swan. They were regarded as patrons of navigation, having suppressed piracy in the Hellespont and quelled a storm during their voyage with Jason and the Argonauts.

6. steed-subduing Castor] Castor was famed for his management of horses.

9. o'er] in *BSM* xviii.

12. prow,] 'poop' in the Gk. (see also *Cyclops* 18).

15   Even then beneath the weltering waters bear
        The staggering ship — they suddenly appear
        On yellow wings rushing athwart the sky,
        And lull the blasts in mute tranquillity,
        And strew the waves o'er the white Ocean's head —
20   Fair omens of the voyage; from the toil and dread
        The sailors rest, rejoicing in the sight,
        And plough the quiet sea in safe delight.

        Farewell Tyndarides who ride [

157
To the Moon

        Daughters of Jove, whose voice is melody!
        Muses, who know and rule all minstrelsy!
        Sing the wide-wingèd Moon. Around the earth
        From her immortal head in Heaven shot forth
5   Far light is scattered — boundless glory springs
        Where'er she spreads her many-beaming wings;
        The lampless air glows round her golden crown.

        But when the Moon divine from Heaven is gone
        Under the sea, her beams within abide:
10   Till, bathing her fair limbs in Ocean's tide,
        Clothing her form in garments glittering far,

---

19. *o'er the white Ocean's head*] Alt. from 'on the white Ocean's bed' (*BSM* xviii reads *on* in both alternatives). The superseded reading suggests the sea-bottom, not its surface. The draft tried 'breast' (*canc.*), and 'plain' (to rhyme with 'pain'; *canc.*) before 'bed'.

20. *omens*] omen *BSM* xviii.

23. *Tyndarides*] i.e. legally, sons of Tyndarus. This half-line exists only in the draft (see headnote), and *ride* is *canc.* The Gk. text continues '. . . on swift horses', before the formula of conclusion.

¶157 Title. The Gk title is 'To Selene'.

3. *wide-wingèd*] wide winged *Nbk 11*. i.e. with wings of wide span (Gk 'with stretched-out wings'). Cp. 'Lines written in the Bay of Lerici' 8–12, of the crescent moon.

5–6. *springs . . . many-beaming wings;*] S.'s own metaphor, following 'wide-wingèd'; the Gk says only 'springs from her shining light'.

8. *Moon divine from Heaven*] Moon, divine from Heaven, *Nbk 11*; but the commas were left over from *Moon, deserting Heaven*, canc.

9. *Under*] Written in pencil next to the original reading *Beneath*; *BSM* xviii reads the pencil as '[?below]'.

10. *fair*] *Nbk 11*; bright *uncanc. alt.*

And having yoked to her immortal car
The beam-invested steeds, whose necks on high
Curve back, she drives to a remoter sky,
15 A western Crescent, borne impetuously.
Then is made full the circle of her light,
And as she grows, her beams more bright and bright
Are poured from Heaven, where she is hovering then
A wonder and a sign to mortal men.

20 The Son of Saturn with this glorious Power
Mingled in love and sleep — to whom she bore
Pandeia, a bright maid of beauty rare
Among the Gods whose lives eternal are.

Hail Queen, great Moon, white-armed Divinity,
25 Fair-haired and favourable, thus with thee
My song beginning, by its music sweet
Shall make immortal many a glorious feat
Of demigods; to those enslaved in song
Whose mouths are sweet as love, such themes belong.

158
To the Sun

Offspring of Jove, Calliope, once more
To the bright Sun thy hymn of music pour;
Whom to the Child of starclad Heaven and Earth
Euryphaëssa, large-eyed Nymph, gave birth;

15. *A western Crescent*] The Gk has 'at evening in the mid-month' (= at full moon).

18. *where she is hovering*] Again S.'s metaphor, following 'wide-wingèd'.

20. *Son of Saturn*] Jupiter.

28–9. *to those enslaved . . . belong*] with lovely lips, so well / Which minstrels, servants of the Muses, tell *Nbk 11*, corrected in pencil; see *BSM* xviii 264 for a different transcription. The earlier reading is closer to the Gk but syntactically distorted.

¶158 *Title* The Gk title is 'To Helios'.

1. *Calliope* The epic Muse.

2. *hymn*] hymns *BSM* xviii.

4. *Euryphaëssa*] Also known as Theia or Thea. *gave birth;*] brought forth *Nbk 11 canc.* The substitution improves the rhyme but confuses the grammar. The sense is that E. bore her child the Sun to her lover Hyperion. Chapman's version using the same construction, 'Whom ox-ey'd Euryphaëssa gave birth / To the bright Seed of starry Heaven and Earth', might possibly have influenced S.; a direct object is however commonly accepted in the phrase 'gave him birth'.

5   Euryphaëssa, divine-famed sister fair
            Of great Hyperion, who to him did bear
            A race of loveliest children: the young Morn
            Whose arms are like twin roses newly born,
            The fair-haired Moon and the immortal Sun
10   Who, borne by heavenly steeds, his race doth run
            Unconquerably, illuming the abodes
            Of mortal men and the eternal Gods.
            Fiercely look forth his awe-inspiring eyes
            Beneath his golden helmet, whence arise
15   And are shot forth afar, clear beams of light:
            His countenance with radiant glory bright
            Beneath his graceful head far shines around,
            And the light vest with which his limbs are bound
            Of woof etherial, delicately twined,
20   Glows in the stream of the uplifting wind.
            His rapid steeds soon bear him to the West
            Where their steep flight his hands divine arrest,
            And the fleet car with yoke of gold, which he
            Sends from bright Heaven beneath the shadowy sea.

25   Hail, King! propitious grant a life serene.
            With thee beginning, [still] my song
            The demigods and heroes shall make known
            Whose deeds to mortals by the Gods were shown.

---

5. *divine-famed sister*] *Nbk 11* has 'the famed sister', with 'the' canc. and 'divine' pencilled in the margin, so S.'s intention could have been either the present reading, or 'divine sister', or 'famèd sister'.

17. *head*] *Nbk 11*; hair locks *uncanc. alt.* The Gk of lines 16–17 means: 'the bright locks streaming from his temples gracefully frame his far-seen face'. S. takes τηλαυγές, 'far-shining', to mean 'throwing light to a distance', as if by a torch, possibly again influenced by Chapman:
            The glorious cheer
      Of his far-shining face up to his crown
      Casts circular radiance, that comes streaming down
      About his temples.

20. *uplifting*] Not in the Gk.

25–8. S's fair copy in *Nbk 11* ends before this invocation with a line-count of '24', but these four lines are then added in pencil.

26. *[still]*] shall *Nbk 11*. Lines 26–7 were left unrevised with a future tense too many, but one of them could be a dittographic slip.

159
To the Earth, Mother of All

O universal Mother, who dost keep
From everlasting thy foundations deep,
Eldest of things, great Earth, I sing of thee.
All shapes that have their dwelling in the Sea,
5   All things that fly, or on the ground divine
Live, move, and there are nourished — these are thine,
These from thy wealth thou dost sustain — from thee
Fair babes are born, and fruits on every tree
Hang ripe and large, revered Divinity.

10   The life of mortal men beneath thy sway
Is held: thy power both gives and takes away.
Happy are they whom thy mild favours nourish,
All things unstinted round them grow and flourish;
For such, endures the life-sustaining field
15   Its load of harvest, and their cattle yield
Large increase, and their house with wealth is filled.
Such honoured dwell in cities fair and free,
The homes of lovely women, prosperously;
Their sons exult in youth's new budding gladness,
20   And their fresh daughters free from care or sadness
With bloom-inwoven dance and happy song
On the soft flowers the meadow grass among
Leap round them sporting — such delights by thee
Are given, rich Power, revered Divinity!

Title. Below the title on both draft and fair copy S. wrote 'See Pliny', perhaps intending a note on the 'Universal Mother'. Pliny's section on the Earth (*Nat. Hist.* II. lxiii) begins: 'Sequiter terra, cui uni rerum naturae partium eximia propter merita cognomen indidimus maternae venerationis. Sic hominum illa ut caelum dei . . .' ('Next comes Earth, the one realm of Nature on which we have for exceptional merit conferred the name of venerable Mother. She is to men what heaven is to God . . .')

2. From everlasting] A Biblical phrase without equivalent in the Gk, recalling *Psalms* xciii 2: 'Thy throne is established of old: thou art from everlasting'.

8–9. fruits . . . large,] Synecdoche for the more comprehensive Gk: 'rich produce'.

12. they] them *BSM* xviii.

13. them] thee *BSM* xviii.

14. such] Nbk 11. them *uncanc. alt.*

16. their] the *BSM* xviii.

25   Mother of Gods, thou wife of starry Heaven,
        Farewell! be thou propitious, and be given
        A happy life for this brief melody.
        Nor thou nor other songs shall unremembered be.

160
To Minerva

        I sing the glorious Power with azure eyes,
        Athenian Pallas, tameless, chaste and wise,
        Tritogenia, town-preserving Maid,
        Revered and mighty; from his awful head
5   Whom Jove brought forth in warlike armour dressed,
        Golden, all-radiant: wonder strange possessed
        The everlasting Gods that shape to see,
        Shaking a javelin keen, impetuously
        Rush from the crest of aegis-bearing Jove:
10   Fearfully Heaven was shaken and did move
        Beneath the might of the Cerulean-eyed;
        Earth dreadfully resounded, far and wide,
        And lifted from its depths, the Sea swelled high
        In purple billows, the tide suddenly
15   Stood still, and great Hyperion's Son long time
        Checked his swift steeds, till where she stood sublime
        Pallas from her immortal shoulders threw
        The arms divine: wise Jove rejoiced to view.

        Child of the Aegis-bearer, hail to thee!
20   Nor thine, nor others' praise shall unremembered be.

25–8. The invocation is added to the fair copy in different ink and writing.

¶160 *Title*. The Gk title is 'To Athena'. Athena/Minerva was goddess of wisdom, war, and the liberal arts. S. wrote '28' adjoining the title, the number of the Hymn in the edition he was using, missing out no. 29.

3. *Tritogenia*] *Nbk 11* appears to read 'Trilogenia' (see *BSM* xviii 252–3); but S. probably left the *t* uncrossed; the reading here adopted means 'Trito-born', i.e. born at Lake Triton, near modern Benghazi in Libya.   *town-preserving*] 'Protectress of the city'. Athena was tutelary goddess of Athens.

6. *wonder strange*] wonder mute *Nbk 11*. No epithet in the Gk.

15. *Hyperion's Son*] the sun (cp. 'To the Sun' 6–12).

16. *till*] that *BSM* xviii.

161
Hymn to Venus

Muse, sing the deeds of Golden Aphrodite
Who wakens with her smile the lulled delight
Of sweet desire, taming the eternal kings
Of Heaven, and men, and all the living things
5   Who fleet along the air, or whom the Sea
Or Earth, with her maternal ministry
Nourish innumerable: thy delight
All seek [   ] O crownèd Aphrodite.

Three spirits canst thou nor deceive nor quell:
10   Minerva, child of Jove, who loves too well
Wide war, and linkèd combat, and the fame
Of glorious deeds, to heed thy gentle flame,
Who first to Earth-born artists [   ] taught
How brass for cart and waggon should be wrought,
15   And to soft virgins gave the noble gift
Of weaving wide and the industrious weft;
Diana, sober-stoled golden-shafted Queen,
Is tamed not by thy smiles — the shadows green

Title. The Gk title is 'To Aphrodite' (no. 5 in the edn used by S.) This incomplete translation exists only in the first draft.

1. Muse, sing] Muse sings *Nbk 11* (an evident slip). *Aphrodite*] Pronounced with three syllables, for the rhyme (also in line 8).

5. Who] *Written over* That *Nbk 11* That *RES.*

7. innumerable:] A word, and cadence, echoing Milton in similar contexts (cp. *Comus* 713: *Paradise Lost* vii 156, 400).

8. Wide space left in *Nbk 11*, though nothing in the Gk is omitted.

11. linkèd] mingling *uncanc. alt. in Nbk 11, RES, BSM* xviii. The distinction is between the fighting of armies and of individuals or small parties. *fame*] name *RES.*

13. Space left in *Nbk 11* although no omission in the Gk.

14. brass for cart] brass – [fair] cart *RES*; brass from cart *BSM* xviii. In *Nbk 11 for* is unclearly shaped, but is the only word that makes sense. The Gk says that she taught craftsmen 'to make war-chariots and cars wrought with brass'.

15. gift] skill *RES.*

16. weft] will *RES*; war *BSM* xviii. The lateral threads on the loom constitute the weft: hence the art of 'weaving wide'. The Gk does not specify any particular domestic art.

17. sober-stoled] *RES* omits these words (*BSM* xviii offers '[?gold] [?hand]'); *sober* seems clear, but *-stoled* could be *-hued* or *-toned* (cp. no. 201, 'Translation of part of Bion's Lament for Adonis' 4). There is no corresponding epithet in the Gk.

18. smiles –] smiles, *Nbk 11*; smiles; *RES.*

Of the wide woods, the bow, the dance, the lute,
20   And piercing cries, amid the swift pursuit
Of beasts among waste mountains, such delight
Is hers, and men who know and do the right.
Nor Saturn's first-born daughter, Vesta chaste,
Whom Neptune and Apollo wooed the last
25   Through the high will of aegis-bearing Jove. —
But sternly then she spurned the ills of love
And touched her mighty father's head and swore
An oath not unperformed, that evermore
A virgin she would live 'mid deities,
30   Divine: her sire for such delightful ties
Renounced, gave glorious [   ]; thus in his hall
She sits and feeds luxuriously: o'er all,
In every fane, her honours first arise;
To men, the eldest of divinities.

35   These spirits she persuades not nor deceives.
But none beside escape, so well she weaves
Her unseen toils; nor mortal men, nor Gods
Who live secure in their serene abodes.
She won the soul of him whose fierce delight
40   Is thunder, first in glory and in might;
And as she willed, his mighty mind deceiving,
With mortal limbs his deathless limbs inweaving,
Concealed him from his spouse and sister fair

---

19. the dance, the lute,] Nbk 11 is confused but these readings seem secure, although they are cramped. BSM xviii does not offer definite alternatives.

22. know] knew BSM xviii.

26. sternly then she] sternly she RES. *then* is *canc.* but is required for the metre.

29. deities,] deities Nbk 11. All deities are divine, but not all virgin.

30. such] own BSM xviii.

31. Above *great recompense, thus* (canc.) S. wrote: *'gave glorious [   ]*, where the bracket represents a tiny hyphen-like mark and one indeterminate letter, perhaps *a* or *e*. S. may have thought momentarily that cancelling *thus* would leave *Renounced, gave glorious recompense; in his hall* metrically acceptable; otherwise a word such as *gain, fee*, or *boon* is required. RES reads: *Renounced, [gave recompense] – thus in his hall.* The Gk says: 'Her father gave her high honour instead of marriage.'

32–4. These three lines are canc. by a wavy line.

37–8. S. made a mark 'x' between theses lines in the left-hand margin, but supplied no corresponding note.

38. This line has no equivalent in the Gk. *secure*] Carefree (Lat. *securus*).

42–3. With mortal limbs . . . sister fair] i.e. Venus caused him to have affairs with mortal women, unbeknown to Juno (Hera), who was both his wife and sister. The Gk is in the present tense.

Whom to wise Saturn ancient Rhea bare,
45 Most glorious and most fair of goddesses:
And Jupiter in deathless counsels wise
Took Juno, a chaste wife . . . with deep devise
In Venus Jove did soft desire awaken,
That by her own enchantments overtaken
50 She might, no more from human union free,
Burn for a nursling of mortality:
For once amid the assembled deities
The laughter-loving Venus from her eyes
Shot forth the light of a soft starlight smile
55 And boasting said that she, secure the while,
Could mix at will with Goddesses or Gods
The mortal tenants of Earth's dark abodes,
And mortal offspring from a deathless stem
She could produce in scorn and spite of them —
60 Therefore he poured desire into her breast
Of young Anchises, [   ]
Folding his herds among the mossy fountains
Of the wide Ida's many-folded mountains,
Whom Venus saw and loved, and the love clung
65 Like wasting fire her senses wild among,
And to [

44. ancient] constant *BSM* xviii.

45. Line canc. in MS.

47. with deep devise] a new device *BSM* xviii.

52–5. For once . . . And boasting said] S. makes the tense first past then conditional, whereas the Gk is the other way round, i.e. 'lest Venus should one day mockingly boast that she had mixed gods with mortals' etc.

56. Goddessess or Gods] Gods [?< >ssemblyd] Gods *BSM* xviii.

61. Line blank after *Anchises* in *Nbk 11* and without a rhyme for *breast*.

62. folding] feeding *BSM* xviii.

63. many-folded] Canc. in *Nbk 11*, with ακροπολοις ('lofty'), the Gk word of the original, written above.

66. And to] Omitted in *RES*.

162
Lament for Bion

This fragment is a translation of the opening lines of Moschus's Idyll iii, which was to become an important source of *Adonais*. Moschus was a Gk Bucolic poet of the 2nd century BC; for S.'s translations of his Idylls iv and v see nos 107 and 204 (Walter Peck (*TLS*, 7 April 1921) has shown that the Gk edition of the Bucolics used by S. was *Theocriti, Bionis et Moschi Carmina Bucolica*, ed. L. C. Valckenaer, Edinburgh 1810). Mary's jnl records that S. read Theocritus and Moschus in Gk in 1816 (*Mary Jnl* i 97), but these lines probably date from January or February 1818 (*SC* v 192–3 suggests vaguer parameters for the date, 'at Marlow', i.e. March 1817– February 1818); Hunt's translation of the Idyll was published in *Foliage* (1818), and as *Forman 1876–7* surmises the two poems may well have originated in a timed competition of the kind that produced 'Ozymandias' and 'To the Nile' (see headnotes to nos 145 and 163; it is curious that Hunt, like S., also translated the same opening lines of Idyll iv, published as 'Sea and Land' in *The Examiner*, 21 January 1816: could these poems also have been written in a competition?). The opening of Hunt's translation of Idyll iii is less free than S.'s:

> Moan with me, moan, ye woods and Dorian Waters,
> And weep, ye rivers, the delightful Bion;
> Ye plants, now stand in tears; murmur, ye groves;
> Ye flowers, sigh forth your odours with sad buds;
> Flush deep, ye roses and anemones;
> And more than ever now, oh hyacinth, show
> Your written sorrows: – the sweet singer's dead.

The poem is not now thought to be by Moschus, but by an unknown pupil of Bion (see *The Greek Bucolic Poets*, trans. J. M. Edmonds (Loeb) 1912, 443). S.'s translation was first published in *Forman 1876–7* from a MS originally in *Hunt MSS* which was subsequently owned by S. R. Townshend Mayer and then H. Buxton Forman. The MS disappeared after its sale in May 1934, and re-entered the public domain only with the publication of *SC* v and vi in 1973, when it emerged that it had been acquired by the Pforzheimer. Forman had described the MS as 'written upon the same paper with the concluding portion of the *Essay on Christianity*' (then assumed to have been written in 1815, but now certainly datable to 1817), although *SC* v 192 explains that at some point between 1920 and 1934 the portion of the sheet containing the conclusion of the 'Essay on Christianity' was removed.

Text from SC 394 (*SC* v 190).

Published in *Forman 1876–7* iv 235.

Ye Dorian woods and waves lament aloud,
Augment your tide, O streams, with fruitless tears,
For the beloved Bion is no more.
Let every tender herb and plant and flower
5   From each dejected bud and drooping bloom
Shed dews of liquid sorrow, and with breath
Of melancholy sweetness on the wind
Diffuse its languid love; let roses blush,
Anemones grow paler for the loss
10   Their dells have known, and thou, O hyacinth,
Utter thy legend now — yet more, dumb flower!
Than 'ah, alas'; thine is no common grief.
Bion the [   ] is no more.

163
To the Nile

Written at Leigh Hunt's house in Lisson Grove on 4 February 1818, in competition
with Keats and Hunt within a time-limit of 15 minutes. Keats told his brothers on
14th: 'The Wednesday before last Shelley, Hunt and I wrote each a Sonnet on the
River Nile, some day you shall read them all' (*Letters of John Keats*, ed. H. E. Rollins,
2 vols, Cambridge, Mass. 1958, i 227–8). S.'s sonnet was drafted on the MS of Keats's

1–2. Cp. Spenser, *Shepheardes Calender*, August, 151–6:

Ye wastefull woodes beare witnesse of my woe,
Wherein my plaints did oftentimes resound:
Ye carelesse byrds are priuie to my cryes,
Which in your songs were wont to make a part:
Thou pleasaunt spring hast luld me oft a sleepe,
Whose streames my tricklinge teares did ofte augment.

1. *Dorian*] dorian *SC*. *aloud,*] aloud *SC*. aloud, – *Forman 1876–7*.

2. *O streams,*] o streams *SC*. *tears,*] tears *SC*. *SC* has *sorrow* at the end of the line as an uncanc.
alt. Apart from the vocative *O streams* this line has no obvious equivalent in the Gk.

3. *more.*] more *SC*.   4. *flower*] flower, *Forman 1876–7*.   5. *bloom*] bloom, *Forman 1876–7*.

6. *dews of liquid*] S. embellishes the Gk, which has no direct equivalent.

7–8. *Of melancholy . . . languid love;*] These lines are S.'s addition.

8. *love;*] love, *SC*. *blush,*] blush *SC*.

9–10. S.'s trans. here is very free, but it does recall νάπαι, 'dells', from line 1 of the Gk.

10. *known,*] known; *Forman 1876–7*. *thou, O*] thou o *SC*.

11. *now –*] now – alas [canc.] – *SC*. *flower!*] flower, *Forman 1876–7*.

12. *'ah, alas';*] ah alas, *SC*. alas!' – *Forman 1876–7*. *grief.*] grief – *Forman 1876–7*. *Thine is no
common grief* is S.'s addition.

13. *more.*] more *SC*. S. left a blank in the MS. *Forman 1876–7* filled it in with '[sweetest singer]',
'which Shelley himself would, surely, have applauded as a substitute for his blank space' (*1975*
358). In fact Forman's interpolation is presumably taken from the Hunt translation quoted
in the headnote; it is possible that S. left a blank because he did not know the Gk word
μελικτάς, 'singer or player, esp. flute-player' (Scott and Liddell).

'Robin Hood'; and until it was published in the *St. James's Magazine* in 1876, his contribution to the contest was believed to have been 'Ozymandias'. Leigh Hunt himself, having forgotten the circumstances, misled Monckton Milnes to that effect in 1847 (*The Keats Circle*, ed. H. E. Rollins, 2 vols, Cambridge, Mass., 2nd edn 1965, ii 181–2). The MS was in *Hunt MSS* (S. apparently having left it with Hunt after composition, without then or afterwards troubling to make a copy), and having passed into the possession of R. Townshend Mayer it was eventually sold by Quaritch in 1886 to Isabella Stewart Gardner. It is now in the Isabella Stewart Gardner Museum in Boston. For a detailed account together with a facsimile and transcript, see *MYR* viii 165–9, 178–9. What prompted the poets' choice of subject is impossible to guess: as Edmund Blunden observed (*Leigh Hunt* (1930) 119) 'It was the period when Egypt was even more in the fashion in London than during the raid on Tutankhamen'. S.'s sonnet is much more regularly Petrarchan than is his usual practice; as Hunt's and Keats's efforts are similarly disciplined, there may have been a formal as well as a time constraint in the competition.

Text from MS Gardner (reproduced in *MYR* viii 178–9).

Published in *St. James's Magazine and United Empire Review*, ii, new series (March 1876) 647; *Forman 1876–7* iii 410–11.

> Month after month the gathered rains descend
> Drenching yon secret Ethiopian dells,
> And from the desert's ice-girt pinnacles
> Where Frost and Heat in strange embraces blend
> 5   On Atlas, fields of moist snow half depend.
> Girt there with blasts and meteors Tempest dwells
> By Nile's aërial urn, with rapid spells
> Urging those waters to their mighty end.
>
> O'er Egypt's land of Memory floods are level,
> 10   And they are thine, O Nile — and well thou knowest
> That soul-sustaining airs and blasts of evil
> And fruits and poisons spring where'er thou flowest.
> Beware, O Man — for knowledge must to thee
> Like the great flood to Egypt, ever be. —

2. *dells,*] dells MS.

3. *desert's ice-girt*] desarts ice girt MS.

5. *Atlas*] The Atlas Mountains are in NW Africa, but Shelley is imagining the effects of late summer in several areas. The melting of the Atlas snows and the Nile flood as metaphors of expanding knowledge anticipate *PU* II iii 37–42. *fields of moist snow half*] loosened snows no more MS *canc. depend.*] depend MS.

7. *Nile's*] Niles MS. *aërial urn*] Mountain source.

9. The Nile flood irrigates the Egyptian plain annually in August. *level,*] level MS.

10. *thine, O Nile –*] thine o Nile – MS.

11. *blasts of evil*] Injurious winds.

12. *flowest.*] flowest MS.

13. *Beware, O Man –*] Beware o Man – MS.

164
'Now Heaven neglected is by Men'

Orally improvised 30 March 1818 during the crossing of the Alps. Claire
Clairmont recorded in her jnl for 8 April: 'Next Morning we begin the ascent of
Mont Cenis and Shelley sung all the way [his lines quoted] and asserted that the
Mountains are God's *Corps de Ballet* of which the Jung fraue is Mademoiselle Milanie'
(Ashley MS 2819 (1), f. 11ᵛ). Shelley's epigram is a parody of Love's words in Peacock's
Rhododaphne (1818) which Shelley had read in manuscript before leaving England
(*L* i 569):

> Flowers may die on many a stem;
> Fruits may fall from many a tree;
> Not the more for loss of them
> Shall this fair world a desert be: (Canto i 182–5)

– conflated with Orlando's lines to Rosalind in *As You Like It*:

> Why should this a desert be?
> For it is unpeopled? No;
> Tongues I'll hang on every tree,
> That shall civil sayings show. (III ii 125–8).

Text from British Museum Ashley MS 2819 (1), f. 11ᵛ (in Claire C's hand).
Published in *Claire Jnl* 88.

> Now Heaven neglected is by Men
> And Gods are hung upon every tree
> But not the more for loss of them
> Shall this fair world unhappy be.

165
'Listen, listen, Mary mine –'

Composed 4 May 1818 (as dated in *1824*) at an inn in the mountains midway
between Modena and Barbarino di Mugello. This was the eve of the fourth
anniversary of Shelley's first meeting with Mary Godwin after her return from
Dundee, which explains the second of her jnl entries: 'May 4 . . . we begin to ascend
the mountains and sleep in a solitary inn among them *Tuesday* May 5 Our day is
passed in passing the mountains' (*Mary Jnl* i 208).

Text from *Nbk 5* f. 41ᵛ rev.

Published in *1824* 206 (lines 1–6, 8–13), with the title 'Passage of the Apennines'.

Listen, listen, Mary mine —
To the whisper of the Apennine —
It bursts on the roof like the thunder's roar
Or like the sea on a northern shore,
5   Heard in its raging ebb and flow
By the captives pent in the cave below,
And raves up the stairs with a long shrill howl.

The Apennine in the light of day
Is a mighty mountain dim and grey
10   Which between the earth and sky doth lay;
But when night comes, a chaos dread
On the dim starlight then is spread
And the Apennine walks abroad with the storm
Shrouding

166
Mazenghi

Dating this poem 'Naples 1818' in *1824*, Mary Shelley wrote: 'This fragment refers to an event, told in Sismo[n]di's Histoire des Republiques Italiennes, which occurred during the war when Florence finally subdued Pisa, and reduced it to a province. The opening stanzas [i.e. lines 36–53 below] are addressed to the conquering city' (*1824* 257). Shelley was in Naples from 1 December 1818 until 28 February 1819, so December 1818 is a plausible date of composition (this is Paul Dawson's assumption in *BSM* iii Introduction xv). But Mary Shelley seems to have been unfamiliar with *Nbk 5*, which contains Shelley's private verses to Constantia as well as many false starts, and she may have assumed the date and place because Shelley had been reading Sismondi with her at about that time (*Mary Jnl* i 247). The nbk indicates an earlier date. *Nbk 5* bridges the move from England to Italy, illustrating Shelley's unsettled state during his first months abroad; except for

4–6. *Or like . . . cave below*] Perhaps a memory of the dungeons of the Castle of Chillon, described by Byron in *The Prisoner of Chillon* (1816) 115–18:

     Below the surface of the lake
     The dark vault lies wherein we lay:
     We heard it ripple night and day;
     Sounding o'er our heads it knocked.

Shelley's own description is in his letter to Peacock of 12 July 1816 (*L* i 485–6).

7. *with a long shrill howl*] *canc.* in *Nbk 5*. Of this part of the journey Claire Clairmont noted: 'The wind is always high here, and it howls dismally' (*SC* v 454).

8,13. *The Apennine*] Classical writers treated the Apennines as a single mountain ridge (*Appenninus*), and the singular was often used in English too.

10. *lay*] Still in 1818 an acceptable alternative for *lie* (*OED* Lay vii 43).

'Ozymandias', which was written in England, the only completed poems in it are translations. This corresponds with Shelley's confession of 25 July that he had lately found himself 'totally incapable of original composition' (*L* ii 26). *Nbk 5* was begun in England from both ends, with 'Ozymandias' (December 1817) and 'Athanase' (October–December 1817) respectively. The 'Mazenghi' draft begins after the sketch for a Tasso drama (April 1818) and immediately after the lines 'Listen, listen, Mary mine' which can be firmly dated 4 May. 'Mazenghi' was therefore most likely written in May 1818 at Leghorn, near the scene of the poem, and abandoned for *The Cyclops* when its author found himself 'still incapable of original composition'. Sismondi's narrative is severely factual, whereas the poem has much local colour, some of it so accurate it must be 'live'. Vada is less than 20 miles from Leghorn, and the challenge in line 5, 'Visit the tower of Vada', with the present tense in line 7, suggests that Shelley had set an example himself. The Maremma Pisana was dangerously malarial (*Claire Jnl* 158 quotes an Italian rhyme warning visitors to Massa that 'Whoever stays too long / Dies here'), but a visit in May would have been thought relatively safe. Failing such a visit, for which there is no other evidence, Shelley could have read this recently-published volume of Sismondi's History in Leghorn and obtained first-hand local details from the Gisbornes, who were Leghorn residents. The misapprehension about the river (see note to line 108) supports this latter alternative. The title is Mary Shelley's. Garnett learned from Sismondi that the hero's real name was Pietro Marenghi, so 'Marenghi' has replaced the name of Shelley's hero in all subsequent *eds*. But *Locock Ex* 43 showed that the Christian name Shelley had considered using was 'Albert'; consequently *Hutchinson* printed '[Albert] Marenghi', a name that is neither authentic nor Shelley's. There is no reason to think that Shelley did not know the real name: he shows a close knowledge of this part of Sismondi's work, correcting his name 'Vado', and did in fact write 'Marenghi' in line 6, but altered the 'r' firmly to 'z' (*Nbk 5*, f. 42ʳ), and then kept constantly to 'Mazenghi', perhaps to avoid associations with Marengo, Italian scene of Napoleon's bloody victory eighteen years earlier. Sismondi's account of the event, which happened in the year 1405, is as follows:

Les Florentins ne croyoient guère possible d'ouvrir une brèche aux murs de Pise, en sorte qu'ils se proposoient de réduire la ville par la famine, tandis que leur armée attaquoit successivement les divers châteaux du territoire. Les Pisans, de leur côté, s'efforçoient de se pourvoir de vivres; ils envoyèrent quelques galères chercher des blés en Sicile, l'une d'elles, surprise à son retour par des vaisseaux que les Florentins avoient fair armer à Gênes, se réfugia sous la tour de Vado. Un Florentin, nommé Pierre Marenghi, qui erroit loin de sa patrie, frappé d'une sentence capitale, saisit cette circonstance pour rendre à ses conçitoyens un service signalé. Il s'élança du rivage, un flambeau à la main, et s'approcha de la galère à la nage, malgré les traits qu'on lançoit contre lui. Percé de trois blessures, il continua longtemps à se tenir sous la proue, en soulevant son flambeau, jusqu'à ce que le feu se fût communiqué à la galère ennemie de manière à ne plus s'éteindre. Elle brûla en face de la tour de Vado, tandis que Pierre Marenghi regagna le rivage. Il fut rappelé ensuite dans sa patrie avec honneur. (J. C. Simonde de Sismondi, *Histoire des Républiques Italiennes du Moyen Âge*, Paris 1818 (2nd edn) viii 142–3.)

The poem has attracted very little critical comment, although there are brief discussions in Timothy Morton, *Shelley and the Revolution in Taste* (1994) 116–18, and Alan Weinberg, *Shelley's Italian Experience* (1991) 98–100.

Text from *Nbk* 5 ff. 42ʳ–49ʳ.

Published in *1824* 257–9 (lines 36–59, 66–95); *1839* iii 70 (lines 171–6, as separate fragment); *Rossetti 1870* ii 314–19 (lines 1–8, 13–23, 25–7, 30–59, 66–170, from Garnett's transcript); *Locock Ex* 43 (lines 60–4); *BSM* iii 168–97 (facsimile and transcription of MS).

166
Mazenghi

Let those who pine in pride or in revenge,
    Or think that ill for ill should be repaid,
Who barter wrong for wrong, until the exchange
    Ruins the merchants of such thriftless trade —
5   Visit the tower of Vada, and unlearn
Such bitter faith beside Mazenghi's urn.

A massy tower yet overhangs the town,
    A scattered group of squalid dwellings now;
Like plague-infected corpses, up and down
10   Men, women, children crawl; and from below
The iron sound of chains clanks up [   ]
    As [   ]

Another scene ere wise Etruria knew
    Its second ruin, through internal strife,
15   And Tyrants through the breach of discord threw

5. *Vada,*] *Nbk 5, 1824*. Vado *eds*, misled by Sismondi. Now a pleasant market town on the coast road from Leghorn to Cecina.

7–11. This stanza must depend partly on eye-witness information. The Torre di Vada is indeed massive, and its ground floor was once used as a prison, but it was never very tall. It is now on shore well away from the town: Shelley cancelled 'town' in *Nbk 5* to make line 7 read 'overhangs the sea', before reverting to his first choice of word (f. 42ʳ). But the later description could have been transferred from early adverse impressions of Pisa, which Mary Shelley described on 13 May 1818 as 'a dull town . . . a tower . . . criminals condemned to labour work publickly in the streets heavily ironed . . . These poor wretches look sallow and dreadfully wretched and you could get into no street but you heard the clanking of their chains' (*Mary L* i 66–7). In Mary S.'s *Valperga* wreckage from the vessel carrying Euthanasia to Sicily is washed up on the shore near 'Vado, a tower on the sea beach of the Maremma' (*MSW* iii 322).

8–11. in its grey rents the wild fig and the brier / Take root *Nbk 5 partially canc.*

9–12. Omitted *Locock 1911*.

10. *Men, women, children,*] The wretched natives *Nbk 5 canc.*

13. *Another scene ere*] 'Conditions were different before . . .' 'Etruria' was the Roman name for a region including modern Tuscany.

15. *threw*] *Nbk 5* canc. 'Chain' seems intended to combine the meanings of 'chain-shot' and 'slave-chains'.

The chain which binds and kills — as death to life,
As winter to fair flowers (though some be poison),
So monarchy succeeds to Freedom's foison.

In Pisa's church a cup of sculptured gold
20   Was brimming with the blood of feuds forsworn:
A sacrament more holy ne'er of old
    Etrurians mingled, 'mid the shades forlorn
Of moon-illumined forests, when the might
Of the [   ]

25   And reconciling factions wet their lips
    With that dread wine, and swear to keep each spirit
Undarkened by their country's last eclipse,
    In liberty; and this [   ] lives yet
In Sismondi's [   ]

30   Was Florence the liberticide? that band
    Of free and glorious brothers, who had planted
Like one green isle 'mid Ethiopian sand
    A nation amid slaveries: disenchanted
Of many impious faiths, true, wise, and just,
35   Doth Florence gorge the sated tyrant's spoil?

O foster-nurse of man's abandoned glory
    Since Athens its great Mother sunk in splendour,
Thou shadowest forth that mighty Shape in story,
    As ocean its wrecked fanes; severe yet tender,

18. foison.] Abundance.   *19. In Pisa's church*] In Pisa's hall *Nbk* 5 canc. The 'hall' was possibly the Baptistry, the 'church' the Duomo.

19–29. Sismondi describes how, after the Florentines had rejected their peace overtures in 1405, the Pisans prepared for further resistance by solemnly abjuring their internal feuds, especially that between the exiled Gambacorti and the ruling Raspanti families: 'l'oubli des injures passées et une réconciliation sans réserve furent jurés sur les autels; les chefs des deux partis firent couler leur propre sang dans la coupe consacrée, avant de la boire en commun; et de nombreux mariages durent sceller la paix entre les deux factions' (Sismondi viii 142).

30–5. 'La politique entière de l'Italie étoit agitée dans les conseils de Florence; et ce peuple, si zélé pour la liberté, maintenoit avec la sienne celle de la nation dont il faisoit partie . . . Florence, pendant tout le quatorzième siècle, eut un gouvernement vraiment démocratique . . . en jetant à présent un coup d'oeil sur tout le siècle . . . nous trouverons sans doute la conduite des Florentins juste, noble et généreuse, pendant le cours de cette période, plus que celle d'aucun autre état' (Sismondi viii 34–6).

34. true, wise, and just,] Omitted Locock 1911. The first two words are canc. in *Nbk* 5.

35. spoil?] prey? *Nbk* 5 canc. Neither word provides a rhyme.

38. that mighty Shape] Man's glory. Florence is seen as inheriting from Athens the task of recreating in art man's past achievements.

40   The light-invested Herald Poesy
             Was drawn from the dim world [   ] by Thee.

        And thou in painting didst transcribe all taught
           By loftiest meditations; marble knew
        The sculptor's fearless soul, and as he wrought,
45   The grace of his own power and freedom grew;
        And more than all heroic, just, sublime,
        Thou wert among the false . . . was this thy crime?

        Yes, for on Pisa's marble walls the twine
           Of desert weeds hangs garlanded: the snake
50   Inhabits its wrecked palaces; in thine
           A beast of subtler venom now doth make
        Its lair, and soils their glories overthrown,
        And thus thy victim's fate is as thine own.

        The sweetest flowers are ever frail and rare,
55   And love and freedom blossom but to wither;
        And good and ill like vines entangled are
           So that their grapes may oft be plucked together.
        Divide the vintage ere thou drink, then make
        Thy heart rejoice for dead Mazenghi's sake.

60   Albert Mazenghi was a Florentine;
           If he had wealth, or children, or a wife,
         Or friends or fame, or cherished thoughts which twine
           The sights and sounds of home with life's own life,

41. [*] by Thee.*] to welcome thee *Nbk 5 canc.* The revision was uncompleted but makes better sense. Lines 40–1 may both be canc. by a wavy line.

42–3. And thou . . . meditations] 'You translated into pictorial art everything established by man's highest thinking'. In the margin is a cryptic (presumably later) note: 'To remember that truth babies to be kept secret from William'. The fourth word is very doubtful and could be 'both' or 'birth'. The phrasing sounds like some educational experiment.

46–7. And . . . false] *1824, eds.* Comma only after *just* in *Nbk 5*; but S. means 'Although you were more heroic [etc.] than any other city state, you still behaved no better in this instance'.

48–50. Yes . . . palaces;] The subjugation of Pisa by Florence in 1406 led to a depopulation and decay from which it had never recovered. Hunt in 1822, however, thought that 'Its desolate aspect is much exaggerated . . . though it is true that grass grows in some of the streets, it is only in the remotest' (*The Liberal* i (1822) 116–17).

51. A beast of subtler venom] Austrian military rule, reimposed by the treaty of Vienna.

56. Mazenghi's action was magnanimous, though it was in a bad cause.

60. Albert Mazenghi] [Pietro] Marenghi *Locock Ex;* [Albert] Marenghi *Hutchinson;* Albert *Nbk 5 canc.* (see headnote).

62. or fame,] [or farm,] *Locock Ex, Hutchinson.*

Of these he was despoiled; and Florence sent
65   Out of the [   ]

No record of his crime remains in story,
    But if the morning bright as evening shone
It was some high and holy deed, by glory
    Pursued into forgetfulness which won
70 From the blind crowd thus made secure and free
The patriot's meed, toil, death and infamy.

For when by sound of trumpet was declared
    A price upon his life, and there was set
A penalty of blood on all who shared
75   So much of water with him as might wet
His lips which speech divided not . . . he went
Alone, as you may guess, to banishment.

'Mid desert mountains, like a hunted beast
    He hid himself, and hunger, toil and cold
80 Month after month endured: it was a feast
    When'er he found those globes of deep red gold
Which in the woods the strawberry tree doth bear,
Suspended in their emerald atmosphere.

And in the roofless huts of vast morasses,
85   Deserted by the fever-stricken serf,
All overgrown with reeds and long rank grasses
    And hillocks heaped of moss-inwoven turf,
And where the huge and speckled aloe made,
Rooted in stones, a broad and pointed shade,

65. *Omitted Locock 1911.*

67. *But if the morning bright as evening shone*] But if we may conjecture from this tale *Nbk 5* canc.

69. *forgetfulness which won*] *Nbk 5*; forgetfulness, which won *1824, eds*. First the deed is forgotten, then its renown; and forgetfulness is what causes the crowd's blind reversal of acclaim.

76. *lips which speech divided not . . .*] i.e. he accepted his sentence in silence.

81–3. *those globes . . . emerald atmosphere.*] Opposite 'Ozymandias' in *Nbk 5* S. noted from 'Gibbon Vol. 8 p. 228': 'A thousand globes of Gold suspended in the dome', and must either have remembered or noticed his quotation when drafting 'Mazenghi'. Gibbon describes 'the thousand globes of gold suspended in the dome, to imitate the motions of the planets and the constellations of the zodiac' in the opulent palace of Chosroes, King of Persia (*Decline and Fall*, ed. J. B. Bury, 7 vols (1896) v 73). S. was reading Gibbon beyond volume 5 in his own edition in December 1817 and January 1818 (*Mary Jnl* i 188–91). See also *PU* III iii 139–40.

82. *strawberry tree*] *Arbutus unedo*, an evergreen of the Maremma scrub.

90   He housed himself. There is a point of strand
            Near Vada's tower and town, and on one side
        The treacherous marsh divides it from the land
            Shadowed by pine and ilex forests wide;
        And on the other, creeps eternally
95   Through muddy weeds the shallow sullen sea.

        Here the Earth's breath is pestilence; and few
            But things whose nature is at war with life,
        Snakes and ill worms, endured its mortal dew:
            The trophies of the clime's victorious strife
100   Among white bones were scattered, yellow hair
        And ringed horns which the buffalo did wear,
        And the wolf's dark grey scalp who tracked him there;

        And at the utmost point [   ] stood there
            The relics of a reed-inwoven cot
105   Thatched with broad flags; an outlawed murderer
            Had lived seven days there; the pursuit was hot
        When he was cold: the birds who were his grave
        Fell dead after their feast in Vada's wave.

        There must have burned within Mazenghi's breast
110   That fire more warm and bright than life and hope,
        Which to the martyr makes his dungeon blest
            More joyous than free Heaven's majestic cope

98. endured] endure *Locock Ex, eds, BSM.*

99–102. The trophies . . . tracked him there;]
            The trophies of the clime's victorious strife –
            White bones, and locks of dun and yellow hair,
            And ringed horns which buffaloes did wear –   *Rossetti 1870*

            The trophies of the clime's victorious strife,
            And ringed horns which the buffalo did wear,
            And the wolf's dark-grey scalp who tracked him there –   *Locock 1911*
There are several possible readings of the MS if an arbitrary selection is made, otherwise the
stanza must be allowed seven lines; see *BSM* iii 180–1 for a photographic reproduction and
transcription. The buffalo's head and the wolf's scalp obviously constitute the trophies won
by the deadly Maremma, so Rossetti's syntax is preferable to Locock's; but & *locks of dun* is
cancelled.

107. the birds who were his grave] i.e. the carrion-eaters that disposed of his corpse.

108. Vada's wave.] These two words are underlined in MS, with a cross between them and a
marginal note, '? the name of the river'. Locock, supposing this to mean that Shelley wanted
a river's name in the text, left a blank, whereas he more probably intended a footnote to
provide local colour. But there is no river anywhere near Vada, only an ancient drainage
ditch known as 'Pozzotto'.

111. blest] *BSM* reads *black* canc., but *blest*, which fits the rhyme, makes much better sense.

To his oppressor, warring with decay,
Or he could ne'er have lived years, day by day.

115 Nor was his state so lone as you might think:
He had tamed every newt and snake and toad,
And every seagull which sailed down to drink
Those freshes ere the death-mist went abroad,
And each one with peculiar talk and play
120 Whiled, not untaught, his silent time away.

And the marsh-meteors, like tame beasts, at night
Came licking with blue tongues his veinèd feet,
And he would watch them as like spirits bright,
In many entangled figures quaint and sweet
125 To some enchanted music, they would dance
Until they vanished at the first moon-glance.

He mocked the stars with grouping on each weed
The summer dew-globes in the golden dawn,
And ere the hoar-frost languished he could read
130 Its pictured path, as on bare spots of lawn
Its delicate brief touch in silver weaves
The likeness of the wood's remembered leaves.

And many a fresh spring morn would he awaken,
While yet the unrisen sun made glow like iron
135 Quivering in crimson fire, the peaks unshaken
Of mountains and blue isles which did environ
With air-clad crags that plain of land and sea,
And feel [   ] liberty.

And in wide moonless nights when the dun sea
140 Heaved underneath the vast Heaven star-impearled,

114. Or he could ne'er have lived years, day by day.] In this dark hut, till three years crawled away *Nbk 5* canc., with no comma after 'decay' (line 113).

118. freshes] Springs.

127–8.   The summer dew globes, & the wild marsh flowers
                The sea herbs & the shells, he numbered oer *Nbk 5 partially canc.*

130. bare] *Nbk 5* canc. *BSM* reads *rare*.

131. delicate brief] *Nbk 5* canc.

138. Blank in *Nbk 5*.

139–41.   [And in] wide [moonless nights] when the dun [sea] Ocean
                [Heaved] underneath the vast Heaven star-impearled,
                [Starting from dreams of   he] *Nbk 5*

                [And in the moonless nights,] when the dun ocean
                [Heaved] underneath wide Heaven, star-impearled,
                He . . . . . .   *Locock 1911*

Starting from dreams of [   ] he
   Communed with the immeasurable world,
And felt his life beyond his limbs dilated
Till his mind grew like that it contemplated.

145   His food was the wild fig and strawberry,
    The milky pine-nuts which the autumn blast
Shaked into the tall grass, or such small fry
    As from the sea by winter storms are cast,
And the coarse bulbs of iris-flowers he found
150   Knotted in clumps under the spongy ground.

And so were kindled powers and thoughts which made
    His solitude less dark. When memory came —
For years gone by leave each a deepening shade —
    His spirit basked in its internal flame,
155   As when the black storm hurries round at night
The fisher basks beside his red fire's light . . .

Yet human hope and cares and faiths and errors
    Like billows unawakened by the wind
Slept in Mazenghi still; but that all terrors,
160   Weakness, and doubt had withered all his mind;
His couch [   ]

And when he saw beneath the sunset's planet
    A black ship walk over the crimson ocean,
Its pennon streaming on the blasts that fan it,
165   Its sails and ropes all tense and without motion,
Like the dark ghost of the unburied even
Striding athwart the orange-coloured Heaven,

The thought of his own kind who made the soul
    Which sped that wingèd shape through night and day,
170   The thought of his own country, [   ]
        . . . .

144. See 'Athanase' Cancelled Sequence 10 and note, and *PU* I 450 and note.

146. pine-nuts] Edible seeds of *Pinus pinea*, the Italian Umbrella-Pine.

151–2.   And his was most unlike a human form
               The squalid air had crusted him all round *Nbk 5 uncanc.*

156. red fire's light . . .] red firelight. *Locock 1911, eds.*

161. Blank in *Nbk 5.*

162. sunset's planet] Venus.

168. the soul] i.e. the animating purpose.

Wealth and dominion fade into the mass
　Of the great sea of human right and wrong
When once from our possession they must pass,
　But love, though misdirected, is among
175　The things which are immortal . . . and surpass
　All that frail stuff which will be, or which was.

167
From Virgil's Tenth Eclogue

Written probably in June 1818, just before, or concurrently with, *The Cyclops* (see headnote to no. 172). S. translated lines 1–16, 22–30, of the 77-line Latin original. His last three lines, spoken by Pan, were adopted a year later as epigraph to *J&M*. Much of the translation is in *terza rima*, but Locock's attempt to establish a regular pattern has to postulate more missing lines than the Latin would allow, and the rhyming is too erratic to justify it. Both S.'s Virgil translations are in rough draft only.

Text from *Nbk* 5 ff. 59ʳ–60ᵛ.

Published in *Rossetti 1870*, ii 458–9 (lines 1–19, 21, 23–7), from a transcript by R. Garnett; revised in *Locock Ex* 49–50 (omitting line 20).

Melodious Arethusa, o'er my verse
Shed thou once more the spirit of thy stream.
Who denies verse to Gallus? So when thou
Glidest beneath the green and purple gleam

171–6. This stanza skips a page and may be an independent fragment, as Mary Shelley first printed it. But though in different ink, it (a) is in the stanza form of this poem; (b) repeats a theme of the story, that power and privilege are short-lived beside virtue; (c) refers back, in 'human right and wrong', to the confusion of 'good and ill' in line 56; and (d) seems in 'love though misdirected' to describe the motivation of Mazenghi's exploit. It could have been intended for the end, or a later part, of the poem.

¶167 *1. Arethusa*] The nymph who changed into water in trying to escape from the river-god Alpheus, but whose stream was united with his to emerge as a fountain near Syracuse in Sicily. She is invoked here as a Sicilian Muse.

3. Gallus] Virgil's friend Cornelius Gallus was a soldier-poet in love with Lycoris, who had deserted him for Mark Antony (lines 22–3).

3–7. So when thou . . . Begin,] The Latin ('sic tibi . . . Doris non intermisceat undam . . . incipe') shows that S.'s syntax is: 'So that . . . you may flow unmingled . . . when you glide beneath the waters, . . . begin –'. Locock's punctuation obscures this sense.

5   Of Syracusan waters mayest thou flow
       Unmingled with the bitter Dorian dew,
       Begin, and whilst the goats are browsing now
       The soft leaves, in our song let us pursue
       The melancholy loves of Gallus — list,
10   We sing not to the deaf; the wild woods knew
       His sufferings and their echoes answer [   ]
       Young Naiades, in what far woodlands wild
       Wandered ye, when unworthy love possessed
       Our Gallus? Nor where Pindus is up-piled,
15   Nor where Parnassus' sacred mount, nor where
       Aonian Aganippe spreads in wastes.
       The laurels and the myrtle copses dim,
       The pine-encircled mountain Maenalus,
       The cold crags of Lycaeus, weep for him.
20   His sheep stand round, and it repents not us
       [
                                                        ]
       'What madness is this, Gallus? thy heart's care,
       Lycoris, 'mid rude camps and Alpine snow
       With willing step, pursues another there.'
       And Sylvan crowned with rustic coronal
25   Came shaking in his speed the budding wands
       And heavy lilies which he bore; we knew
       Pan the Arcadian with bunches red
       [
                                        ] and said
       'Wilt thou not ever cease? Love cares not.
30   The meadows with fresh streams, the bees with thyme,
       The goats with the green leaves of budding spring
       Are saturated not — nor Love with tears.'

---

6. bitter Dorian dew,] Arethusa came from Elis near the northerly mouth of the Alpheus, which rises in the 'Dorian' south (Lat. 'Doris amara', 'bitter Dorian water').

13. unworthy love] Lat. 'indigno amore'. Lycoris was a slave-girl.

16. in wastes.] A doubtful reading; 'in' is apparently written heavily over 'its'. *BSM* iii reads 'its [western *canc.*]'. Aganippe was a spring, sacred to the Muses, on Mount Helicon.

18, 19. Maenalus . . . Lycaeus] Mountains in Arcadia sacred to Pan.

20. This line is canc. in *Nbk 5*, and is omitted in *Locock Ex*. S.'s trans. omits five Latin lines following this line. It is Apollo who speaks lines 21–3.

24. Sylvan] Sylvanus was a forest-god.   *coronal*] coronals *Locock Ex.*

27. with bunches red] A doubtful canc. reading, omitted in *Locock Ex*; *BSM* iii reads '[with *canc.*] [The clear <rose> *canc.*]'. In the Latin, Pan is seen 'sanguineis ebuli bacis minioque rubentum', 'stained with cinnabar and with blood-red elderberries'.

168
From Virgil's Fourth Georgic

Written probably in June 1818, either shortly before, or concurrently with, *The Cyclops* (see headnote to no. 172). The Fourth Georgic is about bee-keeping, and the fable of Aristaeus relates how the practice of getting bees to hive in a dead animal originated. Aristaeus's pursuit of Orpheus's wife Eurydice has led to her death, and Aristaeus is punished by the loss of his bees. He seeks advice from his mother Cyrene, who is daughter of the river Peneus and lives underwater. Cyrene tells him to consult Proteus, who in turn advises a sacrifice of oxen to Orpheus and Eurydice, after which a fresh swarm of bees emerges from the carcasses. S. translated only some opening words of the fable, and the beginning of Aristaeus's underwater visit (*Georgics* iv 317–19 and 360–73). *Webb* 332 observes that the underwater world seems to fascinate S. (cp. 'Ode to the West Wind' 33–42; 'Lines written in dejection' 10–11, etc.), and that by his additions to the Latin (e.g. 'the deep's untrampled fountains' (line 7), and 'groves profaned not by the step of mortal' (line 10), where Virgil has simply 'river', and 'groves') S. is adding to the holy mystery of this underwater paradise into which Aristaeus has penetrated. The lines are in *terza rima*.

Text from *Nbk 5* ff. 61ʳ (lines 1–4), 38ᵛ (lines 5–18), 47ᵛ (lines 19–25).

Published in *Locock Ex* 74 (lines 5–25); *Webb* 331 (lines 5–25).

> The shepherd Aristaeus, as fame tells,
> Losing his bees by hunger, fled
>   Tempe, and to Peneus
>   Mothers Cyrene [
>
>   ]

5   And the cloven waters like a chasm of mountains
> Stood, and received him in its mighty portal
> And led him through the deep's untrampled fountains.

> He went in wonder through the halls immortal
> Of his great Mother and her humid reign,
10   And groves profaned not by the step of mortal

1–5. These lines on a separate page were omitted in *Locock Ex*. S. may first have considered using a form other than *terza rima*, so his arrangement is kept, although lines 3–4 make a regular iambic pentameter.

2. hunger] Partly conjectural; only the first three letters are legible. In Virgil the bees died 'morboque fameque', 'by disease and hunger'.

3–4. The Peneus flows through the Vale of Tempe to the sea, but its 'sacred source' is far inland.

9. her humid reign,] 'Her watery empire' (a literal rendering of 'umida regna').

Which sounded as he passed, and lakes which rain
Replenished not, girt round by marble caves;
By the soft watery motion of the main

Half wildered, he beheld the bursting waves
15   Of every stream, beneath the mighty earth:
Phasis and Lycus which the starred sand paves,

The chasm where old Enipeus has its birth,
And father Tiber, and Aniena's flow,
And whence Caicus', Mysian stream, comes forth

20   And rock-resounding Hypanis, and thou,
Eridanus, who bearest like empire's sign
Two golden horns upon thy taurine brow,

Thou than whom none of the streams divine
Through garden-fields and meads with fiercer power
25   Burst in their tumult to the purple brine.

169
'Heigh ho, wisdom and folly'

These almost unpunctuated lines are in *Nbk* 5, which was in use during S.'s last months at Marlow and first months in Italy, and are apparently an improvise in rhyming, similar to his *bouts rimés* 'It seems to me extremely odd'. Medwin recalled a later more successful occasion (1821) when 'A word was chosen, and all the rhymes to it in the language, and they were very numerous, set down, without regard to their corresponding meanings, and in a few minutes he [Shelley] filled

12. girt round by marble] enclosed in glimmering *uncanc. alt.*

13. the soft watery] the watery *Locock Ex*; 'soft' is doubtful, and *BSM* iii records the word as illegible.

16. Phasis and Lycus] Two rivers now in Georgia. The Enipeus is in Thessaly; the Anieno (Anio) joins the Tiber north of Rome; the Caicus (Grimakli) is in modern Turkey; the Hypanis (Bug) is in Ukraine; Eridanus is the Po in North Italy. Thus S. does not mean that these rivers had a 'chasm' or underground source in common, but that Aristaeus beheld the different sources of all rivers. *starred*] Omitted *Locock Ex*.

18. and Aniena's flow] and Anienas glow *Locock Ex*. These words are now virtually invisible in *Nbk* 5, and *flow* is dubious.

22. Two golden horns] River-gods were traditionally credited with bulls' horns, symbolising virility.

25. to] on *Locock Ex*, *BSM* iii.

in the blanks with a beautifully fanciful poem' (*Medwin (1913)* 372). These lines recall the refrain of Amiens' song in *As You Like It* (II vii 193): 'Hey-ho, sing hey-ho, unto the green holly, / Most friendship is feigning; most loving mere folly', and perhaps also Jacques's melancholy in the same play, which seems always to have been a favourite with S. Here the names seem arbitrary, but the rhyme-name 'Molly' may conceivably be associated with the Olde Rose Inn at Wokingham where, according to one tradition, Gay, with Pope and Swift, wrote the once famous ballad 'Molly Mog: or, the Fair Maid of the Inn' (1726), a poem that has 15 ballad-stanzas all rhyming to 'Mog'. Peacock records how S. and his friends 'took many walks in all directions from Marlow, and saw everything worth seeing within a radius of sixteen miles' (*Peacock Works* viii 107–8). Wokingham is twelve miles from Marlow as the crow flies.

Text from *Nbk 5* f. 47ᵛ.

Published in *Locock 1911* ii 176, *1975* 322.

> Heigh ho, wisdom and folly,
> Heigh ho, Edward and Molly;
> He'll wear the willow and she'll wear the holly —
> There dear Mr. Mug going wild for our Dolly;
> 5   Let us follow him out to his cave in the colly
> And bother him out of his melancholy.

170
Scene for *Tasso*

Composed either between 10 May and 10 June 1818, or (more probably) between 12 June and 8 July at Bagni di Lucca. S. told Peacock on 20 April: 'I have devoted this summer & indeed the next year to the composition of a tragedy on the subject of Tasso's madness, which I find upon inspection is, if properly treated, admirably dramatic & poetical. – But, you will say I have no dramatic talent. Very true in a certain sense; but I have taken the resolution to see what kind of a tragedy a person without dramatic talent could write' (*L* ii 8; ten days later he repeated his intention to Hogg, *L* ii 15). Accordingly, S. had studied August von Schlegel's *Lectures on Dramatic Art and Literature* (1809–11) in J. Black's trans. (1815) on the journey to Italy in March (*Mary Jnl* i 198–9), and read at least two biographies of the poet, Giovanni Manso's *Vita di Torquato Tasso* (Venice 1621) and Pietro Serassi's *La Vita di Torquato Tasso* (Rome 1634) in its 2nd, 2-volume, edition (Bergamo 1790) which was the standard Italian Life in 1818. He read Serassi 6–11 April (*Mary Jnl* i 203–5) and was reading Manso on 11 May (*Mary Jnl* i 209); both biographies appear in a

---

3. To 'wear the willow' was to mourn for a dead or lost sweetheart.

4. There] There's *1975*. The 's' was perhaps intended.

5. cave] Uncertain because written over 'bed'; *BSM* iii reads '<hole>'. *colly*] dirt.

book-list in Mary's hand in *Box 2* f. 156. S. may also have read John Black's English *Life* (2 vols, 1810). On the inside cover of *Nbk 6* facing the opening lines of 'Tasso' is a jotted reference to 'Ariosto, Canto 35 or 36'; Mary S. read these Cantos of *Orlando Furioso* (possibly with S.) on 2–3 July 1818 (*Mary Jnl* i 217). That the jotting is on the cover could mean that page one was by then occupied. The draft is in ink through line 31, and thereafter in pencil, and was probably finally given up on 9 July, when S. turned in frustration to translating Plato's *Symposium*. S.'s jottings in *Nbk 5* f. 41ʳ (April/May 1818) headed 'Drama of Tasso' give no indication of a proposed plot but list suggested conclusions: 'Scene where he reads the sonnet which he wrote to Leonora[,] to herself as composed at the request of another – Scene with his sister – To consider Laura the Poetess – / Sorrentum / Character of M – the mal-vaggio ['the wicked one'] / Opening scene spring – / His disguising himself in the habit of a shepherd & questioning his sister in that disguise concerning himself & then unveiling himself'. Tasso fled from Ferrara in July 1577 to seek refuge with his sister Cornelia in Sorrento, his birthplace (the story of his flight and disguise is in Manso, pp. 87ff.). Tasso's life-story had acquired a European appeal in S.'s day, because it concerned the mysterious love and victimisation of a great poet, who was said to have aspired after Leonora d'Este, a sister of his noble patron the Duke Alfonso, and to have been tyrannously imprisoned for this pretention and driven insane. Manso, who had known Tasso personally and whose biography was the ultimate source of the various legends, had suggested that the poet, though not insane, was confined after fighting a duel with his friend Maddalo, because Maddalo had revealed the secret of Tasso's love for Leonora. Versions of the legend spoke of an impulsive kiss witnessed by the Duke and interpreted as 'madness' justifying restraint, or madness caused in the poet by the oppressions exercised on him, or madness simulated by the poet in order to protect his lady's reputation. S. could not have read Goethe's tragedy *Tasso* (1790) as there was no English translation, but was influenced by Byron's *The Lament of Tasso*, a 247-line soliloquy in couplets, which he read in late summer 1817 soon after its publication (*L* i 548, 556). Byron's Tasso was both sane and steadfast, though mortally shaken by the sufferings imposed by his enemies at court; and S.'s view seems to have been closely similar, judging from his verse fragments and from the attitude expressed to Peacock on 6 November 1818 following his visit to St Anna at Ferrara:

> Tasso's situation was widely different from that of any persecuted being of the present day, for from the depth of dungeons public opinion might now at length be awakened to an echo that would startle the oppressor. But then there was no hope. There is something irresistibly pathetic to me in the sight of Tasso's own hand writing moulding expressions of adulation & entreaty to a deaf & stupid tyrant in an age when the most heroic virtue would have exposed its possessor to hopeless persecution, and – such is the alliance between virtue & genius – which unoffending genius could not escape. (*L* ii 47)

The present text, untitled but headed 'Scen 1', begins on a first page of *Nbk 6*, suggesting that this nbk was once specially intended for the play; but the text peters out on f. 6, and as the principal content of the nbk, *J&M*, was written from the other end, the modern foliation relegates the *Tasso* fragment to the back of the book. Scribbled between lines 2 and 3 of the draft is the note '15 shillings a month', which could refer to the wages the Shelleys had been paying Allegra's nurse Elise Duvillard in England, a sum S. translated into louis for Byron's information when

Elise entered his service with Allegra on 28 April 1818 (*L* ii 13). This note was probably entered before *Tasso* was begun, tending to confirm a summer date.

It is possible that line 31, after which pencil succeeds pen, marks a break of some duration, and that Albano's final speech, like the 'Song for *Tasso*', resulted from a briefly revived interest following S.'s visit to Ferrara in November (see note to lines 42–3). For a short study of the text and its implications see GM, 'A New Text of Shelley's Scene for *Tasso*', *KSMB* xi (1960) 39–47.

Text from *Nbk 6*, ff. 166ʳᵉᵛ–161ʳᵉᵛ. S.'s punctuation in the rough draft has been supplemented lightly at various points; cp. the transcription in *BSM* xv 160–7.

Published in *Relics* 26–7 (lines 3–21, 24–31); *KSMB* xi (1960) 39–42 (complete).

170
Scene for *Tasso*

Pigna	Who denies access to the Duke?
Albano	His Grace Is buried in deep converse with the dead.
Maddalo	No access to the Duke! you have not said That the Count Maddalo would speak with him?
5 *Pigna*	Did you inform his Grace that Signor Pigna Waits with state papers for his signature?
Malpiglio	The Lady Leonora cannot know That I have written a sonnet to her fame In which I [ ] on Venus and Adonis.
10	You should not take my gold and serve me not.

Cast. Pigna. First Secretary to Alfonso, and Historiographer to the Este family whose post, on his death in 1576, passed to Tasso by request. He had been Tasso's rival in love for Lucretia Bendidio.

Vincenzo *Malpiglia* was Duke Alfonso's Treasurer.

Cardinal *Albano.* A friend of Tasso. Garnett (*Relics* 26) identified Albano as 'an Usher', no doubt influenced by S.'s indecision at line 11 as to whether he should assign Albano's words to 'Officer'.

Maddalo. Tasso blamed much of his ill-fortune on an unnamed false friend, suspected by Manso and Serrassi to have been Count Maddalo Fucci, who quarrelled with the poet; and it is generally assumed that he would have been the villain of S.'s drama. But 'the malvaggio' might have described Antonio Montecatino, Pigna's successor as Secretary to the Duke and known to be hostile to Tasso, or even Malpiglio, who is presented as hostile in S.'s scene.

1. His Grace] His grace *Nbk 6* canc.

2. the dead.] Presumably great spirits of the past, such as Dante and Ariosto; cp. 'Letter to the Gisbornes' 160–2, *Adonais* 392–6.

8. written] *Nbk 6* canc. woven *Nbk 6* alt. canc.

9. Blank in *Nbk 6*.

	Albano	In truth I told her, and she smiled, and said:
		'If I am Venus, thou coy Poesy
		Art the Adonis whom I love, and he —
		The Erymanthian boar that wounded him'. —
15		O trust to me, Signor Malpiglio,
		Those words and smiles were favours to thy Zechin.

Malpiglio The words are twisted in some double sense
              That I reach not, the smiles shone not to me.

Pigna   How are the Duke and Princess occupied?

20 Albano   Buried in some strange talk, — the Duke was leaning
              His finger on his brow, his lips unclosed,
              Yet in the pauses of their talk I heard
              No murmur with the breath that parted them.
              The Princess sate within the window seat
25   And so her face was hid, but on her knee
              Her hands were clasped, veinèd and pale as snow
              And quivering, and young Tasso too was there —

Maddalo (to *Malpiglio*)
              Thou seest for whom from thine own chosen Heaven
              Thou drawest down smiles — they did not rain on thee.

30 Malpiglio Would they were parching lightnings for his sake
              On whom they fell.

Pigna   Ye note well, Gentlemen.

Albano   — Tasso, who as I entered ceased to speak,
              But on his form and countenance yet lay plain
              The light of his suspended words — his eyes
35   Inwardly burned, like fire, and seemed to track
              Some half created image through the air,

---

14. Mount Erymanthus in Arcadia was hunting country that produced the boar responsible for the death of Adonis.

16. *Zechin.*] i.e. zecchino, sequin; a gold coin still current in S.'s time.

18–19. Between these two lines the following is canc.: 'When young Torquato languishingly sung'.

22. *of their talk I heard*] of the talk there came *KSMB*. Parts of lines 22–3 are canc. in *Nbk 6*.

28. *(to* Malpiglio*)*] Omitted in *KSMB*. *chosen*] *Nbk 6, BSM* xv; worshipped *KSMB*.

33. *plain*] [?played] *BSM* xv.

35–6. *seemed to track . . . through the air,*] Cp. 'Silence; oh well are Death and Sleep and thou' 7.

Last of the wingèd children of his brain,
Ere yet the soft persuasion of his tongue
Had coloured it to intellectual sight.
40 This was but for a moment, his dark lashes
Soon o'er his eyes fell droopingly, the blood
Glowed in his cheeks like light that went and came,
And rising up with self-deserted mien
He said, 'I will retire.' — 'No, no,' replied the Duke,
45 ''Tis but the babbler Pigna, who will prate
Of his mean self for hours, and Maddalo
The ruined Count, whose cold and gentle smiles
Make me feel ill at ease — sit down, sit down,
And you, Albano, have good care that none
50 Break on my privacy.'

Pigna   I wonder much

171
'Silence; oh well are Death and Sleep and thou'

Probably written between 10 May and 8 July 1818 in connection with S.'s planned *Tasso* drama, the draft of which ends seven pages back in the same *Nbk 6*. The page following the fragment contains some prose lines to a correspondent describing a mountain journey, perhaps the crossing of the Apennines on 5 May (see no. 165; but *BSM* xv 176 cps. a passage from *Mary Jnl* i 201 to imply an earlier date). Like S.'s drama, this fragment is in blank verse, and three cancelled words just above it (*Silent I see*) suggest that it is a speech conceived as part of a dramatic exchange, possibly spoken by Tasso of Leonora d'Este's singing (a sonnet 'Ahi, ben e reo destin ch'invidia e toglie' on the mind-purifying melody of her singing, attributed to Tasso, is quoted in Black ii 80–1; see headnote to preceding poem), or by a listener of Tasso's own verses. The lines have close affinities in tone or phrasing with 'To Constantia' ('Thy voice, slow rising like a Spirit') and with *Tasso* (see note to lines 7–8). The opening recollection of an episode in Ariosto, Tasso's

41. *Soon*] [Down] *BSM* xv.

369

great rival in fame, also supports a dramatic hypothesis. Mary S. made at least four extant transcripts of lines 1–8, all from this original (though she printed none). Text from *Nbk 6* f. 155ʳ.

Published *Relics* 78; *Massey* 252 (transcript of MS). *Hutchinson* 569 used the title 'Apostrophe to Silence' from Mary S.'s transcript in adds. d. 9.

Silence; oh well are Death and Sleep and thou
Three brethren named — the guardians gloomy winged
Of one abyss where life and truth and joy
Are swallowed up — yet spare me, Spirit, o pity me
5 Until the sounds I hear become my soul
And it has left these faint and heavy limbs
To track, along the lapses of the air,
These wandering melodies, until it rest
Among lone mountains in some

2. *Three brethren named*] In Ariosto's *Orlando Furioso* (Canto xiv stanzas 92–4) the Archangel Michael finds a dark grotto in Arabia where Sleep lies, guarded by Oblivion at the entrance and Silence on patrol outside – brethren in the sense of allies.

4. *Spirit, o pity*] o spirit, pity *Mary S. transcripts*.

6,8. *it*] i.e. 'my soul'.

6. *heavy*] weary *Mary S. transcripts, Relics, Massey, BSM* xv (a possible reading, but the *w* seems compounded of a random ink-mark adjoining an *h*).

7–8. *To track . . . melodies*] Cp. *Tasso* 35–6: 'to track / Some half created image through the air'.

8. *These wandering melodies*] This wandering melody *Relics, BSM* xv, *eds*. S. has altered 'This wandering melody' to the plural forms, as the *Nbk 6* spacing of the letters in *These* confirms (all four Mary S. transcripts give the plural reading).

172
The Cyclops

S.'s translation of Euripides' satyr-play *The Cyclops* could conceivably have been written at almost any time between May 1818 and November 1819. As *SC* vi 1086 notes, the positioning of the translation in *Nbk 5* implies that it was written later than 'Listen, listen, Mary mine –' (no. 165), which is firmly dateable to 4 May 1818 (see headnote). And in a letter to Leigh Hunt dated [16] November 1819 S. remarks, in the context of a self-deprecating account of his own efforts as a translator, that he has 'only translated the Cyclops of Euripides when I could do absolutely nothing else, – & the Symposium of Plato' (*SC* vi 1081; see also *L* ii 153). Most *eds* have assumed a date towards the end of this period, i.e. in the summer or even the autumn of 1819, mainly on the grounds that S.'s comment to Hunt would appear to imply that he was speaking of the *Cyclops* translation as a relatively recent effort. Timothy Webb in particular has argued for a date following the death of William Shelley in Rome on 7 June 1819, and probably during the period of intense creative activity which followed S.'s completion of *The Cenci* in August. He further argues that S.'s documented reading in Euripides in 1819 underpins the evidence of his various references to Polyphemus, and of a general interest in the significance of the Cyclops as a character probably originating in discussions with Hunt before the Shelleys left England in March 1818 (see *Webb* 79–87). Other commentators since Webb have followed his dating, and Jennifer Wallace develops a political reading of the translation which proceeds from the confident assertion that it was written 'in 1819 just after the Peterloo Massacre' (*Shelley and Greece* (1997) 71–5). Paul Dawson, however, in his Introduction (xv–xvi) to *BSM* iii is more circumspect and non-committal concerning the likely date of *The Cyclops*, and there are good reasons to propose an earlier date for S.'s translation, in the summer of 1818 at Bagni di Lucca.

S.'s assertion to Hunt that he had translated *The Cyclops* only when he 'could absolutely do nothing else' accords awkwardly with a date between July and October 1819, as by general agreement this was one of the most productive periods of S.'s career, and indeed was by any standards one of the great creative periods of any major English poet. Notwithstanding the death of William and its legacy (see headnotes to nos 199–208), S. completed *The Cenci* by mid-August, together with a number of shorter poems and translations of varying length. Then, after receiving news of the Peterloo Massacre from Peacock on 5 September 1819, he produced a series of powerful political pieces, alongside *The Mask of Anarchy* itself (completed by 23 September). By the end of October a quickening pace of poetic activity had produced *Peter Bell the Third* and the 'Ode to the West Wind', and also the wholly distinctive and brilliantly original fourth act for *PU*, which was probably being composed right through from August to November (see headnote to *PU*).

Against this background, S.'s account of the context of his translation, coupled with the fact that he links it explicitly to his translation of the *Symposium*, points to a date in June 1818. Mary S. noted in her jnl that S. began his translation from Plato on 8 July 1818 at Bagni di Lucca, finishing on 17 July (*Mary Jnl* i 218–9). Her jnl also records that S. was reading intensively in Gk from early May through to his departure from Bagni di Lucca for Venice on 17 August 1818, and that he concentrated in particular on Euripides, Sophocles and Aristophanes (*Mary Jnl* i 209–23). It was of this period that S. remarked to Peacock in a letter of 25 July 1818: 'I have lately found myself totally incapable of original composition'; and he goes on to mention that he had just translated the *Symposium*, and that he had 'been reading scarcely anything but Greek' (*L* ii 26). For arguments that the attempts at 'original composition' which S. found himself unable to bring to fruition were in fact the planned drama on the life of Tasso, and the poem based on Sismondi's account of Pietro Mazenghi, see headnotes to those poems (nos 166 and 170). The arguments advanced in the headnote to 'Mazenghi', that the poem was abandoned in May 1818, carry the further implication that S. proceeded at that time to his translation of *The Cyclops*, as the opening lines of *The Cyclops* in *Nbk 5* clearly follow on immediately from 'Mazenghi' (see *BSM* iii 192–9). A date in June 1818 for S.'s translation is also supported by other considerations. S.'s *Cyclops* employs a versification which alternates between blank verse dramatic exchanges and choric passages in a variety of lyric measures; this offers an experimental model for the much more densely-textured, but essentially similar approach in the writing of *PU*, which S. probably started to think through seriously from July 1818 (see headnote to *PU*). Some passages in *Cyclops*, e.g. the passage beginning at line 46 in a seven-syllable line, more exactly anticipate formal elements which are handled with increasing confidence in the second half of 1818, in the speeches of the Furies in *PU* I, and in 'Lines Written among the Euganean Hills' and 'Stanzas written in dejection – December 1818, near Naples' (see headnotes, nos 183 & 187). Timothy Webb's suggestion that S.'s interest in the play may have been influenced by discussion with Hunt (see above) is plausible, and would fit the summer of 1818 as well as, if not better than the winter of 1819; it would also fit with the period of sustained immersion in Gk reading which characterises the early part of S.'s first Italian summer, and with the series of translations from various sources which he undertook in the first half of 1818 (see nos 156–162 and 167–168, and S.'s translation of the *Symposium*).

It is also perhaps possible that S.'s surprising decision to attempt a translation of *The Cyclops* was related to his belief, articulated in *DMAA*, that 'It is to be lamented that no modern writer has hitherto dared to show [the Greeks] as they were' (*Prose* 219). This essay was planned, and partly written, as an introduction to S.'s translation of the *Symposium*, and would thus have been in his mind through the summer months at Bagni di Lucca. The main emphasis of his discussion in the essay falls on the question of Greek homosexuality, in terms too explicit for Mary to countenance publication in her lifetime (at least of the relevant passages). But there may well be a more general reference to the frankly sexual and ribald character of some Greek dramatic writing in S.'s complaint that 'There is no book which shows the Greeks precisely as they were; they seem all written for children, with the caution that no practice or sentiment highly inconsistent with our present manners should be mentioned, lest those manners should receive outrage and violation. But there are many to whom the Greek language is inaccessible who ought not to be excluded by this prudery to possess an exact and comprehensive conception of the history of man; for there is no knowledge concerning what man has been and may be from partaking of which a person can depart without becoming in some degree more philosophical, tolerant, and just' (*Prose* 219). S. may in attempting his translation of Euripides have been exploring the possibility, and the real difficulties, of producing a translation for adults. His hesitations, at various points in *The Cyclops*, over the translation of sexually or otherwise suggestive passages (see notes) might be explained in the context of a conscious effort to strike a balance between fidelity to the original, and a publicly acceptable English idiom for the early nineteenth century. This might also conceivably explain why Mary apparently remained unaware, in June 1818 or at any other time, that S. was working on his translation.

On the other hand, a date in the second half of 1819 is not only difficult to square with the extent of his other writings at that time. It also presents a problem in accounting for the mood and remarkable fluency of *The Cyclops*, which are quite unlike the anguished and sardonic products of the weeks following William's death (see nos 201–205), or the more worldly and sharply direct political engagement of the post-Peterloo poems. It is indeed almost incredible that the translation could have been produced as late as October, and Jennifer Wallace's reading cited above, while making a good case for those subversive qualities in the satyr-play which no doubt formed part of its attraction and interest for S., offers no substantial evidence, direct or oblique, to link its composition with S.'s own very emphatic and eloquent reactions to the Peterloo Massacre.

Euripides' *Cyclops* is based on the famous episode of Odysseus's encounter with the giant Polyphemus in *Odyssey* ix; see *Euripides: Cyclops, Alcestis, Medea*, trans. David Kovacs (1994; the Loeb translation) 53–7 for discussion of Euripides' treatment of his Homeric source. *The Cyclops* is the only example of a satyr-play that survives complete. A satyr-play was normally the fourth play in a tragic tetralogy, and was characterised by a comic burlesque manner deriving mainly from the behaviour of the pleasure-loving but cowardly and unreliable satyrs; there is a full discussion of the play and its genre in *Euripides: Cyclops*, ed. R. A. S. Seaford (1988). S.'s translation of Euripides is among his most remarkable achievements, and stands among the finest of all English verse-translations from the Gk drama. Swinburne wrote of his 'delight of wonder at its matchless grace of unapproachable beauty, its strength, ease, delicate simplicity and sufficiency' (*Essays and Studies* (1875) 211). It is plainer in style and much more direct than the only other English translation before S.'s, by Michael Wodhull (4 vols 1782; Potter's Euripides of 1781–83 did not include *The Cyclops*). S.'s version sustains a supple and idiomatic verse-texture, but also contrives to preserve an exceptional fidelity to his Gk text; the original 1906 'Everyman' edition of Euripides in English translation gives *The Cyclops* in S.'s version, and describes it as 'the most poetical translation of Euripides in any tongue' (Everyman's Library no. 63, p. xi). The poise and dignity of S.'s translation does however idealise and elevate the ribald tone of the play (see above), and this effect is heightened, and made more anodyne, by the various rewritings and omissions embodied in *1824* (see *Webb* 134–8).

The *Cyclops* was first published in *1824*. The *1824* text differs in various respects from the only known source for S.'s translation, which is the holograph draft in *Nbk 5*. This MS is possibly not itself a first draft; there are some confused and quite heavily corrected passages, but broadly S.'s hand is neat and legible, and the punctuation employs stops, commas, frequent dashes, and suspension points with a care that could suggest an early intermediate stage, somewhat resembling the *PU* fair copy in *Nbks 7, 8*, and *9* (see headnote to *PU*). Mary may well not have been aware of the existence of S.'s translation (let alone its date) until she began work on *1824* (see below); none of the contents of *Nbk 5* were transcribed by Mary during S.'s lifetime, and only two poems in it were finished, 'Ozymandias', which is just inside the back cover, and 'To Constantia', which was a private poem that Mary never saw (see headnote to no. 155). The differences between the text of *The Cyclops* in *Nbk 5* and *1824*, which are relatively extensive, almost certainly derive from the circumstances under which Mary produced *1824*, rather than from S. himself. Soon after S.'s death in July 1822 Mary started, while still in Italy, to collect and transcribe his literary remains, and after her return to England in August 1823 she immediately sought a publisher (see *Taylor* 1–10, and *Mary Jnl* ii 434). *The Cyclops* was evidently among the major unpublished works which she transcribed, and it is clear that she left her copy with Hunt in Italy after her own return to England. She wrote to Hunt from London on 18 September 1823: 'I wish that you w^d send me immediately the Essay on Devils and the Cyclops – particularly the latter – for these were a few lines filled up – besides I should wish to see your correction of it & compare it with the orriginal [*sic*]' (*Mary L* i 384). Presumably Mary made a transcript from *Nbk 5*, and by studying the MS closely was subsequently able to fill in several passages which she had not at first been able to read; she must then have passed this corrected copy to Hunt for his comments on the Gk. Mary's phrase 'the orriginal' in her letter clearly means the original MS of S.'s translation, rather than the Gk text itself from which S. worked. This, as *Webb* 350 shows, was *Euripidis Tragoedie Viginti*, ed. J. Barnes, Oxford 1811 (vol. 3), S.'s copy of which is now in Eton College Library (see note to line 492). The possibility that S. himself had made a corrected fair copy of his translation appears to be excluded by Mary's pointed excepting of *The Cyclops*, in her Preface to *1824*, from the list of those poems in the volume which could be 'considered as having received the author's ultimate corrections' (*1824* vii). Mary again asked Hunt on 2 October 1823 to return her copy ('I want very much the Cyclops and Essay on devils': *Mary L* i 393), and yet again on 3 November ('I want the Cyclops particularly': *Mary L* i 399). But on 27 November she wrote to Marianne Hunt: 'Will you tell Hunt that he need not send any of the MSS that he has (except the Essay on Devils & some lines addressed to himself on his arrival in Italy, if he should choose them to be inserted) as I have re-copied all the rest' (*Mary L* i 404). Mary thus clearly made a second copy, which was no doubt intended for the press; she mentions in a letter to Hunt of 9 February 1824 that 'we have begun to print' (Mary was still attempting – ultimately in vain – to get Hunt to send his 'Notice' of S.'s life for inclusion in *1824*).

Either Hunt returned Mary's original transcript (which is now lost) between the end of November 1823 and February 1824 and Mary used his corrections for *1824*, or she showed her new copy (also now lost) to someone else, perhaps Peacock, and used their corrections. Some details of diction and phrasing in interpolated passages tend to suggest Hunt rather than Peacock; cp. Hunt's comment in a letter of 27 May 1824 to Elizabeth Kent, 'Send me always as many verses to translate as you can. They give me no sort of trouble' (*Hunt Correspondence* ii 218). In either case, the text finally printed in *1824* incorporates not only extensive modification to S.'s punctuation in *Nbk 5*, but also a number of rewritten passages, various changes to individual words, several significant omissions, and some instances where wordings left as undecided alternatives by S. have been decided (presumably by Mary in her transcription). This text, which received further slight revisions in *1839* and *1840*, has remained the received version of S.'s translation in subsequent *eds. Locock 1911* (building on excavatory work in *Locock Ex*) had access to the MS, but its text in fact incorporates from it only a very few and relatively insignificant verbal corrections, while preserving all of the omissions and virtually all of the 'corrections' and modifications in *1824*. The notes below detail all the changes made to *Nbk 5* in *1824*. The text given here follows S.'s own draft in all substantive matters, and the draft's punctuation is preserved wherever possible, although frequent editorial supplement and modification has proved unavoidable.

S. falls in with normal early nineteenth-century practice in Latinising Gk names (see headnote to *PU*), although there are exceptions in *The Cyclops*; his love for the sound of Gk is however nevertheless reflected in several of his transliterations of Gk exclamations (see notes).

Text from *Nbk 5* ff. 49v–58v, 61v–67r, 37r–38r, 67v–68v, 73r, 72v, 73v, 60v–61r.

Published in *1824* 329–61; *BSM* iii 198–235, 246–69, 148–53, 270–5, 292–3, 290–1, 294–5, 242–5.

172

The Cyclops

Silenus

    O Bacchus, what a world of toil both now
    And ere these limbs were overworn with age
    Have I endured for thee; first when thou fledst
    The mountain-nymphs who nursed you, driven afar
5   By the strange madness Juno sent upon you,
    Then in the battle of the sons of earth
    When I stood foot to foot beside thy shield,
    No unpropitious fellow-combatant,
    And driving through his shield my wingèd spear
10 Slew vast Enceladus. — Consider now . . .
    Is it a dream of which I speak to thee?
    By Jove it is not, for you have the trophies —

4. *you,*] thee, *1824*.

5. *strange*] Not in the Gk. *you,*] thee; *1824*.

7. When I stood foot by foot close to thy side, *1824*. S. is closer to the literal meaning of the Gk παρασπιστὴς, 'one who bears a shield beside'.

8. *Webb* 93 notes S.'s trans. here as an example of error as a result of 'confusion of similar words', assuming S. to misunderstand ἐνδέξιος ('on the right-hand side') under the influence of δεξιός ('dexterous'); but ἐνδέξιος perhaps involves a metaphor from augury and could be understood as 'well-omened'.

9. *wingèd*] Not in the Gk.

And now I suffer more than all before.
For when I heard that Juno had devised
15   A tedious voyage for you, and that you sailed
With Tyrcenican pirates rude, I put to sea
With all my children quaint, in search of you;
And I myself stood on the beakèd prow
And fixed the naked mast, and all my boys
20   Leaning upon their oars, with splash and strain
Made white with foam the green and purple sea,
And so we sought you, King. We were sailing
Near Malea, when an eastern wind arose
And drove us to this waste Aetnean rock.
25   The one-eyed children of the Ocean God,
The man-destroying Cyclopses, inhabit
On this wild shore their solitary caves,
And one of these named Polypheme has caught us
To be his slaves; and so, for all delight
30   Of Bacchic sports, sweet dance and melody,
We keep this lawless giant's wandering flocks.
My sons indeed, on far declivities,
Young things themselves, tend on the youngling sheep,
But I remain, filling the water casks
35   Or sweeping the hard floor, or ministering

13. The Gk ἐξαντλῶ πόνον is a metaphor, 'drain my toil to the full'; but S.'s text has πόδον, 'foot', by misprint for πόνον here, which is an incomprehensible reading, and it is therefore puzzling to explain how S. manages his deft trans. Such cases suggest that he may have used a commentary, or perhaps took advice.

15–16. and that . . . pirates rude,] S. was possibly dissatisfied with his rendering of the Gk, which means 'she raised up against you' rather than 'you sailed with'; canc. in *Nbk 5*, and omitted in *1824*. S.'s *Tyrcenican* transliterates the Gk Τυρσηνικὸν (trans. in Loeb as 'Tuscan').

17. quaint] Not in the Gk.

18. prow] The Gk πρύμνηι means 'stern', i.e. where the tiller is.

19. fixed the naked mast] In the Gk literally 'straitened the beam', i.e. steered the ship. *Naked* is not in the Gk.

21. green and purple] A colourful trans. for γλαυκὴν, 'gleaming, silvery' (see note to line 248).

24. waste] Very lightly canc. in *Nbk 5*, and followed by *wild* as an alt.; but *waste* appears to have been reinstated by a subsequent heavier inking (see *BSM* iii 200), perhaps to avoid repetition with *wild* in line 27; neither adj. is in the Gk.

29. for] i.e. 'instead of'.

31. wandering] Not in the Gk.

32. declivities] Perhaps suggesting that S. was using Scapula's Lexicon, which defines κλῖτύς by the Lat. 'declivitas'; S. uses 'declivities' nowhere else in his poetry, but cp. the usage in his letter to Peacock of February 1819, quoted in the note to *PU* II ii 1–23.

34. remain, filling] remain to fill *1824*; *filling the* is canc. in *Nbk 5* (*BSM* iii reads 'th<ese> canc.'), with *to* written in above the preceding comma.

35. hard] Not in the Gk.

Some impious and abominable meal
To the fell Cyclops . . . I am wearied of it —
And now I must scrape up the littered floor
With this great iron rake, so to receive
40   My absent master, and his evening sheep,
In a cave neat and clean . . . even now I see
My children tending the flocks hitherward.
Ha, what is this? — what a Satyric sound!
Are ye not like when the associate band
45   Sought Bacchus [   ]

[*Chorus of Satyrs*]
Where has he of race divine
Wandered in the winding rocks?
Here the air is calm and fine
For the father of the flocks,
50   Here the grass is soft and sweet
And the river eddies meet
In the troughs beside the cave,
Bright as is their fountain wave —
Neither here, nor on the dew
55   Of the lawny uplands feeding?
Oh, you come — a stone at you
Will I throw to mend your breeding.
Get along, you hornèd thing,
Wild, seditious, rambling!

37. *I am wearied of it* –] Not in the Gk.

38. *littered*] Not in the Gk.

43–5. Omitted in *1824*, and replaced with the following:
    Ha! what is this? are your Sicinnian measures
    Even now the same, as when with dance and song
    You brought young Bacchus to Athæa's halls?
These lines are followed in *1824* by a line of asterisks, and like S.'s hesitant rendering, which leaves a space after *Bacchus*, the omissions are probably prompted by the lascivious connotations (see Seaford 106) of the σικινίδων, the satyric dance characterised in line 40 of the Gk as performed in an affectedly effeminate manner (σαυλούμενοι).

46. This speech is not attributed in *Nbk 5*. Here as elsewhere in his trans. S.'s rendering of lyric passages, where the exact meaning is in any case often unclear, is necessarily looser than his treatment of dialogue.

52. *troughs*] trough *1824*.   53. *is*] in *1824*.

59. *seditious*] An understandable mistranslation of the rare στασιωρέ ('watcher of the fold', referring to the satyrs). As *1824* notes, S. omits at this point the whole antistrophe, lines 49–54 in the Gk, perhaps out of delicacy ('Unloose your swollen udders. Take to your teats the young lambs you left behind inside the cave. The little bleating ones, who have slept all day, are missing you. When will you leave the grassy haunts of Aetna behind and enter your vast pen?' Loeb trans.).

60   An Iacchic melody
                    To the golden Aphrodite
                    Will I lift, as thus I fly
                    Seeking her and her delight
                    With the Mænads, whose white feet
65   To the music glance and fleet.
                    Bacchus, o beloved, where
                    Shaking wide thy yellow hair
                    Wanderest thou alone, afar?
                    To the one-eyed Cyclops we,
70   Who by right thy servants are,
                    Minister in misery
                    In the wretched goatskins clad,
                    Far from thy delights and thee.

Silenus
    Be silent, sons, command the slaves to drive
75   The gathered flocks to the rock-roofèd cave.

Chorus
    Go. But what needs this serious haste, o father?

Silenus
    I see a Grecian ship upon the coast,
    And the chief rowers with some general
    Approaching to this cave; around their necks
80   Hang empty vessels, as they wanted food,
    And water-flasks. — O miserable strangers,
    Whence come ye that ye know not what and who
    My master is, and approaching in ill hour
    The inhospitable roof of Polypheme
85   And the Cyclopian jaw-bone, — man-destroying?

60–5. See *PU* III iii 154–5 and note.

62. *thus I fly*] erst did I *1824*.

72. *the*] these *1824*.

75. *to*] into *1824*.

77. *Grecian ship upon*] Greek ship's boat upon *1824*; Grecian vessel on *1839*.

78. *the chief*] thence the *1824*.

79. *cave; around*] cave. About *1824*.

82–7. This passage is all in the third person in the Gk; a mistake which leads to an awkward mistranslation in line 86, and which is corrected in *1824*.

82. *ye . . . ye*] they, . . . they *1824*.

83. *and*] Omitted in *1824*.

Speak low lest we be heard not, while ye tell
Whence coming, ye arrive the Aetnean hill.

Ulysses
Friends, can you show me some clear water spring,
The remedy of our thirst? — will any one
90 Furnish with food seamen in want of it?
Ha! what is this? We are arrived I see
At the blithe court of Bacchus. I observe
A crowd of satyrs peeping from the caves.
First let me greet the elder — hail!

Silenus
                                        Hail thou,
95 O stranger . . . tell thy country and thy race.

Ulysses
The Ithacan Ulysses and the King
Of Cephalonia.

Silenus
                        Oh, I know the man,
Wordy and shrewd, the son of Sisyphus.

Ulysses
I am the same. But be not impudent. —

Silenus
100 Whence sailing do you come to Sicily?

Ulysses
From Ilion, and from the Trojan toils.

---

86. Be silent, Satyrs, while I ask and hear *1824.*

87. *ye*] they *1824.*

91. *are arrived I see*] seem to be arrived *1824.*

92–3. *blithe court . . . peeping*] Details not in the Gk.

92. *court*] courts *BSM* iii.

93. This sportive band of Satyrs near the caves. *1824.*

98. *shrewd,*] Written above *sharp* canc. and *keen* canc. in *Nbk* 5.

99. I am the same, but do not rail upon me. – *1824.*

Silenus
How, touched you not at your paternal shore?

Ulysses
The strength of tempests bore me here, by force.

Silenus
The self-same accident occurred to me.

Ulysses
105 Were you then driven here by stress of weather?

Silenus
Following the pirates who had kidnapped Bacchus.

Ulysses
What land is this, and who inhabit it?

Silenus
Aetna, the loftiest peak of Sicily.

Ulysses
And are there walls and tower-surrounded towns?

Silenus
110 There are not; only these lone mountain tops.

Ulysses
And who possess the land? the race of beasts?

Silenus
Cyclops, who live in caverns, not in houses.

Ulysses
Obeying whom? Is the state popular?

Silenus
Shepherds. No one obeys any in aught.

Ulysses
115 How live they? — do they sow the corn of Ceres?

102. touched you not at] The Gk has 'Don't you know your way to?'
108. of] in *1824*.
110. There are not; – These lone rocks are bare of men. *1824*.
113. Is the state popular?] i.e. 'Is the state a democracy?' *Is*] Or is *1824*.

380

Silenus
On milk and cheese and on the flesh of sheep.

Ulysses
Have they the Bromian drink from the vine's stream?

Silenus
Ah, no, they live in an unhappy land.

Ulysses
And are they just to strangers? hospitable?

Silenus
120 They think the sweetest thing a stranger brings
Is his own flesh.

Ulysses
                    What? do they eat man's flesh?

Silenus
No one comes here who is not eaten up.

Ulysses
The Cyclops now . . . where is he? not at home?

Silenus
Absent on Aetna hunting with his dogs.

Ulysses
125 How shall we 'scape from this [   ] land?

Silenus
I know not. We will help you all we can.

Ulysses
Provide us food, of which we are in want.

Silenus
I have not any thing but meat.

---

118. *unhappy*] ungracious *1824*. S.'s text read ἄχαριν (for which 'unhappy' is at least as apt as *1824*'s correction) where modern texts read ἄχορον, 'without dances'.

125. Space left in *Nbk 5*, presumably for an additional adjective, as S. has trans. all the Gk. *1824* reads 'Know'st thou what thou must do to aid us hence?'

128–9. *Silenus*: Here is not anything, as I said, but meat. / *Ulysses*: But meat is a sweet remedy for hunger. *1824*.

Ulysses

                              Nay, meat
Is a sweet [   ] for a hungry man.

Silenus
130 Cow's milk there is, and a good round of cheese.

Ulysses
Bring out — I would see all before I bargain.

Silenus
But how much gold will you engage to give?

Ulysses
I bring no gold, but Bacchic juice.

Silenus
                              O joy!
'Tis long since these dry lips were wet with wine.

Ulysses
135 Maron, the son of the god, gave it me.

Silenus
Whom I have nursed a baby in my arms?

Ulysses
The son of Bacchus . . .

Silenus
Have you it now, or is it in the ship?

Ulysses
Old man, this skin contains it, which you see.

Silenus
140 Why, this would hardly be a mouthful for me.

---

129. Space left in *Nbk 5.*

130. and a good round of cheese] and store of curdled cheese *1824*; S. presumably did not know the Gk ὀπίας, 'cheese from milk curdled with fig-juice'.

135. Maron] A personification for wine (see Seaford 128).

137. The son of Bacchus, for your clearer knowledge. *1824.*

Ulysses
Nay, twice as much as you can draw from thence.

Silenus
You speak of a fair fountain, sweet to me.

Ulysses
Would you first taste of the unmingled wine?

Silenus
'Tis just — for tasting calls the purchaser.

Ulysses
145 Here is the cup together with the skin.

Silenus
Come then, untie, that I may [   ] drink.

Ulysses
See.

Silenus
          Papaiapax! what a sweet smell it has!

Ulysses
You see it then? —

Silenus
                    By Jove no, but I smell it!

Ulysses
Taste, that you may not praise it in words only.

Silenus
150 Babai, great Bacchus calls me forth to dance!
Joy, joy!

---

141. i.e. the wine is to be diluted with two parts of water; see Seaford 129–30.

144. for tasting calls] tasting invites *1824; Nbk 5* has *invites* in a smaller hand (but still S.'s) above *calls* as an uncanc. alt., presumably preferred by Mary in her transcript.

146. Space left in *Nbk 5. 1824* reads 'Pour: that the draught may fillip my remembrance.'

147. Papaiapax] S.'s transliteration relishingly exaggerates the sound of the Gk exclamation παπαιάξ; cp. *Babai* for βαβαί in line 150.

Ulysses

Did it flow subtly down your throat?

Silenus

So that it tingled to my very nails.

Ulysses

And in addition I will give you gold.

Silenus

Let gold alone . . . only unlock the cask!

Ulysses

155 Bring out some cheeses now, or a young lamb.

Silenus

That will I do, despising any master.
Yes, let me drink one cup, and I will give
All that the Cyclops feed upon their mountains.

[   ]

Silenus

Ye have ta'en Troy and the old widow Helen?

Ulysses

160 And overthrown the realm of Priam old.

Silenus

Why not then, since the girl is caught again,

151. *subtly*] sweetly *1824* (possibly Mary's mistranscription).

152. *tingled*] The Gk has only 'reached'.

155. *lamb.*] goat. *1824* (S.'s trans. is correct).

158. Most of the page in *Nbk 5* is left blank at this point, where S. leaves lines 166–76 of the Gk untranslated; the passage concerns the sexually stimulating properties of drink ('The man who does not enjoy drinking is mad: in drink one can raise *this* to a stand, catch a handful of breast and look forward to stroking her boscage, there's dancing and forgetfulness of cares.' Loeb trans.).

159. Modern texts of *Cyclops* attribute this line to the Chorus, together with lines 161–9, while Silenus is off-stage. S.'s *old widow* mistranslates χειρίαν, 'in your hands', i.e. 'captive', by confusing it with the more common word χήρα, 'widow'; as *Webb* 93 remarks, this is 'a rather unlikely epithet for Helen of Troy'. The line is given to 'Chorus' in *1824*, and reads 'Ye have taken Troy and laid your hands on Helen?'

160. And utterly destroyed the race of Priam. *1824.*

161–3. Omitted in *1824* and *1839* (and replaced with a line of asterisks), obviously on grounds of propriety.

Let the whole army 'taste of her sweet body'
Since she delights in many paramours,
The wanton wretch? — she was bewitched to see
165 The many-coloured anklets, and the chain
Of woven gold which girt his ivory neck
And so she left that good man Menelaus —
There should be no more women in the world
But such as are reserved for me alone.
170 See, here are sheep and here are goats, Ulysses,
Here are unsparing cheeses of pressed milk;
Take them, — depart with what good speed ye may,
First leaving my reward, the Bacchic dew
Of joy-inspiring grapes.

Ulysses
                                    Ah me, alas,
175 What shall we do? . . . the Cyclops is at hand —
Old man, we perish . . . Whither can we fly?

Silenus
Hide yourselves quick within that hollow rock.

Ulysses
'Twere perilous to fly into the net —

Silenus
There are a hundred outlets of the cave,
180 Hide yourselves quick —

Ulysses
                                    That will I never do —
The mighty Troy were space not wide enough
For he who flies one man — how many times

162. *'taste of her sweet body'*] Recalling *Othello* III iii 349–50: 'I had been happy if the general camp, / Pioneers and all, had tasted her sweet body'. The speech marks are in *Nbk 5*.

165. *anklets*] Literally 'bags around his legs', i.e. Persian trousers, in the Gk; S. makes an intelligent guess.

166. *his ivory neck*] the neck of Paris, *1824*.

174–5. Modern texts give these lines to Silenus.

179. The cavern has recesses numberless; *1824*.

180. *Hide yourselves quick* –] Not in the Gk.

181–2. The mighty Troy would be indeed disgraced / If I should fly one man. How many times *1824*. *Mighty* is canc. in *Nbk 5*. S.'s version borders on nonsense, produced by his confusion of στένοι ('Troy would groan') with στενός ('narrow').

Have I withstood, with shield immovable,
Ten thousand Phrygians — if I needs must die,
185 Yet will I die with glory — if I live,
That praise which I have gained shall yet remain.

Silenus
What ho! assistance, cowards! haste, assistance!

Cyclops Silenus Ulysses Chorus

Cyclops
What bacchanals are here? these tympani
And brazen castanets are the wild work
190 Of Bacchus. Ha! my suckling lambs, fresh-dropped
Outside the cave! can they have left so soon
Their mother's side? And this great round of cheese
Packed in a bulrush basket? What? say — speak!
I will beat some of you till you rain tears.
195 Look up, not downwards, when I speak to you.

Silenus
See, I now gape at Jupiter himself,
I stare upon Orion and the stars.

Cyclops
Well, is the dinner fitly cooked and laid?

Silenus
All ready — if your throat is ready too.

186. That] The<n> *BSM* iii. *shall*] will *1824.*

187. cowards!] comrades, *1824*; neither 'cowards' nor 'comrades' corresponds to anything in the Gk. Modern texts give this line to Cyclops.

188–94. These lines are partly mistranslated by S.; the point in the Gk is that there are *no* tympani *here*. The Gk also says 'How are my young lambs in the cavern'; and S.'s *can they have left so soon?* is also wrong. *1824* rewrites:
What is this tumult? Bacchus is not here,
Nor tympanies nor brazen castanets.
How are my young lambs in the cavern? Milking
Their dams or playing by their sides? And is
The new cheese pressed into the bull-rush baskets?
Speak! I'll beat some of you till you rain tears –

190. suckling] sucking *BSM* iii.

198. dinner] S. 'corrects' Euripides, who has ἄριστόν, 'breakfast'; see Seaford 145–7.

Cyclops
200 Are the bowls full of milk besides?

Silenus
                                        O'erbrimming,
So you may drink a tunful if you will.

Cyclops
Is it ewe's milk or cow's milk, or both mixed?

Silenus
Both — either — only pray don't swallow me.

Cyclops
By no means. [
                                        ]
205 What is this crowd I see beside the stalls?
Outlaws or thieves? — for near my cavern-home
I see my young lambs coupled two by two
With willow twigs; mixed with my cheeses lie
Their implements, and this old fellow here
210 Has his bald head broken with stripes. —

Silenus
                                        Ah me!
I have been beaten, till [   ] a fever.

Cyclops
By whom? Who laid his fist upon your head?

Silenus
Those men — because I would not suffer them
To steal your goods.

Cyclops
                        Did not the rascals know
215 I am a God, sprung from the race of Heaven? —

---

204. Space left in *Nbk 5*. S. omits 2 lines of the Gk ('you would be the death of me with
your dance steps, leaping around inside my belly', Loeb trans.).

208. twigs;] bands; *1824*; *bands* is written above *twigs* in a smaller hand by S. in *Nbk 5*, and
was evidently preferred in Mary's transcript.

211. Space left in *Nbk 5*. *1824* reads 'till I burn with a fever.'

214. To steal your goods.] Canc. in *Nbk 5*.

Silenus

I told them so — but they bore off the things
And ate that cheese in spite of all I said,
And carried off the lambs — and said moreover
They'd pin you down with a three cubit collar
220 And pull your vitals out through your one eye,
Furrow your back with stripes, then binding you
Throw you, as ballast, into the ship's hold.
And then deliver you a slave, to move
Enormous rocks, or found a vestibule.

Cyclops

225 In truth? nay, haste, and place in order quickly
The cooking knives, and heap upon the hearth
And kindle it, a great faggot of wood —
As soon as they are slaughtered they shall fill
My belly, broiling warm from the live coals,
230 Or boiled and seethed within the bubbling cauldron.
I am quite sick of the wild mountain game —
Of stags and lions I have gorged enough —
And I grow hungry for the flesh of men.

Silenus

Nay, master, something new is very pleasant
235 After one thing forever . . . and of late
Very few strangers have approached our cave.

Ulysses

Here, Cyclops, a plain tale on the other side:
We, wanting to buy food, came from our ship
Into the neighbourhood of your cave, and here
240 This old Silenus gave us in exchange
These lambs for wine, the which he took and drank,

---

216. the] your *1824*.

217. that] the *1824*.

218. off] out *1824*.

221. Furrow] Torture *1824*; presumably a misreading in Mary's transcript.

224. found a vestibule.] This absurdity is produced by S.'s text, which has πύλωμα ('gateway, gatehouse') where modern texts emend to μυλῶνα ('corn-mill'). Cp. Wodhull's trans.: 'or to the ground / Level some door.'

225. place in order] S.'s mistake for 'sharpen'; θήξεις, 'sharpen', somewhat resembles part of the common irregular vb. τίθημι, 'place'.

235. forever . . .] for ever, *1824*.

And all by mutual compact, without force.
There is no word of truth in what he says,
For slily he was selling all your store.

Silenus

245 I? May you perish, wretch!

Ulysses

— If I speak false.

Silenus

Cyclops, I swear by Neptune who begot thee,
By mighty Triton, and by Nereus old,
Calypso, and the glaucous Ocean Nymphs,
The sacred waves and all the race of fishes —
250 Be these the witnesses, my dear sweet Master,
My darling little Cyclops, that I never
Gave any of your stores to these false strangers.
If I speak false may they whom most I love,
My children, perish wretchedly.

Chorus

There stop.
255 I saw him giving these things to the strangers.
If I speak false then may my father perish,
But let him not wrong hospitality.

Cyclops

You lie — I swear that he is juster far
Than Rhadamanthus — I trust more in him. —
260 But let me ask, whence have ye sailed, o strangers,
Who are you, and what city nourished ye?

Ulysses

Our race is Ithacan . . . having destroyed
The town of Troy, the tempests of the sea
Have driven us on thy land, o Polypheme.

---

242. *compact*,] co<nsent> *BSM* iii (the metre makes this reading unlikely, and there is a clear descender in S.'s admittedly unclear word).

248. *glaucous*] Not in the Gk.

253. *they*] those *1824*.

257. *let him not*] do not thou *1824*; the Gk means 'do not wrong the guests' (perhaps S. took the imperative ἀδίκει as 3rd person sing.).

Cyclops
265 What, have ye shared in the unenvied spoil
Of the false Helen, near Scamander's stream?

Ulysses
The same, having endured a woeful toil.

Cyclops
O basest expedition! — sailed ye not
From Greece to Phrygia for one woman's sake?

Ulysses
270 'Twas the God's work — no mortal was in fault . . .
But, o great offspring of the Ocean King,
We pray thee, and admonish thee with freedom,
That thou dost spare thy friends who visit thee,
And place no impious food within your jaws.
275 For in the depths of Greece we have upreared
Temples to thy great father, which are all
His homes — the sacred bay of Taenarus
Remains inviolate, and each dim recess
Scooped high on the Malean promontory,
280 And aery Sunium's silver-veinèd crag
Which divine Athens keeps unprofaned ever,
And the Gerastian outlets, and whate'er
Within wide Greece our enterprise has kept
From Phrygian contumely, and in which
285 You have a common care, for you inhabit
The skirts of Grecian land, under the roots
Of Aetna, and its crags spotted with fire —
Turn then to converse under human laws,
Receive us shipwrecked suppliants, and provide
290 Food, clothes and fire, and hospitable gifts,
Nor, fixing upon oxen-piercing spits

274. *your*] thy 1824.

275. *upreared*] S.'s text had Stephanus's suggestion ἱδρυσαμέσθα, 'established', where modern texts emend to ἐρρυσάμεσθα, 'rescued, saved'.

278–9. *dim . . . scooped*] Details not in the Gk.

281. *Athens*] Pallas 1824; S.'s mistake (the Gk reads Ἀθάνας).

282. *And the Gerastian outlets,*] The Gerastian asylums, 1824. The correction is more accurate; Geraistos was a safe harbour on the promontory of Euboea.

288. S. translates his text; modern texts emend to produce 'It is the custom of mortals – if you will pay attention to my words – to receive . . .'

Our limbs, so fill your belly and your jaw. —
Priam's wide land has widowed Greece enough
And weapon-wingèd murder heaped together
295 Enough of dead, and wives are husbandless
And ancient women and grey fathers wail
Their childless age — if you should roast the rest
(And 'tis a bitter feast which you prepare)
Where then would any turn? — yet be persuaded,
300 Forego this lust of your jaw-bone . . . prefer
Pious humanity to wicked will . . .
Many have bought too dear their evil joys.

Silenus
Let me advise you . . . do not spare a morsel
Of all that flesh. What, would you eat your words
305 And be a vain and babbling boaster, Cyclops?

Cyclops
Wealth, my good fellow, is the wise man's god,
All other things are a pretence and boast.
What are my father's Ocean promontories,
The sacred rocks whereon he dwells, to me?
310 Stranger, I laugh to scorn Jove's thunderbolt. —
I know not that his strength is more than mine.
As to the rest I care not . . . when he pours
Rain from above, I have a close pavilion
Under this rock, in which I lay supine
315 Feasting on a roast calf, or some wild beast,
And drinking pans of milk, and gloriously
Emulating the thunder of high Heaven;

292. *jaw.* –] jaws. *1824.*

296. *wail*] S.'s trans. is mistaken, perhaps by a confusion of the Gk text's ὤλεσεν (from ὀλλύμι, 'destroy') with ὠλόλυξε (from ὀλολύζω, 'cry aloud').

298. No brackets in *Nbk 5, eds. which*] that *1824.*

300. *this*] the *1824.*

304–5. *1824* rewrites S.'s mistranslation: 'Of all that flesh. If you should eat his tongue / You would become most eloquent, O Cyclops?' Cp. *Webb* 97: 'Shelley misinterpreted the straightforward ἤν τε τὴν γλῶσσαν δάκηις, confusing it with the English idiom *to eat one's words*. As a result the last line of Shelley's version was tailored to suit this sense'.

314. *in which I lay supine*] S.'s trans. invents a plausible meaning for the corrupt text he was using; modern texts emend to produce 'taking my water-tight shelter in this cave' (Loeb trans.). *lay*] lie *1824*. 'Lay' was still in 1818 an acceptable alternative for 'lie' (*OED* Lay vii 43).

317. S. omits the phrase πέπλον κρούω, interpreted by commentators as 'farting', but according to Seaford 166 in fact referring '(hyperbolically) to masturbation'.

And when the Thracian wind pours down the snow
I wrap my body in the skins of beasts,
320 Kindle a fire, and bid the snow whirl on. —
The earth by force, whether it will or no,
Bringing forth grass fattens my flocks and herds
Which, to what other God but to myself
And this great belly, first of deities,
325 Should I be bound to sacrifice? Know this,
That Jupiter himself instructs the wise
To eat and drink during their little day,
Forbidding them to plague him — as for those
Who complicate with laws the life of man,
330 He has appointed tears for their reward.
I will not cheat my soul of its delight
Or hesitate in dining upon you —
And that I may be quit of all demands
These are my hospitable gifts . . . fierce fire
335 And yon ancestral cauldron, which o'erbubbling
Shall finely cook your miserable flesh. —
Creep in! [
                                    ]

Ulysses
Aye! aye! I have escaped the Trojan toils,
I have escaped the sea, and now I fall
340 Under the grasp of one impious man. —
O Pallas, mistress, Goddess sprung from Jove,
Now, now assist me: mightier toils than Troy
Are these . . . I totter o'er the chasms of peril —

325–8. 1824 rewrites:
> Should I be bound to sacrifice? I well know
> The wise man's only Jupiter is this,
> To eat and drink during his little day,
> And give himself no care. And as for those

330. He has appointed] I freely give them *1824*. The Gk line means literally 'I bid them weep' (i.e., as Loeb translates, 'they can go hang').

336. S.'s text had δυσόρητον, emended in modern texts to διαφόρητον, 'chopped up'.

337. Space left in *Nbk 5*, where S. leaves 1½ lines of the Gk untranslated ('in order that you may stand around the altar of the god who dwells within and give me sumptuous entertainment', Loeb trans.).

338. Aye! aye!] Transliterates the Gk αἰαῖ, 'alas'.

340. the grasp] the cruel grasp *1824*; cruel is canc. in *Nbk 5*, but was presumably included in Mary's transcript, perhaps on metrical grounds.

343. I totter o'er] The Gk has simply 'and'. *o'er*] on *1824*; possibly a mistranscription by Mary.

And o thou who inhabitest the thrones
345 Of the bright stars, look, hospitable Jove,
Upon this outrage of thy deity,
Otherwise be considered as no God.

Chorus

For your gaping gulf, and your gullet wide
The ravin is ready on every side,
350 The limbs of the strangers are cooked and done,
There is boiled meat and roast meat and meat from the coal,
You may chop it and tear it and gnash it for fun;
A hairy goatskin contains the whole . . .
Let me but escape and ferry me o'er
355 The stream of your wrath to a safer shore.

The monster, he is cruel and bold,
He murders the strangers
That sit on his hearth
And dreads no avengers
360 To rise from the earth.
He roasts the men before they are cold,
He snatches them broiling from the coal
And from the cauldron pulls them whole,
And minces their flesh, and gnaws their bone
365 With his cursed teeth till all be gone.
Farewell foul pavilion,
Farewell rites of dread —

344. o] Omitted in *1824*, and apparently canc. in *Nbk 5*, but required by the metre.

345. hospitable] i.e. god of guest-friendship.

349. ravin] There is a definite space after this word in *Nbk 5*, but it is not obvious why.

353. A hairy goatskin] An hairy goat's-skin *1824* (alt. back to *A hairy* in *1839*). The suspension points at the end of this line indicate that S. leaves untranslated line 361 of the Gk, 'Do not, do not, I say, give me any share of them!' (Loeb trans.).

354–71. These lines correspond roughly to 363–74 in the original, but not entirely in the same order: S.'s lines 356–65 translate the Gk lines 369–74 (with the details of the eating much expanded); S.'s lines 366–71 translate the Gk lines 363–8.

356. The monster, he] The Cyclops Aetnean *1824*, apparently failing to realise that S. is not taking the Gk in order (S.'s line 368 corresponds to the Gk here).

364. bone] bones *BSM* iii; S. first wrote *bones*, but the word was then canc. and *bone* written again as S. worked out the rhyme with the following line (see *BSM* iii 258).

365. be gone.] begone. *1824* (alt. back to *be gone.* in *1839*). There is a line of space following this line in *1824* and *1839*.

367. rites of dread] S.'s rendering of his corrupt text, which literally means something like 'Farewell feast of the unsacrificing godless Cyclops'.

The Cyclops vermilion
With slaughter uncloying
370   Now feasts on the dead,
In the flesh of strangers joying! —

Ulysses
O Jupiter — I saw within the cave
Horrible things — deeds to be feigned in words
But not to be believed as being done.

Chorus
375 What sawst thou? — is the impious Polypheme
Feasting upon your loved companions now?

Ulysses
Selecting two, the plumpest of the crowd,
He grasped them in his hands.

Chorus
                             Unhappy man!

Ulysses
Soon as we came into this craggy place,
380 Kindling a fire, he cast on the broad hearth
The knotty limbs of an enormous oak,
Three wagon-loads at least, and then he strewed
Upon the ground beside the red firelight
His couch of pine leaves, and he milked the cows,
385 And pouring forth the white milk, filled a bowl
Three cubits wide and four in depth, as much
As would contain ten amphorae, and bound it
With ivy wreaths, then placed upon the fire
A brazen pot to boil, and made red hot
390 The points of spits, not sharpened with the sickle

---

372. saw] Alt. from *see* in *Nbk 5*.

374. to be] Omitted in *1824*.

375. sawst thou? – is] sawest thou *1824*. *BSM* iii reads 's<ee>st', but S. has alt. the tense (as in line 372).

378. grasped] S. probably guesses at κἀπιβαστάσας, 'took them into his hands to feel the weight of them'. Following this line S. leaves a gap (marked by a line of asterisks in *1824*) where one line of the Gk is untranslated ('how came your comrades to suffer this fate', Loeb trans.).

387. ten] four *1824*; *ten* is apparently alt. from *four* in *Nbk 5* (S. translates δεκάμφορον) and Mary presumably read the word as *four* in her transcript.

But with a fruit-tree bough, and with the jaws
Of axes for Aetnean slaughterings;
And when this god-abandoned cook of Hell
Had made all ready, he seized two of us
395 And killed them in a kind of measured manner,
For he flung one against the brazen rivets
Of the huge cauldron-belly, and seized the other
By the foot's tendon and knocked out his brains
Upon the sharp edge of the craggy stone,
400 Then peeled his flesh with a great cooking knife
And put him down to roast. The other's limbs
He chopped into the cauldron to be boiled.
And I, with the tears raining from my eyes,
Stood near the Cyclops ministering to him.
405 The rest, in the recesses of the cave
Clung to the rock like birds, bloodless with fear. —
When he was filled with my companions' flesh
He threw himself upon the ground, and sent
A loathsome exhalation from his maw . . .
410 Then a divine thought came to me. I filled
The cup of Maron, and I offered him
To taste, and said: 'Child of the Ocean God,
Behold what drink the vines of Greece produce,
The exultation and the joy of Bacchus . . .'
415 He, satiated with his unnatural food,
Received it, and at one draught drank it off,
And taking my hand praised me — 'Thou hast given
A sweet draught after a sweet meal, dear guest' —
And I, perceiving that it pleased him, filled
420 Another cup, well knowing that the wine
Would wound him soon, and take a sure revenge . . .

391–2. S. has a marginal note in *Nbk 5* against these lines: 'I confess I do not understand this' (the note is included in *1824* and *1839*). S.'s difficulty is produced by the corrupt Gk text at this point, where there is probably a lacuna; modern emendations of the Gk lines 394–5 give something like 'Spits of hard wood, the tips hardened in the fire, and the rest smoothed with a bill-hook' (see Loeb 104–5, Seaford 180–2).

393. *god-abandoned cook of Hell*] A literal translation.

396. *flung*] In *Nbk 5* flung is canc. and replaced by *knocked*, which is itself canc. with *flung* reinstated by underlining.

397. *cauldron-belly*] The hyphenated *belly*, which is apt for the Gk κύτος, is omitted in *1824*.

406. *birds*] bats *1824*; S. has written *bats* above *birds* in a smaller hand in *Nbk 5*, and Mary evidently preferred the later reading in her transcript. The Gk has ὄρνιθες (birds).

407. *companions'*] *Nbk 5*, *1839*; companions *1824*.

417. *taking my hand*] Literally 'raising his hand' in the Gk.

And the charm fascinated him, and I
Plied him cup after cup, until the drink
Had warmed his entrails, and he sang aloud
425 In concert with my wailing fellow-seamen
A hideous discord — and the cavern rung . . .
I have stolen out, so that if you will
You may assist my safety and your own.
But say, do you desire, or not, to fly
430 This uncompanionable man, and dwell
As was your wont with the Danaides
Within the fanes of your beloved God? —
Your father there within agrees to it,
But he is weak and overcome with wine,
435 And caught as if with bird-lime by the cup
He flaps his wings and crows in doting joy.
You who are young, escape with me and find
Bacchus your ancient friend, unsuited he
To this rude Cyclops.

Chorus

     O my dearest friend,
440 That I could see that day, and leave for ever
The impious Cyclops! [   ]

Ulysses

Listen then what a punishment I have
For this fell monster, how secure a flight
From your hard servitude.

Chorus

     O sweeter far
445 Than is the music of an Asian lyre
Would be the news of Polypheme destroyed.

422. the charm fascinated him] Literally 'he started singing' in the Gk.

428. assist] achieve *1824*; S. has written *achieve* above *assist* in *Nbk 5*, and Mary presumably preferred the later reading in her transcript.

429. But say] By s<k>y *BSM* iii (noting that 'say' is a possible reading); *By* seems clear in *Nbk 5*, giving 'By sky do you desire, or not, to fly', which makes a kind of sense as a line, but corresponds to nothing in the Gk and could only be confusedly linked with the metaphor of bird-lime and wings which follows.

431. with the Danaides] among the Grecian Nymphs *1824*.

436. flaps] claps *1824*.

441. Space left in *Nbk 5*, where S. leaves 2 lines of the Gk untranslated; the omitted passage is probably corrupt in the Gk text, and its sense is unclear, though obviously sexual, meaning something like 'For a long time now my poor siphon here [i.e. penis] has been widowed, with no place to lay its head' (Loeb trans.; cp. Seaford 186–7).

Ulysses
Delighted with the Bacchic drink, he goes
To call his brother Cyclops, who inhabit
A village upon Aetna, not far off.

Chorus
450 I understand . . . catching him when alone
You think with some [   ] measures to despatch him,
Or thrust him from the precipice.

Ulysses
                              O no.
Nothing of that kind . . . my device — is subtle.

Chorus
How then? I heard of old that you were wise.

Ulysses
455 I will dissuade him from this plan — by saying
It were unwise to give the Cyclopses
This precious drink, which if enjoyed alone
Would make life sweeter for a longer time . . .
When vanquished by the Bacchic power he sleeps,
460 There is a trunk of olive wood within,
Whose point having made sharp with this good sword
I will conceal in fire, and when I see
It is alight, will fix it, burning yet,
Within the socket of the Cyclops' eye
465 And melt it out with fire — as when a man
Turns by its handle a great auger round,
Fitting the framework of a ship with beams,
So will I in the Cyclops' fiery eye
Turn round the brand and dry the pupil up . . .

448–9. *who inhabit . . . far off.*] This mistranslates κῶμον, 'a revel', which S. confuses with κώμε, 'village' (see note to line 504).

451. *with some [ ] measures*] S. translates his text's ῥυθμοῖσί, which in modern texts is emended to δρυμοῖσί ('in the woods'); in *Nbk 5* S. has noted the uninflected form ῥυθμος in the margin, presumably with a view to looking it up. *1824* reads 'You think by some measure to dispatch him'.

454. *you were*] thou wert *1824*.

463. *will*] well *BSM* iii.

466. *by its handle*] Literally 'by its pair of straps' in the Gk.

Chorus

470 Joy! I am mad with joy at the device.

Ulysses
And then with you, our friends, and the old man,
We'll load the hollow depth of our black ship,
And row with double strokes from this dread shore.

Chorus
May I, as in libations to a God,
475 Share in the blinding him with the red brand?
I would have some communion in his death.

Ulysses
Doubtless . . . the brand is a great brand to hold.

Chorus
O I would lift a hundred wagon-loads
If like a wasp-nest I could scoop the eye out
480 Of the detested Cyclops.

Ulysses
Silence now —
Ye know the close device . . . and when I call
Look ye obey the masters of the craft. —
I will not save myself and leave behind
My comrades in the cave; I might escape
485 Having got clear from the obscure recess,
But 'twere unjust to leave in jeopardy
The dear companions who sailed here with me.

Chorus
Come — who is first — that with his hand
Will urge down the burning brand
490 Through the lids, and quench and pierce
The Cyclops' eye so fiery fierce.

470. *the*] your *1824.*
471. *our*] my *1824.*
473. *dread*] Not in the Gk.
475. *red*] Not in the Gk.
478. *a*] an *1824* (alt. back to *a* in *1839*).
479. *wasp-nest*] wasp's nest *1824.*
485. *the*] that *1824.*

Semichorus 1

Within is song —
Listen, listen — he is coming,
A most hideous discord humming.
495   Drunken, museless, awkward, yelling,
Far along his rocky dwelling.
Let us with some comic spell
Teach the yet unteachable.
O come along!
500   By all means he must be blinded —
If my counsel be but minded. —

Semichorus 2

Happy those made odorous
With the dew which sweet grapes weep —
To the village hastening thus —
505   Seek the joys that soothe to sleep,
Having first embraced thy friend —
Thou in luxury without end
With the rings of yellow hair
Of thy voluptuous leman fair
510   Shalt sit playing on a bed —
Speak, what door is openèd?

492. This line is a stage direction (the only original example surviving in Gk drama); S. was misled into giving it as a line of the Semichorus by the layout in his copy of Barnes's text (see *Webb* 350). The error is corrected in *1824*.

497. See note to line 504.

499. This line is omitted in *1824*.

501. This line has no equivalent in the Gk.

504. to the village] As in lines 448–9 S. mistakes κῶμον, 'revel', for κώμε, 'village', even though he gets it right in line 497 (Gk line 492); at line 520 (Gk line 508) he ignores the word, and at line 551 (Gk line 537) he correctly has 'mirth'. Puzzlingly, he also actually conflates the two words in line 548 (Gk line 535), 'village mirth', although again there is no mention of villages in Euripides.

505. joys] vines *1824*; the passage has definite sexual overtones, and the 'friend' of line 506 is male in the Gk. The *Nbk 5* reading is debatable, but certainly closer to *joys* than *vines*. Perhaps Mary sought to downplay the indelicate implications of S.'s trans., which itself at first attempted a more neutral rendering in the canc. line (following the received line 505) 'Life's best harvest shalt thou reap'.

507–11. This passage is in the third person sing. in the Gk.

507. Thou] There *1824*. The middle three words of this line are canc. in *Nbk 5*.

508. rings] strings *1824*; the *Nbk 5* reading is difficult and *1824* may originate in Mary's mistranscription.

511. In the Gk this line carries an obvious sexual resonance; S. somewhat clumsily turns it into a 'dramatic' response to the appearance of Polyphemus.

Cyclops
Ha ha ha, I'm full of wine,
Heavy with the joy divine,
With the young feast oversated
515 Like a merchant vessel freighted
To the water's edge, my crop
Laden to the gullet's top.
The fresh meadow grass of spring
Tempts me forth thus wandering
520 To my brothers on the mountains
Who shall share the wine's sweet fountains.
Bring the cask, o stranger, bring!

Chorus
One with eyes the fairest
Cometh from his dwelling —
525 Someone loves thee, rarest,
Bright beyond my telling;
In thy grace thou shinest
Like some Nymph divinest
In her caverns dewy . . .
530 All delights pursue ye,
Soon pied flowers, sweet-breathing,
Shall thy head be wreathing.

Ulysses
Listen, o Cyclops . . . for I am well skilled
In Bacchus, whom I gave thee of to drink.

Cyclops
535 What sort of God is Bacchus then accounted?

Ulysses
The greatest among men for joy of life.

514. young feast] S. literally translates his text, which is probably corrupt at this point.
515. merchant] merchant's *1824*.
516. water's] waters *1824* (alt. back to *water's* in *1839*).
517. Laden] Is laden *1824*.
520. See note to line 504.
521. This line has no equivalent in the Gk.
523–9. The Gk text is corrupt and any trans. conjectural; S.'s Gk text has no verb.
530. ye,] thee, *1824*.

Cyclops
I gulped him down with very great delight.

Ulysses
This is a God who never injures men.

Cyclops
How does the God like living in a cask?

Ulysses
540 He is content wherever he is put.

Cyclops
Gods should not have their body in a skin.

Ulysses
If he gives joy, what is his skin to you?

Cyclops
I hate the skin . . . but love the drink within.

Ulysses
Stay here now, drink and make your spirit glad.

Cyclops
545 Should I not share this liquor with my brothers?

Ulysses
Keep it yourself and be more honoured so.

Cyclops
I were more useful, giving to my friends.

Ulysses
But village mirth breeds contests, broils and blows.

Cyclops
When I am drunk none shall lay hands on me.

---

537. *I gulped him down*] Literally 'I belch him up'; S. has jotted ἐρυγγανω ('I belch') next to this line in *Nbk 5*.

539. *cask?*] Written after *skin?*, and both canc., in *Nbk 5. 1824* reads *skin?*

543. *drink*] wine *1824*.

548, 551. See note to line 504.

Ulysses
550 A drunken man is better within doors.

Cyclops
He is a fool, who drinking loves not mirth.

Ulysses
But he is wise who, drunk, remains at home.

Cyclops
What shall I do, Silenus, shall I stay?

Silenus
Stay — for what need have you of pot companions?

Cyclops
555 Indeed this place is closely carpeted
With flowers and grass.

Silenus
                And in the sunwarm noon
'Tis sweet to drink — lie down beside me now,
Placing your mighty sides upon the ground.

Cyclops
What do you put the cup behind me for?

Silenus
560 That no one here may touch it.

Cyclops
                Thievish one,
You want to drink . . . here, place it in the midst,
And thou, oh stranger, tell how thou art called.

Ulysses
My name is Nobody. What favour now
Shall I receive, to praise you, at your hands?

Cyclops
565 I'll feast on you the last of your companions.

Ulysses
You grant your guest a fair reward, o Cyclops.

---

554. *pot companions*] S.'s deft trans. perhaps echoes the sound of the Gk συμποτῶν.

Cyclops
Ha, what is this? Stealing the wine, you rogue?

Silenus
It was this stranger kissing me because
I look so beautiful.

Cyclops
    You shall repent
570 For kissing the coy wine that loves not you.

Silenus
By Jupiter, you said that I am fair.

Cyclops
Pour out . . . and only give me the cup full.

Silenus
How is it mixed? Let me observe.

Cyclops
       Curse you!
Give it me so.

Silenus
    By Jupiter, while you redress
575 That coronal, I swear I'll have a taste.

Cyclops
An unjust [ ]

Silenus
    But the wine is sweet —
Aye, you will roar if you are caught in drinking.

---

568. *this stranger*] The Gk says 'the wine'.

569. *look*] looked *1824*.

570. *not you.*] you not. *1824*.

571. *you said*] A mistake for 'it says'.

574–6. *By Jupiter . . . unjust [ ]*] Rewritten in *1824*: 'Not till I see you wear / That coronal, and taste the cup to you. *Cyclops*: Thou wily traitor!' S.'s blank leaves untranslated the Gk οἰνοχόος, 'cup-bearer'.

577. S. mistranslates this line, perhaps because his text's ἀπομυκτέον reminds him of the Homeric verb μυκάομαι, 'bellow'; Loeb (using an emended text) gives 'But time to wipe your mouth: here comes a drink'.

Cyclops
See now, my lip is clean, and all my beard.

Silenus
Now put your elbow right, and drink again
580 As you see me drink, so you will not vomit.

Cyclops
How now?

Silenus
                    Oh, what a delicious gulp!

Cyclops
Guest, take it — you pour out the wine for me.

Ulysses
The vine will be distinguished from my hand.

Cyclops
Pour out the wine.

Ulysses
                    I pour . . . only be quiet.

Cyclops
585 Silence is a hard task to him who drinks.

Ulysses
Take it and drink it off — leave not a dreg —
O that the drinker died with his own draught.

Cyclops
Papai! the vine must be a sapient plant.

---

580. so you will not vomit] Omitted in *1824*, no doubt on grounds of propriety. S. mistrans-
lates, and in doing so also misses the joke: Loeb translates 'just as you see me drink – or see
me not!' (i.e. he drinks, tipping the wine cup up so as to conceal his drinking). S. apparently
confuses the pronoun ἐμέ in his text with the verb ἐμεῖν, 'vomit'.

581. Oh,] Ye Gods, *1824.*

583. The wine is well accustomed to my hand. *1824.*

587. S.'s distinctive rendering is a reasonable guess; the Gk, meaning literally something like
'You must be silent and die with the drink', is according to commentators a drinking for-
mula meaning 'You must drink it at one go, even if you pass out' (see Seaford 208).

588. vine] wine *1824.*

Ulysses
If you drink much after a mighty feast,
590 Moistening your thirsty maw, you will sleep well;
If you leave aught, Bacchus will dry you up.

Cyclops
Ho, ho, I can scarce rise . . . What pure delight!
The heavens and earth appear to whirl about
Confusedly . . . I see the throne of Jove
595 And the clear congregation of the Gods . . .
Now if the Graces tempted me to kiss
I would not . . . for the loveliest of them all
I would not leave this Ganymede. 'Tis strange,
Somehow or other I take more delight
600 In boys than women.

Silenus
                O great Polypheme,
I am the Ganymede of Jupiter.

Cyclops
By Jove you are, I bore you off from Dardanus.

Silenus
I perish, boys, I suffer horribly.

Chorus
Do you complain that you are loved, and fallen
605 Into the lap of luxury and delight?

Silenus
Ah me, I soon shall sleep a bitter sleep.

Ulysses
Come, boys of Bacchus, Children of high race,
This man within is folded up in sleep
And soon will vomit flesh from his fell maw.
610 The brand under the shed thrusts forth its smoke,

598–600. 'Tis strange . . . O great] Omitted in *1824* (see note to lines 603–6).
601. This should be a question.
603–6. Omitted in *1824*, obviously because of the frank homosexual reference.
604–5. Modern editors usually give this line to the Cyclops.
606. S.'s *sleep* derives from an emendation in his text, since abandoned by modern editors, who restore 'wine'; Loeb translates 'My glimpse of the wine will soon prove all too bitter!'
610. forth] out *1824*. S.'s *under the shed* seems an odd rendering of the Gk 'within the halls'.

405

No preparation needs, but to burn out
The monster's eye . . . but bear yourselves like men.

Chorus
We will have courage, like the adamant rock.
All things are ready for you here. Go in
615 Before our father shall perceive the noise.

Ulysses
Vulcan, Aetnean King — burn out with fire
The shining eye of this thy neighbouring monster,
And thou, o Sleep, nursling of gloomy Night,
Descend unmixed on this god-hated beast
620 And suffer not Ulysses and his comrades,
Returning from their famous Trojan toils,
To perish by this man, who cares not either
For God or mortal. I of force believe
That chance is a supreme divinity,
625 For things divine are subject to her power.

Chorus
Soon a crab will seize the throat
Of him who feeds upon his guest;
Fire will burn his lamplike eyes
In revenge of such a feast.
630 A great oak stump now is lying
In the ashes yet undying.
Come, Maron, come,

612. In the Gk the brand 'is prepared'; and then '(There is) nothing else (to be done) other than to burn out . . .'. S.'s suspension points perhaps indicate that he had not quite worked this out.

615. *perceive the noise*] This rendering is remote from the Gk. S.'s text has ἀπαλλαγμὸν ('release') where modern texts emend to ἀπάλαμνον (which Loeb translates as 'awful disaster'; Seaford 212 notes the possibility here of 'an obscene overtone'). S.'s 'noise' has no equivalent in the Gk, though his 'perceive' could be a gloss for παθεῖν ('experience'). As *BSM* iii 356 notes, 'Shelley's version evades the point of the original here, namely the Cyclops' homosexual assault on Silenus'.

617. S. omits (perhaps not understanding) 'and get rid of him once for all'.

623. *I of force believe*] or I needs must think *1824*.

625. *For*] And *1824*.

626. *will seize the throat*] the throat will seize *1824*. S.'s uncanc. alt. *fill*, for *seize*, in *Nbk 5* is weaker and less accurate.

629. This line has no equivalent in the Gk.

632. *Maron*] i.e. the wine (cp. line 135 and note).

Raging let him fix the doom,
Let him tear the eyelid up
635   Of the Cyclops . . . that his cup
May be evil.
Oh that I might dance and revel
With sweet Bromius, long desired,
In loved ivy wreaths attired,
640   Leaving this abandoned home.
Will that hour ever come?

Ulysses

Be silent ye wild things — nay, hold your peace
And keep your lips quite close — dare not to breathe
Or spit or e'er wink, lest ye should waken
645   Calamity — until the Cyclops' eye
Be tortured out with sight-destroying fire.

Chorus

Nay, we are silent, and we chaw the air.

Ulysses

Come now, and lend a hand to the great stake
Within — it is delightfully red hot.

Chorus

650   You then command who first should seize the stake
To burn the Cyclops' eye — that all may share
In the great enterprise.

---

633. *Raging*] Modern texts make this word agree with the Cyclops.

637. *Oh that I might*] O, I long to *1824*. *dance and revel*] Simply 'see' in the Gk.

638. *Bromius,*] Bromian, *1824*. Bromius is another name for Dionysus (i.e. Bacchus).

641. *that hour*] the moment *1824*.

644–6. *should waken . . . fire.*] *1824* reads 'wake the monster, / Until his eye be tortured out with fire'; this reading seems a combination of rewriting by a third party (see headnote, and cp. *BSM* iii 292–3) with Mary's rendering of the passage in *Nbk 5*, which leaves *monster* as an uncanc. alt. for *calamity*. The Gk τὸ κακόν, literally 'the evil', could be translated as either 'calamity' or 'monster'. S.'s *sight-destroying* is not (literally) in the Gk.

644. *e'er*] e'en *1824*. Probably Mary's mistranscription; *e'er* is written above *even* canc. in *Nbk 5*.

647. *chaw*] An archaic form for *chew*, common in the sixteenth and seventeenth centuries according to *OED*, but since then the old spelling has connotations of a vulgar idiom, implying to chew roughly, or without swallowing.

650–2. A question in modern texts of the Gk, though not in S.'s.

Semichorus 1
                    We are too far . . .
We cannot from this distance from the doors
Thrust fire into his eye.

Semichorus 2
                         And we just now
655   Have become lame, cannot move hand or foot.

Chorus
The same thing has occurred to us, our ankles
Are sprained with standing here . . . I know not how.

Ulysses
What, sprained with standing still?

Chorus
                              And there is dust
Or ashes in our eyes . . . I know not whence.

Ulysses
[   ]

Chorus
660   With pitying my own back and my backbone,
And with not wishing all my teeth knocked out,
This cowardice comes of itself . . . but stay,
I know a famous Orphic incantation
To make the brand stick of its own accord
665   Into the skull of this one-eyed Son of Earth.

Ulysses
Of old I knew ye thus by nature; now
I know ye better . . . I will use the aid
Of my own comrades . . . yet, though weak of hand,

---

652. *far . . .*] few, *1824.*

653–4. The construction is easier in the Gk: 'we are much too far from the doors to thrust . . .' (the corrections in *1824* look pedantic and are incorrect).

653. *from*] at *1824.*   *doors*] door *1824.*

655. *or*] nor *1839; cannot move hand or foot* is not in the Gk.

656–7. This speech should probably be given to 'Semichorus 1' or to a third division of the Chorus (as should the speech at lines 658–9).

659. S. left the space for a missing line in *Nbk 5; 1824* fills in: 'Cowardly dogs! ye will not aid me then?'

Speak cheerfully, that so I may awaken
670 The courage of my friends with your blithe words.

Chorus
That will I do with peril of my life,
And blind you with my exhortations, Cyclops.
    Hasten and thrust,
    And scorch up to dust
675   The eye of the beast
    Who feeds on his guest.
    Burn and blind
    The Aetnean hind,
    Scoop and draw
680   Till his doom be full,
    But beware lest he claw
    Your limbs near his maw.

Cyclops
Ah me! my eyesight is parched up to cinders.

Chorus
What a sweet paean! sing me that again.

Cyclops
685 Ah me, indeed! What woe has fallen upon me!
But, wretched nothings, think ye not to flee
Out of this rock; I standing at the outlet
Will bar the way and catch you as you pass.

Chorus
What are you roaring out, Cyclops?

Cyclops
                    I perish!

Chorus
690 For you are wicked.

---

669. I] ye *1824*.

671. *That*] This *1824*. The Gk says 'We will incur danger in the person of the Carian', i.e. vicariously (the Carians being notorious as mercenary troops).

674. *scorch*] parch *1824*; *parch* is alt. to *scorch* in *Nbk 5* (*BSM* iii reads '<parch>').

680. Not in the Gk, and omitted in *1824*.

690. *wicked*] The Gk sense is more like 'ugly'; although αἰσχρός can mean 'wicked'.

Cyclops

And besides miserable.

Chorus
What, did you fall upon the coals when drunk?

Cyclops
'Twas Nobody destroyed me.

Chorus

Why, then no one
Can be to blame.

Cyclops

I say 'twas Nobody
Who blinded me.

Chorus

Why, then you are not blind.

Cyclops
695 I wish you were as blind as I am.

Chorus

Nay,
It cannot be that no one made you blind.

Cyclops
You jeer me — where, I ask, is Nobody?

Chorus
Nowhere, o Cyclops.

Cyclops
That stranger 'twas who ruined me — the wretch
700 First gave me wine and then burnt out my eye,

---

691. *upon the coals*] into the fire *1824*; *into the fire* is written above *upon the coals* (which is accurate) as an uncanc. alt. in *Nbk 5*, and was presumably preferred by Mary in her transcript.

695. The Gk is obscure and probably corrupt, saying merely 'so you'.

696. A question in the Gk: 'How could Nobody make you blind?'

699. *That stranger 'twas who*] It was that stranger *1824*; S. at first wrote *That stranger ruined me* – in *Nbk 5*, then added *twas who* above the line; the *1824* reading no doubt derives from Mary's rendering of the line in her transcript.

700. *eye,*] *1839*; eyes *Nbk 5*; eyes, *1824*. The Gk has 'deluged', 'drenched me' for S.'s *burnt out my eye*.

For wine is strong and hard to struggle with —
Have they escaped or are they yet within?

Chorus
They stand under the darkness of the rock
And cling to it.

Cyclops
              At my right hand or left?

Chorus
705 Close on your right.

Cyclops
                Where?

Chorus
                   Near the rock itself
You have them.

Cyclops
            Oh, misfortune on misfortune,
I've cracked my skull.

Chorus
              Now they escape you — there —

Cyclops
Not there, although you say so.

Chorus
                  Not on that side.

Cyclops
Where, then?

Chorus
           They creep about you on your left.

Cyclops
710 Ah, I am mocked, they jeer me in my ills.

---

701. This line is given to the Chorus in modern texts.
706. The Chorus's line is a question in the Gk.
708. The Cyclops's line is a question in the Gk.

Chorus
Not there — he is a little there beyond you.

Cyclops
Detested wretch, where are you?

Ulysses
                              Far from you
I keep with guards this body of Ulysses.

Cyclops
What do you say? You proffer a new name.

Ulysses
715   My father named me so, and I have taken
A full revenge for your unnatural feast.
I should have done ill to have burned down Troy
And not revenged the murder of my comrades.

Cyclops
Ai! ai! — the ancient oracle is accomplished.
720   It said that I should have my eyesight blinded
By you coming from Troy, yet it foretold
That you should pay the penalty for this
By wandering long over the homeless sea.

Ulysses
I bid thee weep . . . consider what I say:
725   I go towards the shore to drive my ship
To mine own land o'er the Sicilian wave.

Cyclops
Not so, if whelming you with this huge stone
I can crush you and all your men together.
I will descend upon the shore — though blind,
730   Groping my way adown this steep ravine.

Chorus
And we, the shipmates of Ulysses, now
Will serve our Bacchus for [   ]

711. Not there –] The Gk sense is rather 'not any more' (i.e. 'we won't mock you').

713. guards] care *1824*; S.'s trans. is correct.

729. descend upon the shore –] The Gk says 'go up onto the hill' (and S.'s *adown* in the following line is simply 'through' in Euripides).

731–2. These lines are not attributed in *Nbk 5*.

732. Space left in *Nbk 5*; *1824* fills in: 'all our happy lives.'

173
Sonnet
('Lift not the painted veil which those who live')

Printed by Mary S. in *1839* with the Poems of 1818; dating is difficult, but possibly composed during the first week of July 1818 (although *eds*, e.g. *Reiman (1977)* generally place the poem somewhat later). Four versions survive: a draft in *Nbk 11* (its position and context in the nbk do not suggest any conclusive dating; see *BSM* xviii 24–5, 281); a holograph fair copy on pages detached from *Harvard Nbk* and now in the Pierpont Morgan Library (see *MYR* v Introduction xxii–xxiv, 76, 170 for discussion of this MS and its implications); and two posthumously-printed texts, *1824* and *1839*. The descent of the text is perplexing, as Mary S. printed in *1824*, and again in *1839* with one entirely different line, a version conspicuously better than S.'s fair copy in *Harvard Nbk*, which itself was copied into that nbk presumably some two years after the poem's composition. Mary S.'s own source or sources are unknown. It is possible that the mood of isolated and disappointed dejection in the second part of the sonnet is related to the vindictive personal attack on S. as author of *RofI* in the *Quarterly*, news of which reached S. in early July 1818 (see headnote to following poem). The poem also shares with the following poem, which is drafted a few pages later in *Nbk 11*, the possible influence of *Barthelemy*, which Mary and S. were reading in June and July 1818 (*Mary Jnl* i 215–21). If a connection with *RofI* is valid, S. might have returned to this sonnet at the time of his proposing a revised edition of *RofI* to Ollier (16 February, 25 September 1821; *L* ii 263, 354). The *Defence of Poetry*, submitted to Ollier at the same time, also introduces the 'veil' symbol ('and whether [poetry] spreads its own figured curtain, or withdraws life's dark veil from before the scene of things, it equally creates for us a being within our being'; *Prose* 295). The sonnet may also, or alternatively, have been revised as one of the accompanying poems sent with *J&M* to Ollier in November 1820 as one of S.'s 'saddest verses [all] raked up into one heap' (*L* ii 246; see headnote to no. 202). Besides improving lines 12–13 S. may perhaps have inserted an alternative version above line 6 and then underlined the original to indicate re-instatement (possibly after realising the awkward repetition of *there* in lines 2 and 6, referring to different locations). If Mary S. mistook the underlining for a cancellation when preparing *1824* she may have realised her error when preparing *1839*. Otherwise it is hard to explain the appearance of line 6 in *1824*, which does not occur either in the draft or in *Harvard Nbk* (or in Mary S.'s own subsequent editions). The text here adopted is *1839*, on the hypothesis that this text probably derives from S.'s own best revised version.

The poem's central symbol has attracted commentary which discerns a heavily Platonic influence; see e.g. *Notopoulos* 230–31, *Rogers* 122ff. But S.'s veil symbol here is probably not from Plato (who appears never to employ it in this form) but from Lucretius, who explains how visual appearances are thrown off from objects as thin films,

And yellow, red, and rust-coloured canopies (*vela*) do this conspicuously, when they flap and billow, spread abroad on poles and crossbeams over a roomy theatre; for then in waves of their own colour they stain the audience in the pit below and the whole face of the stage and the crush of dignitaries. And the more completely enclosed the sides of the theatre, the more the whole interior, flooded with beauty, rejoices in being deprived of daylight. (*De Re. Nat.* iv 75–83)

S. was no doubt reminded of this passage by *Barthelemy*, in which Philocles condoles with an Egyptian priest who, having tried 'to penetrate the origin and end of all things, said to me, with a sigh: Woe to him who shall attempt to lift up the veil of nature! And I will say: Woe to the man who shall refuse to yield to that theatrical illusion which our prejudices and necessities have diffused over all objects! Soon shall his soul, enfeebled and languishing, find itself plunged in the abyss of nihility, the most dreadful of all punishments. At these words, tears fell from his eyes . . .' (*Barthelemy* vi 397–8). The sonnet is formally interesting, in its inversion of the Petrarchan structure, and in its experimental rhymes; commentary however has been relatively slight, but see *Wasserman* 45–6, and Andrew Welburn, *Power and Self-Consciousness in the Poetry of Shelley* (1986) 1–7.

Text from *1839* iii 157.

Published in *1824* 225.

173
Sonnet: 'Lift not the painted veil'

Lift not the painted veil which those who live
Call Life; though unreal shapes be pictured there,
And it but mimic all we would believe
With colours idly spread, — behind, lurk Fear
And Hope, twin Destinies; who ever weave
Their shadows, o'er the chasm, sightless and drear.

I knew one who had lifted it — he sought,
For his lost heart was tender, things to love,

5

1. *the painted veil*] Identical imagery is used in *PU* III iv 190–2, with a quite different meaning (see B. P. Kurtz, *The Pursuit of Death* (New York 1933) 180–3): in *PU* III the veil is a 'loathsome mask' of false creeds and conventions, discarded after social revolution; here the veil divides the living from the dead, as in 'The Voyage' 59–62, 'Mont Blanc' 53–4, and 'The pale, the cold, and the moony smile' 25–8. The passage from *Barthelemy* quoted in the headnote above explicitly distinguishes the two meanings. *those who live*] men deceived *Nbk 11* canc.

4. *spread, –*] spread: – *1824*.

6. The shadows, which the world calls substance, there. *1824*. *Nbk 11*, *Harvard Nbk* and *1839* all read as the text, and the source of *1824*'s line is mysterious; see headnote. The *1824* meaning must be that it is only the speculations of the living that invent the circumstances of an afterlife. *sightless*] 'Impenetrable to vision'.

7–9. *he sought . . . found them not*] 'With a spirit . . . trembling and feeble thro its tenderness, I have every where sought [   ] & found only repulse and disappointment' ('On Love', quoted from *Nbk 6* f. 2; S.'s essay may have been written in the same week of July 1818 as 'Lift not the painted veil').

7. *knew*] met *Nbk 6* canc. *who had lifted*] who lifted *1824* (probably a misprint).

But found them not, alas! nor was there aught
10   The world contains, the which he could approve.
Through the unheeding many he did move,
A splendour among shadows, a bright blot
Upon this gloomy scene, a Spirit that strove
For truth, and like the Preacher found it not.

174
'Alas, this is not what I thought life was'

Difficult to date, but perhaps drafted in the first week of July 1818, possibly at about
the same time as the preceding sonnet 'Lift not the painted veil'. The two pieces
are three pages apart in *Nbk 11*. Mary S.'s inclusion of the lines in her notes to the
Poems of 1820 does not imply their assignation to that date, but was to illustrate
S.'s reaction to the personal abuse of reviewers: 'That he felt these things deeply
cannot be doubted, though he armed himself with the consciousness of acting from
a lofty and heroic sense of right' (*1839* iv 52). Lines 4–5 in the earlier of the two
drafts in *Nbk 11* pp. 26–8 (see *BSM* xviii 28–31) support this connection: 'nor did

11–14. The draft in *Nbk 11* ends:

     Like an unheeded shadow he did move
     Among the careless crowd that marked him not
     I should be happier had I never known
     This mournful man – he was himself alone

As *Wasserman* 181 notes, ' "Being himself alone" was S.'s standard phrase for self-possession,
or for absoluteness and autonomy'; e.g. 'Sonnet to the Republic of Benevento' 10–11, 13–14:
'Man who man would be, / Must rule the empire of himself . . . / . . . quelling the anarchy /
Of hopes & fears, – being himself alone –' (*Harvard Nbk* 152).

12–13. Originally in *Nbk 6*: 'a blight / Cast on the sunny world, – a wave'. Then *blight* was
canc. for *blot*, and *sunny* for *gloomy*; presumably the first cancellation suggested the text's
bright blot. *Wasserman* 67 explains the paradox of *bright blot, a splendour among shadows*, as
expressing the misanthropy of a too-eager idealist; but the imagery can work the other way:
in *Adonais* 280–6, idealism is subduable only by overwhelming despair.

12. A splendour among shadows,] a shadow among shadows – *Harvard Nbk*. S.'s *splendour* is
borrowed from Dante's *splendor*: e.g. *Paradiso* xiii 52–4: 'Ciò che non more e ciò che può
morire / non è se non splendor di quella idea / che partorisce, amando, il nostro sire' ('That
which dies not, / And that which can die, are but each the beam / Of that idea, which our
Sovereign Sire / Engendereth loving', trans. Cary), where it means the light reflected by or
induced in to secondary things by the supreme Light. The word supports a late date for the
revision of the sonnet, as this usage seems confined to the poetry of 1821–22.

13. Cast on this gloomy world – a thing which strove *Harvard Nbk*.

14. the Preacher] Ecclesiastes, who declared that all was vanity, even the search for wisdom:
'Then I beheld all the work of God, that a man cannot find out the work that is done under
the sun: because though a man labour to seek it out, yet he shall not find it; yea further;
though a wise man think to know it, yet shall he not be able to find it' (viii 17).

I hope to pass / Untouched by pain or sorrow, thro this den / Of savage beasts', as do the cancelled first-draft lines of the Sonnet: 'Like an unheeded shadow he did move / Among the careless crowd that marked him not / Except to scoff – and at their scoffing he / Smiled, as if apes had mo[   ]' (see *BSM* xviii 25 for a slightly differing transcription). The ills deplored are not loss or grief, such as his daughter's death caused in September, but neglect, mockery, and hatred. S. did not read the scurrilous article on Leigh Hunt's *Foliage* in the *Quarterly Review* xviii (1818), which contained covert attacks on himself, until August or September (*L* ii 65), but he had been told of it, and Peacock in a letter to S. dated 14 June had quoted the whole footnote in which the reviewer declared that although *RofI* was lying before him and had some beauty, 'we are in doubt whether it would be morally right to lend it notoriety by any comments. We know the Author's history well . . . a man who perverts his ingenuity and knowledge to the attacking of all that is ancient and venerable in our civil and religious institutions' (*Peacock Works* viii 194). Neither S. nor his poem was actually named. Letters to Italy took about fourteen days to arrive. S. replied on 25 July: 'Their notice of me, and their exposure of their true motives for not noticing my book, shows how well understood an hostility must subsist between me and them' (*L* ii 26; Jones confuses *Frankenstein* and *RofI* in a note on p. 23). S. had had great hopes of *RofI* (two years later he still felt that its 'date should have been longer than a day') and was bitterly afflicted by the manner of its reception: in the present fragment he reminds himself of the fortitude he had foreseen would be necessary in the poem itself (see note to lines 6–8 below).

Text from *Nbk 11* ff. 27–8.

Published in *1839* iv 52 (notes); *Massey* 210–11 (Mary S.'s transcript in adds. d. 9 and collation).

Alas, this is not what I thought life was —
I knew that there were crimes and evil men,
Misery and hate — nor did I hope to pass

Untouched by suffering through the rugged glen.
5   In mine own heart I saw as in a glass
The hearts of others . . . so [   ] and when

4. *glen.*] glen *BSM* xviii.

5–6. *In mine own heart . . . others*] 'I was yet unacquainted with men, and imagined I found in their words and actions that innocence and simplicity that reigned in my own heart. I believed them all just, sincere, capable of friendship . . . Under this delusion I entered the world . . . The pretended friends I thus made choice of . . . occasioned me much injury, and abandoned me, some from interest, and others from jealousy and fickleness. The surprise and grief I felt, forced my eyes to overflow with tears' (*Barthelemy* vi 392–3); S. and Mary were reading Barthelemy in June and July 1818 (*Mary Jnl* i 215–21). S. suggested that Southey, his one-time friend at Keswick, had written the *Foliage* review (*L* ii 66).

6–8. *when . . . I armed*] These lines re-state S.'s declaration in the Dedication to *L&C* 40–2: 'I . . . / . . . Wrought linked armour for my soul, before / It might walk forth to war among mankind'.

6. Gap left in *Nbk 11*.

I went among my kind, with triple brass
Of calm endurance my weak heart I armed
To bear scorn, hate and fear, a woeful mass

175
'One sung of thee who left the tale untold'

Date of composition unknown; perhaps mid-July 1818. The lines are not safely dat-
able by their miscellaneous surroundings, but they occur near the beginning of a
nbk in a skeleton framework for stanzas numbered [1]–4, with appropriate spaces
allotted. The spaces left for stanzas 2–3 contain no words except *For though they*
under '2'; lines 5–12 are under '4'; and lines 1–4 at the beginning have no stanza
number but are headed 'Asia γυναικη προμηθεως' ('Asia wife of Prometheus'). It is
not clear whether this is an intended title or an unconnected jotting, or whether
the title is 'Asia' with a Gk notation added. Asia is identified as the wife of Prometheus
only in Herodotus (*Histories* iv 45), and S. read Herodotus through (presumably
the *Histories*) from 16 July to 2 August 1818 (*Mary Jnl* i 219–21). Herodotus can-
not be said to have 'sung' of Asia or anyone else, however; and a possibility is that
the reference is to Aeschylus's partly-lost Prometheus trilogy, which S., for all his
admiration, desired to revise, being 'averse from a catastrophe so feeble as that of
reconciling the Champion with the Oppressor of mankind' (Preface to *PU*; see head-
note and notes). A mountain in 'Indian Scythia' (line 6) must be on the north-
eastern edge of the Hindu Kush, the locale S. adopted two months later for *PU*,
the epigraph to which ironically proclaims his own apostasy from the orthodoxy
of Aeschylus's submissive (lost) solution to the Zeus/Prometheus contest (see note
to *PU* epigraph). Another possibility is that the reference is to Byron, whose short
poem 'Prometheus' had been written in Switzerland and published with 'The Prisoner
of Chillon' in 1816; this expresses only a despondent stoicism that S. doubtless
found unsatisfactory. In any case S.'s scattered lines seem to belong to the period
when he was 'totally incapable of original composition' (25 July 1818; *L* ii 26): the
first two lines, in ink, end '&c', and when (evidently at a later time) lines 3–4 were
added in pencil, the last two words (including the obvious rhyme) were left
unwritten. A similar interruption seems to have occurred between lines 5–9 (ink)
and 10–12 (pencil).

Text from *Nbk 11* ff. 4–6.

Published in *1840* 320 (lines 1–4); *V&P* 8 (lines 5–12).

One sung of thee who left the tale untold —
Like the false dawns which perish in the bursting,

9. *scorn*,] scorn *Nbk 11*.
¶175   1. *One sung of thee*] See headnote.
2. *in*] on *BSM* xviii.   *bursting*,] bursting &c *Nbk 11*; bursting [?&:] *BSM* xviii.

Like empty cups of wrought and daedal gold
Which mock the lips with air when they [are thirsting.]
[

]

* * * * *

5   A mountain in the utmost wildernesses
Of Indian Scythia, whose smooth snowy steepness
Only the footstep of the blast impresses —
Which, on one side, cleft to the very deepness,
Hung high o'er a ravine of waters raging
10   That boiled within their chasmlike path
With stunning roar their toilsome speed assuaging,
And with the struggling rocks a deathless battle waging.

176
'And the fierce beasts of the world's wildernesses'

Written in ink on the inside front cover of *Nbk 11*; date of composition unknown, but the lines may be associated with the previous fragment and with S.'s bathing-place described in a letter to Peacock of 25 July 1818:

> In the middle of the day, I bathe in a pool or fountain, formed in the middle of the forests by a torrent. It is surrounded on all sides by precipitous rocks, and the waterfall of the stream which forms it falls into one side with perpetual dashing . . . The water of this pool . . . is as transparent as the air, so that the stones and sand at the bottom seem, as it were, trembling in the light of noonday . . . My custom is to undress and sit on the rocks, reading Herodotus . . . and then to leap from the edge of the rock into this fountain' (*L* ii 25–6).

3. daedal] 'Of elaborate workmanship'. Usually applied to the earth (from Lucretius, *De Re. Nat.* i 7, 'daedal tellus') as in 'Mont Blanc' 86; but S. uses it of the cups in Jupiter's heaven in *PU* III i 26. In *PU* I 809–11 Prometheus compares Asia to a gold cup: 'Asia! who, when my being overflowed, / Wert like a golden chalice to bright wine / Which else had sunk into the thirsty dust'.

4. [are thirsting.]] Conjectured from the rhyme; not in *Nbk 11* (see headnote).

6. Indian Scythia,] Scythia was a vast and vague region, described in Herodotus (*Histories* iv); India was properly only a southern boundary of *Scythia extra Imaum*. *steepness*] steepnesses *V&P*.

8. deepness,] deepnesses *V&P*.

10. Incomplete line.

11. stunning] streaming *V&P*, *BSM* xviii.

But it is also possible that the lines are associated with *Epipsychidion*, parts of which are drafted in this nbk, for the following reasons: (1) the revised text suggests that they may be couplets; (2) their location on the inside cover could imply late composition; (3) a similar image of erased footprints recurs in *TL* 405–9, though there are others in earlier writing, e.g. 'I visit thee but thou art sadly changed' (no. 137) 15–18. No linkage in rhyme or content, however, has been found in *Epipsychidion* or its draft.

Text from *Nbk 11*, inside front cover.

Published in *Rossetti 1870* ii 312.

> And the fierce beasts of the world's wildernesses
> Track not the steps of him who drinks of it,
> For the light breezes which forever flit
> Around its margin, heap the sands thereon

177
'O Mary dear, that you were here'

Dated in *1824* '*Este, September 1818*'; drafted without title between 24 August and 5 September 1818 (possibly on Mary S.'s birthday, 30 August) when S. was alone at Este awaiting her arrival from the Bagni di Lucca. S. had accompanied Claire Clairmont to Venice so that she might see her daughter Allegra, now with Byron, and Byron had lent him the house, 'I Cappucini', in the belief that his family was also with him. Hence S.'s urgent summons to Mary. The villa, as Mary S. described it,

> was situated on the very over-hanging brow of a low hill at the foot of a range of higher ones [the Euganean Hills] . . . a vine-trellised walk, a Pergola, as it is called in Italian, led from the hall door to a summer-house at the end of the garden, which Shelley made his study . . . a slight ravine, with a road in its depth, divided the garden from the hill, on which stood the ruins of the ancient castle of Este, whose dark massive wall gave forth an echo, and from whose ruined crevices, owls and bats flitted forth at night, as the crescent moon sunk behind the black and heavy battlements. We looked from the garden over the wide plain of Lombardy, bounded to the west by the far Apennines, while to the east, the horizon was lost in misty distance. (*1839* iii 160–1, note to Poems of 1818)

It was presumably in the garden that this and the following fragment were composed (the vine-trellised walk still exists; and a plaque was unveiled on the garden wall facing Este Castle in 1968). Some Italian lines in *Nbk 6* (f. 67), although among the drafts for *J&M*, may belong to the same period: '[Divizione] / [Come] si

1. *And*] Omitted *Rossetti 1870*.   *world's*] woods and *Rossetti 1870*.

2. *it,*] it *Nbk 11*.

3. *flit*] fleet *Rossetti 1870*; [?fleet] *BSM* xviii.

4. *sands*] sand *Rossetti 1870*.

nascondono i pesci nell'onda / convien che cosi nasconda / L'anima mia in te' ('[Separation] As fishes hide in the water, so should my soul hide in thee'). The image recurs in *PU* I 684. All the punctuation in 'O Mary dear' is editorial except after *voice, disconsolate, heard, Mary dear.*

Text from *Nbk 11*, f. 202b rev.

Published in *1824* 207 (entitled 'To Mary –')

O Mary dear, that you were here,
With your brown eyes bright and clear,
And your sweet voice, like a bird
Singing love to its lone mate

5   In the ivy bower disconsolate —
Voice the sweetest ever heard,
And your brow more [   ]
Than the undeceiving sky
Of this azure Italy.

10   Mary dear, come to me soon,
I am not well whilst thou art far:
As sunset to the spherèd moon,
As twilight to the western star
Thou, beloved, art to me.

15   O Mary dear, that you were here;
The Castle's echo whispers 'here'.

2. *brown eyes*] Trelawny, besides others, refers to Mary S.'s 'large grey eyes' (*Recollections* chapter xi); at just this time, however (23 August 1818) S. was reporting to Mary herself that 'Mrs H[oppner] has hazel eyes & sweet looks rather Maryish . . . Her eyes are like a reflection of yours' (*L* ii 37–8), and he probably had Mary in mind when commenting in the following April that the eyes of Italian women 'want the mazy depth of colour behind colour with which the intellectual women of England & Germany entangle the heart in soul-woven labyrinths' (*L* ii 93). Cp. *PU* II i 114–17 and note.

3–5. *like a bird . . . disconsolate* –] Anticipating the *Unfinished Drama* (1822): 'And on a wintry bough the widowed bird / Hid in the deepest night of ivy leaves / Renewed the vigils of her inmost sorrow.' Carlos Baker commented (*MLQ* iv (1943) 208) 'that ivy canopies . . . were almost invariably coincident in Shelley's mind with erotic episodes'.

7. Blank in *Nbk 11*. Many who knew Mary S. admired 'her tall and intellectual forehead' (Thornton Hunt, *Atlantic Monthly* xi (1863) 199). *BSM* xviii reads 'And you [?were] [mine]'.

8. *undeceiving*] Omitted *1824*; *BSM* xviii reads '[?Than] the red evening sky'.

12. *the spherèd moon*] As Mary S.'s note on the Poems of 1818 confirms, the moon was a waxing crescent soon after her arrival at Este; but with a new moon on 1 September the night sky would have been empty when the lines were written – as no doubt the imagery emphasises.

14–15. The physical separation of the last two lines from the rest, reproduced in *1824*, was necessitated in *Nbk 11* only by a blot.

16. *Castle's*] Castles *Nbk 11*; Castle *1824*.

420

178
'I am drunk with the honey-wine'

An untitled fragment isolated amid drafts of *PU* III iv; the ink draft appears to run over a pencil draft of the closing speech of *PU* III, which would indicate a date later than March 1819. But the lines in *Nbk 6* do not appear to be a first draft, but rather an abandoned reworking of an earlier draft; S. is known to have worked on *PU* at Este using loose sheets rather than in a nbk, and these lines were perhaps also similarly drafted at first; see headnote to *PU*. Lines 4–6 establish the locale as Este (see headnote to previous poem). It was probably written soon after Mary S.'s arrival on 5 September and before Clara's death on 24 September. The tone is light-hearted; there is moonlight; the 'summer earth' exhales perfumes. But little can be based on lines so purely fanciful, although they might possibly have influenced *PU* III iii 142–4: 'The flowers whose purple and translucid bowls / Stand ever mantling with aërial dew, / The drink of spirits' (no surviving draft). A comma has been added after *bats*.

Text from *Nbk 6* f. 49.

Published in *1839* iv 181 (untitled; subsequently entitled 'Wine of the Fairies' by Dowden).

> I am drunk with the honey-wine
> Of the moon-unfolded eglantine
> Which fairies catch in hyacinth bowls —
> The bats, the dormice and the moles
> 5   Sleep in the walls, or under the sward
> Of the desolate castle yard,
> And when 'tis spilt on the summer earth
> Or its fumes arise among the dew
> Their jocund dreams are full of mirth
> 10 And they gibber their joy in sleep, for few
> Of the fairies bear those bowls so new
> That [

2. *moon-unfolded*] fresh dew of scented *Nbk 6 canc.* The meaning is presumably 'induced to unfurl by the moonlight' (cp. 'night-folded flowers', *PU* III iii 101). *eglantine*] Sweet-briar (*Rosa rubiginosa*). The season would be too late for flowers, but the foliage itself is scented.

3. *bowls* –] buds: – *1839*.

4. *bats, the*] bats & the *BSM* xv.

179
'Flourishing vine, whose kindling clusters glow'

Date of composition unknown, but probably October 1818 ('autumnal sun') at Este. The draft is among material dating from autumn 1818 to spring 1819. Lines 3–4 might suggest Herculaneum or Pompeii, but leaves of the vines were already in decay when S. travelled south from Este on 5 November (*L* ii 45). No transcript by Mary S. is known.

Text from *Nbk 11*, f. 27.

Published in *Rossetti 1870* ii 313.

> Flourishing vine, whose kindling clusters glow
> Beneath the autumnal sun — none taste of thee —
> For thou dost shroud a ruin, and below
> The rotting bones of dead antiquity.

180
'And where is truth? On tombs?
for such to thee'

Drafted in *Nbk 6*, perhaps in September 1818 after visiting Petrarch's tomb, or after the visit to Ariosto's tomb on 7 November (see *L* ii 43, 46), in either case with possible memories of Harriet Grove. A somewhat later date around April 1819 (making a better fit with surrounding material in the nbk), could be suggested by a connection with S.'s note on 'An Urn' in his 'Notes on Sculptures in Rome and Florence': ' "The memory of the good is ever green." And art thou then forgotten?' (*Prose* 345). Mary S.'s draft is in adds. d. 7 ff. 80–1; she included it among the Poems of 1822 in *1839*, but the draft's position in *Nbk 6* makes an earlier date certain.

Text from *Nbk 6*; punctuation has been added in lines 4 and 6.

Published in *1839* iv 181 (lines 1–4). Given the title 'The Sepulchre of Memory' in *Hutchinson*.

> And where is truth? On tombs? for such to thee
> Has been my heart, and thy dead memory
> Has lain from childhood, many a changeful year

2. *sun* –] Originally followed by *sweet violet* canc. in *Nbk 11*.

4. *rotting bones*] *Nbk 11* canc.

¶180   1. *tombs?*] S. first wrote *tombstones* . . . in *Nbk 6*, then altered to *tombs* and wrote first *and* canc. and then *for* above the suspension points.

Unchangingly preserved and buried there.
5 The scroll of what I lost, and what thou wert
Is folded in the tablets of that heart;
And those who read it know, what few who come
To the vain shadow of a nobler tomb
Can understand,

181
'Behold, sweet Sister mine, once more descend'

These lines, the following poem 'The Two Spirits', and *PU* I 752–800, have strong affinities yet their precise relationship is puzzling. All three are drafted within the first 26 pages of *Nbk 11*; all three are concerned with an apparently ineluctable linkage of good and evil: enlightenment appearing as mental darkness; aspiration that risks calamity; love whose shadow is pain; and all three share similar metaphors, especially that of flight above the earth, and (in the first two cases) a striking phrase. As *Chernaik* 239 suggests, contemporary composition is probable: most likely the last week in September or the first in October 1818. *Forman 1876–7* iii 401 note, followed by *Hutchinson* 548, assign the present lines to *Otho*, for no reason beyond their accidental contiguity with genuine lines from *Otho* printed in *Relics* over the date 1817. Lines 1–2 suggest rather that 'Behold, sweet Sister mine' was drafted for *PU* (which may be why Mary S. did not transcribe the lines, though she transcribed and printed 'The Two Spirits'), but that this prelude led in turn to a dialogue unsuited to the drama. It seems possible that lines 752–88 of *PU* Act I were inserted into the Act after its initial completion. All or most of the Act had been written on separate sheets (*L* ii 39–40; see headnote to *PU*), and the draft lines in *Nbk 11* are the only surviving MS lines of this Act. All three compositions discussed here may therefore have originated in the death of Clara S. on 24 September, which was a disaster resulting from S.'s impulsive good intentions in trying to help Claire C. and Allegra. S. applied the metaphor of flight to his own actions in this matter ('Am I not like a wild swan to be gone so suddenly?': *L* ii 40); and one of the interpolations on f. 13 (see headnote to 'The Two Spirits') is 'the good die first –': unless this quotation, repeating the epigraph to *Alastor*, refers to Clara's death its entry here is obscure. On f. 18 occur three pencilled lines beginning 'How pale and cold thou art in thy despair' (no. 199), which must be addressed to Mary S. after the death either of Clara or of William S. nine months later. The commas after *Behold* and *mankind*, and the full stop, are editorial.
Text from *Nbk 11* f. 12.

Published in *Relics* 76 (omitting the first four words); *Wasserman* 42 note (omitting the first four words).

4. *preserved*] Underlined, or possibly canc. in *Nbk 6*.
9. The line is briefly continued with some illegible words, possibly '[those *canc.*] from less'.

423

Behold, sweet Sister mine, once more descend
The shadows of my soul upon mankind,
For to those hearts with whom they never blend
Thoughts are but shadows, which the flashing mind
5   From the swift clouds which track its flight of fire
Cast on the gloomy world it leaves behind.

182
The Two Spirits. An Allegory

As Charles Robinson demonstrates (*Robinson* 263) this draft must predate those of
PU Act II (spring 1819) in *Nbk 11*. It begins on the page following 'Behold, sweet
Sister mine', to which it relates, and is probably of the same date: late September
or early October 1818 (its inclusion by Mary S. among 'Poems written in 1820' is
an error). At the top of f. 13 is a jotted reminder of the epigraph for *Alastor*: 'the
good die first –'. Between the original opening lines, which are cancelled –

Two genii stood before me in a dream
Seest thou not the shades of even [*BSM* xviii reads *Wert* for *Seest*] –

S. has inserted the present title, evidently after completing the poem and in a
different ink, together with headings '1st Spirit' and '2nd Spirit' to the first and
second stanzas respectively, also in different ink. As these headings were hasty
additions it may be assumed that similar headings were implied, though not added,
for stanzas 3 and 4, and possibly also for 5 and 6; however, the last two stanzas
seem to be detached reflections arising from the Spirits' debate rather than a con-
tinuation of it, or of the Second Spirit's argument, and most *eds* after 1846 rule
them off from the first four. The two Spirits, or genii, are closely akin to the 'two
shapes' of *PU* I 752, the opposite but hitherto inseparable twins Love and Pain (see
headnote to the preceding poem, 'Behold, sweet Sister mine'). On f. 2 of *Nbk 11*
are the draft lines: 'Twin nurslings of the [*BSM* xviii reads *this*] all sustaining air /
Whom one nest sheltered', a version of *PU* I 752–4:

Behold'st thou not two shapes from the east and west
Come, as two doves to one belovèd nest,
Twin nurslings of the all-sustaining air

1. *Behold, . . . mine,*] omitted in *Relics*. In *Nbk 11 Sister* is canc. by vertical strokes; *mine* is inter-
polated into the line. *BSM* xviii reads '[?Sobe canc. mis]' and omits *mine*.

3. *whom*] which *Relics*.

4. *flashing*] restless *Nbk 11* canc.

5. *track its flight of fire*] Cp. 'The Two Spirits' 3.

6. *Cast*] Casts *Relics*; past tense; i.e. those slow of apprehension continue to regard only the
shadows left by the mind's continuing flight. *it*] its *Nbk 11*.

– an image deriving from Dante's *Inferno* v 82–4, where the doves were Paolo and Francesca, whose true love had brought only calamity.

Important discussions of the poem are by *Wasserman* 41–4, who sees it as 'a lyric dialogue between opposing impulses of the human soul'; *Chernaik* 141–4, who terms it 'a metaphysical analysis of human aspiration'; and *Robinson* 263–4, for whom it is 'an exercise in preparation for or in conclusion to his debate [with Byron] in *Julian and Maddalo*'.

Text from *Nbk 11* ff. 13–17. The poem is unpunctuated in MS except at lines 2, 8, 12, 32, 39, 44.

Published in *1824* 179–80; *Chernaik* 239–42.

182
The Two Spirits. An Allegory

First Spirit

Thou who plumed with strong desire
Would float above the Earth — beware!
Shadow tracks thy flight of fire —
    Night is coming.
5   Bright are the regions of the air
And when winds and beams [   ]
It were delight to wander there —
    Night is coming!

Second Spirit

The deathless stars are bright above.
10   If I should cross the shade of night
Within my heart is the lamp of love
    And that is day —
And the moon will smile with gentle light
On my golden plumes where'er they move,
15   The meteors will linger around my flight
    And make night day.

¶182 *1. Thou*] Oh thou *1824*; O Thou *Chernaik*. 'O Thou', 'Floatest' (line 2), and 'A shadow' (line 3) are canc. by similar oblique strokes in *Nbk 11* (although *BSM* xviii does not note the canc. of 'O thou') and 'Thou' is capitalised, so all three cancellations are assumed to stand.

2. Would] 'The auxiliary verb agrees with "who" rather than "thou"' (*Chernaik*). Mary S. first regularised the form to 'Wouldst' in her errata-list to *1824*.

3. Shadow] A shadow *1824*, *Chernaik* (see note to line 1).

6. No rhyme-word in *Nbk 11*.

13. gentle] silver *Nbk 11* canc.

First Spirit

But if the whirlwinds of darkness waken
Eclipse and lightning and stormy rain
See, the bounds of the air are shaken,
20   Night is coming;
And swift the clouds of the hurricane
Yon declining sun have overtaken,
The clash of the hail sweeps o'er the plain —
          Night is coming.

Second Spirit

25 I see the black cloud, I hear the sound —
I'll sail on the flood of the tempest dark
With the calm within and light around
          Which make night day;
And thou when the gloom is deep and stark
30 Look from thy dull earth slumberbound —
My moonlike flight thou then mayst mark
          On high, far away.

Some say there is a precipice
Where one vast pine hangs frozen to ruin
35 O'er piles of snow and chasms of ice
          'Mid Alpine mountains,
And that the leagued storm pursuing

Stanzas 3–6 have no speaker-headings in *Nbk 11*.

18. Eclipse] Hail *1824*, *Chernaik*; in *Nbk 11* S. first wrote 'The hail and the', which is canc. with 'Hail' written in below, either canc. or underlined. 'Eclipse' is written in above.

21. And swift the clouds] The red swift clouds *1824*.

22. declining] [?darkening] *BSM* xviii.

25. I see the black cloud, I] I see the light, and I *1824*; I see the glare and I *Chernaik*; I see & rejoice *Nbk 11* canc.; see *BSM* xviii for a differing transcription.

Stanza 5. S. seems to recall legends of Mount Pilatus in the canton of Lucerne, perhaps read in the guide-book for his Alpine visit of 1816. J. G. Ebel's *Manuel du Voyageur en Suisse*, available in several editions and in three languages in 1816, describes a strange and gigantic pine-tree near Pilatus, and a pool once known as 'la Mare-infernale'; from there a fountain of vapour sometimes rises to the summit of the mountain, 'se dilate, et devient enfin si grande et si formidable qu'elle finit par crever sur les contrées voisines au milieu de l'orage et des plus terribles coups de tonnerre . . . on prétendoit qu'il suffisoit d'en approcher pour mettre *Pilate* en fureur, et que dans ses transports il excitoit la tempête, la grêle et les orages' (Zurich, iv (1811), 36–7). The second legend ('Some say . . .') may be S.'s own invention.

33. is] *1824*; hangs *Nbk 11* uncanc. alt., *Chernaik*; [?hans] *BSM* xviii.

37. leagued] languid *1824*, *Chernaik*, *BSM* xviii. The word is dubious in *Nbk 11*, but the storm's pursuit is unrelaxing, and its banded powers were stressed in lines 17–24.

That winged shape forever flies
Round those hoar branches, aye renewing
40   Its aery fountains.

Some say when the nights are dry and clear
And the death dews sleep on the morass
Sweet whispers are heard by the traveller
Which make night day —
45   And a shape like his early love doth pass
Upborne by her wild and glittering hair,
And when he awakes on the fragrant grass
He finds night day.

183
Lines Written among the Euganean Hills,
October, 1818

The Advertisement to *1819*, dated 20 December 1818, concludes with this paragraph:

> I do not know which of the few scattered poems I left in England will be selected by my
> bookseller, to add to this collection. One, which I sent from Italy, was written after a day's
> excursion among those lovely mountains which surround what was once the retreat, and
> where is now the sepulchre, of Petrarch. If any one is inclined to condemn the insertion
> of the introductory lines, which image forth the sudden relief of a state of deep despond-
> ency by the radiant visions disclosed by the sudden burst of an Italian sunrise in autumn
> on the highest peak of those delightful mountains, I can only offer as my excuse, that they
> were not erased at the request of a dear friend, with whom added years of intercourse only
> add to my apprehension of its value, and who would have had more right than any one
> to complain, that she has not been able to extinguish in me the very power of delineat-
> ing sadness.

Lines 56–112 survive at the Huntington Library as part of Mary S.'s transcript for
the printer (HM331; see *MYR* iii 113–20), so her jnl entries for 18–19 Decem-
ber, 'write out Shelley's Poem . . . Finish Copying his Poem' (*Mary Jnl* i 244–5)
probably refer to this poem, or to *R&H*, or to both, as the volume's other con-
tents were already in England. The date of the Advertisement was presumably the
date of despatch to Ollier. The poem itself is dated pointedly in the title, 'October,
1818'.

41. *dry*] day *BSM* xviii. *and*] Omitted in *Nbk 11*.

45. *a shape*] a silver shape *1824*. *Nbk 11* has canc. alt. adjectives *silver/winged* before *shape*.

45–6. Cp. 'Song for *Tasso*' 15–17: 'Sometimes I see before me flee / A silver-shining form like
thee / O Leonora'.

The poem celebrates a single 'island' of happiness, temporal and geographical, in a sea of calamity, and if the physical descriptions were from life, the day celebrated can be identified. Lines 321–6 describe an autumn sunset with an 'infantine moon' and the planet Venus so close to the moon as to seem to minister light to it. There was a new moon on 30 September, and a striking conjunction of the newborn moon with Venus occurred near the western horizon on 3 October, when about two hours after sunset Venus was passed within less than one diameter of the moon (the editors are indebted to Dr Desmond King-Hele for full statistics and astronomical details). Shelley was at 'I Cappucini' from 30 September through 10 October, and this date accords with S.'s prose description in his next recorded letter (8 October) of Venice 'with its domes & turrets glittering in a long line over the blue waves' and of the view from the Euganean Hills of 'the wide flat plains of Lombardy, in which we see the sun & moon rise & set, & the evening star, & all the golden magnificence of autumnal clouds' (L i 42–3). The 3 October was ten days after Clara Shelley (Mary Wollstonecraft's granddaughter) had died in Venice (24 September); it was, moreover, within a week of the anniversary of Fanny Godwin's suicide, which Fanny herself had timed for the anniversary eve of her mother's second suicide attempt in 1795 (10 October; see Margaret Tims, *Mary Wollstonecraft: a Social Pioneer*, 1976, 293–6). These calamities help to explain the obscure 'introductory lines' of the poem and Mary S.'s special interest in them, revealed in the Advertisement, as well as some of its imagery, such as the mariner (line 3), the 'northern sea' (lines 45–6), the fratricidal King (lines 57–9), and the Norwegian forest fire (lines 269–79). It has been argued that the poem's opening section is heavily autobiographical, but such speculation must be qualified by the implication of lines 45–6, which are taken (as *Chernaik* 80–1 suggests) from Sophocles's famous Chorus deploring human adversity in *Oedipus at Colonus* (1239–44): 'Meanwhile this wretched man, not I alone – as some northern shore struck by waves in winter is shaken on all sides – so him too on the shore the terrible ruinous breakers continually shake'. This reference (here rendered literally) universalises the adversity (οὐκ ἐγὼ μόνος); S.'s introductory lines appear deliberately to generalise from the specific very distressing circumstances of his personal experience during the period of the poem's composition. Peacock had translated some of the Sophoclean lines in 1812–13 (*Peacock Works* vii 228–9), and incorporated into his *Rhododaphne* (v 21–4) earlier lines which (according to Peacock) S. was always repeating to himself at the time of his separation from Harriet; and Mary S. quoted six translated lines in *The Last Man* (1826: iii ch. 4; see *MSW* iv 290). Other elements from this Chorus are echoed in the present poem (see note to line 8). S.'s 'northern sea' probably does have personal as well as universal bearing. Reference to Harriet S. (drowned in London), or to Fanny Godwin (who took poison near the Bristol Channel) is implausible. Clara S. had just been buried on the Lido at Venice, where there were rushes and sea-mews; but although the Adriatic is traditionally stormy (see e.g. Horace, *Odes* II xiv 13–14) its appearance as a sea 'which tempests shake eternally' would invalidate that of the 'level quivering line / Of the waters crystalline' two verse-paragraphs later, and no English refugee could refer to the Adriatic as a 'northern sea'. The personal allusion may rather be the same as that to the 'remote and lonely shore' of 'Her voice did quiver as we parted' (no. 126), and the sea would then be the Baltic or the Skagerrak, where Mary Wollstonecraft in her despair had often longed to die:

How often, passing through the rocks, I have thought, 'But for this child, I would lay my head on one of them, and never open my eyes again!' With a heart feelingly alive to all the affections of my nature – I have never met with one, softer than the stone that I would fain take for my last pillow. (*Posthumous Works* iii 188–9)

In her letters to Imlay she repeatedly compared her life to that of a sailor in a storm ('I am again tossed on the troubled billows of life', 'No poor tempest-tossed mariner ever more earnestly longed to arrive at his port'; *Posthumous Works* iv 5), and this metaphor, based on quotations from her letters, had been taken up in a verse biography which S. is likely to have known, as it went into a second edition in 1816. This was *The Wanderer in Norway, with other Poems*, by Thomas Brown, Professor of Moral Philosophy in Edinburgh University, who was well informed and who based his imagery, as S. does in lines 1–65, on quotations from Mary W.'s letters, such as '. . . how can I expect that she [Fanny] will be shielded, when my naked bosom has had to brave continually the pitiless storm?' (Brown p. 50n):

> Dim on the prow, what form, with bosom bare
> And step disorder'd, haunts the midnight air;
> As tho' with passion's fiercer swell opprest,
> She sought the tempest to her burning breast? (Brown p. 47)

D. H. Reiman ('Structure, Symbol, and Theme in "Lines Written Among the Euganean Hills"', *PMLA* lxxvii (1962) 404–13) takes the whole of lines 1–65 to be about S. himself only, noting that 'The spirit of the dead person is . . . clearly masculine', and identifying the 'One white skull and seven dry bones' as symbolising 'his old self . . . lying dead on a tempest-torn beach', the bones representing 'the seven years between his expulsion from Oxford (March 1811) and his final departure from England (March 1818)'. These dates seem arbitrary, especially for a poem begun in October, and in the light of the Sophocles Chorus little importance attaches to the sex of the mariner or of the dead: S.'s despondency in October 1818 relates to several generations. No exclusive identifications are plausible; but the careful ambiguity of lines 60–5 allows one reading to be that while the remains are mourned by Nature, no lament is deserved by the mere soulless body (the 'sunless vapour') that once inspired the unburied one with emotion and thought. Private miseries are caused by selfish relationships ('Senseless is the breast, and cold, / Which relenting love would fold'), just as social calamity results from distorted social attitudes ('The despot's rage, the slave's revenge'). The 'seven dry bones' could be interpreted as the seven surviving items of Mary Wollstonecraft's wasted potential, in the *Posthumous Works* Godwin published after her death. The one existing leaf of printer's copy, sold from Ollier's papers by Puttick & Simpson (19 July 1877) and now in the Huntington Library, may help to confirm that more than one figure was involved in lines 45–65. It is in Mary S.'s hand, and the verso, containing 30 lines, is numbered 4; presumably p. 1 carried the title so that only the verso pages were numbered. Unfortunately this leaf is damaged, but the first six lines of the recto read:

>]?ter was overblown
>] wrecked limbs – but there came none
> Then he laughed in [blank]

The grey hairs crawled on every limb
Or the whirlwind up an down
Howling, like a slaughtered town (HM331ʳ)

Lines 1–4 are cancelled by a vertical line and by many diagonal erasures, probably in S.'s hand. Mary S. seems to have been transcribing from an early draft (as she could not decipher some of line 3) and inadvertently copied some material S. had discarded. Its meaning is obscure, but it suggests that *unburied bones / sunless vapour* parallels *slaughtered town / king in glory* and *senseless breast / relenting love*; i.e. that a relationship and not a single figure is involved.

The poem depends so entirely on locality, and S. was so soon to be overwhelmed by the scenery of Rome and Naples, that most of it was probably written within a few days of 3 October. But if copied and sent for printing only late in December, parts could have been completed later; in particular, lines 1–65, which have affinities with parts of *J&M*, may have been literally an 'insertion', as the Advertisement hints. The 'Byron' section (lines 167–205) was certainly composed after the despatch of the rest, perhaps in consequence of Peacock's (lost) comments on *Childe Harold* iv, to which S. replied on 17–18 December (*L* ii 57–8): if S. had had the poem in front of him he would not have misquoted the key for the passage's insertion (see note to lines 165–6) – indeed, such a two-line key would not then have been needed.

The seven-syllable lines of S.'s poem suggest various similarities with parts of *PU* I (on which S. was working at the same time), both in thematic organisation (a long-term political optimism; the desire for a peaceful haven from suffering, out of human and social time) and particularly in a formal affinity with some of the Furies' choruses. These choruses themselves recall among other influences some of Coleridge's poems, such as 'Fire, Famine and Slaughter', and 'The Ancient Mariner', whose influence is also evident in the *Lines*. More generally, the poem ultimately derives, like many other influential poems of the period, from the meditative 'prospect poetry' of the eighteenth century, some of which itself deploys the basic device of a hill-top survey, combining personal reflection with historical and political concerns. The use of a short lyric line is not uncommon in the genre, for instance in the poetry of Dyer. More direct influences include the recent meetings with Byron in Venice, together with those poems of Byron which deal with the history and present situation of the city, the famous passage in *Childe Harold* iv, and the 'Ode to Venice'.

The text Mary S. transcribed for publication was apparently not a fair copy, so her punctuation was very erratic, and S. did not trouble to add it himself, though he made verbal corrections; much pointing must therefore have been supplied by the printer or (as Forman conjectured) by Peacock, who probably saw *1819* through the press. But lines 167–205 are printed below from the Yale MS in S.'s own hand (see *MYR* viii 186–93), despite the lack of conformity in accidentals with the rest of the poem; all *eds* since Forman have followed this course, and it would be perverse not to do likewise, especially as the MS corrects an unnoticed error in line 169.

Text from *1819*; lines 56–112 corrected from Huntington Library MS HM331 (*MYR* iii 119–20) and lines 167–205 from Tinker Library MS, Yale University (*MYR* viii 190–3).

Published in *1819*.

183
Lines Written among the Euganean Hills, October 1818

Many a green isle needs must be
In the deep wide sea of misery,
Or the mariner, worn and wan,
Never thus could voyage on
5   Day and night, and night and day,
Drifting on his weary way,
With the solid darkness black
Closing round his vessel's track;
Whilst above the sunless sky,
10   Big with clouds, hangs heavily,
And behind the tempest fleet
Hurries on with lightning feet,
Riving sail, and cord, and plank,
Till the ship has almost drank
15   Death from the o'er-brimming deep;
And sinks down, down, like that sleep
When the dreamer seems to be
Weltering through eternity;
And the dim low line before
20   Of a dark and distant shore
Still recedes, as ever still
Longing with divided will,
But no power to seek or shun,
He is ever drifted on
25   O'er the unreposing wave
To the haven of the grave.
What, if there no friends will greet;
What, if there no heart will meet
His with love's impatient beat;
30   Wander wheresoe'er he may,
Can he dream before that day
To find refuge from distress
In friendship's smile, in love's caress?

---

1. *a green isle*] The Colli Euganei form an isolated mountainous group in the plain west of Padua. S. in Venice described them as 'Those famous Euganean hills, which bear, / As seen from Lido through the harbour piles, / The likeness of a clump of peakèd isles' (*J&M* 77–9).

8. *round*] The adverbs defining the direction of the threats, *round* (8), *above* (9), *behind* (11), *before* (19), correspond generally to the sources of menace in Sophocles, *Oedipus at Colonus* 1245–9: night (encompassing), moon (overhead), evening (West), morning (East).

27. *What, if . . .*] Imitated from the rhetorical questions in Pope's 'Elegy to the Memory of an Unfortunate Lady' (who has committed suicide) 55–62.

Then 'twill wreak him little woe
35   Whether such there be or no:
Senseless is the breast, and cold,
Which relenting love would fold;
Bloodless are the veins and chill
Which the pulse of pain did fill;
40   Every little living nerve
That from bitter words did swerve
Round the tortured lips and brow,
Are like sapless leaflets now
Frozen upon December's bough.
45   On the beach of a northern sea
Which tempests shake eternally,
As once the wretch there lay to sleep,
Lies a solitary heap,
One white skull and seven dry bones,
50   On the margin of the stones,
Where a few grey rushes stand,
Boundaries of the sea and land:
Nor is heard one voice of wail
But the sea-mews, as they sail
55   O'er the billows of the gale;
Or the whirlwind up and down
Howling, like a slaughtered town,
When a king in glory rides
Through the pomp of fratricides:
60   Those unburied bones around
There is many a mournful sound;
There is no lament for him,
Like a sunless vapour, dim,
Who once clothed with life and thought
65   What now moves nor murmurs not.

36. 'Cold is that breast which warm'd the world before' (Pope, 'Elegy' 33).

44–5. There is no space between these lines in 1819.

54. sea-mews] sea-mews' Locock 1911. Reiman (PMLA lxxvii (1962) 407) traces the word (meaning 'seagulls', i.e. the common gull, Larus canus) to Paradise Lost, but it was common in the early nineteenth century and S. had found it in e.g. Eustace i 177–8: 'That bold independence which filled a few lonely islands, the abode of sea-mews and of cormorants, with population and with commerce, is bowed into slavery; and the republic of Venice . . . is now an empty name'.

57–9. a slaughtered town . . . fratricides] Probably based on the bloodbath wreaked by Christian II of Denmark (the 'Christiern' of Q Mab) after his entry into Stockholm on the conquest of Sweden in 1520. pomp] triumphal celebration.

Aye, many flowering islands lie
In the waters of wide Agony:
To such a one this morn was led
My bark by soft winds piloted:
70 'Mid the mountains Euganean
I stood listening to the paean
With which the legioned rooks did hail
The sun's uprise majestical;
Gathering round with wings all hoar,
75 Through the dewy mist they soar
Like grey shades, till th'eastern heaven
Bursts, and then, as clouds of even,
Flecked with fire and azure, lie
In the unfathomable sky,
80 So their plumes of purple grain,
Starred with drops of golden rain,
Gleam above the sunlight woods,
As in silent multitudes
On the morning's fitful gale
85 Through the broken mist they sail,
And the vapours cloven and gleaming
Follow, down the dark steep streaming,
Till all is bright, and clear, and still,
Round the solitary hill.

90 Beneath is spread like a green sea
The waveless plain of Lombardy,
Bounded by the vaporous air,
Islanded by cities fair;
Underneath day's azure eyes
95 Ocean's nursling, Venice lies,
A peopled labyrinth of walls,

68. *this morn*] Probably 4 October 1818 (see headnote).

70. *Euganean*] Not stressed on the second syllable as in Italian, but Anglicised by stressing on the third, as in 'Caribbean'.

71. *paean*] Hymn to Apollo.

72. *the legioned rooks*] In the mist S. mistook the jackdaws which still haunt the ruins of Este Castle for rooks, which are not found in Italy. Rooks are normally birds of good omen.

76. *th'eastern*] The elision is in *1819* and in Mary S.'s transcript for the printer.

82. *sunlight*] The usual contemporary form of mod. 'sunlit'.

89. Round the weird and lonesome hill. *Mary S.'s transcript, alt. in S.'s hand.*

90–3. S. wrote to Peacock from 'I Capuccini' on 8 October: 'We see before [us] the wide flat plains of Lombardy, in which we see the sun & moon rise and set, & the evening star, & all the golden magnificence of autumnal clouds' (*L* ii 43).

Amphitrite's destined halls,
Which her hoary sire now paves
With his blue and beaming waves.
100 Lo! the sun upsprings behind,
Broad, red, radiant, half reclined
On the level quivering line
Of the waters crystalline;
And before that chasm of light,
105 As within a furnace bright,
Column, tower, and dome, and spire,
Shine like obelisks of fire,
Pointing with inconstant motion
From the altar of dark ocean
110 To the sapphire-tinted skies;
As the flames of sacrifice
From the marble shrines did rise,
As to pierce the dome of gold
Where Apollo spoke of old.

115 Sun-girt City, thou hast been
Ocean's child, and then his queen;
Now is come a darker day,
And thou soon must be his prey,
If the power that raised thee here
120 Hallow so thy watery bier.
A less drear ruin then than now,
With thy conquest-branded brow

97. Amphitrite] Daughter of Oceanus, from whom she will inherit the halls of Venice when the sea engulfs them.

100. behind] i.e. behind Venice, to the East.

108. with inconstant motion] i.e. quivering in the heated air-currents.

113. dome of gold] Often taken as referring to Delphi; but if a comma after *gold* has been omitted or displaced, the meaning would be: 'as the flames used to rise from Apollo's marble shrines as if to pierce his very dwelling'. This would provide a more exact simile for lines 106–10. Apollo, god of prophecy, 'spoke' in numberless places besides Delphi, while his palace as sun-god was 'bright with glittering gold' ('Regia Solis erat . . . clara micante auro'; Ovid, *Met.* ii 1–2).

115. Sun-girt] Suggested as a misprint of 'Sea-girt', used e.g. in *Comus*, in Scott's *Marmion* (1808) VI ii 29, and of Venice itself in Thomson's *Liberty* (iv 300) and Byron's *Marino Faliero* (IV i 76), discussed with S. in the city concerned. But S.'s coinage is apt after lines 100–14, and is most unlikely to be an error for the more commonplace 'sea-girt'.

116. Built on the sea, Venice was known as 'regina del Adriatico'.

117. a darker day] At this date it was believed 'almost universally' that the occupying Austrians planned to hasten the destruction of Venice (Lord Broughton, *Italy: Remarks Made in Several Visits from the Year 1816 to 1854*, 2 vols, 1861, ii 118).

Stooping to the slave of slaves
From thy throne, among the waves
125   Wilt thou be, when the sea-mew
Flies, as once before it flew,
O'er thine isles depopulate,
And all is in its ancient state,
Save where many a palace gate
130   With green sea-flowers overgrown
Like a rock of ocean's own,
Topples o'er the abandoned sea
As the tides change sullenly.
The fisher on his watery way,
135   Wandering at the close of day,
Will spread his sail and seize his oar
Till he pass the gloomy shore,
Lest thy dead should, from their sleep
Bursting o'er the starlight deep,
140   Lead a rapid masque of death
O'er the waters of his path.

Those who alone thy towers behold
Quivering through aërial gold,
As I now behold them here,
145   Would imagine not they were
Sepulchres, where human forms,
Like pollution-nourished worms
To the corpse of greatness cling,
Murdered, and now mouldering:
150   But if Freedom should awake
In her omnipotence, and shake
From the Celtic Anarch's hold
All the keys of dungeons cold,
Where a hundred cities lie

123. the slave of slaves] It has been urged (*TLS* 5 June 1919, 313) that this title translates the Pope's 'Servus servorum Dei', but it refers more probably to Austria, 'slave' of the 'slaves' constituting the Congress of Vienna; i.e. the Queen of the Adriatic will be less dishonoured when sunk under Ocean's waves than she is at present under foreign dominion.

139. starlight] An adj. (see note to line 82).

142. 'Any who were to see just your sunlit towers'.

146. human forms] 'Venice which was once a tyrant, is now the next worst thing, a slave . . . I had no conception of the excess to which avarice, cowardice, superstition, ignorance, passionless lust, & all the inexpressible brutalities which degrade human nature could be carried, until I had lived a few days among the Venetians' (S. to Peacock, 8 October 1818, *L* ii 43).

152. the Celtic Anarch] Austria. 'Celtic' corresponded to mod. 'Teutonic'; all tyranny was lawless, so all tyrants were anarchs.

155   Chained like thee, ingloriously,
                   Thou and all thy sister band
                   Might adorn this sunny land,
                   Twining memories of old time
                   With new virtues more sublime;
160   If not, perish thou and they, —
                   Clouds which stain truth's rising day
                   By her sun consumed away,
                   Earth can spare ye: while like flowers,
                   In the waste of years and hours,
165   From your dust new nations spring
                   With more kindly blossoming.

                   Perish — let there only be
                   Floating o'er thy hearthless sea
                   As the garment of the sky
170   Clothes the world immortally,
                   One remembrance, more sublime
                   Than the tattered pall of time
                   Which scarce hides thy visage wan; —
                   That a tempest-cleaving Swan
175   Of the songs of Albion,
                   Driven from his ancestral streams
                   By the might of evil dreams,
                   Found a nest in thee; and Ocean
                   Welcomed him with such emotion

165–6. S.'s key to the printer for his insertion of lines 167–205 (*Yale MS*) was probably from memory:

> From thy dust shall nations spring
> With more kindly blossoming

167–205. The MS of these lines on Byron is now at Yale University. S. sent them to his publisher for insertion into Mary S.'s transcript of the poem, perhaps in consequence of Peacock's (lost) comments on *Childe Harold* iv to which S. replied on 17 or 18 December 1818 (*L* ii 57–8).

168. *hearthless*] Deprived of inhabitants (127) and spiritual life (105–10).

169. *the sky*] *Yale MS*; thy sky *1819, 1839, eds.* A printer's dittography from line 168.

172. *time*] time. *MYR* viii (there is what must be an unluckily placed ink-spot in *Yale MS*; a stop makes no sense); time, *eds.* Line 173 predicates *tattered pall of time*, and not *remembrance*.

174–5. Apparently 'a swan (Byron) whose flight mastered the tempest of British poetry' (see note to line 184). The suggested emendation 'sons' is meaningless; the word is clear in MS. Swans were sacred to Apollo, god of prophecy and poetry (cf. Plato, *Phaedo* 84).

177. *evil dreams*] Scandal aroused by Byron's separation from his wife.

178–82. *Ocean . . . thunder-fit*] S.'s strictures to Peacock on Byron's way of life ended 'But that he is a great poet, I think the address to Ocean proves': i.e. the concluding stanzas 178–84 of *Childe Harold* iv.

180	That its joy grew his, and sprung
	From his lips like music flung
	O'er a mighty thunder-fit
	Chastening terror: — what though yet
	Poesy's unfailing River,
185	Which through Albion winds forever
	Lashing with melodious wave
	Many a sacred Poet's grave,
	Mourn its latest nursling fled?
	What though thou with all thy dead
190	Scarce can for this fame repay
	Aught thine own? oh, rather say
	Though thy sins and slaveries foul
	Overcloud a sunlike soul?
	As the ghost of Homer clings
195	Round Scamander's wasting springs;
	As divinest Shakespeare's might
	Fills Avon and the world with light
	Like Omniscient power which he
	Imaged 'mid mortality;
200	As the love from Petrarch's urn
	Yet amid yon hills doth burn,
	A quenchless lamp by which the heart
	Sees things unearthly; — so thou art
	Mighty spirit — so shall be
205	The City that did refuge thee.

Lo, the sun floats up the sky
Like thought-wingèd Liberty,

---

184. Cf. Gray's Ode 'The Progress of Poesy': 'Now the rich stream of music winds along / Deep, majestic, smooth, and strong / . . . Now rowling down the steep amain, / Headlong, impetuous, see it pour: / The rock and nodding groves rebellow to the roar' (7–12). Much of S.'s lines 174–204 follows the imagery of Gray's Ode, which includes also the prophecy of a successor to the powerful flights of Milton (95–6) Dryden (103–6) and Pindar (113–17), 'Yet shall he mount, and keep his distant way / Beyond the limits of a vulgar fate' (121–2). Verbally S.'s echo is of Thomson's *Autumn* 743–4, '. . . where the numerous wave / For ever lashes the resounding shore'.

187. Poet's] Poets' *Yale MS.*

195. Scamander's wasting springs] A famous river near Troy, 'wasting' because no longer celebrated.

198. Like Omniscient power] i.e. Shakespeare's power gives an impression of superhuman understanding of mortal men and women.

200. Petrarch's urn] urn, *Yale MS.* The village of Arquà Petrárca, where the poet lived and has his tomb ('Petrarch's house & tomb are religiously preserved & visited': *L* ii 43), is near Este on the South edge of the Euganean Hills.

Till the universal light
Seems to level plain and height;
210 From the sea a mist has spread,
And the beams of morn lie dead
On the towers of Venice now,
Like its glory long ago.
By the skirts of that grey cloud
215 Many-domèd Padua proud
Stands, a peopled solitude,
'Mid the harvest-shining plain,
Where the peasant heaps his grain
In the garner of his foe,
220 And the milk-white oxen slow
With the purple vintage strain,
Heaped upon the creaking wain,
That the brutal Celt may swill
Drunken sleep with savage will;
225 And the sickle to the sword
Lies unchanged, though many a lord,
Like a weed whose shade is poison,
Overgrows this region's foison,
Sheaves of whom are ripe to come
230 To destruction's harvest home:
Men must reap the things they sow,
Force from force must ever flow,
Or worse; but 'tis a bitter woe
That love or reason cannot change
235 The despot's rage, the slave's revenge.

Padua, thou within whose walls
Those mute guests at festivals,
Son and Mother, Death and Sin,

208–9. *Wasserman* 202 note quotes *Isaiah* xl 4: 'Every valley shall be exalted, and every mountain and hill shall be made plain' – a vision of social equality.

216. *a peopled solitude*] 'Excepting Ferrara, [Padua] had an air of desolation and desertion more striking than that of any Italian city . . . She had, in 1816, only 25,000 inhabitants' (Lord Broughton, *Italy* i 94–5).

228. *foison*] Abundance.

232. 'Wrong hath but wrong, and blame the due of blame' (Buckingham in *Richard III*, V i 9, going to deserved execution).

238–44. *Death and Sin*] In *Paradise Lost* ii 648–870 Satan and Sin appear as father and mother. The dicing was probably suggested by Coleridge's 'Ancient Mariner' 196–7. Sin's compensation for the loss of Ezzelin is to be made deputy to the Emperor of Austria (with a pun on *Vice*). *Ezzelin*] Eccelino da Romano (1194–1259), an atrocious military hireling who tyrannised Padua for eighteen years. He killed himself by exposing his wounds after final defeat and capture.

Played at dice for Ezzelin,
240   Till Death cried, 'I win, I win!'
And Sin cursed to lose the wager,
But Death promised, to assuage her,
That he would petition for
Her to be made Vice-Emperor,
245   When the destined years were o'er,
Over all between the Po
And the eastern Alpine snow,
Under the mighty Austrian.
Sin smiled so as Sin only can,
250   And since that time, aye, long before,
Both have ruled from shore to shore,
That incestuous pair, who follow
Tyrants as the sun the swallow,
As Repentance follows Crime,
255   And as changes follow Time.

In thine halls the lamp of learning,
Padua, now no more is burning;
Like a meteor, whose wild way
Is lost over the grave of day,
260   It gleams betrayed and to betray:
Once remotest nations came
To adore that sacred flame,
When it lit not many a hearth
On this cold and gloomy earth:
265   Now new fires from antique light
Spring beneath the wide world's might;
But their spark lies dead in thee,
Trampled out by tyranny.
As the Norway woodman quells,

256. *the lamp of learning*] S.'s account of Padua's internationally famous eleventh-century University follows *Eustace* i 154–5: 'Of eighteen thousand students six hundred only remain, a number . . . barely sufficient to shew the deserted state of the once crowded Schools of Padua . . . The decrease of numbers . . . is to be attributed to the establishment of similar institutions in other countries, and to the general multiplication of the means of knowledge over the Christian world'.   258. *a meteor*] Here, an *ignis fatuus*.

260. A line used (of 'Tomorrow') apparently in a draft of 'Lines written in dejection – December 1818, near Naples' (*Nbk 6* ff. 70–71ʳᵉᵛ).

266. *might*] A misprint for 'night' has been suspected; but the intended meaning of 'oppression' is confirmed by lines 279–81.

269–79. *As the Norway woodman . . . down in fear*] Suggested by the scene of a forest fire near Christiania (Oslo) in Mary Wollstonecraft's *Letters Written . . . in Sweden, Norway, and Denmark*, 1796, Letter xv: 'Fires of this kind are occasioned by the wind suddenly rising when the

270   In the depth of piny dells,
One light flame among the brakes,
While the boundless forest shakes,
And its mighty trunks are torn
By the fire thus lowly born:
275   The spark beneath his feet is dead,
He starts to see the flames it fed
Howling through the darkened sky
With a myriad tongues victoriously,
And sinks down in fear: so thou,
280   O tyranny, beholdest now
Light around thee, and thou hearest
The loud flames ascend, and fearest:
Grovel on the earth; aye, hide
In the dust thy purple pride!

285   Noon descends around me now:
'Tis the noon of autumn's glow,
When a soft and purple mist
Like a vaporous amethyst,
Or an air-dissolvèd star
290   Mingling light and fragrance, far
From the curved horizon's bound
To the point of heaven's profound,
Fills the overflowing sky;
And the plains that silent lie
295   Underneath, the leaves unsodden
Where the infant frost has trodden
With his morning-wingèd feet,
Whose bright print is gleaming yet;
And the red and golden vines,
300   Piercing with their trellised lines
The rough, dark-skirted wilderness;
The dun and bladed grass no less,
Pointing from this hoary tower

---

farmers are burning roots of trees, stalks of beans, &c. with which they manure the ground. The devastation must, indeed, be terrible, when this, literally speaking, wild fire, runs along the forest, flying from top to top, and cracking amongst the branches. The soil, as well as the trees, is swept away by the destructive torrent; and the country, despoiled of beauty and riches, is left to mourn for ages' (*MWW* vi 310).

270. piny dells] These words occur in association with the draft of lines 45–6 in *Nbk 3*, f. 215.

289. an air-dissolvèd star] A star whose light is blurred by the atmosphere.

303. this hoary tower] The tower of the Benedictine Monastery of the Olivetani (suppressed in 1767) on Monte Venda, the topmost point of the Euganean Hills. The summit of M. Venda was taken over as a NATO base in the 1960s.

305

310

315

In the windless air; the flower
Glimmering at my feet; the line
Of the olive-sandalled Apennine
In the south dimly islanded;
And the Alps, whose snows are spread
High between the clouds and sun;
And of living things each one;
And my spirit which so long
Darkened this swift stream of song,
Interpenetrated lie
By the glory of the sky:
Be it love, light, harmony,
Odour, or the soul of all
Which from heaven like dew doth fall,
Or the mind which feeds this verse
Peopling the lone universe.

320

325

330

Noon descends, and after noon
Autumn's evening meets me soon,
Leading the infantine moon,
And that one star, which to her
Almost seems to minister
Half the crimson light she brings
From the sunset's radiant springs:
And the soft dreams of the morn
(Which like wingèd winds had borne
To that silent isle, which lies
'Mid remembered agonies,
The frail bark of this lone being)
Pass, to other sufferers fleeing,

306. the olive-sandalled Apennine] The Apennine Mountains with olive-groves at their feet.
Ancient Greek sandals had olive-wood soles.

308. the Alps] The Julian Alps beyond Venice to the north-east, also visible from Monte Venda
in clear weather.

313. The subjects which *interpenetrated lie* include the *plains* (294), the *leaves* (295), the *vines*
(299), the *grass* (302), the *flower* (304), the *line of the . . . Apennine* (305–6), the *Alps* (308), the
livings things (310), and the speaker's *spirit* (311).

318–19. 'Or if the mind that creates this poem is also creating the reality it perceives'. Cp.
'Mont Blanc' 142–4, and *L&C* II xxx 1–2: 'For, before Cythna loved it, had my song / Peopled
with thoughts the boundless universe'. All three quotations recall Richard II in prison: 'And
these same thoughts people this little world' (V v 9).

323. that one star] Venus (see headnote).

327. morn] morn, *1819.*

331. being)] being,) *1819.*

And its ancient pilot, Pain,
Sits beside the helm again.

335　　Other flowering isles must be
In the sea of life and agony:
Other spirits float and flee
O'er that gulf: even now, perhaps,
On some rock the wild wave wraps,
340　　With folded wings they waiting sit
For my bark, to pilot it
To some calm and blooming cove,
Where for me, and those I love,
May a windless bower be built,
345　　Far from passion, pain, and guilt,
In a dell 'mid lawny hills,
Which the wild sea-murmur fills,
And soft sunshine, and the sound
Of old forests echoing round,
350　　And the light and smell divine
Of all flowers that breathe and shine:
We may live so happy there,
That the spirits of the air,
Envying us, may even entice
355　　To our healing paradise
The polluting multitude;
But their rage would be subdued
By that clime divine and calm,
And the winds whose wings rain balm
360　　On the uplifted soul, and leaves
Under which the bright sea heaves,

343–4. An inversion, following 'perhaps' (338): 'where a bower may (already) be awaiting us'.

353–6. . . . the spirits . . . multitude] 'I should have then this only fear, / Lest men, when they my pleasures see, / Should hither throng to live like me, / And so make a City here' (Cowley, 'The Wish' 33–40). The impulse anticipates *Epipsychidion* 407–587.

361. heaves,] heaves; *1819.* The interpretation of lines 357–70 depends on punctuation for which S. was not finally responsible. Bradley (*MLR* i (1905) 36) plausibly suggested that a semicolon after melodies would allow the passage *And the love . . . brotherhood* to be taken in an absolute sense: 'and, since [or while] the love which heals all strife encircles all things in that sweet abode, what would be changed would be the multitude, not the abode'. *Locock 1911* decided that *And the love* depends on *subdued*: 'the rage of the multitude would be subdued by that clime . . . and [by] the winds . . . and [by] the leaves . . . and [by] the love which heals all strife'. This is the reading preferred here. *And the love* cannot coherently depend on *supplies* ('the inspired soul supplies each interval in the music with its own melodies and [with] the love which heals all strife') as this would make the all-embracing love merely intermittent.

While each breathless interval
In their whisperings musical
The inspired soul supplies
365   With its own deep melodies,
And the love which heals all strife
Circling, like the breath of life,
All things in that sweet abode
With its own mild brotherhood:
370   They, not it, would change; and soon
Every sprite beneath the moon
Would repent its envy vain,
And the earth grow young again.

184
'And who feels discord now or sorrow?'

These lines are drafted in *Nbk 6*, in two versions on facing pages (ff. 70–71ʳᵉᵛ); the text given here is that of what appears as the later rewritten version, on f. 70, of rougher and more heavily cancelled lines on f. 71. These read:

And who feels discord now or sorrow
Or loneliness [canc.]; love is god today
And these dark slaves of dim tomorrow
Track that great shade which far away
Beckons, betrayed and to betray
Love

Mary S. transcribed a version in adds. d. 7, and in *1839* assigned the fragment to 1822 (iv 181). The metre and rhyme however suggest connection with 'Stanzas written in dejection' (December 1818), the draft for which surrounds these lines in *Nbk 6*, and *Chernaik* 199 prints them as aborted drafts for a third stanza of that poem. But *BSM* xv 174 proposes a still earlier date of around July 1818, discerning an influence from S.'s translation of the *Symposium*. The metre, and the mood of brief comfort in a long perspective of unhappiness, may alternatively suggest that this fragment is associated with the genesis of 'Lines Written among the Euganean Hills' and therefore dates from early October 1818.

Text from *Nbk 6* f. 70 (punctuation is editorial, except for the question mark).

Published in *1839* iv 181; *Chernaik* 199.

370. They, not it, would change;] *1839, eds*; They, not it would change; *1819*. i.e. 'the multitude would change, not the abode'.

371. 'Every creature subject to transience'.

And who feels discord now or sorrow?
Love is the universe today;
They are the slaves of dim tomorrow
Which on life's labyrinthine way
5   Beckons, betrayed and to betray.

185
'O mighty mind, in whose deep
stream this age'

Addressed to Byron probably in autumn 1818 after renewing contact with him at Venice on 24 August and perhaps after access to *Childe Harold's Pilgrimage* Canto IV which S. had read by 8 October (*L* ii 44). S. had used similar phrasing in his praise of Godwin's *Caleb Williams* and *Mandeville* on 7 December 1817 (*L* i 573–4): '. . . power is in Falkland not as in Mandeville Tumult hurried onward by the tempest, but Tranquillity standing unshaken amid its fiercest rage! But Caleb Williams never shakes the deepest soul like Mandeville. It must be said that in the latter you rule with a rod of iron'. But the appeal for some 'eternal' work cannot have been addressed to the author of *Political Justice*. The lines are difficult to date precisely from their position in *Nbk 11*; they immediately follow 'O Mary dear' (no. 177) of the late summer, yet are apparently written over the first (pencil) draft of lines 145–7 of *PU* II i. The *PU* fragment is isolated, however, and the image of clouds as flocks of sheep may have been recorded before its context in the drama. Following pages contain drafts of the Homeric Hymns translations (early 1818), and lines 126–32 of *The Mask of Anarchy* (1819). S. had admonished Byron for wasting his genius as early as September 1816 (*L* i 506–8), and was still urging him to produce a work worthy of him as late as 1821 (*L* ii 283–4, 309), but in Venice S. was appalled by the dissolute life Byron was leading and attributed the 'contempt & desperation' of *Childe Harold* IV to this cause: '. . . contemplating in the distorted mirror of his own thoughts, the nature & the destiny of man, what can he behold but objects of contempt & despair? But that he is a great poet, I think the address to Ocean proves' (*L* ii 58). Some jotted lines in *Nbk 6* (f. 75) probably also belong to S.'s Venetian visit:

3. They] Alt. from *these* in *Nbk 6*; these *BSM* xv.

4. Which on life's] Dark'ning Life's *1839*.

5. Beckons,] Beckon *BSM* xv. The singular subject is *tomorrow* (a terminal *s* is doubtful in *Nbk 6*, but cp. the alternative version above). At the top of the following page in *Nbk 6* are two further roughly drafted and cancelled lines which may be draft for 'Stanzas written in dejection' but which appear from their position to be earlier: 'And round that cheek once pressed to mine / Health hangs like a fresh atmosphere'.

make
Your spirit as a lamp, & from thy verse
to dissolve unbind [*BSM* xv reads '[?unkind]']
It has dimmed by that it shd disperse

For S.'s opinion of Byron at this time, see his description of Maddalo/Byron in the Preface to *J&M*.

Text from *Nbk 11* f. 204ʳᵉᵛ.

Published in *Relics* 78 (lines 1–3); *Robinson* 106.

O mighty mind, in whose deep stream this age
Shakes like a reed in the unheeding storm,
Why dost thou rule not thine own sacred rage
And clothe thy powers in some eternal form
5   From thine eternal spirit, which might wage

186
Song for *Tasso*

Composed after S.'s visit on 7 November 1818 to the cell exhibited as Torquato Tasso's prison from 1579 to 1586 in the Hospital of St Anne, Ferrara. He was, however, confined under harsh conditions for less than two years. The details in lines 18–19 and 25–6 correspond with the first-hand account S. sent Peacock on 6–7 November: 'The dungeon is low and dark, & when I say it is really a very decent dungeon, I speak as one who has seen the prisons in the Doges palace at Venice . . . It is low, & has a grated window, & being sunk some feet below the level of the earth is full of unwholesome damps' (*L* ii 48). It is possible, though unlikely, that the lyric was drafted earlier, from written accounts. A visitor of 1792, quoted by John Black (*Life of Torquato Tasso* (1810) ii 97 note) described the cell as 'Damp,

1. O mighty mind] The top right-hand corner of the page, conceivably bearing a title, has been torn off. Another apparent attempt at these lines, either contemporary or belonging to late 1819, occurs at f. 57 in the same *Nbk 11* where it interrupts a draft of *PU* IV 424–43:
    Thou Mind, who to our unawakened Nation
    Hast been as is the unseen power which sways
    The moving world, and with thine inspiration
    Hast
These lines replace the italicised cancellations: *O mighty* Mind, *on whom thine inspiration / Hung like a night flowers* unseen power which sways / (etc.)

3. rule] curb *Relics*.

4. And clothe thy powers in some eternal form] And stamp upon thy work [?] *MS canc*. For 'powers' *BSM* xviii reads 'prowess'.

5. Both *spirit* and *depths* (1st choice but unmetrical) are cancelled in *Nbk 11*, without comma. For 'wage' *BSM* xviii reads 'war'. *Robinson* 106 incorporates part of a sixth line, which really belongs to the *PU* draft.

dimly lighted, and too low in many parts to allow me to stand erect'; but John Cam Hobhouse's *Illustrations of the 4th Canto of Childe Harold*, which followed the appearance of Byron's Canto IV on 28 April 1818 and which mentioned the grated window of Tasso's cell, was not read by S. until late September (*Mary Jnl (Jones)* 105). Tasso's reputed cell is illustrated variously in Byron's *Works*, Poetry Vol. vii (1904), ed. E. H. Coleridge, 348, and in *The Italian Journal of Samuel Rogers*, ed. J. R. Hale (1956) 176. S.'s unfinished draft is in pencil; the title is Mary S.'s. Commas have been added in lines 1, 8, 12 (after *fast*), 16, 22; a semicolon in line 3; and stops at stanza-ends.

Text from *Nbk 11* ff. 39–40.

Published in *1824* 264 (lines 1–21); *Julian* iii 202–3; *Massey* 275–6 (transcript of MS).

I loved — alas, our life is love,
But when we cease to breathe and move
I do suppose love ceases too; —
I thought — but not as now I do —
5 Keen thoughts and bright of linkèd lore
Of all that men had thought before
And all that Nature shows, and more. —

And still I love and still I think,
But strangely — for my heart can drink
10 The dregs of such despair and fear
As love [   ]
And if I think, my thoughts come fast,
I mix the present with the past
And each seems uglier than the last.

15 Sometimes I see before me flee
A silver-shining form like thee,
O Leonora, and I sit
In this dark room still watching it

2–3. Leonora d'Este died in 1581, five years before Tasso's release from confinement.

10. *fear*] live, *1824*; ?live *Massey*; pain *canc. BSM* xviii.

11. Blank in MS after *love*.

12–14. Serassi (*La Vita* (Rome 1785) 320 note) quotes a visitor to St Anne's in 1583 who, having asked Tasso what subject he was meditating, received the reply: 'Penso e ripenso, e nel pensare impazzo' ('I think and think again, and in thinking drive myself mad').

14. *each*] i.e. each thought; but the ambiguous syntax involves also 'the present' and 'the past'.

16. A form as silver bright as thee *Nbk 11 canc.* (the *1824* reading 'spirit's' is not in MS). Cp. the *canc.* alt. of 'The Two Spirits: An Allegory' (no. 182) 45: 'And [a silver] shape like his early love doth pass'.

18. The first four words are virtually obliterated under an ink draft for *Epipsychidion* 14: 'Beating thy heavenly wings', which *Massey* introduces into his transcript. *In* and *Dark* seem recognisable in pencil underneath; *this* and *room* are conjectural; cp. *BSM* xviii for a differing transcript.

20	Till by the grated casement's ledge It fades, with such a sigh as sedge Breathes near the breezy streamlet's edge.
25	I knew the image was not thine, And yet I could not but repine To heed 'twas but a vapour hoar Breathed from my sunless dungeon's floor By the unsleeping damps below

187
Stanzas written in dejection – December 1818, near Naples

The rough draft of this poem is in *Nbk 6*, and there are two holograph fair copies, in Bodleian MS Shelley e. 5., and in the Pierpont Morgan Library. Both copies give the date of composition as December 1818, as do Mary S.'s texts in *1824* and *1839*. S. was in Naples from 1 December 1818 to 28 February 1819. The poem's opening description seems to echo phrasing from S.'s letter to Peacock of 23–24 January (see note to lines 1–4) describing the Shelleys' visit to Pompeii on 22 December (*Mary Jnl* i 245), which suggests a more specific date in late December; but S. was impressed by the scenery around Naples from the period of his first arrival, and the dejection articulated in the poem appears to have persisted throughout his stay in the city. Following the death of Clara in Venice Mary's mood was very dark, which in turn strongly affected S. Her 'Note on Poems of 1818' recalls that at this time S. 'suffered greatly in health . . . Constant and poignant physical suffering exhausted him; and though he preserved the appearance of cheerfulness . . . many hours were passed when his thoughts, shadowed by illness, became gloomy, and then he escaped to solitude, and in verses, which he hid from fear of wounding me, poured forth morbid but too natural bursts of discontent and sadness. One looks back with unspeakable regret and gnawing remorse to such periods . . .' (*1839* iii 162; see also e.g. *Mary L* i 85 for Mary's own depression in Naples). The note goes on to make plain the extent of S.'s feelings of isolation and despair. A letter to Peacock of mid-December closes on an uncharacteristically subdued note: 'I have depression enough of spirits & not good health, though I believe the warm air of Naples does me good. We see absolutely no one here' (*L* ii 64), and a few days later he strikes the note again in a letter to Hunt ('I have neither good health or spirits just now': *L* ii 68). According to a story of Trelawny's, S. actually attempted suicide in Naples (see *White* ii 570–1). S.'s chastened sense of responsibility for the

20. *fades,*] *Nbk 11, 1824*; falls, *Massey*; falls / fades *BSM* xviii.

21. *near*] o'er *1824*.   *streamlet's*] streamlet *Massey*.

24. *vapour hoar*] [?vaporous] hour *BSM* xviii.

calamity of Clara's death (see headnotes to 'Behold, sweet Sister mine', and 'The Two Spirits', nos 181–182), and his reaction to Mary's own consequent depression, may also have coincided with a renewed sense of the injustice and malicious distortions of public attacks on him in the *Quarterly Review* and elsewhere (see *L* ii 66, and headnotes to 'Alas, this is not what I thought life was', and 'Lift not the painted veil', nos 173–174). He was also involved at this time in the mysterious affair of the 'Neapolitan baby'. *White* ii 546–50 prints documents from Neapolitan archives which register that a child named 'Elena Adelaide' was born to S. and Mary at their lodgings in the Riviera di Chiaia on 27 December 1818. She was baptised on 27 February 1819, and according to a death certificate died on 10 June 1820. It is obviously impossible that this child could actually have been Mary's, and although scurrilous stories, circulated by a disaffected former servant of the Shelleys, claimed that the child was Claire Clairmont's by S., that too seems under the circumstances entirely incredible, not to say physically impossible. *Mary Jnl* i 249–50 gives a lucid review of the circumstances and known facts of the affair (and see also *Claire Jnl* 97). It has also been suggested that this child was possibly born to the Shelleys' nursemaid Elise, and that S. was the father, but this too seems implausible (see Ursula Orange, 'Elise, Nursemaid to the Shelleys', *KSMB* vi (1955) 24–34). A possible explanation is that S. sought in his desperation to console Mary for the loss of Clara by the adoption of a little girl, and that for unknown reasons the scheme, once in train, was abandoned. A further separate but possibly related story, that S. was followed to Naples by a lady admirer who had conceived a passion for the poet after reading his verses, and who after meeting with S. subsequently died in Naples, lacks any corroborating evidence (see headnote to no. 202). Whatever the true circumstances, it is scarcely surprising against such a background that S. should suffer from depression in December 1818, and that he should during this period produce one of the most openly personal of all his lyrics.

In formal terms S.'s 'Stanzas' adapt the Spenserian stanza by combining its rhyme scheme and final alexandrine with fluent octosyllabics akin to the seven-syllable lines of 'Lines Written among the Euganean Hills'. There is also a marked influence from Wordsworth's 'Ode: Intimations of Immortality', in mood and some details of phrasing but also in the use of the hexameter as an element of a lyric stanza (cp. the Immortality Ode, lines 9, 18). S.'s octosyllabics are, like Milton's in 'Il Penseroso', distinctive in their fusion of light metrical movement with a tone of quiet and sometimes dark reflection, recalling the use of similar effects in Act 1 of *PU*; and this too suggests an influence from the passages including seven-syllable lines in Wordsworth's Ode, particularly 180–7:

> We will grieve not, rather find
> Strength in what remains behind;
> In the primal sympathy
> Which having been must ever be;
> In the soothing thoughts that spring
> Out of human suffering;
> In the faith that looks through death,
> In years that bring the philosophic mind.

There is an attentive reading of S.'s 'Stanzas' in *Chernaik* 74–80, but the poem has otherwise attracted scant critical attention.

'Stanzas written in dejection' was almost certainly one of the poems that S. collected as 'all my saddest verses raked up into one heap' and sent to Ollier on 10 November 1820 for publication with *J&M* (*L* ii 246); see headnote to 'Misery. – A Fragment' (no. 202) for details of the other poems probably included in the collection. Neil Fraistat has shown (*BSM* ix Introduction liii–liv; see also *BSM* xxi 448–53) that the fair copy of 'Stanzas written in dejection' in Bodleian MS Shelley e. 5 came originally from a small MS booklet made up by S. in which his collection of personal lyrics was probably sent to Ollier. This copy is very clean and is punctuated with unusual care, and must be later than the Pierpont Morgan holograph, which is written on leaves originally in *Harvard Nbk* together with 'Lift not the painted veil' (see *MYR* v), probably as a safe-keeping copy. The Pierpont Morgan MS has 'cloudless' for 'stainless' in line 44, according with the draft in *Nbk 6* and presumably therefore closer to it than e. 5, whose readings are identical with *1824* (except for errors of printing; see notes); Pierpont Morgan also has 'cold' in line 37 altered (probably in the hand of Edward Williams) from 'dead', a perplexing circumstance again suggesting a closer relation to the rough draft, which has the same alteration.

Text from Bodleian MS Shelley e. 5 (commas have been added in lines 5, 8, 9, 19, after *power* and *love* in 24, and after *linger* in 45; full stops have been added in lines 9, 18, 27, and 36).

Published in *1824* 164–5, *Chernaik* 198–200.

187
Stanzas written in dejection – December 1818, near Naples

The Sun is warm, the sky is clear,
The waves are dancing fast and bright,
Blue isles and snowy mountains wear
The purple noon's transparent might,
5   The breath of the moist earth is light
Around its unexpanded buds;
Like many a voice of one delight
The winds, the birds, the Ocean-floods;
The City's voice itself is soft, like Solitude's.

1–4. Cp. S.'s description of the scenery near Pompeii, in his letter to Peacock of 23–24 January 1819 (*L* ii 73); 'Above & between the multitudinous shafts of the [?sunshiny] columns, was seen the blue sea reflecting the purple heaven of noon above it, & supporting as it were on its line the dark lofty mountains of Sorrento, of a blue inexpressibly deep, & tinged towards their summits with streaks of new-fallen snow'. The Shelleys visited Pompeii on 22 December 1818 (*Mary Jnl* i 245).

4–5. *1824* reads *light* for *might* in line 4, and omits line 5; a printer's error corrected in an errata slip, and probably accounting for the mistake in line 4.

10   I see the Deep's untrampled floor
           With green and purple seaweeds strown,
           I see the waves upon the shore
           Like light dissolved in star-showers, thrown;
           I sit upon the sands alone;
15   The lightning of the noontide Ocean
           Is flashing round me, and a tone
           Arises from its measured motion,
           How sweet! did any heart now share in my emotion.

           Alas, I have nor hope nor health,
20   Nor peace within nor calm around,
           Nor that content surpassing wealth
           The sage in meditation found,
           And walked with inward glory crowned;
           Nor fame, nor power, nor love, nor leisure —
25   Others I see whom these surround,
           Smiling they live and call life pleasure:
           To me that cup has been dealt in another measure.

           Yet now despair itself is mild
           Even as the winds and waters are;
30   I could lie down like a tired child
           And weep away the life of care
           Which I have borne and yet must bear
           Till Death like Sleep might steal on me,
           And I might feel in the warm air

10–11. Cp. S.'s letter to Peacock of 17 or 18 December 1818 (*L* ii 61): 'We set off an hour after sunrise one radiant morning in a little boat, there was not a cloud in the sky nor a wave upon the sea which was so translucent that you could see the hollow caverns clothed with the glaucous sea-moss, & the leaves & branches of those delicate weeds that pave the unequal bottom of the water'.

13. star-showers] *OED* defines *star-shower* as 'a shower of falling meteors', with S.'s usage here as the only citation. See William Keach, *Shelley's Style* (1984) 125.

19. S.'s draft in *Nbk 6* at first began this stanza 'Alas – that I were not alone'.

21–3. Reiman (1977) notes M. H. Abrams's suggestion that S. is thinking in these lines of the Stoic philosopher Marcus Aurelius (the draft in *Nbk 6* at first read 'empire', with a more Stoic feel than the received reading 'glory'); the passage also perhaps recalls the sage described in the closing lines of Milton's 'Il Penseroso'.

27. The hexameter line, and its particular cadence here, recall Wordsworth's 'Ode: Intimations of Immortality' 9: 'The things which I have seen I now can see no more'.

29. are;] *Pierpont Morgan*; are, *e. S.*

30–1. Cp. *Psalms* cxxxvii 1: 'By the rivers of Babylon, there we sat down, yea, we wept, when we remembered Zion'.

33. Death and Sleep were children of Night in classical mythology; see *Q Mab* i 2 and note, and cp. 'Mont Blanc' 49–52.

35   My cheek grow cold, and hear the sea
              Breathe o'er my dying brain its last monotony.

              Some might lament that I were cold,
              As I, when this sweet day is gone,
              Which my lost heart, too soon grown old,
40   Insults with this untimely moan —
              They might lament, — for I am one
              Whom men love not, and yet regret;
              Unlike this Day, which, when the Sun
              Shall on its stainless glory set,
45   Will linger though enjoyed, like joy in memory yet.

188
'There was a little lawny islet'

The draft in *Nbk 11* is skipped by 'Misery. – A Fragment' and so is presumably earlier than August 1819 (see headnote to no. 202), although Mary S. dates the lines to 1822 in *1839* and *1840*. Some details coincide with the description of scenery in S.'s letter to Peacock of 25 February 1819 (*L* ii 77), quoted in the note to *PU* II ii 1–23. The lines have affinities with the lyrics spoken by the Spirits at the opening of *PU* II ii.

Text from *Nbk 11* f. 107 (commas have been added in lines 5 and 7, an apostrophe in line 5, and a stop in line 8).

Published in *1824* 213 (entitled 'The Isle'), *Massey* 70–1, 238 (Mary's transcript).

              There was a little lawny islet
              By anemone and violet
                Like mosaic, paven —
              And its roof was flowers and leaves

35. There is apparently a full stop after *sea* in *e. 5*, which must be an error.

37. *cold,*] Altered from 'dead' in *Nbk 6* and *Pierpont Morgan*; neither MS has a rhyme-word for 'dead'.

38–45. 'Some might lament were I to die, just as I will lament the passing of this beautiful day (which is insulted by this dejected poem); but whereas my passing will, like my life, cause others regret, the joy of this day will not cease with its passing, but will live again when remembered'.

42. *regret*] i.e. 'feel mental distress on account of' (*OED* v. 2); S. thinks of himself as a cause of regret in both his life and death.

44. *stainless*] *e. 5*, *1824*; cloudless *Nbk 6*, *Pierpont Morgan*.

¶188   1. *lawny*] Written above *mossy* canc. in *Nbk 11*.

3. *mosaic,*] mosaic *BSM* xviii.

5   Which the summer's breath enweaves,
               Where nor Sun nor shower nor breeze
               Pierce the pines and tulip trees,
                   Each a gem engraven.

               Girt by many an azure wave
10   With which the clouds and mountains pave
                   A lake's blue chasm

189
'In the cave which wild weeds cover'

These lines are drafted in *Nbk 10*, and were perhaps composed on S.'s first arrival for his second visit to Rome, in early March 1819; they were possibly at first intended for *PU*. Mary S.'s transcript is in adds. d. 7 f. 76.

Text from *Nbk 10* f. 2r (the draft is unpunctuated).

Published in *1840* 320 (entitled 'A Roman's Chamber' in *eds* from Forman).

               In the cave which wild weeds cover
               Wait for thine etherial lover
               For the pallid moon is waning
               O'er the spiral cypress hanging
5   And the moon no cloud is staining.

               It was once a Roman's chamber
                   Where he kept his [   ] revels
               And the wild weeds twine and clamber
                   It was then a chasm for devils

6. *shower*] showers *1824*.

7. *tulip*] tallest *1824*.

8. *a gem*] Alt. from *gems* in *Nbk 11*. Presumably referring to the flowers of line 2.

11. *A*] Written over *The* in *Nbk 11*. This line is written in pencil, probably at a later date.

¶189   1. *cover*] [cover] *MYR* iv.

2. *thine*] Written *thin* in *Nbk 10*.

5. *moon*] [?morn] *MYR* iv; noon *Huntington Nbks*. The word is debatable, and the context might support *morn* or *noon*; although the meeting of lovers envisaged, recalling in general terms the atmosphere of Coleridge's 'Kubla Khan', seems to suggest moonlight.

6. *Roman's*] Written above *princes* canc. in *Nbk 10*.

7. Space left in *Nbk 10*.

190
'Rome has fallen, ye see it lying'

Drafted in *Nbk 10*, probably around the time of S.'s second visit to Rome in early
March 1819. The fragment may (perhaps together with the preceding and following
lines) be related to S.'s prose fragment 'The Coliseum', written November 1818–
May 1819 (see *Shelley's Guitar* 103).

Text from *Nbk 10* f. 3ʳ.

Published in *1840* 320.

> Rome has fallen, ye see it lying
> Heaped in undistinguished ruin
> Nature is alone undying

191
'Follow to the deep wood, sweetest'

These lines are written in *Nbk 10*, on the same page with the first stanza of 'To
Sophia' ('Thou art fair, and few are fairer'); for the possible adaptation of that poem
from what was originally an unused stanza for Asia's song at the end of *PU* II v,
see headnote to 'To Sophia'. Various suggestions have been made about the proper
context of the present lines (see e.g. *Peck* ii 161, *White* ii 174), and they too may
be a discarded passage for *PU* (perhaps for the end of II i); but they are probably
related to the same impulse which produced other fanciful fragments nearby in
the nbk, and may therefore date from around S.'s arrival in Rome for his second
visit, in early March 1819 (the violet of line 5 suggests spring).

Text from *Nbk 10* f. 2v (unpunctuated).

Published in *Relics* 80.

> Follow to the deep wood, sweetest
> Follow to the wild briar dingle,
> [   ] no eye thou therein meetest
> When we sink to intermingle
5 > And the violet tells no tale

¶**191**   1. *wood, sweetest*] wood's weeds *Relics*.

3. Space left in *Nbk 10*.

4. *when*] where *Relics*.

5. *no*] her *Relics*.

To the odour-scented gale
For they too have enough to do
Of such work as I and you.

192
'How sweet it is to sit and read the tales'

Written in *Nbk 10*, perhaps in March 1819. The lines suggest a public performance; according to *Mary Jnl* (i 255; cp. *Claire Jnl* 104) S. heard the *Miserere* in the Sistine Chapel on 30 March 1819, and as he was also reading Plutarch on that day he possibly read Plutarch during the performance.

Text from *Nbk 10* f. 3ʳ.

Published in *1840* 320.

> How sweet it is to sit and read the tales
> Of mightiest poets, and to hear the while
> Sweet music, which when the attention fails
> Fill the dim pause with

193
'Wake the serpent not – lest he'

Date unknown; but by propinquity with other fragments in *Nbk 10*, and metre (which could even suggest connection or continuity with fragments in the preceding nbk pages; see preceding fragments), possibly March–April 1819 in Rome. The lines are skipped by S.'s draft for the 'Song of Spirits' for *PU* II iii 54–98. Mary's transcript is in adds. d. 7 f. 77. At the top of the same page in *Nbk 10* is a presumably unconnected line 'And from a wilderness of human Crimes [or possibly 'Graves']'.

Text from *Nbk 10* f. 5ʳ (unpunctuated except for the dash in line 1).

Published in *1840* 320.

> Wake the serpent not — lest he
> Should not know which way to go;

7. *too*] two *Relics*.

¶192 2. *mightiest*] mighty *1840*.

4. *Fill*] Fills *1840*.

¶193 2. *which*] the *1840*.

454

Let him crawl while yet he's sleeping
Through the deep grass of the meadow
5   Not a bee shall hear him creeping
Not a worm shall see his shadow
Not a may fly shall awaken
From its cradling bluebell shaken
In the starlight as he's sliding
10   Through the grass with silent gliding

194
'Hold – divine image'

Written in *Nbk 10*; skipped by S.'s draft for the 'Song of Spirits' for *PU* II iii and therefore presumably earlier than April 1819. The blank verse lines perhaps suggest S.'s view of Byron in his Venetian decadence (cp. no. 185, 'O mighty mind, in whose deep stream this age').

Text from *Nbk 10* f. 25r.

Published in *Huntington Nbks* ii 82.

Hold — divine image [   ]
Eclipsed Sun — Planet without a beam
Wilt thou offend the Sun thou emblemest
By blotting out the light of written thought

3. *while yet he's*] which yet lies *1840*.

5. *hear*] [hear] *MYR* iv.

8. *bluebell*] blue bell *Nbk 10*.

¶194   *1*. Space left in *Nbk 10*.

195
Prometheus Unbound
A Lyrical Drama in Four Acts

Composition and Publication

S.'s interest in the Prometheus myth, and its treatment by Aeschylus in *Prometheus Bound*, dates from at least as early as his first term at Oxford (*Hogg Life* i 70), but he doubtless knew the play from schooldays. S. had ordered an Aeschylus from Rickman in 1812 (*L* i 344), and was reading and translating the play with Byron in 1816 (*Medwin* i 268), from which period S.'s interest in writing a poem on the Prometheus theme may well originate (cp. Byron's 'Prometheus' of July 1816). S. was also translating *Prometheus Bound* in July 1817 (*Mary Jnl* i 177). Mary famously recalled in 1823, when retracing the route taken through the Alps on their journey to Italy in March 1818, that S. had conceived the idea of his drama at that time while passing 'la Montagne des Eschelles, whose dark high precipices towering above, gave S— the idea of his Prometheus' (*Mary L* i 357). An entry in S.'s hand in Mary's jnl for 26 March 1818 bears this out:

> After dinner we ascended Les Echelles winding along a road cut thro perpendicular rocks of immense elevation by Charles Emmanuel Duke of Savoy in 1582. The rocks which cannot be less than 1000 feet in perpendicular height sometimes overhang the road on each side & almost shut out the sky. The scene is like that described in the Prometheus of Aeschylus – Vast rifts & caverns in the granite precipices – wintry mountains with ice & snow above – the loud sounds of unseen waters within the caverns, & walls of topling rocks only to be scaled as he describes, by the winged chariot of the Ocean Nymphs. (*Mary Jnl* i 200)

While it is certain that S.'s ideas for *PU* must have originated before this date, it is equally plain that S.'s specific conception of the first three acts owes a great deal to the Shelleys' journey through the wintry Alps in March 1818, and their rapid transition to a warm Italian spring. This experience seems to have prompted a coalescence in S.'s imagination of many diverse literary, philosophical, political, scientific and personal influences, to produce a poem which, in the scale and quality of its achievement, goes far beyond anything S. had hitherto written. His thinking towards the project matured through the first Italian summer of 1818, as he busied himself with translations of Plato's *Symposium*, Euripides' *Cyclops* (see headnote), various other classical translations, and much other reading connected with the conventional tourist sights and activities that the party were anticipating (e.g. *Eustace*, and *Barthelemy*; see notes below). At Bagni di Lucca from June to August S. was also reading in various classical accounts of Greek life, perhaps with a view to an Introduction for his translation of the *Symposium*, the 'Discourse on the Manners of the Ancient Athenians' (as *SC* vi 639 notes, the short essay 'On Love', also written around this time, may represent a false start on this essay). A note in *Nbk 11* p. 4 (see headnote to no. 175), apparently derived from Herodotus, reads 'Asia γυναικη Προμεθεως [i.e. 'wife of Prometheus']'; Herodotus is the only classical source for Asia as Prometheus's wife (*Histories* iv 45), and *Mary Jnl* i 219–21 records S.'s systematic reading of Herodotus at Bagni di Lucca in July and August, suggesting that S. was by then engaged in detailed working out of the characters and action for *PU*. By the end of August, S. had definitely begun work in earnest on his drama.

The composition and publication history of *PU* is exceptionally complex, and constitutes an editorial problem which defies any single completely satisfactory solution. S. states in his Preface to *PU* that the poem was 'chiefly written upon the mountainous ruins of the Baths of Caracalla, among the flowery glades, and thickets of odoriferous blossoming trees, which are extended in ever-winding labyrinths upon its immense platforms and dizzy arches suspended in the air. The bright blue sky of Rome, and the effect of the vigorous awakening of spring in that divinest climate, and the new life with which it drenches the spirits even to intoxication, were the inspiration of this drama'. Mary's jnl for Saturday 13 March 1819 (i 252–3) records a visit to the Baths, and S.'s long letter to Peacock of 23 March (*L* ii 84–7) gives a detailed description suggesting close familiarity. Mary's 'Note on the Prometheus Unbound' (*1839* ii 132) expands on S.'s Preface:

> We spent a month at Milan [on first arriving in Italy] . . . Thence we passed in succession to Pisa, Leghorn, the Baths of Lucca, Venice, Este, Rome, Naples, and back again to Rome, whither we returned early in March 1819. During all this time Shelley meditated the subject of his drama, and wrote portions of it . . . At last, when at Rome, during a bright and beautiful spring, he gave up his whole time to the composition . . . At first he contemplated the drama in three acts. It was not till several months after, when at Florence, that he conceived that a fourth act . . . ought to be added to complete the composition.

This emphasis on the Roman spring of 1819 as the inspiration for the drama is however misleading. Act I was being written from at least the period of S.'s meeting with Byron in Venice in August 1818, and the dramatic structure of the play strongly suggests that Act II was substantially worked out during the visit to Naples at the end of the year, with Act III following in the spring (see *BSM* ix, Introduction lxiii–lxxv, and K. Everest, ' "Mechanism of a kind yet unattempted": The Dramatic Action of *Prometheus Unbound*', *DUJ* lxxxv (1993) 237–46). In her 'Note on Poems of 1818' Mary is more precise about the composition of Act I; at 'I Cappuccini', the villa in Este secured for the Shelleys by Byron, 'a vine-trellised walk, a Pergola, as it is called in Italian, led from the hall door to a summer-house at the end of the garden, which Shelley made his study, and in which he began the Prometheus' (*1839* iii 160). Mary arrived at Este on Saturday 5 September, noting in her jnl for Wednesday 2 to Monday 14 September 'poor Clara is dangerously ill – Shelley is very unwell from taking poison in Italian cakes – He writes his drama of Prometheus' (i 226). S. worked quickly at first, and had probably been writing since at least his own arrival at 'I Cappuccini' at the end of August, for his letter of Tuesday 22 September, written to Mary at Este from Padua, asks her to 'bring . . . the sheets of "Prometheus Unbound" which you will find numbered from 1 to 26 on the table of the pavilion' (*L* ii 39–40). S.'s composition on loose sheets, rather than in a notebook, explains the almost total disappearance of draft materials for Act I; and the mention of *numbered* sheets suggests that Act I may already have been in a relatively advanced state (26 sheets might imply somewhere between 500 and 600 lines). On 8 October S. states in a letter to Peacock that he has 'just finished the first act of a lyric & classical drama to be called "Prometheus Unbound" ' (*L* ii 43). This rapid progress was in spite of the trauma of Clara's illness and death on 24 September, and the hectic travelling and stress occasioned by this catastrophe, and by S.'s efforts to effect a reconciliation between Byron and Claire over their daughter Allegra (the original purpose of his visit to Venice). S. seems to have continued work on Act I after his party left Venice and travelled south from Padua and Este (leaving on Thursday 5 November; *Mary Jnl* i 235) towards Rome and Naples, staying *en route* at Ferrara to visit places associated with Ariosto and Tasso, and at Bologna where S. was impressed by the paintings of Correggio, Raphael, and others (see II i 73–4 and note). The party arrived in Rome on Friday 20 November (*Mary Jnl* i 237), and S. continued on to Naples a week later, where he was joined by Mary, Claire, and the others on Tuesday 1 December (*Mary Jnl* i 241). S.'s mood in Naples was dejected and lonely, and saddened by further difficult personal problems (see headnote to 'Stanzas written in dejection – December 1818, near Naples', no. 187), but his visits to the surrounding areas and his experience of Vesuvius became central to his conception of Acts II and III of *PU*. He wrote to Peacock from Naples, in a letter postmarked 26 January 1819, 'At present I write little else but poetry, & little of that. My 1st Act of Prometheus is complete, & I think you would like it' (*L* ii 70–1). The Shelleys left Naples for Rome on Sunday 28 February, arriving on Friday 5 March 1819 (*Mary Jnl* i 249–51). They remained in Rome until just after William's death on 7 June, leaving for Leghorn (Livorno) on 10 June (*Claire Jnl* 113–14). On 6 April S. wrote to Peacock 'My Prometheus Unbound is just finished [i.e. the first three Acts] & in a month or two I shall send it. It is a drama, with characters & a mechanism of a kind yet unattempted; & I think the execution is better than any of my former attempts' (*L* ii 94). S. presumably copied out his rough drafts for Acts II and III from the notebooks from which he was working (including *Nbk 6*, *Nbk 10*, *Nbk 11* and *Nbk 12*; see *MYR* iv, vi, *BSM* xv, xviii) into the neat fair copy, very lightly punctuated but otherwise quite highly finished, which fills *Nbk 7*, *Nbk 8*, and *Nbk 9*. This fair copy is reproduced with a transcription and excellent commentary by Neil Fraistat (*BSM* ix), whose detailed account of the genesis and composition of *PU* should be consulted. S.'s fair copy was ready before the end of April, as Mary notes in her jnl for Sunday 25 April 'Read Shelley's Drama' (i 260). S. did however continue to alter and add to Acts II and III right up to, and indeed beyond the despatch in December 1819 of Mary's transcription of S.'s fair copy of Act IV (see e.g. II iii 54 and notes, and cp. *SC* vi 1070–1). Other evidence suggests the further inference that by August 1819 at least S. was working simultaneously on the fairly substantial additional passages for Act II ('fairly substantial' judging by the number of insertions in *Nbk 7* and *Nbk 8*; in addition to the Song in II iii, other substantial later passages include Asia's Song at the end of II v, and the exchange between the Fauns at II ii 64–97 (see notes)), and various lyrical passages for Act IV (see notes, and *SC* iv 1070–1). There is strong stylistic evidence that the additional passages in Act II are influenced by the manner of Act IV. There is also clear evidence for S.'s continuing local revision to the fair copy (see below). S. left the first few pages of *Nbk 7* blank when he began his fair copy, presumably to accommodate the as yet unwritten Preface. He then began his copy of Act I on f. 18 and proceeded using verso sides only, leaving recto sides blank for later corrections and additions. Act I is completed on f. 20 of *Nbk 8*; Act II fills the remaining verso pages, and finishes on f. 10 of *Nbk 9*. Act III follows on f. 11 and is completed on f. 36. The first four paragraphs of the Preface were subsequently copied into *Nbk 7* ff. 14–16, but the remaining blank pages in *Nbk 7* were then taken up by other material, so that when S. came to add five more paragraphs to the Preface (see below) these were copied (from his rough draft in *Nbk 10*) into *Nbk 9* turned upside down and reversed, ff. 38–30. Act IV was copied into the remaining blank pages of *Nbk 7*, starting at

f. 2 and continuing up to the start of the Preface (i.e. stopping at the bottom of f. 13), and then covering up those pages not already occupied by corrections and additions to Act I, finishing with the last line of the completed poem written at the top of f. 36.

S. appears to have thought of the three-act version of the poem as its final form, at least up until late August. He wrote to Peacock from Livorno in July 1819 'My Prometheus though ready, I do not send until I know more [about Ollier's activities as S.'s publisher]' (L ii 103). In a letter to Hunt of August 15 he speaks of the poem as finished (L ii 108), and in a letter to Ollier from Livorno written c. 20 August S. writes 'I have two works of some length [PU and The Cenci], one of a very popular character, ready for the press' (L ii 111). But his intention to add a fourth act must have been formed very soon after this. The probability of S.'s work on Acts II and IV together in August is further strengthened by other circumstances. S. informed Ollier on 6 September 'My "Prometheus" which has long been finished, is now being transcribed, & will soon be forwarded to you for publication' (L ii 116–17). S.'s plans for the transcription of the poem to be 'forwarded' were complex and have been the source of much subsequent confusion (e.g. in Zillman Variorum, Introduction). He sent the transcript to Peacock, for him to forward to Ollier at a future time to be communicated by letter from S. (letter to Peacock, 21 September, L ii 120; S.'s letter to Hunt, Monday 27 September, L ii 123, confirms the arrangement). The transcript was to be transported to England personally by Maria Gisborne's husband John, who left for England on business on 12 September (Mary Jnl i 296; see also SC vi 930). Mary's jnl shows that the poem was delivered to the Gisbornes on Friday 10 September, as soon as Mary had finished transcribing it (the entry is dated 'Sunday 12' but may well record activities for the previous few days; there are no entries between September 5 and 12):

Sunday 12
Finish copying my tale [The Fields of Fancy, the first version of Mathilda] – Copy Shelley's Prometheus – work – read Beaumont & Fletcher's plays – on Friday [10 September] – Shelley sends his tragedy to Peacock – on Sunday [12 September] – Mr. G sets out for England.

Evidence from the MS suggests that as soon as Mary had finished with the nbks containing S.'s fair copy (and assuming she transcribed last the first four paragraphs of the Preface, in Nbk 7), S. started work on – or at least started to think of work on – putting together a fourth act to be copied into the blank pages then at the beginning of Nbk 7. At the top of the first page of this Notebook, f. 2, is written in S.'s hand 'Sept 11' (Zillman Variorum and BSM ix both argue that the reading may be either 'Sept 11' or 'Act 4', but the date seems very clear; see facsimile in BSM ix 10). S. perhaps thought to begin copying out a fourth act immediately on Mary's completion of her transcripts of the first three acts, but was prevented from making progress by the more urgent occasion of The Mask of Anarchy (see headnote to The Mask of Anarchy), and then (as Cameron (1974) 651 suggests) by the composition of Peter Bell III (see headnote), the letter in defence of Richard Carlile (dated 3 November 1819; L ii 136–48), and the birth of S. and Mary's son Percy Florence on 12 November. BSM ix (Introduction lxxii–lxxiv), however, points out that MS evidence suggests that Act IV was not composed in the sequence of the received text, and that it is therefore highly unlikely that the opening lines of the fourth act could have been copied on 11 September; but the date may still stand as a strong indication that S. had decided by that date to add a fourth act. The evidence of the nbks suggests that Act IV was drafted in four sections, corresponding to lines 1–179, 194–318 (in *Nbk 11*), 319–502 (the exchange between Earth and Moon, probably the earliest conception for the Act, with various complex drafts in *Nbk 10*, *Nbk 11* and *Nbk 12*), and 519–78 (in *Nbk 12*). Act IV was presumably written out, for the most part, in November and December 1819, after the Shelleys had left Livorno and returned to Florence on 30 September. The Preface to *PU* was written in two parts. The first four paragraphs were copied by S. at the same time as the first three acts, i.e. by September 1819, as is clear from their position in the nbks (see *BSM* ix (Introduction lxxiii)). The last five paragraphs were added by S. in response to the *Quarterly Review*'s attack on him for plagiarism (see notes), and were added to S.'s fair copy by late December 1819 (the first part of the Preface is partly drafted in *Nbk 6*, and the later part is mainly drafted in *Nbk 10*; see *BSM* xv, *MYR* iv).

John Gisborne did not deliver the transcript of Acts I, II, and III on his visit to England because as *BSM* ix (Introduction lxxvi; cp. *SC* vi 930) points out he had fallen ill *en route* in Marseilles and turned back to Italy, bringing the undelivered transcript back with him, as is indicated by S.'s letter to Mrs Gisborne of 13 or 14 October (*L* ii 125–6). S. is 'anxious to hear of Mr Gisborne's return', and asks the Gisbornes to send the transcript of *PU* directly on to England by ship, together with the 250 copies of *The Cenci* which S. had had printed in Italy for publication by Ollier (see headnote to *The Cenci*). S. wrote to Ollier on 15 October informing him that 250 copies of *The Cenci* were on their way, and that 'The "Prometheus", a poem in my best style, whatever that may amount to, will arrive with it, but in MS., which you can print and publish in the season' (*L* ii 127). The ship carrying the copies of *The Cenci* and the transcript of the first three acts of *PU* did not in fact actually leave for England until the middle of December, as S. states to Ollier in a letter of 6 March 1820 (*L* ii 174); and by 13 March S. had still not received confirmation from Ollier of the arrival of the parcel containing the books and MS (letter to Ollier, *L* ii 177–8). In the meantime S. had clearly decided that Ollier should proceed as quickly as possible with the printing of *PU* (but see *BSM* ix (Introduction lxxvii) for the view that S.'s dealings with Ollier up to May 1820 actually served to delay final publication). S.'s letter to Hunt of 14–18 November states that 'The Prometheus I wish to be printed and to come out immediately' (*L* ii 153), and S. had possibly already decided to send the fourth act, when ready, by surface mail so that its arrival would correspond as nearly as possible with the arrival of the shipped material (S. was not yet aware of the delay in the ship's departure). By 15 December S. was still uncertain about the arrival of his consignment to Ollier: 'When the box comes . . . Let Prometheus be printed without delay', adding 'You will receive the additions, which Mrs. S. is now transcribing, in a few days' (*L* ii 163–4). A week later, on Thursday 23 December, S. wrote two letters relating to *PU*. To the Gisbornes he explained that he has 'just finished an additional act to Prometheus which Mary is now transcribing; & which will be enclosed for your inspection before it is transmitted to the Bookseller' (*L* ii 165); that this letter contained the MS of *PU* Act IV is made clear by Gisborne's endorsement of the letter (*L* ii 166), and by Mary's letter to Mrs Gisborne of 28 December: 'I am glad that you are pleased with the Prometheus – the last act though very beautiful is certainly the most mystic of the four –' (*Mary L* i 121). To Ollier, he wrote explaining that the 'additions' to *PU* announced in his previous letter were to be extensive; the whole letter is of great interest (it is not in *L*; the MS is damaged by a burn, and the resulting gaps are here conjecturally reconstructed by GM. For alternatives see *SC* vi 1100):

> My Prometheus I suppose you [have already begun] printing before this letter reaches you – [I am] somewhat doubtful about this said question of pr[oofs.] Who will revise the press? If possible, & if there is time, I should be very glad that the printer could divide the whole poem into two proofs & send it to *me* for the last corrections. – In this case [it ought to be *canc*.] the proofs ought to be taken off on thin paper and sent to me by the Post . . . If there is any difficulty in this, allow me to recommend you the utmost caution in revising the press . . . of course I would *pay* whatever might be necessary for the revision . . . provided it were done correctly. – Mr. Hunt is [revising] Julian & Maddalo, but I will not [burden] him with the Prometheus – [I am the] more anxious because I consider [Prometheus Un] bound as the least imperfect of [my compositions] & because typographical [slips, by confusing fin]e distinctions of the ideal [& philosophical style] in which it is written, cause [errors in the sense p]eculiarly difficult to [seize & adjust corr]ectly – – [Please be kind] enough to give me constant [informatio]n [of the state of *canc*.] as to what Mr. [Hunt] has consigned to you for publication – There is another *Act* written to Prometheus, and some lyrical insertions. They will be prepared for Thursday's Post. (*SC* vi 1099, with facsimile 1097–8; the date 'Dec. '23.' was originally written as 'Dec. '20')

The commentary to SC 554 (*SC* vi 1104–6) notes that S.'s correspondence concerning *PU* provides substantial and conclusive evidence that 'he took all possible pains to insure that his poem was published exactly as he had prepared it for the press and that if any changes of words or significant punctuation were introduced, they be changes he himself had chosen'. It is certainly true that S. was seriously concerned about arrangements for the printing of *PU*, although there is also evidence that S. was inconsistent in his own involvement with the press transcript (see below). No doubt S. had been alerted to possible problems by the printing of *1819* (see headnote to *R&H*, no. 144). His letter to Ollier of 23 December, quoted above, proposes two methods of checking proofs. The best option was to have the proofs sent to Italy so that S. could correct them himself, just as John Murray commonly sent Byron's proofs. Otherwise, S. suggests paying for a careful revising of the press in England by someone he could trust (i.e. a checking of proofs against the copy provided by S.). S. provided a further possibility to Ollier on 13 March 1820:

> I am anxious to hear that you have received the parcel from Leghorn, & to learn what you are doing with the Prometheus. – If it can be done without great difficulty I should be very glad that the *revised* sheets might be sent by the Post to me at Leghorn. – It might be divided into four partitions, sending me four or five sheets at once. – (*L* ii 177–8)

This arrangement would have given two stages of correction, with S. checking already revised sheets. It is also probable that S. wished to add in further detailed alterations which he had made to his own fair copy (see below). But Ollier refused, as is clear from S.'s letter to him of 14 May:

> As to the printing of the 'Prometheus', be it as you will. But, in this case, I shall repose or trust in your care respecting the correction of the press; especially in the lyrical parts, where a minute error would be of much consequence. Mr. Gisborne will revise it; he heard it recited, and will therefore more readily seize any error. (*L* ii 196)

461

Unfortunately even this compromise was to prove unworkable, though S. was still pursuing it later in the month when he wrote on 26 May from Pisa to the Gisbornes in London (they had left Livorno on Tuesday 2 May; *Gisborne Jnl* 19):

> I write to you thus early, because I have determined to accept of your kind offer about the correction of Prometheus. The bookseller makes difficulties about sending the proofs to me, & to whom else can I so well entrust what I am so much interested in having done well, & to whom would I prefer to owe the recollection of an additional kindness done to me? I enclose you two little papers of corrections & additions; – I do not think you will find any difficulty in interpolating them into the proper places. – (*L* ii 201)

In fact the Gisbornes were not eventually involved in the publication of *PU*. Perhaps because of the breach which opened in relations between the Shelleys and the Gisbornes in the course of their visit to London (*Gisborne Jnl* 9–10; see *Mary Jnl* i 334–5 for an excellent account of the circumstances surrounding the rift between the two families), the revision of the press finally fell to Peacock, to whom S. wrote on 12 July 'I make bold to write to you on the news that you are correcting my "Prometheus", for which I return thanks; and I send some things which may be added [presumably the same 'corrections and additions' forwarded to the Gisbornes in May]' (*L* ii 212). By late July S. was expecting publication in England at any moment (see *BSM* ix (Introduction lxxvii–lxxviii) for arguments that Ollier may have been making active arrangements for printing from as early as December 1819). He wrote to Medwin on 20 July expressing his 'wish to present you with "Prometheus Unbound", a drama . . .' and adding 'I hear it is just printed, and I probably shall receive copies from England before I see you' (*L* ii 219). On 27 July he wrote advising Keats to expect a copy of *PU* 'nearly at the same time with this letter' (*L* ii 221), and to Southey he wrote on 17 August that he has 'desired Mr. Ollier to send you those [verses] last published [i.e. *The Cenci* and *PU*]' (*L* ii 231). Zillman shows that it is 'almost certain that the poem was published in August' (see *Zillman Variorum* 7; *BSM* ix argues for 14 August as the actual date). S. did not see a copy of the volume until October, however, when the Gisbornes brought one back from England on their return to Livorno probably on the 5 October (*Mary Jnl* i 333; see also *Gisborne Jnl* 9).

The 1820 printing of *PU* was a complete disaster, as S. immediately realised. He wrote with admirable and even wry restraint to Peacock on 8 November 'Thank you for your kindness in correcting "Prometheus", which I am afraid gave you a great deal of trouble' (*L* ii 244). But to Ollier on 10 November he was much more direct:

> Mr. Gisborne has sent me a copy of the *Prometheus* which is certainly most beautifully printed. It is to be regretted that the errors of the press are so numerous, & in many respects so destructive of the sense of a species of poetry, which I fear even with[out?] this disadvantage very few will understand or like. I shall send you the list of errata in a day or two. (*L* ii 246)

The importance of this errata list is discussed below. S. was still sensitive about the printing of *PU* almost a year later, when he wrote to Ollier on 8 June 1821 explaining why he had decided to take exceptional pains with the printing of *Adonais*: 'My poem [*Adonais*] is finished . . . I shall send it to you, either printed at Pisa, or transcribed in such a manner, as it shall be difficult for the reviser to leave such errors as *assist* the obscurity of the "Prometheus" ' (*L* ii 257; see headnote to *Adonais*).

After *1820*, no further edition of *PU* was published in S.'s lifetime. Except for two pirated editions, published by William Benbow in July 1826 (taking advantage of Sir Timothy Shelley's suppression of *1824*; see *Taylor* 11–17), which have no relevance to the textual transmission of *PU*, the next important witness to the text is *1829*. Galignani's text is based on *1820* but incorporates a number of improvements (as well as some new corruptions; see e.g. II i 171 and note, III iii 126 and note, and cp. *Taylor* 41). At first sight this fact appears to suggest that the errata list, mentioned by S. in his letter to Ollier quoted above, was forwarded to Galignani by Mary for inclusion in *1829*, as her letter to Cyrus Redding, ?3 September 1829, indicates: 'I send you the Errata of the Prometheus' (*Mary L* ii 86). Redding himself later provided an account which seems to confirm the arrangement:

> In Shelley's 'Prometheus', as printed, there were some errata. Those she sent to me . . . Singular enough . . . Galignani's edition contains the errata of the author, as given me by Mrs. Shelley, and not found, I presume, in the English editions of his work, but I have not collated them. (Cyrus Redding, *Fifty Years' Recollections, Literary and Personal, with Observations on Men and Things*, 3 vols, 1858 (2nd edn) ii 352–3)

But the situation is really more complicated, for of the changes between the *1820* and *1829* texts of *PU*, only nine of Galignani's new readings agree with new readings in *1839*, the edition in which, according to Mary's note on *PU*, 'the verbal alterations in . . . Prometheus are made from a list of errata, written by Shelley himself' (*1839* ii 140). Indeed the changes which are in both *1829* and *1839* are all of the type which (as *Taylor* 22 observes), 'any attentive reader might have made', and by no means necessarily imply that Galignani was working from an authoritative list of errata. There is also the problem that the relatively few corrected readings in *1829* hardly correspond to S.'s own description of the errata list he compiled to send to Ollier: 'I send you . . . the Errata of "Prometheus", which I ought to have sent long since – a formidable list, as you will see' (to Ollier, 20 January 1820, *L* ii 257). It is in fact probable, as Taylor cogently argues, that although Mary did indeed send the errata list to Galignani for inclusion in *1829*, the list eventually arrived too late to be incorporated. That she sent the list, and then assumed that it had been incorporated, is suggested by her use of pages from *1829* as printer's copy for *PU* in *1839* (and for the rest of the text of the second of the four volumes of *1839*, i.e. the volume in which *PU* is printed), but not for other poems in *1839*, for which she used pages from Ascham's pirated edition of 1834. But *PU* is printed relatively early in *1829*, and its text was perhaps already set when the errata list arrived; whereas other shorter poems published in *1820* and printed later in *1829*, for which the errata list would have arrived in time to be usable by Galignani's printer, are printed with improved texts in *1829* (see *Taylor* 22). Mary therefore probably remembered in 1839 when preparing copy that *1829* already included the errata she had sent ten years previously, and deliberately chose to use it rather than Ascham as printer's copy for *1839*, only to discover that the errata changes had not in fact been made. She then introduced them herself – *PU* is revised with exceptional care in *1839* – into the *1829* text as printer's copy (at the same time inadvertently perpetuating those errors introduced into the text in *1829*). The relatively small number of substantive variants in the *1829* text of *PU* is then not too difficult to explain. More problematic is Mary's statement in her Note on *PU* that she has incorporated S.'s errata list in *1839*, for the changes between *1820* and *1839*, while very considerable in accidentals and punctuation, do not really

constitute 'a formidable list' of 'verbal alterations' (there are some forty such altera-
tions between *1820* and *1839*; see textual notes for details). The corrections written
into S.'s presentation copy of *1820* to Leigh Hunt (now in the Huntington Library,
catalogue number 22460), about a dozen in number, may well derive from a rel-
atively short errata list. C. D. Locock offers a plausible hypothesis:

> It still remains to explain the continuance of a large proportion of these errors [i.e. the
> errors in *1820*] in Mrs. Shelley's editions, in spite of the 'formidable list' sent by Shelley
> and generally assumed to have been seen by Mrs. Shelley. May we suppose that Mrs. Shelley
> never made use of that particular list at all? that what she did use was a *preliminary* list, –
> the list which Shelley 'hoped to despatch in a day or two' (November 10, 1820) [slightly
> misquoted from Shelley's letter to Ollier, *L* ii 246; see above] – not the 'formidable list'
> which he sent off some ten weeks later (January 20, 1821 [*L* ii 257; see above]), and which
> may in the course of nine years have been mislaid? (*Locock 1911* i 596)

This hypothesis would help to explain the quite small – though significant – number
of substantive changes in *1839*, and the much greater number of substantive dif-
ferences between S.'s fair copy (in *Nbk 7*, *Nbk 8*, and *Nbk 9*) and both *1820* and
1839 (actually it is worth noting that S.'s errata list may have included at least a
few important changes in punctuation as well, e.g. the pointing of II ii 49–51, and
the closing lines of III iv; see notes).

The editorial problem of *PU* thus centres on three different states of the text: the
holograph fair copy, the first edition (*1820*), and Mary's carefully revised text in
her collected edition of the poems (*1839*); and to these we should add for con-
sideration the secondary but still influential text of *1829*. But the textual problems
go further than the mere effort to adjudicate between the claims of these three
candidates for copy text, for it is necessary to explain various features of the rela-
tion between the holograph, *1820*, and *1839* by hypothetical reconstruction of the
lost press transcript (which would of course, had it survived, represent the best
copy text for a modern editor). As we have seen, this was sent to London, and
then presumably used by Peacock in his revision of the press on S.'s behalf. This
crucially important final MS form of *PU* has disappeared (it makes no appearance
in the provenance of Ollier's papers). It is safe to assume that this transcript was
made by Mary: she definitely transcribed Act IV, and S. says of Acts I, II and III in
his letter to Ollier of 6 September 1819 that they are 'being transcribed' (*L* ii 116),
which hardly implies that he was doing it himself. It also seems likely that S. left
Mary not only to transcribe his fair copy, but to *punctuate* it; and a further infer-
ence must be that while S. was very careful in checking and altering the transcript
in important places, he nevertheless missed various errors in Mary's transcript. It
is all but impossible to explain certain features of *PU* in *1820* by any other hypo-
thesis; see e.g. II iii 50 and note, IV 208 and note. The situation is still further
complicated by the fact that Mary's transcript must have been copied from a state
of S.'s fair copy at least as late as many of the corrections made on it by S., includ-
ing not just the many later added and altered passages which take up initially blank
pages, but also the fair number of small (mostly pencil) alterations which are
present throughout S.'s copy (see e.g. III iii 138). It is, on the other hand, equally
clear that a number of S.'s alterations to his fair copy were made *after* Mary's
transcript was copied from it (see e.g. I 157–8). It is probable in fact that S. con-
tinued to make corrections and alterations of this sort, after Mary had copied and
despatched her transcript, because he still hoped to be able to revise the proofs of

PU himself by having Ollier send them to Italy (see above), which would have given him the opportunity to make the alterations. These changes made in the three nbks containing his fair copy were probably also the source of the corrections and additions he later sent to Gisborne and Peacock. There is finally evidence which strongly suggests that, although the points already made about transcription errors in the press transcript indicate that S. did not make an exhaustive check of its accuracy, he nevertheless must have made corrections and alterations to Mary's transcript before it was sent to England, but without entering these changes on to his own fair copy. There are a number of substantive differences between S.'s holograph fair copy and *1820* which are too emphatic to be attributed to either Mary, or to an interfering printer (see e.g. II iii 4 and note). If Mary was responsible for the punctuation of *PU* in the press copy, this would explain what is otherwise very odd, that she failed to make use of the three nbks containing S.'s fair copy of *PU* in her preparation of the poem for *1839*, even though these nbks were at that time in her possession.

Mary's probable responsibility for the punctuation in the lost press copy, taken together with the manifest limitations of *1820*, and the fact that S.'s fair copy in the Bodleian is clearly far too lightly pointed to form a basis for accidentals (particularly in the context of S.'s exceptionally difficult and elaborate syntactical structures in the writing of *PU*), all suggest *1839* as the best choice of copy text for *PU*. No choice can be ideal under the circumstances, and it is sobering to remember that the pointing of *PU* in *1839* includes substantial intervention by Mary (although presumably sanctioned by S. himself), supplemented by possible details in S.'s errata list or lists, modified by three printers (*1820*, *1829*, and *1839*) and by Peacock's alterations made in his correction of proofs. Peacock's 'correction' by his own account involved removing S.'s 'frequent dashes' (see H. B. Forman, *The Shelley Library: An Essay in Bibliography* (1886) 88), and he may well have interfered with the press transcript itself before printing. The copy text in *1839* has therefore been modified to an unusually extensive degree in the text given here. Sometimes this modification is justified on strictly textual grounds, but there are many cases where literary judgement, together with assumptions about probability and articulacy, have come significantly into play. Such cases receive appropriate discussion in the notes.

Sources, Plot, Characters, Commentary

PU draws in an obviously direct way on Aeschylus, in its dramatic conception, and in numerous verbal echoes, particularly in the first act, and to a lesser extent the second act. S. includes an account of Prometheus in his note to *Q Mab* viii 211–12, taken from J. F. Newton's *Return to Nature* (see notes to *Q Mab* in vol. 1); but as in his Preface to *PU*, S.'s explanation of the myth's meaning in his *Q Mab* note (where Prometheus is said to 'represent the human race') is to be understood as a gloss on the meaning of the source myth, and not on S.'s own handling of it. *PU* departs significantly from its source-myth in Aeschylus, as the Preface makes plain. The action and characters of Aeschylus's play are taken from the story of the Titans and the Olympians, as set forth in Hesiod's *Theogony*. In *Prometheus Bound* Prometheus, one of the Titans overthrown by the Olympian gods under Zeus, has helped the new order to victory by advising Zeus to win by intelligence rather than force (the Titans having ignored this advice from Prometheus). But Zeus has aped the overthrown order by himself becoming a tyrant, seeking to dominate by force and looking to destroy primitive mankind. Prometheus takes pity on humanity and improves their condition by showing them the uses of intelligence, and stealing for them from heaven the gift of fire. Zeus punishes him for this by nailing him to the rocky Caucasus. In Aeschylus Prometheus, whose name means 'forethinking', refuses to win his freedom by disclosing the secret he knows of Zeus's future downfall. The secret is that if Zeus marries Thetis he will beget a child stronger than himself, which will lead to his downfall. After being nailed on Caucasus by Hephaestus (encouraged by Might and Force), Prometheus is visited by Oceanus and then by his daughters the Oceanides (anticipating the roles of Panthea and Ione in S.'s drama), whose absent sister Hesione is Prometheus's bride, thus corresponding to S.'s Asia. There is a long dialogue with Io, who like Prometheus suffers under the persecution of Zeus (there is no equivalent character in *PU*), then Hermes (corresponding to S.'s Mercury) arrives and attempts by threats and guile to wheedle the secret out of Prometheus; he refuses to yield, and is cast down to Tartarus, although he is not deserted by the Oceanides. According to various classical sources *Prometheus Bound* was the first play of an otherwise lost trilogy, the second play of which represented Prometheus's reconciliation with Zeus. Prometheus is brought back from Tartarus to Caucasus, where an eagle comes each day to gnaw at his entrails. He is at last freed by Zeus, to whom he discloses his secret, thus enabling the tyrant to avert his fate by marrying Thetis to Peleus. It is this compromise which S. consciously refuses in his own rehandling of the myth (see Preface). S. follows normal early nineteenth-century practice in Latinising Gk names (cp. his practice in the Homeric Hymns, nos 156–161, and in his translation of *The Cyclops*, no. 172). *PU* uses the Roman names Jupiter and Mercury for Zeus and Hermes (and also Hercules for Heracles in III iii); the tyrannical regime represented in the play would anyway bear closer similarity for S. to the Roman imperialism he loathed than to the Greek culture which has such a strong influence on S. (for discussion of contemporary resonances of the Prometheus myth see Stuart Curran, 'The Political Prometheus', *SiR* xxv (1986) 429–55).

PU is of course only in general terms derived from Aeschylus; the 'action' is abstract and operates on many levels, one of which certainly works around the symbolic possibilities of its oblique relation to and various departures from the Aeschylean plot (for telling commentary on S.'s deployment of mythic materials see *Wasserman*). S.'s conception of the marriage of Prometheus and Asia introduces a new dimension into the plot, which enables S. to dramatise a means of breaking the recurrent cycle, embodied in the classical sources, of tyrannous regimes which are overthrown by new generations who promptly reinstall a tyranny in their own conduct (this cycle had immediate and direct resonances for S. and his generation in the failure of the French Revolution; see Preface to *L&C*). While the symbolic meanings of S.'s Prometheus are complex and elusive, it is clear that Asia represents a transcendent form of Love (just as her sisters Panthea and Ione represent lesser and mediated forms of Love), and that Prometheus's victory over Jupiter requires the presence of Asia to avoid reversion to the old cycle of oppression. Prometheus himself seems to approximate to those positive products and potentialities of human intelligence which are not confined to individual minds (although only knowable in and through such minds). The marriage of Asia and Prometheus carries many associations, including the relation of East to West, Oriental to Hellenic cultural traditions, female and male, and also different modes of perception and understanding (Prometheus is locked into a fruitless urge to rational understanding and control, whereas Asia's emotional and intuitive understanding actually leads to change in the second act). Jupiter represents tyranny, but *PU* offers subtle reflection on the close relation of Prometheus to Jupiter, and there is a clear implication that Jupiter has been created and sustained in being by the actions and attitudes of Prometheus himself. Asia's sisters are themselves clearly differentiated in *PU*, and are to be understood as aspects of her larger encompassing significance (cp. S's discussion of 'that profound and complicated sentiment, which we call love', and its relation to 'the sexual impulse', in the closing paragraphs of *DMAA*); Panthea mediates between Prometheus and Asia in their long period of separation, and thus embodies those forms of human love accessible in the dark epoch of pre-revolutionary oppression, particularly sexual love (Panthea is more confident and experienced than Ione, and relates to Prometheus in physical terms); Ione is more timid, shy and inexperienced (she looks to Panthea for explanation of events and characters), and also more sensitive and alert, embodying innocent and purer forms of human love, such as altruism. The sisters appear to begin to merge into each other, and then into Asia, from Act II. The names Panthea and Ione have no obvious significance: S. consistently gives to characters who embody a distinctive departure from the source myth names which cannot be pinned down within any received framework of meaning.

The most strikingly original of S.'s conceptions in *PU* is the figure of Demogorgon. Mary S. characterises him as 'the Primal Power of the world' in her note to *PU* (*1839* ii 134). In Peacock's *Rhododaphne* (1817), reviewed by S. in February 1818 (*Prose* 311–13; see *Mary Jnl* i 194), Demogorgon is described in a note as 'the Genius of the Earth, and the Sovereign Power of the Terrestrial Daemons. He dwelt originally with Eternity and Chaos, till, becoming weary of inaction, he organised the chaotic elements, and surrounded the earth with the heavens. In addition to Pan and the Fates, his children were Uranus, Titaea, Pytho, Eris, and Erebus. This awful Power was so sacred among the Arcadians, that it was held impious to pronounce his name . . . He has been supposed to be a philosophical emblem of the principle of vegetable life' (*Peacock Works* vii 94). Peacock refers to Boccaccio, *Genealogia Deorum*, as his source, and it is probable that S. himself used it. Demogorgon is there described as the primordial god of ancient mythology, mysterious ancestor of all the gods and creator of all things, dwelling in the vaporous depths of the earth, whose name men feared to speak. Boccaccio also suggests Mount Etna or Taenarus as sites for the entrance to Demogorgon's lair, which S. develops into an association with the hundred-headed monster Typhon who was imprisoned beneath Etna by Zeus as a punishment for rebellion. Boccaccio derives the name from δαίμων and γεωργός, 'daemon of the earth'. The actual origins of the name are not classical but medieval; Statius, *Thebaid*, has a pseudo-classical medieval commentary by Lactantius Placidus which glosses iv 514–16, 'Scimus enim et quicquid dici, noscique timetis, / Et turbare Hecaten, ni te, Thymbraee, vererer, / Et triplicis mundi summum quem scire nefastum' as 'Dicit deum Demogorgona summum' (Scholia in Statii Thebaidem iv 516, ed. Jahnke (1898) iii 228). The name appears to originate here as a scribe's error for the Platonic δημιουργός, which in *Timaeus* 28ff. is the power responsible for the material creation. Demogorgon was taken up by demonology and appears in Renaissance literature as an obscurely powerful figure identified variously and loosely with Eternity (his companion in Boccaccio), Chaos, or Fate (cp. *Faerie Queene* I v 22, *Paradise Lost* ii 964, Jonson, *The Alchemist* II i 104, Anon. (Elizabethan drama), *Locrine*, I ii 276). Late medieval and Renaissance conceptions of Demogorgon were frequently read back into classical sources via commentary. Although clearly pseudo-classical, in S.'s presentation Demogorgon has some affinity with the Greek conception of fate as a power of destiny and natural law greater than any god (Cp. *Prometheus Bound* 511–20). S.'s choice of a non-classical character reflects the fact that 'unlike earlier rebels', in *PU* Demogorgon 'genuinely possesses the power to overthrow Jupiter, so that no figure named by Hesiod could have served Shelley's purpose' (GM). Demogorgon's characteristics in *PU* seem especially influenced by Lucan, *Pharsalia*, a great favourite of S.'s, where he found the conjunction of an obscure subterranean god with oracular inspiration and utterance, and the legend of Typhon:

> Which of the immortals is hidden here? What deity, descending from heaven, deigns to dwell pent up in these dark grottoes? What god of heaven endures the weight of earth, knowing every secret of the eternal process of events, sharing with the sky the knowledge of the future, ready to reveal himself to the nations, and patient of contact with mankind? A great and mighty god is he, whether he merely predicts the future or the future is itself determined by the fiat of his utterance. It may be that a large part of the whole divine element is embedded in the world to rule it, and supports the globe poised upon empty space; and this part issues forth through the caves of Cirrha, and is inhaled there, though closely linked to the Thunderer in heaven. When this inspiration has found a harbour in a maiden's bosom, it strikes the human soul of the priestess audibly, and unlocks her lips, even as the crown of Etna in Sicily boils over from the pressure of the flames, where he lies beneath the everlasting mass of Inarime, makes hot the rocks of Campania by his unrest. (v 86–101, Loeb trans.)

See also vi 496–9, 742–9, and cp. Nicholas Rowe's note to vi 794 in his influential trans. (*Lucan's Pharsalia*, 2 vols, 2nd edn (1722) ii 43):

> The Poet seems to allude here to that God whom they called Demogorgon, who was the Father and Creator of all the other Gods; who, though he himself was bound in Chains in the lowest hell, was yet so terrible to all the others that they could not bear the very mention of his name . . . Him Lucan supposes to be the subject of the Power of Magic, as all the other Deities of what kind soever were to him.

In *PU* Demogorgon is the one figure in whom most levels of the poem coincide. He corresponds in the source myth to the secret known only to Prometheus, Zeus's child who will prove stronger than his father. He represents Necessity, 'the mysterious law, that [in S.'s view] no-one *yet* understands, which compels effects to follow causes, whether in the physical or the social or the moral world' (GM; cp. *Q Mab* vi 198 and note, and S.'s note, 'Mont Blanc' 76–83 and note). Demogorgon 'cannot initiate anything on a moral level – this needs the will and purpose of man; he can only operate in terms of a chain of cause and effect: he has to be *activated* . . . On the physical level, he is the volcanic, geological force that inevitably recreates the living earth as it is worn away. He is activated [i.e. into volcanic eruption; see II iv 129] by the entry into his cavern of water in the form of the sea-sisters, the Oceanides Asia and Panthea . . . on the political level he is Historical Necessity, the inevitable causal process that will induce man to rebel, to overthrow his oppressors, to remake himself as a truly human being . . .' (GM). It is likely that S. also associates Demogorgon with 'the people', in the sense of the new 'class' of 'the unrepresented multitude' (see 'Philosophical View of Reform', *Prose* 242), and that the name is to be understood as punning on the Gk δῆμος, 'people', and γοργός, 'grim, terrible'.

As many commentators have shown, the play has a direct relation to the political situation in Europe in the years following the defeat of Napoleon and the Congress of Vienna (see notes, especially to Act I, and *Cameron (1974)* for extensive commentary). There is a significant, strangely conceived and wholly original scientific dimension in *PU*, first discussed in detail in *Grabo (1930)*. Act IV famously embodies a rich variety of scientific allusion without parallel in writings of the period; as the notes below demonstrate, its organisation is informed by an imaginative exploration of contemporary scientific speculation on the nature of time and space. But, in a different and more dramatically focused way, the first three acts build from the metaphoric and symbolic potential of volcanic activity, earthquake and tempest, by which S. was fascinated from boyhood, to elaborate a complex geophysical symbolic narrative first noted and explained in GM, 'A Volcano's Voice in Shelley', *ELH* xxiv (1957) 191–228. Some elements of the play's scientific conception derive from the 'proper machinery for a philosophic poem' in *Darwin* (note to i 73) which embodies natural processes, functions and attributes of the physical world in 'genii'; S.'s use of characters which partly subsume physical, philosophical and historical features of the universe, such as 'Earth', or the Fauns in II ii, is a sophisticated development of Darwin's approach.

The scientific dimension in *PU* is imaginatively fused with an extensive network of allusion to classical lore and literature of volcanic and related activity, which is frequently inseparable from beliefs about oracular prophecy and the power of the Earth to control human affairs. *PU* is steeped in such material, with a richness of detail presumably owing much to S.'s 'Grecian' period at Marlow in 1817, in the company and under the informed influence of Peacock. The Grecian classicism of the play clearly also owes much to S.'s interests in Platonic and Neo-platonic thought and writings, in which he had been closely involved in the eighteen months preceding composition of *PU*. Perhaps most importantly, *PU* is a metaphysical drama, concerned with the nature of good and evil, the relation of the physical and temporally finite to transcendent and abstract modes of existence, and the intersection of moral absolutes with historical and political specifics; this dimension of *PU* is given extended and brilliantly illuminating treatment in *Wasserman*, which remains the most challenging and persuasive single reading of the poem as a whole. The rich cultural and religious syncretism which informs S.'s materials and allusions in the play, and which draws on belief-systems and elements of associated ritual (such as Zoroastrianism) beyond the more obvious Hellenic and Hebraic dimensions of the drama, is powerfully treated in *Curran (1975)*. There is a particular focus in Act II on the relation of individual free will to large movements of historical change, and on the role of poetry in this relation (see notes, especially to II ii), which has close connection with S.'s more concentrated and lyrically impassioned articulation of this problem in 'Ode to the West Wind'. The overall ambition and scale of *PU* is more broadly in the manner established by S. in *Q Mab* and *L&C*; all three poems offer, in their different stylistic idioms, extended treatment of current historical and political questions in a very long-term physical and metaphysical perspective.

The wider range of literary and intellectual influences discernible in *PU* is too extensive and diverse for brief summary; the notes which follow attempt to give at least an indication of the variety and density of the play's cultural reference. *Paradise Lost* is a pervasive influence, as is the Bible; Shakespeare, Spenser, Dante, Lucretius and Virgil are all central, and the Greek tragedians. Plato and Platonic ideas are important, including their mediation in many classical and Renaissance sources. There are marked local influences from many of S.'s contemporaries, particularly Byron, Hunt, Coleridge, Peacock, and Godwin. The play also makes some coded reference to S.'s immediate circle and biographical circumstances; e.g. Mercury suggests Byron's cynical worldliness as S. may recently have experienced it directly in Venice in the late summer of 1818; Prometheus, Asia and Proteus in III iii equate with S., Mary and Godwin; sometimes Panthea and Ione may suggest Mary and Claire Clairmont (see also notes to III i 19, III iii 64–8).

In short, *PU* brings to a focus of extraordinary brilliance the complex diversity of S.'s literary intelligence and cultural inheritance in 1819. In formal terms it is a truly remarkable achievement. There is a mix of blank verse which varies in register from a sometimes almost parodic Miltonising, through a development of the post-Wordsworthian style of *Alastor* and 'Mont Blanc', to a wholly distinctive Shelleyan manner typified for example in the exchanges between Asia and Panthea in II i. The blank verse alternates with an array of lyrical forms which, although they are often individually anticipated in the wide range of stanza forms attempted by S. between 1804 and 1818, occur nowhere else in such profusion of variety and detailed invention (see e.g. headnotes to 'Stanzas written in dejection', no. 187, and 'Misery. – A Fragment', no. 202, for commentary on S.'s developing use of lyric metres in late 1818). This alternation of blank verse with complex lyric passages shadows the dramatic device of an alternation between relatively static dramatic exchanges, and choric elements, which S. adapts from Greek tragic drama (cp. S.'s use of this adaptation from the Gk in his translation of *The Cyclops*, no. 172). *PU* has attracted a vast amount of critical and scholarly commentary. Most book-length studies of S.'s poetry and thought include detailed consideration of the play, and the number of articles and chapters concerned with questions of theme, style and context in *PU* runs into several hundred. In addition to the studies in *Cameron (1974)*, *Curran (1975)*, and *Wasserman*, the reader is directed to the bibliographical listings in *Rognoni* 1506–8, in *Shelley: Poems and Prose*, ed. Timothy Webb (1995) 536–44, and to Stuart Curran's chapter on S. in *English Romantic Poets: A Review of Research and Criticism*, 4th rev. edn, ed. Frank Jordan, 1985.

Text from *1839*; many readings are adopted from the fair copy in *Nbk 7*, *Nbk 8* and *Nbk 9*, and the notes record all such decisions, including all cases where the fair-copy punctuation has been preferred. All other departures from the text of *1839* are also indicated, and explained where necessary. Capitalisation is a vexed issue in *PU*; S.'s capitals in the fair copy are interesting and extensive, but not systematic, and there are numerous divergencies between them, *1820*, and *1839*. Broadly, the text here follows *1839* for capitals, but with many exceptions, sometimes derived from the fair copy, and sometimes based on surmise concerning what S.'s practice might have been, had he consistently observed the intentions that can be inferred from his MSS and printed texts. All variant capitals in the three principle witnesses are recorded in the notes. Patterns of indentation in lyric stanzas are generally more elaborate in *1820* and *1839* than in the fair copy, and its simpler forms are usually followed in the present text. There are substantial draft materials surviving for *PU*, in *Nbk 6*, *Nbk 10*, *Nbk 11*, *Nbk 12*, *Box 1*, British Library (Ashley Manuscript 4086), and CHPL (SC 548, 549).

Published in *1820*.

195
Prometheus Unbound
A Lyrical Drama in Four Acts

AUDISNE HAEC, AMPHIARAE, SUB TERRAM ABDITE?

Epigraph. 'Do you hear this, Amphiaraus, in your home beneath the earth?' Amphiaraus was a seer who fought as one of the Seven against Thebes; he foresaw the failure of the expedition, and Zeus saved him by causing him to be swallowed up by the earth. He became an oracular god. S.'s epigraph appears on the title-page of *1820. S.* quotes it in *Nbk 6,* p. 115 rev., under the heading 'To the Ghost of Æschylus', and with the reference 'Epigon – [Æsch.] ad Cic.' The line is from the *Epigoni,* a lost play by Aeschylus, and its context in Cicero, *Tusculan Disputations* II xxv 69–61, makes for complex irony:

> 'Dionysius of Heraclea, a person certainly of little resolution, after learning from Zeno to be brave was taught by pain to forget his lesson. For upon an attack of kidney trouble, even amid his shrieks, he kept on crying out that the opinions he had himself previously held about pain were false. And on being asked by Cleanthes, his fellow-pupil, what was the reason that had seduced him from his former opinion, he replied: "Because if, after I had given such devoted attention to philosophy, I yet proved unable to bear pain, that would be sufficient proof that pain was an evil. Now I have spent many years in studying philosophy and am unable to bear pain: pain is therefore an evil." Then Cleanthes stamped with his foot upon the ground and, according to the story, recited a line from the *Epigoni:*
> Do you hear this, Amphiaraus, in your home beneath the earth?
> meaning Zeno and grieving that Dionysius was false to his teaching.' (Loeb trans.)

S. adapts the line to turn it against its author Aeschylus: just as Dionysius betrayed the teachings of his Stoic master Zeno by refusing to ignore the reality of pain, so S. in *PU* defiantly rejects the acceptance of pain implicit in the suffering of the Aeschylean hero. 'The protest is to the dead master concerning the living disciple's disagreement: enduring prolonged pain in order to eliminate it (Prometheus's steadfast objective in S.) is quite different from (indeed can be the opposite of) enduring it because it is of no consequence in relation to virtue [the Stoic position]. Pain *is* an evil . . . the pain inflicted by Jupiter is *not* to be deemed unimportant and not an evil. It is *not* to be endured simply as if it did not exist, and eventually accepted because it comes from a god' (GM). See also *Wasserman* 283.

PREFACE

The Greek tragic writers, in selecting as their subject any portion of their national history or mythology, employed in their treatment of it a certain arbitrary discretion. They by no means conceived themselves bound to adhere to the common interpretation, or to imitate in story, as in title,
5   their rivals and predecessors. Such a system would have amounted to a resignation of those claims to preference over their competitors which incited the composition. The Agamemnonian story was exhibited on the Athenian theatre with as many variations as dramas.

    I have presumed to employ a similar license. The 'Prometheus Unbound'
10 of Aeschylus supposed the reconciliation of Jupiter with his victim as the price of the disclosure of the danger threatened to his empire by the consummation of his marriage with Thetis. Thetis, according to this view of the subject, was given in marriage to Peleus, and Prometheus, by the permission of Jupiter, delivered from his captivity by Hercules. Had I framed
15 my story on this model, I should have done no more than have attempted to restore the lost drama of Aeschylus; an ambition, which, if my preference to this mode of treating the subject had incited me to cherish, the recollection of the high comparison such an attempt would challenge might well abate. But, in truth, I was averse from a catastrophe so feeble as that
20 of reconciling the Champion with the Oppressor of mankind. The moral interest of the fable, which is so powerfully sustained by the sufferings and endurance of Prometheus, would be annihilated if we could conceive of him as unsaying his high language and quailing before his successful and perfidious adversary. The only imaginary being resembling in any degree
25 Prometheus, is Satan; and Prometheus is, in my judgement, a more poetical character than Satan, because, in addition to courage, and majesty, and firm and patient opposition to omnipotent force, he is susceptible of being described as exempt from the taints of ambition, envy, revenge, and a desire for personal aggrandisement, which, in the Hero of Paradise Lost,
30 interfere with the interest. The character of Satan engenders in the mind a pernicious casuistry which leads us to weigh his faults with his wrongs, and to excuse the former because the latter exceed all measure. In the minds

---

Pref. 9–12. S. refers to the lost second play by Aeschylus, known only through fragments in classical sources (e.g. Cicero, *Tusculan Disputations* II x 23–5), in the supposed trilogy of which *Prometheus Bound* was thought to be the first part (see headnote, and *Prometheus Bound*, ed. Mark Griffiths (1983) 281–305).

Pref. 9–36. S.'s discussion of Prometheus in this paragraph refers to his character and significance in the source myth, and not in *PU* itself.

Pref. 19. catastrophe] In the Gk sense, i.e. the concluding resolution of a tragic plot.

Pref. 26. majesty,] Nbk 7, *1820*; majesty *1839*.

of those who consider that magnificent fiction with a religious feeling, it engenders something worse. But Prometheus is, as it were, the type of the highest perfection of moral and intellectual nature, impelled by the purest and the truest motives to the best and noblest ends.

This Poem was chiefly written upon the mountainous ruins of the Baths of Caracalla, among the flowery glades, and thickets of odoriferous blossoming trees, which are extended in ever winding labyrinths upon its immense platforms and dizzy arches suspended in the air. The bright blue sky of Rome, and the effect of the vigorous awakening of spring in that divinest climate, and the new life with which it drenches the spirits even to intoxication, were the inspiration of this drama.

The imagery which I have employed will be found, in many instances, to have been drawn from the operations of the human mind, or from those external actions by which they are expressed. This is unusual in modern poetry, although Dante and Shakespeare are full of instances of the same kind: Dante indeed more than any other poet, and with greater success. But the Greek poets, as writers to whom no resource of awakening the sympathy of their contemporaries was unknown, were in the habitual use of this power; and it is the study of their works (since a higher merit would probably be denied me), to which I am willing that my readers should impute this singularity.

One word is due in candour to the degree in which the study of contemporary writings may have tinged my composition, for such has been a topic of censure with regard to poems far more popular, and indeed more deservedly popular, than mine. It is impossible that any one who inhabits the same age with such writers as those who stand in the foremost ranks of our own, can conscientiously assure himself that his language and tone of thought may not have been modified by the study of the productions of those extraordinary intellects. It is true, that, not the spirit of their genius, but the forms in which it has manifested itself, are due less to the peculiarities of their own minds than to the peculiarity of the moral and intellectual condition of the minds among which they have been produced. Thus a number of writers possess the form, whilst they want the spirit of those whom, it is alleged, they imitate; because the former is the

---

Pref. 39. ever winding] Nbk 7, 1820; ever-winding 1839.

Pref. 54. The five paragraphs commencing at this point were added by S. in response to the review of *Rofl* which had appeared in April in the *Quarterly Review* xxi (1819) 460–71, and which S. received in Florence in October 1819 together with Hunt's reply in the *Examiner* for 26 September 1819 (see S.'s letter to Ollier, 15 October 1819, *L* ii 126–8). This exceptionally hostile and indeed vitriolic review, which S. believed to be the work of Southey (it was in fact by J. T. Coleridge) accused S. of plagiarising from Southey and Wordsworth, and offered a savage characterisation of the subversive and immoral nature of his ideas.

Pref. 56. and indeed] Nbk 9, 1820; and, indeed, 1839.

Pref. 61. those extraordinary intellects] S.'s draft in Nbk 10 f. 27r shows that he had Coleridge and Byron specifically in mind.

endowment of the age in which they live, and the latter must be the uncommunicated lightning of their own mind.

70 The peculiar style of intense and comprehensive imagery which distinguishes the modern literature of England, has not been, as a general power, the product of the imitation of any particular writer. The mass of capabilities remains at every period materially the same; the circumstances which awaken it to action perpetually change. If England were divided into forty republics, each equal in population and extent to Athens, there is no

75 reason to suppose but that, under institutions not more perfect than those of Athens, each would produce philosophers and poets equal to those who (if we except Shakespeare) have never been surpassed. We owe the great writers of the golden age of our literature to that fervid awakening of the public mind which shook to dust the oldest and most oppressive form of

80 the Christian religion. We owe Milton to the progress and development of the same spirit: the sacred Milton was, let it ever be remembered, a republican and a bold inquirer into morals and religion. The great writers of our own age are, we have reason to suppose, the companions and forerunners of some unimagined change in our social condition, or the opinions

85 which cement it. The cloud of mind is discharging its collected lightning, and the equilibrium between institutions and opinions is now restoring, or is about to be restored.

As to imitation, poetry is a mimetic art. It creates, but it creates by combination and representation. Poetical abstractions are beautiful and new,

90 not because the portions of which they are composed had no previous existence in the mind of man, or in nature, but because the whole produced by their combination has some intelligible and beautiful analogy with those sources of emotion and thought, and with the contemporary condition of them: one great poet is a masterpiece of nature, which another not only

95 ought to study but must study. He might as wisely and as easily determine that his mind should no longer be the mirror of all that is lovely in the visible universe, as exclude from his contemplation the beautiful which exists in the writings of a great contemporary. The pretence of doing it would be a presumption in any but the greatest; the effect, even in him,

100 would be strained, unnatural, and ineffectual. A poet is the combined product of such internal powers as modify the nature of others; and of such external influences as excite and sustain these powers; he is not one, but both. Every man's mind is, in this respect, modified by all the objects of nature and art; by every word and every suggestion which he ever admit-

105 ted to act upon his consciousness; it is the mirror upon which all forms are reflected, and in which they compose one form. Poets, not otherwise than philosophers, painters, sculptors, and musicians, are, in one sense,

Pref. 105–14. Anticipating similar resonant articulations of S.'s view that poets stand inescapably in a dialectical relation to their historical period, in e.g. the last paragraph of *DP*, and in *PVR* (see *Prose* 240, 297).

the creators, and, in another, the creations, of their age. From this sub-
jection the loftiest do not escape. There is a similarity between Homer
10 and Hesiod, between Aeschylus and Euripides, between Virgil and Horace,
between Dante and Petrarch, between Shakespeare and Fletcher, between
Dryden and Pope; each has a generic resemblance under which their specific
distinctions are arranged. If this similarity be the result of imitation, I am
willing to confess that I have imitated.
15 Let this opportunity be conceded to me of acknowledging that I have,
what a Scotch philosopher characteristically terms, 'a passion for reform-
ing the world:' what passion incited him to write and publish his book,
he omits to explain. For my part, I had rather be damned with Plato and
Lord Bacon, than go to Heaven with Paley and Malthus. But it is a mis-
20 take to suppose that I dedicate my poetical compositions solely to the direct
enforcement of reform, or that I consider them in any degree as contain-
ing a reasoned system on the theory of human life. Didactic poetry is my
abhorrence; nothing can be equally well expressed in prose that is not tedious
and supererogatory in verse. My purpose has hitherto been simply to famil-
25 iarise the highly refined imagination of the more select classes of poetical
readers with beautiful idealisms of moral excellence; aware that until the
mind can love, and admire, and trust, and hope, and endure, reasoned
principles of moral conduct are seeds cast upon the highway of life, which
the unconscious passenger tramples into dust, although they would bear
30 the harvest of his happiness. Should I live to accomplish what I purpose,
that is, produce a systematical history of what appear to me to be the
genuine elements of human society, let not the advocates of injustice and
superstition flatter themselves that I should take Aeschylus rather than Plato
as my model.

Pref. 115–18. Peacock in *Nightmare Abbey* (ch. ii) attributes to Scythrop Glowry (a humorously
satirical representation of S. himself), 'the *passion for reforming the world*'. The phrase refers
to Robert Forsyth's *Principles of Moral Science* (Edinburgh, 1805; see i 291–2) quoted by Peacock
in *Melincourt* (1817) ch. xxi.

Pref. 116–19. See S.'s letter to Peacock of 23–24 January 1819: 'Fortunately Plato is of my
opinion, & I had rather err with Plato than be right with Horace' (*L* ii 75). Cp. Cicero,
Tusculan Disputations I xvii 39: 'Errare mehercule malo cum Platone, quem tu quanti facias
scio et quem ex tuo ore admiror, quam cum istis vera sentire' (I prefer, before heaven, to go
astray with Plato, your reverence for whom I know, and admiration for whom I learn from
your lips, rather than hold true views with his opponents'. Loeb trans.). *Paley and Malthus*]
For Malthus see note to III i 19, and note on *L&C* Preface. William Paley was a well-known
popular theologian, and author of *Evidences of Christianity* (1794), whose complacent
Christianity attracted S.'s especial impatience and scorn; see e.g. *L* i 200, and *Refutation of
Deism* (*Prose Works* i 97, 107).

Pref. 119. Heaven] *Nbk 9, 1820*; heaven *1839*.

Pref. 127–30. Recalling the Parable of the Sower, *Matthew* xiii 3–9.

Pref. 131–2. a systematical history of . . . human society] S. wrote PVR probably in late 1819,
i.e. around the time of the composition of this part of the Preface (see *SC* vi 951–5); but it
remained unpublished until 1920.

135   The having spoken of myself with unaffected freedom will need little apology with the candid; and let the uncandid consider that they injure me less than their own hearts and minds by misrepresentation. Whatever talents a person may possess to amuse and instruct others, be they ever so inconsiderable, he is yet bound to exert them: if his attempt be ineffectual,
140   let the punishment of an unaccomplished purpose have been sufficient; let none trouble themselves to heap the dust of oblivion upon his efforts; the pile they raise will betray his grave, which might otherwise have been unknown.

ACT I

Scene, a ravine of icy rocks in the Indian Caucasus. Prometheus *is discovered bound to the precipice.* Panthea *and* Ione *are seated at his feet. Time, night. During the scene, morning slowly breaks.*

Prometheus
Monarch of Gods and Dæmons, and all Spirits
But One, who throng those bright and rolling worlds
Which Thou and I alone of living things
Behold with sleepless eyes! regard this Earth
5   Made multitudinous with thy slaves, whom thou
Requitest for knee-worship, prayer and praise,
And toil, and hecatombs of broken hearts,
With fear and self-contempt and barren hope;
Whilst me, who am thy foe, eyeless in hate,

SD. Indian Caucasus] The Prometheus story was traditionally placed in the Georgian Caucasus mountains, between the Black Sea and the Caspian, although there is no specific sanction for this in Aeschylus (see *Prometheus Bound*, ed. Mark Griffith (1983) 79–80). S. moves the setting to the Indian Caucasus (i.e. the Hindu Kush), thus placing his action in a region traditionally associated with the birth of civilisation, and away from an area tainted by the presence of reactionary political forces in S.'s contemporary milieu (see *Curran (1975)* 61ff. *et passim*).

1–7. There are dense Miltonic echoes throughout Prometheus's opening speech, often of an elusively composite kind; with these lines cp. e.g. *Paradise Lost* i 84ff., 242ff.

1. Dæmons] Beings which hold 'an intermediate place between what is divine and what is mortal' (S.'s trans. of *Symposium* 202; and cp. Kathleen Raine, 'Thomas Taylor, Plato, and the English Romantic Movement', *Sewanee Review* lxxvi (1968) 230–57, 255).

2. One] Usually identified as Prometheus himself (cp. I 265, III iii 1–4, IV 34); but Demogorgon is a possibility, ironically hinted thus early to Jupiter (the *Monarch* of line 1) as the secret of his downfall which P. refuses to disclose (cp. I 371 and note, II iii 79). The *Spirits . . . who throng those bright and rolling worlds* refers to life on other planets; cp. I 163–5. *worlds*] Worlds *Nbk 7*.

3. Cp. Southey's *Curse of Kehama* (1810) XVIII vii: 'There is it written, Maid, that thou and I, / Alone of human kind a deathless pair . . .'.

4. sleepless] Sleeplessness (conventionally common in tyrants, but shared by Prometheus at line 12) is an element of the curse in *Kehama* II x. Cp. *Prometheus Bound* 32 (ἄϋπνος), Pope's *Iliad* ii 2.

6. Echoing the Miltonic 'knee-tribute', *Paradise Lost* v 782. *prayer*] *Nbk 7*; prayer, *1820, 1839*.

7. hecatombs] Large-scale public sacrifices; cp. S.'s use in the *Letter to Lord Ellenborough* (1812; *Prose Works* i 65), and see his note to *Hellas* 1090–1.

8. hope;] *Nbk 7*; hope. *1820, 1839*.

9–11. 'Blind with hatred, you have made me triumph over my own misery and your revenge' (GM; *eyeless in hate* refers to *thou* in line 10, but the syntax is aptly ambiguous).

10   Hast thou made reign and triumph, to thy scorn,
     O'er mine own misery and thy vain revenge . . .
     Three thousand years of sleep-unsheltered hours
     And moments, aye divided by keen pangs
     Till they seem years, torture and solitude,
15   Scorn and despair, — these are mine empire.
     More glorious far than that which thou surveyest
     From thine unenvied throne, O Mighty God!
     Almighty, had I deigned to share the shame
     Of thine ill tyranny, and hung not here
20   Nailed to this wall of eagle-baffling mountain,
     Black, wintry, dead, unmeasured; without herb,
     Insect, or beast, or shape or sound of life —
     Ah me, alas, pain, pain ever, forever!

11. *revenge . . .*] *Nbk 7*; revenge. *1820, 1839.*

12. *Three thousand years*] The Fall of Troy (understood by antiquarian convention as the beginning of recorded human history) was traditionally dated at 1184 BC, which counting forwards would place the action of the play in S.'s contemporary world of 1816. Plutarch (*Moralia* v 115, 'On Isis and Osiris' 370 BC) says of Zoroaster that he believed 'a time appointed by fate is coming, in which Arimanios . . . must needs be destroyed . . . and utterly vanish; when the earth becoming plain and level there shall be one life and one government for men, all happy and of one language. Theopompus says that, according to the Magi, one of the Gods [i.e. Oromazes and Arimanios] shall conquer, the other be conquered, alternately for 3,000 years, for another 3,000 years they shall fight, war, and undo one the works of the other; but in the end Hades shall fail, and man shall be happy, neither requiring food nor constructing shelter . . .' (Bohn trans.). *hours*] *Nbk 7*; hours, *1820, 1839.*

13–15. Cp. *J&M* 416–19:

> As the slow shadows of the pointed grass
> Mark the eternal periods, his pangs pass
> Slow, ever-moving, – making moments be
> As mine seem – each an immortality!

13. *moments,*] *Nbk 7*; moments *1820, 1839.*

14. *seem*] *Nbk 7*; seemed *1820, 1829, 1839.* Prometheus's torments still continue, as the present tense *are* of line 15 confirms.

17. *O*] *Nbk 7*; O, *1820, 1839.*

20–1. Cp. *Prometheus Bound* 15, φάπαγγι πρὸς δυσχειμέρωι ('by the wintry crag'), and 65, στέρνων διαμπὰξ ('right through the breast').

21–2. Cp. *Prometheus Bound* 20–2, τῶιδ' ἀπανθρώπωι πάγωι, / ἵν' οὔτε φωνὴν οὔτε του μορφὴν βροτων / ὄψηι ('this hill, far from humankind, where no mortal will observe [lit. 'see'] a voice or the shape of something . . .').

22. *life –*] *Nbk 7*; life. *1820, 1839.*

23. Ironically echoed at III i 81. The refrain recalls *Prometheus Bound* 98–100:

> φεῦ φεῦ τὸ παρὸν τό τ' ἐπερχόμενον
> πῆμα στενάχω, πῆι ποτε μόχθων
> χρὴ τέρματα τῶνδ' ἐπιτεῖλαι.

('Woe! Woe! For misery present and misery to come I groan, not knowing where it is fated deliverance from these woes shall rise.'). *Forever*] *Nbk 7*; for ever *1820, 1839.* In S.'s usage 'forever = continually, for ever = eternally' (GM); cp. *Alastor* 209, 357, 407, 425.

No change, no pause, no hope! Yet I endure.
25 I ask the Earth, have not the mountains felt?
I ask yon Heaven — the all-beholding Sun,
Has it not seen? the Sea, in storm or calm
Heaven's ever-changing Shadow, spread below,
Have its deaf waves not heard my agony?
30 Ah me, alas, pain, pain ever, forever!

The crawling glaciers pierce me with the spears
Of their moon-freezing crystals; the bright chains
Eat with their burning cold into my bones.
Heaven's wingèd hound, polluting from thy lips

25–9. Cp. *Prometheus Bound* 88–92:

ὦ δῖος αἰθὴρ καὶ ταχύπτεροι πνοαί,
ποταμῶν τε πηγαὶ ποντίων τε κυμάτων
ἀνήριθμον γέλασμα παμμῆτόρ τε γῆ,
καὶ τὸν πανόπτην κύκλον ἡλίου καλῶ,
ἴδεσθέ η᾽ οἷα πρὸς θεῶν πάσχω θεός.

('O thou bright sky of heaven, ye swift-winged breezes, ye river-waters, and multitudinous laughter of the waves of ocean, O universal mother Earth, and thou, all-seeing orb of the sun, to you I call! Behold what I, a god, endure of evil from the gods.')

26. *Heaven* –] *Nbk 7*; Heaven, *1820, 1839* (*Heaven* and *Sun* are not in apposition).

27. *seen? the*] seen, the *Nbk 7*; seen? The *1820, 1839*.   *calm*] *Nbk 7*; calm; *1820, 1839*.

28. *Shadow*] 'Image, copy' (GM).

31. Cp. *John* xix 34.

32. *moon-freezing*] 'Freezing in the moonlight' (*Locock 1911*).

34–5. 'More venomous by contact with Jupiter than by its own nature' (GM). Cp. *Prometheus Bound* 1016–25:

πρῶτα μὲν γὰρ ὀκρίδα
φάραγγα βροντῆι καὶ κεραυνίαι φλογὶ
πατὴρ σπαράξει τήνδε καὶ κρύψει δέμας
τὸ σόν, πετραία δ᾽ ἀγκάλη σε βαστάσει.
μακρὸν δὲ μῆκος ἐκτελευτήσας χρόνου
ἄψορρον ἥξεις εἰς φάος· Διὸς δέ τοι
πτηνὸς κύων, δαφοινὸς αἰετός, λάβρως
διαρταμήσει σώματος μέγα ῥάκος,
ἄκλητος ἕρπων δαιταλεὺς πανήμερος,
κελαινόβρωτον δ᾽ ἧπαρ ἐκθοινήσεται.

('First, the Father will shatter this jagged cliff with thunder and lightning-flame, and will entomb thy frame, while the rock shall still hold thee clasped in its embrace. But when thou hast completed a long stretch of time, thou shalt come back again to the light. Then verily the winged hound of Zeus, the ravening eagle, coming an unbidden banqueter the whole day long, with savage appetite shall tear thy body piecemeal into great rents and feast his fill upon thy liver till it be black with gnawing.'). *Heaven's wingèd hound*] S. echoes the Aeschylean πτηνὸς κύων; this is the only mention in *PU* of the eagle (or vulture) that in the myth comes every day to consume Prometheus's liver, which then grows again (though III ii 11–17 ironically associate the fallen Jupiter with an eagle, and may themselves recall the Aeschylean lines).

35 His beak in poison not its own, tears up
  My heart; and shapeless sights come wandering by,
  The ghastly people of the realm of dream,
  Mocking me: and the Earthquake-fiends are charged
  To wrench the rivets from my quivering wounds
40 When the rocks split and close again behind;
  While from their loud abysses howling throng
  The genii of the storm, urging the rage
  Of whirlwind, and afflict me with keen hail.
  And yet to me welcome is day and night,
45 Whether one breaks the hoar frost of the morn,
  Or starry, dim, and slow, the other climbs
  The leaden-coloured East; for then they lead
  Their wingless, crawling Hours, one among whom
  — As some dark Priest hales the reluctant victim —
50 Shall drag thee, cruel King, to kiss the blood
  From these pale feet, which then might trample thee
  If they disdained not such a prostrate slave.
  Disdain? ah no, I pity thee. What ruin

35. its] it's *Nbk 7*; his *1820, 1829, 1839* (presumably a transcription error, as the sense is obscured by a personal pronoun at this point, although *its* is clear in the MS).

40. behind;] *Nbk 7*; behind: *1820, 1839.*

42. genii of the storm] 'Genii' is the term in *Darwin* for 'the symbols or personifications of the physical and chemical activities in the various realms of nature' (*Grabo (1930)* 121; see *Economy of Vegetation*, note to i 73, and headnote). *Nbk 7* at first read *spirits*, which is canc. with *genii* written in above.

44–7. Cp. *Prometheus Bound* 23–5: ἀσμένωι δέ σοι
   ἡ ποικιλείμων νὺξ ἀποκρύψει φάος
   πάχνην θ' ἑωιαν ἥλιος σκεδᾶι πάλιν
('And glad shalt thou be when spangled-robed night shall veil his brightness and when the sun shall scatter again the rime of morn.')

44. day and night,] Day and Night *Nbk 7.* *47. East;*] *Nbk 7*; east; *1820, 1839.*

48. Their] *Nbk 7*; The *1820, 1829, 1839.* The image (*wingless, crawling*) is of a caterpillar; cp. II i 16. *Hours*] *Nbk 7*; hours *1820, 1839.*

49. hales] i.e. 'pulls along with violence' (*OED*; now superseded by *hauls*).

53–9. Generally recognised as a crucial turning-point in the poem; Prometheus's changed attitude to Jupiter is a necessary condition for the subsequent action, although there has been much debate about the nature of Prometheus's change. The dominant view is that Prometheus originates the change autonomously (see e.g. I. A. Richards, *Beyond* (New York 1973) 195–9), and that his conversion either takes place at this moment, or has already happened before – probably just before – the action commences (see e.g. *Baker* 97, Milton Wilson, *Shelley's Later Poetry* (New York 1959) 57, *Curran (1975)* 96, and M. H. Abrams, *Natural Supernaturalism* (1971) 304). But Stuart M. Sperry ('Necessity and the Role of the Hero in Shelley's *Prometheus Unbound*', *PMLA* 96 (1981) 242–54) offers an important alternative view: 'S.'s presentation leaves open the view of his hero as the necessary medium and earliest expression of universal change, as distinct from the primary cause of that change' (246; see also Philip Drew, *The Meaning of Freedom* (Aberdeen 1982) 178).

53. Disdain? ah] *Nbk 7*; Disdain! Ah *1820, 1839.*

Will hunt thee undefended through wide Heaven!
55 How will thy soul, cloven to its depth with terror,
Gape like a Hell within! I speak in grief
Not exultation, for I hate no more
As then, ere misery made me wise. The Curse
Once breathed on thee I would recall. Ye Mountains,
60 Whose many-voicèd Echoes, through the mist
Of cataracts, flung the thunder of that spell;
Ye icy Springs, stagnant with wrinkling frost,
Which vibrated to hear me, and then crept
Shuddering through India; thou serenest Air,
65 Through which the Sun walks burning without beams,
And ye swift Whirlwinds, who on poisèd wings
Hung mute and moveless o'er yon hushed abyss,
As thunder louder than your own made rock
The orbèd world — if then my words had power,

54. *through*] Nbk 7; through the *1820, 1829, 1839*; possibly an alteration to the press transcript, but the ametrical effect makes it unlikely.

56. *Hell*] Nbk 7; hell *1820, 1839*. *grief*] Nbk 7; grief, *1820, 1839*.

57. *exultation,*] Exultation, Nbk 7. *more*] Nbk 7; more, *1820, 1839*.

58. *then,*] Nbk 7; then *1820, 1839*. *Curse*] Nbk 7; curse *1820, 1839*.

59–69. *Curran (1975)* 71 points out that this invocation of the elements imitates the Zoroastrian formula of prayer (cp. e.g. Herodotus, *History* i 131, read by S. in the summer of 1818).

59. *recall*] The ambiguity ('remember' or 'revoke') has occasioned much discussion. S.'s usual sense for the word is 'remember', which best fits this context (Prometheus could presumably revoke the curse unaided if he could remember it). See *TLS* 16 December 1955 p. 761; 6 January 1956 p. 7; 20 January 1956 p. 37. *Mountains,*] mountains Nbk 7.

61. *spell;*] Nbk 7; spell! *1820, 1839*. The word recurs at I 184, I 535, II iii 88, II iv 89 (where it seems to mean 'a natural law'), and IV 555. Cp. the note to line 54 of 'March' in Spenser's *Shepheardes Calender*: 'Spell) is a kinde of verse or charme, that in elder tymes they used often to say over every thing, that they would have preserved, as the Nightspel for theeves, and the woodspel. And here hence I thinke is named the gospell, as it were Gods spell or worde. And so sayth Chaucer, Listeneth Lordings to my spells.'

64–5. The upper atmosphere lacks the moisture to refract sunlight into rays; see S.'s note to *Q Mab* i 242–3, and cp. *Paradise Lost* i 594–6.

64. *India;*] Nbk 7; India! *1820, 1839*.

65. *beams,*] Nbk 7; beams! *1820, 1839*.

68–9. Cp. *Prometheus Bound* 1081, χθὼν σεσάλευται ('the earth rocks'); and *Matthew* xxvii 51: 'And, behold, the veil of the temple was rent in twain from the top to the bottom; and the earth did quake, and the rocks rent'.

68. *thunder*] Nbk 7; thunder, *1820, 1839*. *own*] Nbk 7; own, *1820, 1839*.

69. *world – if*] Nbk 7; world! If *1820, 1839*. *then*] 'temporal, and emphatic' (*Locock 1911*).

70   Though I am changed so that aught evil wish
Is dead within; although no memory be
Of what is hate — let them not lose it now!
What was that curse? for ye all heard me speak.

First Voice, from the Mountains
Thrice three hundred thousand years
75   O'er the Earthquake's couch we stood:
Oft, as men convulsed with fears,
We trembled in our multitude.

Second Voice, from the Springs
Thunderbolts had parched our water,
We had been stained with bitter blood,
80   And had run mute, 'mid shrieks of slaughter,
Through a city and a solitude.

Third Voice, from the Air
I had clothed, since Earth uprose,
Its wastes in colours not their own;
And oft had my serene repose
85   Been cloven by many a rending groan.

Fourth Voice, from the Whirlwinds
We had soared beneath these mountains
Unresting ages; nor had thunder,
Nor yon Volcano's flaming fountains,
Nor any power above or under
90   Ever made us mute with wonder.

72. hate –] Nbk 7; hate, *1820, 1839.*

74. S. implies around one million years for the age of the earth. The line recalls Coleridge's 'Fire, Famine, and Slaughter' 23: 'thrice three hundred thousand men'.

78. Grabo (1930) 137 quotes Pliny, *Natural History* ii 52: 'We have accounts of many different kinds of thunderstorms. Those which are dry do not burn objects, but dissipate them. There is a third kind, which is called bright lightning, of a very wonderful nature, by which casks are emptied, without the vessels themselves being injured, or there being any other trace left of their operation.' Meteorites were called thunderbolts in the early nineteenth century, though their origins were known not to be connected with lightning or thunder; see *GM* lxxxviii (1818) 168–9.

80. run] ran Nbk 7; presumably a change to the press transcript.

82–3. Colour is produced by refraction of sunlight in the atmosphere; cp. I 64–5, IV 219–25, and see S.'s note to *Q Mab* i 242–3. *Rognoni* cps. Lucretius, *De Re. Nat.* ii 730–841.

88. Volcano's] Nbk 7; volcano's *1820, 1839.*

First Voice
But never bowed our snowy crest
As at the voice of thine unrest.

Second Voice
Never such a sound before
To the Indian waves we bore.
95   A pilot asleep on the howling sea
Leaped up from the deck in agony
And heard, and cried, 'Ah, woe is me!'
And died as mad as the wild waves be.

Third Voice
By such dread words from Earth to Heaven
100   My still realm was never riven:
When its wound was closed, there stood
Darkness o'er the day like blood.

Fourth Voice
And we shrank back: for dreams of ruin
To frozen caves our flight pursuing
105   Made us keep silence — thus — and thus —
Though silence is as hell to us.

The Earth
The tongueless caverns of the craggy hills
Cried 'Misery!' then the hollow Heaven replied,

95–8. Cp. Coleridge, 'Ancient Mariner' 560–9.   96. *agony*] *Nbk 7*; agony, *1820, 1839*.

102. Suggesting the 'darkness at noon' of the crucifixion; cp. *Matthew* xxvii 45. See also *Q Mab* vii 234 and note. *day*] Day *Nbk 7*.

105. Cp. Coleridge, 'Fire, Famine, and Slaughter' 17: 'Whisper it, sister! so and so!'

106. *as*] *Nbk 7, 1839*; a *1820, 1829*. Possibly corrected in *1839* from S.'s errata list; ink blotting obscures the passage in *Nbk 7*, which could easily have been miscopied. This line is followed in *Nbk 7* by a stage direction: 'they pass with a terrible sound'.

107–11. This speech is entered on the facing page in *Nbk 7*, together with the draft of lines 113–15, and was probably a later addition made before Act IV was copied into the nbk; see *BSM* ix 525. Cp. *Prometheus Bound* 431–5:

> βοᾶι δὲ πόντιος κλύδων
> ξυμπίτνων, στένει βυθός,
> κελαινὸς Ἄιδος ὑποβρέμει μυχὸς γᾶς,
> παγάι θ' ἀγνορύτων ποταμῶν
> στένουσιν ἄλγος οἰκτρόν.

('And the waves of the sea utter a cry as they fall, the deep laments, the black abyss of Hades rumbles in response, and the streams of pure-flowing rivers lament thy piteous pain.')

107. *caverns*] *Nbk 7*; Caverns *1820, 1839*.

108. *Cried 'Misery!' then*] Cried Misery, then *Nbk 7*; Cried 'Misery!' then; *1820, 1839*.

'Misery!' and the Ocean's purple waves,
110 Climbing the land, howled to the lashing winds,
And the pale nations heard it, — 'Misery!'

Prometheus
I hear a sound of voices: not the voice
Which I gave forth. Mother, thy sons and thou
Scorn him, without whose all-enduring will
115 Beneath the fierce omnipotence of Jove
Both they and thou had vanished like thin mist
Unrolled on the morning wind. Know ye not me,
The Titan? he who made his agony
The barrier to your else all-conquering foe?
120 O rock-embosomed lawns, and snow-fed streams,
Now seen athwart frore vapours, deep below,
Through whose o'ershadowing woods I wandered once
With Asia, drinking life from her loved eyes,
Why scorns the spirit which informs ye, now
125 To commune with me? me alone, who checked —

109. and] Nbk 7; And *1820, 1839*.

111. it, – 'Misery!'] it, – Misery! *Nbk 7*; it, 'Misery!' *1820, 1839*.

112ff. The Earth and the elements have two languages, Jupiter and Prometheus only one; see *Wasserman* 267ff. for searching commentary on this sequence.

113–17. Cp. *Prometheus Bound* 234–40:

> καὶ τοῖσιν οὐδεὶς ἀντέβαινε πλὴν ἐμοῦ.
> ἐγὼ δ' ἐτόλμησ'· ἐξελυσάμην βροτοὺς
> τὸ μὴ διαρραισθέντας εἰς Ἀιδου μολεῖν.
> τῶι τοι τοιαῖσδε πημοναῖσι κάμπτομαι,
> πάσχειν μὲν ἀλγειναῖσιν, οἰκτραῖσιν δ' ἰδεῖν

('Against this purpose none dared make stand save I myself – I only had the courage; I saved mortals so that they did not descend, blasted utterly, unto the house of Death. Therefore am I bent by so grievous tortures, painful to suffer, piteous to behold.')

115. Jove] Nbk 7; Jove, *1820, 1839*.   *116. vanished*] Nbk 7; vanished, *1820, 1839*.

117. Know ye not me] Cp. *Paradise Lost* iv 827–9: ' "Know ye not then," said Satan, filled with scorn, / "Know ye not me? Ye knew me once no mate / For you, there sitting where ye durst not soar[.]" '

118. he] Nbk 7; He *1820, 1839*.

120. O] Nbk 7; Oh, *1820, 1839*. *rock-embosomed*] Cp. Mary S.'s letter to Fanny Imlay from the Alps, 17 May 1816: 'no river or rock-encircled lawn relieved the eye, by adding the picturesque to the sublime'(*Mary L* i 18). *lawns*] i.e. grassy clearings (still the usual sense in 1815; cp. *Alastor* 448 and note). *snow-fed*] Cp. Thomson, *Liberty* iv 357, 'The snow-fed torrent', and *Winter* 995, 'snow-fed torrents'.

121. frore] Frozen.

122–3. Asia's eyes are a source of energy; S. assumes an identity of love with electricity. Cp. I 765, III iii 148–52, III iv 17–18. For general comment on the character of Asia, see headnote. *eyes,*] Nbk 7; there is a semicolon in *1820* and *1839*, but this obscures the subject of *ye* in line 124 (i.e. the *lawns* and *streams* of line 120).

125. checked –] Nbk 7; checked *1820*; checked, *1839*.

As one who checks a fiend-drawn charioteer —
The falsehood and the force of Him who reigns
Supreme, and with the groans of pining slaves
Fills your dim glens and liquid wildernesses?
130   Why answer ye not, still? Brethren!

The Earth
                           They dare not.

Prometheus
Who dares? For I would hear that curse again . . .
Ha, what an awful whisper rises up!
'Tis scarce like sound: it tingles through the frame
As lightening tingles, hovering ere it strike —
135   Speak, Spirit! from thine inorganic voice
I only know that thou art moving near
And love. How cursed I him?

The Earth
                    How canst thou hear,
Who knowest not the language of the dead?

Prometheus
Thou art a living spirit; speak as they.

The Earth
140   I dare not speak like life, lest Heaven's fell King
Should hear, and link me to some wheel of pain

126. charioteer –] Nbk 7; charioteer, *1820, 1839.*

127. Him] Nbk 7; him *1820, 1839.*

129. wildernesses?] Nbk 7; wildernesses: *1820, 1839.*

130. Brethren!] brethren! Nbk 7.

131. again . . .] Nbk 7; again. *1820, 1839.*

132. Ha,] Nbk 7, *1820;* Ha! *1839.*

134. As lightening tingles] i.e. like electricity; according to Priestley (*History and Present State of Electricity*, 3rd edn 1775, i 204), lightning and electricity were identical. *strike –*] Nbk 7; strike. *1820, 1839.*

135. inorganic] 'Of the dead'; cp. Mary Shelley, *The Last Man* (1826) ii ch. vii: 'I leapt up precipitately, and escaped from the hut, before nature could revoke her laws, and inorganic words be breathed in answer from the lips of the departed.' (*MSW* iv 203).

137. And love] 'And that thou lovest me' (GM). See *Zillman Variorum* 139–40 for a survey of earlier editorial discussion of this crux.

140ff. Zeus (Jupiter) used a torture-wheel to punish Ixion (Pindar, *Pythia* 2 21ff.); *Wasserman* 262ff., in excellent commentary on this passage, suggests that S. is thinking of the obliquity of the earth's ecliptic, which is responsible for seasonal variation. Cp. also *King Lear* IV vii 45–8.

More torturing than the one whereon I roll.
Subtle thou art and good; and though the Gods
Hear not this voice, yet thou art more than God
145   Being wise and kind: earnestly hearken now.

Prometheus
Obscurely through my brain, like shadows dim,
Sweep awful thoughts, rapid and thick — I feel
Faint, like one mingled in entwining love.
Yet 'tis not pleasure.

The Earth
                No, thou canst not hear:
150   Thou art immortal, and this tongue is known
Only to those who die . . .

Prometheus
                And what art thou,
O melancholy Voice?

The Earth
                I am the Earth
Thy mother, she within whose stony veins,
To the last fibre of the loftiest tree
155   Whose thin leaves trembled in the frozen air,
Joy ran, as blood within a living frame,

---

145. 'At this point it seems that the Earth speaks a few words (perhaps a part of the "Curse") in the "language of the dead," in order to see if Prometheus can understand it.' (*Locock 1911*).

147. *thick* –] *Nbk 7*; thick. *1820, 1839*.

148–51. Cp. III iii 110–12.

148. *love.*] *Nbk 7*; love; *1820, 1839*.

151–2. In *Nbk 7* S. at first wrote *Only to those who die . . . I am the Earth*, then subsequently placed a caret after *die* and wrote in Prometheus's lines in pencil on the facing page.

151. *die . . .*] *Nbk 7*; die. *1820, 1839*.

152. *Earth*] *Nbk 7*; Earth, *1820, 1839*.

153. *mother,*] *Nbk 7*; mother; *1820, 1839*. *stony veins*] Cp. S.'s journal-letter of July 1816 to Peacock from Chamonix: 'One would think that Mont Blanc was a living being & that the frozen blood forever circulated slowly thro' his stony veins' (*L* i 500). See also Pliny, *Natural History* ii 166, and Virgil (attrib.), *Aetna* 98–101: '. . . utque animanti / per tota errantes percurrunt corpora venae / ad vitam sanguis omnis qua commeat eidem, / terra voraginibus conceptas digerit auras' ('As in a living creature veins run through the whole body with wandering course, along which passes every drop of blood to feed life for the selfsame organism, so the earth by its chasms draws in and distributes currents of air').

When thou didst from her bosom, like a beam
From sunrise, leap — a spirit of keen joy!
And at thy voice her pining sons uplifted
160   Their prostrate brows from the polluting dust,
And our almighty Tyrant with fierce dread
Grew pale — until his thunder chained thee here.
Then — see those million worlds which burn and roll
Around us: their inhabitants beheld
165   My spherèd light wane in wide heaven; the sea
Was lifted by strange tempest, and new fire
From earthquake-rifted mountains of bright snow
Shook its portentous hair beneath Heaven's frown;
Lightning and Inundation vexed the plains;
170   Blue thistles bloomed in cities; foodless toads

157–8. like a beam / From sunrise, leap –] *written above* cloud / Of glory arise *canc.* in *Nbk 7* (S. first substituted *burst* for *arise* before cancelling it and settling on *leap*). The cancelled words are printed in *1820* and *1839*, which suggests that S. made this alteration to the fair copy after the despatch of Mary's press transcript (see headnote, and cp. *BSM* ix 528). These lines refer not to Prometheus's birth but to the period of his rebellion.

162. pale –] *Nbk 7*; pale, *1820, 1839*.

163–5. The reference is to life on other planets; cp. I 1–2.

163. Then –] *Nbk 7*; Then, *1820, 1839*.

165. S. wrote *moonlike* in faint pencil above *sphered* in *Nbk 7*; neither word is cancelled. *heaven;*] Heaven; *Nbk 7*; Heaven; *1820; 1839*.

166. lifted by] In *Nbk 7* S. first wrote *shaken with*, then canc. *shaken* and wrote *lifted* above; the change from *with* to *by* in *1820* was presumably made by S. to the fair copy, but he omitted to complete the alteration to *Nbk 7*.

165–8. Prometheus's enslavement was accompanied by earthquake and volcanic fire; cp. I 68–9, II i 196–206, *Matthew* xxvii 51, and also *Prometheus Bound* 1043–50, quoted in the note to lines 266–70 below, and 1080–90. *new fire . . . Shook its portentous hair*] Cp. *Paradise Lost* ii 710, 'horrid hair'. The derivation of 'comet' is from Gk κομήτης, 'long-haired'. Comets are traditionally portents of violent change; cp. II iv 139 and note, IV 317 and note. *Rognoni* suggests cp. with the decriptions of ominous portents in *Julius Caesar* I iii 3–28, II ii 13–24, and Virgil's *Georgics* i 466–88, iii 478–566.

169ff. Suggesting the Biblical flood, and the plagues of Egypt; cp. *Exodus* viii 3: 'And the river shall bring forth frogs abundantly, which shall go up and come into thine house, and into thy bedchamber, and upon thy bed, and into the house of thy servants, and upon thy people, and into thine ovens, and into thy kneadingtroughs'.

170–1. Recalls *Paradise Lost* xi 750–2: '. . . in their palaces / Where luxury late reigned, sea-monsters whelped / And stabled'. See also *Psalms* cv 30, 'Their land brought forth frogs in abundance, in the chambers of their kings' (referring to the passage cited from *Exodus* in preceding note); and *Isaiah* xxxiv 11–13, paraphrased by T. J. Hogg in 'The Fall of Idumea': 'The toad and the adder shall come from the forest, / And dragons pant o'er it [Idumea] when thirst's at the sorest'.

170. Blue thistles] Blue often implies sickness or the unearthly, and has associations with evil; cp. Blair's *The Grave* (1743) 628, 'bluest plague', and Coleridge has 'blue plague' in 'Fears in Solitude' 91.

Within voluptuous chambers panting crawled;
When Plague had fallen on man and beast and worm,
And Famine, and black blight on herb and tree;
And in the corn, and vines, and meadow-grass,
175 Teemed ineradicable poisonous weeds
Draining their growth, for my wan breast was dry
With grief; and the thin air, my breath, was stained
With the contagion of a mother's hate
Breathed on her child's destroyer — aye, I heard
180 Thy curse, the which, if thou rememberest not,
Yet my innumerable seas and streams,
Mountains, and caves, and winds, and yon wide air,
And the inarticulate people of the dead,
Preserve, a treasured spell. We meditate
185 In secret joy and hope those dreadful words,
But dare not speak them.

Prometheus
                    Venerable Mother!
All else who live and suffer take from thee
Some comfort; flowers, and fruits, and happy sounds,
And love, though fleeting; these may not be mine.
190 But mine own words, I pray, deny me not.

The Earth
They shall be told. Ere Babylon was dust,
The Magus Zoroaster, my dead child,

172. *man and beast*] Nbk 7; man, and beast, *1820, 1839*.

173. *Famine,*] Nbk 7; Famine; *1820, 1839*.

176. Cp. III iii 94–5.

178. *contagion*] See note to II iii 10.

179. *destroyer –*] Nbk 7; destroyer; *1820, 1839*.

185. *words,*] words Nbk 7, *1820, 1829, 1839*. The comma was introduced in Foster's first American edition of the *Poetical Works* (Philadelphia 1845) and retained by Rossetti, Forman, and subsequent *eds*.

186. *Mother!*] Nbk 7; mother! *1820, 1839*.

191–218. *Zoroaster* was the Gk name for the ancient Persian prophet Zarathustra. No single specific source for this passage has been identified; cp. J. Duchesne-Guillemin: 'I have searched in vain for a definite source for this particular episode: unless I am mistaken, it is of Shelley's own invention. He appears to have freely combined the account of Zoroaster's visions with that of the faithful soul's encounter with the Daena after death. In order to convey what he thought essential in the Zoroastrian message, namely, a secret correspondence and attraction between visible and spiritual realities, he fashioned a new Zoroaster, thus . . . anticipating Nietzsche's *Unwertung* of Zoroaster' (*The Western Response to Zoroaster* (Oxford 1958) 16). Here as elsewhere in *PU* S. draws on various accounts of Zoroastrian belief and

Met his own image walking in the garden.
That apparition, sole of men, he saw.
195   For know there are two worlds of life and death:
One that which thou beholdest; but the other
Is underneath the grave, where do inhabit
The shadows of all forms that think and live
Till death unite them and they part no more;
200   Dreams and the light imaginings of men,
And all that faith creates or love desires,
Terrible, strange, sublime and beauteous shapes.
There thou art, and dost hang, a writhing shade
'Mid whirlwind-shaken mountains; all the Gods
205   Are there, and all the Powers of nameless worlds,

---

practice, transmitted through Gk sources such as Plutarch and Herodotus, and newly familiar in the general and particular culture in which S. developed, with its imperial interests in the religions of the East. Peacock's Gk interests were no doubt a primary influence. See *Curran (1975)* 68ff. for detailed discussion of Zoroastrian elements and parallels for these lines. *Magus*] Wise man or priest.

193–4. For discussion of 'doubles' in S.'s work and experience see K. Everest, 'Shelley's Doubles: An Approach to "Julian and Maddalo" ', in *Shelley Revalued*.

194. sole of men] i.e. the vision was imaginary.

195ff. These lines have attracted extensive commentary. S.'s 'two worlds' conception implies that life and death exist as opposite poles of one unity; according to conventional wisdom in S.'s view, 'life' is experience as known to the senses, 'death' the realm of abstraction (such that dying out of 'life' is co-instantaneous with birth into the abstract). Cp. the exposition in *Barthelemy* iv 352 of the myth of the cave in Plato's *Republic*: 'Two worlds exist, the one visible and the other ideal. The first, formed on the model of the other, is that which we inhabit. In it every thing, being subject to generation and corruption, changes and passes away incessantly, while we only behold the images and fugitive portions of being. The second contains the essences and prototypes of all visible objects, and these essences are real beings, since they are immutable. Two kings, one of whom is the servant and slave of the other, diffuse their splendour in these two worlds. In the expance of heaven the sun discloses and perpetuates the objects which he renders visible to our eyes. From the most exalted part of the intellectual world, the supreme good produces and preserves the essences which he renders intelligible to our souls.' See also Thomas Taylor's note on Orphic Theology ('. . . there are two worlds, the intelligible and the sensible, the former of which is the source of the latter . . .'), *The Mystical Initiations; or, Hymns of Orpheus*, trans. Thomas Taylor (1787) 134. But S.'s conception does not match the Platonic contrast between the shadow-world in which we live and the reality we may (if we live as philosophers) see when we die; it more closely resembles the Homeric Hades, inhabited by bloodless shadows of those who have lived on earth. *of life and death*] i.e. of life, and of death.

198. shadows] i.e. images.

203. shade] Nbk 7; shade, *1820, 1839*.

204. whirlwind-shaken] Nbk 7; whirlwind-peopled *1820, 1829, 1839*. *shaken* is written above *peopled* canc. in Nbk 7; perhaps changed in the fair copy after Mary S.'s transcription, but the alteration of *shaken* to *lifted* in line 166 may have followed S.'s change here, which would have prompted him to avoid repetition by removing the earlier use of the word. *Gods*] Nbk 7; gods *1820, 1839*.

205. Powers] Nbk 7; powers *1829, 1839*.

Vast, sceptred Phantoms; heroes, men, and beasts;
And Demogorgon, a tremendous Gloom;
And he, the Supreme Tyrant, throned
On burning Gold. Son, one of these shall utter
210 The curse which all remember. Call at will
Thine own ghost, or the ghost of Jupiter,
Hades, or Typhon, or what mightier Gods
From all-prolific evil, since thy ruin
Have sprung, and trampled on my prostrate sons —
215 Ask, and they must reply: so the revenge
Of the Supreme may sweep through vacant shades,
As rainy wind through the abandoned gate
Of a fallen palace.

Prometheus
                    Mother, let not aught
Of that which may be evil, pass again
220 My lips, or those of aught resembling me —
Phantasm of Jupiter, arise, appear!

Ione
My wings are folded o'er mine ears:
My wings are crossed over mine eyes:

206. Phantoms;] *Nbk 7*; phantoms; *1820, 1839.*

207. Gloom;] Gloom *Nbk 7*; gloom; *1820, 1839.* For Demogorgon, see headnote.

208–9. Supreme . . . Gold.] *Nbk 7*; supreme Tyrant, on his throne / Of burning gold. *1820, 1839; on his throne / Of* is canc. in *Nbk 7* with the later version written above. *1820,* and most *eds* opt for the straightfowardly metrical reading; but the effect of S.'s powerful cluster of strong stresses, *Ánd hé, the Supréme Týrant, thróned,* is very striking in context.

212. Hades,] *Nbk 7*; Hades *1820, 1839.* Hades (Gk name for Pluto, god of the underworld) was the brother of Zeus. The Titan Typhon was a hundred-headed dragon who was overthrown by Zeus; according to Virgil (*Aeneid* ix 715–16) he was buried under one of the volcanic islands in the Bay of Naples (Inarime; Aetna in other accounts). Prometheus in *Prometheus Bound* (353ff.) identifies with Typhon's rebellion, which had volcanic associations (see also *Wasserman* 334–6).

213. evil,] Evil, *Nbk 7.*

214. sons –] *Nbk 7*; sons. *1820, 1839.*

216. Supreme] supreme *Nbk 7.*

217–18. The draft of these lines is in *Nbk 11,* p. 23.

220. me –] *Nbk 7*; me. *1820, 1839.*

221. At this point in *Nbk 7* (f. 29ᵛ) there is a cancelled stage direction: 'The sound beneath as of earthquake & the driving of whirlwinds – The Ravine is split, & the Phantasm of Jupiter [appears *canc.*] rises, surrounded by heavy clouds which dart forth lightning'. Panthea's speech at lines 231–2 below includes these descriptive details.

222–3. Cp. *Paradise Lost* iii 380–2: 'Dark with excessive bright thy skirts appear, / Yet dazzle Heaven, that brightest Seraphim / Approach not, but with both wings veil their eyes.'

223. over] *Nbk 7*; o'er *1820, 1839.*

Yet through their silver shade appears,
And through their lulling plumes arise,
A Shape, a throng of sounds;
May it be no ill to thee
O thou of many wounds!
Near whom, for our sweet sister's sake,
Ever thus we watch and wake.

Panthea
The sound is of whirlwind underground,
Earthquake, and fire, and mountains cloven;
The Shape is awful like the sound,
Clothed in dark purple, star-inwoven.
A sceptre of pale gold
To stay steps proud o'er the slow cloud
His veinèd hand doth hold.
Cruel he looks, but calm and strong,
Like one who does, not suffers, wrong.

Phantasm of Jupiter
240 Why have the secret powers of this strange world
Driven me, a frail and empty phantom, hither
On direst storms? What unaccustomed sounds
Are hovering on my lips, unlike the voice
With which our pallid race hold ghastly talk
245 In darkness? And, proud Sufferer, who art thou?

Prometheus
Tremendous Image, as thou art must be
He whom thou shadowest forth. I am his foe,

225 (line 225)
230 (line 230)
235 (line 235)

224–6. i.e. 'A Shape . . . appears, a throng of sounds . . . arise[s]' (attracted into the plural by *sounds*).

229. sweet sister] Asia.

233. Shape] *Nbk 7*; shape *1820, 1839*.

236. stay] i.e. support. *proud*] proud, *Nbk 7, 1820, 1839* (various *eds* omit the comma, e.g. *Rossetti 1870, Locock 1911*). S.'s practice was sometimes to mark an internal rhyme by a comma, but this now appears mannered and can produce grammatical confusion.

237–8. His . . . he] S. was uncertain about the human status of the phantasm; in *Nbk 7 Its* and *it* are uncancelled alternatives to these pronouns.

239. suffers,] suffers *Nbk 7, 1820, eds.* A comma (introduced by Foster in the first American edition, Philadelphia 1845) clarifies the transitive force of *does* (see also *Rossetti 1870*).

245. Sufferer,] Sufferer *Nbk 7*; sufferer, *1820, 1839*.

246. Image,] *1820*; image, *Nbk 7*; Image! *1839*.

247. He] Him *Nbk 7*.

The Titan. Speak the words which I would hear,
Although no thought inform thine empty voice.

The Earth
250   Listen! And though your echoes must be mute,
Grey mountains, and old woods, and haunted springs,
Prophetic caves, and isle-surrounding streams,
Rejoice to hear what yet ye cannot speak.

Phantasm
A spirit seizes me and speaks within:
255   It tears me as fire tears a thunder-cloud.

Panthea
See, how he lifts his mighty looks, the heaven
Darkens above.

Ione
                    He speaks! O shelter me!

Prometheus
I see the curse on gestures proud and cold,
And looks of firm defiance, and calm hate,
260   And such despair as mocks itself with smiles,
Written as on a scroll . . . yet speak — O speak!

Phantasm
Fiend, I defy thee! with a calm, fixed mind,
All that thou canst inflict I bid thee do;
Foul Tyrant both of Gods and Humankind,

---

253. *ye cannot speak.*] *1820, 1839*; after line 252 S.'s fair copy in *Nbk 7* at first read 'Listen, and though ye weep, rejoicing know / That our strong curse cannot be unfulfilled' (f. 31ᵛ); these lines were then cancelled and an alternative line drafted on the blank facing page: 'Rejoice to hear what yet [must be fulfilled *canc.*] ye dare not speak'. The substantive change in *1820* may suggest a correction to the press transcript which was not subsequently copied to *Nbk 7* (see headnote).

256–7. The repetition of Prometheus's curse by the Phantasm of Jupiter (lines 262–301 below) is here preceded by portents similar to those that accompanied the original curse; cp. I 101–2.

256. *heaven*] Heaven *Nbk 7, 1820, 1839*.

258–61. These lines were added later on the facing page in *Nbk 7*. Prometheus appears to recognise not just his own words but his own face and expression in the original act of cursing (cp. line 262).

261. Written as on a scroll . . . yet speak – o speak. *Nbk 7*; Written as on a scroll: yet speak: Oh, speak! *1820, 1839*.

262. *fixed mind*] Cp. *Paradise Lost* i 97, and S. perhaps also recalls *Prometheus Bound* 992–7.

265   One only being shalt thou not subdue.
Rain then thy plagues upon me here,
Ghastly disease, and frenzying fear;
And let alternate frost and fire
Eat into me, and be thine ire
270   Lightning, and cutting hail, and legioned forms
Of furies, driving by upon the wounding storms.

Aye, do thy worst. Thou art Omnipotent.
O'er all things but thyself I gave thee power,
And my own will. Be thy swift mischiefs sent
275   To blast mankind, from yon etherial tower.
Let thy malignant spirit move
Its darkness over those I love:
On me and mine I imprecate
The utmost torture of thy hate;
280   And thus devote to sleepless agony
This undeclining head while thou must reign on high.

But thou who art the God and Lord — O thou
Who fillest with thy soul this world of woe,
To whom all things of Earth and Heaven do bow

266–70. Echoing P.'s defiance of Zeus in *Prometheus Bound* 1043–50:

πρὸς ταῦτ' ἐπ' ἐμοὶ ῥιπτέσθω μὲν
πυρὸς ἀμφήκης βόστρυχος, αἰθὴρ δ'
ἐρεθιζέσθω βροντῆι σφακέλωι τ'
ἀγρίων ἀνέμων χθόνα δ' ἐκ πυθμένων
αὐταῖς ῥίζαις πνεῦμα κραδαίνοι,
κῦμα δὲ πόντου τραχεῖ ῥοθίωι
συγχώσειεν τῶν οὐρανίων
ἄστρων διόδους

('Therefore let the lightning's forked curl be cast upon my head and let the sky be convulsed with thunder and the wrack of savage winds; let the hurricane shake the earth from its rooted base, and let the waves of the sea mingle with their savage surge the courses of the stars in heaven'.)

272. *Omnipotent.*] Nbk 7; omnipotent. 1820, 1839.

273. *I gave thee power*] On Prometheus's responsibility for Jupiter's tyranny, see headnote; in terms of the Gk source myth, Prometheus had helped Zeus (i.e. Jupiter) against his fellow-Titans.

276–7. Cp. *Genesis* i 2: '. . . darkness was upon the face of the deep. And the Spirit of God moved upon the face of the waters.'

277. *Its*] Nbk 7; In 1820, 1839 (probably a mistranscription in the press transcript).

278. *imprecate*] 'To . . . call down (evil or calamity) upon' (OED 1a).

280. *agony*] Nbk 7; agony, 1820, 1839.

282. *God*] Altered from [King *canc.*] in Nbk 7; presumably a correction which preceded despatch of the press transcript, as God is the reading in 1820. *Lord –*] Nbk 7; Lord: O, 1820, 1839.

285   In fear and worship — all-prevailing foe!
                  I curse thee! let a sufferer's curse
                  Clasp thee, his torturer, like remorse,
                  Till thine Infinity shall be
                  A robe of envenomed agony,
290   And thine Omnipotence a crown of pain
                  To cling like burning gold round thy dissolving brain.

                  Heap on thy soul by virtue of this Curse
                  Ill deeds, then be thou damned, beholding good;
                  Both infinite as is this Universe,
295   And thou, and thy self-torturing solitude.
                  An awful Image of calm power
                  Though now thou sittest, let the hour
                  Come, when thou must appear to be
                  That which thou art internally,

285. *worship –*] *Nbk 7*; worship: *1820, 1839.*

287. *remorse,*] *Nbk 7*; remorse; *1820*; remorse! *1839.*

289. Recalling the robe poisoned by the centaur Nessus which killed Hercules (Sophocles, *Trachiniae*), and the poisoned robe used by Medea to murder Creusa (Euripides, *Medea*), but there are also associations with Christ's crown of thorns and the robes with which he was mocked (see e.g. *Luke* xxiii 11, and *Matthew* xxvii 28–9). *agony,*] agony *Nbk 7*; agony; *1820, 1839.*

290. *pain*] *Nbk 7*; pain, *1820, 1839.*

292–4. Cp. *Paradise Lost* i 209–20:
        So stretched out huge in length the Arch-Fiend lay
        Chained on the burning lake; nor ever thence
        Had risen or heaved his head, but that the will
        And high permission of all-ruling Heaven
        Left him at large to his own dark designs,
        That with reiterated crimes he might
        Heap on himself damnation, while he sought
        Evil to others, and enraged might see
        How all his malice served but to bring forth
        Infinite goodness, grace and mercy shown
        On man by him seduced, but on himself
        Treble confusion, wrath and vengeance poured.
Prometheus's curse includes the wish that Jupiter might make his eventual punishment worse by committing more crimes.

292. *soul*] *Nbk 7*; soul, *1820, 1839.* *Curse*] *Nbk 7*; Curse, *1820*; curse, *1839.*

294–5. Rossetti argued that S.'s grammar is radically incoherent in this passage (*Rossetti 1870* 496–7), and prompted a ferocious reply from Swinburne in defence of S. (see *Zillman Variorum* 148–9). S.'s construction is latinate ('Et . . . et'); GM glosses the passage 'May both be infinite – yourself (doing evil), and your agonising isolation (seeing good in others)'.

294. *This*] *Nbk 7*; the *1820, 1839, eds.* *Universe,*] Universe *Nbk 7*; universe, *1820, 1839.*

296. *Image*] *Nbk 7*; image *1820, 1839.*

299. *internally,*] internally *Nbk 7*; internally. *1820, 1839.*

300   And after many a false and fruitless crime
Scorn track thy lagging fall through boundless
space and time.

Prometheus
Were these my words, O Parent?

The Earth
They were thine.

Prometheus
It doth repent me: words are quick and vain;
Grief for awhile is blind, and so was mine.
305   I wish no living thing to suffer pain.

The Earth
Misery, O misery to me
That Jove at length should vanquish thee.
Wail, howl aloud, Land and Sea,
The Earth's rent heart shall answer ye.
310   Howl, Spirits of the living and the dead,
Your refuge, your defence lies fallen and vanquishèd.

First Echo
Lies fallen and vanquishèd?

Second Echo
Fallen and vanquishèd!

Ione
Fear not: 'tis but some passing spasm,
315   The Titan is unvanquished still.
But see, where through the azure chasm
Of yon forked and snowy hill
Trampling the slant winds on high
With golden-sandalled feet, that glow
320   Under plumes of purple dye,
Like rose-ensanguined ivory,

---

300. crime] *Nbk 7, 1820*; crime, *1839*.

301. At this point in *Nbk 7* a stage direction (not cancelled but underlined) reads 'the Phantasm vanishes'.

302–11. Prometheus's renunciation, and Earth's response, sustain the stanza form of the curse.

305. At this point in *Nbk 7* a cancelled stage direction reads: 'he bends his head as in pain'.

310. Spirits] spirits *Nbk 7*.

312. fallen] Fallen *Nbk 7*.

> A Shape comes now,
> Stretching on high from his right hand
> A serpent-cinctured wand.

Panthea

325 'Tis Jove's world-wandering herald, Mercury.

> *Ione*
> And who are those with hydra tresses
> And iron wings that climb the wind,
> Whom the frowning God represses
> Like vapours steaming up behind,

330 Clanging loud, an endless crowd —

> *Panthea*
> These are Jove's tempest-walking hounds,
> Whom he gluts with groans and blood,

324. serpent-cinctured wand] Cp. *Prometheus Bound* 799, δρακοντόμαλλοι ('serpent-haired', said of the Gorgons). A staff twined with snakes was the emblem of Mercury, messenger of the gods (see next note). Peacock uses 'forest-cinctured' (see *The Philosophy of Melancholy* (1812) i 119–20; *Melincourt* (1817) ch. xli).

325. world-wandering] Altered from *heaven-walking* canc. in *Nbk 7*; S. perhaps wished to avoid the repetition with *tempest-walking* at line 331 below, which is cancelled in *Nbk 7* but without alternatives (*tempest-walking* is the reading in *1820*). *Mercury*] Latin name for Hermes, messenger of the gods (especially Zeus) and son of Zeus and Maia (see line 342). S.'s Mercury merges elements from Hephaestus, Oceanus and Hermes in *Prometheus Bound*. In dramatic terms, Mercury's appearance at this point is presumably motivated by Jupiter's assumption that Prometheus's renunciation of his curse means that he is now defeated and ready to reveal his secret (note that in III i Jupiter assumes Prometheus's resistance is over). Mercury is sent to strike a deal. He is akin to Prometheus in the source myth, and here too he has affinities with the hero; but he is an intellectual who uses his powers of intelligence and articulate persuasion in the service of the tyrant with whom he has thrown in his lot. S.'s general conception of the exchanges between Mercury and Prometheus suggests Satan's temptation of Christ in the desert (*Matthew* iv 8–10). *herald*] Herald *Nbk 7*.

326. hydra tresses] 'Hair' consisting of many heads; the Hydra was a many-headed water-snake killed by Hercules. The Erinyes (see below, note to line 331) have snake-hair (e.g. in Aeschylus, *Eumenides*).

330. clanging] A conventional poetic word for the sound of birds' wings, but also used for the harsh scream or screech of a bird (from Gk κεκλάγξομαι). Aeschylus's Furies are wingless.

331. Jove's tempest-walking hounds] The Furies. S.'s Furies derive from the Erinyes of Gk myth, avenging spirits of punishment which worked by disturbing the mind (they are embodiments of mental states, and sometimes more specifically of curses). There are six Furies in *PU* I, balancing the six spirits who speak from line 672 below; Paul Dawson, *The Unacknowledged Legislator: Shelley and Politics* (1980) 116 cps. Aeschylus, *Eumenides*, in which Erinyes (Furies) are transformed to Eumenides (Kindly Ones); in *Eumenides* the Furies support the rule of law, and the pre-Olympian gods whose traditions they support are denounced by Apollo as tyrants. *Wasserman* suggests a contrasting 'Christian ancestry' for the Spirits (see note to 658–61 below). For *tempest-walking* see note to line 325 above.

332. with] on *Nbk 7* (the change is unlikely to be a mistranscription; presumably a correction by S. to the press transcript).

When charioted on sulphurous cloud
He bursts Heaven's bounds.

Ione
335   Are they now led from the thin dead
On new pangs to be fed?

Panthea
The Titan looks as ever, firm, not proud.

First Fury
Ha! I scent life!

Second Fury
        Let me but look into his eyes!

Third Fury
The hope of torturing him smells like a heap
340   Of corpses to a death-bird after battle.

First Fury
Darest thou delay, O Herald? take cheer, Hounds
Of Hell — what if the Son of Maia soon
Should make us food and sport? Who can please long
The Omnipotent?

Mercury
        Back to your towers of iron,
345   And gnash, beside the streams of fire and wail,

---

335. led] Nbk 7; led, *1820, 1839.*

338. into] in *Nbk 7* (presumably a change to the press transcript).

340. corpses] Nbk 7; corpses, *1820, 1839.*

341. Herald?] Nbk 7; Herald! *1820, 1839.*

342. Hell –] Nbk 7; Hell: *1820, 1839.* *Son of Maia*] Mercury.

343. sport? Who] Nbk 7; sport – who *1820, 1839.*

343–4. Cp. *Paradise Lost* ix 948–50: 'Fickle their state whom God / Most favours, who can please him long? Me first / He ruined, now mankind; whom will he next?'

345–6. the streams of fire and wail,] Two of the rivers of Hades were Phlegethon, a river of fire, and Cocytus, a river of tears (Cp. *Paradise Lost* ii 579–81, and see also *Aeneid* vi 265ff., a passage to which S.'s whole conception and introduction of the Furies appears indebted). S.'s syntax can be made ambiguous with adjustments to the punctuation; there is no comma after *fire* in *Nbk 7* and *1820*, but a comma is introduced in *1839*, and omitted after *wail*. E. B. Murray (*KSJ* xxiv (1975) 17–20) has argued that *gnash* and *wail* are both verbs governing

Your foodless teeth! . . . Geryon, arise! and Gorgon,
Chimæra, and thou Sphinx, subtlest of fiends,
Who ministered to Thebes Heaven's poisoned wine,
Unnatural love, and more unnatural hate:
350 These shall perform your task.

First Fury
                                        O mercy! mercy!
We die with our desire — drive us not back!

Mercury
Crouch then in silence. — Awful Sufferer,
To thee unwilling, most unwillingly
I come, by the great Father's will driven down

---

foodless teeth, i.e. that the adverbial phrase qualifying *gnash* is not 'beside the streams of fire
and wail' but 'beside the streams of fire'. This contention is proposed partly on the grounds
that ink marks after *fire* in *Nbk 7* could be read as suspension points. But this is not likely
(see *BSM* ix 152 for a photograph of the MS), and the construction 'wail your foodless teeth'
seems odd and indeed almost meaningless. Murray's reading is adopted in *Reiman (1977)*.

346. teeth! . . .] *Nbk 7*; teeth. *1820*, *1839*.

346–9. Geryon . . . Gorgon, / Chimæra . . . Sphinx] A mainly female group of multiform classical
monsters, recalling *Aeneid* vi 286–9. Geryon was a three-headed monster slain by Hercules;
Dante associates him with Fraud (*Inferno* xvii). The Gorgon was Medusa, a snake-haired
monster whose gaze transformed people to stone; unlike her two sisters she was mortal and
eventually killed by Perseus. Chimæra was a triple-bodied monster (part lion, part serpent,
part goat; see *Iliad* vi 181); S. may have seen the famous bronze Chimæra at Florence *en route*
from Bagni di Lucca to Venice in July 1818. Sphinx was part human, part lion. Oedipus's
liberation of Thebes from the Sphinx (see Sophocles, *Oedipus Tyrannus*) led him into unwit-
ting marriage with his own mother (*unnatural love*), and into cursing his two sons to make
them kill one another (*more unnatural hate*).

351. We die with our desire] 'We are nothing but embodied lust for cruelty, and die if it is
thwarted' (GM). *desire* –] *Nbk 7*; desire: *1820*, *1839*.

352. silence. –] *Nbk 7*; silence. *1820*, *1839*. *Sufferer,*] Sufferer *Nbk 7*, *1820*; Sufferer! *1839*. In
1820 and *1839* this line is broken after *silence.* into two half-lines.

353–7. Cp. *Prometheus Bound* 14–20:

> ἐγὼ δ᾽ ἄτολμός εἰμι συγγενῆ θεὸν
> δῆσαι βίαι φάραγγι πρὸς δυσχειμέρωι.
> πάντως δ᾽ ἀνάγκη τῶνδέ μοι τόλμαν σχεθεῖν·
> εὐωριάζειν γὰρ πατρὸς λόγους βαρύ.
> τῆς ὀρθοβούλου Θέμιδος αἰπυμῆτα παῖ,
> ἄκοντά σ᾽ ἄκων δυσλύτοις χαλκεύμασι
> προσπασσαλεύσω τῶιδ᾽ ἀπανθρώπωι πάγωι

('But for me – I cannot nerve myself to bind amain a kindred god upon this rocky cleft assailed
by cruel winter. Yet, come what may, I am constrained to summon courage to this deed; for
'tis perilous to disregard the commandments of the Father. Lofty-minded son of Themis who
counselleth aright, against my will, no less than thine, I must rivet thee with brazen bonds
no hand can loose to this desolate crag'.)

354. down] *Nbk 7*; down, *1820*, *1839*.

355 To execute a doom of new revenge.
Alas, I pity thee, and hate myself
That I can do no more — aye from thy sight
Returning, for a season Heaven seems Hell,
So thy worn form pursues me night and day,
360 Smiling reproach. Wise art thou, firm and good,
But vainly wouldst stand forth alone in strife
Against the Omnipotent; as yon clear lamps
That measure and divide the weary years
From which there is no refuge, long have taught
365 And long must teach. Even now thy Torturer arms
With the strange might of unimagined pains
The powers who scheme slow agonies in Hell,
And my commission is to lead them here,
Or what more subtle, foul, and savage fiends
370 People the abyss, and leave them to their task.
Be it not so . . . there is a secret known
To thee and to none else of living things
Which may transfer the sceptre of wide Heaven,
The fear of which perplexes the Supreme:
375 Clothe it in words, and bid it clasp his throne
In intercession; bend thy soul in prayer,
And like a suppliant in some gorgeous fane
Let the will kneel within thy haughty heart:

356. Alas,] *Nbk 7*; Alas! *1820, 1839.*

357–8. Cp. *Paradise Lost* i 254–5: 'The mind is its own place, and in itself / Can make a heaven of hell, a hell of heaven'; and iv 75, 'Which way I fly is hell; myself am hell'.

357. can do no more–] can do more *Nbk 7* (an obvious mistake, corrected in the press transcript.) more: *1820, 1839.*

358. season] season, *Nbk 7, 1820, 1839. Heaven seems Hell,*] heaven seems hell *Nbk 7*; heaven seems hell, *1820, 1839.*

359. So] i.e. 'to such a degree'.

364. taught] *Nbk 7, 1820*; taught, *1839.*

367. Hell,] hell, *Nbk 7.*

369. and] *Nbk 7*; or *1820, 1839* (perhaps a mistranscription; the repetition of 'Or . . . or' seems awkward and unlikely).

371. so . . .] *Nbk 7*; so! *1820, 1839. a secret*] In Aeschylus the secret known to Prometheus is that the offspring of Thetis will be greater than his father. The union of Jupiter with Thetis will therefore lead to his overthrow by his son, as Jupiter had overthrown his own father. But S. is never explicit in *PU* concerning the secret of his Prometheus; the forces leading to Jupiter's downfall in *PU* cannot be contained at the level of individual actions.

372. thee] *Nbk 7*; thee, *1820, 1839. things*] *Nbk 7*; things, *1820, 1839.*

377. fane] *Nbk 7*; fane, *1820, 1839.*

For benefits and meek submission tame
380 The fiercest and the mightiest.

Prometheus
Evil minds
Change good to their own nature. I gave all
He has; and in return he chains me here
Years, ages, night and day: whether the Sun
Split my parched skin, or in the moony night
385 The crystal-wingèd snow cling round my hair —
Whilst my belovèd race is trodden down
By his thought-executing ministers.
Such is the tyrant's recompense — 'tis just:
He who is evil can receive no good;
390 And for a world bestowed, or a friend lost,
He can feel hate, fear, shame — not gratitude:
He but requites me for his own misdeed.
Kindness to such is keen reproach, which breaks
With bitter stings the light sleep of Revenge.
395 Submission, thou dost know, I cannot try:
For what submission but that fatal word,
The death-seal of mankind's captivity,

380–98. Cp. *Prometheus Bound* 221–5:

τοιάδ' ἐξ ἐμοῦ
ὁ τῶν θεῶν τύραννος ὠφελημένος
κακαῖσι τιμαῖς ταῖσδέ μ' ἐξημείψατο·
ἔνεστι γάρ πως τοῦτο τῇ τυραννίδι
νόσημα, τοῖς φίλοισι μὴ πεποιθέναι.

('Such profit did the tyrant of Heaven have of me and with such foul return as this did he make requital; for it is the disease that somehow inheres in tyranny to have no faith in friends.')
Lines 380–1 recall *Paradise Lost* ix 122–3: 'all good to me becomes / Bane'.

385. crystal-wingèd] Cp. *Prometheus Bound* 993: λευκοπτέρωι . . . νιφάδι ('white-winged snow').
hair –] Nbk 7; hair: 1820, 1839.

386. trodden] In Nbk 7 *trodden* is written over *trampled*, which is the reading in *1820*. It is possible that S. reinstated *trampled* in the press transcript (see *BSM* ix 548), but a correction to the fair copy after despatch of the press transcript, introducing a pun on 'downtrodden', is also plausible.

387. thought-executing] Cp. *King Lear* III ii 4; S. perhaps intends a pun: 'carrying out orders (as fast as thought itself)', and 'killing (i.e. suppressing or penalising) free thought'.

388 recompense –] Nbk 7; recompense: 1820, 1839.

391. shame –] Nbk 7; shame; 1820, 1839.

395. know,] Nbk 7; know 1820, 1839. *try:*] Nbk 7, 1820; try; 1839.

396. that fatal word] The *secret* of line 371 (cp. note above, and III i 19 and note); the *fatal word* is never specified in S.'s version, but is made rather to carry an abstract symbolic import (see *Wasserman* 287–8).

Like the Sicilian's hair-suspended sword
Which trembles o'er his crown, would he accept
400 Or could I yield? — which yet I will not yield.
Let others flatter Crime where it sits throned
In brief Omnipotence; secure are they:
For Justice when triumphant will weep down
Pity, not punishment, on her own wrongs,
405 Too much avenged by those who err. I wait,
Enduring thus the retributive hour
Which since we spake is even nearer now —
But hark, the hell-hounds clamour: fear delay:
Behold! Heaven lowers under thy Father's frown.

Mercury
410 O that we might be spared — I to inflict,
And thou to suffer! Once more answer me:
Thou knowest not the period of Jove's power?

Prometheus
I know but this, that it must come.

Mercury
                                    Alas,
Thou canst not count thy years to come of pain?

398–9. The *Sicilian* was Damocles, who praised to excess the happiness and wealth of the tyrant Dionysius I, and was rewarded by being feasted beneath a sword hanging above his head by a single hair to symbolise the fear in which rulers live (see Cicero, *Tusculan Disputations* V xxi 61–2).

398. *sword*] Nbk 7; sword, *1820, 1839*.

399. *accept*] Nbk 7; accept, *1820, 1839*.

400. *yield? – which*] Nbk 7; yield? Which *1820, 1839*.

401. *Crime*] Nbk 7; Crime, *1820, 1839*.

402–5. S. held throughout his life to the belief that wrong-doers are made miserable by their own actions, and that this constitutes their worst punishment. Cp. Plato, *Gorgias* sect 508–9: '. . . wrong-doing is the worst harm that can befall a wrong-doer'. See note to II iv 110, and note to Q *Mab* ix 193–5.

402. *Omnipotence;*] Nbk 7, *1840*; Omnipotence: *1820, 1839*.

403. *Justice when triumphant*] Nbk 7; Justice, when triumphant, *1820, 1839*.

406. *thus*] Nbk 7; thus, 1820, 1839.   407. *now –*] Nbk 7; now. *1820, 1839*.

408. *clamour: fear delay:*] *1820*; clamour, fear delay Nbk 7; clamour. Fear delay! *1839*.

409. *lowers*] The sky appears dark and threatening (one of a sequence of references to a storm – probably volcanic – gathering in the background of the dramatic action); 'lours' is presumably intended.

410. *O*] Nbk 7; Oh, *1820, 1839*.   *spared –*] Nbk 7; spared: *1820, 1839*.

413. *Alas,*] Nbk 7; Alas! *1820, 1839*.

414. Cp. *Prometheus Bound* 257, οὐδ' ἐστὶν ἄθλου τέρμα σοι προκείμενον ('And is there no end assigned thee of thine ordeal?').

Prometheus
415   They last while Jove must reign: nor more, nor less
       Do I desire or fear.

Mercury
                    Yet pause, and plunge
       Into Eternity, where recorded time,
       Even all that we imagine, age on age,
       Seems but a point, and the reluctant mind
420   Flags wearily in its unending flight
       Till it sink, dizzy, blind, lost, shelterless;
       Perchance it has not numbered the slow years
       Which thou must spend in torture, unreprieved.

Prometheus
       Perchance no thought can count them — yet they pass.

Mercury
425   If thou might'st dwell among the Gods the while,
       Lapped in voluptuous joy?

Prometheus
                    I would not quit
       This bleak ravine, these unrepentant pains.

Mercury
       Alas! I wonder at, yet pity thee.

Prometheus
       Pity the self-despising slaves of Heaven,
430   Not me, within whose mind sits peace serene

---

415 *reign:*] *1820*; reign, *Nbk 7*; reign; *1839*.
420. *flight*] *Nbk 7, 1840*; flight, *1820, 1839*.
423. *unreprieved.*] *Nbk 7*; unreprieved? *1820, 1839*.
424. *them* –] *Nbk 7*; them, *1820, 1839*.
429–31. Perhaps recalling Portia's famous speech in the trial scene of *The Merchant of Venice*: 'But mercy is above this sceptred sway, / It is enthroned in the heart of kings, / It is an attribute to God himself' (IV i 188–90). In line 429 Prometheus implies that Mercury should save his pity for himself. Cp. also *Prometheus Bound* 966–7: τῆς σῆς λατρείας τὴν ἐμὴν δυσπραξίαν / σαφῶς ἐπίστας', οὐκ ἂν ἀλλάξαιμ' ἐγώ ('For thy servitude, rest thee sure, I'd not barter my hard lot, not I').
430. *serene*] *Nbk 7*; serene, *1820, 1839*.

As light in the sun, throned . . . How vain is talk!
Call up the fiends.

Ione

     O sister, look! White fire
Has cloven to the roots yon huge snow-loaded cedar;
How fearfully God's thunder howls behind!

Mercury

435 I must obey his words and thine — alas!
Most heavily remorse hangs at my heart!

Panthea

See where the child of Heaven with wingèd feet
Runs down the slanted sunlight of the dawn.

Ione

Dear sister, close thy plumes over thine eyes
440 Lest thou behold and die — they come, they come
Blackening the birth of day with countless wings,
And hollow underneath, like death.

First Fury

       Prometheus!

Second Fury
Immortal Titan!

Third Fury

   Champion of Heaven's slaves!

---

431. throned . . . How] throned . . . how *Nbk 7*; throned: how *1820, 1839*. *How vain is talk!*]
Cp. *Job* vi 25: 'How forcible are right words!'; and also *J&M* 472–3, 'How vain / Are words!'

432–4. The storm may at this point suggest Jupiter's angry impatience with Prometheus's
continuing resistance (see Stuart Sperry, *Shelley's Major Verse* (1988) 85); but the forces
involved will prove greater than Jupiter's power to control. In *Nbk 7* a partially canc. stage
direction at line 432 after Prometheus's speech reads '(thunder & lightning)'.

432. O] *Nbk 7*; O, *1820, 1839.*

433. cedar;] Cedar *Nbk 7.*

435. thine –] *Nbk 7*; thine: *1820, 1839.*

437. Heaven] *Nbk 7*; Heaven, *1820, 1839.* *feet*] *Nbk 7*; feet, *1820, 1839.* Cp. *Paradise Lost* iv
555–6, 'Thither came Uriel, gliding through the even / On a sunbeam, swift as a shooting
star', and iv 589–91: 'Uriel to his charge / Returned on that bright beam, whose point now
raised / Bore him slope downward to the sun.'

440. die –] *Nbk 7*; die: *1820, 1839.* *come,*] come *Nbk 7*; come: *1820, 1839.*

442. hollow underneath] i.e. the Furies have no form apart from specific forms of human anguish;
cp. lines 470–2 below. S. recalls *Aeneid* vi 293.

Prometheus
He whom some dreadful voice invokes is here,
445 Prometheus, the chained Titan. Horrible forms,
What and who are ye? Never yet there came
Phantasms so foul through monster-teeming Hell
From the all-miscreative brain of Jove;
Whilst I behold such execrable shapes
450 Methinks I grow like what I contemplate,
And laugh and stare in loathsome sympathy.

First Fury
We are the ministers of pain and fear,
And disappointment, and mistrust, and hate,
And clinging crime; and as lean dogs pursue
455 Through wood and lake some struck and sobbing fawn,

448. all-miscreative] Byron uses 'miscreator' in *Childe Harold's Pilgrimage* iv (1818) st. 125.

449. shapes] *Nbk 7*; shapes, *1820, 1839*.

450. Cp. 'Athanase' (no. 146), cancelled sequence 10: 'The mind becomes that which it contemplates', and see note. The line was adapted by S. in many contexts: see e.g. 'Mazenghi', no. 166, line 144, 'Till his mind grew like that it contemplated'; *Defence of Poetry* (of Petrarch's verses), 'It is impossible to feel them without becoming a portion of that beauty which we contemplate' *(Reiman (1977)* 497). *Notopoulos* 227 points out that the line is adapted from Paine's *Rights of Man*: 'It is the faculty of the human mind to become what it contemplates, and to act in unison with its object' *(Paine Writings* ii 350). *Claire Jnl* 123 notes the sentence in the entry for 9 February 1820; Godwin quotes it in *Political Justice*, and his *Enquirer* 33 would also have been well known to S.: 'When I read Thomson, I become Thomson; When I read Milton, I become Milton. I find myself a sort of intellectual chameleon, assuming the colour of the substances on which I rest.' S. noted in the 'Athanase' draft that the line had been 'said of Shakespeare', presumably with Hazlitt in mind (see note to 'Athanase' cancelled sequence 10). The doctrine (obviously, ironically inverted in this context; cp. IV 573–4) is Platonic; see *Republic* vi 500 quoted in 'Athanase' note, and also e.g. *Republic* iii 401: 'we must seek out those craftsmen who have the happy gift of tracing out the nature of the fair and graceful, that our young men may dwell as in a health-giving region where all that surrounds them is beneficent, whencesoever from fair works of art there smite upon their eyes and ears an affluence like a wind bringing health from happy regions, which, though they know it not, leads them from their earliest years into likeness and friendship and harmony with the principle of beauty' (trans. A. D. Lindsay; cp. also *Timaeus* 90d).

452–4. The First Fury represents personal and domestic forms of mental suffering and anguish.

454–7. Cp. Aeschylus, *Eumenides* 246: τετραυματισμένον γὰρ ὡσ κύων νεβρὸν / πρὸς αἷμα καὶ σταλαγμὸν ἐκματεύομεν ('we track as a dog tracks a wounded fawn, following the dripping blood'); and *Twelfth Night* I i 21–3: 'That instant was I turn'd into a hart, / And my desires, like fell and cruel hounds, / E'er since pursue me'. S.'s lines, like Shakespeare's, evoke the myth of Actaeon, the hunter who was turned to a deer by the goddess Artemis and hunted down by his own hounds in punishment for having seen her naked while bathing. S. also alludes to the story in *Epipsychidion* 272–4, and *Adonais* 274–9.

455. GM noted that *lake* seems a curious word in this context, and that *brake* would make much better sense; but *lake* is clear in *Nbk 7*.

We track all things that weep, and bleed, and live,
When the great King betrays them to our will.

Prometheus
O many fearful natures in one name,
I know ye, and these lakes and echoes know
460 The darkness and the clangour of your wings.
But why more hideous than your loathèd selves
Gather ye up in legions from the deep?

Second Fury
We knew not that: Sisters, rejoice, rejoice!

Prometheus
Can aught exult in its deformity?

Second Fury
465 The beauty of delight makes lovers glad,
Gazing on one another: so are we.
As from the rose which the pale priestess kneels
To gather for her festal crown of flowers
The aerial crimson falls, flushing her cheek,
470 So from our victim's destined agony
The shade which is our form invests us round,
Else are we shapeless as our mother Night.

Prometheus
I laugh your power, and his who sent you here,
To lowest scorn. — Pour forth the cup of pain.

First Fury
475 Thou thinkest we will rend thee bone from bone,
And nerve from nerve, working like fire within?

---

458. O] *Nbk 7*; Oh! *1820, 1839*.

459. *ye,*] *Nbk 7*; ye; *1820, 1839*.

466. *so are we*] i.e. glad.

470–2. i.e. these Furies take their form from specific human anxieties; cp. line 442 above.

471. *form*] Written above *shape* canc. in *Nbk 7*; presumably altered before transcription for the press, and in order to avoid the similarity with *shade* four words earlier.

472. *are we*] *Nbk 7*; we are *1820, 1839*. The Furies are called 'children of the night' in Aeschylus's *Eumenides* 791. *mother Night.*] Mother night *Nbk 7*.

474. *scorn. – Pour*] scorn. – pour *Nbk 7*; scorn. Pour *1820, 1839*.

Prometheus
Pain is my element, as hate is thine;
Ye rend me now: I care not.

Second Fury
                    Dost imagine
We will but laugh into thy lidless eyes?

Prometheus
480   I weigh not what ye do, but what ye suffer,
Being evil. Cruel was the Power which called
You, or aught else so wretched, into light.

Third Fury
Thou think'st we will live through thee, one by one,
Like animal life, and though we can obscure not
485   The soul which burns within, that we will dwell
Beside it, like a vain loud multitude
Vexing the self-content of wisest men:
That we will be dread thought beneath thy brain,
And foul desire round thine astonished heart,
490   And blood within thy labyrinthine veins
Crawling like agony?

---

477. Pain is my element] Cp. Southey's *Curse of Kehama* XIII ix 7–9: 'The pious soul hath framed unto itself / A second nature, to exist in pain / As in its own allotted element'. See also no. 68, 'A Tale of Society as it is', 86 and note.

479. lidless] Unclosed (i.e. unsleeping).

480. Cp. *J&M* 482–3: 'Those who inflict must suffer, for they see / The work of their own hearts'.

481. Power] Nbk 7; power *1820, 1839*.

484. animal life] i.e. 'nervous feeling'; the sensibility that animate creatures possess (Lat. *animalis*, 'of the nerves'). S. uses the phrase in *Q Mab* (see i 142 and note) and *R&H* (825, 1208). 'Animal life' was distinct from 'Brute life' (which informed inanimate Nature), 'Vegetable life' (which moved vegetables), and 'Intellectual life' (Imagination). 'The Animal life, by which [man] has Sensations, Appetites, and Desires, and feels Pleasure and Pain', 'The Animal Principle operates by nerves' (James Burnett, Lord Monboddo, *Ancient Metaphysics; or, the Science of Universals* (Edinburgh 1779) iii 6, 18). See also *Grabo (1930)* 70–1, and Timothy Clark, *Embodying Revolution: The Figure of the Poet in Shelley* (Oxford 1989) ch. 2, esp. p. 50.

485–6. Perhaps recalling Coleridge, *Religious Musings* (1794) 371–5:
> Lo! Priestley there, patriot, and saint, and sage,
> Him, full of years, from his loved native land
> Statesmen blood stained and priests idolatrous
> By dark lies maddening the blind multitude
> Drove with vain hate.

491. agony?] agony Nbk 7; agony. *1820, 1839.*

Prometheus

Why, ye are thus now;
Yet am I king over myself, and rule
The torturing and conflicting throngs within,
As Jove rules you when Hell grows mutinous.

Chorus of Furies

495 From the ends of the Earth, from the ends of the Earth,
Where the night has its grave and the morning its birth,
Come, come, come!
O ye who shake hills with the scream of your mirth
When cities sink howling in ruin; and ye
500 Who with wingless footsteps trample the sea,
And close upon Shipwreck and Famine's track
Sit chattering with joy on the foodless wreck;
Come, come, come!
Leave the bed, low, cold, and red,
505 Strewed beneath a nation dead;
Leave the hatred — as in ashes
Fire is left for future burning,

---

492. king over myself] These words are recalled at III iv 196–7. With lines 492–4, cp. *J&M* 183–5: 'We are assured / Much may be conquered, much may be endured / Of what degrades and crushes us.'

495ff. From the ends of the Earth] A Homeric phrase; cp. *Iliad* xiv 200 (it is recalled at IV 130 below). At this point Prometheus has conquered those Furies embodying merely personal tortures; consequently they call up reinforcements in the shape of Furies embodying larger-scale, external sources of human anguish. The Furies which now arrive (and speak from line 525) suggest S.'s earlier evocation of successive forms of social disaster – war, famine, tyranny, torture and so on – in *L&C* X iv, v, and viii. Note that in both *L&C* and in *PU* I the arrival of a first group is followed by a larger and more inclusive second group (perhaps influenced by the escalation of the French wars in Europe following the British declaration of war in February 1793). *Earth, . . . Earth*] Nbk 7; earth, . . . earth, *1820, 1839*.

497. come, come!] Come, Come *Nbk 7*.

498. O] Nbk 7; Oh, *1820, 1839. mirth*] Nbk 7; mirth, *1820, 1839*. The last line of S.'s fair copy of Act I in *Nbk 7*; the fair copy continues in *Nbk 8* (f. 1ʳ).

500. sea,] Sea *Nbk 8*.

501. track] Nbk 8; track, *1820, 1839*.

503. come, come!] Come, Come *Nbk 8*.

504ff. The verse style of the Furies from this point obviously recalls the Witches in *Macbeth*, and is also generally reminiscent of Coleridge's 'Fire, Famine and Slaughter' (1798); but the sustained complexity of S.'s versification to line 577 is distinctive. For further discussion of S.'s development of versification in this style see headnotes to nos 183, 187 and 202.

506–9. This passage inverts the closing metaphor of 'Ode to the West Wind', which was first published in *1820* (i.e. with *PU*).

506. hatred –] Nbk 8; hatred, *1820, 1839*.

507. burning,] burning, – *Nbk 8*; burning: *1820, 1839*.

It will burst in bloodier flashes
When ye stir it, soon returning;
510   Leave the self-contempt implanted
In young spirits sense-enchanted,
Misery's yet unkindled fuel;
Leave Hell's secrets half-unchanted
To the maniac dreamer: cruel
515   More than ye can be with hate
    Is he with fear.
    Come, come, come!
We are steaming up from Hell's wide gate,
And we burthen the blasts of the atmosphere,
520   But vainly we toil till ye come here.

Ione
Sister, I hear the thunder of new wings.

Panthea
These solid mountains quiver with the sound
Even as the tremulous air: their shadows make
The space within my plumes more black than night.

First Fury
525   Your call was as a wingèd car
Driven on whirlwinds fast and far;
It rapt us from red gulfs of war.

509. *returning;*] *Nbk 8*; returning: *1820, 1839*.

511. *spirits*] *Nbk 8*; spirits, *1820, 1839*.

512. *fuel;*] *Nbk 8*; fuel: *1820, 1839*.

513. *half-unchanted*] *Nbk 8*; half unchanted *1820*; half unchanted, *1839*; *half-unchanted* is S.'s coinage (according to *OED*).

514. *dreamer:*] *Nbk 8*; dreamer; *1820, 1839*.

515. *ye*] i.e. the newly-arriving Furies.

517. *come, come!*] Come come *Nbk 8*.

520. In *Nbk 8* this line is followed by a canc. stage direction: 'Enter rushing by groupes of horrible forms; they speak as they [rush by *canc.*] pass in chorus'. The speeches by Ione and Panthea at lines 521–4, which replace and incorporate this stage direction, were added later by S. on the facing page in *Nbk 8*.

525–31. The four Furies who speak here resume various effects, causes and consequences of war. The socio-historical phenomena they embody echo S.'s more discursive treatments in *L&C*: cp. line 527 with *L&C* VI iv ff., X iv–xi; 528 with *L&C* V iv, X xi ff.; 529 with *L&C* X xxi ff.; and 530–1 with *L&C* X xxxii ff.

525. *car*] *Nbk 8, 1820*; car, *1839*.

527. *rapt us*] 'Carried us away'.

> *Second Fury*
> From wide cities famine-wasted —
>
> *Third Fury*
> Groans half heard, and blood untasted —
>
> *Fourth Fury*
> Kingly conclaves stern and cold
> Where blood with gold is bought and sold;
>
> *Fifth Fury*
> From the furnace white and hot
> In which —
>
> *A Fury*
> Speak not — whisper not:
> I know all that ye would tell,
> But to speak might break the spell
> Which must bend the Invincible,
> The stern of thought;
> He yet defies the deepest power of Hell.

530

535

---

528. *cities famine-wasted –*] *Nbk 8*; cities, famine-wasted; *1820, 1839*.

529. *untasted –*] *Nbk 8*; untasted; *1820, 1839*.

530. *Kingly conclaves*] *Nbk 8, 1820*; Kingly conclaves, *1839*. Often taken as a reference to the Congress of Vienna, where in 1815 the victorious European monarchies parcelled out the defeated Napoleonic empire and sought to create a system of 'buffer' states to contain any future threat of revolutionary insurgence in western Europe. However, *conclave* may suggest a more exclusive and secretive exertion of influence and control. *cold*] *Nbk 7*; cold, *1820, 1839*.

531. *blood with gold*] A recurring collocation in S.'s poetry; see e.g. *Q Mab* iv 195, *L&C* V xiv, *Mask of Anarchy* xvi, lxxii, 'Sonnet: England in 1819', *Witch of Atlas* 190, *Hellas* 1095, *TL* 287. Cp. *Address to the People on the Death of the Princess Charlotte* (1817): 'Kings and their ministers have in every age been distinguished from other men by a thirst for expenditure and bloodshed' (*Prose Works* i 235); and S.'s letter to Peacock, 17 July 1816: 'Leave Mammon and Jehovah to those who delight in wickedness and slavery – their altars are stained with blood or polluted with gold, the price of blood' (*L* i 490). *is*] was *Nbk 8* (presumably an alteration to the press transcript).

532. *furnace*] *Nbk 8*; furnace, *1820, 1839*. *hot*] *Nbk 8*; hot, *1820, 1839*.

533. *not –*] *Nbk 8*; not; *1820*; not; *1839*.

538. This line is followed in *Nbk 8* by a stage direction: '[Another *canc.*] a Fury rushing from the crowd'.

Tear the veil!

A Fury

Another Fury

It is torn!

Chorus
The pale stars of the morn

540 Shine on a misery dire to be borne.
Dost thou faint, mighty Titan? We laugh thee to scorn.
Dost thou boast the clear knowledge thou waken'dst for man?
Then was kindled within him a thirst which outran
Those perishing waters; a thirst of fierce fever,

545 Hope, love, doubt, desire — which consume him for ever.
One came forth of gentle worth
Smiling on the sanguine earth;
His words outlived him, like swift poison
Withering up truth, peace, and pity.

550 Look where round the wide horizon
Many a million-peopled city
Vomits smoke in the bright air —
Hark that outcry of despair!
'Tis his mild and gentle ghost

539–40. These lines imply that morning is beginning to break.

539. Tear the veil! is followed in *Nbk 8* by a stage direction: 'The Furies having mingled in a strange dance divide, & in the background is seen a plain covered with burning cities'. S.'s layout in *Nbk 8* confirms that 539 is a single line, distributed across three speakers, in anapaestic tetrameter. Cp. *J&M* 382–3: 'I must remove / A veil from my pent mind! 'Tis torn aside!' *torn!*] *Nbk 8*; torn. *1820, 1839.*

540. misery] *Nbk 8*; misery, *1820, 1839.*

545. desire –] *Nbk 8*; desire, *1820, 1839.*

546–77. The Furies offer a mocking vision of Christ (cp. *PVR, SC* 546 *SC* vi 963–4), whose words and deeds have been turned against themselves by the perversions of institutional Christianity (546–65), which is followed by a similarly mocking vision of the failure of the French Revolution (566–77). Neither example is explicitly identified; they stand as *types* of experience: cp. S.'s political-historical analyses in 'Ode to Liberty' and 'Lines Written among the Euganean Hills'.

546. worth] *Nbk 8*; worth, *1820, 1839.*

550–2. 'Cities burning in the flames of crusades and persecutions' (GM). Cp. *Q Mab* vii 38–42: 'the smoke / Of burning towns, the cries of female helplessness, / Unarmed old age, and youth, and infancy, / Horribly massacred, ascend to heaven / In honour of his name'. There is a canc. stage direction after line 552 in *Nbk 8*: 'a shadow passes over the scene & a piercing shriek is heard'.

550. Look] *Nbk 8*; Look! *1820, 1839.*

552. air –] *Nbk 8*; air. *1820, 1839.*

553. Hark] *Nbk 8*; Mark *1820, 1829, 1839*; perhaps a printer's error, but more probably a mistranscription in the press transcript.

555   Wailing for the faith he kindled:
                        Look again, the flames almost
                        To a glow-worm's lamp have dwindled:
                        The survivors round the embers
                        Gather in dread.
560   Joy, joy, joy!
Past ages crowd on thee, but each one remembers;
And the future is dark, and the present is spread
Like a pillow of thorns for thy slumberless head.

Semichorus I

Drops of bloody agony flow
565   From his white and quivering brow.
                    Grant a little respite now —
                    See, a disenchanted Nation
                    Springs like day from desolation;
                    To Truth its state is dedicate,
570   And Freedom leads it forth, her mate;
                    A legioned band of linkèd brothers
                    Whom Love calls children —

Semichorus II

                                  'Tis another's —
            See how kindred murder kin!

556. *again,*] Nbk 8, 1820; again! 1839.

559–65. Past, present and future alike torture Prometheus. The Furies identify Prometheus's suffering with Christ's; their image of the present as *a pillow of thorns* for Prometheus recurs at line 598 as Prometheus contemplates the Furies' vision of Christ. With 564–5 Cp. *Luke* xx ii 44: 'And being in agony he prayed more earnestly: and his sweat was as it were great drops of blood falling down to the ground'.

560. *joy, joy!*] Joy, Joy, Nbk 8.

566. *now –*] Nbk 8; now: 1820, 1839.

567. *See,*] See Nbk 8, 1820; See! 1839.   *a disenchanted Nation*] Nbk 8; nation 1820, 1839. Cp. Coleridge, 'France: an Ode' (1798) 28–30: 'when to whelm the disenchanted nation / Like fiends embattled by a wizard's wand, / The Monarchs marched in evil day'. For S.'s use of *disenchanted* in a positive sense – 'released from an evil spell' – see also 'Mazenghi' (no. 166) 33 and note to lines 30–5.

569. *Truth*] truth Nbk 8, 1820.

571. *brothers*] Nbk 8, 1820; brothers, 1839.

572. *another's –*] Nbk 8; another's: 1820; another's 1839. i.e. hatred's; 'the ideals of the Revolution are lost in the bloodshed of internal struggles' (GM).

573–7. Cp. Coleridge, 'France: an Ode' 45–6: 'all the fierce and drunken passions wove / A dance more wild than e'er was maniac's dream!' Cp. also *Isaiah* xliii 2–3: 'Wherefore art thou red in thine apparel, and thy garments like him that treadeth in the winefat? I have trodden the winepress alone; and of the people there was none with me: for I will tread them in mine anger, and trample them in my fury; and their blood shall be sprinkled upon my garments, and I will stain all my raiment'; and *Revelation* xiv 18: 'And another angel came out

575

> 'Tis the vintage-time for Death and Sin:
> Blood, like new wine, bubbles within;
> Till Despair smothers
> The struggling World — which slaves and tyrants win.
>
> [*All the Furies vanish, except one*

Ione

> Hark, sister! what a low yet dreadful groan
> Quite unsuppressed is tearing up the heart

580

> Of the good Titan, as storms tear the deep,
> And beasts hear the sea moan in inland caves.
> Darest thou observe how the fiends torture him?

Panthea

> Alas, I looked forth twice, but will no more.

Ione

> What didst thou see?

Panthea

> A woeful sight — a youth

585

> With patient looks nailed to a crucifix.

Ione

> What next?

Panthea

> The heaven around, the earth below
> Was peopled with thick shapes of human death,

---

from the altar, which had power over fire; and cried with a loud cry to him that had the sharp sickle, saying, Thrust in thy sharp sickle, and gather the clusters of the vine of the earth; for her grapes are fully ripe'.

574. Death] Nbk 8; death *1820, 1839. Sin:*] Sin Nbk 8; sin: *1820*; sin. *1839.*

575. within;] within Nbk 8; within: *1820, 1839.*

577. World –] Nbk 8; world, *1820, 1839.* In Nbk 8 the stage direction after this line reads 'depart but' for 'vanish, except'; cp. note to line 634 below.

583. Alas,] Nbk 8; Alas! *1820, 1839.*

584–654. Panthea recapitulates and meditates on the Furies' visions of Christ (584–5) and the French Revolution (586–93). Prometheus does likewise, 598–615 (Christ), 648–54 (Revolution).

584. sight –] Nbk 8; sight: *1820, 1839.*

586. heaven] Heaven Nbk 8. *earth*] Earth Nbk 8.

All horrible, and wrought by human hands,
Though some appeared the work of human hearts,
590 For men were slowly killed by frowns and smiles:
And other sights too foul to speak and live
Were wandering by — let us not tempt worse fear
By looking forth: those groans are grief enough.

Fury
Behold, an emblem: those who do endure
595 Deep wrongs for man, and scorn, and chains, but heap
Thousandfold torment on themselves and him.

Prometheus
Remit the anguish of that lighted stare;
Close those wan lips; let that thorn-wounded brow
Stream not with blood — it mingles with thy tears!
600 Fix, fix those tortured orbs in peace and death,
So thy sick throes shake not that crucifix,
So those pale fingers play not with thy gore.
O, horrible! Thy name I will not speak,
It hath become a curse. I see, I see
605 The wise, the mild, the lofty, and the just,
Whom thy slaves hate for being like to thee,
Some hunted by foul lies from their heart's home,
An early-chosen, late-lamented home,
As hooded ounces cling to the driven hind;

589. Though] Nbk 8; And *1820, 1829, 1839*; perhaps S.'s change to the press transcript, but the sense seems to require *Though*.

590. Cp. *Henry V* III iv 17–18: 'On whom, as in despite, the sun looks pale, / Killing their fruit with frowns'.

592. by – let] Nbk 8; by. Let *1820, 1839*.

594–6. Cp. *Paradise Lost* i 209–20.

594. Behold,] Nbk 8; Behold *1820, 1839.* *an emblem*] Christ crucified.

596. This line is followed in *Nbk 8* by a stage direction: 'a darkness [*above* shadow *canc.*] floats slowly across the scene'.

599. blood –] Nbk 8; blood; *1820, 1839.*

601ff. Prometheus's vision of the crucifixion may owe something to S.'s recent first exposure to fifteenth- and sixteenth-century Italian paintings; see his letter from Bologna to Peacock, 9 November 1818 (*L* ii 49–53).

608. home,] Nbk 8; home; *1820, 1839.*

609. hooded ounces] Hunting leopards, kept hooded until released at their prey.

513

610 Some linked to corpses in unwholesome cells:
Some — hear I not the multitude laugh loud? —
Impaled in lingering fire: and mighty realms
Float by my feet like sea-uprooted isles,
Whose sons are kneaded down in common blood
615 By the red light of their own burning homes —

Fury
Blood thou canst see, and fire; and canst hear groans;
Worse things unheard, unseen, remain behind.

Prometheus
Worse?

Fury
In each human heart terror survives
The ravin it has gorged: the loftiest fear
620 All that they would disdain to think were true:
Hypocrisy and custom make their minds
The fanes of many a worship, now outworn.
They dare not devise good for man's estate,
And yet they know not that they do not dare.
625 The good want power, but to weep barren tears.
The powerful goodness want: worse need for them.
The wise want love, and those who love want wisdom;
And all best things are thus confused to ill.
Many are strong and rich, — and would be just —

611. hear] Nbk 8; Hear *1820, 1839.*

612. Impaled in lingering fire] S. appears to conflate two barbaric methods of execution, impalement, and burning at the stake.

613. feet] Nbk 8; feet, *1820, 1839.*

615. homes –] Nbk 8; homes. *1820, 1839.*

618–19. 'Superstitious fear lingers in every man's mind after he has stopped believing in the causes of it' (GM).

619. ravin] Prey, spoil. The reading in *1820* and *1829* is *ruin*, perhaps a printer's error, or a mistaken proof correction (*ravin*, with a canc. terminal *e*, is clear in Nbk 8); Mary S. corrected the reading in *1839*, suggesting that the Nbk 8 reading was on S.'s list of errata.

622. fanes] Temples.

627. love,] Nbk 8; love; *1820, 1839.*

628. Cp. *Paradise Lost* iv 201–4:

> So little knows
> Any, but God alone, to value right
> The good before him, but perverts best things
> To worst abuse, or to their meanest use.

629. rich, –] Nbk 8; rich, *1820, 1839.   just –]* Nbk 8; just, *1820, 1839.*

630 But live among their suffering fellow men
    As if none felt: they know not what they do.

Prometheus
Thy words are like a cloud of wingèd snakes;
And yet, I pity those they torture not.

Fury
Thou pitiest them? I speak no more!

[*Vanishes*

Prometheus
                                        Ah woe!
635 Ah woe! Alas! pain, pain ever, forever?
    I close my tearless eyes, but see more clear
    Thy works within my woe-illumèd mind,
    Thou subtle tyrant . . . Peace is in the grave —
    The grave hides all things beautiful and good:
640 I am a God and cannot find it there —
    Nor would I seek it. For, though dread revenge,
    This is defeat, fierce King, not victory!
    The sights with which thou torturest gird my soul
    With new endurance, till the hour arrives
645 When they shall be no types of things which are.

630. *fellow men*] *Nbk 8*; fellow-men *1820, 1839*.

631. The last and subtlest Fury exactly echoes, with cruel irony, Christ's words on the cross (see *Luke* xxiii 34).

633. *yet,*] *Nbk 8*; yet *1820, 1839*.

634. In *Nbk 8* the stage direction 'Vanishes' reads 'Exit'; as *Zillman Text* notes, the change accords with the earlier alteration at line 577 above.

635. *forever?*] *Nbk 8*; for ever! *1820, 1839*.

637. *woe-illumèd*] *Nbk 8 1820*; woe-illumined *1829, 1839* (an error introduced by Galignani and thereafter perpetuated). 'His mind is not *illumined*, but woe-lit' (GM).

638-40. Cp. *Prometheus Bound* 752-4:

> ἦ δυσπετῶς ἂν τοὺς ἐμοὺς ἄθλους φέροις,
> ὅτωι θανεῖν μέν ἐστιν οὐ πεπρωμένον·
> αὕτη γὰρ ἦν ἂν πημάτων ἀπαλλαγή

('Ah, hardly would'st thou bear my agonies to whom it is not foredoomed to die; for death had freed me from my sufferings'.)

638. *tyrant . . .*] *Nbk 8*; tyrant! *1820, 1839*. *grave –*] *Nbk 8*; grave. *1820, 1839*.

640. *there –*] *Nbk 8*; there, *1820, 1839*.

641. *it. For,*] *Nbk 8*; it: for, *1820, 1839*.

642. *defeat, fierce King,*] defeat Fierce King *Nbk 8*; defeat, fierce king, *1820*; defeat, fierce king! *1839*.

515

Panthea
Alas! what sawest thou more?

Prometheus
           There are two woes:
To speak, and to behold; thou spare me one.
Names are there, Nature's sacred watchwords — they
Were borne aloft in bright emblazonry;
650 The nations thronged around, and cried aloud
As with one voice, 'Truth, Liberty, and Love!'
Suddenly fierce confusion fell from Heaven
Among them — there was strife, deceit, and fear;
Tyrants rushed in, and did divide the spoil.
655 This was the shadow of the truth I saw.

The Earth
I felt thy torture, Son, with such mixed joy
As pain and Virtue give. To cheer thy state
I bid ascend those subtle and fair spirits

646. thou more?] *Nbk 8*; thou? *1820, 1839*; obviously an error, creating an ametrical line.

647. 'Don't make me suffer the same pain twice by describing what I saw' (GM). *speak,*] *1820*; speak *Nbk 8, 1839*.

648–54. This account of the failure of the French Revolution echoes a number of similar analyses by S.: see for example *Proposals for an Association of Philanthropists* (1812), *Prose Works* i 51–2; Preface to *L&C*; and *PVR* (*SC* vi 978–81). S. claimed in a letter to Elizabeth Hitchener that he had 'done about 200 pages' of a 'tale', to be entitled *Hubert Cauvin*, 'in which I design to exhibit the cause of the failure of the French revolution' (2 January 1812, *L* i 218, 229; he repeated the claim in a letter to Godwin, 10 January 1812); no further reference to the project is known after January 1812.

648. watchwords –] *Nbk 8*; watch-words, *1820, 1839*.

650. The nations] And nations *Nbk 8*; presumably S.'s change to the press transcript. *aloud*] *Nbk 8*; aloud, *1820, 1839*.

651. voice, 'Truth, Liberty, and Love!'] voice, truth liberty and love – *Nbk 8*; voice, Truth, liberty, and love! *1820, 1839*. Echoing the Revolutionary slogan, *Liberté, Égalité, Fraternité!*

652. Heaven] *Nbk 8*; heaven *1820, 1839*.

653. them –] *Nbk 8*; them: *1820, 1839*. *fear;*] *Nbk 8*; fear: *1820, 1839*.

656. torture, Son,] torture Son, *Nbk 8*; torture, son, *1820, 1839*.

657. Virtue] *Nbk 8*; virtue *1820, 1839*.

658. spirits] *Nbk 8*; spirits, *1820, 1839*.

658–61. The Spirits like birds 'Whose homes are the dim caves of human thought' appear to derive from S.'s reading of Alexandre de Humboldt and Bonpland, *Personal Narrative of travels to the equinoctial regions of the New Continent during the years 1799–1804*, trans. H. M. Williams iii (1818) 119–20, 126. The Spirits represent sources of hope and mental support, in contrast to the mental tortures of the Furies (see note to line 331 above). *Wasserman* 300 suggests a 'Christian ancestry' for the Spirits, contrasting with the Hellenic character of the Furies and deriving from the New Testament angels who minister to Christ (see *Matthew* iv

Whose homes are the dim caves of human thought,
660 And who inhabit, as birds wing the wind,
Its world-surrounding ether: they behold
Beyond that twilight realm, as in a glass,
The future: may they speak comfort to thee!

Panthea
Look, Sister, where a troop of spirits gather,
665 Like flocks of clouds in spring's delightful weather,
Thronging in the blue air!

Ione
                                    And see! more come,
Like fountain-vapours when the winds are dumb,
That climb up the ravine in scattered lines.
And hark! is it the music of the pines?
670 Is it the lake? Is it the waterfall?

Panthea
'Tis something sadder, sweeter far than all.

Chorus of Spirits
From unremembered ages we
Gentle guides and guardians be

11, *Mark* i 13, *Luke* xxii 43). The individual Spirits have been variously identified (see notes to 694–800 below). GM glosses the first four as representing 'qualities that derive only from human minds (*whose homes are the dim caves of human thought*), but that have free access to all humanity throughout the world (thought is an atmosphere that covers the earth as the air does, and these qualities fly in it like birds)'. See W. Hildebrand, 'A Look at the Third and Fourth Spirit Songs' (*KSJ* xx (1971) 87–99) for interesting detailed commentary. The versification of the Spirits' Songs recalls the manner employed for the Furies, but is worked out with a complexity of pattern and variation singular even by S.'s standard in *PU* (e.g. the alternating 14 and 15 line stanzas of the first four Spirits' Songs, with rhymes based on triplets but varied by couplets and an unrhymed line 10, except for the Fourth Spirit whose line 10 is picked up in the closing couplet).

661. world-surrounding] Cp. 'To Constantia Singing' (no. 155) 13 and note. *they behold*] and they see *Nbk* 8; presumably S.'s alteration to the press transcript.

664. Look, Sister,] Look Sister *Nbk* 8; Look, sister, *1820, 1839*.

669. hark!] *Nbk* 8, *1839*; hark? *1820, 1829*; possibly an error in the press transcript (the punctuation is cramped and obscure at this point in *Nbk* 8). The correction in *1839* may derive from S.'s errata list.

671. The Spirits' songs, whose *music* (669) anticipates the sounds that will draw Asia and Panthea towards their destiny in Act II, are both sweet and sad (cp. 756); Vida Scudder (*PU*, ed. V. Scudder, 1892, 150) notes that 'Like the Furies, [the Spirits] fully recognise the evil in the world; unlike the Furies, they do not gloat over it, but lament it'.

672–91. Kathleen Raine ('Thomas Taylor, Plato, and the English Romantic Movement', *Sewanee Review* lxxvi (1968) 230–57, 254–5) cites Apuleius as a source for this Song (253–7).

Of Heaven-oppressed mortality;
675 And we breathe, and sicken not,
The atmosphere of human thought:
Be it dim and dank and grey
Like a storm-extinguished day
Travelled o'er by dying gleams;
680 Be it bright as all between
Cloudless skies and windless streams,
Silent, liquid, and serene —
As the birds within the wind,
As the fish within the wave,
685 As the thoughts of man's own mind
Float through all above the grave,
We make there our liquid lair,
Voyaging cloudlike and unpent
Through the boundless element —
690 Thence we bear the prophecy
Which begins and ends in thee!

Ione
More yet come, one by one: the air around them
Looks radiant, like the air around a star.

First Spirit
On a battle-trumpet's blast
695 I fled hither, fast, fast, fast,

674. Heaven-oppressed] Nbk 8; heaven-oppressed *1820, 1839*.

677. dim and dank and grey] Nbk 8; dim, and dank, and grey, *1820, 1839*.

678. day] Nbk 8; day, *1820, 1839*.

682. serene –] Nbk 8; serene; *1820, 1839*.

686. grave,] grave Nbk 8; grave; *1820, 1839*.

687. there] Nbk 8 *1839*; these *1820, 1829*; probably corrected by Mary S. in *1839* from S.'s errata list; *there* is undoubtedly the correct reading. S. marks the internal rhyme (on *lair*) with a comma in Nbk 8; and *these* misunderstands the sense, as the reference of *there* is to the *atmosphere* of line 676. *liquid*] Clear, transparent.

689. element –] Nbk 8; element: *1820, 1839*.

690. prophecy] Looking forward to the oracular / prophetic elements which come to prominence in the action of Act II (cp. 706, 799); but also presumably here a reference to the hope embodied in Prometheus's 'secret' and in the power of his recall of the curse.

693. radiant, like] radiant like Nbk 8; radiant as *1820, 1839*. Perhaps S.'s alteration to the transcript; but as *BSM* ix 566 notes 'this is the sort of grammatical correction Peacock might have felt licensed to make as proofreader'. The fair copy reading is here preferred.

694–707. The First Spirit, like the Furies and other Spirits, is not explicitly identified. The First Spirit is associated with peace, liberty, 'courage and steadfastness in opposing tyranny' (*Butter (1954)* 179).

'Mid the darkness upward cast —
From the dust of creeds outworn,
From the tyrant's banner torn,
Gathering round me, onward borne,
700   There was mingled many a cry —
Freedom! Hope! Death! Victory!
Till they faded through the sky
And one sound above, around,
One sound beneath, around, above,
705   Was moving; 'twas the soul of love;
'Twas the hope, the prophecy
Which begins and ends in thee.

Second Spirit
A rainbow's arch stood on the sea
Which rocked beneath, immoveably;
710   And the triumphant Storm did flee
Like a conqueror swift and proud,

696. *cast* -] *Nbk 8*; cast. *1820, 1839.*

702. *sky*] *Nbk 8*; sky; *1820, 1839.*

706. *prophecy*] *Nbk 8*; prophecy, *1820, 1839.*

707. After this line in *Nbk 8* is a 14-line song for the second spirit, all of which is canc. by two vertical lines:

I leaped on the wings of the Earth-star damp
As it rose on the steam of a slaughtered camp –
The sleeping newt heard not our tramp
As swift [and silent we did pass *canc.*] as the wing of fire may pass
[Among *canc.*] We threaded the points of long thick grass
Which hide the green pools of the morass
But shook a water-serpents couch
In a cleft skull, of many such
The widest; at the meteors touch
The snake did seem to see in dream
Thrones & dungeons overthrown
Visions how unlike his own . . .
'Twas the hope the prophecy
Which begins & ends in thee

708–22. The Second Spirit is associated with justice (i.e. mercy), and 'the capacity for self-sacrifice' (*Butter (1954)* 179). Cp. Cicero, *De Re Publica* III xx: 'What then would your just man do, if, in a case of shipwreck, he saw a weaker man than himself get possession of a plank? . . . If . . . he prefers death to inflicting unjustifiable injury on his neighbour, he will be an eminently honourable and just man, but not the less a fool, because he saved another's life at the expense of his own'.

708. *sea*] *Nbk 8*; sea, *1820, 1839*; it is the *rainbow's arch* that is immoveable.

710. *Storm*] *Nbk 8*; storm *1820, 1839.*   *flee*] *Nbk 8*; flee, *1820, 1839.*

711. *conqueror*] *Nbk 8*; conqueror, *1820, 1839.*   *proud*] proud, *Nbk 8, 1820, 1839.*

519

       Between, with many a captive cloud,
       A shapeless, dark and rapid crowd,
       Each by lightning riven in half:
715   I heard the thunder hoarsely laugh:
       Mighty fleets were strewn like chaff
       And spread beneath a hell of death
       O'er the white waters. I alit
       On a great ship lightning-split,
720   And speeded hither on the sigh
       Of one who gave an enemy
       His plank — then plunged aside to die.

Third Spirit
       I sate beside a sage's bed,
       And the lamp was burning red
725   Near the book where he had fed,
       When a Dream with plumes of flame
       To his pillow hovering came,
       And I knew it was the same
       Which had kindled long ago
730   Pity, eloquence, and woe;
       And the world awhile below
       Wore the shade its lustre made.
       It has borne me here as fleet
       As Desire's lightning feet:
735   I must ride it back ere morrow,
       Or the sage will wake in sorrow.

Fourth Spirit
       On a Poet's lips I slept
       Dreaming like a love-adept

712. between,] Nbk 8; Between *1820, 1839. cloud,*] *1840*; cloud *Nbk 8, 1820, 1839.*

722. plank –] *Nbk 8*; plank, *1820, 1839.*

723–36. The Third Spirit is associated with wisdom and philosophy.

726. Dream] dream *Nbk 8. flame*] *Nbk 8*; flame, *1820, 1839.*

733. borne] *Nbk 8*; born *1820*; first corrected in *1829.*

737–51. The Fourth Spirit is associated with poetry and the imagination. 'S. sets out . . . from a scientifically-observed piece of reality (the insects and flowers are identified; the source and angle of the lighting defined), but he is not interested in physical details as details (like Clare), nor in bees as bees (like Keats): what he perceives in the natural world gives only a physical basis for what concerns him as a poet – the essence of the human situation reflected in art ("Forms more real than living man"). The bees are on a mission of renewal amid forms of life that spring irrepressibly . . . over the ruins of . . . greatness and oppression' (GM).

737. Poet's] Poets *Nbk 8*; poet's *1820, 1839.*

738. love-adept] i.e. one deeply versed in love (*adept* was originally used for a skilled alchemist).

	In the sound his breathing kept;
740	Nor seeks nor finds he mortal blisses,
	But feeds on the aërial kisses
	Of shapes that haunt thought's wildernesses.
	He will watch from dawn to gloom
	The lake-reflected sun illume
745	The yellow bees i' the ivy-bloom,
	Nor heed nor see what things they be;
	But from these create he can
	Forms more real than living man,
	Nurslings of immortality! —
750	One of these awakened me,
	And I sped to succour thee.

Ione

Behold'st thou not two shapes from the east and west
Come, as two doves to one belovèd nest,
Twin nurslings of the all-sustaining air
755 On swift still wings glide down the atmosphere?
And hark! their sweet sad voices; 'tis despair
Mingled with love, and then dissolved in sound.

Panthea

Canst thou speak, sister? all my words are drowned.

---

745. *i' the*] In *Nbk 8* S. first wrote *in the* and then deleted the *n*. *1820, 1839* and many subsequent *eds* (e.g. *Hutchinson*) read *in the*.

746. *see*] see, *Nbk 8, 1820, 1839*.

747–9. Cp. Byron, 'The Dream' (1816) 19–22: 'The mind can make / Substance, and people planets of its own / With beings brighter than have been, and give / A breath to forms which can outlive all flesh.'

749. *immortality! –*] *Nbk 8*; immortality! *1820, 1839*. Cp. 'Hymn to Venus' (no. 161) 48–51: 'In Venus Jove did soft desire awaken, / That by her own enchantments overtaken / She might, no more from human union free, / Burn for a nursling of mortality.'

752–800. See headnotes to 'Behold, sweet Sister mine' and 'The Two Spirits' (nos 181–2).

753–4. Echoing the description of Paolo and Francesca (whose story, like the Fifth and Sixth Spirits here imaged, mingles love and despair; cp. 756–7) in *Inferno* v 82–4: 'As doves / By fond desire invited, on wide wings / And firm, to their sweet nest returning home, / Cleave the air, wafted by their will along' (trans. Cary).

756. And hark – their sweet sad voices, tis despair *Nbk 8*; And hark! their sweet, sad voices! 'tis despair *1820, 1839*. S.'s punctuation in *Nbk 8* is unclear; he first wrote an exclamation mark after *voices*, then modified it (but without a clarifying cancellation), to either a comma or a semicolon (see *BSM* ix 568).

757. *love,*] *Nbk 8*; love *1820, 1839*.

Ione
Their beauty gives me voice. See how they float
760 On their sustaining wings of skiey grain,
Orange and azure deepening into gold:
Their soft smiles light the air like a star's fire.

Chorus of Spirits
Hast thou beheld the form of Love?

Fifth Spirit
As over wide dominions
I sped, like some swift cloud that wings the wide air's wildernesses,
765 That planet-crested Shape swept by on lightning-braided pinions,
Scattering the liquid joy of life from his ambrosial tresses:
His footsteps paved the world with light — but as I passed 'twas fading,
And hollow Ruin yawned behind: great Sages bound in madness,
And headless patriots, and pale youths who perished unupbraiding
770 Gleamed in the Night I wandered o'er — till thou, O King of sadness,
Turned by thy smile the worst I saw to recollected gladness.

Sixth Spirit
Ah sister, Desolation is a delicate thing:
It walks not on the Earth, it floats not on the air,

760. *skiey grain*] i.e. coloured like the sky (as in 761); cp. *Paradise Lost* v 285: 'Sky-tinctured grain'.

762. *soft*] Changed by S. from *sad* in Nbk 8 f. 16ᵛ (not recorded in *BSM* ix).

763–79. The Fifth and Sixth Spirits are associated with love and despair (cp. 756–7 above), conceived as inseparably linked in pre-revolutionary experience.

765. *planet-crested*] Love wears the crest or badge of Venus. *Shape*] Nbk 8; shape *1820, 1839*. *lightning-braided pinions*] Love's wings are electric; S. was familiar with contemporary scientific thinking which grouped certain phenomena – electricity, magnetism, heat, light – as 'imponderables' which were explained by positing the existence of weightless substances which transmitted cause-and-effect relationships as material operations involving a superfine 'ether'. In the version elaborated by Adam Walker, who taught S. at Eton, the 'imponderables' were considered different forms of one substance, which also took physical forms within humans and included the sensation of love (cp. I 122–3, 133–4, III iii 148–52, III iv 17–18, and see *Walker* 203, and also *Grabo (1930)* ch. 8).

767. *light* –] Nbk 8; light; *1820, 1839*.

768. *Sages*] Nbk 8; sages *1820, 1839*.

769. *perished unupbraiding*] Nbk 8; perished, unupbraiding, *1820, 1839*.

770. *Night*] Nbk 8. Here punctuated as in Nbk 8; this line reads *Gleamed in the night. I wandered o'er, till thou, O King of sadness*, in *1820* and *1839*.

772. *Ah sister,*] Nbk 8; Ah, sister! *1820, 1839*.

773. *Earth,*] Earth Nbk 8; earth, *1820, 1839*.

772–9. Cp. S.'s trans. of Plato, *Symposium* 195: 'There were need of some poet like Homer to celebrate the delicacy and tenderness of Love. For Homer says, that the goddess Calamity

But treads with lulling footstep, and fans with silent wing
775 The tender hopes which in their hearts the best and gentlest bear,
Who, soothed to false repose by the fanning plumes above,
And the music-stirring motion of its soft and busy feet,
Dream visions of aërial joy, and call the monster Love,
And wake, and find the shadow Pain — as he whom now we greet.

Chorus
780 Though Ruin now Love's shadow be,
Following him destroyingly
On Death's white and wingèd steed
Which the fleetest cannot flee —

---

is delicate, and that her feet are tender. "Her feet are soft," he says, "for she treads not upon the ground, but makes her path upon the heads of men." He gives as an evidence of her tenderness, that she walks not upon that which is hard, but that which is soft. The same evidence is sufficient to make manifest the tenderness of Love. For Love walks not upon the earth, nor over the heads of men, which are not indeed very soft; but he dwells within, and treads on the softest of existing things, having established his habitation within the souls and inmost nature of Gods and men; not indeed in all souls – for wherever he chances to find a hard and rugged disposition, there he will not inhabit, but only where it is most soft and tender. Of needs must he be the most delicate of all things, who touches lightly with his feet, only the softest parts of those things which are the softest of all'. Cp. also William Godwin, *Memoirs of Mary Wollstonecraft* (1798): 'we not unfrequently meet with persons, endowed with the most exquisite and refined sensibility, whose minds seem almost of too delicate a texture to encounter the vicissitudes of human affairs, to whom pleasure is transport, and disappointment is agony indescribable. This character is finely pourtrayed by the author of the Sorrows of Werter. Mary was in this respect a female Werter' (*Godwin Novels* i 117).

774. lulling] *Nbk 8*; silent *1820, 1839*. Presumably an error in transcription or printing, probably caused by the occurence of *silent* later in the line. Mathilde Blind misread the MS *lulling* as *killing*, a reading subsequently adopted by Forman, and by *eds* deriving from him, until corrected in *Locock Ex* (see *BSM* ix 570).

775. bear,] bear *Nbk 8*; bear; *1820, 1839*.

778–9. The sense is difficult: *the monster* is presumably *Desolation* (from line 772), misrecognised as *Love* by those, *the best and gentlest*, whose intense idealism drives them when it is disappointed to a special intensity of despair.

778. monster] monster, *Nbk 8, 1820, 1839*.

779. the shadow] their shadow *Nbk 8*; perhaps S.'s alteration to the transcript. *Pain –*] *Nbk 8*; Pain, *1820, 1839*.

779. As *BSM* ix 569–71 notes, the Fifth and Sixth Spirits' Songs appear in early fragmentary draft form in *Nbk 11*. Among these drafts is a possible ninth line for the Sixth Spirit's Song (recorded in *Zillman Variorum* 177), i.e. to follow line 779, which if included would complete the formal matching of stanzaic pattern with the Fifth Spirit's Song: *And wake & die, like early flowers when the winds that waked them, fleet* (*Nbk 11* 25).

781. him destroyingly] *Nbk 8*; him, destroyingly, *1820, 1839*.

782. steed] *Nbk 8*; steed, *1820, 1839*. Cp. *Revelation* vi 8: 'And I looked, and behold a pale horse: and his name that sat on him was Death'.

783. flee –] *Nbk 8*; flee, *1820, 1839*.

523

785   Trampling down both flower and weed,
       Man and beast, and foul and fair,
       Like a tempest through the air;
       Thou shalt quell this Horseman grim,
       Woundless though in heart or limb.

                    Prometheus
       Spirits! how know ye this shall be?

                    Chorus
790   In the atmosphere we breathe,
       As buds grow red when snow-storms flee
       From spring gathering up beneath,
       Whose mild winds shake the elder brake,
       And the wandering herdsmen know
795   That the white-thorn soon will blow:
       Wisdom, Justice, Love, and Peace,
       When they struggle to increase,
       Are to us as soft winds be
       To shepherd-boys — the prophecy
800   Which begins and ends in thee.

Ione
Where are the Spirits fled?

Panthea
                    Only a sense
Remains of them, like the omnipotence
Of music, when the inspired voice and lute
Languish, ere yet the responses are mute
805   Which through the deep and labyrinthine soul,
Like echoes through long caverns, wind and roll.

787. *Horseman*] Nbk 8; horseman 1820, 1839.

789. Prometheus's line here is integrated metrically and by rhyme with the Chorus of Spirits' stanza 789–800.

790. i.e. thought.

791. *snow-storms*] Nbk 8; the snow-storms 1820, 1839; probably a mistake in transcription, though the 1820 reading is not ametrical.

799. *shepherd-boys –*] Nbk 8; shepherd boys, 1820, 1839.

800. This line is followed in Nbk 8 by a stage direction in very light ink: 'They vanish'.

801. *Spirits*] spirits Nbk 8.

802. *omnipotence*] Omnipotence Nbk 8.

804. *responses*] 'Echoes in the mind' (here, as usually in S., stressed on the first syllable).   *mute*] Nbk 8; mute, 1820, 1839.

524

Prometheus
How fair these air-born shapes! and yet I feel
Most vain all hope but love; and thou art far,
Asia! who, when my being overflowed,
810 Wert like a golden chalice to bright wine
Which else had sunk into the thirsty dust.
All things are still: alas! how heavily
This quiet morning weighs upon my heart;
Though I should dream, I could even sleep with grief
815 If slumber were denied not . . . I would fain
Be what it is my destiny to be,
The saviour and the strength of suffering man,
Or sink into the original gulf of things . . .
There is no agony, and no solace left;
820 Earth can console, Heaven can torment no more.

Panthea
Hast thou forgotten one who watches thee
The cold dark night, and never sleeps but when
The shadow of thy spirit falls on her?

Prometheus
I said all hope was vain but love: thou lovest.

Panthea
825 Deeply in truth; but the Eastern star looks white,
And Asia waits in that far Indian vale
The scene of her sad exile — rugged once

807–9. Apparently encouraging an identification of Asia with love; but note that in 765–7 love is clearly male (as he is in S.'s trans. of the *Symposium*).

807. air-born] Born of air (i.e. created by the mind).

809–11. 'An unusually open, and openly sexual simile, reminding us that Prometheus and Asia are in fact man and wife, and that among other things Asia represents the fecundity of the earth, including human fecundity' (GM).

814. Though I should dream,] 'Even at the cost of dreaming'. *dream,*] *Nbk 8*; dream *1820, 1839. grief*] *Nbk 8, 1820*; grief, *1839.*

815. not . . .] *Nbk 8*; not. *1820, 1839.*

818. things . . .] *Nbk 8*; things: *1820, 1839.*

819. agony, and no] agony – no *Nbk 8*; presumably an alteration to the press transcript.

825. Eastern] *Nbk 8*; eastern *1820, 1839. white*] wan *Nbk 8*; probably an alteration by S. to the transcript of a detail about which he remained uncertain, as *Nbk 8* has *looks wan* written above *is pale* canc.

827. exile –] *Nbk 8*; exile; *1820, 1839.*

And desolate and frozen like this ravine;
But now invested with fair flowers and herbs,
830 And haunted by sweet airs and sounds, which flow
Among the woods and waters, from the ether
Of her transforming presence — which would fade
If it were mingled not with thine. Farewell!

End of the First Act

828–30. Cp. Hesiod's account of creation, in which Venus Aphrodite is born on Cythera: 'And out stepped a beautiful goddess, and the grass began to grow all round beneath her slender feet' (*Theogony* 191); also *Iliad* xiv 347–9: 'the son of Cronos took his wife in his arms; and the gracious earth sent up fresh grass beneath them, dewy lotus and crocuses, and a soft and crowded bed of hyacinths, to lift them off the ground'.

828. *frozen*] Nbk 8; frozen, *1820, 1839*.

831. *ether*] See note to line 765 above.

832. *presence –*] Nbk 8; presence, *1820, 1839*.

ACT II

Scene i

Morning. A lovely vale in the Indian Caucasus. Asia, *alone.*

Asia
From all the blasts of heaven thou hast descended:
Yes, like a spirit, like a thought, which makes
Unwonted tears throng to the horny eyes,
And beatings haunt the desolated heart,
5   Which should have learnt repose: thou hast descended
Cradled in tempests; thou dost wake, O Spring!
O child of many winds! As suddenly
Thou comest as the memory of a dream,
Which now is sad because it hath been sweet;
10   Like genius, or like joy which riseth up
As from the earth, clothing with golden clouds
The desert of our life . . .

SD. lovely] *Nbk 8, 1820, 1829*; lonely *1839, 1840* (an uncorrected printer's error). With the setting of this scene cp. the opening Stage Direction for Act I, and note, and see *Alastor* 140–9 and notes.

1–9. No indication is given of the time which has elapsed since the end of Act I; but the implication in Asia's opening lines is that considerable time has elapsed, and that the action is not to be considered as immediately sequential (let alone as simultaneous between the first three acts). See notes to lines 27, 35–8, 92, and 107–8 below. With the opening of Act II cp. Guarini, *Il Pastor fido* (1590) III i 1–6:
    Spring, the yeers youth, fair mother of new flowrs,
    New leaves, new loves, drawn by the winged hours,
    Thou art return'd; but the felicity
    Thou brought'st me last is not return'd with thee.
    Thou art return'd, but nought returns with thee
    Save my lost joyes regretful memory. (trans. Sir Richard Fanshawe, 1647).
S. read *Il Pastor fido* with Claire in early April 1815 (*Mary Jnl* i 74); he had more recently seen a MS of the work in the public library in Ferrara on his journey from Venice to Naples in November 1818 (*L* ii 47).

1. blasts] Cp. *Cratylus* 410 B, where poets call the winds ἀήτας, 'blasts'. *heaven*] Heaven *Nbk 8*.

3. horny] S. twice uses this word in *L&C* (III xxvi 5, VI xlvii 3), where the *Concordance* gloss 'dull, lustreless' might fit the later, but not the earlier occurrence. Here S. may intend 'semi-opaque like horn' as suggested in *Reiman (1977)*, but there is also a possible play on *cornea*; and S. may imply an Oriental appearance for Asia's eyes (i.e. crescent-shaped as in a horned moon). Cp. the illustrations of Indian goddesses in, e.g., Edward Moor, *Hindu Pantheon* (1810). Asia's opening reference here to eyes initiates a recurring motif in this scene.

7–9. Anticipating the exchange of dreams later in the scene.

11. earth,] Earth *Nbk 8*.

12. life . . .] *Nbk 8*; life. *1820, 1839*.

This is the season, this the day, the hour;
At sunrise thou shouldst come, sweet sister mine . . .
15   Too long desired, too long delaying, come!
How like death-worms the wingless moments crawl!
The point of one white star is quivering still
Deep in the orange light of widening morn
Beyond the purple mountains; through a chasm
20   Of wind-divided mist the darker lake
Reflects it — now it wanes — it gleams again
As the waves fade, and as the burning threads
Of woven cloud unravel in pale air . . .
'Tis lost! and through yon peaks of cloud-like snow
25   The roseate sunlight quivers: hear I not
The Æolian music of her sea-green plumes
Winnowing the crimson dawn?
                    Panthea enters.
                    I feel, I see
Those eyes which burn through smiles that fade in tears,
Like stars half quenched in mists of silver dew.
30   Belovèd and most beautiful, who wearest
The shadow of that soul by which I live,

14. *mine* . . .] *Nbk 8*; mine, *1820, 1839*.

16. This line, echoing line 48 of Act I, was inserted on the blank facing page in *Nbk 8*.

17–24. i.e. the ideal fades in intensity as it is transcended by achieved beauty. 'The suggestion could be that what has been aspired to as a distant ideal is now to be brought close, made actual in the light of day' (*Butter (1970)*). Butter cps. *TL* 412–31.

19. *mountains;*] *Nbk 8*; mountains: *1820, 1839*.

21. *it – now it wanes –*] *Nbk 8*; it: now it wanes *1820*; it; now it wanes; *1839*.

23. *air* . . .] *Nbk 8*; air: *1820, 1839*.

25. *sunlight*] sunrise *Nbk 8* (presumably altered in the press transcript).

26–7. Perhaps recalling *Prometheus Bound* 125, πέλας οἰωνῶν; αἰθὴρ δ' ἐλαφραῖς ('The air whirs with the light rush of pinions'); cp. also III iv 107 and note, and *Paradise Lost*:
                    Down thither prone in flight
            He speeds, and through the vast ethereal sky
            Sails between worlds and worlds, with steady wing
            Now on the polar winds, then with quick fan
            Winnows the buxom air. (v 266–70)

26. *Æolian*] eolian *Nbk 8*.

27. *I feel, I see*] Asia's formulation introduces a further new motif; cp. e.g. 109–10 below, II iv 31, and IV 363. On Panthea's entrance in the stage direction at this point, see Susan Hawk Brisman, *SiR* 16 (1977) 81: 'Though critics have stressed the simultaneity of the action in the first three acts, perhaps no other evidence makes a stronger case for sequential action in I and II than the presence of Panthea in both'.

29. *half quenched*] *Nbk 8, 1820*; half-quenched *1839*.

31. As *Butter (1970)* notes, for Asia Panthea is the shadow of Prometheus, and for Prometheus she is the shadow of Asia (cp. line 70).

How late thou art! the spherèd sun had climbed
The sea, my heart was sick with hope, before
The printless air felt thy belated plumes.

Panthea
35 Pardon, great Sister! but my wings were faint
With the delight of a remembered dream,
As are the noontide plumes of summer winds
Satiate with sweet flowers. I was wont to sleep
Peacefully, and awake refreshed and calm
40 Before the sacred Titan's fall, and thy
Unhappy love, had made, through use and pity,
Both love and woe familiar to my heart
As they had grown to thine. Erewhile I slept
Under the glaucous caverns of old Ocean
45 Within dim bowers of green and purple moss,
Our young Ione's soft and milky arms
Locked then, as now, behind my dark, moist hair,
While my shut eyes and cheek were pressed within
The folded depth of her life-breathing bosom . . .

---

33. sea,] *Nbk 8*; sea; *1820, 1839.*

35–8. Panthea mentions nothing about Prometheus's night of torture in Act I, presumably implying that it happened some time ago. Panthea is awake during the action of Act I and so cannot have been dreaming (see also note to line 92 below), although commentators have tended to disregard the inconsistency (see e.g. *Butter (1970)* 281; *Prometheus Unbound*, ed. Vida Scudder (1892) 150; and see James Thomson's discussion of the 'interior time of the poem', 'Notes on the Structure of Shelley's "Prometheus Unbound"', in *Shelley, a Poem: with other Writing relating to Shelley* (1884) 48–70).

38–43. In *Nbk 8* this passage originally read 'satiate with sweet flowers. I slept peacefully / Before thine exile & his grievous woe / Within the glaucous caverns of old Ocean'. S. subsequently cancelled 'I slept . . . grievous woe', and drafted the final version on the blank facing page (f. 24ʳ; see *BSM* ix 260–1, 575). S.'s pencil alterations to this insert represent very late revisions (the lines are not included in S.'s running line count in *Nbk 8*); and there were further alterations to the press transcript, where the *thy* of line 40 was altered from 'thine', presumably because S. also altered the *thine* of line 43 from 'yours'.

42. Both love and woe recalls the Songs of the Fifth and Sixth Spirits in Act I 763–79.

43. thine. Erewhile] The stop after *thine* has been adopted by various *eds* including *Rossetti 1870, Zillman Text,* and *Butter (1970).* S.'s insert (see note to lines 38–43) ends with the line 'as they had grown to yours . . . erewhile I slept'. But S.'s 'yours' (subsequently altered to *thine*) ends an insertion which then picks up at what had been a new sentence; the suspension points introduce a grammatical confusion which is not resolved by the punctuation 'thine: erewhile' introduced in *1820* and *1839.   Erewhile*] i.e. some time ago; Panthea recalls in lines 43–9 a period of innocence with Ione before P.'s fall, now supplanted (lines 50–5) by a more troubled and erotically charged consciousness which is reflected in the first of the remembered dreams (lines 62–91).

44. Under] Alt. *from* within *canc.,* as a result of S.'s insert (see preceding notes).

49. bosom . . .] *Nbk 8*; bosom: *1820, 1839.*

50   But not as now, since I am made the wind
        Which fails beneath the music that I bear
        Of thy most wordless converse; since dissolved
        Into the sense with which love talks, my rest
        Was troubled and yet sweet — my waking hours
55   Too full of care and pain.

        Asia
                                Lift up thine eyes
        And let me read thy dream.

        Panthea
                                As I have said,
        With our sea-sister at his feet I slept.
        The mountain mists, condensing at our voice
        Under the moon, had spread their snowy flakes,
60   From the keen ice shielding our linkèd sleep . . .
        Then two dreams came. One, I remember not.
        But in the other, his pale, wound-worn limbs
        Fell from Prometheus, and the azure night
        Grew radiant with the glory of that form
65   Which lives unchanged within, and his voice fell
        Like music which makes giddy the dim brain,
        Faint with intoxication of keen joy:
        'Sister of her whose footsteps pave the world
        With loveliness — more fair than aught but her
70   Whose shadow thou art — lift thine eyes on me!'
        I lifted them: the overpowering light
        Of that immortal shape was shadowed o'er

50–2. Panthea appears to have become a regular messenger between Asia and Prometheus, although *wordless converse* suggests non-verbal communication (possibly by dreams, or by eye-reading).

54. *sweet* –] *Nbk 8*; sweet; *1820, 1839*.

55. *eyes*] *Nbk 8*; eyes, *1820, 1839*.

56. *said,*] The comma was first introduced in *1840*.

60. *sleep . . .*] *Nbk 8*; sleep. *1820, 1839*.

62–92. For searching commentary on the affinities between the account of Panthea's first dream, and Shelley's earlier lyric 'To Constantia' (no. 155) see *Chernaik* 53–8.

62–5. The Prometheus of Panthea's dream evokes Christ transfigured; cp. *Matthew* xvii 1–6, *Mark* ix 1–8, *Luke* ix 28–36.

62. *other, his pale,*] *Nbk 8*; other his pale *1820, 1839*.

66. *giddy*] dizzy *Nbk 8* (clearly a change to the press transcript).

69. *her*] *Nbk 8*; her, *1820, 1839*.

70. See note to line 31.

By love; which, from his soft and flowing limbs,
And passion-parted lips, and keen, faint eyes,
75   Steamed forth like vaporous fire; an atmosphere
Which wrapped me in its all-dissolving power,
As the warm ether of the morning sun
Wraps ere it drinks some cloud of wandering dew.
I saw not, heard not, moved not, only felt
80   His presence flow and mingle through my blood
Till it became his life, and his grew mine,
And I was thus absorbed — until it passed,
And like the vapours when the sun sinks down,
Gathering again in drops upon the pines,
85   And tremulous as they, in the deep night
My being was condensed; and as the rays
Of thought were slowly gathered, I could hear
His voice, whose accents lingered ere they died
Like footsteps of far melody: thy name
90   Among the many sounds alone I heard
Of what might be articulate; though still
I listened through the night when sound was none.
Ione wakened then, and said to me:

73–4. Cp. S.'s letter to Peacock from Bologna, 9 November 1818, describing a 'Christ Beatified' by Correggio which S. had seen in the picture gallery of a Palazzo: 'It is a half figure rising from a mass of clouds tinged with an ethereal rose-like lustre, the arms are expanded, the whole figure seems dilated with expression, the countenance is heavy as it were with the weight of the rapture of the spirit, the lips parted but scarcely parted with the breath of intense but regulated passion, the eyes are calm and benignant, the whole features harmonized in majesty & sweetness.' (*L* ii 49–50).

75–88. 'Panthea in her dream felt as if she were a drop of dew vaporizing under the warmth of Prometheus's sun-like beams and being somehow absorbed into him. This confused sense of well-being gave way to clarity as she condensed again and focused his light, i.e. heard his words'. (Desmond King-Hele, *Shelley: His Thought and Work* (2nd edn 1971) 177.)

80. mingle] One of S.'s habitual terms for sexual intercourse.

82. absorbed –] Nbk 8; absorbed, *1820, 1839*.

84. Gathering] Written in pencil above *Which hung* canc. in pencil; a change to the fair copy before transcription for the press. For *gathering* in the sense of 'condensing' see *R&H* 1045 and note, and cp. III iii 53 below.

88. ere] as *Nbk 8* (presumably a change to the press transcript).

89–92. S. at first wrote 'Like footsteps of lost music . . . but I heard / Among the many sounds, one word, thy name'; he then cancelled *lost music* and substituted *far melody*, but formed *far* by superimposing it on *weak*; Mary S. presumably misread the word as *weak* in her press transcript, because *weak* is the reading in *1820* and *1839*. The final version of lines 89–92 was written on the blank facing page in *Nbk 8* (f. 26ʳ).

92. This does not seem to refer to the night represented in Act I, which is of course scarcely silent.

93–106. With Panthea's dream of the transformed Prometheus Ione has begun to move beyond the parameters established for her experience in Act I, and to develop intimate affinity with Panthea's kind of experience; innocent love now approaches a natural maturity.

'Canst thou divine what troubles me to-night?
95   I always knew what I desired before,
Nor ever found delight to wish in vain.
But now I cannot tell thee what I seek;
I know not — something sweet, since it is sweet
Even to desire; it is thy sport, false sister!
100   Thou hast discovered some enchantment old,
Whose spells have stolen my spirit as I slept
And mingled it with thine; — for when just now
We kissed, I felt within thy parted lips
The sweet air that sustained me, and the warmth
105   Of the life-blood, for loss of which I faint,
Quivered between our intertwining arms.'
I answered not, for the Eastern star grew pale,
But fled to thee.

Asia

Thou speakest, but thy words
Are as the air. I feel them not . . . Oh, lift
110   Thine eyes, that I may read his written soul!

98. not –] *Nbk 8*; not; *1820, 1839.*

99. sister!] *Nbk 8*; sister; *1820, 1839.*

102. thine; –] *Nbk 8*; thine: *1820, 1839.*

107–8. These lines appear to confirm that the morning after Panthea's night of dreams is a different morning from that which breaks at the end of Act I.

108–10. Cp. S.'s 'On Love': 'if we feel, we would that another's nerves should vibrate to our own, that the beams of their eyes should kindle at once and mix and melt into our own' (*Prose* 170).

109. air.] *Nbk 8*; air: *1820, 1839. not . . .*] *Nbk 8*; not: *1820, 1839.*

110. soul] Written above *spirit* canc. *Nbk 8*. This line is followed by a cancelled line, 'Lift up thine eyes Panthea – they pierce – they burn!' There then follows a cancelled passage, probably continued in the two following leaves which have been torn from the notebook, which as Locock first noted may represent the origin of the 'Life of Life' lyric in 2 v (though *BSM* ix 577 notes that S. included the cancelled passage in his line count for this scene):

> Panthea
> Alas I am consumed – I melt away
> The fire is in my heart –
>
> Asia
> Thine eyes burn burn! – [the second
> burn, required by the metre, is omitted in *BSM* ix 269]
> Hide them within thine hair
>
> Panthea
> O quench thy lips
> I sink I perish
>
> Asia
> Shelter me now – they burn
> It is his spirit in thier orbs . . . my life

Panthea
I lift them, though they droop beneath the load
Of that they would express: what canst thou see
But thine own fairest shadow imaged there?

Asia
Thine eyes are like the deep, blue, boundless heaven
115 Contracted to two circles underneath
Their long, fine lashes; dark, far, measureless, —
Orb within orb, and line through line inwoven.

Panthea
Why lookest thou as if a spirit passed?

Asia
There is a change; beyond their inmost depth
120 I see a shade, a shape: 'tis He, arrayed

Is ebbing fast – I cannot speak –
Panthea
Rest, rest!
Sleep death annihilation pain! aught else

114–17. Cp *L&C* XI v:

Her lips were parted, and the measured breath
Was now heard there; – her dark and intricate eyes
Orb within orb, deeper than sleep or death,
Absorbed the glories of the burning skies,
Which, mingling with her heart's deep ecstasies,
Burst from her looks and gestures; – and a light
Of liquid tenderness like love, did rise
From her whole frame, an atmosphere which quite
Arrayed her in its beams, tremulous and soft and bright.

See also *DMAA* (written in 1818 probably as a prefatory essay to the translation of the *Symposium*), on the limits placed upon women's experience by Greek culture: 'Their eyes could not have been deep and intricate from the workings of the mind, and could have entangled no heart in soul-enwoven labyrinths' (*Prose 220*; for the importance of this essay to S.'s general conception of Asia and Panthea, see headnote). S. adapted the passage in his letter to Peacock from Rome, 6 April 1819, on his impressions of Italian women: 'The only inferior part are the eyes, which though good & gentle, want the mazy depth of colour behind colour with which the intellectual females of England & Germany entangle the heart in soul-inwoven labyrinths' (*L* ii 93). Cp. also Tasso, *Aminta* (1573) I ii 94–5: 'E bevea da' suoi lumi / Un estranea dolcezza' ('and drank from her eyes a strange sweetness'); Mary S. records reading *Aminta* with S. in April 1818 (*Mary Jnl* i 203).

115. to] in *Nbk 8*. Perhaps S.'s alteration to the press transcript; but *to two* introduces a slight verbal awkwardness.

116. measureless, –] *Nbk 8*; measureless, *1820, 1839*.

120–6. Asia sees Panthea's dream (previously described in lines 62–9) in her eyes, and her recapitulation again suggests Christ transfigured (see note to lines 62–5). As *Butter (1970)* notes, Asia is able to *interpret* Panthea's dream; she then sees Panthea's other dream (lines 127–31),

533

In the soft light of his own smiles, which spread
Like radiance from the cloud-surrounded moon.
Prometheus, it is thine! depart not yet!
Say not those smiles that we shall meet again
125   Within that bright pavilion which their beams
Shall build o'er the waste world? The dream is told.
What shape is that between us? Its rude hair
Roughens the wind that lifts it, its regard
Is wild and quick, yet 'tis a thing of air
130   For through its grey robe gleams the golden dew
Whose stars the noon has quenched not.

Dream

Follow, follow!

---

which Panthea herself has been unable to recall (cp. line 61), but which she now recognises in Asia's description (line 132). Panthea's second dream in its turn prompts a recollection by Asia of a prophetic dream (lines 141–62). Such complex interchange of private experience suggests the growing interdependence of Asia and Panthea, or rather the absorption of Panthea into Asia, as their symbolic values begin to merge. Cp. *DMAA*: '[sexual love] soon becomes a very small part of that profound and complicated sentiment which we call love, which is rather the universal thirst for a communion not merely of the senses but of our whole nature, intellectual, imaginative, and sensitive, and which, when individualized, becomes an imperious necessity, only to be satisfied by the complete or partial, actual or supposed fulfilment of its claims . . . The sexual impulse, which is only one and often a small part of these claims, serves from its obvious and external nature as a kind of type or expression of the rest, as common basis, an acknowledged and visible link' (*Prose* 221).

121. S. plays on the ambiguity of Lat. *ridere* (both 'laugh' and 'shine').

122. moon.] moon *Nbk 8*; morn. *1820, 1839* (very probably a misreading by Mary S. in her transcript; the second *o* of *moon* in *Nbk 8* is ill-formed and resembles an *r*).

123. This line has been added on the blank facing page in *Nbk 8*. It is very difficult to determine whether the reading is *thine* or *thou*; *BSM* ix 578 is probably right in preferring *thou*, which could easily have been miscopied in the transcript, but the evidence is not conclusive, and *thine* may coherently refer to the *shade . . . shape* of line 120.

125. pavilion] Pavilion *Nbk 8*.

126. o'er] *Nbk 8*; on *1820, 1839*. Probably a mistranscription; *o'er* has no apostrophe in *Nbk 8*.

127–31. Perhaps recalling the closing lines of Coleridge's 'Kubla Khan'. Panthea's second dream appears to spur to action, in contrast with the reassuring prophetic rapture of the first dream. The dream has been interpreted as a vision of the Spirit of the Hour which will arrive to mark the arrival of revolutionary change and the downfall of Jupiter (see e.g. *Reiman (1969)* 76; *Cameron (1974)* 516; Stuart Sperry, *Shelley's Major Verse* (1988) 98). The *rude hair / Roughens* may imply Demogorgon himself, but there is also a suggestion of maenad-like possession anticipating the more explicit allusions to oracular prophecy in succeeding scenes.

131. i.e. it is not yet noon; 'the noon has not yet arrived so as to quench them' (rather than 'even the noon has not quenched the stars'). The time-scheme here is therefore not inconsistent with II ii 89. *Follow, follow!*] *Nbk 8*; Follow! Follow! *1820, 1839*.

Panthea
It is mine other dream —

Asia
                    It disappears.

Panthea
It passes now into my mind. Methought
As we sate here, the flower-enfolding buds
135   Burst on yon lightning-blasted almond-tree,
When swift from the white Scythian wilderness
A wind swept forth wrinkling the Earth with frost . . .
I looked, and all the blossoms were blown down;
But on each leaf was stamped — as the blue bells
140   Of Hyacinth tell Apollo's written grief —
O, follow, follow!

132. dream –] Nbk 8; dream. *1820, 1839.*

135. almond-tree] Traditionally a symbol of hope and anticipation; cp. *Jeremiah* i 11–12: 'Moreover the word of the Lord came unto me, saying, Jeremiah, what seest thou? And I said, I see a rod of an almond tree. Then said the Lord unto me, Thou hast well seen: for I will hasten my word to perform it' (exegesis understood a Hebrew pun on 'almond' and 'hasten', and interpreted the 'hastening' tree as an anticipatory type of Spring). The almond blossoms in January in Italy, the earliest anticipation of spring (as Pliny notes, *Nat. Hist.* xvi 42); but S.'s *lightning-blasted* almond suggests premature or blasted hope, here redeemed by prophecy.

136. The *Scythian wilderness* provides the setting for Aeschylus's *Prometheus Bound.*

137. frost . . .] Nbk 8; frost: *1820, 1839.*

139–40. Hyacinthus was a beautiful boy loved by Apollo, pre-eminently the god of oracular prophecy (see note to line 141). He was killed by Zephyrus, and as Apollo mourned, a flower sprang from the boy's blood marked with αἰαῖ (Gk 'alas').

139. stamped –] Nbk 8; stamped, *1820, 1839.*

140. grief –] Nbk 8; grief, *1820, 1839.*

141. follow, follow!] Nbk 8; FOLLOW, FOLLOW! *1820, 1839.* The injunction to *Follow*, first announced by the Dream at line 131, is stamped on leaves, and then (lines 151–62) written in nature and humanity (on cloud-shadows, lines 151–3; on herbs, lines 154–5; in the music of the pines, lines 156–9; and in human eyes, lines 161–2). S. borrows the idea from the ancient oracles; the prophetic sybil sometimes wrote her prophecies on leaves to be collected and deciphered. Mary S.'s Preface to *The Last Man* (1826) gives a presumably imaginary account of the accidental discovery by Mary and her 'companion' of the cave of the Cumaean sybil, during a visit to Naples in 1818: 'At length my friend, who had taken up some of the leaves strewed about, exclaimed, "This *is* the Sibyl's cave; these are Sibylline leaves." On examination, we found that all the leaves, bark, and other substances, were traced with written characters. What appeared to us more astonishing, was that these writings were expressed in various languages: some unknown to my companion, ancient Chaldee, and Egyptian hieroglyphics, old as the Pyramids. Stranger still, some were in modern dialects, English and Italian. We could make out little by the dim light, but they seemed to contain prophecies, detailed relations of events but lately passed; names, now well known, but of modern date; and often exclamations of exultation or woe, of victory or defeat, were traced on their thin scant pages. This was certainly the Sibyl's Cave; not indeed exactly as Virgil describes it; but the whole

Asia

As you speak, your words
Fill, pause by pause, my own forgotten sleep
With shapes . . . methought among these lawns together
We wandered, underneath the young grey dawn,
145 And multitudes of dense white fleecy clouds
Were wandering in thick flocks along the mountains,
Shepherded by the slow, unwilling wind;
And the white dew on the new-bladed grass,
Just piercing the dark earth, hung silently —
150 And there was more which I remember not;
But on the shadows of the moving clouds
Athwart the purple mountain slope, was written
Follow, O follow! as they vanished by;
And on each herb, from which Heaven's dew had fallen,
155 The like was stamped as with a withering fire.
A wind arose among the pines; it shook
The clinging music from their boughs, and then
Low, sweet, faint sounds, like the farewell of ghosts,
Were heard: *O, follow, follow, follow me!*

---

of this land had been so convulsed by earthquake and volcano, that the change was not wonderful, though the traces of ruin were effaced by time; and we probably owed the preservation of these leaves, to the accident which had closed the mouth of the cavern, and the swift-growing vegetation which had rendered its sole opening impervious to the storm. We made a hasty selection of such of the leaves, whose writing one at least of us could understand; and then, laden with our treasure, we bade adieu to the dim hypaethric cavern, and after much difficulty succeeded in rejoining our guides.' (*MSW* iv 7–8).

142. my] mine *Nbk 8* (probably altered in the press transcript).

143. shapes . . . methought] *Nbk 8*; shapes. Methought *1820, 1839*. *these*] *Nbk 8*; the *1820, 1839*. Perhaps miscopied in the transcript; *these* is slightly obscure in *Nbk 8* and has possibly been altered from *this*.

146. mountains,] mountains *Nbk 8, 1820, 1839*.

149. silently –] *Nbk 8*; silently; *1820, 1839*.

150. not;] *Nbk 8*; not: *1820, 1839*.

151. moving] *Nbk 8*; morning *1820, 1839*. *Moving* is clear in *Nbk 8*, so *morning* could well be an alteration to the transcript rather than a miscopying, and both *moving* and *morning* fit the context (*Reiman (1977)* reads *morning*); *moving* is preferred here because it appears to fit better with the immediate context of lines 151–3. *clouds*] *Nbk 8*; clouds, *1820, 1839*.

153. Follow, O follow! as] Follow, o follow! as *Nbk 8*; FOLLOW, O, FOLLOW! As *1820, 1839*. *by;*] by, *Nbk 8, 1820, 1839*.

155. stamped] *Nbk 8*; stamped, *1820, 1839*. *Locock 1911* and *Butter (1970)* introduce a stop after *fire*. The comma after *fire* in *Nbk 8, 1820* and *1839* seems definitely too weak for the sense, and a new sentence at this point is judged appropriately to mark a new sequence of thought following the long sentence beginning at line 143.

159. Were heard – Oh, follow, follow, follow me Nbk 8; Were heard: OH, FOLLOW, FOLLOW, FOLLOW ME! *1820, 1839*.

160   And then I said: 'Panthea, look on me.'
But in the depth of those belovèd eyes
Still I saw, *follow, follow!*

Echo

               Follow, follow!

Panthea
The crags, this clear spring morning, mock our voices,
As they were spirit-tongued.

Asia

              It is some being
165   Around the crags. What fine clear sounds! O list!

                   Echoes (unseen).
             Echoes we: listen!
             We cannot stay:
             As dew-stars glisten
             Then fade away —
170   Child of Ocean!

Asia
Hark! Spirits speak! The liquid responses
Of their aërial tongues yet sound.

160. *said:*] *1820*; said *Nbk 8*; said, *1839*.

162. *saw,* follow, follow!] saw *follow, follow. Nbk 8*; saw, FOLLOW, FOLLOW! *1820, 1839*. S. initially intended to call the *Echoes* 'Voices'; their first line here was inserted on the blank facing page in *Nbk 8*, with the speaker identification 'Voice' altered to *Echo* (see note to line 166).

165. *O*] o *Nbk 8*; O, *1820, 1839*.

166ff. The single Echo at line 162 does indeed echo the last words spoken; but from this point to the end of the scene the Echoes articulate on their own account, implying an external agency which draws Asia and Panthea towards their destined meeting with Demogorgon, notwithstanding their assumption that they act under their own desires. See notes to II ii 41–63. As Wasserman notes, echoes traditionally inhabit caves (see e.g. Ovid, *Met.* iii 394); but the mysteriously subterranean hollow caverns to which the Echoes invite Asia and Panthea are specifically volcanic (lines 202–3).

166. In *Nbk 8* S. first wrote *V* for the speaker identification, then cancelled it and wrote *Echoes*, probably then returning to the insert discussed in the preceding note to alter *Voice* there to *Echo*.

171. *Spirits speak!*] spirits speak! *Nbk 8*; Spirits speak. *1820*; Spirits, speak. *1829, 1839*; strong evidence that Mary used *1829* as copy text for *1839* (cp. II v 47 and note; see headnote, and *Taylor* 41).

Panthea
> I hear.

Echoes
> O follow, follow,
> As our voice recedeth
175 > Through the caverns hollow,
> Where the forest spreadeth;

> *[More distant.]*
> O follow, follow
> Through the caverns hollow;
> As the song floats, thou pursue,
180 > Where the wild bee never flew,
> Through the noon-tide darkness deep,
> By the odour-breathing sleep
> Of faint night-flowers, and the waves
> At the fountain-lighted caves,
185 > While our music, wild and sweet,
> Mocks thy gently-falling feet,
> Child of Ocean!

Asia
> Shall we pursue the sound? It grows more faint
> And distant.

Panthea
> List! the strain floats nearer now.

Echoes
190 > In the world unknown
> Sleeps a voice unspoken;
> By thy step alone

175. hollow] Nbk 8; hollow, *1820, 1839.*

176. The stage direction after line 176 is not in *Nbk 8* and was presumably added in the press transcript.

177. follow] Nbk 8; follow, *1820;* follow! *1839.*

178. hollow;] hollow *Nbk 8;* hollow, *1820, 1839.*

179. floats,] floats *Nbk 8, 1820, 1839.*

183. faint] Written in pencil above *sweet* canc. in pencil; a change to the fair copy before transcription for the press.

186. gently-falling] Nbk 8; gently falling *1820, 1839.*

190. Here and at line 196 the choral *Echoes* are altered, presumably in the press transcript, from the singular *Echo* of *Nbk 8.*

Can its rest be broken,
Child of Ocean!

Asia

195   How the notes sink upon the ebbing wind!

Echoes
O follow, follow
Through the caverns hollow;
As the song floats, thou pursue,
By the woodland noon-tide dew,
200   By the forests, lakes and fountains,
Through the many-folded mountains,
To the rents, and gulfs, and chasms,
Where the Earth reposed from spasms
On the day when He and thou
205   Parted — to commingle now,
Child of Ocean!

Asia
Come, sweet Panthea, link thy hand in mine,
And follow, ere the voices fade away.

Scene ii

A forest, intermingled with rocks and caverns. Asia *and* Panthea *pass into it.*
Two young Fauns are sitting on a rock, listening.

193. broken,] broken *Nbk 8*; broken; *1820, 1839*.

196. follow] *Nbk 8*; follow! *1820, 1839*.

197. hollow;] hollow *Nbk 8*; hollow, *1820, 1839*.

198. floats,] *Nbk 8*; floats *1820, 1839*.

199. dew,] dew *Nbk 8*; dew; *1820, 1839*.

201. many-folded] Cp. *J&M 76, Hymn to Venus* (no. 161) 63; and S.'s letter to Peacock from Bologna, 9 November 1818, 'the many folded Apennines' (*L* ii 53). *mountains,*] mountains *Nbk 8*; mountains; *1820, 1839*.

202–5. This summons refers to the earthquake and eruption when Prometheus was chained and Asia exiled (cp. Act I 165–8); see note above to lines 166ff.

203. spasms] *Nbk 8*; spasms, *1820, 1839*.

205. Parted –] *Nbk 8*; Parted, *1820, 1839*. *now,*] now *Nbk 8*; now; *1820, 1839*.

¶ii SD. *Two young fauns . . . listening*] This sentence was added later in *Nbk 8*; see note to lines 64–97.

Semichorus I of Spirits
The path through which that lovely twain
Have passed, by cedar, pine, and yew,
And each dark tree that ever grew,
Is curtained out from Heaven's wide blue;
5   Nor sun, nor moon, nor wind, nor rain
Can pierce its interwoven bowers,
Nor aught, save where some cloud of dew,

1–23. As Asia and Panthea approach the mountains to which the echoes have beckoned them (II i 196–206) they enter 'A forest, intermingled with rocks and caverns' (see stage direction) where 'the lush exuberance of the flora and fauna . . . is neither fanciful nor gratuitous. Asia and her companion have reached an area of volcanic fall-out, long famous for extreme fertility' (GM; see his 'A Volcano's Voice in Shelley' *ELH* 24 (1957) for detailed commentary on the geophysical and especially volcanic symbolism underpinning the action of Act II). S.'s description of the volcanic tract through which Asia and Panthea pass corresponds broadly to the countryside around Naples; cp. his letter to Peacock from Naples, 25 February 1819: 'We are on the point of quitting Naples for Rome. The scenery which surrounds this city is more delightful than any within the reach of civilized man. I dont think I have mentioned to you the lago d'Agnoni & the Caccia d'Astroni . . . They are both the craters of extinguished volcanos, & nature has thrown forth forests of oak & ilex, & spread mossy lawns, & clear lakes over the dead or sleeping fire. The first is a scene of a wider & wilder character with soft sloping wooded hills, & grassy declivities declining to the lake, & cultivated plains of vines woven upon poplar trees bounded by the theatre of hills . . . The other is a royal chase, it is surrounded by steep & lofty hills & only accessible thro a wide gate of massy oak from the vestibule of which the spectacle of precipitous hills hemming in a narrow & circular vale is suddenly disclosed. The hills are covered with thick woods of ilex, myrtle & laurustinus; the polished leaves of the ilex as they move in their multitudes under the partial blasts which rush thro the chasms of the vale glitter above the dark masses of foliage below like the white foam of waves upon a dark blue sea. The plain so surrounded is at most three miles in circumference. It is occupied partly by a lake with bold shores wooded by evergreens, & interrupted by a sylvan promontory of the wild forest whose mossy boughs overhang its expanse of a silent & purple darkness like an Italian midnight; & partly by the forest itself of all gigantic trees, but the oak especially whose jagged boughs now leafless are hoary with thick lichens and loaded with the massy & deep foliage of the ivy. The effect of the dark eminences that surrounded this plain, seen through the boughs is of an enchanting solemnity.' (*L* ii 77) S. was well aware of the special associations of this scenery with Virgil, whose *Eclogue* vi and *Aeneid* vi are pervasive influences on this scene in particular (see note to line 90 below). See *Wasserman* 320ff. for searching commentary on the Virgilian elements in Act II.

2–3. Recalling the wood of error in *Faerie Queene* I i 7–9; and cp. also *Paradise Lost* iv 137–42:
> overhead up grew
> Insuperable highth of loftiest shade,
> Cedar, and pine, and fir, and branching palm,
> A sylvan scene, and as the ranks ascend
> Shade above shade, a woody theater
> Of stateliest view.

5. rain] Nbk 8; rain, *1820, 1839*.

7. where] *1820, 1839* (see also *Butter (1970), Locock 1911*); when *Zillman Text, Reiman (1977)*). It is impossible to decide the reading in *Nbk 8*, which here as at line 14 could be read as either *where* or *when* (see *BSM* ix 294–5, 584). The dominant editorial approach is here adopted on the assumption that S. intends a place / time contrast, but *where / where* and *when / when* are both defensible. The formula *save where*, introducing a series of parallel clauses

Drifted along the earth-creeping breeze
Between the trunks of the great hoar trees,
10   Hangs each a pearl in the pale flowers
Of the green laurel, blown anew;
And bends, and then fades silently,
One frail and fair anenome:
Or when some star of many a one
15   That climb and wander through steep night,
Has found the cleft through which alone
Beams fall from high those depths upon,
Ere it is borne away, away,
By the swift Heavens that cannot stay —
20   It scatters drops of golden light,
Like lines of rain that ne'er unite:
And the gloom divine is all around;
And underneath is the mossy ground.

Semichorus II
There the voluptuous nightingales

(cp. *Or when*, line 14), is a stock convention in English natural descriptive poetry; cp. Gray, 'Elegy in a Country Churchyard' 7–12, Collins, 'Ode to Evening' 9–14.

8. *Drifted*] A participle; 'wafted', 'made to drift'. *breeze*] Nbk 8; breeze, *1820, 1839*.

10. i.e. 'hangs a pearl in each flower'; cp. *Midsummer Night's Dream* II i 14–15: 'I must go seek some dewdrops here / And hang a pearl in every cowslip's ear'.

11. The laurel was sacred to Apollo and traditionally associated with poets; see e.g. *Faerie Queene* I i 9: 'The Laurell, meed of mightie Conquerours / And Poets sage'.

12–13. Inverted syntax; 'save where one anemone bends and fades . . .'

14. *when*] See note to line 7.

15. *climb and wander*] Nbk 8; climbs and wanders *1820, 1839*; *many a one* (line 14) is the plural subject (S.'s verbs are also plural in an earlier draft in *Nbk 11* f. 28).

17. *upon,*] Nbk 8; upon *1820, 1839*.

19. *stay –*] Nbk 8; stay, *1820, 1839*. This line completes an adjectival clause of time qualifying *star* (line 14). Cp. Seneca, *de Brevitate Vitae*: 'Praesens tempus . . . nec magis moram patitur quam mundus aut sidera, quorum inrequieta semper agitatio numquam in eodem vestigio manet' ('Present time . . . can no more brook delay than the firmament or the stars, whose ever unresting movement never lets them abide in the same track.' *Moral Essays* X x 6, Loeb trans.)

20. *It*] i.e. the star.

22. *gloom divine*] Cp. III iii 169.

24. *nightingales*] Nbk 8; nightingales, *1820, 1839*.

24–40. S. appears in these lines to suggest a special agency for the poetic tradition in the movement towards revolutionary change, thus explaining the music and sweet sounds which draw Asia and Panthea on towards Demogorgon. Nightingales are associated in S.'s thought with the poet (see note to line 35); cp. *DP*: 'A poet is a nightingale, who sits in darkness and sings to cheer its own solitude with sweet sounds; his auditors are as men entranced

25   Are awake through all the broad noonday;
     When one with bliss or sadness fails,
     And through the windless ivy-boughs,
     Sick with sweet love, droops dying away
     On its mate's music-panting bosom —
30   Another from the swinging blossom,
     Watching to catch the languid close
     Of the last strain, then lifts on high
     The wings of the weak melody,
     Till some new stream of feeling bear
35   The song, and all the woods are mute;
     When there is heard through the dim air
     The rush of wings, and rising there

---

by the melody of an unseen musician, who feel that they are moved and softened, yet know not whence or why' (*Prose* 283). The idea of successive schools of poetry hinted in this passage may recall Gray's 'Progress of Poesy' which articulates a similar notion; and there is a series of understated puns on terms relating to poetry and music: *catch, close, strain, melody*.

25. noonday;] noonday *Nbk* 8; noon-day, *1820, 1839. When* in the following line is not in apposition with *noonday*.

26–35. Perhaps recalling Orsino's opening speech in *Twelfth Night*:
   If music be the food of love, play on,
   Give me excess of it, that, surfeiting,
   The appetite may sicken and so die.
   That strain again! It had a dying fall;
   O, it came o'er my ear like the sweet sound
   That breathes upon a bank of violets,
   Stealing and giving odour! Enough, no more;
   Tis not so sweet now as it was before.

27. Ivy was sacred to Bacchus (see Ovid, *Fasti* iii 767–70), and by the renaissance was associated with erotic desire; cp. e.g. *Faerie Queene* II v 29:
   And ouer him, art striuing to compair
    With nature, did an Arber greene dispred,
    Framed of wanton Yuie, flouring faire,
   Through which the fragrant Eglantine did spred
    His pricking armes, entrayled with roses red,
    Which daintie odours round about them threw,
    And all within with flowres was garnished,
    That when mild *Zephyrus* emongst them blew,
   Did breathe out bounteous smels, and painted colors shew.
See also *Faerie Queene* III vi 44.

29. bosom –] *Nbk* 8; bosom; *1820, 1839.*

34. stream] Apparently written over *strain* in *Nbk* 8, perhaps to avoid repetition from line 32; the alteration is not very clear and could have been misread, or S. may have made the alteration after completion of the press transcript. *1820* and *1839* read *strain*. Cp. *Q Mab* viii 27–8: 'the pure stream of feeling / That sprung from these sweet notes'.

35. Cp. Milton's Sonnet I ('To the Nightingale') 1–2: 'O nightingale, that on yon bloomy spray / Warbl'st at eve, when all the woods are still'.

Like many a lake-surrounded flute,
Sounds overflow the listener's brain
40 So sweet, that joy is almost pain.

Semichorus I
There those enchanted eddies play
Of echoes music-tongued, which draw,
By Demogorgon's mighty law,
With melting rapture, or sweet awe,
45 All spirits on that secret way,
As inland boats are driven to Ocean
Down streams made strong with mountain-thaw;
And first there comes a gentle sound
To those in talk or slumber bound,
50 And wakes the destined: soft emotion

38. *lake-surrounded*] Nbk 8, 1839; lake-surrounding 1820, 1829. Mary S.'s correction of Galignani suggests that this may have come from S.'s errata list (see headnote). The image is of flute-music heard over encircling water, and refers to a common practice in visiting lakes on picturesque tours.

41–63. 'This extended image expresses the way in which historical change and its human agents (reformers, poets) interact. These agents (*the destined*) are roused from their empty chatter or apathy (*talk or slumber*) by delightful intimations (*echoes music-tongued*) of the task they must accomplish. Destiny inspires them and lures them on, as mountains attract clouds. But they are driven as well as attracted; in following their own wishes they are obeying the dictate of historical necessity' (GM).

41–7. Cp. 'Written on a Beautiful Day in Spring' (no. 77) 12–13 and note.

42. Recalling the closing stanzas of Act II scene i. *echoes*] Nbk 8; echoes, 1820, 1839.

44. *sweet*] deep Nbk 8. Presumably S.'s change to the press transcript.

45. *way,*] Nbk 8; way; 1820, 1839.

46. Anticipating the closing lines of Act II scene v.

48–9. S. repeatedly associates sleep with an unconsciousness of, or unconcern for, pressing social and political realities. Cp. 'Ode to the West Wind' 29–36:

Thou who didst waken from his summer dreams
The blue Mediterranean, where he lay,
Lulled by the coil of his chrystalline streams,

Beside a pumice isle in Baiæ's bay,
And saw in sleep old palaces and towers
Quivering within the wave's intenser day,

All overgrown with azure moss and flowers
So sweet, the sense faints picturing them!

See also *Mask of Anarchy* 1–4:

As I lay asleep in Italy
There came a voice from over the Sea,
And with great power it forth led me
To walk in the Visions of Poesy.

50–1. An important crux, affecting the meaning of the scene, and bearing on the poem's larger thematic preoccupation with human agency in revolutionary change. The lines are

Attracts, impels them; those who saw
Say from the breathing Earth behind
There steams a plume-uplifting wind
Which drives them on their path, while they
55   Believe their own swift wings and feet
The sweet desires within obey:
And so they float upon their way
Until, still sweet, but loud and strong,
The storm of sound is driven along,
60   Sucked up and hurrying: as they fleet

---

mispunctuated in *1820* (and *1829*), and various *eds* (notably *Rossetti 1870* and *Hutchinson*) have compounded the resulting confusion. *Nbk 8* reads:

And wakes the destined – soft emotion
Attracts, impels them: those who saw

In *1820* this appeared as:

And wakes the destinied [sic] soft emotion,
Attracts, impels them: those who saw

Galignani in *1829* perpetuated this reading (while correcting *destinied* to *destined*), but it was corrected in *1839* (presumably following S.'s errata list) to the reading adopted here. *Rossetti 1870* returned to the reading of *1820*, while *Hutchinson* emended the punctuation to:

And wakes the destined soft emotion, –
Attracts, impels them; those who saw

Other *eds* have tinkered in various ways, including *Forman 1876–7* which introduces a stop after *destined* (deriving it, erroneously, from *Nbk 8*).

51. *those who saw*] Perhaps referring to those (such as Godwin) who understand historical causes.

52. *breathing Earth*] *Nbk 8*; earth *1820*, *1839*. S.'s phrase conflates classical and contemporary accounts of volcanic activity, and what it was considered to imply of the earth's interior, with classical ideas concerning the sources of oracular possession and prophecy. Asia and Panthea are descending into Demogorgon's subterranean realm, which itself gives further substance to S.'s distinctive oracular-volcanic conception of the action in the second Act. For classical sources of the connection between oracles and earthly exhalation see *Aeneid* vi, and e.g. Plutarch, *Moralia*, 'de Defectu Oraculorum' l–li; Silius Italicus, *Punica* xii 113–51 (which also associates volcanic activity with the breathing of the buried Titans under the volcanic islands around Naples, which seems to have contributed to S.'s conception of Demogorgon; see headnote).

53. S. is thinking of a fumarole, a hole through which vapour issues from the slopes of a volcano. The associations here include: rising hot vapour which lifts wings; a plume of steam; possibly the plumes characteristically worn on the hats of the French revolutionaries (and as frequently depicted for example in Gillray's cartoons). See GM, 'Shelley's Grasp upon the Actual', *EC* iv (1954) 328–31. Fumaroles were commonly described as emitting 'plumes'; e.g. *Philosophical Transactions* cii (1812) 154, where the birth of Sabrina Island in 1811 caused the sea to erupt jets of vapour like 'innumerable plumes of black and white ostrich feathers'.

56. *desires*] This is the reading in *1820* and *1839*, and also in S.'s draft in *Nbk 11*; *Nbk 8* is unclear but apparently reads *desire*.

57. *way*] *Nbk 8*; way, *1820*, *1839*.

60–3. 'It was observed of volcanoes that they not only generated their own "clouds of fire", but attracted more orthodox clouds from elsewhere' (GM); cp. e.g. an account in the *Edinburgh Review* iii (1804) of a volcanic eruption observed from Naples during which 'every cloud that appeared on the horizon was attracted to Vesuvius'.

60. *hurrying:*] hurrying – *Nbk 8*; hurrying *1820* (perhaps corrected in *1839* from S.'s errata list).

544

> Behind, its gathering billows meet
> And to the fatal mountain bear
> Like clouds amid the yielding air.

First Faun

65
> Canst thou imagine where those spirits live
> Which make such delicate music in the woods?
> We haunt within the least frequented caves
> And closest coverts, and we know these wilds,
> Yet never meet them, though we hear them oft:
> Where may they hide themselves?

Second Faun

> 'Tis hard to tell:
70
> I have heard those more skilled in spirits say,
> The bubbles, which the enchantment of the sun

61. *Behind,*] *1820, 1839*. There is no comma in *Nbk 8* or in e.g. *Reiman (1977)*, but the punctuation is necessary to clarify that the echoes *draw* (line 42) not *drive* the destined spirits.

64–97. This passage was added later on the blank ff. 37ʳ and 38ʳ in *Nbk 8*. The lines are not included in S.'s running line-count, and 'Fawns' was probably the last addition to the list of 'Dramatis Personae' in *Nbk 8* (f. 18r). A stage direction at this point in *Nbk 8* reads 'enter [two young *female* canc.] Fauns [alt. from Fawns]'. *BSM* ix 589 is doubtless correct in surmising that the lines may have been added as late as December 1819. This interlude, 'interpolated so as to give Asia and Panthea time to reach their destination' (GM), derives principally from the speeches of the shepherds in Leigh Hunt's *Descent of Liberty* scene ii (1815). *The Descent of Liberty* was included in volume i of Hunt's *Poetical Works* (3 vols 1819), which S. appears to have asked Hunt to send him in August 1819 (*L* ii 113), and which had apparently been read by S. by December 1819 (*L* ii 164). Cp. Cicero, *de Divinatione* I xlv 101: 'We are told that fauns have often been heard in battle and that during turbulent times truly prophetic messages have been sent from mysterious places.' (Loeb trans.).

64–9. Recalling Ferdinand in *The Tempest* I ii 385–93:
> Where should this music be? I' th' air or th' earth?
> It sounds no more; and sure it waits upon
> Some god o' th' island. Sitting on a bank,
> Weeping again the King my father's wreck,
> This music crept by me upon the waters,
> Allaying both their fury and my passion
> With its sweet air; thence I have follow'd it
> Or it hath drawn me rather. But 'tis gone.
> No, it begins again.

67. *closest*] 'Most secret'.

70. *those more skilled in spirits*] i.e. scientists (such as Erasmus Darwin, or Sir Humphrey Davy).

71. *which the enchantment*] *Nbk 8, 1820*; which enchantment *1829, 1839* (Mary S.'s perpetuation of Galignani's error is evidence for *1829* as copy text for *1839*; see *Taylor* 41).

71–82. Commentators have accepted the explanation of these lines in *Grabo (1930)* 172–4 that they portray the hydrogen cycle as described in Darwin's *Botanic Garden* (*Darwin* i, Additional Note xxxii). But *Butter (1954)* 149–50 and *Butter (1970)* 284–5 offer a more persuasive source in *Walker* 231–2. *Butter (1970)* notes Walker's explanation that 'much "inflammable air" (hydrogen) is released from plants in ponds in hot weather. When the

Sucks from the pale faint water-flowers that pave
The oozy bottom of clear lakes and pools,
Are the pavilions where such dwell and float
75 Under the green and golden atmosphere
Which noontide kindles through the woven leaves;
And when these burst, and the thin fiery air,
The which they breathed within those lucent domes,
Ascends to flow like meteors through the night,
80 They ride on it, and rein their headlong speed,
And bow their burning crests, and glide in fire
Under the waters of the Earth again.

---

bubbles which the sun sucks from the plants come out of the water they burst and the hydrogen which they contain, being very light, ascends to the upper air, which is heavily charged with electricity, and there ignites and appears as meteors or falling stars'. There are however problems even with this explanation as according to Darwin and to Joseph Priestley what the sun raised from *live* conferva in *clear* water (see lines 72–3) was not hydrogen but oxygen (see *Darwin* i, Additional Note xxxiii). The fauns' science in fact seems deliberately old-fashioned; Humphrey Davy had proved by 1817 (see *Philosophical Transactions* cvii (1817) 75–6) that hydrogen raised from the earth and ignited could not be the cause of meteors. Cp. *L* i 201 (?10 December 1811, to Elizabeth Hitchener): 'Yet are we, are these souls which measure in their circumscribed domain the distances of yon orbs, are we but the bubbles which arise from the filth of a stagnant pool, merely to be again reabsorbed into the mass of corruption?'

76. *Which noontide*] In *Nbk 8* S. first wrote *Which the noon kindles* then inserted *tide* with a caret after *noon*, but omitted to cancel *the*, thus creating an ametrical line (which was presumably corrected in the press transcript; *BSM* ix detects a faint cancel-line over part of *the* in *Nbk 8*).

78. *lucent domes*] S. at first wrote *lucid homes* in *Nbk 8*, with *lucent domes* as an alternative written above later, and presumably preferred in the press transcript.

80. *it*] *1820, 1839* and most *eds* read *them*, presumably assuming *meteors* (line 79) as the plural referent of the pronoun. The fair copy in *Nbk 8* is tangled at this point, but it seems to confirm that S. in fact assumes the singular *fiery air* as the referent of what was originally *it* in the fair copy. S. first wrote
> They rein its headlong speed & glide with it
> Into the waters of the Earth again

He then altered the lines by inserting *ride on it* & between *They* and *rein*, and altered the original pronoun *its* to *their*, thus changing the implied referent from *fiery air* to *spirits* (line 70). S. then created a new line by adding *And bow their burning crests* as the first half of a line completed by & *glide with it*, to give:
> They ride on it & rein their headlong speed
> And bow their burning crests & glide in fire
> Under the waters of the Earth again

S.'s alteration of *its* to *their* is however so placed on the page (and with the extra confusion of another *their* messily cancelled) as to suggest that it could easily have been miscopied in the press transcript as a *them* replacing the *it* in *They ride on it*. See *BSM* ix 306–7 for a facsimile and transcript of *Nbk 8* f. 37ʳ, and 589–90 for commentary. Confusion is further compounded by the plausible possibility that S. might have considered *fiery air* to mean 'meteors', and therefore to require a plural pronoun.

82. *Earth*] *Nbk 8*; earth *1820, 1839.*

First Faun
If such live thus, have others other lives,
Under pink blossoms or within the bells
85   Of meadow flowers, or folded violets deep,
Or on their dying odours, when they die,
Or in the sunlight of the spherèd dew?

Second Faun
Ay, many more, which we may well divine.
But should we stay to speak, noontide would come,
90   And thwart Silenus find his goats undrawn,
And grudge to sing those wise and lovely songs
Of fate, and chance, and God, and Chaos old,
And Love, and the chained Titan's woeful doom,
And how he shall be loosed, and make the Earth
95   One brotherhood: delightful strains which cheer
Our solitary twilights, and which charm
To silence the unenvying nightingales.

Scene iii

A pinnacle of rock among mountains. Asia *and* Panthea.

Panthea
Hither the sound has borne us — to the realm
Of Demogorgon, and the mighty portal,

---

85. *folded violets deep*] Written in pencil (and later inked in) above *in the violets heart* canc.; an example of a pencil correction by S. to the fair copy before transcription for the press, as *folded violets deep* is the reading in *1820*.

87. *in*] *Nbk 8*; on *1820, 1839*; perhaps an alteration to the press transcript, but the sense suggests a mistranscription or printing error (possibly a dittography from the preceding line).

88. *more,*] *Nbk 8*; more *1820, 1839*.

90. Silenus, who was tutor to Dionysus, is the subject of Virgil's *Eclogue* vi, where in lines 31–42 he is celebrated for his 'wise and lovely songs' (see lines 91–5). His mention here suggests further volcanic associations, as Silenus is also a principal character in Euripides' *Cyclops* (no. 172), which is set on Mount Etna in Sicily.   *undrawn*] unmilked.

92–5. These lines are added underneath S.'s original version in *Nbk 8*, where the last two lines followed line 91; line 96 at that stage read 'Which cheer our lonesome twilights, & which charm'.

93. *Love,*] love *Nbk 8*.   *doom,*] doom *Nbk 8*; dooms, *1820, 1829*; doom. *1839*; *Forman 1876–7* suggests that the stop in *1839* was accidentally inserted by the printer in correcting *dooms,*.

94. *Earth*] *Nbk 8*; earth *1820, 1839*.

¶iii   *SD*. See note to lines 24–33 below.

    Like a volcano's meteor-breathing chasm,
    Whence the oracular vapour is hurled up
5 Which lonely men drink wandering in their youth,
    And call truth, virtue, love, genius, or joy,
    That maddening wine of life, whose dregs they drain
    To deep intoxication, and uplift,
    Like Mænads who cry loud, Evoe! Evoe!
10 The voice which is contagion to the world.

Asia
Fit throne for such a Power! Magnificent!
How glorious art thou, Earth! and if thou be

3. In early nineteenth-century usage 'meteor' usually meant 'any atmospheric phenomenon'; S. here follows the common ascription of meteoric activity to exhalations of the earth, volcanic in this context (see note to lines 24–33 below). Cp. *Alastor* 651 and note. *volcano's*] Volcano's *Nbk 8*.

4. *oracular vapour*] S. draws in this scene on various classical and contemporary accounts of oracles, particularly the oracle at Delphi; Panthea and, more importantly, Asia, are inspired to prophecy in the manner of a priestess intoxicated by vapour from an oracular cavern. S.'s most direct sources are Plutarch, *Moralia*, 'De defectu oraculorum', xl, xliii, l; Diodorus Siculus xvi 26; Lucan, *Pharsalia* v 82–101 and ix 564–5; and see also *Barthelemy* ii 391–2 and note xx. For analogues with Virgil's account of the Cumaean Sybil cp. *Aeneid* vi 240ff.; S. and Mary visited the landscape of Virgil's poem during their stay in Naples (see *L* ii 61). On S.'s conception of the vapour itself see below, note to line 44. *hurled*] breathed *Nbk 8*. The change from *Nbk 8* cannot be a mistranscription; S. presumably altered the press transcript, perhaps to avoid a repetition of *breathing* from the previous line.

7–10. *That maddening wine . . . contagion to the world.*] S. associates the effects of the oracular vapour with the ambivalent frenzy of Maenads, female followers of the cult of Dionysus whose orgies mingle fertility with destructiveness (see note to lines 43–4 below, and note to III iii 124–47). S.'s Maenads derive from Euripides' *Bacchae*; their cry *Evoe* is the standard transliteration of Gk εὐοῖ, an exclamation used in the cult of Dionysus, which was active at Delphi though the oracle was sacred to Apollo; Dionysus took over in winter, when Apollo visited the Hyperboreans (Apollo inspired to articulate prophecy, Dionysus inspired to ecstasy). See *Bacchae* 142 and Sophocles, *Trachiniae* 216–20. Cp. IV 473–5 and note, and for Maenads see also *The Mask of Anarchy* xii, 'Ode to the West Wind' 20–1, 'The Sensitive Plant' 33 and 589, 'Ode to Liberty' 91, 171 and 200, and 'Orpheus' 51–2.

7. *wine of life*] S. often uses wine imagery in a Dionysian sense; cp. *Athanase*, detached passage c and note. See also II iv 65 and note.

8–10. *intoxication . . . contagion*] Both these words can have either a good or bad sense in S., depending on context.

8. *intoxication,*] *Nbk 8*; intoxication; *1820*, *1839*.

11. *Power!*] power! *Nbk 8*. Cp. 'Mont Blanc' 60ff., 127ff.

12. *and*] *Nbk 8*; And *1820*, *1839*. *be*] beest *Nbk 8* (altered in the press transcript).

12–16. Asia appears to formulate a fundamental Platonic doctrine, that the relation of the phenomenal world to the heavenly world of ideas is as the relation of shadow to reality (see *Republic* x). But the carefully provisional phrasing (recalling *Paradise Lost* v 574–6: 'though what if earth / Be but the shadow of heav'n, and things therein / Each to other like, more than on earth is thought?') is characteristic of the open-minded scepticism of S.'s mature

The shadow of some Spirit lovelier still,
Though evil stain its work, and it should be
15 Like its creation, weak yet beautiful,
I could fall down and worship that and thee —
Even now my heart adoreth — Wonderful!
Look Sister — ere the vapour dim thy brain:
Beneath is a wide plain of billowy mist,
20 As a lake, paving in the morning sky,
With azure waves which burst in silver light,
Some Indian vale . . . Behold it, rolling on
Under the curdling winds, and islanding
The peak whereon we stand — midway, around

thought; cp. *PVR*: 'Berkeley & Hume . . . have clearly established the certainty of our ignorance with respect to those obscure questions which under the name of religious truths have been the watch-words of con[*word incomplete in MS*] and the symbols of unjust power ever since they were distorted by the narrow passions of the immediate followers of Jesus from that meaning to which philosophers are even now restoring them' (*SC* vi 971).

13. shadow] Reflection. The pattern of rhyme, lines 12–17, is presumably intentional. *Spirit*] Nbk 8; spirit *1820, 1839*.

14. should be] S. first wrote *must* in Nbk 8, then cancelled it.

15. Like its creation] *Above* Like all we love *canc. Nbk 8*.

16–18. Dashes after *thee, adoreth,* and *sister* in Nbk 8 were replaced in *1820* by a stop, colon, and comma, and subsequent *eds* have introduced a stop after *adoreth* (e.g. *Rossetti 1870, Woodberry 1893, Locock 1911*). But the dashes in Asia's speech in this scene appear to come more frequently as she approaches the moment of special insight signalled in lines 43–6.

18. Sister –] Nbk 8; sister, *1820, 1839*. Asia anticipates the intoxicating effect of the vapour.

19–27. Cp. *Mary Jnl* i 15,18 August 1814: 'From the summit of one of the hills, we see the whole expanse of the valley, filled with a white undulating mist over which the piny hills p[i]erced like islands. The sun had just risen, & a ray of the red light lay on the waves of this fluctuating vapour.' This entry was included with slight alterations in *1817* (*Prose Works* i 193 lines 374–7). See also C. I. Elton, *An Account of Shelley's Visits to France, Switzerland, and Savoy, in the Years 1814 and 1816* (1894) 29–31. *curdling winds*] Cp. *Athanase*, detached passage b, 27.

22. vale . . . Behold] vale . . . behold Nbk 8; vale. Behold *1820, 1839*.

24–33. '. . . the objective setting seems unchallengeable: the nymphs have been attracted (impelled) to the terminal cone of a colossal volcano'. The setting comprises 'a peak that is naked at the top . . . but belted lower down by the forest through which Asia and Panthea have come. All round them . . . stand mountains, in such a way that "The vale is girdled with their walls" – the idea of a *circle* being insistently enforced by the vocabulary . . . A familiar picture emerges: a cone of rock in the centre of a luxuriant elevated valley, encircled by a mountainous wall . . . Asia and Panthea are conceived as standing in a gigantic *caldera*, the bowl-shaped crater of a quiescent volcano with a tall cinder-cone in the middle' (GM). Cp. S.'s letter to Peacock of 17–20 December 1818 (17 or 18 December by Jones) describing the 'conical hill' of Vesuvius (*L* ii 62–3).

24. stand – midway, around] stand, midway, around, *1820, 1839, Forman 1876–7, Hutchinson*, etc. 'The MS. shows that the line was originally left unfinished, the phrase *midway, around* being inserted with a different pen – clearly as a makeshift . . . the "dash" shows [as does the absence of a comma after "around"] that both words must go with *encinctured'* (*Locock 1911*). For a photographic reproduction of the passage in Nbk 8 see *BSM* ix 308.

25 Encinctured by the dark and blooming forests,
  Dim twilight lawns and stream-illumèd caves,
  And wind-enchanted shapes of wandering mist;
  And far on high the keen sky-cleaving mountains
  From icy spires of sunlike radiance fling
30 The dawn, as lifted Ocean's dazzling spray,
  From some Atlantic islet scattered up,
  Spangles the wind with lamp-like water-drops.
  The vale is girdled with their walls — a howl
  Of cataracts from their thaw-cloven ravines
35 Satiates the listening wind, continuous, vast,
  Awful as silence — Hark! the rushing snow!

26. twilight lawns] Nbk 8; twilight-lawns, *1820, 1839*. *stream-illumèd*] Nbk 8 (not accented); stream-illumined *1820, 1829, 1839* (i.e. 'illuminated by streams').

28–42. A rough draft of these lines is in *Box 1* f. 6; for a photographic reproduction with transcription and commentary see *BSM* xxi 2–3, 438–9. Above the draft S. has written 'This was suggested by the Xterly Review', and Timothy Webb ('"The Avalanche of Ages": Shelley's Defence of Atheism and *Prometheus Unbound'*, *KSMB* 35 (1984) 1–39) has shown that the passage originated in S.'s reaction to the attack on his private life and atheism in the *Quarterly's* review of Leigh Hunt's *Foliage* (1818) in the issue of May 1818, xviii 328–9: '. . . if we were told of a man who, placed on a wild rock among the clouds, yet even in that height surrounded by a loftier amphitheatre of spire-like mountains, hanging over a valley of eternal ice and snow, where the roar of mighty waterfalls was at times unheeded from the hollow and more appalling thunder of the deep and unseen avalanche, – if we were told of a man who, thus witnessing the sublimest assemblage of natural objects, should retire to a cabin near and write atheos after his name in the album, we hope our own feelings would be pity rather than disgust . . .'. S. learned of this attack in Peacock's letter of 14 June 1818 (*Peacock Works* viii 194–5) but actually read it in Venice (presumably at Byron's in September or October 1818), when he wrongly but characteristically assumed Southey to be the author (the review was probably by John Taylor Coleridge); see *L* ii 65–6, and headnotes to nos 173–174. For S.'s entry of αθεος in the album of a Swiss hotel see *White* i 456. S.'s poetic response to the *Quarterly's* attack is developed from the terms of the review, and from S.'s own first reactions to Alpine scenery as he recorded them in a letter to Peacock of 22 July 1816 (*L* i 496–7) which was included in *1817* (*Prose Works* i 222–3). The passage implicitly opposes the Christian spirit of contemporary responses to mountain scenery such as Coleridge's 'Hymn Before Sun-Rise, in the Vale of Chamouni' (1802).

29. icy spires] *Above* pyramids *canc.* Nbk 8; cp. *L* i 496, 'the snowy pyramids which shot into the bright blue sky'.

33. walls –] Nbk 8; walls, *1820, 1839*.

36–42. Cp. S.'s letter to Peacock from Chamounix, 26 July 1816 (*L* i 501; included in *1817, Prose Works* i 228) describing the collapse of Mont d'Anterne in 1751: '. . . the smoke of its fall was seen in Piedmont & people went from Turin to investigate whether a volcano had not burst forth among the Alps. It continued falling for many days spreading with the shock & and the thunder of its ruin consternation thro the neighbouring vales & destroying many persons.' S. actually saw the fallen mountain on 26 July (*Mary Jnl* i 119–20). For the political connotations of *avalanche* (a new word in the early nineteenth century; see Sophie Tucker, *Protean Shape* (1967) 12) cp. *PVR*: 'the government party propose to us the dilemma of submitting to a despotism which is notoriously gathering like an avalanche [sic] year by year; or taking the risk of something which it must be confessed bears the aspect of a revolution' (*SC* vi 997).

36. silence –] Nbk 8; silence. *1820, 1839*.

The sun-awakened avalanche! whose mass,
Thrice sifted by the storm, had gathered there
Flake after flake: in Heaven-defying minds
40 As thought by thought is piled, till some great truth
Is loosened, and the nations echo round,
Shaken to their roots: as do the mountains now.

Panthea
Look, how the gusty sea of mist is breaking
In crimson foam, even at our feet! — it rises
45 As Ocean at the enchantment of the moon
Round foodless men wrecked on some oozy isle.

Asia
The fragments of the cloud are scattered up —
The wind that lifts them disentwines my hair —

39. flake:] *Nbk 8*; flake, *1820, 1839*. S.'s colons here and at line 42 are grammatically irregular, but clarify the structure of the metaphor better than the commas in *1820, 1839*, and most subsequent *eds. Heaven-defying*] *Nbk 8*; heaven-defying *1820, 1839*.

40. ' "You see", said Mr Fax to Mr Sarcastic, "the efficacy of associated sympathies. It is but to give an impulse of cooperation to any good and generous feeling, and its progressive accumulation, like that of an alpine avalanche, though but a snowball at the summit, becomes a mountain in the valley" ' (Peacock, *Melincourt* (1817) ch. xxvii).

42. roots:] *Nbk 8*; roots, *1820, 1839*.

43–4. crimson foam] Perhaps suggesting that S. identifies the oracular vapour with nitrous oxide (N^2O, i.e. laughing gas, and first called nitrous oxide by Sir Humphrey Davy who in *Elements of Chemical Philosophy* (1811) noted its effect of 'transient intoxication'). Nitrous oxide is colourless but early experiments with nitrogen compounds sometimes gave nitrogen peroxide (NO^2), a poisonous orange-red gas, which could be present simultaneously with nitrous oxide (see *Elements of Chemical Philosophy*, and also *Darwin* i, *Economy of Vegetation* (1791) note to ii 143). S. was possibly aware from his reading in these and other scientific sources of the mingled presence of beneficial and harmful substances in the red vapour given by experiments with oxides of nitrogen (thus developing the ambivalent connotations of *intoxication . . . contagion*, lines 8–10 above). See III iii 124–47 and note for a wholly beneficial post-revolutionary *crimson air*.

43. Look,] *Nbk 8*; Look *1820, 1839*.

44. feet! –] *Nbk 8*; feet! *1820, 1839*.

46. some] an *Nbk 8*; presumably a change to the press transcript.

47–50. The unusually frequent dashes in *Nbk 8* are expressive of Asia's heightening excitement as the intoxicating vapour takes effect. *Locock 1911* cps. Byron, *Manfred* (1817) I ii 85–9:
> The mists boil up around the glaciers; clouds
> Rise curling fast beneath me, white and sulphury,
> Like foam from the roused ocean of deep Hell,
> Whose every wave breaks on a living shore,
> Heap'd with the damn'd like pebbles. – I am giddy.

47. up –] *Nbk 8*; up; *1820, 1839*.

48. that] which *Nbk 8*; presumably a change to the press transcript. *hair –*] *Nbk 8*; hair; *1820, 1839*.

Its billows now sweep o'er mine eyes — my brain
50 Grows dizzy — seest thou shapes within the mist?

Panthea
A countenance with beckoning smiles — there burns
An azure fire within its golden locks —
Another and another — hark! they speak!

Song of Spirits
To the Deep, to the Deep,
55   Down, down!

49. *mine*] my *Nbk 8*. Presumably a change to the press transcript; S.'s printed texts normally use *mine* when the pronoun precedes a vowel. *eyes –*] *Nbk 8*; eyes; *1820, 1839*.

50. This line presents an important textual crux. *Nbk 8* at first read:
            Grows dizzy – I see shapes within the mist
S. then cancelled *I*, altered *see shapes* by placing a caret after *see* and writing *st thou* above, and altered *mist* to *mist?*, to give
            Grows dizzy – seest thou shapes within the mist?
In *1820* (and *1829*) the line appeared as
            Grows dizzy; I see thin shapes within the mist.
It is difficult to see how S. himself can have produced this reading, as it appears to be a misreading of the altered MS, which produces an awkward and wholly uncharacteristic ametrical line (the strong pause after *dizzy* makes a possible elision unlikely). The implications are that Mary was not only transcribing the press copy, but that S. did not always carefully check the transcription, and that he may have entrusted punctuation of the press transcript to Mary (this might help to explain why Mary apparently did not consult the MS fair copy, still then in her possession, when preparing *PU* for *1839*; see headnote). In *1839* Mary altered the line to correct the metre, to give
            Grows dizzy; I see shapes within the mist.
There is a photographic reproduction and transcription of the MS in *BSM* ix 314–15, with commentary on 593–4. Neil Fraistat in *BSM* reads S.'s insert as *those* rather than *thou* (but this would have produced a slightly awkward reading), and entertains the possibility that *mist* may at some point have read *mists*.

51–2. *Grabo (1930)* 145 suggests that S. has electricity in mind in these lines, but the Spirit is 'more likely to be gaseous oxide of carbon, described by Davy as burning blue at the base of yellow flames, which – together with what the old mineralogists called "the inflammable breath of the pyrites" – was something suggested among the causes of volcanic activity' (GM). Cp. *Edinburgh Review* xiii (1809) 478: 'There are, in fact, according to Mr Davy, three inflammable gases given out in our fires; – the two we have mentioned, and the gaseous oxide of carbon, which is known by its blue flame . . . the gaseous oxide is occasionally seen near the root of the flame, or in contact with the coal . . .'.

51. *smiles –*] *Nbk 8*; smiles: *1820, 1839*.   52. *locks –*] *Nbk 8*; locks! *1820, 1839*.

53. *another – hark!*] another – hark *Nbk 8*; another: hark! *1820, 1839*.

54. *Deep . . . Deep,*] *Nbk 8*; deep . . . deep, *1820, 1839*.

55. *down!*] Down! *Nbk 8*.

54–98. Scene iii originally ended at line 53 in *Nbk 8* f. 39ᵛ, scene iv following immediately on the same page; but S. wrote on the facing page f. 40ʳ, opposite the gap between scenes iii and iv, *desideratur aliquid*, and subsequently wrote in the Song of Spirits on the blank pages ff. 40ʳ, 41ʳ, and 42ʳ. S.'s draft of this lyric is in *Nbk 10* (see *MYR* iv for photographic repro-

> Through the shade of Sleep,
> Through the cloudy strife
> Of Death and of Life;
> Through the veil and the bar
60   Of things which seem and are,
> Even to the steps of the remotest Throne,
> Down, down!

> While the sound whirls around,
> Down, down!
65   As the fawn draws the hound,
> As the lightning the vapour,
> As a weak moth the taper;
> Death, Despair; Love, Sorrow;

---

ductions and transcription of the MS, with commentary) except for the passage that became lines 86–9 which is on a page torn from *Nbk 10* and now in the Pforzheimer Library (SC 548, *SC* vi 1069–71). *SC* vi 1104 argues that the lyric 'was certainly' one of the lyrical insertions sent by S. to Ollier in December 1819 together with Act IV (see SC 554, *SC* vi 1099, a letter from S. to Ollier dated 23 December 1819). S.'s draft of the Song of Spirits in *Nbk 10* is divided by his rough draft of *The Mask of Anarchy*, which cannot have been written before 6 September when he received news of Peterloo (see headnote to *Mask*). There are stylistic and thematic affinities with Act IV which may suggest a date late in 1819, but for arguments that the Song was composed in September, and possibly sent to England on 12 September with the press transcript of Acts I–III, see *BSM* ix 595, and *Curran (1975)* 209. The lyric has frequently been interpreted in Platonic terms (see e.g. *Grabo (1935)* 69–70, and *Notopoulos* 247) which derive ultimately from Plato's myth of the cave in *Republic* vii; but cp. *Butter (1970)* 287: '. . . Shelley's characters are descending into a cave in order to confront "things that . . . are," whereas in Plato's myth it would be the ascent from the cave into the light of the sun which would represent the attainment of knowledge of the intellectual world. So we must be careful to understand the images as they occur in their contexts in Shelley without bringing in more from Plato than is relevant.' The descent of Asia and Panthea into the realm of Demogorgon is probably modelled primarily on Boccaccio, *Genealogie Deorum Gentilium* i 14, cited in trans. in *Curran (1975)*: '. . . the rustics . . . entered caves in the deepest and most secret recesses of the earth, where in darkness and the grand silence caused by the absence of light, there arose religion and natural fear; and to the ignorant was born the suspicion of a divine presence, a divinity whom they imagined to exist beneath the earth, Demogorgon.'

56. Sleep,] *Nbk 8*; sleep, *1820, 1839.*   *58. Life;*] life *Nbk 8.*

61. Throne,] *Nbk 8*; throne, *1820, 1839.*

62. down!] Down! *Nbk 8.*   *64. down!*] Down! *Nbk 8.*

65–9. The syntax of line 67 is inverted relative to that of lines 65–6: 'as a weak moth is drawn by the taper'. This inversion then makes for difficulty in the following lines because the implied verbs can be understood as passive where they have previously been active, creating ambiguity in which form of the verb is intended in lines 68–9. There is room for argument, but the probable sense is 'as Despair draws Death; as Love draws Sorrow; as Time draws both Death and Sorrow; as today draws tomorrow'.

66. Scientists in S.'s day believed that electricity played a large part in the formation of cloud, and that cloud movement was directed by electrical charge; cp. *Walker* ii 38: 'The water rises [as vapour] through the air flying on the wings of elecricity'. See also notes to 'The Cloud'.

68. Death Despair, Love Sorrow *Nbk 8*; Death, despair; love, sorrow; *1820, 1839.*

Time both; to-day, to-morrow;
70   As steel obeys the Spirit of the stone,
Down, down!

Through the grey void Abysm,
Down, down!
Where the air is no prism,
75   And the moon and stars are not,
And the cavern-crags wear not
The radiance of Heaven,
Nor the gloom to Earth given;
Where there is One pervading, One alone,
80   Down, down!

In the depth of the Deep,
Down, down!
Like veiled lightning asleep,
Like that spark nursed in embers
85   The last look Love remembers,
Like a diamond which shines
On the dark wealth of mines,
A spell is treasured but for thee alone.
Down, down!

69. *to-day*] To-day *Nbk 8.*

70. *Spirit*] *Nbk 8;* spirit *1820, 1839.*

72. *grey*] *Nbk 8;* grey, *1820, 1839. Abysm,*] Abysm *Nbk 8;* abysm, *1820, 1839.*

73. *down!*] Down! *Nbk 8.*

74. 'Where there is no light for the atmosphere to refract into colour'.

78. *given;*] *Nbk 8;* given, *1820, 1839.*

79. *One . . . One*] *Nbk 8;* one . . . one *1820, 1839.*

80. *down!*] Down! *Nbk 8.*

81. *Deep,*] Deep *Nbk 8;* deep; *1820, 1839.*

82. *down!*] Down! *Nbk 8.*

83. *lightning*] Lightning *Nbk 8.*

84. *that*] *Nbk 8;* the *1820, 1839, eds.* Possibly a change to the press transcript, but probably a mistranscription; the difficult draft in *Nbk 10* also appears to read *that* (though Mary Quinn's transcription in *MYR* iv 26–7 is indeterminate), and the reference is obviously to the following line. *embers*] *Nbk 8;* embers, *1820, 1839.*

86–7. Diamonds were thought to be phosphorescent; cp. *Darwin* i, *Economy of Vegetation* (1791) note to ii 228, and see *L&C* I 586–90 and note.

86. *diamond*] *Nbk 8;* diamond, *1820, 1839.*

88. *Treasured*] hidden *above* buried *canc. Nbk 8. for*] from *above* for *canc. Nbk 8;* clearly S. had difficulty with this line, and continued to alter it in the press transcript.

89. *down!*] Down! *Nbk 8.*

90   We have bound thee, we guide thee
               Down, down!
             With the bright form beside thee —
             Resist not the weakness:
             Such strength is in meekness
95   That the Eternal, the Immortal,
             Must unloose through life's portal
         The snake-like Doom coiled underneath his throne
             By that alone!

Scene iv

The Cave of Demogorgon. Asia *and* Panthea.

Panthea
What veilèd form sits on that ebon throne?

90–8. 'The sense may be – "Do not chafe under the helplessness caused by the fetters with which we have bound you; for it is only by your passive obedience now that Demogorgon will be able to send up into the world of life the Doom of Jupiter".' (*Locock 1911*); GM, concurring, adds 'i.e. Freedom is the consciousness of necessity'.

90. *guide thee*] Nbk 8; guide thee; *1820, 1839*.

91. *down!*] Down! Nbk 8.

92. *the*] *over* that, *itself written over* thy Nbk 8. *thee –*] Nbk 8; thee; *1820, 1839*.

93. *weakness:*] weakness – Nbk 8; weakness, *1820, 1839*. Cp. *I Corinthians* i 25, 'the weakness of God is stronger than men'; *I Corinthians* xv 43, 'it [the resurrection of the dead] is sown in weakness; it is raised in power'.

97. *snake-like doom*] Cp. IV 567.

98. *alone!*] Nbk 8; alone. *1820, 1839*.

¶iv *SD.* The arrival of Asia and Panthea at Demogorgon's cave is crucial in relation to the poem's volcanic symbolism: 'It is clear what was to be expected, scientifically speaking, if children of Ocean were drawn into contact with the magma of a volcanic cavern – a violent eruption, accompanied by the classic symptoms: earthquakes; mephitic vapours; the familiar pine-tree cloud; the bursting of a storm, with *ferilli* or volcanic lightning; and of course destruction . . .' (GM). Contemporary scientific opinion entertained the possibility that volcanic eruption was caused by the entry of sea water into magmatic reservoirs, leading to a huge explosion (see e.g. *Quarterly Review* xv (1816) 382, *Edinburgh Review* xxvii (1816) 161); and this view echoed classical accounts of volcanic activity, e.g. in Lucretius, *De Re. Nat.* vi 696–702: 'From this sea, caverns reach underground right to the lofty throat of the mountain. By these we must admit that [wind mingled with water] passes in, and that the nature of the case compels [it often to rise] and to penetrate completely within from the open sea, and to blow out the flame and so to uplift it on high, and cast up the rocks and raise clouds of sand; for on the topmost summit are craters . . . what we speak of as the throat or the mouth.' (Loeb trans.).

1–31. The exchange between Asia and Demogorgon is characteristic of dialogue in alternating single lines in Gk drama (*stichomythia*); cp. e.g. *Prometheus Bound* 515–25.

Asia
The veil has fallen!

Panthea
                    I see a mighty Darkness
Filling the seat of power; and rays of gloom
Dart round, as light from the meridian sun,
5   Ungazed upon and shapeless — neither limb,
Nor form, nor outline; yet we feel it is
A living Spirit.

Demogorgon
                    Ask what thou wouldst know.

Asia
What canst thou tell?

Demogorgon
                    All things thou dar'st demand.

Asia
Who made the living world?

Demogorgon
                    God.

2–7. Cp. *Paradise Lost* ii 666–70:

                    The other shape –
                 If shape it might be called that shape had none
                 Distinguishable in member, joint, or limb
                 Or substance might be called that shadow seemed,
                 For each seemed either – black it stood as Night . . .

See also Mary Wollstonecraft, *Vindication of the Rights of Woman* ch. ix: 'the shapeless void
called – eternity. – For shape, can it be called, "that shape hath none?" ' (*MWW* v 218).

2. *fallen!*] Nbk 8 has the exclamation mark introduced into what were originally three sus-
pension points; fallen. *1820, 1839.*   Darkness] Nbk 8; darkness *1820, 1839.*

3–4. As *Grabo (1930)* 87 has shown, S. attributes to Demogorgon the properties of infra-red
rays as discovered by Herschel in 1800; GM argues that Demogorgon emits infra-red rays
'because he is extremely hot; too hot to be visible. It was known, in Herschel's own words
on the solar spectrum, that "the full red still falls short of the maximum of heat; which per-
haps lies even beyond visible refraction". Demogorgon is, in fact, realised in terms of molten
magma, the obscure and terrible volcanic agent hidden in the depths of the earth'. *Butter
(1954)* 154 suggests a source in Davy's *Elements of Chemical Philosophy* (1811) II ii.

3. *power;*] Nbk 8; power, *1820, 1839.*

4. *sun,*] Sun Nbk 8.

5. *shapeless –*] shapeless – . . Nbk 8; shapeless; *1820, 1839.*

Asia

                              Who made all
10   That it contains — thought, passion, reason, will,
      Imagination?

Demogorgon
                    God: Almighty God.

Asia
      Who made that sense which, when the winds of spring
      In rarest visitation, or the voice
      Of one beloved heard in youth alone,
15   Fills the faint eyes with falling tears which dim
      The radiant looks of unbewailing flowers,
      And leaves this peopled earth a solitude
      When it returns no more?

Demogorgon
                              Merciful God.

Asia
      And who made terror, madness, crime, remorse,
20   Which from the links of the great chain of things

---

10. *contains* –] *Nbk 8*; contains? *1820, 1839.*

12–18. These lines are ungrammatical, as the second and third sub-clauses in the sentence both imply a verb which is not present; the plural *winds* and singular *voice* cannot both govern *Fills*. There may well be a hiatus in the text, although *Nbk 8* does not differ significantly from *1820* or *1839*, so there is no basis for emendation in any witness. Presumably *sense* governs both *Fills* and *leaves*; *as* for *when* in line 12 would give a coherent reading. Asia appears to recall here her own words at the beginning of Act II. Cp. S.'s essay 'On Love' (1818): 'There is eloquence in the tongueless wind, and a melody in the flowing brooks and the rustling of reeds beside them, which by their inconceivable relation to something within the soul awaken the spirits to dance of breathless rapture, and bring tears of mysterious tenderness to the eyes, like the enthusiasm of patriotic success, or the voice of one beloved singing to you alone . . . So soon as this want or power is dead, Man becomes a living sepulchre of himself, and what yet survives is the mere husk of what once he was.' (SC 488; *SC* vi 635).

20. *things*] *Nbk 8*; things, *1820, 1839.*

20–2. Cp. S.'s letter to Peacock from Rome, 6 April 1819: 'In the square of St. Peters there are about 300 fettered criminals at work, hoeing out the weeds that grow between the stones of the pavement. Their legs are heavily ironed, & some are chained two by two. They sit in long rows hoeing out the weeds, dressed in party-coloured clothes. Near them sit or saunter, groupes of soldiers armed with loaded muskets. The iron discord of those innumerable chains clanks up into the sonorous air, and produces, contrasted with the musical dashing of the fountains, & the deep azure beauty of the sky & the magnif[ic]ence of the architecture around a conflict of sensations allied to madness. It is the emblem of Italy: moral degradation contrasted with the glory of nature & the arts' (*L* ii 93–4). See also *Mary L* i 66–7 (qu. in note to no. 166 lines 7–11), *Q Mab* v 51–2 and note, and *J&M* 300–3:

To every thought within the mind of man
Sway and drag heavily — and each one reels
Under the load towards the pit of death;
Abandoned hope, and love that turns to hate;
25 And self-contempt, bitterer to drink than blood;
Pain, whose unheeded and familiar speech
Is howling and keen shrieks, day after day;
And Hell, or the sharp fear of Hell?

Demogorgon
                                        He reigns.

Asia
Utter his name: a world pining in pain
30 Asks but his name: curses shall drag him down.

Demogorgon
He reigns.

Asia
                    I feel, I know it: who?

Demogorgon
                                        He reigns.

                    'Month after month,' he cried, 'to bear this load
                    And as a jade urged by the whip and goad
                    To drag life on, which like a heavy chain
                    Lengthens behind with many a link of pain! –'

22. heavily –] Nbk 8; heavily, *1820, 1839.*

24–5. These lines were added later in Nbk 8 on f. 42ʳ facing the draft on f. 41ᵛ (but before the final stanza of the 'Song of Spirits' from II iii, which is also drafted on f. 42ʳ).

27–8. S. has cancelled three lines at this point in Nbk 8:
                    Or looks which tell that while the lips are calm
                    And the eyes cold, the spirit weeps within
                    Tears like the sanguine sweat of agony;
As various commentators have noted, these lines also appear, slightly modified, in *Athanase* (Detached Passage a, lines 1–3) and *The Cenci* I i 109–13.

27. howling] Nbk 8; howling, *1820, 1839.*

28–31. Demogorgon's answers are in the cryptic manner typical of oracles. 'Asia's exasperating "dialogue" with Demogorgon only makes sense . . . if it is realised that she is talking to herself. She is made to interrogate her own soul; and Demogorgon can supply no answer that she cannot supply herself at this moment of supreme prophetic consciousness, or for which she has insufficient knowledge even to frame the question meaningfully' (GM). With Demogorgon's repeated *He reigns,* cp. Asia's definition of *to reign* at lines 47–8 below.

30. curses] Ironically counterpointing Prometheus's preoccupation with his curse in Act I.

31. Asia becomes conscious that she is about to be inspired to prophecy (in the long speech which follows).

Asia
Who reigns? There was the Heaven and Earth at first,
And Light and Love; then Saturn, from whose throne
Time fell, an envious shadow; such the state
35   Of the earth's primal spirits beneath his sway,
As the calm joy of flowers and living leaves
Before the wind or sun has withered them
And semi-vital worms; but he refused

32–109. Asia's prophetic insight discerns Prometheus's historical role in alleviating the self-imposed miseries of existence, but refuses to identify evil with individual human agency (this perception undermines the tyrant's claim to absolute power and thus paves the way for his downfall). S.'s principal source for this speech is *Prometheus Bound* 436–506, where Prometheus describes the benefits he has contributed to humanity; Asia's speech offers a similarity of general outline and some close verbal parallels (although S. omits the Aeschylean account of divination, *PB* 484–90). There are also marked similarities with the account of Prometheus in Thomas Blackwell, *Letters Concerning Mythology* (1748) 45–8. A further strong influence is from Peacock's Zoroastrian poem 'Ahrimanes', written around 1814 and not published in Peacock's lifetime, but well-known to Shelley (see *SC* iii 211–43). The speech's overview of human progress has parallels in several of S.'s prose and verse writings, notably the 'Ode to Liberty' (published with *PU* in *1820*). Other influences have been noted from Plato's *Statesman* (see L. Winstanley, 'Platonism in Shelley', in *Essays and Studies* iv (1913) 72–100, esp. 98–9), and Rousseau's *Discourse on Inequality*.

32–8. Recalling Hesiod's accounts in *Theogony* and *Works and Days* of a lost Saturnian Golden Age, but S.'s primal period is not here idealised: cp. 'Essay on Christianity' (1817): 'The . . . antient Poets . . . represented equality as the reign of Saturn, and taught that mankind had gradually degenerated from the virtue which enabled them to enjoy or maintain this happy state. Their doctrine was philosophically false . . . uncivilized man is the most pernicious and miserable of beings . . .' (*Prose Works* i 268). Cp. also the opening of Virgil's *Eclogue* iv:

> Ultima Cumaei venit iam carminis aetas;
> magnus ab integro saeculorum nascitur ordo.
> iam redit at Virgo, redeunt Saturnia regna;
> iam nova progenies caelo demittitur alto.

('Now is come the last age of the song of Cumae; the great line of the centuries begins anew. Now the Virgin returns, the reign of Saturn renews; now a new generation descends from heaven on high.' Loeb trans.)

32–3. Time is Saturn's shadow; S. perhaps puns on Saturn's Gk name, Kronos; this was a common Neoplatonic allegory (because it explains why Kronos devours his own children). Cp. 'The Assassins' (1814–15): 'Time was measured and created by the vices and the miseries of men . . .' (*Prose Works* i 130).

34. shadow;] *Nbk 8*; shadow: *1820, 1839*.

35. earth's] *Nbk 8* has *world's* underlined, with *earth* as an alternative written on the facing page; S. evidently decided on *earth's* in the press transcript.

36–8. Line 37 is written as an insert on the page facing the draft in *Nbk 8*; its inclusion produces an ambiguous syntax where the phrase *And semi-vital worms* can be understood either as an instance, with *flowers and living leaves*, of things possessing calm joy, or as one of the subjects, with *wind or sun*, of *withered* in the preceding line. The ambiguity is apt given the transitional and emergent character of Saturnian life in S.'s conception (cp. *semi-vital*, i.e. a transitional form in evolutionary terms; see note to IV 86–7).

37. has] have *Nbk 8*.

The birthrights of their being, knowledge, power,
40 The skill which wields the elements, the thought
Which pierces this dim universe like light,
Self-empire, and the majesty of love;
For thirst of which they fainted. Then Prometheus
Gave wisdom, which is strength, to Jupiter,
45 And with this law alone: 'Let man be free',
Clothed him with the dominion of wide Heaven.
To know nor faith, nor love, nor law; to be
Omnipotent but friendless, is to reign;
And Jove now reigned; for on the race of man
50 First famine, and then toil, and then disease,
Strife, wounds, and ghastly death unseen before,
Fell; and the unseasonable seasons drove,
With alternating shafts of frost and fire,
Their shelterless, pale tribes to mountain caves;
55 And in their desert hearts fierce wants he sent,
And mad disquietudes, and shadows idle
Of unreal good, which levied mutual war,
So ruining the lair wherein they raged.
Prometheus saw, and waked the legioned hopes
60 Which sleep within folded Elysian flowers,
Nepenthe, Moly, Amaranth, fadeless blooms,

39. birthrights] *Nbk 8*; birthright *1820, 1839*. In *Nbk 8 knowledge* is written above *wisdom* canc.

41. universe] Universe *Nbk 8*.

43–6. 'Mankind entrusted the administration and intellectual welfare of society to functionaries who betrayed their office and wielded power in their own interests' (GM).

45. alone:] *Nbk 8* (without quotation marks); alone, *1820, 1839*.

48. friendless,] *Nbk 8*; friendless *1820, 1839*. Cp. *Prometheus Bound* 225, τοῖς φίλοισι μὴ πεποιθέναι ('not to trust in friends').

49–58. Implying that it is not Prometheus's curse which has disordered nature, but Jove's misrule. S. believed that men's moral state and physical environment are not merely correlated but are linked aspects of the same cosmic harmony, and that adverse physical conditions are a function of humanity's moral consciousness. See *Q Mab* viii 145–86 and note, and cp. III iii 115–23.

52. Christian and Classical accounts share the assumption that the golden age enjoyed perpetual spring, and that after the fall the succession of the seasons was produced by the libration of the earth on its axis. See e.g. *Paradise Lost* x 666–70.

54. caves;] caves *Nbk 8*; caves: *1820, 1839*.

55–8. 'Having identified abstract evils amid the data of experience, men began to take arms against their newly-conceived troubles in ways consonant with Jupiter, their primitive self-conception' (*Reiman (1969)* 79).

61. Nepenthe was a drug which brought forgetfulness of trouble, used by Helen to dispel Menelaus's grief (*Odyssey* iv 219–32; cp. *TL* 359). *Moly* was a black-rooted, white-flowered plant of magical properties, given by Hermes to Ulysses as a charm against the sorceries of Circe (*Odyssey* x 302–6). Both are familiar in Spenser and Milton (e.g. *Faerie Queene* IV iii 43, *Comus*

That they might hide with thin and rainbow wings
The shape of Death; and Love he sent to bind
The disunited tendrils of that vine
65 Which bears the wine of life, the human heart;
And he tamed fire which, like some beast of prey,
Most terrible, but lovely, played beneath
The frown of man; and tortured to his will
Iron and gold, the slaves and signs of power,
70 And gems and poisons, and all subtlest forms
Hidden beneath the mountains and the waves.
He gave man speech, and speech created thought
Which is the measure of the universe;
And Science struck the thrones of Earth and Heaven,
75 Which shook, but fell not; and the harmonious mind
Poured itself forth in all-prophetic song;

675–6, 636–7). The *Amaranth* is an unfading flower found only in Paradise, and symbolic of immortality (cp. e.g. *Faerie Queene* III vi 45, *Lycidas* 149, *Paradise Lost* iii 353–7; cp. *R&H* 1308 and note, *Athanase* 131 and note).

63. *Death;*] death, *Nbk 8*.

64. Obviously anticipating *the wine of life* in the following line; but S. perhaps also suggests a visual image of the circulatory blood system.

65. Cp. Euripides, *Bacchae* 773–4:

> οἴνου δὲ μηκέτ' ὄντος οὐκ ἔστιν Κύπρις
> οὐδ' ἄλλο τερπνὸν οὐδὲν ἀνθρώποις ἔτι

('When wine is no more found, then Love is not, / Nor any joy beside is left to men.' Loeb trans.)

66. *prey*] chase *Nbk 8*. Presumably S.'s change to the press transcript; the reading is doubtful, but the word in *Nbk 8* does seem definitely to begin *cha*. See *BSM* ix 330–1, 600.

72. *thought*] *Nbk 8*; thought, *1820*, *1839*. The line appears to imply an extreme materialism in prioritising the physical capacity for speech over thought itself, and commentators have noted the comparison with IV 415–17. But the idea that thought is actually made possible by speech is difficult to reconcile with S.'s discussions of language and mentality elsewhere; cp. e.g. *DMAA* (1818): 'Their very language [i.e. the Athenians] – a type of the understandings of which it was the creation and the image – in variety, in simplicity, in flexibility, and in copiousness, excels every other language of the western world.' (*Prose* 217). Cp. also 'On Life' (1819): 'Thoughts and feelings arise, with or without our will, and we employ words to express them.' (*Prose* 172). The received line could be understood to refer simply to two related Promethean gifts. GM conjectured a hyphen between *speech* and *created*, which together with the absence of a comma after *thought* in *Nbk 8* would imply that thought, usefully articulated and made shareable by speech, is the subject of the following line. For suggestive discussion see *Wasserman* 136–8, and William Keach, *Shelley's Style* (1984) 34–7. In Gk thought λόγος is both thought (reason) and speech, and neither is conceivable without the other.

73. *universe;*] Universe *Nbk 8*. Adapted from the famous dictum of the Sophist Protagoras, 'Man is the measure of all things'.

74. *Earth and Heaven,*] Earth and Heaven *Nbk 8*; earth and heaven, *1820*, *1839*. The last line of S.'s fair copy of Act II in *Nbk 8*; the fair copy continues in *Nbk 9* (f. 1ᵛ).

And music lifted up the listening spirit
Until it walked, exempt from mortal care,
Godlike, o'er the clear billows of sweet sound;
80   And human hands first mimicked and then mocked,
With moulded limbs more lovely than its own,
The human form, till marble grew divine,
And mothers, gazing, drank the love men see
Reflected in their race — behold, and perish.
85   He told the hidden power of herbs and springs,
And Disease drank and slept. Death grew like sleep.
He taught the implicated orbits woven
Of the wide-wandering stars, and how the Sun
Changes his lair, and by what secret spell
90   The pale Moon is transformed, when her broad eye
Gazes not on the interlunar sea;
He taught to rule, as life directs the limbs,

77–9. Suggesting Christ walking on the water, *Matthew* xiv 25–6.

82. till marble] Inserted on the page facing the draft, which originally read *until it grew divine*; S. has cancelled *it* (but not *until*). *divine,*] Nbk 9, *1840*; divine; *1820*; divine *1839*.

83–4. It was generally believed that strong visual or mental impressions during pregnancy could modify an unborn child, hence the resemblance of a child to its father (cp. *R&H* 1218–24 and note, and see Erasmus Darwin, *Zoonomia* (1794–6) ch. 39.6.3). Many *eds* have followed Swinburne's gloss, quoted in *Zillman Variorum* 471: 'Women with child gazing on statues . . . bring forth children like them – children whose features reflect the passion of the gaze and perfection of the sculptured beauty; men, seeing, are consumed with love; "perish" meaning simply "deperire"; compare Virgil's well-worn version, "Ut vidi, ut perii" ["As I saw, how was I lost!" (*Eclogue* viii 41)].' But S.'s sense may more straightforwardly be that women, in gazing on idealised statues, imagine the potentialities of their unborn children; cp. IV 412–14 and note. The subject of *behold, and perish* is presumably the *men* of line 83, but the grammar is dislocated and the sense unclear; S. perhaps intends an ironic contrast between the permanence of ideal representations of humanity, and the transient experience of actual people (a major theme in *PU* as a whole).

84. race –] Nbk 9; race, *1820, 1839*.

87–9. Grabo (1930) 169–70 suggests that the implicated (i.e. 'entangled, mingled together', *Concordance*) orbits might be those of the planets of the solar system, or alternatively might be those of comets, citing a possible source in J. S. Bailly's *Letters to Voltaire* (S. mentions Bailly in his note to *Q Mab* vi 45–6). The sun's changing *lair* probably refers either to the seeming movement of the sun relative to the constellations, or to Herschel's discovery that the solar system is moving towards the constellation Hercules.

88. stars,] Nbk 9; stars; *1820, 1839*. *Sun*] Nbk 9; sun *1820, 1839*.

89. spell] See note to I 61.

90. Moon] moon Nbk 9, *1820, 1839*.

91. interlunar] i.e. between a waning and waxing moon; cp. Milton, *Samson Agonistes* 87–9: 'silent as the moon / When she deserts the night / Hid in her vacant interlunar cave.' *sea;*] Nbk 9; sea: *1820, 1839*.

92–4. i.e. the development of marine navigation in sailing ships enabled inter-continental communication.

The tempest-wingèd chariots of the Ocean,
And the Celt knew the Indian. Cities then
95 Were built, and through their snow-like columns flowed
The warm winds, and the azure ether shone,
And the blue sea and shadowy hills were seen.
Such, the alleviations of his state,
Prometheus gave to man — for which he hangs
100 Withering in destined pain: but who rains down
Evil, the immedicable plague, which, while
Man looks on his creation like a God
And sees that it is glorious, drives him on,
The wreck of his own will, the scorn of Earth,
105 The outcast, the abandoned, the alone?
Not Jove: while yet his frown shook Heaven, aye, when
His adversary from adamantine chains
Cursed him, he trembled like a slave. Declare
Who is his master? Is he too a slave?

94–7. Cp. *L* ii 73: 'Above & between the multitudinous shafts of the [?sunshiny] columns [of Pompeii], was seen the blue sea reflecting the purple heaven of noon above it, & supporting as it were on its line the dark lofty mountains of Sorrento, of a blue inexpressibly deep . . .'

99. man –] *Nbk 9*; man, *1820, 1839*.

100–16. Asia's metaphysical question concerning the origin of evil receives a sceptical answer from S. in the dramatic context. Jove embodies the evil for which humanity is itself collectively responsible; cp. Rousseau, *Émile* (1762), Bk iv, 'The Creed of a Savoyard Priest': 'It is the abuse of our powers that makes us unhappy and wicked. Our cares, our sorrows, our sufferings are of our own making. Moral ills are undoubtedly the work of man, and physical ills would be nothing but for our vices which have made us liable to them . . . O Man! seek no further for the author of evil; thou art he. There is no evil but the evil you do or the evil you suffer, and both come from yourself' (Everyman trans. Barbara Foxley (1911) 244). But Asia's oracular intuition implies deeper questions about ultimate origins which are not susceptible to human inquiry.

100. rains] *Nbk 9, 1839*; reigns *1820* (perhaps deriving from a mistaken proof correction, as a compositor's error seems unlikely); first corrected in *1829*.

101. immedicable] 'Incapable of being healed'. Peacock uses the word in 'Ahrimanes' (*SC* iii 223), and see also Byron, *Childe Harold's Pilgrimage* IV cxxvi. There is also an ironic allusion to the remediable plagues in *Exodus* viii.

102. Cp. *Paradise Lost* iv 32–4: 'O thou that with surpassing glory crowned / Look'st from thy sole dominion like the god / Of this new world . . .'

103. on,] on *Nbk 9, 1820, 1839*.

104. Earth,] *Nbk 9*; earth, *1820, 1839*.

106. Heaven,] *Nbk 9*; heaven *1820, 1839*.

107. Cp. *Prometheus Bound* 6: ἀδαμαντίνων δεσμῶν ἐν ἀρρήκτοις πέδαις ('adamantine chains that cannot be broken').

109–16. Cp. the questions and answers between Philocles and Lysis (a Pythagorean) in *Barthelemy* vi 24–32: 'Philocles: Tell me, Lysis, who formed the world? / Lysis: God. / . . . Philocles: Is God the author of evil? / Lysis: The good Being can only be the cause of good.'

Demogorgon
110 All spirits are enslaved which serve things evil:
Thou knowest if Jupiter be such or no.

Asia
Whom called'st thou God?

Demogorgon
I spoke but as ye speak,
For Jove is the supreme of living things.

Asia
Who is the master of the slave?

Demogorgon
If the Abysm
115 Could vomit forth its secrets: — but a voice
Is wanting, the deep truth is imageless;
For what would it avail to bid thee gaze
On the revolving world? what to bid speak
Fate, Time, Occasion, Chance and Change? To these
120 All things are subject but eternal Love.

Asia
So much I asked before, and my heart gave
The response thou hast given; and of such truths
Each to itself must be the oracle.

---

110. It is a repeated emphasis of S.'s that tyrants, as the agents and perpetrators of evil, are morally as damaged as their victims, and effectively as enslaved as their slaves. Cp. I 50–6, 480–2, 632–4. For the doctrine that it is worse to do than to suffer evil see Plato, *Gorgias*, 469–80 (e.g. 469: 'to do wrong is worse, in the same degree as it is fouler, than to suffer it . . .' Loeb trans.); and cp. note to I 402–5.

114. Abysm] Nbk 9; abysm *1820, 1839.*

115. secrets: – but] Nbk 9; secrets. But *1820, 1839.* As *Wasserman* 345 notes, '*vomere* and *evomere* were the terms most frequently used by the Latin authors to describe volcanic action'.

116. 'All figures from the world of human experience are misleading when applied to ultimates' (F. W. Pottle, in *Shelley: A Collection of Critical Essays*, ed. G. Ridenour (1965) 146).

117–20. 'Love is *human* – not in the sphere of operation of these things' (GM).

118. what] Nbk 9; What *1820, 1839.*

120. Love.] love. Nbk 9.

121–3. Paul Turner (*RES* n.s. x (1959) 274–5) argues that S.'s image of the heart as an oracular shrine is adapted from Lucretius, *De Re. Nat.* i 736–9.

122. response] Stressed on the first syllable; cp. *Alastor* 564 and note, *R&H* 448.

One more demand; and do thou answer me
125 As my own soul would answer, did it know
That which I ask. Prometheus shall arise
Henceforth the Sun of this rejoicing world:
When shall the destined hour arrive?

Demogorgon

Behold!

Asia
The rocks are cloven, and through the purple night
130 I see cars drawn by rainbow-wingèd steeds
Which trample the dim winds: in each there stands
A wild-eyed charioteer, urging their flight.
Some look behind, as fiends pursued them there,
And yet I see no shapes but the keen stars:
135 Others, with burning eyes, lean forth, and drink
With eager lips the wind of their own speed,
As if the thing they loved fled on before,

124–6. S.'s draft in *Nbk 9* at first read:
> One more demand . . . and be thine answer now
> Nor doubtful nor obscure.

He then altered *be* to *do*, *thine* to *thou*, and *now* to *me*, cancelled *Nor doubtful nor obscure*, and wrote *As my own soul would answer, did it know / That which I ask* – on the facing page.

126–8. 'Asia prophesies: ignorantly she triggers off what she announces . . . First Asia breathes the divine vapour and is inspired to be her own oracle, until her ultimate question: *When shall the destined hour arrive?* And at this point she is answered by a volcanic explosion . . .' (GM).

127. Sun] *Nbk 9*; sun *1820, 1839*.

129. The rocks are cloven] A volcanic eruption caused by the meeting of Demogorgon and the sea-sisters. The *purple night* presumably refers to the night of darkness in Demogorgon's realm; see II v 8–11 and note.

132. charioteer,] *Nbk 9*; charioteer *1820, 1839*.

133. Recalling Coleridge, *Ancient Mariner* (1798) 451–6:
> Like one, that on a lonely road
> Doth walk in fear and dread,
> And having once turn'd round, walks on
> And turns no more his head:
> Because he knows, a frightful fiend
> Doth close behind him tread.

135–8. Cp. S.'s description in a letter to Peacock of the Arch of Titus in Rome: 'There are three arches, whose roofs are panelled with fretwork, & their sides adorned with similar reliefs. The keystone of these arches is supported each by two winged figures of Victory, whose hair floats on the wind of their own speed, & whose arms are outstretched bearing trophies, as if impatient to meet . . . Their lips are parted; a delicate mode of indicating the fervour of their desire to arrive at their destined resting place, & to express the eager respiration of their speed.' (To Peacock, 23 March 1819, *L* ii 86, 89). S. also recalls Ariel's 'I drink the air before me, and return', *The Tempest* V i 102.

565

And now, even now, they clasped it. Their bright locks
Stream like a comet's flashing hair: they all
140 Sweep onward.

Demogorgon
These are the immortal Hours,
Of whom thou didst demand. One waits for thee.

Asia
A spirit with a dreadful countenance
Checks its dark chariot by the craggy gulf.
Unlike thy brethren, ghastly charioteer,
145 What art thou? Whither wouldst thou bear me? Speak!

Spirit
I am the shadow of a destiny
More dread than is my aspect: ere yon planet
Has set, the Darkness which ascends with me
Shall wrap in lasting night Heaven's kingless throne.

Asia
150 What meanest thou?

Panthea
That terrible shadow floats
Up from its throne, as may the lurid smoke

138. *locks*] hair *Nbk 9*; altered in the press transcript because of the changes to the following line.

139. *Nbk 9* first read *Streams on the blast like meteors & they all*. S. then cancelled the line and wrote above it *like a comets scattered hair*, and then cancelled *scattered hair*. The received form of the line was presumably written for the press transcript. The derivation of 'comet' is from Gk κομήτης, 'long-haired'; see I 165–8 and note. With S.'s use of *scattered* for hair cp. IV 224–5 and note.

143. *Checks its dark*] *Nbk 9* first read *Waits with its*; S. then cancelled this and wrote *Checks* [above *Stays* canc.] *its dark* on the facing page.

145. *What*] *Nbk 9*; Who *1820, 1839*; perhaps S.'s alteration to the press transcript, but the draft reading makes better sense given the Spirit's answer.

146. *shadow*] *image* is written on the facing page in *Nbk 9*, presumably as an unused alternative.

148. *Darkness*] *Nbk 9*; darkness *1820, 1839*.

149. *Heaven's*] *Nbk 9*; heaven's *1820, 1839*.

151–2. The *lurid smoke / Of earthquake-ruined cities* suggests Pompeii and Herculaneum, both destroyed by Vesuvius. Cp. also Southey, *Letters from England* (1807) Letter xxxvii: 'A heavy cloud of black smoke hung over the city [Birmingham], above which in many places black columns were sent up with prodigious force from the steam-engines . . . Every where around us . . . the tower of some manufactory was to be seen in the distance, vomiting up flames and smoke, and blasting every thing around with its metallic vapours . . .'

Of earthquake-ruined cities o'er the sea.
Lo! it ascends the Car . . . the coursers fly
Terrified: watch its path among the stars
155 Blackening the night!

Asia

Thus I am answered: strange!

Panthea

See, near the verge, another chariot stays:
An ivory shell inlaid with crimson fire,
Which comes and goes within its sculptured rim
Of delicate strange tracery; the young Spirit
160 That guides it has the dove-like eyes of hope.
How its soft smiles attract the soul! — as light
Lures wingèd insects through the lampless air.

Spirit

My coursers are fed with the lightning,
They drink of the whirlwind's stream,
165 And when the red morning is bright'ning

---

151. S. at first wrote *as doth the lurid smoke*, then cancelled *doth* and substituted *may*, and cancelled *smoke* and substituted *dust*; the reversion to *may* and *smoke* in the press transcript was perhaps to avoid the near rhyme on *doth* and *dust*.

153. Car . . .] *Nbk 9*; car; *1820, 1839*.

154–62. S. had difficulty with these lines in *Nbk 9*, which has a number of cancellations and modifications; see *BSM* ix 356–7, 607.

156–9. Asia's shell-chariot associates her with the sea-born Venus Aphrodite, Goddess of Love and associated by Lucretius with the generative principle, whose emblem is a shell; the lines also anticipate the account in II v 20–32 (see note) of Asia's Aphrodite-like birth in a *veinèd* shell (cp. *delicate strange tracery*).

156. verge,] *Nbk 9*; verge *1820, 1839*.

158. comes and goes] S. at first wrote *burns around* in *Nbk 9*, then cancelled it and continued with the received reading.

159. Spirit] *Nbk 9*; spirit *1820, 1839*.

160. hope.] *Nbk 9*; hope; *1820, 1839*. S.'s *dove-like eyes* are adapted from a familiar epithet in English poetry; see III iii 46, and note on *dove-eyed*.

161. soul! –] *Nbk 9*; soul! *1820, 1839*.

163–6. The chariot is powered by electrical energy from the sun. *Grabo (1930)* 130–1 notes that, according to Beccaria, at dawn atmospheric electricity is either non-existent or at its lowest ebb, and that according to Darwin and Davy electrical effects accompany the action of the whirlwind. Cp. II v 1–2, and see commentary in *Cameron (1974)* 523, and King-Hele, *Shelley: His Thought and Work* (1960) 181.

They bathe in the fresh sunbeam;
They have strength for their swiftness I deem:
Then ascend with me, Daughter of Ocean.

170
I desire — and their speed makes night kindle;
I fear — they outstrip the Typhoon;
Ere the cloud piled on Atlas can dwindle
We encircle the earth and the moon:
We shall rest from long labours at noon:
Then ascend with me, Daughter of Ocean.

Scene v

The Car pauses within a cloud on the top of a snowy mountain. Asia,
Panthea, *and the* Spirit of the Hour.

Spirit
On the brink of the night and the morning
My coursers are wont to respire;
But the Earth has just whispered a warning
That their flight must be swifter than fire:
5
They shall drink the hot speed of desire!

Asia
Thou breathest on their nostrils, but my breath
Would give them swifter speed.

Spirit
Alas! It could not.

167. *deem:*] deem Nbk 9; deem, *1820, 1839.*

168. *Daughter*] Daughters Nbk 9; daughter *1820, 1839.* Presumably here and at line 174 below
a change to the press transcript.

169. *desire –*] Nbk 9; desire: *1820, 1839.*

170. *fear –*] Nbk 9; fear: *1820, 1839.*

173. *at*] ere Nbk 9; presumably a change to the press transcript.

174. *Daughter*] daughters Nbk 9; daughter *1820, 1839.*

¶v *1–2.* See II iv 163–6 and note.

2. *respire*] i.e. take breath.

4. i.e. swifter than the fire of Demogorgon's eruption.

Panthea
O Spirit! pause, and tell whence is the light
Which fills this cloud — the sun is yet unrisen.

Spirit
10 The sun will rise not until noon. Apollo
Is held in Heaven by wonder; and the light
Which fills this vapour, as the aërial hue
Of fountain-gazing roses fills the water,
Flows from thy mighty sister.

Panthea
                              Yes, I feel . . .

Asia
15 What is it with thee, sister? Thou art pale.

Panthea
How thou art changed! I dare not look on thee;

8–11. The sun is eclipsed by the eruption, which delays the 'dawn' until noon, when Jupiter has been overthrown. The darkness brought on by volcanic eruption is described in classical and other authors known to S.; cp. e.g. Breislak's eye-witness account of the eruption of Vesuvius in 1794: 'At Caserta, more than ten miles from Vesuvius, torches were obliged to be used at mid-day, and the gloom was only broken by the frequent flashes of lightning which partially displayed the mountain.' (*Edinburgh Review* v (1804) 31). S. also suggests the 'darkness at noon' of the crucifixion: cp. *Matthew* xxvii 45, 'Now from the sixth hour there was darkness over all the land unto the ninth hour'; and *Joshua* x 13: 'And the sun stood still, and the moon stayed, until the people had avenged themselves upon their enemies . . . So the sun stood still in the midst of heaven, and hasted not to go down about a whole day'.

8. O] *Nbk 9*; Oh *1820, 1839*.

9. *this cloud* –] *Nbk 9*; the cloud? *1820, 1839*.

11–14. Cp. *Paradise Lost* vii 243–9:
                    'Let there be light,' said God; and forthwith light
                    Ethereal, first of things, quintessence pure,
                    Sprung from the deep, and from her native east
                    To journey through the airy gloom began,
                    Sphered in a radiant cloud, for yet the sun
                    Was not; she in a cloudy tabernacle
                    Sojourned the while.
From this point Asia increasingly takes on the powers of the sun.

11. *Heaven*] *Nbk 9*; heaven *1820, 1839*.

12. *this vapour*] i.e. the volcanic cloud, now obscuring the light of the sun.

14. *feel . . .*] *Nbk 9*; feel – *1820, 1839*.

16–71. The central instance of a characteristic image in S., of beautiful transformative power radiated from a female presence (cp. e.g. no. 7, 'Henry and Louisa' 112–16 and note, and 'To Jane. The Recollection' 41–52).

I feel, but see thee not. I scarce endure
The radiance of thy beauty. Some good change
Is working in the elements, which suffer
20   Thy presence thus unveiled. The Nereids tell
That on the day when the clear hyaline
Was cloven at thine uprise, and thou didst stand
Within a veinèd shell, which floated on
Over the calm floor of the crystal sea,
25   Among the Aegean isles, and by the shores
Which bear thy name, love, like the atmosphere
Of the sun's fire filling the living world,
Burst from thee, and illumined Earth and Heaven
And the deep ocean and the sunless caves
30   And all that dwells within them; till grief cast
Eclipse upon the soul from which it came:

17–20. See note to lines 48–71 below.

17. feel,] Nbk 9; feel *1820, 1839.*

20–32. Panthea's account of Asia's birth associates her with Venus Aphrodite, born of sea-foam and carried on a shell to the shores of Cythera in the Aegean (Hesiod, *Theogony* 192; the myth of the shell appears in early mythographers). One important direct source for S.'s conception here is probably Botticelli's painting 'The Birth of Venus' in the Uffizi Gallery in Florence. Frederic S. Colwell (*KSMB* xxviii (1977) 32–5) argues that this influence is implausible given the painting's obscurity at that time, and the unlikelihood of S.'s having seen it. But S. could have seen the painting on the morning of 19 August 1818, when he spent at least four hours with Claire Clairmont waiting for the coach to Venice, and when by his own account (*L* ii 32–3) he saw of Florence only the Lung'Arno (the Gallery, which included a 'Venus Temple', is on the Lung'Arno; cp. *Eustace* III i). S.'s evocation of sculpture at II iv 80–2, and an implication in a letter from Bologna of November 1818 (*L* ii 53: 'The Apollo & the Venus are as they were'), together with his habit at other times of visiting galleries with Claire Clairmont, all support the possibility; and there is no other obvious source which brings together so many of the details, and the general conception, of Panthea's description. Other direct contexts include a passage in Darwin's *Origin of Society* i 371–8, in *The Temple of Nature*, which has an interesting note on Venus as 'the beauty of organic nature rising from the sea'; and cp. also Keats, *Endymion* i 624–7: 'Ah, see her hovering feet, / More bluely veined, more soft, more whitely sweet / Than those of sea-born Venus, when she rose / From out her cradle shell.'

20. The Nereids, the fifty (or one hundred) daughters of the old sea-god Nereus, were nymphs of the Aegean; cp. III ii 44–8, which implies that Asia and the Nereids are sisters.

21. hyaline] 'Glassy-surfaced sea'; Milton (*Paradise Lost* vii 619: 'the clear hyaline, the glassy sea') adapts the word from the Gk θάλασσα ὑάλινη of *Revelation* iv 6, 'sea of glass like unto crystal'.

22. thine] Nbk 9 (alt. from *thy*); thy *1820, 1839.*

26–30. S. identifies Asia with love, electricity, and the life-supporting energy of the sun; see I 765 and note, III iv 100–105 and note. Panthea's description of Asia's transformation here recalls her own earlier account at II i 87–91 of a similar change in Prometheus.

26. name,] Nbk 9; name; *1820, 1839.*

28. Earth and Heaven] Nbk 9; earth and heaven *1820, 1839.*

30. dwells] dwell Nbk 9 (perhaps a change by S. to the press transcript).

Such art thou now; nor is it I alone,
Thy sister, thy companion, thine own chosen one,
But the whole world which seeks thy sympathy.
35 Hearest thou not sounds i' the air which speak the love
Of all articulate beings? Feelest thou not
The inanimate winds enamoured of thee? — List!

[*Music*

Asia
Thy words are sweeter than aught else but his
Whose echoes they are: yet all love is sweet,
40 Given or returned. Common as light is love,
And its familiar voice wearies not ever.
Like the wide Heaven, the all-sustaining air,
It makes the reptile equal to the God:
They who inspire it most are fortunate,
45 As I am now; but those who feel it most
Are happier still, after long sufferings,
As I shall soon become.

Panthea
                    List! Spirits speak.

Voice (in the air, singing)
Life of Life! thy lips enkindle
    With their love the breath between them;
50 And thy smiles before they dwindle
    Make the cold air fire; then screen them

37. *thee? – List!*] thee? – list *Nbk 9*; thee? List! *1820, 1839*.

40. Cp. no. 68, 'A Tale of Society as it is: from facts, 1811' 89, 'The sun's kind light feeds every living thing'. For 'Given or returned' cp. *PU* III iii 59–60.

42. *Heaven,*] *Nbk 9*; heaven, *1820, 1839*.

47. *List! Spirits speak.*] *1820*; List, spirits speak *Nbk 9*; List! Spirits, speak. *1829, 1839*. As *Taylor* 41 notes, the perpetuation in *1839* of an obvious error introduced in *1829* is evidence that *1829* was the copy text for *PU* in *1839*; see headnote, and II i 171 and note. The attribution of this half-line to Panthea is canc. in *Nbk 9* but restored in *1820*.

SD. *Nbk 9* has *Voice in the Air* with *Song of an enamoured Spirit* written above and canc. The received SD was presumably included in the press transcript. S.'s Italian trans. of lines 48–71 in *Nbk 16*, probably made in 1821 from a copy of *1820*, is headed 'Una voce nel aere' (see *BSM* iv Pt II 2–5).

48–71. The lyric offers homage to Asia as the embodiment of Absolute Love and Beauty, in a series of invocations which move from high abstraction to an increasingly accessible sensory mode. In strictly dramatic terms, Asia appears by this point to have taken the place of the sun (cp. line 10).

48. *Life!*] life! *Nbk 9*.

571

In those looks where whoso gazes
Faints, entangled in their mazes.

Child of Light! thy limbs are burning
55   Through the vest which seems to hide them,
As the radiant lines of morning
Through the clouds ere they divide them;
And this atmosphere divinest
Shrouds thee wheresoe'er thou shinest.

60   Fair are others; — none beholds thee,
But thy voice sounds low and tender
Like the fairest — for it folds thee
From the sight, that liquid splendour,
And all feel, yet see thee never,
65   As I feel now, lost forever!

52–3. Cp. Dante, *Purgatorio* xxxii 1–6:
    Mine eyes with such an eager coveting
    Were bent to rid them of their ten years' thirst [for sight of Beatrice],
    No other sense was waking: and e'en they
    Were fenced on either side from heed of aught;
    So tangled, in its custom'd toils, that smile
    Of saintly brightness drew me to itself (trans. Cary).
S.'s conception also suggests Dantean influence more generally; cp. e.g. *Paradiso* xxi 1–12.

52. looks] Nbk 9; looks, *1820, 1839*.

54–5. S.'s intensification of a much-used contemporary image, encouraged by prevailing fashion in women's clothes which approached that reported in antiquity of the women of Cos (in the eastern Aegean). S. noted the drapery of a Venus Genetrix in Florence, 'the original of which must have been the "woven wind" of Chios' (*Prose* 346). The literary source was Petronius, *Satyricon* 55–6: 'Aequum est induere nuptam ventum textilem, / palam prostare nudam in nebula linea' ('Your bride might as well clothe herself in woven wind, as stand forth publicly naked under her mist of muslin').

54. limbs] Nbk 9, *1839*; lips *1820, 1829*. S. also corrected the word in his presentation copy of *1820* to Leigh Hunt (see *BSM* ix 610); *lips* for *limbs* does not immediately suggest a printer's error, but it is hard to believe that Peacock or anyone else could have introduced the mistake in checking proof. Such a painfully obvious error will have been in S.'s errata list.

55. them,] them Nbk 9; them; *1820, 1839*.

56–7. Cp. *Romeo and Juliet* III v 7–8: 'Look, love, what envious streaks / Do lace the severing clouds in yonder east'.

57. clouds] Nbk 9, *1820*; clouds, *1839*.

60–4. 'It is still impossible to *see* Absolute Beauty, of course; she is veiled now by her own radiance . . . The suggestion is that the fall of Jupiter allows Love to manifest herself in a form much closer to her essence, as she did once in the form of Aphrodite in the Golden Age. The eclipse is over' (GM).

60. others; –] Nbk 9; others; *1820, 1839*.

62. fairest –] Nbk 9; fairest, *1820, 1839*.

65, 78. forever] Nbk 9; for ever *1820, 1839*; see I 23 and note.

Lamp of Earth! where'er thou movest
Its dim shapes are clad with brightness,
And the souls of whom thou lovest
Walk upon the winds with lightness,
70   Till they fail, as I am failing,
Dizzy, lost . . . yet unbewailing!

Asia
My soul is an enchanted boat
Which, like a sleeping swan, doth float

---

71. Dizzy, lost . . .] *Nbk 9*; Dizzy, lost, *1820, 1839. BSM* ix 610–11 argues that S. has two suspension points preceding Dizzy in *Nbk 9*, 'in order to capture the dizziness and failing he is attempting to convey' (an example of 'a kind of mimetic chirography which occurs elsewhere in PBS's manuscripts'). But the *Nbk 9* reading is debatable, and a comma after *failing* at the end of the previous line is clear in *Nbk 9*, so suspension points at the start of the next line would give an unusual and odd punctuational effect.

71–2. Between these lines in *Nbk 9* is a transitional passage, uncancelled but not included in the press transcript, which makes clear that the preceding lines 48–71 are sung by Prometheus through Panthea's lips, thus providing a climax to her intermediary role between the central characters:

    Asia
You said that Spirits spoke but it was thee
Sweet sister, for even now thy curved lips
Tremble as if the sound were dying there
Not dead

    Panthea
        Alas it was Prometheus spoke
Within me, and I know it must be so
I mixed my own weak nature with his love
and
          And my thoughts
Are like the many forests of a vale
Through which the might of whirlwind and of rain
Had passed they glimmer through the evening light
As mine do now in thy beloved smile.

The passage is given here with light editorial tidying; for a full diplomatic text see *BSM* ix 374–5.

72–110. This lyric was a late addition in *Nbk 9*, probably one of the additional passages for *PU* S. sent to England in December 1819 (see headnote). Its position in the nbk suggests that S. inserted the lines into pages originally left blank during the copying of Act II, and evidence relating to III i 8 (see note) indicates that the lyric, together with the passage given in the preceding note, was copied into the nbk after Act III had been copied for the press. The sole surviving draft for the lyric is in *Nbk 12*, which contains only late work on *PU*. For a full discussion see *BSM* ix 611. S.'s Italian trans. of these lines is in *Nbk 17* (see *BSM* vi 250–5).

72–84. The opening lines of Asia's lyric incorporate concepts and some phrasing from S.'s *terza rima* lines 'My spirit like a charmed bark doth swim' (see no. 153), written probably late in 1817 and themselves related to no. 155, 'To Constantia' ('Thy voice, slow rising like a Spirit, lingers'). See *Chernaik* 55–7 for commentary on the affinities between 'To Constantia' and Asia's lyric.

72. boat] Boat *Nbk 9*; boat, *1820, 1839.*

Upon the silver waves of thy sweet singing;
75   And thine doth like an angel sit
Beside the helm conducting it,
Whilst all the winds with melody are ringing.
It seems to float ever, forever,
Upon that many-winding river,
80   Between mountains, woods, abysses,
A paradise of wildernesses!
Till, like one in slumber bound,
Borne to the ocean, I float down, around,
Into a sea profound of ever-spreading sound.

85   Meanwhile thy spirit lifts its pinions
In Music's most serene dominions,
Catching the winds that fan that happy Heaven.
And we sail on, away, afar,
Without a course, without a star,
90   But by the instinct of sweet music driven;
Till, through Elysian garden islets
By thee, most beautiful of pilots,
Where never mortal pinnace glided,
The boat of my desire is guided:
95   Realms where the air we breathe is Love,
Which in the winds and on the waves doth move,
Harmonizing this Earth with what we feel above.

We have passed Age's icy caves,
Manhood's dark and tossing waves,

81. *paradise*] Paradise *Nbk 9*.

84. *profound*] *Nbk 9, 1820* and *1839* mark the internal rhyme here with a comma.

86. *Music's*] *Nbk 9*; music's *1820, 1839*. *dominions,*] dominions *Nbk 9*; dominions; *1820, 1839*.

87. *Heaven.*] Heaven *Nbk 9*; heaven. *1820, 1839*.

90. *But*] *Nbk 9*; But, *1820, 1839*.

91. *Till,*] *Nbk 9*; Till *1820, 1839*.

95. *Love,*] Love *Nbk 9*; love, *1820, 1839*.

96. *winds and on*] *Nbk 9*; winds on *1820, 1829, 1839* (a transcription error). As *Rossetti 1870* noticed, the error awkwardly affects both sense and metre; but S. may have omitted it from his errata list.

97. *Earth*] *Nbk 9*; earth *1820, 1839*.

98–103. The journey backwards through time, and which reverses the ageing process, derives from Plato, *Statesman* 269–71 (see letter from E. M. W. Tillyard, *TLS* (29 Sept. 1932) 691); cp. also *Phaedrus* 249–50. There is a suggestive account of Orphism in Thomas Taylor, *Dissertation on the Eleusinian and Bacchic Mysteries* (2nd edn 1816) 472–3, which describes how under Saturn souls move from age to youth. S. may be more immediately indebted to Wordsworth's 'Immortality Ode' (1807) 58–84, describing the soul's development from pre-natal existence to manhood in quasi-Platonic terms which are carefully inverted in Asia's lyric.

100   And Youth's smooth ocean, smiling to betray:
    Beyond the glassy gulfs we flee
    Of shadow-peopled Infancy,
    Through Death and Birth, to a diviner day;
    A paradise of vaulted bowers
105   Lit by downward-gazing flowers,
    And watery paths that wind between
    Wildernesses calm and green,
    Peopled by shapes too bright to see,
    And rest, having beheld; somewhat like thee;
110   Which walk upon the sea, and chant melodiously!

End of the Second Act

100. *Youth's*] youth's Nbk 9.

102. *Infancy,*] infancy, Nbk 9.

103. *Death and Birth,*] death and birth Nbk 9.

104. *paradise*] Paradise Nbk 9.

108–10. Cp II iv 77–9 and note.

109–10. The grammar is compressed and difficult: *rest* (line 109) is governed by *we* (lines 98, 101); *Which* in line 110 refers back to the *shapes too bright to see* (line 108); Asia presumably realises, as these shapes become visible to her, that they resemble Prometheus himself (*somewhat like thee*).

ACT III

Scene i

Heaven. Jupiter *on his Throne;* Thetis *and the other Deities assembled.*

Jupiter
Ye congregated Powers of Heaven, who share
The glory and the strength of him ye serve,
Rejoice! henceforth I am omnipotent.
All else has been subdued to me; alone
5   The soul of man, like unextinguished fire,
Yet burns towards Heaven with fierce reproach, and doubt,
And lamentation, and reluctant prayer,
Hurling up insurrection, which might make
Our antique empire insecure, though built
10 On eldest faith, and Hell's coeval, fear;
And though my curses through the pendulous air,
Like snow on herbless peaks, fall flake by flake,
And cling to it; though under my wrath's night
It climb the crags of life, step after step,

1. *Powers of Heaven,*] Powers of Heaven *Nbk 9*; powers of heaven, *1820, 1839.*

3. *I am*] am I *Nbk 9*; presumably S.'s alteration to the press transcript.

4. *has*] Alt. from *had* in *Nbk 9*; had *1820, 1839.*

5–7. Cp. *Revelation* xiv 11: 'And the smoke of their torment ascendeth up for ever and ever: and they have no rest day nor night, who worship the beast and his image, and whosoever receiveth the mark of his name'.

5. *like unextinguished*] *Nbk 9, 1839*; like an unextinguished *1820, 1829*. Perhaps in S.'s errata list. 'What alarms Jupiter at the opening of Act III is that the soul of man ("like unextinguished fire") is busy "Hurling up insurrection", just as the vapour is "hurled up" [cp. II iii 4] from Demogorgon's spiraculum and from Vesuvius itself' (GM).

6. *Heaven*] *Nbk 9*; heaven *1820, 1839.*

8. *Hurling up*] *Nbk 9* at first read *In tameless*. This was cancelled, and S. wrote *the masks of a rebellion* on the facing page as a replacement; this was in its turn cancelled and replaced by *Hurling up* written above in pencil, which was subsequently overwritten by the copy of Asia's lyric at the end of Act II (see note to II v 72–110). Cp. *Paradise Lost* i 669: 'Hurling defiance toward the vault of heaven'.

10. *Hell's*] *Nbk 9*; hell's *1820, 1839.*

11. Recalling *King Lear* III iv 66–7: 'Now all the plagues that in the pendulous air / Hang fated o'er men's faults light on thy daughters!'

13. *night*] *Nbk 9, 1839*; might *1820, 1829*. This last word of the line in *Nbk 9* runs over to the facing page, and was presumably miscopied in the press transcript (or produced by a printer's error); possibly on S.'s errata list.

15   Which wound it, as ice wounds unsandalled feet,
       It yet remains supreme o'er misery,
       Aspiring . . . unrepressed; yet soon to fall:
       Even now have I begotten a strange wonder,
       That fatal child, the terror of the earth,
20   Who waits but till the destined Hour arrive,
       Bearing from Demogorgon's vacant throne
       The dreadful might of ever-living limbs
       Which clothed that awful spirit unbeheld,
       To redescend and trample out the spark . . .

15. unsandalled] Timothy Webb ('Negatives in *Prometheus Unbound*', in *Shelley Revalued* 39) suggests that S. adapts this word from the Gk ἀσάνδἆλος, found for example in Bion, 'Death of Adonis' 21 (trans. by S. in 1819; see no. 201).

17. Aspiring . . . unrepressed;] *Nbk 9*; Aspiring, unrepressed, *1820, 1839*.

18–19. Parodying *Paradise Lost* v 603–4: 'This day I have begot whom I declare / My only Son'. Cp. *Psalms* ii 7: 'I will declare the decree: the Lord hath said unto me, Thou art my Son; this day have I begotten thee'; and *Hebrews* i 5: 'For unto which of the angels said he at any time, Thou art my Son, this day have I begotten thee? And again, I will be to him a Father, and he shall be to me a Son?'

19. child,] Child, *Nbk 9*. *earth,*] Earth, *Nbk 9*. The pun on *fatal*, i.e. both 'destined' and 'destructive', is Miltonic; cp. *Paradise Lost* ii 101–5:

             by proof we feel
    Our power sufficient to disturb his heaven,
    And with perpetual inroads to alarm,
    Though inaccessible, his fatal throne;
    Which if not victory is yet revenge.

C. E. Pulos ('Shelley and Malthus', *PMLA* lxvii (1952) 113–24) has persuasively argued that the *fatal child* represents the ideas of Thomas Malthus as set forth in his *Essay on the Principle of Population* (1798). *Nbk 11* 36 has apparent early drafts for *PU* III i on the same page as jotted notes on 'the principle of population', and S. was reading Malthus in October 1818 (*L* ii 43). The *Essay* was an answer to Godwin's *Political Justice*, and argued that human perfectibility was impossible because the population increases in geometric proportion, while the capacity to produce food increases only arithmetically, thereby ensuring that the population must periodically be checked by war, famine, and other disasters. Thus Jupiter believes that his offspring will help to protect his continuing sway over human development. S. may more specifically recall phrasing from Hazlitt's *Reply to Malthus* (1807): 'Mr Malthus's reputation may, I fear, prove fatal to the poor of this country. His name hangs suspended over their heads, *in terrorem* like some baleful meteor' (*Hazlitt Works* i 181). This would import into S.'s phrase a more definite reference to the controversy surrounding his father-in-law, in keeping with other semi-coded personal allusions in *PU* (see III iii 65–7 and note, and headnote), and of a piece with his overt discussions of Malthus, e.g. in the Preface to *L&C*, and in *PVR* (*Prose* 247–8, *SC* vi 1204). S.'s *terror of the earth* echoes *King Lear* II iv 279–81: 'I will do such things – / What they are yet I know not; but they shall be / The terrors of the earth'.

20. destined] *Nbk 9, 1839*; distant *1820, 1829*. Probably Mary's transcription error (the word is rather ill-written in *Nbk 9*), as a printer's error is unlikely, and S. would presumably have recognised his own writing. Probably on S.'s errata list. *Hour*] *Nbk 9*; hour *1820, 1839*.

24. redescend] *Nbk 9*; redescend, *1820, 1839*. *spark . . .*] *Nbk 9*; spark. *1820, 1839*. In *1820* (and subsequent *eds*) this scene employs line-breaks unusually at several points (lines 24/25, 33, 63, 70, 79), presumably to enhance the dramatic effect of Jupiter's one-sided exchange

25   Pour forth Heaven's wine, Idæan Ganymede,
        And let it fill the daedal cups like fire,
        And from the flower-inwoven soil divine
        Ye all-triumphant harmonies arise,
        As dew from earth under the twilight stars:
30   Drink! be the nectar circling through your veins
        The soul of joy, ye ever-living Gods,
        Till exultation burst in one wide voice
        Like music from Elysian winds.
                                        And thou
        Ascend beside me, veilèd in the light
35   Of the desire which makes thee one with me,
        Thetis, bright Image of Eternity!
        When thou didst cry, 'Insufferable might!
        God! Spare me! I sustain not the quick flames,
        The penetrating presence; all my being,
40   Like him whom the Numidian seps did thaw

---

with Demogorgon. There is no line-break in *Nbk 9* at line 33, or line 79 (and see note to lines 70–4), but it is likely that such a sustained lay-out feature would derive from S.'s change to the press transcript.

25–51. Jupiter's ironically misplaced confidence is exactly the *hubris* of classical Gk tragic drama.

25. Ganymede was the eternally youthful cup-bearer to the gods, taken for his beauty by Zeus from Mount Ida near Troy. *Heaven's*] *Nbk 9*; heaven's *1820, 1839*.

26. daedal] Dædal *1820, 1839*. 'Of elaborate workmanship'; see note to 'One sung of thee who left the tale untold' (no. 175) 3.

27. divine] *Nbk 9, 1820*; divine, *1839*.

29. earth] Earth *Nbk 9*.

34–6. Ironically recalling the transformation of Asia in II v.

36–48. Jupiter's bride Thetis is, like Asia, a Nereid or sea-nymph, and thus develops the pattern by which Prometheus is doubled in his adversary. Thetis was fated to bear a son mightier than his father, which in Aeschylus is the secret known to Prometheus; S. assigns to Jupiter the rape of Thetis that was performed in the myth by Peleus after Zeus had been forewarned (see Ovid, *Met.* xi 229–65). S.'s Jupiter actually has a child by Thetis; in the myth he avoids thus sealing his fate.

36. Image of Eternity!] Image of Eternity – *Nbk 9*; image of eternity! *1820, 1839*. S.'s Thetis appears to represent time (*image of eternity*); i.e. Jupiter as tyranny, when wedded to Thetis as time, begets the conditions for his own downfall (see note to lines 54–5). Cp. *Epipsychidion* 115: 'An image of some bright Eternity'.

37–9. Thetis is here associated with Semele, overwhelmed by the sexual presence of Jove; cp. Ovid, *Met.* iii 308–9: 'corpus mortale tumultus / non tulit aetherios donisque iugalibus arsit' ('Her mortal body bore not the onrush of heavenly power, and by that gift of wedlock she was consumed', Loeb trans.).

40–1. S. recalls the gruesome passage in Lucan, *Pharsalia* ix 762–88, where Sabellus is rapidly decomposed to a pool of venom by a bite from a seps (the highly poisonous snake of fable) in the Numidian desert. The phrasing also perhaps suggests *Hamlet* I ii 129–30: 'O, that this too too solid flesh would melt, / Thaw, and resolve itself into a dew!'

Into a dew with poison, is dissolved,
Sinking through its foundations' — even then
Two mighty spirits, mingling, made a third
Mightier than either, which, unbodied now
45   Between us, floats, felt although unbeheld,
Waiting the incarnation, which ascends
(Hear ye the thunder of the fiery wheels
Griding the winds?) from Demogorgon's throne.
Victory! victory! Feelest thou not, O world,
50   The earthquake of his chariot thundering up
Olympus?

              [The Car of the HOUR arrives. Demogorgon
            descends and moves towards the Throne of Jupiter.
Awful Shape, what art thou? Speak!

Demogorgon
Eternity. Demand no direr name.
Descend, and follow me down the abyss.
I am thy child, as thou wert Saturn's child;

42. *foundations' – even*] foundations' – Even *Nbk 9*; foundations:' even *1820, 1839*.

43–5. In *Nbk 9* S. apparently first left line 44 metrically incomplete at *either*, then wrote two lines as follows: *Even now unbodied and invisible / Between us, floats our mighty Progeny.* He then cancelled the first of these two lines, replacing it with the second half of the received text of line 44 (*which, unbodied now*), and cancelled *our mighty Progeny* to replace it with *felt although unbeheld* written above. There is no punctuation in *Nbk 9* after *now* at the end of line 44, and a comma is very firmly written in after *floats* in line 45 (see *BSM* ix 384–5). In *1820* and *1839* the punctuation *Mightier than either, which, unbodied now, / Between us floats, felt, although unbeheld*, alters the sense. With 43–44 cp. *Prometheus Bound* 768: ἦ τέξεταί γε παῖδα φέρτερον πατρός ('she shall bear a son stronger than his sire').

43. *spirits, mingling,*] *1820*; spirits mingling *Nbk 9*; spirits, mingling *1839*.

46–8. *ascends*] ascends – *Nbk 9*; ascends, *1820, 1839*. The brackets in lines 47–8 appear in *1820*; *Nbk 9* has only a question mark after *winds* in line 48.

48. *Griding*] 'Grating against with a strident sound'; the word was adapted from Middle English by Spenser (see e.g. *Shepheardes Calender, Februarie* 4, *Faerie Queene* III ii 37), and taken up by Milton (*Paradise Lost* vi 329).

49. *world,*] *1820*; World *Nbk 9*; world! *1839*.

50. *earthquake*] Earthquake *Nbk 9*.

SD. The *Car of the Hour* is the first car from II iv 142–4.

51. *Shape,*] *Nbk 9*; shape, *1820, 1839*.

52. The *direr name* is usually taken to be 'Necessity'; although Demogorgon may perhaps simply intend his own name.

54–5. On the historical inevitability of Jupiter's fall, cp. 'Fragment on Reform': 'The distribution of wealth no less than the spirit by which it is upheld and that by which it is assailed render the event inevitable. Call it reform or revolution, as you will, a change must take place; one of the consequences of which will be the wresting of political power from those who are at present the depositories of it' (*Prose* 261).

55   Mightier than thee: and we must dwell together
        Henceforth in darkness. Lift thy lightnings not.
        The tyranny of Heaven none may retain,
        Or reassume, or hold, succeeding thee:
        Yet if thou wilt — as 'tis the destiny
60   Of trodden worms to writhe till they are dead —
        Put forth thy might.

        Jupiter
                        Detested prodigy!
        Even thus beneath the deep Titanian prisons
        I trample thee! thou lingerest?
                                Mercy! mercy!
        No pity, no release no respite! . . . O,
65   That thou wouldst make mine enemy my judge.

55–6. i.e. Jupiter is not destroyed, and he maintains the potential to return; cp. IV 565–9 and note.

55. S. wrote what is probably *He Rhea's* on the blank facing page in *Nbk 9*, as an alternative for *Mightier than thee*, which has been underlined presumably to confirm its inclusion in the press transcript. According to Hesiod (*Theogony* 137–8, 154ff., 453ff.) Rhea was the sister and bride of Kronos, or Saturn; she deceived him by substituting a stone for the infant Zeus and so saved him from being eaten by his father Kronos. Zeus ultimately usurped his father's tyranny.

57. *Heaven*] *Nbk 9*; heaven *1820, 1839*.

59. *wilt –*] *Nbk 9*; wilt, *1820, 1839*.

60. *dead –*] *Nbk 9*; dead, *1820, 1839*.

62. *Titanian*] After their defeat at the hands of Zeus and the gods, the Titans were imprisoned deep underground in Tartarus. The prisons of the Titans were traditionally associated with the volcanic regions of Sicily and the Neapolitan coast.

63–9. Jupiter appeals for mercy to 'mine enemy' as Satan appeals to Christ against the stern justice of God in *Paradise Regained* iii 212–22:

        My error was my error, and my crime
        My crime, whatever for itself condemned,
        And will alike be punished, whether thou
        Reign or reign not; though to that gentle brow
        Willingly I could fly, and hope thy reign,
        From that placid aspect and meek regard,
        Rather than aggravate my evil state,
        Would stand between me and thy Father's ire
        (Whose ire I dread more than the fire of hell),
        A shelter and a kind of shading cool
        Interposition, as a summer's cloud.

64. *respite! . . . O,*] respite! . . . oh *Nbk 9*; respite! Oh, *1820, 1839*.

65. *judge.*] *Nbk 9*; judge, *1820, 1839*. The stop is quite faint and slightly misplaced in *Nbk 9*, but definite.

Even where he hangs, seared by my long revenge
On Caucasus — he would not doom me thus.
Gentle, and just, and dreadless, is he not
The monarch of the world? What then art thou?
70 No refuge! no appeal!
                  Sink with me then —
We two will sink in the wide waves of ruin,
Even as a vulture and a snake outspent
Drop, twisted in inextricable fight,
Into a shoreless sea. Let hell unlock
75 Its moulded oceans of tempestuous fire,
And whelm on them into the bottomless void
This desolated world, and thee, and me,
The conqueror and the conquered, and the wreck
Of that for which they combated.
                        Ai! Ai!
80 The elements obey me not . . . I sink . . .
Dizzily down — ever, forever, down;
And, like a cloud, mine enemy above
Darkens my fall with victory! Ai! Ai!

66. *revenge*] Nbk 9; revenge, *1820, 1839*.

67. *Caucasus –*] Caucasus! *1820, 1839*.

68–9. These lines are inserted on the facing page in Nbk 9, but not at a later date judging from the ink and handwriting.

69. *1820* omits *then*, an obvious error creating an ametrical line. The error was perpetuated in *1829* but corrected in *1839*, suggesting that it was on S.'s errata list.

70–4. *Sink with me then . . . shoreless sea.*] These lines were added later on the facing page in Nbk 9 (see BSM ix 394–5).

70. *then –*] Nbk 9; then, *1820, 1839*.

71. *will*] shall Nbk 9; presumably S.'s alteration to the press transcript.   *in*] Nbk 9; on *1820, 1839*; the *i* of *in* in Nbk 9 is formed slightly to resemble what could be an *o*, but the dot above is clear.

72. A recurring image in S. for the battle of good and evil; cp. L&C I vi–xiv and note, *Alastor* 227–32.

75. *oceans*] Oceans Nbk 9.

77. *This* and *thee* read *The* and *thou* in Nbk 9; presumably S.'s change to the press transcript.

79, 83. *Ai*] In Gk a cry of lamentation.

80. *not . . . I sink . . .*] Nbk 9; not. I sink *1820, 1839*.

81. This line reads *Dizzily down – ever, forever, down* in Nbk 9; *1820* and *1839* read *Dizzily down, ever, for ever, down*. Following this line in Nbk 9 is a canc. line: *Down down down down dizzily, far & deep*.

82–3. Added later on the facing page in Nbk 9; *mine* in Nbk 9 has been canc. and replaced by *the* written above. S. presumably restored the original reading in the press transcript. The imagery in these lines is volcanic.

Scene ii

The mouth of a great river in the Island Atlantis. Ocean *is discovered reclining near the shore;* Apollo *stands beside him.*

Ocean
He fell, thou sayest, beneath his conqueror's frown?

Apollo
Aye, when the strife was ended which made dim
The orb I rule, and shook the solid stars.
The terrors of his eye illumined Heaven
5   With sanguine light, through the thick ragged skirts
Of the victorious Darkness, as he fell:
Like the last glare of day's red agony,
Which, from a rent among the fiery clouds,
Burns far along the tempest-wrinkled Deep.

Ocean
10   He sunk to the abyss? to the dark void?

III.ii. This scene parallels II ii in providing commentary on part of the dramatic action not directly represented, though as various commentators have noted the emphasis here is on the future.

SD. Atlantis was a mythical large island off the Straits of Gibraltar, an earthly paradise where Plato, in the unfinished *Critias*, places his ideal commonwealth. *Ocean* associates with water and thus with Asia (he was also in his mythic origins a river-god; hence the setting at *The mouth of a great river*). *Apollo* as the supreme Gk god of the sun, beauty, prophecy, medicine, and poetry, associates with fire and thus with Prometheus. 'It is fitting . . . that the withdrawal of eclipsing Jupiter from the heavens be reported by the sun-god to Ocean, father of the Oceanids and, according to Aeschylus, Prometheus' sympathizer . . . In effect, heaven has communicated to earth the fact that the false barrier between them has been removed' (*Wasserman* 358). See also III iv 111–21 and note.

2–9. As *Cameron (1974)* 531 notes, these lines imply a considerable passage of time.

2. *dim*] Written after *pale* canc. in *Nbk 9.*

3. *stars.*] *Nbk 9*; stars, *1820, 1839*. *Reiman (1977)* glosses *solid stars* as 'the fixed stars'; but S. probably intends the planets: cp. Herschel, qu. in *Grabo (1930)* 83: 'planets [as distinct from stars] are solid opaque bodies, shining only by superficial light, whether it be innate or reflected'.

4. *Heaven*] *Nbk 9*; heaven *1820, 1839*.

4–6. S. probably recalls descriptions of volcanic eruptions with their power to create artificial night, and perhaps draws on his own night view of Vesuvius in December 1818 (*L* ii 63).

5. *sanguine*] Written under *crimson* canc. in *Nbk 9.*

6. *Darkness,*] *Nbk 9*; darkness *1820, 1839*.

9. *Deep.*] Deep *Nbk 9*; deep. *1820, 1839*.

10. *abyss? to*] *Nbk 9*; abyss? To *1820, 1839*.

Apollo
An eagle so, caught in some bursting cloud
On Caucasus, his thunder-baffled wings
Entangled in the whirlwind, and his eyes
Which gazed on the undazzling sun, now blinded
15 By the white lightning, while the ponderous hail
Beats on his struggling form, which sinks at length
Prone, and the aërial ice clings over it.

Ocean
Henceforth the fields of Heaven-reflecting sea
Which are my realm, will heave, unstained with blood,
20 Beneath the uplifting winds, like plains of corn
Swayed by the summer air; my streams will flow
Round many-peopled continents, and round
Fortunate isles; and from their glassy thrones
Blue Proteus and his humid nymphs shall mark
25 The shadow of fair ships, as mortals see
The floating bark of the light-laden moon
With that white star, its sightless pilot's crest,
Borne down the rapid sunset's ebbing sea;
Tracking their path no more by blood and groans
30 And desolation, and the mingled voice
Of slavery and command — but by the light
Of wave-reflected flowers, and floating odours,
And music soft, and mild, free, gentle voices,
That sweetest music, such as spirits love.

11–16. See Michael O'Neill, *The Human Mind's Imaginings* (1989) 112 for good commentary on this passage. Volcanic activity was known often to be accompanied by violent storms, and S.'s *bursting cloud, thunder, whirlwind, white lightning* and *hail* all suggest that he sustains here the association of Demogorgon's intervention with the phenomena of a major volcanic eruption.

11. so,] *Nbk 9*; so *1820, 1839*; i.e. 'like an eagle', with the verb understood from the preceding line.

19. i.e. there will be no more naval wars or slavery; cp. lines 29–31 and note below.

22. many-peopled] *Nbk 9*; many peopled *1820, 1839*.

24. Proteus] See III iii 65 and note. *nymphs*] Nymphs *Nbk 9*.

26. light-laden] *Nbk 9* (alt. from *unladen*), perhaps with a pun on 'lightly laden' and 'laden with light'; light laden *1820, 1839*.

27–8. 'A star above the tip of a new moon suggests a boat guided by an invisible (*sightless*) pilot with a star as his crest' (*Butter (1970)*).

29–31. Another reference to the conditions of naval service and warfare, and to the slave trade.

29. groans] *Nbk 9*; groans, *1820, 1839*.

31. command –] *Nbk 9*; command; *1820, 1839*.

33. free] Written above *frank* canc. in *Nbk 9*.

Apollo

35 And I shall gaze not on the deeds which make
My mind obscure with sorrow, as eclipse
Darkens the sphere I guide — but list, I hear
The small, clear, silver lute of the young Spirit
That sits i' the morning star.

Ocean
                          Thou must away?
40 Thy steeds will pause at even — till when, farewell.
The loud deep calls me home even now to feed it
With azure calm out of the emerald urns
Which stand forever full beside my throne.
Behold the Nereids under the green sea,
45 Their wavering limbs borne on the wind-like streams,
Their white arms lifted o'er their streaming hair
With garlands pied and starry sea-flower crowns,
Hastening to grace their mighty sister's joy.
                    [*A sound of waves is heard.*
It is the unpastured sea hungering for calm.
50 Peace, monster; I come now! Farewell.

Apollo
                          Farewell!

---

36. *eclipse*] Eclipse *Nbk 9*.   37. *guide* -] *Nbk 9*; guide; *1820, 1839*.

38–9. See *Curran (1975)* 59–60 for commentary on the symbolic patterning of morning and evening stars in *PU*.

39. *i' the*] *Nbk 9* (S. has canc. the *n* of *in*), *1839*; on the *1820, 1829*; probably in S.'s errata list. *morning*] Morning *Nbk 9*. *away?*] *Nbk 9*; away; *1820, 1839*.

40. In *Nbk 9* there is no punctuation after *farewell*, and *even* is written above an illegible canc. word; *even, till when farewell*: is the reading in 1820 and 1839. Following this line in *Nbk 9* is a canc. line: *Hark the loud Deep calls me home too, to feed it.*   43. *forever*] *Nbk 9*; for ever *1820, 1839*.   44–8. This passage implies that Asia and the Nereids are sisters; see II v 20 and note.

45. *streams*] *Nbk 9* (the terminal *s* is poorly formed and could be taken for a comma in transcription); stream *1820, 1839*.   46. Cp. *L&C* II xxix 919–20.   48. The SD following this line reads *The roar of waves is heard*; it has been added later in pencil, and was presumably revised by S. in the press transcript.

49. *unpastured*] 'Unfed'. *OED* cites this usage as the earliest example of the word in the sense of 'not employed for pasture', but this does not fit the context, nor, as Webb (*Shelley Revalued* 39) notes, does it conform to 'S.'s usage elsewhere and to his views on the wastefulness of pasturage'; Webb cps. *the unpastured dragon* (*Adonais* 238), Lat. *impastus* ('unfed', 'hungry'), and S.'s use of the Spenserian word *depasturing* in *Hymn to Mercury* 29 and in his trans. of a passage from Plato, *Republic* (*Notopoulos* 498). S. may alternatively recall the Homeric epithet ἀτρύγετος, 'unfruitful'. *sea*] Sea *Nbk 9*. *calm.*] Calm *Nbk 9*.

50. *now!*] *Nbk 9*; now. *1820, 1839*.

Scene iii

Caucasus. Prometheus, Hercules, Ione, *the* Earth, Spirits, Asia, *and* Panthea, *borne in the* Car with the Spirit of the Hour.

[Hercules *unbinds* Prometheus, *who descends.*

Hercules
Most glorious among Spirits, thus doth strength
To wisdom, courage, and long-suffering love,
And thee, who art the form they animate,
Minister, like a slave.

Prometheus
              Thy gentle words
5   Are sweeter even than freedom long desired
And long delayed.
              Asia, thou light of life,
Shadow of beauty unbeheld; and ye,
Fair sister-nymphs, who made long years of pain
Sweet to remember, through your love and care;
10   Henceforth we will not part. There is a Cave

1–4. Hercules is the Roman name for Gk Heracles; in Aeschylus Heracles rescues Prometheus from the persecution of Zeus by killing the eagle which comes daily to eat his liver. His speech here suggests that strength is subordinate, but still necessary to *wisdom, courage, and long-suffering love*; mind cannot free itself unaided.

1. Spirits,] Nbk 9; spirits, *1820*; spirits! *1839*.

4. Minister,] Nbk 9; Minister *1820, 1839*.

5–6. Cp. II i 15. As various commentators have noted, the reader can presume that Hercules exits at this point.

7. Shadow] i.e. 'image'.

8. sister-nymphs] Nbk 9; sister nymphs *1820, 1839*. *made]* make Nbk 9 (presumably a change to the press transcript).

10. Cave] Nbk 9; cave, *1820, 1839*.

10–24. There has been much disagreement concerning the relation of this cave to the cavern described by the Earth at lines 124–47 below (see *Zillman Variorum* 524–5), some arguing that they are one and the same, others distinguishing between them, and all variously finding merits and demerits in either case. Unlike the cavern described by the Earth, the cave described here is apparently not next to a temple, and does not have obvious connection with Demogorgon's cave described in II iii. The cave described here by Prometheus is a central instance of a symbol ubiquitous in S.'s poetry, and has attracted extensive commentary. Those committed to a Platonic reading of S. have given this passage particular attention as a focal point of the Platonism they see as pervasive in *PU*, understood in these lines to derive specifically from Plato's myth of the cave in *Republic* 514ff. W. B. Yeats ('The Philosophy of Shelley's Poetry', in *Essays and Introductions* (1961) 81–2) argued that 'so good a Platonist as

All overgrown with trailing odorous plants
Which curtain out the day with leaves and flowers,
And paved with veinèd emerald, and a fountain
Leaps in the midst with an awakening sound.
15   From its curved roof the mountain's frozen tears,
Like snow, or silver, or long diamond spires,
Hang downward, raining forth a doubtful light;
And there is heard the ever-moving air
Whispering without from tree to tree, and birds,
20   And bees; and all around are mossy seats,
And the rough walls are clothed with long soft grass;
A simple dwelling, which shall be our own,

Shelley could hardly have thought of any cave as a symbol, without thinking of Plato's cave
that was the world; and so good a scholar may well have had Porphyry on 'the Cave of the
Nymphs' in his mind' (see also e.g. *Grabo (1935)*, *Notopoulos*, and especially *Rogers* 147–68).
But the lines do not appear to offer close parallels with Platonic sources, even in the con-
text of a scene with an unmistakable Platonic dimension (see below, lines 160–75 and notes).
See also *Curran (1975)* 75ff., 217, for possible sources in Zoroastrianism, and in Boccaccio's
Genealogie. The cave fits *PU*'s patterns of geological and volcanic symbolism and imagery,
and its interest in oracular exhalation; there are also hints of actual caves S. knew or may
have known about, not only the classically associated caves around Naples but also caves
such as Poole's Hole and the Devil's Arse, near Buxton, Elden Hole (also in Derbyshire), and
the cavern of Dunmore Park near Kilkenny in Ireland.

11. plants] *Nbk 9*; plants, *1820, 1839*.

13. fountain] *Nbk 9, 1820*; fountain, *1839*.

15. the mountain's frozen tears] i.e. stalactites.

17. light;] *Nbk 9*; light: *1820, 1839*.

18. air] *Nbk 9*; air, *1820, 1839*.

20–1. Cp. *L&C* iv 1428–31:
                    We came at last
        To a small chamber, which with mosses rare
        Was tapestried, where me his soft hands placed
        Upon a couch of grass and oak-leaves interlaced.

22–4. Cp. *King Lear* V iii 8–19:
                    Come, let's away to prison.
        We two alone will sing like birds i' th' cage;
        When thou dost ask me blessing, I'll kneel down
        And ask of thee forgiveness; so we'll live,
        And pray, and sing, and tell old tales, and laugh
        At gilded butterflies, and hear poor rogues
        Talk of court news; and we'll talk with them too –
        Who loses and who wins; who's in, who's out –
        And take upon's the mystery of things
        As if we were God's spies; and we'll wear out
        In a wall'd prison packs and sects of great ones
        That ebb and flow by th' moon.

22. own,] own *Nbk 9*; own; *1820, 1839*.

Where we will sit and talk of time and change,
As the world ebbs and flows, ourselves unchanged —
25   What can hide man from mutability?
And if ye sigh, then I will smile; and thou,
Ione, shall chant fragments of sea-music,
Until I weep, when ye shall smile away
The tears she brought, which yet were sweet to shed.
30   We will entangle buds and flowers, and beams
Which twinkle on the fountain's brim, and make
Strange combinations out of common things,
Like human babes in their brief innocence;
And we will search, with looks and words of love,
35   For hidden thoughts, each lovelier than the last,
Our unexhausted spirits, and like lutes
Touched by the skill of the enamoured wind,
Weave harmonies divine, yet ever new,
From difference sweet where discord cannot be.
40   And hither come, sped on the charmèd winds

23–5. Prometheus is here clearly distinguished from mankind in history; as the poem repeatedly implies, his intercourse with living people is limited by the categorical difference in his mode of existence (i.e. he is of the mind, but not limited to specific minds).

24. *unchanged* –] *Nbk 9*; unchanged. *1820, 1839*.

25. *mutability?*] Mutability? – *Nbk 9*.

27. *shall chant*] *Nbk 9*; shalt chaunt *1820* (perhaps altered by Peacock in proof), *1829*; shall chaunt *1839* (presumably from S.'s errata list).

30. *flowers,*] *Nbk 9*; flowers *1820, 1839*.

34–6. i.e. 'we will search . . . our unexhausted spirits . . . for hidden thoughts'; *with looks and words of love* qualifies *search, each lovelier than the last* qualifies *thoughts*.

34. *search,*] *Nbk 9, 1820*; search *1839*.

36. *spirits,*] *Nbk 9*; spirits; *1820, 1839*.

39. *be.*] *Nbk 9*; be; *1820, 1839*.

40–8. This sentence (like the sentence following, lines 49–56) offers a difficult grammatical complexity (see discussion in Neville Rogers, 'The Punctuation of Shelley's Syntax', *KSMB* xvii (1966) 20–30). In *Nbk 9* S.'s punctuation is very light. *1820* and *1839* make the whole passage 40–56 a single sentence, with a semicolon after *free* in line 48 (the word is not punctuated in *Nbk 9*), after which point their punctuation becomes increasingly confusing. Subsequent *eds* have proposed a wide variety of punctuation. The text here mainly follows *1839* for lines 40–8. There is a history of attempted paraphrase of the passage, inaugurated by Robert Bridges (*Spirit of Man*, rev. impression 1917; see *Zillman Variorum* 238–9); GM and KE offer the following: 'And hither from all directions, like bees homing to their familiar hives, come the echoes of the human world: the whisper of love, the murmur of pity, and the music which is itself an echo of the love and pity of the human heart – echoes of all that alleviates man's condition'. For a long and subtle paraphrase of the whole passage lines 40–62, see I. A. Richards, *Beyond* (1973) 197–9.

40. *hither*] *1820, 1839*; thither *Nbk 9*; presumably S.'s change to the press transcript. *winds*] *Nbk 9*; winds, *1820, 1839*.

Which meet from all the points of heaven, as bees
From every flower aërial Enna feeds
At their known island homes in Himera,
The echoes of the human world, which tell
45   Of the low voice of love, almost unheard,
And dove-eyed pity's murmured pain, and music,
Itself the echo of the heart, and all
That tempers or improves man's life, now free.
And lovely apparitions — dim at first

41–3. The verb is understood from line 41; 'as bees . . . [meet] . . . at their known island homes'. S.'s phrasing probably most directly recalls *Paradise Lost* iv 268–71:

> Not that fair field
> Of Enna, where Proserpine gathering flowers
> Her self a fairer flower by gloomy Dis
> Was gathered, which cost Ceres all that pain
> To seek her through the world . . .

There may also be a recollection of Marvell, 'Upon Appleton House' 291: 'The bee through these known alleys hums'. Proserpina was raped by Dis in a high (*aerial*) flowery meadow near Henna in Sicily (Ovid, *Met.* v 385–96). S.'s bees were perhaps suggested by the abundance of flowers in Ovid's account, more particularly in *Fasti* iv 420ff., where Ceres (mother of Proserpina) is said to have passed through Himera (on the North coast of Sicily) in fleeing from her daughter's distress. Hybla in Sicily was famed for its honey.

41. heaven,] Heaven, *Nbk 9.*   *42. feeds*] *Nbk 9*; feeds, *1820, 1839.*

46. dove-eyed] Cp. *Song of Solomon* v 12, 'His eyes are as the eyes of doves by the rivers of waters, washed with milk, and fitly set'; S.'s epithet (adapted also at II iv 160) is frequent in English poetry, e.g. Chatterton, 'The Complaint', Beattie, 'Ode to Peace' III i 12, Coleridge, 'Ode to the departing Year' 68. See also Emily Brontë, *Wuthering Heights* (1847) ch. 10.

46–7. Echoing *Twelfth Night* II iv 14–21:

> *Duke.*   . . . If ever thou shalt love,
> In the sweet pangs of it remember me;
> For such as I am all true lovers are,
> Unstaid and skittish in all motions else
> Save in the constant image of the creature
> That is belov'd. How dost thou like this tune?
> *Viola.* It gives a very echo to the seat
> Where love is thron'd.

48. free.] free *Nbk 9*; free; *1820, 1839.*

49. apparitions –] apparitions *Nbk 9, Reiman (1977)*; apparitions, *1820, 1839, Rossetti 1870, Butter (1970). first*] *Nbk 9, Reiman (1977)*; first, *1820, 1839, Rossetti 1870, Butter (1970).*

49–56. Another difficult sentence (see note to lines 40–8 above). *Eds* have varied considerably from the early witnesses, and from each other, in their punctuation; the problem centres on which parts of the sentence to mark as parenthetic or relative, either by dashes or brackets (or both). The collation here notes differences with several *eds*. Like the preceding sentence the passage has attracted paraphrase; GM and KE offer the following: 'And lovely imaginings will come, too; vague at first, but growing more vivid as the mind (fresh from intercourse with Beauty, an intercourse which generates the ideal concepts that these imaginings illustrate) realises them in actual works of art: the offspring of painting, sculpture, poetry, and arts not yet invented'.

49–53. The passage is Platonic; the mind's capacity to envisage and comprehend ideals is nourished through intercourse with the beautiful. Cp. *Symposium* 209–12. *Wasserman* 273

50 Then radiant, as the mind, arising bright
  From the embrace of beauty whence the forms
  Of which these are the phantoms, casts on them
  The gathered rays which are reality —
  Shall visit us, the progeny immortal
55 Of Painting, Sculpture, and rapt Poesy,
  And arts, though unimagined, yet to be.
  The wandering voices and the shadows these
  Of all that man becomes, the mediators
  Of that best worship, love, by him and us
60 Given and returned; swift shapes and sounds, which grow
  More fair and soft as man grows wise and kind,
  And veil by veil, evil and error fall . . .
  Such virtue has the cave and place around.
         [Turning to the Spirit of the Hour.
  For thee, fair Spirit, one toil remains. Ione,

---

suggests that the myth of Aurora and Tithonus is 'recognisable behind' this passage; cp. *Odyssey* v 1.

50. *radiant,*] *Nbk 9, 1820, 1839*; radiant, – *Rossetti 1870*; radiant – *Butter (1970), Reiman (1977)*.

51. *beauty whence*] *Nbk 9*; beauty, whence *1820, 1839, Butter (1970)*; beauty (whence *Rossetti 1870, Reiman (1977)*.

52. *phantoms,*] *Nbk 9, 1820, 1839, Butter (1970)*; phantoms), *Rossetti 1870*; phantoms) *Reiman (1977)*.

53. *gathered*] 'Concentrated' (*Concordance*; cp. II i 84 and note). *reality –*] *Butter (1970), Reiman (1977)*; reality, *Nbk 9, 1820, 1839*; reality, – *Rossetti 1870*.

55. *rapt*] *Nbk 9, 1839*; wrapt *1820, 1829*; presumably corrected from S.'s errata list.

60. Cp. II v 40.

62. *fall . . .*] *Nbk 9*; fall: *1820, 1839*.

64–8. This passage appears to include a complex pun on S.'s name and poetic calling, and suggests further implicit references to his immediate family (cp. III i 19 and note). The Shelley family Coat of Arms included three conch shells (see the crest on the cover of *Dowden Life*, and the illustration and catalogue entry in *Shelley's Guitar* 2, 6) and in addition to his known propensity for punning on his own and others' names S. may have in mind a family legend recorded in *Hogg* 3: 'Sir Guyon de Shelley, one of the most famous of the Paladins . . . carried about with him at all times three conchs [sic] fastened to the inside of his shield, tipt respectively with brass, with silver, and with gold. When he blew the first shell, all giants, however huge, fled before him. When he put the second to his lips, all spells were broken, all enchantments dissolved; and when he made the third conch, the golden one, vocal, the law of God was immediately exalted, and the law of the Devil annulled and abrogated, wherever the potent sound reached. Some historians affirm, that the third shell had a still more remarkable effect; that its melting notes instantly softened the heart of every female, gentle or simple, who heard them, to such an extent, that it was impossible for her to refuse whatever its owner might ask.' S.'s lines hint at a fleeting identification between Prometheus and Asia, and himself and Mary (implying that Prometheus and Asia are indeed to be thought of as married in *PU*), with Godwin (humorously) as Proteus; Mary's wedding gift to S. is thought

65   Give her that curvèd shell, which Proteus old
            Made Asia's nuptial boon, breathing within it
            A voice to be accomplished, and which thou
            Didst hide in grass under the hollow rock.

Ione
            Thou most desired Hour, more loved and lovely
70   Than all thy sisters, this is the mystic shell;
            See the pale azure fading into silver
            Lining it with a soft yet glowing light:
            Looks it not like lulled music sleeping there?

Spirit
            It seems in truth the fairest shell of Ocean:
75   Its sound must be at once both sweet and strange.

Prometheus
            Go, borne over the cities of mankind
            On whirlwind-footed coursers: once again
            Outspeed the sun around the orbèd world;
            And as thy chariot cleaves the kindling air,
80   Thou breathe into the many-folded shell,

---

of as S.'s gift of poetry, informed by Godwin's writings. The shell would further identify with S.'s poetic prophecy to the world, and more specifically with *PU* itself in the future moral efficacy envisaged for it by S.

65. that curvèd shell] See preceding note. Asia, like Venus Aphrodite, was born on a shell (see II v 20–32 and note). Shells have a range of symbolic associations with poetry and its effects; the lyre itself was conventionally thought of as originally fashioned from a tortoise shell (see S.'s *Hymn to Mercury*). *Proteus*] A sea god with the power to change shape, and to foretell the future (see Virgil, *Georgic* iv 387ff.). S.'s conception of Proteus, as the informing spirit of the natural human world, appears particularly indebted to Bacon (a favourite of S.'s); cp. *TL* 269–73, *Prose Works* 250 and see *Wasserman* 348–9. Murray's ed. note in *Prose Works* 465 explains that S. thinks of Proteus 'not as the prophetic old man of the sea but, in the Orphic mystical sense, as the source of the elemental material world, a symbolic application of his character derived from his ability to change into whatever shape he pleased until caught in one of them, on which occasion he was obliged to answer truthfully any query put to him.' *old*] Nbk 9, *1820*; old, *1839*.

70. this is the] *1820*, *1829*; this the Nbk 9, *1839*. An odd crux; usually *1839*'s reversion to the nbk reading would imply an erratum noted by S., but here the sense suggests a transcription error in Nbk 9 perhaps coinciding with an uncaught printer's error in *1839*.

71–3. Recalling the shell-chariot of the second spirit at II iv 156–9.

72. light:] *1820*, *1839*; light. Nbk 9; perhaps a change to the press transcript, although the stop in Nbk 9 is faint and could be accidental.

73–5, 80–2. The shell's music strengthens its association with poetry; cp. II ii 24–40 and note.

76–83. The Spirit reports back at the end of III iv.

80. shell,] Shell Nbk 9.

Loosening its mighty music; it shall be
As thunder mingled with clear echoes. Then
Return; and thou shalt dwell beside our cave.

[*Kissing the ground*

And thou, O Mother Earth! —

The Earth

I hear, I feel;
85   Thy lips are on me, and their touch runs down
Even to the adamantine central gloom
Along these marble nerves; 'tis life, 'tis joy,
And through my withered, old, and icy frame
The warmth of an immortal youth shoots down
90   Circling. Henceforth the many children fair
Folded in my sustaining arms — all plants,
And creeping forms, and insects rainbow-winged,
And birds, and beasts, and fish, and human shapes,
Which drew disease and pain from my wan bosom,
95   Draining the poison of despair — shall take
And interchange sweet nutriment; to me
Shall they become like sister-antelopes
By one fair dam, snow-white and swift as wind,
Nursed among lilies near a brimming stream.
100   The dew-mists of my sunless sleep shall float

---

82. *echoes. Then*] echoes – then *Nbk 9*; echoes: then *1820, 1839*.

SD. The SD is in *Nbk 9* but not in *1820* or *1839*, and was presumably omitted or cancelled in the press transcript. *1820* has a gap between lines 83 and 84, which might suggest a printer's error.

84–90. Paralleling the birth of Prometheus at I 154–8.

84. *I hear*] Perhaps implying that until the touch of Prometheus's lips Earth has heard nothing; cp. I 112ff. and note, and see lines 111–12 and note below.

85. *their touch*] *Nbk 9*; thy touch *1820, 1839*; probably a printer's error uncaught by Mary.

88. *And*] *Nbk 9, 1820*; And, *1839*.

91. *arms –*] arms; *Nbk 9, 1820, 1839*; dashes here and at line 95 below clarify that the list from lines 91–5 predicates the *many children* of line 90 above.

93–5. *Grabo (1930)* cites Darwin's view in *Botanic Garden* that 'contagious atoms' sent up from the centre of the earth by volcanic eruption were the source of pestilence: 'Those epidemic complaints, which are generally termed influenza, are believed to arise from vapours thrown out from earthquakes in such abundance as to affect large regions of the atmosphere'. Cp. I 175–7.

95. *despair –*] despair, *Nbk 9, 1820, 1839*; see note to line 91.

96–9. Cp. *Song of Solomon* iv 5: 'Thy two breasts are like two young roes that are twins, which feed among the lilies'.

99. *stream.*] stream; *Nbk 9*.

Under the stars like balm; night-folded flowers
Shall suck unwithering hues in their repose;
And men and beasts in happy dreams shall gather
Strength for the coming day and all its joy:
105   And death shall be the last embrace of her
Who takes the life she gave, even as a mother,
Folding her child, says, 'Leave me not again!'

Asia
O mother! wherefore speak the name of death?
Cease they to love, and move, and breathe, and speak,
110   Who die?

The Earth
      It would avail not to reply:
Thou art immortal, and this tongue is known
But to the uncommunicating dead.
Death is the veil which those who live call life:
They sleep, and it is lifted: and meanwhile

101. *balm;*] balm, *Nbk 9*; balm: *1820, 1839*. Cp. 'I am drunk with the honey-wine' (no. 178) 2 and note.

102. *unwithering*] *Nbk 9, 1839*; unwitting *1820, 1829*. The word is poorly formed in *Nbk 9* and could have been mistranscribed by Mary in the press transcript (though presumably not by S.); probably corrected in *1839* from S.'s errata list. In *Nbk 9* S. first wrote this line *Shall suck unwithering colours as they dream*, then canc. the last four words and replaced them with the received reading written on the facing page. *repose;*] repose *Nbk 9*; repose: *1820, 1839*.

104. *day*] *Nbk 9*; day, *1820, 1839*.

105–14. S. consistently maintained a sceptical position on knowledge of an afterlife; cp. IV 536–8 and note, and see e.g. his note to *Hellas* 197–210, and 'On a Future State', *Prose* 175–8.

111–12. Cp. I 148–51.

113–14. Cp. Milton, Sonnet xiv:
      When faith and love which parted from thee never,
      Had ripened thy just soul to dwell with God,
      Meekly thou didst resign this earthy load
      Of death, called life; which us from life doth sever.
Cp. also F. Salignac de la Mothe-Fénelon, *Adventures of Telemachus* (1699; trans. J. Hawkesworth, 1784) 179, 184: ' "It is here alone," [in Elysium] says he, "that there is life; the shadow only, and not the reality, is to be found upon earth" . . . "These, my son, whom you believe to be dead, these only are the living; those are the dead who languish upon earth the victims of disease and sorrow" . . . "the terms are inverted, and should be restored to their proper place".' The *veil* of line 113 suggests a Platonic context, but there appears to be no direct source in Plato, and S.'s phrasing perhaps implies a more sceptical reserve. The use of the veil image here clearly bears on the question of a life after earthly existence, and is therefore quite different from the image of the 'painted veil' at III iv 190–2, which like the image in S.'s sonnet 'Lift not the painted veil' almost certainly derives from Lucretius (see notes).

115   In mild variety the seasons mild —
       With rainbow-skirted showers, and odorous winds,
       And long blue meteors cleansing the dull night,
       And the life-kindling shafts of the keen sun's
       All-piercing bow, and the dew-mingled rain
120   Of the calm moonbeams, a soft influence mild —
       Shall clothe the forests and the fields — aye, even
       The crag-built deserts of the barren deep —
       With ever-living leaves, and fruits, and flowers.
       And Thou! There is a Cavern where my spirit
125   Was panted forth in anguish whilst thy pain
       Made my heart mad, and those who did inhale it

115–23. The sentence is awkward in comprising two substantial parenthetic passages. Dashes are here introduced in lines 115, 120, and 122, and a dash adopted from *Nbk 9* in line 121. The sense is 'the seasons mild . . . shall clothe the forests and the fields . . . with ever-living leaves, and fruits, and flowers': lines 114–20 qualify *seasons*; lines 121–2, *aye, even / The crag-built deserts of the barren deep*, qualify *the forests and the fields*. The vision of a redeemed physical nature is in keeping with S.'s conviction that humanity's moral state and physical environment are not merely correlated but are linked aspects of the same cosmic harmony; see *Q Mab* viii 145–86 and note, II iv 49–58 and note.

115. mild –] mild *Nbk 9, 1820, 1839.*   *118. sun's*] Sun's *Nbk 9.*

120. mild –] mild; *Nbk 9*; mild, *1820, 1839.*

121. fields –] *Nbk 9*; fields, *1820, 1839.*

122. deep –] deep *Nbk 9*; deep, *1820, 1839.*

123. The arguments of Malthus are implicitly countered in S.'s vision of the possibilities for global food supply (cp. III i 19 and note).

124–47. The Earth's cavern may be the same as the cave described by Prometheus earlier (see lines 10–24 above, and notes), although there are significant differences in the two descriptions. This cavern suggests the oracular cave of Demogorgon in II iii, but now purified of the ill effects associated with its vapours (it may also equate with the 'abyss' into which Jupiter falls in III i; see Paul Dawson, *The Unacknowledged Legislator: Shelley and Politics* (1980) 126). As various commentators have noted, S.'s description suggests the cave at Delphi, especially in the account in Diodorus Siculus (xvi 26) describing the frenzy of those inhaling the oracular vapours (see II iii and notes). The description seems to draw specifically on S.'s impressions of Lake Avernus near Naples, 'once a chasm of deadly & pestilential vapours' and of Solfatara and the area towards Pozzuoli (see *L* ii 61–2). Cp. *Quarterly Review* x (1814) 202: 'of the numerous persons who put their ear to the aperture [in the side of a volcanic mountain], from a curiosity . . . they all became mad, instantly mad, and were never again restored to the light of reason, or the rational government of themselves' (and see note to IV 321). See *Wasserman* 278–82 for excellent commentary on the whole passage lines 124–75. If as noted above, line 84 and note, Earth has heard nothing until kissed by Prometheus, then she will not have heard Prometheus's account of a cave at lines 10–24.

124. Thou! There] Thou . . . there *Nbk 9*; thou! There *1820, 1839. Cavern*] *Nbk 9*; cavern *1820, 1839. where*] whence *Nbk 9*; presumably S.'s change to the press transcript.

126–9. Suggesting sibylline frenzy; but hinting also at the descent into violence, and the subsequent rise of Napoleonic imperialism, following the French Revolution; cp. *Childe Harold's Pilgrimage* III lxxxi, on Napoleon:

Became mad too, and built a temple there,
And spoke, and were oracular, and lured
The erring nations round to mutual war,
130 And faithless faith, such as Jove kept with thee;
Which breath now rises, as among tall weeds
A violet's exhalation, and it fills
With a serener light and crimson air
Intense, yet soft, the rocks and woods around;
135 It feeds the quick growth of the serpent vine,
And the dark linkèd ivy tangling wild,
And budding, blown, or odour-faded blooms
Which star the winds with points of coloured light
As they rain through them, and bright, golden globes
140 Of fruit, suspended in their own green heaven;

> For then he was inspired, and from him came,
> As from the Pythian's mystic cave of yore,
> Those oracles which set the world in flame,
> Nor ceased to burn till kingdoms were no more . . .

126. who] *Nbk 9, 1820*; *that 1829, 1839*; clear evidence that Mary used *1829* as the copy text for *1839* (see *Taylor* 41).

131–4. The exhalation of a crimson air suggests the 'nitrous gas' described by Humphrey Davy and Joseph Priestley (see *Grabo (1930)* 188–90); the Earth now produces a nitrogen-rich *breath* wholly beneficial in its effects, in contrast to the poisonous mixture of gases exhaled in pre-revolutionary time; see II iii 43–4 and note.

131. S. at first began this line *Which now floats upward* in *Nbk 9*, then canc. and replaced these words with *Which breath now rises* written on the facing page. *among*] *Nbk 9*; amongst *1820, 1839*; perhaps S.'s change to the press transcript, but possibly altered by the printer or in proof.

136. Ivy was sacred to Bacchus (Ovid, *Fasti* iii 767–70); S. thus develops the Dionysian associations of the cave, and anticipates the reference of line 154 below.

137–8. Cp. S.'s description of the Astroni crater near Naples: 'The willow trees had just begun to put forth their green & golden buds, and gleamed like points of lambent fire among the wintry forest' (*L* ii 78).

138. Which star] S. at first wrote *Starring* in *Nbk 9*, then cancelled it in pencil and replaced it with *Which star* written in pencil on the facing page; a change to the fair copy which must have been included in the press transcript. *light*] *Nbk 9*; light, *1820, 1839*.

139. bright,] *Nbk 9, 1820*; bright *1839*.

139–40. Cp. 'Mazenghi' (no. 166) 80–3 (and see note):
> it was a feast
> When'er he found those globes of deep red gold
> Which in the woods the strawberry tree doth bear,
> Suspended in their emerald atmosphere.

140. heaven;] *Nbk 9*; heaven, *1820, 1839*; the long sentence lines 124–47 involves from line 135 a series of complex clauses all governed by *It feeds*. S.'s semicolon here (and at line 144) helps better than a comma to control the grammar.

594

And, through their veinèd leaves and amber stems
The flowers whose purple and translucid bowls
Stand ever mantling with aërial dew,
The drink of spirits; and it circles round,
145 Like the soft waving wings of noonday dreams,
Inspiring calm and happy thoughts, like mine
Now thou art thus restored. This Cave is thine.
Arise! Appear!
                    [*A* Spirit *rises in the likeness of a winged child.*
This is my torch-bearer,
Who let his lamp out in old time with gazing
150 On eyes from which he kindled it anew
With love, which is as fire, sweet daughter mine,
For such is that within thine own. Run, wayward!
And guide this company beyond the peak
Of Bacchic Nysa, Mænad-haunted mountain,

141. *And,*] *Nbk 9*; And *1820, 1839.*

142–4. See headnote to 'I am drunk with the honey-wine' (no. 178).

144. *spirits;*] *Nbk 9*; spirits: *1820, 1839.*

146. *mine*] *Nbk 9*; mine, *1820, 1839.*

147. In *Nbk 9* this line reads *Now thou art thus restored . . . that Cave is thine*; presumably altered by S. in the press transcript. *Cave*] *Nbk 9*; cave *1820, 1839.*

SD. The Spirit who appears here *in the likeness of a winged child* is another example in this scene (with the two caves, and the two temples; see below, line 161) of an element which may or may not be identified with another instance in this or the following scene. *Wasserman* 278 offers persuasive commentary on this figure: 'The Spirit of the Earth who appears in Acts III and IV . . . derives from the network of interconnected myths introduced . . . by the identification of Asia with Venus. For this winged child . . . marked by suggestively sexual speech, performs in the poem's special context the role of Eros, or Cupid, son of Venus.'

148. *torch-bearer,*] torch-bearer *Nbk 9*; torch-bearer; *1820, 1839.* A torch was the emblem of Prometheus; cp. line 170 below.

149–52. The Spirit's energy is renewed by the love transmitted from Asia's (i.e. its mother's) eyes; cp. III iv 1–19 and note, 15–19 and note, 24, 95–56.

151. *daughter*] Daughter *Nbk 9*.

152. *own. Run, wayward!*] own – run Wayward! *Nbk 9*; own. Run, wayward, *1820, 1839.*

154–5. Euripides' *The Cyclops* 63–75, trans. by S. probably in June 1818, may be the direct source here ('Nor can I join the Nymphs on Mount Nysa in singing the song "Iacchos Iacchos" to Aphrodite, whom I swiftly pursued in the company of white-footed Bacchants', Loeb trans.), although S.'s trans. of these lines (see no. 172 lines 60–5) does not include the reference to Nysa. Dionysus was born on Mount Nysa (see e.g. *Iliad* vi 133, where the association with Mænads is prominent, and Diodorus Siculus i 15, iii 68). Nysa, variously a mountain, city, or island, was variously situated far to the East of Greece; places were named after the mythic Nysa by adherents of Dionysian cults. S.'s geography implies a journey from the Indian Caucasus westwards and north towards Athens and the Promethean temple of line 161 below (see *Curran (1975)* 91). The details may also recall *Paradise Lost* iv 275–9 (a passage immediately following that recollected in lines 41–3 above):

155   And beyond Indus, and its tribute rivers,
        Trampling the torrent streams and glassy lakes
        With feet unwet, unwearied, undelaying;
        And up the green ravine, across the vale,
        Beside the windless and crystalline pool
160   Where ever lies, on unerasing waves,
        The image of a temple, built above,
        Distinct with column, arch, and architrave,
        And palm-like capital, and over-wrought,
        And populous most with living imagery —
165   Praxitelean shapes, whose marble smiles
        Fill the hushed air with everlasting love.
        It is deserted now, but once it bore

                            that Nyseian isle
              Girt with the river Triton, where old Cham,
              Whom Gentiles Ammon call and Lybian Jove,
              Hid Amalthea and her florid son
              Young Bacchus from his stepdame Rhea's eye . . .

155. Indus,] *Nbk 9*; Indus *1820, 1839.*

157. undelaying;] *Nbk 9*; undelaying, *1820, 1839.*

158–61. Cp. *L* ii 61: '. . . we landed to visit Lake Avernus. We passed thro the cavern of the Sybil (not Virgils Sybil) which pierces one of the hills which circumscribe the lake & came to a calm & lovely basin of water surrounded by dark woody hills, & profoundly solitary. Some vast ruins of the temple of Pluto stand in a lawny hill on one side of it, and are reflected in its windless mirror.'

159–61. S. repeatedly describes reflected buildings in this way; cp. e.g. *Witch of Atlas* 513–15, 'Ode to Liberty' 76–9, 'Euganean Hills' 142–3.

159. pool] *Nbk 9*; pool, *1820, 1839.*

160–7. The temple beside the cavern, to which the Spirit is directed, combines features from western and eastern architectural traditions. Frederic S. Colwell ('Figures in a Promethean Landscape', *KSJ* xlv (1996) 118–31, with photograph) has identified a possible model for S.'s description in the classical temple, certainly well known to S., on an island in the Lago di Borghese on the Roman Pincio. E. B. Hungerford, *Shores of Darkness* (1941) 197–200, since followed by many commentators, noted that the references to the *Lampadephoria* (see lines 168–70 and notes, below) imply that S. is thinking of the temple to Prometheus situated in the Athenian Academy, and that Earth's cavern would therefore be in the nearby grove of Colonus, itself connected with Prometheus and containing an entrance into the Underworld (see Sophocles, *Oedipus at Colonus* 39–40, 50–5). In Sophocles the grove is sacred to the Furies, and S.'s setting would thus imply the victory of Prometheus over their influences (see also *Butter (1970)* 299–300).

163. capital,] capitals, *Nbk 9*; presumably S.'s change to the press transcript, to match the singulars of the preceding line.

164. most with] with most *Nbk 9*; presumably S.'s change to the press transcript. *imagery* –] imagery *Nbk 9*; imagery, *1820, 1839.*

165. Praxiteles was an Athenian sculptor, ranked in antiquity second only to Phidias (see III iv 112 and note). The *marble smiles* suggest early Gk male nude statues, the so-called *kouroi,* copies of which S. would have seen in Florence and Rome.

Thy name, Prometheus; there the emulous youths
Bore to thy honour through the divine gloom
170   The lamp which was thine emblem . . . even as those
Who bear the untransmitted torch of hope
Into the grave, across the night of life,
As thou hast borne it most triumphantly
To this far goal of Time. Depart, farewell.
175   Beside that temple is the destined Cave.

168–70. Opposite these lines in *Nbk 9* S. has written on the facing page 'The beginning of Platos Republic'. The *Republic* opens with references to an Athenian festival involving a race by young men carrying torches, the *Lampadephoria*, run in emulation of Prometheus's feat in bringing fire to humanity. Cp. Pausanias, *Description of Greece* I xxx: 'In the Academy is an altar to Prometheus, and from it they run to the city carrying burning torches. The contest is while running to keep the torch still alight; if the torch of the first runner goes out, he has no longer any claim to victory, but the second runner has. If his torch also goes out, then the third man is the victor. If all the torches go out, no one is left to be the winner' (Loeb trans.). See also Thomas Taylor's trans. of Pausanias (3 vols, 1794) iii 252: 'This custom adopted by the Athenians, of running from the altar of Prometheus to the city with burning lamps, in which he alone was victorious whose lamp remained unextinguished in the race, was intended to signify that he is the true conqueror in the race of life, whose rational part is not extinguished, or, in other words, does not become dormant in the career.' S. ordered Taylor's trans. in July 1817 (*L* i 548). S. would certainly have known the famous passage in Lucretius which uses an image from the *Lampadephoria*:

sic rerum summa novatur
semper, et inter se mortales mutua vivunt:
augescunt aliae gentes, aliae minuuntur,
inque brevi spatio mutantur saecla animantum
et quasi cursores vitai lampada tradunt. (*De Re. Nat.* ii 75–9)

('Thus the sum of things is ever being renewed, and mortal creatures live dependent one upon another. Some species increase, others diminish, and in a short space the generations of living creatures are changed and, like runners, pass on the torch of life', Loeb trans.)

169. divine gloom] Cp. II ii 22.

170. emblem . . .] *Nbk 9*; emblem; *1820, 1839*.

171–5. In *Nbk 9* S. first wrote

Who bear the untransmitted torch of hope
Into the grave across the night of life . . .
Beside it is the destined Cave . . . depart!

He then wrote on the facing page the further lines *As thou hast borne it most triumphantly / To this High* [alt. to *far*] *goal of Time . . . depart, farewell!*, and corrected line 175 to its received form.

175. Cave.] Cave . . . *Nbk 9*; cave. *1820, 1839*.

Scene iv

A forest. In the background, a Cave. Prometheus, Asia, Panthea, Ione, *and the* Spirit of the Earth.

Ione
Sister, it is not earthly . . . how it glides
Under the leaves! how on its head there burns
A light like a green star, whose emerald beams
Are twined with its fair hair! how, as it moves,
5   The splendour drops in flakes upon the grass!
Knowest thou it?

Panthea
It is the delicate spirit
That guides the earth through heaven. From afar
The populous constellations call that light
The loveliest of the planets; and sometimes
10   It floats along the spray of the salt sea,
Or makes its chariot of a foggy cloud,
Or walks through fields or cities while men sleep,

1–19. This description of the Spirit of the Earth combines various effects of electricity as understood by the science of S.'s day, including the electrical character of phosphorescent light in animals and vegetable matter, and the supposed electrical origins of the gases associated with the *ignis fatuus* and related phenomena, such as fogs, gravity and magnetism (see *Grabo (1930)* 123–30, who cites in particular the accounts of electricity in Beccaria, *Treatise upon Artificial Electricity* (English trans. 1776), Davy, *Elements of Chemical Philosophy*, and Darwin, *Botanic Garden*). S.'s implication is that the Earth is guided by electricity in the physical sphere as it is guided by love in the moral sphere, and that the two modes of influence are in a relation not simply of correspondence but of actual identity (see lines 15–19 and note, and cp. e.g. I 122–3 and note). The Spirit identifies in mythic terms with Eros or Cupid to Asia's Venus (see note to stage direction following III iii 147), while in physical terms conforming to contemporary scientific opinion that electricity was emitted from the earth.

1. earthly . . .] Earthly . . . *Nbk 9*; earthly: *1820, 1839.*   *3. light*] *Nbk 9*; light, *1820, 1839.*

2–4. The details here suggest a Leyden Jar, an instrument very familiar to S., which produces a green electric light if the terminals are of copper (see *Grabo (1930)* 126).

5. Cp. Coleridge, *Ancient Mariner* 272–6:
                    Beyond the shadow of the ship
                    I watched the water-snakes:
                    They moved in tracks of shining white,
                    And when they reared, the elfish light
                    Fell off in hoary flakes.
Coleridge is himself thinking here of the phosphorescence of marine life in tropical waters.

7. heaven.] Heaven. *Nbk 9.*

8. The likelihood of life on other planets was a commonplace of scientific speculation in S.'s day; cp. I 2, 163–5.

Or o'er the mountain tops, or down the rivers,
Or through the green waste wilderness, as now,
15   Wondering at all it sees. Before Jove reigned
It loved our sister Asia, and it came
Each leisure hour to drink the liquid light
Out of her eyes, for which it said it thirsted
As one bit by a dipsas; and with her
20   It made its childish confidence, and told her
All it had known and seen, for it saw much,
Yet idly reasoned what it saw; and called her —
For whence it sprang it knew not, nor do I —
'Mother, dear Mother.'

Spirit of the Earth (running to ASIA)
                         Mother, dearest Mother;
25   May I then talk with thee as I was wont?
May I then hide my eyes in thy soft arms,
After thy looks have made them tired of joy?
May I then play beside thee the long noons,
When work is none in the bright silent air?

Asia
30   I love thee, gentlest being, and henceforth
Can cherish thee unenvied. Speak, I pray:
Thy simple talk once solaced, now delights.

Spirit of the Earth
Mother, I am grown wiser, though a child
Cannot be wise like thee, within this day;
35   And happier too; happier and wiser both.
Thou knowest that toads, and snakes, and loathly worms,
And venomous and malicious beasts, and boughs

15–19. The Spirit's energy is renewed from Asia, who is its mother; cp. III iii 148–52.

19. dipsas;] Nbk 9; dipsas, *1820, 1839.* The dipsas (from Gk δυψάω, 'to thirst') was a mythical snake which caused raging thirst by its bite (cp. Lucan, *Pharsalia* ix 699ff., and *Paradise Lost* x 526).   *22. her –*] Nbk 9; her, *1820, 1839.*

23. I –] Nbk 9; I, *1820, 1839.* S.'s underlying scepticism is discernible in Panthea's confessed ignorance of origins here.

24. The caps. are from Nbk 9. Facing this line on the opposite page in Nbk 9 is a stage direction 'Asia & the spirit have entered the cave'; presumably S. decided to omit it in the press transcript, as it appears in no printed witness.

26. my] mine Nbk 9.   *30. being,*] Nbk 9, 1820; being! *1839.*

33–85. This passage effectively reverses Milton's account in *Paradise Lost* xi 423ff. of the growth of evil after the Fall.

36–50. This sentence is phrased as a preliminary (*Thou knowest . . .*) to the information content of the following sentence (*Well . . .*).   *37–9.* Cp. lines 78–82 below.

That bore ill berries in the woods, were ever
An hindrance to my walks o'er the green world:
40 And that, among the haunts of humankind,
Hard-featured men, or with proud, angry looks,
Or cold, staid gait, or false and hollow smiles,
Or the dull sneer of self-loved ignorance,
Or other such foul masks, with which ill thoughts
45 Hide that fair being whom we spirits call man;
And women too, ugliest of all things evil,
(Though fair, even in a world where thou art fair,
When good and kind, free and sincere like thee),
When false or frowning made me sick at heart
50 To pass them, though they slept, and I unseen.
Well, my path lately lay through a great city
Into the woody hills surrounding it.
A sentinel was sleeping at the gate:
When there was heard a sound, so loud, it shook
55 The towers amid the moonlight, yet more sweet
Than any voice but thine, sweetest of all;
A long, long sound, as it would never end:
And all the inhabitants leapt suddenly
Out of their rest, and gathered in the streets,
60 Looking in wonder up to Heaven, while yet
The music pealed along. I hid myself
Within a fountain in the public square,
Where I lay like the reflex of the moon
Seen in a wave under green leaves; and soon

39. *An*] *Nbk 9*, *1820*; A *1829*, *1839*; Mary S. probably overlooked this change introduced by Galignani.

40–50. *Men* in line 41, together with *women* in line 46, are both governed by *made* in line 49; i.e. the sense is 'hard-featured men . . . And women too . . . made me sick at heart . . .'.

41. *or*] Initiating a series of alternative predications of *hard-featured men* which continues to line 45.

42. Cp. *Hamlet* I v 108: 'one may smile, and smile, and be a villain'.

47–8. These lines are not in parenthesis in *Nbk 9*.

52. *it.*] *Nbk 9*; it: *1820*, *1839*.

53. *A*] The *Nbk 9*; presumably S.'s change to the press transcript. The sentinel's relaxed unwariness of threat implies that deep changes are already under way.

54–7. This is the sound of the shell given by Prometheus to the Spirit of the Hour; see III iii 65–82.

61–4. The green light produced by the Spirit's electric phosphorescence allows it to camouflage itself in the fountain within the reflection of the moon shining through trees.

63–4. As O'Neill (*Human Mind's Imaginings* 117) notes, the rhyme here 'seems lax'.

65   Those ugly human shapes and visages
       Of which I spoke as having wrought me pain,
       Passed floating through the air, and fading still
       Into the winds that scattered them; and those
       From whom they passed seemed mild and lovely forms
70   After some foul disguise had fallen; and all
       Were somewhat changed; and after brief surprise
       And greetings of delighted wonder, all
       Went to their sleep again: and when the dawn
       Came — wouldst thou think that toads, and snakes and efts,
75   Could e'er be beautiful? yet so they were,
       And that with little change of shape or hue:
       All things had put their evil nature off.

65–8. S. perhaps recalls Lucretius, *De Re. Nat.* iv 24ff., describing the Epicurean εἴδωλα or 'images', the fine atomic films given off from the surfaces of things:

> esse ea quae rerum simulacra vocamus;
> quae, quasi membranae summo de corpore rerum
> dereptae, volitant ultroque citroque per auras,
> atque eadem nobis vigilantibus obvia mentes
> terrificant atque in somnis, cum saepe figuras
> contuimur miras simulacraque luce carentum,
> quae nos horrifice languentis saepe sopore
> excierunt (30–7)

('there exist what we call images of things; which, like films drawn from the outermost surface of things, flit about hither and thither through the air; it is these same that, encountering us in wakeful hours, terrify our minds, as also in sleep, when we often behold wonderful shapes and images of the dead, which have often aroused us in horror while we lay languid in sleep'; Loeb trans.). These lines immediately precede the passage cited below in relation to lines 190–2; see also III iii 113–14, and headnote and notes to S.'s sonnet 'Lift not the painted veil'.

70. *fallen;*] fallen – *Nbk 9*; fallen, *1820, 1839.*

71. *changed;*] changed – *Nbk 9*; changed, *1820, 1839.*

74–6. Cp. Coleridge, *Ancient Mariner* 277–82:

> Within the shadow of the ship
> I watched their [i.e. the water-snakes'] rich attire:
> Blue, glossy green, and velvet black,
> They coiled and swam; and every track
> Was a flash of golden fire.

> O happy living things! no tongue
> Their beauty might declare:
> A spring of love gushed from my heart,
> And I blessed them unaware:
> Sure my kind saint took pity on me,
> And I blessed them unaware.

74. *Came –*] *Nbk 9*; Came, *1820, 1839.* *snakes*] *Nbk 9*; snakes, *1820, 1839.*

77. *off.*] off *Nbk 9*; off: *1820, 1839.* Following this line in *Nbk 9* is a canc. line: 'Like an old garment soiled & overworn'.

I cannot tell my joy, when o'er a lake,
Upon a drooping bough with nightshade twined,
80   I saw two azure halcyons clinging downward
And thinning one bright bunch of amber berries
With quick long beaks, and in the deep there lay
Those lovely forms imaged as in a sky.
So with my thoughts full of these happy changes,
85   We meet again, the happiest change of all.

Asia
And never will we part, till thy chaste sister
Who guides the frozen and inconstant moon
Will look on thy more warm and equal light
Till her heart thaw like flakes of April snow,
90   And love thee.

Spirit of the Earth
               What! as Asia loves Prometheus?

Asia
Peace, wanton! thou art yet not old enough.
Think ye, by gazing on each other's eyes
To multiply your lovely selves, and fill
With spherèd fires the interlunar air?

78–83. The *halcyons* – i.e. kingfishers, from Gk ἀλκυών – are no longer fish-eating but veget-
arian, and the formerly poisonous berries of the woody nightshade are now edible (see head-
note to no. 66, 'Passion: to the [Woody Nightshade]'). The kingfishers are *thinning* the bunch
because *solanum dulcamara* is peculiar in having ripe (red), half-ripe (amber) and unripe (green)
berries in the same bunch; the birds are taking only the ripe berries. The phrase *downward-
clinging* is odd as kingfishers 'cling upward'; the suggestion may be that the Spirit observes
the scene as reflected in a perfectly calm lake. With the implications of this passage cp. Q
Mab viii 127 and note.   78. *lake,*] Nbk 9; lake *1820, 1839*.

81. *bunch*] In *Nbk 9* this word is written in faint pencil above the original (and uncanc.) read-
ing *mass*; an example of an apparently late change to the fair copy in *Nbk 9* which was never-
theless included in the press transcript. *berries*] Nbk 9; berries, *1820, 1839*.

83. *sky.*] sky *Nbk 9*; sky; *1820, 1839*.

86–96. These lines were added later on the blank facing page in *Nbk 9*, probably to provide
an anticipation of the dialogue between the Earth and Moon in IV 319–502, which S. would
have been working on some time between August and December 1819. As *BSM* ix 637 notes,
the passage was written into *Nbk 9* before the fair copy of S.'s Preface to *PU*, which skips
these lines.   86. *sister*] Sister *Nbk 9*.   90. *What!*] *1840*; What, *Nbk 9*; What; *1820, 1839*.

91. *Peace, wanton!*] *1840*; Peace Wanton – *Nbk 9*; Peace, wanton, *1820, 1839*.

92. *ye,*] Nbk 9; ye *1820, 1839*.

92. Cp. Dante, *Convito* Treatise III Ch. 12: 'In other intelligences she [the divine philosophy]
exists in a lesser way, as though a mistress, of whom no lover has complete enjoyment, but
must satisfy his longing by gazing on her' (trans. Philip Wicksteed).

Spirit of the Earth
95   Nay, Mother, while my sister trims her lamp
'Tis hard I should go darkling.

Asia

                 Listen! look!
                 [*The* Spirit of the Hour *enters.*

Prometheus
We feel what thou hast heard and seen: yet speak.

Sprit of the Hour
Soon as the sound had ceased whose thunder filled
The abysses of the sky, and the wide earth,
100   There was a change . . . the impalpable thin air
And the all-circling sunlight were transformed,
As if the sense of love, dissolved in them,
Had folded itself round the spherèd world.
My vision then grew clear, and I could see
105   Into the mysteries of the universe.

91–7. Asia wryly asks the Spirit of the Earth if he is so naive as to believe that children can be begotten by eye-contact. A lamp cannot give light when it is being trimmed (i.e. cleaned out and made ready for relighting), and is here therefore likened to that 'interlunar' phase when the moon is invisible; prompting the Spirit of the Earth to question why he cannot produce offspring planets whose light would illumine such periods of darkness.

95. Mother,] Mother *Nbk 9*; mother, *1820, 1839.* *trims*] In *Nbk 9* the original reading was *fills*; S. then canc. *fills* and wrote *trims* above, but subsequently underlined *fills* presumably to indicate a return to that reading. But evidently *trims* was preferred in the press transcript.

96–7. These are the last words spoken by Prometheus and Asia in *PU*.

96. Listen!] *Nbk 9*; Listen; *1820, 1839.*

98–204. The Spirit of the Hour reports back on the journey undertaken under Prometheus's order at III iii 64ff., and thus provides a second perspective, following that of the Spirit of the Earth, on the momentous changes following the liberation of Prometheus and his reunion with Asia.

98–9. i.e. the sound of the shell (cp. lines 54–7 above).

99. sky,] *Nbk 9*; sky *1820, 1839.*

100–5. The atmosphere has been cleansed to transparency by Asia as the embodiment of love, electrical energy, and the spirit of animation; cp. I 831–2, II v 26–30.

100. change . . .] *Nbk 9*; change: *1820, 1839.*

105. universe.] Universe *Nbk 9*; universe: *1820, 1839.*

Dizzy as with delight I floated down,
Winnowing the lightsome air with languid plumes,
My coursers sought their birth-place in the sun,
Where they henceforth will live exempt from toil,
110 Pasturing flowers of vegetable fire;
And where my moonlike car will stand within
A temple, gazed upon by Phidian forms
Of thee, and Asia, and the Earth, and me,
And you fair nymphs, looking the love we feel,

106–8. These lines are unpunctuated in *Nbk 9*; the grammar is ambiguous, as the subject of *winnowing* can be understood with equal plausibility as either the *I* of line 106, or the *coursers* of line 108.

107. Cp. II i 27, and Dante, *Purgatorio* (trans. Cary) ii 35: 'Lo! how straight up to Heaven he holds them rear'd, / Winnowing the air with those eternal plumes, / That not like mortal hairs fall off or change.'

108–10. Cp. Ovid, *Met.* iv 214–15: 'Axe sub Hesperio sunt pascua Solis equorum' ('Beneath the western skies lie the pastures of the Sun's horses', Loeb trans.) and Claudian, *De Consulato Stilichonis* ii 467–70:

> Sic fatus croceis rorantes ignibus hortos
> ingreditur vallemque suam, quam flammeus ambit
> rivus et inriguis largum iubar ingerit herbis,
> quas Solis pascuntur equi

('So saying he entered his garden starred with fiery dew, the valley round which runs a river of flame feeding with its bounteous rays the dripping weeds whereon the horses of the sun do pasture', Loeb trans.)

110. fire;] fire – *Nbk 9*; fire. *1820, 1839*; the dash in *Nbk 9* was probably added after the completion of the following lines 111–24.

111–24. These lines were added on the blank facing page in *Nbk 9*; they are heavily corrected and were apparently composed straight into the nbk, presumably around the time of S.'s direct experience of the Roman architecture on which they draw (i.e. in March 1819). D. H. Reiman ('Roman Scenes in *PU* III iv', *PQ* xlvi (1967) 69–78; see also F. S. Colwell, *KSJ* xlv (1996) 118–31) argues persuasively that in this description of a sun-temple of the future S. has specifically in mind 'La Sala della Biga' in the Vatican Museum, modified by some features taken from the Pantheon (for S.'s visits to the Vatican and the Pantheon, on successive days, see *Mary Jnl* i 251 for 8 and 9 March 1819, and cp. *L* ii 87–8). The Biga was a two-horse chariot of the moon (see Lucan, *Pharsalia* i 78), and its sculpture is found in the Vatican in the centre of a roughly circular room, with a fretted domed ceiling, and surrounded by pillars interspersed with statues (see Reiman 71–2 for speculation on S.'s possible adaptations of these statues to the mythic scheme of *PU*). The chariot's two horses are yoked together by an amphisbæna (see line 119 and note). Reiman acknowledges that the Sala is not a temple, is not open to the sky, and has eight rather than twelve columns, and consequently suggests that the idea of an open-roofed temple may derive rather from the Pantheon. The architectural details combine to embody S.'s conception that the Car of the Hour, together with the protagonists in a revolution which has happened in real time, will be commemorated in a temple preserving their representations beyond temporal limit (see line 117 and note). For a different view of the temple, as Zoroastrian in conception, see *Curran (1975)* 78–9, 224–5.

112. Phidian forms] i.e. sculptures like those by Phidias, the supreme master of classical Gk sculpture, assumed to have been responsible for the giant statue of Athena which stood in the Parthenon, and for the metope, frieze, and pedimental figures of the Parthenon.

114. nymphs,] *Nbk 9, 1839*; nymphs *1820, 1829*; perhaps in S.'s errata list.   *feel,*] feel *Nbk 9*; feel; *1820, 1839*.

115   In memory of the tidings it has borne;
        Beneath a dome fretted with graven flowers,
        Poised on twelve columns of resplendent stone,
        And open to the bright and liquid sky.
        Yoked to it by an amphisbænic snake
120   The likeness of those wingèd steeds will mock
        The flight from which they find repose. Alas,
        Whither has wandered now my partial tongue
        When all remains untold which ye would hear?
        As I have said, I floated to the earth:
125   It was, as it is still, the pain of bliss
        To move, to breathe, to be; I wandering went
        Among the haunts and dwellings of mankind,
        And first was disappointed not to see
        Such mighty change as I had felt within
130   Expressed in outward things; but soon I looked,
        And behold! thrones were kingless, and men walked
        One with the other even as spirits do:
        None fawned, none trampled; hate, disdain, or fear,

115. it] i.e. the *car* of line 111 above.

117. The twelve columns perhaps suggest the Zodiac, or alternatively the twelve hours of the classical day, with the implication that in their circular arrangement they image time and its cycles transcended.

118. Cp. S.'s letter to Peacock of 23–24 January 1819, describing the 'upaithric' (i.e. open-roofed) buildings of the Greeks: 'They lived in a perpetual commerce with external nature and nourished themselves upon the spirit of its forms. Their theatres were all open to the mountains & the sky. Their columns that ideal type of a sacred forest with its roof of interwoven tracery admitted the light & wind, the odour & the freshness of the country penetrated the cities. Their temples were mostly upaithric; & the flying clouds the stars or the deep sky were seen above. O, but for that series of wretched wars which terminated in the Roman conquest of the world, but for the Christian religion which put a finishing stroke to the antient system; but for those changes which conducted Athens to its ruin, to what an eminence might not humanity have arrived!' (*L* ii 74–5).

119. The amphisbæna was a snake with a lamp-eyed head at each end (see Lucan, *Pharsalia* ix 719, *Paradise Lost* x 524).

120–1. i.e. the sculpture of the horses will paradoxically catch in its fixity the speed of their headlong flight.

121. flight] Nbk 9, 1839; light 1820, 1829; probably on S.'s errata list.

124. earth:] Earth Nbk 9.

129. change] Nbk 9, 1820; change, 1839. *within*] Nbk 9, 1820: within, 1839.

130–204. Cp. the similar prophetic description in Q Mab ix 93–137.

131. behold!] Nbk 9; behold, 1820, 1839. Cp. no. 86, 'A Retrospect of Times of Old' 1, and Q Mab iii 134–6.

132. do:] do, Nbk 9, 1820, 1839.

133, 137. fawned . . . frowned] In Nbk 9 these epithets are transposed; presumably S.'s change to the press transcript.

Self-love or self-contempt, on human brows
135 No more inscribed, as o'er the gate of hell,
'All hope abandon, ye who enter here';
None frowned, none trembled, none with eager fear
Gazed on another's eye of cold command,
Until the subject of a tyrant's will
140 Became, worse fate, the abject of his own,
Which spurred him, like an outspent horse, to death.
None wrought his lips in truth-entangling lines
Which smiled the lie his tongue disdained to speak;
None, with firm sneer, trod out in his own heart
145 The sparks of love and hope, till there remained
Those bitter ashes, a soul self-consumed,
And the wretch crept, a vampire among men,
Infecting all with his own hideous ill.
None talked that common, false, cold, hollow talk

135. The subject of *inscribed* is the *hate, disdain . . . fear, Self-love . . . self-contempt* of lines 133–4 above; i.e. 'hate [etc] used to be inscribed on human brows just as "All hope abandon [etc]" was inscribed over the gates of hell'.

136. abandon,] *Nbk 9*; abandon *1820, 1839*. Recalling the words written on the gate of Hell in Dante, *Inferno* iii 1–9 (trans. Cary):

> Through me you pass into the city of woe:
> Through me you pass into eternal pain:
> Through me among the people lost for aye.
> Justice the founder of my fabric moved:
> To rear me was the task of Power divine,
> Supremest Wisdom, and primeval Love.
> Before me things create were none, save things
> Eternal, and eternal I endure.
> All hope abandon, ye who enter here.

140. abject] *Concordance* glosses as 'slave', but *OED* (def. B; citing this occurence) 'One cast off . . . an outcast' is better; the sense is that some people become so entirely subjected to the will of a tyrant that they consciously relinquish self-determination, and are 'cast off' by their own will.

145. hope,] *Nbk 9*; hope *1820, 1839*.

147. crept,] *Nbk 9*; crept *1820, 1839*.

148. ill.] *Nbk 9*; ill; *1820, 1839*. Cp. *J&M* 350–6:

> Yet think not though subdued — and I may well
> Say that I am subdued — that the full Hell
> Within me would infect the untainted breast
> Of sacred nature with its own unrest;
> As some perverted beings think to find
> In scorn or hate a medicine for the mind
> Which scorn or hate have wounded —

149–52. The verb in line 150 needs also to be understood in the line following: i.e. 'that . . . talk which makes the heart deny the yes it breathes, yet which also makes the heart question that unmeant hypocrisy . . .'. Cp. Coleridge, *Christabel* 662–5:

150   Which makes the heart deny the *yes* it breathes,
      Yet question that unmeant hypocrisy
      With such a self-mistrust as has no name.
      And women, too, frank, beautiful, and kind
      As the free heaven which rains fresh light and dew
155   On the wide earth, passed; gentle, radiant forms,
      From custom's evil taint exempt and pure;
      Speaking the wisdom once they could not think,
      Looking emotions once they feared to feel,
      And changed to all which once they dared not be,
160   Yet being now, made earth like Heaven; nor pride
      Nor jealousy, nor envy, nor ill shame,
      The bitterest of those drops of treasured gall,
      Spoilt the sweet taste of the nepenthe, love.

      Thrones, altars, judgement-seats, and prisons — wherein,
165   And beside which, by wretched men were borne

    And pleasures flow in so thick and fast
    Upon his heart, that he at last
    Must needs express his love's excess
    With words of unmeant bitterness.

153–63. S. repeatedly insists that the full equality of women is a necessary condition of a good society; see e.g. *L&C* II xxxiv–xlv, VIII xv.

155–9. For S. passion had no necessary conflict with reason, but its expression was distorted by ruling prejudices; cp. lines 193–9 below, and see *Q Mab* v 20–1 and note (for Godwin's influence on S.'s thinking in this respect), viii 231–4.

155. gentle,] Nbk 9; gentle *1820, 1839*.

160. made] make Nbk 9; presumably S.'s change to the press transcript.   *earth like Heaven;*] Earth like Heaven – Nbk 9; earth like heaven; *1820, 1839*.

161. ill shame,] *1820*; ill shame Nbk 9; ill-shame, *1839*.

163. nepenthe] See II iv 60 and note.

164. Cp. *Paradise Lost* v 601: 'Thrones, dominations, princedoms, virtues, powers'; see also *Colossians* i 16, and *Revelation* xx 4: 'And I saw thrones, and they sat upon them, and judgement was given unto them . . .'.   *prisons –*] prisons, Nbk 9; prisons; *1820, 1839*.

164–204. Eds have proposed numerous solutions for the punctuation of this famously difficult passage, which is disastrously mispunctuated in *1820, 1839*, and many subsequent texts, including *Rossetti 1870* and *Hutchinson*. There appears to have been a methodically wrong-headed revision in *1820* of S.'s punctuation, perhaps suggesting an intervention by Peacock in proof-reading deriving from his failure to grasp the sense. *Locock 1911* is the first *ed* to offer satisfactory emendation. S. seems to have taken special pains to punctuate the passage more carefully than usual in Nbk 9, particularly in lines 192–8, possibly supplementing his fair copy punctuation after seeing the effect of the pointing in *1820*. He also corrected the pointing in Leigh Hunt's presentation copy of *1820* (see *BSM* ix 644). The text here follows Nbk 9 in emending *1839* more radically than usual, but also introduces further pointing where necessary. This is another passage for which there is a tradition of paraphrase (see *Zillman Variorum* 256–7), and notwithstanding the obvious pitfalls and complexities the present editors

607

Sceptres, tiaras, swords, and chains, and tomes
Of reasoned wrong, glozed on by ignorance —
Were like those monstrous and barbaric shapes,
The ghosts of a no more remembered fame,
170   Which from their unworn obelisks look forth
In triumph o'er the palaces and tombs
Of those who were their conquerors, mouldering round.

---

offer a paraphrase in support of the pointing here adopted: 'The old oppressive institutions
– which burdened people with the implements of bondage, and with books defending evil
doctrines, interpreted by fools – were now like the hieroglyphics on the Egyptian obelisks in
Rome (relics of a now-forgotten greatness), which stand intact among the decaying ruins of
the city that had conquered Egypt. These obelisks were once emblems of religion and con-
quest to the Egyptian ruling classes, but are now merely something to gape at; in the same
way, the relics of Earth's final bondage stand like museum-pieces among its present inhabi-
tants; and all those hideous forms and expressions of tyranny which men served by means
of war, and imprisonment, and human sacrifice – flattering even while hating what they served
– wither away over the buildings that embodied them. The gaudy pretence which those who
existed under the old régime thought of as "life", and which pretended to be a fulfilment of
the ideals that people really wanted, is destroyed; the pretence is gone, the man himself remains,
no longer oppressed – just simply man; free and equal, without social classes or racial or
national distinctions – just simply man. – Not man without passions, however, yet man free
from guilt or pain; for passion only gave rise to guilt and pain because he imposed these
consequences (or allowed them to be imposed) on himself. And not free, either, from acci-
dent and death (although keeping them under control), because accident and death are the
only ultimate impediments to man's otherwise limitless potentialities.'

167. glozed on] A pun; i.e. 'glossed or explained', but also 'provided with a specious extenuat-
ing commentary'. *ignorance* –] ignorance, *Nbk 9, 1820, 1839.*

168–79. In 1818 there were ten Egyptian obelisks in Rome, mostly of solid granite; S. cer-
tainly knew at least some of them (see his letter to Peacock of 23 March 1819, *L* ii 83–90),
and this passage draws on the associations and implications of their visual presence in the
city. 'Rome, the place of composition of Acts II and III of *PU*, is itself a symbol of the whole
action. From the ruined top of the Baths of Caracalla [where S. actually wrote portions of
the poem; see headnote] S. could look back and see the Coliseum and other ruins, includ-
ing Egyptian obelisks [such as those definitely seen by S. in Piazza Navona, Piazza San Pietro,
and Piazza Quirinale]. S. deploys them in the final speech of Act III as an elaborate image
of historical relativism. The obelisks, with their obscene bird-headed and dog-headed gods,
have, even though their own purpose is long forgotten, physically outlasted the ruins of their
Roman conquerors. In the same way, after Jupiter's fall the monuments of his oppression
stand like museum-pieces among the dwellings of the peopled earth. Human dwellings decay,
and in all likelihood Jupiter's prisons etc will outlast any given set of them, but will even-
tually moulder in their turn. The intellectual activities of new civilisation are however *not*
subject to decay . . .' (GM).

168. monstrous] S. first wrote *hideous*, then crossed it out and wrote *secret* next to it; at some
point *hideous* was then retraced more boldly, and *secret* was underlined. The received read-
ing *monstrous* is written on the facing page. See the passage from Landor, *Gebir* vi 301–8 qu.
in note to IV 556.

170. Which] *Nbk 9*; Which, *1820, 1839. obelisks*] *Nbk 9*; obelisks, *1820, 1839.*

172. conquerors,] *Nbk 9*; conquerors: *1820, 1839. round.*] round *Nbk 9, 1820, 1839.*

These imaged to the pride of Kings and Priests
A dark yet mighty faith, a power as wide
175 As is the world it wasted, and are now
But an astonishment; even so the tools
And emblems of its last captivity,
Amid the dwellings of the peopled earth,
Stand, not o'erthrown, but unregarded now;
180 And those foul shapes, abhorred by God and man,
Which under many a name and many a form
Strange, savage, ghastly, dark, and execrable,
Were Jupiter, the tyrant of the world;
And which the nations, panic-stricken, served
185 With blood, and hearts broken by long hope, and love
Dragged to his altars soiled and garlandless,
And slain amid men's unreclaiming tears,
Flattering the thing they feared, which fear was hate,

173. *These*] Nbk 9; Those *1820, 1839*; The Nbk 9 reading is preferred to avoid confusion over the referent of the pronoun (the *obelisks* of line 170) by repetition of *those* from line 172. *Kings and Priests*] Nbk 9; kings and priests, *1820, 1839*.

175–6. *are now / But an astonishment*] i.e. they are not now meaningful. Reiman ('Roman Scenes' 76; see lines 111–24 and note, 168–79 and note, above; see also *Reiman (1977)* 193) argues that S. has in mind the hieroglyphics on the Egyptian obelisks in Rome, which were not decipherable at the time of S.'s residence in Rome (see 'Ozymandias', headnote and notes). But S. in these lines is referring to the *monstrous and barbaric shapes* of line 168, which is an odd way to describe hieroglyphics; and the passage goes on (lines 171–2) to identify the Romans as the *conquerors* of these shapes, which confirms that S. must be thinking of the Egyptian gods, *which from their unworn obelisks look forth* (line 170).

178. *earth,*] Earth, Nbk 9.

179. *now;*] Nbk 9; now. *1820, 1839*.

180. *God*] Nbk 9; god *1820, 1839*.

181. *Which*] Nbk 9; Which, *1820, 1839*. *form*] Nbk 9, *1820*; form, *1839*.

185–7. The image suggests punishment by sacrificial murder; and as Timothy Webb (*Shelley: A Voice not Understood* (1977) 149–50) has shown, S. probably recalls the account in Lucretius *De Re. Nat.* i 80–101 of Agamemnon's sacrifice of his daughter Iphigenia. Jephthah's sacrifice of his daughter, *Judges* xi 30–40, and Idomeneus's of his son, are also possible echoes. S.'s note to *Q Mab* v 189, 'Even love is sold', declares his conviction that love is degraded and destroyed by institutions and conventions that insist on continued co-habitation when the emotion itself has changed or disappeared: 'A system could not well have been devised more studiously hostile to human happiness than marriage.'

186. *Dragged to*] Written above *Slain at* canc. in Nbk 9 (and also on the facing page).

187. This line has been added on the facing page in Nbk 9; it is not included in S.'s running line count and was presumably a late addition. *amid*] S. first wrote *among*, then altered it to *amid* by cancelling the *g* and changing *on* to *id*; the change was presumably made after the press transcript, because *among* is the reading in *1820* and *1839* (see *BSM* ix 472). *unreclaiming*] 'Passive, unprotesting' (*Concordance*); OED cites only this occurrence.

Frown, mouldering fast, o'er their abandoned shrines:
190 The painted veil, by those who were, called life,
Which mimicked, as with colours idly spread,
All men believed and hoped, is torn aside —
The loathsome mask has fallen, the man remains,
Sceptreless, free, uncircumscribed: — but man:
195 Equal, unclassed, tribeless and nationless,
Exempt from awe, worship, degree, — the King
Over himself; just, gentle, wise: — but man:
Passionless? no — yet free from guilt or pain,
Which were, for his will made, or suffered them,
200 Nor yet exempt, though ruling them like slaves,
From chance, and death, and mutability,

190–2. The painted veil . . .] 'The delusions that were thought to constitute real living by those who existed in the past, before Jupiter's downfall' (GM). The identical image is used in the sonnet 'Lift not the painted veil', but with a different meaning; see headnote and notes to that poem (no. 173).

192. and] or *Nbk 9*; presumably S.'s change to the press transcript, although mistranscription is possible. *aside –*] *Nbk 9*; aside; *1820, 1839*.

193–7. 'The romantic and barbarous distinction of men into Kings and subjects, though it may suit the conditions of courtiers, cannot that of citizens . . . Every citizen is a member of the sovereignty, and, as such, can acknowledge no personal subjection: and his obedience can be only to the laws' (Paine, *Rights of Man* Pt I; *Paine Writings* ii 386).

193. remains,] remains *Nbk 9, 1820, 1839*.

194. uncircumscribed: – but man:] *Nbk 9*; uncircumscribed, but man *1820, 1839*. S. appears to have modified his initial punctuation here, to clarify the sense (see note to lines 164–204 above, and cp. the facsimile and commentary in *BSM* ix 470–1, 644). S. added a semicolon after *man* in Leigh Hunt's presentation copy of *1820*. The *but man* of lines 194 and 197 means 'just simply man'; cp. *Mont Blanc* (B Text) lines 76–83 and notes, *Q Mab* viii 97, *Adonais* 328, *Cyclops* 612. See also *Timon of Athens* IV iii 499–500, *Richard II* V v 39–41, and *Troilus and Cressida* III iii 80–2: 'And not a man for being simply man / Hath any honour, but honour for those honours / That are without him, as place, riches, and favour . . .'

195. tribeless] *Nbk 9*; tribeless, *1820, 1839*.

196–7. Recalling I 492. Cp. S.'s 'Sonnet: To the Republic of Benevento' 10–14:

> Man who man would be,
> Must rule the empire of himself; in it
> Must be supreme, establishing his throne
> On vanquished will, — quelling the anarchy
> Of hopes and fears, — being himself alone.

196. degree, – the King] *Nbk 9*; degree, the king *1820, 1839*.

197. wise: – but man:] *Nbk 9*; wise: but man *1820, 1839*.

198–9. S. is thinking of such things as sexual jealousy, the moral ostracism of 'fallen women', and venereal disease; cp. lines 153–63 above, and see especially *Q Mab* viii 129–30, 230–1, ix 76–92.

198. Passionless? no –] *Nbk 9*; Passionless; no, *1820, 1839*; S. added the question mark in Leigh Hunt's presentation copy of *1820*.

199. made,] *Nbk 9*; made *1820, 1839*.

The clogs of that which else might oversoar
The loftiest star of unascended Heaven,
Pinnacled dim in the intense inane.

End of the Third Act

202. This line is written on the facing page in *Nbk 9*, replacing S.'s original *Which clog that spirit, else which might outsoar* canc. *clogs*] i.e. impediments.

203. *Heaven,*] Heaven *Nbk 9*; heaven, *1820, 1839*.

204. *inane*] From Lat. *inane*, 'Void space'; the word in this sense is frequent in Lucretius, and see also e.g. Virgil, *Eclogue* vi 31. After this line in *Nbk 9*, and at the very foot of the page, S. has written *Prometheus*, centred as if to indicate a further speech.

ACT IV

Scene, – A part of the forest near the Cave of Prometheus. Panthea *and* Ione *are sleeping: they awaken gradually during the first Song.*

> *Voice of Unseen Spirits*
> The pale stars are gone!
> For the Sun, their swift shepherd,
> To their folds them compelling
> In the depths of the dawn,
5 > Hastes, in meteor-eclipsing array, and they flee
> Beyond his blue dwelling,
> As fawns flee the leopard . . .
> But where are ye?

> *A train of dark Forms and Shadows passes by confusedly, singing.*
> Here, oh here!
10 > We bear the bier
> Of the Father of many a cancelled year!
> Spectres we
> Of the dead Hours be,
> We bear Time to his tomb in eternity.

1. S. returned to the beginning of *Nbk 7* for the fair copy of Act IV (see headnote). The 'Voice of Unseen Spirits' which speaks here is identified at line 57 as that of the *Spirits of Air and of Earth. stars*] Stars *Nbk 7.*

2. Sun,] Sun *Nbk 7*; sun, *1820, 1839. shepherd,*] *1820*; Shepherd *Nbk 7*; shepherd, *1839.*

3. compelling] *Nbk 7*; compelling, *1820, 1839.*

4. dawn,] Dawn *Nbk 7.*

7. leopard . . .] *Nbk 7*; leopard. *1820*; leopard, *1839.*

SD. The comma after *confusedly* is in *Nbk 7* and *1820*; *1839* omits it and thus alters the sense. *Nbk 7* at this point has a further SD, 'Panthea wakens'; it was presumably omitted in the press transcript (along with several others).

9. Here, oh here!] Here oh here! *Nbk 7*; Here, oh, here: *1820*; Here, oh! here: *1839.* This line answers the question in line 8, with the implication that lines 9–29 are sung by the 'Train of dark forms and shadows' (the passage perhaps suggests that they are thought of as dead leaves; the dead ages of the past are now blown away to nothingness).

11. Father] *Nbk 7*; father *1820, 1839*; i.e. Jupiter, in apposition with the *Time* of line 14; as *the King of Hours* (line 20) he is buried along with the past ages darkened by his reign, and the hours of those ages here grieve for him (lines 15–20). The identification with Olympian Zeus imports into the figure of Jupiter an association with time, the sky and the calendar. Cp. II iv 32–3 and note.

13. Of the dead] Of dead *Nbk 7*. Presumably a change to the press transcript; the definite article is also in S.'s Italian trans. of these lines in *Nbk 11* 46 (though that trans. may well be of *1820*; see *BSM* ix 494).

14. This line has been taken to indicate that time is now to be thought of as at an end; but it is only the dark time under Jupiter that is finished, as the poem clearly proceeds to a prospect

612

15 Strew, oh strew
  Hair, not yew!
Wet the dusty pall with tears, not dew!
  Be the faded flowers
  Of Death's bare bowers
20 Spread on the corpse of the King of Hours!

  Haste, oh haste!
  As shades are chased,
Trembling, by day, from heaven's blue waste,
  We melt away,
25 Like dissolving spray,
From the children of a diviner day,
  With the lullaby
  Of winds that die
On the bosom of their own harmony.

Ione
30 What dark forms were they?

Panthea
The past Hours weak and grey,
 With the spoil which their toil
  Raked together
From the conquest but One could foil.

---

of future time (following line 56 below). The whole conception of Act IV 1–179 implies not that time has ended but that in S.'s post-revolutionary vision humanity can bring time under a measure of control. Cp. S.'s note to *Q Mab* viii 203–7 and editorial notes.

15. Strew, oh strew] Strew oh strew *Nbk 7*; Strew, oh, strew *1820*; Strew, oh! strew *1839*.

16. Cp. *Adonais* 91–99: 'Another clipped her profuse locks, and threw / The wreath upon him, like an anadem, / Which frozen tears instead of pearls begem;' these lines are based on Bion's 'Lament for Adonis' 80–1: cp. also S.'s trans. of lines 18–21 of the 'Lament' (no. 201): 'The Oread nymphs are weeping – Aphrodite / With hair unbound is wandering through the woods, / Wildered, ungirt, unsandalled –'.

21. oh] Nbk 7; oh, *1820, 1839*.

23. day,] Day, *Nbk 7*. *waste,*] waste *Nbk 7*; waste. *1820, 1839*.

24–9. These lines are adapted from the last six lines of the fragmentary lyric 'The world is dreary' (no. 203).

26. day,] day. *Nbk 7*. The stop marked the original end of this stanza and speech; the next three lines 27–9 were squeezed into *Nbk 7* later, thus exceeding the established stanza pattern.

29. harmony.] harmony *Nbk 7*; harmony! *1820, 1839*. At this point in *Nbk 7* is a stage direction 'they vanish', probably written in before the addition of lines 27–9, and presumably dropped in the press transcript.

31–4. i.e. the past Hours deprived human life of what they could while oppression lasted.

34. but One] Prometheus. The draft in *Nbk 11* 49 at first read *which none*, canc. and replaced with the received reading.

Ione

35   Have they passed?

Panthea

They have passed;
They outspeeded the blast;
While 'tis said, they are fled —

Ione

Whither, oh whither?

Panthea

To the dark, to the past, to the dead.

Voice of Unseen Spirits

40   Bright clouds float in heaven,
Dew-stars gleam on earth,
Waves assemble on ocean,
They are gathered and driven
By the storm of delight, by the panic of glee!
45   They shake with emotion,
They dance in their mirth —
But where are ye?

The pine boughs are singing
Old songs with new gladness,
50   The billows and fountains
Fresh music are flinging,
Like the notes of a spirit, from land and from sea;
The storms mock the mountains
With the thunder of gladness —
55   But where are ye?

36. *blast;*] blast, Nbk 7, 1820, 1839.

37. *fled* –] Nbk 7; fled: 1820, 1839.

38. *oh*] Nbk 7; oh, 1820; oh! 1839.

40. *heaven,*] Heaven, Nbk 7.

41. *earth,*] Earth, Nbk 7.

42. *ocean,*] Ocean, Nbk 7.

44. *storm*] Storm Nbk 7.   *panic*] In the Gk sense, from Pan.

46. *mirth* –] Nbk 7; mirth. 1820, 1839.

52. *spirit,*] spirit Nbk 7, 1820, 1839.

54. *gladness* –] gladness. Nbk 7, 1820, 1839. The first four words of this line in Nbk 7 are written above *Both howl in their* canc.

Ione
What charioteers are these?

Panthea
Where are their chariots?

Semichorus of Hours I
The voice of the Spirits of Air and of Earth
Have drawn back the figured curtain of sleep
Which covered our being and darkened our birth
60   In the deep —

A Voice
In the deep?

Semichorus II
Oh, below the deep.

Semichorus I
An hundred ages we had been kept
Cradled in visions of hate and care,
And each one who waked as his brother slept
Found the truth —

Semichorus II
Worse than his visions were!

57–179. These are the future hours of the new ages awaiting humanity. S.'s conception adapts the classical *Horae*, embodiments of time and the changing seasons and often associated with the Graces; as attendants on Venus they were welcome at marriages and births because of their power to bring gifts and to make things grow, and were frequently figured in a dance.

57. *and of Earth*] and earth *Nbk 7*; presumably a change to the press transcript (S.'s Italian trans. follows the received text; see line 13 and note above).

58. *Have*] Attracted into the plural by *Spirits*; many *eds* have followed *Rossetti 1870* in emending to *has*, but this obviously affects the prosody, and *voice* could be understood as plural. *figured curtain*] Cp. III iv 190 and note.

60. *deep –*] *Nbk 7*; deep. *1820, 1839. Oh,*] *1820*; Oh *Nbk 7*; Oh! *1839*.

61–7. The future hours have existed in potential through the ages of oppression, imagining the evil conditions and sometimes waking to a brief intimation of their actuality; they have also been solaced and encouraged by the hopeful elements which were discernible in human experience.

61. *An*] *Nbk 7, 1820*; A *1829, 1839*.

62. *visions*] Written above *dreams* canc. in *Nbk 7*; cp. line 66 below.

63. *slept*] *Nbk 7*; slept, *1820, 1839*.

615

Semichorus I

65   We have heard the lute of Hope in sleep;
We have known the voice of Love in dreams;
We have felt the wand of Power, and leap —

Semichorus II

As the billows leap in the morning beams.

Chorus

Weave the dance on the floor of the breeze,
70   Pierce with song heaven's silent light,
Enchant the Day that too swiftly flees,
        To check its flight ere the cave of Night.

Once the hungry Hours were hounds
        Which chased the Day like a bleeding deer,
75   And it limped and stumbled with many wounds
        Through the nightly dells of the desert year.

But now — oh weave the mystic measure
        Of music and dance and shapes of light,
Let the Hours, and the Spirits of might and pleasure,
80   Like the clouds and sunbeams, unite.

A Voice

                    Unite!

---

66. *Love*] love *Nbk 7*. *dreams;*] dream *Nbk 7*; dreams, *1820, 1839*; changed in the press transcript together with the rhyme-word *beams* in line 68 (the draft in *Nbk 11* 86 also has plurals; *dream* in *Nbk 7* may be the result of cramped space).

68. *beams.*] beam *Nbk 7*; beams! *1820, 1839*.

69–72. These lines seem implicitly to suggest a change of emphasis: up to this point time has been urged to pass quickly; now it is urged to slow down.

70. *heaven's*] Heaven's *Nbk 7*.

71. *Day*] *Nbk 7*; day *1820, 1839*.

72. *check*] Written below *soothe* canc. in *Nbk 7*. *Night.*] Night; *Nbk 7*; night. *1820, 1839*.

73–6. See I 454–7 and note.

74. *Day*] Day, *Nbk 7*; day *1820, 1839*.

76. *year.*] Year *Nbk 7*.

77. *now – oh*] *Nbk 7*; now, oh *1820*; now, oh! *1839*.

78. *music and dance*] *Nbk 7*; music, and dance, *1820, 1839*.

79. *the Spirits*] all Spirits *Nbk 7*; presumably S.'s change to the press transcript, reverting to the draft reading in *Nbk 11* 89. See line 131 below.

80. *and sunbeams*] and the sunbeams *Nbk 7*; probably changed in the press transcript along with the preceding line. *Unite!*] *Nbk 7, 1820*; Unite. *1839*.

Panthea
See, where the Spirits of the human mind
Wrapped in sweet sounds, as in bright veils, approach.

Chorus of Spirits
We join the throng
Of the dance and the song,
85   By the whirlwind of gladness borne along;
As the flying-fish leap
From the Indian deep,
And mix with the sea-birds half asleep.

Chorus of Hours
Whence come ye, so wild and so fleet,
90   For sandals of lightning are on your feet,
And your wings are soft and swift as thought,
And your eyes are as Love which is veilèd not?

Chorus of Spirits
We come from the mind
Of human kind,

---

81. As various commentators have noted, these *Spirits of the human mind*, which speak in chorus with the future hours to line 179, are akin to or perhaps identical with those which comforted Prometheus in I 672–800, but their potential may now be realised.

82. *as in bright veils,*] like radiant veils, Nbk 7; presumably S.'s change to the press transcript. In Nbk 7 this line first read *Clothed in sweet song, like radiant garments, come*.

83–8. This stanza form, continued in lines 93–128 and 135–58, is that of S.'s 'The world is dreary' (no. 203), drafted in Nbk 11 149–50.

86–7. S. appears to introduce an understated sequence of evolutionary ideas. The fish in their element are repeatedly hinted at in lines 93–128, evolving first into birds (line 120) and ultimately (line 137) into mammals; thus the continuing evolution of mind into future forms is underpinned by celebration of the preceding phases of the evolutionary process. S. was thoroughly familiar with late eighteenth century evolutionary thought, which is repeatedly discussed in e.g. Darwin. See *Botanic Garden*, note to i 101: 'From having observed the gradual evolution of the young animal or plant from its egg or seed; and afterwards its successive advances to its more perfect state, or maturity; philosophers of all ages seem to have imagined, that the great world itself had likewise its infancy and its gradual progress to maturity; this seems to have given origin to the very antient and sublime allegory of Eros, or Divine Love, producing the world from the egg of Night, as it floated in Chaos'. Cp. Akenside, *Pleasures of the Imagination* (1772) ii 257–61:

> The same paternal hand,
> From the mute shell-fish gasping on the shore,
> To men, to angels, to celestial minds,
> Will ever lead the generations on
> Through higher scenes of being.

88. *half asleep.*] Nbk 7, 1820; half-asleep. 1839.

92. *Love*] Nbk 7; love 1820, 1839.

95   Which was late so dusk, and obscene, and blind;
Now 'tis an ocean
Of clear emotion,
A heaven of serene and mighty motion;

     From that deep abyss
100   Of wonder and bliss,
Whose caverns are crystal palaces;
From those skiey towers
Where Thought's crowned Powers
Sit watching your dance, ye happy Hours;

105   From the dim recesses
Of woven caresses,
Where lovers catch ye by your loose tresses;
From the azure isles
Where sweet Wisdom smiles,
110   Delaying your ships with her siren wiles;

     From the temples high
Of Man's ear and eye,
Roofed over Sculpture and Poesy;
From the murmurings
115   Of the unsealed springs
Where Science bedews her daedal wings.

     Years after years,
Through blood and tears,

96. *ocean*] Ocean, *Nbk 7*.

98. *heaven*] Heaven *Nbk 7*. *motion;*] motion. *Nbk 7, 1820, 1839*.

99–116. The Spirits originate in the mind's capacities for wonder (99–101), thought (102–4), love (105–7), wisdom (108–10), art (111–13), and scientific knowledge (114–16).

99. *abyss*] Abyss *Nbk 7*.

103. *Powers*] *Nbk 7*; powers *1820, 1839*.

104. *Hours;*] Hours *Nbk 7*; Hours! *1820, 1839*

105–10. Individual minds will effectively be able to prolong the period of their existence through the 'slowing' of time by a more concentrated exercise of consciousness; see S.'s note to *Q Mab* viii 203–7.

108. *isles*] *Nbk 7*; isles, *1820, 1839*.

110. *wiles;*] wiles *Nbk 7, 1820*; wiles. *1839*.

112. *Man's*] man's *Nbk 7*.

116. *her*] *Nbk 7*; his *1820, 1839*. The reading in *Nbk 7* is not very clear, and Mary possibly mistranscribed; as *Zillman Text* notes, S. elsewhere refers to Science as feminine. *daedal*] Dædal *Nbk 7, 1820, 1839*.

118. *blood and tears,*] blood and tears *Nbk 7*; blood, and tears, *1820, 1839*.

And a thick hell of hatreds, and hopes, and fears,
120   We waded and flew,
And the islets were few
Where the bud-blighted flowers of happiness grew.

Our feet now, every palm,
Are sandalled with calm,
125   And the dew of our wings is a rain of balm;
And beyond our eyes
The human love lies
Which makes all it gazes on, Paradise.

Chorus of Spirits and Hours
Then weave the web of the mystic measure;
130   From the depths of the sky and the ends of the earth,
Come, swift Spirits of might and of pleasure,
Fill the dance and the music of mirth,
As the waves of a thousand streams rush by
To an ocean of splendour and harmony!

Chorus of Spirits
135   Our spoil is won,
Our task is done,
We are free to dive, or soar, or run . . .
Beyond and around,

119. *fears,*] *Nbk 7*; fears; *1820, 1839*.

126. *And beyond our eyes*] *Nbk 7*; And, beyond our eyes, *1820, 1839*.

127. *lies*] *Nbk 7, 1820*; lies, *1839*.

128. *on,*] *Nbk 7*; on *1820, 1839*.

129. Following this line in *Nbk 7* is a canc. line *Of music & dance & shapes of light*.

130. *earth,*] Earth *Nbk 7*.

134. *ocean*] Ocean *Nbk 7*.

135–58. Anticipating interplanetary travel and the colonisation of outer space. As *Cameron (1974)* 544–7 suggests, S.'s interest in astronomy, established since his schooldays, would have familiarised him with contemporary ideas (deriving chiefly from Kant and Herschel) concerning the immensity of the universe and the vast number of stars. Cp. 'On the Devil and Devils' (*Prose* 270): 'The late invention and improvement of telescopes has considerably enlarged the notions of men respecting the bounds of the Universe . . .' See also S.'s notes to *Q Mab* i 242–3, 252–3.

135–40. Cp. *Midsummer Night's Dream* IV i 102–3: 'We the globe can compass soon, / Swifter than the wandering moon'; and see also Milton, *Comus* 1012–16.

137. *run . . .*] *Nbk 7*; run; *1820, 1839*.

138. *and*] In *Nbk 7* S. has overwritten an ampersand with *or*; *1820* and subsequent eds read *and*, which was possibly restored by S. in the press transcript but which could easily be a misreading.

Or within the bound
140   Which clips the world with darkness round.

We'll pass the eyes
Of the starry skies
Into the hoar deep to colonize;
Death, Chaos, and Night,
145   From the sound of our flight
Shall flee, like mist from a tempest's might.

And Earth, Air, and Light,
And the Spirit of Might,
Which drives round the stars in their fiery flight;
150   And Love, Thought, and Breath,
The powers that quell Death,
Wherever we soar shall assemble beneath.

And our singing shall build
In the void's loose field
155   A world for the Spirit of Wisdom to wield;
We will take our plan
From the new world of man,
And our work shall be called the Promethean.

---

140. Cameron (1974) 546 follows *Grabo (1930)* 165–7 in understanding *world* to mean 'the universe' here; but *beyond* in line 138 is incompatible with such a reading, and suggests rather that S. is thinking of the earth's atmosphere. Some Spirits will travel beyond the atmosphere to create new human regions in space (*Semichorus I*, to line 171), while others will create new conditions for human life on earth (*Semichorus II*, to line 174). In line 155 below *world* is clearly used in the modern sense of 'planet'. See *Butter (1954)* 160 for good commentary and convincing arguments against Grabo's interpretation. *clips*] i.e. 'closely surrounds'.

141. eyes] Eyes *Nbk 7*.

143. deep] Deep *Nbk 7. colonize;*] colonize *Nbk 7*; colonize: *1820, 1839*.

145. flight] *Nbk 7*; flight, *1820, 1839*.

146. tempest's] Tempests *Nbk 7*.

147–52. The new human planet will be made out of the elements, controlled by gravity (*the Spirit of Might*), and animated by human attributes (*Love, Thought and Breath*).

147. Earth, Air, and Light,] earth air and light *Nbk 7*.

149. stars] Stars *Nbk 7*.

150. Love, Thought, and Breath,] love, thought, and breath *Nbk 7*.

151. Death,] death, *Nbk 7*.

154. void's] Void's *Nbk 7*.

156–8. Mind is to be the measure of everything.

Chorus of Hours
Break the dance, and scatter the song;
160   Let some depart, and some remain.

Semichorus I
We, beyond heaven, are driven along —

Semichorus II
Us, the enchantments of earth retain —

Semichorus I
Ceaseless and rapid and fierce and free
With the Spirits which build a new earth and sea,
165   And a Heaven where yet Heaven could never be —

Semichorus II
Solemn, and slow, and serene, and bright,
Leading the Day, and outspeeding the Night,
With the Powers of a world of perfect light —

Semichorus I
We whirl, singing loud, round the gathering sphere,
170   Till the trees, and the beasts, and the clouds appear
From its chaos made calm by love, not fear —

---

161. heaven,] Heaven, *Nbk 7. along –*] *Nbk 7*; along: *1820, 1839*.

162. Us,] Superimposed over *We* in *Nbk 7*; the comma is possibly canc., and is omitted in *1820* and *1839*. *retain –*] *Nbk 7*; retain: *1820, 1839*.

163. Nbk 7; Ceaseless, and rapid, and fierce, and free, *1820, 1839*.

165. Heaven where yet Heaven] *Nbk 7*; heaven where yet heaven *1820, 1839*. *be –*] *Nbk 7*; be. *1820, 1839*. The liberated Spirits of the human mind now have the potential to create in space an actual paradise in place of the fabled Christian 'Heaven' conventionally located in the sky. Cp. *Revelation* xxi 1: 'And I saw a new heaven and a new earth: for the first heaven and the first earth were passed away; and there was no more sea'.

167. Day,] day *Nbk 7. Night,*] night *Nbk 7*.

168. Powers] *Nbk 7*; powers *1820, 1839. light –*] *Nbk 7*; light. *1820, 1839*.

169–71. Describing the evolution of a habitable planet; *Cameron (1974)* 546 and *Grabo (1930)* 166 note that *gathering sphere* perhaps alludes specifically to the hypothesis, found in Herschel, Laplace and Erasmus Darwin, that the solid matter of new planets is formed from the stuff of nebulae.

171. fear –] *Nbk 7*; fear. *1820, 1839*.

> *Semichorus II*
> We encircle the oceans and mountains of earth,
> And the happy forms of its death and birth
> Change to the music of our sweet mirth.

> *Chorus of Hours and Spirits*
> 175   Break the dance, and scatter the song —
> Let some depart, and some remain;
> Wherever we fly we lead along
> In leashes, like star-beams, soft yet strong,
> The clouds that are heavy with Love's sweet rain.

> *Panthea*
> 180 Ha! they are gone!

> *Ione*
>   Yet feel you no delight
> From the past sweetness?

> *Panthea*
>   As the bare green hill,
> When some soft cloud vanishes into rain,
> Laughs with a thousand drops of sunny water
> To the unpavilioned sky!

---

172. oceans and mountains of earth,] Oceans and Mountains of Earth *Nbk 7*; ocean and mountains of earth, *1820, 1839*; the *s* of *Oceans* in *Nbk 7* is not well formed and could have been missed in transcription.

175. song –] *Nbk 7*; song, *1820, 1839*.

176. remain;] remain *Nbk 7*; remain, *1820, 1839*.

179. Love's] *Nbk 7*; love's *1820, 1839*. In *Nbk 7* this line is followed by a stage direction, 'they depart', which was presumably dropped in the press transcript.

180–93. Evidence from *Nbk 7* suggests these lines were almost certainly added later, written into a space left by S. to bridge the opening lyric sequence of the Act with the blank verse account of the spheres of Earth and Moon that picks up at line 194 (see *BSM* ix 30–3, 502).

181. hill,] hill *Nbk 7, 1820, 1839*.

184–9. The approaching Spirits of the Earth and the Moon clearly make a sound. S. no doubt has the 'music of the spheres' primarily in mind; but King-Hele, *Shelley: His Thought and Work* (2nd edn 1971) 191, also notes that Adam Walker (*Walker* 406) was impressed by Newton's observation that 'the widths of the spectrum occupied by each of the seven colours correspond exactly with the frequency-differences between the seven musical notes'; S. may be positing a further correspondence with the mathematical relations obtaining between the orbits of the planets. See also Darwin, *Loves of the Plants*, Interlude III.

Ione
                    Even whilst we speak
185 New notes arise . . . What is that awful sound?

Panthea
'Tis the deep music of the rolling world,
Kindling within the strings of the waved air
Æolian modulations.

Ione
                    Listen too,
How every pause is filled with under-notes,
190 Clear, silver, icy, keen, awakening tones,
Which pierce the sense, and live within the soul,
As the sharp stars pierce winter's crystal air
And gaze upon themselves within the sea.

Panthea
But see where, through two openings in the forest
195 Which hanging branches overcanopy,
And where two runnels of a rivulet,
Between the close moss, violet-inwoven,
Have made their path of melody — like sisters

185. arise . . .] *Nbk 7;* arise. *1820, 1839.*

186–7. These lines are unpunctuated in *Nbk 7. 1820* has a comma after *air.* In *1839* the comma after *air* is omitted, and one inserted after *world;* this distinct alteration to the sense may derive from S.'s errata list.

187. waved air] S. was familiar with the wave theory of sound.

190. keen,] *Nbk 7;* keen *1820, 1839.*

194–205. Panthea sees and hears the approach of the spirits of the Moon and the Earth, one within a chariot, the other within a sphere. These symbolic visions of the Spirits offer concentrated complex combinations of qualities and attributes, including a dense scientific allusiveness. The two visions appear through two openings in the forest along two runnels, i.e. small streams or brooklets, formed by the divergence of a rivulet so as to form an island. S. perhaps suggests in symbolic terms the recurrently shifting spatial relations of planets in the solar system, parting and meeting in a pattern dictated by the inter-relation of orbits under gravity. The details of the two elaborate descriptions which follow are conceived in overall terms to associate the Spirit of the Moon with outer space (lines 206–35), and the Spirit of the Earth with atomic space (lines 236–68). The conception of the whole passage, and more particularly the description of the Spirit of the Earth's sphere, derives in part from the apocalyptic vision of God in a machine in *Ezekiel* i, and more specifically from various details of phrasing and diction in Milton's adaptation of *Ezekiel* in *Paradise Lost* vi 749–852 (see Wiltrude L. Smith, 'An Overlooked Source for *Prometheus Unbound*', *SP* xlviii (1951) 783–92, and Ants Oras, 'The Multitudinous Orb: Some Miltonic Elements in Shelley', *MLQ* xvi (1955) 247–57).

197. violet-inwoven,] *1820;* violet-inwoven *Nbk 7;* violet inwoven, *1839.*

198. melody –] melody, *Nbk 7, 1820, 1839. sisters*] Written above *friends* canc. in *Nbk 7.*

Who part with sighs that they may meet in smiles,
200 Turning their dear disunion to an isle
Of lovely grief, a wood of sweet sad thoughts —
Two visions of strange radiance float upon
The ocean-like enchantment of strong sound,
Which flows intenser, keener, deeper yet
205 Under the ground and through the windless air.

Ione
I see a chariot like that thinnest boat
In which the Mother of the Months is borne
By ebbing light into her western cave
When she upsprings from interlunar dreams,
210 O'er which is curved an orblike canopy

201. thoughts –] thoughts *Nbk 7*; thoughts; *1820, 1839.*

203. ocean-like] Ocean-like *Nbk 7.*

206–13. The new moon, appearing as a bright silver crescent with the rest of the moon obscured but still visible (lines 210–13), as in Coleridge's epigraph (from 'The Ballad of Sir Patrick Spence') to the 'Dejection Ode': 'Late, late yestreen I saw the new Moon, / With the old Moon in her arms'. See also *TL* 72–84.

207–9. Cp. *Samson Agonistes* 86–9:

> The sun to me is dark
> And silent as the moon,
> When she deserts the night,
> Hid in her vacant interlunar cave.

207. Mother of the Months] *Nbk 7*; mother of the months *1820, 1839.*

208. light] *Nbk 7*; night *1820, 1839.* The reading in *1820* is obviously wrong (the formation of *li* in *Nbk 7* somewhat resembles an *n*) and implies that S. cannot have made the press transcript, as given his long-standing and informed interest in astronomy it is very unlikely that he would have made this error in copying from his own poem; *ebbing night* would suggest that the new moon sets in the west as the sun rises in the east, when S.'s sense is that the new moon sets with the setting sun (see lines 214–18 and note, below). This crux also suggests that Mary did not use the nbks in her possession to check her revised text of *PU* in *1839.*

209. interlunar] i.e. between a waning and waxing moon.

210–13. S. recalls *Paradise Lost* i 286–91:

> the broad circumference
> Hung on his shoulders like the moon, whose orb
> Through optic glass the Tuscan artist views
> At ev'ning from the top of Fesole,
> Or in Valdarno, to descry new lands,
> Rivers or mountains in her spotty globe.

Milton is thinking of Galileo, whose observations of the moon by telescope (*an enchanter's glass*) first detected lunar equivalents of earthly landscape (here obscured by the *dusk aery veil* of the earth's shadow).

210. curved] *Nbk 7, 1820, 1829*; curbed *1839, 1840*; a misprint.

Of gentle darkness, and the hills and woods,
Distinctly seen through that dusk aery veil,
Regard like shapes in an enchanter's glass;
Its wheels are solid clouds, azure and gold,
215 Such as the genii of the thunderstorm
Pile on the floor of the illumined sea
When the sun rushes under it; they roll
And move and grow as with an inward wind.
Within it sits a wingèd infant, white
220 Its countenance, like the whiteness of bright snow,
Its plumes are as feathers of sunny frost,
Its limbs gleam white, through the wind-flowing folds
Of its white robe, woof of etherial pearl.
Its hair is white, — the brightness of white light

211. woods,] woods Nbk 7, 1820, 1839.

213. Regard] i.e. 'I regard . . .'; the subject is understood in parallel with 'I see . . .' in line 206 above. OED does offer a definition of *regard* as 'To look, appear' (def. 12), but describes this sense as 'rare', and with S.'s usage in this line as the only citation.

214–18. Presumably S. has literally in mind the appearance of storm clouds over the sea at sunset, with the crescent moon low in the west (cp. lines 202–3 above). The intense detail also suggests symbolic meanings: S. perhaps thinks of the moon as having developed a luminous envelope, with sun-spots, like the sun in contemporary astronomical accounts; or he may hint at the processes believed, by Herschel and others, to be involved in the creation and structure of nebulae in outer space.

217. sun] Sun Nbk 7.

218. wind.] Nbk 7; wind; 1820, 1839.

219–23. The whiteness of the Spirit of the Moon is of course in visual terms obvious, but the repeated emphasis here further suggests that with no atmosphere to act as a prism white is the only colour possible on the moon (cp. I 64–5, 82–3, II iii 72–5). Cp. *Revelation* i 14: 'His head and his hairs were white like wool, as white as snow, and his eyes were as a flame of fire'.

219. infant,] Infant, Nbk 7.

224–5. Again the description combines a literal appropriateness with possibilities of scientific or quasi-scientific reference. The moon's beams are likened to hair; cp. e.g. S.'s trans. of the Homeric Hymn 'To the Moon' (no. 157): 'Around the earth / From her immortal head in Heaven shot forth / Far light is scattered'; *Cenci* III i 6–7: 'How comes this hair undone? / Its wandering strings must be what blind me so'; *Alastor* 248–9: 'his scattered hair / Sered by the autumn of strange suffering' (and cp. note to *PU* II iv 139). But the *white light / Scattered in strings* also suggests that 'if the moon has no atmosphere there will be no bending of the light rays, which will be reflected directly without curvature' (*Grabo (1930)* 154, who also proposes the further possibilities that S. is thinking of the light produced in electrical experiments, or of the fancied lunar equivalent of the aurora borealis). Cp. Herschel, 'Observations of a Comet . . .', *Philosophical Transactions* cii (1812) 134: '. . . had the curtain of light, which was drawn over it [the comet], been of any great thickness, the scattered rays of its lustre would have taken away the appearance of its darkness . . .' (see the contents of this volume of the *Transactions* for a good example of the range of contemporary scientific interests variously at work in *PU*).

224. white, –] Nbk 7; white, 1820, 1839.

225 Scattered in strings; yet its two eyes are heavens .
Of liquid darkness, which the Deity
Within seems pouring, as a storm is poured
From jagged clouds, out of their arrowy lashes,
Tempering the cold and radiant air around
230 With fire that is not brightness; in its hand
It sways a quivering moonbeam, from whose point
A guiding power directs the chariot's prow
Over its wheelèd clouds, which as they roll
Over the grass and flowers and waves, wake sounds
235 Sweet as a singing rain of silver dew.

Panthea
And from the other opening in the wood
Rushes, with loud and whirlwind harmony,

225–30. Herschel's discovery of 'dark heat rays' (i.e. infra-red radiation) had been developed by Davy (*Elements of Chemical Philosophy* 221) to explain why the moon's light is apparently without heat (see *Grabo (1930)* 111). S. is here thinking primarily of the dark craters visible on the moon, and attributing to them, speculatively, the emission of invisible rays; but S. is presumably thinking rather of ultra-violet light, because it is clear here and elsewhere that the moon is very cold (see lines 356–61 below). The apparent implication of hot rays in line 230 should therefore be understood in the context of the simile beginning *as a storm is poured* in line 227, i.e. as a predicate of the storm-lightning to which the moon's rays are compared.

225. strings;] strings, *Nbk 7*; string; *1820, 1829*; probably on S.'s errata list. *heavens*] Heavens *Nbk 7*.

229. around] *Nbk 7*; around, *1820, 1839*.

230. that] which *Nbk 7*; presumably S.'s change to the press transcript.

232. The *guiding power* of the moonbeam held by the Spirit presumably embodies the moon's exercise of gravitational and tidal influence.

234. Punctuated as in *Nbk 7*; Over the grass, and flowers, and waves, wake sounds, *1820, 1839.*

236–52. The perspective shifts from telescopic to microscopic. The Spirit of the Earth sits within a sphere consisting of thousands of smaller spheres which, each spinning on its own axis, and visible through and between each other, are all in energetic movement. In literary terms the passage draws as noted above (note to lines 194–205) on *Ezekiel* i and *Paradise Lost* vi 749ff., and perhaps on Dante, *Purgatorio* xxix (which Milton echoes and which itself derives in part from *Ezekiel*). There is little doubt that the sphere also embodies S.'s understanding of contemporary scientific ideas concerning the atomic structure of matter, although the visionary manner does not suggest any closely specific sources. Cp. *Refutation of Deism*: 'Matter, such as we behold it, is not inert. It is infinitely active and subtle. Light, electricity and magnetism are fluids not surpassed by thought itself in tenuity and activity: like thought they are sometimes the cause and sometimes the effect of motion; and, distinct as they are from every other class of substances, with which we are acquainted, seem to possess equal claims with thought to the unmeaning distinction of immateriality.' (*Prose Works* i 116). S. was certainly familiar with recent developments in chemistry; John Dalton's *New System of Chemical Philosophy*, sketching an atomic theory of the elements, began to appear in 1808, by when scientists (such as Davy) and scientific popularisers (such as Darwin and Adam Walker) were engaged in energetic discussion of the implications and nature of

A sphere, which is as many thousand spheres,
Solid as crystal, yet through all its mass
240 Flow, as through empty space, music and light:
Ten thousand orbs involving and involved,
Purple and azure, white and green and golden,
Sphere within sphere; and every space between
Peopled with unimaginable shapes,
245 Such as ghosts dream dwell in the lampless deep,
Yet each inter-transpicuous; and they whirl
Over each other with a thousand motions,
Upon a thousand sightless axles spinning,
And with the force of self-destroying swiftness,
250 Intensely, slowly, solemnly roll on,
Kindling with mingled sounds, and many tones,

---

molecules and atoms, following new research on the constituent nature of solids, liquids and gases (see *Grabo (1930)* 140ff., *Butter (1954)* 155). Here as elsewhere in *PU* these new ideas merge in S.'s description with older scientific ideas such as the notion of 'concentric earths' (see Darwin, *Botanic Garden*, Additional Note xxiv to *Economy of Vegetation*, 'Granite'), although not all efforts of explanation in terms of specific scientific sources are convincing (see e.g. Thomas A. Reisner, 'Some Models for Shelley's Multitudinous Orb' *KSJ* xxiii (1974) 52–9). S.'s orbs even recall in general terms the Epicurean atomism of Lucretius (*De Re. Nat.* ii *passim.*).

238, 243, 247–8. Cp. *Ezekiel* x 10: 'And as for their appearances, they four had one likeness, as if a wheel had been in the midst of a wheel'.

239–52. Cp. *Paradise Lost* v 620–4:

> Mystical dance, which yonder starry sphere
> Of planets and of fixed in all her wheels
> Resembles nearest, mazes intricate,
> Eccentric, intervolved, yet regular
> Then most, when most irregular they seem [.]

See also *Paradise Lost* v 594–9, viii 80–4.

242. white and green] Nbk 7; white, green, *1820, 1839.* Nbk 7 at first read *Purple & azure, golden white & green.* S. then canc. *white & green,* placed a caret after *azure,* and wrote in *white & green* & above. The writing is smudged and the ampersand afer *white* could easily have been missed in transcription. For these colours cp. *Paradise Lost* vii 479, 'spots of gold and purple, azure and green', and see also ix 429.

243–5. Early experiments with the microscope dramatically transformed scientific understanding of the minute bases of matter, which appeared to consist equally of extremely small basic particles, and of previously unimaginably confined space between these basic particles. See e.g. Anthony van Leeuwenhoek, 'Microscopical Observations', *Philosophical Transactions* ix (1674) 378–85.

246. inter-transpicuous;] inter-transpicuous, Nbk 7 (as two unhyphenated words), *1820, 1839.* 'Visible through or between each other'; *OED* gives this occurrence as the only example. Cp. Southey, *Curse of Kehama* vii 9: 'that etherial Lake whose waters lie / Blue and transpicuous, like another sky'.

251–2. These lines were added in the press transcript. A first attempt to draft them is made vertically by this passage in Nbk 7 (f. 9ʳ), and the received reading is worked out in Nbk 9 (f. 37ʳ) on the page facing the closing lines of Act III.

Intelligible words and music wild.
With mighty whirl the multitudinous Orb
Grinds the bright brook into an azure mist
255 Of elemental subtlety, like light;
And the wild odour of the forest flowers,
The music of the living grass and air,
The emerald light of leaf-entangled beams,
Round its intense, yet self-conflicting speed,
260 Seem kneaded into one aërial mass
Which drowns the sense. Within the Orb itself,
Pillowed upon its alabaster arms,
Like to a child o'erwearied with sweet toil,
On its own folded wings, and wavy hair,
265 The Spirit of the Earth is laid asleep,
And you can see its little lips are moving
Amid the changing light of their own smiles,
Like one who talks of what he loves in dream.

Ione
'Tis only mocking the Orb's harmony . . .

253–61. Suggesting the earth's atmosphere, 'ground' out of the ether through which the earth moves.

253. *Orb*] orb *Nbk 7*.

258. *beams,*] beams *Nbk 7, 1820, 1839*.

259. *intense,*] *Nbk 7*; intense *1820, 1839*. *self-conflicting*] i.e. at once moving forward as a whole, and containing innumerable counter-directional movements.

261. *Orb*] orb *Nbk 7*.

262–8. The strikingly precise visualisation perhaps suggests a memory of William Shelley, who died in Rome aged $3\frac{1}{2}$ on 7 June 1819 (between composition of the third and fourth acts of *PU*).

263. *Like to a child o'erwearied*] Like a child overwearied *Nbk 7*; a change to the press transcript. The alteration restores an iambic feel to the pentameter, although the line in its original form gives a metrical effect quite common in S., of a sharply marked counter-rhythm within a blank verse context (cp. e.g. line 221 above).

265. This Spirit of the Earth does not seem identical with the Spirit of the Earth in III iii and iv. Both radiate light from the head, but the Spirit's in Act III is emerald (III iv 3), where this Spirit's is azure or golden (cp. line 271 below). This Spirit also appears not to have the attributes of Eros, and generally to participate less in the poem's network of classical motifs, and to suggest rather a quasi-scientific register.

266. *moving*] *Nbk 7*; moving, *1820, 1839*.

269. *mocking*] i.e. echoing or copying (with no sense of derogation; cp. *Alastor 425*). *Orb's harmony . . .*] *Nbk 7*; orb's harmony. *1820, 1839*.

Panthea
270 And from a star upon its forehead, shoot,
Like swords of azure fire, or golden spears
With tyrant-quelling myrtle overtwined,
Embleming Heaven and Earth united now,
Vast beams like spokes of some invisible wheel
275 Which whirl as the Orb whirls, swifter than thought,

270-9. Cp. Q *Mab* 146-54:

> Yet, human Spirit, bravely hold thy course,
> Let virtue teach thee firmly to pursue
> The gradual paths of an aspiring change:
> For birth and life and death, and that strange state
> Before the naked soul has found its home,
> All tend to perfect happiness, and urge
> The restless wheels of being on their way,
> Whose flashing spokes, instinct with infinite life,
> Bicker and burn to gain their destined goal . . .

The Spirit radiates beams of light *like spokes of some invisible wheel*, which penetrate the earth's strata and lay bare its secrets (cp. II iii 51-2). The beams' association with *lightenings* suggests electricity, and *Grabo (1930)* 144ff. argued that S. had in mind in the Spirit's beams not simply the colours produced in electrical experiments, but specifically the aurora borealis (assumed to be an electrical phenomenon). S.'s *sun-like lightenings, / And perpendicular now, and now transverse* might also suggest the concept, entertained by contemporary scientists, of 'polarised light' (see e.g. Davy, *Elements of Chemical Philosophy* 53). S. was familiar with contemporary scientific opinion that electricity, heat, light, magnetism and love were related substances which existed in different modifications of superfine 'ether' (see notes to I 122-3, 134, 765, II iii 66, iv 163-6, v 26-30, III iv 1-19). Any one specific scientific source here is unlikely; the underlying idea is that natural forces can be used to know and understand the history and true nature of the earth. S.'s overall conception may derive from Addison, *Tatler* 100 (ed. D. Bond, 3 vols (1987) ii 113-19), which describes a morally redemptive vision of a figure resembling 'the Goddess of Justice' who holds a mirror 'endowed with the Same qualities as that which the Painters put into the Hand of *Truth'*. A light streams from the mirror which exposes falsehood and injustice, and which 'pierced into all the dark Corners and Recesses of the Universe, and by that Means detected many Writings and Records which had been hidden or buried by Time, Chance or Design'.

272. tyrant-quelling myrtle] The epithet is from Coleridge, 'France: an Ode' (1798) 37. Myrtle was sacred to Venus and thus associated with love (see Virgil, *Eclogue* vii 61, and Peacock, *Rhododaphne* (1818), note to Canto ii 176). 'Among the Greeks victorious warriors were crowned with myrtle wreaths. There is perhaps a reference here to Harmodius and Aristogeiton who struck down Hipparchus the Tyrant and made Athens free in the year 514 BC. In the hymn of Callistratus to Harmodius there is a refrain which runs – ἐν μύρτου κλαδὶ τὸ ξίφος φορήσω – 'I'll wreathe the sword in the myrtle bough'. To S., tyranny and ignorance were consubstantial powers; the rays of knowledge are weapons to strike down tyrants' (*Hughes 1820*; the reference is persuasive, and S. would doubtless have encountered the Gk refrain, which is among the most famous of Gk drinking-songs, perhaps in a school anthology).

273. Heaven and Earth] *Nbk 7*; heaven and earth *1820, 1839*.

274. spokes] *Nbk 7, 1839*; spoke *1820, 1829*; corrected from S.'s errata list (also corrected by S. in Leigh Hunt's presentation copy of *1820*).

275. Orb] orb *Nbk 7, 1820, 1839*.

Filling the abyss with sunlike lightenings,
And perpendicular now, and now transverse,
Pierce the dark soil, and as they pierce and pass,
Make bare the secrets of the Earth's deep heart;
280   Infinite mines of adamant and gold,

276. *sunlike lightenings,*] sunlike lightenings *Nbk 7*; sun-like lightnings, *1820, 1839.*
279. *Earth's*] Earths *Nbk 7*; earth's *1820, 1839.*
280–314. As in lines 194–269 above, this passage is shaped around specific literary sources, but adapted to provide an imaginative adumbration of various contemporary or older scientific ideas concerning the age, structure, and geological and archaeological evidence of the earth. Cp. Keats, *Endymion* (1818: read by S. between 20 August and 6 September 1819; see *L* ii 110, 117) iii 119–36:

Far had he roam'd,
With nothing save the hollow vast, that foam'd,
Above, around, and at his feet; save things
More dead than Morpheus' imaginings:
Old rusted anchors, helmets, breast-plates large
Of gone sea-warriors; brazen beaks and targe;
Rudders that for a hundred years had lost
The sway of human hand; gold vase emboss'd
With long-forgotten story, and wherein
No reveller had ever dipp'd a chin
But those of Saturn's vintage; mouldering scrolls,
Writ in the tongue of heaven, by those souls
Who first were on the earth; and sculptures rude
In ponderous stone, developing the mood
Of ancient Nox; – then skeletons of man,
Of beast, behemoth, and leviathan,
And elephant, and eagle, and huge jaw
Of nameless monster. A cold leaden awe
These secrets struck into him . . .

Like Keats S. also recalls *Richard III* I iv 21–33:

O Lord, methought what pain it was to drown,
What dreadful noise of waters in my ears,
What sights of ugly death within my eyes!
Methoughts I saw a thousand fearful wrecks,
A thousand men that fishes gnaw'd upon,
Wedges of gold, great anchors, heaps of pearl,
Inestimable stones, unvalued jewels,
All scatt'red in the bottom of the sea;
Some lay in dead men's skulls, and in the holes
Where eyes did once inhabit there were crept,
As 'twere in scorn of eyes, reflecting gems,
That woo'd the slimy bottom of the deep
And mock'd the dead bones that lay scatt'red there.

280. *mines*] *Nbk 7*; mine *1820, 1839. BSM* ix 506 argues that this was a change to the press transcript, and that *infinite mine* is correct because it 'is in apposition to *earth's deep heart* in the line above'. But *infinite mines* is in apposition with *the secrets of the earth's deep heart*, and the following lines make it clear that S. is thinking of several different kinds of hidden subterranean phenomena.

Valueless stones, and unimagined gems,
And caverns on crystalline columns poised
With vegetable silver overspread;
Wells of unfathomed fire, and water-springs
285 Whence the great sea, even as a child, is fed,
Whose vapours clothe Earth's monarch mountain-tops
With kingly, ermine snow. The beams flash on
And make appear the melancholy ruins
Of cancelled cycles; anchors, beaks of ships,
290 Planks turned to marble, quivers, helms, and spears,
And gorgon-headed targes, and the wheels
Of scythèd chariots, and the emblazonry
Of trophies, standards, and armorial beasts,
Round which Death laughed, sepulchred emblems
295 Of dead destruction, ruin within ruin!

281. Valueless] The epithet is ambiguous: both 'priceless' and 'worthless' (depending on whether the stones acquire a value in human terms). Cp. Q *Mab* v 248, and *Richard III* I iv 27, quoted in note to lines 287–96 below.

282. poised] *Nbk 7, 1839*; poured *1820, 1829*; obviously corrected from S.'s errata list, and also corrected in Hunt's presentation copy of *1820*.

283. vegetable silver] i.e. silver in a formation resembling organic growth; Cp. *Paradise Lost* iv 219–20: 'ambrosial fruit / Of vegetable gold', echoed in Southey, *Thalaba* i 31, 'Trees of vegetable gold' (see also Southey's note, citing 'Pietro Martire': 'the vein of gold is a living tree, and that the same, by all waies that it spreadeth and springeth from the root by the softe pores and passages of the earth, putteth forth branches even unto the uttermost parts of the earth . . .'). The whole description of 'Shedad's mighty pile' in Southey (*Thalaba* i 30–1) suggests S.'s descriptive details in lines 280–3, and cp. also the description of the undersea city of Baly in *Curse of Kehama* xvi.

284–7. 'The sea is fed from springs within the earth, and the snow is produced from water vapour sucked up from the sea by the sun' (*Butter (1970)*); see note to II iv, opening stage direction, for S.'s wider symbolic use of water and geological symbolism in *PU*. The theory that the earth contained vast water-filled caverns was associated with Buffon, *La théorie de la terre* (1749) (see also headnote to 'Mont Blanc').

285. child,] *Nbk 7*; child *1820, 1839*.

286. Earth's] *Nbk 7*; earth's *1820, 1839*.

287. The beams flash on] i.e. 'the beams continue to flash'. In *Nbk 7* S. first wrote *see, as they flas*, then canc. that and wrote beneath *as the beams flash*; he then canc. *as* and added *deep*, which is itself canc. and replaced by *on* to give the received reading.

288–95. Suggesting archaeological evidence of ancient, classical and medieval warfare.

289. ships,] ships *Nbk 7*; ships; *1820, 1839*.

290. marble,] *Nbk 7*; marble; *1820, 1839*. S. would have seen examples of petrified wooden artefacts, e.g. in the 'Natural History Cabinet' at Matlock in Derbyshire (see *L* i 501: 'There is a Cabinet d'Histoire Naturelle at Chamouni, just as at Matlock & Keswick & Clifton . . .').

291. targes] Shields.

294. Death] *Nbk 7*; death *1820, 1839*.

The wrecks beside of many a city vast,
Whose population which the Earth grew over
Was mortal, but not human; see, they lie,
Their monstrous works and uncouth skeletons,
300 Their statues, homes, and fanes; prodigious shapes
Huddled in grey annihilation, split,
Jammed in the hard, black deep; and over these

296–302. This passage appears to have in mind the evolutionary gradualism of 'Uniformitarianism', the geological theory developed by James Hutton and set forth in his *Theory of the Earth* (1795; popularised and extended in James Playfair, *Illustration of the Huttonian Theory . . .* (1802)). Hutton established that natural processes were active over enormously long time-spans, and that their cycles of evolution were governed by consistent natural laws. Cp. also S.'s letter from the Lake District to Elizabeth Hitchener, 23 November 1811: 'Imagination is resistlessly compelled to look back upon the myriad ages whose silent change placed them here, to look back when, perhaps this retirement of peace and mountain simplicity, was the Pandemonium of druidical imposture, the scene of Roman Pollution, the resting place of the savage denizen of these solitudes with the wolf. – Still, still further! – strain thy reverted Fancy when no rocks, no lakes no cloud-soaring mountains were here, but a vast populous and licentious city stood in the midst of an immense plain, myriads flocked towards it; London itself scarcely exceeds it in the variety, the extensiveness of [or?] consummateness of its corruption' (*L* i 189).

297. Earth] *Nbk 7*; earth *1820, 1839.*

298. mortal, but not human] Probably referring to speculation, as found for example in Lord Monboddo, *Origin and Progress of Language* (1773–1792; ordered by S. 24 December 1812, *L* i 344) that man had developed from earlier species. Discussion of the idea was frequent in scientific writers, including Cuvier; see S.'s note to *Q Mab* viii 211–12 and notes, and also Darwin's note to *Botanic Garden* i 101. *lie,*] lie *Nbk 7, 1820, 1839.*

299. works] *Nbk 7*; works, *1820, 1839.*

300. homes,] *Nbk 7*; homes *1820, 1839.*

302–14. The implications of the fossil record were the subject of wide debate in S.'s day, particularly under the influence of the anti-evolutionist Georges Cuvier, whose *Recherches sur les ossements fossiles* (1812) argued that the evidence for extinct species pointed to a series of catastrophic events in the earth's history causing massive land upheavals and floods that destroyed entire species. S. was certainly familiar with the debate from at least his Oxford period, and knew e.g. James Parkinson's *Organic Remains of a Former World* (1804–1811), which he was reading in 1812 (*L* i 255); see *Grabo (1930)* 177ff. for details of possible direct influence on this passage from Parkinson. Interest in Cuvier's ideas, and in the meaning of fossils, was however ubiquitous in the period; see e.g. Byron, *Don Juan* ix 37–8, and his Preface to *Cain* (1821), and cp. *GM*, supplement to lxxxiii pt i (1813) 658: 'Fossils have recently been found in the neighbourhood of Brentford, on the side of the Thames, about six miles West from London. The soil, as far as it has been dug, consists of five distinct beds. The uppermost is a gravelly loam; the second, sand and gravel; the third, a calcareous loam; the fourth, sand; and the fifth, blue clay . . . The uppermost bed contains no fossil remains whatever. The next three contain the tusks of elephants, both African and Indian, of the hippopotamus, the horns and jaws of oxen, the horns of deer, pearl-shells, and the shells of fresh-water fish; but no sea animals. The clay contains the fossil remains of sea-animals alone; as echini, shells &c . . .'

302, 308. over these] S.'s strata seem to be going the wrong way; i.e. earlier and earlier deposits appear nearer and nearer to the surface. Perhaps *over* is to be understood as 'next in succession as we go deeper'; or the idea of cyclic evolution, integral to Hutton's ideas and implicit in Cuvier, may be in mind (in which case 'prehistoric' layerings would recur as later deposits than the relics of previous civilisations).

302. these] *Nbk 7*; these, *1820, 1839.*

The anatomies of unknown wingèd things,
And fishes which were isles of living scale,
305 And serpents, bony chains, twisted around
The iron crags, or within heaps of dust
To which the tortuous strength of their last pangs
Had crushed the iron crags; — and over these
The jagged alligator, and the might
310 Of earth-convulsing behemoth, which once
Were monarch beasts, and on the slimy shores
And weed-overgrown continents of Earth
Increased and multiplied like summer worms
On an abandoned corpse, till the blue globe
315 Wrapped deluge round it like a cloak, and they
Yelled, gasped, and were abolished; or some God
Whose throne was in a comet, passed, and cried
'Be not!' — and like my words they were no more.

The Earth
The joy, the triumph, the delight, the madness!
320 The boundless, overflowing, bursting gladness,

304. Cp. *Paradise Lost* vii 412–15: 'There Leviathan, / Hugest of living creatures, on the deep / Stretched like a promontory sleeps or swims, / And seems a moving land'.

308. crags; –] Nbk 7; crags; *1820, 1839.*

310. behemoth] See *Job* xl 15, from which occurrence *behemoth* has typified the notion of a very large and powerful beast; variously interpreted from the Hebrew as either an elephant or a hippopotamus (cp. also *Paradise Lost* vii 471).

311. shores] Nbk 7; shores, *1820, 1839.*

312. Earth] Nbk 7; earth, *1820, 1839.*

314–18. S. entertains two alternative contemporary theories to account for the catastrophes which, judging from the fossil record, had apparently visited the earth in previous ages. Cuvier posited earthly catastrophes such as floods (see note to lines 302–14 above); others hypothesised a catastrophe ensuing from the gravitational disruption of a comet passing close to the earth (e.g. Davy; see *Grabo (1930)* 175–6). Laplace, *System of the World* (1796), trans. J. Pond 2 vols (1809) conjectured the direct impact of a comet, followed by deluge, and a subsequent rebuilding of the moral world 'whose existing monuments do not go much further back than three thousand years' (ii 64).

317. comet,] Comet, Nbk 7. *cried*] cried – Nbk 7; cried, *1820, 1839.*

318. 'Be not!' – and] Be not! – & Nbk 7; Be not! And *1820, 1839.*

319–502. The duet of the Earth and Moon affirms the identity of Love in the moral world with the 'imponderable' forces understood as different modifications of the power in nature for influence between bodies separated in space: electricity, magnetism, gravity, and heat (see note to I 765). Like the Earth in relation to the Sun, the Moon is attracted to the Earth in both physical and overtly sexual senses, and is kindled into life by the influences of Earth, just as Earth is sustained by the light and other influences of the Sun. S.'s primary emphasis is on volcanic activity as the principal mode of the Earth's self-renewing creativity. S.'s myth of the animation of the Moon (not to be understood literally, but nevertheless enriched by an imaginative consciousness of the scientific possibilities) offers a new inflection of the

The vaporous exultation, not to be confined!
Ha! ha! the animation of delight
Which wraps me, like an atmosphere of light,
And bears me as a cloud is borne by its own wind!

The Moon
325   Brother mine, calm wanderer,
Happy globe of land and air,
Some Spirit is darted like a beam from thee,
Which penetrates my frozen frame,
And passes with the warmth of flame,
330   With love, and odour, and deep melody
Through me, through me!

The Earth
Ha! ha! the caverns of my hollow mountains,
My cloven fire-crags, sound-exulting fountains,
Laugh with a vast and inextinguishable laughter.

---

central Golden Age myths in western civilisation, and implicitly acknowledges them (e.g. Virgil's *Eclogue* iv, the biblical accounts such as *Isaiah* xi 1–9, and Milton's re-presentation of classical and biblical acounts). Throughout this exchange the Moon addresses herself rapturously to the Earth, but the Earth appears either self-absorbed, or concerned to celebrate his relation to the Sun; until a change at line 493.

319. The Earth which speaks here is to be understood differently from the 'character' Earth of Act I; this Earth is primarily a planetary body, and brother to the Moon, rather than mother to all life. This Earth, and also the Moon, can equally be distinguished from the Spirits of Earth and Moon described above, who are evidently conceived as young children; the duet of Earth and Moon is definitely adult and frankly sexual (however incestuously). See also line 515 and note.

321. exultation,] *Nbk 7;* exultation *1820, 1839.* The *vaporous exultation* recalls contemporary accounts of volcanic activity; cp. e.g. Sir William Hamilton, 'Account of the Earthquakes which happened in Italy in . . . 1783', *Philosophical Transactions* lxxiii (1783) 169–208: 'the exhalations which issued during the violent commotions of the earth were full of electrical fire, just as the smoke of volcanoes is constantly observed to be during violent eruptions . . . Perhaps . . . the whole destruction I have been describing may have proceeded simply from the exhalations of confined vapours, generated by the fermentation of such minerals as produce volcanos, which have escaped where they meet with least resistance . . .' (194, 197). See also e.g. *Quarterly Review* x (1814) 202: 'Near Ribeira Grande, we are told there is an aperture in the side of a mountain, from whence a light vapour arises, which, if corked up, would generate an earthquake, or cause an explosion that would blow up the mountain' (cp. note to III iii 124–47).

322. animation] Animation *Nbk 7.*

324. wind!] *Nbk 7;* wind. *1820, 1839.*

325. For the Earth as brother of the Moon see Ovid, *Met.* ii 208–9.

332–4. The details are again volcanic; the draft of line 333 in *Nbk 12* (20ʳ rev.) at first read 'My mouthed fire hills' (uncanc.), and S. also tried 'volcanoes' (canc.); see *MYR* vi.

335   The oceans, and the deserts, and the abysses
           Of the deep air's unmeasured wildernesses
           Answer from all their clouds and billows, echoing after.

           They cry aloud as I do: — 'Sceptred Curse,
           Who all our green and azure universe
340   Threatenedst to muffle round with black destruction, sending
           A solid cloud to rain hot thunderstones,
           And splinter and knead down my children's bones,
           All I bring forth, to one void mass battering and blending;

           'Until each crag-like tower, and storied column,
345   Palace, and obelisk, and temple solemn,
           My imperial mountains crowned with cloud, and snow, and fire;
           My sea-like forests, every blade and blossom
           Which finds a grave or cradle in my bosom,
           Were stamped by thy strong hate into a lifeless mire:

350   'How art thou sunk, withdrawn, covered — drunk up
           By thirsty nothing, as the brackish cup

335. The Oceans and the Desarts and the Abysses *Nbk 7*; abysses, *1820, 1839.*

336. Of] *Nbk 7* (and also in the draft, *Nbk 12* f. 20ʳ); And *1820, 1839*; possibly a change to the press transcript, but probably a mistranscription. *wildernesses] Nbk 7*; wildernesses, *1820, 1839.*

338. do: – 'Sceptred Curse] do – Sceptred Curse *Nbk 7*; do. Sceptred curse *1820, 1839*. There are no speech marks around lines 338–55 in *Nbk 7, 1820*, or *1839*. The phrase is a double synecdoche for Jupiter.

339–42. Cp. Sir William Hamilton's account of the 1794 eruption of Vesuvius, *Philosophical Transactions* lxxxv (1795) 91: 'One cloud heaped on another, and succeeding each other incessantly, formed in a few hours such a gigantic and elevated column of the darkest hue over the mountain, as seemed to threaten Naples with immediate destruction, having at one time been bent over the city, and appearing to be much too massive and ponderous to remain long suspended in the air' (the article includes a striking illustration of this cloud).

339. universe] Universe *Nbk 7.*

340–1. Cp. 'Ode to the West Wind' 26–8 (itself a volcanic image): 'vaulted with all thy congregated might / Of vapours, from whose solid atmosphere / Black rain, and fire, and hail will burst'.

343. blending;] blending *Nbk 7*; blending. *1820, 1839.*

345. obelisk, and temple] Obelisk and Temple *Nbk 7.*

348. in] on *Nbk 7*; presumably S.'s change to the press transcript.

349. mire:] mire *Nbk 7*; mire. *1820, 1839.*

350–5. 'Jupiter and all the paraphernalia he stands for are absorbed back into Demogorgon's darkness – into the realm of potentiality (because it will always be possible for him to re-emerge; that depends on man himself). In so far as humanity created Jupiter, and tolerated his thrones and prisons and churches, he is simply a hole in space' (GM).

350. covered –] *Nbk 7*; covered, *1820, 1839.*

Drain'd by a desert-troop, a little drop for all!
And from beneath, around, within, above,
Filling thy void annihilation, Love
355 Bursts in like light on caves cloven by the thunder-ball.'

The Moon
The snow upon my lifeless mountains
Is loosened into living fountains,
My solid oceans flow, and sing, and shine:
A spirit from my heart bursts forth,
360 It clothes with unexpected birth
My cold, bare bosom: oh, it must be thine
On mine, on mine!

Gazing on thee I feel, I know,
Green stalks burst forth, and bright flowers grow,
365 And living shapes upon my bosom move:
Music is in the sea and air,
Wingèd clouds soar here and there,
Dark with the rain new buds are dreaming of:
'Tis Love, all Love!

The Earth
370 It interpenetrates my granite mass,
Through tangled roots and trodden clay doth pass

352. *desert-troop,*] Desart-troop – *Nbk 7. all!*] *Nbk 7*; all; *1820, 1839.*

354. *Love*] *Nbk 7*; love *1820, 1839.*

355. *the thunder-ball*] *Nbk 7, 1839*; thunder-ball *1820, 1829*; presumably on S.'s errata list.

356–61. Contemporary scientific opinion held that the moon had little or no atmosphere, but probably had frozen water which might be a basis for life if heat from the Earth and Sun could be retained, particularly in conjunction with 'air' which might be exhaled by lunar volcanic activity (cp. above, lines 225–30 and note). See Darwin's note to *Botanic Garden* ii 82: '. . . as [the moon] seems to have suffered and to continue to suffer much by volcanos, a sufficient quantity of air may in process of time be generated to produce an atmosphere; which may prevent its heat from so easily escaping, and its water from so easily evaporating, and thence become fit for the production of vegetables and animals. That the moon possesses little or no atmosphere is deduced from the undiminished lustre of the stars, at the instant when they emerge from behind her disk. That the ocean of the moon is frozen, is confirmed from there being no appearance of lunar tides'; see also *Walker* 225–39 for the view that the Earth's own atmosphere had been produced from within by the action of the Sun's heat.

358. *oceans*] Oceans *Nbk 7.*

361. *oh,*] *Nbk 7*; Oh! *1820, 1839.*

363. Cp. II i 27 and note.

369. *Love, all Love!*] *Nbk 7*; love, all love! *1820, 1839.*

370–405. A long and difficult sentence; the main verb, *leave*, explicitly (although ambiguously; see notes below) governs lines 382–93, and is understood to govern lines 394–405.

370. The referent of the pronoun is *Love*, picked up from the Moon's preceding speech.

Into the utmost leaves and delicatest flowers;
Upon the winds, among the clouds 'tis spread,
It wakes a life in the forgotten dead —
375 They breathe a spirit up from their obscurest bowers —

And like a storm, bursting its cloudy prison
With thunder, and with whirlwind, has arisen
Out of the lampless caves of unimagined being,
With earthquake shock and swiftness making shiver
380 Thought's stagnant chaos, unremoved forever,
Till Hate, and Fear, and Pain, light-vanquished shadows, fleeing,

Leave Man — who was a many-sided mirror
Which could distort to many a shape of error

374–5. *dead* –] dead *Nbk 7*; dead, *1820, 1839*. *bowers* –] bowers *Nbk 7*; bowers. *1820, 1839*.
The dashes are necessary to clarify that line 375 is in parenthetic predication of the *forgotten dead* of line 374. The lines are unpunctuated in *Nbk 7*, and in *1820* and *1839* the stop after *bowers* (together with the colon after *being* in line 378) obscures the grammatical relation of this stanza to the stanza following.

375. See note to line 392.

376. *storm,*] *Nbk 7*; storm *1820, 1839*.

377. *has arisen*] i.e. 'it (Love, understood from the pronoun of line 370) has arisen'.

378. *being,*] being *Nbk 7*; being: *1820, 1839*.

379–80. An adverbial sub-clause qualifying *has arisen*.

379. *shock*] *Nbk 7* clearly reads *shook*, but the word sounds oddly in this context and is perhaps a transcription slip on S.'s part.

380. *unremoved forever*] i.e. 'fixed in place up until now'; cp. *Paradise Lost* iv 987, 'Like Teneriffe or Atlas unremoved'. *forever,*] *Nbk 7*; for ever, *1820, 1839*.

381–4. The grammar is ambiguous. The plural subject of *Leave* in line 382 is *Hate, and Fear, and Pain* and the verb is transitive in this occurrence; i.e. 'Hate, Fear and pain, in fleeing from Man, leave him in the condition of being a sea reflecting love'. The *sea reflecting love* is thus placed in contrast with the *many-sided mirror* of line 382. In the following stanza *leave* is again the governing verb, but is understood intransitively (see note to line 388). The following two stanzas, lines 394–405, then return to a transitive understanding of *leave*.

381. *Hate, and Fear, and Pain,*] Hate and Fear and Pain, *Nbk 7*; hate, and fear, and pain, *1820, 1839*.

382–4. Cp. *Ruins* (end ch. 24): '. . . this further truth will then appear . . . That real objects have in themselves an identical, constant, and invariable mode of existence, and that in your organs exists a similar mode of being affected and impressed by them. But at the same time, inasmuch as these organs are liable to the direction of your will, you may receive different impressions, and find yourselves under different relations towards the same objects; so that you are with respect to them, as it were, a sort of mirror, capable of reflecting them such as they are, and capable of disfiguring and misrepresenting them.'

382. *Man* –] Man, *Nbk 7, 1820, 1839*. *mirror*] *Nbk 7*; mirror, *1820, 1839*.

383. *error*] *Nbk 7*; error, *1820, 1839*.

This true fair world of things — a sea reflecting Love;
385 Which over all his kind, as the sun's heaven
Gliding o'er ocean, smooth, serene, and even,
Darting from starry depths radiance and life, doth move:

Leave Man, even as a leprous child is left
Who follows a sick beast to some warm cleft
390 Of rocks, through which the might of healing springs is poured;
Then when it wanders home with rosy smile,
Unconscious, and its mother fears awhile
It is a Spirit — then, weeps on her child restored:

Man, oh, not men! a chain of linked thought,
395 Of love and might to be divided not,
Compelling the elements with adamantine stress;
As the sun rules, even with a tyrant's gaze,

384. *things* –] *Nbk 7*; things, *1820, 1839.   *sea*] Sea *Nbk 7*;   Love;] *Nbk 7*; love; *1820, 1839.* Cp. Young, *Night Thoughts*, Night ix: 'Nature is the glass reflecting God, / As, by the sea, reflected is the sun, / Too glorious to be gaz'd on in his sphere'.

385. *Which* refers to Love, *his* to Man.   *sun's heaven*] Suns Heaven *Nbk 7*.

386. *ocean*,] Ocean *Nbk 7*.   *even*,] *Nbk 7*; even *1820, 1839.*

387. *life*,] *Nbk 7* (also in the draft, *Nbk 12* f. 24ᵛ); light, *1820, 1839*; possibly S.'s change to the press transcript (*radiance & light & life* is canc. in the draft), but a mistranscription is perhaps more likely (*radiance and light* seems tautologous).   *move*:] move *Nbk 7*; move. *1820*; move, *1829, 1839* (probably a mistaken editorial correction in Galignani, left uncorrected or unnoticed by Mary).

388–93. S. has in mind the legend of King Bladud, who was banished from the court of his father Hudibras after contracting leprosy and lived as a swineherd; he saw his swine benefit from bathing in hot marshes, and after bathing himself was cured of his leprosy and founded the City of Bath on the sight of the hot springs. The story is given in most historical accounts of Bath; see e.g. Southey's *Letters from England* (1807) ch. lxxiv.

388. *as a leprous child is left*] i.e. by leprosy.   *left*] *Nbk 7*; left, *1820, 1839.*

392. *its mother fears awhile*] Cp. *Mary L* i 123 (to Maria Gisborne, 28 December 1819): 'If by any chance you have not sent the Prometheus add the word *bowers* after *from their obscurest* & in the other change it to *it's mother fears awhile*'. The first of these might be explained as a doubtful reading (line 375 above) for which Mary had belatedly sought clarification from S. (the word is corrected and obscure in *Nbk 7*); perhaps line 392 had been altered in the press transcript, and S. subsequently decided to restore the received reading, which appears in *Nbk 7*.

393. *Spirit* –] *Nbk 7*; spirit, *1820, 1839.*   *restored*:] restored. *Nbk 7, 1820, 1839.*

394–423. Man will control nature just as the sun controls the planets.

394. *Man, O, not men!*] 'i.e. not sectarian pressure-groups but collective man' (GM).

397–9. Referring to the balanced stress of centrifugal and gravitational forces in the orbits of the solar system.

397. *sun*] Sun *Nbk 7*.

The unquiet republic of the maze
Of planets, struggling fierce towards heaven's free wilderness:

400   Man, one harmonious Soul of many a soul,
Whose nature is its own divine control,
Where all things flow to all, as rivers to the sea;
Familiar acts are beautiful through love;
Labour, and Pain, and Grief, in life's green grove
405   Sport like tame beasts — none knew how gentle they could be!

His will, with all mean passions, bad delights,
And selfish cares, its trembling satellites,
A spirit ill to guide, but mighty to obey,
Is as a tempest-wingèd ship, whose helm
410   Love rules, through waves which dare not overwhelm,
Forcing Life's wildest shores to own its sovereign sway.

All things confess his strength. Through the cold mass
Of marble and of colour his dreams pass —
Bright threads, whence mothers weave the robes their children wear;
415   Language is a perpetual Orphic song,

398. *republic*] Republic *Nbk 7*.

399. *planets,*] Planets, *Nbk 7*. *heaven's*] Heaven's *Nbk 7*. *wilderness:*] wilderness. *Nbk 7, 1820, 1839*.

400. *Soul*] *Nbk 7*; soul *1820, 1839*.

404. *Labour, and Pain, and Grief,*] Labour and Pain and Grief *Nbk 7*; labour, and pain, and grief, *1820, 1839*.

405. *beasts –*] *Nbk 7*; beasts, *1820, 1839*.

408. i.e. the will is bad when in command, but beneficent under the guidance of love.

411. *Life's*] *Nbk 7*; life's *1820, 1839*. *sovereign*] *Nbk 7* reads *sovereigns*, and the draft in *Nbk 12* f. 24ʳ reads *sovereign's*; but all printed witnesses agree on the received reading.

412–14. i.e. sculptors and artists give their ideal visions of man material embodiment; and mothers dream that their children will actually be like that. Cp. II iv 83–4 and note, and see 'The Daemon of the World' (no. 115) i 16–17.

413. *pass –*] pass *Nbk 7*; pass; *1820, 1839*.

414. *threads,*] *Nbk 7*; threads *1820, 1839*. In *Nbk 7* this line originally began *And mothers gazing*, which S. then canc. and replaced with the received reading written above. The canc. reading exactly repeats a phrase from II iv 83–4.

415–18. Like the passage in II iv 72 (see note) this passage has been taken to imply the subordination of thought to language; but *rules* in line 416 suggests that thought exists independently of language, while dependant on it for control and communication; as *Cameron (1974)* 557 notes, S. here refers specifically to Literature (developing the allusions to other arts in this stanza).

415. *Orphic*] Orpheus was the mythical father of Gk poetry; the epithet here suggests in general terms the power of poetry.

Which rules with daedal harmony a throng
Of thoughts and forms, which else senseless and shapeless were.

The lightning is his slave; heaven's utmost deep
Gives up her stars, and like a flock of sheep
420 They pass before his eye, are numbered, and roll on!
The tempest is his steed, — he strides the air;
And the abyss shouts from her depth laid bare,
'Heaven, hast thou secrets? Man unveils me; I have none.'

The Moon
The shadow of white Death has passed
425 From my path in heaven at last,
A clinging shroud of solid frost and sleep;
And through my newly-woven bowers
Wander happy paramours,
Less mighty, but as mild as those who keep
430   Thy vales more deep.

The Earth
As the dissolving warmth of dawn may fold
A half-unfrozen dew-globe, green and gold
And crystalline, till it becomes a wingèd mist,
And wanders up the vault of the blue day,

---

416. Which rules] In *Nbk 7* these words are canc., and *Ruling* is written in pencil to the left; S. probably restored the original reading in the press transcript, but this could be a change made after despatch of the transcript. *daedal*] *Nbk 7*; Dædal *1820, 1839*. Cp. III i 26 and note.

418–23. These lines anticipate specific forms of future productive human control over nature: electricity, astronomy, aviation, and submarine travel.

418. lightning] Lightning *Nbk 7*; *heaven's*] Heavens *Nbk 7*. Cp. Priestley (*History and Present State of Electricity*, 3rd edn 1775) ii 136: '. . . what would Newton himself have said, to see the present race of Electricians imitating in miniature all the known effects of that tremendous power, nay disarming the thunder of its power of doing mischief, and, without any apprehension of danger to themselves, drawing lightning from the clouds into a private room . . .'

421. tempest] Tempest *Nbk 7*. *steed, –*] *Nbk 7*; steed, *1820, 1839*.

423. There are no speech marks in *Nbk 7, 1820,* or *1839*.

424. Death] *Nbk 7*; death *1820, 1839*. *has*] hath *Nbk 7*; presumably a change to the press transcript (perhaps to remove the awkward repetition of *th*).

425. heaven] Heaven *Nbk 7*.

427. bowers] *Nbk 7*; bowers, *1820, 1839*.

431. dawn] Dawn *Nbk 7*.

432. half-unfrozen] *Nbk 7*; half infrozen *1820* (a misprint); half unfrozen *1839*. *green and gold*] *Nbk 7*; green, and gold, *1820, 1839*.

435   Outlives the noon, and on the sun's last ray
Hangs o'er the sea, a fleece of fire and amethyst —

The Moon

Thou art folded, thou art lying
In the light which is undying
Of thine own joy, and heaven's smile divine;
440   All suns and constellations shower
On thee a light, a life, a power
Which doth array thy sphere — thou pourest thine
On mine, on mine!

The Earth

I spin beneath my pyramid of night,
445   Which points into the heavens, dreaming delight,
Murmuring victorious joy in my enchanted sleep;

434. day,] Day *Nbk 7.*

435. sun's] Sun's *Nbk 7.*

436. sea,] sea; *Nbk 7. amethyst –*] *Nbk 7;* amethyst. *1820, 1839.* On this dash, see *Butter (1970):* 'Earth's sentence is unfinished, and we cannot be sure how he would have applied the simile – perhaps to the Moon (as the warmth of the sun has dissolved the cold dewdrop to vapour so the new warmth on the moon has dissolved its snow into fertilizing clouds). But the Moon interrupts and applies it to the Earth (as the cloud of vapour is derived from the earth and is lighted gloriously by the sun, so the light which enfolds the earth comes from his own joy and heaven's smile)'.

439. heaven's] Heavens *Nbk 7.*

442. sphere –] *Nbk 7;* sphere; *1820, 1839.*

444–9. The simile is deceptively complex. In broad terms it likens the earth, when 'sleeping' in the darkness of its own shadow but still cared for by the light and heat of the sun, to a lover, oblivious while asleep of the actual presence of the loved-one who nevertheless keeps a loving watch over the sleeper. It is however difficult to reconcile the details of the astronomical term of the comparison with the term of human relationship. If *Under the shadow of his beauty lying* is understood as 'lying under the shadow of his (the sleeping lover's) own beauty', then the referent of *which* in the line following cannot be 'the Sun', which is however the referent implied by the rest of that line. If *his beauty* in line 448 does indeed refer to the sleeping lover's own beauty, then the simile is analogous to e.g. lines 265–7 above, where the Spirit of the Earth's lips move *Amid the changing light of their own smiles.* This quasi-Platonic notion of a thing irradiated by its own essence, which does occur elsewhere in S., is assumed by Wasserman in his subtle effort of paraphrase (*Wasserman* 352–3), which nevertheless strains to reconcile all the elements in the simile. GM proposes 'The shadow of the lover lies under is the dark security of sleep which his lover's vigilant ever-present love affords him: just as the dark segment of Earth sleeps because the sun invests the rest of Earth with light'. S.'s draft suggests that he hesitated over the terms of the simile, which seems at first to have involved a female sleeper (see *Nbk 12* f. 23ʳ).

444. Pliny, *Nat. Hist.* II vii describes the conical shadow cast by the earth, pointing away from the sun into space.

445. heavens,] Heavens, *Nbk 7;* heavens *1820, 1839.*

As a youth lulled in love-dreams, faintly sighing,
Under the shadow of his beauty lying
Which round his rest a watch of light and warmth doth keep.

The Moon
450 As in the soft and sweet eclipse,
When soul meets soul on lovers' lips,
High hearts are calm, and brightest eyes are dull;
So, when thy shadow falls on me,
Then am I mute and still, by thee
455 Covered; of thy love, Orb most beautiful,
Full, oh, too full!

Thou art speeding round the sun,
Brightest world of many a one,
Green and azure sphere, which shinest
460 With a light which is divinest
Among all the lamps of heaven
To whom life and light is given;
I, thy crystal paramour,
Borne beside thee by a power
465 Like the polar paradise,
Magnet-like, of lovers' eyes;
I, a most enamoured maiden,
Whose weak brain is overladen
With the pleasure of her love,
470 Maniac-like around thee move,
Gazing, an insatiate bride,
On thy form from every side,

447. *love-dreams,*] Nbk 7; love-dreams *1820, 1839.*
448. *lying*] Nbk 7; lying, *1820, 1839.*
450. The Moon picks up and adapts the Earth's simile from the preceding stanza.
455. S. was familiar with the Elizabethan sexual sense of 'covered' (see e.g. *Merchant of Venice* III v 50–3, Donne, 'On his Mistress Going to Bed' 48).
457. *sun,*] Sun Nbk 7.
458. *world*] World Nbk 7. *one,*] one Nbk 7; one; *1820, 1839.*
459. *sphere,*] Nbk 7; sphere *1820, 1839.*
461. *heaven*] Heaven Nbk 7, *1820, 1839.*
465. *paradise,*] Paradise Nbk 7; Paradise, *1820, 1839.*
467–70. Perhaps referring to the apparently eccentric 'libration' of the moon on its axis (caused by the dual gravitational influence of the sun and earth).
470. *move,*] Nbk 7; move *1820, 1839.*
471–2. 'The moon, in circling the earth, always keeps the same side toward the earth because the period of its rotation exactly equals that of its revolution' (*Reiman (1977)*).

<blockquote>

Like a Mænad, round the cup
Which Agave lifted up
475   In the weird Cadmæan forest.
Brother, wheresoe'er thou soarest
I must hurry, whirl and follow
Through the heavens wide and hollow,
Sheltered by the warm embrace
480   Of thy soul from hungry space,
Drinking from thy sense and sight
Beauty, majesty, and might,
As a lover or chameleon
Grows like what it looks upon,
485   As a violet's gentle eye
Gazes on the azure sky
Until its hue grows like what it beholds,
As a grey and watery mist
Glows like solid amethyst
490   Athwart the western mountain it enfolds
When the sunset sleeps
Upon its snow —

</blockquote>

473–5. S. associates the abandonment of Dionysian possession with the fertility of revolutionary upheaval, but retains an awareness of its disturbing and destructive character. The reference is to Euripides, *Bacchae* 1051ff.: Agave was the daughter of Cadmus and mother of Pentheus; together with a group of maenads she unwittingly kills her son in a Bacchic frenzy. Cp. II iii 7–10 and note, and 44 and note, III iii 124–47 and note, 'Ode to Liberty' (published with *PU* in *1820*) 91, 171. See S.'s 'Notes on Sculptures in Rome and Florence', describing a painting of Agave and the maenads: 'Their hair loose and floating seems caught in the tempest of their own tumultuous motion, their heads are thrown back leaning with a strange inanity upon their necks, and looking up to Heaven, while they totter and stumble even in the energy of their tempestuous dance. One – perhaps Agave with the head of Pentheus – has a human head in one hand and in the other a great knife; another has a spear with a pine cone, which was their thyrsus; another dances with mad voluptuousness; the fourth is dancing to a kind of tambourine' (*Prose* 349).

478. heavens] *Heavens* Above *Cavens* [sic] canc. *Nbk 7*; the change 'underscores how closely these lines echo the "follow, follow" lyrics of Act 2' (*BSM* ix 532).

483–4. Cp. 'An Exhortation', published with *PU* in *1820*.

483. or chameleon] or a chameleon *Nbk 7, 1820, 1829*; the *a* has been added later in *Nbk 7*, not very clearly, and S. may have changed his mind about its insertion and deleted it on the errata list.

484. looks upon,] gazes on *Nbk 7*; almost certainly altered at the same time as the inclusion of the following 10 lines, which would have introduced a repetition of *gazes*.

485–94. These lines do not appear in *Nbk 7*, and were either added in the press transcript or sent later. There is an alternative version in draft in *Nbk 12* f. 27ᵛ rev, which Mary published in *1839* iv 123 as 'A Fragment' (see 'Fragments connected with *PU*: I').

487. Cp. I 450 and note.

491–4. The Earth completes the Moon's quatrain, and in so doing responds directly to her words for the first time.

492. snow –] snow. *1820, 1839*.

The Earth
And the weak day weeps
That it should be so.
495   O gentle Moon, the voice of thy delight
Falls on me like thy clear and tender light
Soothing the seaman, borne the summer night
Through isles forever calm;
O gentle Moon, thy crystal accents pierce
500   The caverns of my pride's deep universe,
Charming the tiger Joy, whose tramplings fierce
Made wounds which need thy balm.

Panthea
I rise as from a bath of sparkling water,
A bath of azure light, among dark rocks,
505   Out of the stream of sound.

Ione
                   Ah me! sweet sister,
The stream of sound has ebbed away from us,
And you pretend to rise out of its wave,
Because your words fall like the clear soft dew
Shaken from a bathing wood-nymph's limbs and hair.

Panthea
510   Peace! peace! a mighty Power, which is as darkness,
Is rising out of Earth, and from the sky
Is showered like night, and from within the air
Bursts, like eclipse which had been gathered up
Into the pores of sunlight — the bright Visions,

---

495. gentle Moon] Gentle moon *Nbk 7*.

498. forever] *Nbk 7*; for ever *1820, 1839*.

499. gentle] Gentle *Nbk 7*.

500. pride's deep universe,] Pride's deep Universe *Nbk 7*.

501. Joy,] *Nbk 7*; joy, *1820, 1839*.

503–9. 'Panthea says, "I arise out of the sound." Ione replies, "The sound has gone, it could only have been your own accents which made you think it was still here."' (*Hughes*).

510–14. Demogorgon rises from the Earth. His attributes and effects are again emphasised as volcanic.

510. darkness,] *1820*; Darkness *Nbk 7*; darkness *1839*.

512. night,] Night, *Nbk 7*.

514. sunlight –] *Nbk 7*; sunlight: *1820, 1839*. The phrase *pores of sunlight* (*pores of light* in the draft, *Nbk 12* f. 32ᵛ reverso) suggests that 'the necessitarian power resides in the elemental units of matter' (*Cameron (1974)* 558); *Darwin, Walker* and other contemporary scientific sources use 'pores' to designate the minute spaces between the particles of matter, in which the superfine ether resides (cp. note to lines 270–9 above). *Visions,*] Visions *Nbk 7*; visions, *1820, 1839*.

515   Wherein the singing spirits rode and shone,
      Gleam like pale meteors through a watery night.

Ione
There is a sense of words upon mine ear —

Panthea
An universal sound like words . . . O list!

          Demogorgon
    Thou Earth, calm empire of a happy soul,
520   Sphere of divinest shapes and harmonies,
    Beautiful orb! gathering as thou dost roll
      The Love which paves thy path along the skies:

          The Earth
I hear: I am as a drop of dew that dies!

          Demogorgon
    Thou Moon, which gazest on the nightly Earth
525   With wonder, as it gazes upon thee,
    Whilst each to men, and beasts, and the swift birth
      Of birds, is beauty, love, calm, harmony:

          The Moon
I hear: I am a leaf shaken by thee!

515. This seems to indicate that the preceding sequence of the Earth and Moon has been sung by the spirits described in lines 194–318; but see note to line 319 above.

517. ear –] Nbk 7; ear. *1820, 1839.*

518. An] Nbk 7, 1820; A *1829, 1839.* Presumably carried over by Mary from her copy text in Galignani; modern *eds* preserve the *1839* reading, but Victorian *eds* preferred *1820,* and it is S.'s usual practice to use *an* before a vowel. *words . . . O list!]* Nbk 7; words: Oh, list! *1820, 1839.*

519–53. Demogorgon addresses in turn the Earth (519–23), the Moon (524–8), the stars (529–33), the dead (534–8), the atomic constituents of all things (539–43), all living things and active phenomena (544–9), and mankind (549–53).

519. Thou] Nbk 7; Thou, *1820, 1839. empire]* Empire Nbk 7. *soul,]* Soul, Nbk 7.

522. Love] Nbk 7; love *1820, 1839.*

523. dies!] Nbk 7; dies. *1820, 1839.*

524. Thou] Nbk 7; Thou, *1820, 1839. Earth]* Nbk 7; earth *1820, 1839.*

525. thee,] thee Nbk 7; thee; *1820, 1839.*

526. birth] i.e. race, nation (from Lat. natio).

Demogorgon
Ye Kings of suns and stars, Dæmons and Gods,
530   Etherial Dominations, who possess
Elysian, windless, fortunate abodes
Beyond Heaven's constellated wilderness:

A Voice from Above
Our great Republic hears: we are blest, and bless.

Demogorgon
Ye happy Dead, whom beams of brightest verse
535   Are clouds to hide, not colours to portray,
Whether your nature is that universe
Which once ye saw and suffered —

A Voice from Beneath
    Or as they
Whom we have left, we change and pass away.

Demogorgon
Ye elemental Genii, who have homes
540   From man's high mind even to the central stone
Of sullen lead; from Heaven's star-fretted domes
To the dull weed some sea-worm battens on:

A Confused Voice
We hear: thy words waken Oblivion.

Demogorgon
Spirits whose homes are flesh; ye beasts and birds;
545   Ye worms and fish; ye living leaves and buds;

529–30. Cp. *Paradise Lost* v 600–1: 'Hear, all ye Angels, Progeny of Light, / Thrones, Dominations, Princedoms, Virtues, Powers'.

529. Kings] Nbk 7; kings *1820, 1839.* stars,] Nbk 7, 1820; stars! *1839.*

530. Dominations,] Nbk 7, 1820; Dominations! *1839.*

533. hears:] hears . . . Nbk 7; hears, *1820;* hears; *1839.*

534. Dead,] Nbk 7, 1820 (no cap.); dead! *1839.*

536–8. S. preserves his characteristic sceptical reserve about existence after death; i.e. we do not know whether or not the dead continue to exist and change as living people do, or whether they have simply become reassimilated to the material universe. The whole address to the dead in lines 534–8 anticipates *Adonais.*

536. universe] Universe Nbk 7.

539. elemental Genii] See note to I 42.

544. Spirits] Nbk 7; Spirits, *1820;* Spirits! *1839.* flesh;] flesh – Nbk 7; flesh: *1820, 1839.* birds;] birds Nbk 7; birds, *1820, 1839.*

Lightning and wind; and ye untameable herds,
Meteors and mists, which throng air's solitudes:

A Voice
Thy voice to us is wind among still woods.

Demogorgon
Man, who wert once a despot and a slave;
550   A dupe and a deceiver; a decay;
A traveller from the cradle to the grave
Through the dim night of this immortal day:

All
Speak: thy strong words may never pass away.

Demogorgon
This is the day, which down the void abysm
555   At the Earth-born's spell yawns for Heaven's despotism,
And Conquest is dragged captive through the deep;

---

546. *wind:*] Wind – *Nbk 7.*

547. *throng*] *throng* is canc. in *Nbk 7,* with *feed* written above. The original reading was either restored in the press transcript, or Mary failed to notice the change; or the change may have been made after despatch of the transcript. *air's*] Airs *Nbk 7.*

550. *and*] or *Nbk 7;* presumably a change to the press transcript, but *or* is smudged and could have been misread. *decay;*] Decay *Nbk 7.*

551. *traveller*] Traveller *Nbk 7.*

552. *day:*] Day *Nbk 7.*

554. *This is the day,*] *1820, 1829;* This is the Day *Nbk 7;* This the day, *1839;* presumably a misprint (uncorrected in Mary's subsequent *eds*). Cp. *Psalm* cxviii 24: 'This is the day which the Lord hath made; we will rejoice and be glad in it'. *abysm*] Abysm *Nbk 7.*

555. *Earth-born*] i.e. Prometheus, who as a Titan was the son of Earth and Heaven. *spell*] Cp. I 61 and note. *despotism*] Despotism *Nbk 7.*

556. *Conquest*] conquest *Nbk 7. deep;*] Deep; *Nbk 7;* deep: *1820, 1839.* Cp. Landor, *Gebir* (1798) vi 301–8:

> Time, – Time himself throws off his motley garb
> Figur'd with monstrous men and monstrous gods,
> And in pure vesture enters their pure fanes,
> A proud partaker of their festivals.
> Captivity led captive, War o'erthrown,
> They shall o'er Europe, shall o'er Earth extend
> Empire that seas alone and skies confine,
> And glory that shall strike the crystal stars.

See also *Ephesians* iv 8: 'Wherefore he saith, When he ascended up on high, he led captivity captive, and gave gifts unto men', and cp. *Psalm* lxviii 18, and *Paradise Lost* x 188.

Love, from its awful throne of patient power
In the wise heart, from the last giddy hour
Of dread endurance, from the slippery, steep,
560 And narrow verge of crag-like agony, springs
And folds over the world its healing wings.

Gentleness, Virtue, Wisdom, and Endurance, —
These are the seals of that most firm assurance
Which bars the pit over Destruction's strength;
565 And if, with infirm hand, Eternity,
Mother of many acts and hours, should free
The serpent that would clasp her with his length,
These are the spells by which to re-assume
An empire o'er the disentangled Doom.

570 To suffer woes which Hope thinks infinite;
To forgive wrongs darker than Death or Night;
To defy Power, which seems omnipotent;
To love, and bear; to hope, till Hope creates
From its own wreck the thing it contemplates;

---

557. *throne*] home *Nbk 7*; presumably a change to the press transcript.

559–60. Cp. *Cenci* III i 247–55 and note.

559. *dread*] *Nbk 7, 1839*; dead *1820, 1829*. Probably on S.'s errata list.

560. *agony,*] Agony *Nbk 7*.

562–9. Cp. *Revelation* xx 1–3: 'And I saw an angel come down from heaven, having the key of the bottomless pit and a great chain in his hand. And he laid hold on the dragon, that old serpent, which is the Devil, and Satan, and bound him a thousand years, and cast him into the bottomless pit, and shut him up, and set a seal upon him, that he should deceive the nations no more, till the thousand years should be fulfilled: and after that he must be loosed a little season.'

562. *Endurance, –*] *Nbk 7*; Endurance, *1820, 1839*.

565–9. S. does not envisage that history will ever be at an end; like Huttonian evolution, the processes at work are cyclic and assumed to operate over a vast time-scale, and the over-throw of Jupiter will doubtless eventually need to be repeated.

569. *the*] that *Nbk 7*; presumably a change to the press transcript. *Doom.*] Doom *Nbk 7*; doom. *1820, 1839*.

571. *Death or Night;*] Death or Night *Nbk 7*; death or night; *1820, 1839*.

572. *omnipotent;*] Omnipotent; *Nbk 7*.

573–4. See I 450 and note, and *Athanase* (no. 146), cancelled sequence 10 and note.

573. *hope,*] *Nbk 7*; hope *1820, 1839*.

574. *contemplates;*] *1820*; contemplates *Nbk 7*; contemplates: *1839*. On S.'s distinctively powerful use of the word *own*, here and elsewhere, see G. R. Hamilton, 'Shelley's Own', *English* v (1945) 149–53.

575 Neither to change, nor falter, nor repent:
  This, like thy glory, Titan! is to be
  Good, great and joyous, beautiful and free;
  This is alone Life, Joy, Empire, and Victory.

575. *falter,*] *Nbk 7, 1839*; flatter, *1820, 1829*; probably on S.'s errata list. *repent:*] repent *Nbk 7*; repent; *1820, 1839*. Cp. *Paradise Lost* i 94–6: 'Yet not for those, / Nor what the potent Victor in his rage / Can else inflict, do I repent or change'.

195 Appendix
Fragments connected with
Prometheus Unbound

A: 'For as I fled o'er realm and realm borne on the latest sigh'

Text from *Nbk 11* 35; probably for I *c.* 763.

For as I fled o'er realm and realm borne on the latest sigh
Which a dying lover breathed beneath his lady's bitter sneer
I had a lance of ebony   wreathed round with flowers immortal
Which a genius to my sister gave   when she died for him in passion

B: 'The [living frame which sustains my soul]'

Text from *Nbk 8* f. 1ʳ; for the 'Song of Spirits' in II iii, or possibly for Asia's song in II v (see *BSM* ix 559).

> The [living frame which sustains my soul]
> Is [sinking beneath the fierce control]
> Down through the lampless deep of song
> I am drawn and driven   along —

C: 'The sleepless brooks there ever run'

Conjecturally reconstructed from the very rough, heavily cancelled and unresolved draft in *Nbk 11* pp. 34–5; see *BSM* xviii 36–7 for a facsimile and transcript. Presumably intended for II ii or iii.

> The sleepless brooks there ever run
> From their crystal mines below
> And sink before they see the sun
> To feed great Indus onward flow
> 5   [?These] leap like meteor kindled showers
> And light the pale and starless flowers
> Which overhang their glimmering beams
> From their own sands and lucid streams
> The voice of their immortal springs

3–4. Spaces left in *Nbk 11*.

4. *him*] love *BSM* xviii.

¶B   4. Space left in *Nbk 8*.

650

10   Is heard like [?] thunder
And from their caves to Indus brings
A sound like earthquake stifled under
But here their [?] breathes and moans
In soft and melancholy tones

D: 'All life is glad at thine awakening words'

The first four lines are in *Nbk 6* 52, and suggest a connection with III iii or iv; their continuation by lines 5–7, which are drafted 2 pages later in *Nbk 6*, is conjectural. See *BSM* xv 54–7.

All life is glad at thine awakening words
And the Earth breathes them even as one long pent
In dusky cities amid looks of care
Breathes the thyme-scented mountain atmosphere
5   From thrice ten thousand cities gathering up
The loud acclaim of jubilee and joy
Floats high above their cloud surrounded towers

E: 'Yet look on me – take not thine eyes away'

These lines were first published, as a discrete poem, by Mary S. in her 'Note on Poems of 1817' in *1840* 205 with the comment 'I do not know when it was written, – but it was early' (see *BSM* ii 152–3 for Mary's transcript in adds. d. 7). *Eds* following Rossetti identified the poem as 'an unfinished sonnet' entitled 'To –' and placed the poem even earlier than 1817, often as early as 1814 (e.g. *Dowden Life* i 422, *Woodberry 1893* iii 162). But as *MYR* iv 147 notes, the poem's position early in *Nbk 10*, which is probably of Italian manufacture, implies that a composition date in March 1819 is likely, and the manner and substance of the lines (particularly the interest in reflected light, a recurrent motif in *PU* which recalls S.'s reading in *Walker*) might suggest that they originated as a passage intended for, e.g., the Spirit of the Earth to Asia in III iv 15–24, or 86–9. Other contexts are however possible, e.g. S.'s projected play *Tasso*; but the lines are very unlikely to be earlier than S.'s arrival in Italy in spring 1818. S.'s draft is in pencil, and the text here has been conjectured in lines 7–9 where the rough and cancelled draft is difficult to resolve. Punctuation has been added in lines 1, 4, 9 and 10; see *MYR* iv 4–5 for a facsimile and transcription.

¶D   *2–4.* Recalling *Paradise Lost* ix 445–8: 'As one who long in populous city pent, / Where houses thick and sewers annoy the air / Forth issuing on a summer's morn to breathe / Among the pleasant villages . . .'; and cp. Coleridge, 'Frost at Midnight' 51–2: 'For I was reared / In the great city, pent 'mid cloisters dim'.

4. mountain] Canc. in *Nbk 6*, and then underlined to indicate reinstatement.

5. thrice] twice *BSM* xv.

7. cloud] Canc. in *Nbk 6*, with a word written above and also canc., which *BSM* reads as '[?star]'.

Yet look on me — take not thine eyes away
Which feed upon the love within mine own
Although it be but the reflected ray
Of thy sweet beauty from my spirit thrown.
5   Yet speak to me! thy voice is as the tone
Of my heart's echo, and I think I hear
That thou yet lovest me — yet thou alone
Like one before a mirror, [?take no] care
Of aught but thine own [?form] imaged too truly there.
10   And yet I wear out life in watching thee,
A toil so sweet at times, and thou indeed
Art kind when I am sick, and pity me
And I

F: 'I stood upon a mountain of our land'

Written in *Nbk 11* 91, where it interrupts a draft for *PU* IV (and so must be earlier than November/December 1819); it could be much earlier, but was possibly itself intended for *PU*, perhaps for the Spirit in III iv.

I stood upon a mountain of our land
Which heaves itself into the wintry air
And looked upon the Ocean and its rivers
Its lakes, the mirrors of the eternal Heaven
5   Its cornfields and its meadows and its woods
And saw in

G: 'And who are they'

Written in *Nbk 12* f. 6r; perhaps intended for IV 194–205 and the entrance of the spirits of Earth and Moon. An apostrophe is added in line 2.

And who are they
Bathed in deep luxury of each other's looks
Which flows forth like the inmost light of being
Making the noon obscure? o unforeseeing
Of

H: 'Where lie bare bones, and skeletons'

Written in *Nbk 14* 153, evidently for IV 289.

Where lie bare bones, and skeletons
And anchors and beaks of ships

¶G   *4. o*] [?] *MYR* vi.

I: 'As a violet's gentle eye'

Drafted in *Nbk 12* f. 27ʸrev. (with the first three lines also drafted on f. 7ʸ); an alternative version of the Moon's song at IV 485, although Mary's transcript in adds. d. 9 (see *Massey* 208–9) dates the lines 1821. Cp. *MYR* vi 270–1.

As a violet's gentle eye
Gazes on the azure sky
Until its hue grows like what it beholds,
As a grey and empty mist
5 Lies like solid amethyst
Over the western mountain it enfolds
When the sunset sleeps
Upon its snow —

As a strain of sweetest sound
10 Wraps itself the wind around
Until the voiceless wind grow music too —
As aught dark and vain [and] dull
Basking in what is beautiful
So full of light and love [?]

J: 'Ye Hours, that speed or linger as ye wist'

Written in *Nbk 12* f. 15ʸrev., with the first three lines canc. by three diagonal strokes; probably intended for Demogorgon's closing address in IV. Another, very slight fragment, in *Nbk 12* f. 22ʳrev., may also relate to Demogorgon's closing address: 'Like an eagle hovering / In the golden light of morning / With'.

Ye Hours, that speed or linger as ye wist
Chainless as winds, bright as illumined bees
Which flee from flower to flower to seek their fill
Whose life is
5 Ye spirits who keep watch beside that deep
The human heart, until its frozen prison
Were
Who make their life, with the instinct of [? ?]

11. voiceless] *MYR* vi reads 'voidless', with the last four letters canc.

12. [and]] Omitted in *Nbk 12*.

13–14. The last two words of line 13, and all of line 14, have been added later in rough faint pencil.

¶J *1. wist*] Written above *will* canc. in *Nbk 12*.

4, 7. Spaces left in *Nbk 12*.

8. The line ends on two illegible words; *BSM* xv reads 'th[eir] [?sleep]'.

196
'the weeping willows'

Written in pencil in *Nbk 10*; from the nbk context and content, perhaps *c.* April 1819.

Text from *Nbk 10* f. 5ʳrev.

Published in *Huntington Nbks* ii 83.

the weeping willows
Spread on the lucid wave a green pavilion

197
'The cotton poplar's down'

Written in pencil in *Nbk 10*. Context in the nbk and the content suggest late April or early May 1819; the capsules of *Populus nigra* burst at that time in Italy to distribute their seeds, which show prominently white on and around the female trees.

Text from *Nbk 10* f. 6ʳ.

Published in *Huntington Nbks* ii 19.

The cotton poplar's down
Like snowflakes strewing the dusk ground

¶196   1. Space left in *Nbk 10*.

198
Julian and Maddalo: A Conversation

*Edited by Ralph Pite**

The date of composition has been disputed. S. stated in a letter to Hunt on 15 August 1819 that the poem 'was composed last year at Este' (*L* ii 108); Mary added the date '*Rome, May*, 1819' to the poem's first publication in *1824* (26). S. dated *The Cenci* to the same period in his dedication of the play to Leigh Hunt. (See headnote to no. 209 for the possible significance of the date.) In *1839*, Mary placed the poem among the 'Poems written in 1820' at the end of vol. iii, following the *Letter to Maria Gisborne*. In 1840 she moved it into the poems of 1818. This uncertainty is largely resolved by two pieces of evidence which establish terminal dates: first, S. included a fair copy of the poem, with instructions for publication, in his letter to Hunt on 15 August 1819; secondly, the meeting with Byron which is recalled in the poem's opening occurred on 23 August 1818 (*L* ii 35–6). S. lived at Byron's villa near Este between 25 or 26 August and 5 November 1818 (see headnote to no. 195). He may have completed the poem by the latter date though Mary's initial dating of May 1819 and S.'s delay before sending it to England in August 1819 both suggest it was begun at Este and not completed until the following year. A draft survives in *Nbk 6* ff. 62–117 (*BSM* xv). This includes the bulk of the poem apart from 150 lines of the Maniac's soliloquy (lines 287–93, 300–36, 377–83, 408–510 of the printed text do not appear.) Donald H. Reiman dates the composition of the missing lines to the period after the death of William S. on 7 June 1819 (*SC* vi 865). This cannot be proven. Reiman is too clear-cut when he identifies (*Reiman (1977)* 112) two phases of composition – in early 1819 and June–August 1819. GM's analysis of the nbk reveals that parts of the poem must have been composed after 'Stanzas Written in Dejection – December 1818, near Naples' (which can confidently be dated to December 1818; see headnote to no. 187) and *PU* II (probably begun at the same period (see headnote to no. 195)). GM concludes from his study of the nbk draft that the 'likelihood is . . . that substantial additions were still being made to *Julian and Maddalo* as late as March 1819' ('"Julian and Maddalo": The Draft and the Meaning', *Studia Neophilologica* 35 (1963) 57–84 (67)). The sections of the poem not included in the nbk draft may have been written later still, though whether before or after William S.'s death cannot be decided.

The manuscript that S. sent to Hunt in August 1819 did not provide the text for the poem's first publication in *1824*. It is probable that Mary used a fair copy of her own, made either later in the autumn or in spring 1820. *Harvard Nbk* lists 'Maddalo and Julian' on the contents page but the transcript has been removed, probably to provide press-copy for *1824*. A transcript of lines 1–107 (in Mary's hand and again entitled 'Maddalo and Julian') survives in *Nbk 11* ff. 170–7. The fair copy S. sent to Hunt (*Hunt MS*) became the property of S. R. Townshend Mayer at Hunt's death. Mayer made it available to H. B. Forman who used the MS as copy text in

* *The editor wishes to thank Hester Jones and Diego Saglia for their assistance in editing this text.*

Forman 1876–7. Some time after Mayer's death in 1880, Forman purchased the MS and in 1920, it was bought by J. Pierpont Morgan in whose library it still remains (Pierpont Morgan Library PM MA 974; see *MYR* viii 194–6). *Hunt MS* does not include either the preface or the epigraph from Virgil that appeared in *1824*. It is a strikingly finished version otherwise, although punctuated lightly. Substantive differences between *1824* and *Hunt MS* are relatively minor, though where they occur, *Hunt MS* usually seems superior. S. must have had a copy of the poem in Italy from which Mary made her transcripts in 1819–20 (see *SC* vi 860). The question for the editor is whether S. continued to revise the poem after August 1819 (as he did with the fair copy of *PU*. See headnote to no. 195). Mary perhaps suggests this when in *1824* she describes the poem 'as having received the author's ultimate corrections' (*1824* p. vii). If later revision is accepted, *1824* gains priority over the earlier version of the poem surviving in *Hunt MS*. Differences between *1824* and *Hunt MS* may be the result of Mary's editorial changes and errors in transcription but it is possible they show S.'s revision. On the other hand, S.'s letters of 1819–20 concerning the poem repeatedly urge his London friends to publish it in the form he had sent in August 1819 (S. to Ollier 23 December 1819 (*SC* vi 554) and 14 May 1820 (*L* ii 196)). In transcribing *Hunt MS* from his intermediate fair copy, S. may have made changes which represent his final decisions. If so and if Mary was transcribing the same intermediate fair copy, then her versions become in substance earlier than *Hunt MS* despite being made a few months later. Mary may mean by 'ultimate corrections' the addition of the preface and epigraph or she may be claiming authority for her text over other MSS she knew to be in existence (including *Hunt MS* and others as well: Medwin possessed a version which he read to Washington Irving on 1 February 1824). However, Mary's omission of line 218 suggests she was censoring the poem a little and she may have wished to present these changes as 'ultimate corrections' made by S. There is no supporting evidence for the idea that S. continued to work on the poem itself after August 1819, although he certainly composed the preface after that date, perhaps in response to the *Quarterly Review*'s attack on *RofI* which he first read in October 1819. The reversed form of the title in *Harvard Nbk* and *Nbk 11* may derive from the intermediate fair copy or from revision later and so does not help to decide whether or not Mary's transcripts are superior to *Hunt MS*.

The present edition uses *Hunt MS* as the copy text because it is an exceptionally good fair copy which S. intended for publication. As far as possible the punctuation of *Hunt MS* has been preserved but a small amount has been added (often at the ends of lines – *Hunt MS* is written in a tiny nbk and longer lines in the text are sometimes crushed into the margins). Because later revision (between August 1819 and Mary's transcriptions in 1819–20) remains a possibility, all substantive variants from *1824* have been noted and considered as perhaps indicating later changes made by S. The preface appears only in *1824*; the epigraph appears only in *1824* and *Nbk 11*.

S. initially hoped for anonymous publication in *The Examiner*. When this proved impossible he suggested a separate volume for the poem plus several shorter pieces. When discussions began for *1820*, S. saw the poem as incompatible with *PU* and requiring anonymous publication 'in the first edition of it, in any case' (*L* ii 196). It was announced as being in the press in *1820* but did not appear until *1824* (June 1824), at the head of the volume.

In December 1819 S. told Ollier: 'I mean to write three other poems [similar to *J&M*], the scenes of which will be laid at Rome, Florence, and Naples, but the subjects of which will all be drawn from dreadful or beautiful realities, as that of this was' (*L* ii 164); arguably such poems were written but, if so, there is no sign of S. continuing to have in mind a group. In May 1820, S. suggested *Athanase*: 'I would not print [*J&M*] with "Prometheus". It would not harmonize . . . If you print "Julian and Maddalo", I wish it to be printed in some unostentatious form, accompanied with the fragment of "Athanase" ' (*L* ii 196). Six months later, again to Ollier, S. mentions 'accompanying poems' once more, almost apologetically: 'The Julian & Maddalo & the accompan[y]ing poems are all my saddest verses raked up into one heap. – I mean to mingle more smiles with my tears in future.' (*L* ii 246). Neil Fraistat has shown which poems S. intended to publish with *Julian and Maddalo* (see headnotes to nos 187 and 202). In January 1821 S. assured Claire Clairmont that he had never intended to publish the poem; in February he wrote to Ollier: 'I suppose "Julian and Maddalo" is published. If not, do not add the "Witch of Atlas" ' (*L* ii 254, 269). He sounds willing to let the piece drop for the moment and no more is heard of it in his correspondence.

The location of the poem in Venice, and its portrayal of figures reminiscent of S. and Byron, explicitly recall S.'s and Claire Clairmont's visit to the city (21–25 August 1818). S. went there in order to mediate between Byron and Claire Clairmont about their daughter, Allegra, whom Claire had given into Byron's care in April 1818. Claire regretted the decision and sought some degree of access to the child. Byron refused to speak to her directly on the matter: 'I declined seeing her for fear that the consequence might be an addition to the family' (Byron to Augusta Leigh, 21 September 1818, *Byron L&J* vi 69). S. told Mary: 'he [Byron] often expresses his extreme horror of her [Claire's] arrival, & the necessity it would impose on him of instantly quitting Venise [*sic*]' (*L* ii 36). Byron agreed, however, to lend S. and his family the villa, 'I Capuccini' at Este, about forty miles southwest of Venice, which he had on lease. By this arrangement, Allegra would remain with Byron but be able to visit Claire at the villa. When this plan was accepted, S. asked Mary to travel at once to Este, bringing with her their two children, Clara and William. S. had told Byron that Mary and Claire were both in Padua already, waiting for news of the outcome; in fact Claire was in Venice (staying with the Hoppners) and Mary was still in Lucca. S.'s family arrived on 5 September 1818 and on 24 September, Clara died (*L* ii 40–1). There is some evidence that Mary blamed Clara's death on the hurried journey, and therefore on S.'s concern to placate Byron and arrange things for Claire. S. and the family remained at Este until 5 November, then travelled to Rome and Naples, returning to Rome on 5 March 1819 where William S. died on 7 June. Mary suffered from serious depression after his death and, again, there is evidence of marital unhappiness. The two deaths and the difficulties in S.'s marriage have been linked, in particular, with the Maniac's speeches; there is probably some connection though not as specific or legible as biographical criticism has tried to argue.

The draft in *Nbk 6* reveals that the poem was conceived as a whole: blank pages were left in the nbk for the Maniac's speeches with the frame-narrative drafted before and after. GM remarks: 'the draft shows clear evidence of careful structural planning and of a Soliloquy subordinated to a preconceived overall design' ('The Draft and the Meaning', 63). Although the Maniac voices anguish that may well be linked to S.'s marriage, his speeches should be seen also in the context of the debate between the two other characters. The draft suggests the importance of S.'s friendship with Byron to the poem as a whole (see *Robinson* 91–100). In Venice, the friendship was under strain not only from the tussle over Allegra. S. disapproved of Byron's life in Venice and the poetry he was writing there. Byron recited to S. passages from *Childe Harold* iv and S. wrote to Peacock about it:

> The spirit in which it is written is, if insane, the most wicked & mischievous insanity that ever was given forth. It is a kind of obstinate & selfwilled folly in which he hardens himself. I remonstrated with him in vain on the tone of mind from which such a view of things alone arises . . . He associates with wretches who seem almost to have lost the gait & phisiognomy [sic] of man, & who do not scruple to avow practices which are not only not named but I believe seldom even conceived in England. He says he dissaproves [sic], but he endures (17 or 18 December 1818, *L* ii 58).

S.'s disgust with Byron's life in Venice and his belief that it was destroying Byron's poetic gift underlies much in the Maniac's speech about the endurance of suffering and, in particular, the hardening of the heart that comes from either inflicting or bearing pain (see 350–7, 438–60). The same context informs the debate between Julian and Maddalo and the reader's shifts in sympathy between them.

Biographical readings of the poem have gradually been replaced by ones that emphasise its conversational aspects, seeing in the characters not identifiable persons but projections of personas or aspects of S. and Byron (see *Wasserman* 57: S.'s aim was 'to test in poetry his own insecure meliorism against the resistance of his companion's misanthropic fatalism'). Recent critics have granted S. greater critical and self-critical distance from the poem's characters; Bernard Hirsch emphasises S.'s hostility to Julian: 'Maddalo exposes Julian's naivete and enables us to recognize the spuriousness of his perceptions' ('"A Want of That True Theory": *Julian and Maddalo* as Dramatic Monologue', *Studies in Romanticism* 17 (1978) 19). Similarly, Vincent Newey reads the poem as exposing Julian's naive seriousness in order to elevate 'the imaginative embrace of experience' over 'philosophic speculation' ('The Shelleyan Psycho-Drama: "Julian and Maddalo" ', *Essays on Shelley*, ed. M. Allott (1982) 74). Kelvin Everest argues that the poem's relation to Julian is less straightforwardly hostile (*Shelley Revalued* 63–88) and Timothy Clark argues persuasively that 'the debate between Byron and Shelley . . . is a continuation, on an *inter*personal level, of the *intra*personal debates on the mind's potential power over itself conducted in Shelley's work during 1815–16' (*Embodying Revolution* (1989) 165). The biographical context and Julian's skilful deployment of Byronic opinions (see lines 174–84) support this view of the poem as poised and ambivalent. Neither character is exempt from either criticism or sympathy and neither wins out decisively over the other; in relation to the Maniac, both seem liable to disregard him, either through over-confidence (Julian) or fatalistic resignation (Maddalo).

The poem has no single source; *R&H*, completed in Italy in summer 1818, is similarly structured around a conversation and in Lionel has a character close to the Maniac (see 337–43 and note). 'Conversation' was a frequent topic of eighteenth-century discussion in poetry and prose (Pope, 'The First Satire of the Second Book of Horace, Imitated' (1733); Swift, *A Collection of Polite and Ingenious Conversation* (1738); Fielding, 'An Essay on Conversation' (*c.* 1741–49); Cowper, 'Conversation' (1781); Coleridge, 'The Nightingale: A Conversation Poem', 'Frost at Midnight' (1798)). S.'s subtitle recalls this tradition of refined yet colloquial exchange, in particular as it was employed by Wordsworth in *The Excursion* (1814); there the aftermath of political revolution, personal despondency and human tragedy are debated through conversations held in scenes of natural grandeur. S. read *The Excursion* in 1814 and again the following year. He may also have been influenced by Peacock's novels – particularly *Melincourt* (1817) and *Nightmare Abbey* (1818) – which proceed via pseudo-intellectual conversation and mock the conventions of romantic feeling. S. read and praised the novels in 1818–19 (see *L* i 517, 538, ii 29, 98).

Torquato Tasso (1544–95) wrote many poetic dialogues; *J&M* does not draw on them directly but is in part a reflection on Tasso's life and achievement. S. read Tasso's *Aminta* and *Gerusalemme liberata* first in 1815 and began, when he arrived in Italy in 1818, a more systematic study of him, including his biography. He wrote to Peacock 20 April 1818: 'I have devoted this summer & indeed the next year to the composition of a tragedy on the subject of Tasso's madness, which I find upon inspection is, if properly treated, admirably dramatic and poetical' (*L* ii 8). Scenes of this were written (see nos 170, 186 and *BSM* xv 160–7) and a scenario (see *BSM* iii 165); they include a character named Maddalo, proving the link between projected drama and poem, but the play itself never advanced very far. S. may have been drawn to write on Tasso by Byron's 'The Lament of Tasso' (July 1817) which he read in September 1817. Carlos Baker sees the Maniac's story as 'a semifiction-alized treatment of the poet Tasso's imprisonment for real or alleged madness in the year 1579', having 'nothing probable to do with S.'s domestic affairs' (*Baker* 127, 291). The links between the Maniac and Tasso are convincing but they do not prevent the poem from also having biographical content; Tasso was interest-ing to S. and Byron as a figure of the unjustly persecuted poet, susceptible and possibly driven mad. Their identification with him allowed them to explore their own condition via dramatic monologues either explicitly in Tasso's voice (as in 'The Lament of Tasso') or tacitly so (as in the Maniac's speeches).

S.'s Tasso was in part the product of contemporary images of him. Between 1750 and 1850, Tasso became:

> a prototype of the Romantic poet, loving passionately but hopelessly and beyond his station, the victim of political oppression, maintaining his dignity and essential nobility of heart through intense and prolonged suffering, the hypersensitive artist at odds with society, wandering restlessly from court to court or chained in a lunatic's cell. (C. P. Brand, *Torquato Tasso* (1965) 205)

He is portrayed in S.'s lifetime as a paragon of poetic virtue:

> All his historians concur in their praise of his candour, his inviolable fidelity to his word, his courtesy, his frankness, his freedom from the least tincture of revenge or of malignity . . . his purity of life and manners, his fervent and sincere piety. What was most irksome in his temper was a strange fear he had of being slighted, and a certain suspicious and mistrustful disposition. (J. H. Wiffen, 'The Life of Tasso', *The Jerusalem Delivered of Torquato Tasso* (1826, 1872) xlix)

S.'s most lengthy discussion of Tasso occurs in a letter to Peacock (6 November 1818) written after S. had visited the prison in Ferrara where Tasso was incarcer-ated. S. sees Tasso as someone of 'delicate susceptibilities and elevated fancies' and 'an intense & earnest mind exceeding at times its own depth, and admonished to

659

return by the chillness of the water of oblivion striking upon its adventurous feet' (*L* ii 48, 47). Here, as in the Maniac, S. accepts the conventional image of Tasso and develops it into something closer to himself (see line 385 and note). The poem is written in couplets, in what S. called 'a certain familiar style of language to express the actual way in which people talk with each other whom education and a certain refinement of sentiment have placed above the use of vulgar idioms' (*L* ii 108). The style squares with eighteenth-century and Romantic ideals of 'conversation' (see above); it attracts comparison with Leigh Hunt's *The Story of Rimini* (1816) and Keats's *Endymion* (1818) both of which use couplets in a similar way. All three are drawing on the Della Cruscan poetry of the 1780s and 1790s; S.'s choice of style is appropriate for Julian, therefore, whose behaviour and language is frequently characteristic of eighteenth-century sensibility. The poem is a companion piece to the more optimistic and idealised poetry of *PU* and a precursor of *The Cenci*'s concern with familial turmoil and 'dreadful realities'. Formally, it is nearest to *Letter to Maria Gisborne* and *Epipsychidion* among S.'s other works.

Text from The Pierpont Morgan Library, New York. MA 974 (=*Hunt MS*), except for epigraph and preface from *1824*.

First published in *1824*.

198
Julian and Maddalo: A Conversation

The meadows with fresh streams, the bees with thyme,
The goats with the green leaves of budding spring,
Are saturated not – nor Love with tears.

VIRGIL'S Gallus

Count Maddalo is a Venetian nobleman of ancient family and of great fortune, who, without mixing much in the society of his countrymen, resides chiefly at his magnificent palace in that city. He is a person of the

Epigraph.] S.'s translation of Virgil, *Eclogues* x 29–30; see no. 167. The Latin reads: 'nec lacrimis crudelis Amor nec gramina riuis / nec cytiso saturantur apes nec frondae capellae.' Cp. Tasso, *Aminta* I ii 13–15:

> Pasce l'agna l'erbette, il lupa l'agne;
> Ma il crudo amor di lagrime si pasce,
> Nè se ne mostra mai satollo

Pref. 1. Count Maddalo] To some extent, a portrait of Lord Byron. S. remarked to Leigh Hunt of the poem, 'two of the characters you will recognize' (*L* ii 108), presumably Byron and S. himself as Maddalo and Julian. Byron was living at the Palazzo Mocenigo in Venice when S. visited. Cp. Thomas Medwin, *Conversations of Lord Byron*, ed. Ernest J. Lovell (Princeton, 1966), 119: 'S., I remember, draws a very beautiful picture of the tranquil pleasures of Venice in a poem which he has not yet published, and in which he does not make me cut a good figure. It describes an evening we passed together.' The name is used for a courtier in S.'s drafted scene for a drama on the life of Tasso (see no. 170 and headnote) and may be connected to the French *matelot* (seaman); S. often referred to Byron as Albe and to Allegra as Alba; pseudonyms and nicknames were often used (privately and publicly) by the S. circle.

most consummate genius; and capable, if he would direct his energies to
5 such an end, of becoming the redeemer of his degraded country. But it is
his weakness to be proud: he derives, from a comparison of his own extra-
ordinary mind with the dwarfish intellects that surround him, an intense
apprehension of the nothingness of human life. His passions and his
powers are incomparably greater than those of other men, and instead of
10 the latter having been employed in curbing the former, they have mutu-
ally lent each other strength. His ambition preys upon itself, for want of
objects which it can consider worthy of exertion. I say that Maddalo is
proud, because I can find no other word to express the concentered and
impatient feelings which consume him; but it is on his own hopes and
15 affections only that he seems to trample, for in social life no human being
can be more gentle, patient, and unassuming than Maddalo. He is cheerful,
frank, and witty. His more serious conversation is a sort of intoxication;
men are held by it as by a spell. He has travelled much; and there is an
inexpressible charm in his relation of his adventures in different countries.
20 Julian is an Englishman of good family, passionately attached to those
philosophical notions which assert the power of man over his own mind,

Pref. 4. if he would direct] Cp. S.'s letter to Byron, 29 September 1816, *L* i 507: 'Is there noth-
ing in the hope of being the parent of greatness, and of goodness, which is destined, per-
haps, to expand indefinitely?'

Pref. 5. degraded] Modern sense of 'corrupted, low, debased' co-existing with earlier sense of
'having lost rank or status, dishonoured'; a cliché of protest: soldiers in *L&C* III vi 9 are 'degraded'
by tyranny; Venice in *Childe Harold* iv 134n is 'the degraded capital'. Cp. lines 184, 345.

Pref. 6–8. proud . . . life] Cp. S.'s less charitable account of Byron in a letter to Peacock 17 or
18 December 1818 (*L* ii 58), in particular: 'contemplating in the distorted mirror of his own
thoughts, the nature & the destiny of man, what can he behold but objects of contempt &
despair?'

Pref. 9. men, and instead] men; and, instead *Forman 1876–7*.

Pref. 11–12. His ambition . . . exertion] Cp. Byron to John Murray, 3 November 1821, about
the protagonist of *Cain*: 'the inadequacy of his state to his Conceptions' (*Byron L&J* ix 54).

Pref. 13. concentered] 'Focussed on self as a centre'. A notably Byronic word; see his
Prometheus 55–8: 'a firm will, and a deep sense, / Which even in torture can descry / Its own
concentered recompense, / Triumphant where it does defy' and *Childe Harold* iii 833–5: 'From
the high host / Of stars, to the lull'd lake and mountain-coast / All is concenter'd in a life
intense'.

Pref. 20. Julian] Modelled on S. himself. The name may suggest treachery (because of the Roman
Emperor, Julian the Apostate) and may have been suggested by the Julian Alps, visible from
Venice and mentioned by S. in the letter describing his meeting with Byron (*L* ii 37). S. may
also have had in mind 'Count Julian . . . a powerful Lord among the Wisi-Goths, now a ren-
egade' from Southey's epic, *Roderick, the Last of the Goths* (1814). Scott in *The Vision of Don
Roderick* (1811) and Walter Savage Landor in *Count Julian: A Tragedy* (1812) wrote versions
of the same story in which Julian betrays his country to the Saracens because his daughter
was seduced by Roderick, Julian's King. Arguably, S.'s character similarly puts private inter-
est before the general good when he blithely fails to be of any substantial help to the Maniac.
GM suggests Giulio Segni as a possible source: 'another of Tasso's visitors during his mad-
ness, who was so impressed with him that he became his devoted friend' ('Draft and the
Meaning' 77).

and the immense improvements of which, by the extinction of certain moral superstitions, human society may be yet susceptible. Without concealing the evil in the world, he is for ever speculating how good may be made
25 superior. He is a complete infidel, and a scoffer at all things reputed holy; and Maddalo takes a wicked pleasure in drawing out his taunts against religion. What Maddalo thinks on these matters is not exactly known. Julian, in spite of his heterodox opinions, is conjectured by his friends to possess some good qualities. How far this is possible, the pious reader will deter-
30 mine. Julian is rather serious.

Of the Maniac I can give no information. He seems by his own account to have been disappointed in love. He was evidently a very cultivated and amiable person when in his right senses. His story, told at length, might

Pref. 23. may be yet susceptible] may yet be susceptible *1839*.

Pref. 29. the pious reader] Cp. the less clear-cut irony in S.'s Preface to *Alastor*: 'The picture is not barren of instruction to actual men.'

Pref. 31. the Maniac] S. is coy about his identity in his letter to Hunt (15 August 1819) – he is 'also in some degree a painting from nature, but, with respect to time and place, ideal' (*L* ii 108) – and intended nobody actual. The Maniac has been seen as an aspect of S., distraught because of Mary's coldness in 1818–19, either after the death of Clara S. (September 1818) or the following summer, after William S.'s death (June 1819) – cp. *White* ii 42–50; seen by J. H. Smith as expressing S.'s anguish at conducting an affair with Claire Clairmont ('S. and Claire Clairmont', *PMLA* 54 (September 1939) 785–815); linked by Peck to S.'s memories of Harriet Grove (*Peck* ii 104–7; cp. lines 273–4 note). The Maniac has also been connected with Byron, in his relations with his wife and Augusta (G. W. Knight, *Lord Byron: Christian Virtue* (1952) 251–4 and J. E. Saveson, 'S.'s *Julian and Maddalo*', *KSJ* 10 (1961) 53–8). Ivan Rose, *Shelley: The Last Phase* (1953) 135–58, argues that Hogg's relations with Mary provoked S. to write the Maniac's speeches. News had reached S. of Harriet S.'s suicide on 15 December 1816; Byron reminded S. of the custody battle with Harriet S. when they met in Venice (*L* ii 37) to discuss custody again. The Maniac's soliloquy may, therefore, be in part an expression of S.'s remorse about Harriet also (see H. S. Salt, 'A Study of Shelley's *Julian and Maddalo*', *The Shelley Society Papers*, pt. II (1889) 326). None of the biographical connections is watertight or exclusive; S.'s figure draws on his interest in Tasso (see headnote) and on the literary conventions of sensibility. Contemporary medicine recognised different kinds of mania; Pinel in 1806 gave five: 'Melancholia, or delirium upon one subject exclusively', 'Mania without delirium', 'Mania with delirium', 'Dementia', and 'Ideotism', characterising 'Melancholia' as 'Delirium exclusively upon one subject . . . in some cases, equanimity of disposition . . . in others, habitual depression and anxiety, and frequently a moroseness of character amounting even to the most decided misanthropy, and sometimes to an invincible disgust with life' (Ph. Pinel, *A Treatise on Insanity*, trans. D. Davis (1806) ix–x, 149). Cp. Gordon Spence, 'The Maniac's Soliloquy in *Julian and Maddalo*', *Keats–Shelley Review* iv (1989) 81–93. S.'s maniac seems melancholic, by this definition (though see 424–6 and note). The literature of sensibility used 'maniac' to describe such melancholics, not raving but fixated, and usually gave as the cause heart-break or unrequited love; they were predominantly deserted women, later men as well; the protagonist of *Alastor* and 'Lionel' in *R&H* both fit the type. Where distress is coupled with disgust, however, a revolutionary aspect to the maniac can be found. See Timothy Clark, *Embodying Revolution* (1989) 198: 'The contrast between Julian and the maniac dramatizes opposed aspects of sensibility – the fashionable assumption of a feeling attitude on the one hand, and the revolutionary political force on the other.' Cp. Robert Merry, 'The Pains of Memory' (1796) 329–36:

be like many other stories of the same kind: the unconnected exclama-
5   tions of his agony will perhaps be found a sufficient comment for the text
of every heart.

> I rode one evening with Count Maddalo
> Upon the bank of land which breaks the flow
> Of Adria towards Venice: — a bare strand
> Of hillocks, heaped from ever-shifting sand,
> 5   Matted with thistles and amphibious weeds,

By sharp sensation wounded to the soul,
He ponders on the world . . . abhors the whole;
While black as night, his gloomy thought expands
O'er life's perplexing paths, and barren sands.
In the dire workings of his wakeful dreams
The human race a race of demons seems,
All is unjust, discordant and severe,
He asks not mercy's smiles or pity's tear

Pref. 34–6. the unconnected . . . heart] Possibly linked with John Taylor Coleridge's review of
RofI in the *Quarterly Review* (April 1819) which attacked S.'s private morals: 'if we might with-
draw the veil of private life, and tell what we *now* know about him, it would be indeed a
disgusting picture that we should exhibit, but it would be an unanswerable comment on our
text'. S. drafted a letter to William Gifford, as editor of the *Quarterly* picking up on this phrase,
' "an unanswerable comment["] on the text, either of his review or my poem' (October 1819,
L ii 130 and note). John Coleridge's personal attack may have encouraged S. to write the
preface, which distances the poem from himself and Byron; adapting Coleridge's phrase would
make the preface a pointed rejoinder to biographical criticism. S. continued to be angered
by the review, believing it to be written by Southey and writing to him about it on 26 June
1820. No evidence exists to give a date of composition for the preface (see headnote).

1. I rode one evening] For S's account of the visit to Venice that suggested the poem, see *L* ii
36: 'So he [Byron] took me in his gondola – much against my will for I wanted to return to
Clare at Mrs. Hoppners who was anxiously waiting for me – across the laguna to a long sandy
island which defends Venise [*sic*] from the Adriatic. When we disembarked, we found his
horses waiting for us, & we rode along the sands of the sea talking.'

2. the bank of land] The 'Lido di Malamocco' that acts as a coastal defence for Venice. Clara
was buried on the Lido on 25 September 1818. Cp. *Marino Faliero* IV i 13–15: 'the Adrian
wave / Rose o'er the city's murmur in the night, / Dashing against the outward Lido's bulwark'.

3. Adria] The Adriatic Sea.

3–7. a bare strand . . . Is this] Meaning the Lido but applicable to Venice in decline. Cp. Byron,
'Ode on Venice' 8–10, 12: 'as the slime, / The dull green ooze of the receding deep, / Is with
the dashing of the spring-tide foam . . . Are they to those that were'; and cp. *Marino Faliero*
II ii 111–13: 'Our fathers did not fly from Attila / Into these isles, where palaces have sprung /
On banks redeem'd from the rude ocean's ooze / To own a thousand despots'. Cp. below
lines 219, 275.

5. Matted with thistles] 'Covered with tangled growth' but also, perhaps, 'dulled, deprived of
lustre' (*OED* def. 2). Cp. Goldsmith, *The Deserted Village* 349: 'Those matted woods, where
birds forget to sing', and Dryden's *Virgil's Pastorals* iv 36: 'Through the Matted Grass the
liquid Gold shall creep'. *amphibious*] frequently applied to plants: 'the amphibious tribe as
willow, sallow, withy, osier' (C. Marshall, *Gardening* (1813).) Cp. Coleridge, *Biographia Literaria*,
ch. 1: 'the moderns [sacrifice passion] to an amphibious something, made up, half of image,
and half of abstract meaning'.

Such as from earth's embrace the salt ooze breeds
Is this: — an uninhabitable sea-side,
Which the lone fisher, when his nets are dried,
Abandons, and no other object breaks
10 The waste, but one dwarf tree and some few stakes
Broken and unrepaired, and the tide makes
A narrow space of level sand thereon,
Where 'twas our wont to ride while day went down.
This ride was my delight. — I love all waste
15 And solitary places; where we taste
The pleasure of believing what we see
Is boundless, as we wish our souls to be:
And such was this wide ocean, and this shore
More barren than its billows; — and yet more
20 Than all, with a remembered friend I love
To ride as then I rode; — for the winds drove
The living spray along the sunny air
Into our faces; the blue heavens were bare,
Stripped to their depths by the awakening North,
25 And from the waves, sound like delight broke forth
Harmonizing with solitude, and sent
Into our hearts aërial merriment.
So, as we rode, we talked; and the swift thought,
Winging itself with laughter, lingered not,

7–12. Cp. 'Lines Written among the Euganean Hills' (no. 183) 45–52:

> On the beach of a northern sea
> Which tempests shake eternally,
> As once the wretch lay there to sleep,
> Lies a solitary heap,
> One white skull and seven dry bones,
> On the margin of the stones,
> Where a few grey rushes stand,
> Boundaries of the sea and land:

7. *uninhabitable*] uninhabited *1824, Forman 1876–7*.

23–4. The simplicity of these lines was achieved by considerable redrafting. In *Nbk 6* p. 64 they are heavily corrected, reading first: 'And that divinest depths of Heaven laid bare / To its profoundest Blue by the keen North'.

24. *North,*] North *Hunt MS*; north; *1824*.

27. *aërial merriment.*] 'High spirits', 'elevated cheerfulness'. Cp. 'Euganean Hills' 142–6: 'Those who alone thy towers behold / Quivering through aërial gold . . . would imagine not they were / Sepulchres'; cp. *PU* I 778: 'Dream visions of aërial joy, and call the monster Love'; and III ii 17: 'the aërial ice clings over it'. *merriment.*] merriment . . . *Reiman (1977)*. This ellipsis is recorded in the transcript of *Hunt MS* in *MYR* viii 215 but its existence in the MS is doubtful.

30   But flew from brain to brain, — such glee was ours —
    Charged with light memories of remembered hours,
    None slow enough for sadness; till we came
    Homeward, which always makes the spirit tame.
    This day had been cheerful but cold, and now
35   The sun was sinking, and the wind also.
    Our talk grew somewhat serious, as may be
    Talk interrupted with such raillery
    As mocks itself, because it cannot scorn
    The thoughts it would extinguish: — 'twas forlorn
40   Yet pleasing, such as once, so poets tell,
    The devils held within the dales of Hell
    Concerning God, freewill and destiny:
    Of all that earth has been or yet may be,

30. *glee*] 'Mirth, joy, rejoicing'. The word was revived in the late eighteenth century after falling out of use. Cp. Goldsmith, *Deserted Village* 201: 'Full well they laugh'd with counterfeited glee'. Bowles uses the word frequently as does William Hayley, especially in his ballads. The word has overtones, therefore, of sentimentalism and Della Cruscan poetry, and is reminiscent of Leigh Hunt; cp. Hunt, *Hero and Leander* 116: 'breathed with glee' and *R&H* 88–9: 'laughed with the glee / Of light and unsuspecting infancy.' *ours* –] ours, *1824*. According to the punctuation of *1824* 'glee' is 'Charged with light memories'; in *Hunt MS* 'the swift thought' or the characters' brains are 'charged'. The dash is very clear in *Hunt MS*. In *Nbk 6* p. 64 the draft reads 'But flew from brain to brain / Charged' suggesting that 'such glee was ours' was inserted as a parenthesis.

32. *None slow*] None deep *Nbk 6, Nbk 11*.

36–9. *Our talk . . . extinguish*] 'Our talk grew quite serious, as may be the case when talk is interrupted by the sort of humour which turns its ironies against itself, finding that humour cannot dismiss the thoughts which it is trying to banish from the mind.' In *Nbk 6* 'Our talk . . . mocks itself' is drafted in pencil and a version of the remainder of line 39 added in pen: 'rather than that it scorns'. The passage is redrafted in pen on the same page.

38. *mocks itself*] Cp. *PU* I 260: 'Such despair as mocks itself with smiles'. *scorn*] Frequent in S. and ambivalent. 'Scorn' is both tyrannical and a possible means of resisting tyranny. Cp. lines 354–6 and 'To a Skylark' 91–2: 'Yet if we could scorn / Hate, and pride, and fear'.

40. *tell,*] *1824*; tell *Hunt MS*.

41. *dales*] vales *Nbk 11*.

41–5. *The devils held . . . may achieve*] Cp. *Paradise Lost* ii 555–61:
      In discourse more sweet
  (For eloquence the soul, song charms the sense)
  Others apart sat on a hill retired,
  In thoughts more elevate, and reasoned high
  Of providence, foreknowledge, will, and fate,
  Fixed fate, free will, foreknowledge absolute,
  And found no end, in wand'ring mazes lost.

42. *destiny:*] destiny. *1824*. Mary's punctuation clarifies the syntax, beginning a new sentence at line 43, whose main verb is 'We descanted'. *Hunt MS* is less accurate and more fluid – 'Of all that earth' follows 'freewill and destiny' as a further subject; its relation to 'We descanted' emerges only as one reads on.

All that vain men imagine or believe,
45 Or hope can paint or suffering may achieve,
We descanted, and I (for ever still
Is it not wise to make the best of ill?)
Argued against despondency, but pride
Made my companion take the darker side.
50 The sense that he was greater than his kind
Had struck, methinks, his eagle spirit blind
By gazing on its own exceeding light.
— Meanwhile the sun paused ere it should alight,
Over the horizon of the mountains; — Oh
55 How beautiful is sunset, when the glow
Of Heaven descends upon a land like thee,
Thou Paradise of exiles, Italy!
Thy mountains, seas and vineyards and the towers
Of cities they encircle! — it was ours
60 To stand on thee, beholding it; and then
Just where we had dismounted the Count's men
Were waiting for us with the gondola. —

44. At this point in *Nbk 6* the draft overlaps with drafts of 'Stanzas Written in Dejection – December 1818, near Naples'; 'Stanzas' must have been drafted before *J&M* which is written around them. See GM, 'The Draft and the Meaning', 65–6, arguing from this for a later date of composition, after December 1818. Cp. lines 525–47 and note.

45. may] can *1824.*

46. descanted] Meaning 'discussed freely'; more usually 'descanted upon', not 'descanted of'.

46–7. still . . . ill] Cp. lines 203–4.

50. sense . . . kind] Cp. *Preface* 6ff.: 'he derives, from a comparison' etc.

51. struck . . . blind] Cp. S.'s description of Coleridge in 'Letter to Maria Gisborne' 202–8:

> he who sits obscure
> In the exceeding lustre and the pure
> Intense irradiation of a mind
> Which, with its own internal lightning blind,
> Flags wearily through darkness and despair –
> A cloud-encircled meteor of the air,
> A hooded eagle among blinking owls.

Cp. also Apollo's speech in *PU* III ii 13–14: 'his eyes / Which gazed on the undazzling sun, now blinded'; and Byron, 'The Lament of Tasso' 1–2: 'Long years! – It tries the thrilling frame to bear / And eagle-spirit of a child of Song'.

53. alight,] alight *1824.* In *Nbk 6*, line 53 first read: 'And some such thought I spoke while the [?sunlight]'.

54. Oh] Oh! *1824. MYR* viii 215 transcribes 'oh' but the MS reading (*Hunt MS* 3, line 16) appears to be 'Oh'.

57. Paradise of exiles] S. remembered the phrase; see his letter to Ollier, 6 March 1820 (*L* ii 174).

60. To . . . and] *Nbk 6* first read: 'To stand beneath the dome for ever'.

As those who pause on some delightful way
Though bent on pleasant pilgrimage, we stood
65   Looking upon the evening and the flood
Which lay between the city and the shore
Paved with the image of the sky . . . the hoar
And aery Alps towards the North appeared
Through mist, an heaven-sustaining bulwark reared
70   Between the East and West; and half the sky
Was roofed with clouds of rich emblazonry

63–4. As those . . . we stood] The brief, elegant simile recalls Dante; see *Purgatorio* ii 10–12: 'Noi eravam lunghesso mare ancora, / come gente che pensa a suo cammino, / che va col cuore e col corpo dimora.' Cary translates: 'Meanwhile we linger'd by the water's brink, / Like men, who, musing on their road, in thought / Journey, while motionless the body rests.' (Cary, *The Vision* (1814), 'Purgatory' ii 10–12).

67. Paved with the image of the sky] Cp. *L* ii 42: 'Venice is a wonderfully fine city . . . the silent streets are paved with water', 'Lines Written among the Euganean Hills' 97–9: 'Amphitrite's destined halls / Which her hoary sire now paves / With his blue and beaming waves' and 'Ode to Naples' 106–7: 'The Sea / Which paves the desert streets of Venice'. Other travellers to Venice saw similar effects: 'gliding over the *Lagune*, whose surface unruffled by the slightest breeze, was as smooth as the most polished glass' (*Eustace* i 64); 'There is a glorious City in the Sea. / The Sea is in the broad, the narrow streets, / Ebbing and flowing; and the salt sea-weed / Clings to the marble of her palaces' (Samuel Rogers, *Italy*, 'Venice' 1–4). Lady Morgan sees in Venice 'a gorgeous construction of marble, resting on the undulating surface of the ocean, whose waves impress the tesselated pavements of its mightiest fabrics' (*Italy*, 2 vols (1830) ii 452). *sky . . .*] Ellipses are frequent in *Hunt MS*, especially in the Maniac's speeches. S. uses three dots on most occasions, sometimes four and sometimes only two. This text standardises ellipses to three dots; where S.'s MS variants seem significant, they have been noted.

67–70. the hoar . . . West] The Alps stretch from the eastern to the western horizon. Julian's is a familiar 'station' for the educated traveller; cp. line 87. S. may be suggesting a meeting of contradictory qualities in 'hoar' and 'aery'; cp. W. L. Bowles, 'Shakspeare' 7–8: 'Called by thy magic from the hoary deep, / Aërial forms should in bright troops ascend'.

70–9. and half the sky . . . peakèd isles] Julian turns to the west, towards the setting sun that appears to sink among the 'famous Euganean Hills'. They are a famous tourist attraction because Petrarch is buried there. Cp. the descriptions of sunrise in *PU* II i 18–19: 'the orange light of widening morn / Beyond the purple mountains' and in 'Lines Written among the Euganean Hills' 76–82:

> till th'eastern heaven
> Bursts, and then, as clouds of even,
> Flecked with fire and azure, lie
> In the unfathomable sky,
> So their plumes of purple grain,
> Starred with drops of golden rain,
> Gleam above the sunlight woods,

71. emblazonry] In the period, with a heraldic and military sense; cp. Wordsworth, *The White Doe of Rylstone* iii 91: 'The Banner in all its dread Emblazonry' and *Paradise Lost* ii 511–13: 'him [Satan] round / A globe of fiery seraphim enclosed / With bright emblazonry, and horrent arms'; also with the sense of 'Verbal amplification or embellishment'. The more usual modern sense, 'Display of brilliant colours; brilliant pictorial representation' is first cited by *OED* in 1827.

Dark purple at the zenith, which still grew
Down the steep West into a wondrous hue
Brighter than burning gold, even to the rent
75   Where the swift sun yet paused in his descent
Among the many-folded hills: — they were
Those famous Euganean hills, which bear
As seen from Lido through the harbour piles
The likeness of a clump of peakèd isles —
80   And then — as if the Earth and Sea had been
Dissolved into one lake of fire, were seen
Those mountains towering as from waves of flame
Around the vaporous sun, from which there came
The inmost purple spirit of light, and made
85   Their very peaks transparent. 'Ere it fade,'
Said my companion, 'I will show you soon
A better station' — so, o'er the lagoon
We glided, and from that funereal bark
I leaned, and saw the city, and could mark
90   How from their many isles in evening's gleam
Its temples and its palaces did seem
Like fabrics of enchantment piled to heaven.
I was about to speak, when — 'We are even
Now at the point I meant,' said Maddalo,
95   And bade the gondolieri cease to row.

76. *many-folded*] *Nbk 11, Locock 1911*; many folded *Hunt MS, 1824, Forman 1876–7*. In *Nbk 6* the second word is unclear but there is no hyphen. See, however, *PU* II i 201: 'Through the many-folded mountains'.

79. *peakèd*] Two syllables. A commonplace of eighteenth-century fine writing; cp. Mrs Radcliffe, *The Italian*, ch. 13: 'Its peaked head towered far above every neighbouring summit'; and Caroline Oliphant, 'The Boat Song o' the Clyde': 'How soft an' grand in azure hue / Arran's peakèd hills we view'. The word perhaps creates a clash of register with 'clump'.

83. *vaporous*] Cp. 'Lines Written among the Euganean Hills' 91–2: 'The waveless plain of Lombardy / Bounded by the vaporous air'. Common in S. and generally without derogatory connotation; cp. Coleridge 'Ode to the Departing Year' 160–1: 'the vaporous passions that bedim / God's Image' and Bacon *The Advancement of Learning* II viii §3: 'high and vaporous imaginations . . . shall beget hopes and beliefs of strange and impossible shapes'.

87. *station*] 'A point at which one stands or may stand to obtain a view' (*OED* def. 7c).

88. *that funereal bark*] that most ghastly bark *Nbk 6*. Cp. *L* ii 42: 'The gondolas themselves are things of a most romantic and picturesque appearance; I can only compare them to moths of which a coffin might have been the chrysalis.'

91–2. *Its temples . . . enchantment*] Cp. *Tempest* IV i 151–2: 'the baseless fabric of this vision, / The cloud-capp'd towers, the gorgeous palaces'.

93–5. *We . . . row*] Byron seems to have been fond of showing visitors impressive views of Venice: 'I shall take him [Charles Hanson] to ride at the Lido . . . I will show him the Lazaretto which is not far off you know – & looks nearer than it is' (Byron to Hobhouse, 11 November 1818, *Byron L&J* vii 77).

'Look, Julian, on the West and listen well
If you hear not a deep and heavy bell.'
I looked, and saw between us and the Sun
A building on an island; such a one
100   As age to age might add, for uses vile;
A windowless, deformed and dreary pile
And on the top an open tower, where hung
A bell, which in the radiance swayed and swung.
We could just hear its hoarse and iron tongue.
105   The broad sun sunk behind it, and it tolled
In strong and black relief . . . 'What we behold
Shall be the madhouse and its belfry tower,'
Said Maddalo, 'and ever at this hour
Those who may cross the water hear that bell
110   Which calls the maniacs each one from his cell
To vespers.' — 'As much skill as need to pray

96. *Julian*] Yorick *Nbk 6*. Probably, more closely related to Sterne than *Hamlet*; *Mary Jnl* records S. re-reading *Tristram Shandy* and *A Sentimental Journey* in 1818; cp. *L* ii 114, 'On Love' (drafted July 1818), and *Nbk 6*, p. 9: 'Sterne says that if he were in a desart he would love some cypress'. Sterne evoked sensibility; cp. J. Scott, 'An Essay on Painting', *Poetical Works* (1782) 293, addressing a painter: 'To *Sterne*'s soft Maniac let thy hand impart / The languid cheek, the look that pierc'd his heart, / When to her Virgin Saint the vesper song she rais'd, / Or earnest view'd him as he sat and gaz'd.' Scott refers to the chapter 'Maria' in Sterne, *A Sentimental Journey* vol. ii where Yorick (like Julian and Maddalo) searches out and is moved by a 'disorder'd maid' who pipes an evening-hymn to the Virgin. Cp. *Preface* 31, *The Maniac* and note.

99. *such a one*] such an one *1824*, *Nbk 6*.

100. *as age to age might add*] Meant literally: 'as one age might bequeath to the next'. In *Nbk 6* the draft read first 'As age on age might build'. *uses vile*] See *Childe Harold* iv 91–135.

101. *windowless*] The hospital on San Servolo (see line 214) has many windows; Robert Browning suggested S. was referring to the penitentiary on the islet of San Clemente, lying west of Venice (see *Locock 1911* i 586). Perhaps the uncertainty corresponds to S.'s elision of madness and criminal punishment in *J&M*; cp. 'The Tower of Famine' 5–7: 'built / Upon some prison-homes, whose dwellers rave / For bread, and gold, and blood'. *pile*] Meaning a 'lofty mass of buildings, a large building or edifice' (*OED sb 3*, def. 4a) but drawing attention to Venice's foundations (*OED sb 1* def. 3a). Cp. 78, 92 for S.'s use of the word and its cognates in different senses.

103–4. *bell . . . tongue*] Cp. Wordsworth, *Excursion* viii 167, 169–7, describing a factory: 'an unnatural light / . . . Breaks from a many-windowed fabric huge; / And at the appointed hour a bell is heard, / Of harsher import than the curfew-knoll'.

105. *sunk*] sank *1824*. Hunt MS, *Nbk 6* and *Nbk 11* all read 'sunk'; the vowel echoes not only 'sun' but the rhyme-words 'hung', 'swung' and 'tongue' of lines 102–4.

106. *relief . . .*] *MYR* viii 217 transcribes 'relief. –'. The MS is unclear but appears to have an ellipsis in which two of the dots have run together, forming what looks like a dash. This occurs again at line 357 (Hunt MS 15, *MYR* viii 221). An ellipsis suggests a pause and this suits Maddalo's desire to create an effect.

107. *Shall*] The tense is colloquial ('That'll be the madhouse') and portentous-sounding, as if Maddalo is inviting Julian to imagine it were a madhouse. Cp. lines 120–2.

108. *ever*] even *1824*. Probably Mary's misreading of S.'s hand.

In thanks or hope for their dark lot have they
To their stern maker,' I replied. 'O ho!
You talk as in years past,' said Maddalo.
115 ''Tis strange men change not. You were ever still
Among Christ's flock a perilous infidel,
A wolf for the meek lambs — if you can't swim
Beware of Providence.' I looked on him,
But the gay smile had faded in his eye.
120 'And such, —' he cried, 'is our mortality,
And this must be the emblem and the sign
Of what should be eternal and divine! —
And like that black and dreary bell, the soul
Hung in a heaven-illumined tower, must toll
125 Our thoughts and our desires to meet below
Round the rent heart and pray — as madmen do;
For what? they know not, till the night of death,
As sunset that strange vision, severeth
Our memory from itself, and us from all
130 We sought and yet were baffled.' I recall
The sense of what he said, although I mar
The force of his expressions. The broad star
Of day meanwhile had sunk behind the hill
And the black bell became invisible,
135 And the red tower looked grey, and all between,

115. *Tis strange*] Maddalo was more absolute in *Nbk 6*: 'Men never change – and you were ever still'.

117–18. *A wolf . . . Providence*] Cp. John x 12: 'But he that is an hireling, and not the shepherd, whose own the sheep are not, seeth the wolf coming, and leaveth the sheep, and fleeth: and the wolf catcheth them, and scattereth the sheep', *Lycidas* 114–15: 'such as for their bellies' sake, / Creep and intrude, and climb into the fold' and *Shephearde's Calendar* May 126–7: 'Tho, under colour of shepheards, somewhile / There crept in Wolves, ful of fraude and guile'. Maddalo is teasing Julian with the thought that even such a 'wolf' as he might have to be careful, that his defiance of orthodoxy requires a degree of self-sufficiency he may not possess. This is an autobiographical joke as well because Byron could swim and Shelley could not. In *Nbk 6*, 118 is the last on page 79; the bottom of the sheet is filled with a sketch of a sailing-boat.

119. *in*] from *1824*.

120. *mortality,*] mortality *Hunt MS*; mortality; *1824*.

124. *heaven-illumined*] Cp. James Thomson, 'Seraphina' 13–16: '[her] eyes dispense / A mild and gracious influence; / Such as in visions angels shed / Around the heaven-illumined head.' *toll*] In a transitive sense, 'to summon'; cp. Keats, 'Ode to a Nightingale' 71–2: 'like a bell / To toll me back'.

126. *rent*] 'Torn or ragged'; cp. *R&H* (no. 144) 790–1: 'like flowers delicate and fair, / On its rent boughs'. *do;*] *1824*. do *Hunt MS, Forman 1876–7*. In *Hunt MS*, the line is too long for the page-width and 'do' is inserted below 'madmen'; hence, probably, the lack of punctuation.

The churches, ships and palaces were seen
Huddled in gloom; — into the purple sea
The orange hues of heaven sunk silently.
We hardly spoke, and soon the gondola
140   Conveyed me to my lodgings by the way.

   The following morn was rainy, cold and dim;
Ere Maddalo arose, I called on him
— And whilst I waited, with his child I played:
A lovelier toy sweet Nature never made,
145   A serious, subtle, wild, yet gentle being,
Graceful without design and unforeseeing;
With eyes — oh speak not of her eyes! — which seem
Twin mirrors of Italian heaven, yet gleam
With such deep meaning, as we never see
150   But in the human countenance. With me
She was a special favourite: I had nursed
Her fine and feeble limbs when she came first
To this bleak world; and she yet seemed to know
On second sight her ancient playfellow,
155   Less changed than she was by six months or so —
For after her first shyness was worn out

137. *Huddled in gloom*] Cp. Byron, *Childe Harold* iv 112–14: 'Venice, lost and won . . . Sinks, like a sea-weed, into whence she rose'.

140. *lodgings*] lodging *1824*.

143. *with . . . played*] romped in his saloon *canc. Nbk 6*. The child is usually identified with Allegra, Byron's daughter by Claire Clairmont, whose custody was the reason for S.'s visiting Venice in August 1818. Allegra died on 19 April 1822 of typhus fever, aged five.

145. *serious,*] *1824, Forman 1876–7*; serious *Hunt MS*. S. may have intended a double epithet: 'serious-subtle'. The mixture of qualities recalls S.'s description of Allegra, 15 August 1821: 'she has a contemplative seriousness which, mixed with her excessive vivacity, which has not yet deserted her, has a very peculiar effect in a child' (*L* ii 334). See *PU* II i 114–17 and note.

147. *eyes*] S. often admired Allegra's eyes: 'She yet retains the beauty of her deep blue eyes' (*L* ii 334).

151. *She . . . favourite*] Dear was she as mine own *canc. Nbk 6*. Cp. *Nbk 5*: '[Allegra] better with me than him – Infants dont know their father from a stranger' (*BSM* iii 27).

154. *her ancient playfellow*] S.'s fondness for and success with children is well-documented; see *Peck* ii 237.

155. *Six months or so*] Allegra had been sent from Milan to Venice in April 1818.

155–6. *Less . . . out*] These lines do not appear in *Nbk 6* which reads at this point:
          and now she seemed to know
      On second sight her ancient play fellow
      We sate there rolling billiard balls about
      And as they struck she laughd with sudden shout
      When the Count entered
The fourth line is crossed out.

671

We sat there, rolling billiard balls about,
When the Count entered. — Salutations past,
'The words you spoke last night might well have cast
160   A darkness on my spirit — if man be
The passive thing you say, I should not see
Much harm in the religions and old saws
(Though I may never own such leaden laws)
Which break a teachless nature to the yoke:
165   Mine is another faith' — thus much I spoke
And noting he replied not, added: 'See
This lovely child, blithe, innocent and free;
She spends a happy time with little care
While we to such sick thoughts subjected are
170   As came on you last night — it is our will
That thus enchains us to permitted ill —
We might be otherwise — we might be all
We dream of happy, high, majestical.

157. about,] *1824*; about *Hunt MS*; about. *Reiman (1977)*.

157–8. Hunt MS and *Nbk 6* leave the exact syntax uncertain. *Reiman (1977)* makes 158 the start of a new sentence; *1824* and *Locock 1911* delay the new sentence until after 'entered'. The *Reiman (1977)* punctuation shifts emphasis from the Count's interruption to his dilatoriness: when, finally, he appears, Julian can begin the long-delayed discussion. Line 142 has already indicated Julian's sense of being the earlier riser. The disadvantage of *Reiman (1977)* is a loss of drama; Maddalo's entrance is no longer sudden and unannounced.

158. entered. –] entered – *Hunt MS*; entered. *1824, Locock 1911   past,*] *Locock 1911*; past *Hunt MS*; past: *1824*; o'er *canc. Nbk 6*. In contemporary usage 'past' was a possible spelling of 'passed' but S.'s meaning is clarified by the nbk's cancelled draft: once salutations were over, Julian spoke.

163. I] *I 1824, Locock 1911*.

170. As came on you] As you described *Nbk 6, canc. Hunt MS*.

170–3. it is . . . We dream of] A recurrent thought in S.; cp. *PU* III iv 198–9: 'Passionless? no – yet free from guilt or pain / Which were, for his will made, or suffered them' and 'Ode to Liberty' 241–5:

> He who taught man to vanquish whatsoever
> Can be between the cradle and the grave
> Crowned him the King of Life. Oh, vain endeavour!
> If on his own high will, a willing slave
> He has enthroned the oppression and the oppressor.

173. We dream of happy, high] That we can think high *canc. Nbk 6* We dream of, happy, high *1824*; We dream of happy –, high *Nbk 6*. Punctuation in *Nbk 6* suggests the sense: 'all which we dream of when happy'; *1824* clarifies the lines so they mean: 'all the things we dream of being: happy, high, majestic'. *Hunt MS* punctuation leaves room for the sense suggested by cancelled *Nbk 6* wording that our dreams of happiness, like high thoughts, help create happiness for us.   *majestical*] Kelvin Everest points out the contradictions inherent in Julian's using this word: 'calling into radical service the vocabulary of the very social structure that obstructs the realization of his ideals' (*Shelley Revalued* 74). Cp. 'Lines Written among the Euganean Hills' 73: 'The sun's uprise majestical'.

Where is the love, beauty and truth we seek
175 But in our mind? and if we were not weak
Should we be less in deed than in desire?'
'Aye, if we were not weak — and we aspire
How vainly to be strong!' said Maddalo,
'You talk Utopia.' 'It remains to know,'
180 I then rejoined, 'and those who try may find
How strong the chains are which our spirit bind,
Brittle perchance as straw . . . We are assured
Much may be conquered, much may be endured
Of what degrades and crushes us. We know
185 That we have power over ourselves to do
And suffer — what, we know not till we try;
But something nobler than to live and die —
So taught those kings of old philosophy
Who reigned, before Religion made men blind;
190 And those who suffer with their suffering kind

174–5. Where . . . mind?] Echoing Byron in *Childe Harold* iv 37–43: 'The beings of the mind are not of clay; / Essentially immortal, they create / And multiply in us a brighter ray / And more beloved existence'. S. and Byron had discussed the poem at the meeting which prompted the poem: 'We talked of literary matters, his fourth Canto which he says is very good, & indeed repeated some stanzas of great energy to me' (*L* ii 37). Julian is answering Maddalo with Maddalo's (Byron's) own opinions and this fits, perhaps, with S.'s desire at the time that Byron should live up to his professed ideals. See headnote.

175. mind] minds *1824.*

176. less . . . desire] Cp. Lady Macbeth: 'Art thou afeard / To be the same in thine own act and valour / As thou art in desire?' (*Macbeth* I vii 39–41).

177. if we were not] *1824*; if were not *Hunt MS.*

179. You talk] This is *canc. Nbk 6.* Utopia.' 'It] *1824* inserts a paragraph break between the two speeches here and, from this point on, wherever there is a change of speaker (except lines 544–6). Earlier conversational exchanges remain (in *1824*) within verse-paragraphs. Neither *Hunt MS* nor *Nbk 6* include paragraph-breaks within the poem's passages of dialogue. know] *1824*; see *Hunt MS.*

183. endured] As in lines 174–5, Julian may be echoing *Childe Harold*; cp. iv 186–9: 'if they . . . Endure and shrink not, we of nobler clay / May temper it to bear', and iii 649–66.

184–9. We know . . . blind] Julian's rousing speech recalls Ulysses' 'orazion picciola' in Dante's *Inferno* xxvi 118–20: 'Considerate la vostra semenza: / fatti non foste a viver come bruti, / ma per seguir virtute e canoscenza' ('Call to mind from whence ye sprang: / Ye were not form'd to live the life of brutes, / But virtue to pursue and knowledge high' Cary, *The Vision* (1814), 'Hell' xxvi 115–17).

184. degrades] Cp. *Preface* 5. *degraded* and note, line 345, *The Cenci* III ii 64, and 'Sonnet from Cavalcanti' 9. Apart from these, S. nowhere uses the word as a verb.

186. what] what *1824.*

188. those] the *1824.*

190–1. And those . . . religion] Ambiguous. The principle sense is: 'The same teaching is given by those who are compassionate, even if such people believe their faith in humanity has a religious basis.' Julian claims that truly religious people agree with him and differ only in

Yet feel their faith, religion.' 'My dear friend,'
Said Maddalo, 'my judgment will not bend
To your opinion, though I think you might
Make such a system refutation-tight
195   As far as words go. I knew one like you
Who to this city came some months ago
With whom I argued in this sort, and he
Is now gone mad, — and so he answered me, —
Poor fellow! but if you would like to go
200   We'll visit him, and his wild talk will show
How vain are such aspiring theories.'
'I hope to prove the induction otherwise,
And that a want of that true theory, still
Which seeks a "soul of goodness" in things ill,
205   Or in himself or others has thus bowed
His being — there are some by nature proud,
Who patient in all else demand but this:
To love and be beloved with gentleness,
And being scorned, what wonder if they die
210   Some living death? This is not destiny
But man's own wilful ill.' As thus I spoke
Servants announced the gondola, and we

---

claiming particular religious beliefs to be the source of something universal. S. makes a similar argument about Christian poets in *A Defence of Poetry*: 'The distorted notions of invisible things which Dante and his rival Milton have idealized, are merely the mask and the mantle in which these great poets walk through eternity.' A secondary sense to the lines is made apparent by S.'s drafts: 'To those who feel for their unhappy kind / This creed is as religion' (canc. *Nbk 6*).

191. Yet feel their faith, religion] Find such faith religion *Nbk 6*. *their*] this *1824*.

201. aspiring theories] Cp. the sarcastic use of a similar phrase in J. H. Frere's reactionary poem, 'New Morality' 101–2: 'Shall a name, a word, a sound, control / Th'aspiring thought, and cramp th'expansive soul?' *theories.'*] Cp. line 179 and note.

204. "soul of goodness"] Alluding to *Henry V* IV i 3–4: 'There is some soul of goodness in things evil / Would men observingly distill it out'.

206–10. some . . . living death] Perhaps a memory of Coleridge; see his 'The Pains of Sleep' (1816), 51–2: 'To be beloved is all I need, / And whom I love, I love indeed.' Coleridge's 'Ancient Mariner' focuses on 'The Night-mare LIFE-IN-DEATH' (193).

208–9. To love . . . scorned] Cp.: 'To love, to be beloved suddenly became an insatiable famine of his nature which the wide circle of the universe . . . appeared too narrow and confined to satiate.' (*The Assassins* ch. 1, *Prose Works* i 129).

210. This] *1824*; this *Hunt MS*.

211. But man's] *Nbk 6* has at this point: 'At least tho all the past cd. not have been / Other than as it was – yet things foreseen / Reason and Love may force beneath their yoke / Warned by a fate foregone – as [thus] [?I] spoke'. The exclusion of these lines produced the absence of any rhyme for 'spoke' (211). *As*] *1824*; as *Hunt MS*.

Through the fast-falling rain and high-wrought sea
Sailed to the island where the madhouse stands.
215 We disembarked. The clap of tortured hands,
Fierce yells and howlings and lamentings keen
And laughter where complaint had merrier been,
Moans, shrieks and curses and blaspheming prayers
Accosted us. We climbed the oozy stairs
220 Into an old court-yard. I heard on high
Then, fragments of most touching melody,
But looking up saw not the singer there —
Through the black bars in the tempestuous air
I saw, like weeds on a wrecked palace growing,
225 Long tangled locks flung wildly forth, and flowing,
Of those who on a sudden were beguiled
Into strange silence, and looked forth and smiled

---

214. the island] Identified with San Servolo (also known as San Servilio) used as an asylum from 1725 with a hospital and church built 1734–59.

215–19. The clap of tortured hands . . . Accosted us] Cp. Byron, *The Lament of Tasso* iii 3–4: 'hark! the lash and the increasing howl, / And the half-inarticulate blasphemy', and iv 9–10: 'Where cries reply to curses, shrieks to blows, / And each is tortured in his separate hell'; cp. Dante, *Inferno* iii 22–8:

> quivi sospiri, pianti e alti guai
> risonovan per l'aere sanza stelle [. . . .]
> Diverse lingue, orribili favelle,
> parole di dolore, accenti d'ira,
> voci alte e fioche, e suon di man con elle
> facevano un tumulto

Cary's translation reads:

> Here sighs with lamentations and loud moans
> Resounded through the air pierc'd by no star [. . . .]
> Various tongues,
> Horrible languages, outcries of woe,
> Accents of anger, voices deep and hoarse,
> With hands together smote that swell'd the sounds,
> Made up a tumult (Cary, *The Vision* (1814) 'Hell' iii 21–7)

218. Moans . . . prayers] *1824* omits this line. *Forman 1876–7* suggests the omission is a transcription error but it may have been cautious censorship by Mary.

219. oozy] 'Exuding moisture; damp with exuded or deposited moisture' (*OED* def. 4). This line is cited. Cp. Milton, *Lycidas* 175: 'With nectar pure his oozy locks he laves'; Keats, *Isabella*, 411–12, 'divine liquids come with odorous ooze / Through the cold serpent-pipe'. S. is stressing also the amphibious quality of Venice; see line 5 and 'Ode to the West Wind', 38–40: 'while far below / The sea-blooms and the oozy woods which wear / The sapless foliage of the ocean'.

224. weeds . . . growing] Cp. *Adonais* 435–7: 'where its wrecks like shattered mountains rise, / And flowering weeds, and fragrant copses dress / The bones'.

226–7. those . . . silence] Wordsworthian perhaps; cp. 'There was a Boy' 16–19: 'when there came a pause / Of silence such as baffled his best skill: / Then sometimes, in that silence, while he hung / Listening'.

Hearing sweet sounds. — Then I: 'Methinks there were
A cure of these with patience and kind care
230   If music can thus move . . . but what is he
Whom we seek here?' 'Of his sad history
I know but this,' said Maddalo, 'he came
To Venice a dejected man, and fame
Said he was wealthy, or he had been so;
235   Some thought the loss of fortune wrought him woe;
But he was ever talking in such sort
As you do — far more sadly — he seemed hurt,
Even as a man with his peculiar wrong,
To hear but of the oppression of the strong,
240   Or those absurd deceits (I think with you
In some respects, you know) which carry through
The excellent impostors of this earth
When they outface detection — he had worth,
Poor fellow! but a humourist in his way.' —
245   'Alas, what drove him mad?' 'I cannot say;
A Lady came with him from France, and when
She left him and returned, he wandered then
About yon lonely isles of desert sand
Till he grew wild — he had no cash or land
250   Remaining, — the police had brought him here —
Some fancy took him and he would not bear
Removal; so I fitted up for him

230. move . . .] move . . *Hunt MS*. See line 67 and note.

236–9. But he . . . strong] Cp. Wordsworth, *The Excursion* ii 65–8, characterising the Wanderer: 'the poor man held dispute / With his own mind, unable to subdue / Impatience through inaptness to perceive / General distress in his particular lot'.

237. far] but *1824*.

238. peculiar] Not 'odd' but 'personal, specific, unique'.

243. detection] Cp. Horatio plotting against Claudius: 'If 'a steal aught the whilst this play is playing, / And scape detecting, I will pay the theft' (*Hamlet* III ii 88–9). *worth,*] *1824*; worth *Hunt MS*.

244. humourist] Either someone 'subject to humours . . . fantastical or whimsical' or someone 'facetious or comical' (*OED*). After Maddalo's emphasis on the Maniac's seriousness and sensitivity, 'humourist' concedes that he had a sense of humour (though 'in his way' suggests a hint of condescension).

245. Alas,] *1824*; Alas *Hunt MS*. *1824* places Julian's speech on a separate line; see lines 179, 191, 201.

250. Remaining, –] Remaining: – *1824*. Mary's punctuation here (and at line 252) makes Maddalo more coolly rational whereas *Hunt MS* suggests his kindness is an impulsive reaction to a mass of factors.

251. Some] *1824*; – Some *Hunt MS*.

252. Removal;] Removal, *1824*.

Those rooms beside the sea, to please his whim,
And sent him busts and books and urns for flowers
255 Which had adorned his life in happier hours,
And instruments of music — you may guess
A stranger could do little more or less
For one so gentle and unfortunate,
And those are his sweet strains which charm the weight
260 From madmen's chains, and make this hell appear
A heaven of sacred silence, hushed to hear.' —
'Nay, this was kind of you — he had no claim,
As the world says.' — 'None — but the very same
Which I on all mankind were I as he
265 Fallen to such deep reverse; — his melody
Is interrupted now — we hear the din
Of madmen, shriek on shriek again begin;
Let us now visit him; after this strain
He ever communes with himself again,
270 And sees nor hears not any.' Having said
These words we called the keeper, and he led
To an apartment opening on the sea. —
There the poor wretch was sitting mournfully

252–8. I fitted up . . . unfortunate] Cp. *Epipsychidion* 515–24:
> And I have fitted up some chambers there
> Looking towards the golden Eastern air [. . .]
> I have sent books and music there, and all
> Those instruments with which high spirits call
> The future from its cradle, and the past
> Out of its grave

Cp. also Glenarvon's kindness (also modelled on Byron's) in Lady Caroline Lamb, *Glenarvon*, 3 vols (1816) ii 88–9: 'when a singular and terrific inmate appeared also at the Priory – a maniac! who was however welcomed with the rest of the strange assemblage, and a room immediately allotted for his reception'.

253. whim,] Forman 1876–7; whim *Hunt MS*; whim; *1824*.

263. None – but] None but *1824*; None, but *Nbk 6*.

265. deep] sad *Nbk 6*.

266–7. we hear . . . begin] Cp. Cowper, *The Task* ii 662–5:
> 'tis a fearful spectacle to see
> So many maniacs dancing in their chains.
> They gaze upon the links that hold them fast
> With eyes of anguish, execrate their lot,
> Then shake them in despair, and dance again!

270. nor hears] and hears *1824*.

273–4. sitting . . . piano] Cp. Hogg ii 549–50: '[in 1813, S.] played several times on the piano . . . an exceedingly simple air, which . . . his earliest love was wont to play for him'. Peck suggests from this that in *J&M* 'we have interblended with memories of his first marriage and its tragic consummation, other reminiscences of that earlier love affair [with Harriet Grove], which never wholly faded from his thought' (*Peck* ii 104).

Near a piano, his pale fingers twined
275　One with the other, and the ooze and wind
Rushed through an open casement, and did sway
His hair, and starred it with the brackish spray;
His head was leaning on a music book
And he was muttering, and his lean limbs shook;
280　His lips were pressed against a folded leaf
In hue too beautiful for health, and grief
Smiled in their motions as they lay apart —
As one who wrought from his own fervid heart
The eloquence of passion, soon he raised
285　His sad meek face and eyes lustrous and glazed
And spoke — sometimes as one who wrote and thought
His words might move some heart that heeded not
If sent to distant lands; and then as one
Reproaching deeds never to be undone
290　With wondering self-compassion; then his speech
Was lost in grief, and then his words came each
Unmodulated, cold, expressionless, —
But that from one jarred accent you might guess
It was despair made them so uniform:
295　And all the while the loud and gusty storm
Hissed through the window, and we stood behind

275. *ooze*] rain *canc. Nbk 6.* Cp. lines 3–7, 219, and *Don Juan* II xxv 7–8: 'The waves oozing through the port-hole made / His berth a little damp, and him afraid.'

279. *shook;*] *Nbk 6* inserts 'I could not see his face, but [?thro] dark [?hair] / There gleamed a bloodless cheek, yet it was fair'.

280. *a folded*] the music *Nbk 6.*

280–2. *lips . . . motions*] Cp. S.'s self-portrait in *Adonais* 291–7:
a light spear . . .
Vibrated, as the ever-beating heart
Shook the weak hand that grasped it; of that crew
He came the last, neglected and apart;
A head-abandoned deer struck by the hunter's dart.

281–2. Echoing *Twelfth Night* II iv 111–14:
She pin'd in thought;
And with a green and yellow melancholy
She sat like Patience on a monument,
Smiling at grief.

282–4. *Hunt MS* makes the simile connect both forward and back: the smiling grief visible in the Maniac's lips expresses his passion and so does his raising his eyes and speaking.

287–94. *His . . . uniform:*] Not in *Nbk 6.*

289–90. *Reproaching . . . self-compassion*] Cp. Wordsworth, *The Borderers* 1542: ''Tis done, and in the after vacancy / We wonder at ourselves like men betrayed'.

292. *Unmodulated, cold, expressionless, –*] *Locock 1911*; Unmodulated, cold, expressionless; *Hunt MS*; Unmodulated and expressionless, – *1824.*

Stealing his accents from the envious wind
Unseen. I yet remember what he said
Distinctly: such impression his words made.

300   'Month after month,' he cried, 'to bear this load
And as a jade urged by the whip and goad
To drag life on, which like a heavy chain
Lengthens behind with many a link of pain! —
And not to speak my grief — O not to dare
305   To give a human voice to my despair,
But live and move, and wretched thing! smile on
As if I never went aside to groan
And wear this mask of falsehood even to those
Who are most dear — not for my own repose —
310   Alas, no scorn or pain or hate could be
So heavy as that falsehood is to me —
But that I cannot bear more altered faces
Than needs must be, more changed and cold embraces,
More misery, disappointment and mistrust
315   To own me for their father . . . Would the dust
Were covered in upon my body now!

297. wind] wind, *1824*.

298–9. I yet . . . made] such impression his words made / That I remember them as if just said *Nbk 6*.

299. made.] *1824*, *Forman 1876–7* and *Reiman (1977)* all introduce a line-break here. *Hunt MS* is so small, it is hard to be certain that a space has been left. At lines 319–20 and 343–4 in *Hunt MS* the gap is clearer. The first word is indented however as at lines 320 and 482. In *Nbk 6*, the draft is interrupted at this point; the next two pages are blank and the poem resumes with a version of line 337 (*BSM* xv 97–101).

302–3. To drag . . . pain] Cp. Q *Mab* v 50–2: Commerce brings to an early death 'all that shares the lot of human life, / Which, poisoned body and soul, scarce drags the chain / That lengthens as it goes and clanks behind'; see also *PU* II iv 19–23:

> terror, madness, crime, remorse,
> Which from the links of the great chain of things,
> To every thought within the mind of man
> Sway and drag heavily

Medwin reports that S. (in Pisa, 1818) was 'very much affected by the sight of the convicts fettered two and two, who, escorted by soldiers, sweep the streets, and still more so by the clank of their chains' (*Locock 1911* i 587).

309–12. not for . . . But that] The intervening lines ('Alas . . . to me') are parenthetical; the Maniac says he wears a mask of falsehood not for his own peace of mind but because he could not bear the response of his loved ones to his fully-revealed misery.

310. Alas,] Alas *Hunt MS*; Alas! *1824*.

316. covered in] *OED* gives 'cover in' as a distinct usage: 'To complete the covering of (anything) by adding the upper layer or part; . . . to fill in the earth in a grave' (*v1* def. 18; first use 1726; this line is cited).

That the life ceased to toil within my brow!
And then these thoughts would at the least be fled;
Let us not fear such pain can vex the dead.

320   'What Power delights to torture us? I know
That to myself I do not wholly owe
What now I suffer, though in part I may.
Alas, none strewed sweet flowers upon the way
Where wandering heedlessly, I met pale Pain
325   My shadow, which will leave me not again —
If I have erred, there was no joy in error,
But pain and insult and unrest and terror;
I have not as some do, bought penitence
With pleasure, and a dark yet sweet offence,
330   For then, — if love and tenderness and truth
Had overlived hope's momentary youth,
My creed should have redeemed me from repenting,
But loathèd scorn and outrage unrelenting,
Met love excited by far other seeming
335   Until the end was gained . . . as one from dreaming
Of sweetest peace, I woke, and found my state
Such as it is. — —

318. least] last *1824.*
320. What . . . torture us?] Cp. Asia's question to Demogorgon, *PU* II iv 100–5:
             but who rains down
        Evil, the immedicable plague, which, while
        Man looks on his creation like a God
        And sees that it is glorious, drives him on,
        The wreck of his own will, the scorn of Earth,
        The outcast, the abandoned, the alone?
323. Alas,] Alas *Hunt MS*; Alas! *1824. sweet*] fresh *1824.* S. or Mary may have emended 'sweet' to 'fresh' or *vice versa* because 'sweet' is repeated at line 329 and 'sweetest' used at line 336.
330–7. Cp. the distress in Mary's 'The Fields of Fancy' (1819): 'I saw a wanton malignity in many parts & particularly in the mind of man that baffled me. If knowledge is the end of our being why are passions & feelings implanted in us that hurries [*sic*] us from wisdom to self-concentrated misery & narrow selfish feeling? Is it as a trial?' (*MSW* ii 356–7).
332–5. My creed . . . gained] Cp. the Maniac's beliefs to Julian's (lines 195ff., 236–7). The Maniac speaks here as a rejected lover: if, he says, he had been rejected in such a way that tenderness for the loved one survived, then he would not regret having fallen in love nor look back on it as a mistake; however, his love was met by such violent and unexpected rejection that it was destroyed. By its destruction, he says, 'the end was gained', the aims achieved, of the person whom he loved. Cp. Julian and Maddalo's discussion at lines 525–31.
334. far other seeming] A quite different appearance.
335–7. one from dreaming . . . as it is] Cp. Keats, 'La Belle Dame Sans Merci' 43–4: 'And I awoke and found me here / On the cold hill's side.'
337. Such as it is.] Cp. Julian at lines 15–17.

'O Thou, my spirit's mate
Who, for thou art compassionate and wise,
Wouldst pity me from thy most gentle eyes
340   If this sad writing thou shouldst ever see —
My secret groans must be unheard by thee,
Thou wouldst weep tears bitter as blood to know
Thy lost friend's incommunicable woe.

    'Ye few by whom my nature has been weighed
345   In friendship, let me not that name degrade
By placing on your hearts the secret load
Which crushes mine to dust. There is one road
To peace and that is truth, which follow ye!
Love sometimes leads astray to misery.
350   Yet think not though subdued — and I may well
Say that I am subdued — that the full Hell
Within me would infect the untainted breast
Of sacred nature with its own unrest;

337–43. O Thou . . . woe] The Maniac's grief at broken love recalls Lionel in *R&H* 759–79:

> there were found . . .
> These mournful verses on the ground,
> By all who read them blotted too. . . .
>
> [']I wake to weep,
> And sit through the long day gnawing the core
> Of my bitter heart, and, like a miser, keep,
> Since none in what I feel take pain or pleasure,
> To my own soul its self-consuming treasure.'

Biographical criticism has taken the Maniac to be addressing two women, his 'spirit's mate' here and the 'mockery' of lines 385ff., and then found different identities for these figures from S.'s and Byron's personal lives. N. I. White argues that both are Mary 'turned temporarily into a strange antagonistic personality by her grief' with whom S. is pleading for reconciliation (*White* ii 48). GM, from the evidence of the draft, suggests that the Maniac addresses four or more different women in turn, each of whom is initially conceived as a figure from Tasso's life ('The Draft and the Meaning', 77–82).

341. thee,] thee; *1824*.

342–3. Thou wouldst weep . . . woe] Cp. the situation reversed in *Epipsychidion* 19–20: 'I weep vain tears: blood would less bitter be, / Yet poured forth gladlier, could it profit thee.'

344. Ye] *1824* does not begin a new paragraph here.

350. Yet think not] Lines 344 to 350 appear in *Nbk 6*. Here the draft diverges, reading 'Yet think not thou subdued, as [?I] [?] / That I make peace with the worlds [tyranny]'. In the final version, the Maniac vows instead that he will not project his suffering onto the blameless, external world. *subdued*] frequent in S.; cp. 'Scenes from the "Magico Prodigioso" of Calderon' iii 134–5: 'Woman, thou hast subdued me, / Only by not owning thyself subdued.' Cp. Wordsworth, *The Excursion* i 283–4: 'by the turbulence subdued / Of his own mind' and 795 (of Margaret in the 'Ruined Cottage' section): 'Her body was subdued. In every act / . . . appeared / The careless stillness of a thinking mind / Self-occupied' and Byron, *Childe Harold* iv 199–200: 'But ever and anon of griefs subdued / There comes a token like a scorpion's sting'.

351. full] deep *canc. Hunt MS.*

As some perverted beings think to find
355   In scorn or hate a medicine for the mind
Which scorn or hate have wounded — O how vain!
The dagger heals not but may rend again . . .
Believe that I am ever still the same
In creed as in resolve, and what may tame
360   My heart, must leave the understanding free
Or all would sink in this keen agony —
Nor dream that I will join the vulgar cry,
Or with my silence sanction tyranny,
Or seek a moment's shelter from my pain
365   In any madness which the world calls gain,
Ambition or revenge or thoughts as stern
As those which make me what I am, or turn
To avarice or misanthropy or lust . . .
Heap on me soon O grave, thy welcome dust!
370   Till then the dungeon may demand its prey,
And poverty and shame may meet and say —

354–6. S.'s view that ridicule or satire were intrinsically ineffective is expressed in 'Fragment of a Satire on Satire' 36–7: 'Suffering makes suffering, ill must follow ill. / Rough words beget sad thoughts'. Cp. James Woodhouse (1735–1820), 'Ridicule' (1787) 331–4:

> True wisdom knows no raillery can restrain
> Or conquer error, by inflicting pain.
> True policy perceives that jibe and joke
> Never conciliate, constantly provoke.

See 38–9 and note. Cp. Nora Crook and Derek Guiton, *S.'s Venomed Melody* (1986) 137: 'S. refers here to the homeopathic principle, but warns against a single-minded application of it.'

356. have] hath *1824.*

357. again . . .] again. . . . *Hunt MS.*

361. in this keen] under this *1824.*

362. cry] eye *1824.*

365. gain,] gain; *1824.* Ambition, revenge and stern thoughts (366) are other kinds of 'madness', no different essentially from 'gain'.

366–7. thoughts as . . . what I am] Recalling lines 333–7. The Maniac will not adopt the same sternness or harshness as his lover displayed.

368. lust . . .] lust. . . . *Hunt MS.*

371. poverty and shame] Poverty and Shame *1824.* Cp. *Nbk 6*: 'I seem to [wander] linger on the public way / And hear Oblivion whisper Death, & say / That love-devoted youth'. The first half of both lines is cancelled; S. seems to have kept the rhyme but changed the personifications. Cp. *R&H* 473–9:

> Thou knowest what a thing is Poverty
> Among the fallen on evil days:
> 'Tis Crime, and Fear, and Infamy,
> And houseless Want in frozen ways
> Wandering ungarmented, and Pain,
> And, worse than all, that inward stain
> Foul Self-contempt

Halting beside me on the public way —
That love-devoted youth is ours — let's sit
Beside him — he may live some six months yet.
375   Or the red scaffold, as our country bends,
May ask some willing victim, or ye, friends!
May fall under some sorrow which this heart
Or hand may share or vanquish or avert;
I am prepared: in truth with no proud joy
380   To do or suffer aught, as when a boy
I did devote to justice and to love
My nature, worthless now! . . .
                  'I must remove
A veil from my pent mind. 'Tis torn aside!
O, pallid as death's dedicated bride,
385   Thou mockery which art sitting by my side,
Am I not wan like thee? at the grave's call
I haste, invited to thy wedding-ball
To greet the ghastly paramour, for whom

372. on] in *1824.*

375. bends] The country tends or inclines towards capital punishment and this tendency is a decline, a yielding or giving way to ignoble tendencies (see *OED* defs 10, 14).

376. ye, friends!] *1824;* ye friends *Hunt MS.*

380–2. as when . . . My nature] S. describes a similar act of self-dedication in the 'Dedication to Mary —— ——', 31–3, prefaced to *L&C:* 'So without shame, I spake: – "I will be wise, / And just, and free, and mild, if in me lies / Such power. . . ."' Cp. 'Hymn to Intellectual Beauty', text B 59–72 and note.

384. death's dedicated bride] *Nbk 6,* heavily corrected, reads here: 'And [o] thou Laura, sitting at my side? / [Pale] [?are] [You] deaths dedicated bride' *(BSM* xv 103). The reference to Laura supports the connection between the poem and the life of Tasso (see headnote). Cp. *Romeo and Juliet* V iii 102–9:

> Shall I believe
> That unsubstantial Death is amorous,
> And that the lean abhorred monster keeps
> Thee here in dark to be his paramour?
> For fear of that I still will stay with thee,
> And never from this palace of dim night
> Depart again. Here, here will I remain
> With worms that are thy chambermaids.

385. Tasso was subject while in prison to delusions that a familiar spirit was beside him whom he could address. 'And it was no wonder, both from the injured state of his nerves, and the long over-activity which the direction of his studies had given to the faculty of fiction, that with Tasso illusions should have become stronger than external impressions, and that he should have mistaken realities for his own diseased perceptions. . . . he was employed at leisure in the frequent composition of Socratic dialogues, and his mischievous sprite was converted into a familiar spirit' (John Black, *Life of Torquato Tasso* 2 vols (1810) ii 242).

386. at] At *1824.*

388. greet] meet *1824.*

Thou hast deserted me . . . and made the tomb
390   Thy bridal bed . . . but I beside your feet
Will lie and watch ye from my winding-sheet —
Thus . . . wide awake though dead . . . yet stay O stay!
Go not so soon — I know not what I say —
Hear but my reasons . . . I am mad, I fear,
395   My fancy is o'erwrought . . . thou art not here . . .
Pale art thou, 'tis most true . . . but thou art gone,
Thy work is finished . . . I am left alone! —

           *   *   *   *   *   *

'Nay, was it I who wooed thee to this breast
Which, like a serpent, thou envenomest
400   As in repayment of the warmth it lent?
Didst thou not seek me for thine own content?
Did not thy love awaken mine? I thought
That thou wert she who said "You kiss me not
Ever, I fear you cease to love me now" —
405   In truth I loved even to my overthrow
Her, who would fain forget these words: but they
Cling to her mind, and cannot pass away.

           *   *   *   *   *   *

'You say that I am proud — that when I speak
My lip is tortured with the wrongs which break
410   The spirit it expresses . . . Never one
Humbled himself before, as I have done!

389–90. made . . . bed] Cp. *Romeo & Juliet* III v 202–3: 'make the bridal bed / In that dim monument where Tybalt lies.' The phrase intervenes into the speech like a murmured quotation, recalling Ophelia in *Hamlet* IV v 21–74. Ophelia was a frequent example of madness in the poetry of sensibility; cp. Bowles, 'Shakspeare' 45–6: 'A maid, a beauteous maniac, wildly sings: / They laid him in the ground so cold'.

394. reasons . . .] reasons . . *Hunt MS*. In *Hunt MS* lines 394–6, two-dot ellipses may be being used to suggest the Maniac's increasing agitation. See line 434.

395. o'erwrought . . .] o'erwrought . . *Hunt MS*.

396. true . . .] true . . *Hunt MS*.

397–8. The asterisks here and below are indicated in *Hunt MS* by a row of crosses between the lines.

398. Nay,] *1824*; Nay *Hunt MS*.

399. Which,] Which *1824*. *serpent,*] serpent *Hunt MS, 1824*.

404. cease to] do not *1824*.

407. pass away] Cp. *Adonais* 432: 'And of the past are all that cannot pass away.' This line ends the fragmentary drafts of the Maniac's speech in *Nbk 6*; it is followed by line 511 (*BSM* xv 107).

Even the instinctive worm on which we tread
Turns, though it wound not — then with prostrate head
Sinks in the dust and writhes like me — and dies?
415 No: wears a living death of agonies!
As the slow shadows of the pointed grass
Mark the eternal periods, his pangs pass
Slow, ever-moving, — making moments be
As mine seem — each an immortality!

* * * * * *

420 'That you had never seen me — never heard
My voice, and more than all had ne'er endured
The deep pollution of my loathed embrace —
That your eyes ne'er had lied love in my face —
That, like some maniac monk, I had torn out
425 The nerves of manhood by their bleeding root
With mine own quivering fingers, so that ne'er
Our hearts had for a moment mingled there
To disunite in horror — these were not
With thee, like some suppressed and hideous thought

412–14. Cp. Goethe, *Faust* I 653–5:
> Dem Wurme gleich' ich, der den Staub durchwühlt,
> Den, wie er sich im Staube nährend lebt,
> Des Wandrers Tritt vernichtet und begräbt.

('I am like the worm tunnelling through soil which, while it lives nourished by dust, is crushed and buried by the foot of a passer-by.')

414. dies?] dies: *1824*.

416–19. slow shadows . . . immortality] Cp. S. to Godwin, 7 December 1817: 'I find the very blades of grass & the boughs of distant trees present themselves to me with microscopical distinctness' (*L* i 572), *Alastor* 528–9: 'tall spires of windlestrae / Threw their thin shadows down the rugged slope' and *PU* I 13–14: 'And moments, aye divided by keen pangs / Till they seem years'.

417. his] its *1824*.

420–8. 'That . . . these] The Maniac remembers in these lines what he later terms 'those curses' (line 435); each of these possibilities is something his lover wished for and told him that she wished for. The punctuation of *Hunt MS* clarifies this syntax.

424–6. Self-castration was observed as a symptom of mania; cp. Cabanis, 'Rapports du physique et du moral de l'homme', *Oeuvres Complètes* 5 vols (Paris 1823–25) iii 343: 'On voit souvent ces malheureux [maniacs] s'arracher les testicules' ('These patients are often observed gouging out their testicles').

428. disunite] Cp. *R&H* 984: '[two strains of harmony] slowly disunite'; and cp. Southey's *Wat Tyler* II i: 'They will use every art to disunite you . . . Whom in a mass they fear'. *horror –* *these*] horror! These *1824*; horror: – These *Locock 1911*.

429–30. some . . . musings] Cp. *Lament of Tasso* v 8–10: 'The vivid thought still flashes through my frame, / And for a moment all things as they were / Flit by me; they are gone – I am the same.'

430   Which flits athwart our musings, but can find
                No rest within a pure and gentle mind . . .
                Thou sealedst them with many a bare broad word
                And ceredst my memory o'er them, — for I heard
                And can forget not . . . they were ministered
435   One after one, those curses. Mix them up
                Like self-destroying poisons in one cup,
                And they will make one blessing, which thou ne'er
                Didst imprecate for, on me, — death.

            *   *   *   *   *   *

                                  'It were
                A cruel punishment for one most cruel
440   If such can love, to make that love the fuel
                Of the mind's hell — hate, scorn, remorse, despair:
                But *me* — whose heart a stranger's tear might wear
                As water-drops the sandy fountain-stone,

432–4. Cp. *Adonais* 453–5: 'and if the seal is set, / Here, on one fountain of a mourning mind, / Break it not thou!' and *Childe Harold* ii 73–6:

> There, thou! – whose love and life together fled,
> Have left me here to love and live in vain –
> Twined with my heart, and can I deem thee dead
> When busy Memory flashes on my brain?

433. ceredst my memory o'er] cearedst my memory oer *Hunt MS*; seard'st my memory o'er *1824*; searedst my memory o'er *Forman 1876–7*. Cp. line 614 where *Hunt MS* reads 'ceared over their memory' and *1824* 'cered over their memory'. S.'s spelling 'ceared' is an alternative for both seared and cered. Emendation has obscured the parallel between the two lines. To cere means to anoint with spices, to embalm; to shut up (a corpse in a coffin), to seal up in lead. To sear means to dry up; to wither or blight; or to cauterize (cp. *1 Tim.* iv 2 where St Paul warns of those 'whose consciences are seared with a hot iron'). This meaning for 'cear' is reinforced by the rhyme with 'sere'. The Maniac complains that his memory has been forcibly restricted to his lover's curses: 'for I heard / And can forget not'. It is a context more appropriate to cere than to sear. His imprisonment suggests blight and dryness but 'cere' gives a more precise sense of living death (see lines 206–10). Editors may have emended the word to 'sear' because of the sealing process referred to in 432. Cp. *Cymbeline* I i 116–17: 'Seare up my embracements from a next, / With bonds of death' and *Alastor* 248–9: 'his scattered hair / Sered by the autumn of strange suffering'.

434. not . . .] not. . . . *Hunt MS*. S. may be using four dots to indicate a fractionally longer pause. *ministered*] This rhyme closes one of the few triplets in the poem; cp. lines 102–4, 447–9.

438. imprecate for] Meaning to pray for or call down (*OED* def. 1); *OED* does not give 'for' as a preposition for imprecate.

438–42. It were . . . me] The Maniac says that his treatment would be a cruel punishment if inflicted on a cruel person (supposing such a person could love at all) but is even worse when dealt out to him.

441. hell –] *1824*; hell; *Hunt MS*.

443. Cp. *R&H* 721–3: 'Many then wept, not tears, but gall / Within their hearts, like drops which fall / Wasting the fountain-stone away.'

Who loved and pitied all things, and could moan
445   For woes which others hear not, and could see
The absent with the glance of fantasy,
And with the poor and trampled sit and weep,
Following the captive to his dungeon deep;
Me — who am as a nerve o'er which do creep
450   The else unfelt oppressions of this earth
And was to thee the flame upon thy hearth
When all beside was cold — that thou on me
Shouldst rain these plagues of blistering agony —
Such curses are from lips once eloquent
455   With love's too partial praise — let none relent
Who intend deeds too dreadful for a name
Henceforth, if an example for the same
They seek . . . for thou on me lookedst so, and so —
And didst speak thus . . . and thus . . . I live to shew
How much men bear and die not!

*   *   *   *   *   *

460   'Thou wilt tell
With the grimace of hate how horrible
It was to meet my love when thine grew less;
Thou wilt admire how I could e'er address
Such features to love's work . . . this taunt, though true,
465   (For indeed nature nor in form nor hue
Bestowed on me her choicest workmanship)
Shall not be thy defence . . . for since thy lip

---

444. Cp. 'The Sensitive Plant' 70–4:
> But the Sensitive-plant which could give small fruit
> Of the love which it felt from the leaf to the root,
> Received more than all – it loved more than ever,
> Where none wanted but it, could belong to the giver.

Peck compares the whole paragraph (lines 438–60) to the later poem (*Peck* ii 104–7).

446. glance] glass *1824*.

447. with] near *1824*.

449. creep] This rhyme-word completes another triplet; cp. lines 432–4.

450. else unfelt] else-unfelt *1824*.

450. Cp. *Ecclesiastes* iv 1: 'So I returned, and considered all the oppression's that are done under the sun'.

452–5. that thou . . . let none] This punctuation follows *Hunt MS*; it has been variously edited. *Hunt MS*'s pointing gives a sense of hectic and relentless speed in the Maniac's train of thought and emphasises the pause in line 458, 'They seek . . .'

459. speak thus . . .] speak thus . . *Hunt MS*. Cp. lines 394–6.

467. lip] life *1824*.

Met mine first, years long past, since thine eye kindled
With soft fire under mine, I have not dwindled
470 Nor changed in mind or body, or in aught
But as love changes what it loveth not
After long years and many trials.

                              'How vain
Are words! I thought never to speak again
Not even in secret, — not to my own heart —
475 But from my lips the unwilling accents start
And from my pen the words flow as I write,
Dazzling my eyes with scalding tears . . . my sight
Is dim to see that charactered in vain
On this unfeeling leaf which burns the brain
480 And eats into it . . . blotting all things fair
And wise and good which time had written there.

'Those who inflict must suffer, for they see
The work of their own hearts and this must be
Our chastisement or recompense — O child!
485 I would that thine were like to be more mild
For both our wretched sakes . . . for thine the most
Who feelest already all that thou hast lost
Without the power to wish it thine again;
And as slow years pass, a funereal train
490 Each with the ghost of some lost hope or friend

467–70. lip . . . body] Cp. *PU* II v 48–51:
                  Life of Life! thy lips enkindle
                    With their love the breath between them
                  And thy smiles before they dwindle
                    Make the cold air fire

471. 'Except as Love alters those whom it does not favour'.

471. not] not, *Locock 1911*. The comma stresses that the Maniac has 'not dwindled' after the long years and many trials; without the comma, emphasis falls on how love through many years alters the unloved.

472. Echoed by Julian at lines 583–4. Cp. *PU* II v 45–6: 'those who feel it most / Are happier still, after long sufferings'.

472. trials.] *1824* inserts a row of asterisks here.

481. there.] *1824* does not insert a line-break. In *Hunt MS*, the gap is small but the first word of line 482 is indented. Cp. line 299.

482. 'Those] Those *1824*.

483. this] that *1824*.

490. lost] dead *canc. Hunt MS*. S. may have wished to avoid echoing 'dead memory' (492). See line 323 and note.

Following it like its shadow, wilt thou bend
No thought on my dead memory?

*   *   *   *   *   *

                  'Alas, love!
Fear me not . . . against thee I would not move
A finger in despite. Do I not live
495   That thou mayst have less bitter cause to grieve?
I give thee tears for scorn and love for hate
And that thy lot may be less desolate
Than his on whom thou tramplest, I refrain
From that sweet sleep which medicines all pain.
500   Then, when thou speakest of me, never say
He could forgive not. Here I cast away
All human passions, all revenge, all pride;
I think, speak, act no ill; I do but hide
Under these words like embers, every spark
505   Of that which has consumed me — quick and dark
The grave is yawning . . . as its roof shall cover
My limbs with dust and worms under and over
So let oblivion hide this grief . . . the air
Closes upon my accents, as despair
510   Upon my heart — let death upon despair!'

    He ceased, and overcome leant back awhile
Then rising, with a melancholy smile
Went to a sofa, and lay down, and slept

493. I would] I'd *1824.*

496. hate] hate; *1824, Forman 1876–7.*

498. tramplest] Frequent in S.: see line 447, *Preface* and *TL* 387–8: 'and she, thought by thought / Trampled its fires into the dust of death'. Cp. Byron, 'Ode on Venice' 131–3: 'For tyranny of late is cunning grown, / And in its own good season tramples down / The sparkles of our ashes.'

501–5. In idea and imagery, cp. Rousseau's speech in *TL* 199–204:
                Before thy memory

      I feared, loved, hated, suffered, did, and died,
  And if the spark with which Heaven lit my spirit
    Earth had with purer nutriment supplied

    Corruption would not now thus much inherit
        Of what was once Rousseau
503–5. hide . . . consumed me] Reminiscent of Ulysses in Dante's *Inferno* xxvi 48 who 'si fascia di quel ch'elli è inceso' ('is wrapped or swathed in what burns him').

504. words] words, *1824.* 'The sense of course being "as embers hide sparks"' (*Locock 1911*).

510. despair] my care *1839.*

511. awhile] awhile; *1824, Locock 1911* awhile, *Forman 1876–7.*

A heavy sleep, and in his dreams he wept
515 And muttered some familiar name, and we
Wept without shame in his society.
I think I never was impressed so much;
The man who were not, must have lacked a touch
Of human nature ... then we lingered not,
520 Although our argument was quite forgot,
But calling the attendants, went to dine
At Maddalo's; yet neither cheer nor wine
Could give us spirits, for we talked of him
And nothing else, till daylight made stars dim;
525 And we agreed his was some dreadful ill
Wrought on him boldly, yet unspeakable,
By a dear friend; some deadly change in love
Of one vowed deeply which he dreamed not of;
For whose sake he, it seemed, had fixed a blot
530 Of falsehood on his mind which flourished not
But in the light of all-beholding truth,
And having stamped this canker on his youth
She had abandoned him ... and how much more
Might be his woe, we guessed not — he had store
535 Of friends and fortune once, as we could guess
From his nice habits and his gentleness;
These were now lost ... it were a grief indeed

518. *were*] was *1839*.

525. *his*] it *1824, Nbk 6*.

525–47. Lines 525–6 occur at the foot of p. 103 of *Nbk 6*; a version of lines 527–30 is written, very small, at the foot of the preceding, facing page. The section (lines 525–33) is redrafted on p. 109, continued (lines 533–46) on p. 116. Lines 547ff. begin at the top of p. 104 (*BSM* xv 107, 113, 121, 109). This suggests S. wrote lines 547ff. first, before the Maniac's speeches, and left blank pages (perhaps pp. 94–103) in the nbk for the Maniac. When these were full, he added to the Maniac's speeches on later pages; first, on p. 109, a blank page opposite the concluding lines of the draft; later on p. 116 – the drafts on this page are closer to the printed text. Morever, pp. 110–15 contain drafts of *PU* II i 163–208, which must, therefore, have been written before the drafts of *J&M* 525–46 were complete, though not necessarily before *J&M* 547ff. GM dates the *PU* stanzas after March 1819 ('The Draft and the Meaning', 63, 66). Cp. headnote, line 44 and note.

525–6. his was ... Wrought] 'that it was secret love / Inflicted' *canc. Nbk 6*.

527. some deadly change] some unrequited *Nbk 6*.

528. vowed] perhaps 'loved' in *Nbk 6* but the MS is unclear.

529. he, it seemed,] he it seemed *Hunt MS*.

529–31. fixed a blot ... truth,] 'The Maniac had practised falsehoods against his own mind which could remain healthy only if it remained candid'.

530. on] in *1824*.

537. were now] now were *1824*.

If he had changed one unsustaining reed
For all that such a man might else adorn.
540   The colours of his mind seemed yet unworn
For the wild language of his grief was high
Such as in measure were called poetry,
And I remember one remark which then
Maddalo made. He said: 'Most wretched men
545   Are cradled into poetry by wrong,
They learn in suffering what they teach in song.'
If I had been an unconnected man
I, from this moment, should have formed some plan
Never to leave sweet Venice, — for to me
550   It was delight to ride by the lone sea;
And then, the town is silent — one may write
Or read in gondolas by day or night
Having the little brazen lamp alight,
Unseen, uninterrupted; books are there,
555   Pictures, and casts from all those statues fair
Which were twin-born with poetry, and all
We seek in towns, with little to recall
Regrets for the green country. I might sit
In Maddalo's great palace, and his wit
560   And subtle talk would cheer the winter night

539. adorn.] 1824; adorn: *Hunt MS.*

540. unworn] unworn; *1824, Forman 1876-7.* Because in *Hunt MS* the lower dot of the colon after 'adorn' (line 539) stands above the upstroke of 'n' in 'unworn', there seems to be a semicolon.

542. 'Such as would have been called poetry if it had been in metre' (GM, 'Draft and the Meaning', 75). One draft reads: 'As writers who transcribe call poetry' (*BSM* xv 113), recalling Dante, *Purgatorio* xxiv 52–3: 'un che, quando / Amor mi spira, noto', translated by Cary: 'but as one / Who am the scribe of love; that, when he breathes, / Take up my pen, and, as he dictates, write' (Cary, *The Vision* (1814), 'Purgatory' xxiv 52–4).

544–6. Most . . . song.] There are several versions in *Nbk 6,* some at a distance separate from their context in the final version: 'And learn in suffering what they speak in song' (p. 69) and 'It is because they act the parts themselves / And learn through suffering what they speak in song' (p. 156; *BSM* xv 71, 159). Within drafts of this section, there are three versions; 1: '[For] this is what to poets shall belong / They learn in suffering what they'; 2: 'Poets he said are men whose [nurse] is wrong / They learn by suffering what they teach in song'; 3: 'Their minds are made sublime & keen [by] wrong / They learn [thro]'; (*BSM* xv 111, 113, 120). It is impossible to know the order of composition. See GM, 'Draft and the Meaning', 68–9.

547. If I] All *eds* begin a new paragraph here. *Hunt MS* begins a new page with this line which is indented. Cp. lines 300, 320 and 511.

551–3. write . . . alight] Another triplet; cp. lines 432–4, 449–51.

554. Unseen,] Unseen *Hunt MS.*

558. Regrets] Regret *1824. I might]* One might *Nbk 6.*

And make me know myself, and the firelight
Would flash upon our faces, till the day
Might dawn and make me wonder at my stay.
But I had friends in London too: the chief
565   Attraction here, was that I sought relief
From the deep tenderness that maniac wrought
Within me — 'twas perhaps an idle thought —
But I imagined that if day by day
I watched him, and but seldom went away
570   And studied all the beatings of his heart
With zeal, as men study some stubborn art
For their own good, and could by patience find
An entrance to the caverns of his mind,
I might reclaim him from his dark estate: —
575   In friendships I had been most fortunate —
Yet never saw I one whom I would call
More willingly my friend; and this was all
Accomplished not; such dreams of baseless good

---

561. *me know myself*] one know oneself *Nbk 6.* Cp. *Adonais* 415–16: 'come forth / Fond wretch! and know thyself and him aright' and *TL* 211–12: 'their lore / Taught them not this – to know themselves'.

563. *stay.*] *1824*; stay: *Hunt MS.*

564. *in London*] elsewhere *canc. Nbk 6.* *too:*] too. *1824.*

565. *here,*] here *1824.* In *Nbk 6* 'Attraction here was' is cancelled; S. may have felt 'here' was a little confusing if set against 'London' instead of 'elsewhere' (line 564). The word jars also with 'there' (line 554).

568. *that if day by day*] that, if day by day *Nbk 6;* that if, day by day, *1824.* The *Nbk 6* comma begins the parenthesis ending at line 574.

569. *and but seldom*] and seldom *1824.*

570. *beatings of his heart*] Cp. *R&H* 1026–34:
            You might hear the beatings of his heart,
            Quick, but not strong; and with my tresses . . .
            Alas! the unquiet life did tingle
And cp. Mary Robinson, 'The Maniac' 79–84, *Poetical Works* (1806):
            From mine own heart through every vein
            Oh! tell me, tell me all thy pain,
            Pour to mine ear thy frenzied strain
          And I will share thy pangs and soothe thy woes!
            Poor Maniac! I will dry thy tears
            And bathe thy wound and calm thy fears,
          And with soft Pity's balm enchant thee to repose.

571. *stubborn*] difficult *Nbk 6.* 'secret' and 'stubborn' are inserted above 'difficult'.

573. *mind,*] mind *Hunt MS.*

574. Cp. *Athanase* 34: 'Pitying the tumult of their dark estate.' *his*] this *Forman 1876–7.*

578. *Accomplished not;*] Vain imagery – *Nbk 6.* 'talk' is inserted above the dash.

<pre>
          Oft come and go in crowds and solitude
580   And leave no trace — but what I now designed
          Made for long years impression on my mind.
          The following morning urged by my affairs
          I left bright Venice.

                              After many years
          And many changes I returned; the name
585   Of Venice, and its aspect was the same;
          But Maddalo was travelling far away
          Among the mountains of Armenia.
          His dog was dead. His child had now become
          A woman; such as it has been my doom
590   To meet with few, a wonder of this earth
          Where there is little of transcendent worth
          Like one of Shakespeare's women: kindly she
          And with a manner beyond courtesy
          Received her father's friend; and when I asked
595   Of the lorn maniac, she her memory tasked
          And told as she had heard the mournful tale:
          That the poor sufferer's health began to fail
          Two years from my departure, but that then
</pre>

579. crowds and] crowds or *1824*.

582. The] – The *1824*.

583–4. The draft reads: 'Venice I left for five & twenty years / After this period I returned, & found / That Maddalo'. '& . . . Maddalo' is cancelled and replaced by 'the name / Of Venice'.

584. changes] In *Hunt MS* 'wanderings' is cancelled and 'changes' inserted above.

587. mountains of Armenia] mountains tribes of India *Nbk 6*. 'tribes of India' is cancelled; 'of Armenia' inserted above. The 's' of 'mountains' was probably added when S. altered the line.

588–92. An early draft of these lines appears on p. 115 of *Nbk 6*, after the drafted stanzas of *PU* II i. This implies that the frame-narrative of the poem (as well as the Maniac's speeches) was completed after the *PU* stanzas. Cp. lines 525–47 and note.

588. His child] Peck suggests that Thomas Medwin connected the grown-up child with Harriet Grove, S.'s early love (*Peck* ii 106). Cp. lines 273–4 and note.

591. transcendent] uncommon *Nbk 6*.

595. lorn] poor *Nbk 6*.

596–606. tale: . . . him'] It is unclear where precisely the text changes from indirect to reported speech. *Hunt MS* places quotation marks before lines 598ff. This does not resolve the difficulty of 'my departure' (line 598) – which must refer to Julian – unless direct speech is seen as beginning at 'but' or 'then' (line 598). *Locock 1911* begins direct speech at line 602: ' "Her coming"; other *eds* follow *1824* in beginning direct speech at line 597. *Nbk 6*, followed here, begins direct speech at line 600. Cp. lines 608, 610.

596. tale:] *1824. Hunt MS* is unclear.

597. That] "That *1824, Forman 1876–7*.

598. Two] "Two *Hunt MS*.

The Lady who had left him, came again.
600 'Her mien had been imperious, but she now
Looked meek — perhaps remorse had brought her low.
Her coming made him better, and they stayed
Together at my father's — for I played
As I remember with the lady's shawl —
605 I might be six years old — but after all
She left him.' . . . 'Why, her heart must have been tough:
How did it end?' 'And was not this enough?
They met — they parted.' — 'Child, is there no more?'
'Something within that interval which bore
610 The stamp of *why* they parted, *how* they met:
Yet if thine agèd eyes disdain to wet
Those wrinkled cheeks with youth's remembered tears,
Ask me no more, but let the silent years
Be closed and cered over their memory
615 As yon mute marble where their corpses lie.'
I urged and questioned still, she told me how
All happened — but the cold world shall not know.

599. *again.*] *1824*; again *Hunt MS*.

600. *'Her*] *Nbk 6* begins direct speech here.

607. *was*] is *Nbk 6*.

608. *more?'*] more? *Hunt MS*.

609–10. These lines are assigned in all *eds* to the Maniac's daughter. They would sound just as appropriate coming from Julian, however. In *Hunt MS* the speaker remains uncertain because 'met' (line 610) runs into the join of the notebook, leaving any punctuation obscure.

611–12. Cp. line 31 and a similar caution in *R&H* 592–4: 'Weep not at thine own words, though they must make / Me weep. What is thy tale? I fear 'twill shake / Thy gentle heart with tears.'

611. *Yet*] In *Hunt MS* and *Nbk 6* 'Yet' replaces a cancelled 'But'. If lines 609–10 were assigned to Julian, 'Yet' (rhyming with the preceding word, 'met') might enforce a pause and help suggest a change of speaker. *disdain*] Frequent in S.; cp. *PU* I 51–3: 'these pale feet, which then might trample thee / If they disdained not such a prostrate slave. / Disdain? Ah no! I pity thee' and *TL* 204–5: 'nor this disguise / Stain that within which still disdains to wear it.' The word has some of the ambiguity of 'scorn' in S.'s lexicon; cp. line 38 and note.

614. *cered*] ceared *Hunt MS*, cered *1824*. Cp. line 433 and note.

199
'How pale and cold thou art in thy despair'

Drafted in pencil in *Nbk 11*; the lines may date from the days following the death of William Shelley in Rome on 7 June 1819, and would then refer to Mary's deep depression following that event. S. wrote to Peacock two months after William's death that 'Poor Mary's spirits continue dreadfully depressed' (*L* ii 109) and there is no doubt that the shock of this second death affected Mary's spirits profoundly, and quite possibly throughout the remainder of her life with S. (see *Mary Jnl* i 291–2). These lines may alternatively date from September 1818 and the death of Clara in Venice; S.'s letter to Claire Clairmont of 25 September, giving her the news, describes Mary 'in the most dreadful distress' (*L* ii 41).

Text from *Nbk 11* p. 18.

Published in *V&P* 7.

> How pale and cold thou art in thy despair
> One who from many mourners might be chosen
> To imitate the very peak of grief

200
Retribution: from Moschus

These lines are a relatively close translation of Moschus's Idyll v. Moschus was a Gk Bucolic poet of the second century BC, and S. also translated his Idylls iii and iv (see nos 107 and 162). A date for this translation is difficult to establish. Mary's jnl records that S. read Theocritus and Moschus in Gk in 1816 (*Mary Jnl* i 97), but none of his three translations from Moschus can be comfortably dated to that period, and it is likely that he carried his copy of the Greek bucolic poets with him to Italy (as Walter Peck (*TLS*, 7 April 1921) has shown, the Gk edition of the Bucolics used by S. was *Theocriti, Bionis et Moschi Carmina Bucolica*, ed. L. C. Valckenaer, Edinburgh 1810). *Eds* have usually dated the poem in 1818 or earlier; *Webb* 87–8 appears to imply a very early date for the poem, and a context in the S., Harriet and Hogg situation. It is certainly possible that the lines might date from at least as early as December 1817–July 1818; S. produced various translations, particularly from Gk, in that period. The poem might alternatively date from the period of the Shelleys' stay in Naples, December 1818–February 1819, and might conceivably be connected with the strange story of S.'s lady admirer who, so Medwin claimed, had fallen in love with S. through reading his verses (see headnote to no. 202).

¶199   1. *despair*] despair! *V&P*.
3. *peak*] breath *V&P*.

The lines are drafted on the back of one of two sheets also containing S.'s draft for his translation of part of the 'Lament for Adonis' (see headnote to no. 201), which are now in the British Library (see *MYR* viii 257–70). This obviously suggests that the two translations were written around the same time; according to *MYR* viii 257 the paper on which these drafts are written is probably of Italian manufacture, and the headnote to no. 201 argues that the 'Lament for Adonis' was probably written in Rome in June 1819, after the death of William Shelley. This would imply that the present poem also dates from that period, and in stylistic terms the translation does seem definitely later in manner than S.'s other translations from Moschus; its grammatically compressed expression of a complex emotional situation, fitted with unshowy skill to the demands of a lyric form, points forward to the powerful short lyrics of S.'s later writing. But a date in June 1819 is apparently challenged by the fact that S.'s fair copy of the poem, which was presumably made from the rough draft now in the British Library, is in *Nbk 11* p. 31, immediately following the last few lines of 'That time is dead forever, child'. This is the second of the two poems (nos 127 and 128) which the present edition argues must have been written into *Nbk 11* before spring 1819, because they, together with the Moschus translation, are apparently skipped by S.'s draft for *PU* II ii (see headnote to nos 127 and 128). But the nbk evidence does not in fact preclude a later date for S.'s copying of this translation into *Nbk 11*; it is not impossible that S. originally left most of p. 31 blank after copying the last five lines of 'That time is dead forever, child' at the top, and the draft of *PU* II ii that is interrupted at p. 28, and resumes at p. 32, may have been skipping two full pages *and* one partly blank page (for whatever reason; the physical evidence of the nbk is in other words not in itself conclusive). Ink colour and the condition of the pen used for the fair copy of the translation from Moschus are also not incompatible with copying at a later date than the other lines on the page. The title 'Retribution from Moschus' has apparently been added, by S., after the copy of the translation, as it is slightly cramped for space (see *BSM* xviii 32–3). The British Library MS is headed 'Pan, Echo & The Satyr', in a hand other than S.'s. *Forman 1876–7* uses this title; in *1824* the lines were headed 'Translation from Moschus'.

There is a transcript of this translation by Mary S. in *Box 2* f. 131r, on a single sheet torn from *Harvard Nbk* (see *MYR* v 160–1); this copy was no doubt made from *Nbk 11*, and is probably itself the source of the first published text in *1824*. S.'s fair copy is virtually unpunctuated apart from dashes, and the text here follows Mary S.'s pointing in *1824* except where indicated.

Text from *Nbk 11* p. 31.

Published in *1824* 362.

> Pan loved his neighbour Echo — but that child
>   Of Earth and Air, pined for the Satyr leaping;
> The Satyr loved with wasting madness wild
>   The bright nymph Lyda — and so three went weeping.

2. *Air,*] *Nbk 11*; Air *1824*.

3. *madness*] madness madness *BSM* xviii.

4. *Lyda –*] *Nbk 11*; Lyda, – *1824*.

5   As Pan loved Echo, Echo loved the Satyr;
         The Satyr, Lyda — and so love consumed them.
         And thus to each — which was a woeful matter —
         To bear what they inflicted Justice doomed them;
         For inasmuch as each might hate the lover,
10   Each loving, so was hated. — Ye that love not
         Be warned — in thought turn this example over,
         That when ye love, the like return ye prove not.

201
Translation of part of Bion's Lament for Adonis

These lines are a translation of the first 47 lines of Bion's Lament for Adonis (for S.'s text of the Bucolic poets, see headnotes to nos 162 and 200). Their source is a rough draft on two leaves, which also contain the rough draft of S.'s translation of Moschus's idyll v (which is the preceding poem in this edition). This MS was given by the Shelley family to Richard Garnett, who sold it to T. J. Wise; it subsequently passed with Wise's collection to the British Museum (MS Ashley 5031; see *MYR* viii 257–70). S.'s translation of the 'Lament' was first published in *Forman 1876–7* 232–4 as 'Fragment of the Elegy on the Death of Adonis. From the Greek of Bion'. There is a transcript by Mary S. in adds. d. 7 which was almost certainly made from the Ashley MS (see *BSM* ii 209–13). The date of S.'s translation is not known, but it is probably contemporary with the translation from Moschus in the same MS, like that poem may conceivably be as early as at least 1816, and could certainly date from the period December 1817–July 1818 when S. made several translations, mainly from Gk. The draft is however on paper probably of Italian manufacture, and there are no circumstances bearing on the dating of the translation from Moschus which preclude a somewhat later date for both poems (see headnote to preceding poem). The translation has an emotional intensity and darkness of tone which are unlike the translations of 1817 and 1818 (cp. no. 162), and may well date from summer 1819 and the period of despair endured by S. and Mary following the death of their son William, aged 3½, on 7 June 1819. There also seems

¶200   *6. so*] Altered from *thus* in *Nbk 11*; thus *Box 2, 1824*. *BSM* xviii reads 'then / so'. The draft in the British Library reads *so*. S. was presumably trying to avoid a repetition of *thus* in the following half line (where the word may also have been altered in *Nbk 11*), although *so* in line 6 itself initiates a repetition of *so* from line 4.   *them.*] them *Nbk 11*; them. – *1824*.

8. inflicted Justice] *Nbk 11*; inflicted, justice *1824*.

9. inasmuch] in as much *1824*. *BSM* xviii and *MYR* viii both read *in as much*, as does Mary's transcript in *Box 2* (altered from 'as much'); but in both holograph MSS S.'s spacing seems clearly to indicate that he intends one word here; according to *OED inasmuch* is the normal form from the seventeenth century onwards.

to be some specific influence from that part of Bion's Lament here translated on lines 15–20 of *PU* IV (see notes), a passage which must have been composed in the second half of 1819 and which itself looks forward to *Adonais*; and that poem has significant connection with both the Lament for Adonis, and the death of William Shelley.

In general terms S.'s translation of the 'Lament' uses more varied and less obvious repetitions than the Gk, which is more mannered and patterned in style; and he tends to a more highly-coloured and expressive vocabulary than the relatively plain diction of Bion's Gk. There are instances where S. appears to have preferred variant readings rejected by Valckenaer (see notes to lines 12 and 18). His rendering of the Gk λέγε πᾶσιν in line 5, 'Tell everyone', as "Tis Misery calls', perhaps suggests more particularly a context in the distressing impact of William's death.

Text from British Library MS Ashley 5031 (S.'s rough draft is almost unpunctuated apart from dashes, and the pointing here is mostly editorial).

Published in *Forman 1876–7* 232–4.

> I mourn Adonis — dead, loveliest Adonis,
> Dead. Dead Adonis — and the Loves lament. —
> Sleep no more, Venus, wrapped in purple woof:
> Wake, violet-stoled queen, beat your breast,
> 5 'Tis Misery calls — for he is dead,
> The lovely one lies wounded in the mountains,
> His white thigh struck with the white tooth; he scarce
> Yet breathes; and Venus hangs in agony there.
> The dark blood wanders o'er his snowy limbs,
> 10 His eyes beneath their lids are lustreless,

1. S. apparently first wrote 'I mourn Adonis –', then wrote a word which is possibly 'dead' or 'loved' and cancelled it, writing above another now illegible word (possibly 'loved' or 'lost') which he then also cancelled; and 'dead' was then written to the left of this cancelled word and above the original dash. But see *MYR* viii for a different reading. *Forman 1876–7* reads 'I mourn Adonis dead – loveliest Adonis –'.

4–5. The MS at first read 'Wake violet stoled queen, and weave the crown / Of Death, tis Misery calls – for he is dead'. S. cancelled 'and weave the crown / Of Death', wrote in 'beat your breast' above, and left the second line short of one metrical foot. *Forman 1876–7* gives the original reading on metrical grounds.

4. S. omits the Gk δειλαία, 'miserable, wretched'. *violet-stoled*] The Gk has κυανόστολα, 'blue- or black-robed'.

5. *'Tis Misery calls –*] See headnote; the Gk λέγε πᾶσιν means 'Tell everyone' (an imperative addressed to Aphrodite).

6. S. omits the Gk refrain καλὸς Ἄδωνις here, and again after line 14 below.

7–8. Line 7 at first ended '& she', followed by 'Hangs over him to catch his fading breath'. This line was cancelled, and 'he scarce' written above the cancelled '& she'. S.'s trans. omits the repetition in the Gk text of ὀδόντι (tooth).

9. *wanders o'er*] Literally 'drips down' in the Gk, εἴβεται.

10. *are lustreless*] Literally 'grow numb' in the Gk, ναρκῇι.

The rose has fled from his wan lips, and there
That kiss is dead which Venus gathers yet

Deep, deep wounds, Adonis;
A deeper Venus bears within her heart . . .
15   See, his beloved dogs are gathering round,
The Oread nymphs are weeping — Aphrodite
With hair unbound is wandering through the woods
Wildered, ungirt, unsandalled — the thorns pierce
Her hastening feet and drink her sacred blood;
20   Bitterly screaming out she is driven on
Through the long vales; and her Assyrian boy,
Her love, her husband calls — the purple blood
From his struck thigh stains her white navel now,
Her bosom, and her neck before like snow.

25   'Alas for Cytherea', the Loves mourn.
The lovely, the beloved is gone — and now
Her sacred beauty vanishes away —

11. wan] Not in the Gk.

12. Venus gathers yet] Cancelled in MS. S.'s trans. here may be influenced by rejected variants discussed in a textual note in the edition he was using (see headnote, and cp. note to line 18 below). S. leaves two lines untranslated at this point.

13. A deep deep wound Adonis . . . *Forman 1876–7.* The Gk line is literally 'Adonis has in his thigh a savage savage wound'; S.'s abbreviated grammar is alien to Gk.

14. S. omits the repetition of ἕλκος (wound).

15. are gathering round] Noted as a mistranslation in *Webb* 93; the Gk ὠρύσαντο means 'howled'.

17. With hair unbound] Written under 'Loosening her hair' canc. in MS.

18. wildered] The Gk πενθαλέα is a rare and late word for 'sad' (πένθος). *ungirt*] Canc. in MS. S.'s *pierce* may derive from a rejected variant mentioned in a textual note in the edition he was using.

19. hastening] The Gk ἐρχομέναν, 'going / as she goes', is plainer than S.'s word, and not a transferred epithet as S. makes it. *feet*] Canc. in MS.

22. S. adds *Her love.* S.'s *purple blood* elaborates the Gk μέλαν, 'black' rather than 'purple' and a standard poetic word for blood.

23–4. S.'s pronouns in these lines are puzzling. The MS unambiguously reads 'her' for all four possessive pronouns, where the Gk plainly requires 'his'; while the pronouns in Gk grammar are potentially ambivalent, their context here makes it obvious that the referent is Adonis. The first of S.'s pronouns, *her struck thigh*, is here emended to *his* as this must be a slip of the pen (Venus has not herself been wounded by the boar); the others stand, on the assumption that they are a mistranslation.

25, 34–5, 40. There are no speech marks in the MS, in Mary's transcript, or in *Forman 1876–7.*

25. S. adds *Alas.*

For Venus whilst Adonis lived was fair;
Alas, her loveliness is dead with him.
30   The oaks and mountains cry, 'Ai, ai, Adonis!'
The streams their murmurs turn to groans for him,
The springs their waters change to tears and weep,
The flowers are withered up with grief

'Ai, ai [   ] Adonis is dead';
35   Echo resounds: [   ] 'Adonis dead'.
Who will weep not thy dreadful woe, o Venus?
Soon as she saw and knew the mortal wound
Of her Adonis — saw the life-blood flow
From his fair thigh, now wasting, wailing loud
40   She clasped him and cried [   ] 'Stay, Adonis,
Stay, dearest one, [
                    ] and mix my lips with thine;
Wake yet a while, Adonis — oh, but once
That I may kiss thee now for the last time —
45   But for so long as one short kiss may live
O let thy breath flow from thy dying soul
Even to my mouth and heart, that I may suck
That

31. Cp. the facsimile in *MYR* viii 264. The line is very difficult to make out in MS and the reading here is conjectural (the line is omitted in *Forman 1876–7*). Mary's transcript in adds. d. 7 reads 'The streams change their harmonious tune & groan for him', and the transcript in *MYR* viii implies a line reading 'The streams change their harmonious tune & groan'. The Gk has no equivalent for 'harmonious tune'; and S.'s notion of change, here and in the following line, is also absent from the Gk.

33. are withered up] Webb 92 notes this as an instance of mistranslation by S. because of his ignorance of the Gk word, here ἐρυθαίνεται, 'blush'. But S.'s trans. could be understood as an exegetical gloss; the Gk text is obviously itself metaphorical. S. leaves 1½ lines untranslated at this point.

34–5. As elsewhere in his trans., S. here varies what is an exact repetition in the Gk.

35. resounds] Written after 'replies' canc. in MS.

38. life-blood] The Gk has φοίνιον, 'red'; S. adds *flow*.

39. S. adds *fair*.

40. She clasped him] The Gk has πάχεας ἀμπετάσασα, 'lifting up her hands' (as a gesture of grief).

41. dearest one] The Gk δύσποτμε means 'wretched-fated one'.

43. S. adds *oh, but once*.

44. S. inverts the Gk, i.e. 'that you may kiss me now'.

47. As Webb 98 suggests, S.'s *suck* may have been suggested by the sound of the Gk ἀποψύχῃς.

202
Misery. – A Fragment

Difficult to date with confidence, but most probably written in June 1819 in Livorno, following the death of William Shelley aged 3½ in Rome on 7 June and prompted at least in part by the severe effect of that catastrophe on Mary's spirits and on her attitude to S. (see e.g. *Mary Jnl* i 291–2). The poem is drafted in *Nbk 11*, on scattered pages which offer no securely determining context for a date of first conception. There is an intermediate fair copy in *Nbk 8* on leaves left blank after the fair copy of *PU* II ii, which must therefore be at least later than March 1819 (see headnote to *PU*). There is also an exceptionally careful holograph fair copy of the poem in *Box 1*, entitled 'Misery. – A Fragment' in S.'s hand, which as *BSM* ix demonstrates was originally part of the booklet that S. made up containing a collection of all his 'saddest verses raked up into one heap', and sent 10 November 1820 to Ollier for publication (*L* ii 246). This collection, which for unknown reasons was never in fact published, was to have accompanied publication of *J&M* and *Athanase*, and was also to have included 'The cold Earth slept below' (no. 127), 'Stanzas written in dejection – December 1818, near Naples' (no. 187), and 'To a Faded Violet', together probably with other personal lyrics (see *BSM* ix Introduction liii–lv).

The present poem was first published by Medwin in the *Athenaeum* 8 September 1832 and subsequently included without significant modification in his *Shelley Papers* in 1833, as 'Invocation to Misery' (by which title it has usually been known). Mary S. did not include it in *1824*. The painfully personal and bitter tone of the poem, and its almost explicit references to her attitude to S., may well have dictated Mary's omission, although it is possible that she was unaware of any usable fair copy to hand for *1824*, as she appears not to have consulted *Nbk 8* (presumably assuming it to contain nothing but a superseded copy of *PU*; see headnote to *PU*), and the fair copy in *Box 1* may still have been with Hunt, who published 'The cold earth slept below' from the same MS in the *Literary Pocket Book* for 1823 (see headnote to nos 127–128). The poem's inclusion in *1839* was doubtless prompted by Medwin's earlier publication of the version in his possession. Mary places it among the 'Poems of 1818' in *1839* iii 153–5, but given the poem's subject this may be disingenuous, or genuinely confused, as it is perfectly possible that Mary never saw the lines in S.'s lifetime; but as *SC* vi 863–4 cogently argues, the serious breakdown in relations between S. and Mary took place not in 1818 (though it came under great strain with the death of Clara), but in Rome after the death of William, and Mary's possible unwillingness to publish the poem in *1824* may itself suggest that the poem dates from that period. The cancelled reference in 'Fragment A' (see the following appendix) to a mother clasping her dying 'boy' seems to confirm an unnervingly direct personal reference for the poem. The summer references in lines 21–30, especially the willow, the 'fresh grass newly mown', and also the 'same lone home' (line 13), might suggest the countryside around Livorno, where the Shelleys arrived 17 June, or perhaps the Villa Valsovano just outside Livorno, where they moved a week after their arrival from Rome (*Claire Jnl* 113–14, *Mary L* i 100–1, *Mary Jnl* i 291). Medwin's story (*Medwin I* 324–9), that the lines are connected with the mysterious unknown lady admirer who followed S. to Italy and died after a confessional meeting with him at Naples, lacks plausibility or any substantial corroborating evidence (but see *Cameron (1974)* 72). It is possible that the poem actually echoes at one point some phrasing from *PU* II i (see notes); but the echo may of course run the other way.

There are also stylistic grounds for placing the poem in the summer of 1819; the stanza is based on five seven-syllable lines, with some octosyllabic alternation, rhyming *aabbb*, and may be regarded as in transition from the metrically similar manner of 'Lines written among the Euganean Hills', 'Stanzas written in dejection – December 1818, near Naples', and some of the Furies' choruses from *PU* I, towards the more sardonic voice of *Mask of Anarchy*, which uses a four-line seven-syllable stanza with some octosyllabic variation, and which also occasionally introduces the exact stanza of 'Misery. – A Fragment' (*Mask* lines 11–14, 130–4, 151–5, 221–5, 270–4, 331–5, 368–72). The poem's possible role in S.'s developing poetic voice may also bear on Neil Fraistat's argument in *BSM* ix that the textual history of 'Misery. – A Fragment' has involved suppression of a political dimension in the poem. He suggests that various drafts in *Nbk 11*, which are in the same stanza as the poem itself but which are overtly political in character, were 'suppressed' by S. himself in a way which compounds what he describes as the different attempted suppressions on personal grounds by Mary (see *BSM* ix Introduction xlvii–lx for a very full and thoughtful discussion). Other commentators have subsequently spoken of the poem as S. himself proposed to publish it as the 'apolitical' or 'depoliticized version' (*BSM* xviii 296–7). But it can hardly be doubted that S. intended to publish the poem as a personal document; and while there are good reasons to suppose that the passages in the same stanza in *Nbk 11* and *Nbk 8* (which are given here in an appendix) are indeed rejected drafts for 'Misery. – A Fragment', it must be remembered that they are in themselves no more than fragmentarily unresolved and inconclusive, and that they may have been discarded because S. had moved to a new development of a political inflection for this bitter personal voice, under the stimulus of the Peterloo Massacre and the composition of *Mask of Anarchy* in September 1819. The subsequent appearance of these unused stanzas under various more or less misleading guises, as S.'s MSS have entered the public domain, has certainly furthered confusion, but does not affect the question of S.'s original intention, which seems clearly enough to have been to leave them out of the poem. It is however the case that the fair copy – effectively a press copy – in *Box 1* uses a pattern of crosses after the last stanza as if to indicate the omission of material; but whether this implies omitted personal material, or an entire political dimension omitted under pressures now unknown, it is impossible to say.

S.'s fair copy in *Box 1* probably derives from the intermediate fair copy in *Nbk 8*, which is based in turn on *Nbk 11*. Medwin's text presumably derives from the copy that he claims (*Medwin* i 331) S. showed him in 1821, and which he allowed him to copy; as *BSM* ix shows this Medwin copy seems to be based on a copy of S.'s, now lost, apparently intermediate between *Nbk 11* and *Nbk 8*. Mary's text in *1839* is probably based on Medwin's in *Shelley Papers*, corrected from *Box 1*, which while evidently the best text has clearly not been used as press copy. See *BSM* ix Introduction xlvii–xlix, and *BSM* xxi 448–53, for detailed discussion and collations, and also Joseph Raben, 'Shelley's "Invocation to Misery": An Expanded Text', *JEGP* lxv (1966) 65–74. As noted above, there are various fragmentary drafts which are probably unused stanzas for this poem, and these are given in the following appendix. For further detailed discussion of the poem's various contexts, and its possible composition dates, see *BSM* xviii Introduction xxxix–xlviii.

Text from *Box 1* ff. 79v–81r.

Published in *The Athenaeum* 8 September 1832 (as 'Invocation to Misery'); *1839* iii 153–5.

202
Misery. – A Fragment

    Come, be happy, sit near me
    Shadow-vested Misery,
    Coy, unwilling, silent bride,
    Mourning in thy robe of pride,
5   Desolation deified.

    Come, be happy; sit near me:
    Sad as I may seem to thee
    I am merrier yet than thou,
    Lady, whose imperial brow
10   Is endiademed with woe.

    Misery! — we have known each other
    Like a sister and a brother
    Living in the same lone home
    Many years: we must live some
15   Hours or ages yet to come. —

    'Tis an evil lot, and yet
    Let us make the best of it —
    If love can live when pleasure dies
    We two will love; till in our eyes
20   This heart's Hell seem Paradise.

1. near] by *1832*.

2. Misery,] Misery. *BSM* xxi.

3. unwilling,] unwilling *Box 1*.

8. merrier yet] happier still *Nbk 11*; happier far *1832*, *1839*.

11. we] We *BSM* xxi.

15. Hours or] Years and *1832. come. –*] come – *Box 1*.

17. best] most *1832*.

18. can live] lives *Nbk 11*, *Nbk 8*, *1832*.

19. two] Omitted in *1832*.

20. Paradise.] Paradise *Box 1*.

Come, be happy — lie thee down
On the fresh grass newly mown
While the grasshopper doth sing
Merrily — one joyous thing
25   In a world of sorrowing.

There our tent shall be the willow
And mine arm shall be thy pillow:
Sounds and odours, sorrowful
Because they once were sweet, shall lull
30   Us to slumber deep and dull. —

Ha! thy frozen pulses flutter
With a love thou dar'st not utter —
Thou art murmuring — thou art weeping —
Is thine icy bosom leaping
35   While my burning heart lies sleeping?

Kiss me; — oh, thy lips are cold —
Round my neck thine arms enfold: —
They are soft, but chill and dead,
And thy tears upon my head
40   Burn like points of frozen lead.

Hasten to the bridal bed —
Underneath the grave 'tis spread;
In darkness may our love be hid,
Oblivion is our coverlid —
45   We may rest, and none forbid. —

21–30. The descriptive details in these lines suggest a setting in early summer; see headnote.

23. While] Altered from *where* in Nbk 8; *where* Nbk 11, *1832*, *1839*.

25. sorrowing.] sorrowing *Box 1*.

27. mine . . . thy] thine . . . my *1832*.

28–9. Cp. *PU* II i 8–10: 'As suddenly / Thou comest as the memory of a dream, / Which now is sad because it hath been sweet'.

30. All but the first word of this line is omitted in *Nbk 8*, perhaps because S. had run into the bottom of the page. *dull. –*] dull – *Box 1*.

32. A row of asterisks follows this line in *1832*, doubtless to cover the fact that in conflating lines 34–5 below Medwin's copy had dropped a line in this stanza; see *BSM* ix 583.

34–5. These lines are conflated in *1832* to read 'Whilst my burning bosom's leaping'.

36–40. There is a cancelled slightly different version of this stanza in *Nbk 8*, which is followed by the received stanza.

36. oh,] oh *Box 1*.

38. dead,] dead *Box 1*.

44. is] be *Nbk 11, 1832, 1839. coverlid –*] coverlid *Box 1. coverlid*] i.e. 'coverlet', in the general sense of 'covering'.

Clasp me, till our hearts be grown
Like two shadows into one —
Till this dreadful transport may
Like a vapour fade away
50   In the sleep which lasts alway:

We may dream in that long sleep
That we are not those who weep;
Even as Pleasure dreams of thee
Life-deserting Misery,
55   Thou mayest dream of her with me. —

Let us laugh and make our mirth
At the shadows of the Earth —
As dogs bay the moonlight clouds
Which like spectres wrapped in shrouds
60   Fleet o'er Night in multitudes.

All the wide world, beside us
Shows like multitudinous
Puppets passing from a scene —
What but mockery can they mean
65   Where I am — where thou hast been?

*   *   *   *   *

*   *   *   *   *

*   *   *   *   *

46–50. This stanza has been added in *Nbk 8* at a later date, although the draft is in *Nbk 11* p. 128 (see *BSM* ix 288–9).

47. *shadows*] lovers' *Nbk 8*; lovers *Nbk 11, 1832*.

50. *which*] that *1832, 1839*. *alway:*] alway. *BSM* xxi (the reading is debatable, as the lower point of what is here taken as a colon is set below the line).

57. *the . . . of*] all . . . on *Nbk 8*.

59. *Which*] That *1832*.

60. *Fleet*] Pass *Nbk 11, Nbk 8, 1832, 1839*.

62. *Shows*] Are *Nbk 11, Nbk 8, 1832*; Show *1839*.

63. *Puppets*] Altered from *Shadows* in *Box 1*; Shadows Nbk 8, 1832; figures *Nbk 11*. *passing*] shifting *1832*.

64. *can*] may *1832*.

65. *I am*] am I *1832*. The asterisks following the last line presumably indicate omitted material; see headnote.

202 Appendix
Unused stanzas for 'Misery. – A Fragment'

A: 'When a lover clasps his fairest'

Text from *Nbk 11* p. 108; first published in *1840* as a two-stanza fragment. There are transcriptions in both *BSM* xviii and *BSM* ix Introduction li, and in Raben, *JEGP* lxv (1966) 65–74. See *BSM* ix Introduction lv for the publication history of these two stanzas.

When a lover clasps his fairest
Then be our dread sport the rarest
Their caresses   like chaff
In the tempest, and be our laugh
5   His despair — her epitaph

When a mother clasps her child
Watch till dusty Death has piled
Its cold ashes on the clay —
She has loved it many a day
10   She remains . . . it fades away

When a mighty

B: 'When a King ascends a throne'

Text from *Nbk 11* p. 119; first published in *Julian* iii 305–6, in confused relation with the preceding item. See *BSM* ix Introduction lv, *BSM* xviii 298–9, for discussion of the publication history; both vols of *BSM* offer transcriptions, as does Raben, *JEGP* lxv (1966).

When a King ascends a throne
Blood and gold have made his own
When a hundred Kings bestride
Mighty nations, in their pride
5   Spurning in their deadly ride;

3. The gap is produced by a cancellation, possibly of 'it were'; see *BSM* ix and xviii for alternative possible readings.

5. There is a false start following this line, apparently picked up and developed a few pages later in *Nbk 11*, as the item following.

6. *child*] Written after *boy* canc. in *Nbk 11* (see main headnote).

8. *Its*] Written in before the original cancelled reading, which was possibly 'His'; *BSM* ix reads '[K] [His *canc.*]', *BSM* xviii 'His / His *canc.*'.

11. *mighty*] Smighty *BSM* xviii.

¶B 2. *Blood and gold*] See *PU* I 531 and note.

And liars [?knaves] [?tyrants] murderers
At their heels like yelping curs —
Pontiffs, warriors, [?combatants], [?treading]

C: 'When soft winds and sunny skies'

Text from *Nbk 11* p. 181; first published in *1839* as a fragment. See *BSM* ix Introduction lv–lvi for transcription and discussion of the publication history, and also *BSM* xviii 307, and Raben, *JEGP* lxv (1966).

When soft winds and sunny skies
With the green earth harmonize
And the young and dewy dawn
Bold as an unhunted fawn
5   Up the windless Heaven is gone

Laugh — for ambushed in the day
Clouds and whirlwinds watch their prey —

Smile like thee a dying

D: 'When a Nation screams aloud'

Text from *Nbk 8* f. 23ʳrev.; see *BSM* ix 256–7, 573–4; these fragments may possibly be connected with *Mask of Anarchy* rather than 'Misery. – A Fragment'.

When a Nation screams aloud
Like an eagle from the cloud
When a

Watch the look askance and cold —
5   See neglect, and falsehood fold

203
'The world is dreary'

Drafted in pencil in *Nbk 11* pp. 148–9; when Mary published the first six lines as a fragment in *1840* she dated them 'July 1819', and their mood strongly suggests the period of Mary's deep depression following William's death in Rome on 7 June 1819. S. adapted the last six lines for *PU* IV 24–9 (which are drafted in *Nbk 11*

6–8. These lines are confused and very difficult to read in *Nbk 11*; see *BSM* ix Introduction lii and *BSM* xviii 149 for differing transcriptions.

pp. 84–5, 88). For further detailed discussion of this fragment's possible contexts see *BSM* xviii Introduction xlvi–xlvii.

Text from *Nbk 11* pp. 148–9 (all punctuation is editorial).

Published in *1840* (lines 1–6), *Julian* iii 297 (a version of lines 7–8, 10).

The world is dreary,
And I am weary
Of wandering on without thee Mary;
A [?soul] was erewhile
In thy voice and thy smile
But 'tis gone when I should be gone too, Mary.

O why do we rest
On the world's cold breast
When the warmth has gone which made us blest?
Thy [?name] is like the [?violet's] [?scent]
[?Suddenly] floating past upon the wind

O that I may
Be melted away
Like a mist in the [?grasp] of the [?burning] [?day]
With the lullaby
Of birds that die
On the bosom of their own harmony.

5

10

15

204

'What dost thou here Spirit of glowing life'

Written in *Nbk 11* p. 180 rev.; *BSM* xviii 307 conjectures an association with *PU* I, but in mood the lines match other poems and fragments written by S. in the period following the death of William, June–August 1819.

Text from *Nbk 11* p. 180 rev.   Published in *BSM* xviii 217.

What dost thou here Spirit of glowing life
In this decaying bosom

¶203   4. *[?soul]*] joy *1840*; A/[?feast] joy *BSM* xviii.

6. The line takes up too much space in *Nbk 11*, and the last three words are written by S. as a turn-over line, aligned to the right. The transcript in *BSM* xviii reads a capital for *gone*, which gives the appearance of two lines of verse.   *But*] And *1840*; OBut *BSM* xviii.

9–11. Difficult to read in *Nbk 11*; see *BSM* xviii for a differing transcription.

14. Like a mist in the [?warmth] of [?] *BSM* xviii.   16. *birds*] winds *BSM* xviii.

¶204   1. *glowing*] Very difficult to read; 'fiery' is possible (*BSM* xviii reads 'frozen').

2. *decaying*] Also difficult; *BSM* xviii reads 'terrifying'.

205

'My dearest Mary, wherefore hast thou gone'

Drafted in pencil, with some ink insertions, in *Nbk 11* (the lines are now badly faded); Mary's two transcripts are both dated 'Livorno, August 1819', although when she published the fragment in *1840* she revised her date to July (see *BSM* ii 90–1, 230, and *Massey* 88–9). The transcript in adds. d. 9 is entitled 'To M –'. The lines clearly belong to the period of Mary's continuing deep depression following the death of William Shelley in June. S. wrote for example to Amelia Curran from Livorno on 5 August 1819 that 'Mary's spirits still continue wretchedly depressed – more so than a stranger . . . could imagine' (*L* ii 107). Bruce Barker-Benfield places these lines in the context of the extraordinary series of letters sent by Godwin to his daughter in response to the news of William's death, which coldly urge on Mary a stoical resolve which was so ill-judged that S. felt obliged by mid-August to start intercepting his letters (see *Shelley's Guitar* 117–18, which gives a transcript of the draft, and *L* ii 109).

Text from *Nbk 11* p. 179 rev. (punctuation has been added in lines 1 and 2).

Published in *1840* 320 (lines 1–8), *Chernaik* 149, 247 (lines 1–9).

> My dearest Mary, wherefore hast thou gone
> And left me in this dreary world alone?
> Thy form is here indeed, a lovely [?   ]
>
> But thou art fled, — gone down the dreary road
5 > Which leads to Sorrow's most obscure abo[de]
> Thou sittest on the hearth of pale despair
> If [   ] where
> For thine own sake I cannot follow the[e]
> Do thou return for mine —

---

1. Mary,] M. *Nbk 11.*

3. lovely [?   ]] lovely one – *1840.* S. has inked over the word *lovely* in *Nbk 11*, and then apparently left a blank; *BSM* xviii reads 'lovely [? s]', and *Chernaik* reads 'lovely . . .'. There is a space following this line in *Nbk 11.*

7. Space left in *Nbk 11. If*] It *Chernaik, Shelley's Guitar.* Both words appear to have been added later, in ink.

8. the[e]] the<?re> *BSM* xviii.

9. Added later, in ink (first published in *Chernaik*).

206
'Wilt thou forget the happy hours'

This poem is written in *Nbk 11* among drafts for *PU* IV and 'Misery. – A Fragment' and other pieces dating probably from 1819. Mary published it in *1824* as 'The Past', and in *1839* and *1840* she added the date '1818'. But the poem's mood, together with its nbk context, suggest that these lines, like the preceding items, were written in the difficult period following William's death and Mary's resulting depression and distance from S. Mary's subsequent scattered datings of several such poems may be calculated to draw attention away from their true context in the Shelleys' strained relations in the summer of 1819. A more specific date for this poem in the second half of August 1819 might be suggested by its thematic affinity with some passages in S.'s surviving letters from that period. After remarking to Hunt in a letter of 15 August that 'Poor Mary's spirits continue dreadfully depressed' (*L* ii 109), S. wrote to Peacock from Livorno on 24 August 'How we prize what we despised when present! So the ghosts of our dead associations rise & haunt us in revenge for our having let them starve, & abandoned them to perish' (*L* ii 114).

Text from *Nbk 11* p. 104 (the draft is sparsely punctuated; the text here follows the pointing in *1824* except where indicated).

Published in *1824* 208.

> Wilt thou forget the happy hours
> Which we buried in Love's sweet bowers,
> Heaping over their corpses cold
> Blossoms and leaves instead of mould?
> 5   Blossoms which were the joys that fell,
> And leaves, the hopes that yet remain.
>
> Forget the dead, the past? o yet
> These are ghosts that may take revenge for it,
> Memories that make the heart a tomb,

1. *happy*] Written above *buried* canc. in *Nbk 11*.

3. *corpses cold*] balmy ruin *Nbk 11* canc.

4. *leaves*] leaves, *1824*.

5. *joys*] Written under *hopes* canc. in *Nbk 11*.

6. Following this line S. left a blank and then began the second stanza with two canc. lines: 'They who forget the dead will die / And their ghosts be without a memory'.

7–12. Cp. S.'s letter to Peacock of 24 August 1819, quoted in the headnote.

8. *These*] There *1824*. *These* is altered from *They* in *Nbk 11*; the final reading is not clear and *There* is possible (and would fit the context equally well, perhaps better).

10   Regrets which glide through the spirit's gloom
         And with ghastly whispers tell
         That joy, once lost, is pain.

207
'The babe is at peace within the womb'

Written out neatly in ink in the midst of miscellaneous materials in *Nbk 11*. The lines fit the period between the death of William Shelley in June and the birth of Percy Florence Shelley on 12 November 1819; the calmed tone perhaps points to late August or September (see *Shelley's Guitar* 118 for comment and a transcript).

Text from *Nbk 11* p. 180.

Published in *1840* 321.

         The babe is at peace within the womb
         The corpse is at rest within the tomb
         We begin in what we end —

208
'There is a warm and gentle atmosphere'

Written in ink in *Nbk 10*, where it is skipped by the draft for 'People of England, ye who toil and groan'. That poem is a product of S.'s reaction to the news of the Peterloo Massacre, which reached him in early September (see headnote to *Mask of Anarchy*), and these lines are therefore presumably earlier than that, and are perhaps connected with S.'s feelings for Mary after the death of William. The idea in these lines of identity characterised as an enwrapping atmosphere occurs in various contexts in S.'s poetry; see e.g. *L&C* IX v 8, 'The Sensitive Plant' I 69, and *PU* I 676, II i 75, IV 323.

Text from *Nbk 10* f. 59v rev.

Published in *1840* 321 (given the title 'Love's Atmosphere' by Forman).

10. *gloom*] gloom, *1824*.
11. *ghastly*] [?parting] *BSM* xviii.   *whispers*] Written above *accents* canc. in *Nbk 11*.
12. *lost,*] left/lost, *BSM* xviii.

There is a warm and gentle atmosphere
About the form of one we love, and thus
As in a tender mist our spirits are
Wrapped in the [   ] of that which is to us
5   The breath of life's own life, without which we
Is as a tomb vacant and [   ] our

4. Space left in *Nbk 10*.
5. In *1840* the lines end here with the reading 'The health of life's own life'.
6. Space left in *Nbk 10*.

712

209
The Cenci
A Tragedy in Five Acts

Edited by Michael Rossington*

According to Mary, 'When in Rome, in 1819, a friend put into our hands the old manuscript account of the story of the Cenci' (*1839* ii 274). However, the MS account to which she refers here was in fact communicated to Mary, S. and Claire by John and Maria Gisborne the previous year in Livorno. Claire's jnl entry for 25 May 1818 (which covers the period since 1 May) includes the statement, 'We are much with the Gisbornes. Read the manuscrit [*sic*] History of the *Cenci* family' (*SC* v 455). In her entry for 23 May, Mary notes, 'Copy Mʳ G's M.S.', and for 25 May, 'Finish Copying the Cenci M.S.' (*Mary Jnl* i 211). Interest was revived a year later in Rome possibly through the *conversazioni* in the salon of Signora Marianna Candida Dionigi whom they saw regularly in March and April 1819 (see *Mary Jnl* i 254–61 and *White* ii 88–91; Dionigi and her salon are referred to in Lady Morgan, *Italy*, 2 vols. (London, 1821) ii 273). On 22 April 1819 the three saw a portrait in the Palazzo Colonna believed to be of Beatrice Cenci and attributed to Guido Reni (*Mary Jnl* i 259 and *Claire Jnl* 108; see Appendix B). Mary's involvement in the composition of *C* is recorded in *1839*, where she states that as a direct result of seeing the portrait,

Shelley's imagination became strongly excited, and he urged the subject to me as one fitted for a tragedy. More than ever I felt my incompetence; but I entreated him to write it instead; and he began and proceeded swiftly, urged on by intense sympathy with the sufferings of the human beings whose passions, so long cold in the tomb, he revived and gifted with poetic language. This tragedy is the only one of his works that he communicated to me during its progress. We talked over the arrangement of the scenes together (*1839* ii 274).

The ménage moved to no. 65 Via Sestina from the Corso on 5 May. S., Mary and Claire visited 'yᵉ Casa Cenci' (i.e. the Palazzo Cenci) on the afternoon of 11 May (*Mary Jnl* i 262). Mary first notes that S. 'writes his Tragedy' on 14 May (*Mary Jnl* i 263), and it seems likely that it was between 22 April and 14 May that S. consulted Mary's copy of 'Mʳ G's M.S.' and made the notes on the Cenci story in *Nbk 10* (see *MYR* iv xxxii). On 14 May Claire records 'Read Manuscript of the Cenci Family' (*Claire Jnl* 111), which could suggest that the MS was read aloud. At this time S. was ordered by a Scottish surgeon, Mr Bell, to spend the summer in Naples on account of his consumptive symptoms. But, after the onset of William's fever at the end of May, it was decided that they would move to the Bagni di Lucca instead, within riding distance of the Gisbornes at Livorno. The intended date of departure of 7 June was delayed by the tragic death of their three-year old son William and his subsequent burial in the Cimitero Acattolico. They left Rome on

* *Michael Rossington wishes to acknowledge the help and support of the following in preparing this edition: Linda Anderson, Bruce Barker-Benfield, Rowena Bryson, Marilyn Butler, Tom Cain, Eric Cross, Joan Frayn, Desmond Graham, Paul Hamilton, Claire Lamont, Maryse Morton L'Hoste, Justin Philips, Michael Pincombe, Robert Parks, John Pitcher, Francesco Rognoni, Freda Rossington, Rowland Smith, Maria Pia Wilkins, and, especially, Annabel Hayward, Rosanna, Jessamyn, and Thomas.*

10 June for Livorno where they arrived on 17 June (*Claire Jnl* 113–14). Having visited the Gisbornes, they moved into Villa Valsovano near the village of Monte Nero, within walking distance of Livorno. As Holmes remarks, 'The summer of 1819 at Monte Nero was a time of great unhappiness in Shelley's household' (*Holmes* 519; and see 202 headnote), but the Villa turned out a congenial setting for S. to write. Mary comments that S. made its glass tower his study: 'the dazzling sunlight and heat made it almost intolerable to every other; but Shelley basked in both, and his health and spirits revived under their influence. In this airy cell he wrote the principal part of the Cenci' (*1839* ii 276). S. described his tower as 'like Scythrop's' (*L* ii 100, 105) in which a tragedy is composed in Peacock's *Nightmare Abbey* (1818). S. appears to have worked steadily on the play from the end of June until the middle of August but there is no evidence for Holmes's neat division of the writing of the play into two stages, a first draft completed by 29 May, and a second draft written at Villa Valsovano (see *Holmes* 517, 521). The bulk of the play, or a version of it, seems to have been written by the middle of July; in his letter to Peacock of ?25 July 1819 (for dating of this letter, see *SC* vi 897n.1), S. refers to it as almost 'ready to be sent' (*L* ii 103). This impressively brief period of composition accords with S.'s later statement to Peacock in a letter of ?24 August that 'my work on the Cenci . . . was done in two months' (*L* ii 115). In a letter to Amelia Curran of 5 August, S. states 'I have nearly finished my Cenci – which Mary likes' (*L* ii 107) and Mary records that S. 'finishes his tragedy' on 8 August (*Mary Jnl* i 294). But S.'s letter to Hunt of 15 August (SC 531), in which covert reference to *C* is made, indicates that he was still at work: 'My Prometheus is finished, and [I] am also on the eve of completing another work, totally different from any thing you might conjecture that I should write, of a more popular kind, &, if any thing of mine c^d deserve attention, of higher claims. – "Be innocent of the knowledge dearest chuck till thou approve the performance"' (text from *SC* vi 851), the latter a play on *Macbeth* III ii 45–6: 'Be innocent of the knowledge, dearest chuck, / Till thou applaud the deed'. S.'s reference here to imminent completion suggests that a fair copy of the play was probably made, with Mary's help, between 11–20 August (*Mary Jnl* i 294, *L about S* 32). The Preface seems to have been drafted in mid-August. A passage in the Preface ('In a dramatic composition . . . shadow of its own greatness', lines 116–23), drafted in *Nbk 10* ff. 15^{v}rev–16^{r}rev, contains echoes of a draft fragment explaining the poetic language of *J&M* also in *Nbk 10* (ff. 1^{r}rev–1^{v}rev) polished in S.'s letter to Hunt of 15 August (*SC* vi 851–2, ll. 18–29) which contained *J&M* (see headnote to no. 198).

It is possible to date S.'s decision to dedicate *C* to Hunt between 16 and 19 August, when S. finally received the parcel from Ollier containing Hunt's portrait by John Wildman along with a letter from the Hunts in which the portrait is discussed at length (see *SC* vi 605–18). The Hunts' letter had been written between the middle of July and 4 August 1818 (for dating, see *SC* vi 614) but Hunt only registers that Ollier's parcel might still not have reached its destination a year later, in his letter to S. of 8 July 1819: 'Is it possible that you have never received even Ollier's first packet yet, with the portrait in it, which I thought, in my egotism, was to gratify you so? I guess as much by your silence about it. –' (*SC* vi 840–1). Whereas S. informs Hunt in his letter dated 15 August, that 'no [portraits] are yet arrived?' (*SC* vi 852–3), Mary's journal entry of 20 August (the first since 11 August) notes its recent arrival (*Mary Jnl* i 295). S.'s letter of ?17–19 August acknowledging receipt of the portrait suggests that he conceived of dedicating the tragedy to Hunt the preceding evening: 'I have written something & finished it – different from anything else & a new attempt for me, – & I mean to dedicate it to you. I should not *have done* so without your approbation, but I asked your picture last night & it smiled assent. If I did not think it in some degree worthy of you I would not make you a public offering of it – I expect to have to write to you soon about it –' (*L* ii 112). However, as against the view advanced in *SC* vi 871–2 that the actual drafting of the Dedication took place between 16 and 19 August, a later date is possible. The draft of the Dedication in *Nbk 10* begins directly after the draft of the passage from the Song in *PU* II iii that became ll. 86–9 (see photograph and transcription of *Nbk 10*, f. 6⁽ᵃ⁾ʳ in *MYR* iv 28–9), and both *BSM* ix 595 and *Curran (1975)* 209 suggest that the draft of the Song in *Nbk 10* may be dated to early September (see note to *PU* II iii 54–98). It is possible that the news of Peterloo which had reached S. by 6 September (see headnote to *Mask*) informs the explicitly political reference of the drafts of the final paragraph of the Dedication (see *Nbk 10*, f. 6⁽ᶜ⁾ʳ in *MYR* iv 36–7). Though not always reliable in matters of chronology, it is significant that Mary states that S. was 'writing the Cenci, when the news of the Manchester Massacre reached us' (*1839* iii 205). The published version of the Dedication ends: 'ROME, May 29, 1819'. The reason why S. wanted to record his presence in the city in which the events recounted in *C* occurred, and in which he conceived and began work on it, are easy to understand but the significance of retrospectively appending this precise date to the Dedication remains a matter of conjecture. Mary adds '*Rome, May*, 1819' to *J&M* in *1824* (26) (see headnote to no. 201). In each case, a private reference to the days prior to the calamity of William's death seems possible. Reiman speculates that 29 May 'was one of the last days when William Shelley's health seemed to be improving from the illness that struck on Tuesday May 25' (*SC* vi 873).

Relatively few MS sources of *C* survive though a forged MS of part of the play was in circulation in the early 1950s according to *Cameron (1974)* 636n.11. *Box 1* f. 198ᵛ contains a draft fragment of V i 77–8, and three lines not included in the final text of the play (see *BSM* xxi 228–9). Barker-Benfield notes that 'these few scraps suggest at least some drafting [of *C*] in a notebook which he later discarded after tearing out his fair copy of *The Coliseum*' (*Shelley's Guitar* 113). The phrase 'Then they must be' and various calculations on f. 201ᵛ also probably belong with the drafting of *C* as do fragments of S.'s writing on the stubs of *Box 1* f. 199ʳ and f. 200ʳ and *Box 2* f. 16ʳ. For a reconstruction of 'the original notebook quire (or portion of quire)' from which *The Coliseum* was torn, containing these draft fragments of *C*, see *BSM* xxii (Part II) 17. S.'s notes on the Cenci story in *Nbk 10* ff. 2ʳrev–5ʳrev re-work material in 'Mʳ G's M.S.' for *C*, a process examined by Paul Smith in 'Restless Casuistry: Shelley's Composition of *The Cenci*', *KSJ* xiii (1964) 77–85. S.'s draft of the Preface in *Nbk 10* ff. 7ʳrev–18ᵛrev is followed by the 'Note on Shakespeare' (ff. 19ʳrev–20ʳrev). Forman seems right to say that the latter was 'unquestionably a part of the original scheme of the Preface' excluded because 'it was too long an *excursus*' (*Huntington Nbks* ii 99). A version of one part of the 'Note' (f. 19ʳrev, ll. 14–22, f. 19ᵛrev, and f. 20ʳrev, ll. 1–8) was published by Mary in her 'Note on the Prometheus Unbound' (*1839* ii 136–7) and of the other (f. 19ʳrev, ll. 1–10) as 'Fragment XIX' in *Relics* 81. For commentary on material relating to *C* in *Nbk 10* see *Huntington Nbks* ii 84–103 and *MYR* iv. S.'s draft of the Dedication is in CHPL (for a facsimile, with a transcription and commentary, see *SC* vi 865–74). The three leaves containing the draft of the Dedication, probably removed from *Nbk 10* by Mary or Lady Shelley and given to Hunt are restored to their original position in *Nbk 10* (ff. 6(a)ʳ–6(c)ʳ) by Quinn in *MYR* iv 28–37. For *C*'s relationship to *Relation*, see Appendix B.

The text of the play was printed probably by the firm of Glauco Masi of Livorno (see *Dowden Life* ii 279) in late August or early September (in his letter to Peacock of 9 September S. says that *C* 'was then already printing when I received your letter' (*L* i 118) which implies that Peacock's response to S.'s letter about *C* of ?25 July was communicated after 24 August when S. had last written to him). Mary's 'Note' states that S. 'printed a small edition at Leghorn to insure its correctness; as he was much annoyed by the many mistakes that crept into his text, when distance prevented him from correcting the press' (*1839* ii 279). S.'s letter to Peacock of 21 September 1819 mentions other considerations, both financial ('I have printed in Italy 250 copies', because it costs, with all duties & freightage about half what it wd. cost in London') and strategic ('My other reason, was a belief that the seeing it in print wd. enable the people at the theatre to judge more easily' (*L* ii 119)). The printed text of the play probably without the Dedication, Preface, and title-page was sent to Peacock on 10 September (*Mary Jnl* i 296). S. had earlier enjoined Peacock to secrecy concerning its authorship: 'I wish to preserve a complete incognito, & can trust to you, that whatever else you do, you will at least favour me on this point. Indeed this is essential, deeply essential to it's success. After it had been acted & successfully (could I hope such a thing) I would own it if I pleased, & use the celebrity it might acquire to my own purposes. –' (*L* ii 102). The 250 copies of *Cenci (1819)* were ready to be shipped to England by 21 September but were not sent until much later (see headnote to *PU*). In his letter from Florence of 14 October (for dating of this letter, see *SC* vi 929n.8), S. tells Maria Gisborne that 'I should be very much obliged to you if you would contrive to send the Cenci's which are at the printers to England by the next ship – I forgot it in the hurry of departure' (*L* ii 126). A few weeks later, in a letter of 4 November, Mary thanks Maria Gisborne 'for your trouble about the Cenci' (*Mary L* i 111). S. believed the ship to have sailed 'in the middle of December' (*L* ii 174). An interval between printing and publication had been intended by S. so as to allow Peacock time to get the play accepted by a London theatre but such a delay in publication was not anticipated. S.'s letter to Ollier of 15 October in which he acknowledges receipt of J. T. Coleridge's review of *RofI* (see headnote to *PU* and note to *PU* Preface line 54), shows how anxious he was to keep the project, in Mary's words, '*a deep secret*' (see *Mary L* i 106):

> I am on the point of sending to you 250 copies of a work which I have printed in Italy; which you will have to pay four or five pounds duty upon, on my account. Hunt will tell you the *kind of thing* it is, and in the course of the winter I shall send directions for its publication, *until the arrival of which directions I request that you would have the kindness not to* open the box, *or, if by necessity it is opened, to abstain from observing yourself, or permitting other to observe, what it contains.* I trust this confidently to you, it being of consequence. Meanwhile, assure yourself that this work has no reference, direct or indirect, to politics, or religion, or personal satire, and that this precaution is merely literary. (*L* ii 127)

On the previous day S. had told Maria Gisborne, 'I have just heard from Peacock saying that he dont think my tragedy will do & and that he dont much like it' (*L* ii 126), and was clearly beginning to interpret Peacock's silence, correctly, to indicate that the play was not going to be staged. S. had requested Peacock 'to procure for me its presentation at Covent Garden' (*L* ii 102 and *Peacock Works* viii 119) and contemplated Edmund Kean in the role of the Count and Eliza O'Neill as Beatrice. The latter's performance as Bianca in Milman's *Fazio* (1815) had impressed him at Covent Garden on 16 February 1818 (see *Mary Jnl* i 193), though Milman is named in S.'s denunciation of contemporary English tragedy as 'miserable trash' in a letter to Byron of 4 May 1821 (*L* ii 290). Of O'Neill, S. commented that the part of Beatrice 'might even seem to have been written for her' (*L* ii 102) and, though contradicted by Medwin (*Medwin (1913)* 219), Mary's statement that O'Neill was 'often in his thoughts as he wrote' (*1839* ii 277) is echoed by Peacock (*Peacock Works* viii 81). Hazlitt viewed her as the greatest tragic actress since Mrs Siddons and his reviews of her in the role of Belvidera in Otway's *Venice Preserved* demonstrate why S. would have considered her ideally suited to the role of Beatrice (see *Hazlitt Works* xviii 196, 265–7). But Thomas Harris, the manager of Covent Garden 'pronounced the subject to be so objectionable, that he could not even submit the part to Miss O'Neil [*sic*] for perusal' (*1839* ii 279). S.'s later statement that *C* 'was refused at Drury Lane' (*L* ii 178) appears to be an error as there is no evidence that Peacock showed *C* to any theatre manager other than Harris. S. effectively instructed Ollier in a letter of 15 December 1819 to proceed with publication on receipt of the copies of *Cenci (1819)*: 'When the box comes, you may write a note to Mr. Peacock; or it would be better to call on him, and ask if *my tragedy is accepted*? If not, publish what you find in the box. I think it will succeed as a publication' (*L* ii 163). News of Harris's rejection of *C* is recorded in Mary's letter to Amelia Curran of 19 January 1820 (*Mary L* i 127) in which she also acknowledges that the recently married O'Neill had just retired from the stage. On 6 March, having apparently had no acknowledgement of receipt from Ollier, S. provided instructions on recovering the items sent (*L* ii 174). A week later he is still anxious to hear that Ollier has 'received the parcel from Leghorn' (*L* ii 177).

Cenci (1819) had in fact been advertised as 'just published' in *The Examiner* (5 March 1820) 160, though the title-page of *Cenci (1819)* bears the date 1819: THE CENCI.| A TRAGEDY,| IN FIVE ACTS.| *By* PERCY B. SHELLEY.| ITALY.| PRINTED FOR C. AND J. OLLIER| VERE STREET, BOND STREET.| LONDON.| 1819. It is worth noting that his earlier idea, expressed to Peacock, that anonymity would be 'essential, deeply essential to [the play's] success' (*L* ii 102) had been abandoned, and that the word 'ITALY.' allows itself to be read not simply as a statement of the provenance of the printed text but as a pointed reference to *C*'s relevance to the contemporary nationalist struggle in the Italian peninsula. *Cenci (1819)* was briefly noticed in *The Examiner* (19 March 1820) 190 and the first reviews are dated 1 April. Sales of *Cenci (1819)* were reportedly good. Hunt's letter to the Shelleys of 6 April (SC 724) states that S.'s 'tragedy is out & flourishing' and reports Ollier telling Henry Hunt that the first edition 'had almost all gone off already' (*SC* viii 931), a claim repeated in *The Examiner* (30 April 1820) 278: '*The Cenci*, we understand, had nearly gone through the first edition some weeks ago'. Hogg wrote to S. on 21 May, 'I . . . am glad that you have begun to write upon some story, and the public seem as glad too, as I heard some time since that all but twelve copies had been disposed of' (*Shelley and Mary*, 4 vols (1882) iii [Bod. Pr. Shelley adds. e. 7] 502). Ollier's letter to Mary of 17 November 1823 (*Shelley and Mary* iv [Bod. Pr. Shelley adds.

e. 8] 990–1) in which he enumerates 'such copies of Mr. Shelley's works as remained in my possession' lists just three unsold copies of *Cenci (1819)*. *Cenci (1819)*'s reasonable sales were apparently not communicated to S. who told Peacock on 15 February 1821 that 'if my play of 'The Cenci' found none or few [readers], I despair of producing anything that shall merit them' (*L* ii 262) and to Byron on 4 May 1821 wrote, 'My "Cenci" had, I believe, a complete failure – at least the silence of the bookseller would say so' (*L* ii 290). Its success was commercially insignificant: Charles E. Robinson suggests that 'Even the sales on *The Cenci* would not have netted the poet much more than £40' ('Percy Bysshe Shelley, Charles Ollier, and William Blackwood: the contexts of early nineteenth-century publishing', in *Shelley Revalued* 199).

C is the only one of S.'s works to be published in an authorised second edition in his lifetime. S. contemplated a second edn as a result of his mistaken belief that Galignani had pirated *Cenci (1819)* in Paris (see *L* ii 188, 189, 191, 193, 216) an episode to which Mary refers in *Mary L* i 155–6. As Forman suggests, 'such an impression may have arisen from Galignani's having obtained and advertised for sale copies of Shelley's own edition' (*Shelley Library* (1886) 93). The advertisement possibly appeared in *Galignani's Weekly Repertory or Literary Gazette*. Evidence that S. was dissatisfied with *Cenci (1819)* is apparent from his letter to Ollier of 30 April 1820:

> I observe that an edition of *The Cenci* is advertised as published in Paris by Galignani. This, though a piracy both upon the author and the publisher, is a proof of an expectation of a certain demand for sale that probably will soon exhaust the small edition I sent you. In your reprint you will be guided of course by the apparent demand. I send a list of errata; the incorrectness of, the forms of typography, etc., which are considerably numerous, you will be so obliging as to attend to yourself. I cannot describe the trouble I had with the Italian printer (*L* ii 188).

The list of *errata* referred to (hereafter identified as *Errata*), appears to be the one in Mary's hand, first published by Forman (*Shelley Library* (1886) 91), and pasted into a copy of *Cenci (1819)* now in the Bodleian Library (Bod. shelfmark: Don. d. 130). This copy, once owned by Forman, contains an endorsement of *Errata* apparently in Ollier's hand on a paste-in, thus: '(No date)| Mrs Shelley| [Corrections for "The Cenci"]'. S. asked of Ollier on 14 May that a 'new edition of "The Cenci" . . . by all means . . . be instantly urged forward' (*L* ii 196), and on 12 July expected Peacock to be able to send him 'Six copies of the 2nd edit. of "Cenci"' (*L* ii 214). S. intended 'Corpses are Cold in the Tomb' to be published 'at the end of the second edition of the Cenci' (see *L* ii 246 and the headnote to no. 131). *Cenci (1821)* was published by Ollier and printed by Reynell in London apparently in the spring of 1821 (the first public notice of *Cenci (1821)* is the review in *The British Review and London Critical Journal* xvii (June 1821) 380–9). In his letter to Mary of 17 November 1823, referred to above, Ollier records having sent twelve unsold copies of *Cenci (1821)* to Hunt. That *Cenci (1821)* did not sell well is evident from its inclusion in a made-up set issued by the publishers Simpkin and Marshall, *Poetical Pieces, by the Late Percy Bysshe Shelley* (1823), comprising, as Ollier puts it, 'the unsold stock of those [works] which were printed at our sole expense . . . disposed of in the general sale of our property' in 1823 (*Shelley and Mary* iv [Bod. Pr. Shelley adds. e. 8] 990), i.e.: *1820, Hellas, Cenci (1821)*, and *1819*. The twelve unsold copies of *C* in quires to which Ollier refers in this letter (991) are presumably *Cenci (1821)*. An unauthorised edition of *C*, based on *Cenci (1821)*, was published by

William Benbow in 1827 (for a bibliographical description, see Forman, *Shelley Library* (1886) 93).

There are several areas of biographical reference in *C*. Mary suggests in *1839* ii 275n. that V ii 49–54 alludes to William's death, described by S. as a 'sacred loss' (*1839* iii 210). S.'s reflections on fatherhood as a result of losing custody of his children by Harriet (see no. 131 and 'Declaration in Chancery', *Prose Works* i 166–9), also seem to inform *C* (see note to I iii 105–6). Claire's mischievous suggestion of similarities between Cenci and Byron in a cancelled portion of a letter to the latter of ?18 May 1819 cannot be dismissed given the strongly 'Byronic' cast of much of the Count's language: 'Did you ever read the history of the Cenci's a most frightful & horrible story? [I am sorely afraid to say that in the elder Cenci you may behold [yourse]lf some twenty years hence but if I live Allegra shall never be a Beatrice. *canc.*]' (*Clairmont Correspondence* i 127). But Holmes's suggestion that *C* commemorates the dates of birth of children borne to Claire and Elise Foggi, allegedly fathered by S., is dubious (see note to I iii 68). Otto Rank makes the questionable assertion that *C* manifests S.'s 'own complexes' (*Das Incest-Motiv in Dichtung und Sage* (1912), trans. Gregory C. Richter, *The Incest Theme in Literature and Legend* (1992) 327–9 (327)).

For the Cenci story and the sources of S.'s knowledge of it, see Appendix B.

With the exception of the song in V iii, *C* is written in blank verse and is the only work of S.'s, apart from 'Alastor', 'entirely without end-rhyme' (Keach, *Shelley's Style* (1984) 165) except for the Song in V iii. In terms of Aristotelian poetics, *C* does not observe the unities of time and place though *hamartia* and *anagnorisis* are recognisable in it. *C* was conceived as a play to be performed (see *L* ii 102, 178) and represents a conscious decision on S.'s part to experiment with a genre which he had hitherto avoided and with which, in its contemporary form, he was impatient (see *1839* ii 276 and *Peacock Works* viii 81–2). *C* was first staged by the Shelley Society in a private performance with Alma Murray playing Beatrice before an audience of over 2,400 including Browning, Lowell, Meredith, Shaw, and Wilde at the Grand Theatre, Islington in May 1886 (reviewed engagingly by George Bernard Shaw, in *Our Corner* vii (1886) 370–3; for other reviews, see *The Shelley Society's Note-book* i [1886] 50–80). Censorship of the public staging of *C* on the grounds of its blasphemous and incestuous content was annulled in 1920, one hundred years after the play's publication. The first legal and public staging of *C* in England, by Lewis Casson and Sybil Thorndike (the latter in the role of Beatrice), was at the New Theatre, London, in 1922 (for reviews and notices, see *Shelley: After One-Hundred Years*, 9 vols (1922) ix), a production revived briefly in 1926. Casson and Thorndike were also involved in a dramatisation of *C* broadcast by the BBC on the Third Programme in 1947 and repeated in 1948 (see Bert O. States, Jr., 'Addendum: The Stage History of Shelley's *The Cenci*', *PMLA* lxxii (1957) 633–44 (635–6)). Other notable productions for English-speaking audiences include one for The Industrial Theatre, Leeds (1923), the Lenox Hill Players directed by Vladimir Nelidoff, New York (1926), Michael Benthall's for the Old Vic, London (1959), Debbie Sherwell's for the Bristol Old Vic Company at the Almeida Theatre, London (1985), Syndee Blake's for the Damned Poets Theatre Company at the Lyric Studio, London (1993) and the rehearsed reading directed by David Farr and produced by Reeve Parker at Queen's College, Cambridge (1993). In Europe, *C* lent itself to symbolist and expressionist interpretations in productions in Paris (in 1891, and in a significant adaptation by Artaud discussed in Appendix B, in 1935), Coburg (1919), Moscow (1919–20), Prague (1922), Rome (1923), and Frankfurt-am-Main (1924). For discussion of productions of C, see: Kenneth N. Cameron and Horst Frenz, 'The Stage History of Shelley's *The Cenci*', *PMLA* lx (1945) 1080–105; States, 'Addendum'; *Curran (1970)* 183–256; and Richard Allen Cave, 'Romantic Drama in Performance', in *The Romantic Theatre: An International Symposium*, ed. Richard Allen Cave (1986) 79–104 (86–95).

The principal literary influences on C are classical tragedy (e.g. the trilogies of Aeschylus and Sophocles which portray the working out of a curse in the destruction of a noble family), Shakespeare's plays, especially the tragedies (for a summary list of the main parallels see *Curran (1970)* 38n. and for critical comment see below), Renaissance drama (e.g. Webster and Marlowe though some of the parallels with *Tamburlaine the Great* identified by Else von Schaubert in her *Shelley's Tragödie The Cenci und Marlowe's Doppeldrama* Tamburlaine (Paderborn, 1965) seem somewhat forced), and the Gothic genre in fiction and drama with its repeated attacks on the corrupt and repressive practices of the Church. In addition to the felicitous coincidence of the first names of the historical figure of '*La Cenci*' (Preface line 39) and the female protagonist of the *Divina Commedia*, the sustained reading of Dante with Mary in 1818–19 (see *Mary Jnl* ii 643–4) results in an influence so deep that 'allusions to Dante form part of the design [of C]' (Ralph Pite, *The Circle of our Vision: Dante's Presence in English Romantic Poetry* (1994) 163n.). C embodies S.'s comment to Peacock in a letter of 25 February 1819: 'What is terror without a contrast with a connection with loveliness? How well Dante understood this secret' (*L* ii 80). Despite Mary's claim (*1839* ii 276) that 'none of [Calderón's] peculiarities crept into the composition of the Cenci', it should be noted that S.'s routine during the summer of 1819 included an intensive, enthusiastic reading of Calderón's plays with Maria Gisborne (see *L* ii 105, 115 and 120). There is some evidence of Calderón's influence in S.'s critical analysis in the Preface of the ideological form of the Catholic faith in the culture of southern Europe, and Beatrice's long yet concentrated speeches in Act V could be argued to draw on a characteristic feature of Calderón's dramaturgy (for a summary of parallels between Calderón's plays and C, see Eunice Joiner Gates, 'Shelley and Calderon', *PQ* xvi (1937) 49–58 (49–52)). In terms of characterisation, Francesco Cenci's excesses have models in the Gothic novel and drama (e.g. Ambrosio in M. G. Lewis's *The Monk* (1796) and Osmond in the same author's hugely popular *The Castle Spectre: A Drama* (1798), Shakespeare (e.g. Richard III), Renaissance tragedy (e.g. Malefort Senior in Massinger's *The Unnatural Combat* (?1639) and Lodovico Enio in Calderón's *El Purgatorio de San Patricio*), and the Bible (e.g. Herod). His defiant isolation finds echoes in solitary figures in poems by Wordsworth (e.g. *The Excursion*) and Byron (e.g. *Manfred*) as is noted in *Rognoni* 1556. His pursuit of an aesthetic or even ethic of parental cruelty has models in literature (e.g. the works of the Marquis de Sade) and in the reputations of historical figures such as Cesare Borgia and Peter the Great. Orsino's sly dissemblance owes much to Satan in *Paradise Lost*, Spenserian allegory (see *Rognoni* 1556), Iago, and through this Shakespearean progenitor parallels Rivers in Wordsworth's *The Borderers* (composed in 1796–7 but published, and then in revised form, in 1842). The distinctive characterisation of Beatrice draws on heroines of classical tragedy, especially Sophocles' Antigone, for S. an abidingly exemplary figure who 'acted in direct in noble violation of the laws of a prejudiced society' (*L* i 81, see also *L* ii 364), and of recent historical poetry (e.g. Southey's *Joan of Arc: An Epic Poem* (1796)). Beatrice's madness in III i has parallels in popular heroines of the English stage e.g. Belvidera in Otway's *Venice Preserved* (1682), Bianca in Milman's *Fazio*, and Imogine in Maturin's *Bertram; Or, The Castle of St. Aldobrand* (1816). But the portrayal of her distress also owes much to Richardson's *Clarissa* which Mary had read in an Italian translation in April 1818 and was read again by her during the period S. was writing *C* (see *Mary Jnl* i 205, 293) and Coleridge's *Christabel* (1816). The banquet scene (I iii) has many possible models including *Macbeth* III iv, Seneca's *Thyestes* 908ff., and *The Unnatural Combat* III iii. The justification of revenge is the central theme of *Marino Faliero* (1821), a play Byron had meditated since 1817.

That incest was an inflammatory topic for his contemporary audience S. knew from *L&C* but the Preface to *C* suggests that its combination of incest and parricide makes the Cenci story particularly suitable material for tragedy. S. was aware that *C* calls to mind tragic treatments of incest in drama (see *L* ii 118–19, 200), e.g. Sophocles' *Oedipus* plays, *Hamlet*, Voltaire's *Sémiramis* (1746), Walpole's *The Mysterious Mother. A Tragedy* (1768), and Byron's *Manfred: A Dramatic Poem* (1817). S.'s comments on Calderón's *Cabellos de Absalón*, a dramatisation of the story of Amnon and Tamar in 2 *Samuel* 13, in a letter of 16 November 1819 are instructive in respect of the incest in *C*:

> Incest is like many other *incorrect* things a very poetical circumstance. It may be the excess of love or of hate. It may be that defiance of every thing for the sake of another which clothes itself in the glory of the highest heroism, or it may be that cynical rage which confounding the good & bad in existing opinions breaks through them for the purpose of rioting in selfishness & antipathy. (*L* ii 154)

Mary had been encouraged by S. in September 1818 (see *Mary Jnl* i 226 and *L* ii 39–40) to translate Alfieri's *Mirra* published in *Tragedie di Vittorio Alfieri*, 6 vols. (Paris, 1787–89) v [1789] 97–183, trans. as *Myrrha* in Charles Lloyd, *The Tragedies of Vittorio Alfieri*, 3 vols (1815) iii 292–353. *Mirra*, based on Ovid's account of Myrrha's incestuous love for her father Cinyras (*Metamorphoses* x 298–502), influenced *The Fields of Fancy*, the first draft of *Matilda*, which Mary began in August 1819 (see *Mary Jnl* i 294 n. 1, 296 and n. 3 and *MSW* ii 2). Moreover Alfieri's description of the adaptation of this story for tragedy in *Memoirs of the Life and Writings of Victor Alfieri Written by Himself*, trans., 2 vols (1810) ii 168–9 bears comparison with S.'s account of his conception of *C* in the Preface. As in Euripides' *Hippolytus*, Massinger's *The Unnatural Combat*, and Racine's *Phèdre*, in *Mirra* and *Matilda* the tragedy lies in the nature of the incestuous love depicted (daughter for father and father for daughter respectively) whereas in *C* it is the victim's recourse to revenge as a result of violent incestuous hatred which is tragic. Though there is no evidence that S. knew details of the defence of Beatrice at her trial, her lawyer, Prospero Farinacci (1544–1618), cited precedents of defensible parricide in classical literature: Cyane and Medullina both killed the fathers who raped them (see Plutarch) and Semiramis's incestuous advances towards Ninyas resulted in her death (see Justin, Book I). Farinacci also cited Cicero's *Pro Milone* 7–11 which includes among examples of defensible homicide Orestes' murder of his mother Clytemnestra (see 'Consilium LXVI' in Prosperi Farinacci Jcti Romani, *Operum Criminalium*, 2nd edn, 9 vols (Nuremberg, 1682) iv 396–8 and George Bowyer, 'Translation of the

Pleading of Prospero Farinacio in Defence of Beatrice Cenci and Her Relatives' in *A Dissertation on the Statutes of the Cities of Italy* (1838) 73–115). Parricide figures overtly in political discourse of the 1790s (e.g. Burke's *Reflections*) and in Clarendon's *History of the Rebellion* (see note to V iv 20–4). Medwin's comment that 'In Beatrice we behold the Angel of Parricide, to make use of an expression applied to Charlotte Corday by a poet historian' (*Medwin (1913)* 217) connects Beatrice with one of S.'s earlier tragically flawed revolutionary heroines (see no. 33 and headnote).

C has an interesting status within S.'s artistic development and canon. It can be seen as a venture in line both with his early experiments with the Gothic such as *Zastrozzi* and *St Irvyne* and, more significantly, as the logical outcome of an interest in writing drama which began in April 1818 when he announced plans for a tragedy on Tasso (see no. 170 and headnote) and contemplated a drama 'founded on the book of Job' (*1839* ii 131). S. must have realised that the events dramatised in C occurred soon after the death of Tasso in 1595 though whether he was aware of reports that Francesco Cenci sought to attend Tasso's planned coronation in Rome in 1595 and that Beatrice's will assigned part of her legacy to a widow who lived with Margherita Sarrochi Birago, a poetess and friend of Tasso and Galileo is unknown (see *Ricci* i 102, ii 185–7). S.'s dramatic interests continued with a translation of Euripides' *Cyclops* (for dating see headnote to no. 172), his encouraging Mary to begin a tragedy about Charles the First (*L* ii 39–40; see headnote to *Charles the First*), and, in late August, the start of *PU* (see headnote to 195 and, for discussion of C in relation to *PU, Curran (1975)* 120–36). Mary (*L* ii 107, *1839* ii 279–80, *1839* iv 51), Hunt (*Lord Byron and some of his contemporaries* (1828) 218–19), Horace Smith (see *Shelley and Mary* iii [Bod. Pr. Shelley adds. e. 7] 535–6, 690), and John Taaffe (*L* ii 253) all praised C but Byron's ambivalence (see *Byron L&J* vii 174 and viii 103, *Medwin's Conversations of Lord Byron*, ed. Ernest J. Lovell, Jr. (Princeton, 1966) 97 and *L* ii 345) and Keats's criticism merit attention. C elicited from the latter, an apparently engrossed reader (see Hyder E. Rollins, 'A Fanny Brawne Letter of 1848', *Harvard Library Bulletin* v (1951) 372–5 (375)), a poised injunction to 'be more of an artist' (Letter to S., 16 August 1820 in Hyder E. Rollins, ed., *The Letters of John Keats*, 2 vols (1958) ii 322–3 (322)). S.'s constant diffidence about his abilities as a dramatist (see, e.g., *Nbk 10* f. 18^{v}rev; *L* ii 8, 189, 290; *1839* ii 273, *Recollections* 76 and *Records* i 117) is combined with a wish to see C as merely his first attempt at an unfamiliar genre, a marker on the way towards greater dramatic work (*L* ii 219–20, 258, 380). The Preface's references to Plato (see note to lines 70–4) suggest how seriously S. took the artistic and moral responsibilities of writing drama and it is possible that he felt a certain amount of anxiety if not self-reproach at C by his own admission being 'calculated to produce a very popular effect' (*L* ii 116).

C had a not entirely unfavourable contemporary critical reception (see *Unextinguished Hearth* 167–216) with several reviewers condemning the subject-matter while praising its language and acknowledging its dramatic power. Particularly interesting interpretation and analysis may be found in the following: Swinburne's Preface to *Les Cenci: Drame de Shelley*, trans. 'Tola Dorian' (Paris, 1883), i–xviii, reprinted in his *Studies in Prose and Poetry* (1894) 146–57; Wilhelm Wagner, *Shelley's 'The Cenci'* (Rostock, 1903); *Bates; Curran (1970); Wasserman* 84–128; *Rognoni* xliv–xlvii and 1552–67. Critical debate has focused on whether Beatrice is to be seen as having been corrupted into behaving like her father; Robert F. Whitman, 'Beatrice's

Pernicious Mistake' in *The Cenci*', *PMLA* lxxiv (1959) 249–53 provides a standard account of the case against her while Hunt in *The Indicator* xlii (26 July 1820) 331–2 and in *Lord Byron and Some of His Contemporaries* (1828) 219 and *Curran (1970)* see C's morality as encompassing a defence of her actions. There are deeply instructive critical meditations on C by Walter Savage Landor ('Five Scenes' in *Fraser's Magazine* xliii (1851), 59–74 (the fourth scene, 'Beatrice Cenci and Pope Clement VIII' was published in *The Keepsake for 1851* (London, 1851 [1850]) 2–8), reprinted in *The Last Fruit off an Old Tree* (1853) 487–520) and Robert Browning ('Cenciaja' in *Pacchiarotto And How He worked in Distemper: With Other Poems* (1876) 162–83, and 'Mr Browning on the Santa Croce case and on Farinacci's failure in the defence of the Cenci', in *Forman 1876–7* ii 418–20). For useful summaries of recent secondary material on C, see Stuart Curran's chapter on S. in *The English Romantic Poets: A Review of Research and Criticism*, 4th edn, ed. Frank Jordan (1985) 646–8, and *Rognoni* 1566–7. Despite GM's comment that 'Except in the most trivial ways [C] is quite un-Shakespearian, in versification as in content' (*Shelley* (1970) 22), critics have found C's relationship to Shakespeare an absorbing topic. For comment other than in the critical works cited above, see: J. B. B., 'Imitations of Shakespeare by Shelley, in his Tragedy of "The Cenci", *The Shakespeare Society's Papers* i (1844) 52–4; [John James Elmes], 'Some Notes on Othello', *The Cornhill Magazine* xviii (1868) 419–40 (430–3); [T. S. Baynes], Review of *The Poetical Works of Percy Bysshe Shelley*, ed. W. M. Rossetti, 2 vols (1870), *Edinburgh Review* cxxxiii (1871) 426–59 (445–8); Edward Aveling, 'The Cenci', *Progress* vi (1886) 260–5; *Woodberry (1909)* xxvi–xxx; F. R. Leavis, 'Shelley', in *Revaluation: Tradition and Development in English Poetry* (1936) 203–40 (223–7); David Lee Clark, 'Shelley and Shakespeare', *PMLA* liv (1939) 261–87 (277–86); Sara Ruth Watson, 'Shelley and Shakespeare: An Addendum – A comparison of *Othello* and *The Cenci*', *PMLA* lv (1940) 611–14; Beach Langston, 'Shelley's Use of Shakespeare', *Huntington Library Quarterly* xii (1949) 163–90 (167–70); Paul A. Cantor, ' "A Distorting Mirror": Shelley's *The Cenci* and Shakespearean tragedy', *Shakespeare: Aspects of Influence*, ed. G. B. Evans, *English Studies* vii (1976) 91–108; D. Harrington-Lueker, 'Imagination versus Introspection: *The Cenci* and *Macbeth*', *KSJ* xxxii (1983) 172–89; Jonathan Bate, *Shakespeare and the English Romantic Imagination* (1986) 202–21.

The copy-text here is *Cenci (1821)*. While most *eds* have taken *Cenci (1819)* as copy-text incorporating the substantive emendations in *Errata*, the requirement that the accidentals of the first edition be retained is, in the case of *Cenci (1819)*, virtually unworkable because the instances of apparent error and inconsistency in respect of punctuation, capitalisation and typography are so prolific. Forman judged that 'there was probably much less deviation from the MS. [in *Cenci (1819)*] than in the works printed in England, because the compositors would not know *how* to deviate' (*Forman 1876–7* ii [4]), and his view that *Cenci (1819)* is 'a text more like the absolute production of Shelley' (*Shelley Library* (1886) 91; see also 92–3) is correct in that in respect of pointing *Cenci (1819)* is characteristic of S., for example, in its abundant use of dashes. But the editors believe that the claims of *Cenci (1819)* are outweighed by S.'s letter of 30 April 1820 (referred to above), in which Ollier is authorised to make changes to *Cenci (1819)* in respect of accidentals as well as substantives. *Woodberry (1909)*, which, like *Hutchinson*, takes *Cenci (1821)* as copy-text, defends the choice on just these grounds (xxxvi), and even Forman acknowledges that *Cenci (1821)* 'is far less suspect than most of the books printed in England in Shelley's absence, probably because it was printed from a slightly revised copy of the first edition, in which case there would not be the many questionable places that a MS. presents for a printer to exercise his ingenuity on' (*Forman 1876-7* ii [4]). Further support for not following *Cenci (1819)* is found in a recently-auctioned presentation copy of *Cenci (1819)* inscribed on the fly-leaf with the name 'J. Taaffe Esq.'' in S.'s hand, described in 'Lot 172', *Bloomsbury Book Auctions*, Catalogue for Sale 110 (15 December 1988) 30-2. The catalogue suggests that 'In the absence of the copy actually sent to Ollier, [Taaffe's copy of *Cenci (1819)*] must lay claim to being the copy-text of the play in its final form and as Shelley wished it to be published' (31). Seen by the present editors before its sale, Taaffe's copy of *Cenci (1819)* contains alterations in respect of accidentals as well as substantives in the hands of S. and Mary (referred to below as *Taaffe*), some though not all of which correspond to those listed in *Errata*. This edition records only those variants in *Cenci (1819)* judged to be of significance. It does not note unambiguous errors of the press in *Cenci (1819)* nor does it record routinely such features of *Cenci (1819)* as the use of three suspension points where *Cenci (1821)* employs a dash except in those cases where a significant alternative reading is offered to the copy-text in an edition other than *Cenci (1819)*. Concerning variants recorded here, it should be noted that *1829*, which follows *Cenci (1819)*, served as copy for the second volume of *1839* in which C was published, and that *1839* frequently does not follow *Errata* (see *Taylor* 39-42).

Text from *Cenci (1821)*; the several readings from *Errata* and *Taaffe* not in *Cenci (1821)* are adopted, as are many readings from other editions, especially *Cenci (1819)*, where their punctuation is preferred. Where readings in editions other than *Cenci (1821)* are felt to observe the metrical requirements of the verse more effectively (e.g. in respect of the setting of lines split between speakers), they too are adopted. Decisions to depart from *Cenci (1821)* are recorded in the notes with explanation where necessary. Variants in other editions are recorded selectively.

Published in *Cenci (1819)*.

209
The Cenci
A Tragedy in Five Acts

Dedication
To LEIGH HUNT, Esq.

My Dear Friend,

I inscribe with your name, from a distant country, and after an absence whose months have seemed years, this the latest of my literary efforts. Those writings which I have hitherto published, have been little else than visions which impersonate my own apprehensions of the beautiful and the just. I can also perceive in them the literary defects incidental to youth and impatience; they are dreams of what ought to be, or may be.

Dedication. The structure and tone of what Mary describes as S.'s 'warm and just eulogium' to Hunt (*Essays, Letters from Abroad, Translations and Fragments*, 2 vols (1840) i xxiii–iv) bears comparison with Hunt's Dedication to Byron in *The Story of Rimini* (1816) v–vi. *C*, with a tale of incontinent hatred comparable to the story of Ugolino (*Inferno* xxxiii) may be seen to reciprocate the rendition of the incontinent love of Paolo and Francesca (*Inferno* v) in Hunt's poem which S. admired warmly (see headnote to 'Lines to Leigh Hunt', no. 118).

Ded. 6–12. Those writings which I have hitherto published . . . that which has been.] Cp. William Godwin's withdrawn Preface to the first edition of *Things as They Are; Or, The Adventures of Caleb Williams* 3 vols (1794) in which he contrasts his novel with *Enquiry Concerning Political Justice* (1793): 'What is now presented to the public, is no refined and abstract speculation; it is a study and delineation of things passing in the moral world' (*Godwin Novels* iii 279). A rejected paragraph concerning the portrait of Hunt which S. had recently received (see headnote) precedes the draft of this paragraph in *Nbk 10* ff. 6(a)ʳ–6(a)ᵛ (see *MYR* iv 28–31).

Ded. 6. published,] presented to the world *Nbk 10.*

Ded. 7. visions] a [visions of ideal ex *canc.*] cellence *Nbk 10* (cp. Preface to *PU*).

Ded. 7–8. which impersonate . . . the just.] have [been the *canc.*] contained impersonations of My own persuasion of what is beautiful & just; *Nbk 10.*

Ded. 8–9. the literary defects incidental to youth] They have many literary defects. But I am yet young. *Nbk 10.*

Ded. 9. they are dreams of what ought to be, or may be.] In *Nbk 10* there are several attempts at this summary characterisation of S.'s earlier work including '[the picture of should & may be *canc.*]' and 'they are a kind of visions, which are not, but should be'.

Ded. 9–10. dreams . . . sad reality.] For this collocation, cp. Crabbe, 'Tale II: The Parting Hour' in *Tales* (1812) line 433: 'Sad as realities, and wild as dreams'; Byron, *The Prisoner of Chillon, and other Poems* (1816) esp. 'The Dream' and 'Prometheus' lines 1–5: 'Titan! to whose immortal eyes / The sufferings of mortality, / Seen in their sad reality, / Were not as things that gods despise; / What was thy pity's recompense?'; Byron, *Childe Harold's Pilgrimage Canto the Fourth* (1818) stanzas vi–vii: 'Yet there are things whose strong reality / Outshines our fairy-land . . . / I saw or dreamed of such, – but let them go – / They came like truth, and disappeared like dreams'; *Frankenstein* (1818): 'they appeared like a dream, yet distinct and oppressive as a reality' (*MSW* i 131). Cp. also the phraseology of S.'s letter to Ollier of 15 December 1819: 'Have you seen my poem, *Julian and Maddalo*? . . . I mean to write three other poems, the scenes of which will be laid at Rome, Florence, and Naples, but the subjects of which will be all drawn from dreadful or beautiful realities, as that of this was' (*L* ii 164).

10 The drama which I now present to you is a sad reality. I lay aside the presumptuous attitude of an instructor, and am content to paint, with such colours as my own heart furnishes, that which has been. Had I known a person more highly endowed than yourself with all that it becomes a man to possess, I had solicited for this work the ornament
15 of his name. One more gentle, honourable, innocent, and brave; one of more exalted toleration for all who do and think evil, and yet himself more free from evil; one who knows better how to receive, and how to confer a benefit, though he must ever confer far more than he can receive; one of simpler, and, in the highest sense of the word, of purer life and man-
20 ners, I never knew: and I had already been fortunate in friendships when your name was added to the list. In that patient and irreconcilable enmity with domestic and political tyranny and imposture which the tenor of your life has illustrated, and which, had I health and talents, should illustrate mine, let us, comforting
25 each other in our task, live and die.
All happiness attend you!

Your affectionate friend,
PERCY B. SHELLEY

ROME,
30 May 29, 1819.

Ded. 9–12. what ought to be or may be . . . that which has been.] Traditional contrasts between poetry and history appear to be invoked here, e.g. Aristotle, *Poetics* ix: 'it is not the poet's function to relate actual events, but the *kinds* of things that might occur and are possible in terms of probability or necessity' (Loeb trans. rev. edn 1995), and Philip Sidney, *A Defence of Poetry* (1595) in K. Duncan-Jones and J. van Dorsten (eds) *Miscellaneous Prose of Sir Philip Sidney* (1973) 102: 'He [the poet] citeth not authorities of other histories, but even for his entry calleth the sweet Muses to inspire into him a good invention; in truth, not labouring to tell you what is or is not, but what should or should not be'. Cp. also August Wilhelm Schlegel, *A Course of Lectures on Dramatic Art and Literature*, trans. John Black, 2 vols (1815) i 144: 'This is the meaning of Sophocles, when he said that he himself painted men as they ought to be, and Euripides as they actually were.'

Ded. 10. The drama . . . sad reality.] It [This *canc.*] is a [dark *canc.*] picture of human nature; *Nbk 10.*

Ded. 13. Had I known a person . . .] S.'s draft of this paragraph in *Nbk 10* ff. 6(b)ʳ–6(c)ᵛ is preceded by rejected material in praise of Hunt (see *MYR* iv 32–7).

Ded. 14. ornament] honour *Nbk 10.*

Ded. 15. brave] brave & true *Nbk 10.*

Ded. 20. I had already been fortunate in friendships] Cp. *J&M* line 575.

Ded. 22–5. In that patient and irreconcilable enmity . . . live and die.] Hunt's imprisonment is alluded to here. Cp. 'Lines to Leigh Hunt', no. 118, lines 25–7. S. also seems to identify himself and Hunt with Satan and the fallen angels in *Paradise Lost* i 120–2: 'We may with more successful hope resolve / To wage by force or guile eternal war / Irreconcilable to our grand foe'. The first draft of this paragraph in *Nbk 10* f. 6(c)ʳ is less restrained than the second on which the published text is based (see *MYR* iv 36–7).

Ded. 23. imposture] *Cenci (1819)*; imposture, *Cenci (1821)*.

PREFACE

A manuscript was communicated to me during my travels in Italy, which was copied from the archives of the Cenci Palace at Rome, and contains a detailed account of the horrors which ended in the extinction of one of the noblest and richest families of that city, during the Pontificate of Clement VIII, in the year 1599. The story is, that an old man having spent his life in debauchery and wickedness, conceived at length an implacable hatred towards his children; which showed itself towards one daughter under the form of an incestuous passion, aggravated by every circumstance of cruelty and violence. This daughter, after long and vain attempts to escape from what she considered a perpetual contamination both of body and mind, at length plotted with her mother-in-law and brother to murder their common tyrant. The young maiden, who was urged to this tremendous deed by an impulse which overpowered its horror, was evidently a most gentle and amiable being, a creature formed to adorn and be admired, and thus violently thwarted from her nature by the necessity of circumstance

Preface. 1. manuscript] Manuscript *Cenci (1819)*; MANUSCRIPT *Cenci (1821)*.

Pref. 4–5. the Pontificate of Clement VIII,] *Cenci (1819)*; Clement VIII. *Cenci (1821)*. Clement VIII (Ippolito Aldobrandini, b. 1536) was Pope from 1592 until his death in 1605 as is noted in Bod. MS Shelley adds. e. 13 p. 78 (see *BSM* x 252–3 though Bennett's transcription of the latter date as 1615 is questionable). His orchestration of the invasion of Ferrara from which the House of Este were ejected by his nephew in 1598 is criticised by Edward Gibbon in *The History of the Decline and Fall of the Roman Empire*, ed. J. B. Bury, 7 vols (1896–1900) vii 296n., and by J. C. L. Simonde de Sismondi, in *Histoire des Républiques Italiennes du Moyen Âge*, Seconde Édition Parisienne, 16 vols (Paris, 1818) xvi 197–8.

Pref. 9–12. This daughter . . . their common tyrant.] Cp. Hazlitt, 'The Times Newspaper[:] On the Connection Between Toad-Eaters and Tyrants', *The Examiner* (12 January 1817) 27: '[Tyranny] does not satisfy the enormity of the appetite for servility, till it has slain the mind of a nation, and becomes like the evil principle of the universe, from which there is no escape' (*Hazlitt Works* vii 150). *after long and vain attempts to escape from*] found no escape[d *canc.*] from his attempts, & from the horror which she felt at being compelled to live [as *canc.*] in *Nbk 10*. *mind*] soul *Nbk 10*. *mother-in-law*] i.e. step-mother (also used in this sense in *Oedipus Tyrannus* II ii 85). Lucretia is described as 'mother-in-law' in *Relation* 17, 35 and 49 but is referred to as 'step-mother' in 'Dramatis Personae' and at III i 355. *murder*] kill *Nbk 10*. *common tyrant.*] After this sentence there is the following cancelled and unfinished passage in *Nbk 10* ff. 16ʳrev–17ʳrev in which S. appears to be about to refer to Guerra's role in the plotting of the murder described in *Relation* 13–17: 'She had a lover also who appears by the story to b'.

Pref. 12–16. The young maiden . . . opinion.] Cp. Godwin's description of Mary Wollstonecraft's reaction to her father's violent temper: 'She was not formed to be the contented and unresisting subject of a despot . . . The blows of her father . . . instead of humbling her, roused her indignation' (*Memoirs of the Author of A Vindication of the Rights of Woman* (1798), in *Godwin Novels* i 89). *maiden*] creature *canc. Nbk 10*. *urged*] impelled *canc. Nbk 10*. *the necessity of circumstance and opinion.*] Cp. S.'s 'On Frankenstein; Or, the Modern Prometheus': 'Nor are the crimes and malevolence of a single Being, tho' indeed withering and tremendous, the offspring of any unaccountable propensity to evil, but flow inevitably from certain causes fully adequate to their production. They are the children, as it were, of Necessity and Human Nature' (*Prose Works* i 283).

and opinion. The deed was quickly discovered, and, in spite of the most earnest prayers made to the Pope by the highest persons in Rome, the criminals were put to death. The old man had, during his life, repeatedly bought his pardon from the Pope for capital crimes of the most enormous and
20 unspeakable kind, at the price of a hundred thousand crowns; the death therefore of his victims can scarcely be accounted for by the love of justice. The Pope, among other motives for severity, probably felt that whoever killed the Count Cenci deprived his treasury of a certain and copious source of revenue.* Such a story, if told so as to present to the reader all
25 the feelings of those who once acted it, their hopes and fears, their confidences and misgivings, their various interests, passions and opinions, acting upon and with each other, yet all conspiring to one tremendous end, would be as a light to make apparent some of the most dark and secret caverns of the human heart.
30 On my arrival at Rome, I found that the story of the Cenci was a subject not to be mentioned in Italian society without awakening a deep and

* The Papal Government formerly took the most extraordinary precautions against the publicity of facts which offer so tragical a demonstration of its own wickedness and weakness; so that the communication of the MS. had become, until very lately, a matter of some difficulty.

Pref. 17–18. *the criminals were put to death.*] the[y are executed *canc.*] – they are led to execution *Nbk 10*. The detailed account of the execution of the Cenci family in 'M' G's M.S.' (see *Relation* 48–68) probably reminded S. of reports of the hangings of Jeremiah Brandreth, Isaac Ludlam and William Turner in *The Examiner* (9 November 1817) 715–17 and 721–3 on which he drew in 'An Address to the People on The Death of the Princess Charlotte' (1817) (*Prose Works* i 231–9, esp. 237–8). For interesting discussion of 'An Address' in relation to *C*, see Barbara Groseclose, 'The Incest Motif in Shelley's *The Cenci*', *Comparative Drama* xix (1986) 222–39 (232).

Pref. 18–20. *The old man . . . a hundred thousand crowns;*] Francesco Cenci was fined this sum on three occasions for the crime of sodomy, not murder, according to *Relation* 3 and 7.

Pref. 23. *Count Cenci*] *Cenci (1819)*; Count Cenci, *Cenci (1821)*.

Pref. 24. *S.'s note. The Papal Government . . .*] *Errata* and *Taaffe* instruct that this sentence, in the body of the text in *Cenci (1819)*, is 'to be printed as a note'.

Pref. 24–9. *Such a story . . . would be as a light . . . the human heart.*] Cp. *J&M* lines 568–74 and the final sentence of its Preface. The phrase 'the most dark and secret caverns of the human heart' has echoes in a review which S. may have read of Vincenzo Pieracci's play *Beatrice Cenci* (1816) in *Gazzetta di Firenze* cx (12 September 1816) 4: 'Il nostro autore ha cercato nello stile di secondare i vari argomenti e d'imitar la natura, per facilitarsi l'ingresso nelle recondite strade del cuore uomo' ('Our author has searched for a style to favour various arguments and to imitate nature by making possible an entry into the hidden ways of the human heart' (my trans.)). For discussion of S.'s probable debt to Pieracci's play, see George Yost, *Pieracci and Shelley: An Italian Ur-Cenci* (1986) and Appendix B. Cp. Hazlitt's essay on *Othello* in *Characters of Shakespear's Plays* (1817): 'Tragedy . . . opens the chambers of the human heart' (*Hazlitt Works* iv 200). See the draft of this sentence in *Nbk 10* f. 17'rev and a related, rejected passage on f. 17'rev. (*MYR* iv 404–7).

Pref. 30–5. *On my arrival at Rome . . . common dust.*] Cp. Hunt's comment on the tale of Paolo and Francesca in the Preface to *The Story of Rimini* (1816) ix: 'The Italians have been very fond of this little piece of private history'. Beatrice Cenci's iconic status in the late eighteenth and early nineteenth centuries as a symbol of heroic resistance to the Papacy is discussed in breathless interest; and that the feelings of the company never failed to incline to a romantic pity for the wrongs, and a passionate exculpation of the horrible deed to which they urged her, who has been mingled two centuries with the common dust. All ranks of people knew the outlines of this history, and participated in the overwhelming interest which it seems to have the magic of exciting in the human heart. I had a copy of Guido's picture of Beatrice, which is preserved in the Colonna Palace, and my servant instantly recognised it as the portrait of La Cenci.

This national and universal interest which the story produces and has produced for two centuries, and among all ranks of people in a great City, where the imagination is kept for ever active and awake, first suggested to me the conception of its fitness for a dramatic purpose. In fact it is a tragedy which has already received, from its capacity of awakening and sustaining the sympathy of men, approbation and success. Nothing remained, as I imagined, but to clothe it to the apprehensions of my countrymen in such language and action as would bring it home to their hearts. The deepest and the sublimest tragic compositions, King Lear and the two plays in which the tale of Oedipus is told, were stories which already existed in tradition, as matters of popular belief and interest, before Shakespeare and Sophocles made them familiar to the sympathy of all succeeding generations of mankind.

This story of the Cenci is indeed eminently fearful and monstrous: any thing like a dry exhibition of it on the stage would be insupportable.

Appendix B. See the following rejected passage apparently relating to this sentence and the next in *Nbk 10* f. 8'rev which provides an insight into S.'s view of Beatrice's actions: 'Perhaps [*canc.*] they appeared to me, even to think [too with too much *canc.*] lenity of the [monstrous action *canc.*] [unnatural action *canc.*] [dreadful alternative *canc.*] of the [action which *canc.*] of the dreadful side of the alternative chosen by the heroine of the tale' (see also *MYR* iv 442–3). *romantic pity*] powerful compassion *canc. Nbk 10. wrongs*] sufferings *canc. Nbk 10. her*] Beatrice the chief victim of a *canc. Nbk 10. dust.*] earth *Nbk 10.*

Pref. 37–8. I had a copy of Guido's picture . . .] See Appendix B for discussion of the portrait on which this copy was based.

Pref. 44–5. awakening and sustaining the sympathy of men,] Cp., e.g., Hazlitt, 'On Shakspeare and Milton': 'The objects of dramatic poetry affect us by sympathy, by their nearness to ourselves, as they take us by surprise, or force us upon action, "while rage with rage doth sympathise" ' (*Hazlitt Works* v 52).

Pref. 46–7. to clothe it . . . in such language] Cp. Schlegel, *Lectures*, trans. Black (1815) i 327: 'poetry, that art which is absolved from every aim but the unconditional one of creating the beautiful by means of free invention and clothing it in a suitable language'.

Pref. 47–8. The deepest and the sublimest tragic compositions, King Lear . . .] Cp. *DP*: '*King Lear* . . . may be judged to be the most perfect specimen of the dramatic art existing in the world' (*Prose* 284).

Pref. 54. dry] 'Feeling or showing no emotion, impassive; destitute of tender feeling; wanting in sympathy or cordiality' (*OED* 13).

55 The person who would treat such a subject must increase the ideal, and diminish the actual horror of the events, so that the pleasure which arises from the poetry which exists in these tempestuous sufferings and crimes may mitigate the pain of the contemplation of the moral deformity from which they spring. There must also be nothing attempted to make the
60 exhibition subservient to what is vulgarly termed a moral purpose. The highest moral purpose aimed at in the highest species of the drama, is the teaching the human heart, through its sympathies and antipathies, the knowledge of itself; in proportion to the possession of which knowledge, every human being is wise, just, sincere, tolerant and kind. If dogmas can
65 do more, it is well: but a drama is no fit place for the enforcement of them. Undoubtedly, no person can be truly dishonoured by the act of another; and the fit return to make to the most enormous injuries is kindness and forbearance, and a resolution to convert the injurer from his dark passions by peace and love. Revenge, retaliation, atonement, are pernicious mistakes.

Pref. 55–9. The person who would treat . . . from which they spring.] The concept of the 'ideal' in tragic poetry is much discussed by Schlegel, e.g. *Lectures*, trans. Black (1815) i 370: 'In tragedy, men are opposed to each other in the most dreadful strife, and in a close struggle with misfortune; we can only exact an ideal dignity from them.' *pleasure . . . pain*] Cp. *DP*: 'Sorrow, terror, anguish, despair itself are often the chosen expressions of an approximation to the highest good. Our sympathy in tragic fiction depends on this principle; tragedy delights by affording a shadow of the pleasure which exists in pain' (*Prose* 292).

Pref. 59–60. There must also be . . . moral purpose.] Cp. 'Didactic poetry is my abhorrence' (Preface to *PU* lines 122–3).

Pref. 62. the teaching the human heart] the teaching of the human heart *1839*.

Pref. 64–5. If dogmas . . . of them.] For the view that a criticism of Calderón is intended here, see Susana Hernández Araico, 'The Schlegels, Shelley, and Calderón', *Neophilologus* lxxi (1987) 481–8 (484).

Pref. 66–9. Undoubtedly . . . peace and love.] Cp. Godwin, *Caleb Williams* (1794): 'I am unable to cope with you: what then? Can that circumstance dishonour me? No; I can only be dishonoured by perpetrating an unjust action. My honour is in my own keeping, beyond the reach of all mankind. Strike! I am passive. No injury that you can inflict shall provoke me to expose you or myself to unnecessary evil' (*Godwin Novels* iii 87). Laurence S. Lockridge, 'Justice in *The Cenci*', *The Wordsworth Circle* xix (1988) 95–8 (96) cps. this sentence and the following to *J&M* lines 182–7 ('We are assured . . . to live and die'). *dishonoured*] depraved *canc. Nbk 10*. *fit*] just *Nbk 10*. *forbearance*] endurance *Nbk 10*. *by*] to *Nbk 10*.

Pref. 69. Revenge, retaliation, atonement, are pernicious mistakes.] On S.'s view of the iniquity of revenge, see *Zastrozzi, A Romance* (1810); 'On Christianity' (1817) (*Prose Works* i 246–71); the letter to the Gisbornes of 10 July 1818 in which he describes revenge as 'the most deadly superstition that ever infested the world' (*L* ii 20); and the Preface to *PU* in which Prometheus is described as 'exempt from the taints of ambition, envy, revenge'. Cp. *Political Justice* ii 327: 'To punish [a guilty man], upon any hypothesis for what is past and irrecoverable, and for the consideration of that only, must be ranked among the most pernicious exhibitions of an untutored barbarism'; Robert Southey, *Thalaba the Destroyer* 2 vols (1801) ii 286 (Book XI): 'This is no time to harbour in my heart / One evil thought . . . here I put off revenge, / The last rebellious feeling'; *Frankenstein* (1818) (*MSW* i 130 and 153). On atonement, cp. Coleridge, *Remorse* (1813), esp. V i 254–94, and Byron, *Manfred: A Dramatic Poem* (1817) III i esp. 78–98.

) If Beatrice had thought in this manner she would have been wiser and
better; but she would never have been a tragic character: the few whom such
an exhibition would have interested, could never have been sufficiently
interested for a dramatic purpose, from the want of finding sympathy in
their interest among the mass who surround them. It is in the restless and
anatomizing casuistry with which men seek the justification of Beatrice,
yet feel that she has done what needs justification; it is in the supersti-
tious horror with which they contemplate alike her wrongs and their revenge,
that the dramatic character of what she did and suffered, consists.

) I have endeavoured as nearly as possible to represent the characters as
they probably were, and have sought to avoid the error of making them
actuated by my own conceptions of right or wrong, false or true, thus under

Pref. 70–4. If Beatrice . . . who surround them.] Cp. Plato, *Republic* x 604e–605a: ' "And does not
the fretful part of us present many and varied occasions for imitation, while the intelligent
and temperate disposition, always remaining approximately the same, is neither easy to imi-
tate nor to be understood when imitated, especially by a nondescript mob assembled in the
theatre? For the representation imitates a type that is alien to them." "By all means." "And
is it not obvious that the nature of the mimetic poet is not related to this better part of the
soul and his cunning is not framed to please it, if he is to win favour with the multitude,
but is devoted to the fretful and complicated type of character because it is easy to imitate?"
"It is obvious." ' (Loeb trans.). For discussion, see Joan Rees, 'The Preface to *The Cenci*', *RES*
n.s. viii (1957) 172–3. Schlegel, *Lectures*, trans. Black (1815) i 141 refers to this passage.

Pref. 74–8. It is in the restless and anatomizing casuistry . . . consists.] Cp. Preface to *PU* lines
30–2: 'The character of Satan engenders in the mind a pernicious casuistry which leads us
to weigh his faults with his wrongs and to excuse the former because the latter exceed all
measure'. *anatomizing*] See I ii 85 and II ii 110 and note. *casuistry*] Cp. S.'s 'On "Godwin's
Mandeville" ', *The Examiner* (28 December 1817) 827: 'The interest of this novel is undoubt-
edly equal, in some respects superior, to that of *Caleb Williams*. Yet there is no character like
Falkland, whom the author, with that sublime casuistry which is the parent of toleration and
forbearance, persuades us personally to love, whilst his actions must for ever remain the theme
of our astonishment and abhorrence' (*Prose Works* i 277). William H. Marshall cps. Falkland's
murder of Tyrrel to Beatrice's of her father: 'In each case the murder of the tyrant would
seem . . . to be a form of personal vengeance rather than an act of justice', ' "Caleb Williams"
and "The Cenci" ', *N&Q* ccv (1960) 260–3 (262).

Pref. 79–83. I have endeavoured . . . impersonations of my own mind.] See S.'s letter to Medwin
of 1 May 1820: 'My chief endeavour [in *C*] was to produce a delineation of passio[ns] which
I had never participated in, in chaste language, & according to the rules of enlightened art'
(*L* ii 189; see also *L* ii 102, *L* ii 190–2, and *Recollections* 76 for similar statements). Cp. *DP*:
'A poet would therefore do ill to embody his own conceptions of right and wrong, which
are usually those of his place and time, in his poetical creations which participate in neither'
(*Prose* 283), and S.'s comment on this passage in *Nbk 13* Quire III f. 13v: 'This [is *canc*.] was
Mr Shelley's error in the Revolt of Islam. He has attempted to cure himself in subsequent
publications but, except in the tragedy of the Cenci, with little effect' (see *BSM* vii 188–9).
Cp. also Schlegel, *Lectures*, trans. Black (1815) i 36: 'From the nature of the dramatic art, the
poet must put much into the mouths of his characters of which he does not himself approve
. . .'. Rognoni 1554–5 cps. Coleridge on Shakespeare's genius in *Venus and Adonis* in Chapter
XV of *Biographia Literaria*, 2 vols (1817) ii 15–16: 'It is throughout as if a superior spirit . . .
were placing the whole before our view; himself meanwhile unparticipating in the passions'.
as they probably were] as acting & speaking, as they really would have spoken *canc. Nbk 10*.
sixteenth] seventeenth *Nbk 10*. *true*,] true *Cenci (1819)*; true: *Cenci (1821)*.

a thin veil converting names and actions of the sixteenth century into cold
impersonations of my own mind. They are represented as Catholics, and
as Catholics deeply tinged with religion. To a Protestant apprehension there
85   will appear something unnatural in the earnest and perpetual sentiment
of the relations between God and man which pervade the tragedy of the
Cenci. It will especially be startled at the combination of an undoubting
persuasion of the truth of the popular religion with a cool and determined
perseverance in enormous guilt. But religion in Italy is not, as in Protestant
90   countries, a cloak to be worn on particular days; or a passport which those
who do not wish to be railed at carry with them to exhibit; or a gloomy
passion for penetrating the impenetrable mysteries of our being, which
terrifies its possessor at the darkness of the abyss to the brink of which it
has conducted him. Religion coexists, as it were, in the mind of an Italian
95   Catholic, with a faith in that of which all men have the most certain know-
ledge. It is interwoven with the whole fabric of life. It is adoration, faith,
submission, penitence, blind admiration; not a rule for moral conduct.
It has no necessary connection with any one virtue. The most atrocious
villain may be rigidly devout, and without any shock to established faith,
100 confess himself to be so. Religion pervades intensely the whole frame of
society, and is, according to the temper of the mind which it inhabits, a
passion, a persuasion, an excuse, a refuge; never a check. Cenci himself
built a chapel in the court of his Palace, and dedicated it to St. Thomas
the Apostle, and established masses for the peace of his soul. Thus in the
105 first scene of the fourth act Lucretia's design in exposing herself to the con-
sequences of an expostulation with Cenci after having administered the
opiate, was to induce him by a feigned tale to confess himself before death;
this being esteemed by Catholics as essential to salvation; and she only

Pref. 84. tinged with religion] religious *Nbk 10.*

Pref. 86. between God and man which pervade] between God and man which pervades *Rossetti
1870*; between God and men which pervade *Forman 1876-7.*

Pref. 88. persuasion] faith *canc. Nbk 10.*

Pref. 93. the darkness of the abyss] Cp. III i 254.

Pref. 96. It is interwoven with the whole fabric of life.] See S.'s letter to Medwin of July 1820:
'Your objections to "The Cenci" as to the introduction of the name of God is good, inas-
much as the play is addressed to a Protestant people; but *we* Catholics speak eternally and
familiarly of the first person of the Trinity; and amongst *us* religion is more interwoven with,
and is less extraneous to, the system of ordinary life' (*L* ii 219).

Pref. 98-9. The most atrocious villain may be rigidly devout . . .] This sentence serves as a gloss
on Count Cenci in *C.*

Pref. 98. any one] moral *Nbk 10.*

Pref. 102-4. Cenci himself built a chapel . . . to St. Thomas the Apostle,] *Relation* 4 states that
Francesco's intention in building the chapel 'was to bury there all his children'. S. exploits
the irony of his source's identification of Cenci with Thomas the Apostle, a notorious doubter
(see *John* x 24-9), at I i 105.

relinquishes her purpose when she perceives that her perseverance would
10 expose Beatrice to new outrages.

I have avoided with great care in writing this play the introduction of
what is commonly called mere poetry, and I imagine there will scarcely
be found a detached simile or a single isolated description, unless Beatrice's
description of the chasm appointed for her father's murder should be judged
15 to be of that nature.*

In a dramatic composition the imagery and the passion should inter-
penetrate one another, the former being reserved simply for the full devel-
opment and illustration of the latter. Imagination is as the immortal God
which should assume flesh for the redemption of mortal passion. It is thus

* An idea in this speech was suggested by a most sublime passage in *El Purgatorio de San Patricio* of Calderon;
the only plagiarism which I have intentionally committed in the whole piece.

Pref. 110. new outrages.] a repetition of the unutterable horror which is the subject of the
drama *Nbk 10*.

Pref. 114. the chasm appointed for her father's murder] the spot designed for the ass *Nbk 10* (S.
appears to have begun to write 'assassination').

Pref. 115. S.'s note. the only plagiarism . . . in the whole piece.] For precedents for this disavowal
of 'intentional' plagiarism, see: M. G. Lewis, Advertisement to *The Monk* (1796) i viii: 'I have
now made a full avowal of all the plagiarisms of which I am aware myself'; the same author's
The Castle Spectre (1798) 28 (note at the end of Act II, scene i): 'When I wrote the foregoing
scene, I really believed the invention to be entirely my own: But the situations of Angela,
Osmond and Percy, so closely resemble those of Isabella, Manfred, and the animated por-
trait in The Castle of Otranto that I am convinced the idea must have been suggested to me
by that beautiful Romance. – Wherever I can trace any plagiarisms, whether wilful or invol-
untary, I shall continue to point them out to the reader without reserve'; and Byron, Preface
to *Hours of Idleness* (1807) vii: 'I have not been guilty of intentional plagiarism.' For the source
of the 'plagiarism' see note to III i 247–57. *which I have intentionally committed*] to which I
can plead guilty *Nbk 10*.

Pref. 116–19. In a dramatic composition . . . mortal passion.] S.'s use of biblical language to express
aesthetic theory in this sentence drew from *The Literary Gazette, and Journal of Belles Lettres,
Arts, Sciences* clxvii (1 April 1820) 209 an accusation of 'treating of dramatic imagery . . . blas-
phemously and senselessly'. On 'passion' cp. the Preface to Joanna Baillie, *A Series of Plays:
in which it is attempted to delineate the stronger passions of the mind* (1798), e.g.: 'amidst all this
decoration and ornament, all this loftiness and refinement, let one simple trait of the human
heart, one expression of passion genuine and true to nature, be introduced, and it will stand
forth alone in the boldness of reality, whilst the false and unnatural around it, fades away upon
every side, like the rising exhalations of the morning' (21). *mortal passion*] passion *Nbk 10*.

Pref. 119–23. It is thus that the most remote . . . shadow of its own greatness.] S. appears here
and in the next two sentences to draw upon a draft fragment in *Nbk 10* explaining the poetic
language of *J&M* (see headnote). S. wrote 'The works of Shakespeare are a perpetual illustra-
tion of this doctrine' following the draft of this sentence in *Nbk 10* f. 16'rev (see *MYR* iv
410–11) and illustrated further in the 'Note on Shakespeare' (see headnote) with reference
to Sonnet 111, *Oedipus Tyrannus*, and *Agamemnon. which raises what is low, and levels . . .
that which is lofty,*] Cp. Ezekiel xxi 26, 'exalt him that is low, and abase him that is high',
and Luke i 52, 'He hath put down the mighty from their seats, and exalted them of low degree'
which S. described as 'Jacobinism' in *Nbk 15* f. 1 (see *BSM* xiv 6–7). Both Schlegel (*Lectures*,
trans. Black (1815) ii 147–9) and Hazlitt (*Hazlitt Works* v 53–5) comment on Shakespeare's
language in comparable terms. *fit*] impressive *canc. Nbk 10. dramatic*] dramatic [& sublime
canc.] *Nbk 10. feeling*] passion *Nbk 10*.

120 that the most remote and the most familiar imagery may alike be fit for
dramatic purposes when employed in the illustration of strong feeling, which
raises what is low, and levels to the apprehension that which is lofty, casting
over all the shadow of its own greatness. In other respects I have written
more carelessly; that is, without an over-fastidious and learned choice of
125 words. In this respect I entirely agree with those modern critics who assert
that in order to move men to true sympathy we must use the familiar lan-
guage of men; and that our great ancestors the ancient English poets are
the writers, a study of whom might incite us to do that for our own age
which they have done for theirs. But it must be the real language of men
130 in general, and not that of any particular class to whose society the writer
happens to belong. So much for what I have attempted; I need not be assured
that success is a very different matter; particularly for one whose attention
has but newly been awakened to the study of dramatic literature.

I endeavoured whilst at Rome to observe such monuments of this story
135 as might be accessible to a stranger. The portrait of Beatrice at the Colonna
Palace is admirable as a work of art: it was taken by Guido during her

Pref. 123–5. In other respects . . . learned choice of words.] Cp. a rejected passage in *Nbk 10*
f. 18ʳrev: '[The lan *canc.*] My caution to avoid the ever intruding faults of youthful com-
position, diffuseness, a profusion of inapplicable imagery, vagueness, generality, & as Hamlet
says, <u>words</u> – <u>words</u>, has [cast *canc.* ?stamped *canc.*] I fear some of the scenes of the two first
acts with defects of an opposite nature. – [I feared that they have *canc.*] These defects if they
exist are however those which, as they proceed rather from diffidence than presumption the
[most *canc.*] best deserve, & the most easily receive, forgiveness.' (see *MYR* iv 400–1). The
reference is to *Hamlet* II ii 191.

Pref. 125. modern critics] Hunt appears to be foremost of those to whom S. refers. See Preface
to *The Story of Rimini* (1816) xv–xvi: 'But the proper language of poetry is in fact nothing
different from that of real life, and depends for its dignity upon the strength and sentiment
of what it speaks. It is only adding musical modulation to what a fine understanding might
actually utter in the midst of its griefs or enjoyments'.

Pref. 127. men; and] *1829*; men. And *Cenci (1819), Cenci (1821)*; men, and *Forman 1876–7*.

Pref. 128–9. and that our great ancestors . . . have done for theirs.] Cp. Hunt, Preface to *The Story
of Rimini* (1816) xvi: 'The poet therefore should do as Chaucer or Shakspeare did, – not copy
what is obsolete or peculiar in either, any more than they copied from their predecessors, –
but use as much as possible an actual, existing language, –'.

Pref. 129–31. But it must be the real language of men . . . to belong.] The phrase 'the real lan-
guage of men' is a direct borrowing from Wordsworth, Preface to *Lyrical Ballads*, 2nd edn,
2 vols (1800) i v and xxxvi–xxxvii. S. appears here to acknowledge Coleridge's criticism of
Wordsworth's phrase yet to resist the alternative theory of the *lingua communis* put forward
in Chapter XVII of *Biographia Literaria* (1817) ii 53–4.

Pref. 132–3. for one whose attention . . . dramatic literature.] A cryptic sentence since S. had
obviously studied drama seriously since at least 1810; possibly a reference to his reading of
Calderón with Maria Gisborne (see headnote).

Pref. 136. is admirable] *Errata*; is most admirable *Cenci (1819)*.

Pref. 136–7. during her confinement in prison.] as the procession past in which she was led to
execution. – *Nbk 10*. On the myth that Reni painted Beatrice just before her execution, see
Barbara Groseclose, 'A Portrait not by Guido Reni of A Girl Who is Not Beatrice Cenci', *Studies
in Eighteenth-Century Culture* xi (1982) 107–32 (125), and *Ricci* ii 280–1.

confinement in prison. But it is most interesting as a just representation of one of the loveliest specimens of the workmanship of Nature. There is a fixed and pale composure upon the features: she seems sad and stricken down in spirit, yet the despair thus expressed is lightened by the patience of gentleness. Her head is bound with folds of white drapery from which the yellow strings of her golden hair escape, and fall about her neck. The moulding of her face is exquisitely delicate; the eyebrows are distinct and arched; the lips have that permanent meaning of imagination and sensibility which suffering has not repressed and which it seems as if death scarcely could extinguish. Her forehead is large and clear; her eyes, which we are told were remarkable for their vivacity, are swollen with weeping and lustreless, but beautifully tender and serene. In the whole mien there is a simplicity and dignity which united with her exquisite loveliness and deep sorrow are inexpressibly pathetic. Beatrice Cenci appears to have been one of those rare persons in whom energy and gentleness dwell together without destroying one another: her nature was simple and profound. The crimes and miseries in which she was an actor and a sufferer are as the mask and the mantle in which circumstances clothed her for her impersonation on the scene of the world.

The Cenci Palace is of great extent; and though in part modernized, there yet remains a vast and gloomy pile of feudal architecture in the same state

Pref. 137. just] faithful *canc. Nbk 10.*

Pref. 138–50. There is a fixed and pale composure . . . inexpressibly pathetic.] Cp. S.'s descriptions of paintings by Guido he saw in Bologna in November 1818 (*L* ii 50–1, 53).

Pref. 140–1. lightened by the patience of gentleness.] tempered with patience & sorrow *Nbk 10.*

Pref. 142. the yellow strings of her golden hair escape] Cp. *Relation* 68–9: 'Her hair appeared like threads of gold and because they were [not *canc.*] extremely long she used to tie [curl *canc.*] it up & when afterwards she loos[t *canc.*]ened it [their *canc.*] the splendid ringlets dazzled the eyes of the spectator' (see *BSM* x 242–3).

Pref. 142–6. The moulding of her face . . . extinguish.] S.'s description anticipates some of his notes on statuary in the Uffizi Gallery which he saw in October 1819 (see *Prose* 343–53).

Pref. 146–8. her eyes . . . serene.] Cp. Charlotte Eaton's description of the painting in *Rome in the Nineteenth Century* (1820) iii 19–20: 'There is a settled sorrow, a wildness, and a prophetic melancholy in her eye, that is inexpressibly touching'. *her eyes,*] *1829*; her eyes *Cenci (1819), Cenci (1821). which we are told were remarkable for their vivacity,*] See *Relation* 69: 'Her eyes were of a deep blue – pleasing & [filled with a warm *canc.*] and [muted by a commanding vivacity *canc.*] full of fire' (see *BSM* x 242–3). *tender*] gentle *Nbk 10.*

Pref. 149. loveliness] beauty *Nbk 10.*

Pref. 152–5. The crimes . . . the scene of the world] Cp. the cancelled opening sentence of the Preface in *Nbk 10* f. 7'rev: 'The Story upon which the "Family of the Cenci" is written is perhaps fearful domestic tragedy which was ever acted on the scene of real life' (see *MYR* iv 446–7), a passage which reveals S.'s working title for his play. *the mask and the mantle*] Cp. *DP*: 'The distorted notions of invisible things which Dante and his rival Milton have idealized are merely the mask and the mantle in which these great poets walk through eternity enveloped and disguised' (*Prose* 289–90).

Pref. 156–8. The Cenci Palace . . . tragedy.] Cp. Charles Dickens, *Pictures from Italy* (1846) 212: 'The guilty palace of the Cenci: blighting a whole quarter of the town, as it stands withering

as during the dreadful scenes which are the subject of this tragedy. The
Palace is situated in an obscure corner of Rome, near the quarter of the
160   Jews, and from the upper windows you see the immense ruins of Mount
Palatine half hidden under their profuse overgrowth of trees. There is a
court in one part of the Palace (perhaps that in which Cenci built the Chapel
to St. Thomas), supported by granite columns and adorned with antique
friezes of fine workmanship, and built up, according to the ancient Italian
165   fashion, with balcony over balcony of open-work. One of the gates of the
Palace, formed of immense stones, and leading through a passage dark
and lofty, and opening into gloomy subterranean chambers, struck me
particularly.

Of the Castle of Petrella, I could obtain no further information than that
170   which is to be found in the manuscript.

---

away by grains: had that face [i.e. the face portrayed in the alleged Reni painting], to my
fancy, in its dismal porch, and at its black blind windows, and flitting up and own its dreary
stairs, and growing out of the darkness of its ghostly galleries'. However an American visitor
later in the century, James Henry Dixon, accuses S. of exaggeration in making the Palazzo
Cenci into 'a sort of Roman Udolpho' ('Shelley's Beatrice Cenci' in *The American Bibliopolist*
vii (1875) 165–7 (166)). *modernized*] rebuilt *Nbk 10*. *a vast and gloomy pile of feudal archi-
tecture*] 'The description reminds one of the madhouse in *Julian and Maddalo* [line] 101' (Alan
Weinberg, *Shelley's Italian Experience* (1991) 266).

Pref. 159. obscure] remote & obscure *Nbk 10*.   *near*] in *Nbk 10*.

Pref. 160–1. the immense ruins of Mount Palatine . . . trees.] the ruins and the trees of the Palatine
Mount *Nbk 10*. On the ruins on the Palatine hill, cp. *Paradise Regained* iv 50–4: 'and there
Mount Palatine / The imperial palace, compass huge, and high / The structure, skill of noblest
architects, / With gilded battlements, conspicuous far, / Turrets and terraces, and glittering
spires'; Byron, *Childe Harold's Pilgrimage Canto the Fourth* (1818) stanzas cvi and cvii and note;
Hobhouse, *Historical Illustrations of the Fourth Canto of Childe Harold* (1818) 206–14; and *Eustace*
i 378–81.

Pref. 162–3. (perhaps that in which Cenci built the Chapel to St. Thomas),] As *Rognoni* 1567 points
out, S. confuses the description of an inner courtyard of the Palazzo Cenci with the nearby
square in which is to be found the Church of San Tommaso de' Cenci, built by Bishop Cenci
in 1112 according to Richard Davey, 'Beatrice Cenci', *The Antiquary* lxxiv (1886) 68.

Pref. 164. built up,] *Cenci (1819)*; built up *Cenci (1821)*.

Pref. 165. gates] gateways *Rossetti 1878*.

Pref. 166. formed of] built of *Nbk 10*.   *passage*] *1839*; passage, *Cenci (1819), Cenci (1821)*.

Pref. 166–7. dark and lofty] dark vast *Nbk 10*.

DRAMATIS PERSONAE

COUNT FRANCESCO CENCI.

GIACOMO,
BERNARDO, } his Sons.

CARDINAL CAMILLO.

ORSINO, a Prelate.

SAVELLA, the Pope's Legate.

OLIMPIO,
MARZIO, } Assassins.

ANDREA, Servant to Cenci.

Nobles, Judges, Guards, Servants.

LUCRETIA, Wife of Cenci, and Step-mother of his Children.

BEATRICE, his Daughter.

The SCENE lies principally in Rome, but changes during the Fourth Act to Petrella, a castle among the Apulian Apennines.

TIME. During the Pontificate of Clement VIII.

Dramatis Personae Petrella, a castle among the Apulian Apennines.] The ruin of the Castle of Petrella (Rocca di Petrella), now known as the Rocca Cenci, is situated *c.* 90km NE of Rome above the medieval village of Petrella Salto. In S.'s day it was in the Kingdom of Naples as it was in the late sixteenth century. Though Petrella is in the Apennines, S. was mistaken in locating it in Apulia, the furthermost SE region of the Italian peninsula. *During the Pontificate of Clement VIII*] See note to Preface lines 4–5.

ACT I

Scene i

An Apartment in the Cenci Palace. Enter Count Cenci, *and* Cardinal Camillo.

    Camillo
    That matter of the murder is hushed up
    If you consent to yield his Holiness
    Your fief that lies beyond the Pincian gate.
    It needed all my interest in the conclave
5   To bend him to this point: he said that you
    Bought perilous impunity with your gold;
    That crimes like yours if once or twice compounded
    Enriched the Church, and respited from hell
    An erring soul which might repent and live;
10   But that the glory and the interest
    Of the high throne he fills, little consist
    With making it a daily mart of guilt
    As manifold and hideous as the deeds
    Which you scarce hide from men's revolted eyes.

    Cenci
15   The third of my possessions — let it go!
    Aye, I once heard the nephew of the Pope

---

1. That matter of the murder] i.e. the murder referred to at I i 23. Gibbon (*Decline and Fall* vii 295–8) and J. C. L. Simonde de Sismondi (*Histoire des Républiques Italiennes du Moyen Âge*, Seconde Édition Parisienne, 16 vols (Paris, 1818) xvi 191–3) comment on the violent feuds of powerful families in sixteenth-century Rome in which the Papacy was frequently embroiled.

3. Pincian gate.] An entrance to Rome from the North.

7. compounded] i.e. 'paid for'. See *OED*: 'compound' *v.* (13a) 'To come to terms and pay *for* an offence or injury; to substitute a money payment in lieu of any other liability or obligation; to pay.' See note to Preface lines 18–20.

13. As] *Errata*; So *Cenci (1819)*.

16. nephew] On Clement VIII's notorious nepotism see Lodovico Muratori, *Annali d'Italia*, 12 vols (Milan, 1744–9) xi [1749] 16: 'Lascio ancora in grande auge, e con illustri parentele, e con grande lucrosi, e con fabbriche sontuose i suoi Nipoti e Pronipoti, tre de' quali fregiati della Sacra Porpora' ('he left also his nephews and grand-nephews in great felicity, with illustrious connections, and lucrative posts, and sumptuous dwellings. Three of them were adorned with the sacred Purple' (*Ricci (1926)* ii 247–8)). 'Nephew' may be 'euphemistically applied to the illegitimate son of an ecclesiastic' (*OED* 1b) but in this scene (see also I i 28, 57) it is used to point to the historical origin of the word 'nepotism' (*OED* 2), 'The practice, on the part of the Popes . . . of showing special favour to nephews . . . in conferring offices.'

Had sent his architect to view the ground,
Meaning to build a villa on my vines
The next time I compounded with his uncle:
20   I little thought he should outwit me so!
Henceforth no witness — not the lamp — shall see
That which the vassal threatened to divulge
Whose throat is choked with dust for his reward.
The deed he saw could not have rated higher
25   Than his most worthless life: — it angers me!
Respited me from Hell! — So may the Devil
Respite their souls from Heaven. No doubt Pope Clement,
And his most charitable nephews, pray
That the Apostle Peter and the saints
30   Will grant for their sake that I long enjoy
Strength, wealth, and pride, and lust, and length of days
Wherein to act the deeds which are the stewards
Of their revenue. — But much yet remains
To which they show no title.

Camillo
                                    Oh, Count Cenci!
35   So much that thou mightst honourably live
And reconcile thyself with thine own heart

---

19. compounded with his uncle] i.e. 'came to a settlement with the Pope by paying him money' (see *OED*: 'compound' *v*. (8b): 'to settle (any matter) by a money payment, in lieu of other liability'). Cp. note to I i 7.

22. divulge] *Cenci (1819)*; divulge, *Cenci (1821)*.

24–5. The deed . . . worthless life:] 'The sense is, "I could hardly have been made to pay more for the crime which he saw, than I have to pay for killing him. Consequently the murder was not worth my while"' (*Locock 1911*).

24. rated higher] i.e. 'been worth more' (cited in *OED*, 'rate' *v*. 6b).

25. Than] *1839*; That *Cenci (1819)*, *Cenci (1821)*.

26. Respited me from Hell! –] *Errata, Taaffe*; Respited from Hell! – *Cenci (1819)*.

28. nephews,] See note to I i 16.

29. Peter, like Thomas, the Apostle invoked by Cenci at I i 105 (see also Preface lines 102–4 and note), is accused by Christ of lacking faith (see *Matthew* xiv 31, xvi 23, xxvi 69–75).

31. Ann McWhir, 'The Light and the Knife: Ab/Using Language in *The Cenci'*, *KSJ* xxxviii (1989) 152 notes that this catalogue 'ironically echoes' *Proverbs* iii 1–2: 'My son, forget not my law; but let thine heart keep my commandments: For length of days, and long life, and peace, shall they add to thee.' *lust,*] G. H. Lewes, Review of *1839* and other works, *The Westminster Review* xxxv (1841) 303–44 (336) cps. Cenci to Crispinus in Juvenal, *Satires* iv lines 2–3: 'monstrum nulla virtute redemptum / a vitiis, aegrae solaque libidine fortis' ('monster! in whose tainted heart / Not one atoning virtue claims a part: / Diseased, emaciate, weak in all but lust' (William Gifford, trans., *The Satires of Decimus Junius Juvenalis* (1802))).

35. thou mightst] *Taaffe*; thou migh'st *Cenci (1819)*.

And with thy God, and with the offended world.
How hideously look deeds of lust and blood
Through those snow-white and venerable hairs!
40   Your children should be sitting round you now,
But that you fear to read upon their looks
The shame and misery you have written there.
Where is your wife? Where is your gentle daughter?
Methinks her sweet looks, which make all things else
45   Beauteous and glad, might kill the fiend within you.
Why is she barred from all society
But her own strange and uncomplaining wrongs?
Talk with me, Count, — you know I mean you well.
I stood beside your dark and fiery youth
50   Watching its bold and bad career, as men
Watch meteors, but it vanished not; I marked
Your desperate and remorseless manhood; now
Do I behold you, in dishonoured age,
Charged with a thousand unrepented crimes.
55   Yet I have ever hoped you would amend,
And in that hope have saved your life three times.

Cenci
For which Aldobrandino owes you now
My fief beyond the Pincian. Cardinal,
One thing, I pray you, recollect henceforth,
60   And so we shall converse with less restraint.
A man you knew spoke of my wife and daughter:
He was accustomed to frequent my house;
So the next day *his* wife and daughter came
And asked if I had seen him; and I smiled:
65   I think they never saw him any more.

Camillo
Thou execrable man, beware! —

49–54. *I stood beside your . . . unrepented crimes.*] Cp. *Richard III* IV iv 168–72: 'Tetchy and way-
ward was thy infancy; / Thy school-days frightful, desp'rate, wild, and furious; / Thy prime
of manhood daring, bold, and venturous; / Thy age confirm'd, proud, subtle, sly, and
bloody, / More mild, but yet more harmful – kind in hatred'.

50–1. *as men / Watch meteors, but it vanished not;*] Cp. Webster, *The White Devil* I i 24–6: 'as
fore-deeming you / An idle meteor which drawn forth the earth / Would be soon lost i' th'air.'

51. *not;*] *Rossetti 1870*; not – *Cenci (1819)*; not: *Cenci (1821)*.

57. *Aldobrandino*] The 'nephew' of the Pope referred to at I i 16. Clement VIII's family name
was Aldobrandini (see Sismondi, *Histoire des Républiques Italiennes* xvi 197) as is noted in Bod.
MS. Shelley adds. e. 13, p. 78 (see *BSM* x 252–3).

Cenci
                                              Of thee?
Nay, this is idle: we should know each other.
As to my character for what men call crime,
Seeing I please my senses as I list,
70   And vindicate that right with force or guile,
It is a public matter, and I care not
If I discuss it with you. I may speak
Alike to you and my own conscious heart;
For you give out that you have half reformed me,
75   Therefore strong vanity will keep you silent
If fear should not; both will, I do not doubt.
All men delight in sensual luxury,
All men enjoy revenge; and most exult
Over the tortures they can never feel;
80   Flattering their secret peace with others' pain.
But I delight in nothing else. I love
The sight of agony, and the sense of joy,
When this shall be another's and that mine.
And I have no remorse and little fear,

72–3. *I may speak . . . conscious heart;*] i.e. 'I may speak as openly to you as if I were talking to myself.' *Locock 1911* cps. I i 119. *conscious*] 'Knowing, witting, well aware' (cited in *OED* as a *poetical* usage, 'conscious' *a*. 6e). Cp. Byron, *Don Juan* (1819) Canto I stanza cvi: 'How beautiful she look'd! her conscious heart / Glow'd in her cheek, and yet she felt no wrong.'

78–91. Eunice Joiner Gates, 'Shelley and Calderon', *PQ* xvi (1937) 51–2 cps. the following speech by Lodovico Enio in Calderón, *El Purgatorio de San Patricio* II i: 'Baste que tan malo sea, / que aún no me arrepiento agora / de mis cometidas culpas, / y que quiera intentar otras. / Pues, ¡vive Dios!, que mi vida, / si fuese posible cosa / escaparse hoy, fuera asombro / del Asia, Africa y Europa. / Hoy empezara a tomar / venganza tan rigurosa, / que en estas islas de Egerio / no me quedara persona / en quien no satisfaciera / la pena, la sed rabiosa / que tengo de sangre . . . No, no me pesa morir / por morir muerte afrentosa, / sino porque acabarán, / con mi edad temprana y moza, / mis delitos. Vida quiero / para empezar desde agora / mayores temeridades, / no, cielos, para otra cosa' (text from *El Purgatorio de San Patricio*, ed. J. M. Ruano de la Haza (1988)) (''Tis enough to be so wicked / As even now to feel no sorrow, / No repentance for past sins, / Rather a desire for others. / Yes, by God! for if escape / Fortune now my life would offer, / Europe, Africa, and Asia / I would fill with fear and horror; / First exacting here the debt / Of a vengeance so enormous, / That these islands of Egerius / Would not hold a single mortal / Who should not appease the thirst, / The insatiable longing / That I have for blood . . . / No, it is not death that grieves me, / Even a death of such dishonour, / 'Tis because at last are ended, / In my youth's fresh opening blossom, / My offences. Life I wish for / To begin from this day forward / Greater and more dread excesses. / Heavens! 'tis for no other object.' (trans. Denis Florence Mac-Carthy, *Calderon's Dramas* (1873)).

80. *peace*] G. Wilson Knight, *The Golden Labyrinth: A Study of British Drama* (1962) 215 cps. Wordsworth, *The Borderers: A Tragedy* (1842) III 1468–9: 'In terror, / Remembered terror, there is peace and rest', and V 2186: 'The extremes of suffering meet in absolute peace.'

84. Cp. III i 209. *no remorse*] Remorse, or its absence, becomes the locus of a contrast between Cenci and Beatrice on the one hand, and Giacomo and Lucretia on the other. For the influence

85   Which are, I think, the checks of other men.
This mood has grown upon me, until now
Any design my captious fancy makes
The picture of its wish, and it forms none
But such as men like you would start to know,
90   Is as my natural food and rest debarred
Until it be accomplished.

Camillo
                    Art thou not
Most miserable?

Cenci
                Why miserable? —
No. I am what your theologians call
Hardened; which they must be in impudence,
95   So to revile a man's peculiar taste.
True, I was happier than I am, while yet
Manhood remained to act the thing I thought;
While lust was sweeter than revenge; and now
Invention palls: aye, we must all grow old:
100   And but that there yet remains a deed to act
Whose horror might make sharp an appetite
Duller than mine — I'd do, — I know not what.

---

of La Mettrie on S.'s views concerning remorse, see Seamus Deane, *The French Revolution and Enlightenment in England 1789–1832* (1988) 95–129.

84–5. Cp. Byron, *Manfred, A Dramatic Poem* (1817) I i 24–7: 'I have no dread, / And feel the curse to have no natural fear, / Nor fluttering throb, that beats with hopes or wishes, / Or lurking love of something on the earth. –'

86–91. Cp. the description of Napoleon in Byron, *Childe Harold's Pilgrimage, Canto the Third* (1816) stanza xlii: 'But quiet to quick bosoms is a hell, / And *there* hath been thy bane; there is a fire / And motion of the soul which will not dwell / In its own narrow being, but aspire / Beyond the fitting medium of desire; / And, but once kindled, quenchless evermore, / Preys upon high adventure, nor can tire / Of aught but rest; a fever at the core, / Fatal to him who bears, to all who ever bore.' Cp. also Ordonio in Coleridge, *Remorse* (1813) IV i 124–7: 'With his human hand / He gave a substance and reality / To that wild fancy of a possible thing. – / Well it was done!'

87. captious] 'designed to entrap or entangle by subtlety' (*OED* 1). S. possibly also includes an obsolete usage meaning 'capacious' (*OED* 3a) as in: 'Yet in this captious and intenible sieve / I still pour in the waters of my love, / And lack not to lose still.' (*All's Well* I iii 193–5).

97. the thing I thought.] *OED* ('think' v, 8b) cps. this transitive usage with *Paradise Lost* i 660–1: 'peace is despaired, / For who can think submission?'

100. Errata; But that there yet remains a deed to act *Cenci (1819)*; And but that there remains a deed to act *Woodberry 1893*. 'My own impression is that [S.] meant to cancel *yet*.' (Forman, *Shelley Library* (1886) 92).

102. Cp. III i 86–7.

When I was young I thought of nothing else
But pleasure; and I fed on honey sweets:
105   Men, by St. Thomas! cannot live like bees,
And I grew tired: yet, till I killed a foe,
And heard his groans, and heard his children's groans,
Knew I not what delight was else on earth,
Which now delights me little. I the rather
110   Look on such pangs as terror ill conceals:
The dry, fixed eyeball; the pale, quivering lip,
Which tell me that the spirit weeps within
Tears bitterer than the bloody sweat of Christ.
I rarely kill the body, which preserves,
115   Like a strong prison, the soul within my power,
Wherein I feed it with the breath of fear
For hourly pain.

Camillo

              Hell's most abandoned fiend
Did never, in the drunkenness of guilt,
Speak to his heart as now you speak to me;
120   I thank my God that I believe you not.

Enter Andrea.

103–6. When I was young . . . / And I grew tired:] For the significance of the invocation to St Thomas in line 105, see Preface lines 102–4 and note. The terms in which Cenci epitomises his sexuality in these and earlier lines (cp. I i 95, 98, 101) contrast markedly with the description of the disciplined republic of the bee-hive in *Georgics* iv (see also no. 168). *Relation* states that Cenci was fined for sodomy not murder (see note to Preface lines 18–20).

109–13. I the rather . . . sweat of Christ.] These lines draw on a passage in *Nbk 5* (see *Athanase*, Detached Passage (a) 1–3 and note), and a cancelled passage in the draft of *PU* in *Nbk 8* after II iv 27 (see note to *PU* II iv 27–8).

113. the bloody sweat of Christ.] Cp. *Luke* xxii 44: 'his sweat was as it were great drops of blood falling down to the ground.'

114–15. 'The body as the prison of the soul is an echo of *Phaedo* 62b, 67d, 82e' (*Notopoulos* 262). Cp. esp. Plato, *Phaedo* 82d–e: ' "The lovers of knowledge," said he, "perceive that when philosophy first takes possession of their soul it is entirely fastened and welded to the body and is compelled to regard realities through the body as through prison bars, not with its own unhindered vision, and is wallowing in utter ignorance. And philosophy sees that the most dreadful thing about the imprisonment is the fact that it is caused by the lusts of the flesh, so that the prisoner is the chief assistant in his own imprisonment. The lovers of knowledge, then, I say, perceive that philosophy, taking possession of the soul when it is in this state, encourages it gently and tries to set it free . . ." ' (Loeb trans.). Cp. also *Matthew* x 28: 'And fear not them which kill the body, but are not able to kill the soul: but rather fear him which is able to destroy both soul and body in hell.'

115. strong] i.e. 'impossible to escape from' (cited in *OED*, 'strong' *a.* 8b).

Andrea
My Lord, a gentleman from Salamanca
Would speak with you.

Cenci
              Bid him attend me in
The grand saloon.

                                 [*Exit* Andrea.

Camillo
              Farewell; and I will pray
Almighty God that thy false, impious words
125   Tempt not his spirit to abandon thee.   [*Exit* Camillo.

Cenci
The third of my possessions! I must use
Close husbandry, or gold, the old man's sword,
Falls from my withered hand. But yesterday
There came an order from the Pope to make
130   Fourfold provision for my cursèd sons;
Whom I had sent from Rome to Salamanca,
Hoping some accident might cut them off;
And meaning if I could to starve them there.
I pray thee, God, send some quick death upon them!
135   Bernardo and my wife could not be worse
If dead and damned: then, as to Beatrice —
                  [*Looking around him suspiciously.*

122–3. Bid him attend me in / The grand saloon.] *Rossetti 1870*; Bid him attend me in the grand saloon. *Cenci (1819), Cenci (1821)*; Bid him attend me / In the grand saloon. *Woodberry 1893*.

124. words] *Cenci (1819)*; words, *Cenci (1821)*.

126–8. The third . . . withered hand.] Michael Worton, 'Speech and Silence in *The Cenci*' in *Essays on Shelley*, ed. Miriam Allott (1982) 105–24 (117) points out that the dramatic irony of IV iv is explained in these lines: 'the Pope's decision [i.e. to send Savella to the Castle of Petrella with a warrant for Cenci's death] would therefore seem to find its justification in revenge against a disobedient subject who has cut off a major source of income.'

127. gold, the old man's sword,] Cp. 'England in 1819' lines 9–10: 'Make as a two-edged sword to all who wield; / Golden and sanguine laws which tempt and slay.'

131. See *Relation* 4. The University of Salamanca was a common destination for sons of the Catholic nobility in the Renaissance. Don Raymond and Don Lorenzo are educated there in M. G. Lewis, *The Monk: A Romance*, 3 vols (1796) i 169. *had*] *Errata, Taaffe*; have *Cenci (1819)*.

132. Cp. *Richard III* I iii 212–14: 'God, I pray him, / That none of you may live his natural age, / But by some unlook'd accident cut off!'

135–6. could not be worse / If dead and damned:] i.e. 'they could not be worse off dead and damned than they are alive'. 'The point seems to be that Cenci actually takes credit to himself for praying for the death of his wife and son' (*Locock 1911*).

I think they cannot hear me at that door;
What if they should? And yet I need not speak,
Though the heart triumphs with itself in words.
140 O, thou most silent air, that shalt not hear
What now I think! Thou, pavement, which I tread
Towards her chamber, — let your echoes talk
Of my imperious step, scorning surprise,
But not of my intent! — Andrea!

Enter Andrea.

Andrea
                                        My Lord!

Cenci
145 Bid Beatrice attend me in her chamber
This evening: — no, at midnight, and alone.

                                        [*Exeunt.*

Scene ii

A Garden of the Cenci Palace. Enter Beatrice *and* Orsino, *as in conversation.*

Beatrice
Pervert not truth,
Orsino. You remember where we held
That conversation; — nay, we see the spot
Even from this cypress; — two long years are past
5 Since, on an April midnight, underneath
The moonlight ruins of Mount Palatine,
I did confess to you my secret mind.

---

140. *shalt*] *Errata*; shall *Cenci (1819).*

141-4. *Thou, pavement, . . . not of my intent!*] Cp. *Macbeth* II i 56–8: 'Thou sure and firm-set earth, / Hear not my steps which way they walk, for fear / Thy very stones prate of my where-about'; Milman, *Fazio* (1815) Act I scene iii: 'The stones whereon I tread do grimly speak, / Forbidding echoes, aye with human voices.'; the fifteenth chapter of *La Vita Nuova* in Dante, *Opere* 5 vols (Venice, 1760) v 23: 'Le pietre par, che gridin: mora, mora!' ('The very stones I walk on echo "Die!"' ' (*La Vita Nuova*, trans. Barbara Reynolds (1969))).

144. *intent! –*] *Cenci (1819)*; intent! *Cenci (1821).*   *My Lord!*]. My lord? *Cenci (1819)*; My lord! *Cenci (1821).*

¶ii   *1–8.* A possible explanation of the markedly ametrical first line of this scene is that 'Orsino.' in line 2 was originally intended as a stage direction. The language of lines 2–8 would seem appropriate to Orsino, and to make line 1 the sum of Beatrice's first speech in the play would give her opening three words singular dramatic force.

6. *Mount Palatine,*] *1829*; mount Palatine, *Cenci (1819)*, *Cenci (1821).* See Preface lines 160–1 and note.

Orsino
You said you loved me then.

Beatrice
                          You are a priest,
Speak to me not of love.

Orsino
                         I may obtain
10   The dispensation of the Pope to marry.
Because I am a priest do you believe
Your image, as the hunter some struck deer,
Follows me not whether I wake or sleep?

Beatrice
As I have said, speak to me not of love;
15   Had you a dispensation, I have not;
Nor will I leave this home of misery
Whilst my poor Bernard, and that gentle lady
To whom I owe life and these virtuous thoughts,
Must suffer what I still have strength to share.
20   Alas, Orsino! All the love that once
I felt for you, is turned to bitter pain.
Ours was a youthful contract, which you first
Broke, by assuming vows no Pope will loose.
And thus I love you still, but holily,

8. *priest,*] Priest, *Cenci (1819)*.

9–10. *I may obtain / The dispensation of the Pope to marry.*] Cp. Don Raymond's assurance to Agnes that he will 'easily obtain a dispensation from her vows' from the Pope so that they can marry in Lewis, *The Monk* (1796) ii 109–10.

11. *priest*] Priest *Cenci (1819)*.

12–13. *Your image, . . . wake or sleep?*] An allusion to the myth of Actaeon is discernible in Orsino's portrayal of Beatrice as a huntress and himself as a wounded deer. Cp. *PU* I 454–7 and note.

12. *struck deer*] A commonplace image of helpless affliction (see e.g. *Aeneid* iv 68–73; *Fairie Queene* II i 12; *Hamlet* III ii 265; Cowper, *The Task* (1785) iii 108–9).

15. *dispensation,*] Taaffe; dispensation *Cenci (1819)*.

18. *To whom I owe life*] To whom I owe life, *Cenci (1819)*. i.e. 'who preserved my life' (see II i 89–93).

23. *loose.*] An apparently archaic usage in S.'s day (cited in *OED*, 'loose' *v*. 7b; *OED* cps. the usage with *Lat.* 'solvere', to dissolve).

24. *thus*] *Errata*, Taaffe; yet *Cenci (1819)*.

25 Even as a sister or a spirit might;
And so I swear a cold fidelity.
And it is well perhaps we shall not marry.
You have a sly, equivocating vein
That suits me not. — Ah, wretched that I am!
30 Where shall I turn? Even now you look on me
As you were not my friend, and as if you
Discovered that I thought so, with false smiles
Making my true suspicion seem your wrong.
Ah! no, forgive me; sorrow makes me seem
35 Sterner than else my nature might have been;
I have a weight of melancholy thoughts,
And they forbode, — but what can they forebode
Worse than I now endure?

Orsino
                All will be well.
Is the petition yet prepared? You know
40 My zeal for all you wish, sweet Beatrice;
Doubt not but I will use my utmost skill
So that the Pope attend to your complaint.

Beatrice
Your zeal for all I wish; Ah me, you are cold!
Your utmost skill — speak but one word —   [*Aside.*
                           Alas!
45 Weak and deserted creature that I am,
Here I stand bickering with my only friend!

                       [*To* Orsino.

This night my father gives a sumptuous feast,
Orsino; he has heard some happy news
From Salamanca, from my brothers there,
50 And with this outward show of love he mocks
His inward hate. 'Tis bold hypocrisy,
For he would gladlier celebrate their deaths,
Which I have heard him pray for on his knees:

---

29. *not.* −] *Cenci (1819)*; not. *Cenci (1821).*

33. *your wrong.*] i.e. 'a wrong done to you.' The word 'wrong' is used in this sense throughout C: e.g. Preface line 33, I iii 108, II i 2 etc.

34. *Ah! no,*] *Taaffe*; Ah! No, *Cenci (1819), Cenci (1821).*

41. *skill*] *Cenci (1819)*; skill, *Cenci (1821).*

Great God! that such a father should be mine!
55 But there is mighty preparation made,
And all our kin, the Cenci, will be there,
And all the chief nobility of Rome.
And he has bidden me and my pale mother
Attire ourselves in festival array.
60 Poor lady! She expects some happy change
In his dark spirit from this act; I none.
At supper I will give you the petition:
Till when — farewell.

Orsino
　　　　　　　　Farewell.

　　　　　　　　　　　　　　　　　　[Exit Beatrice.

　　　　　　　　I know the Pope
Will ne'er absolve me from my priestly vow
65 But by absolving me from the revenue
Of many a wealthy see; and, Beatrice,
I think to win thee at an easier rate.
Nor shall he read her eloquent petition:
He might bestow her on some poor relation
70 Of his sixth cousin, as he did her sister,
And I should be debarred from all access.
Then as to what she suffers from her father,
In all this there is much exaggeration:
Old men are testy and will have their way;
75 A man may stab his enemy, or his vassal,
And live a free life as to wine or women,
And with a peevish temper may return
To a dull home, and rate his wife and children;
Daughters and wives call this foul tyranny.

69–71. 'These three lines are the key to the whole tragedy' (*Locock 1911*).

69–70. Cp. *Relation* 7–8: 'The eldest of these [i.e. Francesco Cenci's daughters] being unable any longer to support the cruelty of her father exposed her miserable condition to the Pope & supplicated him either to marry him according to his choice or to shut her up in a monastery that by any means she might be liberated from [miserable *canc.*] the cruel oppression of her parent. Her prayer was heard and the Pope in pity to her unhappiness bestowed [her as *canc.*] her in marriage to Sig. Carlo Gabrielli one of the first gentlemen of the city of Gabbio & obliged Francesco to give her a fitting dowry of some thousand crowns' (*BSM* x 178–81). Luzio Savelli, who married Antonina, Beatrice's sister, 'in obedience to a suggestion of the Pope' (*Ricci (1926)* i 75), was wealthy.

75. vassal,] *Errata, Taaffe*; slave, *Cenci (1819)*. The word 'vassals' is used in *Relation* 17 to describe Marzio's and Olympio's relationship to Francesco Cenci. See also V ii 82.

80   I shall be well content if on my conscience
There rest no heavier sin than what they suffer
From the devices of my love — A net
From which she shall escape not. Yet I fear
Her subtle mind, her awe-inspiring gaze,
85   Whose beams anatomize me, nerve by nerve,
And lay me bare, and make me blush to see
My hidden thoughts. — Ah, no! A friendless girl
Who clings to me, as to her only hope: —
I were a fool, not less than if a panther
90   Were panic-stricken by the antelope's eye,
If she escape me.

                                         [*Exit.*

80–2. I shall be well content . . . the devices of my love -] i.e. 'My conscience will be clear so long as my designs on Beatrice result in nothing worse than the continuation of what she, her step-mother, and brother already suffer.'

80. content] *Cenci (1819)*; content, *Cenci (1821)*.

84. her awe-inspiring gaze] Cp. Gray, *The Bard. A Pindaric Ode* (1757) 117: 'her awe-commanding face', and Wordsworth, *The Excursion* (1814) iv 886–7: '["] Pan himself / The simple Shepherd's awe-inspiring God."'

85. anatomize] i.e. 'to lay open minutely; to analyse' (*OED* 3); cp. *King Lear* III vi 75–6: 'Then let them anatomize Regan; see what breeds about her heart.'

89–91. An inversion of the hunting image in I ii 12. Orsino now identifies himself with the predatory panther, itself a symbol of various evils including lust in *Inferno* i 31–3: 'Ed, ecco quasi al cominciar dell'erta, / Una lonza leggiera e presta molto, / Che di pel maculato era coperta' ('Scarce the ascent / Began, when, lo! a panther, nimble, light, / And cover'd with a speckled skin, appear'd' (trans. Cary)). Yet, in the repetition in 'panic-stricken' of the Greek prefix παν, 'pan' (signifying the terror associated with the invisible God of that name), a further allusion to the Actaeon myth seems intended (cp. note to I ii 12). The image of the antelope identifies Beatrice with vulnerable prey; cp. Belford's letter to Lovelace of 22 August in Richardson, *Clarissa. Or, the History of a Young Lady*, 7 vols (1748) vii 2: 'Canst thou thyself say, on reflection, that it has not the look of a wicked and hardened sportiveness, in thee, for the sake of a wanton humour only, (since it can answer no end that thou proposest to thyself, but the direct contrary) to hunt from place to place a poor lady, who, like a harmless deer, that has already a barbed shaft in her breast, seeks only a refuge from thee, in the shades of death?'; the description of the ounce hunting the antelope in Southey, *Thalaba*, 2 vols (1801) Book IX, ii 159–61; and *Frankenstein* (1818): 'I could have torn him limb from limb, as the lion rends the antelope' (*MSW* i 101). But the implied coldness of her gaze calls to mind a contrast referred to in Lucretius, *De Rerum Natura* iii 296–301: 'quo genere in primis vis est violenta leonum, / pectora qui fremitu rumpunt plerumque gementes / nec capere irarum fluctus in pectore possunt. / at ventosa magis cervorum frigida mens est / et gelidas citius per viscera concitat auras, / quae tremulum faciunt membris existere motum' ('A notable instance of this is the violent fury of the lion, which so often bursts his breast with roaring and growling, nor can he find room in his heart for the storm of passion. But the cold mind of the stag has more of wind, and more speedily sends currents of cold breath through his flesh, which cause a tremulous movement to pervade the limbs' (Loeb trans., rev. edn 1992)). *Curran (1975)* 125 cps. *PU* I 609: 'Ironically, the priest exactly applies Prometheus' figure for the priesthood that has perverted Christ's vision and persecuted its true adherents.'

Scene iii

A magnificent Hall in the Cenci Palace. A Banquet. Enter Cenci, Lucretia, Beatrice, Orsino, Camillo, Nobles.

Cenci
Welcome, my friends and kinsmen; welcome ye,
Princes and Cardinals, pillars of the church,
Whose presence honours our festivity.
I have too long lived like an anchorite,
5   And, in my absence from your merry meetings,
An evil word is gone abroad of me;
But I do hope that you, my noble friends,
When you have shared the entertainment here,
And heard the pious cause for which 'tis given,
10   And we have pledged a health or two together,
Will think me flesh and blood as well as you;
Sinful indeed, for Adam made all so,
But tender-hearted, meek and pitiful.

1. Guest
In truth, my Lord, you seem too light of heart,
15   Too sprightly and companionable a man,
To act the deeds that rumour pins on you.

                                       [*To his companion.*

I never saw such blithe and open cheer
In any eye!

2. Guest
           Some most desired event,
In which we all demand a common joy,
20   Has brought us hither; let us hear it, Count.

Cenci
It is indeed a most desired event.
If, when a parent from a parent's heart

1. *ye,*] *Cenci (1819)*; ye *Cenci (1821)*.

2. *Princes*] i.e. 'noblemen' (cited in *OED*, 'prince' *sb.* 7a).

5. Cp. *Richard III* I i 7: 'Our stern alarums chang'd to merry meetings'.

6. *me;*] *Cenci (1819)*; me: *Cenci (1821)*.

12. To use the doctrine of original sin as a means of justifying evil is blasphemy. Cp. *Romans* vi 1–2: 'What shall we say then? Shall we continue in sin, that grace may abound? God forbid. How shall we, that are dead to sin, live any longer therein?'

22. *If, when a parent from a parent's heart*] If when a parent from a parent's heart *Cenci (1819)*; If, when a parent, from a parent's heart, *Cenci (1821)*.

Lifts from this earth to the great father of all
A prayer, both when he lays him down to sleep
25   And when he rises up from dreaming it;
One supplication, one desire, one hope,
That he would grant a wish for his two sons,
Even all that he demands in their regard —
And suddenly, beyond his dearest hope,
30   It is accomplished, he should then rejoice,
And call his friends and kinsmen to a feast,
And task their love to grace his merriment,
Then honour me thus far — for I am he.

Beatrice   [*To* Lucretia.
Great God! How horrible! Some dreadful ill
35   Must have befallen my brothers.

Lucretia
                              Fear not, child,
He speaks too frankly.

Beatrice
                      Ah! My blood runs cold.
I fear that wicked laughter round his eye,
Which wrinkles up the skin even to the hair.

Cenci
Here are the letters brought from Salamanca;
40   Beatrice, read them to your mother. God,
I thank thee! In one night didst thou perform,
By ways inscrutable, the thing I sought.
My disobedient and rebellious sons
Are dead! — Why, dead! — What means this change of cheer?
45   You hear me not, I tell you they are dead;
And they will need no food or raiment more:
The tapers that did light them the dark way
Are their last cost. The Pope, I think, will not
Expect I should maintain them in their coffins.
50   Rejoice with me, my heart is wondrous glad.

41–4. In one night . . . Are dead!] Cp. Creon's description of the death of Oedipus's sons, Eteocles and Polyneices, in Sophocles, *Antigone* 170: πρὸς διπλῆς μοίρας μίαν / καθ᾽ ἡμέραν ὤλοντο ('perished by twofold ruin on a single day' (Loeb trans. rev. edn 1994)). Cenci's view that his prayers have been answered in respect of his sons' deaths parallels the fulfilment of Oedipus's curse of his sons. The sense in which the Cenci family is accursed mirrors, in turn, the working out of the curse on the House of Labdacus.

44. Are dead! – Why, dead! –] *Taaffe*; Are dead! – Why dead! – *Cenci (1819), Cenci (1821).*

Beatrice   [Lucretia *sinks, half fainting*; Beatrice *supports her.*
It is not true! — Dear lady, pray look up.
Had it been true, there is a God in Heaven,
He would not live to boast of such a boon.
Unnatural man, thou knowest that it is false.

Cenci
55   Aye, as the word of God; whom here I call
To witness that I speak the sober truth;
And whose most favouring Providence was shown
Even in the manner of their deaths. For Rocco
Was kneeling at the mass, with sixteen others,
60   When the church fell and crushed him to a mummy;
The rest escaped unhurt. Cristofano
Was stabbed in error by a jealous man,
Whilst she he loved was sleeping with his rival;
All in the self-same hour of the same night;
65   Which shows that Heaven has special care of me.
I beg those friends who love me, that they mark
The day a feast upon their calendars.
It was the twenty-seventh of December:
Aye, read the letters if you doubt my oath.
[*The assembly appears confused; several of the guests rise.*

58–64. Contrast 'the manner of their deaths', though not Cenci's reaction, in *Relation* 9: 'In the mean ensued the death of two of his sons, Rocco & Cristofero – one being assassinated by a surgeon and the other by Paolo Corso while he was attending Mass – the inhuman father shewed every sign of joy on hearing this news –'. *Ricci* (i 81–2, 142ff.) states that Rocco was killed in a duel in March 1595 and that Cristoforo was murdered in June 1598.

58–61. For Rocco . . . escaped unhurt.] A possible allusion to the Conspiracy of the Pazzi (1478) to murder the Medici brothers in church, during Mass itself described in William Roscoe, *Life of Lorenzo de' Medici*, 2nd edn, 2 vols (1796) i 176 as 'a transaction that has seldom been mentioned without emotions of the strongest horror and detestation; and which, as has justly been observed, is an incontrovertible proof of the practical atheism of the times in which it took place'.

60. mummy;] i.e. 'a pulpy substance or mass' but with a possible play on an earlier jocular usage 'dead flesh; body in which life is extinct' (see *OED* 'mummy', *sb.* 1b and 1c).

66–7. Cp. *Macbeth* IV i 133–4: 'Let this pernicious hour / Stand aye accursed in the calendar!'

68. The date functions as a further reminder of Cenci's impious behaviour. December 27 is the eve of Innocents' Day (also known as Childermas) which commemorates the slaughter of all male children two years old or under ordered by Herod, noted in *Matthew* ii 16 (see Fred L. Milne, 'Shelley's *The Cenci*, I iii 55–69', *The Explicator* xxxv (1976) 30–1). 'This may mean that Cenci even outdoes Herod by one day' (GM). *Holmes* 483 suggests, implausibly, that the date is S.'s way of commemorating the deaths through miscarriage of two babies sired by him, one born to Claire the other to Elise Foggi (for Holmes's revised views see his *Footsteps: Adventures of a Romantic Biographer* (1985) 170–7). For further discussion of the significance of the date of 27 December in S.'s work, see Nora Crook and Derek Guiton, *Shelley's Venomed Melody* (1986) 53–5.

1. Guest

70   Oh, horrible! I will depart.

2. Guest

And I.

3. Guest

No, stay!
I do believe it is some jest; though faith,
'Tis mocking us somewhat too solemnly.
I think his son has married the Infanta,
Or found a mine of gold in El Dorado;

75   'Tis but to season some such news; stay, stay!
I see 'tis only raillery by his smile.

Cenci   *[Filling a bowl of wine, and lifting it up.*
Oh, thou bright wine, whose purple splendour leaps
And bubbles gaily in this golden bowl
Under the lamplight, as my spirits do,

80   To hear the death of my accursèd sons!
Could I believe thou wert their mingled blood,
Then would I taste thee like a sacrament,
And pledge with thee the mighty Devil in Hell;

---

70. An alexandrine.

73. Infanta,] i.e. the daughter of the king and queen of Spain or Portugal.

74. El Dorado;] The legendary city of Manoa (or Omoa) in Guiana to which several sixteenth-century explorers, including Raleigh, led expeditions in search of gold. See *Paradise Lost* xi 409–11: 'and yet unspoiled / Guiana, whose great city Geryon's sons / Call El Dorado', and Voltaire, *Candide, ou l'Optimisme* (1759) chs xvii and xviii.

77–90. [Filling a bowl of wine, and lifting it up. . . . *Bear the bowl around.*] A profanation of the Eucharist and Holy Communion. The bowl recalls the visionary cup of death which Christ calls on God to remove in *Luke* xxii 42 ('Father, if thou be willing, remove this cup from me: nevertheless not my will, but thine, be done'), and thus symbolically heralds the destruction of the Cenci family. On the association of the cup with death in S.'s work, cp. *R&H* lines 1118–30, 'Mazenghi' lines 19–26, *J&M* lines 435–8.

77–81. Oh, thou bright wine . . . mingled blood,] For the similarity between bubbling wine and human blood, cp. *PU* I 575.

77. bright wine,] Cp. *PU* I 810.   *purple splendour*] The wine is described in terms of the colour associated with Roman tyranny. See e.g. Horace, *Odes* I xxxv line 12: 'purpurei metuunt tyranni' ('tyrants clad in purple, fearing' (Loeb trans.)); Thomson, *Summer* 758: 'the purple Tyranny of Rome'; Gray, 'Ode to Adversity' (1753) 7: 'And purple tyrants vainly groan'.

78. golden bowl] Another sacrilegious reference. Cp. *Ecclesiastes* xii 6: 'Or ever the silver cord be loosed, or the golden bowl be broken.'

81. mingled blood,] Cp. Seneca, *Thyestes* 917: 'mixtum suorum sanguinem genitor bibat' ('His sons' mingled blood let the father drink' (Loeb trans.)).

Who, if a father's curses, as men say,
85   Climb with swift wings after their children's souls,
And drag them from the very throne of Heaven,
Now triumphs in my triumph! — But thou art
Superfluous; I have drunken deep of joy,
And I will taste no other wine tonight.
90   Here, Andrea! Bear the bowl around.

A Guest   *[Rising.*
                                 Thou wretch!
Will none among this noble company
Check the abandoned villain?

Camillo
                              For God's sake
Let me dismiss the guests! You are insane,
Some ill will come of this.

2. Guest
                            Seize, silence him!

1. Guest
95   I will!

3. Guest
        And I!

Cenci   *[Addressing those who rise with a threatening gesture.*
              Who moves? Who speaks?
                                [Turning to the company.
                               'Tis nothing,

85. their] his *Rossetti 1878.*

86. throne of Heaven,] Cp. M. G. Lewis, *The Love of Gain: A Poem* (1799) lines 336–7: 'Oh! think, when summoned to the throne of Heaven, / As thou forgav'st, so thou shalt be forgiven!'; Southey, *Madoc* (1805) Part II xvii: 'With a smile, / Sweet as good Angels wear when they present / Their mortal charge before the throne of Heaven, / She showed where little Hoel slept below'; Coleridge, *Zapolya: A Christmas Tale* In Two Parts (1817) Scene 1 (Prelude): 'Thou tyrant's den, be call'd no more a palace! / The orphan's angel at the throne of heaven / Stands up against thee'.

94. Some ill will come of this.] Cp. I iii 151 and note.

Enjoy yourselves. — Beware! For my revenge
Is as the sealed commission of a king,
That kills, and none dare name the murderer.
[*The banquet is broken up; several of the guests are departing.*

Beatrice
I do entreat you, go not, noble guests;
100 What, although tyranny and impious hate
Stand sheltered by a father's hoary hair?
What, if 'tis he who clothed us in these limbs
Who tortures them, and triumphs? What, if we,
The desolate and the dead, were his own flesh,
105 His children and his wife, whom he is bound
To love and shelter? Shall we therefore find
No refuge in this merciless wide world?
Oh, think what deep wrongs must have blotted out
First love, then reverence in a child's prone mind,
110 Till it thus vanquish shame and fear! O, think!

96. Beware! . . .] Cenci appears to address those who have risen as opposed to those who are still seated.

96–8. For my revenge . . . the murderer.] Cp. V iv 2–4.

100–3. What, although tyranny . . . triumphs?] Cp. Byron, 'Prometheus' in *The Prisoner of Chillon and Other Poems* (1816) lines 15–20: 'Titan! to thee the strife was given / Between the suffering and the will, / Which torture where they cannot kill; / And the inexorable Heaven, / And the deaf tyranny of Fate, / The ruling principle of Hate'.

102–6. What, . . . To love and shelter?] 'The phrase, "What if 'tis he" would naturally be followed by the phrase "What if we *are* his own flesh." Taking into account this point, and also the expression "he who *clothed* us in these limbs," I strongly suspect that the word "were" ought to be "wear"' (*Rossetti 1878*). The word 'flesh' signals kinship but also has sinister and unnatural overtones, as in III i 22, III i 48, no. 172, *The Cyclops* lines 121, 233, 336; Coleridge, 'The Rime of the Ancyent Marinere' (1798) lines 487–8: 'But soon I saw that my own flesh / Was red as in a glare'; and the pleas of Ugolino's children in *Inferno* xxxiii 61–3: '"Padre, assai ci fia men doglia, / Se tu mangi di noi: tu ne vestisti / Queste misere carni, e tu le spoglia."' ('"Father, we should grieve / "Far less, if thou wouldst eat of us: thou gav'st / "These weeds of miserable flesh we wear, / "And do thou strip them off from us again."' trans. Cary). Ralph Pite comments: 'Cenci has just rejoiced in the death of his sons and assumes that he has every right to demand what Ugolino's children offer their father. From here, Ugolino's example begins to inform Cenci's behaviour . . .' (*The Circle of our Vision: Dante's Presence in English Romantic Poetry* (1994) 164n).

105–6. whom he is bound / To love and shelter?] Cp. S.'s description of fatherhood as 'the most sacred of human duties, and the most inestimable of human rights' in 'Declaration in Chancery' (*Prose Works* i 166).

109. prone] i.e. 'ready in mind (for some action expressed or implied); eager.' (cited in OED, 'prone' *a.* 7). An apparently archaic usage in S.'s day. Cp. *Cymbeline* V iv 197: 'Unless a man would marry a gallows and beget young gibbets, I never saw one so prone', and *Measure for Measure* I ii 175–7: 'for in her youth / There is a prone and speechless dialect / Such as move men'.

110. Till . . . fear!] I.e. 'until shame and fear thus vanquish [i.e. overcome] it' (where 'it' refers to 'love' in line 109.)

I have borne much, and kissed the sacred hand
Which crushed us to the earth, and thought its stroke
Was perhaps some paternal chastisement!
Have excused much, doubted; and when no doubt
115 Remained, have sought by patience, love and tears,
To soften him; and when this could not be,
I have knelt down through the long sleepless nights,
And lifted up to God, the father of all,
Passionate prayers: and when these were not heard
120 I have still borne; — until I meet you here,
Princes and kinsmen, at this hideous feast
Given at my brothers' deaths. Two yet remain,
His wife remains and I, whom if ye save not,
Ye may soon share such merriment again
125 As fathers make over their children's graves.
Oh! Prince Colonna, thou art our near kinsman;
Cardinal, thou art the Pope's chamberlain;
Camillo, thou art chief justiciary;
Take us away!

Cenci   [*He has been conversing with* Camillo *during the first part of*
               Beatrice's *speech; he hears the conclusion, and now advances.*
               I hope my good friends here
130 Will think of their own daughters — or perhaps
Of their own throats — before they lend an ear
To this wild girl.

111–12. kissed . . . to the earth,] Cp. S.'s account of Tasso in his letter to Peacock of
6 November 1818: 'Some of those Mss of Tasso were sonnets to his persecutor which con-
tain a great deal of what is called flattery. If Alfonso's ghost were asked how he felt these
praises now I wonder what he would say. But to me there is much more to pity than to
condemn in these entreaties and praises of Tasso. It is as a Christian prays to [and] praises
his God whom he knows to [be] the most remorseless capricious & inflexible of tyrants, but
whom he knows also to be omnipotent.' (*L* ii 47).

118–19. And lifted . . . prayers:] Cp. I iii 23–4.

126. Prince Colonna,] The Colonna are 'one of the most ancient and most distinguished
families in Rome, ennobled by its heroic achievements' (*Eustace* ii 34). Stefano Colonna
(?1257–?1350) is celebrated by Petrarch, see *Rime di Francesco Petrarca* (Parma, 1799), Parte
Prima, Sonetto x: 'Gloríosa Colonna, a cui s'appoggia / Nostra speranza, e'l gran nome
Latino, / Ch'ancor non torse dal vero cammino / L'ira di Giove per ventosa pioggia'
('Glorious Colonna! still the strength and stay / Of our best hopes, and the great Latin name /
Whom power could never from the true right way / Seduce by flattery or by terror tame'
(trans. R. G. MacGregor (1854) in *The Sonnets of Petrarch*, ed. Thomas G. Bergin (Verona, 1965))).
See also Muratori, Dissertazione xlii in *Dissertazioni sopra le Antichità Italiane*, 3 vols (Milan,
1751) ii 577–8; and Gibbon, *Decline and Fall* vii 250–54.

Beatrice   [*Not noticing the words of* Cenci.
Dare no one look on me?
None answer? Can one tyrant overbear
The sense of many best and wisest men?
135 Or is it that I sue not in some form
Of scrupulous law, that ye deny my suit?
Oh, God! That I were buried with my brothers!
And that the flowers of this departed spring
Were fading on my grave! And that my father
140 Were celebrating now one feast for all!

Camillo
A bitter wish for one so young and gentle;
Can we do nothing?

Colonna
Nothing that I see.
Count Cenci were a dangerous enemy:
Yet I would second any one.

A Cardinal
And I.

Cenci
145 Retire to your chamber, insolent girl!

Beatrice
Retire thou, impious man! Aye, hide thyself
Where never eye can look upon thee more!
Wouldst thou have honour and obedience,
Who art a torturer? Father, never dream,
150 Though thou mayst overbear this company,
But ill must come of ill. — Frown not on me!
Haste, hide thyself, lest with avenging looks

132. *Dare no one*] *Errata, Taaffe*; Dare not one *Cenci (1819).*
137. Another identification of Beatrice with the heroine of Sophocles' *Antigone* 71–3: κεῖνον
δ' ἐγὼ / θάψω. καλόν μοι τοῦτο ποιούσῃ θανεῖν. / φίλη μετ' αὐτοῦ κείσομαι, φίλου μέτα ('but
I shall bury him! It is honourable for me to do this and die. I am his own and I shall lie
with him who is my own' (Loeb trans. rev. edn 1994)).
151. *But ill must come of ill.* –] Cp. Aeschylus, *Agamemnon* 758–60: τὸ δυσσεβὲς γὰρ ἔργον /
μετὰ μὲν πλείονα τίκτει, / σφετέρᾳ δ' εἰκότα γέννᾳ. ('It is the deed of iniquity that thereafter
begetteth more iniquity and like unto its own breed' (Loeb trans.)); and *Macbeth* V i 68–9:
'Unnatural deeds / Do breed unnatural troubles'. Cp. also IV iv 134. Similar kinds of state-
ment pervade S.'s works; see e.g. no. 183, 'Lines Written among the Euganean Hills' lines
231–5 and note to line 232, and *L* ii 324–5 (in which the lines from *Agamemnon* above are
cited).

My brothers' ghosts should hunt thee from thy seat!
Cover thy face from every living eye,
155 And start if thou but hear a human step:
Seek out some dark and silent corner, there
Bow thy white head before offended God,
And we will kneel around, and fervently
Pray that he pity both ourselves and thee.

Cenci
160 My friends, I do lament this insane girl
Has spoilt the mirth of our festivity.
Good night, farewell; I will not make you longer
Spectators of our dull domestic quarrels.
Another time. —

> [*Exeunt all but* Cenci *and* Beatrice.

My brain is swimming round;
165 Give me a bowl of wine!

> [*To* Beatrice.

Thou painted viper!
Beast that thou art! Fair and yet terrible!
I know a charm shall make thee meek and tame,
Now get thee from my sight!

> [*Exit* Beatrice.

Here, Andrea,
Fill up this goblet with Greek wine. I said
170 I would not drink this evening, but I must;
For, strange to say, I feel my spirits fail
With thinking what I have decreed to do.

> [*Drinking the wine.*

Be thou the resolution of quick youth
Within my veins, and manhood's purpose stern,

165–72. Give me . . . decreed to do.] Cp. *Richard III* V iii 72–4: 'Give me a bowl of wine. / I have not that alacrity of spirit / Nor cheer of mind that I was wont to have'.

168. Now get thee from my sight!] Cp. *Cymbeline* V v 236: 'O, get thee from my sight', *Titus Andronicus* III i 284: 'As for thee, boy, go, get thee from my sight', and, esp., Lear to Cordelia (*Lear* I i 123): 'Hence, and avoid my sight! –'

169. Greek wine.] Though *Mary Jnl* ii 634 records S. as reading Athenaeus, *Deipnosophistai* in February 1820, he may already have been aware of the catalogue of Greek wines to which it refers along with extensive citations from ancient authorities (I 27d. ff.)

170. evening,] *1829*; evening; *Cenci (1819), Cenci (1821).*

171–8. For, . . . I swear!] Cp. Byron, *Manfred, A Dramatic Poem* (1817) II ii 199–205: 'Within few hours I shall not call in vain – / Yet in this hour I dread the thing I dare: / Until this hour I never shrunk to gaze / On spirit, good or evil – now I tremble, / And feel a strange cold thaw upon my heart, / But I can act even what I most abhor, / And champion human fears. –'

173–5. See I i 49–54 and note.

758

175   And age's firm, cold, subtle villainy;
      As if thou wert indeed my children's blood
      Which I did thirst to drink. The charm works well;
      It must be done; it shall be done, I swear!

[Exit.

End of the First Act

---

175. See Fred L. Milne, 'Shelley's *The Cenci*: The Ice Motif and the Ninth Circle of Dante's Hell', *Tennessee Studies in Literature* xxii (1976) 117–32. With reference to *Inferno* xxxii–xxxiv, Milne argues, 'Cold and hard become the defining attributes of the evil force which is dramatically centered in Cenci but which spreads until everything is tinged by its iciness' (117).

176–7. *As if thou wert indeed my children's blood / Which I did thirst to drink.*] Cp. I iii 81–2 and note. The suggestion of vampirism here and elsewhere in the play is explored in James B. Twitchell, 'Shelley's Use of Vampirism in *The Cenci*', *Tennessee Studies in Literature* xxiv (1979) 120–33.

177–8. *The charm works . . . it shall be done,*] Cp. *Macbeth* I iii 37: 'The charm's wound up'; and II i 62: 'I go, and it is done'.

ACT II

Scene i

An Apartment in the Cenci Palace. Enter Lucretia *and* Bernardo.

Lucretia
Weep not, my gentle boy; he struck but me,
Who have borne deeper wrongs. In truth, if he
Had killed me, he had done a kinder deed.
O, God Almighty, do thou look upon us,
5   We have no other friend but only thee!
Yet weep not; though I love you as my own,
I am not your true mother.

Bernardo
                    Oh more, more,
Than ever mother was to any child,
That have you been to me! Had he not been
10 My father, do you think that I should weep?

Lucretia
Alas! Poor boy, what else couldst thou have done?

                    Enter Beatrice.

Beatrice   [*In a hurried voice.*
Did he pass this way? Have you seen him, brother?
Ah! no, that is his step upon the stairs;
'Tis nearer now; his hand is on the door;
15 Mother, if I to thee have ever been
A duteous child, now save me! Thou, great God,
Whose image upon earth a father is,
Dost thou indeed abandon me? He comes;
The door is opening now; I see his face;
20 He frowns on others, but he smiles on me,
Even as he did after the feast last night.

                    Enter a Servant.

II i. The time is the morning after I iii (see II i 21, II i 106, II i 152).

13. Ah! no,] *Taaffe*; Ah! No, *Cenci (1819), Cenci (1821).*

18ff. He comes; . . .] On S.'s use here of the dramatic device of false suspense, see St. John
Ervine, 'Shelley as a Dramatist' in *Essays by Diverse Hands, Transactions of the Royal Society of
Literature of the United Kingdom* n.s. xv (1936) 77–106 (96–7).

Almighty God, how merciful thou art!
'Tis but Orsino's servant. — Well, what news?

Servant
My master bids me say, the Holy Father
25 Has sent back your petition thus unopened.

[*Giving a paper.*

And he demands at what hour 'twere secure
To visit you again?

Lucretia
                    At the Ave Mary.

[*Exit Servant.*

So, daughter, our last hope has failed; Ah me,
How pale you look; you tremble, and you stand
30 Wrapped in some fixed and fearful meditation,
As if one thought were over-strong for you:
Your eyes have a chill glare; O, dearest child!
Are you gone mad? If not, pray speak to me.

Beatrice
You see I am not mad; I speak to you.

Lucretia
35 You talked of something that your father did
After that dreadful feast? Could it be worse
Than when he smiled, and cried, 'My sons are dead!'
And every one looked in his neighbour's face
To see if others were as white as he?
40 At the first word he spoke I felt the blood
Rush to my heart, and fell into a trance;
And when it passed I sat all weak and wild;
Whilst you alone stood up, and with strong words

27. *At the Ave Mary.*] i.e. at the hour when a bell is rung for the recitation of the angelic salutation to the Virgin, the Ave Maria (or *Hail Mary!*).

34. *You see I am not mad;*] Cp. *King John* III iv 45: 'I am not mad.'

37. *and cried, 'My sons are dead!'*] *Woodberry 1893*; and cried, My sons are dead! *Cenci (1819)*, *Cenci (1821)*.

38. The conception is Shakespearean. Cp. e.g. *Macbeth* I iv 11–12: 'There's no art / To find the mind's construction in the face'; *Macbeth* I v 59–60: 'Your face, my thane, is as a book where men / May read strange matters'; *Othello* IV ii 25: 'Let me see your eyes; Look in my face'.

43–4. *Whilst you alone . . . his unnatural pride;*] Cp. *Lear* II i 49–50: 'Seeing how loathly opposite I stood / To his unnatural purpose.'

Checked his unnatural pride; and I could see
45   The devil was rebuked that lives in him.
Until this hour thus you have ever stood
Between us and your father's moody wrath
Like a protecting presence: your firm mind
Has been our only refuge and defence:
50   What can have thus subdued it? What can now
Have given you that cold melancholy look,
Succeeding to your unaccustomed fear?

Beatrice
What is it that you say? I was just thinking
'Twere better not to struggle any more.
55   Men, like my father, have been dark and bloody,
Yet never — O! before worse comes of it
'Twere wise to die: it ends in that at last.

Lucretia
Oh, talk not so, dear child! Tell me at once
What did your father do or say to you?
60   He stayed not after that accursèd feast
One moment in your chamber. — Speak to me.

Bernardo
Oh, sister, sister, prithee, speak to us!

Beatrice   *[Speaking very slowly with a forced calmness.*
It was one word, mother, one little word;
One look, one smile.   *[Wildly.*
          Oh! He has trampled me
65   Under his feet, and made the blood stream down
My pallid cheeks. And he has given us all
Ditch-water, and the fever-stricken flesh
Of buffaloes, and bade us eat or starve,
And we have eaten. He has made me look
70   On my beloved Bernardo, when the rust
Of heavy chains has gangrened his sweet limbs,

46–50. Until this hour . . . subdued it?] Rognoni 1568 cps. *PU* I 306–11.

48. a protecting presence:] An e.g. of Beatrice's christological significance (as noted in Bryan Shelley, *Shelley and Scripture* (1994) 83). Cp. *1 Tim* ii 5: 'For there is one God, and one mediator between God and men, the man Christ Jesus.'

63. mother,] Mother, *Cenci* (1819).

69. eaten.] eaten. – *Cenci* (1819).

71. gangrened] i.e. 'mortified' (cited in *OED* 'gangrene' *v.* 2).

And I have never yet despaired — but now!
What would I say?

[*Recovering herself.*]

Ah! no, 'tis nothing new.
The sufferings we all share have made me wild:
75   He only struck and cursed me as he passed;
He said, he looked, he did, — nothing at all
Beyond his wont, yet it disordered me.
Alas! I am forgetful of my duty,
I should preserve my senses for your sake.

Lucretia
80   Nay, Beatrice; have courage, my sweet girl.
If any one despairs it should be I,
Who loved him once, and now must live with him
Till God in pity call for him or me.
For you may, like your sister, find some husband,
85   And smile, years hence, with children round your knees;
Whilst I, then dead, and all this hideous coil,
Shall be remembered only as a dream.

Beatrice
Talk not to me, dear lady, of a husband.
Did you not nurse me when my mother died?
90   Did you not shield me and that dearest boy?
And had we any other friend but you
In infancy, with gentle words and looks,
To win our father not to murder us?
And shall I now desert you? May the ghost
95   Of my dead mother plead against my soul
If I abandon her who filled the place
She left, with more, even, than a mother's love!

Bernardo
And I am of my sister's mind. Indeed
I would not leave you in this wretchedness,

---

73. *Ah! no,*] *Taaffe*; Ah! No, *Cenci (1819), Cenci (1821)*.

76. *He said, he looked, he did* –] *1839*; He said, he look'd, he did, – *1829*; He said, he looked, he did; – *Cenci (1819), Cenci (1821)*.

77. *disordered*] i.e. 'disturbed'. An apparently archaic usage in S.'s day (cited in *OED* 'disorder' *v.* 3).

86–7. The nuances of these lines have a specific source in *Hamlet* III i 66–8: 'For in that sleep of death what dreams may come, / When we have shuffled off this mortal coil, / Must give us pause.'

763

100   Even though the Pope should make me free to live
        In some blithe place, like others of my age,
        With sports, and delicate food, and the fresh air.
        Oh, never think that I will leave you, mother!

Lucretia
My dear, dear children!

                    Enter Cenci, suddenly.

Cenci
              What, Beatrice here!
105   Come hither!   *[She shrinks back, and covers her face.*
        Nay, hide not your face, 'tis fair;
        Look up! Why, yesternight you dared to look
        With disobedient insolence upon me,
        Bending a stern and an inquiring brow
        On what I meant; whilst I then sought to hide
110   That which I came to tell you — but in vain.

Beatrice   *[Wildly, staggering towards the door.*
Oh, that the earth would gape! Hide me, oh God!

Cenci
Then it was I whose inarticulate words
Fell from my lips, and who with tottering steps

100–2. An e.g. of the proleptic irony which pervades this scene (see also II i 130–48). The Pope's pardon makes Bernardo 'free to live' rather than die with Lucretia in Act V (see *Relation* 45 (*BSM* x 218–19)).

103. mother!] Mother! *Cenci (1819)*.

105. Nay,] *Taaffe*; Nay *Cenci (1819)*.

111. Cp. Aeschylus, *Persae* 915–17: εἴθ᾽ ὄφελεν, Ζεῦ, κἀμὲ μετ᾽ ἀνδρῶν / τῶν οἰχομένων / θανάτου κατὰ μοῖρα καλύψαι. ('Ah, Zeus, would that the doom of death had buried me, too, together with the men who are laid low!' (Loeb trans.)); *Aeneid*. x 675–6: 'aut quae iam satis ima dehiscat / terra mihi?' ('What earth could now gape deep enough for me?' (Loeb trans.)); *Aeneid* xii 883–4: 'o quae satis ima dehiscat / terra mihi' ('O what deepest earth can gape enough for me . . .' (Loeb trans.)); Seneca, *Thyestes* 1006–9: 'sustines tantum nefas / gestare, Tellus? non ad infernam Styga / tenebrasque mergis rupta et ingenti via / ad chaos inane regna cum rege abripis?' ('Canst thou endure, O Earth, to bear a crime so monstrous? Why dost not burst asunder and plunge thee down to the infernal Stygian shades and, by a huge opening to void chaos, snatch this kingdom with its king away?' (Loeb trans.)); Ugolino in *Inferno* xxxiii 66: 'Ahi dura terra, perché non t'apristi?' ('Ah, obdurate earth! Why open'dst not upon us?' (trans. Cary)); Marlowe, *Doctor Faustus* (1604) V ii 88: 'Earth, gape!'; Imogine in Maturin, *Bertram; Or, The Castle of St. Aldobrand* (1816) IV ii: 'Oh, that I could into the earthy centre / Sink and be nothing.'

113. and who with tottering steps] who with tottering steps *1829, 1839, 1840*. Strictly, a hypermetrical line but see Swinburne's comment, 'Note on the Text of Shelley', *Essays and Studies* (1875) 202: 'The later copies drop the word *and*, thus breaking down the metre.'

Fled from your presence, as you now from mine.
115   Stay, I command you: — from this day and hour
Never again, I think, with fearless eye,
And brow superior, and unaltered cheek,
And that lip made for tenderness or scorn,
Shalt thou strike dumb the meanest of mankind;
120   Me least of all. Now get thee to thy chamber!
Thou too, loathed image of thy cursèd mother,

[*To* Bernardo.

Thy milky, meek face makes me sick with hate!

[*Exeunt* Beatrice *and* Bernardo.
[*Aside.*

So much has passed between us as must make
Me bold, her fearful. — 'Tis an awful thing
125   To touch such mischief as I now conceive:
So men sit shivering on the dewy bank,
And try the chill stream with their feet; once in —
How the delighted spirit pants for joy!

Lucretia   [*Advancing timidly towards him.*
Oh, husband! Pray forgive poor Beatrice,
130   She meant not any ill.

Cenci
                    Nor you perhaps?
Nor that young imp, whom you have taught by rote
Parricide with his alphabet? Nor Giacomo?
Nor those two most unnatural sons, who stirred

---

115. *you:* -] *Locock 1911*; you – *Cenci (1819)*; you: *Cenci (1821)*.

117. *superior*] i.e. 'unmoved' (cited in *OED*, 'superior' *a.* and *sb.* 7). Also implied is the sense 'too great to be overcome' (*OED* 6b), the gloss supplied by Christopher Ricks in his edn of *Paradise Lost* (1968) to the instance of the word in the description of Abdiel (*Paradise Lost* v 903–5): 'From amidst them forth he passed, / Long way through hostile scorn, which he sustained / Superior, nor of violence feared aught'.

118. Cp. 'Ozymandias' line 5.

122. *sick with hate!*] Cp. *A Midsummer Night's Dream* II ii 211–12: 'Tempt not too much the hatred of my spirit; / For I am sick when I do look on thee.'

123–4. *as must make / Me bold, her fearful*-] Cp. *Macbeth* II i 1: 'That which hath made them drunk hath made me bold'.

124. *fearful.* -] *Cenci (1819)*; fearful. *Cenci (1821)*.

128. *pants*] The word has unmistakably sexual overtones. Cp. II ii 140 and *Othello* II i 80: 'Make love's quick pants in Desdemona's arms'.

133–4. See *Relation* 5: 'the hatred & contempt of their father towards them was so aggravated that he refused to dress or maintain them so that they were obliged to have recourse to the Pope who caused Cenci to make them a fit allowance with which they withdrew from his house' (*BSM* x 176–7).

Enmity up against me with the Pope?
135 Whom in one night merciful God cut off:
Innocent lambs! They thought not any ill.
You were not here conspiring? You said nothing
Of how I might be dungeoned as a madman;
Or be condemned to death for some offence,
140 And you would be the witnesses? — This failing,
How just it were to hire assassins, or
Put sudden poison in my evening drink?
Or smother me when overcome by wine?
Seeing we had no other judge but God,
145 And he had sentenced me, and there were none
But you to be the executioners
Of his decree enregistered in heaven?
Oh, no! You said not this?

Lucretia
So help me God,
I never thought the things you charge me with!

Cenci
150 If you dare speak that wicked lie again
I'll kill you. What! It was not by your counsel
That Beatrice disturbed the feast last night?
You did not hope to stir some enemies
Against me, and escape, and laugh to scorn
155 What every nerve of you now trembles at?
You judged that men were bolder than they are;
Few dare to stand between their grave and me.

Lucretia
Look not so dreadfully! By my salvation,
I knew not aught that Beatrice designed;
160 Nor do I think she designed any thing
Until she heard you talk of her dead brothers.

136. *Innocent lambs!*] The children murdered by Herod were often described as such. See note to I iii 68 and Fred L. Milne, 'Shelley's *The Cenci*, I iii 55–69', *The Explicator* xxxv (1976) 31 which suggests that S. would have seen such a symbolic depiction in the Basilica of Santa Maria Maggiore in Rome (which he visited in November 1818 according to *Mary Jnl* i 238).

142. sudden] i.e. 'Prompt in its effect' (cited in *OED*, 'sudden' *a.* 6). Cp. *Romeo and Juliet* III iii 44–6: 'Hadst thou no poison mix'd, no sharp-ground knife, / No sudden mean of death, though ne'er so mean, / But "banished" to kill me?'

150. dare speak] dare to speak *Woodberry 1893*.

156. are;] *Cenci (1819)*; are: *Cenci (1821)*.

Cenci
Blaspheming liar! You are damned for this!
But I will take you where you may persuade
The stones you tread on to deliver you:
165 For men shall there be none but those who dare
All things; not question that which I command.
On Wednesday next I shall set out: you know
That savage rock, the Castle of Petrella:
'Tis safely walled, and moated round about:
170 Its dungeons underground, and its thick towers
Never told tales; though they have heard and seen
What might make dumb things speak. Why do you linger?
Make speediest preparation for the journey!

[*Exit* Lucretia.

The all-beholding sun yet shines; I hear
175 A busy stir of men about the streets;
I see the bright sky through the window-panes:
It is a garish, broad, and peering day;
Loud, light, suspicious, full of eyes and ears;
And every little corner, nook, and hole,

---

168. See note to *Dramatis Personae*. S.'s poetical description here and at III i 239 appears to be rooted in a misunderstanding of his Italian source (as is noted in *Rossetti 1878*). Since the word 'rocca' means 'fortress, or stronghold', not 'rock', 'Rocca di Petrella' is fully translated as 'the Castle of Petrella'. The error can also be found in *Relation* 17 where Olimpio is described as formerly 'Castelan of the Rock of Petrella' (*BSM* x 188–9).

170. towers] *Cenci (1819)*; towers, *Cenci (1821)*.

171–2. though they have heard and seen / What might make dumb things speak.] The collocation is Shakespearean. Cp. *Hamlet* I i 171: 'This spirit, dumb to us, will speak to him'.

174–93. Cp. Osmond in M. G. Lewis, *The Castle Spectre* (1798) III ii: 'Oh! fly from my eyes, bright Day! Speed thy pace, Darkness! thou art my Love! Haste to unfold thy sable mantle, and robe the world in the colour of my soul!'

174. The all-beholding sun] Cp. Sophocles, *Oedipus at Colonus* 869–70: ὁ πάντα λεύσσων Ἥλιος δοίη βίον / τοιοῦτον οἷον κἀμὲ γηρᾶναί ποτε. ('Therefore may the all-seeing Sun grant that your old age is like mine!' (Loeb trans. rev. edn 1994)); *Romeo and Juliet* I ii 92–3: 'The all-seeing sun / Ne'er saw her match since first the world begun'. Cp. also IV i 134.

174–5. I hear . . . streets;] Cp. *L'Allegro* lines 117–18: 'Towered cities please us then, / And the busy hum of men'; Gray, 'Sonnet on the Death of Mr Richard West' lines 9–10: 'Yet morning smiles the busy race to cheer, / And new-born pleasure brings to happier men'.

176–81. This passage is marked with a line in the margin of Taaffe's copy of *Cenci (1819)* (see headnote).

177. Cp. *Romeo and Juliet* III ii 24–5: 'That all the world will be in love with night, / And pay no worship to the garish sun'; *Il Penseroso* line 141: 'Hide me from day's garish eye'. *broad,*] *Cenci (1819)*; broad *Cenci (1821)*.

178. Cp. IV i 5.

180   Is penetrated with the insolent light.
        Come, darkness! Yet, what is the day to me?
        And wherefore should I wish for night, who do
        A deed which shall confound both night and day?
        'Tis she shall grope through a bewildering mist
185   Of horror: if there be a sun in heaven
        She shall not dare to look upon its beams,
        Nor feel its warmth. Let her then wish for night;
        The act I think shall soon extinguish all
        For me: I bear a darker deadlier gloom
190   Than the earth's shade, or interlunar air,
        Or constellations quenched in murkiest cloud,
        In which I walk secure and unbeheld
        Towards my purpose. — Would that it were done!

                                                 [Exit.

181–3. Cp. *John* iii 19: 'And this is the condemnation, that light is come into the world, and men loved darkness rather than light, because their deeds were evil.'

181. Come, darkness!] Cp. *Macbeth* I v 47–51: 'Come, thick night, / And pall thee in the dunnest smoke of hell, / That my keen knife see not the wound it makes, / Nor heaven peep through the blanket of the dark / To cry, "Hold, hold".'

183. For the consequence of evil being to confound the distinction between night and day, cp.: *Macbeth* II ii 8–10: 'Is't night's predominance, or the day's shame, / That darkness does the face of earth entomb, / When living light should kiss it?'; *Macbeth* III iv 126–7: 'What is the night? / Almost at odds with morning, which is which'.

184–93. Cp. *Aeneid* ii 355–62: 'inde, lupi ceu / raptores atra in nebula, quos improba ventris / exegit caecos rabies catulique relicti / faucibus exspectant siccis, per tela, per hostis / vadimus haud dubiam in mortem mediaeque tenemus / urbis iter; nox atra cava circumvolat umbra. / quis cladem illius noctis, quis funera fando / explicet aut possit lacrimis aequare labores?' ('Then, like ravening wolves in a black mist, when the belly's lawless rage has driven them blindly forth, and their whelps at home await them with thirsty jaws; through swords, through foes we pass to certain death, and hold our way to the city's heart; black night hovers around with sheltering shade. Who could unfold in speech that night's havoc? Who its carnage? Or who could match our toils with tears?' (Loeb trans.))

184. a bewildering mist] A commonplace image of evil. Cp. Marlowe, II *Tamburlaine* II iv 14: 'All dasled with the hellish mists of death.'; Webster, *The White Devil* V vi 256: 'O I am in a mist.'

190. the earth's shade,] A precise, scientific usage referring to the cone or pyramid of shadow cast by the earth, pointing away from the sun out into space (cp. *PU* IV 444 and note). *Rognoni* 1463, in a note to no. 182, 'The Two Spirits. An Allegory' line 10, cites comparable instances in S.'s works of such descriptions of night. *interlunar*] Cp. *PU* II iv 91 and note. Cp. also *PU* III iv 94, and *PU* IV 209.

191–3. constellations . . . purpose.] Cenci's wish to embody total darkness is unnatural. On the moral significance of stellar illumination see *Paradise Lost* iv 634–88 and vii 340–52, esp. iv 674–5: 'These then, though unbeheld in deep of night, / Shine not in vain'.

193. Would that it were done!] Cp. I iii 178 and note to I iii 177–8.

Scene ii

A Chamber in the Vatican. Enter Camillo *and* Giacomo, *in conversation.*

Camillo
There is an obsolete and doubtful law
By which you might obtain a bare provision
Of food and clothing —

Giacomo
      Nothing more? Alas!
Bare must be the provision which strict law
5 Awards, and agèd, sullen avarice pays.
Why did my father not apprentice me
To some mechanic trade? I should have then
Been trained in no high-born necessities
Which I could meet not by my daily toil.
10 The eldest son of a rich nobleman
Is heir to all his incapacities;
He has wide wants, and narrow powers. If you,
Cardinal Camillo, were reduced at once
From thrice-driven beds of down, and delicate food,
15 An hundred servants, and six palaces,
To that which nature doth indeed require? —

Camillo
Nay, there is reason in your plea; 'twere hard.

Giacomo
'Tis hard for a firm man to bear: but I
Have a dear wife, a lady of high birth,
20 Whose dowry in ill hour I lent my father,
Without a bond or witness to the deed:
And children, who inherit her fine senses,
The fairest creatures in this breathing world;
And she and they reproach me not. Cardinal,
25 Do you not think the Pope would interpose,
And stretch authority beyond the law?

14. thrice-driven beds of down,] Cp. *Othello* I iii 231: 'My thrice-driven bed of down.'

24. 'I strongly suspect that "not" should be omitted, for the sake of the metre and a more obvious sense. That Giacomo's family did in fact reproach him is clear from III i 326 etc.' (*Locock 1911*).

25–6. Cp. *Merchant of Venice* IV i 209–12: 'Wrest once the law to your authority; / To do a great right do a little wrong, / And curb this cruel devil of his will.'

26. stretch] A pun. Cp. V ii 74.

Camillo
Though your peculiar case is hard, I know
The Pope will not divert the course of law.
After that impious feast the other night
30   I spoke with him, and urged him then to check
Your father's cruel hand; he frowned and said,
'Children are disobedient, and they sting
Their fathers' hearts to madness and despair,
Requiting years of care with contumely.
35   I pity the Count Cenci from my heart;
His outraged love perhaps awakened hate,
And thus he is exasperated to ill.
In the great war between the old and young,
I, who have white hairs and a tottering body,
40   Will keep at least blameless neutrality.'

Enter Orsino.

You, my good Lord Orsino, heard those words.

Orsino
What words?

Giacomo
          Alas, repeat them not again!
There then is no redress for me; at least
None but that which I may achieve myself,
45   Since I am driven to the brink. But, say,
My innocent sister and my only brother
Are dying underneath my father's eye.
The memorable torturers of this land,
Galeaz Visconti, Borgia, Ezzelin,

---

29. the other night] An instance of S.'s seemingly casual attitude to the time-scheme in *C*. II ii would seem to be set on the same day as II i which (see note to II i 1) takes place the morning after the feast.

33. fathers'] *1839*; father's *Cenci (1819)*, *Cenci (1821)*.

48. torturers] *Cenci (1819)*; tortures *Cenci (1821)* (a printing error).

49. Gian Galeazzo Visconti (1351–1402), leader of the famous Milanese family from 1378, succeeded in bringing much of Italy under his control (see J. C. L. Simonde de Sismondi, *Histoire des Républiques Italiennes du Moyen Âge*, Seconde Édition Parisienne, 16 vols (Paris, 1818) vii 254–432 *passim*). On the exploits of Cesare Borgia (1476–1507), son of Pope Alexander VI, Duke of Valentinois and Romagna, see Sismondi, *Histoire des Républiques Italiennes* xiii 82–380. For the exceptional cruelties of the tyrant Eccelino (or Ezzelino) da Romano (1194–1259), a leader of the Ghibellines, see Sismondi, *Histoire des Républiques Italiennes* iii 7–213 *passim*, and Villani, *Croniche* (1537) Book VI ch. lxxiv. Eccelino is recognised in *Inferno* xii 110 and is referred to in *Paradiso* ix 30–1. See also 'Lines Written among the Euganean Hills' line 239 and note.

50   Never inflicted on their meanest slave
      What these endure; shall they have no protection?

Camillo
Why, if they would petition to the Pope
I see not how he could refuse it — yet
He holds it of most dangerous example
55   In aught to weaken the paternal power,
      Being, as 'twere, the shadow of his own.
I pray you now excuse me. I have business
That will not bear delay.

                                     [*Exit* Camillo.

Giacomo
                       But you, Orsino,
Have the petition: wherefore not present it?

Orsino
60   I have presented it, and backed it with
      My earnest prayers, and urgent interest;
It was returned unanswered. I doubt not
But that the strange and execrable deeds
Alleged in it (in truth they might well baffle
65   Any belief) have turned the Pope's displeasure
      Upon the accusers from the criminal:
So I should guess from what Camillo said.

Giacomo
My friend, that palace-walking devil, Gold,
Has whispered silence to his Holiness:
70   And we are left, as scorpions ringed with fire,

50. *their*] the *Forman 1876–7.* *slave*] As is evident from the emendation to *Cenci (1819)* at
I ii 75, S. was apparently aware that such a usage is not strictly appropriate to sixteenth-
century Italy.

64–5. *it (in . . . belief) have*] it – in . . . belief – have *Cenci (1819).*

68–71. See William Keach's comment in *Shelley's Style* (1984) 106: 'Cencian self-anatomy,
like Promethean self-knowledge, is often represented in circular figures. Internally *The Cenci*
offers no escape from the circle of negative reflexiveness; corrupt self-consciousness can only
finally reconfigure itself as self-destruction.'

70. *fire,*] fire. *1829.*

70–1. *as scorpions . . . to death?*] Cp. *Declaration of Rights* (1812) (*Prose Works* i 57); *Q Mab* vi
36–8; *L&C* Canto XI stanza viii. See also Byron, *The Giaour, A Fragment Of A Turkish Tale*,
7th edn (1813) lines 422–38: 'The Mind, that broods o'er guilty woes, / Is like the Scorpion
girt by fire, / In circle narrowing as it glows / The flames around their captive close, / Till
inly search'd by thousand throes, / And maddening in her ire, / One sad and sole relief she

What should we do but strike ourselves to death?
For he who is our murderous persecutor
Is shielded by a father's holy name,
Or I would —   [*Stops abruptly.*

Orsino
                    What? Fear not to speak your thought.
75 Words are but holy as the deeds they cover:
A priest who has forsworn the God he serves;
A judge who makes truth weep at his decree;
A friend who should weave counsel, as I now,
But as the mantle of some selfish guile;
80 A father who is all a tyrant seems,
Were the profaner for his sacred name.

Giacomo
Ask me not what I think; the unwilling brain
Feigns often what it would not; and we trust
Imagination with such fantasies
85 As the tongue dares not fashion into words;
Which have no words, their horror makes them dim
To the mind's eye. My heart denies itself
To think what you demand.

Orsino
                    But a friend's bosom
Is as the inmost cave of our own mind,

knows, / The sting she nourish'd for her foes, / Whose venom never yet was vain, / Gives but one pang, and cures all pain, / And darts into her desperate brain. – So do the dark in soul expire, / Or live like Scorpion girt by fire; / So writhes the mind Remorse hath riven, / Unfit for earth, undoom'd for heaven, / Darkness above, despair beneath, / Around it flame, within it death! –' and note to line 434. Giacomo's use of the scorpion image anticipates the precise terms of his later affliction with remorse (see e.g. V i 2–4). For another kind of figuring of its poisonous self-destructiveness, see the epigraph to Coleridge, *Remorse* (1813) (from I i): 'REMORSE is as the heart, in which it grows: / If that be gentle it drops balmy dews / Of true repentance, but if proud and gloomy, / It is a poison-tree, that pierced to the inmost / Weeps only tears of poison!'

77. makes truth weep] makes the truth weep *Cenci (1819)*; makes Truth weep *Rossetti 1870*.

80–1. A father . . . his sacred name.] Cp. note to I iii 105–6.

88–91. But a friend's . . . all-communicating air.] Orsino's language may be understood both to invite Giacomo to use him as a mirror in which to see his thoughts reflected (cp. V i 19–21) and to expose the illusion of this seductive possibility. On the limitations of introspection and for a parallel to line 89, see the prose fragment in *Box 1* ff. 184ʳ–184ᵛ (*BSM* xxii 192–5), dated to Spring 1817 by E. B. Murray (*BSM* xxii 488) and titled 'On a Science of Mind' in *Webb* 83–4: 'If it were possible that a person should give a faithful history of his being from the earliest epochs of his recollection, a picture would be presented such as the world has never contemplated before. [It is that which is best *canc.*] A mirror would be held up to all

90   Where we sit shut from the wide gaze of day,
And from the all-communicating air.
You look what I suspected —

Giacomo

                  Spare me now!
I am as one lost in a midnight wood,
Who dares not ask some harmless passenger
95   The path across the wilderness, lest he,
As my thoughts are, should be — a murderer.
I know you are my friend, and all I dare
Speak to my soul, that will I trust with thee.
But now my heart is heavy, and would take
100   Lone counsel from a night of sleepless care.
Pardon me, that I say farewell — farewell!
I would that to my own suspected self
I could address a word so full of peace.

Orsino
Farewell! — Be your thoughts better or more bold.

                                  [*Exit* Giacomo.
105   I had disposed the Cardinal Camillo
To feed his hope with cold encouragement:
It fortunately serves my close designs

---

men in which [their recollections *canc*.] they might behold their own recollections, & in dim perspective thier shadowy hopes & fears, – all that they dare not, or that daring and desiring, they could not expose to the open light of day – But [Let *canc*.] thought can with difficulty visit the intricate & winding chambers which it *inhabits*. – [Let it *canc*.] It is like a river whose rapid & perpetual stream flows outwards; – like one in dread who speeds thro the recesses of some haunted pile & dares not look behind. The caverns of the mind are obscure & shadowy, or pervaded with a lustre, beautifully bright indeed, but shining not beyond their portals. If it were possible to be where we have been, vitally & indeed – if at the moment of our presence there we could [describe *canc*.] define the results of our experience – if the passage from sensation to reflexion – from a state of [passivene *canc*.] to voluntary contemplation were not so dizzying & so tumultuous – this attempt would be less difficult. –'

89. *cave of our own mind*,] Cp. *J&M* line 573 and 'caverns of the mind' in 'On a Science of Mind' (cited in the note to II ii 88–91).

90–1. Cp. Orsino's image of the conditions for introspection with Cenci's description of the conditions required for his 'act' at II i 177–8.

92. *suspected –*] *Cenci (1819)*; suspected: *Cenci (1821)*.

93. Cp. *Inferno* i 2–3: 'Mi ritrovai per una selva oscura, / Che la diritta via smarrita' ('I found me in a gloomy wood, astray / Gone from the path direct' (trans. Cary)).

107–18. *It fortunately . . . half reconciled*.] Cp. *PU* I lines 380–1 (as Keach, *Shelley's Style* (1984) 105 observes, lines which 'could serve as an epigraph for *The Cenci*'). Cp. also the anonymously published essay by Julius Charles Hare (1795–1855) on the Danish poet Adam Oehlenschlaeger, 'On the German Drama. No. I. Oehlenschlaeger' in *Olliers Literary Miscellany in Prose and Verse* i (1820) 90–153. Hare's essay is instructive in its criticism of

That 'tis a trick of this same family
To analyse their own and other minds.
110 Such self-anatomy shall teach the will
Dangerous secrets: for it tempts our powers,
Knowing what must be thought, and may be done,
Into the depth of darkest purposes:
So Cenci fell into the pit; even I,
115 Since Beatrice unveiled me to myself,
And made me shrink from what I cannot shun,
Show a poor figure to my own esteem,
To which I grow half reconciled. I'll do
As little mischief as I can; that thought
120 Shall fee the accuser conscience.

[After a pause.

Now what harm
If Cenci should be murdered? — Yet, if murdered,

---

the poetry of Byron and Wordsworth for indulging excessively in self-reflection (102–6
and notes) and for its praise of S. and specific identification of *C* II ii 108–13 in the follow-
ing passage concerning the evils of introspection: 'But, besides, Hindbad [a character in
Oehlenschlaeger's play *Aladdin*] is a thoroughly evil character, and is therefore appropriately
described as poring over the musty pages of his own mouldered heart, as indulging in that
brooding self-reflection which springs from the source of all evil, the separation which the
individual consciousness establishes between itself and the rest of the creation. For though
the perception of a separated existence be the necessary result of the development of the
human mind, where the heart is pure and humble, such a perception will be merged in the
higher perception of the union of all the insulated existences into one co-operating harmon-
izing whole by the spirit of love; and where this is not the case, it is because the indi-
vidual looks upon himself as separated by hatred from and at war with the universe, and
consequently as the one sole object of self-regard, to the will and lusts of which it is his busi-
ness and his wisdom to render all other things subservient. Unable to attain to the height
of self-sacrifice, he would sacrifice every thing unto self. And then, in such a spirit, the whole
order of nature is reversed; the place of love is occupied by hatred, that of peace by strife,
that of hope by fear: instead of confiding in man, he suspects him; instead of trusting in
God, he believes in nothing save the devil. Shakespeare accordingly has made all his evil
characters, Edmund, Iago, Richard, all more or less self-reflective. In the words of a great mod-
ern poet, whose genius, when he has bowed down his neck and received into himself the
purifying and sanctifying influence of the Spirit, if such be his earthly fate, must assuredly
prove a cherisher of innocent thoughts and a kindler of noble thoughts unto many: [the
passage, "'tis a trick . . . darkest purposes', is then quoted, not altogether accurately].' (148–9).
For S.'s interest in Hare's essay, see *L* ii 258–9, and G. F. McFarland, 'Shelley and Julius Hare:
A Review and A Response', *Bulletin of the John Rylands University Library of Manchester* lvii
(1974–75) 406–29.

110. self-anatomy] Cp. I ii 85. *Rognoni* 1568 cps. S.'s letter to Mary of 10 August 1821 in which,
referring to his relations with Byron, S. comments 'What is passing in the heart of another
rarely escapes the observation of one who is a strict anatomist of his own –' (*L* ii 324). For
an influential discussion of 'self-anatomy', see *Wasserman* 110–22.

120. fee] i.e. 'to induce by a fee to go away' (see *OED*, 'fee' *v.* 2). *conscience.*] Conscience.
Rossetti 1870.

Wherefore by me? And what if I could take
The profit, yet omit the sin and peril
In such an action? Of all earthly things
125   I fear a man whose blows outspeed his words;
And such is Cenci: and while Cenci lives
His daughter's dowry were a secret grave
If a priest wins her. — Oh, fair Beatrice!
Would that I loved thee not, or loving thee
130   Could but despise danger and gold, and all
That frowns between my wish and its effect,
Or smiles beyond it! There is no escape:
Her bright form kneels beside me at the altar,
And follows me to the resort of men,
135   And fills my slumber with tumultuous dreams,
So when I wake my blood seems liquid fire;
And if I strike my damp and dizzy head,
My hot palm scorches it: her very name,
But spoken by a stranger, makes my heart
140   Sicken and pant; and thus unprofitably
I clasp the phantom of unfelt delights
Till weak imagination half possesses
The self-created shadow. Yet much longer
Will I not nurse this life of feverous hours:
145   From the unravelled hopes of Giacomo
I must work out my own dear purposes.
I see, as from a tower, the end of all:
Her father dead; her brother bound to me

127. *grave*] *Cenci (1819)*; grave, *Cenci (1821)*.

130-1. *and all / That frowns between my wish and its effect,*] Cp. *Macbeth* I v 42-4: 'That no compunctious visitings of nature / Shake my fell purpose nor keep peace between / Th'effect and it.'

132. *escape:*] escape . . . *Cenci (1819)*.

134. *resort*] *Locock 1911* suggests this 'may be a slip for "resorts"'. Cp. *L&C* Canto I stanza xxx.

136-43. *So when I wake . . . shadow.*] This passage draws on no. 154, 'To thirst and find no fill', in *Nbk* 5. Cp. esp. lines 141-3 with lines 5-7.

136. *So when I wake*] *Cenci (1819)*; So, when I wake, *Cenci (1821)*. *So*] i.e. 'so that'.

140. *Sicken and pant;*] Cp. II i 126-8 and note to II i 128.

141. *delights*] *Cenci (1819)*; delights, *Cenci (1821)*.

145. *unravelled*] The sense is 'disclosed' (see *OED* 'unravel' *v.* 3).

147. Cp. Plato, *Republic* iv 445c: ' "And truly," said I, "now that we have come to this height of argument I seem to see as from a point of outlook that there is one form of excellence" ' (Loeb trans.); *Richard III* II iv 53-4: 'Welcome, destruction, blood, and massacre! / I see, as in a map, the end of all'.

> By a dark secret, surer than the grave;
150 Her mother scared and unexpostulating
> From the dread manner of her wish achieved:
> And she! — Once more take courage, my faint heart;
> What dares a friendless maiden matched with thee?
> I have such foresight as assures success:
155 Some unbeheld divinity doth ever,
> When dread events are near, stir up men's minds
> To black suggestions; and he prospers best,
> Not who becomes the instrument of ill,
> But who can flatter the dark spirit, that makes
160 Its empire and its prey of other hearts,
> Till it become his slave — as I will do.

[*Exit.*

End of the Second Act

150–1. *unexpostulating . . . achieved:*] i.e. 'unexpostulating, because her wish is achieved, and scared at the dread manner of its achievement' (*Locock 1911*).

155–61. Joan Rees, 'Shelley's Orsino: Evil in "The Cenci"', *KSMB* xii (1961) 3–6 glosses this passage thus: 'In other words Orsino, though the story requires him to be a priest of the Roman church, acknowledges no Christian god but a "dark spirit" whose evil suggestions he intends to use in order to bring others under his domination' (4).

161. *slave* –] slave . . . *Cenci (1819).*

ACT III

Scene i

An Apartment in the Cenci Palace. Lucretia, *to her enter* Beatrice.

Beatrice   [*She enters staggering, and speaks wildly.*
Reach me that handkerchief! — My brain is hurt;
My eyes are full of blood; just wipe them for me —
I see but indistinctly: —

Lucretia
                    My sweet child,
You have no wound; 'tis only a cold dew
5   That starts from your dear brow — Alas! Alas!
What has befallen?

Beatrice
              How comes this hair undone?
Its wandering strings must be what blind me so,
And yet I tied it fast. — O, horrible!
The pavement sinks under my feet! The walls
10   Spin round! I see a woman weeping there,
And standing calm and motionless, whilst I
Slide giddily as the world reels — My God!
The beautiful blue heaven is flecked with blood!
The sunshine on the floor is black! The air
15   Is changed to vapours such as the dead breathe
In charnel-pits! Pah! I am choked! There creeps

1. My brain is hurt;] Cp. *R&H* line 589.

2. Curran (1970) 116 suggests that Beatrice uses the word 'blood' as 'a euphemism for her father's semen' in this scene (see also III i 13, 95).

6-7. How comes . . . blind me so,] Cp. *PU* IV 224-5 and note.

13. Cp. Marlowe, *Doctor Faustus* (1604) V ii 78: 'See, see where Christ's blood streams in the firmament!' and Coleridge, *Remorse* (1813) IV iii: 'And all the hanging drops of the wet roof / Turn'd into blood – I saw them turn to blood!'

14-16. The air . . . I am choked!] Cp. Coleridge, *Remorse* (1813) I ii: 'The black air, / It was a toil to breathe it!'

16-23. There creeps . . . spirit of life!] *Curran (1975)* 128-9 describes this as 'syphilitic imagery' in which Beatrice 'images her father's semen' in terms of Ahrimanic pestilence. However there are many precedents for such imagery in Jacobean drama e.g. Bianca after her seduction in Middleton, *Women Beware Women* (?1621) II ii 420-6: 'Now bless me from a blasting; I saw that now / Fearful for any woman's eye to look on. / Infectious mists and mildews hang at's eyes, / The weather of a doomsday dwells upon him. / Yet since mine honour's leprous, why should I / Preserve that fair that caused the leprosy? / Come poison all at once.'

A clinging, black, contaminating mist
About me — 'tis substantial, heavy, thick,
I cannot pluck it from me, for it glues
20   My fingers and my limbs to one another,
And eats into my sinews, and dissolves
My flesh to a pollution, poisoning
The subtle, pure, and inmost spirit of life!
My God! I never knew what the mad felt
25   Before; for I am mad beyond all doubt!

                                      [More wildly.

No, I am dead! These putrefying limbs
Shut round and sepulchre the panting soul
Which would burst forth into the wandering air!

                                       [A pause.

What hideous thought was that I had even now?
30   'Tis gone; and yet its burden remains here
O'er these dull eyes — upon this weary heart!
O, world! O, life! O, day! O, misery!

Lucretia
What ails thee, my poor child? She answers not:
Her spirit apprehends the sense of pain,
35   But not its cause; suffering has dried away
The source from which it sprung.

  Beatrice   *[Franticly.*
                  Like Parricide —

17. Cp. the description of Satan, *Paradise Lost* ix 180: 'Like a black mist low creeping'.

24–5. Cp. Bianca's madness in Milman, *Fazio* (1815) Act III scene ii: 'Mad! mad! – aye, that it is! – aye, that it is! / Is't to be mad to speak, to move, to gaze, / But not know how, or why, or whence, or where? / To see that there are faces all around me, / Floating within a dim discolour'd haze, / Yet have distinction, vision, but for one? / To speak with rapid and continuous flow, / Yet know not how the unthought words start from me? – / Oh, I am mad, wildly, intensely mad.' Joseph W. Donohoe cps. *C* and *Fazio* in 'Shelley's Beatrice and the Romantic Concept of Tragic Character', *KSJ* xvii (1968) 53–73 esp. 64–8.

26–8. Cp. *Richard II* I iii 194–6: 'By this time, had the King permitted us, / One of our souls had wand'red in the air, / Banish'd this frail sepulchre of our flesh . . .' See also note to I i 114–15.

27. soul] *Cenci (1819)*; soul, *Cenci (1821)*.

29. hideous thought] Cp. Coleridge, 'Christabel' Part II in *Christabel: Kubla Khan, A Vision; The Pains of Sleep* (1816): ' "Sure I have sinned!" said Christabel, / "Now heaven be praised if all be well!" / And in low faltering tones, yet sweet, / Did she the lofty lady greet / With such perplexity of mind / as dreams too lively leave behind.' Terry Otten, 'Christabel, Beatrice, and the Encounter with Evil', *Bucknell Review* xvii (1969) 19–31 (27–8) cps. the reactions of Beatrice and Christabel to contamination by evil.

36. Parricide –] *1829*; Parricide . . . *Cenci (1819)*; parricide – *Cenci (1821)*; Parricide, *Rossetti 1870*. A personification.

36–8. Like Parricide – . . . like mine –] G. H. Lewes, *The Westminster Review* xxxv (1841) 303–44

Misery has killed its father: yet its father
Never like mine — O, God! What thing am I?

Lucretia
My dearest child, what has your father done?

Beatrice   [*Doubtfully.*
40   Who art thou, questioner? I have no father.

                                              [*Aside.*

She is the madhouse nurse who tends on me,
It is a piteous office.
                    [*To* Lucretia, *in a slow, subdued voice.*
              Do you know
I thought I was that wretched Beatrice
Men speak of, whom her father sometimes hales
45   From hall to hall by the entangled hair;
At others, pens up naked in damp cells
Where scaly reptiles crawl, and starves her there,
Till she will eat strange flesh. This woeful story
So did I overact in my sick dreams,
50   That I imagined — no, it cannot be!
Horrible things have been in this wild world,
Prodigious mixtures, and confusions strange

(338–9) comments: 'We do not agree with Leigh Hunt's explanation here, that she personifies herself as misery, and has killed her father in thought [see *The Indicator* xlii (26 July 1820) 332, 334]; we think she means that the intensity of her misery has absorbed all consciousness of its cause (father), and therefore she is mad. This seems borne out by the previous remark of Lucretia: – "Her spirit apprehends the sense of pain, / But not its cause".'

38. What thing am I?] Cp. Imogine in Maturin, *Bertram* (1816) IV ii: 'If I run mad, some wild word will betray me, / Nay – let me think – what am I? – no, what was I?'

41. me,] me *Cenci (1819)*; me: *1829*; me; *Rossetti 1870.*

43–56. I thought . . . As –] Cp. Clarence's description of his dream in *Richard III* I iv 2–74.

44. hales] i.e. 'drags' (see *OED*, 'hale' v. 1b).

46–50. Ralph Pite, *The Circle of our Vision* (1994) 164n. comments that Beatrice thinks of her treatment here in terms similar to that of Ugolino's children. See note to I iii 102–4.

48. strange flesh.] Cp. *Jude* 7: 'Even as Sodom and Gomorrah, and the cities about them in like manner, giving themselves over to fornication, and going after strange flesh, are set forth for an example, suffering the vengeance of eternal fire.' *Antony and Cleopatra* 1 iv 67: 'It is reported thou didst eat strange flesh'.

49. my sick dreams,] Cp. Horace, *De Arte Poetica* lines 7–8: 'velut aegri somnia, vanae / fingentur species' ('whose idle fancies shall be shaped like a sick man's dreams' (Loeb trans.)). Cp. also Montaigne, *Essais* (1580), ed. Albert Thibaudet (1950), Book I ch. viii ('De L'Oisiveté') in which these lines are cited: 'Et n'est folie ny rêverie, qu'ils ne produisent en cette agitation'. Mary was reading Montaigne in Rome in March 1819 (*Mary Jnl* i 252–5).

52. Prodigious] i.e. 'unnatural, abnormal', as in *Paradise Lost* ii 625–6: 'all monstrous, all prodigious things, / Abominable, inutterable'.

Of good and ill; and worse have been conceived
Than ever there was found a heart to do.
55 But never fancy imaged such a deed
As —

[*Pauses, suddenly recollecting herself.*

Who art thou? Swear to me, ere I die
With fearful expectation, that indeed
Thou art not what thou seemest — Mother!

Lucretia
                                        Oh!
My sweet child, know you —

Beatrice
                        Yet speak it not:
60 For then if this be truth, that other too
Must be a truth, a firm enduring truth,
Linked with each lasting circumstance of life,
Never to change, never to pass away.
Why so it is. This is the Cenci Palace;
65 Thou art Lucretia; I am Beatrice.
I have talked some wild words, but will no more.
Mother, come near me: from this point of time,
I am —

[*Her voice dies away faintly.*

Lucretia
            Alas! What has befallen thee, child?
What has thy father done?

Beatrice
                    What have I done?

59. 'This line lacks a syllable. In Lucretia's mouth, "know you not" would seem the right phrase, rather than "know you." Perhaps Shelley had first written the "not"; then cut it out, observing the other "not" closing the line; and forgot to put an extra syllable elsewhere' (*Rossetti 1878*).

69–76. *What have I done? . . . even despair?*] *Curran (1975)* 130–3 cps. Io in Aeschylus, *Prometheus Bound* 578–82:

τί ποτέ μ', ὦ Κρόνιε παῖ, τί ποτε ταῖσδ'
ἐνέζευξας εὑρὼν ἁμαρτοῦσαν ἐν
πημοναῖσιν; ἒ ἔ,
οἰστρηλάτῳ δὲ δείματι
δειλαίαν παράκοπον ὧδε τείρεις;

70   Am I not innocent? Is it my crime
      That one with white hair, and imperious brow,
      Who tortured me from my forgotten years,
      As parents only dare, should call himself
      My father, yet should be! — Oh, what am I?
75   What name, what place, what memory shall be mine?
      What retrospects, outliving even despair?

      Lucretia
      He is a violent tyrant, surely, child:
      We know that death alone can make us free;
      His death or ours. But what can he have done
80   Of deadlier outrage or worse injury?
      Thou art unlike thyself; thine eyes shoot forth
      A wandering and strange spirit. Speak to me,
      Unlock those pallid hands whose fingers twine
      With one another.

      Beatrice
                          'Tis the restless life
85   Tortured within them. If I try to speak
      I shall go mad. Aye, something must be done;
      What, yet I know not — something which shall make
      The thing that I have suffered but a shadow
      In the dread lightning which avenges it;
90   Brief, rapid, irreversible, destroying
      The consequence of what it cannot cure.

('Wherein, O son of Cronus, wherein hast thou found offence in me that thou hast bound me to this yoke of misery – ah me! and dost thus harass a wretched maiden to frenzy by the terror of the pursuing gad-fly?' (Loeb trans.)). Cp. also Massinger, *The Unnatural Combat* (?1639) V ii 207–11 in *The Plays and Poems of Philip Massinger*, ed. Philip Edwards and Colin Gibson, 5 vols (1976) ii: 'What offence / From my first infancie did I commit / That for a punishment you should give up / My Virgin chastity to the trecherous guard / Of Goatish *Montreville*?'

86–7. something must be done; / What, yet I know not –] Cp. Procne in Ovid, *Metamorphoses* vi 618–19: ' "magnum quodcumque paravi; / quid sit, adhuc dubito" ' (' "I am prepared for some great deed; but what it shall be I am still in doubt" ' (Loeb trans.)); Atreus in Seneca, *Thyestes* 267–70: 'Nescio quid animo maius et solito amplius / supraque fines moris humani tumet / instatque pigris manibus – haud quid sit scio, / sed grande quiddam est.' ('Some greater thing, larger than the common and beyond the bounds of human use is swelling in my soul, and it urges on my sluggish hands – I know not what it is, but 'tis some mighty thing.' (Loeb trans.)); *Lear* II iv 279–80: 'I will do such things – / What they are yet I know not'; *The Examiner* (3 January 1819) 1: 'all classes feel that something, as the phrase is, must be done.' In his letter to Ollier of 6 September 1819, S. quotes Beatrice's words here in reacting to 'the Manchester work' (i.e. 'Peterloo') (*L* ii 117), and he uses a similar wording to Peacock on the same subject in a letter of 21 September 1819 (*L* ii 120). Cp. I i 102. *yet*] i.e. 'at present' (*Locock 1911*).

88–9. a shadow . . . which avenges it;] Cp. *PU* III i 19 ('the terror of the earth') and note.

Some such thing is to be endured or done:
When I know what, I shall be still and calm,
And never any thing will move me more.
95 But now! — Oh blood, which art my father's blood,
Circling through these contaminated veins,
If thou, poured forth on the polluted earth,
Could wash away the crime, and punishment
By which I suffer — no, that cannot be!
100 Many might doubt there were a God above
Who sees and permits evil, and so die:
That faith no agony shall obscure in me.

Lucretia
It must indeed have been some bitter wrong;
Yet what, I dare not guess. Oh, my lost child,
105 Hide not in proud impenetrable grief
Thy sufferings from my fear.

Beatrice
                                    I hide them not.
What are the words which you would have me speak?
I, who can feign no image in my mind
Of that which has transformed me: I, whose thought
110 Is like a ghost shrouded and folded up
In its own formless horror: of all words,

97–9. *If thou, . . . I suffer –*] Cp. the Chorus on the deaths of Eteocles and Polyneices in Aeschylus, *Seven Against Thebes* 734–41:

ἐπεὶ δ' ἂν αὐτοκτόνως
αὐτοδάικτοι θάνωσι,
καὶ γαῖα κόνις πίῃ
μελαμπαγὲς αἷμα φοίνιον,
τίς ἂν καθαρμοὺς πόροι,
τίς ἂν σφε λούσειεν; ὧ
πόνοι δόμων νέοι παλαι-
οῖσι συμμιγεῖς κακοῖς.

('But when they shall have perished, slain by kindred hands in mutual slaughter, and the dust of earth hath drunk their black and clotted gore, who can provide wherewith to purify? Who can wash away their stain? O house of misery, wherein new woes are blent with woes of old!' (Loeb trans.)).

98. *Could*] Couldst *Rossetti 1870* (an emendation justified in *Rossetti 1870* 502n.).

100–2. Cp. 'Mont Blanc' lines 76–7.

101. *so*] i.e. 'thus doubting'.

108. *image*] i.e. 'idea' or 'conception' (see Keach, *Shelley's Style* (1984) 45).

109. *me:*] me. *Cenci (1819)*.

111. *horror: of*] horror. Of *Cenci (1819)*.

That minister to mortal intercourse,
Which wouldst thou hear? For there is none to tell
My misery; if another ever knew
115 Aught like to it, she died as I will die,
And left it, as I must, without a name.
Death! Death! Our law and our religion call thee
A punishment and a reward. — Oh, which
Have I deserved?

Lucretia
                              The peace of innocence;
120 Till in your season you be called to heaven.
Whate'er you may have suffered, you have done
No evil. Death must be the punishment
Of crime, or the reward of trampling down
The thorns which God has strewed upon the path
125 Which leads to immortality.

Beatrice
                              Aye, death —
The punishment of crime. I pray thee, God,
Let me not be bewildered while I judge.
If I must live day after day, and keep
These limbs, the unworthy temple of thy spirit,
130 As a foul den from which what thou abhorrest
May mock thee, unavenged — it shall not be!
Self-murder? no, that might be no escape,
For thy decree yawns like a Hell between
Our will and it. O! in this mortal world
135 There is no vindication and no law
Which can adjudge and execute the doom
Of that through which I suffer.

                              Enter Orsino.

                              [*She approaches him solemnly.*
                              Welcome, friend!

---

114. misery;] misery: *Cenci (1819).*
118. reward. –] reward ... *Cenci (1819);* reward – *1829;* reward. *1839.*
129. the unworthy temple of thy spirit,] Alan M. Weinberg, *Shelley's Italian Experience* (1991) 86 and 268 cps. I *Corinthians* vi 19–20: 'know ye not that your body is the temple of the Holy Ghost which is in you, which ye have of God, and ye are not your own? For ye are bought with a price: therefore glorify God in your body, and in your spirit, which are God's.'

I have to tell you that, since last we met,
I have endured a wrong so great and strange,
140   That neither life nor death can give me rest.
Ask me not what it is, for there are deeds
Which have no form, sufferings which have no tongue.

Orsino
And what is he who has thus injured you?

Beatrice
The man they call my father: a dread name.

Orsino
145   It cannot be —

Beatrice
                        What it can be, or not,
Forbear to think. It is, and it has been;
Advise me how it shall not be again.
I thought to die, but a religious awe
Restrains me, and the dread lest death itself
150   Might be no refuge from the consciousness
Of what is yet unexpiated. Oh, speak!

Orsino
Accuse him of the deed, and let the law
Avenge thee.

Beatrice
                        Oh, ice-hearted counsellor!
If I could find a word that might make known
155   The crime of my destroyer; and that done,

---

140. *nor*] or *Cenci (1819)*.

142. sufferings which have no tongue.] Cp. Philomela's fate and Procne's reaction to it in Ovid, *Metamorphoses* vi 583–6: 'dolor ora repressit, / verbaque quaerenti satis indignantia linguae / defuerunt, nec flere vacat, sed fasque nefasque / confusura ruit poenaeque in imagine tota est.' ('Grief chokes the words that rise to her lips, and her questing tongue can find no words strong enough to express her outraged feelings. Here is no room for tears, but she hurries on to confound right and wrong, her whole soul bent on the thought of vengeance' (Loeb trans.)).

148. die,] die; *Cenci (1819)*.

155. done,] done *Cenci (1819)*.

My tongue should, like a knife, tear out the secret
Which cankers my heart's core; aye, lay all bare,
So that my unpolluted fame should be
With vilest gossips a stale-mouthed story;
160   A mock, a byword, an astonishment: —
If this were done, which never shall be done,
Think of the offender's gold, his dreaded hate,
And the strange horror of the accuser's tale,
Baffling belief, and overpowering speech;
165   Scarce whispered, unimaginable, wrapt
In hideous hints — Oh, most assured redress!

Orsino
You will endure it then?

Beatrice
               Endure! Orsino,
It seems your counsel is small profit.
        [Turns from him, and speaks half to herself.
                   Aye,
All must be suddenly resolved and done.
170   What is this undistinguishable mist

---

156. should, like a knife,] should like a knife *Cenci (1819).*

157. bare,] bare *Cenci (1819).*

159. stale-mouthed] *1829*; stale mouthed *Cenci (1819), Cenci (1821)*; stale mouthèd *Forman 1876–7*; stale-mouthèd *Rossetti 1870.* The accent supplied by Forman and Rossetti is, strictly speaking, metrically superfluous, but the insertion of a hyphen usefully enforces the compound sense which S. appears to have intended. As is pointed out in Nora Crook and Derek Guiton, *Shelley's Venomed Melody* (1986) 201, the meaning of 'stale' here, obsolete in S.'s day, is 'a prostitute of the lowest class' (see *OED*, 'stale' *sb.* 4) as in *Much Ado* II ii 21–3: 'he hath wronged his honour in marrying the renowned Claudio – whose estimation do you mightily hold up – to a contaminated stale, such a one as Hero.'

160. Locock 1911 cps. V iii 33 and *PU* III iv 176. *byword*] Cp. *Deuteronomy* xxviii 37: 'And thou shalt become an astonishment, a proverb, and a byword, among all nations whither the LORD shall lead thee'; and Richardson, *Clarissa. Or, the History of a Young Lady,* 7 vols (1748) ii 267: 'For I have no doubt, that I am the talk, and perhaps the by-word of half the county.'

165. wrapt] wrapped *Rossetti 1870.* Not modernised here so as not to conceal a pun which suggests the sense of being entranced (i.e. 'rapt') as well as covered ('wrapped'). However the word is used in a not dissimilar sense with the spelling 'Wrapped' at II i 30 in *Cenci (1821)* (and in *Cenci (1819)*) so it is possible that the alternative spelling here is simply a matter of orthographical inconsistency to which S. would have been indifferent. Cp. V iv 148.

167. Endure!] Endure? – *Cenci (1819)*; Endure! – *1839.*

170. Cp. II i 184 and note. A sense continued in Orsino's 'until thou mayest become / Utterly lost' at III i 175–6.

Of thoughts, which rise, like shadow after shadow,
Darkening each other?

Orsino

           Should the offender live?
Triumph in his misdeed? and make, by use,
His crime, whate'er it is, dreadful no doubt,
175   Thine element; until thou mayest become
Utterly lost; subdued even to the hue
Of that which thou permittest?

Beatrice   *[To herself.*
                  Mighty death!
Thou double-visaged shadow! Only judge!
Rightfullest arbiter!

                  [She retires absorbed in thought.

Lucretia

             If the lightning
180   Of God has e'er descended to avenge —

Orsino

Blaspheme not! His high Providence commits
Its glory on this earth, and their own wrongs
Into the hands of men; if they neglect
To punish crime —

---

175. *Thine element;*] Cp. *PU* I 477. *mayest*] Pronounced as a monosyllable (see also V iv 155).

176–7. *subdued even to the hue / Of that which thou permittest?*] Cp. Shakespeare, Sonnet cxi lines 6–7: 'And almost thence my nature is subdu'd / To what it works in, like the dyer's hand'. S. cites this passage from Sonnet cxi in the 'Note on Shakespeare' in *Nbk 10* f. 19ʳrev. (see *MYR* iv 396–7), part of the draft of the Preface to *C* composed in August 1819, i.e. after III i 176–7 was drafted (see headnote). The lines from Sonnet cxi seem to have had some currency in the Romantic period. See e.g. Lamb's 'On the Tragedies of Shakspeare, considered with reference to their Fitness for Stage Representation' (first published in 1812) in *The Works of Charles Lamb*, 2 vols (1818) ii 1–36 (19), a work which S. refers to as having read by August 1819 (see *L* ii 110–12, 117), and Byron, *Don Juan, Cantos III, IV, and V* (1821) Canto III stanza lxxxvii: 'And feeling, in a poet, is the source / Of others' feeling; but they are such liars, / And take all colours – like the hands of dyers.' Ralph Pite, *The Circle of our Vision* (1994) 170 cps. S.'s letter to Horace Smith of 29 June 1822: 'all, more or less, subdue themselves to the element that surrounds them, & contribute to the evils they lament by the hypocrisy that springs from them' (*L* ii 442).

178. *double-visaged*] Satan describes Sin, mother of Death, as 'double-formed' (*Paradise Lost* ii 741).

Lucretia
                              But if one, like this wretch,
185   Should mock, with gold, opinion, law, and power?
      If there be no appeal to that which makes
      The guiltiest tremble? If, because our wrongs,
      For that they are unnatural, strange, and monstrous,
      Exceed all measure of belief? Oh, God!
190   If, for the very reasons which should make
      Redress most swift and sure, our injurer triumphs?
      And we, the victims, bear worse punishment
      Than that appointed for their torturer?

Orsino
                              Think not
      But that there is redress where there is wrong,
195   So we be bold enough to seize it.

Lucretia
                              How?
      If there were any way to make all sure,
      I know not — but I think it might be good
      To —

Orsino
            Why, his late outrage to Beatrice;
      For it is such, as I but faintly guess,
200   As makes remorse dishonour, and leaves her
      Only one duty, how she may avenge:
      You, but one refuge from ills ill endured;
      Me, but one counsel —

Lucretia
                              For we cannot hope
      That aid, or retribution, or resource,

---

185. Should mock with gold, opinion law and power? *Cenci (1819)*; Should mock with gold opinion, law, and power? *Rossetti (1870)*.

187. If,] If *Cenci (1819)*.

188. *are unnatural, strange, and*] are, unnatural, strange and *Cenci (1819)*.

192. *we,*] we *Cenci (1819)*.

204. *resource,*] resource *Cenci (1819)*.

205   Will arise thence, where every other one
            Might find them with less need.

                                        [Beatrice *advances.*

Orsino

                        Then —

Beatrice

                             Peace, Orsino!
            And, honoured Lady, while I speak, I pray,
            That you put off, as garments overworn,
            Forbearance and respect, remorse and fear,
210   And all the fit restraints of daily life,
            Which have been borne from childhood, but which now
            Would be a mockery to my holier plea.
            As I have said, I have endured a wrong,
            Which, though it be expressionless, is such
215   As asks atonement, both for what is past,
            And lest I be reserved, day after day,
            To load with crimes an overburdened soul,
            And be — what ye can dream not. I have prayed
            To God, and I have talked with my own heart,
220   And have unravelled my entangled will,
            And have at length determined what is right.
            Art thou my friend, Orsino? False or true?
            Pledge thy salvation ere I speak.

Orsino

                         I swear
            To dedicate my cunning, and my strength,
225   My silence, and whatever else is mine,
            To thy commands.

Lucretia

                    You think we should devise
            His death?

---

205. thence,] i.e. 'from the Law' (*Locock 1911*).

208–9. That you put off, . . . remorse and fear,] Cp. Satan in *Paradise Lost* iv 108–9: 'So farewell hope, and with hope farewell fear, / Farewell remorse'. Cp. I i 84.

214. be expressionless,] i.e. 'finds no expression' (cited in *OED*, 'expressionless' *a.* 2). The only such usage given in *OED*.

215. atonement,] atonement; *Cenci (1819)*. See Preface line 69 and note.

219. Cp I i 72–3 and I i 119.

220. unravelled] Cp. II ii 145 and note. Here the sense is of 'disentangling'.

222. friend,] friend *Cenci (1819)*.

Beatrice
                    And execute what is devised,
And suddenly. We must be brief and bold.

Orsino
And yet most cautious.

Lucretia
                    For the jealous laws
230   Would punish us with death and infamy
For that which it became themselves to do.

Beatrice
Be cautious as ye may, but prompt. Orsino,
What are the means?

Orsino
                    I know two dull, fierce outlaws,
Who think man's spirit as a worm's, and they
235   Would trample out, for any slight caprice,
The meanest or the noblest life. This mood
Is marketable here in Rome. They sell
What we now want.

Lucretia
                    Tomorrow, before dawn,
Cenci will take us to that lonely rock,
240   Petrella, in the Apulian Apennines.
If he arrive there —

Beatrice
                    He must not arrive.

Orsino
Will it be dark before you reach the tower?

Lucretia
The sun will scarce be set.

232. *Orsino,*] Orsino; *Cenci (1819).*
233. *I know two dull, fierce outlaws,*] i.e. Marzio and Olimpio. See note to III ii 62–4.
236–7. *This mood . . . Rome.*] See note to I i 1.
239–40. *that lonely rock, / Petrella,*] See note to II i 168.
240. *Apulian*] See note to *Dramatis Personae.*

>   *Beatrice*
>   But I remember
>   Two miles on this side of the fort, the road
> 245   Crosses a deep ravine; 'tis rough and narrow,
>   And winds with short turns down the precipice;
>   And in its depth there is a mighty rock,
>   Which has, from unimaginable years,
>   Sustained itself with terror and with toil
> 250   Over a gulf, and with the agony
>   With which it clings seems slowly coming down;
>   Even as a wretched soul hour after hour,
>   Clings to the mass of life; yet clinging, leans;
>   And leaning, makes more dark the dread abyss
> 255   In which it fears to fall: beneath this crag,
>   Huge as despair, as if in weariness,
>   The melancholy mountain yawns; below,

247–57. And in its depth . . . The melancholy mountain yawns;] The 'most sublime passage' referred to in the second footnote of the Preface is Calderón, *El Purgatorio de San Patricio*, Act II (lines 2019–26): '¿No ves ese peñasco que parece / que se está sustentando con trabajo, / y con el ansia misma que padece / ha tantos siglos que se viene abajo? / Pues mordaza es que sella y enmudece / el aliento a una boca, que debajo / abierta está, por donde con pereza / el monte melancólico bosteza' (text from *El Purgatorio de San Patricio*, ed. J. M. Ruano de la Haza (1988)) ('See ye not here this rock some power secureth, / That grasps with awful toil the hill-side brown, / And with the very anguish it endureth / Age after age seems slowly coming down? / Suspended there with effort, it obscureth / A mighty cave beneath, which it doth crown; / – / An open mouth the horrid cavern shapes, / Wherewith the melancholy mountain gapes' (trans. Denis Florence Mac-Carthy, *Calderon's Dramas* (1873))). For comment on this passage and its relationship to the argument of the Preface, see *Curran (1970)* 120–1, Keach, *Shelley's Style* (1984) 64–5 and *Webb* 382–3. Cp. comparable descriptions of overhanging rocks in Thomson, *Spring* 755–7: 'High from the Summit of a craggy Cliff, / Hung o'er the Deep, such as amazing frowns / On utmost *Kilda's* Shore', and Gray, 'The Bard. A Pindaric Ode' lines 15–16: 'On a rock, whose haughty brow, / Frowns o'er old Conway's foaming flood'. Cp. also *L* i 496–7 (cited in the headnote to no. 124, 'Mont Blanc') and *PU* IV 558–60.

249. Sustained itself] i.e. 'held itself in check'. Cp. 'sustinet' in *Pervigilium Veneris* v: 'emicant lacrimae trementes de caduco pondere, / gutta praeceps orbe parvo sustinet casus suos' ('Sparkling tears quiver in a heavy drip, the little splashing dew-bead holds together in its fall' (Loeb trans.)), and 'sustain' in Charlotte Dacre, *Zofloya; or, The Moor: A Romance of the Fifteenth Century*, 3 vols (1806) iii 135: 'At length a deep hollow presented itself – they descended its almost perpendicular sides, and reached the rocky valley below; – a rude projecting mass of rock, (seeming to sustain itself in mid air, as it were) became, by the winding of the path, presently visible; it extended nearly to the opposite side of the mountain, forming thereby a kind of huge irregular arch. –'. Medwin states that *Zofloya* 'enraptured' S. as a child (*Medwin* i 30). Cp. also the negative usage in *Paradise Lost* ix 430: 'Hung drooping unsustained'.

252. soul] soul, *Locock (1911)*. *after hour,*] after hour *1840*.

253. yet] yet, *1840*.

254. And] And, *1840*.

255. crag,] crag *Cenci (1819)*.

257. yawns;] yawns . . . *Cenci (1819)*; yawns – *1829*; yawns. *Rossetti (1870)*; yawns: *Locock (1911)*.

You hear but see not an impetuous torrent
Raging among the caverns, and a bridge
260 Crosses the chasm; and high above there grow,
With intersecting trunks, from crag to crag,
Cedars, and yews, and pines; whose tangled hair
Is matted in one solid roof of shade
By the dark ivy's twine. At noonday here
265 'Tis twilight, and at sunset blackest night.

Orsino
Before you reach that bridge make some excuse
For spurring on your mules, or loitering
Until —

Beatrice
　　　　What sound is that?

Lucretia
Hark! No, it cannot be a servant's step;
270 It must be Cenci, unexpectedly
Returned — Make some excuse for being here.

258–62. impetuous torrent . . . Cedars,] The diction of these lines ('impetuous', 'Raging', 'caverns', 'chasm', 'Cedars') recalls the second verse paragraph of Coleridge, 'Kubla Khan: Or, A Vision in a Dream' in *Christabel: Kubla Khan, A Vision; The Pains of Sleep* (1816), esp. lines 12–13: 'But oh that deep romantic chasm which slanted / Down the green hill athwart a cedarn cover!' *an impetuous torrent / Raging*] Cp. Thomson, *Summer* 590–3: 'SMOOTH to the shelving Brink a copious Flood / Rolls fair, and placid; where collected all, / In one impetuous Torrent, down the Steep / It thundering shoots, and Shakes the Country round.'

260–5. and high above . . . blackest night.] Locock 1911 cps. *PU* II ii 1–6, *Scenes from the 'Magico Prodigioso' of Calderon* (see *1824* 372: 'These toppling rocks and tangled boughs, / Impenetrable by the noonday beam, / Shall be the sole witnesses of what we –'), and the description of the 'valley of Bethzatanai' in *The Assassins: A Fragment of a Romance* (1814–15): 'The immensity of those precipitous mountains with their starry pyramids of snow excluded the sun, which overtopped not even in its meridian their overhanging rocks.' (*Prose Works* i 127). Beatrice's evocation recalls both earlier confoundings of light and dark in *C* (e.g. II i 183) and the moral danger of wooded seclusion alluded to in *Fairie Queene* I i 7–9 and, by Adam, in *Paradise Lost* ix 1084–90: 'O might I here / In solitude live savage, in some glade / Obscured, where highest woods impenetrable / To star or sunlight, spread their umbrage broad / And brown as evening: cover me ye pines, / Ye cedars, with innumerable boughs / Hide me, where I may never see them more.'

262. Cedars, and yews, and pines;] Cp. *PU* II ii 2 and note, and the letter-journal to Peacock of 17 or 18 December 1818 about Rome: 'The gardens of the modern palaces are like wild woods of cedar & cypress & pine' (*L* ii 59). *tangled hair*] Cp. III i 45. This image is also applied to plants in *R&H* line 208.

268. A markedly ametrical line.

269ff. Cp. II i 18ff. and note.

Beatrice   [*To* Orsino, *as she goes out.*
That step we hear approach must never pass
The bridge of which we spoke.
                    [*Exeunt* Lucretia *and* Beatrice.

Orsino
                    What shall I do?
Cenci must find me here, and I must bear
275   The imperious inquisition of his looks
As to what brought me hither: let me mask
Mine own in some inane and vacant smile.

        Enter Giacomo, *in a hurried manner.*

How! Have you ventured hither? Know you then
That Cenci is from home?

Giacomo
                    I sought him here;
280   And now must wait till he returns.

Orsino
                    Great God!
Weigh you the danger of this rashness?

Giacomo
                            Aye!
Does my destroyer know his danger? We
Are now no more, as once, parent and child,
But man to man; the oppressor to the oppressed;
285   The slanderer to the slandered; foe to foe.
He has cast Nature off, which was his shield,
And Nature casts him off, who is her shame;
And I spurn both. Is it a father's throat
Which I will shake, and say, I ask not gold;
290   I ask not happy years; nor memories
Of tranquil childhood; nor home-sheltered love;
Though all these hast thou torn from me, and more;
But only my fair fame; only one hoard

278. *hither?*] thither? *Cenci* (1819).   *Know*] know *Cenci* (1819).
284. *the oppressor to the oppressed;*] Cp. V iii 75, and *Peter Bell the Third* line 253.
285. *foe to foe.*] foe to foe: *Cenci* (1819).
289. *shake,*] shake? 1839.
293. *fair*] I.e. 'unblemished' (cited in *OED*, 'fair' *a.* and *sb.* 9).

295   Of peace, which I thought hidden from thy hate,
Under the penury heaped on me by thee;
Or I will — God can understand and pardon,
Why should I speak with man?

Orsino
                        Be calm, dear friend.

Giacomo
Well, I will calmly tell you what he did.
This old Francesco Cenci, as you know,
300   Borrowed the dowry of my wife from me,
And then denied the loan; and left me so
In poverty, the which I sought to mend
By holding a poor office in the state.
It had been promised to me, and already
305   I bought new clothing for my ragged babes,
And my wife smiled; and my heart knew repose;
When Cenci's intercession, as I found,
Conferred this office on a wretch, whom thus
He paid for vilest service. I returned
310   With this ill news, and we sate sad together
Solacing our despondency with tears
Of such affection and unbroken faith
As temper life's worst bitterness; when he,
As he is wont, came to upbraid and curse,
315   Mocking our poverty, and telling us
Such was God's scourge for disobedient sons.
And then, that I might strike him dumb with shame,
I spoke of my wife's dowry; but he coined
A brief yet specious tale, how I had wasted
320   The sum in secret riot; and he saw
My wife was touched, and he went smiling forth.
And when I knew the impression he had made,
And felt my wife insult with silent scorn
My ardent truth, and look averse and cold,
325   I went forth too: but soon returned again;

295. thee;] thee, *Cenci (1819).*

306. repose;] repose. *Cenci (1819).*

318–20. but he coined . . . secret riot;] Cp. Jesus' parable of the Prodigal Son in *Luke* xv 13:
'And not many days after the younger son gathered all together, and took his journey into
a far country, and there wasted his substance with riotous living.'

321. he went smiling forth.] Cp. I i 64.

Yet not so soon but that my wife had taught
My children her harsh thoughts, and they all cried,
'Give us clothes, father! Give us better food!
What you in one night squander were enough
330   For months!' I looked, and saw that home was hell;
And to that hell will I return no more
Until mine enemy has rendered up
Atonement, or, as he gave life to me
I will, reversing nature's law —

Orsino

                     Trust me,
335   The compensation which thou seekest here
Will be denied.

Giacomo

            Then — Are you not my friend?
Did you not hint at the alternative,
Upon the brink of which you see I stand,
The other day when we conversed together?
340   My wrongs were then less. That word parricide,
Although I am resolved, haunts me like fear.

Orsino

It must be fear itself, for the bare word
Is hollow mockery. Mark, how wisest God
Draws to one point the threads of a just doom,
345   So sanctifying it: what you devise
Is, as it were, accomplished.

Giacomo

                  Is he dead?

Orsino

His grave is ready. Know that since we met
Cenci has done an outrage to his daughter.

328. See III ii 81–3 and note.

330. hell;] hell. *Cenci (1819).*

333. Cp. III i 215.

337–8. the alternative, / . . . I stand,] Orsino's effect on Giacomo here is telling in that it recalls both Beatrice's description of the abyss (III i 243ff.) and the terms of the Preface's assertion (in lines 89–94) that 'religion in Italy is not, as in Protestant countries . . . a gloomy passion for penetrating the impenetrable mysteries of our being, which terrifies its possessor at the darkness of the abyss to the brink of which it has conducted him.' Giacomo's 'self-anatomy' seems thus to take the form of a 'Protestant apprehension'.

Giacomo
What outrage?

Orsino
                    That she speaks not, but you may
350   Conceive such half conjectures as I do,
       From her fixed paleness, and the lofty grief
       Of her stern brow, bent on the idle air,
       And her severe unmodulated voice,
       Drowning both tenderness and dread; and last
355   From this; that whilst her step-mother and I,
       Bewildered in our horror, talked together
       With obscure hints; both self-misunderstood,
       And darkly guessing, stumbling, in our talk,
       Over the truth, and yet to its revenge,
360   She interrupted us, and with a look
       Which told before she spoke it, he must die: —

Giacomo
       It is enough. My doubts are well appeased;
       There is a higher reason for the act
       Than mine; there is a holier judge than me,
365   A more unblamed avenger. Beatrice,
       Who in the gentleness of thy sweet youth
       Hast never trodden on a worm, or bruised
       A living flower, but thou hast pitied it
       With needless tears! Fair sister, thou in whom
370   Men wondered how such loveliness and wisdom
       Did not destroy each other! Is there made
       Ravage of thee? O, heart, I ask no more
       Justification! Shall I wait, Orsino,
       Till he return, and stab him at the door?

Orsino
375   Not so; some accident might interpose
       To rescue him from what is now most sure;
       And you are unprovided where to fly,

351–2. lofty grief . . . stern brow,] Cp. 'brow superior' in II i 117 and note.

352. brow,] brow *Cenci (1819).*

354. last] I.e. 'lastly' (cited in *OED*, 'last' B *adv.* 3)

361. he must die: –] he must die . . . *Cenci (1819);* he must die. *1829;* he must die – *1839;* 'He must die' – *Rossetti (1870).* Cp. *Measure for Measure* II i 31: 'Sir, he must die.'

377. unprovided] i.e. 'unprepared' or 'unready' (cited in *OED*, 'unprovided' *ppl. a.* 2).

How to excuse or to conceal. Nay, listen:
All is contrived; success is so assured
380   That —

Enter Beatrice.

Beatrice
    'Tis my brother's voice! You know me not?

Giacomo
My sister, my lost sister!

Beatrice
    Lost indeed!
I see Orsino has talked with you, and
That you conjecture things too horrible
To speak, yet far less than the truth. Now, stay not,
385   He might return: yet kiss me; I shall know
That then thou hast consented to his death.
Farewell, farewell! Let piety to God,
Brotherly love, justice, and clemency,
And all things that make tender hardest hearts,
390   Make thine hard, brother. Answer not: farewell.

                           [Exeunt severally.

Scene ii

A mean Apartment in Giacomo's *House.* Giacomo *alone.*

Giacomo
'Tis midnight, and Orsino comes not yet.
                 [Thunder, and the sound of a storm.
What! can the everlasting elements
Feel with a worm like man? If so, the shaft
Of mercy-wingèd lightning would not fall
5   On stones and trees. My wife and children sleep:

---

381. *lost . . . Lost*] A word used of Beatrice throughout this scene (see III i 104, 176).
387. *Farewell, farewell!*] Farewell, Farewell! *Cenci (1819).*
388. *justice,*] justice *Cenci (1819).*
389–90. *And all things . . . Make thine hard, brother.*] Cp. note to I iii 175.
390. *not:*] not . . . *Cenci (1819)*; not – *1829.*

They are now living in unmeaning dreams:
But I must wake, still doubting if that deed
Be just, which was most necessary. O,
Thou unreplenished lamp! whose narrow fire
10   Is shaken by the wind, and on whose edge
Devouring darkness hovers! Thou small flame,
Which, as a dying pulse rises and falls,
Still flickerest up and down, how very soon,
Did I not feed thee, wouldst thou fail, and be
15   As thou hadst never been! So wastes and sinks
Even now, perhaps, the life that kindled mine:
But that no power can fill with vital oil
That broken lamp of flesh. Ha! 'tis the blood
Which fed these veins, that ebbs till all is cold:
20   It is the form that moulded mine, which sinks
Into the white and yellow spasms of death:
It is the soul by which mine was arrayed
In God's immortal likeness, which now stands
Naked before Heaven's judgement-seat!

                                         [*A bell strikes.*

---

8. *just,*] just *Cenci (1819).*

8–18. *O, / Thou unreplenished lamp! . . . That broken lamp of flesh.*] Cp. *Othello* V ii 7–15: 'Put out the light, and then put out the light. / If I quench thee, thou flaming minister, / I can again thy former light restore, / Should I repent me; but once put out thy light, / Thou cunning'st pattern of excelling nature, / I know not where is that Promethean heat / That can thy light relume. When I have pluck'd thy rose, / I cannot give it vital growth again; / It needs must wither.' *Locock 1911* cps. the scene entitled 'Nacht' in which Valentine dies in Goethe, *Faust*, Part I (1808): 'Wie von dem Fenster dort der Sakristei / Aufwärts der Schein des ew'gen Lämpchens flämmert / Und schwach und schwächer seitwärts dämmert, / Und Finsternis drängt ringsum bei! / So sieht's in meinem Busen nächtig.' (text from *Faust*, ed. Albrecht Schöne, in Goethe, *Sämtliche Werke* (Frankfurt am Main, 1994)) ('How, from the windows of yon sacristy, / The ever-lighted lamp its flickering ray / Shoots out, and then in darkness fades away, / With powers still weaken'd, 'till at last they die! – / So in my breast, round virtue's lessening light / Deep grow the shades of guilt, till all is night.' (trans. Lord Francis Leveson Gower (1823) 217). Cp. also Coleridge, *Remorse* (1813) I ii 'the lamp's red flame / Cower'd as it enter'd and at once sunk down.'

14. *fail,*] fail *Cenci (1819).*

17. *oil*] *Cenci (1819)*; oil, *Cenci (1821)*; oil, – *Woodberry 1893.* A crux. *Cenci (1819)* makes 'But' in line 17 equivalent to 'With this difference', *Cenci (1821)* to 'except' (and, thereby, 'that' in line 17 refers back to 'the life that kindled mine' in line 16). Although *Rossetti 1878* describes the pointing in *Cenci (1819)* as 'more energetic and impressive', *Forman 1876–7* is right to suggest that *Cenci (1819)* is 'the more characteristic' of S.

19. *veins,*] veins *Cenci (1819).*

20. *mine,*] mine *Cenci (1819).* *which*] *Taaffe;* that *Cenci (1819), Cenci (1821).*

21. Cp. 'Ode to the West Wind' line 4.

23. *likeness,*] likeness *Cenci (1819).*

One! Two!

25 The hours crawl on; and, when my hairs are white,
My son will then perhaps be waiting thus,
Tortured between just hate and vain remorse;
Chiding the tardy messenger of news
Like those which I expect. I almost wish
30 He be not dead, although my wrongs are great;
Yet — 'tis Orsino's step —

Enter Orsino.

Speak!

Orsino
I am come

To say he has escaped.

Giacomo
Escaped!

Orsino
And safe

Within Petrella. He passed by the spot
Appointed for the deed an hour too soon.

Giacomo
35 Are we the fools of such contingencies?
And do we waste in blind misgivings thus
The hours when we should act? Then wind and thunder,
Which seemed to howl his knell, is the loud laughter
With which Heaven mocks our weakness! I henceforth
40 Will ne'er repent of aught designed or done,
But my repentance.

Orsino
See, the lamp is out.

24. *One! Two!*] Cp. *Macbeth* V i 33–4: 'One; two; why, then 'tis time to do't.'

25. *white,*] white *Cenci (1819)*.

32. *To say he has escaped.*] Cp. *Macbeth* III iv 20: 'Fleance is 'scap'd'. The authority for the failure of the scheme to murder the Count discussed in III i may be found in *Relation* 18–19: 'But the affair did not succeed for as the [information of his *canc.*] banditti were not informed of his approach time enough Francesco arrived safe & sound at Petrella' (see *BSM* x 190–1).

40. *aught designed or done,*] *1839*; aught designed or done *Cenci (1819)*; aught, designed or done, *Cenci (1821)*.

Giacomo
If no remorse is ours when the dim air
Has drank this innocent flame, why should we quail
When Cenci's life, that light by which ill spirits
45   See the worst deeds they prompt, shall sink for ever?
No, I am hardened.

Orsino
                    Why, what need of this?
Who feared the pale intrusion of remorse
In a just deed? Although our first plan failed,
Doubt not but he will soon be laid to rest.
50   But light the lamp; let us not talk i' the dark.

Giacomo   [Lighting the lamp.
And yet, once quenched, I cannot thus relume
My father's life: do you not think his ghost
Might plead that argument with God?

Orsino
                              Once gone,
You cannot now recall your sister's peace;
55   Your own extinguished years of youth and hope;
Nor your wife's bitter words; nor all the taunts
Which, from the prosperous, weak misfortune takes;
Nor your dead mother; nor —

43. *drank*] drunk *Woodberry 1893*. The reading supplied by Woodberry is to be found in several nineteenth-century editions of S.'s works and derives from that given in John Ascham's two-volume pirated edition of S.'s *Works* of 1834 (discussed in the Introduction to Volume I of this edition, p. xvi).

45. *worst*] *Cenci (1819)*; worse *Cenci (1821)* (apparently a printer's error).

46. *I am hardened.*] Cp. III i 389–90.

48. *failed,*] failed *Cenci (1819)*.

51–60. *once quenched, . . . Must quench the life*] Cp. III ii 11–18 and note.

51. *yet, once quenched,*] yet once quenched *Cenci (1819)*.

53–8. *Once gone, . . . nor –*] Cp. *Hamlet* III i 68–76: 'There's the respect / That makes calamity of so long life; / For who would bear the whips and scorns of time, / Th'oppressor's wrong, the proud man's contumely, / The pangs of despis'd love, the law's delay, / The insolence of office, and the spurns / That patient merit of th'unworthy takes, / When he himself might his quietus make / With a bare bodkin?'

53. *gone,*] gone *Cenci (1819)*.

54. *recall*] i.e. 'bring back' (cited in *OED*, 'recall' *v.* 4 and used in this sense in *Paradise Lost* iv 94–5: 'how soon / Would highth recall high thoughts'). However a different sense, 'revoke' or 'undo' (see *OED* 5) appears to govern lines 56–7.

Giacomo

                      O, speak no more!
I am resolved, although this very hand
60   Must quench the life that animated it.

Orsino

There is no need of that. Listen: you know
Olimpio, the castellan of Petrella
In old Colonna's time; him whom your father
Degraded from his post? And Marzio,
65   That desperate wretch, whom he deprived last year
Of a reward of blood, well earned and due?

Giacomo

I knew Olimpio; and they say he hated
Old Cenci so, that in his silent rage
His lips grew white only to see him pass.
70   Of Marzio I know nothing.

Orsino

                  Marzio's hate
Matches Olimpio's. I have sent these men,
But in your name, and as at your request,
To talk with Beatrice and Lucretia.

61. know] *Cenci* (1819); know, *Cenci* (1821).

62-4. Olimpio, the castellan . . . Degraded from his post?] Cp. *Relation* 16–17: 'The appartments of Monsignore Guerra was the place in which the circumstances of the crime about to be committed [was *canc.*] were concerted & determined on – Here Giacomo with the understanding of his sister & mother in law held various consultations & finally resolved to commit the murder of Francesco to two of his vassals who had become his inveterate enemies one called Marzio & the other Olympio – the latter by means of Francesco had been deprived of his post [and *canc.*] as Castelan of the Rock of Petrella' (see *BSM* x 188–9). S. follows the sequence of events described in *Relation* in which Marzio and Olympio are charged with organising both plans for the murder, the first of which was unsuccessful (see III ii 32 and note) but makes Orsino rather than Giacomo the instigator of the means (see III ii 72 and note). Orsino began to explain the role of Marzio and Olimpio to Beatrice at III i 233.

62. castellan] 'The governor or constable of a castle' (*OED*).

63. In old Colonna's time;] See note to I iii 126. Petrella was part of the Colonna family's estate as is noted in *Relation* 17–18: 'It was already well known that Francesco with the permission of Sig. Marzio di Colonna, Baron of that feud, had resolved to retire to Petrella & to pass the summer there with his family –' (see *BSM* x 188–91). 'Feud' means 'estate' (see *OED*, 'fee' *sb.* 3).

64. Degraded] See *OED* 'degrade' v. 2a: 'To depose (a person) formally from his . . . position of honour as an act of punishment'. See *J&M* line 184 and note.

66. reward of blood,] An obscure expression but the sense seems to be 'money or goods paid in return for committing a murder' (i.e. 'blood-money').

72. Note Orsino's careful dissociation of himself from the murder, and his implication of Giacomo as instrumental in it.

Giacomo
Only to talk?

Orsino
                    The moments which even now
75 Pass onward to tomorrow's midnight hour
    May memorize their flight with death: ere then
    They must have talked, and may perhaps have done,
    And made an end —

Giacomo
                    Listen! What sound is that?

Orsino
    The house-dog moans, and the beams crack: nought else.

Giacomo
80 It is my wife complaining in her sleep:
    I doubt not she is saying bitter things
    Of me; and all my children round her dreaming
    That I deny them sustenance.

Orsino
                    Whilst he
    Who truly took it from them, and who fills
85 Their hungry rest with bitterness, now sleeps
    Lapped in bad pleasures, and triumphantly
    Mocks thee in visions of successful hate
    Too like the truth of day.

Giacomo
                    If e'er he wakes
    Again, I will not trust to hireling hands —

---

76. *memorize*] 'cause to be remembered' (see *OED*, 'memorize' v. 1; used in this sense in *Macbeth* I ii 40–1: 'Except they meant to bathe in reeking wounds, / Or memorize another Golgotha'.)

77–9. *have done, . . . nought else.*] Cp. the exchange between Macbeth and Lady Macbeth in *Macbeth* II ii 14–15: 'I have done the deed. Didst thou not hear a noise?' / 'I heard the owl scream and the crickets cry.'

81–3. *I doubt not . . . sustenance.*] Ralph Pite, *The Circle of Our Vision* (1994) 164n. comments: 'Giacomo's alienation from his family recalls Ugolino'. See note to I iii 102–4.

Orsino

90 Why, that were well. I must be gone; good night!
When next we meet may all be done —

Giacomo

And all

Forgotten — Oh, that I had never been!

[*Exeunt.*

End of the Third Act

90–2. *Errata*; *Ors.* Why, that were well. I must be gone; good night! / When next we meet
. . . *Giac.* May all be done – and all / Forgotten – Oh, that I had never been! *Cenci (1819)*;
Ors. Why, that were well. I must be gone; good night: / When next we meet may all be done!
Giac. And all / Forgotten: Oh, that I had never been! *Cenci (1821)*. A crux. In *Forman 1876–7*
Forman comments that the reading in *Cenci (1819)* 'seems to me a much more likely way
for Shelley to have left the text: it is quite in the subtle vein of Orsino to elicit such a wish
from Giacomo rather than express it himself.' But his opinion is contradicted both by *Errata*,
and by *Taaffe* which instructs that 'May all be done' be spoken by Orsino. *Forman 1892* acknowl-
edges the substantive changes recommended in *Errata* but does not follow its punctuation.

ACT IV

Scene i

An Apartment in the Castle of Petrella. Enter Cenci.

Cenci
She comes not; yet I left her even now
Vanquished and faint. She knows the penalty
Of her delay: yet what if threats are vain?
Am I not now within Petrella's moat?
5   Or fear I still the eyes and ears of Rome?
Might I not drag her by the golden hair?
Stamp on her? Keep her sleepless till her brain
Be overworn? Tame her with chains and famine?
Less would suffice. Yet so to leave undone
10   What I most seek! No, 'tis her stubborn will,
Which, by its own consent, shall stoop as low
As that which drags it down.

Enter Lucretia.

                  Thou loathèd wretch!
Hide thee from my abhorrence; fly, begone!
Yet stay! Bid Beatrice come hither.

Lucretia
                  Oh,
15   Husband! I pray, for thine own wretched sake,
Heed what thou dost. A man who walks like thee
Through crimes, and through the danger of his crimes,
Each hour may stumble o'er a sudden grave.
And thou art old; thy hairs are hoary grey;
20   As thou wouldst save thyself from death and hell,
Pity thy daughter; give her to some friend

4–5. Petrella, in the Kingdom of Naples, would not have come under the jurisdiction of the Court of Rome as is made clear in *Relation* 26.

4. *not now*] now not *Cenci (1819)*.

5. Cp. II i 178.

6. *drag her by the golden hair*] On Beatrice's golden hair, see Preface line 142 and note. One of the Judges during her trial ordered that Beatrice be subject to 'the torture of the hair' according to *Relation* 35. Cp. III i 44–5 and IV i 30.

8. *Tame her with chains and famine?*] See notes to I iii 102–4 and III i 46–50.

In marriage: so that she may tempt thee not
To hatred, or worse thoughts, if worse there be.

Cenci
What! like her sister who has found a home
25   To mock my hate from with prosperity?
Strange ruin shall destroy both her and thee
And all that yet remain. My death may be
Rapid, her destiny outspeeds it. Go,
Bid her come hither, and before my mood
30   Be changed, lest I should drag her by the hair.

Lucretia
She sent me to thee, husband. At thy presence
She fell, as thou dost know, into a trance;
And in that trance she heard a voice which said,
'Cenci must die! Let him confess himself!
35   Even now the accusing angel waits to hear
If God, to punish his enormous crimes,
Harden his dying heart!'

Cenci
                                    Why — such things are:
No doubt divine revealings may be made.
'Tis plain I have been favoured from above,
40   For when I cursed my sons they died — Aye — so —
As to the right or wrong, that's talk — repentance —
Repentance is an easy moment's work,
And more depends on God than me. Well — well —

24-5. See I ii 69-70 and note. 'If this is the sister whom Cenci bestowed on a poor relation of his sixth cousin, the use of the word "prosperity" is rather strange. Possibly it may be equivalent to "impunity"' (*Locock 1911*). *Lat.* 'prosperitas' means 'good fortune' as well as 'success' so Locock's surmise is tenable.

34. Cp. Preface lines 104-10. Lucretia's obsession with religious observance in this scene and the next (IV ii 12) is manifest in a different form in *Relation* 21 which states that Marzio and Olympio 'were secretly admitted into the Castle the 8ᵗʰ of September 1598; but because this day was the anniversary of the birth of the Blessed Virgin – the Sigᵃ Lucretia held by [a *canc.*] her veneration for so holy a time desired with the consent of her daughter-in-law that the execution of the murder should be put off untill the following day' (see *BSM* x 194-5).

35. angel] Angel *Cenci (1819)*.

36. enormous] i.e. 'excessively wicked' (see *OED*, 'enormous' *a.* 2). John Carey's gloss of Milton's usage in his 1968 edn of *Paradise Lost* (v 297, 'Wild above rule or art; enormous bliss') is instructive: '"deviating from ordinary rule" (Lat. *norma*); but probably influenced also by the modern meaning "immense".' Cp. 'enormous deeds' (used to describe Julius Caesar's crimes) in 'On Christianity' (*Prose Works* i 254).

41. wrong,] 1829; wrong *Cenci (1821)*; *Cenci (1819)*.

I must give up the greater point, which was
45   To poison and corrupt her soul.

                         [A pause; Lucretia *approaches anxiously, and then shrinks*
                                               back as he speaks.

                          One, two;
Aye — Rocco and Cristofano my curse
Strangled: and Giacomo, I think, will find
Life a worse Hell than that beyond the grave:
Beatrice shall, if there be skill in hate,
50   Die in despair, blaspheming: to Bernardo,
He is so innocent, I will bequeath
The memory of these deeds, and make his youth
The sepulchre of hope, where evil thoughts
Shall grow like weeds on a neglected tomb.
55   When all is done, out in the wide Campagna
I will pile up my silver and my gold;
My costly robes, paintings, and tapestries;
My parchments and all records of my wealth;
And make a bonfire in my joy, and leave
60   Of my possessions nothing but my name;
Which shall be an inheritance to strip
Its wearer bare as infamy. That done,
My soul, which is a scourge, will I resign
Into the hands of him who wielded it;
65   Be it for its own punishment or theirs,
He will not ask it of me till the lash
Be broken in its last and deepest wound;
Until its hate be all inflicted. Yet,
Lest death outspeed my purpose, let me make
70   Short work and sure —   *[Going.*

Lucretia   *[Stops him.*
                     Oh, stay! It was a feint:
She had no vision, and she heard no voice.
I said it but to awe thee.

---

55. *the wide Campagna*] the wide Campagna, *Cenci (1819)*; i.e. the 'Campagna di Roma', the flat area to the south east of the Tiber. 'Campagnia' derives from the Latin word 'campania' meaning 'plain and level country' hence 'wide'. On its barren and unhealthy environment, see *Eustace* iii 241–57.

59. *And make a bonfire in my joy,*] Cp. 'the feelings of revenge and hatred' which make the Creature set fire to De Lacey's cottage in *Frankenstein* (1818) vol. ii ch. viii: 'I lighted the dry branch of a tree, and danced with fury around the devoted cottage' (*MSW* i 103–4).

64. *him*] Him *Woodberry 1893.*

Cenci

                    That is well.
Vile palterer with the sacred truth of God,
Be thy soul choked with that blaspheming lie!
75   For Beatrice, worse terrors are in store,
To bend her to my will.

Lucretia

                    Oh! to what will?
What cruel sufferings, more than she has known,
Canst thou inflict?

Cenci

                    Andrea! Go call my daughter,
And if she comes not, tell her that I come.
80   What sufferings? I will drag her, step by step,
Through infamies unheard of among men:
She shall stand shelterless in the broad noon
Of public scorn, for acts blazoned abroad,
One among which shall be — What? Canst thou guess?
85   She shall become (for what she most abhors
Shall have a fascination to entrap
Her loathing will) to her own conscious self
All she appears to others; and when dead,
As she shall die unshrived and unforgiven,
90   A rebel to her father and her God,
Her corpse shall be abandoned to the hounds;
Her name shall be the terror of the earth;
Her spirit shall approach the throne of God

---

79. not,] *1829*; not *Cenci (1819)*, *Cenci (1821)*.

85–8. She shall become . . . to others;] Cp. IV i 148 and note. Michael O'Neill, *The Human Mind's Imaginings: Conflict and Achievement in Shelley's Poetry* (1989) 82 cps. Byron, *Manfred, A Dramatic Poem* (1817) Act II scene ii: 'But I can act even what I most abhor, / And champion human fears. –'.

87. her own conscious self] Cp. I i 73 and note.

89–91. Cp. Antigone on Creon's treatment of Polyneices's corpse in Sophocles, *Antigone* 29–30: ἐὰν δ᾽ ἄκλαυτον, ἄταφον, οἰωνοῖς γλυκὺν / θησαυρὸν εἰσορῶσι πρὸς χάριν βορᾶς. ('they should leave it unwept for, unburied, a rich treasure house for birds as they look out for food' (Loeb trans.)) and 1197–8: ἔκειτο νηλεὲς / κυνοσπάρακτον σῶμα Πολυνείκους ἔτι ('the unpitied corpse of Polynices still lay, torn by the dogs.' (Loeb trans.)). Cp. also 2 *Kings* ix 10: 'And the dogs shall eat Jezebel in the portion of Jezreel, and there shall be none to bury her. And he opened the door and fled.'

89. die] die, *Locock 1911*.

92. the terror of the earth;] Cp. *PU* III i 19 and note.

95 Plague-spotted with my curses. I will make
Body and soul a monstrous lump of ruin.

Enter Andrea.

Andrea
The Lady Beatrice —

Cenci
                              Speak, pale slave! What
Said she?

Andrea
          My Lord, 'twas what she looked; she said:
'Go tell my father that I see the gulf
Of Hell between us two, which he may pass,
100 I will not.'

                                        [*Exit* Andrea.

Cenci
               Go thou quick, Lucretia,
Tell her to come; yet let her understand
Her coming is consent; and say, moreover,
That if she come not I will curse her.

                                        [*Exit* Lucretia.
                              Ha!
With what but with a father's curse doth God
105 Panic-strike armèd victory, and make pale
Cities in their prosperity? The world's Father
Must grant a parent's prayer against his child,

---

95. *monstrous lump of ruin.*] Incest is referred to as a 'monstrous curse' in *R&H* line 157, although the context is ironical (see note to *R&H* line 155). Cp. Byron, 'Darkness' in *The Prisoner of Chillon, and Other Poems* (1816) lines 69–72: 'The world was void, / The populous and the powerful was a lump, / Seasonless, herbless, treeless, manless, lifeless – / A lump of death – a chaos of hard clay.'

96. *Lady*] *Rossetti 1870*; lady *Cenci (1819)*, *Cenci (1821)*.

97. *looked; she*] *Cenci (1819)*; looked she *Cenci (1821)*; looked. She *Rossetti 1870*.

98–9. Cp. *Luke* xvi 26: 'And beside all this, between us and you there is a great gulf fixed: so that they which would pass from hence to you cannot; neither can they pass to us, that would come from thence.'

99. *he*] *he Rossetti 1870*.

102. *consent;*] consent: *Cenci (1819)*.

105. *armèd*] *Rossetti 1870*; armed *Cenci (1819)*, *Cenci (1821)*. Rossetti's reading is metrically correct.

Be he who asks even what men call me.
Will not the deaths of her rebellious brothers
110   Awe her before I speak? For I on them
Did imprecate quick ruin, and it came.

                Enter Lucretia.

Well; what? Speak, wretch!

Lucretia
            She said, 'I cannot come;
Go tell my father that I see a torrent
Of his own blood raging between us.'

Cenci   *[Kneeling.*
            God!
115   Hear me! If this most specious mass of flesh,
Which thou hast made my daughter; this my blood,
This particle of my divided being;
Or rather, this my bane and my disease,
Whose sight infects and poisons me; this devil
120   Which sprung from me as from a hell, was meant
To aught good use; if her bright loveliness
Was kindled to illumine this dark world;
If, nursed by thy selectest dew of love,
Such virtues blossom in her as should make

---

114. blood] See III i 2 and note.

114–67. Cenci's curse of Beatrice builds upon both the earlier curse of his sons and the wider sense of a father's curse, as in Sophocles' Theban Trilogy, fulfilling the divinely ordained destruction of a family (see note to I iii 41–4). It also echoes other set-piece curses in S.'s works (e.g. of Lord Eldon in no. 131, 'To the [Lord Chancellor]' and *PU* I 262ff.) Cp. *Lear* I iv 275–89 (esp. IV i 141ff. with I iv 281–9: 'If she must teem, / Create her child of spleen, that it may live / And be a thwart disnatur'd torment to her. / Let it stamp wrinkles in her brow of youth, / With cadent tears fret channels in her cheeks, / Turn all her mother's pains and benefits / To laughter and contempt, that she may feel / How sharper than a serpent's tooth it is / To have a thankless child.'), I iv 299–301 ('Blasts and fogs upon thee! / Th'untented woundings of a father's curse / Pierce every sense about thee! –'), and II iv 160–2 ('All the stor'd vengeances of heaven fall / On her ingrateful top! Strike her young bones, / You taking airs, with lameness'). See S.'s comment in a letter to Medwin of 20 July 1820: 'As to Cenci's curse – I know not whether I can defend it or no. I wish I may be able, since, as it often happens respecting the worst part of an author's work, it is a particular favourite with me.' (*L* ii 219).

119. Whose sight infects and poisons me;] One of several images of the basilisk in *C* (cp. e.g. IV iv 174–5). βασιλίσκος (Gk. 'Basiliskos', 'little king') is a kind of goldcrested serpent whose breath or gaze is fatal. Cp. *PU* III iv 148.

123. If,] *1829*; If *Cenci (1819), Cenci (1821). love,*] *1829*; love *Cenci (1819), Cenci (1821).*

125 The peace of life, I pray thee, for my sake,
As thou the common God and Father art
Of her, and me, and all; reverse that doom!
Earth, in the name of God, let her food be
Poison, until she be encrusted round
130 With leprous stains! Heaven, rain upon her head
The blistering drops of the Maremma's dew,
Till she be speckled like a toad; parch up
Those love-enkindled lips, warp those fine limbs
To loathèd lameness! All-beholding sun,
135 Strike in thine envy those life-darting eyes
With thine own blinding beams!

Lucretia
                              Peace! Peace!
For thine own sake unsay those dreadful words.
When high God grants, he punishes such prayers.

Cenci   [*Leaping up, and throwing his right hand towards Heaven.*
He does his will, I mine! This in addition,
140 That if she have a child —

Lucretia
                              Horrible thought!

Cenci
That if she ever have a child — and thou,
Quick Nature! I adjure thee by thy God,

125. *thee,*] thee *Cenci (1819).*

128–34. *Earth . . . lameness!*] Cp. *PU* III i 40–1 and note.

131. *Maremma's dew,*] The Maremma, a corruption of 'Marittima' (meaning 'situated on the sea'), a marshy region on the Tuscan coast stretching from the south of Livorno to Orbetello, was renowned for its noxious, malarial atmosphere. It is the location of no. 166, 'Mazenghi'.

134. Cp. II i 174 and note.

136. A line of four feet. However, there is no basis for Rossetti's conjecture that 'Perhaps we ought to read – "Peace, *husband!* peace!" ' (*Rossetti 1870*).

137. *unsay*] Cp. the use of this verb, meaning 'to retract', in the Preface to *PU*.

139. *He does his will, I mine!*] *Baker* 151 cps. usefully Cenci's *hubris* and ensuing demise with Jupiter's in *PU* III i.

140. *That if she have a child –*] The 'Note on The Cenci. By The Editor' in *1840* 159 contains the following footnote (not in *1839*): 'In speaking of his mode of treating this main incident, Shelley said that it might be remarked that, in the course of the play, he had never mentioned expressly Cenci's worst crime. Every one knew what it must be, but it was never imaged in words – the nearest allusion to it being that portion of Cenci's curse, beginning, "That if she have a child," &c.'

141. *child –*] *Woodberry 1893*; child; child; *Cenci (1819), Cenci (1821)*; child, – *Rossetti 1870*; child; – *Locock 1911.*

That thou be fruitful in her, and increase
And multiply, fulfilling his command,
145 And my deep imprecation! — may it be
A hideous likeness of herself; that, as
From a distorting mirror, she may see
Her image mixed with what she most abhors,
Smiling upon her from her nursing breast.
150 And that the child may from its infancy
Grow, day by day, more wicked and deformed,
Turning her mother's love to misery:
And that both she and it may live, until
It shall repay her care and pain with hate,
155 Or what may else be more unnatural, —
So he may hunt her through the clamorous scoffs

145. imprecation! – may] *Woodberry 1893*; imprecation! May *Cenci (1819), Cenci (1821);* imprecation, – may *Rossetti 1870*; imprecation! – May *Woodberry (1909).*

145–9. may it be . . . breast.] Cp. 'On Love' (July 1818): 'We dimly see within our intellectual nature a miniature as it were of our entire self, yet deprived of all that we condemn or despise, the ideal prototype of every thing excellent or lovely that we are capable of conceiving as belonging to the nature of man. Not only the portrait of our external being but an assemblage of the minutest particles of which our nature is composed; a mirror whose surface reflects only the forms of purity and brightness; a soul within our soul that describes a circle around its proper paradise which pain, and sorrow, and evil dare not overleap.' (*Prose* 170). Milton Wilson, *Shelley's Later Poetry: A Study of His Prophetic Imagination* (1959) 85 cps. III i 108–11.

147. a distorting mirror,] Cp. *PU* IV 382–3.

148. most abhors,] Cp. IV i 85 and note. Curran in *Curran (1970)* 137–8, and in Stuart Curran and Joseph Anthony Wittreich, Jr., 'The Dating of Shelley's "On the Devil, and Devils"', *KSJ* xxi–xxii (1972–73) 83–94 (89–90)) cps. 'On the Devil and Devils' (?1820): 'the benevolent and amiable disposition which distinguished his adversary furnished God with the true method of executing an enduring and a terrible vengeance. He turned his good into evil, and, by virtue of his omnipotence, inspired him with such impulses as, in spite of his better nature, irresistibly determined him to act what he most abhorred and to be a minister of those designs and schemes of which he was the chief and the original victim' (*Prose* 270).

154–5. The relationship between love and hate fascinated S.; see note to Dedication, and S.'s gloss to Mercury's 'Unnatural love, and more unnatural hate' (*PU* I 349) in *Nbk 7*, f. 38ʳ: 'The contrast would have been completeter if the sentiment had been transposed: but wherefore sacrifize the philosophical truth, that love however monstrous in its expression is still less worthy of horror than hatred – [the *canc.*] perhaps in whatever degree' (see *BSM* ix 154–5).

155. unnatural, –] *Locock 1911*; unnatural. *Cenci (1819), Cenci (1821);* unnatural, *1829;* unnatural – *Rossetti 1870*; unnatural; *Woodberry 1893.* '[I]t seems likely that "So" [in line 156] stands for "So that," and, if so, that the full stop is wrong' (*Locock 1911*).

156–7. There is a vampiric suggestion in the idea that the child will consume his mother. Cp. Byron, *The Giaour, A Fragment Of a Turkish Tale*, 7th edn (1813) lines 755–66: 'But first, on earth as Vampire sent, / Thy corse shall from its tomb be rent; / Then ghastly haunt thy native place, / And suck the blood of all thy race, / There from thy daughter, sister, wife, / At midnight drain the stream of life; / Yet loathe the banquet which perforce / Must feed thy livid living corse; / Thy victims ere they yet expire / Shall know the dæmon for their sire, / As cursing thee, thou cursing them, / Thy flowers are wither'd on the stem.' Cp. I iii 176–7 and note.

Of the loud world to a dishonoured grave.
Shall I revoke this curse? Go, bid her come,
Before my words are chronicled in heaven.

[*Exit* Lucretia.

160   I do not feel as if I were a man,
But like a fiend appointed to chastise
The offences of some unremembered world.
My blood is running up and down my veins;
A fearful pleasure makes it prick and tingle:
165   I feel a giddy sickness of strange awe;
My heart is beating with an expectation
Of horrid joy.

Enter Lucretia.

What? Speak!

Lucretia
She bids thee curse;
And if thy curses, as they cannot do,
Could kill her soul —

Cenci
She would not come. 'Tis well,
170   I can do both: first take what I demand,
And then extort concession. To thy chamber!
Fly ere I spurn thee: and beware this night
That thou cross not my footsteps. It were safer
To come between the tiger and his prey.

[*Exit* Lucretia.

175   It must be late; mine eyes grow weary dim
With unaccustomed heaviness of sleep.
Conscience! Oh, thou most insolent of lies!

---

162. *some unremembered world.*] *Notopoulos* 263 suggests this is an allusion to Plato's doctrine of the pre-existence of the soul in *Phaedo* 72e–77a and *Meno* 81ff.

163. Cp. IV iii 44.

173–4. *It were safer . . . the tiger and his prey.*] Cp. *Lear* I i 121: 'Come not between the dragon and his wrath.'

175–6. The opiate referred to as having been administered by Lucretia (see IV ii 30) begins to take effect. Cp. *Relation* 21–2: 'They [i.e. Beatrice and Lucretia] dexterously mixed opium with the drink of Francesco who upon going to bed was soon oppressed by a deep sleep' (see *BSM* x 194–7).

175. *weary dim*] weary, dim *Rossetti 1878*.

      They say that sleep, that healing dew of heaven,
      Steeps not in balm the foldings of the brain
180   Which thinks thee an impostor. I will go,
      First to belie thee with an hour of rest,
      Which will be deep and calm, I feel: and then —
      O, multitudinous Hell, the fiends will shake
      Thine arches with the laughter of their joy!
185   There shall be lamentation heard in Heaven
      As o'er an angel fallen; and upon Earth
      All good shall droop and sicken, and ill things
      Shall, with a spirit of unnatural life,
      Stir and be quickened — even as I am now.

                                             [Exit.

Scene ii

Before the Castle of Petrella. Enter Beatrice *and* Lucretia *above on the Ramparts.*

    Beatrice
    They come not yet.

    Lucretia

                   'Tis scarce midnight.

    Beatrice

                         How slow
    Behind the course of thought, even sick with speed,
    Lags leaden-footed time!

178. sleep, that healing dew of heaven,] Cp. *Paradise Lost* iv 614: 'the timely dew of sleep'.

179. foldings] Glossed by Locock as 'convolutions' (*Locock 1911*).

183. multitudinous] Cp. *PU* I line 5.

186. Earth] earth *Rossetti 1870*.

187–9. All good shall droop . . . as I am now.] Cp. *Macbeth* III ii 52–5: 'Good things of day begin to droop and drowse, / Whiles night's black agents to their preys do rouse. / Thou marvell'st at my words; but hold thee still: / Things bad begun make strong themselves by ill.'

189. quickened –] *1839*; quickened . . . *Cenci (1819)*; quickened; *Cenci (1821)*; quicken'd – *1829*.

¶ii *1.* The almost identical opening of this and the previous two scenes is noted in *Julian* ii 418. *'Tis scarce midnight.*] This time is specified in *Relation* 22 though the location of Beatrice and Lucretia is different: 'About midnight his daughter herself led the two assassins into the appartment of her father & left [that *canc.*] them there that they might [excu *canc.*] execute the deed they had undertaken, and retired to a chamber close by where Lucretia remained also expecting the return of the murderers & the relation of their success' (see *BSM* x 196–7).

3. leaden-footed time!] leaden-footed Time! *Rossetti 1870*. Cp. *All's Well That Ends Well* V iii 41: 'Th' inaudible and noiseless foot of Time'.

Lucretia

The minutes pass —
If he should wake before the deed is done?

Beatrice

5   O, mother! he must never wake again.
What thou hast said persuades me that our act
Will but dislodge a spirit of deep hell
Out of a human form.

Lucretia

'Tis true he spoke
Of death and judgement with strange confidence
10   For one so wicked; as a man believing
In God, yet recking not of good or ill.
And yet to die without confession!

Beatrice

Oh!
Believe that Heaven is merciful and just,
And will not add our dread necessity
15   To the amount of his offences.

Enter Olimpio *and* Marzio *below.*

Lucretia

See,
They come.

Beatrice

All mortal things must hasten thus
To their dark end. Let us go down.

[*Exeunt* Lucretia *and* Beatrice *from above.*

Olimpio
How feel you to this work?

12–15. Cp. IV i 34 and note. *Webb* 382 cps. *Hamlet* III iii 80–96: "A took my father grossly, full of bread, / With all his crimes broad blown, as flush as May; / And how his audit stands who knows save heaven? / But in our circumstance and course of thought / 'Tis heavy with him; and am I then reveng'd / To take him in the purging of his soul, / When he is fit and season'd for his passage?'

17. This line is a foot short.

Marzio

As one who thinks
A thousand crowns excellent market-price
20 For an old murderer's life. Your cheeks are pale.

Olimpio
It is the white reflection of your own,
Which you call pale.

Marzio

Is that their natural hue?

Olimpio
Or 'tis my hate, and the deferred desire
To wreak it, which extinguishes their blood.

Marzio
25 You are inclined then to this business?

Olimpio

Aye,
If one should bribe me with a thousand crowns
To kill a serpent which had stung my child,
I could not be more willing.

Enter Beatrice *and* Lucretia *below.*

Noble ladies!

Beatrice
Are ye resolved?

Olimpio

Is he asleep?

Marzio

Is all
30 Quiet?

Lucretia

I mixed an opiate with his drink:
He sleeps so soundly —

Beatrice

That his death will be
But as a change of sin-chastising dreams,

A dark continuance of the Hell within him,
Which God extinguish! But ye are resolved?
35   Ye know it is a high and holy deed?

Olimpio
We are resolved.

Marzio
                 As to the how this act
Be warranted, it rests with you.

Beatrice
                              Well, follow!

Olimpio
Hush! Hark! What noise is that?

Marzio
                     Ha! some one comes!

Beatrice
Ye conscience-stricken cravens, rock to rest
40   Your baby hearts. It is the iron gate,
Which ye left open, swinging to the wind,
That enters whistling as in scorn. Come, follow!
And be your steps like mine, light, quick, and bold.
                              [*Exeunt.*

Scene iii

An Apartment in the Castle. Enter Beatrice *and* Lucretia.

Lucretia
They are about it now.

---

33. *the Hell within him,*] Cp. *Paradise Lost* iv 18–23: 'horror and doubt distract / His troubled thoughts, and from the bottom stir / The hell within him, for within him hell / He brings, and round about him, nor from hell / One step no more than from himself can fly / By change of place'.

¶iii   *1–35.* This exchange follows closely the language of *Relation* 22–3 and, as such, does not derive exclusively from *Macbeth* II i 1–18: 'Soon after the Assassins entered and told the ladies that pity had held them back and that they could not overcome their repugnance to kill in cold blood a poor sleeping old man. These words filled Beatrice with anger and after having bitterly reviled them as cowards & traitors she exclaimed – since you have not courage

Beatrice

Nay, it is done.

Lucretia
I have not heard him groan.

Beatrice

He will not groan.

Lucretia
What sound is that?

Beatrice

List! 'tis the tread of feet
About his bed.

Lucretia
My God!
5   If he be now a cold stiff corpse.

Beatrice

O, fear not
What may be done, but what is left undone:
The act seals all.

Enter Olimpio *and* Marzio.

Is it accomplished?

Marzio

What?

Olimpio
Did you not call?

_____

enough to [kill *canc.*] murder a sleeping man. I will kill my father myself but your lives shall
not be long secure – The assassins hearing this short but terrible threat feared that if they
did not commit the deed the [n *canc.*] tempest would burst over their own heads – took courage
& reentered the chamber where Francesco slept' (see *BSM* x 196–7).

3–5. A series of ametrical lines.

5. *cold*] cold, *Woodberry 1893.*

8. This line is three syllables too long. Cp. *Macbeth* II ii 16: 'Did not you speak?' 'When?'
'Now.' *over?*] over. *Rossetti 1870*

Beatrice

When?

Olimpio

Now.

Beatrice

I ask if all is over?

Olimpio
We dare not kill an old and sleeping man;
10   His thin grey hair, his stern and reverent brow,
His veinèd hands crossed on his heaving breast,
And the calm innocent sleep in which he lay,
Quelled me. Indeed, indeed, I cannot do it.

Marzio
But I was bolder; for I chid Olimpio,
15   And bade him bear his wrongs to his own grave
And leave me the reward. And now my knife
Touched the loose wrinkled throat, when the old man
Stirred in his sleep, and said, 'God! hear, O, hear
A father's curse! What, art thou not our father?'
20   And then he laughed. I knew it was the ghost
Of my dead father speaking through his lips,
And could not kill him.

Beatrice

Miserable slaves!
Where, if ye dare not kill a sleeping man,
Found ye the boldness to return to me
25   With such a deed undone? Base palterers!
Cowards and traitors! Why, the very conscience
Which ye would sell for gold and for revenge
Is an equivocation: it sleeps over
A thousand daily acts disgracing men;

---

10. *reverent*] reverend *Hutchinson, Locock 1911.*

11. *veinèd*] *Forman 1876–7*; veined *Cenci (1819), Cenci (1821).* Forman's reading allows for the pentameter to be fully observed.

15. *his wrongs*] Cp. III ii 63–4.

16. *me*] *me Rossetti 1870.*

19. *What, art*] *1829*; What art *Cenci (1819), Cenci (1821).*

30 And when a deed where mercy insults heaven —
Why do I talk?

[Snatching a dagger from one of them and raising it.
Hadst thou a tongue to say,
She murdered her own father, I must do it!
But never dream ye shall outlive him long!

Olimpio
Stop, for God's sake!

Marzio

I will go back and kill him.

Olimpio
35 Give me the weapon, we must do thy will.

Beatrice
Take it! Depart! Return!

[Exeunt Olimpio *and* Marzio.
How pale thou art!
We do but that which 'twere a deadly crime
To leave undone.

Lucretia

Would it were done!

Beatrice

Even whilst
That doubt is passing through your mind, the world
40 Is conscious of a change. Darkness and hell
Have swallowed up the vapour they sent forth
To blacken the sweet light of life. My breath

---

31. *Hadst thou a tongue*] Beatrice addresses the dagger.

32. *She murdered her own father,*] 'She murdered her own father,' *Rossetti 1870.*

33. *ye*] ye *Rossetti 1870.*

37. *deadly crime*] The sense seems to be 'mortal sin' (see *OED*, 'deadly' a 5).

39–40. *the world / Is conscious of a change.*] Cp. *PU* II v 16–20 and *PU* III iv 70–1.

40–2. *Darkness and hell . . . light of life.*] Cp. the pestilential imagery of III i 14–23.

42. *light of life.*] Cp. *John* viii 12: 'Then spake Jesus again unto them, saying, I am the light of the world: he that followeth me shall not walk in darkness, but shall have the light of life.' Cp. *PU* III iii 6.

Comes, methinks, lighter, and the jellied blood
Runs freely through my veins. Hark!

Enter Olimpio *and* Marzio.

He is —

Olimpio

Dead!

Marzio
45   We strangled him that there might be no blood;
And then we threw his heavy corpse i' the garden
Under the balcony; 'twill seem it fell.

---

43. jellied] *1829, Rossetti 1878*; gellyed *Cenci (1819)*; gellied *Cenci (1821)*; gelid *Rossetti 1870*.
Rossetti's first edition states 'it is impossible to determine whether Shelley really meant "gelid,"
frozen, or "jellied," coagulated. As I think "gelid" the preferable word, I give that' (*Rossetti
1870*). But the context suggests clearly that S. intended Beatrice to say that her blood is now
flowing freely having been 'jellied' (i.e. congealed), as Rossetti acknowledges in his second
edition. Forman is rightly dubious of the *Rossetti 1870* reading on other grounds: 'The fact
is that, had Shelley written *gelid*, no foreign compositor could have transformed the word to
gellyed, the main mistake of which is wholly English. I have hardly a doubt that what Shelley
really wrote was *jellyed*, the *y* instead of *i* being a very common type of lapse in such words,
of which lapse there are such instances in Shelley's works; and there would be no difficulty
in the transformation of *j* to *g*, whether the compositor were Italian or English' (*Forman 1876–7*).
Cp. *Faerie Queene* III iv 40: 'They softly wiped away the gelly blood / From th'orifice'.

45–7. S. departs from significant details concerning the means of the murder and the dis-
posal of the body described in *Relation*. *Relation* 23–4 states that the assassins 'with a ham-
mer drove a nail into his head making it pass by his eye and another they drove into his
neck – After a few struggles the unhappy Francesco breathed his last' (see *BSM* x 196–9).
Relation 24–5 states that 'the two ladies after drawing out the two nails, invelopped the body
in a fine sheet & carried it to an [? *canc.*] [Galery *canc.*] open gallery that overhung a garden
and had underneath an Elder tree – From thence they threw it down [th *canc.*] so that it
might be believed that Francesco attending a call of nature [had *canc.*] was traversing this
galery [which *canc.*] when being only supported by feeble beams [he had fallen down *canc.*]
it had given way, & thus had lost his life –' (see *BSM* x 198–9). It was a bloody sheet which
eventually incriminated Beatrice and the others according to *Relation* (see note to IV iv 103–4
and Appendix B). In dramatic terms, Marzio's avoidance of bloodshed contrasts dramatically
with Beatrice's earlier snatching of the dagger (line 31); the same contrast between what Marzio
did and Beatrice's figuring of the murder as bloody is apparent later (cp. V ii 13 with V ii
99–100). *Ricci* i 172–3 offers the intriguing suggestion that the seventh novella in the third
decade of Giraldo Cinthio's *Hecatommithi* (1565), Shakespeare's source for *Othello*, could have
provided the suggested means of Cenci's death. In it, the Moor approves of the Ensign's sug-
gested method of murder: 'the house where you are staying is very old, and the ceiling of
your room has many cracks in it. I suggest that we beat Disdemona with a stocking filled
with sand until she dies. When she is dead, we shall make part of the ceiling fall; and we'll
break the Lady's head, making it seem that a rafter has injured it in falling, and killed
her. In this way nobody will feel any suspicion of you, for everyone will think that she died
accidentally.' (Cited from Appendix 3 of *Othello*, ed. E. A. J. Honigmann, 'The Arden
Shakespeare' 3rd edn (1997) 383.)

Beatrice   [*Giving them a bag of coin.*
Here, take this gold, and hasten to your homes.
And, Marzio, because thou wast only awed
50   By that which made me tremble, wear thou this!
                                        [*Clothes him in a rich mantle.*
It was the mantle which my grandfather
Wore in his high prosperity, and men
Envied his state: so may they envy thine.
Thou wert a weapon in the hand of God
55   To a just use. Live long and thrive! And, mark,
If thou hast crimes, repent: this deed is none.
                                        [*A horn is sounded.*

Lucretia
Hark! 'tis the castle horn; my God! it sounds
Like the last trump.

Beatrice
                        Some tedious guest is coming.

Lucretia
The drawbridge is let down; there is a tramp
60   Of horses in the court; fly, hide yourselves!
                                        [*Exeunt* Olimpio *and* Marzio.

Beatrice
Let us retire to counterfeit deep rest;
I scarcely need to counterfeit it now:
The spirit which doth reign within these limbs
Seems strangely undisturbed. I could even sleep
65   Fearless and calm: all ill is surely past.
                                                [*Exeunt.*

48–53. See *Relation* 24: 'The murderers departed after having received the remainder of the promised reward besides which Beatrice gave Marzio a mantle trimmed with gold' (see *BSM* x 198–9). *Relation* 1–2 notes that 'Monsignor Cenci . . . having been treasurer during the Pontificate of Pius V left [him *canc.*] [his ow only son *canc.*] immense wealth to Francesco his only son' (see *BSM* x 172–5).

50. me] *me Rossetti 1870.*

56. none] done *Rossetti 1870* (a mistaken emendation acknowledged in *L about S* 53–4).

57–8. Hark! . . . trump.] Cp. *Macbeth* II i 78–81: 'What's the business / That such a hideous trumpet calls to parley / The sleepers of the house?'

58. tedious] i.e. 'late' or 'tardy' (see *OED* 4).

65. Fearless and calm:] Cp. the 'calm' of Cenci's sleep referred to in IV i 182, IV iii 12, IV iv 57.

Scene iv

Another Apartment in the Castle. Enter on one side the Legate Savella, *introduced by a Servant, and on the other* Lucretia *and* Bernardo.

Savella
Lady, my duty to his Holiness
Be my excuse that thus unseasonably
I break upon your rest. I must speak with
Count Cenci; doth he sleep?

Lucretia   [*In a hurried and confused manner.*
                    I think he sleeps;
5   Yet, wake him not, I pray, spare me awhile,
He is a wicked and a wrathful man;
Should he be roused out of his sleep tonight,
Which is, I know, a hell of angry dreams,
It were not well; indeed it were not well.
10   Wait till day break —
                                        [*Aside.*
            O, I am deadly sick!

Savella
I grieve thus to distress you, but the Count
Must answer charges of the gravest import,
And suddenly; such my commission is.

Lucretia   [*With increased agitation.*
I dare not rouse him: I know none who dare:
15   'Twere perilous; — you might as safely waken
A serpent; or a corpse in which some fiend
Were laid to sleep.

Savella
            Lady, my moments here
Are counted. I must rouse him from his sleep,
Since none else dare.

---

6. *and a wrathful man;*] and wrathful man *Cenci (1819).*

10. *day break –*] day-break, – *1840;* daybreak. – *Rossetti 1870.* The metre of the line requires 'day break' not to be understood as a noun.

13. *suddenly;*] i.e. 'immediately'.

18. *I*] I *Rossetti 1870.*

Lucretia [*Aside.*

O, terror! O, despair!

[*To* Bernardo.

20   Bernardo, conduct you the Lord Legate to
Your father's chamber.

[*Exeunt* Savella *and* Bernardo.

Enter Beatrice.

Beatrice

    'Tis a messenger
Come to arrest the culprit who now stands
Before the throne of unappealable God.
Both Earth and Heaven, consenting arbiters,
25   Acquit our deed.

Lucretia

    Oh, agony of fear!
Would that he yet might live! Even now I heard
The Legate's followers whisper, as they passed,
They had a warrant for his instant death.
All was prepared by unforbidden means,
30   Which we must pay so dearly, having done.
Even now they search the tower, and find the body;
Now they suspect the truth; now they consult
Before they come to tax us with the fact:
O, horrible, 'tis all discovered!

Beatrice

    Mother,
35   What is done wisely, is done well. Be bold
As thou art just. 'Tis like a truant child
To fear that others know what thou hast done,
Even from thine own strong consciousness, and thus
Write on unsteady eyes and altered cheeks
40   All thou wouldst hide. Be faithful to thyself,
And fear no other witness but thy fear.

28. On the irony, see note to I i 126–8. As is noted in Appendix B, there is no authority in *Relation* nor in any other known source of the story for the Pope having issued a warrant for Cenci's death. Such dramatic irony pervades Gothic drama (e.g. Walpole, *The Mysterious Mother* (1768)) and fiction e.g. Lucifer to Ambrosio in Lewis, *The Monk* (1796) iii 311: 'Had you resisted me one minute longer, you had saved your body and soul. The guards whom you heard at your prison-door, came to signify your pardon.'

36. *child*] child, *1839*.

For if, as cannot be, some circumstance
Should rise in accusation, we can blind
Suspicion with such cheap astonishment,
45   Or overbear it with such guiltless pride,
As murderers cannot feign. The deed is done,
And what may follow now regards not me.
I am as universal as the light;
Free as the earth-surrounding air; as firm
50   As the world's centre. Consequence, to me,
Is as the wind which strikes the solid rock
But shakes it not.

[*A cry within and tumult.*]

Voices

Murder! Murder! Murder!

Enter Bernardo *and* Savella.

Savella   [*To his followers.*]
Go search the castle round; sound the alarm;
Look to the gates that none escape!

Beatrice
                    What now?

Bernardo
55   I know not what to say: my father's dead!

Beatrice
How, dead? he only sleeps: you mistake, brother.
His sleep is very calm, very like death;

44. *cheap*] *Concordance*'s gloss is 'common, ordinary', *Locock 1911*'s 'easy, simple'. The sense seems to be 'easily accomplished'.

47. *regards not me.*] i.e. 'does not concern me' (cited in *OED*, 'regard' *v.* 7a).

49. *Free as the earth-surrounding air;*] Cp. *Macbeth* III iv 23: 'As broad and general as the casing air' and *Richard III* I iv 39: 'empty, vast, and wand'ring air'.

51. *rock*] rock, *1839*.

54. *gates*] gates, *1840*.

55. *dead!*] dead. *Cenci (1819)*.

56. *How, dead?*] *1839*; How; dead! *Cenci (1819)*; How? dead? *Cenci (1821)*; How, dead! *1829*. *sleeps:*] sleeps; *Cenci (1819)*. Beatrice's and Lucretia's feigned grief in *C* (to which Bernardo refers in lines 68–9) appears to be more pronounced in *Relation* 25: 'the feigned lamentations of Lucretia & Beatrice who appeared inconsolable spread the news of Francesco's death' (see *BSM* x 198–9).

'Tis wonderful how well a tyrant sleeps.
He is not *dead?*

Bernardo
                    Dead! murdered!

Lucretia   [*With extreme agitation.*
                              Oh, no, no,
60   He is not murdered, though he may be dead;
        I have alone the keys of those apartments.

Savella
Ha! Is it so?

Beatrice
                My Lord, I pray excuse us;
        We will retire; my mother is not well:
        She seems quite overcome with this strange horror.
                              [*Exeunt* Lucretia *and* Beatrice.

Savella
65   Can you suspect who may have murdered him?

Bernardo
I know not what to think.

Savella
                              Can you name any
        Who had an interest in his death?

Bernardo
                                    Alas!
        I can name none who had not, and those most
        Who most lament that such a deed is done;
70   My mother, and my sister, and myself.

Savella
'Tis strange! There were clear marks of violence.
I found the old man's body in the moonlight,

---

59. dead?] dead? *Cenci (1819)*; dead. *Rossetti 1870.   Dead! murdered!*] Dead; murdered. *Cenci (1819).* Dead; murdered! *1839*; Dead, murdered! *Rossetti 1870.*

60. *murdered,*] murdered *Cenci (1819).*

72. *moonlight,*] *1829*; moonlight *Cenci (1819), Cenci (1821).*

Hanging beneath the window of his chamber,
Among the branches of a pine: he could not
75 Have fallen there, for all his limbs lay heaped
And effortless; 'tis true there was no blood.
Favour me, Sir, (it much imports your house
That all should be made clear) to tell the ladies
That I request their presence.

[*Exit* Bernardo.

Enter Guards, bringing in Marzio.

Guard

We have one.

Officer
80 My Lord, we found this ruffian and another
Lurking among the rocks; there is no doubt
But that they are the murderers of Count Cenci:
Each had a bag of coin; this fellow wore
A gold-inwoven robe, which, shining bright
85 Under the dark rocks to the glimmering moon,
Betrayed them to our notice: the other fell
Desperately fighting.

Savella

What does he confess?

Officer
He keeps firm silence; but these lines found on him
May speak.

73. *chamber,*] chamber *Cenci (1819)*.

76. *effortless;*] i.e. 'without strength' or 'lifeless'. S.'s usage negates in a literal way the Latin root of the word 'effort' (*fortis* 'strong').

77–8. *Sir, (it . . . clear) to*] Sir; it . . . clear; to *Cenci (1819)*; Sir – it . . . clear – to *1829*.

77. *house*] The first of several references to the family's noble lineage. Cp. IV iv 145, V ii 147, V iii 30.

79. *We have one.*] Marzio was captured in January 1599, four months after the murder. According to *Relation* 28–9 he was 'imprisoned at Naples where he confessed the whole' (see *BSM* x 202–3). For details of his arrest and confession, see *Ricci* i 267–98.

86–7. *the other fell / Desperately fighting.*] As with Marzio's capture, Olympio's assassination occurred long after the murder of Francesco Cenci (in May 1599). According to *Relation* 28, 'Monsignore Guerra having heard of the notification made by the Court of Naples to that of Rome fearing that Marzio & Olympio might fall into the hands of justice & be induced to confess their crime suddenly [sent pe *canc.*] hired men [hired canc.] to murder them but succeeded only in assassinating Olympio at the city of Terni' (see *BSM* x 202–3). For details of Olympio's assassination, see *Ricci* ii 29–55.

Savella

Their language is at least sincere.

[*Reads.*

'TO THE LADY BEATRICE.

That the atonement of what my nature sickens to conjecture
may soon arrive, I send thee, at thy brother's desire, those who
will speak and do more than I dare write —

Thy devoted servant,

Orsino.'

Enter Lucretia, Beatrice, *and* Bernardo.

90   Knowest thou this writing, Lady?

Beatrice

No.

Savella

Nor thou?

Lucretia   [*Her conduct throughout the scene is marked by
extreme agitation.*

Where was it found? What is it? It should be
Orsino's hand! It speaks of that strange horror
Which never yet found utterance, but which made
Between that hapless child and her dead father
95   A gulf of obscure hatred.

Savella

Is it so?
Is it true, Lady, that thy father did
Such outrages as to awaken in thee
Unfilial hate?

Orsino's letter. This edition follows *Locock 1911* in not lineating Orsino's letter. *Cenci (1821)*
sets the letter as prose whereas *Cenci (1819)* sets it in lines thus:

TO THE LADY BEATRICE.
"That the atonement of what my nature
"Sickens to conjecture may soon arrive,
"I send thee, at thy brother's desire, those
"Who will speak and do more, than I dare
"Write . . . Thy devoted servant,
ORSINO.

As Forman points out of the arrangement in *Cenci (1819)*: 'curiously enough each of the lines
except one consists of ten syllables, though plain prose enough' (*Forman 1876–7*).

Orsino's letter. at thy brother's desire,] Cp. III ii 72 and note.

Beatrice
               Not hate, 'twas more than hate:
This is most true, yet wherefore question me?

Savella
100   There is a deed demanding question done;
Thou hast a secret which will answer not.

Beatrice
What sayest? My Lord, your words are bold and rash.

Savella
I do arrest all present in the name
Of the Pope's Holiness. You must to Rome.

Lucretia
105   O, not to Rome! Indeed we are not guilty.

Beatrice
Guilty! Who dares talk of guilt? My Lord,

---

100. i.e. 'there is a deed done which demands questioning'.

101. i.e. 'you have a secret which refuses to be divulged'. Cp. the structure of *PU*. Beatrice's dialogue with Savella echoes Prometheus's with Mercury in *PU* Act I.

103–4. As with the fates of Marzio and Olympio noted above, S. condenses the time-scheme of events in *Relation* significantly here. After Francesco's burial *Relation* 25–7 describes the family as returning 'to Rome to enjoy the fruits of their crime – They passed some time there in tranquillity – but divine Justice which would not allow so atrocious a wickedness to remain hid & unpunished so ordered it that the Court of Naples [tw *canc.*] to which the account of the death of Cenci was forwarded began to entertain doubts concerning the mode by which he came by it and sent a Commissary to examine the body & to take informations; among other things this man [t *canc.*] discovered [some *canc.*] a circumstances to the prejudice of the family of the deceased.' Having mentioned the discovery of an incriminating bloody sheet (discussed in Appendix B), the passage continues: 'These informations were instantly forwarded to the Court of Rome but nevertheless several months passed without any step being taken in disfavour of the Cenci family' (see *BSM* x 198–201).

106. dares] Rossetti comments: 'My own sense of rhythm would dictate the insertion of "to" in this line after "dares"' (*Rossetti 1870*). But, as Swinburne points out, 'Note on the Text of Shelley' [1869], *Essays and Studies* (1875) 202: 'the insertion of "to" before "talk," . . . indeed rather weakens the force of emphasis in this sudden outbreak of passionate protest.' Locock suggests that, '*dares* has the value of a whole foot' (i.e. that it is disyllabic) and that such 'license here is extremely effective' (*Locock 1911*).

106–24. On Beatrice's defiant refusal to admit guilt, cp. S.'s account of the murder of Julius Caesar in 'On Christianity': 'His assassins understood justice better. They saw the most virtuous and civilized community of mankind under the insolent dominion of one wicked man, and they murdered him. They destroyed the usurper of the liberties of their countrymen, not because they hated him, not because they would revenge the wrongs which they had sustained. Brutus, it is said, was his most familiar friend. Most of the conspirators were habituated to domestic intercourse with the man whom they destroyed. It was in affection, in

I am more innocent of parricide
Than is a child born fatherless. Dear mother,
Your gentleness and patience are no shield
110   For this keen-judging world, this two-edged lie,
Which seems, but is not. What! will human laws,
Rather will ye who are their ministers,
Bar all access to retribution first,
And then, when heaven doth interpose to do
115   What ye neglect, arming familiar things
To the redress of an unwonted crime,
Make ye the victims who demanded it
Culprits? 'Tis ye are culprits! That poor wretch
Who stands so pale, and trembling, and amazed,
120   If it be true he murdered Cenci, was
A sword in the right hand of justest God.
Wherefore should I have wielded it? Unless
The crimes which mortal tongue dare never name
God therefore scruples to avenge.

Savella

                              You own
125   That you desired his death?

Beatrice

                      It would have been
A crime no less than his, if, for one moment,
That fierce desire had faded in my heart.

---

inextinguishable love for all that is *venerable and dear* to the human heart in the names of country, liberty and virtue, it was in serious and solemn and reluctant mood that these holy patriots murdered their *father and their friend.' (Prose Works* i 254).

107–8. I am more innocent . . . fatherless.] There are legal precedents for this statement. See Bowyer, 'Translation of the Pleading of Prospero Farinacci' 78 (discussed in headnote): 'Therefore much more is the paternal quality and privilege forfeited by a father who attempts the chastity of his daughter, for by that outrage he makes himself not her father, and shows himself not to be truly her father'.

110. keen-judging] keen judging *Cenci (1819). two-edged*] two edged *Cenci (1819). Curran (1975)* 133 cps. the Chorus on Io's fate in Aeschlyus, *Prometheus Bound* 691–2, which has ἀμφάκει, 'double-pronged'; but 'two-edged' is a common compound adjective in S.'s work (see e.g. V ii 98 and 'the two-edged sword' in line 9 of 'England in 1819') and there are other sources with which S. would have been familiar for ἀμφίΘήγης ('two-edged' or 'sharpened on both sides'), e.g. *Iliad* x 256, Sophocles, *Ajax* 286.

113–16. Locock suggests that Beatrice alludes first to the failure of the petition to the Pope (line 113) then to Olimpio and Marzio who desired revenge on Cenci for their own wrongs (lines 115–16) (*Locock 1911*).

124. therefore] i.e. 'because men dare not name them' (*Locock 1911*).

126. if, for one moment,] if for one moment *Cenci (1819)*.

'Tis true I did believe, and hope, and pray,
Aye, I even knew — for God is wise and just,
130 That some strange sudden death hung over him.
'Tis true that this did happen, and most true
There was no other rest for me on earth,
No other hope in Heaven: now what of this?

Savella
Strange thoughts beget strange deeds; and here are both:
135 I judge thee not.

Beatrice
                                And yet, if you arrest me,
You are the judge and executioner
Of that which is the life of life: the breath
Of accusation kills an innocent name,
And leaves for lame acquittal the poor life
140 Which is a mask without it. 'Tis most false
That I am guilty of foul parricide;
Although I must rejoice, for justest cause,
That other hands have sent my father's soul
To ask the mercy he denied to me.
145 Now leave us free: stain not a noble house
With vague surmises of rejected crime;
Add to our sufferings and your own neglect
No heavier sum; let them have been enough;
Leave us the wreck we have.

Savella
                                I dare not, Lady.
150 I pray that you prepare yourselves for Rome:
There the Pope's further pleasure will be known.

Lucretia
O, not to Rome! O, take us not to Rome!

Beatrice
Why not to Rome, dear mother? There as here
Our innocence is as an armèd heel

---

134. Cp. I iii 151 and note.

146. rejected] i.e. 'denied' (cited in *OED*, 'rejected' *ppl. a.* a.).

148. sum;] sum: *Cenci (1819). enough;*] enough: *Cenci (1819).*

154. armèd] *Rossetti 1870*; armed *Cenci (1819), Cenci (1821).* Cp. IV i 105 and note.

155 To trample accusation. God is there
   As here, and with his shadow ever clothes
   The innocent, the injured, and the weak;
   And such are we. Cheer up, dear Lady, lean
   On me; collect your wandering thoughts. My Lord,
160 As soon as you have taken some refreshment,
   And had all such examinations made
   Upon the spot, as may be necessary
   To the full understanding of this matter,
   We shall be ready. Mother, will you come?

   Lucretia
165 Ha! they will bind us to the rack, and wrest
   Self-accusation from our agony!
   Will Giacomo be there? Orsino? Marzio?
   All present; all confronted; all demanding
   Each from the other's countenance the thing
170 Which is in every heart! O, misery!
                              [*She faints, and is borne out.*

   Savella
   She faints: an ill appearance this.

   Beatrice
                              My Lord,
   She knows not yet the uses of the world.
   She fears that power is as a beast which grasps
   And loosens not: a snake, whose look transmutes
175 All things to guilt which is its nutriment;
   She cannot know how well the supine slaves
   Of blind authority read the truth of things

---

159. collect your wandering thoughts.] Cp. Adam in *Paradise Lost* viii 180–7: 'How fully hast thou satisfied me, pure / Intelligence of heaven, angel serene, / And freed from intricacies, taught to live, nor with perplexing thoughts / To interrupt the sweet of life, from which / God hath bid dwell far off all anxious cares, / And not molest us, unless we our selves / Seek them with wandering thoughts, and notions vain'.

169. other's] *1829*; others *Cenci (1819), Cenci (1821).*

173. power] Power *Rossetti 1870.*

174–5. a snake, whose look transmutes / All things to guilt] Cp. IV i 119 and note.

174. snake,] snake *Cenci (1819), Rossetti 1870.*

175. guilt] guilt, *Rossetti 1870. nutriment;*] nutriment. *Cenci (1819), Rossetti 1870.*

177. authority] Authority *Locock 1911.*

When written on a brow of guilelessness:
She sees not yet triumphant Innocence
180 Stand at the judgement-seat of mortal man,
A judge and an accuser of the wrong
Which drags it there. Prepare yourself, my Lord;
Our suite will join yours in the court below.

[Exeunt.

End of the Fourth Act

ACT V

Scene i

An Apartment in Orsino's Palace. Enter Orsino *and* Giacomo.

Giacomo
Do evil deeds thus quickly come to end?
O, that the vain remorse which must chastise
Crimes done, had but as loud a voice to warn
As its keen sting is mortal to avenge!
5   O, that the hour when present had cast off
The mantle of its mystery, and shown
The ghastly form with which it now returns
When its scared game is roused, cheering the hounds
Of conscience to their prey! Alas! Alas!
10   It was a wicked thought, a piteous deed,
To kill an old and hoary-headed father.

Orsino
It has turned out unluckily, in truth.

Giacomo
To violate the sacred doors of sleep;
To cheat kind nature of the placid death
15   Which she prepares for over-wearied age;
To drag from Heaven an unrepentant soul
Which might have quenched in reconciling prayers
A life of burning crimes —

Orsino
                    You cannot say
I urged you to the deed.

---

3. *warn*] warn, *1840*.

12. Cp. *Romeo and Juliet* III iv 1: 'Things have fall'n out, sir, so unluckily'.

13. Cp. *Paradise Lost* iv 882–3: 'thy bold entrance on this place; / Employed it seems to violate sleep'.

14. *nature*] Nature *Rossetti 1878, Locock 1911*.

15. *over-wearied*] overwearied *Cenci (1819)*.

16. *soul*] soul, *1840*.

Giacomo
O, had I never
20   Found in thy smooth and ready countenance
The mirror of my darkest thoughts; hadst thou
Never with hints and questions made me look
Upon the monster of my thought, until
It grew familiar to desire —

Orsino
'Tis thus
25   Men cast the blame of their unprosperous acts
Upon the abettors of their own resolve;
Or any thing but their weak, guilty selves.
And yet, confess the truth, it is the peril
In which you stand that gives you this pale sickness
30   Of penitence; confess 'tis fear disguised
From its own shame that takes the mantle now
Of thin remorse. What if we yet were safe?

Giacomo
How can that be? Already Beatrice,
Lucretia, and the murderer, are in prison.
35   I doubt not officers are, whilst we speak,
Sent to arrest us.

Orsino
I have all prepared
For instant flight. We can escape even now,
So we take fleet occasion by the hair.

19–24. O, had . . . desire –] Cp. *King John* IV ii 219–48 esp. 231–41: 'Hadst thou but shook thy head or made a pause, / When I spake darkly what I purposed, / Or turn'd an eye of doubt upon my face, / As bid me tell my tale in express words, / Deep shame had struck me dumb, made me break off, / And those thy fears might have wrought fears in me. / But thou didst understand me by my signs, / And didst in signs again parley with sin; / Yea, without stop, didst let thy heart consent, / And consequently thy rude hand to act / The deed which both our tongues held vile to name'; and Valdez to Ordonio in Coleridge, *Remorse* (1813) Act III scene ii: 'O that I ne'er had yielded / To your entreaties!'

19. I urged you] *I* urged you *Rossetti 1870.*

25. unprosperous] i.e. 'unfortunate' or 'unlucky'. Cp. IV i 24–5 and note.

27. any thing] anything *Rossetti 1870.*

30. confess] Confess *Cenci (1819). fear*] Fear, *Rossetti 1870, Locock 1911.*

32. remorse.] Remorse. *Rossetti 1870, Locock 1911.*

34. Lucretia, and the murderer,] Lucretia and the murderer *Cenci (1819);* Lucretia and the murderer, *1829.*

38. Cp. *Othello* III i 49: 'To take the safest occasion by the front'. *occasion*] Occasion *Rossetti 1870.*

Giacomo
Rather expire in tortures, as I may.
40 What! will you cast by self-accusing flight
Assured conviction upon Beatrice?
She, who alone in this unnatural work,
Stands like God's angel ministered upon
By fiends; avenging such a nameless wrong
45 As turns black parricide to piety;
Whilst we for basest ends — I fear, Orsino,
While I consider all your words and looks,
Comparing them with your proposal now,
That you must be a villain. For what end
50 Could you engage in such a perilous crime,
Training me on with hints, and signs, and smiles,
Even to this gulf? Thou art no liar? No,
Thou art a lie! Traitor and murderer!
Coward and slave! But, no, defend thyself;

[*Drawing.*

55 Let the sword speak what the indignant tongue
Disdains to brand thee with.

Orsino
                    Put up your weapon.
Is it the desperation of your fear
Makes you thus rash and sudden with a friend,
Now ruined for your sake? If honest anger
60 Have moved you, know, that what I just proposed
Was but to try you. As for me, I think
Thankless affection led me to this point,
From which, if my firm temper could repent,
I cannot now recede. Even whilst we speak
65 The ministers of justice wait below:

42. She, who alone] She who alone, *1840.*

46. ends –] ends . . . *Cenci (1819).*

52. liar?] liar; *1829.*

54. no,] no – *1829.*

55–6. Let the sword . . . thee with.] Cp. the exchange between Floro and Lelio in *Scenes from the 'Magico Prodigioso' of Calderon* lines 219–23 (see *1824* 372–3): 'Floro. "Draw! / If there were words, here is the place for deeds." / Lelio. "Thou needest not instruct me; well I know / That in the field the silent tongue of steel / Speaks thus." '

58. a friend,] your friend, *1829, 1839, 1840.*

61. I think] I think, *Cenci (1819), 1829.*

63. could] *could Rossetti 1870.*

They grant me these brief moments. Now if you
Have any word of melancholy comfort
To speak to your pale wife, 'twere best to pass
Out at the postern, and avoid them so.

Giacomo

70   O, generous friend! how canst thou pardon me?
Would that my life could purchase thine!

Orsino

                                    That wish
Now comes a day too late. Haste; fare thee well!
Hear'st thou not steps along the corridor?

                                    [*Exit* Giacomo.

I'm sorry for it; but the guards are waiting
75   At his own gate, and such was my contrivance
That I might rid me both of him and them.
I thought to act a solemn comedy
Upon the painted scene of this new world,
And to attain my own peculiar ends
80   By some such plot of mingled good and ill
As others weave; but there arose a Power
Which grasped and snapped the threads of my device,
And turned it to a net of ruin — Ha!

                                    [*A shout is heard.*

Is that my name I hear proclaimed abroad?

---

66. *Now*] Now, 1829.

67. *word*] words *Woodberry (1909).*

77–8. These are the only lines of the play itself extant in MS (see headnote).

80. *mingled good and ill*] Cp. 'Mazenghi' line 56.

82. Cp. Coleridge, 'The Rime of the Ancient Mariner' in *Sibylline Leaves* (1817) line 442: 'this spell was snapt'.   *device*] device *Cenci (1819).*

84*ff.* Orsino's final soliloquy repeats his original self-portrayal as prey (cp. I ii 12–13 and note). The comparison of Orsino to the figure described in *PU* III iv 142–8 in Charles L. Adams, 'The Structure of *The Cenci*', *Drama Survey* iv (1965) 146 is particularly apposite here.

84–91. In *Relation*, Guerra is implicated after the murderers of Olympio are captured (and confess that they were hired by him) but S. draws on *Relation* 31–3 for his adoption of a 'vile disguise' (line 85) in order to effect his escape from Rome: 'Fortunately for this prelate he [had *canc.*] received prompt information of the [inform *canc.*] testimony given against him and was able to hide himself [& plan *canc.*] for a time & to plan his escape which was very difficult for his stature, the fairness & beauty of his countenance, & his light hair made him conspicuous for discovery – he changed his dress for that of a charcoal man, blackening his face & shaving his head & thus disguised – driving two asses before him with some bread & onions in his hands he passed freely through Rome under the eyes of the ministers of

85   But I will pass, wrapped in a vile disguise;
        Rags on my back, and a false innocence
        Upon my face, through the misdeeming crowd
        Which judges by what seems. 'Tis easy then
        For a new name and for a country new,
90   And a new life, fashioned on old desires,
        To change the honours of abandoned Rome.
        And these must be the masks of that within,
        Which must remain unaltered. Oh, I fear
        That what is past will never let me rest!
95   Why, when none else is conscious but myself
        Of my misdeeds, should my own heart's contempt
        Trouble me? Have I not the power to fly
        My own reproaches? Shall I be the slave
        Of — what? A word? which those of this false world
100   Employ against each other, not themselves;
        As men wear daggers not for self-offence.
        But if I am mistaken, where shall I
        Find the disguise to hide me from myself,
        As now I skulk from every other eye?

                                                        [*Exit.*

---

justice who sought him everywhere and [1 *canc.*] without being recognized by any one passed out of one of the gates of the City where after a short time he was met by the sbirri who were searching the country and passed unknown by them not without suffering great fear at his risk of being discovered & arrested – [and *canc.*] by means of this ingenious disguise he effected his escape to a safe country.' (see *BSM* x 204–207). For the mistranslation of 'bocca' ('mouth') as 'hands', see Appendix B.

85. *wrapped*] wrapt *Cenci (1819)*, *Cenci (1821)*. Modernised because the sense is unambiguous. See III i 165 and note. *vile*] i.e. 'mean' or 'wretched' (cited in *OED*, 'vile' *a. adv.* and *sb.*, 3b).

87. *misdeeming*] i.e. 'misjudging' (cited in *OED*, 'misdeeming' *ppl. a.*). Cp. *Faerie Queene* iv 2: 'Who after that he had faire *Vna* lorne, / Through light misdeeming of her loialtie', and *Paradise Regained* i 424–5: 'What but thy malice moved thee to misdeem / Of righteous Job'. *crowd*] crowd, *1840*.

88. *then*] then, *1840*.

89. *name*] name, *1840*.

91. *abandoned Rome.*] A suitable pun on Orsino's indifference to his vocation (see note to II ii 155–61).

94. *past*] pass'd *1829*.

95. *conscious but myself*] conscious, but myself, *Cenci (1819)*.

99. *A word?*] A word! *1839*.

101. *self-offence.*] self offence. *Cenci (1819)*. Cp. *Samson Agonistes* 514–15: 'self-displeased / For self-offence, more than for God offended'.

Scene ii

A Hall of Justice. Camillo, *Judges, & c. are discovered seated.* Marzio *is led in.*

1st Judge
Accused, do you persist in your denial?
I ask you, are you innocent, or guilty?
I demand who were the participators
In your offence? Speak truth and the whole truth.

Marzio
5   My God! I did not kill him; I know nothing;
Olimpio sold the robe to me from which
You would infer my guilt.

2nd Judge
                   Away with him!

1st Judge
Dare you, with lips yet white from the rack's kiss,
Speak false? Is it so soft a questioner,
10   That you would bandy lover's talk with it
Till it wind out your life and soul? Away!

Marzio
Spare me! O, spare! I will confess.

1st Judge
                 Then speak.

Marzio
I strangled him in his sleep.

1st Judge
                 Who urged you to it?

Marzio
His own son Giacomo, and the young prelate
15   Orsino sent me to Petrella; there
The ladies Beatrice and Lucretia

---

4. *truth*] truth, *1829.*
8. *kiss,*] kiss *Cenci (1819).*
10. *lover's*] lovers' *1839.* *it*] it, *1829.*

Tempted me with a thousand crowns, and I
And my companion forthwith murdered him.
Now let me die.

1st Judge
20 This sounds as bad as truth. Guards, there,
Lead forth the prisoners.

     Enter Lucretia, Beatrice, *and* Giacomo, *guarded.*

        Look upon this man;
When did you see him last?

Beatrice
        We never saw him.

Marzio
You know me too well, Lady Beatrice.

Beatrice
I know thee! How? where? when?

Marzio
        You know 'twas I
25 Whom you did urge with menaces and bribes
To kill your father. When the thing was done
You clothed me in a robe of woven gold
And bade me thrive: how I have thriven, you see.

19–22. *Now let me die. /* 1st Judge *This sounds as bad as truth. Guards, there, / Lead forth the prisoners. Look upon this man; / When did you see him last? /* Beatrice *We never saw him. /* Marzio *You know me too well, Lady Beatrice.*] Now let me die. 1st Judge This sounds as bad as truth. / Guards there, lead forth the prisoners. Look upon / This man. When did you see him last? *Beatrice* We never / Saw him. *Marzio* You know me too well, Lady Beatrice. *Rossetti 1870*; Now let me die. *1st Judge* This sounds as bad as truth. / Guards, there, lead forth the prisoners. Look upon this man; / When did you see him last? *Beatrice* We never saw him. / *Marzio* You know me too well, Lady Beatrice. *Woodberry 1893.* The alternative lineation of this passage offered by Rossetti and Woodberry cannot overcome its metrical awkwardness.

21. *prisoners.*] prisoners! *Cenci (1819), 1829.*

22–180. The source of Marzio's behaviour may be found in *Relation* 29–30: 'all constantly denied the crime & particularly Beatrice who also denied being given [the *canc.*] to Marzio the mantle trimmed with gold of which mention before was made: And Marzio overcome & moved by the presence of mind and courage of Beatrice retracted all that he had deposed at Naples & rather than again confess obstinately died under his torments.' (see *BSM* x 202–5).

24. *How?*] How! *1839.*

26. *done*] done, *1840.*

27. *gold*] gold, *1840.*

You, my Lord Giacomo, Lady Lucretia,
30   You know that what I speak is true.

> [Beatrice *advances towards him; he covers his face,*
> *and shrinks back.*

                    O, dart
The terrible resentment of those eyes
On the dead earth! Turn them away from me!
They wound: 'twas torture forced the truth. My Lords,
Having said this, let me be led to death.

Beatrice
35   Poor wretch, I pity thee: yet stay awhile.

Camillo
Guards, lead him not away.

Beatrice
                    Cardinal Camillo,
You have a good repute for gentleness
And wisdom: can it be that you sit here
To countenance a wicked farce like this?
40   When some obscure and trembling slave is dragged
From sufferings which might shake the sternest heart,
And bade to answer, not as he believes,
But as those may suspect or do desire,
Whose questions thence suggest their own reply;
45   And that in peril of such hideous torments
As merciful God spares even the damned. Speak now
The thing you surely know, which is, that you
If your fine frame were stretched upon that wheel,
And you were told: 'Confess that you did poison

30–3. *O, dart . . . They wound:*] On the power of Beatrice's gaze, see I ii 84–5, V ii 177, and on her specifically basilisk qualities, see note to IV i 119.

32. *dead earth!*] dread earth! *1829, 1839, 1840.* Forman comments: 'There can be no possible doubt that *dead* is the right word, – the dead earth, which could not be wounded and tortured, as Marzio was, by the gaze of Beatrice. The thought corresponds precisely with that in Beatrice's speech further on [i.e. V ii 86–7]' (*Forman 1876–7*).

34. *this,*] this *Cenci (1819).*

40. *obscure*] obscure, *Cenci (1819).*

41. *heart,*] heart *Cenci (1819).*

43. *desire,*] desire *Cenci (1819).*

44. *reply;*] reply: *Cenci (1819).*

47. *which is, that you*] which is that you, *Cenci (1819);* which is, that you, *1839, 1840.*

49–51. *told: 'Confess . . . life:' – and*] told: Confess . . . life: and *Cenci (1819);* told, Confess . . . life; and *1829;* told, 'Confess . . . life;' and *1839;* told, 'Confess . . . life;' – and *Rossetti 1870.*

50   Your little nephew; that fair blue-eyed child
        Who was the lodestar of your life:' — and though
        All see, since his most swift and piteous death,
        That day and night, and heaven and earth, and time,
        And all the things hoped for or done therein
55   Are changed to you, through your exceeding grief,
        Yet you would say, 'I confess any thing:'
        And beg from your tormentors, like that slave,
        The refuge of dishonourable death.
        I pray thee, Cardinal, that thou assert
60   My innocence.

        Camillo   [*Much moved.*
        What shall we think, my Lords?
        Shame on these tears! I thought the heart was frozen
        Which is their fountain. I would pledge my soul
        That she is guiltless.

        Judge
                        Yet she must be tortured.

        Camillo
        I would as soon have tortured mine own nephew
65   (If he now lived he would be just her age;
        His hair, too, was her colour, and his eyes
        Like hers in shape, but blue and not so deep)
        As that most perfect image of God's love

50. nephew;] nephew: *1829.*

50–5. that fair blue-eyed . . . exceeding grief,] Mary comments in *1839* that these lines allude to S.'s pain at the loss of William (see headnote). See also V ii 65–7. Cp. *PU* IV 262–8 and note.

54. therein] therein, *1840.*

56. say, 'I confess any thing:'] say I confess any thing. *Cenci (1819)*; say, I confess any thing – *1829*; say, 'I confess anything' – *1839.*

59. thee,] you, *Rossetti 1870. thou*] you *Rossetti 1870.*

61–2. I thought . . . fountain.] See note to V iii 109–11. Cp. Bosola in Webster, *The Duchess of Malfi* IV ii 364–6: 'where were / These penitent fountains while she was living? / O, they were frozen up!' See Richard Allan Davison, 'A Websterian Echo in "The Cenci" ', *American N&Q* vi (1967) 53–4.

61. the heart was frozen] Cp. *R&H* line 399.

64. nephew] *1829*; nephew: *Cenci (1819), Cenci (1821).*

65. lived] lived, *1840.*

67. but blue and not so deep)] As is pointed out in *Locock 1911*, an apparent slip on S.'s part since Beatrice's eyes are described as of 'a deep blue' (*Relation* 69). *blue*] blue, *1829. deep)*] deep): *1829*; deep:) *1840.*

That ever came sorrowing upon the earth.
70 She is as pure as speechless infancy!

Judge
Well, be her purity on your head, my Lord,
If you forbid the rack. His Holiness
Enjoined us to pursue this monstrous crime
By the severest forms of law; nay, even
75 To stretch a point against the criminals.
The prisoners stand accused of parricide
Upon such evidence as justifies
Torture.

Beatrice
           What evidence? This man's?

Judge
                                    Even so.

Beatrice   [*To* Marzio.
Come near. And who art thou thus chosen forth
80 Out of the multitude of living men
To kill the innocent?

Marzio
           I am Marzio,
Thy father's vassal.

Beatrice
           Fix thine eyes on mine;
Answer to what I ask.
                              [*Turning to the Judges.*
                    I prithee mark
His countenance: unlike bold calumny
85 Which sometimes dares not speak the thing it looks,

---

74. *severest forms of law;*] Cp. *Romeo and Juliet* V iii 268: 'the rigour of severest law.' *nay, even*] nay even *Cenci (1819).*

75. *stretch*] Cp. II ii 26 and note.

76. *parricide*] parricide, *1829*.

78. *What evidence?*] Cp. Clarence in *Richard III* I iv 178–9: 'What is my offence? / Where is the evidence that doth accuse me?'

79. *thou*] thou, *1829*.

80. *men*] men, *1840*.

84. *calumny*] calumny, *1840*; Calumny *Rossetti 1870, Locock 1911.*

He dares not look the thing he speaks, but bends
His gaze on the blind earth.
                                                    [*To* Marzio.
                            What! wilt thou say
That I did murder my own father?

Marzio
                                    Oh!
Spare me! My brain swims round — I cannot speak —
90   It was that horrid torture forced the truth.
Take me away! Let her not look on me!
I am a guilty, miserable wretch;
I have said all I know; now, let me die!

Beatrice
My Lords, if by my nature I had been
95   So stern, as to have planned the crime alleged,
Which your suspicions dictate to this slave,
And the rack makes him utter, do you think
I should have left this two-edged instrument
Of my misdeed; this man, this bloody knife
100   With my own name engraven on the heft,
Lying unsheathed amid a world of foes,
For my own death? That with such horrible need
For deepest silence, I should have neglected
So trivial a precaution, as the making
105   His tomb the keeper of a secret written
On a thief's memory? What is his poor life?
What are a thousand lives? A parricide
Had trampled them like dust; and see, he lives!
                                        [*Turning to* Marzio.
And thou —

Marzio
                    Oh, spare me! Speak to me no more!
110   That stern yet piteous look, those solemn tones,

---

91. *Let her not look on me!*] Cp. Belvidera to Jaffeir in Otway, *Venice Preserved* Act IV scene ii:
'Oh, do not look so terribly upon me, / How your Lips shake, and all your Face disorder'd!'

92. *guilty,*] guilty *Cenci (1819)*.   *wretch;*] wretch! *1840*.

98. *two-edged*] two edged *Cenci (1819)*. Cp. IV iv 110 and note.

99. *man,*] man; *1840*.   *knife*] knife, *1840*.

100. *heft,*] *Cenci (1819)*; heft *Cenci (1821)*.

108. *and*] and, *Cenci (1819)*.

Wound worse than torture.

[*To the Judges.*

      I have told it all;
For pity's sake lead me away to death.

Camillo
Guards, lead him nearer the Lady Beatrice,
He shrinks from her regard like autumn's leaf
115 From the keen breath of the serenest north.

Beatrice
Oh, thou who tremblest on the giddy verge
Of life and death, pause ere thou answerest me;
So mayst thou answer God with less dismay:
What evil have we done thee? I, alas!
120 Have lived but on this earth a few sad years
And so my lot was ordered, that a father
First turned the moments of awakening life
To drops, each poisoning youth's sweet hope; and then
Stabbed with one blow my everlasting soul;
125 And my untainted fame; and even that peace
Which sleeps within the core of the heart's heart.
But the wound was not mortal; so my hate
Became the only worship I could lift
To our great father, who in pity and love,
130 Armed thee, as thou dost say, to cut him off;
And thus his wrong becomes my accusation;
And art thou the accuser? If thou hopest
Mercy in heaven, show justice upon earth:
Worse than a bloody hand is a hard heart.
135 If thou hast done murders, made thy life's path
Over the trampled laws of God and man,
Rush not before thy Judge, and say: 'My Maker,
I have done this and more; for there was one
Who was most pure and innocent on earth;

114. *autumn's*] Autumn's *Locock 1911.*
116–58. Cp. IV iv 107–8 and note.
118. *mayst*] mayest *Cenci (1819), 1829.*
120. *years*] years, *1829.*
124. *soul;*] soul, *1839.*
126. *heart.*] heart; *Cenci (1819);* heart, *1829.*
129. *father,*] Father, *1829.*
131. *accusation;*] accusation: *1829;* accusation *Rossetti 1870;* accusation. *Woodberry 1893.*
137. *Maker,*] maker, *Cenci (1819).*

140 And because she endured what never any
Guilty or innocent, endured before;
Because her wrongs could not be told, not thought;
Because thy hand at length did rescue her;
I with my words killed her and all her kin.'
145 Think, I adjure you, what it is to slay
The reverence living in the minds of men
Towards our ancient house, and stainless fame!
Think what it is to strangle infant pity,
Cradled in the belief of guileless looks,
150 Till it become a crime to suffer. Think
What 'tis to blot with infamy and blood
All that which shows like innocence, and is,
Hear me, great God! I swear, most innocent,
So that the world lose all discrimination
155 Between the sly, fierce, wild regard of guilt,
And that which now compels thee to reply
To what I ask: Am I, or am I not
A parricide?

Marzio
                Thou art not!

Judge
                What is this?

Marzio
I here declare those whom I did accuse
160 Are innocent. 'Tis I alone am guilty.

---

140. any] any, *1840.*

141. innocent,] innocent *Cenci (1819). before;*] before: *Cenci (1819).*

142. not thought;] nor thought, *Rossetti 1870.*

145. you,] thee, *Rossetti 1870.*

148. pity,] Pity, *Rossetti 1870, Locock 1911.*

152. is,] is, – *1840.*

153. innocent,] innocent, – *1840.*

159–60. Cp. Caleb Williams who feels guilt at having revealed the truth about Falkland committing murder in the 'Postscript' to *Caleb Williams (Godwin Novels* iii 275): 'I proclaim to all the world that Mr Falkland is a man worthy of affection and kindness, and that I am myself the worst of villains! Never will I forgive myself the iniquity of this day. The memory will always haunt me, and embitter every hour of my existence. In thus acting I have been a murderer, a cool, deliberate, unfeeling murderer. – I have said what my accursed precipitation has obliged me to say. Do with me as you please! I ask no favour. Death would be a kindness, compared to what I feel!'. For cp. of Marzio with Caleb Williams, see Stephen Behrendt, *Shelley and his Audiences* (1989) 156.

Judge
Drag him away to torments; let them be
Subtle and long drawn out, to tear the folds
Of the heart's inmost cell. Unbind him not
Till he confess.

Marzio
                    Torture me as ye will:
165 A keener pain has wrung a higher truth
From my last breath. She is most innocent!
Bloodhounds, not men, glut yourselves well with me;
I will not give you that fine piece of nature
To rend and ruin.
                    [*Exit* Marzio, *guarded.*

Camillo
                    What say ye now, my Lords?

Judge
170 Let tortures strain the truth till it be white
As snow thrice sifted by the frozen wind.

Camillo
Yet stained with blood.

Judge   [*To* Beatrice.
                    Know you this paper, Lady?

Beatrice
Entrap me not with questions. Who stands here

162–3. *folds / Of the heart's inmost cell.*] The construction is similar to 'the foldings of the brain' (IV i 179).

165. *pain*] Cenci (1819), 1829, 1839; pang Cenci (1821). Since there is no authority for the reading in Cenci (1821) in Errata or Taaffe, Cenci (1819) is followed here. However, Forman describes Cenci (1821) as 'a variation which commends itself to me as probably Shelley's own.' (Forman 1876–7). The word 'pangs' is used later (V iii 65, 75).

167. *Bloodhounds,*] Donohue, KSJ xvii (1968) 68 cps. the Duke's reproof of Bianca in Milman, *Fazio* (1815) Act III scene ii 'Oh, but 'gainst thy husband, / Thy bosom's lord, flesh of thy flesh! – To set / The bloodhounds of the law upon his track!'. *glut yourselves well with me;*] Cp. the passage from Caleb Williams cited in the note to V ii 159–60. *me;*] me! 1829.

168. Locock cps. Scenes from the 'Magico Prodigioso' of Calderon line 211 (see 1824 372): 'A piece of excellent beauty'.

170. *strain*] The sense is of sifting or filtering (cited in OED, 'strain' v. 14a, but see also 9a).

171. *thrice sifted*] thrice-sifted 1829.

173–6. *Entrap me not . . . all in one?*] Cp. Vittoria in Webster, The White Devil III ii 225–6: 'if you be my accuser / Pray cease to be my judge'.

173–80. On Beatrice's effectiveness in outfacing her Judges, see Relation 34–5: 'But the Signora Beatrice being young – lively – and [robust canc.] strong neither with good or ill treatment

845

As my accuser? Ha! wilt thou be he,
175 Who art my judge? Accuser, witness, judge,
What, all in one? Here is Orsino's name;
Where is Orsino? Let his eye meet mine.
What means this scrawl? Alas! Ye know not what,
And therefore on the chance that it may be
180 Some evil, will ye kill us?

Enter an Officer.

Officer
Marzio's dead.

Judge
What did he say?

Officer
Nothing. As soon as we
Had bound him on the wheel, he smiled on us,
As one who baffles a deep adversary;
And holding his breath, died.

Judge
There remains nothing
185 But to apply the question to those prisoners,
Who yet remain stubborn.

Camillo
I overrule
Further proceedings, and in the behalf
Of these most innocent and noble persons
Will use my interest with the Holy Father.

Judge
190 Let the Pope's pleasure then be done. Meanwhile
Conduct these culprits each to separate cells;

– With menaces or fear of torture would allow a single word to pass her lips which might inculpate her; and even by her lively eloquence confused the judges who examined her – The Pope being informed of all that passed by Sig^re Ulysse Moraci the judge employed in this affair became suspicious that the beauty of Beatrice had softened the mind of this Judge and committed the cause to another' (see *BSM* x 208-9).

174. accuser?] accuser! *1840.*

190. the Pope's pleasure] Cp. IV iv 151.

And be the engines ready: for this night,
If the Pope's resolution be as grave,
Pious, and just as once, I'll wring the truth
195   Out of those nerves and sinews, groan by groan.

                                                [Exeunt.

Scene iii

The Cell of a Prison. Beatrice *is discovered asleep on a Couch. Enter* Bernardo.

Bernardo
How gently slumber rests upon her face,
Like the last thoughts of some day sweetly spent
Closing in night and dreams, and so prolonged.
After such torments as she bore last night,
5   How light and soft her breathing comes. Aye, me!
Methinks that I shall never sleep again.
But I must shake the heavenly dew of rest
From this sweet folded flower, thus — wake! awake!
What, sister, canst thou sleep?

Beatrice
                                        [Awaking.
                        I was just dreaming
10   That we were all in Paradise. Thou knowest
This cell seems like a kind of Paradise
After our father's presence.

Bernardo
                     Dear, dear sister,
Would that thy dream were not a dream! O, God!
How shall I tell?

192. night,] night *Cenci (1819);* night – *Rossetti 1870.*

194. Pious,] Pious *Cenci (1819). once,]* once – *Rossetti 1870.*

¶iii   *1. face,]* face! *1829.*

2. spent] spent, *1840.*

5. comes.] comes! *1829. Aye, me!]* Ah, me! *1829, 1839, 1840;* Ah me! *Rossetti 1870;* Ay me! *Rossetti 1878.*

7. the heavenly dew of rest] Cp. *Richard III* IV i 84: 'the golden dew of sleep' and *Julius Caesar* II i 230: 'the honey-heavy dew of slumber', and IV i 178 and note.

8. wake! awake!] wake; awake; *1840.*

10. Paradise.] paradise. *1840.*

11. Paradise] paradise *1840.*

Beatrice

What wouldst thou tell, sweet brother?

Bernardo

15 Look not so calm and happy, or, even whilst
I stand considering what I have to say,
My heart will break.

Beatrice

See now, thou mak'st me weep:
How very friendless thou wouldst be, dear child,
If I were dead. Say what thou hast to say.

Bernardo

20 They have confessed; they could endure no more
The tortures —

Beatrice

Ha! What was there to confess?
They must have told some weak and wicked lie
To flatter their tormentors. Have they said
That they were guilty? O, white innocence,
25 That thou shouldst wear the mask of guilt to hide
Thine awful and serenest countenance
From those who know thee not!

Enter Judge, *with* Lucretia *and* Giacomo, *guarded.*

Ignoble hearts!
For some brief spasms of pain, which are at least

14. *wouldst*] would'st *1839.*

15. *or,*] *1829, 1839;* or *Cenci (1819), Cenci (1821).*

16. *say,*] *1829, 1839;* say *Cenci (1819), Cenci (1821).*

18. *wouldst*] would'st *Cenci (1819).*

20-1. *They have confessed . . . tortures* -] Cp. *Relation* 33-4 which suggests that Bernardo as well as Giacomo was tortured: 'The flight of Mons.ᵣᵉ [Gurr *canc.*] Guerra joined to the confession of the murderer of Olympio aggravated the other proofs so much that the Cenci were re-transfered from Castello to Corte Savella, and were condemned to be put to the torture – The two sons sunk vilely under their torments and became convicted – Lucretia being of advanced age, having completed her fiftieth year and being [o *canc.*] of a fat make was not able to resist the torture of the cord –' (see *BSM* x 206–9).

24. *O, white innocence,*] O white innocence! *1829;* O white innocence, *1839;* O white Innocence, *Rossetti 1870.*

28. *at least*] Rossetti comments: 'I think this should be "at *most.*" The utmost harms which the spasms of pain can do lasts no longer than the limbs which they affect.' *(Rossetti 1878)* but 'at least' makes sense if understood as 'merely'.

As mortal as the limbs through which they pass,
30   Are centuries of high splendour laid in dust?
And that eternal honour which should live
Sun-like, above the reek of mortal fame,
Changed to a mockery and a byword? What!
Will you give up these bodies to be dragged
35   At horses' heels, so that our hair should sweep
The footsteps of the vain and senseless crowd,
Who, that they may make our calamity
Their worship and their spectacle, will leave
The churches and the theatres as void
40   As their own hearts? Shall the light multitude
Fling, at their choice, curses or faded pity,
Sad funeral flowers to deck a living corpse,
Upon us as we pass to pass away,
And leave — what memory of our having been?
45   Infamy, blood, terror, despair? O thou,
Who wert a mother to the parentless,
Kill not thy child! Let not her wrongs kill thee!
Brother, lie down with me upon the rack,
And let us each be silent as a corpse;
50   It soon will be as soft as any grave.
'Tis but the falsehood it can wring from fear
Makes the rack cruel.

Giacomo

                 They will tear the truth
Even from thee at last, those cruel pains:
For pity's sake say thou art guilty now.

---

30. The source of Beatrice's view that her family's reputation has been destroyed by the confessions of Giacomo and Lucretia is in *Relation* 36 (see note to V iii 84–9).

32. *Sun-like*,] Sunlike, *Cenci (1819)*.

33. *a mockery and a byword?*] Cp. III i 160.

34–5. *these bodies to be dragged / At horses' heels*,] Cp. *Relation* 37: 'The Pope after having seen all the examinations & the entire confessions ordered that the delinquents should be drawn through the streets at the tails of horses and afterwards decapitated –' (see *BSM* x 210–11).

35. *horses'*] horse's *Cenci (1819)*.

36–45. *the rain . . . despair?*] Cp. *TL* lines 41ff.

43. *pass to*] pass, to *1840*.

46. *parentless*,] parentless *Cenci (1819)*.

52–60. *They will tear . . . And all be well.*] Cp. *Relation* 35: 'and when she was already tied under this torture [th *canc.*] he brought before her her mother-in-law & [bl. *canc.*] brothers – They began altogether to exhort her to confess saying that since the crime had been committed that they must suffer the punishment.' (*BSM* x 208–9).

Lucretia
55　O, speak the truth! Let us all quickly die;
　　And after death, God is our judge, not they;
　　He will have mercy on us.

Bernardo
　　　　　　　　　　　If indeed
　　It can be true, say so, dear sister mine;
　　And then the Pope will surely pardon you,
60　And all be well.

Judge
　　　　　　　　　Confess, or I will warp
　　Your limbs with such keen tortures —

Beatrice
　　　　　　　　　　　　　　Tortures! Turn
　　The rack henceforth into a spinning wheel!
　　Torture your dog, that he may tell when last
　　He lapped the blood his master shed — not me!
65　My pangs are of the mind, and of the heart,
　　And of the soul; aye, of the inmost soul,
　　Which weeps within tears as of burning gall
　　To see, in this ill world where none are true,
　　My kindred false to their deserted selves.
70　And with considering all the wretched life
　　Which I have lived, and its now wretched end,
　　And the small justice shown by Heaven and Earth
　　To me or mine; and what a tyrant thou art,
　　And what slaves these; and what a world we make,
75　The oppressor and the oppressed — such pangs compel
　　My answer. What is it thou wouldst with me?

Judge
　　Art thou not guilty of thy father's death?

Beatrice
　　Or wilt thou rather tax high-judging God

62. *spinning wheel!*] spinning-wheel! *1829.*

69. *selves.*] selves, *1829.*

71. *end,*] end; *1840.*

75. *The oppressor and the oppressed* –] Cp. III i 284 and note.

78. *high-judging*] *1829;* high judging *Cenci (1819),* Cenci *(1821).* Cp. *Lear* II iv 227: 'high-judging Jove'.

That he permitted such an act as that
80   Which I have suffered, and which he beheld;
Made it unutterable, and took from it
All refuge, all revenge, all consequence,
But that which thou hast called my father's death?
Which is or is not what men call a crime,
85   Which either I have done, or have not done;
Say what ye will. I shall deny no more.
If ye desire it thus, thus let it be.
And so an end of all. Now do your will;
No other pains shall force another word.

Judge
90   She is convicted, but has not confessed.
Be it enough. Until their final sentence
Let none have converse with them. You, young Lord,
Linger not here!

Beatrice
          O, tear him not away!

Judge
Guards, do your duty.

Bernardo   *[Embracing* Beatrice.
                Oh! would ye divide
95   Body from soul?

Officer
               That is the headsman's business.
             [Exeunt all but Lucretia, Beatrice *and* Giacomo.

84–9. Cp. *Relation* 35–6: 'Beatrice after some resistance said – "So you all wish to die and to disgrace & ruin our house? – This is not right; But since it so pleases you so let it be." – & turning to the Gaolors she told them to [untie her *canc.*] unbind her & that all the examinations might be brought to her saying – "That which I ought to confess that will I confess – that to which I ought [to cons *canc.*] [approve *canc.*] [that will *canc.*] to assent, to that will I assent – & that which I ought to deny that will I deny" –' (see *BSM* x 208–11). Cp. *Othello* V ii 306–7: 'Demand me nothing. What you know, you know / From this time forth I never will speak a word.'

87. *be.*] be, *Cenci (1819)*.

90. Cp. *Relation* 36–7: 'in this manner she was convicted without having confessed –' (see *BSM* x 210–11).

94. *Guards,*] Guards *Cenci (1819)*; Guards! *1829*.

Giacomo
Have I confessed? Is it all over now?
No hope! No refuge! O weak, wicked tongue,
Which hast destroyed me, would that thou hadst been
Cut out and thrown to dogs first! To have killed
100 My father first, and then betrayed my sister;
Aye, thee! the one thing innocent and pure
In this black guilty world, to that which I
So well deserve! My wife! my little ones!
Destitute, helpless, and I — Father! God!
105 Canst thou forgive even the unforgiving,
When their full hearts break thus, thus? —

                                         [*Covers his face, and weeps.*

Lucretia

                                        O, my child!
To what a dreadful end are we all come!
Why did I yield? Why did I not sustain
Those torments? Oh, that I were all dissolved
110 Into these fast and unavailing tears,
Which flow and feel not!

Beatrice

                                What 'twas weak to do,
'Tis weaker to lament, once being done;

97. No hope!] No hope? *Rossetti 1870.   No refuge!*] No refuge? *1840*; no refuge? *Rossetti 1870.*
O weak, wicked tongue,] O, weak, wicked tongue *Cenci (1819).*

98. me,] me *Cenci (1819).*

99. first!] *1829, 1839*; first? *Cenci (1819), Cenci (1821).*

102. black] black, *1839.*

104. helpless,] helpless *Cenci (1819)*; helpless; *1829.*

106. thus, thus? –] *1839*; thus, thus! . . . *Cenci (1819)*; thus, thus! *Cenci (1821)*; thus, thus! –
1829; thus? – thus! . . . *Locock 1911.*

109–11. Oh, that . . . feel not!] *Rognoni* cps. Lucretia to Niobe who was transformed into a
fountain of tears after her children were killed (see *Iliad* xxiv 599–620 and *Metamorphoses* vi
146–312). For S.'s response to the statue of Niobe in the Uffizi Gallery, Florence (which he
saw in October 1819) see *Prose* 352–3, and his letter to Hogg of 20 April 1820: 'No produc-
tion of sculpture . . . ever produced on me so strong an effect as this Niobe' (*L* ii 186). Lucretia's
'feel not' (line 111) suggests she is frozen. Contrast her language of release at V iv 95–6 with
Camillo's description of the issue of a fountain of tears from what was thought to be their
frozen source, the heart, at V ii 61–2. The imagery is Dantesque (cp. I iii 175 and note).

111–13. What 'twas weak . . . Take cheer!] The contrast between the calm fortitude of Beatrice
and the nervous remorse of Giacomo and Lucretia bears a marked similarity to the contrast
between Jeremiah Brandreth on the one hand and William Turner and Isaac Ludlam on the
other, noted in *The Examiner*'s accounts of the trial and execution of the latter in 1817 (see
note to Preface lines 17–18).

Take cheer! The God who knew my wrong, and made
Our speedy act the angel of his wrath,
115 Seems, and but seems to have abandoned us.
Let us not think that we shall die for this.
Brother, sit near me; give me your firm hand,
You had a manly heart. Bear up! Bear up!
O, dearest Lady, put your gentle head
120 Upon my lap, and try to sleep awhile:
Your eyes look pale, hollow, and overworn,
With heaviness of watching and slow grief.
Come, I will sing you some low, sleepy tune,
Not cheerful, nor yet sad; some dull old thing,
125 Some outworn and unused monotony,
Such as our country gossips sing and spin,
Till they almost forget they live: lie down!
So, that will do. Have I forgot the words?
Faith! They are sadder than I thought they were.

Song

130 False friend, wilt thou smile or weep
When my life is laid asleep?
Little cares for a smile or a tear,
The clay-cold corpse upon the bier!

115. seems] seems, *1839.*

121. hollow,] hollow *Cenci (1819).*

123–7. Cp. Iphigenia who sings to her mother on hearing of her imminent sacrifice by her father in Euripides, *Iphigenia in Aulis* 1279–81: οἲ 'γώ, μᾶτερ ταὐτὸν γὰρ δὴ / μέλος εἰς ἄμφω πέπτωκε τύχης, ('Alas for me, mother! / One song for us twain / Fate finds us – none other / But this sad strain' (Loeb trans.)) and *Twelfth Night* II iv 41–5: 'O, fellow, come, the song we had last night. / Mark it, Cesario; it is old and plain; / The spinsters and the knitters in the sun, / And the free maids that weave their thread with bones, / Do use to chant it'.

123. low,] i.e. 'quiet' as in *Lear* V iii 272–3: 'Her voice was ever soft, / Gentle, and low –'.

125. unused monotony,] 'Monotony' is used here in its literal Greek sense of 'sameness of tone', i.e. without change of pitch; *Concordance* glosses 'unused' as 'forgotten'.

128. So,] So; *1840.*

130–45. The 'Song' is balladic in form. Francesco Rognoni has kindly supplied the following note which supersedes the note in *Rognoni 1570*: 'Beatrice's song consists of two strophes of catalectic trochaic tetrameters, with occasional iambic substitutions, the first strophe with three and the second with four different rhymes (AABBcCBB; DDEEfFGG). The refrain is made up of an iambic dipody, followed by an iambic tripody (line 135) or a trochaic tetrapody (line 143)'. In *Relation* 48, after the sentence has been communicated, Beatrice and Lucretia 'passed some time in the Conforteria reciting psalms & litanies and other prayers with so much fervour that it well appeared that they were assisted by the peculiar grace of God.' (see *BSM* x 222–3).

133. bier!] bier; *1840.*

                        Farewell! Heigho!
135   What is this whispers low?
                        There is a snake in thy smile, my dear;
                        And bitter poison within thy tear.

                        Sweet sleep, were death like to thee,
                        Or if thou couldst mortal be,
140   I would close these eyes of pain;
                        When to wake? Never again.
                        O, World! Farewell!
                        Listen to the passing bell!
                        It says, thou and I must part,
145   With a light and a heavy heart.

                                                    [*The scene closes.*

Scene iv

A Hall of the Prison. Enter Camillo *and* Bernardo.

        Camillo
        The Pope is stern; not to be moved or bent.
        He looked as calm and keen as is the engine
        Which tortures and which kills, exempt itself
        From aught that it inflicts; a marble form,
5   A rite, a law, a custom: not a man.
        He frowned, as if to frown had been the trick

134. Heigho!] Heigh ho! *1829.*

138. Sweet sleep,] Sweet Sleep! *1829*; Sweet sleep! *1839.   death*] Death *1829.*

142. O, World! Farewell!] O World! farewell! *1829, 1839.*

¶**iv**   *1–27.* Camillo's entreaty (mooted in V ii 186–9) has its basis in the reaction to the Pope's injunction concerning the method of the prisoners' execution (see note to V iii 34–5) in *Relation* 37–8: 'Many Cardinals & Princes interested themselves and entreated that at least they might be allowed to draw up their defence. The Pope at first refused to comply – replying with severity – and asking these intercessors what defence had [F *canc.*] been allowed to Francesco when he had been so barbarously murdered in his sleep' (see *BSM* x 212–13). Camillo's pleading draws on that of the advocates, including Farinacci, who defended the family, cited in *Relation* 38–41 (*BSM* x 212–15).

2–4. He looked . . . it inflicts;] Cp. I iii 96–8.

4–5. a marble form, . . . not a man.] See Bianca's address to the Duke in Milman, *Fazio* (1815) Act III scene ii: 'Die! Fazio die! – / Ye grey and solemn murderers by charter! / Ye ermined manslayers! when the tale is rife / With blood and guilt, and deep and damning, oh, / Ye suck it in with cold insatiate thirst: / But to the plea of mercy ye are stones, / As deaf and hollow as the unbowell'd winds. / Oh, ye smooth Christians in your tones and looks, / But in your hearts as savage as the tawny / And misbelieving African!'.

5. custom:] custom; *1839.*

Of his machinery, on the advocates
Presenting the defences, which he tore
And threw behind, muttering with hoarse, harsh voice:
10 'Which among ye defended their old father,
Killed in his sleep?' Then to another: 'Thou
Dost this in virtue of thy place; 'tis well.'
He turned to me then, looking deprecation,
And said these three words, coldly: 'They must die.'

Bernardo
15 And yet you left him not?

Camillo
                            I urged him still;
Pleading, as I could guess, the devilish wrong
Which prompted your unnatural parent's death.
And he replied: 'Paolo Santa Croce
Murdered his mother yester evening,
20 And he is fled. Parricide grows so rife,

10–11. '*Which . . . sleep?*'] For the source of this question in *Relation* 38, see note to V iv 1–27.

10. *father,*] father *Cenci (1819)*.

14. '*They must die.*'] Cp. III i 361 and note.

18–24. '*Paolo Santa Croce . . . crimes capital.*] *Ricci* ii 192–3 provides authority for the fact that the Pope, 'noting with great care the most exculpating passages of the writing of the advocate Farinacci – with which he became so satisfied that he gave hope of granting a pardon to the criminals' (*Relation* 41, see *BSM* x 214–15), reverted to his original uncomprising stance on hearing of the Santa Croce murder. *Relation* 42–3 makes the incident an act of divine intervention: 'But since by the high dispensation of Providence it was resolved that they should incur the just penalty of Parricide it so happened that at this time Paolo Santa Croce killed his mother in the town of Subiaco because she refused to give up her inheritance to him – And the Pope upon the occurrence of this second crime of this nature resolved to punish those guilty of the first and the more so because the Matricide Santa Croce had escaped from the vengeance of the law by flight.' (*BSM* x 216–17). Browning's 'Cenciaja' is based upon these lines (see headnote).

18. *replied:*] replied. *Cenci (1819)*; replied, *1829*.

20. *rife,*] rife *Cenci (1819)*.

20–4. *Parricide . . . capital.*] On the sense that the murder of a father is an offence against divine law as well as a threat to the wider social order, S. possibly had in mind the Earl of Clarendon's account of the 'unparalleled Murder and Parricide' of Charles I on 30 January 1648 in Book XI of *The History of the Rebellion and Civil Wars in England Begun in the Year 1641*, 12 vols (Basil [*sic*], 1798) ix 309. Mary had read Clarendon's work in 1816 and it no doubt influenced S.'s plans for a tragedy about Charles in 1818 (see headnote). S. also seems to draw parallels between the trial of Beatrice and Clarendon's account of the 'deplorable Tragedy' of Charles's trial (*History* ix 304–5): 'The several unheard of insolencies which this excellent Prince was forced to submit to, at the other times he was brought before that odious Judicatory, his Majestic behaviour, and resolute insisting upon his own dignity, and defending it by manifest Authorities in the Law, as well as by the clearest deductions from Reason, the pronouncing that horrible sentence upon the most innocent Person in the world, the

That soon, for some just cause no doubt, the young
Will strangle us all, dozing in our chairs.
Authority, and power, and hoary hair,
Are grown crimes capital. You are my nephew,
25   You come to ask their pardon; stay a moment;
Here is their sentence; never see me more
Till, to the letter, it be all fulfilled.'

Bernardo
O, God, not so! I did believe indeed
That all you said was but sad preparation
30   For happy news. O, there are words and looks
To bend the sternest purpose! Once I knew them,
Now I forget them at my dearest need.
What think you if I seek him out, and bathe
His feet and robe with hot and bitter tears?
35   Importune him with prayers, vexing his brain
With my perpetual cries, until in rage
He strike me with his pastoral cross, and trample
Upon my prostrate head, so that my blood
May stain the senseless dust on which he treads,
40   And remorse waken mercy? I will do it!
O, wait till I return!

[Rushes out.

Execution of that Sentence by the most execrable Murder that was ever committed since that of our Blessed Saviour; and the circumstances thereof; the Application and Interposition that was used by some noble Persons to prevent that woeful Murder, and the hypocrisy with which that interposition was eluded, the Saint-like behaviour of that Blessed Martyr, and his Christian courage and patience at his death, are all particulars so well known, and have been so much enlarged upon in a Treatise peculiarly writ to that purpose, that the farther mentioning it in this place would but afflict and grieve the Reader, and make the Relation itself odious as well as needless; and therefore no more shall be said here of that deplorable Tragedy, so much to the dishonor of the Nation, and the Religion professed in it, though undeservedly.'

23. hair,] hair *Cenci* (1819).

24–7. There is some authority for the manner of the Pope's communication of his judgement in *Relation* 44: 'on the 10th of May he called into his presence Monsig^r Terrante Taverna Governor of Rome & said to him: "I give up into your hands the Cenci cause, that you may as soon you may execute the justice alotted to them." ' (see *BSM* x 218–19).

24. You are my nephew,] See I i 16 and note.

25. pardon;] pardon: *1840. moment;*] moment! *1840.*

32. dearest] i.e. 'direst' with the sense also of 'heartfelt' (cited in *OED*, 'dear, dere' *a. poetic. Obs.* or *arch.* 2). An archaic usage in S.'s day but common in Spenser, Shakespeare and Milton as *OED* notes. Cp. Shakespeare, Sonnet xxxvii, line 3: 'So I, made lame by Fortune's dearest spite', and *Lycidas*, line 6: 'Bitter constraint, and sad occasion dear'.

Camillo
　　　　　　Alas! poor boy!
A wreck-devoted seaman thus might pray
To the deaf sea.

　　　　Enter Lucretia, Beatrice, *and* Giacomo, *guarded.*

Beatrice
　　　　　　　I hardly dare to fear
That thou bring'st other news than a just pardon.

Camillo
45　May God in heaven be less inexorable
To the Pope's prayers, than he has been to mine.
Here is the sentence and the warrant.

Beatrice　　　　　　　　　　　　　　　　　　　　[*Wildly.*
　　　　　　　　　　　　Oh,
My God! Can it be possible I have
To die so suddenly? So young to go
50　Under the obscure, cold, rotting, wormy ground!
To be nailed down into a narrow place;
To see no more sweet sunshine; hear no more
Blithe voice of living thing; muse not again

47–75. *Oh, . . . whither?*] Cp. Euripides, *Iphigenia in Aulis* 1218–19: μή μ' ἀπολέσῃς ἄωρον ἡδὺ γὰρ τὸ φῶς / λεύσσειν τὰ δ' ὑπὸ γῆς μή μ' ἰδεῖν ἀναγκάσῃς. ('Ah, slay me not untimely! Sweet is light: Constrain me not to see the nether gloom!' (Loeb trans.)); *Measure for Measure* III i 119–33: 'Ay, but to die, and go we know not where; / To lie in cold obstruction, and to rot; / This sensible warm motion to become / A kneaded clod; and the delighted spirit / To bathe in fiery floods or to reside / In thrilling region of thick-ribbed ice; / To be imprison'd in the viewless winds, / And blown with restless violence round about / The pendent world; or to be worse than worst / Of those that lawless and incertain thought / Imagine howling – 'tis too horrible. / The weariest and most loathed worldly life / That age, ache, penury, and imprisonment, / Can lay on nature is a paradise / To what we fear of death.'; Margaret in the final Prison scene ('Kerker') in Goethe, *Faust*, Part I (1808): 'Bin ich doch noch so jung, so jung! / Und soll schon sterben!' (text from *Faust*, ed. Albrecht Schöne, in Goethe, *Sämtliche Werke* (Frankfurt am Main, 1994)) ('And I am yet so young – so young! / And yet so soon to perish by your laws.' trans. Lord Francis Leveson Gower (1823) 255).

47–9. *Oh, My God! . . . To die so suddenly?*] The wording follows closely Beatrice's reaction to the sentence in *Relation* 46: 'Beatrice on hearing it broke into a piercing lamentation and into passionate gesture exclaiming – "How is it possible – oh my God – that I must so suddenly die!"' (see *BSM* x 220–1).

53–5. *muse not again . . . To be nothing!*] Cp. *Paradise Lost* ii 146–51: 'sad cure; for who would lose, / Though full of pain, this intellectual being, / Those thoughts that wander through eternity, / To perish rather, swallowed up and lost / In the wide womb of uncreated night, / Devoid of sense and motion?'

Upon familiar thoughts, sad, yet thus lost —
55   How fearful! To be nothing! Or to be —
What? O, where am I? Let me not go mad!
Sweet Heaven, forgive weak thoughts! If there should be
No God, no Heaven, no Earth in the void world;
The wide, grey, lampless, deep, unpeopled world!
60   If all things then should be — my father's spirit,
His eye, his voice, his touch, surrounding me;
The atmosphere and breath of my dead life!
If sometimes, as a shape more like himself,
Even the form which tortured me on earth,
65   Masked in grey hairs and wrinkles, he should come
And wind me in his hellish arms, and fix
His eyes on mine, and drag me down, down, down!
For was he not alone omnipotent
On Earth, and ever present? Even though dead,
70   Does not his spirit live in all that breathe,
And work for me and mine still the same ruin,
Scorn, pain, despair? Who ever yet returned
To teach the laws of death's untrodden realm?
Unjust perhaps as those which drive us now,
75   O, whither, whither?

Lucretia

                Trust in God's sweet love,
    The tender promises of Christ: ere night,
    Think we shall be in Paradise.

54. lost –] lost *Cenci (1819)*; lost, *1829*; lost! *1839*.

56–7. Let me . . . thoughts!] Cp. *Lear* I v 42: 'O, let me not be mad, not mad, sweet heaven!'

57–60. If there . . . world!] Cp. IV i 94–5 and the passage from Byron's 'Darkness' cited in the note to IV i 95.

59. deep,] deep *1829*.

60–75. There are broad parallels here, as some critics have noted, with Asia's questioning of Demogorgon in *PU* II iv 19–30. But Beatrice is fearful where Asia senses victory (cp. line 67 with *PU* II iv 30.)

60. then] Locock suggests 'it may be suspected that Shelley wrote "there."' (*Locock 1911*). *spirit,*] spirit *Cenci (1819)*; spirit: *Locock 1911*.

61. touch,] touch *Cenci (1819)*. *me;*] me, *Locock 1911*.

65. come] come, *1840*.

67. See note to V iv 60–75.

72–3. Who . . . realm?] Cp. *Hamlet* III i 78–80: 'death – / The undiscover'd country, from whose bourn / No traveller returns –'.

73. death's] Death's *Rossetti 1870, Locock 1911*.

75–7. Trust . . . in Paradise.] A reference to *Luke* xxiii 43: 'And Jesus said unto him, Verily I say unto thee, To day shalt thou be with me in paradise'. On Lucretia's relative calm on hear-

Beatrice
                                'Tis past!
Whatever comes, my heart shall sink no more.
And yet, I know not why, your words strike chill:
80 How tedious, false, and cold seem all things. I
Have met with much injustice in this world;
No difference has been made by God or man,
Or any power moulding my wretched lot,
'Twixt good or evil, as regarded me.
85 I am cut off from the only world I know,
From light, and life, and love, in youth's sweet prime.
You do well telling me to trust in God,
I hope I do trust in him. In whom else
Can any trust? And yet my heart is cold.
        [*During the latter speeches* Giacomo *has retired conversing*
            with Camillo, *who now goes out.* Giacomo *advances.*

Giacomo
90 Know you not, mother — sister, know you not?
Bernardo even now is gone to implore
The Pope to grant our pardon.

Lucretia
                            Child, perhaps
It will be granted. We may all then live
To make these woes a tale for distant years:
95 O, what a thought! It gushes to my heart
Like the warm blood.

Beatrice
                        Yet both will soon be cold.
O, trample out that thought! Worse than despair,

---

ing the sentence, cp. *Relation* 46–7: 'Lucretia as prepared & already resigned to her fate lis-
tened without terror to the reading of this terrible sentence and with gentle exhortations
induced her daughter-in-law to enter the chapel with her, and the latter whatever excesses
she might have [i *canc.*] indulged in on the first intimation of a speedy death so much the
more now courageously supported herself & gave everyone certain proofs of a humble
resignation' (see *BSM* x 220–1).

76. *night*,] night *1829*.

77. *Paradise.*] *paradise. Rossetti 1870.*   'Tis past!] . . . 'Tis past! *Rossetti 1870.*

78. *comes,*] comes *Cenci (1819).*

80. *How . . . things.*] Cp. *Hamlet* I ii 133–4: 'How weary, stale, flat, and unprofitable, / Seem
to me all the uses of this world!' *false,*] false *Cenci (1819).* *things.*] things! *1840.*

90. *mother – sister,*] Mother . . . Sister *Cenci (1819)*; Mother – Sister, *1829.*

96. *cold.*] cold, *1829*; cold: *1840.*

Worse than the bitterness of death, is hope:
It is the only ill which can find place
100 Upon the giddy, sharp and narrow hour
Tottering beneath us. Plead with the swift frost
That it should spare the eldest flower of spring:
Plead with awakening earthquake, o'er whose couch
Even now a city stands, strong, fair and free;
105 Now stench and blackness yawn, like death. O, plead
With famine, or wind-walking pestilence,
Blind lightning, or the deaf sea, not with man!
Cruel, cold, formal man! righteous in words,
In deeds a Cain. No, mother, we must die:
110 Since such is the reward of innocent lives;
Such the alleviation of worst wrongs.
And whilst our murderers live, and hard, cold men,
Smiling and slow, walk through a world of tears
To death as to life's sleep; 'twere just the grave
115 Were some strange joy for us. Come, obscure Death,
And wind me in thine all-embracing arms!
Like a fond mother hide me in thy bosom,

---

98. See S.'s letter to Peacock of 6 November 1818: 'Tasso's situation was widely different from that of any persecuted being of the present day, for from the depth of dungeons public opinion might now at length be awakened to an echo that would startle the oppressor. But then there was no hope.' (*L* ii 47) Cp. note to I iii 111–12.

99–101. *It is ... beneath us.*] Cp. the description of the abyss at III i 245ff.

100. *giddy, sharp and narrow hour*] Cp. *PU* IV 558. *sharp*] sharp, *1839. narrow*] i.e. 'short, brief' (cited in *OED*, 'narrow' *adj.* 3. c. as a rare usage).

101–7. *Plead ... man!*] Cp. *Merchant of Venice* IV i 71–80: 'You may as well go and stand upon the beach / And bid the main flood bate his usual height; / You may as well use question with the wolf, / Why he hath made the ewe bleat for the lamb; / You may as well forbid the mountain pines / To wag their high tops and to make no noise / When they are fretten with the gusts of heaven; / You may as well do anything most hard / As seek to soften that – than which what's harder? – / His Jewish heart.'

102. *eldest*] i.e. 'earliest' or 'first'. *spring:*] Spring: *Rossetti 1870, Locock 1911.*

103–6. *earthquake, ... pestilence,*] Cp. Byron, *Manfred, A Dramatic Poem* (1817) Act II scene iv lines 8–10: 'earthquakes rend the world asunder. / Beneath his footsteps the volcanos rise; / His shadow is the Pestilence'.

103. *earthquake,*] Earthquake, *Cenci (1819).*

104. *fair*] fair, *1829.*

105. *yawn,*] yawns, *Cenci (1819), 1829, 1839.*

106. *wind-walking pestilence,*] Cp. *Psalms* xci 6: 'Nor for the pestilence that walketh in darkness; nor for the destruction that wasteth at noonday.'; the winds described in *Paradise Lost* x 693–5: 'sideral blast, / Vapour, and mist, and exhalation hot, / Corrupt and pestilent'. *wind-walking*] Cp. 'tempest-walking' in *PU* I 331. *pestilence,*] Pestilence, *Cenci (1819).*

108. *man!*] man; *Cenci (1819).*

108–9. *Cruel, ... Cain.*] Cp. the passage from *Fazio* cited in the note to V iv 4.

And rock me to the sleep from which none wake.
Live ye, who live, subject to one another
120   As we were once, who now —

                Bernardo rushes in.

Bernardo
                Oh, horrible!
That tears, that looks, that hope poured forth in prayer,
Even till the heart is vacant and despairs,
Should all be vain! The ministers of death
Are waiting round the doors. I thought I saw
125   Blood on the face of one — what if 'twere fancy?
Soon the heart's blood of all I love on earth
Will sprinkle him, and he will wipe it off
As if 'twere only rain. O, life! O, world!
Cover me! let me be no more! To see
130   That perfect mirror of pure innocence
Wherein I gazed, and grew happy and good,
Shivered to dust! To see thee, Beatrice,
Who made all lovely thou didst look upon —
Thee, light of life — dead, dark! while I say, sister,
135   To hear I have no sister; and thou, Mother,
Whose love was a bond to all our loves —
Dead! The sweet bond broken!

            Enter Camillo *and Guards.*

               They come! Let me
Kiss those warm lips before their crimson leaves
Are blighted — white — cold. Say farewell, before
140   Death chokes that gentle voice! O, let me hear
You speak!

---

119. *Live ye,*] Live, ye *Rossetti 1870.*

129–33. Cp. Cenci's image of Beatrice's hideous reflection in IV i 146–52.

133. *made*] mad'st *Rossetti 1870.*

134. *light of life* –] Cp. IV iii 42 and note. *say, sister,*] say 'Sister,' *Rossetti 1870.*

136. *was a bond*] was as a bond *Rossetti 1870, Forman 1876–7, Woodberry 1893, Locock 1911.*
Rossetti states: 'I have inserted "*as*," conceiving it to be a necessity of metre which Shelley
can only by inadvertence have neglected.' (*Rossetti 1870*); Forman writes 'I have . . . no hes-
itation in following Mr. Rossetti. Compare this line with [V iv 150]' (*Forman 1876–7*). The
case for emendation is convincing but lacks authority.

140. *O,*] O *1829.*

Beatrice
            Farewell, my tender brother. Think
Of our sad fate with gentleness, as now:
And let mild pitying thoughts lighten for thee
Thy sorrow's load. Err not in harsh despair,
145   But tears and patience. One thing more, my child,
For thine own sake be constant to the love
Thou bearest us; and to the faith that I,
Though wrapt in a strange cloud of crime and shame,
Lived ever holy and unstained. And though
150   Ill tongues shall wound me, and our common name
Be as a mark stamped on thine innocent brow
For men to point at as they pass, do thou
Forbear, and never think a thought unkind
Of those, who perhaps love thee in their graves.
155   So mayest thou die as I do; fear and pain
Being subdued. Farewell! farewell! farewell!

Bernardo
I cannot say, farewell!

Camillo
                      O, Lady Beatrice!

Beatrice
Give yourself no unnecessary pain,
My dear Lord Cardinal. Here, Mother, tie

143. mild] mild, *Cenci (1819).*

145. child,] child: *1840.*

146–9. For thine . . . unstained.] Locock cps. *Faerie Queene* II i 37: 'Live thou; and to thy mother dead attest / That cleare she dide from blemish criminall.' (*Locock 1911*).

148. wrapt] Not modernized for the same reason as is given in the note to III i 165.

154. Of those,] Of those *1829.*

156. Farewell! farewell! farewell!] Farewell! Farewell! Farewell! *Cenci (1819).*

157. say,] say *1829.*

159–61. Here, Mother . . . simple knot;] Cp. S.'s note on 'The Niobe' (October 1819): 'The child is clothed in a thin tunic of delicatest woof, and her hair is gathered on her head into a knot, probably by that mother whose care will never gather it again.' (*Prose* 352). See note to V iii 109–11.

159–63. Here, Mother, . . . one another!] Cp. *Relation* 49–50: 'Beatrice considering that it was not [decourous *canc.*] decorous to appear before the Judges & [to *canc.*] on the scaffold with their splendid dresses ordered two dresses one for herself & the other for her mother-in-law made in the manner of the nuns – gathered up & with long sleeves of black cotton for Lucretia & of common silk for herself, with a large cord girdle – When these dresses came Beatrice rose & turning to Lucretia "-Mother" – said she – "the hour of our departure is drawing near let us dress therefore in these clothes & let us mutually aid one another in this last office".

160 My girdle for me, and bind up this hair
In any simple knot; aye, that does well.
And yours I see is coming down. How often
Have we done this for one another! now
We shall not do it any more. My Lord,
165 We are quite ready. Well, 'tis very well.

The End

Lucretia readily complied with this invitation & they dressed each helping the other shew-
ing the same indifference & [ca *canc.*] pleasure as if they were dressing for a feast.' (see *BSM*
x 222–5).

161. knot;] knot: *1840.*

163. another!] another; *Cenci (1819).*

APPENDIX A:
THE CONTENTS OF SHELLEY'S
COLLECTIONS OF *1819* AND *1820*

1819

Rosalind and Helen, a Modern Eclogue
'Lines written among the Euganean Hills'
'Hymn to Intellectual Beauty'
'Ozymandias'

1820

Prometheus Unbound
'The Sensitive Plant'
'A Vision of the Sea'
'Ode to Heaven'
'An Exhortation'
'Ode to the West Wind'
'An Ode [Written, October, 1819, before the Spaniards had recovered their
   Liberty]'
'The Cloud'
'To a Skylark'
'Ode to Liberty'

APPENDIX B:
AN HISTORICAL NOTE ON THE CENCI STORY AND THE SOURCES OF SHELLEY'S KNOWLEDGE OF IT

by Michael Rossington

Bod. MS Shelley adds. e. 13, and the translation of the Cenci story

Bod. MS Shelley adds. e. 13, a nbk containing several items relating to *C*, has been edited and transcribed by Betty T. Bennett (*BSM* x 157–272), though the present ed. offers some readings which differ from hers. *Relation* is a translation in Mary's hand of an account in Italian of the Cenci story of about 7,500 words in length (the leaves of the notebook are paginated not foliated). *Relation* contains several sets of emendations, some in S.'s hand, some done by Mary apparently in 1819 and others by her as she was preparing *Relation* for the press in 1839 for its first publication in *1840* (see *BSM* x 167). A subsequent section of adds. e. 13 in Italian (73–4) refers to the location of the alleged portrait of Beatrice, the end of the Cenci family line, and the whereabouts of Paolo Santa Croce. A further section in Italian, headed 'Variazione' (74–83), suggests that either the source of *Relation* contained variations in the story derived from other sources, or that S. and Mary had access to more than one source of the story: a cancelled passage in S.'s draft of the Preface in *Nbk 10* refers to 'a number of variations in the story all corresponding however in all points of importance' (ff. 8ʳrev–8ᵛrev). Finally the notebook contains a sketch (86) attributed to Mary Shelley by Emily W. Sunstein, described as a 'drawing of a man lying on a pallet . . . possibly meant to be the murdered father of Beatrice Cenci' (reprinted in *Mary Shelley: Romance and Reality* (1989) in the Illustrations facing 210).

It seems certain that *Relation* is a translation of 'Mʳ G's M.S.' which Mary had copied in 1818 (see 209 headnote). 'Mʳ G's M.S.' has never been identified and is presumed to be lost. Mary's 1818 copy of it has also been lost. It is just possible that Mary's copy was sent to Hunt who used it as the basis of a translation of the Cenci story which appeared in *The Indicator* in July 1820 (see below). Both 'Mʳ G's M.S.' and Mary's copy of it seem to have disappeared by 1839 when Mary appears to have made an unsuccessful attempt to obtain the former in the course of preparing *Relation* for publication in *1840* (see *BSM* x 161). Bennett is right to be sceptical about claims made by two American auction houses that they had 'Mʳ G's M.S.' in their possession (*BSM* x 162–3). 'Sale of the Library of C. W. Frederickson', Bangs & Co., New York, 24–28 May 1897, 150–1, and 'Sale of the Library of H. B. Forman', Anderson Galleries, Part I, 15 March 1820, lot 772 describe two different documents each of which is claimed to be the original Italian MS on which S. based *C* (see *BSM* x 162–3 and *SC* v 464 for further details of the catalogue entries).

It is not certain who is responsible for the translation. Forman asked Richard Garnett in a letter of 3 September 1876 'whether Shelley made the translation of the Cenci "Relazione" ' (*Letters about Shelley from the Richard Garnett Papers, University of Texas*, ed. William Richard Thurman, Jr. (1972) 312 cited in *BSM* x 169) and Browning in his letter to Forman of 25 October 1876 appears to be replying to this same question: 'I believe I have seen somewhere that the translation was made by Mrs Shelley – the note appended to an omitted passage seems a womanly performance' (*Letters of Robert Browning*, ed. T. L. Hood (1933) 176). *Forman 1876–7* ii 399n. studiously avoids attributing authorship. It has never been claimed as part of S.'s canon, and though T. G. Steffan suggests that the core translation was done by someone other than the Shelleys ('The phrasing is frequently so awkward that one doubts that Mary or Percy was the translator' ('Seven Accounts of the Cenci and Shelley's Drama', *SELit* ix (1969) 601–18 (603))), Bennett presents the overwhelmingly compelling case that it is Mary's (*BSM* x 167–8).

There is disagreement about the dating of *Relation*. In a strict sense, it cannot be regarded with certainty as a source, or a version of a source, of S.'s knowledge of the Cenci story since it has been argued that it could have been composed after the play was printed in September 1819. Although 'a translation of the Italian Mss. on which my play is founded', now lost, was apparently enclosed in S.'s letter to Peacock of ?25 July 1819 (*L* ii 102), S. cannot be referring to *Relation* itself, since the folds of the letter cannot have enclosed adds. e. 13 nor were the postal fees for the letter commensurate with the notebook's weight (see *SC* vi 897n.3 and *Shelley's Guitar* 112n. and 114n.). However, Reiman's conjecture that *Relation* is therefore 'a second translation done late in 1819 or 1820, perhaps for inclusion in a later edition of *The Cenci*' (*SC* vi 898) seems hardly credible. It seems highly unlikely that Mary and S. would have translated 'Mʳ G's M.S.' on two separate occasions. It is true that S. appears to have used adds. e. 13 after 1819 since there is a subtraction of 1598 from 1821 in his hand in the back cover (a calculation which he appears to have made in order to establish the length of time since the murder of Francesco Cenci, said to have taken place in September 1598 in *Relation* 21–4). But this calculation does not in itself help to date *Relation*. The translation enclosed in the letter to Peacock of ?25 July is also lost but it seems likely that it was a polished and probably abridged version of *Relation*. Though she does not actually date *Relation*, Bennett seems right to say that it is 'Mary Shelley's working text, and likely served as the basis for the fair copy of the text Shelley sent to Peacock in 1819 with the intention that it be appended to the *Cenci*' (*BSM* x 167). Neil Fraistat states that the translation was 'first written into adds. e. 13 in 1818'(*KSJ* xlii (1993) 250) but late April or May 1819 when Mary visited locations in Rome associated with the Cenci story is a more likely date.

It seems almost certain, given the emendations by both S. and Mary, that *Relation* or the version of it sent to Peacock, was intended as an integral part of the tragedy as a publication up until August; but did practicalities preclude its appearance in *Cenci (1819)* and *Cenci (1821)* or did S. abandon the idea perhaps on Peacock's advice? It has been argued that S.'s directions to Peacock in his letter of ?25 July, 'The translation which I send you is to be prefixed to the play' (*L* ii 103), are consistent with the last sentence of the Preface as published which Reiman believes may be read as implying that a translation of the 'manuscript' referred to in its opening sentence will follow (*SC* vi 897). Barker-Benfield's argument that, 'The fact that no translation was included in the September printing of *The Cenci*, though required by the Preface, implies that no translation was then available' (*Shelley's*

Guitar 112n.) supports Reiman's notion that *Relation* was not composed until after September 1819 but also relies on a somewhat ingenious intepretation of the Preface's final sentence. A dating of *Relation* between May and July 1819 still holds if the explanation of the translation's absence from *Cenci (1819)* is that S. in fact changed his mind on the matter at some point in August. It seems at least plausible that S., having sent an abridged version of *Relation* in his letter of ?25 July, anticipating at this time that the tragedy would be printed in England and its publication overseen by Peacock, was discouraged from printing *Relation* or a version of it by the latter's obviously negative view of the whole enterprise of C communicated in a letter now lost though probably received in late August or early September to which S. refers in his letter of 9 September 1819: 'You will see that the subject has not been treated as you suggested, and why it was not susceptible of such treatment' (*L* ii 118). Strategically, then, S. seems to have come round to the view, as Forman notes, that inclusion of the translation would be a mistake: 'The omission of the literal version of the story from the two editions of *The Cenci* published during Shelley's life may perhaps have arisen from the consideration that, to the public of that day, the bare horrors of the story might, if given, negative that very delicacy and reticence to which S. refers [in his letter to Peacock of ?25 July]' (*Forman 1876-7* ii 399). Moreover the Preface as published may be interpreted as signalling that S. had discovered a more effective rhetorical technique for communicating the story than his original idea of presenting a translation of the MS account which he anyway may have come to see as dubious in its aesthetic value as a piece of writing and because it is not, as Alan M. Weinberg points out, anti-clerical (*Shelley's Italian Experience* (1991) 83). It seems likely that S. drafted the Preface in mid-August (see 209 headnote) after receiving Peacock's apparently negative response to his letter of ?25 July. In the Preface he engages the reader's attention immediately by first sketching the main elements of the narrative before proceeding in his characteristically effective essayistic manner to a broader interpretation of the story's significance and its suitability for dramatisation. However, it is to Peacock, in a letter of 21 September 1819, that S. repeats his view that a published translation of the MS of the narrative in some form would assist the prospects of his play. S. clearly had in mind that the historical veracity of the story be enforced upon the public from an independent source just before the play's first performance: 'If my Play should be accepted don't you think it would excite some interest, & take off the unexpected horror of the story by shewing that the events are real, if it could appear in some Paper in some form. –' (*L* ii 120).

It was Hunt who fulfilled S.'s intentions by proclaiming the historical veracity of the Cenci story to an English audience. In *The Examiner* (19 March 1820) he announced that C 'is founded on a most terrific family story, which actually took place in Italy' (190). Then, in the first of two articles entitled 'The Destruction of the Cenci Family, and Tragedy on that Subject' in *The Indicator* xl (19 July 1820) 321–8, and xlii (26 July 1820) 329–36, he introduced the historical basis of S.'s tragedy in terms that seem to follow closely the wording of S.'s letter to Peacock of 21 September 1819, cited above: 'It has been supposed by some, we understand, that the author of the Cenci has overcharged his story; and these and other persons think that it is too horrible to tell' (321). The first of *The Indicator* articles begins, 'We lay before our readers in the present number the substance of a remarkable document, containing the authorities for the tragedy which has lately appeared on the same subject, and which we shall afterwards proceed to notice' (321). Hunt's phraseology here, 'the substance of a remarkable document', is important to note for his article is not a literal translation of a documentary source so much as his own freely edited and abridged version of the Cenci story which contains much authorial interjection by way of comment. Reiman suggests that 'Hunt may actually have used the translation Shelley had sent to Peacock as the basis of his account, perhaps sending parts of it to press as copy' (*SC* vi 898). There is some evidence to support the idea that Hunt was familiar with *Relation* or a version of it (this might explain, e.g., why both *Relation* 32 and *The Indicator* 325 apparently mistranslate 'la bocca' as 'hands' and 'hand'). But collation of the account in *The Indicator* (322–8) with *Relation* suggests that each contains distinct translations of the same passage in an original Italian source (e.g., cp. *The Indicator* 324: 'She had blue eyes, very pleasing, of a sprightliness mixed with dignity: and in addition to all these graces, her conversation, as well as all that she did, had a spirit in it, and a sparkling polish (un brio signorile) which made every one in love with her. She was then under twenty years of age' with *Relation* 69: 'Her eyes were of a deep blue – pleasing & [filled with a warm *canc*.] and [muted by a commanding vivacity *canc*.] full of fire [& *canc*.] to all these beauties she[d *canc*.] added both in words & actions a spirit & a [m *canc*.] majestic vivacity that captivated everyone. She was twenty years of age when she died.'). The way in which Hunt sometimes quotes directly from the Italian original (e.g. in the passage on 324 cited above and on 326), uses expressions such as 'says the manuscript' (326), and introduces errors (e.g. the lawyer Farinacci is given as 'Tarinacci' and 'Tarrinacci' in *The Indicator* 326), strongly suggests that he was working directly from a source that was both in Italian and in MS form. Hunt's letter to S. of 23 August 1820, 'You will see that I made an *Indicator* out of the MS. about the *Cenci*, as a preface to what I said of your noble play' (*The Correspondence of Leigh Hunt*, ed. Thornton Hunt (1862) i 157–8) allows for the possibility that S. had sent him either Mary's copy of 'Mʳ G's M.S.' or a copy of her copy in the autumn of 1819. Furthermore Hunt's description of the MS, 'The Manuscript was copied by an Italian gentleman from a library at Rome, and is entitled, "An Account of the Death of the Cenci Family" ' (322), tallies broadly with S.'s description of 'Mʳ G's M.S.' in the first sentence of the Preface to *C*. Certainly S. would have known that Hunt's Italian was up to the task of translating and abridging the narrative for an English audience and that one of Hunt's periodicals would be the best (ostensibly) independent source for corroborating S.'s Preface's assertion that his tragedy was based on historical fact.

Relation signals the omission of two passages from its source with a series of crosses and, in the case of the first (*Relation* 11), a note: 'The details here are horrible. & unfit for publication' (see Browning's comment on this note, cited above). The emended version of *Relation* with the MS expurgations intact in *1840* (160–5), titled 'Relation of the Death of the Family of the Cenci', was prefaced by the following paragraph, appended to the 'Note on the Cenci': 'Finding among my papers the account of the case of the Cenci family, translated from the old Roman MS., written at the period when the disastrous events it commemorates occurred, I append it here, as the perusal must interest every reader' (*1840* 160). Forman, in his edition of 'Relation' (*Forman 1876–7* ii 399–417), added the first of the omitted passages, which refers to Cenci's attempt to persuade Beatrice 'by an enormous heresy, that children born of the commerce of a father with his daughter were all saints' (401–2).

Forman's authority for his insertion was possibly the MS account in his possession referred to above. *Forman 1876–7* ii 406n. refers the reader to a passage in Italian in *Mélanges publiés par la Société des Bibliophiles Français* (Paris, 1822) 41–2, partially reproduced and translated in *BSM* x 264, to supply the second omitted passage (*Relation* 27) in which reference is made to the laundress's deposition that the heaviness of blood on the sheets at Petrella could not have been a consequence of Beatrice's menstruation. In fact by the time *Relation* was published in 1840, both expurgated passages had already been identifiable by the curious for some time in a printed version of the Cenci story which was published in London soon after the appearance of *Cenci (1819)* and *Cenci (1821)*, *Narrazione della morte di Giacomo e Beatrice Cenci* (J. Moyes, 1821), discussed below.

Manuscript accounts of the Cenci story

'Mʳ G's M.S.' was one of many versions of the most common source of the Cenci story circulating in MS form in the early nineteenth century, the so-called 'Relatione'. Several nineteenth-century writers including Medwin claimed that 'There is scarcely a public library in Italy that does not contain such a MS.' (*Medwin* i 345). The bibliography of the MS and printed accounts of the Cenci story in *Ricci* ii 287–317 contains a list of over fifty MS versions of the 'Relatione' mostly dating from the seventeenth and eighteenth centuries (293–7). Ricci argues that the original 'Relatione' on which subsequent versions including 'Mʳ G's M.S.' were based, was written in the first quarter of the seventeenth century and usefully details the falsifications of the historical facts it introduced (see *Ricci* ii 195–6). Though of the Cenci story S. wrote 'the facts are [a] matter of history' (*L* ii 102) those 'facts' were communicated to him via *Relation* through a version of a widely known but by no means historically accurate source.

It is possible that 'Mʳ G's M.S.' itself dated from the late eighteenth century rather than earlier. Barbara Groseclose in 'A Portrait Not by Guido Reni of a Girl Who Is Not Beatrice Cenci', *Studies in Eighteenth-Century Culture* xi (1982) 107–32 offers a possible *terminus ante quem* (111–12). If 'Mʳ G's M.S.' and not some other source contained the statement 'Il più ritratto di Beatrice esiste nel Palazzo della Villa Pamfili' (Bod. MS Shelley adds. e. 13, p. 73) then the *terminus ante quem* of 'Mʳ G's M.S.' would seem to be 1783. The portrait referred to could be found in the collection of the 'prince Pamfilio', i.e. the Villa Pamfili, in 1749 according to James Russel's anonymously published, *Letters from a Young Painter Abroad to his Friends in England*, 2nd edn, 2 vols (1750) ii 236. But by 1783 it is listed in a catalogue of paintings in the Palazzo Colonna where S. and Mary saw it in 1819 (see *Catalogo dei quadri, e pitture esistenti nel palazzo dell'ecc. Casa Colonna in Roma* (Rome, 1783) 11 no. 847 cited in Groseclose 129n.19). If 'Mʳ G's M.S.' contained the reference cited in adds. e. 13, 'vide Muratori Annali d'Italia – v.10 – P.511' (74), which is to the tenth volume of the Monaco edition of Muratori's *Annali d'Italia* of 1761–64, published in 1764, then the latter is the *terminus post quem* of 'Mʳ G's M.S.'.

It should be noted that the extensive list of versions of 'Relatione' in *Ricci* referred to above is not comprehensive (e.g. it omits a seventeenth-century MS in the Bodleian: Ms. Rawl. D.596.143, pp. 143–64). Steffan in 'Seven Accounts' collates an arbitrary selection of MS accounts including one in English, now in the Stark Library of the University of Texas, dated by watermark to 1821. The proliferation of MS accounts testifies both to the public appetite for the story and its clandestine status. S.'s account of the effective suppression of the 'facts' by the government of the Papal States 'so that the communication of the MS. had become, until very lately, a matter of some difficulty' (note to Preface line 24) implies that MS accounts of the story surfaced in the early nineteenth century as a result of the legacy of the Napoleonic occupation of Italy during which, according to many observers, the authority of the Church had been challenged, especially in Rome (see, e.g., Stendhal [Marie-Henri Beyle], *Rome, Naples, et Florence, en 1817* (Paris, 1817) 41: 'Bon trait dans le centre de la religion, qui prétend retenir les hommes par le moral! Que l'on sente cependant la nécessité de la baïonnette, plus qu'à Paris, où l'on nous dit que nous sommes impies'). S. registers his anxiety that an English rival might appropriate the dramatic potential of the story through reference to an increasing awareness of its content on the part of the English expatriate community in Rome: 'Write to me as soon as you can on this subject because it is necessary that I should present it, or if rejected by the Theatre, print it this coming season lest some body else should get hold of it, as the story which now exists only in Mss begins to be generally known among the English' (*L* ii 103). It is not difficult to see how liberal English sympathisers felt that the story, combined with the status of the MS forms in which it was mediated, served as an allegory of the struggle for an Italian nation-state in the Napoleonic and post-Napoleonic periods, thwarted, as always in the history of the Italian peninsula, by the Papacy and foreign, imperial interests. As an early twentieth-century critic remarked, for Italians, 'this tragedy means the beginning of Italian liberty' (Clarence Stratton, 'The Cenci Story in Literature and in Fact', *Studies in English Drama*, First Series, ed. A. Gaw (1917) 130–60 (130)).

Printed accounts of the Cenci story

Emil Koeppel's thesis in *Quellen-Studien zu den Dramen George Chapman's, Philip Massinger's und John Ford's* (1897) 85–9 that Malefort's incestuous passion for his daughter Theocrine in Massinger's *The Unnatural Combat* is based on the Cenci story was refuted convincingly by R. S. Telfer in his edition of the play (Princeton, 1932). Indeed there is no conclusive evidence that the Cenci story was either known to or utilised by early seventeenth-century English dramatists. From the mid-eighteenth century the most widely known printed authority for the story was Lodovico Muratori, *Annali d'Italia*, 12 vols (Milan, 1744–49) x [1749] 565–7. As noted above, this source, though with a page reference to the tenth volume of the Monaco edition of 1761–64, is referred to in adds. e. 13, p. 74. Muratori's emphasis on 'l'iniquità del Padre, cagione di tanto disordine, e massimamente in considerare l'età, la bellezza, e lo straordinario coraggio della giovinetta Beatrice' (566), could be said to have set the terms for the cult of Beatrice as tragic heroine in the late eighteenth and early nineteenth centuries. Muratori, a leading figure in the Italian Enlightenment, can be seen as a modern consciousness reflecting critically on Italian history, particularly in respect of the Church. The following accounts seem to draw on Muratori: [Anon. i.e. James Russel], *Letters from a Young Painter Abroad to his Friends in England*, 2nd edn, 2 vols (London, 1750) ii 235–9; Giuseppe Abate Piatti, *Storia Critico-Cronologica De' Romani Pontefici*, 12 vols (Naples, 1765–68) xii [1768] 30–1; [Anon.], *Nuovo Dizionario Istorico*, 27 vols (Naples, 1791) vi 260–2; Giuseppe de Novaes, *Elementi Della Storia De' Sommi Pontefici*, 2nd edn, 16 vols (Siena, 1802–15) ix [1805] 51–3. Friedrich Johann Lorenz Meyer mentions the story by reference to the portrait in *Darstellungen aus Italien* (Berlin, 1792) 244–6. According to several published reports, Beatrice Cenci's tomb in the Church of San Pietro in Montorio had been desecrated in 1798 by sympathisers with the French Revolution (see Carlo Falconieri, *Vita di Vincenzo Camuccini* (Roma, 1875) 309–10). S. could conceivably have been acquainted with two recent Italian literary renditions of the story. Especially significant given S.'s preoccupation with melancholy topics in 1818–19 is 'Beatrice Cenci', chapter 18 of *Canti Melanconici* (Pisa: Dalla Tipografia della Società Letteraria, 1802) 121–4 by the Genoese Bernardo Laviòsa (1736–1810), a series of *terza rima* poems on sacred and profane subjects modelled on Dante and Young. A further possible printed source for *C* is *Beatrice Cenci*, a tragedy based on the Cenci story by Vincenzo Pieracci (1768–1834). George Yost, in *Pieracci and Shelley: An Italian Ur-Cenci* (Potomac, Md., 1986) argues, in effect, that S. drew with a deliberate lack of acknowledgement on Pieracci's play (which Yost gives in the Italian original and in his own translation). The play was published in *Tragedie di Vincenzio Pieracci di Turicchi* (Firenze: Presso Niccolo Carli, 1816), and noticed in *Gazzetta di Firenze* cx (12 September 1816) 4. Though Pieracci appears to have been a minor dramatist derivative of Alfieri, Yost suggests (8n.13) that S. was alerted to *Beatrice Cenci* in the salon of Signora Dionigi (see headnote to 209). Yost's hypothesis that 'A reading of both plays puts it beyond reasonable doubt . . . that Shelley did draw upon Pieracci's *Beatrice Cenci*' (7) is argued exhaustively, and centres on numerous examples of features common to the two plays but not to be found in *Relation* (for a summary of parallels see Yost, 29). Though there are major differences of characterisation (Beatrice commits suicide at the end of Pieracci's play and is less forcefully realised than in *C*), that S. drew on relatively incidental features of *Beatrice Cenci* in *C* could be construed from such facts as that both plays have a similar character by the name of Camillo (spelt 'Cammillo' in Pieracci's play) whereas neither such a character nor this name are to be found in *Relation* nor in any other known source of the Cenci story.

Several printed accounts published between 1820 and 1822, while clearly not sources of *C*, demonstrate the contemporary currency of the story in Europe. It is to be found in further editions of Muratori's *Annali d'Italia*, 18 vols (Milano: Società Tipografica de' Classici Italiani, 1818–21) xv [1820] 155–8, and Novaes' *Elementi della Storia De' Sommi Pontefici*, 17 vols (Rome, 1822) ix 48–50. Charlotte Ann Eaton in *Rome in the Nineteenth Century; in a series of letters written during a Residence at Rome in the Years 1817 and 1818* (1820) iii 18–20 uses the portrait in the Palazzo Colonna as a pretext for recounting a version of the story recognisable in many of its nuances in *C*. *Narrazione della morte di Giacomo e Beatrice Cenci* (1821) is a printed version, in pamphlet form, of an MS account which appears to follow closely the source on which *Relation* is based, to be roughly of the same length, and to contain a statement about the provenance of its MS source (24) which accords broadly with the opening sentence of S.'s Preface to *C* in which the MS is described as 'copied from the archives of the Cenci Palace at Rome' and with Hunt's statement that the basis of his *Indicator* xl article is a MS 'copied by an Italian gentleman from a library at Rome' (322). The copy in the British Library is bound with a copy of *Cenci (1821)*. Both A. Bertolotti, who comments 'La rivoluzione del 1821 deve aver prodotto la seguente clandestina pubblicazione' (*Francesco Cenci e la sua famiglia: studi istorici*, 2nd edn (Firenze, 1879) 305) and F. Marion Crawford, who claims it was 'published in London, doubtless in order to escape being placed on the "Index"' ('Beatrice Cenci: The True Story of a Misunderstood Tragedy', *The Century Illustrated Monthly Magazine* lxxv (1908) 449–66 (461)) ascribe the publication of this, the first full-length unexpurgated version of the narrative to the climate of political instability in the Italian peninsula in 1821. Though it is purely speculative to suggest that either Hunt or Peacock was involved in the publication of *Narrazione*, both were apparently sent versions of the Cenci story by S. (see above). It would be satisfying to believe that if, as argued above, *The Indicator* article is derived from a copy of Mary's copy of 'M^r G's M.S.' sent to Hunt by S., then it could be that *Narrazione* is based on 'M^r G's M.S.' though Bennett does not allow for this (*BSM* x 163) and it has to be acknowledged that there are differences in points of fact between *Relation* and *Narrazione* (e.g. in respect of the ages of the various family members at their deaths).

A French translation, 'Relation de la mort de Giacomo et de Béatrix Cenci' by the Marquis de Fortia d'Urban, is introduced by 'Malartic' (Alphonse de Malartic) in *Mélanges publiés par la Société des Bibliophiles Français* (Paris, 1822) 1–28 with the following: 'Le morceau suivant est la traduction d'un manuscrit italien trouvé dans une bibliothèque de Rome par M. le comte de Fortia.' The original Italian narrative on which the translation is based, 'La Funesta Morte di Giacomo, e Beatrice Cenci Fratelli, e di Lucrezia Petroni, loro matregna', follows (33–62) to which is appended a brief quotation from Piatti.

Since the early nineteenth century a vast secondary literature concerning the historical basis of the Cenci story has developed, some of it, unsurprisingly, superficial, but much of it motivated by a serious scholarly desire to disentangle fact from legend. Bertolotti is probably the most influential if not accurate presentation of the available historical evidence in the nineteenth century. Richard Davey, 'Beatrice Cenci', *The Antiquary: A Magazine Devoted to the Study of the Past* lxxiv–lxxvii (1886) 67–71, 119–22, 163–6, 197–203, Crawford, and Stratton, the last two of which draw on Bertolotti's scholarship, are useful but not altogether reliable. *Encyclopaedia Britannica*, 11th edn, 29 vols (1910–11) v [1910], 660–1, gives a brief, clear account of the facts as against the embellishments. *Ricci* (English trans. *Ricci (1926)*) supersedes Bertolotti and has not been surpassed as the most comprehensive if somewhat prolix account of the historical evidence so far. There appears to be much historical evidence to affirm Francesco's criminality and the Papacy's complicity with it as well as Beatrice's legendary if not saint-like status during and after her trial in Rome in 1599. But, as indicated above, historical accounts of the Cenci story differ sharply from the source of *Relation* and *The Indicator* article. One common view is that Beatrice had her father murdered in order to pre-empt his knowledge of her bearing a child to Olimpio, the keeper of the castle of Petrella (for discussion of 'The Son of Beatrice', see *Ricci* ii 171–91). It must be remembered, however, that S.'s Preface makes it clear that he views *C* as a dramatisation of a popular legend communicated through various samizdat MS accounts of which 'M^r G's M.S.' is one, not as a forum for adjudicating between various interpretations of historical evidence of which he may, anyway, have been unaware.

Since *C*, there have been a vast number of renditions of the story. Scott is reported to have 'had once a thought of applying the history of the Cenci to romance, but that he had found it too atrocious and too disgusting to be rendered available in the drawing room at the present day' (*Reminiscences of Sir Walter Scott's Residence in Italy* 1832 by Sir William Gell, ed. James C. Corson (1957) 30). Stendhal's 'Les

Cenci' was first published in *Revue Des Deux Mondes* (1 July 1837) 5–32, and reprinted in *L'Abbesse de Castro* (Paris, 1839) 265–329. Though he states that 'J'ai acheté la permission de copier un récit contemporain' in 1823 (*Revue* 11), he probably did not do so until after 1831 and 'Les Cenci' was conceived and written after 1834. T. W. Earp refutes convincingly a traditional view that Stendhal knew S. in Italy and communicated the Cenci story to him ('Shelley and Stendhal', *TLS* (29 July 1944) 367). Stendhal's essay consists of a translation of the story, preceded by an introduction in which Francesco Cenci is analysed as a grotesque version of a Don Juan figure (*Rossetti 1878* ii 435 briefly compares *Relation* on points of fact with 'Les Cenci'). Alexandre Dumas, though he does not mention S.'s play, provided an account of the story, 'Les Cenci', in *Crimes Célèbres*, 8 vols (Paris, 1840) i 1–57, trans. in *Celebrated Crimes* (London, 1843) 266–81. Nineteenth-century dramas based upon, or heavily influenced, by *C* include Prosper Merimée's 'La Famille de Carvajal' in his anonymously published *La Jaquerie, scènes féodales* (Paris, 1828) 339–422, which Mary described in a review as 'a tremendous domestic tragedy, founded on the same story as the Cenci' (*The Westminster Review* x (1829) 71–81 (80) and *MSW* ii 172–81 (180)), La Marquis de Custine's *Beatrix Cenci, Tragédie en Cinq Actes et en Vers* (Paris, 1833) and G.-B Niccolini's *Beatrice Cenci*, in *Opere di G.-B. Niccolini*, 3 vols (Firenze, 1844) ii 357–448 which N. I. White, in 'An Italian "Imitation" of Shelley's *The Cenci*', *PMLA* xxxvii (1922) 683–90, argues is a straightforward plagiarism of *C*. The Italian radical F. D. Guerrazzi produced a substantial work of historical fiction, *Beatrice Cenci: storia del secolo XVI* (1854). The Italian Expressionist Mario Caserini (1874–1920) directed a film entitled *Beatrice Cenci* (1909) shown by James Joyce at the opening of the first cinema in Dublin in 1909 (see Richard Ellmann, *James Joyce* (1982) 303). Antonin Artaud's *Les Cenci: Tragédie en quatre actes et dix tableaux d'après Shelley et Stendhal*, first performed in Paris in May 1935, is a creative translation of Shelley's play into the idiom of the Theatre of Cruelty. The text of the play is in Artaud, *Oeuvres complètes*, Nouvelle édition revue et augmentée (Paris, 1978) iv 147–210, an edition which summarises usefully Artaud's borrowings and departures from *C* (iv 336), as well as providing related documents, 'Dossier des Cenci' (iv 257–71) and 'A Propos des Cenci' (v [1979], 35–49). The play is trans. by Simon Watson-Taylor (London, 1969). Alberto Moravia's *Beatrice Cenci* in *Botteghe Oscure* xvi (1955) 363–461 reprinted in *Opere complete di Alberto Moravia*, x, *Teatro* (Milan, 1958) 141–267 and trans. Angus Davidson (London, 1965), is an existentialist drama focusing on Beatrice's relationship with Olimpio.

The Portrait

Along with the translation referred to above, S. originally considered 'a print of Beatrice' (*L* ii 103) as an integral part of *C* as a publication. S. wrote to Amelia Curran, who had been their neighbour in Rome, on 5 August 1819 about the possibility of obtaining an engraving of the portrait in the Palazzo Colonna 'to place as a frontispiece to his tragedy' (*Mary L* i 105), though nothing materialised despite further correspondence (see *L* ii 107, 159 and *Mary L* i 159). For a reproduction of the painting, now in the Galleria Nazionale d'Arte Antica, Palazzo Corsini, Rome, see Groseclose, 'A Portrait' 108. Its attribution to Guido Reni, whose work S. admired (see, e.g., the letter of 9 November 1818 to Peacock, *L* ii 50–1), has been challenged with increasing force since the beginning of the twentieth century (see

G. C. Cavalli, *Mostra di Guido Reni* (Bologna, 1954) 103–4). D. S. Pepper classes it as a 'rejected attribution' and says it 'is perhaps by Elisabetta Sirani, based on a tradition of turbaned sibyls derived from Guido and his studio' (*Guido Reni: A Complete Catalogue of his Works* (Phaidon, 1984) 304). Equally questionable is the subject of the painting. The view that it is 'certain that neither the identification of the subject with Beatrice nor its attribution to Guido go farther back than the eighteenth century' (*Ricci* ii 283, quotation from *Ricci (1926)*), is confirmed by Groseclose in 'A Portrait' who suggests that the belief it depicted Beatrice Cenci derived primarily from a need in the mid-eighteenth century for a visual symbol which would correspond to written accounts of her beauty and suffering in Muratori and elsewhere. A copy of this portrait hung in S.'s room in Via Sestina (see *L* ii 103). The nature of his enchantment with it, expressed in the Preface, is directly in line with the dominant terms of the contemporary cultural construction of Beatrice, to be found, for example, in Charlotte Eaton's discussion of 'the only painting in this suite of rooms [in the Palazzo Colonna] that had power to interest me – Guido's Portrait of Beatrice Censi [*sic*]' (*Rome in the Nineteenth Century* (1820) iii 18ff.), referred to above. Mary's recollection that 'We visited the Colonna and Doria Palaces, where the portraits of Beatrice were to be found' (*1839* ii 274) reflects the widespread belief that there were at least two portraits of Beatrice in the collections of two families 'whose houses were historically associated with the ill-fated Cencis' (Groseclose, 'A Portrait' 112). S. refers to the better-known portrait as 'now in the Colonna Palace' (*L* ii 103), suggesting that he was aware that it had until the late eighteenth century been in the Villa Pamfili (Palazzo Doria), its location in *Relation* (73). Dickens comments on the portrait in *Pictures from Italy* (1846) 211–12 and both Herman Melville in *Pierre: Or, The Ambiguities* (1852) and Nathaniel Hawthorne in *The Marble Faun* (1860) allude to the story by reference to the portrait. On portraits of Beatrice inspired by *C*, see Barbara Groseclose, 'The Incest Motif in Shelley's *The Cenci*', *Comparative Drama* xix (1986) 221–39 (234–6).

The relationship between *C* and Relation

C ends before the execution which, along with its aftermath, is described in great detail in *Relation* 45–68. The other principal differences between *C* and *Relation* are as follows (for further comparison of *C* and *Relation*, see *Bates* 49–51 and Paul Smith, 'Restless Casuistry: Shelley's Composition of *The Cenci*', *KSJ* xiii (1964) 77–85). *C* excises references to Cenci's sodomy (*Relation* 2, 3, 6) and has him punished through fines for murder instead (see, e.g., I i 1–3). Cenci is a Catholic in *C* where *Relation* 3 refers to 'Atheism' as 'the greatest, of his vices'; Hunt registers the significance of this alteration in *The Indicator* with a characteristic flourish: 'the atheism of such men as Cenci is the only real atheism' (320). The time-scheme of *C* appears to span a period of about a week and is therefore more compressed than that of *Relation*, as S. noted in a cancelled portion of the draft of the Preface: 'The story is much the same in the tragedy as in the manuscrit [*sic*], except that the action is more hurried in the latter' (*Nbk 10* f. 14ᵛ[rev.]; S. presumably meant 'former' rather than 'latter'). *Relation* itself condenses the three-year period of the 'core' events of the story (from the deaths of Rocco and Cristofero in 1596 to the trial and execution in 1599) to about one year. For useful discussion of the sometimes seemingly inconsistent time-scheme of *C*, see *Bates* 50–2; Smith, 'Restless Casuistry' 82–3; and, most helpful of all, *Robinson* 146. *Relation* contains no reference to the banquet in *C* I iii, Bernardo appears to be an adolescent in *C* (e.g., V iii 18) whereas in *Relation* (71) he is said to be twenty-six years old (the legal defence of Bernardo claimed he was mentally retarded, see *Ricci* ii 164). Cristoforo, referred to as 'Cristofero' in *Relation* 9, is called Cristofano in *C* (I iii 61, IV i 46). The use of the name 'Orsino' in *C* for the character whose basis is Guerra in *Relation*, appears to be purposive. The Orsini were a powerful Roman family of the Guelphic faction. Dante refers to the simoniac Nicholas III (Giovanni Gaetano Orsini), Pope from 1277 to 1280, and to the common designation of the Orsini as *filii ursae*, the bear symbolising voraciousness (see *Inferno* xix 69–70, and Villani, *Croniche* (1537) Book VII ch. liv). S.'s sophisticated characterisation of Orsino owes little to *Relation*, as he admits in a cancelled and rejected sentence in the draft of the Preface, 'Orsino – whose real name was Guerra – plays a more conspicuous part' (*Nbk 10* f. 14^{v}rev.), a development ably discussed in *Bates* (68), Smith, 'Restless Casuistry' (81), and Charles L. Adams, 'The Structure of *The Cenci*', *Drama Survey* iv (1965) 139–48 (143–6). There is also a revealing sketch of the priest in another rejected portion of the draft Preface in *Nbk 10* f. 18^{r}rev.: 'A young [ple *canc*.] prelate, [of the *canc*.] in love with [Beatrice acts according to the *canc*.] Beatrice assists them in their design, & so soon as their deed is discovered abandons them [If he had posessed any thing like virtue or courage & *canc*.]' (see *MYR* iv 402–3). The characterisation of Giacomo in *C* also owes little to *Relation*, as Smith points out ('Restless Casuistry' 83–4). There is no authority in *Relation* nor in any other known source for the dramatic irony of Savella's 'commission' in IV iv. Finally, the Count's rape of Beatrice in *C* has no authority in *Relation*, although this statement requires very careful qualification. Though Francesco Cenci's 'incestuous passion' is referred to in the Preface (line 8), the act of incestuous rape is never actually referred to directly in *C*, but it is worth noting that it was recognised and named as such by at least one contemporary reviewer (see *The British Review and London Critical Journal* xvii (1821) 382). It is clearly meditated from the opening scene (I i 100) and occurs prior to III i (see also the note to 'That if she have a child –' (IV i 140)). *Relation*, in which it is stated that Francesco 'often endeavoured by force & threats to debauch his daughter Beatrice who was now grown up & exceedingly beautiful' (11, after which there follows the omitted passage referred to above), however, does not refer to his designs as having been realised. S.'s notes on the Cenci story in *Nbk 10* employ similarly allusive language to that of *Relation* suggesting that for dramatic purposes as well as to avoid censorship S. adopted the silence about incest in *Relation* to his own ends. The sentence 'He thinks by mild means to bring her to his will' (*Nbk 10* f. 2^{v}rev.) is preceded by 'He [?cr *canc*.] tempts Beatrice' where the word 'tempts' is written above three words, the last of which is 'with' (see *MYR* iv 468–9). The first two of these words are cancelled and indecipherable though Quinn offers the unlikely reading of 'has larks' (*MYR* iv 230). The question of whether or not incestuous rape did occur is, as a matter of historical fact, contested. Farinacci's defence of Beatrice states that Francesco 'endeavoured to overcome her chastity' (see Bowyer, 'Translation of the Pleading of Prospero Farinacci' 74 and headnote) but Ricci, in the face of what he regards as insufficient evidence, is doubtful (see *Ricci* ii 150–70). Whatever the historical facts, in the light of comparing *C* and *Relation*, it is disingenuous to state as do some critics, including, e.g., Groseclose, that 'incest was not . . . an aspect of the original story', 'The Incest Motif' (222).

INDEX OF TITLES

INDEX OF FIRST LINES